lonely

KOH RONG

Southeast Asia

on a shoestring

Myanmar
(Burma)
p480

Laos
p311

Thailand
p643

Vietnam
p812

Cambodia
p64

Philippines
p547

Brunei
Darussalam
p50

Malaysia
p378

Singapore
p613

Indonesia
p149

Timor-
Leste
p791

THIS EDITION WRITTEN AND RESEARCHED BY

China Williams,

Greg Bloom, Celeste Brash, Stuart Butler, Shawn Low, Simon Richmond,
Daniel Robinson, Iain Stewart, Ryan Ver Berkmoes, Richard Waters

PLAN YOUR TRIP

HOI AN, VIETNAM P862

BORACAY, PHILIPPINES
P576

ON THE ROAD

Contents

ON THE ROAD

KYLIE MCLAUGHLIN/GETTY IMAGES ©

SONGKRAN FESTIVAL,
THAILAND P785

Contents

UNDERSTAND

SURVIVAL GUIDE

SPECIAL FEATURES

Welcome to Southeast Asia

Friendly and intense, historic and devout, Southeast Asia is a warm embrace, from its sun-kissed beaches and steamy jungles to its modern cities and sleepy villages.

Elemental Forces

Water has sculpted many Southeast Asian landscapes. The jungle-topped islands of the Malay peninsula are cradled by coral reefs that tame the ocean into azure pools. The languorous Vietnamese coastline greets the South China Sea from tip to tail, while inland there are karst mountains – evidence of long-vanished oceans. And the muddy Mekong River lopes through tightly knit mountains to flat rice baskets. The traditional 'highways' of Borneo are tannin-stained rivers. And the volcanoes of Indonesia and the Philippines provide a glimpse into the earth's blacksmithing core.

Spiritual Spaces

Southeast Asia bathes in spirituality. With the dawn, pots of rice come to a boil and religious supplications waft from earth to sky. Barefoot monks collect food alms from the faithful; the call to worship bellows from mosques summonsing devotees to prayer; family altars are tended like thirsty house plants. And the region's great monuments were built for the divine, from Angkor's heaven incarnate to Bagan's temples. This is a region in close communication with the divine. Visitors can join the conversation at meditation retreats or by hiking to a golden-spired temple or sacred mountain.

A Marriage of Old & New

Southeast Asian cities grabbed on to the future long before it became the present. Bangkok's masses zip between shopping malls aboard suspended trains; Singapore shows off its multicultural heritage like a fashion show; and Ho Chi Minh City (Saigon) is in a race to the top of the commercial heap. In between these modern marvels are rickety wooden villages filled with yawning dogs and napping water buffaloes, where the agricultural clock measures out the seasons. These rural landscapes are best visited by bike or on foot, so that you're close enough to wave and chit-chat with the sandal-clad locals.

A Bountiful Harvest

With the absence of winter, the earth here is always pregnant with ambrosial fruits, spices once as prized as gold and the staple of rice, which is concocted into three square meals and dessert. Grazing is a Southeast Asian art, cultivated in the hawker centres of Penang and Singapore or by itinerant vendors in Thailand and Vietnam. From Indian curries to Chinese dim sum, cuisine tells a tale of migration and intermingling, and the flavours flirt with the climate, balancing spicy, sweet, salty and sour.

Why I Love Southeast Asia

By China Williams

People always have time for a chat in Southeast Asia. Be it a political brainstorm or personal exposé, this is a region where people will eclipse the common tourist attractions. All of my memories involve wandering around some city, making friends. I was the pied piper of a parade of kids in Penang, adopted by a bored civil servant in Sumatra, invited to share a picnic in Thailand and escorted around town by a Hanoi uni student. I've posed for a million pictures with strangers, mostly as a prop, but sometimes we were temporary besties.

For more about our authors, see page 976.

Above: Buddhist monks, Bagan (p522), Myanmar

Southeast Asia

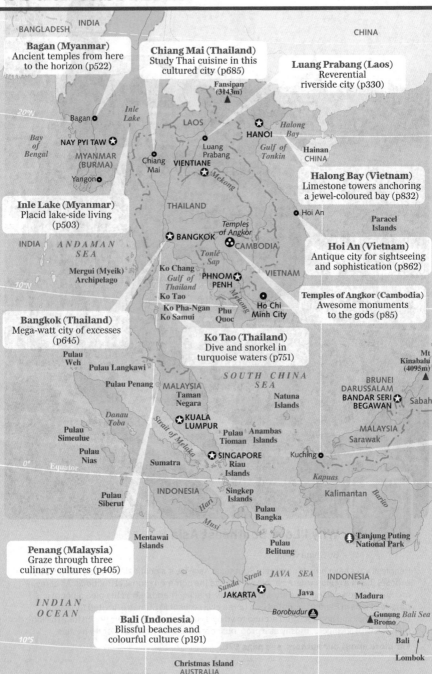

Bagan (Myanmar)
Ancient temples from here
to the horizon (p522)

Chiang Mai (Thailand)
Study Thai cuisine in this
cultured city (p685)

Luang Prabang (Laos)
Reverential
riverside city (p330)

Halong Bay (Vietnam)
Limestone towers anchoring
a jewel-coloured bay (p832)

Inle Lake (Myanmar)
Placid lake-side living
(p503)

Hoi An (Vietnam)
Antique city for sightseeing
and sophistication (p862)

Temples of Angkor (Cambodia)
Awesome monuments
to the gods (p85)

Bangkok (Thailand)
Mega-watt city of excesses
(p645)

Ko Tao (Thailand)
Dive and snorkel in
turquoise waters (p751)

Penang (Malaysia)
Graze through three
culinary cultures (p405)

Bali (Indonesia)
Blissful beaches and
colourful culture (p191)

BANGLADESH

INDIA

CHINA

Fansipan
(3143m)

Bagan

Inle
Lake

20°N

Bay
of
Bengal

NAY PYI TAW

LAOS

Luang
Prabang

HANOI

Halong
Bay

Gulf
of
Tonkin

Hainan
CHINA

MYANMAR
(BURMA)

Chiang
Mai

VIENTIANE

Yangon

Mekong

THAILAND

Hoi An

Paracel
Islands

INDIA

ANDAMAN
SEA

Temples
of Angkor

BANGKOK

CAMBODIA

Mergui (Myeik)
Archipelago

Tonlé
Sap

10°N

Ko Chang

Gulf of
Thailand

PHNOM
PENH

VIETNAM

Ko Tao

Mekong

Ho Chi
Minh City

Ko Pha-Ngan
Ko Samui

Phu
Quoc

Pulau
Weh

Pulau Langkawi

Pulau Penang

Mt
Kinabalu
(4095m)

SOUTH CHINA
SEA

Natuna
Islands

BRUNEI
DARUSSALAM

BANDAR SERI
BEGAWAN

Sabah

MALAYSIA

Taman
Negara

KUALA
LUMPUR

MALAYSIA

Sarawak

Danau
Toba

Pulau
Simeulue

Pulau
Nias

Strait of Melaka

Pulau
Tioman

Anambas
Islands

SINGAPORE

Riau
Islands

Kuching

0°

Equator

Sumatra

INDONESIA

Singkep
Islands

Kapuas

Kalimantan

Barito

Pulau
Siberut

Hari

Musi

Pulau
Bangka

Mentawai
Islands

Pulau
Belitung

Tanjung Puting
National Park

JAVA
SEA

INDONESIA

INDIAN
OCEAN

Sunda Strait

JAKARTA

Java

Madura

Borobudur

Gunung
Bromo

Bali Sea

10°S

Bali

Christmas Island
AUSTRALIA

100°E

110°E

Lombok

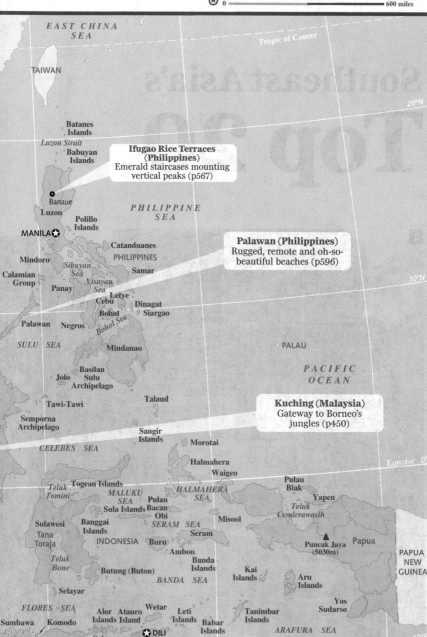

N 0 — 1000 km
0 — 600 miles

EAST CHINA
SEA

Tropic of Cancer

TAIWAN

Batanes
Islands

Luzon Strait

Babuyan
Islands

20°N

**Ifugao Rice Terraces
(Philippines)**
Emerald staircases mounting
vertical peaks (p567)

Banaue

Luzon

Polillo
Islands

*PHILIPPINE
SEA*

MANILA

Catanduanes

Palawan (Philippines)
Rugged, remote and oh-so-
beautiful beaches (p596)

Mindoro

PHILIPPINES

*Sibuyan
Sea*

Calamian
Group

Samar

Panay

*Visayan
Sea*

Letye

Cebu

10°N

Dinagat

Bohol

Siargao

Bohol Sea

Palawan

Negros

SULU SEA

Mindanao

PALAU

Jolo

Basilan

Sulu
Archipelago

*PACIFIC
OCEAN*

Tawi-Tawi

Talaud

Kuching (Malaysia)
Gateway to Borneo's
jungles (p450)

Semporna
Archipelago

Sangir
Islands

Morotai

CELEBES SEA

Equator 0°

*Teluk
Tomini*

Togean Islands

*MALUKU
SEA*

*HALMAHERA
SEA*

Halmahera

Waigeo

Pulau
Biak

Pulau
Sula Islands Bacan

Yapen

Banggai
Islands

Obi

*Teluk
Cenderawasih*

Sulawesi

SERAM SEA

Misool

Tana
Toraja

Buru

Seram

Papua

Ambon

Puncak Jaya
(5030m)

*Teluk
Bone*

Butung (Buton)

Banda
Islands

Kai
Islands

PAPUA
NEW
GUINEA

BANDA SEA

Aru
Islands

Selayar

Yos
Sudarso

FLORES SEA

Alor Atauro Wetar Leti
Islands Island Islands

Babar
Islands

Tanimbar
Islands

Sumbawa Komodo

ARAFURA SEA

10°S

Solor
Flores Islands

DILI

TIMOR-LESTE

**Komodo National
Park (Indonesia)**
Idyllic beaches, beautiful diving
and komodo dragons (p238)

SAWU SEA

West
Timor

TIMOR SEA

Sumba

Sawu Rote

120°E

AUSTRALIA

140°E

Southeast Asia's
Top 20

Temples of Angkor (Cambodia)

1 One of the world's most magnificent sights, the temples of Angkor (p94) are so much better than the superlatives. Angkor Wat is the world's largest religious building; Bayon is the world's weirdest spiritual monument with its immense four-sided stone faces; and at Ta Prohm nature has run amok. Siem Reap is the base to explore this collection of temples and is a buzzing destination with superb restaurants and bars. Beyond the temples are cultural attractions, such as floating villages and cooking classes. Bayon (p98)

Bali (Indonesia)

2 Indonesia's 17,000 islands may offer myriad cultural and exploration adventures, but the one island not to miss is Bali (p191). The original backpackers' haven, you can surf epic breaks by day and rub shoulders with supermodels at legendary clubs by night. With one of Southeast Asia's richest cultures, Bali also offers a chance to escape party glitz and stay in a family homestay in and around the arts centre of Ubud, where the sounds of traditional dance and music echo over the rice fields at night. Legian Beach (p195)

Luang Prabang (Laos)

3 Hemmed in by the Mekong and Nam Khan rivers, this ancient city boasts history, religious devotion and natural beauty. Once a royal capital, Luang Prabang (p330) is populated by temples and Buddhist monks on their morning alms routes. In between are forested river views and world-class French cuisine. Hire a bike and explore the backstreets, take a cooking workshop or elephant trek, or just ease back with a restful massage at one of a dozen affordable spas. Prepare to adjust your timetable and stay a little longer than planned. Wat Xieng Thong (p332)

Bangkok (Thailand)

4 This superstar city (p645) has it all in super-sized proportions: food, shopping, fun and then some... It might be a pressure cooker for new arrivals, but it will be a needed dose of civilisation after weeks of dusty back roads. Build in plenty of time to load up on souvenirs, refresh your wardrobe, be plucked and kneaded, and recount tall tales over a sweaty bottle of beer. Don't forget a sunset river ferry ride, an evening noodle tour of Chinatown and one final round of temple spotting.

Halong Bay (Vietnam)

5 More than 3000 limestone-peaked islands sheltered by shimmering seas make Halong Bay (p832) one of Vietnam's top tourist draws as well as a Unesco World Heritage Site. An overnight cruise allows you to adore the scenery through the day's dramatic changes of light: rise early for an ethereal misty morn, kayak into the tidal-carved grottoes and lagoons and track the pastel parade of the sinking sun. If you're still hankering for more karst action, move on to less touristy Lan Ha Bay (p833).

BRIAN RAISBECK/GETTY IMAGES ©

Ko Tao (Thailand)

6 The dive-master's island, Ko Tao (p751) is the cheapest and easiest spot to learn how to strap on a tank and dive into the deep. The water is warm and gentle and the spectacles are not to be missed. Just offshore are rocky coves and coral reefs frequented by all manner of fish, providing a snorkelling aperitif. Its small size means that the island is a diving 'university', with a lively social scene after class. There's also free-diving if you're too cool for tanks.

AAR STUDIO/GETTY IMAGES ©

Chiang Mai (Thailand)

7 Bestowed with charm, Chiang Mai (p685) is a cultural and artistic magnet for Thais and tourists alike. The old city is framed by a time-preserving moat and is chock-a-block with antique teak temples displaying northern Thailand's distinct art and architecture. It is one of Asia's most liveable places where visitors come to study language, massage, meditation or just chat with a monk for a bit. Guarding the city is Doi Suthep, a sacred peak bejewelled with a temple, and beyond the city limits are high-altitude valleys, hill-tribe treks and mountain vistas. Wat Phra That Doi Suthep (p689)

Hoi An (Vietnam)

8 Antique Hoi An (p862) was once Vietnam's most cosmopolitan port, as evidenced by the genteel shophouses that survive today. These have been repurposed into modern-day businesses: gourmet restaurants, hip bars and cafes, quirky boutiques and expert tailors. This is a sightseeing city offering historical wanderings through the warrens of the Old Town, religious exultation in grandiose pagodas, and cooking courses to transform you into a knowledgeable chef. Wash off the hot day at nearby An Bang beach (p867).

KIMBERLEY COOLE/GETTY IMAGES ©

ANDERS BLOMQVIST/GETTY IMAGES ©

HOLGER LEUE/GETTY IMAGES ©

LAURIE NOBLE/GETTY IMAGES ©

KIMBERLEY COOLE/GETTY IMAGES ©

Kuching (Malaysia)

9 Borneo's most stylish and sophisticated city (p450) brings together an atmospheric old town, romantic waterfront, fine cuisine for all budgets and chic nightspots that would be right at home in London. But the city's biggest draw is what's nearby: some of Sarawak's finest natural sights that are easy to visit on day trips. You can spot orang-utans or search out a giant *Rafflesia* flower in the morning, or look for proboscis monkeys and wild crocs on a sundown cruise in the South China Sea. Finish off the evening by dining on fresh seafood or crunchy *midin* (jungle fern tips).
Semenggoh Wildlife Centre (p458)

Penang (Malaysia)

10 The colonial Southeast Asian experience is still tangible on this steamy port island (p405) where Malaysian, Chinese, Indian and British cultures collide. The capital of Georgetown has been designated a Unesco World Heritage Site and the once-tumbledown Chinese shophouses, clan houses and colonial buildings are being painted and primped up. Wander a maze of streets where joss smoke and the call to prayer mingle with Bollywood tunes and fragrant street food on every corner. Outside the city are beaches, jungles and endless shopping malls.
Georgetown (p406)

Si Phan Don (Laos)

11 The Mekong River sheds its characteristic muddy hue for a more tropical turquoise blue as it eddies around four thousand islands, known collectively as Si Phan Don (p365). This is Laos at its most quintessential: a sleepy, riverside idyll. The villages host a whole lot of hammock hanging as well as meandering cycling trips and late-night carousing. Kayakers and tubers take to the water, giving this hang-out haven a bit of a pulse. And the rare Irrawaddy dolphin makes seasonal appearances. Don Det (p367)

Bagan (Myanmar)

12 More than 4000 Buddhist temples are scattered across the plains of Bagan (p522), the site of the first Burmese kingdom and an architectural complement to the temples of Angkor. Dating to between the 11th and 13th centuries, the vast majority have been renovated, as Bagan remains an active religious site and place of pilgrimage. Yes, there are tour buses and crowds at the most popular sunset-viewing spots, but they can be avoided. Pedal off on a bike and have your own adventure amid the not-so-ruined temples.

Inle Lake (Myanmar)

13 Surrounded by an enormous carpet of greenery, Inle Lake (p503) is so awe-inspiring and large that everybody comes away with a different experience. If you're counting days, you'll most likely be hitting the hot spots: water-bound temples, shore-bound markets and floating gardens. If you have more time, you can consider day hikes or exploring the more remote corners of the lake. The cool weather, friendly folks and that placid pool of inklike water are bound to find a permanent place in your memory.

JOHNNY HAGLUND/GETTY IMAGES ©

AWL IMAGES/GETTY IMAGES ©

KIMBERLEY COOLE/GETTY IMAGES ©

ANDERS BLOMQVIST/GETTY IMAGES ©

Singapore

14 This small city-state (p613) excels in the art of 'multi-culti' cuisine served in the approachable hawker centres. Over the generations, descendants from China, Malaysia, Indonesia and India joined their cooking pots, importing, creating and tweaking dishes from their homelands. In between meals visit Gardens by the Bay, a plant conservatory without Victorian-era stuffiness, or Baba House, a restored Straits-Chinese home that provides a free history and culture lesson surprisingly crowd-free. If a couple of hours have passed, it is time for another meal. Gardens by the Bay (p615)

Gunung Mulu National Park (Malaysia)

15 From caves to karsts, this Unesco World Heritage park (p466) packs in many spectacular sights. The caves are like subterranean cathedrals with ribbed walls and calcified sculptures and were once classified as the world's largest cave passages but have lost out to a new discovery in Vietnam. In the evenings, swarming clouds of bats escape from the cave's mouth for the day's hunt. Then there are rainforest treks to the razorlike pinnacles and canopy skywalks. Make your reservations in advance during the European summer months.

Palawan (Philippines)

16 Rugged and remote, Palawan (p596) has sky-rocketed in popularity as travel magazines rush to add it to their lists of the world's best islands. The crown jewel is the Bacuit Archipelago (p599) near El Nido, a surreal seascape of brooding limestone cliffs where you can kayak among sea turtles. Further south, the heavenly beaches of Port Barton and Sabang beckon. To the north, make the eerie descent to the sunken Japanese ships in Coron Bay. Overnight island-hopping trips around Coron or El Nido are unbeatable.

Ifugao Rice Terraces (Philippines)

17 These incredible terraces (p567) were hand-hewn centuries ago by the Ifugao tribe in the remote Cordillera mountains of the northern Philippines. The result was arable land where there had been only vertical impediments. Referred to as one of the wonders of the world, the rice terraces ring the towns of Banaue and Batad, but adventurous travellers will find terraces ribbing most of the spiny Cordillera – and sleeping among them in idyllic Batad – is an experience not to be missed.

TROPICALPIX/GETTY IMAGES ©

LAURIE NOBLE/GETTY IMAGES ©

18

19

20

Phnom Penh (Cambodia)

18 The Cambodian capital (p68) is the 'phoenix risen' of modern-day history, signalled by the onset of urban chaos (a regional speciality) and influx of urbane businesses (watch out Bangkok). Its beautiful riverfront is an enclave for welcoming designer restaurants, funky bars and hip hotels. Meanwhile the atrocities of the Khmer Rouge regime – remembered at the inspiring National Museum and the depressing Tuol Sleng Museum – require an emotional sense of adventure and historical civic duty.

National Museum of Cambodia (p69)

Atauro Island (Timor-Leste)

19 Get a group together, hire a dive boat and head to the incredible dive sites of Atauro (p799). The diving in Timor-Leste is world class, thanks to a perfect mix of cool, deep water, undamaged reefs, under-fished marine life and its prime location in the Coral Triangle. Atauro, some 30km off the coast of Dili, has strong tides (you'll be drift diving) and is one of the few places you can dive and spot small reef-dwelling creatures as well as large pelagic creatures including turtles, hammerhead sharks, whales and dolphins.

Komodo National Park (Indonesia)

20 More than 5000 namesake dragons stalk the arid beaches of Komodo National Park (p238), a Unesco World Heritage Centre, looking menacing for camera-toting tourists. These pre-historic-looking creatures are found nowhere else on the planet. Park trips are best arranged from nearby Labuanbajo on the volcano-studded island of Flores. This is the next 'it' spot in Indo with half a dozen nearby islands with beaches of varying hues (including the rare pink beach), near-shore diving and snorkelling and a cool, ditch-the-watch vibe.

Need to Know

For more information, see Survival Guide (p929)

Planes
Affordable flights for Indonesian island-hopping or cutting out long-haul buses.

Buses
The region's primary intra-country mode of travel; reliability and road conditions vary.

Trains
Slow but scenic alternative to buses for some destinations.

Ferries
Services connect islands and archipelago nations; quality and safety varies.

Bikes
Motor or cycle; easy and convenient for in-town travel.

Cars
Rentals available in most tourist towns, though road rules are confusing; better to hire a driver.

Local Transport
Taxis and chartered vehicles plentiful; bargain before climbing aboard.

When to Go

Hanoi
GO Dec–May

Bangkok
GO Nov–Mar

Boracay
GO Jan–Sep

Ko Tao
GO Dec–Sep

Kuching
GO Jun–Sep

Bali
GO Apr–Aug

Tropical climate, rain year round
Tropical climate, wet & dry seasons
Highland areas, warm summers, cool winters

High Season
(Jun–Aug & Dec–Feb)
➡ Dry, cool
➡ Chilly in mountains
➡ Travel is difficult during Tet in Vietnam
➡ Rain in Indonesia

Shoulder
(Mar & Nov)
➡ Hot, dry season begins in March
➡ Dry season begins in Indonesia (Apr–May)

Low Season
(Apr–Jun & Sep–Oct)
➡ Travel difficult for April's water festivals
➡ Easter festivities in the Philippines
➡ Wet season (Sep–Oct); flooding, typhoons, transport cancellations
➡ Indonesia's dry season

Useful Websites

Lonely Planet (www.lonelyplanet.com) Read country profiles, post questions to the traveller community on the Thorn Tree forum and make travel reservations.

CNN Travel (travel.cnn.com/asia) Travel trends, news and top 10 lists.

Agoda (www.agoda.com) Regional online hotel booking site.

Asia Times (www.atimes.com) In-depth analysis of current events in Southeast Asia.

Time Zones

GMT+ 6hr Myanmar

GMT+ 7hr Thailand, Cambodia, Vietnam, Laos, parts of Indonesia (Sumatra, Java, and west and central Kalimantan)

GMT+ 8hr Malaysia, Singapore, Brunei, Philippines, parts of Indonesia (Bali, Nusa Tenggara, south and east Kalimantan and Sulawesi)

GMT+ 9hr Timor-Leste, parts of Indonesia (Irian Jaya, Maluku)

Money

Each country has its own currency. ATMs are widely available in most of mainland Southeast Asia and the Philippines. ATMs are limited to major cities in Indonesia, Laos, Myanmar and Timor-Leste; stock up on local currency or have a supply of cash or travellers cheques before travelling to small towns or remote areas. Check with your bank to determine international withdrawal fees and to notify them of your travel plans.

Daily Costs

**Budget:
less than US$50**

➡ Cheap guesthouse US$10–20

➡ Local meal or street eats US$1–5

➡ Local transport US$1–5

➡ Beer US$1–5

**Midrange:
US$50–100**

➡ Hotel room US$21–75

➡ Restaurant meal US$6–10

➡ Motorcycle hire US$6–10

**Top end:
more than US$100**

➡ Boutique hotel or beach resort US$100+

➡ Dive trip US$50–100

➡ Car hire US$50

Visas

Visas on arrival in Cambodia, Laos, Thailand, Indonesia, Philippines and Timor-Leste. Most arrival visas are valid for about a month, though there are exceptions. Travel with a ready supply of passport photos for visa applications.

Verify that the border offers arrival visas; some land and sea borders do not.

You must arrange visas prior to arrival for Vietnam and Myanmar.

Be aware that overland border crossings are often fraught with minor rip-offs.

Staying in Touch

Most of Southeast Asia is globally wired with modern communication technologies, including internet cafes, wi-fi networks and some 3G capabilities. Tourist centres have more options, better rates and faster connectivity than remote villages.

Mobile Phones Local, pre-paid SIM cards and mobile phones are available throughout the region. International roaming is prohibitively expensive.

Wi-fi & Internet Access Internet cafes are common in tourist centres and wi-fi is often free in guesthouses in some countries. 3G networks common in large cities.

Calling Home International calling rates are fairly affordable. To call home on a mobile phone, dial an international access code + country code + subscriber number. Internet cafes are often equipped with headsets and Skype as an alternative. With mobile wireless capability, you can also make Skype calls from a mobile phone.

Arriving In...

Suvarnabhumi International Airport (Bangkok, Thailand) Taxis (one hour) and rail (15 to 30 minutes) to the centre

Kuala Lumpur International Airport (Kuala Lumpur, Malaysia) KLIA Ekspres rail (15 minutes) to centre

Soekarno-Hatta International Airport (Jakarta, Indonesia) Taxis and buses (one hour) to centre

For much more on **getting around**, see p940

First Time Southeast Asia

For more information, see Survival Guide (p929)

Checklist

➡ Make sure your passport is valid for at least six months past your arrival date.

➡ Apply for an extended visa if visiting a country for longer than the standard visa allows.

➡ Organise travel insurance, diver's insurance and international driving permit.

➡ Visit a doctor for check-up and suggested vaccines.

➡ Inform your bank and credit-card provider of your travel plans.

What to Pack

➡ A week's worth of lightweight clothes

➡ Rain gear (jacket, breathable poncho, dry pack for electronics)

➡ Comfortable sandals

➡ Earplugs

➡ Medicine/first aid kit

➡ USB drive

➡ GSM mobile phone

➡ Refillable water bottle

➡ Sunscreen and heavy-duty deodorant

Top Tips for Your Trip

➡ Know the scams: border crossings, dodgy transport, touts.

➡ Be prepared for crazy driving; pedestrians have no rights.

➡ Most supplies (mosquito repellent, umbrella) can be bought locally.

➡ Ladies, dare to wear more.

➡ Take digital pictures of important documents and cards in case of theft or loss.

➡ Know your passwords! Extra security measures will be triggered by your new location.

➡ Carry your valuables in a waist pack to prevent theft; keep them secure on overnight journeys, in dorms and in rooms with insufficient locks.

➡ Pay for accommodation first thing in the morning, or the night before if you have an early morning departure.

What to Wear

In general, lightweight, loose-fitting clothes will be the most comfortable options. Bring a jacket for cool temperatures in the mountains and overly air-conditioned buses. Wear clothes that cover to your elbows and knees for visits to temples and rural villages.

Sleeping

➡ **Hotels** From snazzy to stodgy, hotels have modern amenities (refrigerators, TVs, air-con) and private bathrooms.

➡ **Guesthouses** These backpacker faves have a range of rooms from basic to plush and loads of local information.

➡ **Homestays** Live like a villager in a family home; simple set-up but a cultural immersion.

➡ **Hostels** Dormitories provide cheap and social lodging for solo travellers. Amenities sometimes include pool, restaurant or hang-out space.

Money

Most businesses deal only in cash. You can withdraw cash (in the local currency) directly from your home account through local ATMs. Have a mix of cash and travellers cheques as back-up. Currency exchanges accept US dollars, Australian dollars, British pounds and the euro.

➡ Keep your money in a money belt worn on your person.

➡ Don't use your ATM card for point-of-sale purchases.

➡ Determine your bank's fee system for overseas banking and obtain a 24-hour international customer-service phone number in case of card loss or theft.

➡ Monitor credit-card activity to avoid missing payments and to protect against fraudulent charges.

➡ Bring cash in crisp, untorn bills. Some money changers will reject old or ripped bills.

➡ Get travellers cheques in large denominations (US$100 or US$50) to avoid per cheque commissions and record which cheques you've cashed to protect against theft or loss.

For more information, see p935.

Bargaining

It is acceptable to bargain for goods and services when there isn't a posted price. You can't bargain for food, at shopping malls or wherever a price is posted.

Tipping

Tipping is not standard, but it is appreciated as wages are very low. Always buy your guide lunch plus add a little extra at the end.

Etiquette

➡ **Modesty** Though fashions are changing in the cities, modesty is still important in traditional areas, especially Muslim-dominated places. Avoid baring too much skin in general and no topless sunbathing. Cover up when visiting religious buildings.

➡ **Taboos** Politics and religion are often sensitive topics. Always treat both with deference and avoid being critical. Many Southeast Asian cultures are superstitious; it is wise to learn about these beliefs and act accordingly. Muslims don't drink alcohol or eat pork. Women shouldn't touch Buddhist monks or their belongings.

➡ **Save Face** Southeast Asians, especially Buddhist cultures, place a high value on harmonious social interactions. Don't get visibly angry, raise your voice or get into an argument – it will cause you and the other person embarrassment. When in doubt, smile.

➡ **Take Off Your Shoes** When entering a private home, religious building and certain businesses. If there is a pile of shoes at the door, it means you're entering a shoe-free zone.

Language

Towns are well-stocked with English speakers, though bus drivers, market vendors and taxi drivers tend to be less fluent. Thailand, Laos, Cambodia and Myanmar have their own script. Learn to say hello, thank you and how much in each language. Counting is also helpful. If you like taking pictures of people, learn how to ask their permission.

JUDY BELLAH/GETTY IMAGES ©

Hoi An (p862), Vietnam

If You Like...

Fabulous Food

Bangkok (Thailand) Food glorious food! Fresh, tasty meals are everywhere in this 24-hour grazing city (p662)

Hanoi (Vietnam) Be an urban forager among Hanoi's rice and noodle stalls (p823)

Luang Prabang (Laos) Cafes and bakeries with a French flair preserve a delicious colonial connection (p335)

Chiang Mai (Thailand) Learn how to slice and dice like the Thai wok masters at a cooking school (p690)

Singapore Savour Asia old and new, from 50-year-old chicken-rice stalls to swish international outposts (p631)

Penang (Malaysia) Malaysia's multi-culti melting pot is an edible journey through Indian curries, Chinese dim sum and Malay desserts (p409)

Temples, Tombs & Towers

Angkor (Cambodia) An architectural wonder of the world built by the great Khmer empire (p85)

Bagan (Myanmar) Hundreds of ancient temples stretch out towards the horizon like a grazing herd (p522)

Borobudur (Indonesia) A stunning stupa ringed by mist and mountains (p179)

Wat Phra Kaew (Thailand) A dazzling royal temple and home to the revered Emerald Buddha (p645)

Ho Chi Minh Mausoleum (Vietnam) Come face to face with history in Ho Chi Minh's austere mausoleum (p818)

Shwedagon Paya (Myanmar) A golden hilltop temple that gleams with heavenly splendour (p483)

Petronas Towers (Malaysia) For superlative seekers, this skyscraper is one of the world's top 10 tallest buildings (p383)

Spectacular Treks

Sapa (Vietnam) Dirt paths wind through verdant rice terraces tended by ethnic minorities in this toothy mountain range (p840)

Nam Ha NPA (Laos) Eco-oriented treks through an old-growth forest and high-altitude hill-tribe villages (p347)

Cordillera Mountains (Philippines) Ancient hand-hewn rice terraces are carved into jagged mountains (p563)

Gunung Bromo (Indonesia) An active volcano hiked up at night for a sunrise view of its moonscape summit (p187)

Taman Negara National Park (Malaysia) Old-growth rainforest conveniently close to civilisation (p430)

Mt Kinabalu (Malaysia) Borneo's highest mountain is a two-day march to the sky (p440)

Gibbon Experience (Laos) Trek up to the canopy at this zipline course outfitted with tree-top lodging (p351)

Khao Yai National Park (Thailand) Wild patch of jungle close to Bangkok and filled with elephants, birds and monkeys (p721)

Kalaw (Myanmar) Follow the undulating landscape through forested hills and minority villages to lovely Inle Lake (p507)

Beautiful Beaches

Ko Pha-Ngan (Thailand) Full-on Full Moon parties and hammock-hanging on the original beach-bum island (p745)

Bali (Indonesia) Justifiably famous for its beach bliss, lush volcanic interior and colourful culture (p191)

Krabi/Railay (Thailand) Rock-climbers scale the karst cliffs, while kayakers slice the jewel-hued waters (p770)

Sihanoukville (Cambodia) Good times rule at Cambodia's premier seaside hang-out (p114)

Nha Trang (Vietnam) Plenty of R&R is available at this mainland beach city (p868)

(Above) Shwedagon Paya (p483), Yangon, Myanmar
(Below) Street food, Kuala Lumpur (p381), Malaysia

Mui Ne (Vietnam) Squeaky sands, towering dunes and kitesurfing galore (p874)

Boracay (Philippines) Party paradise in a small package (p576)

Gili Islands (Indonesia) A collection of three nonmotorised islands ranging from party to pastoral (p229)

Ko Lipe (Thailand) Backpackers claim one last roost before sliding across the Malaysian border (p775)

Diving & Snorkelling

Ko Tao (Thailand) Cheap dive certifications, shallow waters and year-round good conditions (p751)

Sipadan (Malaysia) Legendary 'Coral Triangle' with visiting turtles and large pelagics (p447)

Surin & Similan Islands National Marine Parks (Thailand) These Andaman islands are global faves visited on live-aboards, so start saving up (p762)

Pulau Weh (Indonesia) Experience drift, wreck and drop-off dives on a relaxed Sumatran island (p271)

Coron (Philippines) Sunken battleships, matey! (p601)

Togean Islands (Indonesia) Dive hot spot, with diverse reefs and fish aplenty (p284)

Pulau Perhentian (Malaysia) Low-key islands with near-shore pinnacle and shipwreck dives (p425)

> **IF YOU LIKE RIVERS & LAKES**
> ....
> Enjoy the liquid life on Si Phan Don (Laos; p364), Inle Lake (Myanmar; p503) and Vang Vieng (Laos; p325).

Month by Month

January

Peak tourist season; cool and dry weather in mainland Southeast Asia and Philippines. The east coast of the Malay peninsula (Samui Archipelago, Pulau Perhentian) and Indonesia are wet due to the northeast monsoon; low season on Bali.

✦ Ati-Atihan

The mother of all Filipino fiestas, Ati-Atihan celebrates Santo Niño (Infant Jesus) with colourful, Mardi Gras–like indigenous costumes and displays in Kalibo on the island of Panay.

✦ Prophet Mohammed's Birthday

The birthday of Islam's holy prophet is celebrated in the third month of the lunar-based Islamic calendar (January 2015, December 2016) with religious prayers and processions.

✦ Myanmar's Independence Day

The end of colonial rule in Burma is celebrated as a national holiday on 4 January.

✦ Sultan of Brunei's Birthday

Colourful official ceremonies are held on 15 January to mark the birthday of Sultan Hassanal Bolkiah.

February

Peak season continues on mainland Southeast Asia and the beaches are abuzz with snowbirds. The east coast of the Malay peninsula starts to dry as the rains move east; still raining in Bali.

✦ Tet

Vietnam's lunar New Year (sometimes occurring in late January) is the country's biggest holiday and coincides with Chinese New Year. The festival recognises the first day of spring and involves family reunions, ancestor worship, exchanges of presents and lots of all-night luck-inducing noise. Travel is difficult and businesses close.

✦ Chinese New Year

This lunar festival (sometimes occurring in January) is celebrated in Chinese-dominated towns. In Penang, it's a family affair and businesses close for one to two weeks. In Bangkok, Singapore, Phnom Penh and Kuching, there are dragon-dancing parades, food festivities, fireworks and noise.

✦ Bun Pha Wet

This Lao-Buddhist festival commemorates the story of the Buddha-to-be (Prince Vessantara or Pha Wet). It is considered an auspicious time to enter the monastery.

LUNAR CALENDAR
....

Buddhist and Hindu religious festivals follow the lunar calendar so dates vary each year, typically within a two-week period. Muslim holidays are pegged to the Islamic calendar; dates move forward about 11 days each year.

Makha Bucha

One of three Buddhist holy days, Makha Bucha falls on the full moon of the third lunar month and commemorates Buddha preaching to 1250 enlightened monks who came to hear him 'without prior summons'.

March

Mainland Southeast Asia is hot and dry and the beaches start to empty out. The winds kick up, ushering in kiteboarding season. The northwest monsoon rains are subsiding to afternoon showers in Bali.

Nyepi

Bali's 'day of silence' is marked by fasting and mediation; businesses and beach access close. The next day is New Year's Day, welcomed with night-time racket.

Easter Week

A Christian holiday (sometimes in April) is observed in the Philippines, Vietnam, Indonesia, Melaka and Timor-Leste. Holy Week (Semana Santa) in the Philippines starts on the Wednesday prior to Easter Sunday; Spanish-influenced observances, such as fasting, rituals of penance and church attendance, ensue.

April

The hottest time of year in mainland Southeast Asia makes inland sightseeing a chore. Buddhist countries (except Vietnam) celebrate their traditional New Year; make transport reservations in advance, as everyone is going somewhere else. Good shoulder season in Bali.

(Above) Dragon dance, Chinese New Year (p629), Singapore
(Below) Buddhist monks, Bun Pha That Luang festival (p319), Vientiane

✿ Buddhist New Year/Water Festival

In mid-April, Buddhist countries celebrate their lunar New Year with water-throwing and religious observances.

✿ Vietnamese Liberation Day

The day US troops withdrew from Saigon (30 April) as North Vietnamese forces entered the city. Also called reunification day and less complimentary names by overseas Vietnamese.

✿ Hué Festival (Biennial)

Vietnam's biggest cultural event is held every two years (2016, 2018...). Art, theatre, music, circus and dance, including domestic and international acts, are held inside Hué's Citadel.

May

Still hot in mainland Southeast Asia but with an end in sight. May hosts preparations for the upcoming rains and the start of rice-planting season. There is spring-like weather in northern Vietnam, and Bali is not yet crowded.

✿ Royal Ploughing Ceremonies

In Thailand and Cambodia, this royal ceremony employs astrology and ancient Brahman rituals to kick off the rice-planting season.

✿ Rocket Festival

Villagers craft bamboo rockets and fire them into the sky to provoke rainfall for the rice harvest. Mainly celebrated in northeast Thailand and Laos; dates vary.

✿ Visaka Bucha

This Buddhist holy day falls on the 15th day of the waxing moon in the sixth lunar month and commemorates Buddha's birth, enlightenment and *parinibbana* (passing away). Activities centre around the temple.

✿ Independence Day (Timor-Leste)

One of the planet's youngest nations celebrates Independence Day (20 May) with cultural events and sporting competitions.

June

The southwest monsoon brings rain, usually an afternoon downpour, to most of mainland Southeast Asia and most parts of the Philippines. As summer in Europe and China approaches, there is another high season, especially in Bali.

✿ Gawai Dayak

The end of the rice-harvest season is celebrated the first two days of June in the Malaysian Borneo state of Sarawak. City-dwelling Dayaks return to their longhouses to socialise, eat and down shots of *tuak* (rice wine).

✿ Rainforest World Music

Sarawak (Malaysian Borneo) celebrates tribal music from around the world during this three-day music festival.

✿ Ramadan

The Muslim fasting month is observed in Malaysia, Indonesia, Brunei and parts of southern Thailand in the ninth month of the Islamic calendar (June to July 2015 and 2016). Muslims abstain

from food, drink, cigarettes and sex between sunrise and sunset. Idul Fitri marks the end of Ramadan.

July

Mainland Southeast Asia prepares for Buddhist Lent, a period of meditation that coincides with the rainy season (southwest monsoon). Despite the drizzle, this is an ideal time for rural sightseeing as rice planting begins. The Samui Archipelago often stays dry during the southwest monsoon.

✿ Asanha Bucha

The full moon of the eighth lunar month commemorates Buddha's first sermon.

✿ Khao Phansaa

Marking the rainy season, Buddhist monks retreat into monasteries. This is the traditional time for young men to be ordained. Worshippers offer candles and donations to the temples.

August

Mini high season still in effect during Europe and China's summer holiday period. Afternoon showers in most of mainland Southeast Asia; a few all-day soakers. Weather in Indonesia (especially Bali) is just right.

✿ Independence Day (Indonesia)

The country celebrates its liberation on 17 August with large parades in Jakarta.

✿ HM the Queen's Birthday

Thailand wishes its queen a happy birthday on 12

August. The day is also recognised as Mother's Day.

September

One of the wettest parts of the wet season for mainland Southeast Asia, when flooding and boat cancellations are common. Occasional typhoons sweep in across Vietnam and the Philippines, wreaking havoc. Shoulder season in Bali.

🎊 Pchum Ben

In Cambodia, respects are paid to the dead through temple offerings. Many Khmers visit their home villages and try to pack in seven temples in seven days. Sometimes celebrated in October.

October

Mainland Southeast Asia prepares for the end of the rainy season and the end of Buddhist Lent. The northeast monsoon (which affects the east coast of the Malay peninsula and Indonesia) begins. Bali has occasional showers.

🎊 Festival of the Nine Emperor Gods

In Thailand, this Taoist event is called the Vegetarian Festival, marked by abstinence from meat and other purification rituals. The most extreme is Phuket's parade of entranced and pierced worshippers. Variations occur in Singapore, Malaysia and Myanmar.

🎊 Ork Phansaa

The end of Buddhist Lent occurs three lunar months after Khao Phansaa. Merit-makers present new robes to the monks. The Mekong River's mysterious 'naga fireballs' coincides with Ork Phansaa. Localities in Thailand and Laos celebrate with traditional longtail boat races.

🎊 Islamic New Year

This lunar New Year (known as Awal Muharram) in Indonesia and Malaysia is marked by fasting, self-reflection and commemoration of the martyrdom of Hussein ibn Ali.

November

Early in the month is a shoulder season in mainland Southeast Asia, with cool, dry days and a lush landscape. In northern altitudes there are chilly nightly temperatures. The east coast of the Malay peninsula and Indonesia are in the midst of the rainy season.

🎊 Bon Om Tuk

This Cambodian festival (sometimes in October) celebrates Jayavarman VII's victory over the Chams in 1177 and the reversal of the Tonlé Sap river. Boat races stir local patriotism, with huge crowds descending on Phnom Penh. A smaller event takes place in Siem Reap.

🎊 Deepavali

The most important festival in the Hindu calendar is this festival of lights that celebrates the triumph of good over evil. Tiny oil lamps are ceremoniously lit in Malaysia. Singapore's Little India hosts public festivities. Sometimes occurs in October.

🎊 Loi Krathong

During November's full moon, Thais launch banana-leaf boats decorated with candles in honour of the river goddess. In Chiang Mai, floating paper lanterns are made as offerings as well. A similar tradition is practised in the Shan State of Myanmar during the fire-balloon competitions in Taunggyi.

🎊 Bun Pha That Luang

Laos pays tribute to its iconic stupa in Vientiane with a weeklong festival coinciding with the full moon.

December

This is mainland Southeast Asia's busiest tourism season and the weather is fine. Rain is tapering off in the Samui Archipelago but still in effect in Bali.

🎊 Christmas

Most of the region has adopted Christmas in some form, but for Catholic communities in the Philippines, Timor-Leste, Indonesia and Vietnam, it is a serious business with important religious services and ceremonies.

🎊 Lao National Day

This 2 December holiday celebrates the 1975 victory over the monarchy and the establishment of the Lao People's Democratic Republic.

🎊 HM the King's Birthday

This Thai holiday (5 December) hosts parades and merit-making events in honour of the king; it is also recognised as Father's Day.

Plan Your Trip
Itineraries

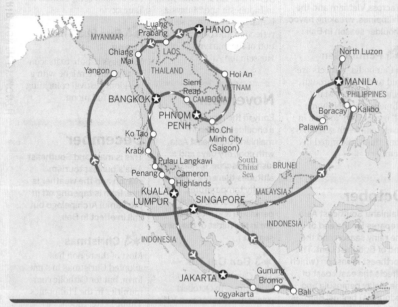

The Best of Southeast Asia

This 'sampler plate' of Southeast Asia will have you jetting between countries to hit the highlights: cool cities, ancient kingdoms, beautiful beaches and smoldering volcanoes.

Most international airlines fly to **Bangkok**, a chaotic but fantastic city filled with fun and food. Take the direct bus to **Siem Reap** to see Angkor's magnificent temples. Bus to charming **Phnom Penh** to study Cambodia's tragic not-so-distant past and on to Vietnam's bustling **Ho Chi Minh City**, a study in resiliency. Work your way north with a stop in adorable **Hoi An**, for bespoke fashions and atmospheric strolls, and on to the antique streets of **Hanoi**. Air-lift out of Vietnam to laid-back **Luang Prabang**, Laos' world-heritage city filled with temples and French colonial fragments, and then fly to chic **Chiang Mai** for elephant and hill-tribe adventures, Thai cooking courses and loads of temple-spotting.

Return to Bangkok (plane, train or bus) and work your way south to **Ko Tao** to learn how to dive before hitting the

Tea estate, Cameron Highlands (p400), Malaysia

seaside rock-climbing retreat of **Krabi** and other beachy hotspots, such as Ko Phi Phi, Ko Lanta and Ko Lipe, on Thailand's Andaman coast. Scoot across the border from Ko Lipe to Malaysia's **Pulau Langkawi** – high season only. Then take the ferry to the foodie's paradise of **Penang** and overland to Malaysia's multi-ethnic capital **Kuala Lumpur** with a stop in the green-tea plantations of the **Cameron Highlands**.

Catch a flight from Kuala Lumpur to **Jakarta**, Indonesia's capital, and soak up Java's renowned culture in **Yogyakarta**.

Then bus to **Gunung Bromo**, an active volcano, visited on pre-dawn hikes for sunrise summits. Leapfrog to **Bali** for sun, fun and the island's unique Hindu culture.

Catch a cheap flight to sophisticated **Singapore**, which has air connections to everywhere else, including Myanmar's **Yangon**, where you can explore the temples and villages of this formerly cloistered country. Or fly from Singapore to **Kalibo** (Philippines), then bask on **Boracay's** party beaches, transit through **Manila** to trek the rice terraces of **North Luzon** or just chill on the rustic beaches of **Palawan**.

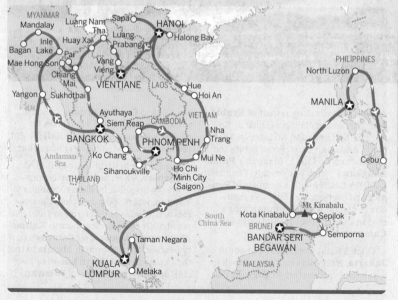

Mainland to Borneo & Philippines

8 WEEKS

Cruise around mainland Southeast Asia, hitting the beaches and the highlands, and then bound over to Borneo and the Philippines to climb into the heavens and dive under the sea.

From **Bangkok**, head to **Ko Chang** and then slide into **Sihanoukville** for lots of sand and suds. Scoot to shabby-chic **Phnom Penh**. Adore the architectural wonder of the Angkor temples from the base town of **Siem Reap**. Fly to full-throttle **Ho Chi Minh City**. Migrate to the beaches of **Mui Ne** or **Nha Trang**, the antique city of **Hoi An** and imperial **Hue**. Rest in **Hanoi**, a mature, manicured capital. Cruise karst-filled **Halong Bay** and detour to **Sapa** and its highland communities of ethnic minorities. Return to Hanoi.

Fly to **Vientiane** (Laos), bus to **Vang Vieng** and on to **Luang Prabang**, a riverside city. Continue to the trekking centre of **Luang Nam Tha**. Ride the Mekong River south to the Laos–Thailand border at **Huay Xai**.

Slide into **Chiang Mai**. Escape to the mountains of **Pai** or **Mae Hong Son** for stunning mountain vistas and intriguing border cultures. Return to the lowlands for the ancient Thai capitals at **Sukhothai** and **Ayuthaya** before returning to **Bangkok**.

Fly to Myanmar's **Yangon** and continue to the island monasteries of **Inle Lake**, the ancient capital of **Mandalay** and the ruins of **Bagan**.

From Yangon, fly to **Kuala Lumpur**. Explore **Taman Negara**, an ancient wilderness. Cruise through **Melaka**, a colonial port of call. Return to KL for a well-planned, well-funded tour of Malaysian Borneo. Fly to **Kota Kinabalu**, Sabah, and ascend **Mt Kinabalu**, Borneo's highest peak. Head east to **Sepilok**'s orangutan sanctuary. Swing over to **Semporna**, the gateway to dive sites. Culture vultures: detour to oil-rich Brunei and its unassuming capital, **Bandar Seri Begawan** (BSB), surrounded by pristine rainforests and water villages.

Cheap flights link Kota Kinabalu with **Manila** (Philippines). Bus to the mountains of **North Luzon**, then fly to **Cebu**, gateway to the Visayas beaches.

Top: Mt Kinabalu (p440), Malaysia
Bottom: Beach at Boracay (p576), Philippines

6 WEEKS — Mainland Beaches to Indonesia

PLAN YOUR TRIP ITINERARIES

Become a certified beach connoisseur by tracing the coastline of Thailand, Malaysia and Indonesia. In-between, grab a few slices of culture to keep things balanced.

From **Bangkok**, make a beeline for the islands in the Gulf of Thailand: dive-crazy **Ko Tao** and hippie **Ko Pha-Ngan**. Get certified on Tao, then follow the herd to the Andaman coast. **Khao Lak** is the base for live-aboard dive trips to the world-class Surin and Similan islands. Skip down to adrenalin-charged **Krabi**, home to rock climbing and cave exploring, and then island-hop to Rasta-vibed **Ko Lipe**. Cross the border at **Pulau Langkawi** for **Penang**'s famous hawker centres.

From Penang, bus to **Kota Bharu**, the jumping-off point for the fabulous jungle islands of **Pulau Perhentian**. Head south to **Mersing**, the mainland port for sleepy **Pulau Tioman**, before returning to civilisation in **Kuala Lumpur**, for flights to Indonesia.

From Indonesia's tip in **Medan**, on the island of Sumatra, visit the orang-utan outpost of **Bukit Lawang** and go volcano hiking in **Berastagi**. From Medan fly to lovely Banda Aceh for dive-tastic **Pulau Weh**.

Say goodbye to rugged Sumatra and buzz over to Java, touching down in **Jakarta**, Indonesia's intense capital. Cruise **Yogyakarta** and its culture trail. Day trip to the giant stupa of **Borobudur** or huff-and-puff up **Gunung Bromo** volcano for a sunrise spectacle.

Leapfrog to **Denpasar**, in Bali, to nuzzle the sandy beaches of the Bukit Peninsula or get cultured in Ubud. Party in **Gili Trawangan**, spot dragons on **Komodo** and go rustic on the beaches of **Flores**.

Check your visa and apply for an extension back in Denpasar before flying to **Makassar** on the island of Sulawesi. Pay your respects in **Tana Toraja**, where funeral rituals are ancient and bloody. Travel to the Togean Islands and the northern diving board of **Pulau Bunaken**; it might feel faraway, but it is worth it. Fly from **Manado** to Kuala Lumpur.

Alternatively, from Denpasar hop over to Timor-Leste's capital of **Dili** to tour old colonial towns and uncrowded reefs.

Top: Longtail boats, Ko Lipe (p775), Thailand
Bottom: Religious ceremony, Ubud (p208), Indonesia

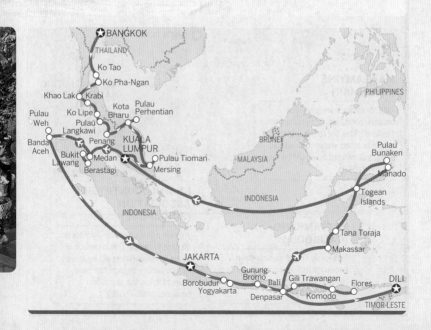

Off the Beaten Track: Southeast Asia

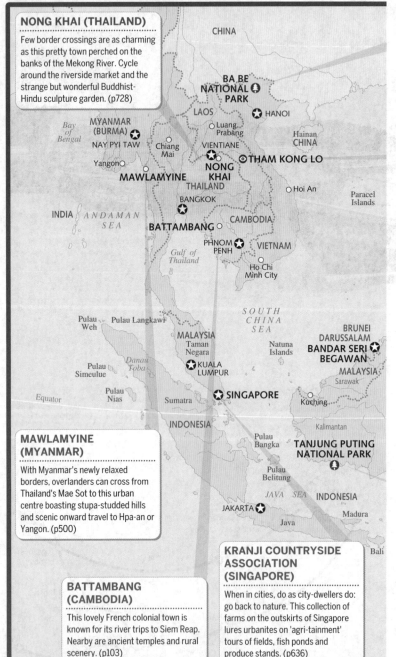

NONG KHAI (THAILAND)

Few border crossings are as charming as this pretty town perched on the banks of the Mekong River. Cycle around the riverside market and the strange but wonderful Buddhist-Hindu sculpture garden. (p728)

MAWLAMYINE (MYANMAR)

With Myanmar's newly relaxed borders, overlanders can cross from Thailand's Mae Sot to this urban centre boasting stupa-studded hills and scenic onward travel to Hpa-an or Yangon. (p500)

BATTAMBANG (CAMBODIA)

This lovely French colonial town is known for its river trips to Siem Reap. Nearby are ancient temples and rural scenery. (p103)

KRANJI COUNTRYSIDE ASSOCIATION (SINGAPORE)

When in cities, do as city-dwellers do: go back to nature. This collection of farms on the outskirts of Singapore lures urbanites on 'agri-tainment' tours of fields, fish ponds and produce stands. (p636)

N 0 ─── 500 km
0 ─── 300 miles

Tropic of Cancer

BA BE NATIONAL PARK (VIETNAM)

A stunning landscape of limestone mountains, sloping valleys, mist-shrouded lakes and evergreen forests provides a full dose of nature exploration. For a cultural hook, ethnic minorities host rustic homestays. (p837)

THAM KONG LO (LAOS)

A watery underworld awaits at this 7.5km-long cave explored by longtail boat. Daylight recedes as you putter deep into the darkness and bulbous-shaped calcified sculptures decorate the vaulted ceiling. (p353)

SIARGAO ISLAND (PHILIPPINES)

Famous for its surf break, this Catholic island in northern Mindanao is blessed with pretty coves, fine blonde beaches and laid-back villages. Nearby Camiguin has volcano hikes, reef dives and scenic wandering. (p593)

BANDAR SERI BEGAWAN (BRUNEI DARUSSALAM)

Shoestringers mistakenly assume that they can't afford to visit the capital of this oil-rich sultanate. But it is a modest and traditional city, kind to visitors of all budgets. (p53)

TAIWAN

O Banaue
Luzon
PHILIPPINE SEA
★ MANILA
Catanduanes
PHILIPPINES
Mindoro
Samar
Panay
Cebu
Bohol   SIARGAO
Palawan
SULU SEA   Mindanao
Mt
Kinabalu
(4095m)   · Jolo
PACIFIC
OCEAN
Sabah   · Tawi-Tawi
Talaud
Sangir
Islands   Morotai
CELEBES SEA
Waigeo
Togean Islands
Sula Islands
Sulawesi   SERAM SEA   Misool
Tana
Toraja   INDONESIA   Seram
Buru
Puncak Jaya   Papua
(5030m)
Butung (Buton)   Kai
Islands
Selayar   BANDA SEA   Aru
Islands
FLORES SEA   Wetar   Yos
Bali   Sudarso
Sea   SUMBAWA   ★ DILI   Tanimbar
Flores   Babar   Islands
Lombok   Islands   ARAFURA SEA
Sumba   TIMOR-LESTE
Sawu   TIMOR SEA
AUSTRALIA

PAPUA NEW GUINEA

SUMBAWA (INDONESIA)

Surfers brave the poor infrastructure and conservative Islamic culture for this island's year-round breaks. It is easy to get to from Lombok, but hard to get around. (p236)

TANJUNG PUTING NATIONAL PARK (INDONESIA)

Riverboats glide into a deep and dark Borneo jungle where orang-utans perch in the trees and fireflies light up the night. Join forces with other travellers to cut costs. (p275)

Pulau Langkawi (p413), Malaysia

Plan Your Trip

Big Adventures, Small Budget

You don't need to be a high-roller in Southeast Asia. In fact you can live like a pauper and still bask on beautiful beaches, visit magnificent temples and explore stunning landscapes. But you do need to watch your spending and plan wisely.

Planning & Costs

Planning Timeline

12 months before Calculate a trip budget and start saving.

6 months Pick which countries to visit, when and for how long.

6 to 4 weeks Get vaccinations and travel insurance.

4 weeks Start booking flights; make visa and passport arrangements.

2 weeks Reserve high-season transport and accommodation for popular destinations, live-aboard dive trips and Borneo trekking tours.

1 week Book accommodation for international arrival city; start packing.

Average Costs

Bottle of beer US$1–3

Long-distance bus ticket US$15–30

Food-stall meal US$2–5

Guesthouse bed US$10–25

Internet access per hour US$1–6

Domestic flight US$50–100

Admission to Angkor Wat US$20–60

Cooking course in Chiang Mai US$35

When to Go

The monsoon rains and peak tourist season are two factors determining how to plot your trip. You might also want to plan a trip around famous festivals or avoid public holidays when everything is closed or when the local population is on the move.

Monsoon Seasons

Southeast Asia is always hot and humid, but sometimes it is also hot, humid and wet. The region is affected by two monsoons. The southwest monsoon (June/July to September/October) brings rain to most of mainland Southeast Asia and the west coast of the Malay peninsula (Phuket and Langkawi). Following the rainy season, there is dry, cool weather (November to February) and then it turns hotter than usual (March to June). Most of the Philippines follows this same weather pattern, so steer clear of the country if there is a typhoon brewing; check Typhoon 2000 (www.typhoon2000.ph) before making travel plans.

The northeast monsoon starts in September, bringing rain to the east coast of the Malay peninsula (Ko Samui, Pulau Perhentian) and then migrating east through Indonesia, hitting Timor-Leste by December. In many parts of Indonesia, especially rainforest belts, it's a little rainy most of the year but less so from June to September.

Beaches & Islands

It is a fine art to hit the right beach at the right time: nice weather and not too many topless Western matrons. Shoulder seasons for the beaches usually bookend the rainy season (start and end), when there are short afternoon showers. Another shoulder season is the first few months of the hot, dry season when the natural air-conditioning of the ocean is a relief from harsh interior temperatures.

Best Times

March to May Hot, dry season; good for mainland Southeast Asia's beaches and both coasts of the Malay peninsula; Bali gets some rain, dries out by April.

October to November End of rainy season for mainland Southeast Asia and the west coast of the Malay peninsula (Phuket and friends); rainy on east coast of Malay peninsula and parts of Vietnamese coast.

September Dry season for Bali; Ko Samui and the east coast of the Malay peninsula turn soggy. Whale migration begins in Timor-Leste.

Times to Avoid

June to August High season in Bali and Ko Samui; great weather but crowded and expensive.

September to October Wettest months for mainland Southeast Asia and the west coast of the Malay peninsula (Phuket and friends). On small islands, hotels shut down and boat travel is interrupted by storms.

December to February Peak tourist season for mainland Southeast Asia and west coast of Malay peninsula. Some showers in Bali.

Surfing & Kiteboarding

When the weather is too crummy for sunbathing, it is just right for hanging ten. May to September brings prime swells to Indonesia's Lombok and Sumbawa, while Bali always has a good surf spot somewhere. In the Philippines surf season coincides with the typhoons (August to November). Good for beginners, Phuket has swells from April to September, and Cherating from November to March.

Kiteboarding is popular on Boracay (Philippines), the east and west coast of Thailand (Hua Hin and Phuket) and in Vietnam (Mui Ne). These beaches tend to have a long windy season through most of the year.

Diving

Diving depends on visibility and visibility depends on calm waters and storm-free days. Most diving locations have sub-par conditions during the rainy season. Luckily the double monsoon means that you'll find high visibility somewhere. The Gulf of Thailand can be dived most of the year.

Trekking

Rain, not temperature, is the primary consideration when planning a trekking trip.

Most of mainland Southeast Asia's forests are classified as deciduous, meaning they shed their leaves in an attempt to conserve water during the dry season. When the rains come, the forests spring to life, the rivers transform from sluggish troughs into watery bulldozers and remote roads are prone to flooding. Trekking is obviously at its best in the months following the rainy season when the forest is lush and flooding is not a concern.

The Malay peninsula and Indonesia get two monsoon seasons that feed their dense canopies. These equatorial forests are classified as tropical rainforests because they have a longer rainy season of at least nine months. In some cases the differences in seasons vary between a little rain and a lot of rain.

Kitesurfing, Mui Ne (p874), Vietnam

Best Times

November to February Just after the rainy season is ideal for mainland Southeast Asia; in higher elevations frost is possible. December to January is high season for international and domestic tourists.

April to June A shoulder season for Indonesia when the weather is drier.

Times to Avoid

September to October The wettest months of the southwest monsoon.

January to February The wettest months of the northeast monsoon.

June to August Peak tourist season.

Sightseeing

The ideal time to tour Southeast Asia's historic monuments and cities is when the weather is driest and coolest (relatively speaking). But the best weather also coincides with high season. The beginning of the rainy season is a recommendable shoulder season as rain is minimal and rural areas are busy with rice planting (a splendid sight). The hot months, especially

Gunung Mulu National Park (p466), Malaysia

for mainland Southeast Asia, make sightseeing difficult, as temperatures can climb as high as 40°C and humidity is stifling.

Best Times

November to February Cool and dry high season in mainland Southeast Asia.

June to August Beginning of rainy season in mainland Southeast Asia.

April to June Indonesia's driest months.

Times to Avoid

September to October/November Wettest part of the rainy season in mainland Southeast Asia.

March to June Hottest time of year in mainland Southeast Asia.

January to February Wettest part of the rainy season in Indonesia.

Budget Guide

Western currencies enjoy a favourable exchange rate in Southeast Asia, giving you greater purchasing power. The cost of living is also cheaper in Southeast Asia and shoestringers can skimp their way to a budget of about US$30 to US$40 a day. This covers the basics: food, shelter, local transport and a few beers. This budget will vary by country, the popularity of the destination and the time of year (high versus low season).

In addition to this base rate, factor in the costs of long-distance travel – by bus, boat or air. Add any special activities, such as diving, rock climbing, hill-tribe trekking or a sightseeing tour. Then allow for unexpected expenses, such as increased transport or accommodation costs due to holidays or needing to get somewhere in a hurry.

Accommodation costs occupy the largest portion of your budget and luckily the region is filled with simple lodging that charges simple prices. The more creature comforts (air-con, hot water, en suite) you can forsake, the more money you'll save.

Public transport within each country is generally affordable. Costs rise with boat and air travel and wherever road conditions are rough. Local public transport

Rice terraces (p567), Philippines

won't stretch the budget, but hiring private taxis is pricey. Getting around individual islands can often be expensive because of price-fixing or lack of competition. You can save on local transport costs if you know how to ride a motorbike before arriving. Much cheaper is bicycle hire, which is a lovely way to tour the region's towns and countryside.

Budget Tips

We posed the following question to our *Southeast Asia* authors: What is the cheapest place in which to have the best time in your country? Here are their answers:

Brunei Darussalam Tiny, oil-rich Brunei can be a great budget destination if you arrive by bus from Malaysian Borneo. Stay in a hostel (from US$7), dine in the open-air markets and tour the free cultural sights, national parks and opulent mosques.

Cambodia You can have a great, cheap time in Sihanoukville, where you can score dorm beds for around US$5 and a beer for US$0.50.

Indonesia Do Bali on the cheap by opting for an Ulu Watu homestay (US$16 to US$20). You can enjoy a surfer-chic scene and epic views with enough spare cash to wash it all down with several Bintangs.

Laos Muang Ngoi Neua is a great shoestring escape. It has towering karst cliffs, sleepy riverine character, cheap digs and scenic country walks. Si Phan Don (Four Thousand Islands) is the quintessential lotus-eating country: hammock-hanging, a happening traveller scene, laid-back island life, tubing down the river and dolphin-spotting.

Malaysia Pulau Perhentian is an awesome deal and has some of the cheapest diving in Asia, comparable to Ko Tao. Cherating is another budget-friendly beach. In pricey Malaysian Borneo, Kuching could accommodate shoestringers with inexpensive dorms (US$5) and national parks and beaches accessible via public transport (instead of expensive charter taxis).

Myanmar It is a little bit of a schlep, but Mrauk U is one of the country's best value spots. It is an ancient capital of temples and carvings that doesn't cost a fortune to visit and has fewer package tourists than Bagan.

Philippines A proliferation of budget flights is opening up the Philippines to backpackers. North Luzon and Palawan are inexpensive, off-the-beaten-track options. Sleep amid Batad's rice terraces or beach camp in Coron or El Nido.

Singapore You can't afford to be a high-flyer in Singapore on a budget, but you can soak up culture with the Singapore Symphony Orchestra's free concerts.

Thailand The budget impediments in Thailand are the beaches, which are decidedly upscale (rooms starting at US$25) and it is expensive to get around the islands. Ko Tao is still a cheap place for an open-water diving certificate. The east side of Ko Pha Ngan remains a bargain. On the Andaman side, Railay still has cheap digs.

Timor-Leste Getting to the beaches can be slow (on public transport) or expensive (in private transport). Instead catch a *microlet* (local bus) heading to Liquica (US$1) and hop off at the rocky point near the Pope's monument. Welcome to Dili Rock West. There's no need for a boat, just jump in with your snorkel to see amazing coral and fish.

Vietnam With some of the cheapest beer in the region (as little as US$0.25 a glass), Vietnam might win the budget showdown. Nha Trang is the backpackers' beach with a rocking nightlife and affordable lodging.

Above: Wat Phra That Doi Suthep (p689), Chiang Mai, Thailand

Right: Diving in the Semporna Archipelago (p447), Malaysia

WEATHER OR NOT? PICKING A BEACH BY SEASON

BEACH	JAN–FEB	MAR–APR	MAY–JUN	JUL–SEP	OCT–NOV	DEC
Ko Tao (Thailand)	dry, high season	dry, shoulder season	dry, shoulder season	dry until Sep, high season	rain, low season	end of rains, high season
Phuket (Thailand)	dry, high season	dry, shoulder season	start of rains, shoulder season	rain, low season	dry, shoulder season	dry, high season
Bali (Indonesia)	rain, low season	end of rains, shoulder season	dry, shoulder season	dry, high season	start of rains, shoulder season	rain, low season
Nha Trang (Vietnam)	dry, high season	dry, high season	dry, high season	dry, high season	rain, low season	end of rains, low season
Sihanoukville (Cambodia)	dry, high season	dry, shoulder season	start of rains, shoulder season	rain, low season	rain, shoulder season	end of rains, high season
Boracay (Philippines)	dry, high season	dry, high season	dry, shoulder season	rain, low season	end of rains, shoulder season	end of rains, high season
Timor-Leste	rain, low season	dry, high season	dry, high season	dry, high season	dry, high season	rain, low season

Sticking to a Budget

→ Eat like a local at street stalls or markets.

→ Opt for dorm rooms or share a room with a buddy.

→ Stay in fan (non-air-con) rooms with shared bathroom.

→ Travel overland instead of flying.

→ Book flights online rather than paying a travel agent's commission.

→ Snorkel instead of dive.

→ Hire a bicycle instead of a motorbike.

→ Stick to small towns instead of big cities.

→ Be discriminating about which national parks to visit.

→ Avoid package deals (transport, lodging, touring).

→ Know how much local transport should cost and bargain accordingly.

→ Don't forget to factor in the costs of visas.

→ Do souvenir shopping at the end of your trip with surplus funds.

→ Track all of your daily expenses so you know your average costs.

Accommodation Tips

Lodging will be one of your primary expenses. Here are some tips for keeping this line item lean:

→ If the price is too high, ask if the hotel or guesthouse has anything cheaper. We list independent businesses that can alter their prices without notifying us.

→ Unless it is the low season, most rates are non-negotiable.

→ Once you've paid for a room, there is no chance of a refund, regardless of the size of the rat that scurried across the floor.

→ Pay per day rather than all at once. This gives you the option of changing hotels if the conditions are unsuitable.

→ Advance reservations (especially with advance deposits) are generally not necessary.

→ If you do make a booking, don't rely on an agent, who will charge a commission.

TIMOTHY HULIOS/GETTY IMAGES ©

Railay (p770), Krabi, Thailand

Packing

Take as little as possible because you're going to have to carry it everywhere. Pack your bag once and then repack it with a third less stuff. Repeat until your pack is small enough to fit into the aircraft's overhead locker, which represents the average size of most stowage areas on Southeast Asia's buses and trains. The smaller your pack the easier it will be to climb on and off public transport (which doesn't always come to a complete stop), the easier it will be to walk if taxi drivers are asking too much money, and you'll look like less of a target for touts and hustlers.

Going with Gadgets

More and more travellers are taking multiple gadgets – phones, tablets, laptops, cameras – with them on their trips, but the risk of theft or damage is high. Southeast Asia is hot and dusty, bags get dropped or tossed, thieves and pickpockets want what you have and you or your stuff could easily get caught in a rainstorm long enough for a short-circuit.

Here are some tips for travelling smartly with technology:

➡ Limit yourself to one or two versatile devices: a tablet or iPad that can read books and check emails or a smartphone (like an iPhone) that can do it all.

➡ Store your electronics in dry packs and separate the batteries in case of rain.

➡ Use a volt converter, as some destinations have power surges that can fry sensitive equipment.

➡ USB roaming sticks, available through local mobile-phone providers, enable near-universal internet access from your computer.

➡ Get a travel insurance policy that covers theft or damage to your equipment.

TOURIST SEASONS

High season Ideal weather but crowded and prices are high.

Shoulder season Iffy weather but affordable prices and fewer crowds.

Low season Crummy weather, cheap prices, few visitors.

Countries at a Glance

Thailand

Culture/History
Beaches
Food

Monarchs & Monuments
Thais are devoted royalists and their architectural treasures are kingly creations. Bangkok's glittering royal temples continue the tradition of fusing royalty and religion. In the northeast, the Khmer empire built mini-Angkors, while the Thais crafted their own versions in the central plains.

Coastal Loafing
With their jewel-hue waters and blond strands of sand, Thailand's southern beaches have tropical-island proportions and a party personality. The Samui sisters are hang-out buddies, Krabi is a karst cathedral and diving abounds.

Curries & Chillies
A global culinary legend, Thai food combines four elemental flavours (spicy, sweet, sour and salty) into radioactive-coloured curries, vegetable-studded stir-fries and steaming bowls of noodles.

p643

Brunei Darussalam

Culture/History
Outdoor Activities
River Journeys

Model Citizen
This oil-rich sultanate balances Islamic devotion with a high standard of living. Citizens receive free pensions, schooling and medical care. It's often described as a model for modern Islam and thanks to its friendly people it is an 'abode of peace' *(darussalam)*.

Between Earth & Sky
Brunei's rainforests are safeguarded as precious natural habitats. Visitors can experience a pristine wilderness with low impact infrastructure and a bird's-eye view of the canopy.

Watery Veins
Glimpse Brunei's culture at the world's largest stilt village on the banks of Sungai Brunei, or experience a watery obstacle course aboard a longtail boat.

p50

Cambodia

Culture/History
Outdoor Activities
Beaches

Mighty Empire, Modern Tragedy
No journey here is complete without visiting the Temples of Angkor, an architectural rendering of the heavens. The not-so-distant past is a tale of genocide memorialised in Phnom Penh's museums.

Activities for a Cause
Community-based tourism projects are turning former poachers into guides and creating rural villages of affable hosts. Give back and do good while just being a tourist.

Beaches Better Than Thailand?
Budget sun-seekers are second-class citizens in Thailand's expensive beaches. But coastal Cambodia has got squeaky clean stretches of sand, young revellers and not as many package tourists.

p64

Indonesia

Culture/History
Outdoor
Activities
Beaches

So Many Spice Islands

A huge archipelago spanning two oceans, Indonesia is mythical and magical, with smoking volcanoes, vibrant cultures and deep jungles. So many places, too little time.

Smoking Giants

A quintessential Indonesia experience is to huff and puff up a cone behind a local guide wearing sandals and smoking a cigarette. At the summit is a smouldering pot of foul-smelling gases that inspires a serious study of earth sciences.

Beach Buffet

Charming Bali is a cultured beach bum. Just across the channel are the Gili islands for diving, Sumbawa for surfing, and the dragon-guarded Komodo and backpacker delight of Flores.

p149

Laos

Culture/History
Outdoor
Activities
River Journeys

Temples & Tribes

The former royal capital of Luang Prabang is dominated by temples and remnants of Indochina. More than 65 tribal groups (and counting) call Laos home. Hill tribes host village homestays that provide a face-to-face cultural (and economic) exchange.

Leafy Laos

With around 20 protected areas, Laos has an abundance of undisturbed wilderness. Programs, such as the Gibbon Experience, turns trekkers into zipline fliers and treetop sleepers.

River Reverie

Almost every attraction in Laos features a river, providing an easygoing pace of life. You can laze beside the muddy waters, party like a red-neck in Vang Vieng and traverse the liquid highway.

p311

Malaysia

Food
Beaches
Outdoor
Activities

Laksa Luck

Malaysia is a multicultural success story. The diversity is evident at the hawker stalls where noodles and dumplings are served alongside coconut-milk curries and steamed-rice dishes.

Below the Surface

Diving in Borneo's Semporna archipelago or in Pulau Perhentian puts Malaysia on the scuba crowd's watch-list. Malaysia's beaches are blessedly not as boozy as Thailand's.

Borneo Bound

The fabled jungles of Borneo are sliced open by tannin-coloured rivers. The granite spire of Mt Kinabalu is a two-day pilgrimage and orang-utan sanctuaries provide refuge for our hairier cousins.

p378

Myanmar

Culture/History
Outdoor
Activities
Festivals

History in the Making

The new government in this once cloistered country has made peace with its political enemies and now welcomes outsiders. The old sites are just as marvellous, but the new-found optimism is history you can touch.

Mountain Dew

Inle Lake hugs a rugged mountainous landscape where the water's surface has been transformed into fertile farmland. Boats are more important than shoes and puttering from place to place is a peaceful pastime.

Elemental Celebrations

Myanmar brightens up during its festival of lights (Tazaungdaing), and it douses the hot season during Burmese New Year (Thingyan).

p480

Philippines

Culture/History
Outdoor
Activities
Beaches

Maritime Madonna

Wanderers have long visited Filipino shores: the Spanish planted forts and towns as well as Catholicism, the Americans marched behind leaving an inheritance of now-vintage US cars and English as a secondary language. And the Filipinos sewed it up into an intriguing cultural quilt.

Coughing Cones

Volcanoes make lush, statuesque landscapes and the Philippines boasts still-smouldering specimens and dormant peaks, since carved into rice terraces.

Coastal Jigsaw

The myth of deserted palm-fringed beaches is a reality among the 7000-plus islands, and creates a playground for divers, kiteboarders and even surfers, as well as beach-combers.

p547

Singapore

Culture/History
Food
Shopping

Super Singapore

The best of East and West formed lovable Singapore. It features a host of well-curated, well-funded museums, atmospheric colonial houses and oh-so modern shopping malls.

Hawk Me a Meal

Ever-efficient Singapore corralled its roaming vendors into hawker centres, where appetites and meals could be happily united. These open-air pavilions are the centre of a community and meals that turn into nightcaps.

Malls & More

Shopping is more than just bargain- or fashion-hunting here. Malls and hawker centres (an inseparable duo) form the nucleus of every area. Orchard Rd is a retail phenomenon, with two dozen malls.

p613

Timor-Leste

Culture/History
Outdoor
Activities
Beaches

History in Motion

It might be one of the youngest nations in the world, but Timor-Leste has lived many lives. Colonial-era architecture, hilltop crowning statues of Jesus Christ and habit-wearing nuns embody the Portuguese legacy, while Dili's cemeteries and museums memorialise the struggle for independence from Indonesia.

Vistas

Climb to the top of sacred Mt Ramelau for a sunrise view of the front and back of the island.

Coral Monogamy

Not even a blip on the global dive radar, the Atauro Islands have healthy reefs mere steps from the shore and more sea critters than scuba creatures.

p791

Vietnam

Culture/History
Beaches
Food

Small Country, Big History

Be it neighbouring China, colonial France or anti-communist USA, foreign powers couldn't keep their hands off Vietnam. There are epic tales of occupation, resistance and the home-grown heroes of ancient Hanoi, imperial Hué and entrepreneurial Ho Chi Minh City.

Dunes, Dudes & Dudettes

Vietnam has a voluptuous coastline and a young, sociable vibe in the old R&R haunt of Nha Trang and towering dunes of Mui Ne, to name two.

Nuoc Mam to You

Vietnam's cuisine is a legend thanks to the zesty dishes of the south and the hearty soups of the north. The legacy of colonialism bestowed chewy cups of coffee and crusty baguettes.

p812

On the Road

Brunei Darussalam

☑ 673 / POP 415,000

Best Places to Eat

➡ Taman Selera (p56)

➡ Wisma Setia Food Court (p56)

➡ Tamu Kianggeh (p56)

➡ Lim Ah-Siaw Pork Market (p56)

Best Places to Stay

➡ Empire Hotel & Country Club (p56)

➡ KH Soon Resthouse (p55)

➡ Youth Hostel (p55)

Why Go?

The tiny sultanate of Brunei, last remnant of a naval empire that once ruled all of Borneo and much of the Philippines, is famous for its almost unimaginable oil wealth, but it should be no less renowned for having had the foresight and wisdom to preserve its rainforests. Today the country is blessed with some of the most pristine jungle habitats in all of Borneo – you can get a sense of their verdant vastness in Temburong District. And if you take the time to slow down and engage with the locals – in the mellow capital, Bandar Seri Begawan (BSB), as well as in outlying districts – you may find that there's more than first meets the eye in this quiet, verdant and remarkably welcoming *darussalam* (Arabic for 'abode of peace').

When to Go
Bandar Seri Begawan

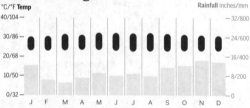

Oct–Dec The rainiest, if coolest, months of the year.

Feb–Mar February and March are the driest months. National Day is celebrated on 23 February.

Jun–Aug It's *hot*. The sultan's birthday (15 July) is marked with festivities around the country

Don't Miss

Spending time surrounded by the rustling, buzzing, chirping rainforests of Ulu Temburong National Park is one of the highlights of a visit to Brunei Darussalam. After whizzing along *nipa-* (traditional hut) and palm-lined waterways on a turbo-charged speedboat from BSB, you board a *temuai* (shallow-draft Iban longboat), dodging submerged boulders and hanging vines as you make your way upriver through the early morning mist. A steep, slippery climb through virgin jungle takes you to a towering wall of scaffolding: the park's famous canopy walk. Held steady by guy wires, the structure creaks as you make your way up into the jungle canopy, passing bird's nest ferns, orchids and (if you're lucky) the flash of a hornbill's plumage.

ITINERARIES

Two Days

Spend your first day exploring BSB: visit the water village of Kampung Ayer in the morning, learn about the sultanate's rich history and culture at the Brunei Museum, and then explore central BSB and the Royal Regalia Museum's regal bling. Take a water taxi excursion at sunset. Spend your second day on a tour of Ulu Temburong National Park.

Five Days

In addition to the two-day itinerary, spend another day in BSB visiting Omar Ali Saifuddien Mosque and more excellent food stalls, followed by a day soaking up the gilded atmosphere of the Empire Hotel & Country Club; add a day relaxing at a beach (eg Muara) or exploring the Temburong District.

Essential Food & Drink

If there's one word you should learn during a visit to Brunei, it's *makan,* meaning 'eat' in Bahasa Malaysia. *Makan* isn't just a word, it's a way of life – because, the locals joke, there's nothing else to do!

BSB's hawker centres serve up some superb – and remarkably inexpensive – local dishes. In the city centre, Tamu Kianggeh has Malay-style chicken mains for just B\$1 as well as mouth-watering pastries, while in the evening you can't beat Taman Selera for BBQ specialities such as satay. Wisma Setia Food Court offers *ambuyat* (gooey sago paste), a local speciality, as well as scrumptious Thai and Indonesian dishes.

AT A GLANCE

➡ **Currencies** Brunei dollar (B\$), Singapore dollar (S\$)

➡ **Language** Bahasa Malaysia, Melayu Brunei (Brunei Malay), English

➡ **Money** ATMs easy to find in towns, but not in Temburong District

➡ **Visas** Available to most nationalities. Free for most nationalities, except Australians.

➡ **Mobile phones** Prepay local SIM B\$30

Fast Facts

➡ **Area** 5765 sq km

➡ **Capital** Bandar Seri Begawan (BSB)

➡ **Emergency** ambulance 🖉 991, police 🖉 993, fire 🖉 995

Exchange Rates

Australia	A\$1	B\$1.15
Euro Zone	€1	B\$1.75
Malaysia	RM10	B\$3.85
Singapore	S\$1	B\$1.00
UK	UK£1	B\$2.10
USA	US\$1	B\$1.25

Set Your Budget

➡ **Dorm bed** B\$10–18

➡ **Food stall meal** from B\$1

➡ **Museum admission** free

➡ **Beer** Brunei is dry

Entering the Country

Daily buses link Sabah (KK) and Sarawak (Miri) with BSB. Ferries connect Pulau Labuan with Brunei (Muara).

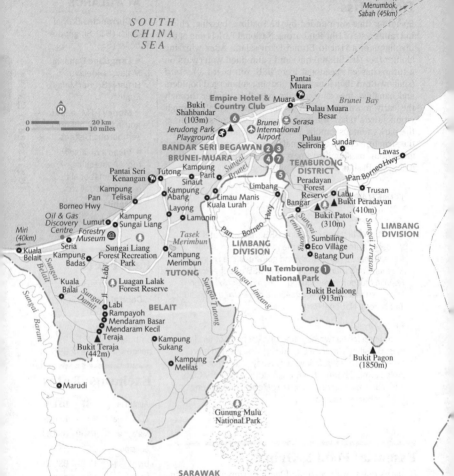

Brunei Darussalam Highlights

① Climb high into the rainforest canopy and swim in a cool jungle river at **Ulu Temburong National Park** (p60)

② Take a water taxi to the water village of **Kampung Ayer** (p53) and then a boardwalk stroll

③ Sight proboscis monkeys and the sultan's palace on a **water-taxi cruise** (p53)

④ Visit the opulent **mosques** (p53) of Brunei's capital, Bandar Seri Begawan

⑤ Tear along mangrove-lined waterways on a **speedboat** (p59) from Bandar Seri Begawan to Bangar

⑥ Marvel at the over-the-top luxury of the **Empire Hotel & Country Club** (p56), a sparkling monument to world-class profligacy

⑦ Enjoy a delicious BBQ dinner at **Taman Selera** (p56) night market

BANDAR SERI BEGAWAN

POP 140,000

If you're expecting some kind of lavish mini-Dubai, think again – Brunei may be a super-rich oil state, but BSB (as the capital is known) has little nouveau riche ostentation. In fact, it's remarkably quiet and relaxed, with picturesque water villages, two opulent mosques, some great food stalls and a vibe as polite and unassuming as its people. Despite the almost total lack of nightlife, there's something quietly alluring about BSB, whose mellow pace can definitely grow on you.

◉ Sights & Activities

◎ Central BSB

Kampung Ayer   WATER VILLAGES
Founded at least 1000 years ago, Kampung Ayer is considered the largest stilt settlement in the world and has its own schools, mosques, police stations and fire brigade. When Venetian scholar Antonio Pigafetta, who accompanied Ferdinand Magellan on his last voyage, visited Kampung Ayer in 1521, he grandly dubbed it the 'Venice of the East'.

While Kampung Ayer, which runs along both banks of Sungai Brunei, is far from squalid, be prepared for boardwalks without safety rails and the low-tide trash that carpets the intertidal mud, home to mudskippers and crabs.

A good place to start a visit – and get acquainted with Brunei's pre-oil culture – is the **Kampung Ayer Cultural & Tourism Gallery** (⊘ 9am-5pm Sat-Thu, 9-11.30am & 2.30-5pm Fri) **FREE**, whose displays focus on the history, lifestyle and crafts of the Kampung Ayer people. A film shows scenes from the 1950s – notice that the women are not wearing headscarves. A square, glass-enclosed **viewing tower** offers panoramic views of the watery scene below.

From BSB's **Riverfront Promenade**, getting across the river to Kampung Ayer (B\$0.50 for locals, B\$1 for tourists, more for a diagonal crossing) is a breeze. Just stand somewhere a water taxi – BSB's souped-up version of the gondola – can dock and chances are a boatman will spot you before you even have time to wave. Some of the quayside landings are very slippery.

Omar Ali Saifuddien Mosque   MOSQUE
(Jln Stoney; ⊘ interior 8.30am-noon, 1.30-3pm & 4.30-5.30pm Sat-Wed, 4.30-5pm Fri, closed Thu, exterior compound 8am-8.30pm daily except prayer times) Built between 1954 and 1958, gold-domed Masjid Omar Ali Saifuddien – named after the 28th sultan of Brunei (the late father of the current sultan) – is surrounded by a sublime reflecting pool. The ceremonial stone boat sitting in the lagoon is a replica of a 16th-century *mahligai* (royal barge). Inside, the floor and walls are made of the finest Italian marble, the stained-glass windows and chandeliers were crafted in England, and the luxurious carpets were flown in from Saudi Arabia and Belgium.

Water-Taxi Cruise   BOAT TOUR
(1hr circuit B\$25-30) The best way to see BSB's water villages, the sultan's fabled palace, Istana Nurul Iman, and leaf-munching proboscis monkeys is from a hand-crafted wooden water taxi, which can be chartered along the waterfront. The best time to head out is very late afternoon (about 5.30pm or 6pm), as monkeys are easiest to spot around sunset.

Royal Regalia Museum   MUSEUM
(Jln Sultan; ⊘ 9am-5pm Sun-Thu, 9-11.30am & 2.30-5pm Fri, 9.45am-5pm Sat, last entry 4.30pm) **FREE** What do you give a man who has everything? To find out how various heads of state have solved this conundrum, drop by the Royal Regalia Museum (hint: you're pretty safe with gilded knick knacks). Other highlights include the golden chariot used for the present sultan's 1968 coronation and the text of the first treaty of friendship between Brunei and the USA, signed way back in 1850. Bags, cameras and mobiles (cellphones) must be checked at the entrance.

◎ East of Central BSB

Brunei Museum   MUSEUM
(Jln Kota Batu; ⊘ 9am-5pm Sat-Thu, 9-11.30am & 2.30-5pm Fri, last entry 30min before closing; P) **FREE** Brunei's national museum is a great place to get acquainted with the sultanate's rich history and culture. Ceramics and blown glass from as far back as the 9th and 10th centuries are featured in the Islamic Art Gallery, while the recently renovated Natural History Gallery offers a concise but informative introduction to Borneo's extraordinary biodiversity. The Oil & Gas

Bandar Seri Begawan

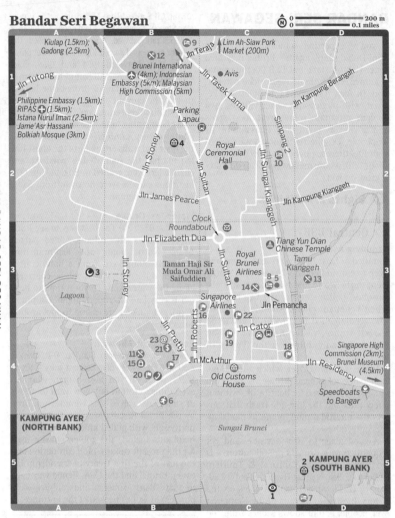

Gallery features ravishing photos of the oil platforms that have made Brunei what it is.

Situated 4.5km east of central BSB along the coastal road, on a bluff overlooking Sungai Brunei. To get there, take bus 39 (B$1, twice an hour) or a taxi (B$10 one way).

Malay Technology Museum   MUSEUM
(Jln Kota Batu; ⊙ 9am-5pm Sun-Thu, 9-11.30am & 2.30-5pm Fri, 9.45am-5pm Sat, last entry 30 min before closing) **FREE** Linked to the neighbouring Brunei Museum by a short, steep path, this museum has informative, well-presented exhibits on life in an old-time Malay water

village and in Dusun and Murut (Lun Bawang) longhouses, and on the traditional technologies used to fish, weave, cook and make *ambuyat*.

◉ North & West of Central BSB

**Jame'Asr Hassanil
Bolkiah Mosque**   MOSQUE
(Sultan Hassanal Bolkiah Hwy, Kampung Kiarong; ⊙ 8am-noon, 2-3pm & 5-6pm Mon-Wed & Sat, 5-6pm Fri, 10.30am-noon, 2-3pm & 5-6pm Sun, closed Thu; 🅿) Built in 1992 to celebrate the 25th year of the current sultan's reign, Bru-

Bandar Seri Begawan

nei's largest mosque and its four terrazzo-tiled minarets dominate BSB's northwestern suburbs. Because the sultan is his dynasty's 29th ruler, the complex is adorned with 29 golden domes. The interior is best described as jaw-droppingly over-the-top.

Situated about 3km northwest of the city centre towards Gadong. To get there, take buses 01C or 20 or a taxi (B$10 one way).

Istana Nurul Iman   PALACE
(Jln Tutong) FREE More than four times the size of the Palace of Versailles and three times larger than Buckingham Palace, Istana Nurul Iman (Palace of the Light of the Faith), the sultan's official residence, has 1788 rooms, including 257 bathrooms. Designed by Filipino architect Leandro Locsin, it mixes Malay and Islamic elements with the sweep and oversized grandeur of an airport terminal.

Situated 3km southwest of the centre of town, Istana Nurul Iman is open to the public for three days during the Hari Raya Aidilfitri festivities at the end of Ramadan. Come to the palace gates well-dressed and with both your passport and an appetite (there's a buffet). Women shake hands with the queen and princesses, men with the sultan and princes.

☞ **Tours**

Borneo Guide   TOUR
(☑718 7138, 876 6796, 242 6923; www.borneo guide.com; Unit 204, Kiaw Lian Building, Jln Pemancha; ⊙9am-5pm Mon-Fri, 9am-1pm Sat & Sun) Has

excellent ecotours and very friendly staff. Destinations include day trips to Ulu Temburong National Park (B$125 per person). Situated one floor below KH Soon Resthouse.

🛏 **Sleeping**

Contrary to what you may have heard, cheap beds *are* available in BSB. Upscale places often offer big online discounts.

KH Soon Resthouse   GUESTHOUSE $
(☑222 2052; khsoon-resthouse.tripod.com; 2nd fl, 140 Jln Pemancha; dm B$18, s/d B$40/45, with shared bathroom B$35/40; ❄) This old-time cheapie offers a super-central location, 29 spartan (but huge) rooms and heaps of low-budget character – oh, and a bell that sounds like a gecko. Recent addition: dorm beds in single-sex rooms.

Youth Hostel   HOSTEL $
(Pusat Belia; ☑899 8852, 222 2900, 887 3066; Jln Sungai Kianggeh; dm B$10; ❄❄) Gets rave reviews from backpackers. The 28 spacious, strictly sex-segregated rooms, with four or 10 beds (all bunks), have functional furnishings and decent bathrooms. The adjacent swimming pool costs B$1.

Situated at the southern end of the Youth Centre complex, behind the cylindrical staircase. Reception is supposed to be open from 7.45am to 4.30pm Monday to Thursday, with someone on call til 10pm, but staffing can be sporadic. If the office is locked, hang around and someone should find you. Closed to travellers when official guests move in for sports events.

SPLURGE

Dubaian in its proportions and opulence, the 523-room **Empire Hotel & Country Club** (☑ 241 8888; www.theempirehotel.com; Muara-Tutong Hwy, Kampung Jerudong; r incl breakfast from B$400, villas B$1300-2900; 🏧 @ 🛜 🏊) was commissioned by Prince Jefri – get this – as lodging for guests of the royal family. To recoup at least part of the US$1.1 billion investment, the property was quickly transformed into an upscale resort, so now anyone with a thing for bling can hang out in the lobby and enjoy a US$500,000 lamp made of gold and Baccarat crystal (an identical lamp lives in the Emperor Suite and can be appreciated privately for B$16,600 per night). Fun for an over-the-top honeymoon! It's worth a visit just to take in the gilded spectacle; tea in the Lobby Lounge costs a mere B$5 a pot. The hotel is 26km northwest of BSB's city centre. To get there, take bus 57 (B$1) from central BSB or Gadong (on the way back, book at the hotel's Transport desk), or a taxi (B$30 one way).

Kampung Ayer Homestay HOMESTAY $
(Water Village Malay Modern House; ☑ 881 6873; wv.malaymodernhouse@gmail.com; No 2, B1 Skim Perintis, Jambatan Laila Menchanai, Kampung Ayer; r per person incl breakfast B$30; 🏧 🛜) Kampung Ayer's first (and so far only) homestay is run by an enthusiastic and friendly water village headman named Ahmad bin Hajji Bujang. Upstairs, four spacious bedrooms share two huge bathrooms, while in the living room two gilded thrones replicate a Malay wedding. Situated in a new duplex, built in 2011, right behind the Kampung Ayer Cultural & Tourism Gallery.

Terrace Hotel HOTEL $$
(☑ 224 3557, 224 3555, 224 3554; www.terracebrunei.com; Jln Tasek Lama; d B$65-75; 🏧 @ 🛜 🏊) The 84 dowdy rooms were undergoing a much-needed renovation when we visited. Near central BSB's best night market dining.

🍴 Eating

In the city centre, restaurants are sprinkled along the waterfront and on Jln Sultan south of Jln Pemancha. Shopping malls, in-cluding the Yayasan Complex and those out in Gadong, have food courts.

Taman Selera HAWKER $
(cnr Jln Tasek Lama & Jln Stoney; mains B$2-4; ⊙ 5pm-midnight) Feast on cheap, excellent Malay, Indonesian and Indian dishes at this old-fashioned evening hawker centre. Options include satay (four skewers for B$1), *roti canai* (B$1), fried chicken (B$3) and iced drinks (from B$1). Fish are sold by weight and can be expensive. Mizu Restaurant, at the far northern end, is open 24 hours. Situated in the middle of a grassy park 1km north of the waterfront, across from the Terrace Hotel.

Wisma Setia Food Court HAWKER $
(2nd fl, Wisma Setia, Jln Pemancha; ⊙ 7am-5pm) Sunisma (stall 05) is the only place in central BSB that serves *ambuyat* (unbelievably gooey sago paste dipped in sauces; B$8), Mari-Mari (stall 03) cooks up outstanding halal Thai dishes, and stall 06 specialises in Indonesian favourites. Situated between KH Soon Resthouse and the HSBC bank.

Tamu Kianggeh HAWKER $
(Jln Sungai Kianggeh; mains from B$1; ⊙ 5am-5pm) The food stalls, most numerous early in the morning, serve Brunei's cheapest meals, including *nasi lemak* (rice cooked in coconut milk and served with chicken, beef or prawn, and cucumber slices; also B$1), as well as local pastries. A great place to pick up a snack for the bus ride to KK.

Lim Ah-Siaw Pork Market HAWKER $
(☑ 222 3963; Jln Teraja; mains B$2-7; ⊙ 6:30am-10pm Sat-Thu, 6.30am-noon Fri) Bruneian law prohibits the consumption of pig products, but only for Muslims – so Chinese are free to feast on pork, as long as they do so very discreetly. The result is Lim Ah-Siaw, a cheerful pavilion with the vibe of a speakeasy. Situated in BSB's 'pork-light district', 400m behind the Terrace Hotel.

Hua Ho Supermarket SUPERMARKET $
(western bldg, Yayasan Complex, Jln Pretty; ⊙ 10am-10pm) Dozens of kinds of absolutely scrumptious Bruneian cookies and snacks (B$3 to B$5) can be found in this four-storey department store's basement supermarket, in a case next to the fruit section. Some of the sweets are dusted with powdered sugar; many simply melt in your mouth. Among the highlights: *kuih lenggang*, a green, coconut-filled crepe.

🔒 Shopping

Shopping is Brunei's national sport. Locals bop through the shopping malls scouting out the best deals while bemoaning the fact that their micronation doesn't have as much variety as Singapore.

Escape the heat at the ritzy **Yayasan Complex** (Kompleks Yayasan Sultan Haji Hassanal Bolkiah; Jln Pretty), the city centre's main shopping mall, whose courtyard is aligned with Omar Ali Saifuddien Mosque. Crafts are sold along the river at **Tamu Kianggeh** (Jln Sungai Kianggeh), but prices are higher than in Malaysia.

The malls of Gadong, Brunei's main shopping district, are about 3km northwest of the city centre. To get there, take buses 01C or 20; a cab costs B$10 one way.

ℹ️ Information

INTERNET ACCESS
Several internet cafes are hidden away inside the buildings along Jln McArthur.
Paul & Elizabeth Cyber Cafe (Shop 1.18, 1st fl, Block B, Yayasan Complex, Jln Pretty; per hr B$1; ⊗9am-9pm) Has about a dozen computers.

MEDICAL SERVICES
RIPAS Hospital (📞224 2424; www.moh.gov.bn/medhealthservices/ripas.htm; Jln Tutong; ⊗24hr) Brunei's main hospital, with fully equipped, modern facilities. Most of the senior staff are Western trained. Situated about 2km west of the centre (across the Edinburgh Bridge). Served by buses 01C and 20.

MONEY
Banks and international ATMs are sprinkled around the city centre, especially along Jln McArthur and Jln Sultan. The airport has ATMs, too.
Isman Money Changer (Shop G.14, ground fl, Block B, Yayasan Complex, Jln Pretty; ⊗10am-8pm) Changes 12 flavours of cash but not travellers cheques.

POST
Main Post Office (cnr Jln Sultan & Jln Elizabeth Dua; ⊗8am-4.30pm Mon-Thu & Sat, 8-11am & 2-4pm Fri) Displays colourful local stamps from as far back as 1895.

TELEPHONE
Internet cafes offer international calls for as little as B$0.10 a minute.
DST Communications (www.dst-group.com; ground fl, western bldg, Yayasan Complex, Jln McArthur; ⊗9am-4pm Mon-Thu & Sat, 9am-11am & 2.30-4pm Fri, closed Sun) Sells SIM cards. Bring your passport.

TOURIST INFORMATION
Borneo Guide (p55) serves as a very welcoming, if unofficial, tourist guide.
Kampung Ayer Cultural & Tourism Gallery (Kampung Ayer; ⊗9am-5pm Sat-Thu, 9-11am & 2.30-5pm Fri) Has free glossy brochures on the sultanate.

ℹ️ Getting Around

TO/FROM THE AIRPORT
The airport, about 8km north of central BSB, is linked to the city centre by buses 23, 24 and 34 (B$1) and the Express Bus Service (B$2).

A taxi to/from the airport should cost B$20 (50% more after 9pm); taxis are not metered so agree on a price before you get in.

BUS
BSB's public bus system is remarkably cheap, but because it's run by five independent companies it can be hard to figure out. Another problem: buses don't have fixed timetables.

Buses (B$1 regardless of distance) operate daily from about 6.30am to (theoretically) 8pm at some point, but after that your options are taking a taxi or hoofing it. Finding stops can be a challenge – some are marked by black-and-white striped uprights or a shelter, others by a yellow triangle painted on the pavement and yet others by no discernible symbol whatsoever.

The carbon-monoxide-choked BSB **Bus Terminal** (Jln Cator), on the ground floor of a multistorey parking complex two blocks north of the waterfront, lacks an information office or a ticket counter. However, a new colour-coded bus route map (included in some tourist brochures) was erected in 2013. Signs next to each numbered berth indicate the route of each line.

Many places in or near central BSB (eg Gadong) are served by Circle Line buses 01C and 01A, which follow the same circular route in opposite directions.

CAR
Brunei has Southeast Asia's cheapest fuel – petrol is just B$0.53 a litre and diesel goes for only B$0.35!

Hiring a car is a good way to explore Brunei's hinterland. Prices start at about B$75 (plus B$15 for insurance) a day. Most agencies will bring the car to your hotel and pick it up when you've finished.

Local rental companies, most with offices at the airport, tend to be cheaper than the international biggies.

GETTING TO MALAYSIA

BSB to Miri

Getting to the border Two buses a day link BSB with Miri's Pujut Bus Terminal (B$18, 3½ hours, 7am and 1pm).

At the border Most travellers to Malaysia are granted 30- or 90-day visas on arrival. Border posts are open from 6am to 10pm.

Moving on Miri's Pujut Bus Terminal is linked to the city centre (4km) by infrequent local buses (RM1.60 or RM2.60) and taxi (RM15).

BSB to Labuan & Kota Kinabalu

Getting to the border One bus a day links BSB with Kota Kinabalu's (KK's) Jalan Tugu Bus Station (B$45, eight hours, 8am), but you can avoid standing in seven visa queues (and having precious passport pages filled up with stamps) by taking a ferry from Muara (20km north of BSB) to Pulau Labuan (B$17, 1¼ hours, four a day). The cheapest and fastest way to get from BSB to KK is to take an early morning speedboat to Bangar (B$6, 45 minutes) and then catch the daily bus to KK (B$25, 6½ hours), which stops in front of the youth hostel sometime between 10am and 11.30am.

At the border Most travellers to Malaysia are granted 30- or 90-day visas on arrival. Border posts are open from 6am to 10pm.

Moving on From Labuan, there are onward ferries to Kota Kinabalu (RM40, 3¼ hours, two a day) and the mainland port of Menumbok (RM12, one hour, two a day), linked with KK by bus. In KK, buses from BSB stop at the Jalan Tugu Bus Station and ferries from Pulau Labuan dock at the Jesselton Point ferry terminal – both are right in the city centre.

Avis (☑ Radisson Hotel 222 7100, airport 876 0642; www.avis.com)

Hertz (☑ airport 872 6000; www.hertz.com)

TAXI

Taxis are a convenient, if expensive, way of exploring BSB – if you can find one, that is: the entire country has only 55 official cabs and it's well nigh impossible to flag one down on the street. Most taxis have yellow tops; a few serving the airport are all white.

Brunei's taxis are owned and operated by independent drivers so there is no centralised dispatcher. Hotels can provide drivers' mobile phone numbers; if you're going to need a ride back, get your driver's number on the trip out. BSB's only **taxi rank** (Jln Cator) is in front of the Bus Terminal (p57).

Taxis do not have meters so always agree on a price before getting in. A ride to the malls and restaurants of Gadong or Kiulap (3km or 4km) should cost about B$10. Fares go up by 50% between 9pm and 6am.

WATER TAXI

If your destination is along Sungai Brunei, water taxis are a good way of getting there. You can hail one anywhere along the BSB waterfront that a boat can dock, as well as along Venice-themed

Sungai Kianggeh (Jl Sungai Kianggeh). Crossing straight across the river is supposed to cost B$0.50 per person (tourists usually pay B$1); diagonal crossings cost more.

AROUND BANDAR SERI BEGAWAN

Jerudong

In its heyday, **Jerudong Park Playground** (Jerudong; admission free, rides under 5/over 5 B$8/10; ⊘ 4-10.30pm Wed, Thu & Sun, 2-10pm Fri & Sat, closed Mon & Tue except during school holidays), a B$1 billion amusement park opened by Prince Jefri in 1994, was hugely popular with local children – as one Bruneian born in the late 1980s put it: 'This was the highlight of our childhood.' For adults, the concert venue hosted free performances by the likes of Whitney Houston and Michael Jackson, the latter to celebrate the sultan's 50th birthday. Most of the rides were eventually sold off to repay debts, but 10 still operate, including a merry-go-round. At press time, new attractions, including minigolf, were planned.

The park is about 20km northwest of BSB, near the coast. It is served by bus 55 (B$1, 50 minutes, twice an hour); a taxi will cost B$30 one way (B$45 after 9pm).

Muara

Not many people come to Brunei for sun 'n' sand, but if you have some spare time to stretch out on the seashore, there are a couple of options about 25km northeast of BSB around the port town of Muara, site of an Australian amphibious landing in April 1945.

Attractive **Pantai Muara** (Muara Beach), near the tip of the peninsula, is a popular weekend retreat, with food stalls, picnic tables, toilets and a children's playground. Watch out for the undertow, particularly after storms, and be prepared for sand flies (bring repellent). Women should wear rather more than a bikini or risk unwanted attention.

Muara's town centre is served by buses 37 and 39 (B$1); bus 33 will take you from there to Pantai Muara.

Temburong District

POP 10,000

Possibly the most pristine tract of primary rainforest in all of Borneo covers much of Brunei's 1288-sq-km Temburong District, which is separated from the rest of the country by a strip of Malaysia's Limbang Division. The area's main draw is the brilliant Ulu Temburong National Park, accessible only by longboat.

The speedboat ride from BSB out to Bangar, the district capital, is the most fun you can possibly have for B$6.

Bangar

Bangar, a three-street town on the banks of Sungai Temburong, is the gateway to (and administrative centre of) the Temburong district. It can easily be visited as a day trip from BSB.

🛏 Sleeping

Youth Hostel   HOSTEL $
(Pusat Belia; ☑ 522 1694; www.bruneiyouth.org.bn; dm B$10; ⊘ office staffed 7.30am-4.30pm, closed

Fri & Sat) Part of a youth centre, this basic hostel, painted pastel orange, sits in a fenced compound between the market and the highway. Rooms, each with six beds (bunks), are clean and fan-cooled. If no one's around, try phoning or looking helplessly at passers by – worked for us.

Rumah Persinggahan
Kerajaan Daerah Temburong   GUESTHOUSE $
(☑ 522 1239; Jln Batang Duri; s/d/tr/q B$25/30/40/50, 4-person chalets B$80; ❋ 🛜) Set around a grassy courtyard, this government guesthouse has friendly, helpful staff. The six spacious rooms are slightly frayed but the bathrooms are new. Situated a few hundred metres west of the town centre, across the highway from the two mosques.

🍴 Eating

Food Court   HAWKER CENTRE $
(1st fl, Kompleks Utami Bumiputera; mains B$1-3; ⊘ 6/7am-8pm, closed noon-2pm Fri) Head up the stairs from the small fruit and vegie market to find half-a-dozen good-value Malay food stalls.

ℹ Information

3 in 1 Services (Shop A1-3, 1st fl, Kompleks Utami Bumiputera; per hr B$1; ⊘ 8am-5pm, closed Sun) Internet access across the pedestrian bridge from the food court.
Bank Islam Brunei Darussalam (⊘ 8.45am-3.45pm Mon-Thu, 8.45-11am & 2.30-4pm Fri, 8.45-11.15am Sat) The only bank in town – but the ATM does not accept international cards. Changes US dollars and pounds sterling but not Malaysian ringgits.
Chop Hock Guan Minimarket (⊘ 8am-8pm) Exchanges Malaysian ringgits for Brunei dollars. Situated in the second row of shops from the youth hostel.

ℹ Getting There & Away

Getting to/from Bangar from BSB is a breeze in more ways than one. Speedboats (adult B$6, 45 minutes) run from 6am to at least 4.30pm, later on Sunday and holidays. In BSB, the dock is on Jln Residency about 200m east of Sungai Kianggeh. Boats depart at a scheduled time or when full, whichever comes first. Services are run by **Ampuan** (☑ 522 1985) and **Koperasi** (☑ 522 628); check at the ticket counters to see which company's boat will be the next to leave. Peak-hour departures can be as frequent as every 15 minutes.

The **Jesselton** (☑ 719 3835, 717 7755, in BSB 718 3838) bus from BSB to Lawas and Kota

Kinabalu (B$25) stops in front of Bangar's Youth Hostel sometime between 10am and 11.30am, depending on traffic.

Ulu Temburong National Park

Ulu Temburong National Park (admission B$5) is in the heart of the pristine rainforests that blanket southern Temburong. Only about 1 sq km of the park is accessible to tourists – in order to protect it for future generations, the rest is off-limits to *Homo sapiens* – except scientists, who flock here from around the world.

☥ Activities

Longboat Trip BOAT

The only way to get to park HQ is by *temuai* (shallow-draft Iban longboat). The exhilarating trip, which takes 25 to 40 minutes from Batang Duri, is challenging even for experienced skippers. When it rains, the water level can quickly rise by up to 2m, but if the river is low you might have to get out and push. All tours to the park include the boat ride and it is a highlight of any visit to Ulu Temburong.

Canopy Walk ADVENTURE

The park's main attraction is a delicate aluminium walkway, secured by guy ropes, that takes you through (or, more accurately, near) the jungle canopy, up to 60m above the forest floor. In primary rainforests, only limited vegetation can grow on the ground because so little light penetrates, but up in the canopy all manner of life proliferates: orchids; bird's nest ferns and other epiphytes; ants and myriad other insects; amphibians and snakes; and many species of bird. Unfortunately, there are no explanatory signs.

☞ Tours

For all intents and purposes, the only way to visit the park is by booking a tour. BSB-based Borneo Guide (p55), which charges B$125 per person (minimum two) for a day trip (slightly cheaper if you start from Bangar), is a good bet.

🛏 Sleeping

★ Sumbiling Eco Village GUESTHOUSE **$$**
(☑ 718 7138, 242 6923; borneoguide.com/eco village; tent/room per person incl meals B$60/70; ℗ @) This ecofriendly camp, about 14km south of Bangar near Batang Duri, offers rustic accommodation, great Iban cuisine and plenty of outdoor activities, including visits to Ulu Temburong National Park. Nearby is a five-door Iban longhouse. Prices do not include transport or activities. Run by Borneo Guide (p55) in cooperation with the local community.

UNDERSTAND BRUNEI DARUSSALAM

Brunei Darussalam Today

Brunei's oil and gas wealth affords its citizens one of the highest standards of living in the world, with per capita GDP over US$55,000. Literacy stands at 95%, average life expectancy is 76 years, and there are pensions for all, free medical care, free schooling, free sport and leisure centres, cheap loans, subsidies for many purchases (including cars), short work weeks, no income tax and the highest minimum wages in the region. Economic diversification – including significant sovereign wealth investments overseas – and deep-sea exploration for yet more oil aim to keep the cash rolling in, and as long as it does, the people of Brunei should stay happy (though in some cases slightly bored) with their felicitous lot.

History

The earliest recorded references to Brunei concern China's trading connections with 'Pu-ni' in the 6th century, during the Tang dynasty. Prior to the region's embrace of Islam in the 1400s, Brunei was within the boundaries of the Sumatran Srivijaya Empire, then the Majapahit Empire of Java. By the late 15th and early 16th centuries, the so-called Golden Age of Sultan Bolkiah (the fifth sultan), Brunei Darussalam had become a considerable regional power, with its sea-faring rule extending throughout Borneo and deep into the Philippines.

The Spanish and Portuguese arrived in the 16th century and at times confronted the sultanate with force, though in the long term the European powers' disruption of traditional patters of trade proved more damaging. In the mid- and late 19th century, internal divisions and the bold salami strategy of Sarawak's first White Rajah, a British adventurer named James Brooke, led to a series of treaties ceding land and power. To save itself from oblivion, Brunei became a British protectorate in 1888. Despite this, two years later, with a final dash of absurdity, Limbang was lost to Sarawak, dividing the sultanate into two parts.

In 1929 oil was discovered, turning the tiny state into an economic power overnight. The present sultan's father, Sultan Omar Saifuddien, kept Brunei out of both the Federation of Malaya and Malaysia, preferring that his country remain a British protectorate – and that oil revenues stay on home soil.

Saifuddien abdicated in 1967, leaving the throne to his popular son and heir, Sultan Hassanal Bolkiah. Early in 1984 he reluctantly led his tightly ruled country to complete independence from Britain. As a former public-school boy and graduate of the Royal Military Academy Sandhurst, the sultan rather enjoyed British patronage and the country still has very close political, economic and military ties to Britain.

After independence Brunei adopted a national ideology known as Melayu Islam Beraja (MIB; Malay Islamic Monarchy), which stresses Malay culture, Islam (the official religion) and the legitimacy of the sultan.

People & Culture

Brunei is the most observant Islamic country in Southeast Asia, with Sharia strictures increasingly enforced in recent years. However, Bruneians embrace integration into the global economy, striving to strike a balance between international trends and traditionalist Sunni Islam.

Ethnic Malays make up two-thirds of the sultanate's 415,000 inhabitants, people of Chinese heritage account for 11%, and Iban, Kelabit and other Dayak groups constitute around 3.4%. Temporary workers make up the rest.

The state religion is Islam. The Ministry of Religious Affairs actively promotes Islam and, in some cases, limits the freedom of other religious groups, for example when it comes to building churches or hiring clergy.

Traditional crafts have almost disappeared in modern Brunei. In its heyday, Brunei produced lost-wax brassware – gongs, kettles, betel containers and, most famously, ceremonial cannons – that was prized throughout Borneo and beyond. The sultanate's silversmiths were also celebrated. *Jong sarat* sarongs, handwoven using gold thread, are still worn at formal ceremonial occasions.

THE VIRTUE OF MODESTY

Bruneians are quite conservative when it comes to what they wear. Though non-Muslims, including visitors, aren't expected to adopt Islamic standards, it is best to cover up a bit. Sleeveless T-shirts and ripped jeans are inappropriate for men, bikini tops and shorts too revealing for women.

Environment

Brunei (5765 sq km) consists of two non-contiguous areas separated by the Sarawak's Limbang District. The larger, western part of the country includes the main towns: Bandar Seri Begawan (BSB), the oil town of Seria and the commercial centre of Kuala Belait. The eastern sliver of Brunei, the hilly, mostly forested Temburong District, is much less developed.

Away from the coast, Brunei is mainly jungle, with about 75% of the country still covered by virtually untouched forests. As you can see if you fly over the sultanate (or check out Google Earth), clear cutting, 'selective' logging, road building and palm-oil plantations – the most serious threats to Borneo's incredibly rich ecosystems – stop at the sultanate's borders.

SURVIVAL GUIDE

❶ Directory A–Z

ACCOMMODATION

A handful of excellent budget options make shoestring travel eminently possible.

The following price ranges refer to a double room with bathroom.

$ less than B$60 (US$50)
$$ B$60 to B$150 (US$50 to US$120)
$$$ more than B$150 (US$120)

EMBASSIES & CONSULATES

All of the following embassies, high commissions and consulates are located within Bandar Seri Begawan.

Australian High Commission (☑222 9435; www.bruneidarussalam.embassy.gov.au; 6th fl, Dar Takaful IBB Utama, Jln Pemancha)

British High Commission (☑222 2231; www.ukinbrunei.fco.gov.uk; Unit 2.01, 2nd fl, Block D, Yayasan Complex, Jln Pretty)

Canadian High Commission (222 0043; www.brunei.gc.ca; 5th fl, Jalan McArthur Bldg, 1 Jln McArthur)

French Embassy (222 0960; www.ambafrance-bn.org; Units 301-306, Kompleks Jalan Sultan, Jln Sultan)

German Embassy (222 5547; www.bandar-seri-begawan.diplo.de; Unit 2.01, 2nd fl, Block A, Yayasan Complex, Jln Pretty)

Indonesian Embassy (233 0180; www.kemlu.go.id/bandarseribegawan; Lot 4498, Simpang 528, Jln Muara, Kampung Sungai Hanching)

Malaysian High Commission (238 1095; www.kln.gov.my; No 61, Simpang 396, Jln Kebangsaan)

New Zealand Consulate (222 5880, 222 2422; www.mfat.govt.nz; c/o Deloitte & Touche, 5th fl, Wisma Hajjah Fatimah, 22-23 Jln Sultan) Honorary consul.

Philippine Embassy (224 1465/6; www.philippine-embassybrunei.com; Simpang 336-17, Diplomatic Enclave, Jln Kebangsaan)

Singapore High Commission (226 2741; www.mfa.gov.sg/brunei; No 8, Simpang 74, Jln Subok)

US Embassy (238 4616; http://brunei.usembassy.gov; Simpang 336-52-16-9, Diplomatic Enclave, Jln Kebangsaan) About 5km northeast of downtown BSB.

FOOD

Brunei's delicious cuisine is similar to the Malay dishes popular in nearby Malaysia, though with local variations. One uely Bruneian speciality is *ambuyat*, an extraordinary white goo made from the pith of the sago plant. Market stalls serve remarkably cheap meals.

The following price ranges refer to the cost of the cheapest nonvegetarian main dish on the menu.

$ less than B$6 (US$5)
$$ B$6 to B$16 (US$5 to US$13)
$$$ more than B$16 (US$13)

GAY & LESBIAN TRAVELLERS

According to www.smartraveller.gov.au, 'consensual homosexual acts between adults of either sex are illegal and penalties include prison sentences'.

INTERNET ACCESS

All hotels have internet connections, as do many places that serve food and drinks. BSB has a number of internet cafes.

LEGAL MATTERS

When entering Brunei you'll see signs reading 'Warning: Death for drug traffickers under Brunei law'.

The sale and public consumption of alcohol is forbidden. Non-Muslim visitors 18 or older are allowed to import 12 cans of beer and two bottles of wine or spirits for personal consumption.

MEDIA

The *Borneo Bulletin* (http://borneobulletin.brunei-online.com; B$0.80) is filled with local and international news, most of it from news agencies, none of it locally controversial.

MONEY

Brunei dollars (B$ or BND) and Singapore dollars (S$ or SGD) are legal tender and accepted virtually everywhere, in both countries.

OPENING HOURS

All offices, businesses and shops – including restaurants and food stalls – are now required to close from noon to 2pm on Friday, when Muslims traditionally go to the mosque to pray. During Ramadan, business and office hours are shortened and many Muslim-owned restaurants and food stalls are closed. Those that are open (so people can buy break-the-fast food) are prohibited from serving eat-in food during fast hours, even to non-Muslims. Standard hours at other times are as follows:

Banks Approximately 8.45am to 3.30pm or 4pm Monday to Friday and 8.45am to 11am on Saturday.

Government offices 7.45am to 12.15pm and 1.30pm to 4.30pm Monday to Thursday and Saturday. Closed Friday and Sunday.

Shops Approximately 10am to 6pm. Shopping malls generally 9am or 10am to 10pm.

TELEPHONE

Prepaid SIM cards (B$30, including B$5 credit) are issued by DST Communications (p57) and B-Mobile.

TOURIST INFORMATION

Brunei's national tourist authority, **Brunei Tourism** (www.bruneitourism.travel), has an office at the airport. Its website is sumptuous and informative but not always up-to-date.

VISAS

Most travellers are issued free visas on arrival: 90 days for Americans, 14 or 30 days for most other Westerners. Three-day transit visas are available for almost everyone except Israelis.

Australians receive on-arrival visas but have to pay: B$20/30 for a single-/multiple-entry visa and B$5 for a transit visa. If you'll be travelling overland through Brunei, make sure to ask for a multiple-entry visa.

WOMEN TRAVELLERS

Women are rarely hassled, and report being able to converse freely with both women and men.

Some Muslim women do not shake hands with men.

🛈 Getting There & Away

Brunei is an easy stopover if you are travelling between the Malaysian states of Sabah and Sarawak.

AIR

Brunei International Airport (☏233-1747, flight enquiries 233-6767; www.civil-aviation. gov.bn) About 8km north of central BSB.

AirAsia (www.airasia.com) Inexpensive flights from BSB to KL.

Cebu Pacific Air (www.cebupacificair.com) BSB to Manila.

Malaysia Airlines (www.malaysiaairlines.com) BSB to KL.

MASwings (www.maswings.com.my) BSB to Kota Kinabalu and Kuching.

Royal Brunei Airlines (www.flyroyalbrunei. com) BSB to London, Dubai, Hong Kong, Shanghai, Bangkok, Manila, Melbourne, Singapore, Surabaya, Jakarta, Kota Kinabalu and Kuala Lumpur. Flights are alcohol free.

Singapore Airlines (www.singaporeair.com) BSB to Singapore.

BOAT

Passenger ferries from the Terminal Feri Serasa in Muara, about 20km northeast of BSB, to Pulau Labuan (B$17, 1¼ to 1¾ hours) are scheduled for 8am, 8.30am, 1pm and 4.30pm. Departures from Labuan (RM35) are at 9am, 1.30pm, 3.30pm and 4pm.

The only way to make it all the way to Kota Kinabalu (KK), Malaysia, in one day, with a change of boats in Labuan, is to take the earliest ferry of the day, and even then the trip takes about 10 hours (including the bus ride from central BSB to Muara). The bus is a bit faster but not nearly as much fun. KK to BSB by ferry takes about eight hours.

To get from the bus station in central BSB to the ferry terminal in Muara, you can either take the Express Bus Service (B$2, 30 min) which goes via the airport, or buses 37 o. (one hour) to Muara town and then bus 33 (fare B$1). Leave *plenty* of time – we've heard o. travellers missing ferries because of bus delays. A taxi should cost B$30, though from Muara some drivers ask for B$40.

BUS

The only bus company authorised to transport passengers between Brunei and Malaysia has three names: Jesselton Express and Sipitang Express for services eastward towards Kota Kinabalu, and PHLS for services westward towards Miri. For details on services, contact **Danny Hardini** (☏ in Brunei 880 1180, in Malaysia 016 585 9814; danny25174@yahoo.com), an ebullient tourist guide and all-round character who helps out with bus boarding each morning.

Buses depart from Parking Lapau, the parking lot across the street from the Royal Regalia Museum (p53).

Jesselton Express (☏ in BSB 714 5734, in KK 016 836 0009; www.sipitangexpress.com. my) sends a bus to Kota Kinabalu (B$45, eight hours), via Limbang, Bangar and Lawas, daily at 8am. In the other direction, the bus leaves Kota Kinabalu's Jalan Tugu Bus Station at 8am. Reservations can be made online at www. busonlineticket.com. Make sure your passport has plenty of pages – the trip between BSB and Sabah will add eight 'chops' (stamps)!

PHLS Express (☏ in BSB 714 5735, in BSB 714 5734) links BSB with Miri (B$18 from BSB, RM40 from Miri, 3½ hours) daily at 7am and 1pm; tickets are sold onboard. Departures from Miri's Pujut Bus Terminal, where ticketing is handled by Bintang Jaya, are about 8.15am and 3.45pm. Booking ahead is not necessary.

Another option for travel between BSB and Miri is to go by private minivan (RM60 per person, 2½ hours). To reserve, contact **Mr Foo** (☏ in Brunei 878 2521, from noon to 1pm, in Malaysia 013 833 2231, from 7am to 9am and 5pm to 7pm). In Miri, reservations can be made via the Dillenia Guesthouse (p464).

Cambodia

📞 855 / POP 14.9 MILLION

Best Temples

➡ Angkor Wat (p94)
➡ Bayon (p98)
➡ Ta Prohm (p99)
➡ Banteay Srei (p102)
➡ Prasat Preah Vihear (p108)

Best Places for Cultural Connections

➡ Temples of Angkor (p94)
➡ Ratanakiri Province (p131)
➡ Battambang (p103)
➡ Mondulkiri Province (p134)
➡ National Museum of Cambodia (p69)

Why Go?

Ascend to the realm of the gods at Angkor Wat, a spectacular fusion of spirituality, symbolism and symmetry. Descend into the darkness of Tuol Sleng to witness the crimes of the Khmer Rouge. This is Cambodia, a country with a history both inspiring and depressing, a captivating destination that casts a spell on all those who visit.

Fringed by beautiful beaches and tropical islands, sustained by the mother waters of the Mekong River and cloaked in some of the region's few remaining emerald wildernesses, Cambodia is an adventure as much as a holiday. This is the warm heart of Southeast Asia, with everything the region has to offer packed into one bite-sized chunk.

Despite the headline attractions, Cambodia's greatest treasure is its people. The Khmers have been to hell and back, but thanks to an unbreakable spirit and infectious optimism they have prevailed with their smiles and spirits largely intact.

When to Go
Phnom Penh

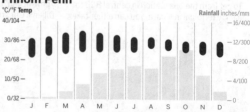

Nov–Feb The best all-round time to visit with relatively cool climes.

Apr–May Khmer New Year falls in mid-April and the mercury regularly hits 40°C.

Jul–Sep Green season: rice paddies shimmer, clouds bring heat relief and prices plummet.

Don't Miss

Cambodia's nightlife is the stuff of legend. While other cities in the region tuck themselves into bed for the night, thanks to curfews and closing times, Phnom Penh and Siem Reap rumble on from dusk till dawn. Phnom Penh has a vibrant bar and club culture. The riverfront area is a good hunting ground for bars, but as the night wears on it is time to try other haunts such as popular St 278 or buzzin' St 51, home to Pontoon and the Heart of Darkness.

Up in sublime Siem Reap, one street boasts so many bars it's earned itself the moniker 'Pub St'. There is no easier place for a crawl in the region and draught beer is almost a giveaway at US$0.50 a glass. Try alternative backpacker bars Angkor What? or the Warehouse, or something a little more refined such as Miss Wong.

ITINERARIES

One Week

Soak up the sights, sounds and smells of Phnom Penh, Cambodia's dynamic and fast-changing capital. Travel by road to Siem Reap, gateway to the majestic temples of Angkor, passing by the pre-Angkorian temples of Sambor Prei Kuk or taking a longer detour via the charming colonial-era city of Battambang. Explore Angkor in depth, as nowhere does temples quite like Cambodia.

Two Weeks

After exploring Phnom Penh and Siem Reap for a week, hit the provinces. Those heading to Thailand should head south to Cambodia's up-and-coming coastline. Soak up the languid charms of Kampot and Kep, then head to Sihanoukville, where dreamy islands lurk offshore. Try some adrenalin adventures around Koh Kong before exiting the country. Laos- or Vietnam-bound travellers can easily spend a week in the wild east, trekking in Ratanakiri or Mondulkiri and tracking rare Irrawaddy dolphins on the Mekong River around Kratie or Stung Treng.

Essential Adventures

➡ **Chi Phat** Mountain bikes, treks, kayaks, birdwatching – it's all here at this pioneering ecotourism project.

➡ **Stung Treng** Kayak with rare Irrawaddy dolphins then continue down the Mekong amid enchanting flooded forests.

➡ **Veun Sai-Siem Pang Conservation Area** Trek into the jungle to observe rare gibbons in their element in Ratanakiri.

➡ **Koh Rong Island** Beachcomb the deserted sands and shores of this tropical island near the city of the same name.

➡ **Phnom Prich Wildlife Sanctuary** Walk with elephants, mountain bike and trek in this WWF-supported program in Mondulkiri.

AT A GLANCE

➡ **Currency** Riel (r)

➡ **Language** Khmer

➡ **Money** ATMs common in major cities

➡ **Visas** Available on arrival for most nationalities

➡ **Mobile phones** Prepaid SIM cards are cheap, but you need a passport to register

CAMBODIA

Fast Facts

➡ **Area** 181,035 sq km

➡ **Capital** Phnom Penh

➡ **Emergency** Police 117

Exchange Rates

Australia	A$1	3580r
Euro Zone	€1	5440r
Laos	1000K	495r
Thailand	10B	1220r
UK	£1	6595r
USA	US$1	3960r
Vietnam	10,000d	1880r

Set Your Budget

➡ **Budget guesthouse room** US$3–8

➡ **Local restaurant meal** US$1.50–3

➡ **Beer in backpacker bar** US$0.50–1

➡ **Moto ride** US$0.50–1

Entering the Country

Fly into Phnom Penh or Siem Reap. Land borders with Laos, Thailand and Vietnam.

Cambodia Highlights

1 Discover the eighth wonder of the world, **Angkor** (p94)

2 Enjoy the 'Pearl of Asia', **Phnom Penh** (p68), with striking museums, a sublime riverside setting and happening nightlife

3 Island hop around **Sihanoukville** (p114) and soak up the city's hedonistic vibe

4 Wander around the lush **Battambang** (p103) countryside, climbing hilltop temples and exploring caves

5 Explore wild **Mondulkiri** (p134), a land of rolling hills, thundering waterfalls and indigenous minorities

6 Slip into the soporific pace of riverside **Kampot** (p122)

7 Make the pilgrimage to the awe-inspiring hilltop temple of **Prasat Preah Vihear** (p108)

8 Explore the bucolic Mekong islands and dolphin pools around **Kratie** (p128) by bicycle and boat

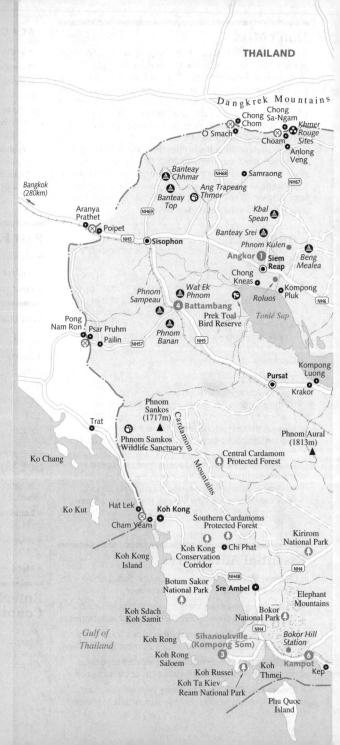

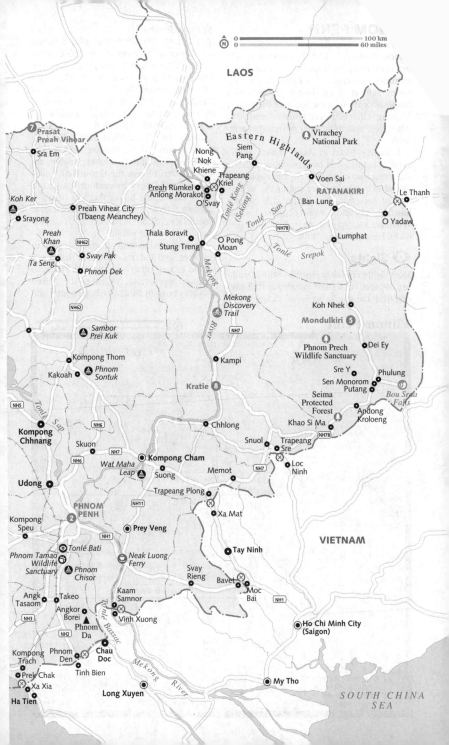

ពេញ): the name can't help
an image of the exotic. The
es of the Royal Palace, flut-
...iron of the monks' robes and a
...scious location on the banks of the mighty
Mekong – this is the Asia many dreamed of
when first imagining their adventures overseas.

Once the 'Pearl of Asia', Phnom Penh's
shine was tarnished by war and revolution.
But that's history and the city has risen from
the ashes to take its place among the 'in' capitals of Asia, with an alluring cafe culture,
bustling bars and a world-class food scene.
Whatever your flavour, no matter your taste,
it's all here in Phnom Penh.

◉ Sights

Most sights are fairly central – within walking distance or a short *remorque* (túk-túk)
ride from the riverfront Sisowath Quay.

★ **Royal Palace**   PALACE

(ព្រះវិហារព្រះកែវមរកត; Map p70; Sothearos
Blvd; admission incl camera/video 25,000r, guide
per hr US$10; ◷ 8-11am & 2-5pm) With its classic
Khmer roofs and ornate gilding, the Royal
Palace dominates the diminutive skyline of
Phnom Penh. It is a striking structure near
the riverfront, bearing a remarkable likeness
to its counterpart in Bangkok.

Being the official residence of King Si-
hamoni, parts of the massive palace compound are closed to the public. Visitors are
only allowed to visit the throne hall and a
clutch of buildings surrounding it. Adjacent
to the palace, the **Silver Pagoda** (Map p74;
Samdech Sothearos Blvd; included in admission to
Royal Palace; ◷ 07.30-11am & 2.30-5pm) complex
is also open to the public.

Visitors need to wear shorts that reach to
the knee, and T-shirts or blouses that reach
to the elbow; otherwise they will have to
rent an appropriate covering. The palace
gets very busy on Sundays when countryside

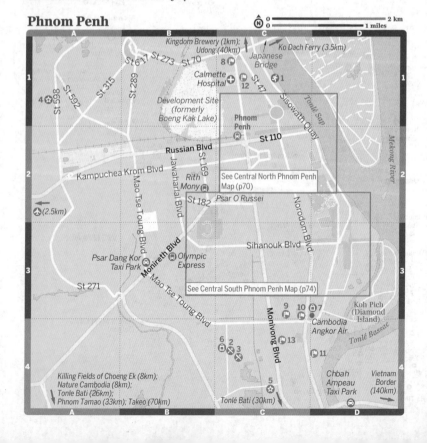

Khmers come to pay their respects, but this can be a fun way to experience the place, thronging with locals.

⭐**National Museum of Cambodia** MUSEUM
(សារមន្ទីរជាតិ; Map p70; www.cambodiamuseum. info; cnr St 13 & St 178; admission US$5; ⊙8am-5pm) The National Museum of Cambodia is home to the world's finest collection of Khmer sculpture, a millennium's worth and more of masterful Khmer design. Housed in a graceful, traditionally designed terracotta structure (built 1917–20), it provides the perfect backdrop to an outstanding array of delicate objects.

The museum comprises four pavilions facing the beautiful central courtyard. Start left and continue in a clockwise, chronological direction. Most interesting are the pre-Angkorian and Angkorian collections, which include an imposing eight-armed Vishnu statue from the 6th century found at Phnom Da; several striking statues of Shiva from the 9th, 10th and 11th centuries; a giant pair of wrestling monkeys (Ko Ker, 10th century); and the sublime, oft-copied statue of a seated Jayavarman VII (r 1181–1219) meditating. No photography is allowed except in the central courtyard.

⭐**Tuol Sleng Museum** MUSEUM
(សារមន្ទីរទួលស្លែង; Map p74; cnr St 113 & St 350; admission US$2, guide US$6; ⊙7am-5.30pm) In 1975, Tuol Svay Prey High School was taken over by Pol Pot's security forces and turned into a prison known as Security Prison 21 (S-21). This soon became the largest centre of detention and torture in the country. At the height of its activity, some 100 victims were killed every day.

S-21 has been turned into the Tuol Sleng Museum, which serves as a testament to the crimes of the Khmer Rouge. Like the Nazis, the Khmer Rouge leaders were meticulous in keeping records of their barbarism. Each prisoner who passed through S-21 was photographed, sometimes before and after torture. The long corridors are hallways of ghosts containing haunting photographs of the victims, their faces staring back eerily from the past. Tuol Sleng is not for the squeamish.

French-Cambodian director Rithy Panh's powerful 1996 film *Bophana*, which tells the true story of a beautiful young woman and a regional Khmer Rouge leader who fall in love and are consequently executed at S-21 prison, screens here at 10am and 3pm daily.

For a greater insight into the methodical machine of death that was Tuol Sleng, pick up *Voices from S-21* by David Chandler, a chilling and incisive description of life in the prison, pieced together from accounts from the tortured and the torturers.

Killing Fields of Choeung Ek MUSEUM
(វាលពិឃាតជើងឯក; admission incl audio tour US$5; ⊙7.30am-5.30pm) Most of the 17,000 detainees held at the S-21 prison were executed at Choeung Ek, 14km southwest of Phnom Penh. Prisoners were often bludgeoned to death to avoid wasting precious bullets. It is hard to imagine the brutality that unfolded here when wandering through this peaceful, shady, former longan orchard, but the memorial stupa soon brings it home, displaying more than 8000 skulls of victims and their ragged clothes.

A trip out here will cost US$5 round trip on a moto (motorcycle taxi) or about US$10 by *remorque* (drivers will start at US$15 to US$20).

Wat Phnom BUDDHIST TEMPLE
(វត្តភ្នំ; Map p70; temple admission US$1, museum admission US$2; ⊙7am-6.30pm, museum 7am-6pm) Wat Phnom, meaning Hill Temple, is appropriately set on the only hill (more like a mound at 27m) in Phnom Penh. The wat

Phnom Penh

CAMBODIA PHNOM PENH

Central North Phnom Penh

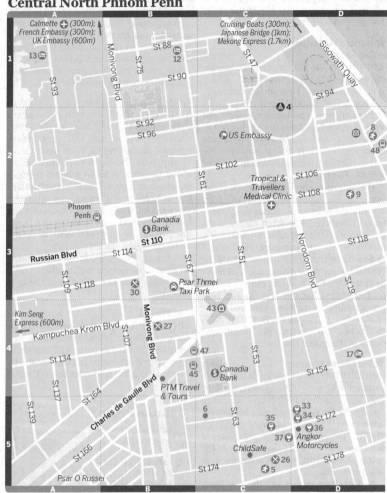

is revered by locals, who flock here to pray for good luck. Legend has it that in 1373 the first temple was built by a lady named Penh to house four Buddha statues that she found floating in the Mekong. A statue of a smiling and rather plump Lady Penh is in a pavilion behind the *vihara* (temple sanctuary).

Independence Monument MONUMENT
(វិមានឯករាជ្យ; Map p74; cnr Norodom & Sihanouk Blvds) Soaring over the city's largest roundabout is the grand Independence Monument, built in 1958 to commemorate Cambodia's 1953 independence from France and now also a memorial to Cambodia's war dead.

Modelled on the central tower of Angkor Wat, it was designed by leading Khmer architect Vann Molyvann.

Wat Ounalom BUDDHIST TEMPLE
(វត្តឧណ្ណាលោម; Map p70; Sothearos Blvd; ⊙6am-6pm) FREE This wat is the headquarters of Cambodian Buddhism. It received a battering during the Pol Pot era, but today the wat has come back to life. Behind the main building is a stupa containing an eyebrow hair of Buddha with an inscription in Pali (an ancient Indian language) over the entrance.

Boat Cruises

Sunset boat trips on the Tonlé Sap and Mekong Rivers are highly recommended. A slew of **cruising boats** (Map p68) are available for hire on the riverfront about 500m north of the tourist boat dock. Just rock up and arrange one on the spot for US$15 to US$20 an hour, depending on negotiations and numbers. Bring your own drinks.

Public river cruises are another option. They leave every 30 minutes from 5pm to 7.30pm from the **tourist boat dock** (Map p70; 93 Sisowath Quay) and last about 45 minutes (US$5 per head).

Cooking Classes

Cambodia Cooking Class   COOKING COURSE
(Map p74; ☑ 012 524801; www.cambodia-cooking-class.com; booking office 67 St 240, classes near Russian embassy; half/full day US$15/23) Learn the art of Khmer cuisine through Frizz Restaurant. Reserve ahead.

Cycling

Vicious Cycle   CYCLING
(Map p70; ☑ 012 430622; www.grasshopper adventures.com; 23 St 144; road/mountain bike per day US$4/8) Plenty of excellent mountain and other bikes available here. Kiddie seats can be attached to your mountain bike for US$3. Vicious represents well-respected Grasshopper Adventures in Phnom Penh.

Massage & Meditation

Free one-hour Vipassana meditation sessions take place in the central *vihara* of **Wat Langka** (Map p74; cnr St 51 & Sihanouk Blvd) at 6pm on Monday, Thursday and Saturday, and on Sunday at 8am.

Daughters   SPA
(Map p70; ☑ 077 657678; www.daughtersof cambodia.org; 65 St 178; 1hr foot spa US$10; ⊙ 9am-5.30pm Mon-Sat) Hand and foot massages are administered by participants in this NGO's vocational training program for at-risk women. Shorter (15- to 30-minute) treatments available.

Nail Bar   MASSAGE
(Map p70; www.mithsamlanh.org; Friends n' Stuff store, 215 St 13; 30/60min massages US$4/7; ⊙ 11am-9pm) Cheap manicures, pedicures, foot massages, hand massages and nail painting, all to help Mith Samlanh train street children in a new vocation.

Seeing Hands Massage   MASSAGE
(Map p70; 12 St 13; ⊙ 7.30am-10pm) Helps you ease those aches and pains; helps blind

🏃 Activities

Don't miss the quirky and colourful **aerobics** sessions that take place in parks around the city at dawn and again at dusk. The riverfront opposite Blue Pumpkin and Olympic Stadium are two good places to jump in and join the fun.

Most pool-equipped boutique hotels will let you **swim** for about US$5 and/or with the purchase of food. The great pool at the **Himawari Hotel** (Map p74; ☑ 023-214555; 313 Sisowath Quay; admission weekday/weekend US$7/8) is another option.

Central North Phnom Penh

masseurs stay self-sufficient. Massages average US$7 per hour, making it one of the best-value massages in the capital. There are several other cooperatives around town including **St 108** (Map p70; 34 St 108; ⊙8am-9pm).

ⓖ Tours

Cyclo Centre TOUR
(Map p70; ☏097 700 9762; www.cyclo.org.kh; 95 St 158; per hour/day from US$3/12) Dedicated to supporting *cyclo* (pedicab) drivers in Phnom Penh, the tours are a great way to see the sights.

Kingdom Brewery TOUR
(☏023-430180; 1748 NH5; tours US$6; ⊙1-5pm Mon-Fri) Tours include two beers and you don't have to book ahead – just show up. It's exactly 1km north of the Japanese Bridge on NH5.

🛏 Sleeping

Phnom Penh's traditional backpacker area around Boeng Kak ('The Lake') all but died when the lake was filled in with sand in 2011. Four miniature Khao San Rd backpacker colonies have emerged in its wake, with additional options scattered around the centre.

🛏 St 172 & Around

With the downfall of Boeng Kak, St 172 between St 19 and St 13 has emerged as the most popular area for budget accommodation. For walk-in guests, this is a great area to target.

Royal Guesthouse HOTEL $
(Map p70; ☏023-218026; hou_leng@yahoo.com; 91 St 154; s US$6-13, d US$8-15, tr from US$15; ❄@🛜) This old-time high-rise is getting a bit tired, but it's priced right and the family in charge is super friendly and doles out travel info aplenty.

Natural House Boutique Hotel   HOTEL $$
(Map p70; ☑ 097 263 4160; www.naturalhouse.asia;
52-54 St 172; r incl breakfast US$20-35; ❀ 🖂) The
best-looking US$20 rooms in the St 172 area
are here. Plush bedding and kitchenettes in
all rooms are the highlights. Roughly oppo-
site is Natural House's newly opened **Natu-
ral Inn Backpacker Hostel** (Map p70; ☑ 097
263 4160; www.naturalhouse.asia; off St 172; dm
US$3-8; ❀ 🖂).

Sundance Inn & Saloon   GUESTHOUSE $$
(Map p70; ☑ 016 802090; www.sundancecambo-
dia.com; 61 St 172; r US$25-30; ❀ @ 🖂 🖂) Sun-
dance separates itself from the pack on St
172 with positively giant beds, designer
bathrooms, a popular bar with a pool, and
computers that hook up to flat-screens in
every room.

🛏 St 258

South of St 172 and closer to the river, St 258
has a clutch of guesthouses with rooms in
the US$5 to US$10 range.

Lazy Gecko Guesthouse   GUESTHOUSE $
(Map p74; ☑ 078 786025; lazygeckocafe@gmail.
com; St 258; r with fan US$6-10, with air-con US$14-
18; ❀ 🖂) Best known as a cafe, Lazy Gecko's
rooms are a mixed bag. The air-con doubles
are nondescript but do have flat-screen TVs
and plenty of space, while the fan rooms are
mostly dark and grotty.

Same Same Backpackers   HOSTEL $
(Map p74; ☑ 077 717174; theatoch@yahoo.com; 5
St 258; dm US$4, d with fan/air-con from US$7/10;
❀ @ 🖂) Nothing fancy, just simple rooms
priced right. The air-conditioned dorm room
has no bunks, just 10 beds in close proximity
to each other and a single bathroom.

🛏 Psar O Russei Area

In this area west of busy Monivong Blvd
you'll find a mix of high-rise hotels and
backpacker-oriented guesthouses. The hotels are particularly appealing – you won't
come close to finding better US$15 air-con
rooms elsewhere in the centre.

★Narin Guesthouse   GUESTHOUSE $
(Map p74; ☑ 099 881133; www.naringuesthouse.
com; 50 St 125; r with fan/air-con US$12/17;
❀ @ 🖂) One of the stalwarts of the Phnom
Penh guesthouse scene. Rooms are smart,
bathrooms smarter still and there is a super-

SPLURGE

★Blue Lime (Map p70; ☑ 023-222260;
www.bluelime.asia; 42 St 19z; r incl breakfast
US$45-80; ❀ @ 🖂 🖂) is a popular bou-
tique hotel offering smart, minimalist
rooms and a leafy pool area done just
right. The pricier rooms are true gems,
with private plunge pools, four-poster
beds and contemporary concrete love
seats. No kids allowed.

---

relaxed open-air restaurant-terrace for taking some time out.

Smiley's Hotel   HOTEL $
(Map p74; ☑ 012 365959; smileyhotel.pp@gmail.
com; 37 St 125; s with fan US$6, d US$15-20;
❀ @ 🖂) A migrant from Siem Reap, Smiley's
is a huge seven-storey hotel with a choice of
40 spacious rooms that border on chic. The
US$20 rooms have big flat-screen TVs. In-
cludes a lift.

Sunday Guesthouse   GUESTHOUSE $
(Map p74; ☑ 023-211623; gech_sundayguest
house@hotmail.com; 97 St 141; d/tr from US$7/11;
❀ @ 🖂) This is a *real* guesthouse, a three-
storey walk-up affair run by an amiable family that can cook meals and help with travel
arrangements.

Tat Guesthouse   GUESTHOUSE $
(Map p74; ☑ 012 921211; tatcambodia@yahoo.com;
52 St 125; s without bathroom US$4, d with bathroom
US$7-12; ❀ @ 🖂) A super-friendly spot with a
breezy rooftop hang-out that's perfect for
chilling. The rooms aren't going to wow you,
but they're functional. For US$12 you get air-
con – not bad.

🛏 Golden St & Around

The trendy Boeng Keng Kang (BKK) district south of Independence Monument is
the flashpacker zone. Most budget accommodation here is centred on St 278, dubbed
'Golden St' because of the preponderance of
hotels that feature 'Golden' in their name.

★Mad Monkey   HOSTEL $
(Map p74; ☑ 023-987091; www.phnompenhhostels.
com; 26 St 302; dm US$7, r without/with bathroom
US$15/20; ❀ @ 🖂) This colourful and arty
hostel is justifiably popular. The spacious
dorms have air-con and sleep six to 20; the
smaller ones have double-wide bunk beds

Central South Phnom Penh

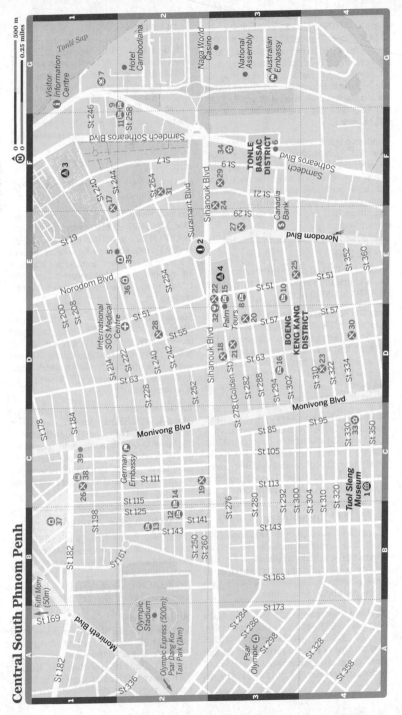

CAMBODIA

Central South Phnom Penh

◎ **Top Sights**
1 Tuol Sleng Museum C4

◎ **Sights**
2 Independence Monument E2
3 Silver Pagoda F1
4 Wat Langka E3

◎ **Activities, Courses & Tours**
5 Cambodia Cooking Class E1
6 Cambodian Living Arts F3
7 Himawari Hotel G1

◎ **Sleeping**
8 Blue Dog Guesthouse E3
9 Lazy Gecko Guesthouse G2
10 Mad Monkey E3
Narin Guesthouse .... (see 14)
11 Same Same Backpackers F2
12 Smiley's Hotel B2
13 Sunday Guesthouse B2
14 Tat Guesthouse C2
15 Top Banana Guesthouse E3
16 White Rabbit D3

◎ **Eating**
17 ARTillery F1
18 ARTillery D3
19 Asian Spice C2
20 Blue Pumpkin D3
21 Café Soleil D3
22 Dosa Corner E3
23 Hagar D4
24 Java Café F3
25 Le Lotus Blanc E3
26 Mama Restaurant C1
27 Red Cow E3
28 Sonivid D2
29 Sovanna F3
30 Thai Huot D4
31 The Vegetarian F2

◎ **Drinking & Nightlife**
32 Equinox D3
Top Banana .... (see 15)

◎ **Entertainment**
33 Flicks C4
34 Meta House F3

◎ **Shopping**
35 D's Books E2
36 Monument Books E2
37 Psar O Russei B1

◎ **Transport**
38 Capitol Tour C1
39 Lucky! Lucky! C1
New! New! .... (see 39)

that can sleep two (US$9 per couple). The private rooms vary, so check out a few.

Top Banana Guesthouse HOSTEL $
(Map p74; ☏ 012 885572; www.topbanana.biz; 9 St 278; dm US$6, r US$7-20; ❄@🗢) Great bar, so-so hostel has long been the mantra here. Now a facelift has seen the rooms improved and three dorm rooms added. The brilliant location high above Golden St and comfy open-air chill-out area remain the top selling points, however. Book way ahead.

White Rabbit HOSTEL $
(Map p74; www.whiterabbitguesthouse.com; 40A St 294; dm with fan/air-con US$4/5, d US$12-15; ❄🗢) This convivial hostel is a hidden gem, with an attractive ground-level bar and hang-out area, comfortable dorms with wide bunk beds, and good food.

Blue Dog Guesthouse HOSTEL $
(Map p74; ☏ 012 658075; bluedogguesthouse@gmail.com; 13 St 51; dm US$5-6, s/d US$6/10; @🗢) Location and price are right, plus there's a cosy common area and a popular bar downstairs, so you don't have to spend too much time in the clean but basic rooms.

🏠 Around Town

★**Eighty8 Backpackers** HOSTEL $
(Map p70; ☏ 023-500 2440; www.88backpackers.com; 98 St 88; dm US$5-7, d US$20-24; ❄@🗢🏊) The swimming pool and the premises – a magnificent, rambling villa – set this place apart from the rest of Phnom Penh's hostels. The courtyard is anchored by a big, sturdy bar, with billiards and plenty of places to lounge. Dorm rooms come in air-con and fan varieties, plus there's a female dorm.

Osaka Ya GUESTHOUSE $
(Map p70; ☏ 023-650 9423; www.osakayaguesthouse.com; 171 Sisowath Quay; r US$15-25; ❄🗢) This Japanese-run high-rise raises the bar for budget riverside lodging. Osaka Ya is allergic to the stank and mould that plague other hotels of this ilk. Here you swathe yourself in imported linens and watch crisp flat-screen TVs. Tasteful and spotless.

Grand View Guesthouse GUESTHOUSE $
(Map p70; ☏ 023-430766; www.grandview.netfirms.com; 4 St 93; r US$5-8; ❄@🗢) A few super-budget holdouts remain on the sandlot formerly known as Boeng Kak, including this

LOCAL FLAVOURS

Khmer Barbecues

After dark, Khmer eateries scattered across town illuminate their Cambodia Beer signs, hailing locals in for grilled strips of meat or seafood and generous jugs of draught beer. Khmer barbecues are literally all over the place, so it won't be hard to find one. A few recommended local eateries:

Sovanna (Map p74; 2C St 21; mains US$2-3; ☺6-11am & 3-11pm) Always jumping with locals and even a smattering of expats who have made this their barbecue of choice.

Red Cow (Map p74; 126 Norodom Blvd; mains US$2.50-7; ☺4-11pm) Grills up everything imaginable – eel, eggplant, frog, pig intestine, quail – along with curries and other traditional Khmer dishes.

Sonivid (Map p74; 39 St 242; meals US$5-10; ☺3pm-midnight) Steamed or fried crab, squid, fish and shellfish are the specialities at this wildly popular corner eatery.

Markets

Phnom Penh's many markets all have large central eating areas where stalls serve up local faves like noodle soup and fried noodles duing daylight hours. Most dishes cost a reasonable 4000r to 6000r. The best market for eating is Russian Market (p80), with an interior food zone that's easy to find and with a nice variety of Cambodian specialities. Psar Thmei (p80) and Psar O Russei (p80) are other great choices. **Psar Kandal** (Map p70; btwn Sts 144 & 154) gets going a little later and is an early evening option.

tall, skinny structure with basic rooms and unrivalled views of the lake-cum-beach.

✖ Eating

For foodies, Phnom Penh is a real delight, boasting a superb selection of restaurants that showcase the best in Khmer cooking, as well as the greatest hits from the region and the world.

✖ Centre North

★**Sam Doo Restaurant** CHINESE $
(Map p70; 56-58 Kampuchea Krom Blvd; mains US$2.80-5; ☺7am-2am) Many Chinese Khmers swear that this upstairs eatery near Central Market has the best food in town. The signature 'Sam Doo fried rice', hotpots and dim sum are recommended.

Beirut MIDDLE EASTERN $
(Map p70; ☐023-720011; 117 Sisowath Quay; dishes US$3-7; ☺11am-10.30pm; ☏🖋) Lilliputian eatery with super deals on wraps, kebabs and saucy appetisers like hummus with pita bread, plus *shisha* pipes (hookahs) for US$6 to US$8. Keep in mind that river views are obstructed up here.

Laughing Fatman CAMBODIAN $
(Map p70; St 172; mains US$2.50-6.50; ☺7am-midnight) A welcoming backpacker cafe with cheap food and big breakfasts. Formerly Oh

My Buddha – 'new name, same body', the corpulent owner joked.

¡Viva! MEXICAN $
(Map p70; 111 Sisowath Quay; dishes US$4-6; ☺10am-11pm; ☏) This Siem Reap import has raised the bar for Mexican food in Phnom Penh. A bucket of margaritas costs US$5.

Thai Huot SUPERMARKET $
(Map p70; 103 Monivong Blvd; ☺7.30am-8.30pm) This is the place for French travellers who are missing home, as it stocks many French products, including Bonne Maman jam and Hénaff pâté. Additional location in BKK (Map p74; cnr Sts 63 & 352; ☺7.30am-8.30pm).

★**Chat n' Chew** CAMBODIAN $$
(Map p70; 54 St 172; mains US$3-10; ☺7.30am-11pm; ☏) This is kind of like an upscale backpacker cafe, popular with expats and serving a range of Cambodian and international dishes.

Blue Pumpkin CAFE $$
(Map p70; 245 Sisowath Quay; mains US$3-7; ☺6am-11pm; ☏) An alluring cafe serving healthy breakfasts, pastas, sandwiches and ice cream. Other branches in BKK (Map p74; 12A St 57; ☺6am-10pm; ☏) and at Kids City (Sihanouk Blvd; ☺8am-9.30pm) and Monument Books (p80).

Happy Herb Pizza PIZZERIA **$$**
(Map p70; ☎ 012 921915; 345 Sisowath Quay; medium pizzas US$6-8.50; ☺8am-11pm; ☎) No, happy doesn't mean it comes with free toppings; it means pizza à la ganja. The non-marijuana pizzas are also pretty good, but don't involve the free trip. Delivery available.

Sher-e-Punjab INDIAN **$$**
(Map p70; ☎023-216360; 16 St 130; mains US$3-7; ☺11am-11pm; ☑) The capital's top spot for a curry fix; the tandoori dishes are particularly good. Even the prawn dishes cost under US$6.

🍴 Centre South

★**Dosa Corner** INDIAN **$**
(Map p74; 5E St 51; mains US$1.50-3; ☺8.30am-2pm & 5-10pm) Fans of Indian dosas will be pleased to discover this place does just what it says on the label, namely a generous variety of savoury pancakes from the south. Great value.

★**Asian Spice** ASIAN **$**
(Map p74; 79 St 111; mains US$2.30-2.80; ☺6am-9pm; ☎) The house speciality is the zesty Singapore laksa (yellow curry noodles), but

you'll also find spicy Indonesian, Malaysian and Cambodian fare. One of Phnom Penh's best bargains.

The Vegetarian CAMBODIAN **$**
(Map p74; 158 St 19; mains US$1.75-2.50; ☺10.30am-8.30pm Mon-Sat; ☑) All dishes at this vegetarian spot are US$2.50 or under and it doesn't skimp on portions either. Noodles and fried rice are the specialities.

Café Soleil VEGETARIAN **$**
(Map p74; 22D St 278; mains US$2-4; ☺7am-10pm; ☎☑) Cheap-as-chips vego dishes such as fried noodles, pumpkin curry, hummus and salads.

Mama Restaurant CAMBODIAN **$**
(Map p74; 10C St 111; mains US$1.50-4; ☺7.30am-8.30pm) This long-running backpacker cafe in the heart of the Psar O Russei area serves tasty French-influenced Khmer food.

Java Café CAFE **$$**
(Map p74; www.javaarts.org; 56 Sihanouk Blvd; mains US$4-8; ☺7am-10pm; ☎☑) Consistently popular thanks to a breezy balcony and a creative menu that includes crisp salads, delicious homemade sandwiches and burgers. The downstairs doubles as a bakery.

CAMBODIA PHNOM PENH

TOP FIVE: GOOD-CAUSE DINING

These fantastic eateries act as training centres for young staff and help fund worthy causes in the capital.

Friends (Map p70; ☎ 012 802072; www.friends-international.org; 215 St 13; tapas US$4-7, mains from US$6; ☺11am-9pm; ☎) One of Phnom Penh's best-loved restaurants, this place is a must, with tasty tapas bites, heavenly smoothies and creative cocktails. It offers former street children a headstart in the hospitality industry.

Sugar 'n Spice Cafe (Map p70; www.daughtersofcambodia.org; 65 St 178; sandwiches US$3.50-7; ☺9am-6pm Mon-Sat; ☎) This fantastic cafe on the top floor of the Daughters visitors centre features soups, smoothies, coffee drinks and fusion-y mains served by former sex workers being trained by Daughters to reintegrate into society.

Romdeng (Map p70; ☎ 092 219565; 74 St 174; mains US$5-8; ☺11am-9pm; ☎) Part of the Friends' extended family, this elegant restaurant specialises in Cambodian country fare, including a famous *amok* (fish baked with coconut and lemon grass in banana leaves). *The* place to sample deep-fried tarantulas or stir-fried tree ants with beef and holy basil.

Hagar (Map p74; 44 St 310; lunch/dinner buffet US$6.50/11; ☺7am-2pm & 6-9pm Thu-Sat, 7am-2pm Sun-Wed) Proceeds from the all-you-can-eat buffets here go towards assisting destitute or abused women. The spread is usually Asian fusion or barbecue, except for Wednesday lunches and Thursday dinners, when Hagar lays out its legendary Italian buffet.

Le Lotus Blanc (Map p74; 152 St 51; mains US$4-8.50; ☺7am-10pm Mon-Sat; ☎) This suburban restaurant acts as a training centre for youths who previously scoured the city dump. Run by French NGO Pour un Sourire d'Enfant (For the Smile of a Child), it serves classy Western and Khmer cuisine.

ARTillery CAFE $$
(Map p74; St 240½; mains US$4-6; ⊙7.30am-9pm Tue-Sun, to 5pm Mon; ⊛🖋) Healthy salads, sandwiches, shakes and snacks like hummus and felafel are served in this creative space on an artsy alley off St 240. Also has a small raw-food menu. Another **branch** (Map p74; 13 St 278; ⊙7.30am-5pm) is on St 278.

🍴 Russian Market Area

⭐ **Café Yejj** CAFE $
(Map p68; www.cafeyejj.com; 170 St 450; mains US$3.50-6; ⊙8am-9pm; ⊛🖋) 🖉 An air-con escape a half-block south of Russian Market, this cafe uses many organic ingredients to prepare pastas, salads, wraps and soups. Promotes fair trade and responsible employment.

Sumatra INDONESIAN $
(Map p68; 35 St 456; mains US$1.50-3.50; ⊙11am-8pm; ⊛🖋) A block east of Russian Market, Sumatra is fantastic value, although big eaters may have to order two dishes like spicy *balado* (tomato and chilli sauce).

🍸 Drinking & Nightlife

Phnom Penh has some great bars and clubs and it's definitely worth planning at least one big night on the town. Many venues are clustered around the intersection of St 51 and St 172, where seemingly everybody ends up late at night. 'Golden St' (St 278) is popular and the riverfront also has its share of bars. Two-for-one happy hours are a big thing in Phnom Penh, so it pays to get started early.

For the lowdown on club nights, check out **Phnom Penh Underground** (www.phnom-penh-underground.com), a roving party of sorts that promotes gigs for various electro troupes in Phnom Penh and beyond.

⭐ **FCC** BAR
(Foreign Correspondents' Club; Map p70; 363 Sisowath Quay; ⊙6am-midnight; ⊛) A Phnom Penh institution, the FCC is housed in a colonial gem with great views and cool breezes. One of those must-see places in Cambodia. Happy hours run from 5pm to 7pm.

⭐ **Heart of Darkness** NIGHTCLUB
(Map p70; 26 St 51; ⊙8pm-late) Everybody should stop in at least once just to bask in the aura and history of the legendary 'Heart'. It has evolved into a nightclub more than a bar over the years, attracting all – and we mean *all* – sorts.

Equinox BAR
(Map p74; 3A St 278; ⊙8am-late; ⊛) At the heart of the action on St 278, this is a popular place with a lively outdoor bar downstairs and bands upstairs from Thursday to Saturday.

Slur BAR
(Map p70; 28 St 172; ⊙11am-2am) Slur consistently draws some of Phnom Penh's best musical talent. Worth stopping by to see who's on stage and throw back a Jägerbomb.

Zeppelin Café BAR
(Map p70; 109 St 51; ⊙6.30pm-late) Who says vinyl is dead? It lives on here thanks to this old-school rock bar with a serious '60s and '70s music collection.

Howie Bar BAR
(Map p70; 32 St 51; ⊙7pm-6am) Friendly, fun and unpredictable, 'way-cool' Howie is the perfect spillover when the famous Heart of Darkness is packed.

Pontoon NIGHTCLUB
(Map p70; www.pontoonclub.com; 80 St 172; admission weekends US$3-5, weekdays free; ⊙9.30pm-late) The city's premier nightclub often sees big foreign acts on the decks. Thursday is gay-friendly night, with a 1am lady-boy show.

Top Banana BAR
(Map p74; 9 St 278) There's no question where the top backpacker party spot in Phnom Penh is. The rooftop bar of this guesthouse goes off practically every night of the week.

Eighty8 Backpackers BAR
(Map p70; 98 St 88) A well-stocked, perfectly oval bar commands the courtyard of this villalike hostel. Great tunes, great ambience and regular first-Friday parties see the expat and backpacker worlds collide.

Blue Chili BAR
(Map p70; 36 St 178; ⊙6pm-late) The owner of this gay-friendly bar stages his own drag show every Friday and Saturday at 10.30pm.

☆ Entertainment

For the ins and outs of the entertainment scene, grab a copy of the free listings newspaper the *Advisor,* or check out '7 Days' in the Friday issue of the *Phnom Penh Post*. Online, try www.ladypenh.com, http://khmer440.com or www.lengpleng.com.

★**Meta House** CINEMA
(Map p74; www.meta-house.com; 37 Sothearos Blvd; ☺4pm-midnight Tue-Sun; 🐾) This German-run open-air theatre screens art-house films, documentaries and shorts from Cambodia and around the world most evenings at 4pm (admission free) and 7pm (admission US$2). Films are sometimes followed by Q&As with those involved.

Flicks CINEMA
(Map p74; www.theflicks-cambodia.com; 39B St 95; tickets US$3.50; 🐾) It shows at least two movies a day in an ubercomfortable air-conditioned screening room. You can watch both on one ticket. A second **Flicks** (Map p70; 90 St 136) is at 11 Happy Backpacker.

★**Plae Pakaa** PERFORMING ARTS
(Fruitful; Map p70; ✐ 023-986032; www.cambodian livingarts.org; National Museum, St 178; adult/child US$15/6; ☺7pm Mon-Sat Oct-Mar, Fri & Sat May-Sep, closed Apr) Plae Pakaa is a series of three rotating, hour-long performances put on by **Cambodian Living Arts** (CLA; Map p74; ✐ 017 998570; www.cambodianlivingarts.org; 128

Sothearos Blvd) that showcase various Khmer traditional arts and customs.

Apsara Arts Association DANCE
(Map p68; ✐ 012 979335; www.apsara-art.org; 71 St 598; tickets US$6-7) ✐ Alternate performances of classical dance and folk dance most Saturdays at 7pm (call to confirm). It's in Tuol Kork district, in the far north of the city.

**Sovanna Phum
Arts Association** PERFORMING ARTS
(Map p68; ✐ 023-987564; www.shadow-puppets.org; 166 St 99, btwn Sts 484 & 498; adult/child US$5/3) ✐ Traditional shadow-puppet, classical dance and traditional drum shows are held here at 7.30pm every Friday and Saturday night.

 Shopping

An affirmation of identity, the *krama* (chequered scarf) is worn around the necks, shoulders and waists of nearly every Khmer. The scarves make superb souvenirs, as do Cambodia's sculptures and handicrafts.

RESPONSIBLE TRAVEL IN CAMBODIA

Cambodia has been to hell and back and there are many ways that you can put a little back into the country. Staying longer, travelling further and avoiding package tours is obvious advice. For those on shorter stays, consider spending money in local markets and in restaurants and shops that assist disadvantaged locals. If visiting minority villages, pay attention to a few basic rules such as those in the Responsible Trekking Around Ratanakiri boxed text (p134).

The looting of stone carvings from Cambodia's ancient temples has devastated many temples. Don't contribute to this cultural rape by buying antiquities of any sort – classy reproductions are available in Phnom Penh and Siem Reap, complete with export certificates.

Cambodians dress very modestly and are offended by skimpily dressed foreigners. Just look at the Cambodians frolicking in the sea – most are fully dressed. Wearing bikinis on the beach is fine but cover up elsewhere. Topless or nude bathing is a definite no-no.

The sexual exploitation of children is now taken very seriously in Cambodia. Report anything that looks like child-sex tourism to the ChildSafe hotlines in **Phnom Penh** (✐ 012 311112), **Siem Reap** (✐ 017 358758) or **Sihanoukville** (✐ 012 478100), or to the national **police hotline** (✐ 023-997919). Tourism establishments that sport the ChildSafe logo have staff trained to protect vulnerable children and, where necessary, intervene.

Organisations with lots of practical ideas for responsible travel:

Cambodia Community-Based Ecotourism Network (www.ccben.org) The official website promoting community-based ecotourism in Cambodia. Browse here for more on projects and initiatives across the country.

ConCERT (Map p87; ✐ 063-963511; www.concertcambodia.org; 560 Phum Stoueng Thmey Siem Reap; ☺9am-5pm Mon-Fri) Siem Reap–based organisation 'connecting communities, environment and responsible tourism'.

Friends International (www.friends-international.org) Supports marginalised children and their families and runs the global **ChildSafe** (Map p70; ✐ 023-986601, hotline 012 311112; www.childsafe-cambodia.org; 71 St 174, Phnom Penh; ☺8am-5pm Mon-Fri) network to encourage travellers to behave responsibly with children.

TOP FIVE: GOOD-CAUSE SHOPPING

The stores here sell high-quality silk items and handicrafts to provide the disabled and disenfranchised with valuable training for future employment, plus a regular flow of income to improve lives.

Daughters (Map p70; www.daughtersofcambodia.org; 65 St 178; ⊘ 9am-6pm Mon-Sat) Fashionable clothes, bags and accessories made with eco-friendly cotton and natural dyes by former prostitutes and victims of sex trafficking.

Friends n' Stuff (Map p70; 215 St 13; ⊘ 11am-9pm) The closest thing to a charity shop or thrift store in Phnom Penh, with a good range of new and secondhand products sold to generate money to help street children.

KeoK'jay (Map p70; www.keokjay.com; cnr St 110 & Sisowath Quay; ⊘ 11am-10pm) Original women's clothing and accessories stitched by HIV-positive women.

Rajana (Map p70; www.rajanacrafts.org; 170 St 450; ⊘ 7am-6pm Mon-Sat, 10.30am-5pm Sun) One of the best all-around handicraft stores, Rajana aims to promote fair wages and training. It has a beautiful selection of cards, some quirky metalware products, quality jewellery, bamboo crafts, lovely shirts, gorgeous wall hangings, pepper, candles – you name it. Has a second **market store** (Russian Market; ⊘ 10am-6pm).

Watthan Artisans (Map p68; www.wac.khmerproducts.com; 180 Norodom Blvd; ⊘ 8am-6.30pm) Silk and other products, including wonderful contemporary handbags, made by landmine and polio victims.

Markets

Bargains galore can be found at Phnom Penh's vibrant markets. Navigating the labyrinths of shoes, clothing, bric-a-brac and food is one of the most enjoyable ways to earn a foot massage.

Russian Market   MARKET

(Psar Tuol Tom Pong; Map p68; ⊘ 6am-5pm) The Russians' retail outlet of choice back in the 1980s, this is the one market all visitors should explore during a trip to Phnom Penh. It includes designer clothing labels hot out of the factory, bootleg music and films, and carvings in wood, stone or bronze. Bargain hard, as hundreds of tourists pass through here every day. It is located in the far south of the city, about four blocks south of Mao Tse Toung Blvd.

Psar Thmei   MARKET

(ផ្សារធំថ្មី, Central Market; Map p70; ⊘ 6.30am-5.30pm) Often referred to as Central Market, this art-deco landmark resembles a Babylonian ziggurat. It houses an array of stalls selling jewellery, clothing and curios. The food section is enormous, with produce spilling onto the streets.

Psar O Russei   MARKET

(Map p74; ⊘ 6.30am-5.30pm) Much bigger than either Psar Thmei or Russian Market, Psar O Russei sells foodstuffs, costume jewellery, imported toiletries, secondhand clothes and everything else you can imagine from hundreds of stalls.

Night Market   MARKET

(Psar Reatrey; Map p70; cnr St 108 & Sisowath Quay; ⊘ 5-11pm Fri-Sun) The Night Market is a cooler, alfresco version of Russian Market and sells souvenirs, silks and knick-knacks. Bargain vigorously, as prices can be on the high side.

Bookshops

Monument Books   BOOKS

(Map p74; 111 Norodom Blvd; ⊘ 7am-8.30pm; ☎) The best-stocked bookshop in town, with every Cambodia-related book available, a superb maps and travel section, plus a wi-fi-enabled branch of Blue Pumpkin cafe.

D's Books   BOOKS

(Map p70; 7 St 178; ⊘ 9am-9pm) The largest chain of secondhand bookshops in the capital, with a good range of titles. There's a second **branch** (Map p74; 79 St 240; ⊘ 9am-9pm) on trendy St 240.

❶ Orientation

Phnom Penh's sequentially numbered streets may be a paragon of logic, but when it comes to house numbering, utter chaos reigns. It's not uncommon to find a row of adjacent buildings numbered, say, 13A, 34, 7, 26. Worse, several buildings on the same street, blocks apart, may have adopted the same house number! When you're given an address, try to get a cross-street, such as 'on St 240 near St 51'.

ℹ Information

EMERGENCY
Ambulance (📞119, in English 023-724891)
Fire (📞in Khmer 118)
Police (📞117)

INTERNET ACCESS
Internet cafes are everywhere and usually charge US$0.50 to US$1 per hour. Pretty much all hotels and most cafes and restaurants offer wi-fi connections, usually free.

MEDICAL SERVICES
Calmette Hospital (Map p68; 📞023-426948; 3 Monivong Blvd; ⊘24hr) The best of the local hospitals, with the most comprehensive services and an intensive-care unit.

International SOS Medical Centre (Map p74; 📞012 816911, 023-216911; www.international sos.com; 161 St 51; ⊘8am-5.30pm Mon-Fri, 8am-noon Sat, emergency 24hr) Top clinic with a host of Western doctors, and with prices to match.

Tropical & Travellers Medical Clinic (Map p70; 📞023-306802; www.travellersmedical clinic.com; 88 St 108; ⊘9.30-11.30am & 2.30-5pm Mon-Fri, 9.30-11.30am Sat) Well-regarded clinic run for more than a decade by a British general practitioner.

U-Care Pharmacy (Map p70; 26 Sothearos Blvd; ⊘8am-10pm) International-style pharmacy with a convenient location near the river.

MONEY
Phnom Penh's airport has a few ATMs. The city has plenty of banks and exchange services, including the following:

ANZ Royal Bank (Map p70; 265 Sisowath Quay; ⊘8.30am-4pm Mon-Fri, 8.30am-noon Sat) With multiple locations, it offers cash advances and ATM withdrawals at US$4 per transaction.

Canadia Bank Canadia Bank ATMs around town incur no transaction charges. This flagship branch (Map p70; cnr St 110 & Monivong Blvd; ⊘8am-3.30pm Mon-Fri, 8-11.30am Sat) changes travellers cheques of several currencies for a 2% commission. Additional branches at Sorya Shopping Centre (Map p70; cnr St 63 & St 154) and Norodom Blvd (Map p74).

POST
Central Post Office (Map p70; St 13; ⊘8am-6pm) A landmark, it's in a charming building just east of Wat Phnom.

WARNING: BAG SNATCHING

Bag and phone-snatching has become a real problem in Phnom Penh. Hot spots include the riverfront and busy areas around popular markets, but there is no real pattern and the speeding motorbike thieves, usually operating in pairs, can strike any place, any time. Countless expats and tourists have been injured falling off their bikes in the process of being robbed. Keep your valuables close or concealed and be prepared to let go rather than be dragged into the road. Keep shoulder bags in front of you when riding on motos. These people are real pros and only need one chance.

TOURIST INFORMATION
There is not much in the way of official tourist information in the Cambodian capital, but private travel agencies are everywhere and are usually happy to dispense advice. The *Phnom Penh Visitors' Guide* (www.canbypublications. com) has good maps and is brimming with useful information on the capital.

Visitor Information Centre (Map p74; Sisowath Quay; ⊘8am-5pm Mon-Sat) Located on the riverfront near the Chatomuk Theatre. While it doesn't carry a whole lot of information, it does offer free internet access, free wi-fi, air-con and clean public toilets.

TRAVEL AGENCIES
Reliable travel agencies include the following:

Palm Tours (Map p74; 📞023-726291; www. palmtours.biz; 1B St 278; ⊘8am-9pm) Efficient Volak and her team are a great option for bus tickets (no commission) and the like. In the heart of all the action on St 278.

PTM Travel & Tours (Map p70; 📞023-219268; www.ptmcambodia.com; 200 Monivong Blvd; ⊘8am-5.30pm Mon-Sat) Good bet for outgoing air tickets.

ℹ Getting There & Away

AIR
Many international air services run to/from Phnom Penh. Domestically, **Cambodia Angkor Air** (Map p68; 📞023-666 6786; www.cambodia angkorair.com; 206A Norodom Blvd) flies four to six times daily to Siem Reap (about US$100, 30 minutes).

BOAT
Between August and March, speedboats depart daily to Siem Reap (US$35, five to six hours) at 7.30am from the tourist boat dock at the eastern

BUSES FROM PHNOM PENH

DESTINATION	COMPANY	PRICE (US$)	DURATION (HR)	FREQUENCY
Bangkok	Mekong Express, PP Sorya, Virak Buntham	18-23	12	daily per company
Battambang (day bus)	GST, PP Sorya, Rith Mony, Virak Buntham	5-10	6	several per company
Ho Chi Minh City	Capitol Tour, Giant Ibis, Mekong Express, PP Sorya	13	7	several per company until about 3pm
Kampot (direct)	Capitol Tour, Rith Mony	5.50-6	3	2 daily per company
Kampot (via Kep)	PP Sorya	5.50	4	7.30am, 9.30am, 2.45pm
Koh Kong	Olympic Express, PP Sorya, Virak Buntham	5	5½	2-3 per company until noon
Kratie	PP Sorya	8	6-8	6.45am, 7.15am, 7.30am, 9.30am, 10.30am
Pakse via Don Det (Laos)	PP Sorya	28	12-14	6.45am
Siem Reap (day bus)	most companies	5.50-17	6	frequent
Sihanoukville	Capitol Tour, GST, Mekong Express, PP Sorya, Rith Mony, Virak Buntham	5-6	5½	frequent
Stung Treng	PP Sorya	12.50	9	6.45am, 7.30am

end of St 104, but the tickets are overpriced compared with the bus.

Following the river to Chau Doc in Vietnam is a gorgeous way to go; see the boxed text, 'Getting to Vietnam: Mekong Delta Borders'.

BUS

All major towns in Cambodia, plus regional hubs Bangkok, Ho Chi Minh City and Pakse, are accessible by air-conditioned bus from Phnom Penh. Most buses leave from company offices, which are generally clustered around Psar Thmei or located near the corner of St 106 and Sisowath Quay.

Not all buses are created equal. Buses run by Capitol Tour and Phnom Penh Sorya are usually among the cheapest; Giant Ibis runs upscale 'VIP' buses with plenty of legroom and dysfunctional wi-fi, but they are about double the average price. Virak Buntham is the night bus specialist.

Express vans are an option to most cities. These shave hours off average trip times, but are cramped and often travel at ulcer-inducing speeds.

Main bus companies:

Capitol Tour (Map p74; ☎023-724104; 14 St 182)

Giant Ibis Map p70; ☎023-999333; www. giantibis.com; 3 St 106; 🛜)

GST (US Liang Express Bus; Map p70; ☎023-218114; 13 St 142)

Mekong Express 2020 NH5 (☎023-427518; www.catmekongexpress.com) Also a riverside booking office (Map p70; Sisowath Quay)

Olympic Express (Map p68; ☎092 868782; 70 Monireth Blvd)

Phnom Penh Sorya (Map p70; ☎023-210359; Psar Thmei area)

Rith Mony St 169 (Map p68; ☎097 888 9447). Also a riverfront terminal (Map p70; ☎017 525388; 24 St 102)

Virak Buntham (Kampuchea Angkor Express; Map p70; ☎016 786270; St 106)

CAR & MOTORCYCLE

Guesthouses and travel agencies can arrange a car and driver for US$25 to US$60 a day, depending on the destination.

SHARE TAXI, PICK-UP & MINIBUS

Share taxis serve most destinations. They save time and offer flexible departure times. Local minibuses and pick-ups tend to be slow and packed, but they will save you a buck or two if you're pinching pennies and offer a true 'local' experience (especially if somebody vomits on you).

Taxis to Kampot, Kep and Takeo leave from **Psar Dang Kor** (Map p68; Mao Tse Toung Blvd), while local minibuses and share taxis for most other places leave from the northwest corner of **Psar Thmei** (Map p70). Vehicles for the Vietnam border leave from **Chbah Ampeau taxi park** (Map p68;

Hwy 1) on the eastern side of Monivong Bridge in the south of town.

ℹ Getting Around

Phnom Penh International Airport is 7km west of central Phnom Penh. An official booth outside the airport arrivals area arranges taxis/*remorques* to anywhere in the city for a flat US$12/7. You can get a *remorque* for US$4 and a moto for half that if you walk one minute out to the street. Heading to the airport from central Phnom Penh, a taxi/*remorque*/moto will cost about US$10/4/2. The journey usually takes about 30 minutes.

If you arrive by bus, chances are you'll be dropped off near Psar Thmei (aka Central Market), a short ride from most hotels and guesthouses. Figure on US$0.50 to US$1 for a moto, and US$2 to US$3 for a *remorque*. Prices are about the same from the tourist boat dock on Sisowath Quay, where arriving boats from Vietnam and Siem Reap incite moto-madness.

GETTING TO VIETNAM: MEKONG DELTA BORDERS

Phnom Penh to Ho Chi Minh City

The original Bavet/Moc Bai land crossing between Vietnam and Cambodia has seen steady traffic for two decades.

Getting to the border The easiest way to get to Ho Chi Minh City (HCMC; Saigon) is to catch an international bus (US$12, seven hours) from Phnom Penh. Numerous companies make this trip.

At the border Long lines entering either country are not uncommon, but otherwise it's straightforward provided you purchase a Vietnamese visa in advance.

Moving on If you are not on the international bus, it's not hard to find onward transport to HCMC or elsewhere. For more information on making this crossing in the other direction see boxed text, p891.

Phnom Penh to Chau Doc

The most scenic way to end your travels in Cambodia is to sail the Mekong to Kaam Samnor, about 100km south-southeast of Phnom Penh, cross the border to Vinh Xuong in Vietnam, and proceed to Chau Doc on the Tonlé Bassac River via a small channel or overland. Chau Doc has onward land and river connections to points in the Mekong Delta and elsewhere in Vietnam.

Various companies do trips all the way through to Chau Doc using a single boat (US$21 to US$35, about four hours) or a cheaper bus/boat combo. Prices vary according to speed and level of service. Departures are from the tourist boat dock in Phnom Penh. Pick up tickets there or at any travel agent.

You can go it alone, but it won't save you much money (if any). Make your own way overland to Neak Luong, on the Mekong east of Phnom Penh, and look for the pier about 300m south of the ferry landing on the west bank of the Mekong. From the pier a slow morning passenger boat departs around 9am for Kaam Samnor. Or hire a speedboat (US$50, one hour). In Vinh Xuong, local Vietnamese transport will transfer you to Chau Doc, an hour away. For more information on making this crossing in the other direction see boxed text, p898.

Takeo to Chau Doc

The remote and seldom-used Phnom Den/Tinh Bien border crossing (open 7am to 5pm) between Cambodia and Vietnam lies about 60km southeast of Takeo town in Cambodia and offers connections to Chau Doc.

Getting to the border Take a share taxi (10,000r), a chartered taxi (US$25) or a moto (US$10) from Takeo to the border (48km).

At the border Formalities are minimal here, provided you have a Vietnamese visa.

Moving on On the other side, travellers are at the mercy of Vietnamese *xe om* (moto) drivers and taxis for the 30km journey from the border to Chau Doc. Prepare for some tough negotiations. Expect to pay somewhere between US$5 and US$10 by bike, more like US$20 for a taxi. For more information on making this crossing in the other direction see boxed text, p898.

BICYCLE

Simple bicycles can be hired from some guest-houses and hotels from US$1 a day, or contact Vicious Cycle (p71) for something more sophisticated.

MOTO, REMORQUE & CYCLO

Motos are everywhere and the drivers of those hanging out around tourist areas can generally speak good street English. Short rides around the city cost 2000r; it's US$1 to venture out a little further. At night these prices double. To charter one for a day, expect to pay around US$7 to US$10. *Remorques* usually charge double the price of a moto, possibly more if you pile on the passengers. *Cyclos* can be tougher to find but cost about the same as motos.

MOTORCYCLE

Exploring Phnom Penh and the surrounding area on a motorbike is a very liberating experience if you are used to chaotic traffic conditions. You generally get what you pay for when choosing a steel steed.

Angkor Motorcycles (Map p70; ☑ 012 722098; 92 St 51) Huge selection of trail bikes (day/week rentals US$15/100), plus motorbikes at US$5 to US$7 per day.

Lucky! Lucky! (Map p74; ☑ 023-212788; 413 Monivong Blvd) Motorbikes are US$4 to US$7 per day, less for multiple days. Trail bikes from US$12.

New! New! (Map p74; ☑ 012 855488; 417 Monivong Blvd) Motorbikes start at US$4 per day, trail bikes from US$12.

Vannak Bikes Rental (Map p70; 46 St 130) Has high-performance trail bikes up to 600cc for US$15 to US$30 per day, and smaller motorbikes for US$5 to US$7.

TAXI

Taxis are cheap at 3000r per kilometre but don't expect to flag one down on the street. Call **Global Meter Taxi** (☑ 011 311888) or **Choice Taxi** (☑ 010 888010, 023-888023) for a pick-up.

AROUND PHNOM PENH

There are several sites close to Phnom Penh that make for interesting excursions.

Tonlé Bati, Phnom Tamao and Phnom Chisor are all near each other on NH2 and make a great full-day *remorque* excursion (US$35) or motorbike ride.

Koh Dach   កោះដាច់

Known as 'Silk Island' by foreigners, this is actually a pair of islands lying in the Mekong River about 5km northeast of the Japanese Friendship Bridge. They make for an easy half-day DIY excursion for those who want to experience the 'real Cambodia'. The hustle and bustle of Phnom Penh feels light years away here. The name derives from the preponderance of silk weavers who inhabit the islands, and you'll have plenty of chances to buy from them.

Remorque drivers offer half-day tours to Koh Dach; US$12 should do it, but be ready to negotiate. Daily boat tours from the tourist boat dock, departing at 8.30am, 9.30am and 1pm, are another option (minimum four people). If self-driving, cross the Japanese Bridge and follow NH6 for a few kilometres before turning right and picking up a dirt road that's parallel to the river, which leads right to the ferry landing.

WORTH A TRIP

KOMPONG LUONG

Kompong Luong (កំពង់លួង) has all the amenities you'd expect to find in a large fishing village – cafes, mobile-phone shops, chicken coops, ice-making factories, a pagoda, a church – except that here everything floats. The result is an ethnic-Vietnamese Venice without the dry land. In the dry season, when water levels drop and the Tonlé Sap shrinks, the entire aquapolis is towed, boat by boat, a few kilometres north.

The way to explore Kompong Luong, naturally, is by boat. The official tourist rate to charter a four-passenger wooden motorboat is US$9 per hour for one to three passengers. **Homestays** (per night not incl boat ride US$6) are available with local families and meals are available for US$1 to US$2 per person. This is an interesting way to discover what everyday life is really like on the water.

The jumping-off point to Kompong Luong is the town of Krakor, 32km east of Pursat. From Krakor to the boat landing where tours begin is 1.5km to 6km, depending on the time of year. From Pursat, a moto/*remorque* costs about US$10/20 return. From Phnom Penh, take any Pursat- or Battambang-bound bus.

Udong ឧដុង្គ

Another popular offering among Phnom Penh touts, Udong (the Victorious) served as the capital of Cambodia under several sovereigns between 1618 and 1866. The hill temple of Phnom Udong has several interesting stupas and sanctuaries, plus a 20m-high Buddha. At the base of the hill the sprawling **Cambodia Vipassana Dhura Buddhist Meditation Centre** (⊡ contact Mr Um Sovann 016 883090; www.cambodiavipassana-center.com) offers meditation retreats.

Udong is 37km north of the capital. Take a Phnom Penh Sorya bus bound for Kompong Chhnang (10,000r, one hour to Udong). To return to Phnom Penh flag down a bus on NH5 or take a moto/taxi for US$10/40.

Tonlé Bati ទន្លេបាទី

Locals love to come to this **lake** (admission US$3) for picnics, as along the way they can stop off at two 12th-century temples: **Ta Prohm** and **Yeay Peau**. Ta Prohm is the more interesting of the two; it has some fine carvings in good condition, depicting scenes of birth, dishonour and damnation.

The well-marked turn-off to Tonlé Bati is on the right 33km south of central Phnom Penh. The Takeo-bound Phnom Penh Sorya bus (8000r, four daily – shoot for the 7am or 10.30am one) can drop you here; find a moto to the temples (1.8km from the highway). Returning to Phnom Penh can be problematic. The best advice is to buy a ticket in advance on Sorya's Takeo–Phnom Penh bus. Otherwise, hire a moto.

Phnom Tamao Wildlife Sanctuary ភ្នំតាម៉ៅ (សួនសត្វ)

This **sanctuary** (adult/child US$5/2; ⊘ 8am-5pm) for rescued animals is home to gibbons, sun bears, elephants, tigers, deer and a bird enclosure. All were taken from poachers or abusive owners and receive care and shelter here as part of a sustainable breeding program.

The access road to Phnom Tamao is clearly signposted on the right 6.5km south of the turn-off to Tonlé Bati on NH2. If coming by bus, have the driver let you off at the turn-off, where motos await to whisk you the final 5km to the sanctuary.

Phnom Chisor

Some spectacular views of the cou **86** are on offer from the summit of Phnom Chisor, although the landscape screams Gobi Desert during the dry season. A laterite-and-brick **temple** (admission levied at the summit US$2), dating from the 11th century, with carved sandstone lintels, guards the hilltop's eastern face. From atop the temple's southern stairs, the sacred pool of **Tonlé Om** is visible below.

The access road to Phnom Chisor is signposted (in Khmer) on the left 12km south of the Phnom Tamao turn-off on NH2. The temple is 4.5km from the highway – motos wait at the turn-off.

SIEM REAP & THE TEMPLES OF ANGKOR

⊡ 063 / POP 119,500

Siem Reap is the life-support system for the temples of Angkor, the eighth wonder of the world. Although in a state of slumber from the late 1960s until a few years ago, the town has woken up with a jolt and is now one of the regional hot spots for wining and dining, shopping and schmoozing.

The ultimate fusion of creative ambition and spiritual devotion, the temples of Angkor are a source of inspiration and profound pride to all Khmers. No traveller to the region will want to miss their extravagant beauty and spine-tingling grandeur. One of the most impressive ancient sites on earth, Angkor has the epic proportions of the Great Wall of China, the detail and intricacy of the Taj Mahal and the symbolism and symmetry of the pyramids, all rolled into one.

Angkor is a place to be savoured, not rushed, and Siem Reap is the perfect base from which to plan your adventures.

ℹ Getting Around

There are endless options when it comes to exploring Angkor. Bicycles are a great way to get to and around the temples, which are linked by flat roads in good shape. Just make sure you glug water at every opportunity.

Another environmentally friendly option is to explore on foot. There are obvious limitations, but exploring Angkor Thom's walls or walking to and from Angkor Wat are both feasible. Don't forget to buy an entrance ticket.

...ppy and inexpensive motos (about US$10 per day, more for distant sites) are the most popular form of transport around the temples. Drivers accost visitors from the moment they set foot in Siem Reap, but they often end up being friendly and knowledgeable. Guesthouses are also a good source of experienced driver-guides.

Remorques (around US$15 a day, more for distant sites) take a little longer than motos but offer protection from the rain and sun.

Even more protection is offered by cars, though these tend to isolate you from the sights, sounds and smells. Hiring a car in Siem Reap costs about US$30 for a day cruising around Angkor; US$50 to Kbal Spean and Banteay Srei; US$70 to Beng Mealea; and US$90 out to Koh Ker.

As in days of old, it's possible to travel by elephant between the south gate of Angkor Thom and the Bayon (US$10; available 8am to 11am) and, for sunset, from the base to the summit of Phnom Bakheng (US$15; from about 4pm).

Siem Reap សៀមរាប

Siem Reap is the comeback kid of Southeast Asia. It has reinvented itself as the epicentre of the new Cambodia, with more guesthouses and hotels than temples, world-class wining and dining, and sumptuous spas.

At its heart, Siem Reap remains a charming town with rural qualities. Old French shophouses, shady tree-lined boulevards and a gentle winding river are attractive remnants of the past, while five-star hotels, air-conditioned buses and international restaurants point to a glitzy future.

◉ Sights

★ Angkor National Museum MUSEUM
(សារមន្ទីរអង្គរ; Map p87; ☏ 063-966601; www.angkornationalmuseum.com; 968 Charles de Gaulle Blvd; adult/child under 1.2m US$12/6; ⊗ 8.30am-6pm, to 6.30pm 1 Oct-30 Apr) A worthwhile introduction to the glories of the Khmer empire, the state-of-the-art Angkor National Museum will help clarify Angkor's history, religious significance, and cultural and political context. Displays include 1400 exquisite stone carvings and artefacts.

Les Chantiers Écoles SCHOOL
(កសិដ្ឋានស្សត្រ; Map p87; www.artisansdangkor. com; ⊗ 7.30am-5.30pm) FREE Siem Reap is the epicentre of the drive to revitalise Cambodian traditional culture, which was dealt such a harsh blow by the Khmer Rouge and the years of instability that followed its rule.

Les Chantiers Écoles is a school specialising in teaching wood- and stone-carving techniques, traditional silk painting, lacquerware and more to impoverished youngsters. Tours of the workshops are possible when school is in session. On the premises is an impressive shop, **Artisans d'Angkor** (Map p87; www. artisansdangkor.com; ⊗ 7.30am-6.30pm), that specialises in silks and sculptures.

To see the entire silk-making process, from mulberry trees to silk worms and spinning to weaving, visit Les Chantiers Écoles' **silk farm** (⊗ 7.30am-5.30pm), 16km west of town. Shuttle buses leave the school daily at 9.30am and 1.30pm for a three-hour free tour.

Cambodia Landmine Museum MUSEUM
(☏ 012 598951; www.cambodialandminemuseum. org; admission US$2; ⊗ 7.30am-5pm) Popular with travellers thanks to its informative displays on one of the country's postwar curses, the nonprofit Cambodia Landmine Museum has a mock minefield where visitors can search for deactivated mines. It's situated about 25km from Siem Reap and 6km south of Banteay Srei temple.

Angkor Butterfly Centre WILDLIFE RESERVE
(សួនមេអំបៅបន្ទាយស្រី; ☏ 097 852 7852; www. angkorbutterfly.com; adult/child US$4/2; ⊗ 9am-5pm) 🐾 This is a worthwhile place to include on a trip to Banteay Srei and the Landmine Museum. The largest fully enclosed butterfly centre in Southeast Asia, there are more than 30 species of Cambodian butterflies fluttering about. It is located about 7km before Banteay Srei on the right-hand side of the road.

Khmer Ceramics Centre ARTS CENTRE
(មជ្ឈមណ្ឌលកុលាលភាជន៍; Map p87; ☏ 017 843014; www.khmerceramics.com; Charles de Gaulle Blvd; ⊗ 8am-7.30pm) 🐾 Located on the road to the temples, this ceramics centre is dedicated to reviving the Khmer tradition of pottery, which was an intricate art during the time of Angkor. It's possible to visit and try your hand at the potter's wheel, and courses in traditional techniques are available from US$15 to US$25.

Wat Thmei BUDDHIST TEMPLE
(វត្តថ្មី; Map p96; ⊗ 6am-6pm) FREE On the left fork of the road to Angkor Wat, Wat Thmei has a small memorial stupa containing the skulls and bones of victims of the Khmer Rouge. It also has plenty of young monks eager to practise their English.

Siem Reap

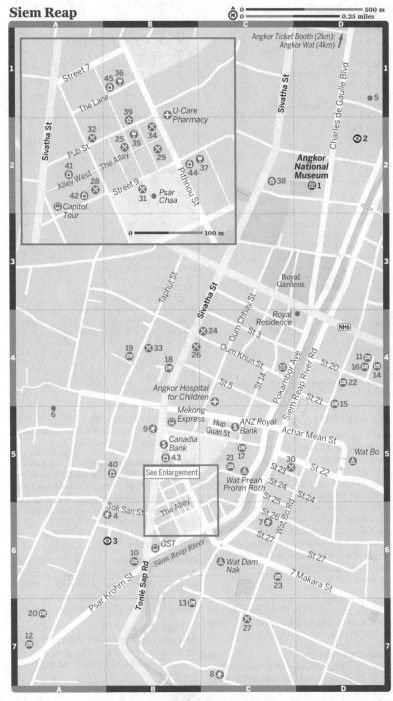

CAMBODIA

Map labels (clockwise / by area):

0   500 m
0   0.25 miles

Angkor Ticket Booth (2km);
Angkor Wat (4km)

Street 7
The Lane
45 36
39
U-Care
Pharmacy
32
Pub St
25 34
35
Sivatha St
41
Alley West 28
29
37
44
42
Capitol
Tour
Street 9
31
Psar
Chaa
Pithnou St
The Alley

0   100 m

Sivatha St
Charles de Gaulle Blvd
5
2
Angkor
National
Museum
38
1

Taphul St
Sivatha St
Royal
Gardens
24
Oum Chhay St
Royal
Residence
St 3
NH6
19 33
18
26
Oum Khun St
St 20
11
16
14
22
St 5
St14
Pokambor Ave
Siem Reap River Rd
St 21
15
Angkor Hospital
for Children
Mekong
Express
9
Canadia
Bank
6
Hup
Guan St
ANZ Royal
Bank
Achar Mean St
Wat Bo
43
40
21 17
30
St 23
St 22
See Enlargement
Wat Preah
Prohm Roth
St 24
St 24
Sok San St
4
The Alley
St 25
St 26
Wat Bo Rd
3
GST
7
St 27
10
Siem Reap River
Psar Krohm St
Tonlé Sap Rd
Wat Dam
Nak
23
7 Makara St
St 27
20
13
27
12
8

Siem Reap

🏃 Activities

Foot massage is a big hit in Siem Reap, hardly surprising given all those steep stairways at the temples. There are half a dozen or more places offering a massage for about US$6 to US$8 an hour on the strip running northwest of Psar Chaa. Some are more authentic than others, so dip your toe in first before selling your sole. For an alternative foot massage, try a **fish spa**, which sees cleaner fish nibble away at your dead skin – heaven for some, tickly as hell for others. Places have sprung up all over town, including along Pub St.

Krousar Thmey   MASSAGE
(Map p96; massage US$7) Massage by the blind in the same location as its free Tonlé Sap Exhibition.

Peace Cafe Yoga   YOGA
(Map p87; ☑063-965210; www.peacecafeangkor. org; St 26; per session US$6) Popular commu-

nity centre-cum-cafe that has daily yoga sessions at 8.30am and 6.30pm, including ashtanga and hatha sessions.

Seeing Hands Massage 4   MASSAGE
(Map p87; ☑012 836487; 324 Sivatha St; per br fan/air-con US$5/7) 🌿 Seeing Hands trains blind people in the art of massage. Watch out for copycats, as some of these are just exploiting the blind for profit.

🍽 Courses

Cooks in Tuk Tuks   COOKING COURSE
(Map p87; ☑063-963400; www.therivergarden.info; per person US$25) Starts at 10am daily with a visit to Psar Leu market, then returns to the River Garden hotel for a professional class.

Le Tigre de Papier   COOKING COURSE
(Map p87; Pub St; per person US$12) 🌿 Starts at 10am daily and includes a visit to the market. Proceeds are used to support Sala Bai (p91).

Tours

Happy Ranch
HORSE RIDING
(Map p87; ☑ 012 920002; www.thehappyranch. com; 1hr/half-day US$25/56) Take the chance to explore Siem Reap on horseback, taking in surrounding villages and secluded temples. Book direct for the best prices.

Quad Adventure Cambodia
ADVENTURE TOUR
(Map p87; ☑ 092-787216; www.quad-adventure-cambodia.com; sunset ride US$30, full day US$170) Offers sunset rides through the rice fields or longer rides to pretty temples following back roads through traditional villages. Quad Adventure Cambodia is well signposted in the Wat Dam Nak area.

Sleeping

While accommodation is spread throughout town, three areas hold the bulk of budget choices: the Psar Chaa area; the area to the west of Sivatha St; and north of Wat Bo on the east bank of the river. Most of these places offer free pick-up from the airport, port or bus station: email or call ahead. Commission scams abound in Siem Reap so keep your antennae up.

Psar Chaa Area

This is the liveliest part of town, brimming with restaurants, bars and boutiques. Staying here can be a lot of fun, but it's not the quietest part of town.

★ Ivy Guesthouse 2
GUESTHOUSE $
(Map p87; ☑ 012 800860; www.ivy-guesthouse. com; r US$6-15; ✳@⌂) An inviting guesthouse with a chill-out area and bar, the Ivy is a lively place to stay. The restaurant is as good as it gets among the guesthouses in town, with a huge vegetarian selection.

Downtown Siem Reap Hostel
HOSTEL $
(Map p87; ☑ 012 675881; www.downtownsiemreap hostel.hostel.com; Wat Damnak area; dm US$4-6, r US$13-17; ✳⌂⌕) Also sometimes known as

---

SPLURGE

The Siem Reap outpost of the growing Frangipani empire, the **Frangipani Villa Hotel** (Map p87; ☑ 063-999930; www.frangipanihotel.com; Wat Bo Rd; r US$40-60; ✳@⌂⌕) is chic boutique on the cheap. Rooms include stylish touches such as flat-screen TVs. There's an inviting pool.

Bamboo Garden, the rates here are particularly attractive when you consider there is a small pool in the garden. Chill out with air-con in the more expensive dorms or rooms.

Prohm Roth Guesthouse
GUESTHOUSE $
(Map p87; ☑ 012 466495; www.prohmroth-guesthouse.com; near Wat Preah Prohm Roth; r US$12-30; ✳@⌂) Central, yet tucked away down a side street that runs parallel to Wat Preah Prohm Roth, this is a friendly place.

Angkor Park Guesthouse
GUESTHOUSE $
(Map p87; ☑ 063-761663; www.angkorparkguest house.com; off Sivatha St; r with fan/air-con US$8/13; ✳⌂) A no-frills good-value guesthouse that has 22 rooms, including TV and attached bathroom with hot water.

Sivatha St Area

The area to the west of Sivatha St includes a good selection of budget guesthouses and midrange boutique hotels.

My Home Tropical Garden Villa
GUESTHOUSE $
(Map p87; ☑ 063-760035; www.myhomecambodia. com; r US$12-30; ✳@⌂⌕⌕) Offering hotel standards at guesthouse prices, this is a fine place to rest your head. The decor includes some soft silks and the furnishings are tasteful, plus there's an inviting little swimming pool.

Mad Monkey
HOSTEL $
(Map p87; www.madmonkeyhostels.com; Sivatha St; dm US$5-6, r US$8-17; ✳@⌂) The Siem Reap outpost of an expanding Monkey business, this is a classic backpacker crashpad with several dorms, good-value rooms for those wanting privacy, and the statutory rooftop bar, only this one's a beach bar!

Cashew Nut Guesthouse
GUESTHOUSE $
(Map p87; ☑ 063-765015; http://thecashewnut. com; Psar Krom Rd; r incl breakfast US$13-20; ✳@⌂) A lively little place run by a self-proclaimed 'nutter' who previously worked as a tour leader for Intrepid. Artful decoration and slick service propel this into boutique backpacker orbit.

Mommy's Guesthouse
GUESTHOUSE $
(Map p87; ☑ 012 941755; mommy_guesthouse@ yahoo.com; r US$5-15; ✳@⌂) A warm and welcoming family-run place, this 13-room villa has large rooms with air-con, as well as cheap digs with cold showers. The owners really go out of their way to assist travellers.

Wat Bo Area

There is a great guesthouse ghetto in a back-street running parallel to the north end of Wat Bo Rd, which is good for on-the-spot browsing.

Seven Candles Guesthouse GUESTHOUSE $
(Map p87; ☎063-963380; www.sevencandles guesthouse.com; 307 Wat Bo Rd; r US$10-20; ❄@🛜) ✎ A good-cause guesthouse: its profits help a local foundation that seeks to promote education to rural communities. Rooms include hot water, TV and fridge.

Babel Guesthouse GUESTHOUSE $
(Map p87; ☎063-965474; http://babel-siemreap. com; r incl breakfast US$15-27; ❄@🛜) ✎ An upmarket guesthouse with a relaxing tropical garden. The service and presentation are a cut above the nearby budget places.

Happy Guesthouse GUESTHOUSE $
(Map p87; ☎063-963815; www.happyangkorguest house.com; r US$3-12; ❄@🛜) This place will really make you happy thanks to welcoming owners who speak very good English *et un peu de Français*. Great-value rooms and free internet.

European Guesthouse GUESTHOUSE $
(Map p87; ☎012 582237; www.european-guest house.com; d US$3-5, r US$15-28; ❄@🛜) ✎ Fun and friendly, the rooms here are well presented, the dorms are a bargain and the garden is a good place to relax. The European is a member of local NGO networks Childsafe and ConCERT and supports projects like the White Bicycles, whose proceeds go to local development projects.

Siem Reap Hostel HOSTEL $
(Map p87; ☎063-964660; www.thesiemreap hostel.com; 10 Makara St; dm US$6-8, r incl breakfast US$20-39; ❄@🛜☰) Angkor's original full-on backpacker hostel is pretty slick. The dorms are well tended and the rooms are definitely flashpacker, plus there's a covered pool.

✗ Eating

Worthy restaurants are sprinkled all around town but Siem Reap's culinary heart is the Psar Chaa area, whose focal point, the Alley, is literally lined with mellow eateries offering great atmosphere. It is wall-to-wall with good Cambodian restaurants, many family owned.

Cheap eats can be found in the small eateries (Map p87; mains US$1.50-4; ⊙7am-9pm) lining Psar Chaa. For self-caterers,

markets sell fruit and veg. **Angkor Market** (Map p87; Sivatha St), a supermarket, can supply international treats.

★Green Star CAMBODIAN $
(Map p87; www.greenstarrestaurant.org; mains US$2-5; ⊙11.30am-2pm & 5.30-10.30pm Mon-Sat; 🛜) ✎ Tucked away in a quiet street behind Wat Damnak is this appealing not-for-profit restaurant supporting former street kids in Siem Reap. Authentic Khmer dishes include spicy duck, lemon-grass eel and succulent frog.

Blue Pumpkin CAFE $
(Pithnou St; cones US$1.50; ⊙6am-10pm; 🛜) Upstairs is a world of white minimalism with beds to lounge on and free wi-fi. Light bites, great sandwiches, divine shakes and superb cakes keep them coming.

Khmer Kitchen Restaurant CAMBODIAN $
(Map p87; www.khmerkitchens.com; The Alley; mains US$2-5; ⊙11am-10pm) Can't get no (culinary) satisfaction? Then follow in the footsteps of Sir Mick Jagger and try this popular place, which offers an affordable selection of Khmer and Thai favourites.

Le Café CAFE $
(Map p87; French Cultural Centre; snacks US$2-4; ⊙7.30am-9pm; 🛜) ✎ Run in partnership with the Paul Dubrule Hotel & Tourism School, this cafe brings five-star sandwiches, salads and shakes to the French Cultural Centre.

Red Piano ASIAN, INTERNATIONAL $
(Map p87; www.redpianocambodia.com; Pub St; mains US$3-6; 🛜) Strikingly set in a restored colonial gem, Red Piano has a big balcony and a reliable selection of Asian and international food, all at decent prices.

Curry Walla INDIAN $
(Map p87; Sivatha St; mains US$2-5; ⊙10.30am-11pm) For good-value Indian food, this place is hard to beat. The *thalis* (set meals) are a bargain and the owner knows his share of spicy specials from the subcontinent.

Joe-to-Go CAFE $
(Map p87; near Psar Chaa; mains US$2-5; ⊙7am-9.30pm) ✎ Gourmet coffees, shakes and light bites, with proceeds supporting street children.

Sala Bai Hotel &
Restaurant School INTERNATIONAL $$
(Map p87; www.salabai.com; set lunch US$8; ⊙7-9am & noon-2pm Mon-Fri) This school trains

young Khmers in the art of hospitality and serves an affordable menu of Western and Cambodian cuisine.

Soup Dragon
ASIAN, INTERNATIONAL **$$**

(Map p87; Pub St; Vietnamese mains US$2-10; ⏰6am-11pm; 🕿) This three-level restaurant has a split personality: the ground floor serves up cheap, classic Asian breakfasts, while upstairs serves a diverse menu of Asian and international dishes, including Italian and Moroccan.

Cambodian BBQ
BARBECUE **$$**

(Map p87; www.angkorw.com; The Alley; mains US$5-9; ⏰11am-11pm; 🕿) Crocodile, snake, ostrich and kangaroo meat add an exotic twist to the traditional *phnom pleung* (hill of fire) grills. It has spawned a dozen copycats in the surrounding streets.

Le Tigre de Papier
INTERNATIONAL **$$**

(Map p87; www.letigredepapier.com; Pub St; mains US$2-9; ⏰24hr; 🕿🖉) Established spot with a wood-fired oven and a great menu of Italian, French and Khmer food. Its 24-hour opening means it's a good place if the midnight munchies strike.

 Drinking & Nightlife

Siem Reap is now firmly on the nightlife map of Southeast Asia. The Psar Chaa area is a good hunting ground, and one street is now known as 'Pub St': dive in, crawl out.

Angkor What?
BAR

(Map p87; Pub St; ⏰5pm-late; 🕿) Siem Reap's original bar claims to have been promoting irresponsible drinking since 1998. The happy hour (to 9pm) lightens the mood for later, when everyone's bouncing along to indie anthems, sometimes on the tables, sometimes under them.

Warehouse
BAR

(Map p87; Pithnou St; ⏰10.30am-3am; 🕿) A popular bar opposite Psar Chaa, offering indie anthems, table football, a pool table and devilish drinks. Charity quiz night on Thursday.

Laundry Bar
BAR, NIGHTCLUB

(Map p87; St 9; ⏰4pm-late; 🕿) One of the most alluring bars in town thanks to discerning decor, low lighting and a laid-back soundtrack. Happy hour is 5pm to 9pm.

Miss Wong
BAR

(Map p87; The Lane; ⏰5pm-late; 🕿) Miss Wong carries you back to the chic of 1920s Shanghai. The cocktails are the draw here. A gay-friendly bar.

Asana
BAR

(Map p87; www.asana-cambodia.com; The Lane; ⏰11am-late; 🕿) A traditional Cambodian

CAMBODIA SIEM REAP

WORTH A TRIP

FLOATING VILLAGES

The famous floating village of **Chong Kneas** is an easy excursion to arrange yourself. The village moves depending on the season and you will need to rent a boat to get around it properly. Unfortunately, large tour groups tend to take over and Sou Ching, the company that runs the tours, has fixed boat prices at an absurd US$20 per person, plus a US$3 entrance fee. In practice it may be possible to pay just US$20 for the boat shared between several people, or contact **Tara Boat** (☑092 957765; www.taraboat.com) for an all-inclusive trip. The small, floating **Gecko Centre** (www.tsbr-ed.org; ⏰7am-4pm) has displays on the Tonlé Sap's remarkable annual cycle.

To get to Chong Kneas from Siem Reap costs US$2 by moto each way (more if the driver waits), or US$15 by taxi. The trip takes 20 minutes. Alternatively, you can rent a bicycle in town, as it's a leisurely 11km ride through pretty villages and rice fields.

More memorable than Chong Kneas, but also harder to reach, is the friendly village of **Kompong Pluk**, an other-worldly place built on soaring stilts. In the wet season you can explore the nearby flooded forest by canoe.

Rather like Chong Kneas, prices have been fixed at US$20 per person for a boat, plus there is a US$1 entry fee, but again it may be possible to negotiate this as a per-boat cost split between a group.

To get here, either catch a boat at Chong Kneas (US$55 return, 1¼ hours) or come via the small town of Roluos by a 60- to 90-minute combination of road (about US$7 return by moto) and boat (US$8 per person).

countryside dwelling dropped into the back-streets of Siem Reap, which makes for an atmospheric place to imbibe.

☆ Entertainment

Classical dance shows take place all over the town, but only a few are worth considering.

★ Phare   CIRCUS

(Cambodian Circus; Map p87; ☎ 015 499480; www.pharecambodiancircus.org; behind Angkor National Museum; adult/child US$15/8, premium seats US$35/18; ⊘ 7.30pm daily) The revered Battambang circus troupe opened a big top in Siem Reap in 2013 and the results have been spectacular. Besides stunningly daring and original acts, Phare's shows carry a subtle yet striking social message. Not to be missed.

Beatocello   CLASSICAL MUSIC

(Map p96; www.beatocello.com; ⊘ 7.15pm Thu & Sat) ⏵ Better known as Dr Beat Richner, Beatocello performs cello compositions at Jayavarman VII Children's Hospital. Entry is free, but donations are welcome, as they assist the hospital in offering free medical treatment to the children of Cambodia.

Temple Club   DANCE

(Map p87; Pub St) Free traditional dance show upstairs from 7.30pm, providing punters order some food and drink from the very reasonably priced menu.

🛍 Shopping

Siem Reap has an excellent selection of Cambodian-made handicrafts. Psar Chaa is well stocked. There are bargains to be had if you haggle patiently and humorously. **Angkor Night Market** (Map p87; www.angkor nightmarket.com; ⊘ 4pm-midnight) is packed with silks, handicrafts and souvenirs. Up-and-coming **Alley West** is also a great strip to browse socially responsible fashion boutiques.

Several shops support Cambodia's disabled and disenfranchised, including exquisite Artisans d'Angkor (p86).

Three Seasons   CLOTHING

(Map p87; The Lane; ⊘ 10am-10pm) Three shops in one, including Elsewhere, Zoco and KeoK'jay, a fair-trade fashion enterprise helping HIV-positive women earn a living.

Rajana   ARTS & CRAFTS

(Map p87; ☎ 063-964744; www.rajanacrafts.org; Sivatha St; ⊘ 9am-9pm Mon-Sat) Sells quirky wooden and metalware objects, silver jewellery and handmade cards. Rajana promotes fair trade and employment opportunities for Cambodians.

Bambou Indochine   CLOTHING

(Map p87; Alley West; ⊘ 10am-10pm) Original clothing designs inspired by Indochina. A cut above the average souvenir T-shirts.

Senteurs d'Angkor   HANDICRAFTS

(Map p87; ☎ 063-964860; Pithnou St; ⊘ 8.30am-9.30pm) Has a wide-ranging collection of silk, stone carvings, beauty products, massage oils, spices, coffees and teas, all sourced locally.

Blue Apsara   BOOKS

(Map p87; St 9; ⊘ 9am-9pm) Used books in several languages.

ℹ Information

Hotels, restaurants and bars can provide the free *Siem Reap Angkor Visitors Guide* (www.canbypublications.com) and two handy booklets produced by **Pocket Guide Cambodia** (www.cambodiapocketguide.com).

There are ATMs at the airport and in banks and minimarts all over central Siem Reap, especially along Sivatha St. The greatest concentration of internet shops is along Sivatha St and around Psar Chaa. Free wi-fi is available at many of the leading cafes, restaurants and bars, not forgetting most guesthouses and hotels.

Angkor Hospital for Children (Map p87; ☎ 063-963409; http://angkorhospital.org; cnr Oum Chhay & Achar Mean Sts; ⊘ 24hr) A paediatric hospital supported by donors. It's free for anyone under 16, tourists included.

ANZ Royal Bank (Map p87; Achar Mean St) Plus ATMs (US$5 per withdrawal) conveniently dotted about town.

SUPPORTING RESPONSIBLE TOURISM IN SIEM REAP

Many travellers passing through Siem Reap are interested in contributing something to the communities they visit as they explore the temples and surrounding areas. ConCERT (p79) is a Siem Reap–based organisation that is working to build bridges between tourists and good-cause projects in the Siem Reap–Angkor area. It offers information on anything from ecotourism initiatives to volunteering opportunities.

GETTING TO THAILAND: SIEM REAP TO BANGKOK

The original land border crossing (open from 7am to 8pm) between Cambodia and Thailand is by far the busiest and the one most people take when travelling between Bangkok and Siem Reap. It has earned itself a bad reputation over the years, with scams galore to help tourists part with their money, especially coming in from Thailand.

Getting to the border Frequent buses and share taxis run from Siem Reap and Battambang to Poipet. Buying a ticket all the way to Bangkok (usually involving a change of buses at the border) can expedite things and save you the hassle of finding onward transport on the Thai side. The 8am through bus to Mo Chit bus station in Bangkok run by Nattakan in Siem Reap costs an inflated US$28, but is the only bus service that allows you to continue to Bangkok on the same bus you board in Siem Reap.

At the border Be prepared to wait in sweltering immigration lines on both sides – waits of two or more hours are not uncommon, especially in the high season. Show up early to avoid the crowds. You can pay a special 'VIP fee' (aka a bribe) of 200B on either side to skip the lines. There is no departure tax to leave Cambodia despite what Cambodian border officials might tell you. Entering Thailand, most nationalities are issued 15-day visa waivers free of charge.

Moving on Minibuses wait just over the border on the Thai side to whisk you to Bangkok (B300, four hours, every 30 minutes). Or make your way 7km to Aranya Prathet by túk-túk (80B) or *sŏrngtăaou* (pick-up truck; 15B), from where there are regular buses to Bangkok's Mo Chit station (223B, five to six hours) between 4am and 6pm. Make sure your túk-túk driver takes you to the main bus station in Aranya Prathet for your 80B, not to the smaller station about 1km from the border (a common scam). The 1.55pm train is another option to Bangkok.

For information on making the crossing in the other direction, see p735.

Canadia Bank (Map p87; Sivatha St) International ATM with no transaction fees.

Main Post Office (Map p87; Pokambor Ave; ☺7am-5.30pm) Offers EMS express international postal service.

Royal Angkor International Hospital (Map p96; ☑063-761888; www.royalangkorhospital.com; Airport Rd) A new international facility affiliated with the Bangkok Hospital, so very expensive.

Tourist Police (Map p96; ☑097-778 0013) At the main Angkor ticket checkpoint.

U-Care Pharmacy (Map p87; ☑063-965396; Pithnou St; ☺8am-9pm) Smart pharmacy and shop, like Boots in Thailand (and the UK). English spoken.

Getting There & Away

AIR

Siem Reap International Airport (Map p96; ☑063-761261; www.cambodia-airports.com) is a work of art set 7km west of the centre and offers regular connections to most neighbouring Asian cities, plus domestic flights to Phnom Penh and Sihanoukville.

BOAT

Boats for the incredibly scenic trip to Battambang (US$20, five to nine hours depending on water levels) and the faster ride to Phnom Penh (US$35, six hours, August to March only) depart at 7am from the tourist boat dock at Chong Kneas, 11km south of town. Tickets are sold at guesthouses, hotels and travel agencies, including pick-up from your hotel or guesthouse around 6am.

BUS

All buses arrive in and depart from the bus station, which is 3km east of town and about 200m south of NH6. Upon arrival, be prepared for a rugby scrum of eager moto drivers greeting the bus.

Tickets are available at guesthouses, hotels, bus offices, travel agencies and ticket kiosks. Some bus companies send a minibus around to pick up passengers at their place of lodging. Most departures to Phnom Penh are between 7am and 1pm, but there are also some night buses available. Buses to other destinations generally leave early in the morning.

Tickets to Phnom Penh via NH6 cost anywhere from US$5 for basic air-con buses to US$17 for the business-class buses run by Giant Ibis, which feature plenty of legroom, hosts and dysfunctional wi-fi.

Several companies offer direct services to Kompong Cham (US$6, five or six hours), Battambang (US$3.75, three hours) and Poipet

CAMBODIA SIEM REAP

TRANSPORT FROM SIEM REAP

DESTINATION	CAR/MOTORBIKE	BUS	BOAT	AIR
Bangkok	8hr	US$12-15, 10hr, frequent	N/A	from US$90, 1hr, 5 daily
Battambang	3hr	US$4-5, 4hr, mostly morning	US$20, 7hr, 7am	N/A
Kompong Thom	2hr	US$5, 2½hr, frequent	N/A	N/A
Phnom Penh	5hr	US$5-17, 6hr, frequent	US$35, 5hr, 7am	from US$90, 30min, 4 daily
Poipet	3hr	US$4-5, 4hr, regular	N/A	N/A
Sihanoukville	9hr	US$10, 12hr, mostly night buses	N/A	from US$90, 45min, 4 weekly

(US$3.75, three hours). GST has a bus to Anlong Veng (US$4, two hours) and on to Sra Em (for Prasat Preah Vihear; US$10, four hours, 7am). There are no through buses to Ho Chi Minh City, but it is possible to change in Phnom Penh.

Bus companies that serve Siem Reap:

Capitol Tour (Map p87; ☏ 063-963883)

Giant Ibis (www.giantibis.com)

GST (Map p87; ☏ 092 905016)

Mekong Express (Map p87; ☏ 063-963662)

Neak Kror Horm (☏ 063-964924)

Phnom Penh Sorya (Map p96; ☏ 012 235618)

Rith Mony (☏ 012 344377)

SHARE TAXI

Share taxis stop along NH6 just north of the bus station. Destinations include Phnom Penh (US$10, five hours), Kompong Thom (US$5, two hours), Sisophon (US$5, two hours) and Poipet (US$7, 2½ hours).

❶ Getting Around

From the airport, an official moto/taxi will cost US$2/7; *remorques* (US$5) are available on the road outside the terminal's parking area.

If arriving by boat, a moto into town should cost about US$3 from the dock in Chong Kneas.

From the bus station a moto/*remorque* to the city centre should cost about US$1/2. If you're arriving on a bus service sold by a guesthouse, the bus will head straight to a partner guesthouse.

Short moto trips around the centre of town cost 2000r or 3000r, more at night. A *remorque* is double again.

Most guesthouses and small hotels can usually help with bicycle rental for about US$2 per day. Look out for guesthouses and hotels supporting the **White Bicycles** (www.thewhite bicycles.org) project, whose proceeds go to local development projects. Motorbike hire is currently prohibited in Siem Reap.

Temples of Angkor
ប្រាសាទអង្គរ

Where to begin with Angkor? There is no greater concentration of architectural riches anywhere on earth. Choose from the world's largest religious building, Angkor Wat, one of the world's weirdest, Bayon, or the riotous jungle of Ta Prohm. All are global icons and have helped put Cambodia on the map as the temple capital of Asia.

Beyond the big three are dozens more temples, each of which would be the star were it located anywhere else in the region: Banteay Srei, the art gallery of Angkor; Preah Khan, the ultimate fusion temple uniting Buddhism and Hinduism; or Beng Mealea, the *Titanic* of temples suffocating under the jungle. The most vexing part of a visit to Angkor is working out what to see, as there are simply so many spectacular sites. One day at Angkor? Sacrilege! Don't even consider it.

The hundreds of temples surviving today are but the sacred skeleton of the vast political, religious and social centre of the ancient Khmer empire. Angkor was a city that, at its zenith, boasted a population of one million when London was a small town of 50,000. The houses, public buildings and palaces of Angkor were constructed of wood – now long decayed – because the right to dwell in structures of brick or stone was reserved for the gods.

Angkor Wat
អង្គរវត្ត

The traveller's first glimpse of **Angkor Wat** (Map p96; admission to all of Angkor 1 day/3 days/ 1 week US$20/40/60), the ultimate expression of Khmer genius, is simply staggering and is matched by only a few select spots on earth such as Machu Picchu or Petra.

Angkor is heaven on earth, namely the symbolic representation of Mt Meru, the Mt Olympus of the Hindu faith and abode of ancient gods. It is the perfect fusion of creative ambition and spiritual devotion. The Cambodian 'god-kings' of old each strove to better their ancestors in size, scale and symmetry, culminating in the world's largest religious building, Angkor Wat.

Angkor Wat is the Khmers' national symbol, the epicentre of their civilisation and a source of fierce national pride. Unlike the other Angkor monuments, it was never abandoned to the elements and has been in virtually continuous use since it was built.

The temple is surrounded by a moat, 190m wide, which forms a giant rectan-gle measuring 1.5km by 1.3km. Stretching around the outside of the central temple complex is an 800m-long series of bas-re-liefs, designed to be viewed in an anticlock-wise direction. Rising 31m above the third level is the central tower, which gives the whole ensemble its sublime unity.

Angkor Wat was built by Suryavarman II (r 1113–52), who unified Cambodia and extended Khmer influence across much of mainland Southeast Asia. He also set himself apart religiously from earlier kings by his devotion to the Hindu deity Vishnu, to whom he consecrated the temple, built around the same time as European Gothic heavyweights such as Westminster Abbey and Chartres.

EXPLORING THE TEMPLES

One Day

If you've got only one day to spend at Angkor, that's unfortunate, but a good itinerary would be Angkor Wat for sunrise, after which you can explore the mighty temple before the crowds arrive. From there, drop by Ta Prohm before breaking for lunch. In the afternoon, explore the temples within the walled city of Angkor Thom and the enigmatic faces of the Bayon in the late afternoon light. Biggest mistake: trying to pack in too much.

Three Days

With three days to explore the area, start with some of the smaller temples and build up to the big hitters. Visit the early Roluos group on the first day for some chronological consistency and try the stars of the Grand Circuit, including Preah Khan and Preah Neak Poan. Day two might include Ta Prohm and the temples on the Small Circuit, plus the distant but stunning Banteay Srei. Then the climax: Angkor Wat at dawn and the immense city of Angkor Thom in the afternoon.

One Week

Angkor is your oyster, so relax, enjoy and explore at will. Make sure you visit Beng Mealea and Kbal Spean. Do at least one overnight trip further afield, to Koh Ker, Banteay Chhmar, Sambor Prei Kuk or even Prasat Preah Vihear. For a change of pace, take a boat to the floating village of Kompong Pluk.

Tickets

The Angkor **ticket booth** (Map p96; 1-day/3-day/1-week tourist pass US$20/40/60, children under 12 free; ☺5am-5.30pm) is on the road from Siem Reap to Angkor. Three-day passes can be used on any three days over a one-week period, and one-week passes are valid over the course of a month. Tickets issued after 5pm (for sunset viewing) are valid the next day. Tickets are not valid for Phnom Kulen or Beng Mealea. Get caught ticketless in a temple and you'll be fined US$100.

Eating

There are dozens of local **noodle stalls** just near the Terrace of the Leper King, and a village with a cluster of **restaurants** opposite **Sra Srang** (Pool of Ablutions; Map p96), the former royal bathing pond. Angkor Wat has full-blown cafes and restaurants.

Try to be patient with the hordes of children selling food, drinks and souvenirs, as they're only doing what their families have asked them to do to survive. You'll find that their ice-cold bottled water and fresh pineapples are heavenly in the heat.

Temples of Angkor

CAMBODIA

ANGKOR THOM

Angkor Thom
North Gate

♨ 6

Angkor
Thom
Victory
Gate

Preah Palilay ●

🏛 10

Royal Enclosure & 🏯
Phimeanakas

🏛 9

BAYON

Angkor Thom
West Gate ●

BAPHUON

Angkor
Thom
East
Gate

Bayon ♨ 2

Western
Baray
ẘ Western
Mebon

Angkor Thom
South Gate ●

Baksei
Chamkrong

ẘ Ak Yom

5 ẘ

ẘ Western
Mebon

**ANGKOR
WAT**

*Angkor
Wat* 1

Siem Reap
International ✈
Airport

Little Circuit

NH6

Dykes

Charles de Gaulle Blvd

Ticket
Booth ●

Airport Rd

Royal Angkor
✚ International
Hospital

11 ♨

12 ★

13 🏯

4

**SIEM
REAP**

Airport Rd

See Siem Reap
Map (p87)

Psar
Chaa

Makara St

Sivatha St

Wat Bo Rd

Wat
Athvea ♨

Phnom
Krom ẘ

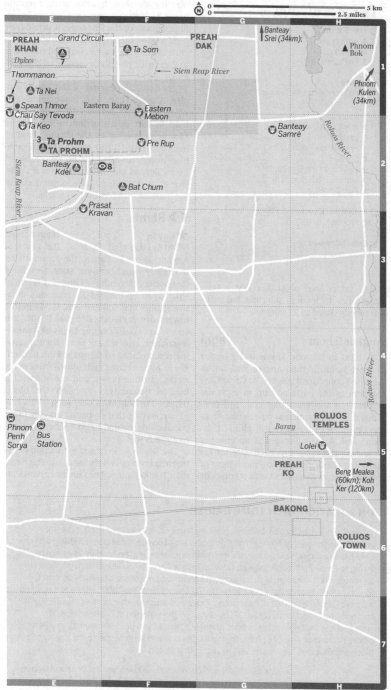

N 0 ____ 5 km
0 ____ 2.5 miles

CAMBODIA

PREAH KHAN
Dykes
7
Grand Circuit

Thommanon

Ta Som

PREAH DAK

Banteay Srei (34km);

Phnom Bok

Siem Reap River

Phnom Kulen (34km)

Ta Nei

Chau Say Tevoda

Ta Keo

Eastern Baray

Eastern Mebon

Roluos River

3 Ta Prohm
TA PROHM

Pre Rup

Banteay Samré

Banteay Kdei

8

Bat Chum

Prasat Kravan

Siem Reap River

ROLUOS TEMPLES

Baray

Lolei

Phnom Penh Sorya

Bus Station

PREAH KO

Beng Mealea (60km); Koh Ker (120km)

BAKONG

ROLUOS TOWN

Roluos River

Temples of Angkor

The upper level of Angkor Wat is once again open to modern pilgrims, but visits are strictly timed to 20 minutes.

Angkor Thom   អង្គរធំ

It is hard to imagine any building bigger or more beautiful than Angkor Wat, but in Angkor Thom (Great Angkor, or Great City) the sum of the parts add up to a greater whole. It is the gates that grab you first, flanked by a monumental representation of the Churning of the Ocean of Milk, 54 demons and 54 gods engaged in an epic tug of war on the causeway. Each gate towers above the visitor, the magnanimous faces of the Bodhisattva Avalokiteshvara staring out

over the kingdom. Imagine being a peasant in the 13th century approaching the forbidding capital for the first time: it would have been an awe-inspiring yet unsettling experience to enter such a gateway and come face to face with the divine power of the god-kings.

The last great capital of the Khmer empire, Angkor Thom took monumental to a whole new level, set over 10 sq km. It was built in part as a reaction to the surprise sacking of Angkor by the Chams. Jayavarman VII (r 1181–1219) decided that his empire would never again be vulnerable at home. Beyond the formidable walls is a massive moat that would have stopped all but the hardiest invaders in their tracks.

⦿ Sights

★ Bayon   BUDDHIST TEMPLE
(បាយ័ន; (Map p96) Right at the heart of Angkor Thom is Bayon, the mesmerising if slightly mind-bending state temple of Cambodia's legendary king, Jayavarman VII. Bayon epitomises Jayavarman's creative genius and inflated ego. Its 54 gothic towers are famously decorated with 216 enormous, coldly smiling **faces of Avalokiteshvara**, which bear more than a passing resemblance to the great king himself. These huge visages glare down from every angle, exuding power and control with a hint of humanity – precisely the blend required to hold sway over such a vast empire, ensuring that disparate and far-flung populations yielded to the monarch's magnanimous will.

The Bayon is decorated with 1.2km of extraordinary **bas-reliefs** incorporating more than 11,000 figures. The famous carvings on

---

ON LOCATION WITH TOMB RAIDER

Several sequences for *Tomb Raider*, starring Angelina Jolie as Lara Croft, were shot around the temples of Angkor. The Cambodia shoot opened at Phnom Bakheng with Lara looking through binoculars for the mysterious temple. The baddies were already trying to break in through the East Gate of Angkor Thom by pulling down a giant poly-styrene apsara. Reunited with her custom Landrover, Lara made a few laps around the Bayon before discovering a back way into the temple from Ta Prohm, where she plucked a sprig of jasmine and fell through into... Pinewood Studios. After battling a living statue and dodging Daniel Craig (aka 007) by diving off the waterfall at Phnom Kulen, she emerged in a floating market in front of Angkor Wat, as you do. She came ashore here before borrowing a mobile phone from a local monk and venturing in to the gallery of a thousand Buddhas, where she was healed by the abbot.

By Lonely Planet author Nick Ray, who worked as Location Manager for Tomb Raider *in Cambodia*

TOP ANGKOR EXPERIENCES

➡ See the sun rise over the holiest of holies, **Angkor Wat**, the world's largest religious building.

➡ Contemplate the serenity and splendour of the **Bayon**, its 216 enigmatic faces staring out into the jungle.

➡ Witness nature reclaiming the stones at the mysterious ruin of **Ta Prohm**, the *Tomb Raider* temple.

➡ Stare in wonder at the delicate carvings adorning **Banteay Srei**, the finest seen at Angkor.

➡ Trek deep into the jungle to discover the River of a Thousand Lingas at **Kbal Spean**.

the outer wall of the first level vividly depict everyday life in 12th-century Cambodia.

Baphuon HINDU TEMPLE
(បាពួន; Map p96) Some have called this the 'world's largest jigsaw puzzle'. Before the civil war the Baphuon was painstakingly taken apart piece-by-piece by a team of archaeologists, but their meticulous records were destroyed during the Khmer Rouge madness. Now, after years of excruciating research, this temple is being restored. On the western side, the retaining wall of the second level was fashioned – apparently in the 15th or 16th century – into a reclining Buddha 60m in length.

Terrace of the Elephants HISTORIC BUILDING
(ទីលានជល់ដំរី; Map p96) The 350m-long Terrace of the Elephants – decorated with parading elephants towards both ends – was used as a giant viewing stand for public ceremonies and served as a base for the king's grand audience hall. As you stand here, try to imagine the pomp and grandeur of the Khmer empire at its height, with infantry, cavalry, horse-drawn chariots and, of course, elephants parading across the Central Square in a colourful procession, pennants and standards aloft.

Terrace of the Leper King HISTORIC BUILDING
(ទីលានព្រះគម្លង់; Map p96) This 7m-high terrace, which once supported a pavilion made of lightweight materials, is topped by a (replica) statue once believed to be that of a leprous king. Researchers now believe it's

Yama, the god of death, and that this site served as a royal crematorium.

The terrace's front retaining walls are decorated with at least five tiers of meticulously executed carvings of seated *apsaras* (celestial nymphs). At the base on the southern side, there is narrow access to a hidden terrace that was covered up (and thus protected from the elements) when the outer structure was built. The figures look as fresh as if they had been carved yesterday.

Around Angkor Thom

◉ Sights

★**Ta Prohm** BUDDHIST TEMPLE
(តាព្រហ្ម; Map p96) If Angkor Wat and the Bayon are testimony to the genius of the ancient Khmers, the 12th-century Mahayana Buddhist temple of Ta Prohm reminds us equally of the awesome fecundity and power of the jungle. Looking much the way most Angkor monuments did when European explorers first set eyes upon them, this temple – built by Jayavarman VII from 1186 – is cloaked in dappled shadow, its crumbling towers and walls locked in the muscular embrace of centuries-old trees.

Bas-reliefs on bulging walls are carpeted with moss and creeping plants, shrubs sprout from the roofs of monumental porches, and many of the corridors are impassable. Indiana Jones would feel right at home, and, in fact, Ta Prohm was used as a location for both *Tomb Raider* and *Two Brothers*.

Phnom Bakheng HINDU TEMPLE
(ភ្នំបាក់ខែង; Map p96) The first of a succession of Angkor temples designed to represent mythical Mt Meru, this hill's main draw is the sunset view of Angkor Wat, although late afternoons here have turned into something of a circus, with hundreds of shutterbugs jockeying for space. Built by Yasovarman I (r 889–910), the temple has five tiers, with seven levels (including the base and the summit). Phnom Bakheng is about 400m south of Angkor Thom.

Preah Khan BUDDHIST TEMPLE
(ព្រះខ័ន; Sacred Sword; Map p96) One of the largest complexes at Angkor, Preah Khan (Sacred Sword), constructed by Jayavarman VII, once housed more than 1000 teachers and may have been a Buddhist university. The temple itself, a cruciform maze of vaulted corridors, fine carvings and lichen-clad stonework, is

Temples of Angkor

THREE-DAY EXPLORATION

The temple complex at Angkor is simply enormous and the superlatives don't do it justice. This is the site of the world's largest religious building, a multitude of temples and a vast, long-abandoned walled city that was arguably Southeast Asia's first metropolis, long before Bangkok and Singapore got in on the action.

Starting at the Roluos group of temples, one of the earliest capitals of Angkor, move on to the big circuit, which includes the Buddhist-Hindu fusion temple of ❶ **Preah Khan** and the ornate water temple of ❷ **Preah Neak Poan**.

On the second day downsize to the small circuit, starting with an atmospheric dawn visit to ❸ **Ta Prohm**, before continuing to the temple pyramid of Ta Keo, the Buddhist monastery of Banteay Kdei and the immense royal bathing pond of ❹ **Sra Srang**.

Next venture further afield to Banteay Srei temple, the jewel in the crown of Angkorian art, and Beng Mealea, a remote jungle temple.

Saving the biggest and best until last, experience sunrise at ❺ **Angkor Wat** and stick around for breakfast in the temple to discover its amazing architecture without the crowds. In the afternoon, explore ❻ **Angkor Thom**, an immense complex that is home to the enigmatic ❼ **Bayon**.

Three days around Angkor? That's just for starters.

TOP TIPS

» **Dodging the Crowds** Early morning at Ta Prohm, post sunrise at Angkor Wat and lunchtime at Banteay Srei does the trick.

» **Extended Explorations** Three-day passes can now be used on non-consecutive days over the period of a week but be sure to request this.

Bayon
The surreal state temple of legendary king Jayavarman VII, where 216 faces bear down on pilgrims, asserting religious and regal authority.

Terrace of the Leper King
Preah Palilay
Phimeanakas Temple
Tep Pranam
West Gate Angkor Thom
Baphuon Temple
Terrace of the Elephants
❼
South Gate Angkor Thom
Phnom Bakheng
Baksei Chamrong
❺

Angkor Wat
The world's largest religious building. Experience sunrise at the holiest of holies, then explore the beautiful bas-reliefs – devotion etched in stone.

Angkor Thom
The last great capital of the Khmer empire conceals a wealth of temples and its epic proportions would have inspired and terrified in equal measure.

Preah Khan
A fusion temple dedicated to Buddha, Brahma, Shiva and Vishnu; the immense corridors are like an unending hall of mirrors.

Preah Neak Poan
If Vegas ever adopts the Angkor theme, this will be the swimming pool; a petite tower set in a lake, surrounded by four smaller ponds.

North Gate, Angkor Thom

Preah Pithu

Thommanon Temple

1

Preah Neak Poan **2**

Prasat Suor Prat

6

Victory Gate Angkor Thom

East Gate Angkor Thom

Chau Say Tevoda

Ta Keo Temple

Ta Nei Temple

Banteay Srei

3

Banteay Kdei Temple

Roluos, Beng Mealea

Prasat Kravan

4

Bat Chum Temple

Ta Prohm
Nicknamed the *Tomb Raider* temple; *Indiana Jones* would be equally apt. Nature has run riot, leaving iconic tree roots strangling the surviving stones.

Sra Srang
Once the royal bathing pond, this is the ablutions pool to beat all ablutions pools and makes a good stop for sunset.

within a rectangular wall of around 700m by 800m. The southern corridor is a wonderfully atmospheric jumble of vines and stones, while near the eastern entrance stands a curious two-storey structure that would look more at home in Greece.

Preah Khan is a genuine fusion temple, the eastern entrance dedicated to Mahayana Buddhism with equal-sized doors, and the other cardinal directions dedicated to Shiva, Vishnu and Brahma with successively smaller doors, emphasising the unequal nature of Hinduism.

Preah Neak Poan   BUDDHIST TEMPLE
(ព្រះនាគព័ន្ធ; Temple of the Intertwined Nagas; Map p96) Another late-12th-century work of – no surprises here – Jayavarman VII, this petite temple has a large square pool surrounded by four smaller square pools, with a circular 'island' in the middle. Water once flowed into the four peripheral pools via four ornamental spouts in the form of an elephant's head, a horse's head, a lion's head and a human head.

Roluos Temples   រលួស

The monuments of Roluos, which served as the capital of Indravarman I (r 877–89), are among the earliest large, permanent temples built by the Khmers and mark the dawn of Khmer classical art. **Preah Ko**, dedicated to Shiva, has elaborate inscriptions in Sanskrit on the doorposts of each tower and some of the best surviving examples of Angkorian plasterwork. The city's central temple, **Bakong**, with its five-tier central pyramid of sandstone, is a representation of Mt Meru.

Roluos is 13km east of Siem Reap along NH6 and can be easily combined with a visit to the stilted village of Kompong Pluk.

Further Afield

◉ Sights

★**Banteay Srei**   HINDU TEMPLE
(បន្ទាយស្រី) Considered by many to be the jewel in the crown of Angkorian art, Banteay Srei is cut from pinkish stone and includes some of the finest stone carving anywhere on earth. Begun in AD 967, it is one of the few temples around Angkor not to be commissioned by a king, but by a Brahman, perhaps a tutor to Jayavarman V.

Banteay Srei means 'Citadel of the Women' and it is said that it must have been built by women, as the elaborate carvings are too fine for the hand of a man.

Banteay Srei, 21km northeast of the Bayon and about 32km from Siem Reap, can be visited along with Kbal Spean, the Angkor Butterfly Centre and the Cambodia Landmine Museum. Transport here will cost a little more than the prices quoted for the central temples of Angkor.

Kbal Spean   HINDU SHRINE
(ក្បាលស្ពាន) A spectacularly carved riverbed set deep in the jungle, Kbal Spean lies about 50km northeast of Siem Reap. More commonly referred to in English as the 'River of a Thousand Lingas', it's a 2km uphill walk to the carvings, which include phallic lingas and Hindu deities. From the carvings you can work your way back down to the **waterfall** to cool off. Carry plenty of water.

Kbal Spean was only 'discovered' in 1969, when École française d'Extrême-Orient (EFEO) ethnologist Jean Boulbet was shown the area by a local hermit; the area was soon

---

BANTEAY CHHMAR

The temple complex of **Banteay Chhmar** (បន្ទាយឆ្មារ; admission US$5) was constructed by Cambodia's most prolific builder, Jayavarman VII (r 1181–1219), on the site of a 9th-century temple. One of a handful of Angkorian sites to feature the towering heads of Avalokiteshvaras, with their enigmatic smiles, the 12th-century temple is also renowned for its intricate carvings.

A pioneering community-based **homestay project** (☑ 012 237605; info@visitbanteay chhmar.org; r US$7) 🅟 makes it possible to stay in and around Banteay Chhmar. Rooms come with mosquito nets, fans that run when there's electricity (6pm to 10pm) and downstairs bathrooms. Bikes can be rented for US$2 a day. Near the temple's eastern entrance, rustic **Banteay Chhmar Restaurant** (mains US$1.50-4) serves tasty Khmer food.

Banteay Chhmar can be visited on a long day trip from Siem Reap, or base youself in Sisophon, 61km south of the temple, where a moto/taxi costs US$20/50 return. You *may* be able to find a morning share taxi from Sisophon's Psar Thmei to the temple (15,000r, one hour).

BITTER RIVALRY

Much of Thailand's culture is linked to the Cambodian artisans, dancers, scholars and fighters with whom the Thais made off after they sacked Angkor in 1432. Have a peek at the bas-reliefs at Bayon and you'll see something that looks much like the 'Thai' kickboxing of today. The history of Angkor remains a seriously sensitive topic between the two cultures, fuelling a bitter rivalry that's lasted centuries.

off-limits due to the civil war, only becoming safe again in 1998.

At the nearby **Angkor Centre for Conservation of Biodiversity** (Map p96; www. accb-cambodia.org; donation US$3; ⊙ tours 1pm Mon-Sat) trafficked animals are nursed back to health. Free tours generally begin at 1pm daily, except Sunday.

Phnom Kulen   MOUNTAIN
(ភ្នំគូលែន; admission US$20) The most sacred mountain in Cambodia, the 487m Phnom Kulen is where Jayavarman II proclaimed himself a *devaraja* (god-king) in AD 802, giving birth to the Khmer empire. A popular place of pilgrimage during weekends and festivals, the views are spectacular. Attractions include a large **waterfall**, a **reclining Buddha** and riverbed **carvings**.

Phnom Kulen is 50km from Siem Reap and 15km from Banteay Srei. The private road charges a hefty US$20 toll per foreign visitor, but none of this goes towards preserving the site. It is possible to buy a cheaper entrance ticket to Phnom Kulen for US$12 from the City Angkor Hotel in Siem Reap.

Beng Mealea   BUDDHIST TEMPLE
(បឹងមាលា; admission US$5) Built by Suryavarman II to the same floor plan as Angkor Wat, Beng Mealea is Angkor's ultimate Indiana Jones experience. Nature has well and truly run riot here and jumbled stones lie like forgotten jewels swathed in lichen. Beng Mealea is about 65km northeast of Siem Reap on a sealed toll road. It can be visited on the way to Koh Ker.

Koh Ker   HINDU TEMPLE
(កោះកេរ៍; admission US$10) Abandoned to the forests of Preah Vihear Province to the north, Koh Ker, capital of the Angkorian empire from AD 928 to AD 944, is now within day-trip distance of Siem Reap. Most visitors

start at **Prasat Krahom**, where impressive stone carvings grace lintels, doorposts and slender window columns. The principal monument is Mayan-looking **Prasat Thom**, a 55m-wide, 40m-high sandstone-faced pyramid whose seven tiers offer spectacular views across the forest. However, access to the top of Prasat Thom is currently prohibited for safety reasons.

Koh Ker is 127km northeast of Siem Reap (car hire is around US$90, 2½ hours).

NORTHWESTERN CAMBODIA

Offering highway accessibility and outback adventure in equal measure, northwestern Cambodia stretches from the Cardamom Mountains to the Dangkrek Mountains, with Tonlé Sap lake at its heart. Battambang attracts the most visitors thanks to an alluring blend of mellowness, colonial-era architecture and excellent day tripping.

Northwestern Cambodia's remote plains and jungles conceal some of the country's most inspired temples, including spectacular Prasat Preah Vihear, declared a World Heritage Site in 2008; 12th-century Banteay Chhmar, with its trademark Avalokiteshvara faces; and the pre-Angkorian temples of Sambor Prei Kuk near Kompong Thom.

Battambang   បាត់ដំបង
☑ 053 / POP 140,000
The elegant riverside town of Battambang is home to Cambodia's best-preserved French-period architecture. The stunning boat trip from Siem Reap lures travellers here, but it's the remarkably chilled atmosphere that makes them linger. Battambang is an excellent base for exploring nearby temples and villages that offer a real slice of rural Cambodia.

⊙ Sights

Colonial-Era Architecture   NOTABLE BUILDINGS
Much of Battambang's special charm lies in its early-20th-century French architecture. Some of the finest colonial buildings are along the waterfront (St 1), especially just south of **Psar Nath**, itself an architectural monument, albeit a modernist one. The two-storey **Governor's Residence**, with its balconies and wooden shutters, is another handsome legacy of the early 1900s.

Battambang

N 0 ————— 500 m
0 ————— 0.25 miles

St 501

8

Vietnamese
Consulate

24

NH5

Pepsi Bottling Plant (1km);
Slaket Crocodile
Farm (2km)

Phare
Ponleu
Selpak
(1.5km)

St 101

27 31 19
29
30 26

St 102

NH5

Wat
Phiphétaram

Handa Emergency Centre &
Medical Clinic (700m)

28

St 115 11

Canadia
Bank

5

B2B 14
23 @
21 13 15

ANZ Royal
Bank

CITY
CENTRE

12
1

9

St 4

St 119

EAST
BANK

St 201

St 102

25

7

St 121

17

16 20

St 203

St 3

St 2½

St 2

St 1½

St 1

Wat
Kandal

Battambang 6
3

St 123

Sangkei River

Riverside Rd

St 102

St 125

St 209

Wat
Damrey
Sar

2

St 127

18

10

Old NH5

Riverside Rd

Psar Thmei (1km);
Share Taxis to
Pursat (1km)

Tourist
Information
Office

4

St 1

St 139

Taxi Station (300m);
Psar Leu (400m)

22

CAMBODIA

Battambang

CAMBODIA BATTAMBANG

Arts Quarter — NEIGHBOURHOOD
(St 2½) The block of St 2½ that runs south of Psar Nath is Battambang's unoffical arts district. A gaggle of galleries, funky bars and shops have set up, including **Lotus Bar** (St 2½; ⊙11am-late) and **Make Maek Art Space** (66 St 2½), with more expected to follow. Make a point to have a stroll here and check out the latest happenings.

Battambang Museum — MUSEUM
(សារមន្ទីរបាតដំបង; St 1; admission US$1; ⊙8-11am & 2-5.30pm) This small museum displays fine Angkorian lintels and statuary from all over Battambang Province, including Phnom Banan.

Train Station — HISTORIC BUILDING
Here the time is always 8.02. Just along the tracks to the south, you can explore a treasure trove of derelict **French-era train repair sheds**, warehouses and rolling stock.

🏃 Activities

Heritage Walking Trail — WALKING TOUR
(http://battambang-heritage.org/downloads.htm) **FREE** Phnom Penh-based **KA Architecture Tours** (www.ka-tours.org) has two half-day heritage walks in the historic centre of Battambang available for free on its website. If you're short on time you can do it by bicycle.

Soksabike — CYCLING
(⊡012 542019; www.soksabike.com; depending on group size, half day US$19-27, full day US$29-40; ⊙departures 7.30am) 🚴 Based at the cafe Kinyei, Soksabike is a social enterprise aiming to connect visitors with the Cambodian countryside and its people. The daily half-day trip covers about 30km. It includes a fresh coconut, seasonal fruits and a shot of rice wine.

Green Orange Kayaks — KAYAKING
(⊡017 736166; feda@online.com.kh; half day US$12) 🚣 One- to three-person kayaks can be rented from Green Orange Kayaks, run by an **NGO** (www.fedacambodia.org) that offers free English classes. The half-day trip begins at the Green Orange Cafe in Ksach Poy, 8km south of Battambang on the road to Phnom Banan.

Seeing Hands Massage — MASSAGE
(⊡078 337499; St 121; per hr US$6; ⊙7am-10pm) 🙌 Trained blind masseurs and masseuses offer soothing work-overs.

🛏 Sleeping

★ Ganesha Family Guesthouse — GUESTHOUSE $
(⊡092 135570; www.ganeshaguesthouse.com; St 1½; dm US$4, r US$10-16; ☎) This is sort of an upscale backpacker (but not quite flashpacker) place. The en-suite private rooms

LE CIRQUE

Battambang's signature attraction is this internationally acclaimed **Phare Ponleu Selpak circus** (053-952424; www.phareps.org; adult/student US$10/5), a multiarts centre for disadvantaged children. Even though they are now running shows in Siem Reap, it's worth timing your visit to Battambang to watch this amazing spectacle where it all began. Performances are at 6.15pm on Monday, Thursday and Saturday, with a Friday show added during the high season.

Guests are welcome to walk in during the day to **tour** (admission US$5; 8-11am & 2-5pm) the Phare complex and observe circus, dance, music, drawing and graphic-arts classes.

To get here from the Vishnu Roundabout on NH5, head west for 900m and then turn right (north) and continue another 600m.

have attractively tiled bathrooms and plump beds, while the dorms have double-wide beds hung with privacy-protecting linens.

Here Be Dragons HOSTEL $
(089 264895; www.herebedragonsbattambang. com; Riverside East; dm US$2, r US$8-10;) Here bedraggled backpackers find comfy dorm beds and, if they're looking to get their drink on, like-minded souls to swap yarns with at the popular bar. The clean private rooms are a dandy deal.

Banan Hotel HOTEL $
(012 739572; www.bananhotel.com; NH5; r without/with breakfast from US$15/20;) A modern high-rise hotel with Khmer-style wooden decor, immaculate rooms and extremely friendly service.

Tomato Guesthouse GUESTHOUSE $
(012 853639; www.luxguesthouse.com; St 119; dm/d US$1.50/3;) This place has very few frills but the odd thrill. No funky smells, no layers of mould, no tattered sheets – great value at this absurd price.

Royal Hotel HOTEL $
(016 912034; www.royalhotelbattambang.com; St 115; r with fan US$6-15, with air-con US$10-20;) Deservedly popular with independent travellers, the Royal has somewhat faded rooms that are nonetheless clean and spacious. It's near the bus offices.

✖ Eating

Cheap dining is available in and around Psar Nat. There's a **riverside night market** (St 1; 3pm-midnight) opposite the Battambang Museum.

★ Lonely Tree Cafe CAFE $
(www.thelonelytreecafe.com; St 121; mains US$2-4; 10am-10pm;) Upstairs from the shop of the same name, this uber-cosy cafe serves Khmer food and a few Spanish dishes like *huevos rotos* (broken eggs). Proceeds support cultural preservation and the disabled.

Kinyei CAFE $
(www.kinyei.org; 1 St 1½; mains US$3-4; 7am-7pm;) The home base of Soksabike, this tiny cafe hidden at the end of St 1½ offers light bites and what many believe is the best coffee in town. National barista champs have been crowned here.

Fresh Eats Café CAMBODIAN $
(www.mpkhomeland.org; St 2½; mains US$2.50-4; 9am-9pm Mon-Sat;) Run by an NGO that helps children whose families have been affected by HIV/AIDS, this little place complements its Khmer specialities with build-your-own baguettes (including a Philly cheesesteak) and pasta.

Vegetarian Foods Restaurant VEGETARIAN $
(St 102; mains 1500-3000r; 6.30am-5pm;) This hole-in-the-wall eatery serves some of the most delicious vegetarian dishes in Cambodia, including rice soup, homemade soy milk and 1000r dumplings. Tremendous value.

Lan Chov Khorko Miteanh NOODLES $
(145 St 2; mains 4000-6000r; 9am-9pm) More conveniently known as Chinese Noodle by resident foreigners, the Chinese chef here does bargain dumplings and serves fresh noodles a dozen or more ways, including with pork or duck soup.

★ Jaan Bai FUSION $$
(078 263144; jaanbaibtb@gmail.com; cnr Sts 1½ & 2; tapas US$3-4; 5-11pm) Battambang deserves a contemporary eating space like Jaan Bai ('rice bowl' in Khmer). The mainly tapas menu and decor are each successfully bold. Trains and employs vulnerable youth through the **Cambodia Childrens Trust** (www.cambodianchildrenstrust.org).

Cafe Eden CAFE $$
(www.cafeedencambodia.com; 85 St 1; mains US$4-7; 7.30am-9pm, closed Tue, happy hour 3-7pm;)

Located in an old colonial block on the riverfront, this is a social enterprise offering a relaxed space for breakfast or an afternoon drink, great food and an original boutique out the back.

🍺 Drinking

Riverside Balcony Bar BAR
(cnr St 1 & St 149; mains US$3.50-7.50; ⊙4-11pm Tue-Sun) Set in a gorgeous wooden house high above the riverfront, Australian-run Riverside is Battambang's original bar and a mellow place for a sundowner. The small menu mixes pub grub and Khmer classics.

★Choco l'art Café CAFE
(www.chocolartcafe.com; St 117; ⊙9am-midnight; 🛜) This inviting gallery-cafe sees foreigners and locals alike gather to drink, eat and sometimes listen to live music.

ℹ Information

Most backpacker-oriented guesthouses can help arrange guides, transport and just about anything else. The city map that the tourist office hands out details scenic routes to the bamboo train and other attractions outside of town.

ANZ Royal Bank (St 1; ⊙8.30am-4pm Mon-Fri) Full international ATM, plus the usual currency services.

B2B (St 2½; ⊙24hr) Fast, air-conditioned internet on Battambang's arty strip.

Canadia Bank (Psar Thom; ⊙7.30am-3.30pm Mon-Fri, 7.30-11.30am Sat) Free cash withdrawals and cash advances on plastic.

Handa Emergency Centre & Medical Clinic (⊡070 810812, 012 674001; NH5; ⊙clinic 9am-3.30pm, emergency 24hr) Has two ambulances and usually a Western doctor or two in residence.

Tourist Information Office (⊡012 534177; www.battambang-town.gov.kh; St 1; ⊙8-11am & 2-5pm Mon-Fri) Moderately useful office with a great map of Battambang.

ℹ Getting There & Away

BOAT
The riverboat to Siem Reap (US$20, 7am) squeezes through narrow waterways and passes by protected wetlands, taking from five hours in the wet season to nine or more hours at the height of the dry season. Cambodia's most memorable boat trip, it's operated on alternate days by **Angkor Express** (⊡012 601287) and **Chann Na** (⊡012 354344). In the dry season, passengers are driven to a navigable section of the river.

BUS
Most bus companies are clustered in the centre just south of the intersection of NH5 and St 4.

Sleeper buses run by Kampuchea Angkor Express are popular to Phnom Penh, but keep in mind it's not a very long trip so arrival at an ungodly hour is a virtual certainty.

For quicker day travel to the capital, consider express minivans run by Golden Bayon Express (US$10, 4½ hours) or Mekong Express (US$12, 4½ hours).

Golden Bayon Express (⊡070 968966; St 101)

Mekong Express (⊡088 576 7668; St 3)

Kampuchea Angkor Express (⊡017 535015; St 4)

Rith Mony (⊡011 575572; St 102)

Phnom Penh Sorya (⊡053-953904; St 4)

Ponleu Angkor Khmer (⊡053-952366; St 4)

TAXI
At the **taxi station** (NH5), share taxis to Phnom Penh (40,000r, 4½ hours) leave from the southeast corner, while taxis to Poipet (20,000r, 1¾ hours) and Siem Reap (26,000r, three hours) leave from north of the market out on NH5.

BUSES FROM BATTAMBANG

DESTINATION	COMPANIES	PRICE (US$)	DURATION (HR)	FREQUENCY
Bangkok	Sorya	13-14	9	7.45am, 1pm
Kompong Cham	Sorya, Rith Mony	7.5-10	7½	both 9.30am
Pailin	Ponleu Angkor, Rith Mony	33	1½	1.30pm (PA), 3pm (RM)
Phnom Penh	all companies	regular/sleeper 5/10	6	frequent
Poipet	Kampuchea Angkor, Sorya, Rith Mony	3.25	2¼	7.45am, 6.30am (KA), 1pm (Sorya), noon (RM)
Siem Reap	most companies	4-5	4	frequent to 2pm

ALL ABOARD THE BAMBOO TRAIN

Battambang's **bamboo train** (1hr ride for 2-plus passengers per person US$5, for 1 passenger US$10; ⊘7am-dusk) is one of the world's all-time classic rail journeys. From O Dambong, on the East Bank 3.7km south of Battambang's old French bridge (Wat Kor Bridge), the train bumps 7km southeast to O Sra Lav along warped, misaligned rails and vertiginous bridges left by the French.

Each bamboo train – known in Khmer as a norry (nori) or lorry – consists of a 3m-long wooden frame, covered lengthwise with slats made of ultralight bamboo, that rest on two barbell-like bogies, the aft one connected by fan belts to a 6HP gasoline engine. Pile on 10 or 15 people or up to three tonnes of rice, crank it up and you can cruise along at about 15km/h.

Share taxis to Pailin (US$6, 1¼ hours) near the Psar Pruhm–Pong Nam Ron border leave from the east edge of Psar Leu.

❶ Getting Around

English- and French-speaking *remorque* drivers are commonplace in Battambang, and all of them are eager to whisk you around on day trips. Figure on US$12 for a half-day trip and US$16 to US$20 for a full day, depending on your haggling skills and the destinations. A moto costs about half as much.

A moto ride in town costs around 2000r, while a *remorque* ride starts from US$1.

Gecko Moto (☑089 924260; www.geckocafe cambodia.com; St 3; ⊘8am-7pm) and Royal Hotel rent out motorbikes for US$7 to US$8 per day. Bicycles are a great way to get around; these can be rented at the Royal Hotel, Soksabike and several other guesthouses for about US$2 per day.

Around Battambang

The countryside around Battambang is littered with old temples, bamboo trains and other worthwhile sights. Admission to Phnom Sampeau, Phnom Banan and Wat Ek Phnom costs US$3. If you purchase a ticket at one site, it's valid all day long at the other two.

Phnom Sampeau   ភ្នំសំពៅ

At the summit of this fabled limestone outcrop, 12km southwest of Battambang (towards Pailin), a complex of **temples** affords gorgeous views. Some of the macaques that live here, dining on bananas left as offerings, are pretty cantankerous.

Between the summit and the mobile-phone antenna, a deep canyon descends steeply through a natural arch to a 'lost world' of stalactites, creeping vines and bats. Nearby, two government artillery pieces still point west towards **Phnom Krapeu** (Crocodile Mountain), a one-time Khmer Rouge stronghold.

About halfway up the hill, a turn-off leads 250m up to the **Killing Caves of Phnom Sampeau**. An enchanted staircase, flanked by greenery, leads into a cavern where a golden reclining Buddha lies peacefully next to a glass-walled memorial filled with the bones and skulls of some of the people bludgeoned to death by Khmer Rouge cadres, before being thrown through the overhead skylight. Every evening at dusk, a thick column of bats pours out of a massive cave high up on the north side of the cliff face – the mesmerising display lasts a good 30 minutes.

Phnom Banan   ភ្នំបាណន់

Exactly 358 stone steps lead up a shaded slope to 11th-century **Wat Banan**, 28km south of Battambang, whose five towers are reminiscent of the layout of Angkor Wat. The views are well worth the climb.

From the temple, a narrow stone staircase leads south down the hill to three caves, which can be visited with a local guide.

Wat Ek Phnom   វត្តឯកភ្នំ

This atmospheric, partly collapsed, 11th-century **temple** is 11km north of Battambang. A lintel showing the Churning of the Ocean of Milk can be seen above the east entrance to the central temple, whose upper flanks hold some fine **bas-reliefs**. This is a great place for a shady picnic.

On the way from Battambang by bicycle or moto, it's possible to visit a 1960s **Pepsi bottling plant** (1.2km north of Battambang's ferry landing), frozen in time since 1975 and, 1km further out, the **Slaket crocodile farm**.

Prasat Preah Vihear
ប្រាសាទព្រះវិហារ

This 800m-long **temple** (suggested donation US$2-5) – not to be confused with Preah

Vihear City (Tbeng Meanchey) some 110km southeast – is the most dramatically situated of all the Angkorian monuments. It sits high atop the Dangkrek escarpment on the Thai border, with stupendous views of Cambodia's northern plains.

Prasat Preah Vihear consists of a series of four cruciform *gopura* (sanctuaries) decorated with exquisite carvings, including some striking lintels. Starting at the **Monumental Stairway**, a walk south takes you to the **Gopura of the Third Level**, with its early rendition of the Churning of the Ocean of Milk, and finally, perched at the edge of the cliff, the **Central Sanctuary**. Stick to well-marked paths, as the Khmer Rouge laid huge numbers of landmines around Prasat Preah Vihear as late as 1998.

Driving in from Sra Em, your first stop should be the **information centre** (☉7am-5.30pm) in the village of Kor Muy. This is where you pay your donation, secure an English-speaking guide if you want one (US$15), and arrange transport via moto (US$5 return) or 4WD (US$25 return, maxi-mum six passengers) up the 6.5km temple access road, the final 1.5km of which is extremely steep. Another option is to ascend the hill on foot via the **Eastern Staircase**.

Budget lodging is plentiful in the burgeoning town of Sra Em, 23km south of the information centre – try neighbouring **Sok San** (☑097 715 3839; s/d with fan US$10/11, with air-con from US$14/15; ✳ @ 🛜) or **Raksmey** (☑077 516255; r with fan/air-con from US$12/16; ✳🛜), 1km west of Sra Em's central roundabout. Eat at **Limy Restaurant** (mains US$3-4.50; ☉6am-10pm), the last in a row of restaurants on the right just north of the roundabout (towards Prasat Preah Vihear).

❶ Getting There & Away

With a private car you can get to Prasat Preah Vihear in about 2½ hours from Siem Reap (about US$140 round-trip).

It makes much more sense to break up the long trip with a night in Sra Em, which is just 30km from the temple. Share taxis (US$10, 2½ hours) link Sra Em with Siem Reap. **Liang US Express** has a morning bus from Sra Em to Phnom Penh (US$10, 10 hours) via Preah Vihear City and Kompong

---

GETTING TO THAILAND: REMOTE NORTHERN BORDERS

There are a couple of seldom-used crossings along Cambodia's northern border with Thailand. The usual 15-day Thai waivers and Cambodian visas-on-arrival are available at both borders.

Anlong Veng to Chong Sa-Ngam

The remote Choam/Chong Sa-Ngam crossing (open from 7am to 8pm) connects Anlong Veng in Oddar Meanchey Province with Thailand's Si Saket Province.

Getting to the border A moto from Anlong Veng to the border crossing (16km) costs US$3 or US$4 (more like US$5 in the reverse direction). Share taxis link Anlong Veng with Siem Reap (20,000r, 1½ hours).

At the border Formalities here are straightforward.

Moving on On the Thai side, it should be possible to find a motorcycle taxi or taxi to take you to the nearest town, Phusing (30 minutes), where buses and *sŏrngtǎaou* (pick-up trucks) head to Si Saket and Kantharalak. Or try to hop on a casino shuttle from the border to Phusing, Ku Khan or Si Saket.

Samraong to Surin

The remote O Smach/Chong Chom crossing connects Cambodia's Oddar Meanchey Province and Thailand's Surin Province.

Getting to the border Share taxis link Siem Reap with Samraong (30,000r, two hours) via NH68. From Samraong, take a moto (US$5) or a charter taxi (US$15) for the smooth drive to O Smach (40km, 30 minutes) and its frontier casino zone. A private taxi from Siem Reap all the way to the border should cost US$40 to US$50.

At the border The crossing itself is easy.

Moving on On the Thai side walk to the nearby bus stop, where regular buses depart to Surin throughout the day (60B, 70km, 1½ hours). For information on making the crossings in the other direction, see p735.

THE FIGHT FOR PRASAT PREAH VIHEAR

Prasat Preah Vihear and the lands surrounding it were ruled by Thailand for several centuries, but were returned to Cambodia during the French protectorate, under the treaty of 1907. In 1959 the Thai military seized the temple from Cambodia and the then prime minister Sihanouk took the dispute to the International Court of Justice (ICJ) in the Hague, gaining worldwide recognition of Cambodian sovereignty in a 1962 ruling.

In July 2008, Prasat Preah Vihear was declared Cambodia's second Unesco World Heritage Site. Within a week, Thai troops crossed into Cambodian territory, sparking an armed confrontation that has taken the lives of several dozen soldiers and some civilians on both sides. The Cambodian market at the bottom of the Monumental Stairway, which used to be home to some guesthouses, burned down during an exchange of fire in April 2009. In 2011, exchanges heated up once more and long-range shells were fired into civilian territory by both sides.

In July 2011, the ICJ ruled that both sides should withdraw troops from the area to establish a demilitarised zone. Then in November 2013, the ICJ confirmed its 1962 ruling that the temple belongs to Cambodia, although it declined to define the official borderline, leaving sovereignty of some lands around the temple open to dispute. With a pro-Thaksin (therefore Hun Sen–friendly) government tenuously hanging on to power in Bangkok since August 2011, the border dispute has died down in recent years, but tensions can reignite at any time, especially if the Yellow Shirts regain control in Thailand.

Thom. **Rith Mony** (📞 097 865 6018) has a morning bus to Phnom Penh (US$10, 10 hours) via Siem Reap (20,000r, 3½ hours). Note that buses from Siem Reap or Phnom Penh marked 'Preah Vihear' go only as far as Preah Vihear City and do not continue on to Prasat Preah Vihear.

From Sra Em's central roundabout, you can find a moto to the information centre in Kor Muy (US$10 return).

It used to be possible to get to Prasat Preah Vihear from Thailand, where paved roads from Kantharalak lead almost up to the Monumental Stairway. However, due to the long stand-off between Thailand and Cambodia, access from the Thai side has been forbidden since mid-2008.

Kompong Thom ក្ំពង់ធំ

📞 062 / POP 66,000

A bustling commercial centre, Kompong Thom is mainly a base from which to explore dazzling Sambor Prei Kuk.

🛏 Sleeping & Eating

Arunras Hotel HOTEL $
(📞 062-961294; NH6; s/d with fan US$5/8, d with air-con US$15; ❋ 🛜) Dominating the accommodation scene in Kompong Thom, this seven-storey corner establishment has 58 smart, good-value rooms, as well as Kompong Thom's only lift. Also operates the slightly cheaper, 53-room **Arunras Guesthouse** (📞 012 865935; NH6; s/d with fan US$6/8, with air-con US$10/13; ❋ 🛜) next door.

Prum Bayon Restaurant CAMBODIAN $
(Prachea Thepatay St; mains incl rice 6000-10,000r; ⏰ 5am-9pm) Lacking English signs but with an English menu, this immensely popular feeding station is where locals come for flavourful Khmer cooking.

Psar Kompong Thom
Night Market CAMBODIAN $
(NH6; mains 2000-4000r; ⏰ 4pm-2am) Sit on a plastic chair at a neon-lit table at Kompong Thom's main market and dig into chicken rice soup, chicken curry noodles, Khmer-style baguettes or a *tukalok* (fruit shake).

ℹ Information

Canadia Bank (NH6; ⏰ 8am-3.30pm Mon-Fri, 8-11.30am Sat) ATM cash withdrawals fee-free.

Chamroeun Rith Pharmacy (NH6; ⏰ 6.30am-8pm) Internet access as well as medications.

ℹ Getting There & Around

Dozens of buses travelling between Phnom Penh (US$5, four hours) and Siem Reap (US$5, two hours) pass through Kompong Thom and can easily be flagged down outside the Arunras Hotel.

Heading north to Preah Vihear City, share taxis (US$5, two hours) depart in the morning only.

Im Sokhom Travel Agency (📞 012 691527; St 3) rents bicycles (US$1 a day) and motorbikes (US$5 a day).

Around Kompong Thom

Sambor Prei Kuk   សំបូរព្រៃគុក

Cambodia's most impressive group of pre-Angkorian monuments, **Sambor Prei Kuk** (www.samborpreikuk.com; admission US$3) encompasses more than 100 brick temples scattered throughout the forest. Originally called Isanapura, it served as the capital of Chenla during the reign of the early-7th-century King Isanavarman.

Forested and shady, Sambor Prei Kuk has a serene and soothing atmosphere. The main temple area consists of three complexes, each enclosed by the remains of two concentric walls. The principal group, **Prasat Sambor**, is dedicated to Gambhireshvara, one of Shiva's many incarnations (the other groups are dedicated to Shiva himself). **Prasat Yeay Peau** (Prasat Yeai Poeun) feels lost in the forest, its eastern gateway both held up and torn asunder by an ancient tree.

Prasat Tao (Lion Temple), the largest of the Sambor Prei Kuk complexes, boasts excellent examples of Chenla carving in the form of two large, elaborately coiffed stone lions.

Isanborei (☑017 936112; www.samborpreikuk.com; dm/d US$4/6) runs a community-based homestay program, offers cooking courses, rents bicycles (US$2 per day) and organises ox-cart rides. It also operates a stable of *remorques* to whisk you safely to/from Kompong Thom (US$15 one-way).

You'll find plenty of **restaurants** (mains US$2-4) serving local fare around the large open-air handicrafts market near the temple entrance.

Sambor Prei Kuk is 30km northeast of Kompong Thom via smooth roads. A round-trip moto ride out here should cost US$10, a *remorque* about US$20.

SOUTH COAST

Cambodia's south coast is an alluring mix of clear blue water, castaway islands, pristine mangrove forests, time-worn colonial towns and jungle-clad mountains, where bears and elephants lurk. Adventurers will find this region of Cambodia just as rewarding as sunseekers.

Koh Kong City   ក្រុងកោះកុង
☑ 035 / POP 35,000

Once Cambodia's Wild West, its frontier economy dominated by smuggling, prostitution and gambling, the city of Koh Kong, capital of the province of the same name, is

---

GETTING TO THAILAND: WESTERN BORDERS

Pailin to Chanthaburi

Laid-back Psar Pruhm/Pong Nam Ron border (open from 7am to 8pm) is 102km southwest of Battambang and 18km northwest of Pailin via good sealed roads.

Getting to the border From Battambang, the daily Ponleu Angkor and Rith Mony buses to Pailin continue on to this border. Alternatively, take a share taxi to Pailin from Psar Leu in Battambang, then continue to the border by moto (US$5) or private taxi (US$10).

At the border Formalities are extremely straightfoward and quick on both sides.

Moving on Onward transport on the Thai side dries up midmorning so cross early. In the morning you should be able to find a motorcycle taxi (50B) to the nearby *sŏrngtăaou* (pick-up truck) station, where two morning minibuses head to Chanthaburi (150B, 1½ hours). Otherwise, you're looking at a private taxi from the border to Chanthaburi bus station (1200B), where you'll find frequent buses to Bangkok.

Koh Kong to Trat

Getting to the border To cross at Cham Yeam/Hat Lek border, take a taxi (US$10 plus toll) or moto (US$3 plus toll) from Koh Kong across the toll bridge to Cham Yeam at the border.

At the border Departing Cambodia via the Hat Lek border is actually pretty straightforward, as there are no visa scams for immigration to benefit from.

Moving on Once in Thailand, catch a minibus to Trat (120B), where there are regular buses to Bangkok (from 225B, five to six hours). Arrange onward transport to Ko Chang in Trat. For information on making the crossings in the other direction, see p738.

Koh Kong City

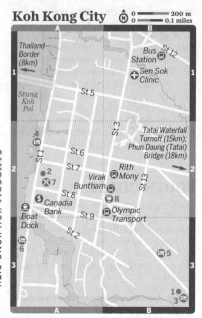

N
0 — 200 m
0 — 0.1 miles

CAMBODIA KOH KONG CITY

Koh Kong City

☉ Activities, Courses & Tours
1 Blue Moon Guesthouse.........................B3
2 Koh Kong Eco Adventure Tours A2

⬤ Sleeping
3 Blue Moon Guesthouse.........................B3
4 Koh Kong City Hotel.............................A2
5 Paddy's Bamboo Guesthouse..............B3
6 PS Guesthouse.......................................A3

⬤ Eating
7 Bob's Ice..A2
Café Laurent.................................(see 4)

⬤ Drinking & Nightlife
8 Fat Sam's...B2

ⓘ Transport
Phnom Penh Sorya......................(see 8)

striding towards respectability as ecotourists scare the sleaze away.

☉ Sights & Activities

Koh Kong's main draw is for those seeking adventure in and around the Cardamom Mountains and the Koh Kong Conservation Corridor.

Peam Krasaop Mangrove Sanctuary   WILDLIFE RESERVE

(ជម្រកសត្វព្រៃបឹងក្រឃាំក នៅព្រោមក្រសោម; mangrove walk admission 5000r; ☉ mangrove walk 6.30am-6pm) ☞ Anchored to alluvial islands – some no larger than a house – this 260-sq-km sanctuary's millions of magnificent mangroves protect the coast from erosion, serve as a vital breeding and feeding ground for fish, shrimp and shellfish, and provide a home to myriad birds (see www.ramsar.org).

The best way to visit the sanctuary is on a boat tour out of Koh Kong. Alternatively, ride a bicycle or moto (return US$5) out to the park entrance, 5.5km southeast of the city centre, where a 600m-long concrete mangrove walk wends its way above the briny waters to a 15m observation tower.

☞ Tours

Boat tours are an excellent way to view Koh Kong's many coastal attractions. English-speaking **Teur** (☏ 016 278668) hangs around the **boat dock** (cnr Sts 1 & 9) and can help you hire six-passenger (40-horsepower) and three-passenger (15-horsepower) outboards (speedboats). Destinations include Koh Kong Island's western beaches (big/small boats US$80/50), around Koh Kong Island (US$120/90) and Peam Krasaop Mangrove Sanctuary (US$40/30).

Recommended operators for boat and other tours:

Koh Kong Eco Adventure Tours   TOUR
(☏ 012 707719; www.kohkongecoadventure.com; St 1) Excursions include excellent Koh Kong Island boat tours, bird-watching and jungle treks in the Cardamoms.

Blue Moon Guesthouse   TOUR
(☏ 012 946079; bluemoonkohkong@yahoo.com) Mr Neat offers boat trips and rainforest overnights in a hammock.

🛏 Sleeping

Some places pay moto drivers a commission, leading to a whole lot of shenanigans.

★**Koh Kong City Hotel**   HOTEL $
(☏ 035-936777; http://kkcthotel.netkhmer.com; St 1; r US$15-20; ❈ @ 🛜) Ludicrous value for what you get, rooms include a huge bathroom, two double beds, 50 TV channels, a full complement of toiletries, free water and – in the US$20 rooms – glorious river views.

Paddy's Bamboo Guesthouse GUESTHOUSE $
(☏ 015 533223; ppkohkong@gmail.com; r US$4-8;
☞) Paddy's targets backpackers with basic
rooms, a balcony for chillin', tours and a pool
table. Shoot for the wood-floored rooms upstairs with shared bathrooms.

Blue Moon Guesthouse GUESTHOUSE $
(☏ 012 575741; bluemoonkohkong@yahoo.com;
r with fan/air-con US$6/10; ❄☞) Nine neat,
clean rooms with spiffy furnishings and hot
water line a long, narrow courtyard.

PS Guesthouse GUESTHOUSE $
(☏ 097 729 1600; St 1; r with fan/air-con US$7/12;
❄☞) A single-storey hotel backing on to
the riverfront, the 18 rooms here are well-
furnished with large beds, flat-screen TVs
and tastefully decorated bathrooms. PS. We
recommend it.

🍴 Eating & Drinking

The best cheap food stalls are in the southeast corner of Psar Leu, the main market.
Riverfront food carts sell noodles and cans
of beer for 2000r to 3000r.

Bob's Ice CAFE $
(St 1; mains US$2-5; ⊘ 7am-10pm; ☞) Popular
Bob's has a lively location near the riverfront.
Don't be fooled by the name, though: the
ice cream is great, but most people here are
drinking chilled beers.

Crab Shack SEAFOOD $
(Koh Yor Beach; mains US$4-8; ⊘ 11am-9pm) A
family-run place over the bridge on Koh
Yor, it's known for perfect sunsets and heaping portions of fried crab ▪
request).

★ Café Laurent INTE.
(http://cafelaurent.asia; St 1; mains
⊘ 11am-10pm; ☞) This chic, French-sty.
and restaurant offers refined Khmer cui.
and Western dishes like lamb stew.

Fat Sam's BAR
(St 3; ⊘ 7am-11pm) An informal, Welsh-run
bar-restaurant with a decent selection of
beers, fish and chips, pasta, chilli con carne
and more.

ℹ Information

Guesthouses, hotels and pubs are the best places to get the local low-down. You can also look
for the free **Koh Kong Visitors Guide** (www.koh-
kong.com), which is mostly advertisements.

Canadia Bank (St 1; ⊘ 8am-3.30pm Mon-Fri,
to 11.30am Sat) The ATM here accepts most
international plastic and there's no local charge
for withdrawals.

Sen Sok Clinic (☏ 012 555060; kkpao@
camintel.com; St 3, cnr St 5; ⊘ 24hr) Has
doctors who speak English and French.

ℹ Getting There & Away

Most buses drop passengers at Koh Kong's
unpaved **bus station** (St 12), on the northeast
edge of town, where motos and *remorques*
await, eager to overcharge tourists. Don't pay
more than US$1/2 for the three-minute moto/
remorque ride into the centre.

Rith Mony (☏ 012 640344; St 3), **Phnom
Penh Sorya** (☏ 077 563447; St 3), **Olympic
Transport** (☏ 011 363678; St 3) and **Virak
Buntham** (☏ 089 998760; St 3) each runs two

CHI PHAT

Once notorious for its loggers and poachers, Chi Phat (សហគមន៍ទេសចរណ៍ជីផាត) is
now home to a pioneering **community-based ecotourism project** offering hardy
travellers a unique opportunity to explore the Cardamoms ecosystem while contributing
to its protection. Visitors can take day treks through the jungle, go sunrise bird-watching
by boat, mountain bike to several sets of rapids, and look for monkeys and hornbills with a
former poacher as a guide. Also possible are one- to four-night mountain-bike safaris and
jungle treks deep into the Cardamoms. In the village, visitors can relax by playing volleyball, badminton or pool with the locals.

Basic accommodation options in Chi Phat include 13 CBET-member guesthouses
(doubles US$5) and 10 homestays (singles/doubles US$3/4). Reserve through the **CBET
office** (☏ 035-675 6444) in Chi Phat.

Chi Phat is on the Preak Piphot River 17km upriver from Andoung Tuek, which is 98km
east of Koh Kong on the NH48. Any Koh Kong–bound bus can drop you in Andoung Tuek.
From Andoung Tuek to Chi Phat it's a two-hour boat (about US$30 for the whole boat) or
a 45-minute motorbike ride (US$7) on an unpaved but smooth road. Call the CBET office
to arrange a boat or moto in advance.

...enh (US$7, six hours,
...and one or two trips
...hours). Most Siha-
...sfer, but Rith Mony
...ct buses around 8am.

...IS$12, five hours)
...ith Rith Mony and
...le change or two.
...midday trips to
...ge at the border (US$20,
...). There are also trips to Koh Chang
(US$14, including ferry) with a change of bus at
the border, plus a local ferry to the island. See the
corresponding boxed text in the Thailand chapter
(p738) for tips on navigating this border from the
Thai side.

From the taxi lot next to the bus station, share
taxis head to Phnom Penh (US$11, five hours) and
occasionally to Sihanoukville (US$10, four hours).

ⓘ Getting Around

Paddy's Bamboo Guesthouse and Koh Kong Eco
Adventure Tours rent out bicycles for US$1 to
US$2 per day. Motorbike hire is available from
Fat Sam's and from Koh Kong Eco Adventure
Tours for US$5 a day.

Koh Kong Conservation Corridor របៀងអភិរក្សខេត្តកោះកុង

Stretching along both sides of NH48 from
Koh Kong to the Gulf of Kompong Som, the
Koh Kong Conservation Corridor encompasses many of Cambodia's most outstanding natural sites, including the most
extensive mangrove forests on mainland
Southeast Asia and the southern reaches of
the fabled Cardamom Mountains, an area
of breathtaking beauty and astonishing
biodiversity.

The next few years will be critical in
determining the future of the Cardamom
Mountains. NGOs such as Conservation International (CI; www.conservation.
org), Fauna & Flora International (FFI;
www.fauna-flora.org) and Wildlife Alliance
(www.wildlifealliance.org) are working to help
protect the region's 16 distinct ecosystems
from loggers and poachers. Ecotourism is
playing a huge role in their plans – Wildlife Alliance is promoting several enticing
projects in the Southern Cardamoms Protected Forest (1443 sq km).

Tatai Waterfall ស្ទឹងទឹកធ្លាក់តាតៃ

About 18km east of Koh Kong on the NH48,
the Phun Daung (Tatai) Bridge spans the
Tatai River. Nestled in a lushly forested
gorge upstream from the bridge is the Tatai
Waterfall, a thundering set of rapids in the
wet season, plunging over a 4m rock shelf.
Water levels drop in the dry season but you
can swim year-round in refreshing pools
around the waterfall.

The turn-off to Tatai is about 15km southeast of Koh Kong, or 2.8km northwest of the
Tatai Bridge. From the highway it's about 2km
to the falls along a rough access road. From
Koh Kong, a half-day moto/remorque excursion to Tatai Waterfall costs US$10/15 return.

Sihanoukville ក្រុងព្រះសីហនុ

🎵 034 / POP 155,000

Surrounded by white-sand beaches and relatively undeveloped tropical islands, Sihanoukville (aka Kompong Som) is Cambodia's
premier seaside resort. While backpackers
flock to the party zone of Serendipity Beach,
the gorgeous Otres Beach, south of town,
has made an incredible comeback and is
now equally popular for a more relaxed stay.
Meanwhile, the southern islands off Sihanoukville continue to blossom as cradles of
castaway cool.

⊙ Sights & Activities

Coastal Ream National Park, 15km east of
Sihanoukville, offers invigorating boat trips
through coastal mangroves and long stretches of unspoilt beach, not to mention trekking
in primary forest.

Beaches

Sihanoukville's beaches all have wildly different characters, offering something for just
about everyone. Most central is Occheuteal
Beach (ឆ្នេរអូរឈើទាល; Map p118), lined with
ramshackle restaurants, whose northwestern
end – a tiny, rocky strip – has emerged as a
happy, easy-going travellers' hang-out known
as Serendipity Beach.

South of Occheuteal Beach, beyond a
small headland, lies Otres Beach (ឆ្នេរអូរ
ត្រ៎:), lined by dozens of bungalow-style
restaurants and resorts. Otres has cleaner
water and is more relaxed than anything in
Sihanoukville proper, and is lengthy enough
that finding your own patch of private sand is
not a challenge...just walk south. Otres Beach
is about 5km south of the Serendipity area.
It's a US$2/5 moto/remorque ride to get here
(more at night).

 NATIONAL $$
IS$4-15;
cafe
ne
pepper (on

IS$4-15;
113

Sihanoukville

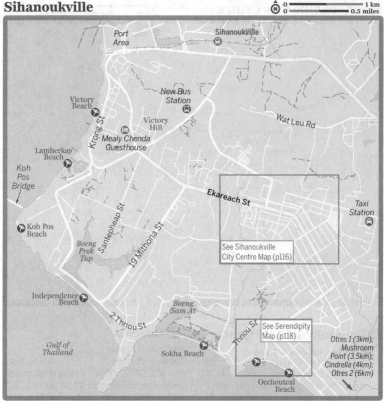

See Sihanoukville
City Centre Map (p116)

See Serendipity
Map (p118)

Otres 1 (3km);
Mushroom
Point (3.5km);
Cindrella (4km);
Otres 2 (6km)

One beach north of Serendipity lies Sihanoukville's prettiest beach, 1.5km-long **Sokha Beach** (ឆ្នេរសុខា; Map p115). Its fine, silicon-like sand squeaks loudly underfoot. The tiny eastern end of Sokha Beach is open to the public and rarely crowded. The rest is part of the exclusive Sokha Beach Resort.

Moving north from Sokha Beach, you'll hit pretty **Independence Beach** (ឆ្នេរឯករាជ្យ; Map p115) near the classic Independence Hotel, and the original backpacker beach, **Victory Beach** (ឆ្នេរជ័យជំនះ; Map p115), now under Russian management. The latter is clean, orderly and devoid of buzz.

Diving

The diving near Sihanoukville isn't terrific. It gets better the further you go out, although you still shouldn't expect anything on a par with the western Gulf of Thailand or the Andaman Sea. Most serious trips will hit **Koh Rong Samloem**, while overnight trips target the distant islands of **Koh Tang** and Koh

Prins. Overnight trips cost about US$100 per day including two daily dives, food, accommodation on an island and equipment. Two-tank dives out of Sihanoukville average US$80 including equipment. PADI open-water courses average about US$400 to US$450 – pretty competitive by world standards.

Dive Shop DIVING
(Map p118; ☑034-933664; www.diveshopcambodia.com; Rd to Serendipity) PADI five-star dive centre offering National Geographic Diver certification.

Scuba Nation DIVING
(Map p118; ☑012 604680; www.divecambodia.com; Serendipity St) Longest-running operator in town, Scuba Nation has a comfortable boat for liveaboard trips.

Massage

NGO-trained blind and disabled masseurs deftly ease away the tension at **Seeing**

CAMBODIA SIHANOUKVILLE

Sihanoukville City Centre

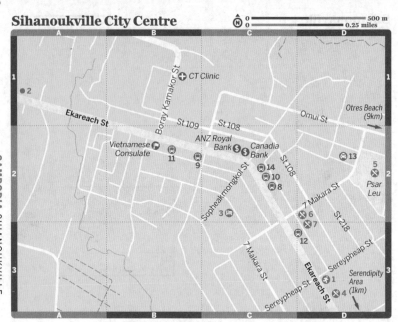

Ⓝ 0 _____ 500 m
0 _____ 0.25 miles

CAMBODIA SIHANOUKVILLE

Sihanoukville City Centre

Ⓐ Activities, Courses & Tours

ⓢ Sleeping

ⓧ Eating

ⓘ Transport

Hands Massage 3 (Map p116; 95 Ekareach St; per hr US$6; ⊙8am-9pm) ∥ and **Starfish Bakery & Café** (Map p116; No 62, 7 Makara St; per hr US$6-10; ⊙7am-6pm).

🎓 Courses

Traditional Khmer
Cookery Classes   COOKING COURSE
(Map p116; ☎092 738615; www.cambodiacookery classes.com; 335 Ekareach St; per person US$23; ⊙10am-2pm Mon-Sat) Teaches traditional culinary techniques in classes with no more than eight participants. Reserve a day ahead.

☞ Tours

Popular day tours go to some of the closer islands and to Ream National Park. Booze cruises are popular.

Eco-Trek Tours   TOUR
(Map p118; ☎012 987073; ecotrektourscambodia@ yahoo.com; Rd to Serendipity; ⊙8am-10pm) Associated with the knowledgeable folks at Mick and Craig's restaurant, this travel agency has information on just about anything. Mountain bikes (per day US$4) available.

Party Boat   BOAT TOUR
(Map p118; www.thepartyboat.asia; Serendipity Beach Pier; per person US$25) The Party Boat heads out daily to Koh Rong Samloem, departing at 9.30am. The trip includes snacks, lunch, snorkelling and a free drink.

Ravuth Travel BOAT TOUR
(Map p118; 012 439292; www.ravuthtravel.blog
spot.com; Otres Beach) Located at Otres Beach
Resort, Ravuth is one of several operations
running daily trips to Koh Ta Kiev/Koh
Russei (per person US$12/15).

Sleeping

Most backpackers shoot for the Serendipity
area if they want to party, Otres Beach if they
want to chill. Other decent options exist in
the town centre (for those who want to escape tourists) and on long-running Victory
Hill, a former backpacker ghetto that is now
one of Sihanoukville's sleazier strips. There
are popular bungalow resorts popping up all
over the islands off Sihanoukville.

Sihanoukville Proper

The Road to Serendipity is the main backpacker hang-out, while down the hill Serendipity Beach offers a string of mellow midrange
resorts perched on the rocky shoreline.

★**Monkey Republic** HOSTEL $
(Map p118; 012 490290; http://monkeyrepublic.
info; Rd to Serendipity; r US$10-12; @ 🛜) Self-pro-
claimed 'backpacker central', established in
2005, Monkey Republic quickly rose from the
ashes in 2013 following a dramatic fire (no
casualities). Smart dorms and an immensely
popular bar-restaurant with a happy hour
from 6pm to 9pm.

Big Easy HOSTEL $
(Map p118; 081 943930; www.thebigeasy.asia; Rd
to Serendipity; dm US$3, r US$6-10; 🛜) The Big
Easy is a classic backpacker pad with accommodation, comfort food and a lively bar all
rolled into one.

New Sea View Villa HOTEL $
(Map p118; 092 759753; www.sihanoukville-hotel.
com; Serendipity St; r US$10-35; ❀🛜) Known
more for its food, New Sea View also has
popular rooms in a central (almost beachfront) location in the heart of Serendipity.

Utopia HOSTEL $
(Map p118; 034-934319; www.utopia-cambodia.
com; Rd to Serendipity; dm US$1-2.50, r US$6-7;
@🛜❀) Dorm beds don't come any cheaper
than at this backpacker mecca, including 'luxury' air-con options. The bar is party central.

Mealy Chenda Guesthouse GUESTHOUSE $
(Map p115; 034-933472; Victory Hill; r with fan
US$7-9, with air-con US$15-25; ❀🛜) The clean

and spacious air-con rooms in this old classic are a fine deal on Victory Hill. Check out
the popular BBQ nights on Wednesday and
Saturday.

Geckozy Guesthouse GUESTHOUSE $
(Map p116; 012 495825; www.geckozy-guest
house.com; r US$6-10; 🛜) For a slice of
old-fashioned Sihanoukville hospitality,
check out these basic rooms in an old wood-
en house on a quiet side street in the city
centre.

Otres Beach

Most guesthouses are in a cluster about 1km
south of Queen Hill Resort, an area known
as Otres 1. About 2.5km of empty beach
separates this cluster from a smaller, more
isolated colony of resorts at the far southern
end of the beach, known as Otres 2.

Mushroom Point HOSTEL $
(078 509079; mushroompoint.otres@gmail.
com; Otres 1; dm US$7-10, r US$20-30; 🛜) The
open-air dorm over the restaurant, with
mosquito-net-draped pods good for two, is
a creative masterpiece. The mushie-shaped
private bungalows and food get high
marks too. There is also now a small annex
on the beach.

Otres Orchid GUESTHOUSE $
(034-633 8484; otres.orchid@yahoo.com; Otres
1; r US$15-20) Cracking value for this popu-
lar Otres strip, the Orchid offers a mix of 20
rooms and bungalows at sensible prices.

SPLURGE

For US$35 you'll be sitting pretty in a
huge, modern room with a huge pool and
borderline four-star amenities at **Serendipity Beach Resort** (Map p118; 034-
938888; www.serendipitybeachresort.com;
Serendipity St; US$35-100; ❀@🛜❀). It's
downright perfect if you're looking to
dial up a night of creature comforts after
hard weeks on the hostel trail.

One of the smarter bungalow resorts
on Serendipity Beach, the **Cove** (Map
p118; 034-638 0296; www.thecovebeach.
com; Serendipity Beach; r US$21-129; ❀🛜)
has a variety of hillside bungalows and
a bar lapped by waves. Most bungalows
face the sea and all have balconies and
hammocks.

Serendipity

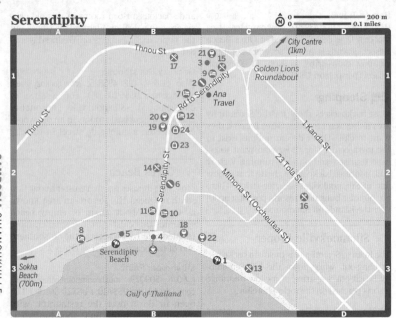

N 0 —— 200 m
0 —— 0.1 miles

Thnou St

City Centre
(1km)

Golden Lions
Roundabout

Rd to Serendipity

Ana
Travel

Thnou St

Serendipity St

Mithona St (Occheuteal St)

1 Kanda St

23 Tola St

Serendipity
Beach

Sokha
Beach
(700m)

Gulf of Thailand

Wish You Were Here HOSTEL $

(☎ 097 241 5884; http://wishotres.com; Otres 1; r US$10-12, bungalows US$15) The rooms are pretty standard Otres fare, but the bar-restaurant is one of the hippest hang-outs in the Otres area. Lounge around listening to top tunes or order one of the popular wish burgers or barra burgers.

Cinderella RESORT $

(☎ 092 612035; www.cinderella-cambodia.com; Otres 2; bungalows US$15-25; ☎) Way down south in Otres 2, this is your spot if you just want some alone time. The beach is a bit dishevelled here and the A-frame cottages basic, but you can't argue with the beach-front setting.

🍴 Eating

Sihanoukville's centre of culinary gravity is in the Serendipity area.

🍴 Serendipity Area

For romance, nothing beats dining on the water, either at one of the resorts at Serendipity Beach or – more cheaply – in one of the shacks along adjacent Occheuteal Beach. Of the resorts, the best food is found at New Sea Villa (good for candlelight dinners) and Reef Resort.

Nyam CAMBODIAN $

(Map p118; www.nyamsihanoukville.com; 23 Tola St; US$2-4.25; ☉ 5-10pm; ☎) Translating as 'eat' in Khmer, this is a great spot for a contemporary Cambodian dinner. All the favourites are here such as *amok* (baked fish curry).

Cafe Mango ITALIAN $

(Map p118; Serendipity St; US$3-6; ☉ 7am-10pm; ☎) A cracking little Italian cafe turning out wood-fired pizzas, homemade pasta and delicate gnocchi, plus generous US$5 set meals before 6.30pm.

Beachys BARBECUE $

(Map p118; Occheuteal Beach; mains US$2.50-5; ☉ 7am-10pm; ☎) The generous mixed seafood grill at this barbecue shack is fantastic value at US$4. If you aren't up for surf, order turf, a heaped platter of various grilled meats.

★ Sandan CAMBODIAN $$

(Map p118; 2 Thnou St; mains US$4-10; ☉ 7am-9pm Mon-Sat; ☎) 🍴 This superb eatery is loosely modelled on the beloved Phnom Penh restaurant Romdeng. It's an extension of the vocational-training programs for at-risk Cambodians run by local NGO M'lop Tapang. The menu features creative Cambodian cuisine.

Serendipity

Mick & Craig's   INTERNATIONAL **$$**
(Map p118; www.mickandcraigs.com; Road to Ser-endipity; mains US$4-7; ⊘7am-10pm; 🤳) This long-running guesthouse and restaurant is a great place for classic comfort food from around the globe. Two-course Indian meals are just US$6. Thursday and Friday barbe-cue nights include a rack of ribs.

✗ Around the City

For Sihanoukville's cheapest dining, head to the food stalls in and around **Psar Leu** (Map p116; 7 Makara St; ⊘7am-9pm). The vendors across the street, next to the Kampot taxis, are open 24 hours.

★**Holy Cow**   ORGANIC **$**
(Map p116; 83 Ekareach St; mains US$2.50-5; ⊘8.30am-11pm; 🤳💻) Options at this chic and funky cafe-restaurant include pasta, sandwiches on homemade bread and two vegan desserts, both involving chocolate.

Starfish Bakery & Café   ORGANIC **$**
(Map p116; www.starfishcambodia.org; sandwiches US$2.50-4.50; ⊘7am-6pm; 🤳💻) 🌀 This relaxing, NGO-run garden cafe specialises in filling West-ern breakfasts and healthy, innovative sandwiches heavy on Mexican and Middle Eastern flavours. Sells silks and other gifts in a shop upstairs. Income goes to sustain-able development projects.

Samudera Supermarket   SUPERMARKET **$**
(Map p116; No 64, 7 Makara St; ⊘6am-10pm) Has a good selection of fruit, vegies and Western favourites, including cheese and wine.

Drinking

The party tends to start up on the Road to Serendipity before heading downhill (liter-ally and figuratively) to the all-night beach discos along Occheuteal Beach. A few long-standing regular bars remain amid the hostess bars of Victory Hill, but the overall impression is Sinville rather than the more relaxed beach vibe of Sihanoukville.

Some of the aforementioned guesthouses have lively bars, including Monkey Re-public (happy hour 6pm to 9pm), the Big Easy (sport and live music) and hedonistic Utopia, with regular US$0.25 beer promo-tions: yes, that does equal 20 beers for US$5.

Led Zephyr   BAR
(Map p118; Road to Serendipity; ⊘7am-midnight) Sihanoukville's premier live-music venue, the house band (and friends from time to time) are rockin' here most nights.

Sessions   BAR
(Map p118; Occheuteal Beach; ⊘5pm-1am) An as-sorted music selection makes Sessions the top sundowner bar on Occheuteal Beach, with the drinking clientele usually lingering well into the evening.

Dolphin Shack   BAR
(Map p118; Occheuteal Beach; ⊘5pm-late) Long-running beach shack with a host of specials designed to get you drunk fast, and bevies of beautiful backpackers pouring drinks and passing out flyers.

Reggae Bar   BAR
(Map p118; Thnou St; ⊘5pm-1am) It has more Marley on the walls than we've seen in quite

CAMBODIA SIHANOUKVILLE

some time (owner Dell is an avid collector) and a clientele diligently paying homage.

Elephant
BAR

(Map p118; Serendipity St; ⊙5pm-late) This quirky little bar is Cambodia's leading drum 'n' bass venue. Blink and you'll miss it.

🛍 Shopping

Tapang
HANDICRAFTS

(Map p118; www.mloptapang.org; Serendipity St; ⊙10am-8pm) 🖉 Run by a local NGO that works with at-risk children, this shop sells bags, scarves and good-quality T-shirts. Several other handicrafts shops are nearby.

Let Us Create
ARTS & CRAFTS

(Map p118; www.letuscreate.org; Serendipity St; ⊙10am-6pm) Another NGO that works with underprivileged kids; you can buy small paintings and postcards here. The volunteer backpackers are happy to tell you more about the project.

ℹ Information

Internet cafes (per hour 4000r) are sprinkled along the road to Serendipity and, in the city centre, along Ekareach St near Sopheakmongkol St. Theft is a problem, especially on Occheuteal Beach, so leave your valuables in your room. As in Phnom Penh, drive-by bag snatchings occasionally happen and are especially dangerous when you're riding a moto. Hold your shoulder bags tightly in front of you. At night, both men and women should avoid walking alone along dark, isolated beaches and roads.

Ana Travel (Map p118; ☑016 499915; www.anatravelandtours.com; Road to Serendipity; ⊙8am-10pm) Handles Cambodia visa extensions and arranges Vietnam visas the same day.

ANZ Royal Bank (Map p116; 215 Ekareach St; ⊙8am-3.30pm Mon-Fri, to 11.30am Sat) Has a 24-hour ATM. Also offers ATMs at Victory Hill and Serendipity Beach.

Canadia Bank (Map p116; 197 Ekareach St; ⊙8am-3.30pm Mon-Fri, to 11.30am Sat) No fees on ATM withdrawals.

CT Clinic (Map p116; ☑034-936666, 081 886666; 47 Boray Kamakor St; ⊙emergencies 24hr) The best medical clinic in town. Can administer rabies shots and snake antivenene.

ℹ Getting There & Away

AIR

Cambodia Angkor Airlines (www.cambodiaangkorair.com) has direct flights to Sihanoukville from Siem Reap (daily). The airport is 15km east of town, just off the NH4. Figure on US$5/10 for a one-way moto/*remorque*.

BUS

All of the major bus companies have frequent connections with Phnom Penh (US$3.75 to $6, four hours) from early morning until at least 2pm, after which trips are sporadic.

Kampot Tours & Travel runs minibuses to Kampot (US$6, 1½ hours), which continue to Kep (US$10, 2½ hours) and Ha Tien in Vietnam (US$16, five hours). Travel agents can arrange hotel pick-ups.

Virak Buntham and Rith Mony have morning buses to Bangkok (US$25, change buses on the Thai side) via Koh Kong (US$7, four hours). GST has a night bus to Siem Reap and day buses to Battambang and Ho Chi Minh City (Saigon). Virak Buntham also has a night bus to Siem Reap (US$17, nine hours) with departures at 7pm and 8pm.

Most bus departures originate at the company terminals on Ekareach St and stop at the **new bus station** (Map p115; Mittapheap Kampuchea Soviet St) on the way out of town.

Capitol Tour (Map p116; ☑034-934042; Ekareach St)

Giant Ibis (www.giantibis.com)

GST (Map p116; ☑034-633 9666; Ekareach St)

Kampot Tours & Travel (☑in Kampot 092 125556)

Mekong Express (Map p116; ☑034-934189; Ekareach St)

Phnom Penh Sorya (Map p116; ☑034-933888; Ekareach St)

Rith Mony (Map p116; ☑012 644585; Ekareach St)

Virak Buntham (Map p116; ☑016 754358; Ekareach St)

SHARE TAXI

Cramped share taxis (US$6 per person, US$45 per car) and minibuses (15,000r) to Phnom Penh depart from the new bus station until about 8pm. Avoid the minibuses if you value things like comfort and your life.

Share taxis to Kampot (US$5, 1½ hours) leave mornings only from an open lot on 7 Makara St, across from Psar Leu. This lot and the new bus station are good places to look for rides to Koh Kong or the Thai border. If nobody's sharing, expect to pay US$45 to US$60 to the Thai border.

ℹ Getting Around

Arriving in Sihanoukville, most buses these days terminate at the new public bus terminal and do not continue to their central terminals. Prices to the Serendipity Beach area from the new bus station are fixed at a pricey US$2/6 for a moto/*remorque*. You can do better by walking out to the street. A moto/*remorque* should cost about US$1/2 from the city centre to Serendipity.

Motorbikes can be rented from many guesthouses for US$5 to US$7 a day. For fundraising purposes, the police sometimes 'crack down' on foreign drivers. Common violations: no driver's licence, no helmet, and no wing mirrors and driving with the lights on during the day.

Bicycles can be hired from many guesthouses for about US$2 a day, or try Eco-Trek Tours at Mick & Craig's for mountain bikes.

The Southern Islands

They may lack the cachet of Southern Thailand, but the two dozen or so islands that dot the Cambodian coast offer the chance to see what places such as Koh Samui were like back in the early days of Southeast Asia overlanding. This is paradise the way you dreamt it: endless crescents of powdered sugary-soft sand, hammocks swaying in the breeze, photogenic fishing villages on stilts, technicolour sunsets and the patter of raindrops on thatch as you slumber. It seems too good to last – bits of Koh Rong are already getting a tad rowdy. Enjoy it while you can.

❶ Getting There & Away

The logical jumping-off point for the most popular islands is Sihanoukville. Scheduled boat services link Sihanoukville with Koh Rong, Koh Rong Samloem and Koh Sdach. Other islands are reached by private boats, usually owned by the resort you're visiting.

Koh Rong & Koh Rong Samloem
កោះរុង និងកោះរុងសន្លឹម

These deceptively large neighbouring islands are the rapidly emerging pearls of the South Coast. They boast isolated white-sand beaches and heavily forested interiors populated by an incredible variety of wildlife.

Plans to turn Koh Rong into a Cambodian version of Thailand's Koh Samui, complete with ring road and airport, have stalled, allowing DIY developers to move in with rustic resorts targeting backpackers. The epicentre of the action is rapidly developing Koh Tui Beach on Koh Rong's southeast foot.

Koh Rong Samloem is also slowly taking off. Several colonies of bungalows have sprung up on **Saracen Bay** on the east coast, and more isolated options exist around the island. Saracen Bay is also the venue for monthly full-moon parties at the Beach Resort, accessible via the Party Boat from Sihanoukville.

🛏 Sleeping

Most island resorts from about 6pm to 10.

Bunna's Place
(☑086 446515; Koh Tui; d classic backpacker crash beach bar and the chea Tui, plus some cheap ro ....who want a modicum of privacy.

Island Boys/Vagabonds   HOSTEL $
(Koh Tui; dm US$6, r from US$10) Two different places under the same ownership offering a similar vibe. Island Boys has a popular bar; Vagabonds has more of a chilled cafe vibe.

M'Pay Bay   RESORT $
(☑016 596111; www.mpaybay.com; Koh Rong Samloem; s/d tents US$ 5/7, bungalows US$20) 🌿 A cluster of simple bungalows in a fishing village on the north side of the island. The friendly owners bill it as a more ecofriendly option.

Monkey Island   RESORT $$
(☑081 830992; www.monkeyisland-kohrong. com; Koh Tui; bungalows without/with bathroom US$25/35) One of the first resorts to plant its flag on this stretch of Koh Rong, centrally located Monkey Island has a nice mix of stand-alone bungalows, and a great bar and restaurant specialising in Thai food.

Treehouse Bungalows   BUNGALOW $$
(☑081 830992; Koh Rong; beach/tree bungalow US$20/30) Service is indifferent but the bungalows are big and comfortable and the secluded location around the headland northeast of Koh Rong's main beach is highly appealing.

The Beach Resort   RESORT $$
(☑034-666 6106; www.thebeachresort.asia; Saracen Bay; dm US$5, r US$15-85) Koh Rong Samloem's funkiest place to stay. Located on up-and-coming Saracen Bay, the Beach Resort offers breezy open-air dorms with mozzie nets, plus a range of beachfront bungalows.

❶ Getting There & Away
Koh Rong Island Travel (☑034-934744; http:// kohrong-islandtravel.com) runs two daily boats to/from the port area in Sihanoukville (one-way US$10, 2½ hours); these continue on to Koh Rong Samloem if there's demand.

The new **SEA Cambodia Fastcat** (www. seacambodia.com) departs four times a day from the Serendipity Beach jetty, arriving at Koh Rong in less than one hour (one-way US$13).

ᴵsland   កោះកុង

᷅ coast of Cambodia's largest island ᷅s seven pristine beaches fringed with ᷅onut palms and lush vegetation, just as you'd expect in a true tropical paradise. At the sixth beach from the north, a narrow channel leads to a Gilligan's Island–style lagoon.

About 25km south of Koh Kong, the island is not part of any national park and is thus susceptible to rampant development. The island recently got its first resort. The best way to get here is on a tour from Koh Kong (full day per person including lunch and snorkelling equipment US$25, or overnight for US$55).

Other Islands

Closer to Sihanoukville **Koh Ta Kiev** and **Koh Russei** appear on most island itineraries out of Sihanoukville, with day trips running from US$12 to US$15 depending whether you launch from Otres Beach or Serendipity Beach. Both islands have accommodation, although both are slated for development.

Kampot   កំពត

☏ 033 / POP 33,000

There is something about this little charmer that encourages visitors to linger. It might be the lovely riverside setting or the ageing French buildings, or it could be the great little guesthouses and burgeoning bar scene. Whatever the magic ingredient, this is the perfect base from which to explore nearby caves and tackle Bokor National Park.

◉ Sights & Activities

This is not a town where you come and do, but a place to come and feel. Sit on the riverbank and watch the sun set beneath the mountains, or stroll among the town's fine **French shophouses** (in the triangle delineated by 7 Makara St, the central roundabout and the post office).

**Kampot Traditional
Music School**   SCHOOL

(⊙ 6-9pm Mon-Fri) Visitors are welcome to observe training sessions and/or performances every weekday evening at this school that trains orphaned and disabled children in traditional music and dance.

Seeing Hands Massage 5   MASSAGE

(per hr US$5; ⊙ 7am-11pm) Blind masseurs and masseuses offer soothing bliss.

☞ Tours

The big tour is **Bokor Hill Station** (see Bokor National Park, p124), which everybody and their grandmother offers. Excursions also hit the pepper farms and other sights in the countryside around Kampot and nearby Kep.

Some of the riverside places send boats out on evening firefly watching tours. Many a sceptic has returned from these trips in awe.

Bart the Boatman   BOAT TOUR

(☏ 092 174280) Known simply as Bart the Boatman, this Belgian expat runs original boat tours along the small tributaries of the Kampong Bay River.

Sok Lim Tours   TOUR

(☏ 012 796919; www.soklimtours.com) Kampot's longest-running outfit, well regarded all round. Has trained pepper-plantation guides.

Captain Chim's   BOAT TOUR

(☏ 012 321043) Sunset cruises on a traditional boat cost US$5 per head and include a cold beer – a real bargain. Also offers half-day kayaking trips for US$9.

🛏 Sleeping

You can stay in the centre of the old town, or stay a little out of town in one of several places strung out along the riverbank.

★ Bodhi Villa   HOSTEL $

(☏ 012 728884; www.bodhivilla.com; Tuk Chhou Rd; dm US$2.50-3, r US$5-12; 🛜) Bodhi is a peaceful hideaway on the opposite bank of the river 2km north of town. There's a good waterfront chill-out bar and a variety of rooms, including one floating bungalow. Live music every Friday from 7.30pm, plus a speedboat for hire.

Hour Kheang Guesthouse   GUESTHOUSE $

(☏ 033-210351; hourkheang_gh@yahoo.com; Old Market; dm US$3, fan r US$8, air-con room US$15-20; ❄🛜) The host family are very helpful and the rooms are very well looked after, including flat-screen TVs and hot-water bathrooms. Downstairs is a handy minimart, and everything from bicycles to motorbikes are available for rent.

Kampot

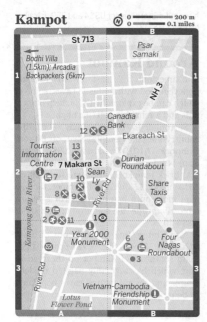

CAMBODIA KAMPOT

🍴 Eating

Quite a few restaurants line River Rd south of the old French bridge. There are **fruit stalls and little eateries** (⊙7am-10pm) next to the Canadia Bank and, nearby, a **night market** (7 Makara St; ⊙4pm-midnight), with both mains and desserts.

Arcadia Backpackers HOSTEL $
(☎077 219756; www.arcadiabackpackers.com; Tuk Chhou Rd; dm US$3-4, r US$9-10, bungalow US$15-30; 🅦) In a secluded riverside setting northwest of town, there is a large bar-restaurant jutting out into the water, plentiful dorms, thatched private bungalows, a rope swing and tubing.

Magic Sponge GUESTHOUSE $
(☎017 946428; www.magicspongekampot.com; dm US$3, r US$9-15; 🅦) This popular backpacker place has a rooftop dorm with impressive through breezes and personalised fans and reading lights. There's well-regarded Indian food and even minigolf in the garden.

Titch's Place GUESTHOUSE $
(☎033-650 1631; titchs.place@yahoo.com; River Rd; dm US$3, r US$10; 🅦) The only budget crashpad on the riverfront, there are dorm beds aplenty here, including single-sex dorms.

Blissful Guesthouse GUESTHOUSE $
(☎092 494331; www.blissfulguesthouse.com; dm US$2-3, r US$4-8; 🅦) An old-time backpacker vibe lives on at this atmospheric wooden house. Cheaper rooms involve a shared bathroom.

★**Epic Arts Café** CAFE $
(www.epicarts.org.uk; mains US$2-4; ⊙7am-4pm; 🅦) 🍃 A great place for breakfast, homemade cakes or tea, this mellow eatery is staffed by deaf and disabled young people. Profits fund arts workshops for disabled Cambodians.

Espresso CAFE $
(near Old Market; mains US$3-6; ⊙7am-9pm) A blink-and-you'll-miss-it cafe – we advise you don't blink. The Aussie owners are real foodies and offer fresh specials and the best coffee in town.

Indo Bar INTERNATIONAL, ASIAN $
(St 726; meals US$2-6; ⊙11am-11pm) A fun and friendly place just up from the river, Indo Bar offers eclectic regional cuisine and the strongest Long Island iced tea in Kampot.

Captain Chim's CAFE $
(mains US$1-3; ⊙7am-10pm; 🅦) Best known for breakfast, Khmer faves like *loc lak* (peppery stir-fried beef cubes) will fill you up at any time of day. Ask about Cambodian

KAMPOT PEPPER

In the years before the Cambodian civil war took its toll, no self-respecting French restaurant in Paris would be without Kampot pepper on the table. Pepper plantations are once again a common sight in the Kampot region and come in a variety of colours, including white, black, green and red.

cooking classes or join its bargain booze cruise for sunset every day.

ⓘ Information

The free and often hilarious *Kampot Survival Guide* takes a tongue-in-cheek look at local expat life, and there's also the free guide *Coastal* (www.coastal-cambodia.com), with heaps of info on local businesses in Kampot and Kep.

Canadia Bank (⊘ 8am-3.30pm Mon-Fri, to 11.30am Sat) Has an ATM with no transaction fees and turbo air-con.

Tourist Information Centre (⌨ 033-655 5541; lonelyguide@gmail.com; River Rd; ⊘ 7am-7pm) The main point of contact for assembling groups for Bokor National Park trips. Also doles out free advice and can arrange transport to area attractions like caves, falls and Kompong Trach.

ⓘ Getting There & Away

Kampot is 105km from Sihanoukville and 148km from Phnom Penh.

Rith Mony, Phnom Penh Sorya and Hua Lian sell tickets from offices opposite the Total petrol station near the Four Nagas Roundabout. All three have daily trips to Phnom Penh (US$4 to US$5, 2½ hours) until 1pm or so. Phnom Penh Sorya's buses go via Kep so they take longer.

Across the street you can catch share taxis (US$6), packed-to-the-gills local minibuses (16,000r) and private taxis (US$40) to Phnom Penh. Giant Ibis and Kampot Express run express vans to Phnom Penh (US$8, two hours).

For Sihanoukville, ask your guesthouse to set you up with a minibus service, which can also get you to Koh Kong (usually with at least one bus/van transfer).

A moto/*remorque* to Kep should cost about US$8/12.

ⓘ Getting Around

Bicycles are offered to guests for free by many guesthouses, which can also arrange motorbike hire. **Sean Ly** (⌨ 012 944687; ⊘ 7am-9pm)

hires out motorbikes for US$4 and 250cc trail bikes for US$12.

Around Kampot

The limestone hills east towards Kep are honeycombed with fantastic caves, some of which can be explored with the help of local kids and a reliable torch (flashlight).

Surrounded by blazingly beautiful countryside, the temple cave of **Phnom Chhnork** (ភ្នំឆ្នោក; admission US$1; ⊘ 7am-6pm) is known for its 7th-century (Funanera) brick temple. To get there turn left off NH33 about 5.5km east of Kampot, then go 6km more on a bumpy road. For a return moto/*remorque* ride count on paying about US$6/10.

Also interesting is **Phnom Sorsia** (ភ្នំសរសៀរ, Phnom Sia; ⊘ 7am-6pm) **FREE**, 13km southeast of Kampot on the road to Kep, which has a gaudily painted modern temple and several natural caves populated by dense bat colonies.

Bokor National Park

ឧទ្យានជាតិបូកគោ

This 1581-sq-km **national park** (ឧទ្យានជាតិ បូកគោ; Preah Monivong National Park; admission US$5) has impressive wildlife, lush primary forests and a refreshingly cool climate, but is most famous for its once-abandoned French hill station, established atop Phnom Bokor (1080m) in the 1920s.

Unfortunately it is now becoming more famous for the ugly casino that blights the summit, part of a massive development project that has sadly destroyed the atmosphere of bygone Bokor.

At the park entrance, 7km west of Kampot, an informative **ranger station** has displays about Bokor's fauna, which includes leopards, elephants, bears, gibbons, macaques, slow loris and pangolins. Don't expect to see much wildlife, however, as most of the animals survive by staying in more remote areas and, in addition, are nocturnal.

◎ Sights

Until recently the main attraction here was the old French hill station and its grand, four-storey hotel, the **Bokor Palace**, opened in 1925. The hill station was abandoned to the howling winds in the 1970s when Khmer Rouge forces infiltrated the area. The once-grand buildings became eerie, windowless shells.

Bokor Palace was undergoing renovations when we visited and will become part of the new resort city. Other buildings of interest include the squat belfry of the Romanesque-style **Catholic church**, which still holds aloft its cross; and lichen-caked **Wat Sampeau Moi Roi**, which offers tremendous views over the jungle to the coastline below. Wild monkeys like to hang out around the wat. From the wat an 11km trail (four or five hours) leads to two-tiered **Popokvil Falls**.

Getting There & Away

To visit the park you can take private transport up the new road, or join an organised tour. Trekking trips used to be very popular, but treks were recently banned due to all the development underway, a rather surreal scenario, as we have not heard of banning trekking in national parks before. Standard day trips still operate for around US$10 to US$15 per person depending on numbers. Many travellers prefer to rent a motorbike and travel under their own steam.

Kep កែប

☎ 036 / POP 13,300

The seaside resort of Kep-sur-Mer is a province-level municipality that consists of little more than a small peninsula facing Bokor National Park and Vietnam's Phu Quoc Island. Famed for its spectacular sunsets and splendid seafood, it was founded as a colonial retreat for the French elite in 1908.

Some find Kep a bit soulless because it lacks a centre and accommodation options are spread out all over the place. Others revel in its sleepy vibe, content to relax at their resort, nibble on crab at the famed Crab Market and poke around the mildewed shells of modernist villas, which still give the town a sort of post-apocalyptic feel.

Sights & Activities

Kep National Park PARK
(ឧទ្យានជាតិកែប; admission 4000r) The interior of Kep peninsula is occupied by Kep National Park, degraded in recent years by illegal logging but finally guarded by a complement of rangers. An 8km circuit around the park, navigable by foot or mountain bike, starts at the park entrance behind Veranda Natural Resort. Fuel up and grab a map of the park at the **Led Zep Cafe** (9.30am-6pm), which is on the trail 300m into the walk. The map is also reprinted in the Kep and Kampot guide, *Coastal*.

Koh Tonsay (Rabbit Island) ISLAND
(កោះទន្សាយ) Offshore, rustic Koh Tonsay has a lovely beach with several family-run clusters of rudimentary bungalows where you can overnight for US$8. Boats to the island (30 minutes) leave from a pier 2.7km east of the Kep Beach roundabout. Your guesthouse can arrange to get you on a boat for around US$7 one-way or US$10 per person return. A private boat arranged at the pier costs US$30 one-way for up to seven passengers.

Beaches BEACH
Most of Kep's beaches are too shallow and rocky to make for good swimming. The best is centrally located **Kep Beach**, but it's still somewhat pebbly and tends to fill up with locals on weekends. The best place for sunset viewing is the long wooden pier in front of Knai Bang Chat's **Sailing Club**, where there's also a small but shallow beach.

Sleeping

★**Botanica Guesthouse** GUESTHOUSE $
(☎097 801 9071; www.kep-botanica.com; NH33A; r with fan US$15-19, with air-con US$23-29;) A little way from the action (if Kep can be said to have any action), Botanica offers exceptional value for money with attractive bungalows boasting contemporary bathrooms. There is a small swimming pool and guests can use free bicycles to hit the beach.

Bacoma GUESTHOUSE $
(☎088 411 2424; bacoma@live.com; r US$10-36;) Cheap and cheerful *rondavels* (round huts) are available in the lush garden and include high ceilings, mosquito nets and a fan, with a generous helping of shared bathrooms.

SPLURGE

About 2.5km in from the Rabbit Island pier, **Jasmine Valley Eco-Resort** (☎097 791 7635; www.jasminevalley.com; r incl breakfast US$24-64;) has funky bungalows raised dramatically amid dense jungle foliage. Green credits include solar power and a natural swimming pool complete with pond critters.

Tree Top Bungalows
GUESTHOUSE $

(📞 012 515191; khmertreetop@hotmail.com; r US$5-45; 🌐🤶) The highlights here are the towering, stilted, bamboo 'treehouse' bungalows with sea views; each pair shares a bathroom.

Kukuluku Beach Club
GUESTHOUSE $

(📞 036-630 0150; www.kukuluku-beachclub.com; NH33A; dm US$5-7, r US$15-35; 🤶💺) The rooms are nothing special and the pool is tiny, but it's a great place to meet other travellers.

✗ Eating

Eating fresh crab fried with Kampot pepper at the Crab Market – a row of wooden waterfront shacks next to a wet fish market – is a quintessential Kep experience. There are lots of great places to choose from. Kimly (📞 info 036-904077; Crab Market; mains US$2.50-7; ⌚ 9am-10pm) has a good reputation with crab prepared 27 different ways, or try the memorably named Holy Crab. The crab shacks also serve prawns, squid, fish and terrestrial offerings. You can also buy fresh crab at the Crab Market and have your guesthouse fry it up.

★ Sailing Club
FUSION $$

(mains US$5-12; ⌚ 10am-10pm; 🤶) With a small beach, a breezy wooden bar and a wooden jetty poking out into the sea, this is one of Cambodia's top sundowner spots. The Asian fusion food is excellent and you can get your crab fix here too. Happy hour is two-for-one.

❶ Getting There & Away

Kep is 25km from Kampot and 41km from the Prek Chak/Xa Xia border crossing to Vietnam.

Phnom Penh Sorya and Hua Lian buses link the town with Kampot (US$2, 45 minutes) and Phnom Penh (US$4, four hours, last trips at 2pm). A private taxi to Phnom Penh (three hours) costs US$40 to US$45.

A moto/remorque to Kampot costs about US$8/12. Guesthouses can arrange minibus/bus combos to Sihanoukville and Koh Kong.

Motorbike rental is US$5 to US$7 per day; ask your guesthouse or any travel agency.

Around Kep

For an enchanting mixture of dramatic natural beauty and Buddhist piety, it's hard to beat Wat Kiri Sela (វត្តគិរីសិលា; ⌚ 7am-6pm), 23km northeast of Kep. Built at the foot of a karst formation riddled with over 100 caverns and passageways, this Buddhist temple is linked by an underground passage to the centre of the hill, where the vine-draped cliffs of a hidden valley unfold before you. This is the sort of place where you'd hardly be surprised to see a dinosaur munching on foliage or, à la *Jurassic Park*, chewing on a lawyer. Friendly local kids with torches, eager to put their evening-

---

GETTING TO VIETNAM: KEP TO HA TIEN

The Prek Chak/Xa Xia border crossing (open 6am to 5.30pm) has become a popular option for linking Kampot and Kep with Ha Tien and the popular Vietnamese island of Phu Quoc.

Getting to the border The easiest way to get to Prek Chak and on to Ha Tien, Vietnam, is on a bus or van from Sihanoukville (US$16, five hours), Kampot (US$10, two hours) or Kep (US$8, 1½ hours). Several companies ply the Sihanoukville–Kampot–Kep–Ha Tien route.

A more flexible alternative from Phnom Penh or Kampot is to take any bus to Kompong Trach, then a moto (about US$3) for 15km to the border. In Kep, tour agencies and guesthouses can arrange a direct moto (US$8, 40 minutes), remorque (US$13, one hour) or taxi (US$20, 30 minutes). Rates and times are almost double from Kampot.

At the border As always, it's necessary to have a Vietnamese visa for travel to Phu Quoc, the Mekong Delta and on to Ho Chi Minh City. Pick up motos on the Vietnamese side of the border to Ha Tien (7km). You'll save money walking across no-man's land and picking up a moto on the other side for US$2 to US$3.

Moving on Travellers bound for Phu Quoc should arrive in Ha Tien no later than 12.30pm to secure a ticket on the 1pm ferry (230,000d or about US$11, 1½ hours). Extreme early risers may be able to make it to Ha Tien in time to catch the (slower) 8.20am car ferry to Phu Quoc. For infomration on making this trip in the opposite direction, see p898.

school English to use, are happy to serve as guides; make sure your tip covers the cost of batteries.

To get to Wat Kiri Sela from Kep, take a moto/*remorque* (return US$5/10) or grab a Phnom Penh–bound bus or minibus. From the town of Kompong Trach, take the dirt road opposite the Acleda Bank for 2km.

EASTERN CAMBODIA

If it is a walk on the wild side that fires your imagination, then the northeast is calling. It's home to rare forest elephants and freshwater dolphins, and peppering the area are thundering waterfalls, crater lakes and meandering rivers. Trekking, biking, kayaking and elephant adventures are all beginning to take off. The rolling hills and lush forests provide a home to many ethnic minority groups. Do the maths: it all adds up to an amazing experience.

Kompong Cham កំពង់ចាម

🖉 042 / POP 45,400

This quiet Mekong city, an important trading post during the French period, serves as the gateway to Cambodia's northeast. Most action is on the riverfront.

◉ Sights & Activities

Koh Paen   ISLAND
For a supremely relaxing bike ride, it's hard to beat Koh Paen, a rural, traffic-free island that's connected to the mainland about 600m south of the Mekong bridge by a motorised ferry in the wet season and an elaborate bamboo toll bridge – totally rebuilt from scratch each December – in the dry season.

Wat Nokor   BUDDHIST TEMPLE
(វត្តនគរ; admission US$2) The ultimate fusion temple, Wat Nokor is a modern Buddhist pagoda squeezed into the walls of an 11th-century temple of sandstone and laterite. Located about 2.5km west of the bridge over the Mekong in Kompong Cham.

🛏 Sleeping

Mekong Sunrise   GUESTHOUSE $
(🖉011 449720; bong_tho@yahoo.com; Sihanouk St; r with fan US$5-8, with air-con US$12; 🕸 🛜) A backpacker crashpad over a popular riverfront bar-restaurant, Mekong Sunrise has spacious upper-floor rooms with access to a

sprawling rooftop. Furnishings are sparse, but it's cheap enough.

Mekong Hotel   HOTEL $
(🖉042-941536; Sihanouk St; r with fan/air-con US$8/16; 🕸 🛜) This old timer has a prime riverfront locale, *Shining*-esque corridors and big, bright, relatively well-maintained rooms.

🍴 Eating

Stalls line the waterfront, selling snacks and cold beers until late in the evening.

★**Smile Restaurant**   CAMBODIAN $
(www.bdsa-cambodia.org; Sihanouk St; mains US$3-5; ⊙6.30am-9pm; 🛜) 🍴 This nonprofit restaurant run by the Buddhism and Society Development Association is a big hit with the NGO crowd for its big breakfasts, healthy menu and free wi-fi.

Destiny Coffee House   CAFE $
(12 Vithei Pasteur; mains US$3-5; ⊙7am-5.30pm Mon-Sat; 🛜🍴) This stylish cafe has relaxing sofas and a contemporary look. The international menu includes delicious hummus with dips, lip-smacking homemade cakes, breakfast burritos, salads and wraps.

Lazy Mekong Daze   INTERNATIONAL $
(Sihanouk St; mains US$3-5.50; ⊙7.30am-last customer; 🛜) Run by Frank, a Frenchman, this is the go-to place to assemble after dark thanks to a mellow atmosphere, a pool table and a big screen for sports and movies. The menu parades a range of Khmer, Thai and Western food, including chilli con carne, pizza baguettes and delicious Karem ice cream.

❶ Information

Lazy Mekong Daze hands out a decent map that highlights the major sights in and around Kompong Cham.

Canadia Bank (Preah Monivong Blvd; ⊙8am-3.30pm Mon-Fri, 8-11.30am Sat) Free ATM withdrawals, plus free cash advances on credit card.

Mekong Internet (Vithei Pasteur; per hr 1500r; ⊙6.30am-10pm) Among a gaggle of internet cafes on Vithei Pasteur.

❶ Getting There & Around

Phnom Penh is 120km southwest. If you are heading north to Kratie or beyond, secure transport via the sealed road to Chhlong rather than taking a huge detour east to Snuol on NH7.

Phnom Penh Sorya, located on Preah Monivong Blvd, is the most reliable bus company operating

BUSES FROM KOMPONG CHAM

DESTINATION	PRICE	DURATION (hr)	FREQUENCY
Ban Lung	36,000r	7	10am
Kratie via Chhlong	20,000r	2	9.30am
Kratie via Snuol	21,000r	4	10.30am, 2pm
Pakse (Laos)	US$22	12	10am
Phnom Penh	19,000r	3	hourly to 3.45pm
Sen Monorom	31,000r	5	noon
Siem Reap	24,000r	5	7.30am, noon

out of Kompong Cham. It serves all of the locales listed in the Buses from Kompong Cham table.

Share taxis dash to Phnom Penh (US$3.50, 2½ hours) from the **taxi park** near the New Market (Psar Thmei). Overcrowded local minibuses also do the run (10,000r).

Morning share taxis and minibuses to Kratie (US$5, 1½ hours) depart when full from the **Caltex station** (NH7) at the main roundabout, and there are morning minibuses from the taxi park as well.

Kratie   ក្រចេះ

☑ 072 / POP 30,000

The most popular place in Cambodia to glimpse Southeast Asia's remaining freshwater Irrawaddy dolphins, Kratie (pronounced 'kra-cheh') is a lively riverside town with a rich legacy of French-era architecture and some of the best Mekong sunsets in Cambodia. A thriving travel hub, Kratie is the natural place to break the journey when travelling overland between Phnom Penh or Siem Reap and Champasak in southern Laos.

◉ Sights & Activities

Koh Trong   ISLAND

Lying just across the water from Kratie is the island of Koh Trong, an almighty sandbar in the middle of the river. Cross here by boat and enjoy a slice of rural island life. Catch the little ferry from the port or charter a local boat (around US$2) to get here. Bicycle rental is available on the island near the ferry landing for US$1, or do the loop around the island on a moto (US$2.50) steered by a female *moto-dup* (moto driver) – a rarity for Cambodia.

Dolphin Viewing   WILDLIFE

Less than 85 critically endangered freshwater Irrawaddy dolphins *'trey pisaut'* in Khmer remain in the Mekong between Kratie and the Lao border. For more on this rare creature, see www.panda.org/greater mekong.

These gentle mammals can be seen at Kampi, about 15km north of Kratie (on the road to Sambor). A return moto/*remorque* ride costs about US$7/10, depending on how long the driver has to wait and whether you stop off at Phnom Sombok, a 70m-high hill with an active wat and fine Mekong views. Cycling is also an option.

Motorboats shuttle visitors out to the middle of the river to view the dolphins at close quarters. It costs US$9 per person for one to two persons and US$7 per person for groups of three or more. Encourage the boat driver to use the engine as little as possible once near the dolphins, as the noise is sure to disturb them. The best viewing times are in the morning and late afternoon.

☞ Tours

CRDTours   TOUR

(☑ 099 834353; www.crdtours.org; Tonlé Traning Centre, St 3; ⊗ 8am-noon & 2-5.30pm; ☎) ☞ Run by the Cambodian Rural Development Team, this company focuses on sustainable tours along the Mekong between Kratie and Stung Treng, plus homestays.

Sorya Kayaking Adventures   KAYAKING

(☑ 090 241148; www.soryakayaking.com; Rue Preah Suramarit) Run by a socially conscious American woman, Sorya has a fleet of eight kayaks and runs half-day and multiday trips (with homestay accommodation) on the Mekong north of Kratie or on the Te River to the south.

⌂ Sleeping

There are also homestays on the island of Koh Trong opposite Kratie town.

Silver Dolphin Guesthouse   HOSTEL $

(☑ 012 999810; silver.dolphinbooking@yahoo.com; 48 Rue Preah Suramarit; dm/s/tr US$2/4/12, d

Kratie

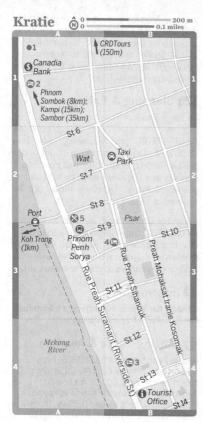

US$6-14; ❋@🛜) Even the cheapest doubles here have a TV, bathroom and some furniture, and the dorm is plenty big, with a soaring ceiling. You can drink and eat both downstairs and upstairs on the riverfont balcony.

Balcony Guesthouse   GUESTHOUSE $
(☑016 604036; www.balconyguesthouse.net; Rue Preah Suramarit; s/d without bathroom US$3/6, r with bathroom US$7-20; ❋@🛜) This long-running backpacker place has good-value rooms and impressive food. Doubles up as a popular little bar by night and is gay-friendly.

Star Backpackers   GUESTHOUSE $
(☑097 455 3106; starbackpackerskratie@gmail.com; Rue Preah Sihanouk; dm US$2, d US$5-6; ❋🛜) Young Spanish managers have revived this once-faded backpacker stalwart with colourful paint and a rooftop bar and hammock lounge. It's above Tokae Restaurant.

✗ Eating

When in Kratie keep an eye out for two famous specialities, sold on the riverfront: *krolan* (sticky rice, beans and coconut milk steamed inside a bamboo tube) and *nehm* (tangy, raw, spiced river fish wrapped in banana leaves). The south end of the *psar* (market) turns into a carnival of **barbecue stands** hawking meat-on-a-stick by night.

Red Sun Falling   INTERNATIONAL $
(Rue Preah Suramarit; mains 7000-14,000r; ⊙7am-9pm; 🛜) One of the liveliest spots in town, with a relaxed cafe ambience, a supreme riverfront location, used books for sale and a good selection of Asian and Western meals.

Tokae Restaurant   CAMBODIAN $
(St 10; mains US$2-3; ⊙6am-11pm; 🛜) Although French-run, the focus at this lively restaurant underneath Star Backpackers is very much on cheap Cambodian food.

❶ Information

All of the recommended guesthouses are pretty switched on to travellers' needs. Silver Dolphin Guesthouse has public internet access (per hour 3000r).

Canadia Bank (Rue Preah Suramarit) ATM offering free cash withdrawals, plus currency exchange.

❶ Getting There & Away

Kratie is 348km northeast of Phnom Penh (250km via Chhlong) and 141km south of Stung Treng.

Phnom Penh Sorya (☑081 908005) operates three buses per day to Phnom Penh (US$8, eight hours) along the slow route (via Snuol); Sorya's bus from Laos comes through at roughly 3.30pm and goes to Phnom Penh via the much-shorter Chhlong route (six hours). Sorya buses to Siem Reap involve a change in Suong.

Going the other way, Sorya's bus from Phnom Penh to Pakse, Laos (US$20, eight hours) via Stung Treng collects passengers in Kratie at about 11.30am. Sorya also has a 1pm bus to Ban Lung (US$8, five hours), and a 3pm bus to Stung Treng (US$5, three hours).

Share taxis (US$10) head to Phnom Penh between 6am and 8am, with possible additional departures after lunch. Other destinations include Snuol (10,000r), Kompong Cham (30,000r) and Stung Treng (25,000r). The **taxi park** is just north of the market.

Most guesthouses can arrange bicycle (from US$1) and motorbike hire (from US$5). An English-speaking *motodup* will set you back US$10 to US$15 per day, a *remorque* about US$25.

Stung Treng   ស្ទឹងត្រែង

📞 074 / POP 24,500

Located on the Tonlé San near its confluence with the Mekong, Stung Treng is a dusty city with not much to offer, but perhaps this will change when a new bridge over the Mekong is completed in 2015. The bridge will feed into a new highway running west to Preah Vihear City, cutting about four hours off the journey from northeast Cambodia or southern Laos to Siem Reap.

Loaded with largely untapped tourist potential, Stung Treng could benefit hugely from the increased traffic. The main attractions are up near the Lao border, where you can kayak out to a pod of Irrawaddy dolphins then continue downstream along a heavenly stretch of the Mekong known as the flooded forest. Talk to **Xplore-Asia** (📞 074-973456, 011 433836; www.xplore-cambodia.com) to arrange this trip.

🛏 Sleeping & Eating

Le Tonlé Tourism Training Centre   GUESTHOUSE **$**

(📞 074-973638; http://letonle.org; s/d from US$6/8; 📶) On the riverfront about 500m west of the ferry dock, this small guesthouse doubles as a training centre to help under-privileged locals. Delicious meals can be ordered in advance.

Riverside Guesthouse   GUESTHOUSE **$**

(📞 012 257207; timtysou@gmail.com; r US$5-8; @) Overlooking the riverfront area, the Riverside is a long-time travellers' crossroads with basic rooms and a popular bar-restaurant.

ℹ Information

Canadia Bank (near market) Has a full international ATM with free withdrawals.

ℹ Getting There & Away

Phnom Penh Sorya (📞 092 181805) has a 6.30am bus to Phnom Penh (40,000r, nine hours) via Kratie (20,000r, three hours). Sorya's bus from Laos to Phnom Penh comes through Stung Treng around 11.30am. There is a comfortable tourist van to Ban Lung (US$6,

---

GETTING TO LAOS: STUNG TRENG TO SI PHAN DON

The remote Trapeang Kriel/Nong Nok Khiene border (open 6am to 6pm) is 60km north of Stung Treng.

Getting to the border Sorya Phnom Penh, in partnership with Pakse-based Lao operator Sengchalean, has buses from Phnom Penh straight through to Pakse's 2-Kilometre (VIP) bus station (US$27, 12 to 14 hours). This bus leaves Phnom Penh at 6.45am, with pick-ups possible in Kompong Cham (around 9.30am), Kratie (around 11.30am) and Stung Treng (around 3pm). The only other option to the border from Stung Treng is a private taxi (US$35 to US$45) or moto (US$15 to US$20). Services to Laos from Siem Reap are also possible, with a bus change in Suong.

At the border Both Lao and Cambodian visas are available on arrival. Entering Laos, you'll pay US$30 to US$40 for a visa, depending on nationality, plus a US$2 fee (dubbed either an 'overtime' or a 'processing' fee, depending on when you cross). The bus company wants its cut too, so it charges an extra US$1 to US$2 to handle your paperwork with the border guards. To avoid this fee, insist on doing your own paperwork and go through immigration alone.

Moving on Aside from the Sorya bus, there's virtually zero traffic on either side of the border. If you're dropped at the border, expect to pay 150,000r/50,000K (US$12/4) for a taxi/sǎhmlór heading north to Ban Nakasang (for Don Det). For information on making this crossing in the other direction, see p369.

THE MEKONG DISCOVERY TRAIL

It's well worth spending a couple of days exploring the various bike rides and activities on offer along the Mekong Discovery Trail (www.mekongdiscoverytrail.com), an initiative to open up stretches of the Mekong River around Stung Treng and Kratie to community-based tourism. Once managed by the government with foreign development assistance, the project is now being kept alive by private tour companies – mainly Xplore-Asia in Stung Treng and CRDTours in Kratie. It intends to provide fishing communities an alternative income in order to protect the Irrawaddy dolphin and other rare species on this stretch of river.

The various tour routes can be tackled by bicycle or motorbike. They range in length from a few hours to several days, with optional overnights in village homestays. Routes criss-cross the Mekong frequently by ferry and traverse several Mekong islands, including Koh Trong and Koh Pdao, 20km north of Kampi.

two hours, 8am), with additional morning trips in cramped local minibuses from the market (15,000r, three hours).

Riverside Guesthouse does minivan trips to Siem Reap via the new highway to Preah Vihear City when there's demand (US$25 per person).

Riverside Guesthouse also rents out motorbikes (from US$8) and bicycles (US$1 to US$2).

Ratanakiri Province

Popular Ratanakiri Province is a diverse region of outstanding natural beauty that provides a remote home for a mosaic of minority peoples – Jarai, Tompuon, Brau and Kreung – with their own languages, traditions and customs.

Adrenalin activities abound. Swim in clear volcanic lakes, shower under waterfalls, or trek in the vast Virachey National Park – it's all here. Tourism is set to take off.

Ban Lung   បានលុង

📞 075 / POP 25,000

Affectionately known as 'dey krahorm' (red earth) after its rust colour, Ban Lung provides a popular base for a range of Ratanakiri romps. It is one of the easiest places in Cambodia to arrange a jungle trek and has several beautiful lakes and waterfalls nearby.

◉ Sights & Activities

Boeng Yeak Lom   LAKE

(បឹងយក្សឡោម; admission US$1) Boeng Yeak Lom is one of the most serene and sublimely beautiful sites in Cambodia. This clear blue crater lake, surrounded by dark-green jungle, is sacred to the indigenous Tompuon peoples. It's a great place to take a dip, although Cambodians jump in fully clothed. A small **Cultural & Environmental Centre** has a modest display on ethnic minorities in the province and hires out life jackets for the young'uns.

To get to Boeng Yeak Lom from Ban Lung, head east towards Vietnam for 3km, turn right at the minorities statue and proceed 2km or so. Motos charge US$3 return (more if you make them wait), while *remorques* charge up to US$10 return.

Waterfalls   WATERFALL

Tucked amid the sprawling cashew and rubber plantations just west of Ban Lung are three waterfalls worth visiting: **Chaa Ong** (admission 2000r), **Ka Tieng** (admission 2000r) and **Kinchaan** (Kachang; admission 2000r). These falls are booming in the wet season but dry up to a trickle in the dry season. One-hour **elephant rides** (one/two riders US$15/20) are available near Ka Tieng waterfall.

The turn-offs to all three waterfalls are 200m west of the new bus station, just beyond a Lina petrol station. The Chaa Ong turn-off is on the right (north) side of NH19; the waterfall is 5.5km from the highway along a dirt road. The turn-off to Ka Tieng and Kinchaan is on the left side of NH19; proceed 5.5km to a fork in the road. Go left 200m to Kinchaan, or right 2.5km to Ka Tieng.

Motos (return US$6 for one waterfall, or US$10 for all three) and *remorques* (US$10/20 for one/three waterfalls) can get you here safely. Visits to all three falls are usually included in tour companies' half- and full-day excursions.

Virachey National Park   TREKKING

In this Asean Heritage Park, one of the largest and wildest protected areas in

Ban Lung

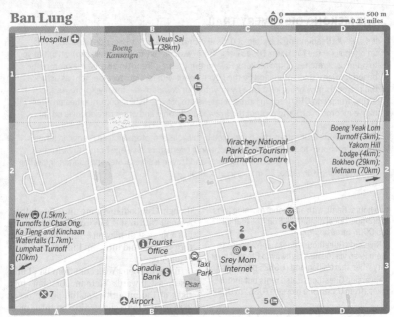

Cambodia, ecotourism is playing an important role in protecting the park from development (Cambodian authorities have already sold more remote regions of the park to Vietnamese rubber plantations). The **Virachey National Park Eco-Tourism Information Centre** (☑097 896 4995, 075-974013; virachey@camintel.com; ☺8am-noon & 2-5pm) is the exclusive operator of tours within the park boundaries, offering two-to eight-day treks led by English-speaking, park-employed rangers. The signature trek is an eight-day, seven-night **Phnom Veal Thom Wilderness Trek** (per person one/two people US$400/350). Prices drop the larger the group.

☞ Tours

Overnight treks with nights spent camping or staying in minority villages north of Voen Sai or Ta Veng are popular. Figure on US$45 or US$50 per person per day for a couple (less for bigger groups).

Backpacker Pad, Tree Top Ecolodge and Yaklom Hill Lodge are good at arranging tours, but we recommend using one of the following dedicated tour companies.

Highland Tours TOUR
(☑088 870 3080, 097 658 3841; highland.tour@yahoo.com) Kimi and Horng are husband-wife graduates of the Le Tonlé Tourism Training Centre (p130) in Stung Treng who have moved to the highlands to run a range of tours. Horng is the only female guide in Ratanakiri.

Khieng TOUR
(☑097 923 0923; khamphaykhieng@yahoo.com) Bespectacled Khieng is an indigenous Tompuon guide who runs unique one- to two-night trips in some fairly well-preserved jungle around Lumphat, with overnights in minority villages.

DutchCo Trekking Cambodia TOUR
(☑097 679 2714; www.trekkingcambodia.com)
One of the most experienced trekking operators in the province, run by – wait for it – a
friendly Dutchman.

🛏 Sleeping

★**Tree Top Ecolodge** BUNGALOW $
(☑012 490333; www.treetop-ecolodge.com; d US$7,
cottage with cold/hot water US$12/15; 🛜) Sets the
standard for budget digs in the northeast.
Here rough-hewn walkways lead to all-wood
bungalows with mosquito nets, thatch roofs
and verandahs with verdant valley views.

Banlung Balcony GUESTHOUSE $
(☑097 911 0989; www.balconyguesthouse.net;
d US$4-7; @🛜) Ban Lung's best deal at the
bargain-basement end. The rooms are basic
but have high ceilings and odour-combating
wood floors.

Backpacker Pad HOSTEL $
(☑092 785259; banlungbackpackerpad@yahoo.
com; dm US$2, d without/with bathroom US$4/5;
🛜) Penny pinchers rejoice: it doesn't get
cheaper than this. Owner Sophat is a great
source of info and runs a tour company.

Yaklom Hill Lodge LODGE $
(☑011 725881; www.yaklom.com; s/d/tr
US$10/15/20) 🏊 Ratanakiri's only true
ecolodge, staffed by Tompuon, is set amid
lush forest near Boeng Yeak Lom, 5km east
of Ban Lung's central roundabout. It will appeal to those who like camping, down to the
minimal electricity available.

🍴 Eating

★**Sal's Restaurant & Bar** INTERNATIONAL $
(mains US$1.75-5) This welcoming restaurant-
bar, popular with Ban Lung's small expat
community, is the place to come for comfort
food from home, including Indian curries,
spicy Mexican and great burgers.

Cafe Alee INTERNATIONAL $
(mains US$1.50-5.50; ☺7am-last customer) Cafe
Alee's menu features the full spectrum
of Khmer food plus a few token Western
dishes – veggie burgers, lasagne, pizza, baguettes, and hearty breakfasts and breads
for trekkers. Do try the homemade potato
crisps.

Gecko House INTERNATIONAL $
(mains 10,000-20,000r; ☺8am-10pm; 🛜) A
charming little restaurant-bar with soft

lighting and famously frosty beer mugs. This
is a great place by day or night.

ℹ Information

Canadia Bank Full-service bank with fee-free
ATM.
Srey Mom Internet (☑097 295 9111; per hr
4000r; ☺6.30am-10pm) Fan-cooled internet
access, plus hires out motorbikes (from US$5).

ℹ Getting There & Away

Ban Lung's new **bus station** (NH19) is on the
western outskirts of town, 2.5km west of Ban
Lung's main roundabout. All buses and most long-
distance minibus services depart from here. Tour
companies in town usually offer free rides out here
with the purchase of a ticket.

Phnom Penh Sorya, Rith Mony and Thong Ly operate early-morning buses to Phnom Penh (US$9
to US$10, 11 hours) via Kratie and Kompong Cham.

Quicker are the speedy express vans that pick
you up at your guesthouse and head to Phnom
Penh (US$15, eight hours, 6am and 4pm) and
Stung Treng (US$6, two hours, around 7.30am).
Call Tree Top Ecolodge to arrange an express van
pick-up if coming from Phnom Penh. Tree Top is
also an expert regarding the ins and outs of getting to Laos and Vietnam.

Long a dirt cattle track known as the 'Death
Hwy', the road south to Mondulkiri has been upgraded to a sealed highway. It should be ready for
prime time upon completion of a bridge over the
Srepok River in Lumphat (estimated finish date
late 2014). Until that opens, the easiest way to get
to Mondulkiri by public transport is to backtrack
to Snuol or Kratie and pick up transportation
there.

ℹ Getting Around

Motodups hang out around the market and some
double as guides. Figure on US$15 to US$20 per
day for a good English-speaking driver-guide. A
moto to Yeak Lom costs US$3 to US$4 return;
to Voen Sai is US$15 return; to any waterfall is
about US$6 return.

Cheng Heng (☑088 851 6104; ☺6am-8pm)
has some 250cc trail bikes for rent (US$25) in

WARNING

The Ho Chi Minh Trail once passed
through the hills of Ratanakiri where it was
nicknamed the Sihanouk Trail in reference
to Cambodia's then head of state. This
region was heavily bombed by the Americans and there is still some unexploded
ordnance (UXO) around. Never touch
anything that looks vaguely like UXO.

RESPONSIBLE TREKKING AROUND RATANAKIRI

Treks taking in the remote forests and minority villages of Ratanakiri are very popular these days. Where possible, we recommend using indigenous guides for organised treks and other excursions around Ban Lung. They speak the local dialects, understand tribal taboos and can secure permission to visit cemeteries that are off-limits to Khmer guides. Their intimate knowledge of the forests is another major asset.

Tour companies listed in this section can all hire indigenous guides on request. A loose association of Tompuon guides is based at Boeng Yeak Lom. They have neither a phone number nor an email address so you'll just have to rock up. They can take you on an exclusive tour of several Tompuon villages around Boeng Yeak Lom. You can observe weavers and basket makers in action, learn about animist traditions and eat a traditional indigenous meal of bamboo-steamed fish, fresh vegetables, 'minority' rice and, of course, rice wine.

More tips on visiting indigenous communities responsibly:

➡ Try to spend some real time in minority villages – at least several hours if not an overnight. If you don't have a few hours to invest, don't go.

➡ Travel in small, less disruptive groups.

➡ Do not photograph without asking permission first – this includes children. Some hill tribes believe the camera will capture their spirit.

➡ Dress modestly.

➡ Taste traditional wine if you are offered it, especially during a ceremony. Refusal will cause offence.

➡ Individual gifts create jealousy and expectations. Instead, consider making donations to the local school, medical centre or community fund.

➡ Honour signs discouraging outsiders from entering a village, for instance during a spiritual ceremony. A good local guide will be able to detect these signs.

➡ Never give children sweets or money.

➡ Don't buy village treasures, such as altar pieces or totems, or the clothes or jewellery they are wearing.

addition to a stable of well-maintained smaller motorbikes (US$6 to US$8).

Mondulkiri Province

Mondulkiri (Meeting of the Hills), the original Wild East of the country, is a world apart from the lowlands with not a rice paddy or palm tree in sight. Home to the hardy Bunong people and their noble elephants, this upland area is a seductive mix of grassy hills, pine groves and rainforests of jade green. Conservationists have grand plans for the sparsely populated province but are facing off against loggers, poachers, prospectors and well-connected speculators.

Sen Monorom   សែនមនោរម្យ

♫ 073 / POP 10,000 / ELEV 800M

Sen Monorom, the best base for exploring Mondulkiri, has the feel of a remote outpost town. Many Bunong people from nearby villages come to Sen Monorom to trade; the distinctive baskets they carry on their backs make them easy to spot.

◉ Sights & Activities

As in Ratanakiri, multiday forest treks taking in minority villages are the big draw. We recommend securing indigenous Bunong guides for these trips. They know the forests intimately and can break the ice with the locals in any Bunong villages you visit.

Monorom Falls   WATERFALL
FREE A 10m drop into a popular swimming hole, Monorom Falls is lovely if you can beat the crowds. From the west side of the airstrip, head northwest for 2.3km, turn left and proceed 1.5km. A return moto costs US$3.

Elephant Valley Project   WILDLIFE RESERVE
(♫099 696041; www.elephantvalleyproject.org; ⊙Mon-Fri) This popular initiative entices lo-

cal mahouts to bring their overworked or injured elephants in for some down time or to live permanently. You are not allowed to ride the elephants here. Instead, you simply walk through the forest with them and observe them in their element, learning about elephant behaviour, Bunong culture and forest ecology in the process.

There are two options for visiting the Elephant Valley Project. Option one is a day trip (half/full day US$40/70) on which half the day is spent observing the elephants, the other half, washing them and doing other tasks around the project site. The second option is an overnight stay (dorm US$20, double US$30 to US$50) in exquisite bungalows tucked into the jungle on a ridge overlooking the valley. Prices include full board.

It's popular so book well in advance. The maximum amount of day trippers allowed per day is 12. Short- and long-term volunteers who want to help the project while learning mahout skills are welcome.

☞ Tours

Elephant Rides   TOUR
You can ride elephants in the villages of Phulung, 7km northeast of Sen Monorom, and Putang, 9km southwest of town. Treks arranged in Sen Monorom cost US$25 to US$30 per person, including lunch and transport to and from the village.

Green House   TOUR
(📞017 905659; www.greenhouse-tour.blogspot. com) Offers the most comprehensive tour program around the province. Besides the normal trekking it also runs full-day mountain-bike tours (about US$20). Has internet access too.

Bunong Place   TOUR
(📞012 474879; www.bunongcenter.org; ⏱6am-6pm) This NGO-run 'drop-in centre' for Bunong people provides trained Bunong guides for local tours, costing US$15/25 per half/full day, including motorbike. Also sells handicrafts.

🛏 Sleeping

★Nature Lodge   GUESTHOUSE **$**
(📞012 230272; www.naturelodgecambodia.com; r US$10-30; 🛜) Located on a windswept hilltop near town, this quirky resort has attractive, comfortable bungalows with hot showers. The magnificent restaurant/common area has comfy nooks, a pool table and an enviable bar.

Tree Lodge   BUNGALOW **$**
(📞097 723 4177; www.treelodge-senmonorom. blogspot.com; r with cold/hot water from US$3/5; 🛜) Run by a nice, helpful young family, Tree Lodge targets backpackers with rote-basic (think bed, floor, mozzie net) A-frame huts made from native materials.

Happy Elephant   GUESTHOUSE **$**
(📞097 616 4011; motvil@hotmail.com; d from US$5; 🛜) This backpacker special features a half-dozen sturdy cold-water bungalows on a hill behind the pleasingly simple wooden restaurant.

Sovankiri   HOSTEL **$**
(📞097 474 4528; dm US$3, r US$5-8) This central guesthouse offers clean, no-nonsense budget rooms, plus the best Western food in town (fine Khmer food as well).

CAMBODIA MONDULKIRI PROVINCE

THE REAL GIBBON EXPERIENCE

Conservation International Cambodia (CI; 📞in Phnom Penh 023-214627; www. conservation.org) has set up a new project to observe semihabituated yellow-cheeked crested gibbons in the **Veun Sai-Siem Pang Conservation Area** (VSSPCA), just outside the border of Virachey National Park north of Veun Sai. This colony was only discovered in 2010 and is believed to be one of the world's largest at about 500 groups. Hearing their haunting dawn call echo through the jungle and seeing them swing through the canopy is memorable.

You stay at least one night in the jungle sleeping in hammocks or in a community-based homestay, rising well before dawn to spend time with the gibbons. CI has an exclusive arrangement with the village near the gibbon site to run these tours. The gibbon-viewing season runs from November to mid-June – it's too wet at other times – and the maximum group size is six. The tours cost US$100 to US$200 per person. Most companies in Ban Lung can arrange these trips on behalf of CI.

The VSSPCA is highly susceptible to the types of illegal and legal logging that have ravaged most of the forests around Ban Lung.

✖ Eating & Drinking

Khmer Kitchen
CAMBODIAN **$**

(mains US$2-4; ⊙ 6am-10pm; 🛜) This unassuming street-side eatery whips up some of the most flavoursome Khmer food in the hills. The *kari saik trey* (fish coconut curry) and other curries are particularly scrumptious.

Hefalump Cafe
CAFE **$**

(🛜) 🍃 A collaboration of various NGOs and conservation groups in town, this cafe doubles as a training centre for Bunong people in hospitality. Coffee, tea, cake and sandwiches.

❶ Information

The guesthouses listed are all very good sources of information and run the full gamut of tours.

Acleda Bank (NH76) Changes major currencies and has a Visa-only ATM.

❶ Getting There & Away

Phnom Penh Sorya runs a 7.30am bus to Phnom Penh (US$8, eight hours). Express vans run by Chim Vuth Mondulkiri Express and Kim Seng Express do the trip in 5½ hours (US$10).

Vehicles to Phnom Penh go via Kompong Cham. Any advertised trip to Siem Reap usually involves a change in Suong.

Local minibuses (departing from the taxi park) are the way forward to Kratie (30,000r, four hours). Count on at least one early-morning departure and two or three departures around 12.30pm.

See Ban Lung's Getting There & Away (p133) section for information on the new direct route

---

GETTING TO VIETNAM: EASTERN BORDERS

Kompong Cham to Tay Ninh

The Trapeang Plong/Xa Mat crossing (open 7am to 5pm) is convenient for those using private transport to travel between northeast Cambodia or Siem Reap and Ho Chi Minh City.

Getting to the border From Kompong Cham take anything heading east on NH7 toward Snuol, and get off at the roundabout in Krek (Kraek) on NH7 55km east-southeast of Kompong Cham. From there, it's 13km south by moto (US$3) along NH72 to snoozy Trapeang Plong, marked by a candy-striped road barrier and a few tin shacks.

At the border This border is a breeze; just have your Vietnamese visa ready.

Moving on On the Vietnamese side, motorbikes and taxis go to Tay Ninh, 45km to the south.

Snuol to Binh Long

The Trapeang Sre/Loc Ninh crossing (open 7am to 5pm) is useful for those trying to get straight to Vietnam from Kratie or points north.

Getting to the border First get to Snuol by bus, share taxi or minibus from Sen Monorom, Kratie or Kompong Cham. In Snuol catch a moto (US$5) for the 18km trip southeastward along smooth NH74.

At the border As always you'll need a prearranged visa to enter Vietnam, and US$20 for a visa-on-arrival to enter Cambodia.

Moving on On the Vietnamese side, the nearest town is Binh Long, 40km to the south. Motorbikes wait at the border.

Ban Lung to Pleiku

The O Yadaw/Le Thanh crossing (open 7am to 5pm) is 70km east of Ban Lung along smooth NH19.

Getting to the border From Ban Lung, guesthouses advertise a 6.30am van to Pleiku (US$12, 3½ hours) involving a change of vehicles at the border. These pick you up at your guesthouse.

At the border Formalities are straightforward and lines nonexistent; just make sure you have a Vietnamese visa.

Moving on On the Vietnamese side of the frontier, the road is nicely paved. Motos await to take you to Duc Co (20km), where there are buses (15,000d) to Pleiku, Quy Nhon and Hoi An. For information on making this trip in the opposite direction, see p883.

to Ratanakiri. Until that's ready, backtrack to Snuol or Kratie and pick up transportation there.

ⓘ Getting Around

English-speaking moto drivers cost about US$15 to US$20 per day. Most guesthouses rent out motorbikes for US$6 to US$8 and a few have bicycles for US$2. **Adventure Rider Asia** (☑ 078 250350; www.adventureriderasia.com; NH76; tours per day from US$65) has well-maintained 250cc dirt bikes (US$25) for rent.

Around Sen Monorom

BOU SRAA WATERFALL ទឹកជ្រោះប៊ូស្រា
This two-tiered waterfall admission 5000r) 33km east of Sen Monorom is famous throughout the country. It's a double-drop waterfall with an upper tier of some 10m and a spectacular lower tier with a thundering 25m drop.

PHNOM PRICH WILDLIFE SANCTUARY
WWF (☑ 073 690 0096; www.panda.org) has recently helped two villages in this wildlife sanctuary launch projects geared towards giving tourists a glimpse into traditional Bunong lifestyles while improving local livelihoods and protecting the forest.

About 55km north of Sen Monorom on the road to Koh Nhek, the village of **Dei Ey** offers homestays, traditional meals, trekking, and walking with elephants owned by the local Bunong. Prices for a two-day trip start at US$135 for one person and go down substantially with each additional person. Included are transport, meals cooked by Bunong, guides and accommodation in the Dei Ey Community Lodge.

There's a similar program in **Sre Y**, about 30km northwest of Sen Monorom. Day trips here involve walking with elephants, followed by a trek to a waterfall, then returning to Sen Monorom on mountain bikes.

Contact Nimith at WWF for details on both projects, which can also be booked through tour operators in Sen Monorom.

UNDERSTAND CAMBODIA

Cambodia Today

Cambodia is at a crossroads in its road to recovery from the brutal years of Khmer Rouge rule. Compare Cambodia today with the dark abyss into which it plunged under the Khmer Rouge and the picture looks optimistic, but look to its more successful neighbours and it's easy to be pessimistic. Cambodia must choose its path: pluralism, progress and prosperity or intimidation, impunity and injustice. The jury is still very much out on which way things will go.

Prime Minister Hun Sen and his Cambodian People's Party (CPP) have dominated the politics of Cambodia since 1979 when the party was installed in power by the Vietnamese. However, in a result that shocked many observers, the 2013 national election saw the united opposition make significant gains in the national assembly.

Or did they win it outright? They claim they did, and have refused to take their seats in the assembly until a fair investigation of

---

MONKEY BUSINESS IN MONDULKIRI
··

A recent Wildlife Conservation Society (WCS) study estimated populations of 30,500 black-shanked doucs in Mondulkiri's **Seima Protected Forest**, and 2600 yellow-cheeked crested gibbons – the world's largest concentration of both species. You can trek into the wild and possibly spot these primates, along with other wild beasts, thanks to an exciting new project supported by the WCS near the Bunong village of Andong Kraloeng, which lies on the highway just 20km west of Sen Monorom. The project site is just a few kilometres north of the highway, so access is relatively easy.

Day treks and overnight trips wind their way through mixed evergreen forest and waterfalls with an excellent chance of spotting the doucs along the way (the gibbons were still being habituated at the time of research).

Registered guides accompany visitors together with local Bunong guides to identify the trails. Sample prices: about US$50 per person for a one-day tour, or US$100 for an overnight tour, including all guides, equipment for overnight stays in hammocks, and food.

For information and booking, contact Green House (p72) in Sen Monorom.

widespread election irregularities – some alleged, some proven – takes place. Six months of sometimes-violent street protests continued to drag on as we went to print. Leading the protests are long-standing opposition leader Sam Rainsy and his one-time rival, Kem Sokha. The two leaders brought their parties together to form the Cambodia National Rescue Party (CNRP) before the 2013 elections.

Many Cambodians hope that both sides will reach a compromise and that in time this surprise result will put pressure on the CPP to introduce much-needed political and electoral reform. The next five years will be very interesting indeed.

History

The good, the bad and the ugly is a simple way to sum up Cambodian history. Things were good in the early years, culminating in the vast Khmer empire, unrivalled in the region during four centuries of dominance. Then the bad set in, from the 13th century, as ascendant neighbours steadily chipped away at Cambodian territory. In the 20th century it turned downright ugly, as a brutal civil war culminated in the genocidal rule of the Khmer Rouge (1975–79), from which Cambodia is still recovering.

Funan & Chenla

The Indianisation of Cambodia began in the 1st century AD as traders plying the sea route from the Bay of Bengal to southern China brought Indian ideas and technologies to what is now southern Vietnam. The largest of the era's nascent kingdoms, known to the Chinese as Funan, embraced the worship of the Hindu deities Shiva and Vishnu and, at the same time, Buddhism.

From the 6th to 8th centuries Cambodia seems to have been ruled by a collection of competing kingdoms. Chinese annals refer to 'Water Chenla', apparently the area around the modern-day town of Takeo, and 'Land Chenla', further north along the Mekong and around Sambor Prei Kuk.

The Rise & Fall of Angkor

The Angkorian era lasted from AD 802 to 1432, encompassing periods of conquest, turmoil and retreat, revival and decline, and fits of remarkable productivity.

THE KHMER ROUGE TRIAL

The Vietnamese ousted the Khmer Rouge on 7 January 1979, but it wasn't until 1999 – after two decades of civil war – that serious discussions began about a trial to bring those responsible for the deaths of about two million Cambodians to justice. After lengthy negotiations, agreement was finally reached on establishing a war crimes tribunal to try the surviving leaders of the Khmer Rouge.

It took another decade for the first verdict in the Extraordinary Chambers in the Courts of Cambodia (ECCC) trial. In that time one of the key suspects, the one-legged general Ta Mok ('The Butcher'), died in custody. Case 001, the trial of Kaing Guek Eav, aka Comrade Duch, finally began in 2009. Duch was seen as a key figure as he provided the link between the regime and its crimes in his role as head of S-21 prison. Duch was sentenced to 35 years in 2010, a verdict that was later extended on appeal to life imprisonment.

Case 002 began in November 2011, involving the most senior surviving leaders of the Democratic Kampuchea (DK) era: Brother Number 2 Nuon Chea (age 84), Brother Number 3 and former foreign minister of DK Ieng Sary (age 83), and former DK head of state Khieu Samphan (age 79). Justice may prove elusive, however, due to the slow progress of court proceedings and the advancing age of the defendants. Ieng Sary died in 2013, and his wife and former DK Minister of Social Affairs Ieng Thirith (age 78) was ruled unfit to stand trial because of dementia. Verdicts in Case 002 were due some time in 2014.

Case 003 against head of the DK navy, Meas Muth, and head of the DK air force, Sou Met, is meant to follow Case 002. However, investigations into this case stalled back in 2009 under intense pressure from the Cambodian government, which wanted to draw a line under proceedings with the completion of Case 002. Prime Minister Hun Sen in particular is strongly opposed to Case 003, and few observers give any chance of a third trial actually taking place.

In 802, Jayavarman II (reigned c 802–50) proclaimed himself a *devaraja* (god-king). He instigated an uprising against Javanese domination of southern Cambodia and, through alliances and conquests, brought the country under his control, becoming the first monarch to rule most of what we now call Cambodia.

In the 9th century, Yasovarman I (r 889–910) moved the capital to Angkor, creating a new centre for worship, scholarship and the arts. After a period of turmoil and conflict, Suryavarman II (r 1113–52) unified the kingdom and embarked on another phase of territorial expansion, waging successful but costly wars against both Vietnam and Champa (an Indianised kingdom that occupied what is now southern and central Vietnam). His devotion to the Hindu deity Vishnu inspired him to commission Angkor Wat.

The tables soon turned. Champa struck back in 1177 with a naval expedition up the Mekong, taking Angkor by surprise and putting the king to death. But the following year a cousin of Suryavarman II – soon crowned Jayavarman VII (r 1181–1219) – rallied the Khmers and defeated the Chams in another epic naval battle. A devout follower of Mahayana Buddhism, it was he who built the city of Angkor Thom.

During the twilight years of the empire, religious conflict and internecine rivalries were rife. The Thais made repeated incursions into Angkor, sacking the city in 1351 and again in 1431, and from the royal court making off with thousands of intellectuals, artisans and dancers, whose profound impact on Thai culture can be seen to this day.

From 1600 until the arrival of the French, Cambodia was ruled by a series of weak kings whose intrigues often involved seeking the protection of either Thailand or Vietnam – granted, of course, at a price.

French Colonialism

The era of yo-yoing between Thai and Vietnamese masters came to a close in 1864, when French gunboats intimidated King Norodom I (r 1860–1904) into signing a treaty of protectorate. An exception in the annals of colonialism, the French presence really did protect the country at a time when it was in danger of being swallowed up by its more powerful neighbours. In 1907 the French pressured Thailand into returning the northwest provinces of Battambang, Siem Reap and Sisophon, bringing Angkor under Cambodian control for the first time in more than a century.

Led by King Norodom Sihanouk (r 1941–55 and 1993–2004), Cambodia declared independence on 9 November 1953.

Independence & Civil War

The period after 1953 was one of peace and prosperity, and a time of creativity and optimism. Dark clouds were circling, however, as the war in Vietnam began sucking in neighbouring countries. As the 1960s drew to a close, the North Vietnamese and the Viet Cong were using Cambodian territory in their battle against South Vietnam and US forces, prompting devastating American bombing and a land invasion into eastern Cambodia.

In March 1970 Sihanouk, now serving as prime minister, was overthrown by General Lon Nol, and took up residence in Beijing. Here he set up a government-in-exile that allied itself with an indigenous Cambodian revolutionary movement that Sihanouk had dubbed the Khmer Rouge. Violence engulfed large parts of the country.

Khmer Rouge Rule

Upon taking Phnom Penh on 17 April 1975 – two weeks before the fall of Saigon – the Khmer Rouge implemented one of the most radical and brutal restructurings of a society ever attempted. Its goal was to transform Cambodia – renamed Democratic Kampuchea – into a giant peasant-dominated agrarian cooperative, untainted by anything that had come before. Within days, the entire populations of Phnom Penh and provincial towns, including the sick, elderly and infirm, were forced to march into the countryside and work as slaves for 12 to 15 hours a day. Intellectuals were systematically wiped out – having glasses or speaking a foreign language was reason enough to be killed. The advent of Khmer Rouge rule was proclaimed Year Zero.

Leading the Khmer Rouge was Saloth Sar, better known as Pol Pot. Under his rule, Cambodia became a vast slave labour camp. Meals consisted of little more than watery rice porridge twice a day, meant to sustain men, women and children through a backbreaking day in the fields. Disease stalked the work camps, malaria and dysentery striking down whole families.

MUST SEE

The Killing Fields (1984) is a poignant film about American journalist Sydney Schanberg and his Cambodian assistant both during and after the Khmer Rouge takeover.

Khmer Rouge rule was brought to an end by the Vietnamese, who liberated the almost-empty city of Phnom Penh on 7 January 1979. It is estimated that at least 1.7 million people perished at the hands of Pol Pot and his followers. The **Documentation Center of Cambodia** (DC-Cam; www.dccam. org) records the horrific events of the period.

A Sort of Peace

The Vietnamese installed a new government led by several former Khmer Rouge officers, including current Prime Minister Hun Sen, who had defected to Vietnam in 1977. In the dislocation that followed liberation, little rice was planted or harvested, leading to a massive famine.

The Khmer Rouge continued to wage civil war from remote mountain bases near the Thai border throughout the 1980s. In February 1991 all parties – including the Khmer Rouge – signed the Paris Peace Accords, according to which the UN Transitional Authority in Cambodia (UNTAC) would rule the country for two years before elections were held in 1993. But the Khmer Rouge boycotted the elections and re-established a guerrilla network throughout Cambodia.

The last Khmer Rouge hold-outs, including Ta Mok, were not defeated until the capture of Anlong Veng and Prasat Preah Vihear by government forces in the spring of 1998. Pol Pot cheated justice by dying a sorry death near Anlong Veng during that year; he was cremated on a pile of old tyres.

People & Culture

Population

Nearly 15 million people live in Cambodia. With a rapid growth rate of about 2% a year, the population is predicted to reach 20 million by 2025. More than 40% of the population is under the age of 16. According to official statistics, around 96% of the people are ethnic Khmers, making the country the most homogeneous in Southeast Asia, but in reality anywhere between 10% and 20% of the population is of Cham, Chinese or Vietnamese origin. Cambodia's diverse Khmer Leu (Upper Khmer) or Chunchiet (minorities), who live in the country's mountainous regions, probably number between 75,000 and 100,000.

The official language is Khmer, spoken by 95% of the population. English has taken over from French as the second language of choice, although Chinese is also growing in popularity. Life expectancy is currently 62 years.

Lifestyle

For many older Cambodians, life is centred on faith, family and food, an existence that has stayed the same for centuries. Faith is a rock in the lives of many older Cambodians, and Buddhism helped them to survive the terrible years and then rebuild their lives after the Khmer Rouge. Family is more than the nuclear family we now know in the West; it's the extended family of third cousins and obscure aunts – as long as there is a bloodline, there is a bond. Families stick together, solve problems collectively, listen to the wisdom of the elders and pool resources. The extended family comes together during times of trouble and times of joy, celebrating festivals and successes, mourning deaths and disappointments. Whether the Cambodian house is big or small, there will be a lot of people living inside.

However, the Cambodian lifestyle is changing as the population gets younger and more urbanized. Cambodia is experiencing its very own '60s swing, as the younger generation stands ready for a different lifestyle to the one their parents had to swallow. This creates plenty of friction in the cities, as rebellious teens dress as they like, date whoever they wish and hit the town until all hours. More recently this generational conflict spilled over into politics as the Facebook generation helped deliver a shock result that saw the Cambodian Peoples' Party majority slashed in half in the 2013 general elections.

Corruption remains a way of life in Cambodia. It is a major element of the Cambodian economy and exists to some extent at all levels of government. Sometimes it is overt, but increasingly it is covert, with private companies often securing very favourable business deals on the basis of their connections. It seems everything has a price, including ancient temples, national parks and even genocide sites.

Religion

The majority of Khmers follow the Theravada branch of Buddhism. Buddhism in Cambodia draws heavily on its predecessors, incorporating many cultural traditions from Hinduism for ceremonies such as birth, marriage and death, as well as genies and spirits, such as Neak Ta, which link back to a pre-Indian animist past.

Under the Khmer Rouge, the majority of Cambodia's Buddhist monks were murdered and nearly all of the country's wats (more than 3000) were damaged or destroyed. In the late 1980s, Buddhism once again became the state religion.

Other religions found in Cambodia include: Islam, practised by the Cham community; animism, among the hill tribes; and Christianity, which is making inroads via missionaries and Christian NGOs.

Arts

The Khmer Rouge regime not only killed the living bearers of Khmer culture, it also destroyed cultural artefacts, statues, musical instruments, books and anything else that served as a reminder of a past it was trying to efface. The temples of Angkor were spared as a symbol of Khmer glory and empire, but little else survived. Despite this, Cambodia is witnessing a resurgence of traditional arts and a growing interest in cross-cultural fusion.

Cambodia's royal ballet is a tangible link with the glory of Angkor and includes a unique *apsara* (heavenly nymphs) dance. Cambodian music, too, goes back at least as far as Angkor. To get some sense of the music that Jayavarman VII used to like, check out the bas-reliefs at Angkor Wat.

In the mid-20th-century a vibrant Cambodian pop-music scene developed, but it was killed off by the Khmer Rouge. After the war, overseas Khmers established a pop industry in the USA and some Cambodian-Americans, raised on a diet of rap, are now returning to their homeland. The Los Angeles–based sextet Dengue Fever, inspired by 1960s Cambodian pop and psychedelic rock, is the ultimate fusion band.

The people of Cambodia were producing masterfully sensuous sculptures – much more than mere copies of Indian forms – in the age of Funan and Chenla. The Banteay Srei style of the late 10th century is regarded as a high point in the evolution of Southeast Asian art.

Food & Drink

Some traditional Cambodian dishes are similar to those of neighbouring Laos and Thailand (though not as spicy), others closer to Chinese and Vietnamese cooking. The French left their mark, too.

Thanks to the Tonlé Sap, freshwater fish – often *ahng* (grilled) – are a huge part of the Cambodian diet. The legendary national dish, *amok,* is fish baked with coconut and lemon grass in banana leaves. *Prahoc* (fermented fish paste) is used to flavour foods, with coconut and lemon grass making regular cameos.

A proper Cambodian meal almost always includes *samlor* (soup), served at the same time as other courses. *Kyteow* is a rice-noodle soup that will keep you going all day. *Bobor* (rice porridge), eaten for breakfast, lunch or dinner, is best sampled with some fresh fish and a dash of ginger.

Tap water *must* be avoided, especially in rural areas. Bottled water is widely available but coconut milk, sold by machete-wielding street vendors, is more ecological and may be more sterile.

Beer is immensely popular in the cities, while rural folk drink palm wine, tapped from the sugar palms that dot the landscape. *Tukaloks* (fruit shakes) are mixed with milk, sugar and sometimes a raw egg.

CAMBODIA FOOD & DRINK

BOTTOMS UP

When Cambodians propose a toast, they usually stipulate what percentage must be downed. If they are feeling generous, it might be just *ha-sip pea-roi* (50%), but more often than not it is *moi roi pea-roi* (100%). This is why they love ice in their beer, as they can pace themselves over the course of the night. Many a *barang* (foreigner) has ended up face down on the table at a Cambodian wedding when trying to outdrink the Khmers without the help of ice.

Environment

The Land

Cambodia's two dominant geographical features are the mighty Mekong River and a vast lake, the Tonlé Sap. The rich sediment deposited during the Mekong's annual wet-season flooding has made central Cambodia incredibly fertile. This low-lying alluvial plain is where the vast majority of Cambodians live, fishing and farming in harmony with the rhythms of the monsoon.

In Cambodia's southwest quadrant, much of the land mass is covered by the Cardamom Mountains and, near Kampot, the Elephant Mountains. Along Cambodia's northern border with Thailand, the plains collide with the Dangkrek Mountains, a striking sandstone escarpment more than 300km long and up to 550m high. One of the best places to get a sense of this area is Prasat Preah Vihear.

In the northeastern corner of the country, in the provinces of Ratanakiri and Mondulkiri, the plains give way to the Eastern Highlands, a remote region of densely forested mountains and high plateaus.

Wildlife

Cambodia's forest ecosystems were in excellent shape until the 1990s and, compared with its neighbours, its habitats are still relatively healthy. The years of war took their toll on some species, but others thrived in the remote jungles of the southwest and northeast. Ironically, peace brought increased threats as loggers felled huge areas of primary forest and the illicit trade in wildlife targeted endangered species.

Still, with more than 200 species of mammal, Cambodia has some of Southeast Asia's best wildlife-watching opportunities. Highlights include spotting gibbons and black-shanked doucs in Ratanakiri and Mondulkiri provinces, and viewing some of the last remaining freshwater Irrawaddy dolphins in Kratie and Stung Treng provinces. The country is a birdwatcher's paradise – feathered friends found almost exclusively in Cambodia include the giant ibis, Bengal florican, sarus crane and three species of vulture. The marshes around Tonlé Sap are particularly rich in bird life. The Siem Reap–based Sam Veasna Center runs bird-watching trips.

Globally threatened species that you stand a slight chance of seeing include the Asian elephant, banteng (a wild ox), gaur, clouded leopard, fishing cat, marbled cat, sun bear, Siamese crocodile and pangolin. Asian tigers were once commonplace but are now exceedingly rare – the last sighting was in about 2007.

Environmental Issues

Cambodia's pristine environment is a big draw for adventurous ecotourists, but much of it is currently under threat. Ancient forests are being razed to make way for plantations, rivers are being sized up for major hydroelectric power plants and the south coast is being explored by leading oil companies. Places like the Cardamom Mountains are in the front line and it remains to be seen whether the environmentalists or the economists will win the debate.

The greatest threat is illegal logging, carried out to provide charcoal and timber, and to clear land for cash-crop plantations. The environmental watchdog **Global Witness** (www.globalwitness.org) publishes meticulously documented exposés on corrupt military and civilian officials and their well-connected business partners.

In the short term, deforestation is contributing to worsening floods along the Mekong, but the long-term implications of deforestation are mind-boggling. Siltation, combined with overfishing and pollution, may lead to the eventual death of Tonlé Sap lake, a catastrophe for future generations of Cambodians.

TONLÉ SAP: THE HEARTBEAT OF CAMBODIA

During the wet season (June to October), the Mekong River rises dramatically, forcing the Tonlé Sap river to flow northwest into Tonlé Sap (Great Lake). During this period, the lake swells from around 3000 sq km to almost 13,000 sq km, and from the air Cambodia looks like one almighty puddle. As the Mekong falls during the dry season, the Tonlé Sap river reverses its flow, and the lake's floodwaters drain back into the Mekong. This unique process makes Tonlé Sap one of the world's richest sources of freshwater fish.

Throughout the country, pollution is a problem, and detritus of all sorts, especially plastic bags and bottles, can be seen in distressing quantities everywhere.

The latest environmental threat to emerge are dams on the Mekong River. Environmentalists fear that damming the mainstream Mekong may disrupt the flow patterns of the river and the migratory patterns of fish (including the critically endangered freshwater Irrawaddy dolphin). Work on the Don Sahong (Siphandone) Dam just north of the Cambodia–Laos border has begun, and plans under consideration include the Sambor Dam, a massive 3300MW project 35km north of Kratie.

SURVIVAL GUIDE

 **Directory A–Z**

ACCOMMODATION

Accommodation in Cambodia is terrific value. In popular tourist destinations, budget guesthouses generally charge US$5 to US$8 for a room with a cold-water bathroom. Double rooms go as low as US$3 for a room with shared facilities. Dorm beds usually cost US$2 to US$3. Rooms with air-con start at US$10. Spend US$15 or US$20 and you'll be living in style. Spend US$30 and up and we're talking boutque quality with a swimming pool.

Accommodation is busiest from mid-November to March. There are substantial low-season rates available at major hotels in Phnom Penh, Siem Reap and Sihanoukville (although you can only discount a US$5 room so much).

Homestays are popular in more rural areas and on Mekong islands. These are a good way to meet the local people and learn about Cambodian life.

Price Ranges

The following price ranges refer to the cheapest double room on offer, with or without a bathroom, in the high season.

$ less than 80,000r (US$20)
$$ 80,000r to 320,000r (US$20 to US$80)
$$$ more than 320,000r (US$80)

ACTIVITIES

Cambodia is steadily emerging as an ecotourism destination. Activities on offer include the following:

➤ Rainforest trekking in Ratanakiri, Mondulkiri and the Cardamom Mountains of the south coast;

➤ Elephant treks or walking with elephants in Mondulkiri;

➤ Scuba diving and snorkelling near Sihanoukville;

➤ Cycling around Phnom Penh, in Mondulkiri, along the Mekong Discovery Trail between Kratie and Stung Treng, and around the temples of Angkor; and

➤ Adventurous dirt biking all over the country (for those with some experience).

BOOKS

A whole bookcase-worth of volumes examine Cambodia's recent history, including the French colonial period, the spillover of the war in Vietnam into Cambodia, the Khmer Rouge years and the wild 1990s. The best include the following:

➤ *Cambodia's Curse*, by Joel Brinkley (2011). Pulitzer Prize–winning journalist pulls no punches in his criticism of the government and donors alike.

➤ *Cambodia Now*, by Karen Coates (2005). A no-holds-barred look at contemporary Cambodia through the eyes of its diverse population.

➤ *Golden Bones* by Sichan Siv (2010). Describes the author's remarkable story from Cambodian refugee in New York to US ambassador to the UN.

➤ *River of Time* by John Swain (1995). Takes readers back to an old Indochina, lost to the madness of war.

➤ *The Gate* by François Bizot (2003). Bizot was kidnapped by the Khmer Rouge, and later held by them in the French embassy.

➤ *First They Killed My Father* by Loung Ung (2001). Covers the destruction of an urban Cambodian family through execution and disease during the Khmer Rouge period.

CUSTOMS REGULATIONS

A 'reasonable amount' of duty-free items is allowed into the country. Alcohol and cigarettes are on sale at well below duty-free prices on the streets of Phnom Penh. It is illegal to take antiquities out of the country.

ELECTRICITY

The usual voltage is 220V, 50 cycles, but power surges and power cuts are common, particularly in the provinces. Electrical sockets are usually two-prong, mostly flat but sometimes round pin.

EMBASSIES & CONSULATES

Australian Embassy (Map p74; ☑ 023-213413; 16 National Assembly St, Phnom Penh)

French Embassy (Map p68; ☑ 023-430020; 1 Monivong Blvd, Phnom Penh)

German Embassy (Map p74; ☑ 023-216381; 76-78 St 214, Phnom Penh)

Lao Embassy (Map p68; ☑ 023-982632; 15-17 Mao Tse Toung Blvd, Phnom Penh)

Myanmar Embassy (Map p68; ☑ 023-223761; 181 Norodom Blvd, Phnom Penh)

Thai Embassy (Map p68; 023-726306; 196 Norodom Blvd, Phnom Penh)

UK Embassy (Map p68; 023-427124; 27-29 St 75, Phnom Penh)

US Embassy (Map p70; 023-728000; 1 St 96, Phnom Penh)

Vietnamese Embassy (Map p68; 023-726274; 436 Monivong Blvd, Phnom Penh) Fifteen-day visas cost US$60 for one-day processing or US$70 on the spot. Bring a passport photo.

Vietnamese Consulate (053-688 8867; St 3, Battambang; 8-11.30am & 2-4.30pm Mon-Fri)

Vietnamese Consulate (Map p116; 034-934039; 310 Ekareach St, Sihanoukville; 8am-noon & 2-4pm Mon-Sat)

FOOD

The following price ranges refer to the average price of a main course.

$ less than 20,000r (US$5)

$$ 20,000r to 40,000r (US$5 to US$10)

$$$ more than 40,000r (US$10)

GAY & LESBIAN TRAVELLERS

Cambodia is a very tolerant country when it comes to sexual orientation and the scene is slowly coming alive in the major cities. But as with heterosexual couples, displays of public affection are a basic no-no. Handy websites:

Cambodia Out (www.cambodiaout.com) Promoting the GLBT community in Cambodia and the gay-friendly Adore Cambodia campaign.

Sticky Rice (www.stickyrice.ws) Gay travel guide covering Cambodia and Asia.

INSURANCE

Make sure your medical insurance policy covers emergency evacuation: limited medical facilities mean that you may have to be airlifted to Bangkok for problems such as an accident or dengue fever.

Worldwide travel insurance is available at www. lonelyplanet.com/travel_services. You can buy, extend and claim online anytime, even if you're already on the road.

INTERNET ACCESS

Internet access is widespread and there are internet shops in all provincial capitals. Charges range from 1500r to US$2.50 per hour.

Free wi-fi is pretty much ubiquitous at hotels, guesthouses and cafes in tourist hubs like Phnom Penh, Siem Reap and Battambang and is usually easy to find in all but the most remote locales.

LEGAL MATTERS

All narcotics, including marijuana, are illegal in Cambodia. However, marijuana is traditionally used in food preparation, so you may find it sprinkled across some pizzas.

Many Western countries have laws that make sex offences committed overseas punishable at home.

MAPS

The best all-round map is Gecko's *Cambodia Road Map* at a 1:750,000 scale.

MONEY

➡ Cambodia's currency is the riel, abbreviated in our listings to a lower-case 'r' written after the sum.

➡ The US dollar is accepted everywhere and by everyone, though change may arrive in riel (handy when paying for things such as moto rides and drinks).

➡ When calculating change, the US dollar is usually rounded off to 4000r.

➡ Near the Thai border, many transactions are in Thai baht.

➡ Avoid ripped banknotes, which Cambodians often refuse.

ATMs

ATMs that accept debit cards and credit cards are found in all major cities and a growing number of provincial towns and at border crossings. Machines dispense US dollars or riel. Canadia Bank ATMs charge no transaction fees, although they limit withdrawals on most cards to US$150 per day. ANZ Royal Bank ATMs are friendly to Western plastic, but charge US$5 per transaction.

Bargaining

Bargaining is expected in local markets, when travelling by share taxi or moto and, sometimes, when taking a cheap room. The Khmers are not ruthless hagglers, so a persuasive smile and a little friendly quibbling is usually enough to get a good price.

Tipping

Tipping is not traditionally expected here, but in a country as poor as Cambodia, a dollar tip (or 5% to 10% on bigger bills) can go a long way.

OPENING HOURS

Most Cambodians get up very early and it's not unusual to see people out exercising at 5.30am if you're heading home – ahem, sorry, getting up – at that time.

Banks Most keep core hours of 8am to 3.30pm Monday to Friday, plus Saturday morning.

Government offices Open from Monday to Friday and on Saturday mornings. They theoretically begin the working day at 7.30am, break for a siesta from 11.30am to 2pm, and end the day at 5pm.

Local markets Operate seven days a week and usually open and close with the sun, running from 6.30am to 5.30pm. They close for a few days during major holidays.

Shops Tend to open from about 8am until 6pm, sometimes later.

POST

➡ The postal service is hit-and-miss. Letters and parcels sent further afield than Asia can take up to two or three weeks to reach their destination.

➡ Send anything valuable by courier service, such as **EMS** (☎ 023-723511; www.ems.com.kh; Main Post Office, St 13) in Phnom Penh, or from another country.

➡ Ensure postcards and letters are franked before they vanish from your sight.

➡ Phnom Penh's main post office has the most reliable poste restante service.

PUBLIC HOLIDAYS

It is widely believed that Cambodia has more public holidays than any other country on earth.

In addition to the following, the whole country basically shuts down for an entire week for Chaul Chnam Khmer (Khmer New Year, usually in April) and P'chum Ben (Festival of the Dead, in September or October).

Chinese New Year (January or February) and Bon Om Tuk (Water Festival, October or November) usually mean several days off for the masses as well (although the primary Bon Om Tuk celebration, in Phnom Penh, was cancelled from 2011 to 2013 after a stampede killed hundreds in 2010).

International New Year's Day 1 January
Victory over Genocide Day 7 January
International Women's Day 8 March
International Labour Day 1 May
King's Birthday 13-15 May
International Children's Day 1 June
King Mother's Birthday 18 June
Constitution Day 24 September
Coronation Day 29 October
King Father's Birthday 31 October
Independence Day 9 November
International Human Rights Day 10 December

SAFE TRAVEL
Mines & Mortars

Cambodia is one of the most heavily mined countries in the world, especially in the northwest of the country near the Thai border. Many mined areas are unmarked, so *do not* stray from well-worn paths and *never, ever* touch any unexploded ordnance (UXO) you come across, including mortars and artillery shells. If you find yourself in a mined area, retrace your steps only if you can clearly see your footprints. If not, stay where you are and call for help. If someone is injured in a minefield, do not rush in to help even if they are crying out in pain – find someone who knows how to enter a mined area safely.

Crime

Given the number of guns in Cambodia, there is less armed theft than one might expect. Still, hold-ups and motorcycle theft are a potential danger in Phnom Penh and Sihanoukville. There is no need to be paranoid, just cautious. Walking or riding alone late at night is not ideal, certainly not in rural areas.

Bag snatching has become an increasing problem in Phnom Penh in recent years and the motorbike thieves don't let go, dragging passengers off motos and endangering lives. If riding a moto carry your shoulder bag in front of you and be careful when riding on *remorques* as well.

Should anyone be unlucky enough to be robbed, it is important to note that the Cambodian police are the best that money can buy! Any help, such as a police report, is going to cost you. The going rate depends on the size of the claim, but anywhere from US$5 to US$50 is a common charge.

Scams

Most scams are fairly harmless, involving a bit of commission here and there for taxi or moto drivers, particularly in Siem Reap.

There have been one or two reports of police set-ups in Phnom Penh, involving planted drugs. This seems to be very rare, but if you fall victim to the ploy, it may be best to pay them off before more police get involved at the local station, as the price will only rise when there are more officials to pay off.

Beggars in places such as Phnom Penh and Siem Reap are asking for milk powder for an infant in arms. Some foreigners succumb to the urge to help, but the beggars usually request

HOW TO AVOID A BAD TRIP

Watch out for *yama* (known as *yaba* in Thailand), which ominously shares its name with the Hindu god of death. Known as ice or crystal meth back home, it's not the usual diet pills but instead homemade methamphetamines often laced with toxic substances, such as mercury and lithium. It is more addictive than many users would like to admit, provoking reactions such as powerful hallucinations, sleep deprivation and psychosis.

Also be wary of buying 'cocaine'. Most of what is sold as coke, particularly in Phnom Penh, is actually pure heroin and far stronger than any smack found on the streets back home. Bang that up your hooter and you'll be doing impressions of Uma Thurman in *Pulp Fiction*.

the most expensive milk formula available and return it to the shop to split the proceeds after the handover.

Moto and *remorque* drivers will always try to get an extra buck or two out of you. Some price inflation for foreigners is natural, but you are being gouged if they charge three times the prices quoted in this chapter. Fares are pretty cheap and don't tend to rise much year on year.

TELEPHONE

Landline area codes appear under the name of each city but in many areas service is spotty. Mobile phones, whose numbers start with 01, 06, 07, 08 or 09, are hugely popular with both individuals and commercial enterprises. Buying a local SIM card is highly recommended to avoid expensive roaming charges. SIM cards are widely available and cost almost nothing. Mobile phone calls and 3G internet access are also quite cheap. Foreigners usually need to present a valid passport to purchase a local SIM card.

If you don't have a phone, the easiest way to make a local call in most urban areas is to head to one of the many small private booths on the kerbside, with prices around 300r.

For listings of businesses and government offices, check out www.yp.com.kh.

TIME

Cambodia, like Laos, Vietnam and Thailand, is seven hours ahead of Greenwich Mean Time or Universal Time Coordinated (GMT/UTC).

TRAVELLERS WITH DISABILITIES

Although Cambodia has one of the world's highest rates of limb loss (due to mines), the country is not designed for people with impaired mobility. Few buildings have lifts/elevators, footpaths and roads are riddled with potholes, and the staircases and rock jumbles of many Angkorian temples are daunting even for the able-bodied. Transport-wise, chartering is the way to go and is a fairly affordable option. Also affordable is hired help if you require it, and Khmers are generally very helpful should you need assistance.

VISAS

See the various border-crossing boxes within this chapter for tips on crossing specific borders.

Visas on Arrival

➤ For most nationalities, one-month tourist visas (US$20) are available on arrival at Phnom Penh and Siem Reap airports and all land border crossings. If you are carrying an African, Asian or Middle Eastern passport, there are some exceptions.

➤ One passport-sized photo is required and you'll be 'fined' US$2 if you don't have one. Citizens of Asean member countries do not require a visa.

➤ Visas are issued extremely quickly at the airports and lines are usually minimal, so it's not really worth paying US$5 extra for an e-visa. However, you might consider the e-visa option if you plan to cross at the Poipet or Koh Kong land borders. Overcharging for visas is rampant at these crossings, and with an e-visa you'll avoid these potential charges.

E-Visas

➤ One-month tourist e-visas cost US$20 plus a US$5 processing fee.

➤ E-visas are available from www.mfaic.gov.kh and take three business days to process.

➤ E-visas can be used at all airports and at the Bavet, Koh Kong and Poipet land border crossings. They cannot be used at the more remote land crossings, so you are on your own dealing with corrupt border officials at remote Thai and Lao land borders (corruption is less of a problem at Vietnamese borders).

Visa Extensions

➤ Tourist visas can be extended once for one month. If you're planning a longer stay, upon arrival request a one-month business visa (US$25), which can be extended for up to a year through any travel agent in Phnom Penh. Bring a passport photo.

➤ Extensions for one/three/six/12 months cost about US$45/75/155/285 and take three or four business days.

➤ For one-month extensions, it may be cheaper to do a 'visa run' to Thailand, getting a fresh visa when you cross back into Cambodia.

➤ Overstayers are charged US$5 per day at the point of exit.

Visa Regulations for Neighbouring Countries

Vietnam One-month single-entry visas cost US$60/70 for one-day/one-hour processing in Phnom Penh, Sihanoukville or Battambang.

Laos Most visitors can obtain a visa on arrival.

Thailand Most visitors do not need a visa.

VOLUNTEERING

Cambodia hosts a huge number of NGOs, some of whom require volunteers from time to time. The best way to find out who is represented in the country is to drop in on the **Cooperation Committee for Cambodia** (CCC; Map p70; ☎ 023-214152; www.ccc-cambodia.org; 9-11 St 476) in Phnom Penh.

Professional Siem Reap–based organisations helping to place volunteers include ConCERT (p79) and **Globalteer** (☎ 063-761802; www.globalteer.org); the latter program involves a weekly charge.

WORK

Jobs are available throughout Cambodia, but apart from teaching English or helping out in guesthouses, bars or restaurants, most are for professionals and are arranged in advance. There is a lot of teaching work available for English-speakers; anyone with an English-language teaching certificate can earn considerably more than those with no qualifications. Places to look for work include the classifieds sections of the *Phnom Penh Post* and the *Cambodia Daily,* and notice boards at guesthouses. For information about work opportunities with NGOs, call into the CCC, which posts vacant positions.

❶ Getting There & Away

AIR

Cambodia's two major international airports, Phnom Penh International Airport and Siem Reap International Airport, have frequent flights to destinations all over eastern Asia.

Airlines

Air Asia (☏023-356011; www.airasia.com) Serves Bangkok and Kuala Lumpur.

Asiana Airlines (☏023-890440; www.asiana.co.kr) Serves Seoul from Phnom Penh.

Bangkok Airways (☏023-722545; www.bangkokair.com) Flights to Bangkok from Phnom Penh and Siem Reap.

Cambodia Angkor Air (☏023-212564; www.cambodiaangkorair.com) Serves Bangkok, Hanoi and Ho Chi Minh City from Siem Reap and Phnom Penh.

Cebu Pacific Air (www.cebupacificair.com) Flight to Manila.

China Eastern Airlines (☏063-965229; www.ce-air.com) Siem Reap to Kunming.

China Southern Airlines (☏023-430877; www.cs-air.com) Phnom Penh to Guangzhou.

Dragon Air (☏023-424300; www.dragonair.com) Phnom Penh to Hong Kong.

Eva Air (☏023-219911; www.evaair.com) Phnom Penh to Taipei.

Jetstar (☏023-220909; www.jetstar.com) Phnom Penh and Siem Reap to Singapore.

Korean Air (☏023-224047; www.koreanair.com) Phnom Penh and Siem Reap to Seoul.

Lao Airlines (☏023-216563; www.laoairlines.com) Serves Vientiane, Luang Prabang and Pakse.

Malaysia Airlines (☏023-426688; www.malaysiaairlines.com) Phnom Penh to Kuala Lumpur.

AIRPORT TAXES

There's a tax of US$25 on all international flights out of Cambodia. The airport tax for domestic flights is US$6. Both are now included in the ticket price, so you do not need cash at the airport.

Myanmar Airways International (☏023-881178; www.maiair.com) Siem Reap to Yangon.

Shanghai Airlines (☏023-723999; www.shanghai-air.com) Siem Reap to Shanghai.

Silk Air (☏023-426807; www.silkair.com) To Singapore and Danang.

Thai Airways (☏023-214359; www.thaiair.com) Phnom Penh to Bangkok.

Tigerair (☏023-551 5888; www.tigerair.com) Phnom Penh to Singapore.

Vietnam Airlines (☏023-363396; www.vietnamair.com.vn) Serves Hanoi, Ho Chi Minh City, Vientiane and Luang Prabang.

LAND
Border Crossings

There are land border crossings to Laos, Thailand and Vietnam. See p941 for more information.

❶ Getting Around

AIR

All domestic routes are operated by Cambodia Angkor Air, a monopolistic joint venture with Vietnam Airlines. The only scheduled domestic flights at the time of writing were:

➡ Phnom Penh–Siem Reap (from US$75, several daily)
➡ Siem Reap–Sihanoukville (from US$110, daily)

BICYCLE

Some guesthouses and hotels rent out bicycles for US$1 to US$2 per day. If you'll be doing lots of cycling, bring along a bike helmet, which can also provide some protection on a moto.

Cambodia is a great country for cycle touring as travelling at gentle speeds allows for lots of inter-action with locals. Much of Cambodia is pancake flat or only moderately hilly. Safety, however, is a considerable concern on paved roads as trucks, buses and cars barrel along at high speed. Usually flat unpaved trails run roughly parallel to the highways, allowing for a more relaxed journey and much more interaction with the locals.

Cycling around Angkor is an awesome experience, as it really gives you a sense of the size and scale of the temple complex. Adventure mountain biking is likely to take off in the Cardamom Mountains and in Mondulkiri and Ratanakiri provinces over the coming years.

BOAT

Long-distance public boats are increasingly rare as the roads improve, but fast boats still ply the Tonlé Sap from Phnom Penh to Siem Reap, while smaller boats take on the sublime stretch between Siem Reap and Battambang.

BUS & MINIBUS

About a dozen bus companies serve all populated parts of the country. Comfort levels and prices vary wildly, so shop around. Booking bus tickets through guesthouses and travel agents is convenient, but often incurs a commission. Also note that travel agents tend to work with only a handful of preferred companies, thus won't always offer your preferred company and/or departure time.

Express vans – usually modern Ford Transits or Toyota Hiaces – are an option between most major cities. They operate a one seat/one passenger policy. They cost about the same as the big buses, but are much faster – often too fast for many people's taste. Also, they don't have much legroom; big buses are considerably more comfortable.

Older local minibuses serve most provincial routes and are not widely used by Western visitors. They are very cheap but often uncomfortably overcrowded (you are almost guaranteed to be vomited on) and sometimes driven by maniacs. Only really consider them if there is no alternative.

CAR & MOTORCYCLE

Renting a (self-drive) motorbike is a great way to get around provincial cities and their surrounding sights (although tourists are forbidden from renting motorbikes in Siem Reap). Basic 100cc to 125cc motorbikes are widely available and cheap (about US$5 per day). No one will ask you for a driver's licence except, occasionally, the police. Make sure you have a strong lock and always leave the bike in guarded parking where possible.

For longer-distance travel, motorcycles and cars offer travellers flexibility to visit out-of-the-way places and to stop when they choose. Cambodia's main national highways (NH) are generally in good shape but can be quite dangerous due to the prevalence of high-speed overtaking/passing.

While major national highways are too heavily trafficked for happy motorcycling, many of Cambodia's less travelled tracks are perfect for two-wheeled exploration. However, forays on motorcycles into the remote and diabolical roads of the northwest and northeast should only be attempted by experienced riders. In all cases, proceed cautiously, as outside Phnom Penh and Siem Reap medical facilities are rudimentary and ambulances are rare.

CYCLO

A few cyclos (pedicabs) can be seen on the streets of Phnom Penh and Battambang. They are a charming and environmentally friendly, if slow, way to get around, and cost about the same as a moto.

MOTO, REMORQUE & TAXI

Motos, also known as motodups (meaning moto driver), are small motorcycle taxis. They are a quick way of making short hops around towns and cities. Prices range from 1000r to US$1 or more, depending on the distance and the town. Chartering a moto for the day costs between US$7 and US$10, but can cost more if a greater distance is involved or the driver speaks English.

The vehicle known in Cambodia as a remorque (túk-túk) is, technically speaking, a remorque-moto, a roofed, two-wheeled trailer hitched to the back of a motorbike. These generally cost a bit more than double what a moto costs. Still, for two or more people a remorque can be cheaper than a moto, not to mention safer and much more comfortable if you've got luggage or it's raining.

Although locals rarely agree on a price in advance for a moto or remorque, it's best for tourists to agree to a price beforehand. Many optimistic drivers have gotten into the habit of overcharging foreigners, or trying to charge per passenger (you should never let them do this, although paying an extra dollar or two is fair if you are stuffing six or seven people into a remorque).

Taxis can be ordered via guesthouses and hotels to get around Phnom Penh, Siem Reap and Sihanoukville, and usually cost a bit more than a remorque.

SHARE TAXIS & PICK-UPS

Share taxis (usually Toyota Camrys) are faster, more flexible in terms of departure times and a bit more expensive than buses. They leave when full, which is usually rather quickly on popular routes. For less-travelled routes, you may have to wait a while (possibly until the next day if you arrive in the afternoon) before your vehicle fills up, or pay for the vacant seats yourself.

Share taxis can be pretty cramped. In addition to the driver, each one carries four to seven passengers, with the price fluctuating according to how many people are in the car. It's not uncommon to see two in the front seat, four in the back, and a seventh passenger squished between the driver and his door! Pay double the regular fare and you get the front seat all to yourself; pay six fares and you've got yourself a private taxi. Haggle patiently, with a smile, to ensure fair prices.

Pick-up trucks, which are favoured by country folk with oversized luggage (some of it alive), continue to take on the worst roads in Cambodia. Squeeze in the air-con cab or, if you feel like a tan and a mouthful of dust, sit in the back. They leave when seriously full. Bring a krama (scarf), sunscreen and, in the wet season, rain gear.

Indonesia

Best Beaches

➡ Kuta Beach, Lombok (p227)

➡ Gili Air (p231)

➡ Komodo National Park (p238)

➡ Pulau Ai (p291)

➡ Raja Ampat, Papua (p296)

Best Places for Cultural Connections

➡ National Museum (p157)

➡ Dance, Ubud (p214)

➡ Funeral rites, Ubud (p243)

➡ Banda Islands (p290)

➡ Tribal culture, Papua (p291)

Why Go?

Indonesia defines adventure: the only limitation is how many of its 17,000 islands you can reach before your visa expires. Following the equator, Indonesia stretches between Malaysia and Australia in one long intoxicating sweep. The nation's natural diversity is staggering, alluring and inspiring, from the snow-capped peaks in Papua, sandalwood forests in Sumba, dense jungle in Borneo and impossibly green rice paddies in Bali and Java. Indonesian reefs are a diver's fantasy while the surf breaks above are the best anywhere.

But even as the diversity on land and sea run like a traveller's fantasy playlist, it's the mash-up of people and cultures that's the most appealing. Bali justifiably leads off, but there are also Papua's stone-age folk, the many cultures of Flores, the artisans of Java, mall-rats of Jakarta and much more. Whether it's a dreamy remote beach, an orang-utan encounter or a Bali all-nighter, Indonesia scores.

When to Go
Jakarta

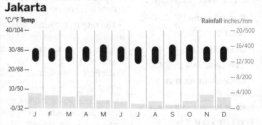

| Sep–Mar Wet season; starts later in the southeast. Rain everywhere in January & February. | Apr–Jun Dry days & highs that aren't withering. Hill towns such as Bali's Ubud can be chilly at night. | Aug High season. Prices peak on Bali & the Gilis; book ahead. Remote spots may also fill up. |

AT A GLANCE

➡ **Currency** Rupiah (Rp); 100,000Rp notes can be hard to break

➡ **Language** Bahasa Indonesia; English in tourist areas

➡ **Money** ATMs in major centres; carry rupiah for remote islands

➡ **Visas** Complicated!

➡ **Mobile phones** SIMs (around 30,000Rp) sold everywhere; cheap call/text rates

Fast Facts

➡ **Area** 1.92 million sq km

➡ **Capital** Jakarta

➡ **Emergency** Ask the nearest local for advice

Exchange Rates

Australia	A$1	10,500Rp
Euro Zone	€1	15,955Rp
Malaysia	RM1	3530Rp
Singapore	S$1	9180Rp
UK	£1	19,355Rp
USA	US$1	11,620Rp

Set Your Budget

➡ **Budget room** 150,000Rp

➡ **Meal** 30,000Rp

➡ **Beer** 15,000Rp

➡ **Two-tank dive** US$80

➡ **Long-distance bus** 100,000Rp

Entering the Country

Fly into Jakarta or Bali; flights to Sulawesi, Lombok etc also available. Ferries to Sumatra from Malaysia and Singapore are popular.

Don't Miss

With so many islands, it would be a shame not to get a sense of this vast archipelago by limiting your visit to only one or two; rather, see as many as possible. Ferries – never luxurious, often a bit squalid – provide myriad links and truly adventurous island-hopping. Shorten distances with flights on any of the many discount airlines and connect overland dots with buses bombing down the middle of the road at breakneck speeds.

ITINERARIES

One Week

This is a tough one, but Bali is the obvious choice. Spend a couple of days in the south, possibly partying in Seminyak and/or surfing and chilling on the Bukit Peninsula. Head up to Ubud for rice-field walks and intoxicating culture. Catch a fast boat to/from the nearby Gili Islands for a heaving travellers' scene.

One Month

Include your week on Bali and the Gilis, but start on Java and cross through the cultural city of Yogyakarta and the Unesco treasure of Borobudur. From Lombok catch ferries and buses across Sumbawa to Flores with stops at beaches and dragon-filled Komodo. Optionally finish your time following the spine of Sulawesi or head further east for Maluku's idyllic Banda Islands or track down orang-utans on Kalimantan or Sumatra.

Essential Outdoor Activities

➡ **Diving & Snorkelling** Diving highlights include western Flores and Komodo, the Gili Islands, Pulau Menjangan in Bali, Pulau Bunaken and the Togean Islands in Sulawesi, Pulau Weh in Sumatra, the Banda Islands in Maluku and the incredible Raja Ampat Islands in Papua.

➡ **Spas & Treatments** Bali leads the way, with a multitude of salons and spas in all the main travellers' centres.

➡ **Surfing** All the islands on the southern side of the Indonesian archipelago – from Sumatra to Timor – get reliable, often exceptional, and sometimes downright frightening surf. Many start at the legendary breaks of Bali's Bukit Peninsula, such as Ulu Watu.

➡ **Trekking** In Java, organised trekking centres on some spectacular volcano hikes such as Gunung Merapi. There's more variety in Bali, the location of the wonderful Gunung Batur region and the hills around Munduk, which offer walks amid cool hillside forests, spice plantations and waterfalls. Gunung Rinjani on Lombok is a dramatic and rewarding trek. On Sumatra, try the jungles of Bukit Lawang. The Baliem Valley in Papua is popular and Tana Toraja has fabulous trekking opportunities through Sulawesi's spectacular traditional villages.

JAVA

The heart of the nation, Java is an island of megacities and mesmerising natural beauty. It's the economic powerhouse of Indonesia, as well as the political epicentre, an island with complex, profound cultural traditions in art, dance, spiritualism and learning.

On first impressions many of the cities come across as pretty uninspiring; their pollution levels are high and they're plagued by environmental issues. That said, it's the cities, with their vibrant art and culture, that'll start you down the path to falling in love with Java.

Leaving the cities, you'll find an island of bewitching landscapes – iridescent rice paddies, gurgling streams, villages of terracotta-tiled houses and patches of dense jungle-clad hills. Verdant and fecund, this is one of the most fertile parts of Earth, with three annual crops possible in some regions. And with over 40 volcanoes forming a spiky central backbone, it's safe to say almost every journey in Java passes a succession of giant, often smoking cones.

ℹ Getting There & Away

AIR

Jakarta is Indonesia's busiest international arrival point and has numerous international connections on national and low-cost airlines to cities throughout Asia and beyond. Surabaya is the next-busiest airport for international flights while Yogyakarta, Solo (Surakarta) and Bandung all receive a few flights from other Southeast Asian cities.

BOAT

Java is a major hub for shipping services. Jakarta and Surabaya are the main ports for **Pelni ships** (www.pelni.co.id) although very few travellers get around Indonesia by long-distance ferry nowadays.

INDONESIA JAVA

Indonesia Highlights

① Surf by day, party at night and absorb the amazing culture in **Bali** (p191)

② Ascend the ancient Buddhist stupa of **Borobudur** (p179) before trawling the batik markets of bustling **Yogyakarta** (p171)

③ Peek at komodo dragons near booming **Labuanbajo** (p240) in Nusa Tenggara

④ Pay primate-to-primate respects to the 'man of the jungle', the **orang-utans** (p301) native to Sumatra and Kalimantan

⑤ Dive the pristine walls and coral canyons beneath seas of dimpled glass at **Pulau Bunaken** (p287) in Sulawesi

⑥ Explore the lovely time capsule that is Maluku's **Banda Islands** (p290)

⑦ Hike along raging rivers and scale exposed ridges to reach interior Papua's remote tribal villages in the **Baliem Valley** (p294)

Java

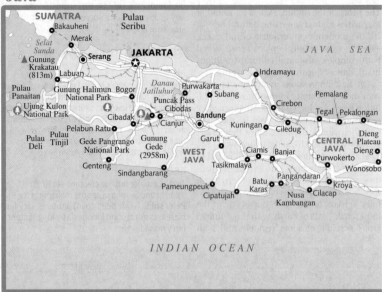

There are very frequent ferries between Java and Bali, and from Java to Sumatra.

ⓘ Getting Around

AIR

Domestic flight routes in Java are continuing to expand rapidly and can be quite inexpensive. Surabaya and Yogyakarta to Jakarta is very popular and is covered by several airlines.

BUS

Travel is often slow and nerve-racking; night buses are a little faster and a little more dangerous! Trains are better for the long hauls, but bus departures are more frequent.

Public buses, 'cooled' by a flow of sooty air from an open window, are very frequent, but they also stop for passengers every five minutes. Better air-con buses (known as Express) also run the major routes and are well worth paying the extra 25% for.

Small minibuses that cover shorter routes and back runs are commonly called *angkot* and shouldn't be confused with the door-to-door minibuses *(travel)*. The latter are air-con minibuses that travel all over Java and pick you up at your hotel and drop you off wherever you want to go in the destination city. These sound good in theory, but you can spend hours driving around the departure and arrival cities picking people up and dropping them off again.

LOCAL TRANSPORT

Dream up a way of getting around and you will find it somewhere on the streets of Java. *Ojek* (motorcycle taxis) are very widely available. *Dokar* (brightly coloured, horse-drawn cart, awash with jingling bells and psychedelic motifs) are a highlight.

TRAIN

Trains are usually quicker, more comfortable and more convenient than buses for getting between the main centres and are many a sensible backpackers' preferred means of transport.

Having said that, *Ekonomi* trains are dirt cheap, slow, crowded and often run late. Seats can be booked on the better *ekonomi plus* services. For a little extra, express trains with *bisnis* (business) and *eksekutif* (executive) sections are much better and seating is guaranteed. For air-con and more comfort, go for the top-of-the-range *argo* (luxury) trains; don't expect anything luxurious – cracked windows and semi-swept aisles are the norm – though compared to bus travel they are heaven indeed. Meals are available on the better class of trains.

For basic *ekonomi* trains, tickets go on sale an hour before departure. *Bisnis* and *eksekutif* trains can be booked weeks ahead, and the main stations have efficient, computerised booking offices for *eksekutif* trains. Try to book at least a day in advance, or several days beforehand, for travel on public holidays and long weekends.

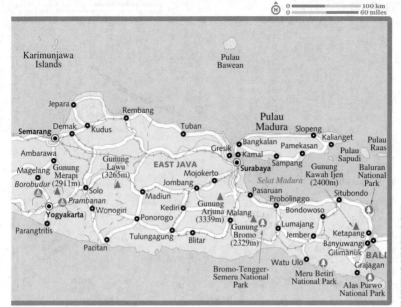

INDONESIA JAKARTA

The railway's **Train Information Service** (www.kereta-api.co.ide; in Indonesian) has more information (on the website, *Jadwal* means schedule).

Jakarta

☑ 021 / POP 10.19 MILLION

First impressions of Jakarta are not good. One of the world's greatest megalopolises, its grey, relentlessly urban sprawl spreads for tens of traffic-snarled kilometres across a flood-prone plain with barely a park to break the concrete monotony.

And yet beneath the unappealing facade of high-rises, slums and gridlocked streets, this is a city of surprises and many faces. From the steamy, richly scented streets of the old quarter to the city's riotous, decadent nightlife, Jakarta is filled with unexpected corners. Spend a Sunday on the pedestrianised streets of the old colonial Kota neighbourhood laughing over street performers, enjoying a *wayang* (leather puppet) performance and mingling with locals and tourists at the venerable Café Batavia and you'll start to see that the 'Big Durian' is actually a highly cultured and artistic city with a huge amount going for it.

Metropolitan Jakarta sprawls 28km from the docks to the southern suburbs. Soekarno's national monument in Lapangan Merdeka (Freedom Sq) is an excellent central landmark. North of the monument is the older part of Jakarta, which includes Chinatown, the former Dutch area of Kota and the old port of Sunda Kelapa. Tanjung Priok, the main harbour, is several kilometres further east. The sprawling modern suburbs of Jakarta are south of the monument.

Jl Thamrin is the main north–south street of the new city and has Jakarta's big hotels and banks. A couple of blocks east along Jl Kebon Sirih Raya is Jl Jaksa, the cheap accommodation centre of Jakarta.

◉ Sights & Activities

◎ Kota

Jakarta's crumbling historic heart is Kota, home to the remnants of the Dutch capital of Batavia. **Taman Fatahillah**, the old town square, features cracked cobblestones, postcard vendors, fine colonial buildings, a flurry of museums and, on weekends, masses of locals enjoying a carnival-like atmosphere. Trains from Gondangdia, near Jl Jaksa, run here. A taxi will cost around 50,000Rp from Jl Thamrin. In and around Taman Fatahillah are a number of interesting buildings and monuments including the **Gereja Sion**

Jakarta

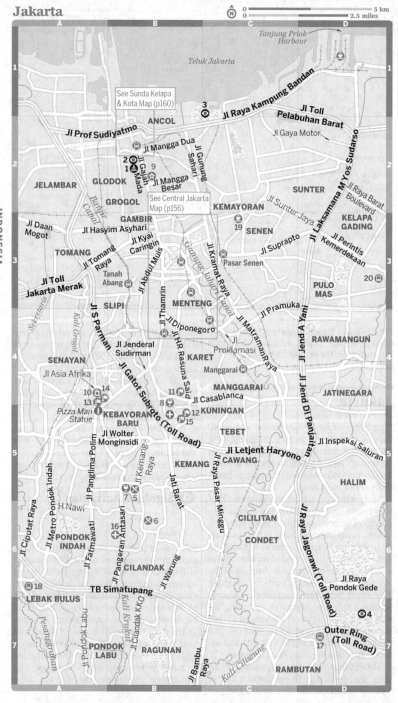

N

0 ———————————— 5 km
0 ———————————— 2.5 miles

INDONESIA

Tanjung Priok Harbour

Teluk Jakarta

Jl Raya Kampung Bandan

Jl Toll Pelabuhan Barat

See Sunda Kelapa & Kota Map (p160)

3

ANCOL

Jl Prof Sudiyatmo

Jl Gaya Motor

Jl Mangga Dua

Jl Gunung Sahari

2
1
9

Jl Gajah Mada

GLODOK

JELAMBAR

Jl Mangga Besar

GROGOL

See Central Jakarta Map (p156)

KEMAYORAN

SUNTER

Jl Laksamana M Yos Sudarso

Jl Raya Barat Boulevard

KELAPA GADING

GAMBIR

Jl Daan Mogot

Jl Hasyim Asyhari

Jl Sunter Jaya

19

SENEN

Jl Suprapto

Jl Perintis Kemerdekaan

Jl Kyai Caringin

Jl Tomang Raya

TOMANG

Tanah Abang

Jl Abdul Muis

Jl Kramat Raya

Pasar Senen

20

PULO MAS

Jl Toll Jakarta Merak

SLIPI

Jl S Parman

Jl Thamrin

MENTENG

Jl Diponegoro

Gunung Jati Canal

Jl Pramuka

Jl Jend A Yani

RAWAMANGUN

Jl Jenderal Sudirman

Jl HR Rasuna Said

KARET

Jl Proklamasi

Jl Mataram Raya

SENAYAN

Jl Asia Afrika

Jl Gatot Subroto (Toll Road)

Manggarai

MANGGARAI

Jl Casablanca

11

JATINEGARA

10 14
13
Pizza Man Statue

KEBAYORAN BARU

8

12
15

KUNINGAN

TEBET

Jl Jend DI Panjaitan

Jl Inspeksi Saluran

Jl Wolter Monginsidi

Jl Pangeran Antasari

Jl Panglima Polim

Jl Kemang Raya

KEMANG

Jl Letjent Haryono

CAWANG

HALIM

Jl Raya Pasar Minggu

Jati Barat

7 5

Jl Metro Pondok Indah

H Nawi

16

CILILITAN

CONDET

Jl Raya Jagorawi (Toll Road)

6

Jl Ciputat Raya

PONDOK INDAH

Jl Fatmawati

CILANDAK

Jl Warung

Jl Raya Pondok Gede

18

TB Simatupang

LEBAK BULUS

Jl Pondok Labu

Jl Cilandak KKO

Kali Krukut

4

Outer Ring (Toll Road)

17

PONDOK LABU

RAGUNAN

Jl Bambu Raya

Kali Ciliwung

RAMBUTAN

Pesanggrahan

Jakarta

(Map p160; Jl Pangeran Jayakarta), which is the oldest remaining church in Jakarta. It was built in 1695 for the 'black Portuguese' brought to Batavia as slaves and given their freedom if they joined the Dutch Reformed Church.

The old Portuguese cannon **Si Jagur** (Mr Fertility; Map p160; Taman Fatahillah) was believed to be a cure for barrenness because of its suggestive clenched fist, and women sat astride it in the hope of bearing children. It's in the courtyard of the Museum Sejarah Jakarta.

Some fine Dutch architecture lines the grotty Kali Besar canal, including the **Toko Merah** (Map p160; Jl Kali Besar Barat, Red Shop), formerly the home of Governor General van Imhoff. Further north, the last remaining Dutch drawbridge, the **Chicken Market Bridge**, spans the canal.

Also don't miss a drink at the Café Batavia, which drips with colonial nostalgia.

Museum Bank Indonesia   MUSEUM
(Map p160; Pintu Besar Utara III; audio guides 50,000Rp; ⊙8.30am-3.30pm Tue-Fri, 8am-4pm Sat & Sun) **FREE** One of the nation's best, this museum is dedicated to the history of Indonesia from a loosely financial perspective, in a grand, expertly restored, neoclassical former bank headquarters that dates from the early 20th century. All the displays (including lots of zany audiovisuals) are slickly presented and engaging, with exhibits about the spice trade, the financial meltdown of 1997 (and subsequent riots) and a gallery dedicated to currency, with notes from virtually every country in the world.

Museum Wayang   MUSEUM
(Map p160; ☑021-692 9560; Taman Fatahillah; admission 5000Rp; ⊙9am-3pm Tue-Sun) This puppet museum has one of the best collections of *wayang* puppets in Java and its dusty cabinets are full of a multitude of characters from across Indonesia, as well as China, Vietnam, India, Cambodia and Europe. The building itself dates from 1912. There are free *wayang* performances here on Sunday at 10am.

Museum Sejarah Jakarta   MUSEUM
(Map p160; Taman Fatahillah; admission 5000Rp; ⊙9am-3pm Tue-Sun) The Jakarta History Museum is a poorly presented museum of peeling plasterwork and lots of heavy, carved ebony and teak furniture from the Dutch period (plus a disparate collection of exhibits collected from across the nation). But you will find the odd exquisite piece, such as the stunning black granite sculpture of Kali, a Hindu goddess associated with death and destruction.

Maybe a bigger highlight than the contents is the building the museum is housed in: it's the old town hall of Batavia, a stately Dutch colonial structure that was once the epicentre of an empire. This bell-towered building, built in 1627, served the administration of the city and was also used by the city law courts.

Balai Seni Rupa   MUSEUM
(Map p160; Taman Fatahillah; admission 5000Rp; ⊙9am-3pm Tue-Sun) Built between 1866 and 1870, the former Palace of Justice building is now a Fine Arts Museum. It houses contemporary paintings with works by prominent artists, including Affandi, Raden Saleh and Ida Bagus Made. Part of the building is also a ceramics museum, with Chinese ceramics and Majapahit terracottas.

INDONESIA JAKARTA

Central Jakarta

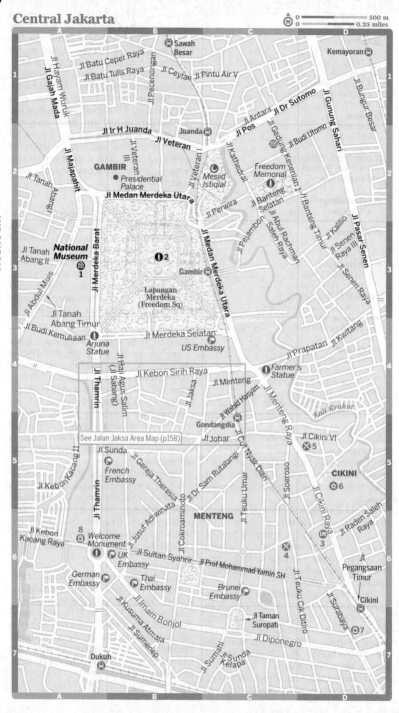

0   500 m
0   0.25 miles

Central Jakarta

◎ Sunda Kelapa

Among the hubbub, floating debris and oil slicks, the old Dutch **port** (Sunda Kelapa harbour; admission 2000Rp) is still used by magnificent Buginese *pinisi* (fishing boats), their cargo unloaded by teams of porters walking along wobbly gangplanks. Someone can normally be found to take the old sea-dogs among you out onto the waters in a **rowing boat** (Sunda Kelapa harbour; very negotiable 40,000Rp for 30min). Go at dawn or dusk when water-borne activity reaches the crest of a wave. The port is a 1km walk from Taman Fatahillah, or take one of the area's unique push-bike taxis known as *ojek sepeda* (2500Rp).

Museum Bahari   MUSEUM
(Map p160; www.museumbahari.org; admission 2000Rp; ◷9am-4pm Tue-Sun) Near the entrance to Sunda Kelapa, several old Dutch East India Company (VOC) warehouses (dating back to 1652) have been converted into the Museum Bahari. This is a good place to learn about the city's maritime history, and though the wonderful old buildings (some renovated) are echoingly empty there are some good information panels (in English and Bahasa Indonesia).

Pasar Ikan   MARKET
(Market; Map p160) The early-morning Pasar Ikan, or fish market, is an intense, colourful scene of busy crowds around dawn, when the day's catch is sold. Later in the day you'll find souvenir sellers here.

◎ Lapangan Merdeka

★ **National Museum**   MUSEUM
(Map p156; Jln Merdeka Barat 12; admission 10,000Rp; ◷8am-4pm Tue-Thu, 8am-11.30am & 1-4pm Fri, 8am-5pm Sat & Sun) The sensational National Museum has an excellent collection of ethnographic displays from across the archipelago, which brings home just how utterly diverse this nation is. Upstairs is a glittering, jewel-encrusted treasure room while the impressive new wing houses displays related to prehistoric life in Indonesia and includes a tiny skull of a 'Flores Hobbit' – the tiny hominoid unearthed on Flores island in 2004.

Other highlights include fine exhibits of Han ceramics, ancient Hindu statuary and magnificent *kris* (traditional dagger) handles studded with rubies.

This museum is also known as Gedung Gajah (Elephant House) on account of the bronze elephant outside, which was donated by the king of Thailand in 1871. At the time of research half the museum was closed for renovations.

National Monument   MONUMENT
(Map p156; admission 5000Rp; ◷8am-3pm, closed last Mon of every month) Soekarno attempted to tame Jakarta by giving it a central space, Lapangan Merdeka (Freedom Sq), and topping it with a gigantic monument to his machismo. The towering, 132m-high column, capped with a gilded flame, has been dubbed 'Soekarno's last erection' and one look at it and you'll see why – what was the architect thinking? For an extra 5000Rp you can whiz up the 'shaft' for a shot of the city.

◎ Other Areas

Taman Mini Indonesia Indah   AMUSEMENT PARK
(Map p154; ☏021-545 4545; www.tamanmini.com; Jl Raya Jagorawi; adult/child 9000/6000Rp; ◷8am-6pm) In the city's southeast, Taman Mini Indonesia Indah is a 'whole country in one park'.

This 100-hectare park has full-scale traditional houses for each of Indonesia's provinces, with displays of regional handicrafts and clothing. Museums, theatres and an IMAX cinema are scattered throughout the grounds, which all command additional entrance fees. Free cultural performances are staged (around 10am); Sunday is the big

INDONESIA JAKARTA

Jalan Jaksa Area

day for cultural events, but shows are also held during the week.

You can walk, drive, take a shuttle bus or use the monorail or cable car to get around the park. Taman Mini is about 18km from the city centre. To get there, take a Koridor 7 bus to the Kampung Rambutan terminal and then a T15 metro-mini to the park entrance. A taxi from central Jakarta costs about 85,000Rp.

Taman Impian Jaya Ancol   AMUSEMENT PARK
(Map p154; ☑ 021-6471 0497; www.ancol.com; basic admission incl entry to Pasar Seni 17,500Rp; ☉ 24hr) On Jakarta's bay front, the people's 'Dreamland' is a landscaped recreation complex. It has amusement rides and sporting and leisure facilities.

Prime attractions include the Pasar Seni (Art Market), which has sidewalk cafes, a host of craft shops, cable-car rides, art exhibitions, and live jazz every Friday (at 8.30pm)

and **Seaworld** (Map p154; ☑ 021 641 0080; www.seaworldindonesia.com; 60,000Rp; ☉ 9am-6pm), with its 'sharkquarium', bored looking manatees and turtles.

Koridor 5 of the busway runs to Ancol. A taxi will cost around 50,000Rp from Jl Thamrin.

✯ Festivals & Events

Jakarta has a packed calendar of festivals, fairs and other events. These are only some of the biggest or more tourist-friendly. For the full run-down get hold of a copy of the free *Jakarta Calendar of Events*, published annually and available from the tourist office.

Java Jazz Festival   FESTIVAL
(www.javajazzfestival.com) Held sometime between late February and early March at the Jakarta Convention Center in Senayan. Attracts acclaimed international artists.

CULTURAL CONSIDERATIONS

Generally Indonesians are a relaxed lot, but that's no reason to go rudely trampling their sensibilities.

➡ Indonesia is a conservative, largely Muslim country, and while bikinis and Speedos are tolerated in the beach resorts of Bali, try to respect local clothing traditions wherever possible. This is particularly true near a mosque.

➡ Couples should avoid canoodling or kissing in public.

➡ You have to haggle in Indonesia, but it's important to do so respectfully and learn when to draw the line. It's very bad form to shout or lose your temper. Remember that a few extra rupiah may make a great deal of difference to the other party.

➡ A little Bahasa Indonesia, which is very easy to pick up, will get you a long way. Not only will you delight the locals, but it'll save you cash when it comes to dealing with stall owners, hoteliers and becak drivers.

Jakarta Anniversary   EVENT

The 22nd of June marks the establishment of the city in 1527. Celebrated with fireworks and the Jakarta Fair.

Jalan Jaksa Street Fair   FESTIVAL

Features Betawi dance, theatre and music, art and photography. Held for one week in August.

Independence Day   EVENT

Indonesia's independence is celebrated on 17 August and the parades in Jakarta are the biggest in the country.

🛏 Sleeping

Jl Jaksa is Jakarta's budget-hotel enclave and there are plenty of cheap beds (and beers) on offer. There's a cosmopolitan atmosphere, as the area is also a popular place for Jakarta's young intelligentsia and artistic types to socialise. Jaksa is a short stroll from the main drag, Jl Thamrin, close to Gambir train station and even closer to Gondangdia train station, though not all trains stop there.

Cikini (south) and Menteng (southeast) of Jaksa have a selection of decent midrange hotels, a guesthouse or two and some excellent restaurants and cafes.

All but one of the following budget places are found in and around Jl Jaksa.

★Six Degrees   HOSTEL $

(Map p156; ☎ 021-314 1657; www.jakarta-backpackers-hostel.com; Jl Cikini Raya 60 B-C, Cikini; dm 120,000-135,000Rp, s/d 170,000/250,000Rp; ☀❄@🛜) This hostel, run by a helpful, friendly, informative Irish/English/Sumatran team, is putting a smile on the face of many a backpacker. There's a relaxed, sociable atmosphere thanks to the pool table

and large-screen TV and you'll find plenty of bathrooms and toilets, a guests' kitchen and roof garden.

The dorms are a bit of a squeeze, but clean and the more expensive ones are like Japanese-style 'pod' hotels. Breakfast is included. It's tricky to find, but located next to Texas Chicken and close to the 7-11 Supermarket in Cikini.

★Hostel 35   GUESTHOUSE $

(Map p158; ☎ 021-392 0331; Jl Kebon Sirih Barat I 35; r with fan/air-con 150,000/250,000Rp; ☀❄🛜) Boasting charm, character and comfort, this is an excellent budget hotel, located just off the main Jaksa drag. The lobby/lounge area with rattan sofas is very inviting and decorated with fine textiles and tasteful photography. The sixteen rooms are neat and attractive (all but two have private bathrooms).

Borneo Hostel   GUESTHOUSE $

(Map p158; ☎ 021-314 0095; Jl Kebon Sirih Barat Dalam 37; r with fan & share bathroom 100,000Rp, with fan/air-con 130,000/200,000Rp; ❄) A cheerful place with a warm, family atmosphere and polished rooms (see those bathrooms sparkle) set around a plant-filled courtyard. The tiny fans won't do much to keep you cool at night, though. It's on a peaceful side street.

Alinda Hotel   HOTEL $

(Map p158; ☎ 021-314 0373; www.alinda-hotel.com; Jl Kebon Sirih Barat VI 9; r with fan/air-con 180,000/290,000Rp; ❄@🛜) Well-organised, clean and welcoming this large place definitely feels like a 'proper' hotel not a backpackers' crash pad. The rooms are clean and quite spacious, with a wardrobe and decent beds, and the location is quiet.

Bloem Steen Homestay   GUESTHOUSE $

(Map p158; ☎ 021-3192 5389; Gang I 173; s/d with fan 70,000/90,000Rp, with air-con 150,000Rp; ❄🛜) Age-old place with 18 no-frills rooms, all with shared bathrooms, and a pleasant front terrace for chilling with a beer or a tea. It's clean enough (shoes off at the door, folks!) and staff are reasonably welcoming.

Memories   GUESTHOUSE $

(Map p158; ☎ 021-316 2548; Jl Jaksa 17; r with fan 100,000Rp, with air-con 175,00-200,000Rp; ❄🛜) Right above one of Jaksa's most popular backpacker bar-restaurants, these small and fairly uninspiring rooms are ideal if you want to sink a Bintang or two and not worry about getting lost on the way home. Just don't fall down the stairs.

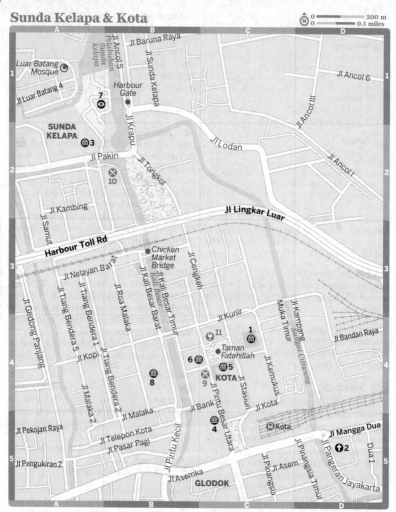

Wisma Delima GUESTHOUSE **$**
(Map p158; ☑ 021-319 04157; Jl Jaksa 5; s/d with shared mandi 75,000/85,000Rp) The original guesthouse on Jl Jaksa, with poky, ultra-basic rooms, but it's secure and dirt cheap.

Ristana Ratu Hotel HOTEL **$$**
(Map p158; ☑ 021-314 2464; Jl Jaksa 7-9; r 210,000-325,000Rp; ✳ ☎) Standards have remained quite high at this small hotel, which is set off the street. The large rooms offer style and comfort with great beds, bright duvets and soft pillows. You'll find a little cafe downstairs for your breakfast (included for the more expensive accommodation).

✗ Eating

✗ Jl Jaksa Area

Jl Jaksa is fine for no-nonsense, inexpensive, but toned down, Indonesian fare as well as sloppy Western dishes of the classic backpacker ilk. For something more authentic, head to the night-hawker stalls grouped around the southern end of Jl Hagi Agus Salim (also known as Jl Sabang), which is famous for its street food (including satay).

Sunda Kelapa & Kota

KL Village MALAY, INDONESIAN **$**
(Map p158; ✆021-3192 5219; Jl Jaksa 21-23; mains from 17,000Rp; ⊙7am-11pm Sun-Wed, 24hr Thu-Sat; 🛜) Ever-popular Malaysian-style place that serves up inexpensive grub such as black-pepper chicken, *canai* (Malay-Indian bread) and *murtabak* (stuffed pancake). If you're suffering after a long flight (or a long night), try one of the health-kick juices: 'heart and the brain' or 'sugar balance'.

Sate Khas Senayan SATE, INDONESIAN **$**
(Map p158; ✆021-3192 6238; Jl Kebon Sirih Raya 31A; mains 30,000-50,000Rp; ⊙11.30am-10pm; 🛜) Upmarket air-conditioned restaurant at the northern end of Jl Jaksa. It is renowned for its superb *sate* – sticked-up in chicken, beef and lamb forms – plus Indonesian favourites such as *ayam goreng kremes* (fried chicken in batter) and *gurame bakar* (grilled fish).

Daoen Sirih INDONESIAN **$**
(Map p158; Jl Kebon Sirih 41-43; meals 12,000-25,000Rp; ⊙11am-10pm; 🌿) A short stroll northwest of Jalan Jaksa, this large bamboo-roofed, open-sided food court has a wide selection of Indonesia cook-shacks offering Indonesian noodles, and dishes such as *nasi goreng kambing* (spicy rice with goat) and *sate madura* (skewered meat with sweet soy sauce), as well as espresso coffee. It's non touristy and a great place to mingle with locals.

Memories INTERNATIONAL **$**
(Map p158; Jl Jaksa 17; mains 14,000Rp; ⊙24hr) A classic Jaksa haunt of fresh-in-town backpackers and seen-it-all expats. There are plenty of local dishes, lots of Chinese flavours and some ho-hum Western food, including popular set breakfasts. There's also a book exchange and lots of traveller talk.

🍴 Other Areas

The upmarket suburb of Kemang, with plenty of stylish bars, clubs and restaurants, is popular with expats, but backpackers are a rare species here. It does, however, have a couple of food courts where you can chow down on the cheap before clubbing till dawn. A taxi from Jl Jaksa area (45,000Rp to 80,000Rp depending on traffic) can easily take over an hour thanks to the crazy traffic, and Kemang doesn't sit on any handy TransJakarta busway route.

The Kota neighbourhood has a few options. Most are aimed at the tourist market (both domestic and international) but they're generally very pleasant places for a slow lunch in-between bouts of sightseeing.

D'Fest FOOD COURT **$**
(Map p154; Jl Kemang Raya 19C; ⊙5pm-midnight) Very sociable and popular open-air food court complete with stylish sofa seating and lots of international and local food stalls. It has Middle Eastern kebab joints, lots of Japanese options, *soto* (soup) places, *roti canai* (Malay-Indian flaky flat bread), plus a beer hall. There's often live music here on weekend nights.

LARA DJONGGRANG & KINARA

If a never-ending diet of *nasi goreng* is leaving you a little jaded, Jakarta is a great place to splash out on something that'll make your taste buds love you again. **Lara Djonggrang** (Map p156; ✆315 3252; www.tuguhotels.com/lara djonggrang; Jl Teuku Cik Ditiro 4; mains 48,000-170,000Rp; ⊙12.30pm-11pm; 🛜), where you dine surrounded by museum-worthy statues, antiques and temple treasures, is a very civilised setting for sublime Imperial Javanese cuisine. For the spice girls (and boys) among you, **Kinara** (Map p154; ✆719 2677; www. kinara.co.id; Jl Kemang Raya 78B; mains 60,000-80,000Rp; ⊙11.30am-11pm; 🛜), with its mock medieval doors and an opulent interior of grand arches, is an impressive setting for some of the finest Indian dishes in Jakarta – plump samosas, sublime chicken tikka and plenty of vegetarian choices.

VOC Galangan INDONESIAN $

(Map p160; 021-667 8501; Jl Kakap I; snacks & meals from 15,000Rp; ⊙9am-5pm) This atmospheric cafe occupies the premises of a beautifully restored warehouse dating back to 1628. Enjoy a drink or meal inside the beamed interior or on the terrace, which overlooks a grassy courtyard containing a vintage car and horse-buggy carriage. Prices are reasonable for dishes such as *gado gado* (vegetables with peanut sauce) or *sup buntut* (oxtail soup).

Djakarté Kedai Senai INDONESIAN $

(Map p160; Jl Pintu Besar Utara 17; mains 20,000-40,000Rp) One of several similar places around Taman Fatahillah, this is in the ground floor basement of an old Dutch building. You can eat inside under the cool of the ceiling fans or sweat it out on the outdoor tables. The cheap and tasty dishes are of the *nasi goreng*–style Indonesian comfort food.

Vietopia VIETNAMESE $$

(Map p156; 021-391 5893; Jl Cikini Raya 33; mains 35,000-60,000Rp; ⊙11.30am-10.30pm; ☎) A highly enjoyable, stylish and relaxing destination for a meal, this authentic Vietnamese place offers delicious moderately priced and delicately spiced cooking, including flavoursome *pho bo* (beef broth) and other classics from Indochina.

 Drinking & Nightlife

If you're expecting Jakarta, as the capital of the world's largest Muslim country, to be a pretty sober city with little in the way of drinking culture, think again. From expat pubs to gorgeous lounge bars with cocktail lists set at (near) London or New York prices, and far more beautiful people, Jakarta has it all. The bar zone on Jl Falatehan near Blok M (6km southwest of Jl Jaksa) is a good all-round bet, with everything from European-style pubs, where you can shoot pool and sip wine, to raucous bar-clubs with heaving dance floors.

Jakarta is the clubbing mecca of Southeast Asia. The city has some great venues (from dark 'n' sleazy to polished and pricey), internationally renowned DJs, world-class sound systems and some of the planet's longest party sessions (some clubs open around the clock for entire weekends). Entrance is typically 50,000Rp to 100,000Rp, but includes a free drink. Clubs open around 9pm, but don't really get going until midnight; most close around 4am.

If you're young enough to backpack but too old and sleepy to party the night away,

Jakarta has plenty of more-civilised nightlife options from theatre to dance and cinema.

★**Potato Head** BAR

(Map p154; www.ptthead.com/Jakarta; Pacific Place Mall, Jl Sudirman 52-53; ☎) Brilliant warehouse-style bar-bistro with remarkable artistic decor (including a living green wall, lots of statement art and vintage seating) that also promotes music and cultural events. The food recieves mixed reviews so come for the liquid instead.

Café Batavia BAR

(Map p160; Jl Pintu Besar Utara 14) This historic, classy (but frankly overpriced) restaurant, inside an old Dutch era building with teak floors and art-deco furnishings, doubles as an evocative place for a cocktail, a cool Bintang or a coffee.

Eastern Promise PUB

(Map p154; 021-7179 0151; www.easternpromise-jakarta.com; Jl Kemang Raya 5; ☎) A classic British-style pub in the heart of Kemang, with a pool table, welcoming atmosphere and filling Western and Indian grub. Service is prompt and friendly, the beer's cold and there's live music on weekends. It's a key expat hang-out and rammed at weekends.

★**Stadium** CLUB

(Map p154; 021-626 3323; www.stadiumjakarta.com; Jl Hayum Waruk III FF-JJ) This hardcore club is a Jakartan institution, drawing the world's leading DJs (such as Sasha and Derek May) and a loyal crowd of regulars with tribal house and techno.

 Entertainment

Check the entertainment pages of *Time Out Jakarta* or *Jakarta Kini* for films, concerts and special events.

Taman Ismail Marzuki PERFORMING ARTS

(TIM; Map p156; 021-3193 7325; www.tamanismailmarzuki.com; Jl Cikini Raya 73) Jakarta's premier cultural centre, the Taman Ismail Marzuki, or TIM, has a great selection of cinemas, theatres and exhibition spaces. Performances (such as Sundanese dance and *gamelan* music events) are always high quality and the complex has a couple of good casual restaurants too.

🔒 **Shopping**

Given the climate, it's not surprising that Jakartans love their air-conditioned malls – there are over 100 in the metropolitan area.

Periplus   BOOKS
(Map p154; ☑ 021-718 7070; level 3, Jl Asia Afrika, Plaza Senayan; ⊙9am-7pm) Excellent selection of English-language magazines and books: fiction and nonfiction (including Lonely Planet guides). You'll find branches in Kemang and Plaza Indonesia too.

Plaza Indonesia   MALL
(Map p156; www.plazaindonesia.com; Jl Thamrin; 🛜) This mall is centrally located and very classy, with a wide selection of stores that include leading Indonesian design boutiques and the likes of Cartier and Lacroix. In the basement there's an excellent, inexpensive food mall.

Pasar Seni   MARKET
(Art Market; Jl Raya Kampung Bandan; ⊙10am-10pm) For arts and crafts. Also check out Pasar Seni, at Taman Impian Jaya Ancol.

Flea Market   MARKET
(Map p156; Jl Surabaya) Jakarta's famous flea market is in Menteng. It has woodcarvings, furniture, textiles, jewellery, old vinyl records and many (dubious) antiques. Bargain like crazy.

ℹ Information

DANGERS & ANNOYANCES
Considering its size and the scale of poverty, Jakarta is generally a safe city and security incidents are rare. That said, you should be careful late at night in Glodok and Kota – muggings do occasionally occur – and only use reputable taxi companies, such as the citywide Bluebird group. Keep your eyes open on buses and trains, which are a favourite haunt of pickpockets. It's wise to steer clear of political and religious demonstrations. In the past some high-profile Western chain hotels have been targeted by terrorists.

Dengue fever outbreaks occur in the wet season, so come armed with mosquito repellent.

EMERGENCY
Fire (☑ 113)
Police (☑ 110)
Medical Help (☑ 119, 118)
Tourist Police (Map p158; ☑ 021-566000; Jl Wahid Hasyim) On the 2nd floor of the Jakarta Theatre.

INTERNET ACCESS
Internet cafes are scattered all over Jakarta and generally charge between 4000Rp and 10,000Rp per hour. There are several places in and around Jl Jaksa, although as almost every backpacker is now travelling with an internet-enabled device and all but the very cheapest doss house hotels

WORTH A TRIP

CHINA TOWN
· ·

The neighbourhood of Glodok, the traditional enclave of the Chinese, is a district full of bustling lanes, street markets and a shabby mall or two.

Most of the fun here is simply experiencing the (very) Chinese vibe of the place, eating some dumplings and browsing the myriad stalls and stores selling everything from traditional medicines to dodgy DVDs.

Be sure to wander around the **Petak Sembilan Street Market** (Map p154) with its skinned frogs and live bugs for sale next to an open sewer.

A few steps from Petak Sembilan Street Market is the **Jin de Yuan** (Dharma Bhakti Temple; Map p154; www.jindeyuan.org; Jl Kemenangan III 13) Chinese Buddhist temple. Dating from 1755 its incense- and candle-smoke-scented interior is crammed with statues of the Buddha and there's some wonderful calligraphy.

have wi-fi access, internet cafes are becoming less and less of a concern for many a traveller.

MEDICAL SERVICES
Hospital (Map p154)
SOS Medika Klinik (Map p154; ☑ 021-750 6001; www.sosindonesia.com; Jl Puri Sakti 10, Cipete) Offers English-speaking GP appointments, dental care, and emergency and specialist healthcare services.

MONEY
There are banks all over the city, and you're never far from an ATM in Jakarta.

POST
Main Post Office (Map p156; Jl Gedung Kesenian 1; ⊙8am-7pm Mon-Fri, to 1pm Sat)

TOURIST INFORMATION
Jakarta Visitor Information Office (Map p158; ☑ 316 1293, 021-314 2067; www.jakarta-tourism.go.id; Jl Wahid Hasyim 9; ⊙9am-7pm Mon-Fri, to 4pm Sat) Inside the Jakarta Theatre building. A helpful office; the staff here can answer many queries and set you up with tours of West Java. Practical information can be lacking but it does have a good stock of leaflets and publications and a colour map. There's also a desk at the airport.

ℹ Getting There & Away

Jakarta is the main travel hub for Indonesia, with flights and ships to destinations all over the archipelago. Buses depart for cities across Java, and for Bali and Sumatra, while trains are an excellent way to get across Java.

AIR

Soekarno-Hatta International Airport (www.jakartaairportonline.com) is 35km northwest of the city.

For onwards domestic travel, you can fly from Jakarta to almost every major Indonesian city on a daunting array of airlines.

BOAT

The **Pelni ticket office** (Map p154; ☎ 021-6385 0960; www.pelni.com; Jl Angkasa 18; ⊗ 8am-4pm Mon-Fri, to 1pm Sat) is 13km northeast of the city centre in Kemayoran. Tickets (plus commission) can be bought through numerous Pelni agents (many travel agents sell them).

Pelni ships all arrive at and depart from Pelabuhan Satu (Dock No 1) at Tanjung Priok, 13km northeast of the city centre. When they are (eventually) completed, Busway Koridor 10 and 12 should provide the fastest connection to the port. A taxi from Jl Jaksa costs about 70,000Rp to 90,000Rp.

BUS

So many buses leave Jakarta's bus stations that you can usually just front up at the station and join the chaos, though it pays to book ahead. Travel agencies on Jl Jaksa sell tickets and usually include transport to the terminal, which saves a lot of hassle, though they'll charge a commission for this. Jakarta has four main bus stations, all well out of the city centre. There are buses that will take you to each station from the city centre.

Kalideres Bus Terminal Located 15km northwest of the city centre and has frequent buses to destinations west of Jakarta. Take a Koridor 3 TransJakarta bus to get here.

Kampung Rambutan Bus Terminal (Map p154) This terminal is 18km south of the city and primarily handles buses to destinations south and southeast of Jakarta, such as Bogor (normal/air-con 8000/10,00Rp, one hour) and Cianjur (25,000Rp, three hours). Koridor 7 TransJakarta buses serve this terminal.

Pulo Gadung Bus Terminal (Map p154) Located 12km east of the city centre, serves central and eastern Java, Sumatra and Bali. Destinations include Yogyakarta (normal/air-con 110,000/175,000Rp, 12 hours). Koridor 4 or 2 TransJakarta buses serve here.

Lebak Bulus Bus Terminal (Map p154) Lebuk Bulus is 16km southwest of the city and also handles some deluxe buses to Yogyakarta, Surabaya and Bali. Most departures are in the late afternoon or evening. When completed Koridor 8 TransJakarta buses will whisk you out here.

MINIBUS

Door-to-door *travel* minibuses are not a good option in Jakarta because it can take hours to pick up or drop off passengers in the traffic jams. Some travel agencies book them, but you may have to go to a depot on the city outskirts.

TRAIN

Jakarta's four main train stations are quite central, making trains the easiest way out of the city. The most convenient and important is Gambir train station, on the eastern side of Merdeka Sq, a 15-minute walk from Jl Jaksa. Gambir handles express trains to Bogor, Bandung, Yogyakarta, Solo, Semarang and Surabaya. Some Gambir trains also stop at Kota train station in the north

---

WORTH A TRIP

BANDUNG

Big and burly, Bandung is not a place for those who crave peace and tranquillity. Once dubbed the 'Paris of Java', this is one of Indonesia's megacities (the Bandung conurbation has more than seven million inhabitants), with a city centre that's prone to Jakarta-style congestion. Few travellers make a concerted effort to come here, but rummage through the concrete sprawl and odd pockets of interest remain, including some Dutch art-deco monuments, the quirky fibreglass statues of Jeans St and some cool cafes popular with the thousands of students who call this city home.

The main drag, Jl Asia Afrika, runs through the heart of the city centre past the *alun alun* (main public square). Many of Bandung's cheapest places are close to the train station on Jl Kebonjati and are looking quite run down these days, plus the area is very dark after nightfall. Backpackers should up their budgets in this prosperous city. The most popular hotel with travellers is **Hotel Kenangan** (☎ 022-421 3244; www.kenanganhotel.com; Jl Kebon Sirih 4; r incl breakfast with fan/air-con from 195,000/245,000Rp; ❋ ☎) which is very central and has modern, comfortable rooms.

of the city. The Pasar Senen train station is to the east and mostly has *ekonomi*-class trains. Tanah Abang train station has *ekonomi* trains to the west.

There's a (slightly pricey) taxi booking desk inside Gambir train station; the fare to Jl Jaksa is 35,000Rp.

For express trains, tickets can be bought in advance at the booking offices at the northern end of Gambir train station, while the ticket windows at the southern end are only for tickets bought on the day of departure. Check timetables online at www.kereta-api.co.id (in Bahasa Indonesian), or consult the helpful staff at the station's **information office** (☑ 021-386 2363).

Bogor

No frills commuter trains (5000Rp, 1¼ hours) leave from Cikini train stations roughly every hour. They can be horribly crowded during rush hours (watch your gear).

Surabaya

Most trains between Jakarta and Surabaya take the shorter northern route via Semarang, though a few take the longer southern route via Yogyakarta. *Eksekutif* class trains from Gambir leave four times daily (450,000Rp, eight to 10 hours). Cheaper, and slower, *ekonomi* trains leave from Pasar Senen station (55,000Rp to 350,000Rp).

Yogyakarta & Solo

Luxury trains depart from Gambir station several times daily (380,000Rp, 8¼ hours). These trains go to Solo and stop at Yogyakarta, 45 minutes before Solo, but cost the same to either destination. Cheaper trains leave from Pasar Senen station (180,000 Rp to 210,000Rp).

ℹ Getting Around

Taxis and the TransJakarta busway network are most travellers' normal way of getting about the city. Other buses are not very useful for visitors, as they are much slower, hotter (they have no air-conditioning) and crowded (pickpockets can be a problem). Nevertheless, you may come across regular city buses, *patas* (express) buses and orange Metro minibuses from time to time; fares generally cost between 2000Rp and 3000Rp.

TO/FROM THE AIRPORT

Soekarno-Hatta International Airport is 35km northwest of the city – 50 minutes away via a toll road when traffic is light and the taxi driver inspired, but up to two hours away during rush hour/traffic-jam hour (which to be honest seems to be most of the time).

Damri (☑ 550 1290, 021-460 3708; www.damri.co.id) buses (20,000Rp, every 30 minutes, 5am to 7pm) run between the airport and Gambir train station (near Jl Jaksa) and points in the city, including Blok M.

Taxis from the airport to Jl Thamrin/Jl Jaksa cost about 250,000Rp including tolls. Book via the official taxi desks to be safe, rather than using the unlicensed drivers outside. Going in the opposite direction is much cheaper at around 20,000Rp to 60,000Rp depending on traffic.

BUS

Jakarta has a network of clean air-conditioned buses called TransJakarta that run on busways (designated lanes that are closed to all other traffic). They represent, by far, the quickest way to get around the city.

Most busways have been constructed in the centre of existing highways, and stations have been positioned (roughly) at 1km intervals. Access is via elevated walkways, each station has a shelter and many are manned, which means someone can normally point you towards your destination. Ten busway lines (called *koridor*) were up and running at the time of research, with a total of 15 planned, which should eventually form a network from Tanjung Priok south to Kampung Rambutan.

Tickets cost 3500Rp (2000Rp between 5am and 7am), payable before you board, which covers you to any destination in the network (regardless of how many *koridor* you use). Buses (5am to 10pm) are well maintained and not too crowded, as conductors (usually) ensure that maximum passenger numbers are not exceeded.

LOCAL TRANSPORT

Bajaj (pronounced ba-jai) are Indonesian túk-túk. There are few about now in central Jakarta. If you hire one, it's worth remembering that they are not allowed on many major thoroughfares.

TAXI

Metered taxis cost 6000Rp for the first kilometre and 250Rp for each subsequent 100m. Make sure the *argo* (meter) is used.

Bluebird cabs (☑ 021-794 1234; www.bluebirdgroup.com) can be booked ahead and have the best reputation; do *not* risk travelling with the less reputable firms.

Typical taxi fares from Jl Thamrin are 20,000Rp to Kota and 30,000Rp for Blok M. Any toll-road charges are extra and are paid by the passengers.

Bogor

☑ 0251 / POP 949,000 / ELEV 265M

Known throughout Java as *kota hujan* (city of rain) for having more than 300 storms a year, Bogor became a home away from home for Sir Stamford Raffles during the British interregnum, a respite for those mad dogs and Englishmen who preferred *not* to go out in the midday sun. These days, this once-quiet town is almost a suburb of Jakarta, with the traffic and hubbub to match. But while Bogor itself

Bogor

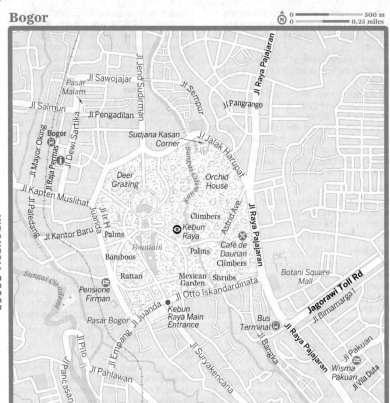

clogs up with bemos (three-wheeled pick-up trucks) and mopeds, the real oasis remains untouched. Planted at the very hub of the city, with chaos all around, the town's world-class botanical gardens remain – in the words of one upstanding British visitor – 'a jolly fine day out'. They are perhaps the best possible day trip from Jakarta, one hour away by train, that you can make.

Try and get to Bogor and the gardens reasonably early in the morning because by mid to late afternoon the heavens usually open and it rains. And when we say it rains we don't mean a short, sharp shower. We mean a Biblical-style, build a big boat and gather up two of every animal kind of rain storm.

◉ Sights

Kebun Raya   GARDENS
(Great Garden; www.bogor.indo.net.id/kri; admission 26,000Rp; ◎8am-5pm) At the heart of Bogor are the fabulous botanical gardens, known as

the Kebun Raya. There are more than 15,000 species of trees and plants here including 400 types of palms. There's a good stock of graceful pandanus (look out for their unusual aerial roots) and some huge agave (used to make tequila) and cacti in the Mexican section.

Other highlights include the Orchid House (Indonesia is a hotbed of orchid diversity) and the lovely ponds, which have giant Victoria water lilies over a metre across.

Crowds flock here on Sunday but the gardens are quiet at most other times. The southern gate is the main entrance; other gates are only open on Sunday and holidays. Don't miss wonderful Café de Daunen, the perfect spot for lunch. Allow yourself at least half a day to enjoy Kebun Raya.

⌷ Sleeping

Most people just make a day trip from Jakarta.

Pensione Firman GUESTHOUSE **$**
(📞 0251-832 3246; Jl Paledang 48; r 75,000-
200,000Rp; ❄ @ 🛜) For years this rambling
place was a backpackers' stronghold though
it's now something of a last resort due to lack
of maintenance – expect very basic rooms. It's
friendly enough though, and there's free tea
and coffee.

Wisma Pakuan GUESTHOUSE **$$**
(📞 0251-831 9430; wismapakuanbogor@yahoo.com;
Jl Pakuan 12; r with fan 225,000Rp, with air-con
270,000-355,000Rp; ❄ 🛜) This excellent,
welcoming guesthouse, a short stroll from
the bus terminal, has 12 spacious, well-
maintained rooms with flat-screen TV and
good beds. Those at the rear have views over a
garden, where breakfast is served.'

The owners aren't always present so it's
a very good idea to call in advance and give
them an estimated arrival time.

🍴 Eating

Cheap *warung* (food stalls) appear at night
along Jl Dewi Sartika and Jl Jend Sudirman.
During the day you'll find plenty of *warung*
and good fruit at Pasar Bogor, the market
close to the main Kebun Raya gates.

Café de Daunan INTERNATIONAL **$$**
(📞 0251-835 0023; inside Kebun Raya; meals
30,000-70,000Rp; ⊗ 10am-8pm Mon-Thu, 10am-
10pm Fri-Sun) The cafe-restaurant in the botanical gardens is a wonderfully civilised place for
a bite or a drink, with sweeping views down to
the water lily ponds. It's a little pricey, but the
tasty Western and Indonesian food and sublime setting make it an essential stop.

When the gardens are closed you can
access the restaurant via Gate 3 (on the eastern side of the gardens).

ℹ️ Information

Tourist Office (📞 081 61953838; Jl Dewi Sar-
tika 51; ⊗ 7am-6pm) The team here can help out
with most queries, provide a city map and offer
excellent, well-priced tours around the town
and out into the stunning countryside. Opening
hours can be a little elastic.

ℹ️ Getting There & Away

Bogor is a good place to hire a car and driver for
a trip around the countryside; ask the tourist
board to recommend someone. Prices are around
500,000Rp to 800,000Rp per day depending on
car type and destination.

BUS
Every 15 minutes or so, buses depart from Jakarta's Kampung Rambutan bus terminal (normal/
air-con 8000/12,000Rp, one hour), but you're far
better off taking the train.

All buses leave from the main bus station on Jl
Raya Pajajaran, departing frequently to Bandung
(normal/air-con 30,000/50,000Rp, 3½ hours).
At weekends these buses are not allowed to go via
the scenic Puncak Pass and therefore travel via
Sukabumi.

TRAIN
No frills commuter trains (5000Rp, 1¼hrs) leave
roughly every hour for Jakarta.

ℹ️ Getting Around

Angkot (minibuses; 3000Rp) make slow circuits
of the gardens, taking in most central locations en
route. Number 2 goes from the train station to the
gardens and number 3 from train to bus station.

Pangandaran

📞 0265

Situated on a narrow isthmus, with a broad
sweep of sand on either side and a thickly forested national park on the nearby headland,
Pangandaran is Java's premier beach resort.
Most of the year Pangandaran is quiet, but
the town fills up on holidays (and weekends).
Swimming is dodgy, with heavy dumping
surf and strong currents, but it's not a bad
place to get out on a board, or to learn how,
on small swells. When the waves are maxed
out (which is often), head an hour up the
coast to sheltered Batu Karas.

🅾️ Sights & Activities

**Taman Nasional
Pangandaran** NATIONAL PARK
(Pangandaran National Park; admission 7000Rp;
⊗ dawn-dusk) The Taman Nasional Pangandaran, which fringes the southern end of Pangandaran, is a stretch of not quite untouched
forest that's populated by barking deer,
hornbills and Javan gibbons, and features
some spectacular white-sand beaches. Various trails meander through the forest: guides
charge 100,000Rp to 200,000Rp (for a group
of four), depending on the length of the walk.

Numerous deer and monkeys gather next
to the ticket offices and car parks, meaning
that those with wallets sewn firmly shut can
see some of the animals without actually entering the park.

Pangandaran

Pangandaran Ⓝ
0 ——— 400 m
0 ——— 0.2 miles

🛏 Sleeping

As Pangandaran has close to 100 hotels you should have no bother finding a bed, except during Christmas and Lebaran (the end of Ramadan) when half of Java seems to head here and prices skyrocket. Many of Pangandaran's best homestays and *losmen* (basic accommodation) are crowded along the northern stretch of the town's western beach. Most places don't have hot water.

★**Mini Tiga Homestay**   GUESTHOUSE $
(📞0265-639436; katmaja95@yahoo.fr; s/d/tr incl breakfast 100,000/150,000/180,000Rp; @🛜) A simply excellent backpackers' centre with very reasonable rates considering the quality of the accommodation. The nine rooms are very clean, spacious and have nice decorative touches – including bamboo walls and batik wall hangings – all have en-suite bathrooms and Western toilets. From the moment you arrive you're made to feel welcome: the French owner provides free tea/coffee, wi-fi, DVDs to watch and even homemade yoghurt. Good tours and transport tickets are also offered.

Rinjani Homestay   GUESTHOUSE $
(📞0265-639757; s/d 80,000/120,000Rp; 🛜) A very solid choice, this welcoming family-run place with 10 clean, tiled rooms with TV, fan, porch or balcony and private cold-water bathroom. Excellent discounts available for long-term guests.

Adam's Homestay   HOTEL $$
(📞0265-639396; www.adamshomestay.com; Jl Pamugaran; r 250,000-550,000Rp; ❄🛜⛱) A veritable oasis, this is a wonderfully relaxed, enjoyable place to stay with artistically presented rooms (many with balconies, beamed ceilings and outdoor bathrooms) spread around a verdant tropical garden that's

Surfing Lessons   SURFING
(per half-day incl board hire 200,000Rp) Surfing lessons are offered at the northern end of the beach. Pangandaran is a good place to learn, and local instructors have 'soft' boards ideal for beginners. The friendly staff from **Pangandaran Surf** (📞0813 2354 4583; www.pangandaransurf.com; beachside, Mungil Steak House) are all lifesavers, speak English and understand local conditions.

☞ Tours

Paradise Island   BOAT TOUR
(📞0265-639180; Jl Kidang Pananjung 123; Rp300,000 per person, minimum 4 persons) There are tours to Paradise Island, an uninhabited nearby island with good beaches (including a 5km white-sand beach) and surfing. For food, make an early-morning trip to Pangandaran's fish market (p169) and fire up a barbecue when you get to the island.

just bursting with exotic plants, ponds and birdlife. There's good Western and local food available too.

Eating

Pangandaran is famous for its excellent seafood. For cheap Indonesian nosh, the town has many *warung*.

Green Garden Cafe INDONESIAN $
(Jl Kidang Pananjung 116; snacks & meals 10,000-20,000Rp; 🖉) There's not much of a garden in evidence but you must try the delicious *batagor* (crispy tofu) here, which is fried in cassava flour and served with spicy peanut sauce – it's the house speciality. Other Indonesian dishes including *gado gado* and *cap cai* – and great fresh juices are available.

★ Pasar Ikan SEAFOOD $$
(Fish Market; Jl Raya Timor; large fish 40,000-70,000Rp) Pangandaran's terrific fish market consists of more than a dozen large open-sided restaurants just off the east beach. They all operate on exactly the same basis – select your fish or seafood from the glistening iced displays, decide which sauce (usually garlic, oyster or sweet-and-sour) you fancy and it'll arrive in minutes.

ℹ Information

A 3500Rp admission charge is levied at the gates on entering Pangandaran.
BRI Bank (Jl Kidang Pananjung) Changes cash dollars and major brands of travellers cheques.

ℹ Getting There & Away

Pangandaran lies roughly halfway between Bandung and Yogyakarta. Most people get here by road, as there's no train station, but it's perfectly possible to arrive by rail and bus. Speak to staff at the Mini Tiga Homestay (p168) for impartial transport advice and possible routes, and you can book tickets there too.

BUS

Local buses run from Pangandaran's bus station, north of town, to Sidareja (15,000Rp, 1¼ hours) and Cijulang (7000Rp, 40 minutes). Express buses leave for Bandung (45,000Rp to 60,000Rp, six hours) and Jakarta's Kampung Rambutan terminal (70,000Rp to 85,000Rp, 8½ hours).

MINIBUS

The most comfortable way to travel to Bandung (normal/air-con 100,000/130,000Rp) is aboard a door-to-door *travel* minibus. Minibuses also run to Jakarta's Kampung Rambutan terminal (normal/ air-con 135,000/150,000Rp, nine hours) and to Yogyakarta (150,000Rp, seven hours).

TRAIN

To get to Yogyakarta by train you first need to get to Sidareja, from where there are train services to Yogya (150,000Rp to 300,000Rp) a couple of times daily; there's a fast train leaving Sidareja at noon, which takes 3½ hours.

Batu Karas

☑ 0265 / POP 3000

The idyllic fishing village and emerging surfing hot spot of Batu Karas, 32km west of Pangandaran, is one of the most enjoyable places to kick back in Java. It's a tiny one-lane settlement, bisected by a wooded promontory, and it has a low key, relaxed charm (except on weekends and holidays when it's jammed with Javanese visitors). There are two fine black-sand beaches, with sheltered sections that are usually calm enough for swimming, but most visitors are here for the waves, and there's a lot of surf talk. The long right pointbreak here is a very mellow sand-bottom wave that's seriously sheltered from all but the biggest swells. This makes it one of the best places in Java to learn to surf. More experienced wave riders will probably rate the main pointbreak a fairly dull ride compared to most Indonesian waves, but 15 minutes' walk north of the village is a marginally more interesting and consistent right reef. The locally run surf co-op charges 80,000Rp per person per day for lessons; board hire is extra (around 35,000Rp).

🛏 Sleeping & Eating

In addition to restaurants at the following hotels, there are a few cheap eating spots on the waterfront. Try **Kang Ayi** (mains 10,000-20,000Rp) or, at the junction by the entrance to the village, **Bayview Seafood** (meals 35,000-70,000Rp). We probably don't need to tell you that you'll be eating seafood at both these places.

Bonsai Bungalows BUNGALOW $
(☑ 081 5466 4177; www.bonsaibungalows.com; dm 100,000Rp, r 150,000-300,000Rp, bungalows 500,000Rp; 🌬) A good choice, with well-constructed, clean, thatched-roof accommodation – neat little wooden rooms (some with air-conditioning), family bungalows or an excellent dorm that has six beds with good-quality mattresses and fresh linen. There's a cafe at the front for a beer or coffee. Prices rise by 25% in high season.

Jesfa GUESTHOUSE $
(📞 0813 2306 8358; weekday/weekend incl breakfast 100,000/150,000Rp) Above a little restaurant at the far end of the beach, these three rooms (all en suite) are highly attractive with exposed brick walls and lovely chunky wooden beds with thick mattresses.

★ **Java Cove** BOUTIQUE HOTEL $$
(📞 0265-708 2020; www.javacovebeachhotel.com; r with fan 434,000Rp, luxury r 749,000-1,249,000Rp, meals around 90,000Rp; ⊖ ❋ @ ✿) 🍃 Yeah okay so it's not a bare bones budget option, but sometimes it's worth paying the extra. Established by a welcoming, knowledgable Australian couple who have spent years in Indonesia, this beautiful beachfront hotel has gorgeous contemporary-chic rooms, most with sea views. The cheaper, fan-cooled options make it a welcoming treat for backpackers.

There's a decked garden and chillout zone with a pool. The bistro-style restaurant serves excellent Western food including healthy breakfasts, pasta and tapas, as well as mocktails and cocktails. Book online for significant discounts.

ℹ Getting There & Away

You have to pay a toll of 5000Rp to enter the village. Batu Karas can be reached from Pangandaran by taking a bus to Cijulang (5000Rp to 10,000Rp depending on bus type) and then an *ojek* (15,000Rp to 20,000Rp) on to Batu Karas. It's sometimes possible to charter a motorbike direct from Pangandaran for around 30,000Rp.

Around Batu Karas

About 6km inland from Batu Karas, pleasure boats run upriver to **Green Canyon**, a lush river valley where you can swim in surging emerald currents and take a natural power shower under the streams that tumble into the gorge (don't look up!). Boats cost 75,000Rp and run between 7.30am and 4pm. Day trips can be organised from Pangandaran for 150,000Rp, but it's easy enough to get here on a hired motorbike, as the route to the canyon is very well signposted.

Wonosobo

📞 0286 / POP 110,000 / ELEV 790M
Wonosobo is the main gateway to the Dieng Plateau. At 800m above sea level in the central mountain range, it has a comfortable climate and is a typical country town with a busy market.

★ **Wisma Duta Homestay** (📞 0286-321674; dutahomestay@yahoo.com; Jl Rumah Sakit III; r incl breakfast 300,000Rp; P ❋ 🛜) is one of the best homestays in the central mountains, occupying a lovely suburban house and garden. It's worth staying just to see the massive gold Harley Davidson that sits in pride of place in the front room! At the time of research the owner was renovating and constructing a new block of cheaper rooms.

If the Wisma Duta Homestay is full, alternative lodgings can be found at the large, concrete, motel-like **Hotel Sri Kencono** (📞 0286-321522; Jl A Yani 81; r 150-400,000Rp), which has well-kept, spacious rooms with hot-water bathrooms and Western-style toilets.

Shanti Rahayu (Jl A Yani 122; meals 9000-22,000Rp) is considered by locals to be among the best cheap eateries in the town centre, and its chicken curry certainly made us believers. For something a little more upmarket (and we do only mean a little more) the **Asia Restaurant** (Jl Angkatan 45; mains 25,000-55,000Rp), with its large and often forlorn dining room, is the place to go if you want to impress.

Wonosobo's bus station is 4km out of town on the Magelang road, but only very long distance depart from here. From Yogyakarta take a bus to Magelang (13,000Rp, 1½ hours) and then another bus to Wonosobo (15,000Rp, two hours). **Rahayu Travel** (📞 0286-321217; Jl A Yani 95) has door-to-door minibuses to Yogyakarta (45,000Rp, three hours).

Frequent buses to Dieng (8000Rp, one hour) leave from Jl Rumah Sakit.

Dieng Plateau

📞 0286 / ELEV 2000M
A startling contrast from the heat and fecundity of the lowlands, the plateau of Dieng (Abode of Gods) is another world: a windswept volcanic landscape of swirling clouds, green hills, mist and damp punctuated with ancient ruins.

You can see all the main sights, including the temples, on foot in a morning or afternoon, though to really explore the plateau and its crater lakes, allow a couple of days.

◉ Sights

Arjuna Complex TEMPLE
(admission incl Candi Gatutkaca & Kawah Sikidang 25,000Rp) The five main temples that form the Arjuna Complex are clustered together on the central plain. They are Shiva temples, but

like the other Dieng temples they have been named after the heroes of the *wayang* stories of the Mahabharata epic: Arjuna, Puntadewa, Srikandi, Sembadra and Semar. All have mouth-shaped doorways and strange bell-shaped windows and some locals leave offerings, burn incense and meditate here.

On our last visit to the temples we bumped into the Teletubbies, which was rather unexpected but not at all unwelcome. Indonesian children believe that Dipsy, Laa-Laa and whatever the hell the other ones are called live in the hills surrounding the temples. They are now frequently found hanging out posing for photos around the temples.

Considerably less colourful than the Teletubbies is Candi Gatutkaca, a small Shiva temple (a yoni was found inside) with a square base, south of the main complex.

Natural Attractions   LAKE, VOLCANO
The plateau's natural attractions and remote allure are as much a reason to visit as the temples. From the village, you can do a two-hour loop walk that takes in the turquoise lake of **Telaga Warna** (admission 15,000Rp; ☺8am-4.30pm) and the steaming vents and frantically bubbling mud pools of **Kawah Sikidang** (admission incl in ticket for Arjuna temples) volcanic crater.

The walk to Sembungan village (2300m) to see the sunrise is heavily touted by the guesthouses, though having to pay to get up at 4.30am is a dubious privilege (particularly on cloudy mornings). All the guesthouses can arrange transport and guides (per person 50,000Rp to 110,000Rp depending on group size) and hire out warm clothing.

🛏 Sleeping & Eating

Dieng's several dozen guesthouses are notoriously poor value. Spartan conditions and draughty, semi-clean rooms are the norm. Beware that hot water is not always forthcoming.

Homestay Bougenville   GUESTHOUSE $
(Jl Pandawa; r with/without bathroom 150,000/100,000Rp) The tiny rooms here, some with even smaller bathrooms, have been given a recent lick of paint and are now decidely cute and cosy. It's opposite the main entrance to the temple complex.

Hotel Gunung Mas   HOTEL $
(☎0286-334 2017; d 125,000-375,000Rp) This solidly built hotel has a wide choice of well-scrubbed rooms, from a clean crash pad

for the night to quite spacious rooms with private hot-water bathrooms. All are decent value and there's a shared upper-level balcony for *those* plateau views.

❶ Getting There & Away

Dieng is 26km from Wonosobo, which is the usual access point. Buses run frequently (8000Rp, one hour).

Yogyakarta

📞 0274 / POP 396,000 / ELEV 125M

From an all-night shadow-puppet performance to the bold and socially aware graffiti that covers many a wall throughout the city, Yogyakarta is, above all else, a city of art and culture and a hotbed of Javanese intellectual and political thought. Although still headed by its sultan, whose *kraton* (palace) remains the hub of traditional life, contemporary Yogya is as much a city of cybercafes, lounges and traffic jams as batik, *gamelan* and ritual.

But while the process of modernisation homogenises many of Java's cities, Yogya continues to juggle past and present with relative ease, sustaining a slower, more conservative way of life in the quiet *kampung* (villages) that thrive only a stone's throw from the throbbing main streets.

Yogya's potency has long outweighed its size, and it remains Java's premier tourist city, with countless hotels, restaurants and attractions of its own. The city is also an ideal base for exploring Borobudur and Prambanan.

Jl Malioboro is the main drag, running south from the train station to become Jl A Yani at its southern end (where you'll find the *kraton*). Jl Malioboro is lined with stores, and you'll find the main budget accommodation enclave of Sosrowijayan just off it. A second swankier hotel and restaurant district lies to the south around Jl Prawirotaman.

◎ Sights

Kraton   PALACE
(Map p172; ☎0274-373321; admission 12,500Rp, camera 1000Rp, guided tour by donation; ☺8am-1.30pm Sat-Thu, to noon Fri) Traditions hold firm in Yogya, and nowhere is this more evident than in the *kraton*, a walled royal enclave and the cultural and political heart of the city. Effectively a city within a city, over 25,000 people live within the compound. Sadly, unless you take a guide, information about

Yogyakarta

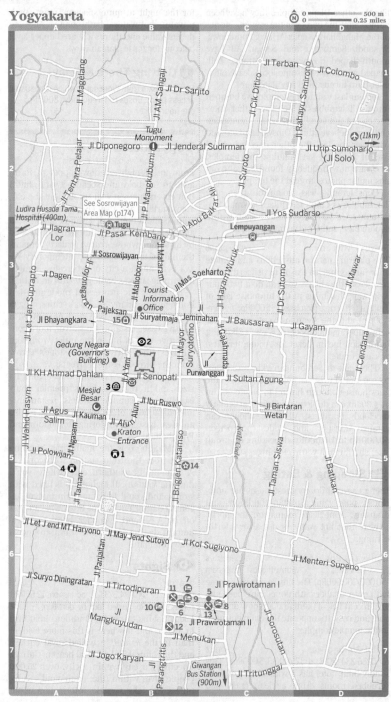

N 0 ———— 500 m
0 ———— 0.25 miles

Jl Terban
Jl Colombo

Jl Magelang
Jl AM Sangaji
Jl Dr Sarjito
Jl Cik Ditiro
Jl Rahayu Samirono

Jl Tentara Pelajar

Tugu Monument
Jl Diponegoro
Jl Jenderal Sudirman

(11km)
Jl Urip Sumoharjo (Jl Solo)

Jl P Mangkubumi
Jl Suroto
Jl Abu Bakar Ali
Jl Yos Sudarso

See Sosrowijayan Area Map (p174)

Ludira Husada Tama Hospital (400m)
Tugu
Lempuyangan

Jl Jlagran Lor
Jl Pasar Kembang

Jl Sosrowijayan
Jl Mataram
Jl Mas Soeharto
Jl Hayam Wuruk
Jl Dr Sutomo
Jl Mawar

Jl Dagen
Jl Let Jen Suprapto
Jl Jogonegaran
Jl Maliboro
Jl Pajeksan

Tourist Information Office
Jl
Jeminahan
Jl Bausasran
Jl Gayam
Jl Cendana

Jl Bhayangkara
15
Jl Suryatmaja
Jl Mayor Suryotomo
Jl Gajahmada

2

Gedung Negara (Governor's Building)
Jl A Yani
Jl Senopati
Jl Purwanggan
Jl Sultan Agung

Jl KH Ahmad Dahlan
Mesjid Besar
3
Jl Ibu Ruswo
Jl Bintaran Wetan

Jl Agus Salim
Jl Kauman
Jl Ngasem
Jl Alun Alun
Jl Wahid Hasym

Kraton Entrance
Kali Code

Jl Polowijan
1

4
14
Jl Brigjen Katamso
Jl Taman Siswa
Jl Batikan

Jl Taman

Jl Let J end MT Haryono
Jl May Jend Sutoyo
Jl Kol Sugiyono
Jl Menteri Supeno

Jl Suryo Diningratan
Jl Panjaitan

Jl Tirtodipuran
11
7
Jl Prawirotaman I
5

10
9
6
8
13

Jl Mangkuyudan
12
Jl Prawirotaman II
Jl Sorosutan

Jl Menukan

Jl Jogo Karyan
Jl Parangtritis
Giwangan Bus Station (900m)
Jl Tritunggal

Yogyakarta

the glittering palaces, temples and treasures is lacking, but that's because the *kraton* primarily remains the sultan's home and a centre of political power, and is only secondly a tourist attraction.

The golden pavilion, the official reception hall of the sultans, boasts a marble floor and showcases a host of free cultural events. Other highlights include the souvenir house, textile room and the small museum dedicated to Hamengkubuwono IX, the current sultan's father. Daily events (normally held around 10am to noon, but confirm at the ticket office) include *gamelan*, classical dance, *wayang kulit,* poetry and *wayang gohek.*

Try and visit the *kraton* during the week – at weekends the complex becomes a menagerie of tour buses, screeching children, dripping ice-creams and 'hello missterrrs!'

Taman Sari & Pasar Ngasem PALACE, GARDENS
(Water Castle; Map p172; Jl Taman; admission 10,000Rp, camera/video 1000/2000Rp; ⊙8am-3pm) The Taman Sari was a complex of canals, pools and palaces built within the *kraton* between 1758 and 1765 by a Portuguese architect who was allegedly later executed to keep the sultan's hidden 'pleasure rooms' secret. Damaged first by Diponegoro's Java War and then further by an earthquake, it is today a mass of ruins, crowded with small houses and batik galleries. The main bathing pools have been restored.

Sono-Budoyo Museum MUSEUM
(Map p172; ⊘0274-376775; admission 5000Rp; ⊙8am-3.30pm Tue-Thu & Sat-Sun, to 2.30pm Fri) This is the pick of Yogya's museums, even if it is dusty and dimly lit, with a first-class collection of Javanese art, including *wayang*

kulit puppets, *topeng* (masks), *kris* and batik. It also has a courtyard packed with Hindu statuary and artefacts from further afield, including superb Balinese carvings. *Wayang kulit* performances are held here.

Bird Market MARKET
(Ring Rd Selatan; ⊙9am-4pm) Yogya's main bird market is a fascinating place in which to pick up a pet finch or owl. Or maybe you need a dark-as-night raven (traditionally used in black magic), a fluffy bunny, a smelly mongoose or a sweet terrapin? If you're not here to buy, the market is still an interesting place to explore.

Pasar Beringharjo MARKET
(Map p172; Jl A Yani; ⊙8am-4.30pm) Yogya's main market, 800m north of the *kraton*, is a lively and fascinating place. The front section has a wide range of batik – mostly inexpensive *batik cap* (stamped batik) – while the 2nd floor is dedicated to cheap clothes and shoes. Most interesting of all, though, is the old section towards the back. Crammed with *warungs* and stalls selling a huge variety of fruit and vegetables, this is still very much a traditional market. The range of *rempah rempah* (spices) on the 1st floor is quite something.

Affandi Museum MUSEUM
(⊘0274-562593; www.affandi.org; Jl Laksda Adisucipto 167; admission incl a soft drink & souviner 50,000Rp, camera 20,000Rp, mobile phone with camera 10,000Rp; ⊙9am-4pm except holidays) One of Indonesia's most celebrated artists, Affandi lived and worked in a wonderfully quirky riverside house-cum-studio, about 6km east of the town centre. Today his former home is the Affandi Museum, which has an extensive collection of his paintings,

Sosrowijayan Area

Sosrowijayan Area

Sleeping
1 105 Homestay C2
2 Andrea Hotel B2
3 Bladok Losmen & Restaurant B2
4 Dewi Homestay B2
5 Losmen Lucy C2
6 Losmen Setia Kawan...........................C2
7 Tiffa Losmen..B2

Eating
8 Atap B2
9 Bedhot Resto..B2
10 Mi Casa es Tu Casa B2

Drinking & Nightlife
11 Hell's Kitchen......................................B2

Entertainment
12 Bintang Resto......................................B2

Shopping
13 Lucky Boomerang C2

including some astonishing self-portraits and personal items. Check out his car, a real boy racer's dream: a lime-green and yellow customised 1967 Galant with an oversized rear spoiler.

☞ Tours

Tour agents on Jl Prawirotaman and in the Sosrowijayan area offer a host of tour options at similar prices. Typical day tours and per-person rates (excluding entrance fees) are Borobudur (60,000Rp to 100,000Rp), Dieng (275,000Rp), Prambanan 75,000Rp,

Prambanan and Parangtritis 180,000Rp, and Solo and Candi Sukuh 200,000Rp.

Operators also arrange cars with driver, with rates starting at 350,000Rp to 400,000Rp per day.

Via Via Tours TOUR
(Map p172; www.viaviajogja.com; Jl Prawirotaman I 30) This famous cafe-restaurant (p176) offers dozens of tours, including some really creative options such as a backroad trip to Prambanan (180,000Rp), a *jamu* (herbal medicine) and massage tour (200,000Rp) that takes in a visit to a specialist market and a behind-the-scenes tour of a travelling Javanese theatre (190,000Rp to 390,000Rp).

Jogja Trans TOUR
(☑ 081 6426 0124, 0274-439 8495; www.jogja trans.com; Gang 04/09, Madurejo, Prambanan) A highly professional agency that can provide cars (around 400,000Rp per day) with reliable drivers and also arrange bespoke tours throughout Java.

★★ Festivals & Events

The three Gerebeg festivals – held each year at the end of January and April and the beginning of November – are Java's most colourful and grand processions.

🛏 Sleeping

Yogya has dozens of good guesthouses and hotels and intense competition keeps prices low and standards high. Sosrowijayan is the main budget zone, while the Prawirotaman area, 2km south of the *kraton,* also has some cheap places as well as midrange options.

🛏 Sosrowijayan Area

Situated within a short walk of the Tugu train station, Sosrowijayan is a fascinating traditional neighbourhood of narrow *gang* (alleyways), lined with backpacker-geared accommodation, eateries, laundries and the like. (Although be aware that Gang III is something of a red-light district and, though safe enough, women travellers may prefer to avoid this alleyway at night.) Few of the guesthouses here include breakfast in their rates.

★ Andrea Hotel   GUESTHOUSE $
(Map p174; ☑ 0274-563502; www.andreahoteljogja. wordpress.com; Sosrowijayan I/140 Gang II; r incl breakfast 125,000-250,000Rp; ❋ 🖵) Excellent guesthouse owned by an informative, helpful Swiss guy and his Indonesian wife. Immaculately clean, if smallish, rooms with good quality beds, fresh linen and compact, well-designed bathrooms. There's a slim street terrace where you can watch the Sosrowijayan world go by with a drink or snack.

Bladok Losmen & Restaurant   HOTEL $
(Map p174; ☑ 0274-560452; www.bladok.web.id; Jl Sosrowijayan 76; s with fan 100,000Rp, d with fan 180,000-240,000Rp, d with air-con 320,000Rp; ❋ 🖵 ❋) A dependable, well-run place that looks vaguely like an Austrian mountain chalet. Bladok's rooms won't disappoint with lovely chunky wooden beds and furniture, high cleanliness standards and crisp, fresh linen; some rooms have balconies. The (small) pool is a real bonus and the cafe-restaurant serves reliably good European food and homemade bread.

Losmen Setia Kawan   GUESTHOUSE $
(Map p174; ☑ 0274-560966; www.bedhots.com; r with fan 135,000-150,000Rp, with air-con 160,000-350,000Rp; ❋ @) Inviting, well-run place that occupies a fine artistically decorated house. There are nice touches evident everywhere, with classic Vespa scooters in the lobby, a lounge area with TV/DVDs, computers for internet access and a good information board. Rooms are smallish but very attractive, though the swirling, hippyish murals could be a bit much after a heavy night.

Dewi Homestay   HOMESTAY $
(Map p174; ☑ 0274-516014; dewihomestay@ hotmail.com; Jl Sosrowijayan GT I 115; s/d 100,000/150,000Rp) An attractive long-running place with character and a leafy, shady garden and spacious, charming rooms – many have four-poster beds draped with mosquito nets.

Tiffa Losmen   GUESTHOUSE $
(Map p174; ☑ 0274-512841; tiffaartshop@yahoo. com; Jl Sosrowijayan Wetan Gt II 12; s/d incl breakfast 125,000/150,000Rp) A tidy little *losmen* owned by a hospitable family, with smallish rooms, each with private *mandi* (basin for washing) above an art shop. There's a communal balcony where you can tuck into your free breakfast and slurp tea or coffee. The nearby Mosque will have you up and about with the cockerals.

105 Homestay   GUESTHOUSE $
(Map p174; ☑ 0274-582896; homestay_105@yahoo. co.id; r with fan 80,000-150,000Rp, with air-con 100,000-190,000Rp; ❋) A lobby complete with Gaudiesque tiles and a welcoming owner sets a nice introduction at this guesthouse, which has no less than seven classes of tidy, neat rooms. It's in the heart of Sosrowijayan's souk-like backstreets.

Losmen Lucy   GUESTHOUSE $
(Map p174; ☑ 0274-513429; r with fan/air-con 120,000/175,000Rp; ❋) One of the best *losmen* in the area this place is run by a house-proud lady and has 12 tidy, very clean rooms with good beds; all have en-suite *mandi*.

🛏 Jl Prawirotaman Area

This area used to be the centre for midrange hotels in Yogya, but many have slashed their prices in recent years and there are bargains to be had. Breakfast is normally included in the hotel room rates.

Via Via Guest House   BOUTIQUE HOTEL $
(☑ 0274-374748; www.viaviajogja.com; Jl Prawirotaman mg 3; r 175,000-225,000Rp; ❋ 🖵) This stylish little guesthouse down a quiet side street has immaculate whitewashed rooms adorned in superb photographic works of art. If you don't like one room, ask to see another, as they're all slightly different. Breakfast is eaten in the small courtyard.

Kampoeng Djawa Hotel   GUESTHOUSE $
(Map p172; ☑ 0274-378318; www.kampoengdjawa hotel.com; Jl Prawirotaman I 40; r with with/without bathroom 190,000-135,000Rp, with air-con 250,000Rp; ❋ 🖵) Occupying a long, thin house, this place really has some local character. The rooms (in several price categories) have artistic touches including exposed brick walls, mosaic tiling and pebble-walled bathrooms. There's a peaceful little rear garden for your complimentary tea or coffee (available all day) and afternoon snack. Staff are eager to help here and breakfast is included.

INDONESIA YOGYAKARTA

Rumah Eyang
GUESTHOUSE $

(Map p172; ☑ 0812 2711 7439; www.rumaheyangjogja. com; Jl Parangtritis, Gang Sartono 823; r incl breakfast from 150,000Rp, with air-con 200,000Rp; ❋ @) A stylish suburban house that's been converted into a guesthouse. Rooms are simple and comfortable, but the real benefit here is that Atik, the lovely Javanese owner is a fount of knowledge about the region and offers great tours.

Delta Homestay
GUESTHOUSE $

(Map p172; ☑ 0274-327051; www.dutagardenhotel. com; Jl Prawirotaman II 597A; r with shared mandi 125,000-165,000Rp, r 175,000-200,000Rp; ❋ 🛜 🏊) A great little hideaway with a selection of small but perfectly formed rooms built from natural materials, each with a little porch, grouped around a pool. It's very peaceful here, staff are welcoming and breakfast is included.

Prambanan Guesthouse
HOTEL $$

(Map p172; ☑ 0274-376167; www.prambanangh. be; Jl Prawirotaman I 14; s/d with fan & cold shower 205,000/225,000Rp, with air-con & hot shower 340,000/370,000Rp; ❋ 🛜 🏊) A peaceful place to stay with a small pool and attractive gardens in which to eat your free breakfast, this little guesthouse enjoys a prime location. Many of the rooms have been recently redecorated and the better options are very comfortable with *ikat*-style textiles draped on good-quality beds.

Gading Resto Cafe & Bed
GUESTHOUSE $$

(Map p172; ☑ 0274-383987; www.guesthousegading. com; Jl Pawirotaman 9; r 350,000Rp; ❋ 🛜 🏊) This realitively new place mixes greys, blacks and whites into tidy and style-aware rooms. Mattresses are of a very high quality and there are stone sinks in the otherwise small bathrooms. The unusual wall of foilage, which separates guesthouse from restaurant is a nice touch.

✖ Eating & Drinking

🍴 Sosrowijayan Area

For cheap and cheerful Indonesian and Western nosh, this area fits the bill nicely. It's also the place to join locals for a bite to eat; after 10pm the souvenir vendors along the northern end of Jl Malioboro pack up and a *lesahan* area (where diners sit on straw mats) comes alive. Here you can try Yogya's famous *ayam goreng* (deep-fried chicken soaked in coconut milk) and listen to young Indonesians strumming their guitars into the wee hours.

A host of good *warung* also line Jl Pasar Kembang, beside the train line.

Mi Casa es Tu Casa
SPANISH, INDONESIAN $

(Map p174; www.micasaestucasa.mye.name; Sosrowijayan Wetan GT I/141; meals 15,000-40,000Rp; 🛜) This stylish place is Spanish owned and has a small selection of Spanish dishes amongst a host of other international flavours. It even has an Indonesian version of a *paella* (100,000Rp for two, order well ahead). You won't have to wait long for the Indo grub, however, and if you want to try snake – this is the place.

Bedhot Resto
INTERNATIONAL $

(Map p174; Gang II; mains 25,000-40,000Rp; 🛜 🖉) Bedhot means 'creative' in old Javanese and this place is one of the more stylish eateries in Sosrowijayan. There's reasonable Indonesian and Western food, good juices and internet access upstairs.

Atap
INDONESIAN, INTERNATIONAL $

(Map p174; Jl Sosrowijayan GT I/113; meals 16,000-30,000Rp; ⊘ 5.30-10pm) Quirky, boho restaurant with a great little outdoor terrace and tables made from car tyres. The menu is strong on grilled meat, with daily specials including spicy Balinese chicken and Cajun-style barbecued beef.

Hell's Kitchen
CAFE, BAR

(Map p174; Jl Sosrowijayan; meals 30,000-40,000Rp; ⊘ noon-1am) Open-sided bar-cafe with quirky decor that's a great bet for a beer, as the street-terrace tables offer the best people-watching perch in Sosrowijayan. Also hosts live bands (everything from punk to acoustic) in the evenings and has filling Western (salads, sandwiches and pasta) and Indonesian dishes.

🍴 Jl Prawirotaman Area

★ Via Via
INTERNATIONAL, INDONESIAN $

(Map p172; ☑ 0274-386557; www.viaviajogja.com; Jl Prawirotaman I 30; mains 18,000-45,000Rp; 🛜) Setting the bar high for both Western and Indonesian food, this hip cafe-restaurant has a fresh, inventive menu and always some tempting daily specials and great breakfasts. The decor mixes exposed concrete and bamboo screens, and there's a great outdoor terrace and art exhibitions.

Also hosts daily yoga sessions and offers lots of tours and courses (p174). It's as popular with locals as travellers.

Milas   INDONESIAN $
(Map p172; 🖅 0274-742 3399; Jl Prawirotaman IV 127; meals from 24,000Rp; ☺ from 3pm Tue-Fri, lunch and dinner Sat & Sun; 🖉) A great retreat from the streets, this secret garden restaurant is a part of a project centre for street youth. Offers tasty vegetarian cooking including healthy snacks, sandwiches and salads, and many of the ingredients are bio and locally grown. It's very popular, so be prepared to wait for a table or book ahead.

Easy Goin'   INTERNATIONAL $
(Map p172; Jl Prawirotaman 12; Mains 25,000-55,000Rp) Very much a classic 'traveller restaurant', this is one of the current hot tickets in this part of town. No doubt that's because of a menu that looks beyond the normal and includes regional dishes. Happy 'hour' lasts a head spinning five hours (2pm to 7pm).

Hanis Restaurant & Bakery   INTERNATIONAL $$
(Map p172; Jl Prawirotaman I 14; mains 40,000-56,000Rp) A cool, bright and modern cafe-restaurant with a fantastic range of well-prepared Indonesian and Italian dishes. The Balinese chicken curry is the establishment's culinary highlight, and if you're sensible you'll follow up with one of their homemade cakes and desserts, which are so good that, oh, we just ate them all.

☆ Entertainment

Dance, *wayang* or *gamelan* are performed most mornings at the *kraton* (admission free).

Most dance performances in and around town are based on the Ramayana or at least billed as 'Ramayana ballet' because of the famed performances at Prambanan.

Wayang kulit performances can be seen at several places around Yogya every night of the week.

Purawisata   TRADITIONAL DANCE
(Map p172; 🖅 0274-375705; Jl Brigjen Katamso; 300,000Rp) This amusement park stages Ramayana performances nightly at 8pm. You can dine here and watch the show and although it's no match for the spectacular version at the Prambanan temples (p179) it's a more than worthy alternative if you can't catch its big brother.

Sono-Budoyo Museum   PUPPETRY
(Map p172; 🖅 0274-376775; admission 20,000Rp, camera 3000Rp; ☺ 8-10pm Mon-Sat) Runs popular two-hour performances; the first half-hour

involves the reading of the story in Javanese, so most travellers skip this and arrive later.

Bintang Resto   LIVE MUSIC
(Map p174; Jl Sosrowijayan 54; ☺ to 1am) This popular travellers cafe in Sosrowijayan has live blues, reggae or rock on Wednesday, Friday and Saturday nights from 9pm. It also serves a very standard menu of Indo classics and traveller favourites.

🛍 Shopping

Yogya is a great place to shop for crafts and artefacts; try the Beringharjo (p173) market first for bargains, or the Prawirotaman area, which has several fine antique stores.

Jl Malioboro is one great, long, throbbing bazaar of souvenir shops and stalls selling cheap cotton clothes, leatherwork, batik bags, *topeng* masks and *wayang golek* puppets.

Most of the batik workshops and several large showrooms are along Jl Tirtodipuran, south of the *kraton*. Many give free guided tours of the process. These places cater to tour groups, so prices are high. Batik is cheapest in the markets, especially Pasar Beringharjo, but quality is questionable. Jl Malioboro and Jl A Yani have good fixed-price places.

Fine filigree work is a Yogya speciality, but many styles and designs are available. **Kota Gede** (sacred tomb admission 1000Rp; ☺ sacred tomb around 9am-noon Sun, Mon & Thu, around 1-3pm Fri), a couple of kilometres east of the city, has some very attractive jewellery, boxes, bowls, cutlery and miniatures, and there are dozens of smaller silver shops on Jl Kemesan and Jl Mondorakan, where you can get some good buys if you bargain.

Batik Keris   CLOTHING
(Map p172; www.batikkeris.co.id; Jl A Yani 71) Excellent-quality batik at fixed prices. Best for traditional styles – men's shirts start at about 200,000Rp.

Lucky Boomerang   BOOKS
(Map p174; Gang I 67) Has used guidebooks and fiction, Periplus maps and books, plus souvenirs.

ℹ Information

Yogya has more than its fair share of thieves; the Prambanan and Borobudur buses are favourites for pickpockets. Wandering batik or art salesmen, posing as guides or instant friends, can be a pain, especially around the Taman Sari and the *kraton*.

Internet cafes can be found all over Yogyakarta, although many of the cheaper cafes (which charge around 3000Rp per hour) are located north of Jl Diponegoro. There are numerous banks (and a few money changers) in the tourist areas; ATMs are widespread throughout the city.

Ludira Husada Tama Hospital (☑ 0274-620333; Jl Wiratama 4; ☉ 24hr)

Main Post Office (Map p172; cnr Jl Senopati & Jl A Yani; ☉ 7am-8pm Mon-Sat)

Mulia (Map p174; Jl Malioboro 60, Inna Garuda Hotel) This has the best exchange rates in Yogya.

Tourist Information Office (Map p172; ☑ 0274-566000; Jl Malioboro 16; ☉ 8am-7pm Mon-Thu, to 6pm Fri & Sat) A very helpful office; staff here can provide excellent information and tips. Tugu train station and the airport also have desks.

❶ Getting There & Away

AIR

Yogyakarta airport (code JOG), 10km east of the city centre, has frequent flights to Jakarta, Surabaya, Bali, Bandung and elsewhere, as well as connections to Singapore and Kuala Lumpur.

Buses 3A and 1A (3000Rp) serve Jl Malioboro from the airport. Taxis cost 60,000Rp to 70,000Rp to the city centre.

BUS

Yogyakarta's **Giwangan Bus Station** (☑ 0274-378288; Jl Imogiri) is 5km southeast of the city centre, on the ring road.

Buses also operate regularly to towns in the immediate area, including Borobudur (15,000Rp, 1½ hours) and Kaliurang (10,000Rp, one hour).

For really long trips take a luxury bus. It's cheaper to buy tickets at the bus terminal, but it's less hassle to simply check fares and departures with the ticket agents along Jl Mangkubumi, Jl Sosrowijayan or Jl Prawirotaman.

Local bus 4 leaves from Jl Malioboro (2000Rp) for Giwangan.

MINIBUS

Door-to-door *travel* service to all major cities from Yogyakarta, including Pangandaran (150,000Rp, eight hours), Semarang (30,000Rp, four hours), Surabaya (115,000Rp to 125,000Rp), Malang (100,000Rp) and Jakarta (175,000Rp, 12 hours). Most *travel* will pick you up from your hotel. Hotels

and travel agencies can arrange tickets for the minibuses, or you can book directly through **Dinda** (Map p172; ☑ 0274-447015; Jl Prawirotaman 14).

TRAIN

Yogya's main **Tugu train station** (☑ 0274-514270) is conveniently central, although some *ekonomi* trains run to/from the Lempuyangan station, 1km further east.

The comfortable *Taksaka* (from 350,000Rp, eight hours) departs twice daily for Jakarta at 10am and 7.45pm. The best train is the *eksekutif Argo Lawu* (from 400,000Rp, seven hours), which leaves at 8.56am.

Very regular trains run to Solo, including *Prameks* (10,000Rp to 15,000Rp, one hour), which depart six times daily from Tugu.

For Surabaya, the best option is the *eksekutif Argo Wilis* (from 200,000Rp, 5½ hours), which leaves at 3.15pm.

❶ Getting Around

BIKE

Rent motorbikes for around 60,000Rp a day, and bicycles for 25,000Rp a day. The Sosrowijayan area has a number of rental companies, including **Hotel Kartika** (Map p174; Jl Sosrowijayan 8; per day bicycle/moped 25,000/60,000Rp).

BUS

Yogya has a reliable new bus system called the TransJogja busway. The modern air-conditioned buses run from 6am to 10pm on six routes around the city to as far away as Prambanan. Tickets cost 3000Rp per journey, or 27,000Rp for a carnet of 10. Bus 1A is a useful service, running from Jl Malioboro as far as Jl Senopati, then northeast past the Affandi Museum, Ambarukmo Plaza and airport, to the ruins of Prambanan. Bus 3B connects Giwangan bus terminal with the airport and Prambanan before heading west to Jl Malioboro.

LOCAL TRANSPORT

Becaks cost around 5000Rp minimum, but will generally ask for more – around 20,000Rp from tourist accommodation to the *kraton*. Bargain hard or catch an air-conditioned, metered taxi for less money and hassle!

BUSES FROM YOGYAKARTA

DESTINATION	PRICE ECONOMY/AIR-CON (RP)	DURATION (HR)
Bandung	90,000/125,000-175,000	10
Jakarta	100,000/175,000	12
Semarang	45,000/88,000	4
Solo	15,000/35,000	2
Surabaya	55,000/165,000	8

TAXI

Taxis have meters and are quite efficient, costing 5500Rp for the first kilometre, then 2500Rp for each subsequent kilometre.

Prambanan

The grandest, most evocative Hindu temple complex in Java, **Prambanan** (www.borobudur park.co.id; admission 171,000Rp) features some 50 temple sites. Many suffered extensive damage in a 2006 earthquake. Though the temples survived, hundreds of stone blocks collapsed or were cracked (479 in the Shiva temple alone). Parts of the complex are now fenced off (although the Shiva temple is now once again partially open to the public) and some temples are partially covered in scaffolding. It will take years to fully restore Prambanan. That said, Prambanan is still one of the unmissable historical sites of Indonesia.

The **Shiva temple** is the largest and most lavish, towering 47 dizzy metres above the valley and decorated with a pantheon of carved deities. The statue of Shiva stands in the central chamber and statues of the goddess Durga, Shiva's elephant-headed son Ganesh, and Agastya the teacher stand in the other chapels in the upper part of the temple. The Shiva temple is flanked by the **Vishnu** and **Brahma temples**, the latter carrying further scenes from the Ramayana. In the small central temple, opposite the Shiva temple, stands a statue of the bull Nandi, Shiva's mount.

Built in the 9th century AD, the complex at Prambanan was mysteriously abandoned soon after its completion. Many of the temples had collapsed by the 19th century and only in 1937 was any form of reconstruction attempted. A guide to the complex costs 75,000Rp.

Ramayana ballet (☑021-496408; www. borobudurpark.com) is performed here from May to October several nights a week (tickets from 100,000Rp to 350,000Rp depending on seat location; hotels and tourist offices in Yogya can provide exact timetables). Based on the ancient Indian epic, one of the cornerstones of traditional Indian culture and Hindu religion, the 250 dancers, elaborate costumes and extravagant dance routines, all set in front of a floodlit temple complex, make this one of the most memorable cultural shows in Indonesia. The smaller (50 dancers) **indoor version** (admission 100,000-200,000Rp; ⊙7.30-9.30pm) is held year-round – again check exact schedules with tourist offices and hotels.

There are many other temples in the vicinity of Prambanan that are generally overlooked by backpackers, which is a real shame as most are almost as impressive as the main Prambanan temple complex and far more peaceful. Closest to Prambanan is the large **Plaosan Temple** (admission 10,000Rp) complex, 3km to the northeast. Built around the same time as Prambanan the Plaosan group combine Hindu and Buddhist religious motifs. This site was very badly damaged by the earthquake but reconstruction is underway.

To the south of Prambanan is **Kraton Ratu Boko** (Palace of King Boko) which is a partially ruined Hindu palace complex dating back to the 9th century. Its hill-top perch offers memorable views over the Prambanan plains and it's espically beautiful at sunset.

The so called **Western Group** (per temple 2000Rp) of temples lies closer to Yogya: **Candi Kalasan** (close to Kalasan village) is one of the oldest Buddhist temples in the area. A Sanskrit inscription fromAD 778 refers to a temple dedicated to a female Bodhisattva. A few hundred metres away is **Candi Sari**, another Buddhist temple that dates from about the same period. Ten minutes' drive away is **Candi Sambisari**, an isolated Shiva temple discovered by a farmer digging in his field in 1966.

Most backpacker hotels in Yogyakarta can organise transport to and from Prambanan for both a temple tour or for the ballet.

The main temples face Prambanan village on the highway, while others are scattered across the surrounding fields. The site is 17km east of Yogya on the Solo road. From Yogyakarta, take TransJogja bus 1A (3000Rp, 40 minutes) from Jl Malioboro. Solo-bound buses also stop here. A motorbike or bicycle is a good way to explore all the temples in the area via the back roads.

Borobudur

☑0293

The bustling little village of Borobudur, 42km northwest of Yogya, may at first seem to be nothing but a fairly inconsequential farming village, but looks deceive because it's actually home to one of the most important Buddhist sites in the world and one of the finest temple complexes in Southeast Asia; the breathtaking Borobudur temple complex – a poignant epitaph to Java's Buddhist heyday.

◉ Sights

Borobudur Temple   BUDDHIST TEMPLE
(admission 191,000Rp, sunrise 280,000Rp,
90min guided tour 1-5 people 75,000Rp; ⊘6am-
5.15pm) Borobudur, one of Asia's most magnificent temples, is built from two million stone
blocks in the form of a symmetrical stupa, literally wrapped around a small hill. Standing
on a 118m by 118m base, its six square terraces
are topped by three circular ones, with four
stairways leading up through carved gateways to the top. The paintwork is long gone,
but it's thought that the grey stone of Borobudur was once coloured to catch the sun.

Viewed from the air, the structure resembles a colossal three-dimensional tantric
mandala (symbolic circular figure). It has
been suggested, in fact, that the people of
the Buddhist community that once supported Borobudur were early Vajrayana or
Tantric Buddhists who used it as a walk-
through mandala.

The monument was conceived as a Buddhist vision of the cosmos in stone, starting
in the everyday world and spiralling up to
nirvana, the Buddhist heaven. At the base of
the monument is a series of reliefs representing a world dominated by passion and desire,
where the good are rewarded by reincarnation as a higher form of life, while the evil are
punished by a lowlier reincarnation. These
carvings and their carnal scenes are covered
by stone to hide them from view, but they are
partly visible on the southern side.

Starting at the main eastern gateway, go
clockwise (as one should around all Buddhist monuments) around the galleries of the
stupa. Although Borobudur is impressive for
its sheer bulk, the delicate sculptural work

when viewed up close is exquisite. The pil-
grim's walk is about 5km long and takes you
along narrow corridors past nearly 1460 richly
decorated narrative panels and 1212 decorative panels in which the sculptors have carved
a virtual textbook of Buddhist doctrines as
well as many aspects of Javanese life 1000
years ago – a continual procession of ships
and elephants, musicians and dancing girls,
warriors and kings.

Admission to the temple includes entrance
to **Karmawibhangga** archaeological museum, which is just east of the monument and
contains 4000 original stones and carvings
from Borobudur and some interesting photographs. The ticket also includes admission to
the **Samudraraksa Museum**, which is dedicated to the importance of the ocean and sea
trade in Indonesia.

**Mendut Temple
& Monastery**   BUDDHIST TEMPLE, MONASTERY
(admission 3300Rp; ⊘8am-4pm) This exquisite
temple, around 3.5km east of Borobudur, may
look insignificant compared with its mighty
neighbour, but it houses the most outstanding statue in its original setting of any temple
in Java. The magnificent 3m-high figure of
Buddha is flanked by Bodhisattvas: Lokesvara
on the left and Vairapana on the right. The
Buddha is also notable for his posture: he sits
Western-style with both feet on the ground.

⌷ Sleeping & Eating

Most places to stay also rustle up meals and
most people end up eating in their hotels (in
general, though, hotel restaurants are open to
all). Otherwise there are several cheap food
stalls and basic restaurants scattered along
the main road.

★Lotus II   GUESTHOUSE $
(☑0293-788845;   jackpriyana@yahoo.com.sg;
Jl Balaputradewa 54; r incl breakfast 200,000-
225,000Rp; ✳@☎) This very popular, friendly
place is owned by one of the founders of Jaker,
so there's great local information and everyone speaks good English. Most of the rooms
here are exceptionally large, with mosquito
nets draped from high ceilings and lovely
comfy beds, plus huge bathrooms (with tubs).

The long rear balcony, overlooking rice
fields, is perfect for your breakfast or an afternoon tea or beer.

Rajasa Hotel & Restoran   GUESTHOUSE $
(☑0293-788276; Jl Badrawati II; r incl breakfast with fan & cold water/air-con & hot water

---

BOROBUDUR GUIDES

Jaker (☑0293-788845; jackpriyana@
yahoo.com.sg) is a group of guides and
local activists based in the small settlement of Borobudur.

If you want to explore the region
around Borobudur, Jaker can provide
expert local knowledge. Many guides
speak fluent English. Backpacking rates
are charged for trips to Selogriyo (towering rice terraces and a small Hindu temple), Tuksongo (a centre of glass-noodle
production), tofu and pottery villages,
and to Mahitan hill for sunrise over the
Borobudur monument.

KALIURANG & GUNUNG MERAPI

On the flanks of Gunung Merapi (Mountain of Fire), Kaliurang is a pleasant mountain resort, with crisp air and some spectacular views of one of Java's most boisterous volcanoes. Outside of weekends, when half of Yogya seems to head up here, the spread-out town can seem virtually devoid of humanity and as such makes a perfect place to recharge the batteries and remember what air without carbon monoxide tastes like. Serious hikes up the slopes of Merapi are the main attraction but you could do nothing more strenuous than a clamber up and down the town's green country lanes.

Gunung Merapi is Indonesia's most active volcano and has been in a near constant state of eruption for hundreds of years. People living on its conical flanks are regularly killed by pyroclastic flows. In 2006, 28,000 villagers had to be evacuated after intense seismic activity, and in 2010 Merapi erupted again in spectacular fashion, resulting in 353 fatalities and thousands left homeless.

To learn more Gunung Merapi don't miss the impressive **Museum Gunungapi Merapi** (Jl Kaliurang Km25.7; admission 3000Rp, film 5000Rp; ⏱ 8.30am-3.30pm Tue-Sun), which is 3km south of Kaliurang. You'll find exhibits dedicated to Merapi (including a scale model that demonstrates previous eruptions), a fascinating film and lots of information about other volcanoes around the world, as well as an earthquake simulation room. To get closer to the action jump in one of the jeeps that depart from the museum for a **lava tour** (Jl Kaliurang Km25.7, Museum Gunungapi Merapi; per 4WD 300,000Rp), which will get you up close and personal with the leftovers from the 2010 eruption.

Check the latest situation in Kaliurang, but at the time of writing the climb to the peak from Kaliurang had been strictly off limits since 1994 because of volcanic activity. However, you can hike to **Kali Aden**, a viewpoint that's about as close as most people would actually want to get to a bad tempered, fire-breathing volcano. Treks last around five hours, but in times of increased volcanic activity it might not be possible to do even this hike. Christian Awuy, owner of **Vogels Hostel** (📞 0274-895208; www.vogelshostel. blogspot.com; Jl Astamulya 76; dm 25,000Rp, tw without bathroom 50,000Rp, bungalows with bathroom & hot water 100,000-200,000Rp, meals 15,000-25,000Rp; @ 🛜), in Kaliurang, has organised climbs for years and is an essential first reference point. He charges US$15 per person with a departure time of 4.30am. The price includes a gut-busting breakfast. Vogels itself is a travellers' institution and has been serving up the same mixture of cheap, and very spartan, accommodation and hearty food for just as long.

Kaliurang is 26km north of Yogya. *Angkot* from Yogyakarta's Terban station to Kaliurang cost 8000Rp; the last leaves at 4pm. A taxi from Jl Malioboro will cost around 100,000Rp.

200,000/400,000Rp, meals 20,000-25,000Rp; ❄ 🛜) A deservedly popular, welcoming guesthouse, with rooms that face rice fields (through railings), about 1.5km south of the bus terminal. The fan-cooled rooms are the best value, as you pay a lot more for air-conditioning and slightly smarter furniture. Meals are well priced here.

Pondok Tinggal Hotel   HOTEL $
(📞 0293-788145; www.pondoktingal.com; Jl Balaputradewa 32; dm 25,000Rp, r 150,000-225,000Rp; ❄ 🛜) First impressions of this large hotel constructed of bamboo and timber are that it looks far too grand for budget travellers, but actually there's an excellent choice of inexpensive rooms around an attractive, peaceful garden, and even a couple of dorms.

Don't expect much in the way of atmosphere, but there's a small *wayang* 'museum' and an okay restaurant too.

Lotus Guesthouse   GUESTHOUSE $
(📞 0293-788281; Jl Medang Kamulan II; r incl breakfast 100,000-300,000Rp, meals 15,000Rp) Bare, basic rooms scattered over a rambling building but a very hospitable local family and the authentic local food here is very cheap and tasty.

🛈 Getting There & Away

Direct buses between Borobudur and Yogyakarta cost 15,000Rp and the last one from Borobudur leaves around 6pm. If there are no direct buses, take a bus from Yogyakarta to Muntilan (10,000Rp), where you can change for Borobudur (10,000Rp). There are numerous half-day tours from Yogya which are very popular with travellers but we think it's better to stay in the village and savour the atmosphere a little longer.

Solo (Surakarta)

☑ 0271 / POP 520,000 / ELEV 128M

Arguably the epicentre of Javanese identity and tradition, Solo is one of the least Westernised cities on the island. An eternal rival to Yogyakarta, this conservative city hasn't gone out of its way to attract visitors. However, Solo rewards those with time on their hands who are willing to dig around a little. The city has hidden, backstreet *kampung* and elegant *kraton*, traditional markets and gleaming malls, all of which more than warrant at least an overnight visit.

In many ways, Solo is also Java writ small, incorporating its vices and virtues and embodying much of its heritage. On the downside, the island's notoriously fickle temper tends to flare in Solo first – the city has been the backdrop for some of the worst riots in Java's recent history, especially in 1998. And Solo retains a reputation as a hotbed of radicalism. On the upside, most citizens are extremely hospitable and welcome visitors.

◉ Sights & Activities

Kraton Surakarta PALACE, MUSEUM
(Kraton Kasunanan; ☑ 0271-656432; admission 15,000Rp, guide 25,000Rp; ⊙ 9am-2pm Mon-Thu & Sat, 9am-3pm Sun) Once the hub of an empire, today the Kraton Surakarta is a faded memorial of a bygone era. It's worth a visit, but much of the *kraton* was destroyed by fire in 1985 and today the allure of this once-majestic palace has largely vanished and its structures left bare and unloved.

The main sight for visitors is the **Sasono Sewoko Museum**. Its exhibits include a array of silver and bronze Hindu-Javanese figures, weapons, antiques and other royal

Solo (Surakarta)

heirlooms, plus the mother of all horse-carriage collections. Labelling is poor or nonexistent and termites, woodworm and rot are serious issues.

Dance practices are held here on Sundays at 1pm.

Istana Mangkunegaran PALACE, MUSEUM
(admission 18,000Rp; ☺8.30am-2pm Mon-Sat, 8.30am-1pm Sun) Dating back to 1757, the Istana Mangkunegaran is the second house of Solo. A guided tour of the complex is nothing short of fascinating.

The centre of the compound is the *pendopo*, a pavilion built in a mix of Javanese and European architectural styles. Its high, rounded ceiling was painted in 1937 and is intricately decorated with a central flame surrounded by figures of the Javanese zodiac, each painted in its own mystical colour.

Behind here is the *dalem* (residence), which forms the delightful palace museum. Most exhibits are from the personal collection of Mangkunegara VII. On display are gold-plated dresses for royal dances, a superb mask collection, jewellery and a few oddities, including huge Buddhist rings and gold genital covers.

A guide is mandatory (and worthwhile) for the museum. Most guides are very informative and speak English (a tip of 25,000Rp is appreciated).

At the pavilion, there's *gamelan* music, singing and dance-practice sessions on Wednesday from 10am until 12.30pm.

Danar Hadi MUSEUM
(☑0271-722042; www.houseofdanarhadi.com; Jl Slamet Riyadi 261; admission 25,000Rp; ☺9am-4pm, showroom to 9pm) Danar Hadi is one of the world's best batik museums, with a terrific collection of antique and royal textiles from Java, China and beyond. Entry includes an excellent guided tour (around 1½ hours, in English), which explains the history of the 10,000-piece collection.

✵ Festivals & Events

Kirab Pusaka CULTURAL
(Heirloom Procession) Since 1633, these colourful processions have been held on the first day of the Javanese month of Suro (between March and May). They start at Istana Mangkunegaran in the early evening and continue late into the night.

🛏 Sleeping

Solo has plenty of great value budget hotels.

Cakra Homestay HOMESTAY $
(☑0271-634743; Jl Cakra II 15; r incl breakfast with/without mandi 150,000/100,000Rp, with air-con 175,000Rp; ☀☎☀) In the last edition we said how it wouldn't take much to turn this into one of Java's better backpacker hotels. It seems the management has taken heed. Rooms have been cleaned up and facilities improved, but what hasn't changed are the beautiful gardens and the magnificent *gamelan* room with free performances.

It also has a pleasant pool area.

Warung Baru Homestay GUESTHOUSE $
(☑0815 6763 1000; Jl Ahmad Dahlan 23; r incl breakfast with fan/air-con from 100,000/150,000Rp; ☀) This guesthouse, run by the people of the restaurant with the same name, offers great-value rooms set around a courtyard garden. The homely rooms are well cared for and have colourful art on the walls. The more expensive rooms have hot water and bathtubs.

Istana Griya GUESTHOUSE $
(☑0271-632667; Jl Ahmad Dahlan 22; r incl breakfast with fan/air-con from 100,000/175,000Rp; ☀☎) Istana Griya is popular with backpackers thanks to its sociable atmosphere and clean if unexciting rooms (many don't have outside windows). Staff are knowledgable and friendly enough, but their tours are expensive.

Istana Griya 2 GUESTHOUSE $$
(☑0271-661118; Jl Imam Bonjol 35; r incl breakfast 225,000-300,000Rp; ☀☎) 'One small step up

INDONESIA SOLO (SURAKARTA)

in price. One giant leap in quality.' Words, we feel sure, Neil Armstrong would have uttered if he'd seen this smart, central and modern place with quality mattresses, hot water and earthy toned rooms. The English-speaking manager is very helpful.

✗ Eating

Solo has a superb street-food tradition and a fine traffic-free area called **Galabo** (Jl Slamet Riyadi; ☉5-11pm), where you can sample it. Galabo is a kind of open-air food court with around 90 stalls – tuck into local specialities like *nasi gudeg* (unripe jackfruit served with rice, chicken and spices), *nasi liwet* (rice cooked in coconut milk and eaten with a host of side dishes) or the beef noodle soup *timlo solo* here.

Warung Maksan Es Masuk   INDONESIAN $
(Jl Honggowongso 78; mains from 10,000Rp) One of a couple of branches across the city, this is a 'posh' *warung* and, if the hectic crowds of locals who flock here are anything to go by, it's also one of the best *warung* in town. There's lots of excellent local specialities.

Adem Ayem   INDONESIAN $
(☏0271-716992; Jl Slamet Riyadi 342; meals 20,000-30,000Rp) Huge canteen-like place with swirling fans and photos of ye olde Surakarta. Grab one of the plastic-fantastic chairs and order the chicken – fried, or served up *gudeg*-style – which is what everyone's here for.

Warung Baru   INTERNATIONAL $
(☏0271-656369; Jl Ahmad Dahlan 23; mains from 15,000Rp; ✎) Old school backpackers' hangout, the Baru bakes great bread and caters quite well to vegetarians but the rest of the enormous menu is a bit forgettable. Still, the friendly owners arrange tours and batik classes.

Omah Sinten   INDONESIAN $$
(Jl Diponegoro 34-54; mains 17,000-40,000Rp) Right opposite the entrance to the Istana Mangkunegaran; at this restaurant you can dine on quality Javanese fare (including lots of local specialities) while listening to the tinkle of fountains and the calming notes of classical music.

☆ Entertainment

Solo does offer a few opportunities to see traditional Javanese performing arts, although they're nowhere near as well advertised as similar events in Yogyakarta; contact the tourist office for the latest schedules.

Sriwedari Theatre   THEATRE
(admission 3000Rp; ☉performances 8-10pm Tue-Sat) At the back of Sriwedari Amusement Park, Sriwedari Theatre has a long-running *wayang orang* troupe – it's well worth dropping by to experience this masked dance-drama; you can come and go as you please.

ℹ Information

BCA Bank (cnr Jl Dr Rajiman & Jl Gatot Subroto) Has currency-exchange facilities.
Main Post Office (Jl Jenderal Sudirman)
Tourist Office (☏0271-711435; Jl Slamet Riyadi 275; ☉8am-4pm Mon-Sat) Staff are well-informed here and have maps, brochures and reliable information on cultural events. They also peddle (slightly pricey) tours.

ℹ Getting There & Away

AIR
Air Asia (☏021 2927 0999; www.airasia.com) connects Solo to Kuala Lumpur daily. On Thursday's **Silk Air** (☏724604, 0271-724605; www.silkair.com; Jl Slamet Riyadi 272, Novotel Hotel) flies to/from Singapore.

Domestic services include frequent flights to Jakarta with all the normal players.

BUS & MINIBUS
The Tirtonadi Bus Station is 3km from the centre of the city. Only economy buses leave from here to destinations such as Prambanan (8000Rp, 1½ hours), Yogyakarta (15,000Rp to 35,000Rp, two hours) and Semarang (20,000Rp to 25,000Rp, 3¼ hours). Buses also travel to a number of destinations in East Java including Surabaya (48,000Rp to 70,000Rp, seven hours, and Malang (90,000Rp, nine hours).

Directly behind the bus terminal, the Gilingan Minibus Terminal has express air-con minibuses to almost as many destinations as the larger buses.

Minibus destinations include Yogyakarta (40,000Rp), Semarang (40,000Rp), Surayaba (115,000Rp), Blitar (120,000Rp) and Melang (120,000Rp).

TRAIN
Solo is on the main Jakarta–Yogyakarta–Surabaya train line and most trains stop at Solo **Balapan** (☏714 039), the main train station.

Seventeen daily trains connect Solo with Yogyakarta. The *pramek* (bisnis 10,000Rp, one hour) trains are reasonably comfortable but not air-conditioned.

Express trains to Jakarta include the 8am *Argo Lawu* (*eksekutif* 400,000Rp, eight hours), which is the most luxurious day train.

The *Lodaya* (*bisnis* from 210,000Rp, *eksekutif* from 240,000Rp, nine hours) departs for Bandung at 7am and 3.41pm daily, while the *Sancaka* (*bisnis* from 180,000Rp, *eksekutif* from 200,000Rp, five hours) heads for Surabaya twice daily.

There are several trains to Malang (125,000Rp to 315,000Rp) but they all leave Solo at some ungodly hour of the morning (normally around 2am) so you're better off taking a bus. Jebres train station in the northeast of Solo has a few very slow *ekonomi*-class services to Surabaya and Jakarta.

❶ Getting Around

A taxi to/from Adi Sumarmo airport, located 10km northwest of the city centre, costs around 60,000Rp; otherwise you can take a bus to Kartosuro and then another to the airport. For a taxi, metered **Kosti Solo taxis** (✆ 0271-856300) are reliable. Becak cost about 10,000Rp from the train station or bus terminal into the centre. Public buses run up and down Jl Slamet Riyadi and cost 3000Rp.

Around Solo

The fascinating and remote temple complex **Candi Sukuh** (admission 10,000Rp; ⊙ 7am-5pm) on the slopes of Gunung Lawu (3265m), some 36km east of Solo, is well worth a visit. Dating from the 15th century, Sukuh was one of the last temples to be built in Java by Hindus, who were on the run from Muslims and forced to isolated mountain regions (and Bali).

The main pyramid resembles an Incan or Mayan monument, with steep sides and a central staircase; at its base are flat-backed turtles that may have been sacrificial altars. It's clear a fertility cult built up around the temple, as there are all manner of erotic carvings, including a *yoni-lingga* (vagina-phallus) representation and a figure clasping his erect penis.

Higher still up the mountain (and further around the northern slope) is **Candi Cetho** (admission 10,000Rp; ⊙ 7am-5pm), a large Hindu temple complex dating from the 13th century. Unlike Candi Sukuh this is more of a 'living' temple with buses of Balinese Hindu pilgrims arriving most days. Architecturally though it's less interesting than Candi Sukuh.

There are a number of homestay options around Candi Sukuh and Nglorok and this area is a lovely place to relax for a few days and enjoy the slow and quiet village pace, the cool climate and the lush greenery.

Coming by public transport to either temple is very tricky. Take a bus bound for Tawangmangu from Solo as far as Karangpandan (6000Rp), then a Nglorok minibus (3000Rp) to the turn-off to Candi Sukuh; from here it's a steep 2km walk uphill to the site or a 10,000Rp *ojek* ride. For around 35,000Rp, *ojek* will take you to both Sukuh and Cetho. Hiring a motorbike and guide/driver in Solo costs around 250,000Rp, but it's a very long ride if you're not used to being on the back of a motorbike!

Malang & Around

✆ 0341 / POP 760,000 / ELEV 476M

With leafy, colonial-era boulevards and a breezy climate, Malang moves at a far more leisurely pace than the regional capital, Surabaya. It's a cultured city with several important universities and is home to a large student population.

City life revolves around the *alun alun* (main square) and the busy streets flowing into Jl Agus Salim and Jl Pasar Besar near the central market. This is where you'll find the main shopping plazas, restaurants, cinemas and many of Malang's hotels. Banks are northwest of the *alun alun* along Jl Basuki Rahmat. Many of Malang's best restaurants are in the west of the city. For more historical wanderings, start with the circular Jl Tugu.

⊙ Sights

Hotel Tugu Malang   MUSEUM
(www.tuguhotels.com/malang; Jl Tugu III; 🛜)
Malang's most impressive museum isn't actually a museum at all but a hotel – the five-star

---

MALANG KEMBALI

Held in late May, **Malang Kembali** is a colourful festival celebrating *ludruk*, an old-time music-hall tradition that was very popular in Java in the last century. Jl Ijen, home to many wonderful old Dutch villas, is closed to traffic for five days and there's street theatre, shows and actors in period costumes. Outside of the festival, Jl Ijen is also the home of colourful Sunday mornings. Every Sunday from around 6am until 11am the street is closed to traffic and fills instead with food stalls, sellers of plastic knick-knacks and street artists.

Hotel Tugu Malang. This hotel acts as a showcase for its culturally obsessed owners and their astonishing collection of art, sculpture and treasures, including 10th-century ceramics, ancient *wayang*, antique teak furniture, glassware and even the complete facade of a Chinese temple.

The portrait of a lady in the mirror is one of Java's most famous paintings. Visitors are welcome to browse the collection, which is spread throughout the hotel premises (though you might consider it polite to buy a drink while you're here).

Colonial Architecture   NOTABLE BUILDINGS

Malang has some wonderful colonial architecture. Just northwest of the centre, Jl Besar Ijen is Malang's millionaire's row, a boulevard lined with elegant whitewashed mansions from the Dutch era. Many have been substantially renovated, but there's still much to admire.

Close to the city centre, the Balai Kota (Town Hall; Jl Tugu) is an immense Dutch administrative building, built in a hybrid of Dutch and Indonesian architectural styles with a tiered central roof that resembles a Javanese mosque.

🛏 Sleeping

There's some superb budget accommodation in Malang.

★ Kampong Tourist   HOSTEL $

(☎ 0341-351801; www.kampongtourist.com; Hotel Helios, Jl Patimura 37; dm 50,000-90,000Rp; r 110,000-125,000Rp; ☎) 🍃 The owners of this superb new backpacking place have fashioned an excellent hostel on the rooftop of

Hotel Helios. The vision is impressive, with top-quality mattresses in the dorm (though it does have a *lot* of beds), lovely gazebo-style private rooms, a great shower block and guests' kitchen.

You can tour the town and then socialise in the bar-cafe, with commanding city views, cold beer and snacks.

Jona's Homestay   HOMESTAY $

(☎ 0341-324678; Jl Sutomo 4; r 210,000-280,000Rp; ※ ☎) This long-running homestay in a huge old Dutch villa is run by a sweet family who look after guests well and offer tours. The location is convenient and quiet but the ageing rooms could do with a little more TLC.

Hotel Helios   HOTEL $$

(☎ 0341-362741; www.hotelhelios-malang.com; Jl Pattimura 37; r with fan 100,000-200,000Rp, with aircon 280,000-450,000Rp; ※ ☎) Behind the flash reception you'll find a selection of great value clean, comfortable rooms, most with flat-screen TV and modern bathrooms grouped around a rear garden (and cafe). The economy options are tiny and very spartan. Helios Tours is based here. Breakfast included.

🍴 Eating & Drinking

Agung   INDONESIAN $

(☎ 0341-357061; Jl Basuki Rahmat 80; meals 12,000-18,000Rp) A kind of modern *warung*, this stylish little place has very tasty, inexpensive local food including *martabak* (meat, egg and vegetable pancake-like dish), rice and fish dishes, plus great juices.

Toko Oen   INTERNATIONAL $

(☎ 0341-364052; Jl Basuki Rahmat 5; mains 22,000-60,000Rp) Boasting an imposing art deco frontage that dates from 1930, Toko Oen is a throwback to ye olde days, with rattan furniture, waiters in starched whites and Sinatra on the stereo. In truth it's looking a tad tired, and the Indonesian and Western food could be better. So you could just down a Bintang or a coffee.

ℹ Information

Malang has plenty of banks with ATMs; most are congregated along Jl Basuki Rahmat, including BCA; or try Lippo Bank, opposite the *alun alun*.

Gunung Bromo National Park Head Office (☎ 0341-490885; tn-bromo@malang. wasantara.net.id; Jl Raden Intan 6; ⊙8am-3pm Mon-Thu, to 11am Fri) For Bromo info.

Tourist Information Kiosk (In the *alun alun*) This small kiosk is staffed by students.

TEMPLES AROUND MALANG

The beautiful countryside around Malang is littered with the debris of times past. It's worth getting a group together and hiring a car for a half-day temple exploration (you can also arrange a drop off in the Bromo area afterwards). **Helios Tours** (☑0341-362741; www.heliostour.net; Jl Pattimura 37) are the best people to talk to about doing this. The Singosari temples are mostly funerary temples dedicated to the kings of the Singosari dynasty (AD 1222–92), the precursors of the Majapahit kingdom.

Candi Singosari (⊙7am-5pm) Situated right in the village of Singosari, 12km north of Malang, this temple stands 500m off the main Malang–Surabaya road. This temple – one of the last monuments erected to the Singosari dynasty – was built in 1304 in honour of King Kertanegara, the fifth and last Singosari king, who died in 1292 in a palace uprising.

To reach Singosari, take a green *angkot* (4000Rp) from Malang's Arjosari bus terminal and get off at the Singosari market on the highway.

Candi Sumberawan (⊙7am-5pm) This small, squat Buddhist stupa lies in the foothills of Gunung Arjuna, about 5km northwest of Singosari. Originating from a later period than the Singosari temples, it was built to commemorate the visit of Hayam Wuruk, the great Majapahit king, who visited the area in 1359.

Candi Jago (Jajaghu; admission 5000Rp; ⊙7am-5pm) Along a small road near the market in Tumpang, 22km from Malang, Candi Jago was built between 1268 and 1280 and is thought to be a memorial to the fourth Singosari king, Vishnuvardhana.

Candi Kidal (admission 5000Rp; ⊙24hr) This graceful temple, 7km south of Candi Jago, was built around 1260 as the burial shrine of King Anusapati (the second Singosari king, who died in 1248).

Tourist Information Office (☑0341-558919; Jl Gede 6; ⊙8am-4pm Mon-Fri) Helpful, but 3km northwest of the *alun alun*.

ⓘ Getting There & Away

BUS

Malang has three bus terminals. Arjosari, 5km north of town, is the main one, with regular buses to destinations such as Surabaya (every 20 minutes, normal/air-con 7000/15,000Rp, two to three hours), Probolinggo (normal/air-con 17,000/27,000Rp, 2½ hours) and Banyuwangi (45,000Rp, six hours). Luxury long-haul buses also run to Solo and Yogyakarta (from 80,000Rp) and Jakarta (around 180,000Rp), mostly leaving in the early evening. Gadang bus terminal is 5km south of the city centre and has buses along the southern routes to destinations such as Blitar (13,000Rp, two hours). The third station, Landungsari, is 5km northwest of the city and has buses to destinations heading west.

MINIBUS

Plenty of door-to-door travel companies operate from Malang, and hotels and travel agencies can book them. Minibuses travel to Solo (120,000Rp), Yogyakarta (100,000Rp) and Probolinggo (45,000Rp), among other destinations.

TRAIN

Malang train station is centrally located but not well connected to the main network. The best train to Surabaya is the *Malang Ekspres* (*eksekutif* 20,000Rp, two hours). For Jakarta, the *eksekutif*-class *Gajayana* (from 450,000Rp, 15 hours) leaves Malang at 3pm bound for Jakarta's Gambir station, stopping at Blitar, Solo and Yogyakarta en route.

ⓘ Getting Around

Mikrolet (small minibuses) run all over town. Most run between the bus terminals via the town centre. These are marked A-G (Arjosari to Gadung and return), A-L (Arjosari to Landungsari) or G-L (Gadang to Landungsari). Trips cost 2000Rp to 3000Rp.

Gunung Bromo

☑0335

A lunaresque landscape of epic proportions and surreal beauty, Gunung Bromo is one of Indonesia's most breathtaking sights. Bromo is the Javanese translation of Brahma, the Hindu God of creation. It's an apt name because, with each of the volcano's eruptions it reshapes the surrounding landscape.

The exploding cone of Bromo is just one of three peaks to emerge from a vast caldera, the Tengger Massif (which stretches 10km across), its steep walls plunging down to a vast, flat sea of lava and sand. This desolate landscape has a distinctly end-of-the-world feeling, particularly at sunrise.

An even larger cone – Java's largest mountain, the fume-belching Gunung Semeru (3676m) – oversees Bromo's supernatural beauty, and the entire volcanic wonderland forms the Bromo-Tengger-Semeru National Park.

The usual jumping-off point for Bromo is the town of Probolinggo, which is served by trains and buses from Surabaya and Banyuwangi, but it's also easily reached via Malang.

◉ Sights & Activities

It's all about the sunrise here. The best vantage point over this bewitching landscape is from the viewpoint known as **Gunung Penanjakan** (2770m). All the hotels, and several freelance guides, can put together 4WD trips (125,000Rp per person in a group of four to six people), leaving around 4am to catch the sunrise from Penanjakan. Is it worth the early start? Well, the views of Bromo, the Tengger crater and towards smoking Gunung Semeru are certainly spellbinding. However, don't expect to be the only admirer. Every single morning in season hundreds of people gather to await the sunrise. In fact, it's now so busy that traffic jams (hey, you're in Java – what do you expect?!) form on the access road to Penanjakan and once there it can be hard to actually see anything over the heads of masses of other people and cameras flashing. (Turn it off – your camera flash is not going to light up the entire galaxy!)

After you've seen the sunrise, you'll be driven back down the lip of the caldera and across the crater bed and the **Sand Sea** towards the squat grey cone of Gunung Bromo itself. From here you can often climb to the summit and gaze into Bromo's steaming guts, however, access will vary by the day depending on local wind directions and the amount of ash being thrown forth.

If you don't want to pay for a jeep tour, it's a straightforward 3km hike (around an hour) from Cemoro Lawang to Gunung Penanjakan or just over a kilometre down onto the Sand Sea itself. The **Hindu temple** at the foot of Bromo and Gunung Bator is only open for religious ceremonies.

🛏 Sleeping & Eating

🛏 Cemoro Lawang

At the lip of the Tengger crater and right at the start of the walk to Bromo, Cemoro Lawang is the most popular place to stay and has plenty of cheap accommodation, although all of it's overpriced.

Cafe Lava Hostel   HOTEL $
(☑ 0335-541020; r without bathroom from 178,500Rp, with bathroom & breakfast from 396,000Rp; 🛜) With a sociable vibe thanks to its streetside cafe and attractive layout, this is first choice for most travellers. Economy rooms are small but neat, and have access to a shared verandah and clean communual bathrooms (fitted with all-important hot showers). More expensive rooms are attractive; all have little porches with great views and furniture.

The restaurant serves up very average Indonesian and Western grub and cold Bintang.

Lava View Lodge   HOTEL $$
(☑ 0335-541009; www.globaladventureindonesia.com; r/bungalows from 713,000/792,000Rp; 🛜) This is a well-run hotel located 500m along a side road on the eastern side of the village. As it's almost on the lip of the crater, you can virtually stumble out of your door to magnificent Bromo views. The wooden rooms and bungalows are comfortable enough (if dated) and staff are very friendly and helpful.

🛏 Ngadisari

Another 3km back towards Probolinggo is the tiny village of Ngadisari.

Yoschi's Guesthouse   GUESTHOUSE $
(☑ 0335-541018; yoschi.bromo@gmail.net; r with/without shower 420,000/215,000Rp, cottages from 720,000Rp; @ 🛜) This rustic place has lots of character, with little bungalows and small rooms dotted around a large, leafy garden compound. However, many lack hot water and cleanliness standards could be better. There's a huge restaurant that serves up pricey Western and Indonesian food (subject to a stiff 20% service charge).

🛏 Probolinggo

On the highway between Surabaya and Banyuwangi, this is the jumping-off point for Gunung Bromo. Most travellers only see the bus or train station, but the town has hotels if you get stuck.

SURABAYA

Surabaya's airport is the second busiest in the country and many travellers transit through the city. The airport is served by numerous airlines which link it to Singapore, Kuala Lumper, Penang, Hong Kong and destinations within Indonesia.

Surabaya is not an easy place to love. It's a big, noisy, polluted and commerce-driven city that's not well set up for visitors or pedestrians – just crossing the eight-lane highways that rampage through the centre is a challenge in itself. But though Surabaya's sheer size seems intimidating at first, it does have the odd curious attraction, including the **Qubah**, the city's labyrinthine Arab quarter. Centred upon the imposing **Mesjid Ampel** (Jl Ampel Suci), this fascinating quarter begs exploration. The mosque itself marks the burial place of Sunan Ampel, one of the *wali songo* (holy men) who brought Islam to Java; pilgrims chant and present rose-petal offerings at his grave behind the mosque. The warren of surrounding lanes are reminiscent of a Middle Eastern souk, with stalls selling perfumes, sarongs, prayer beads, *peci* (black Muslim felt hats) and other religious paraphernalia.

Chinatown, just south of here, bursts into life at night when Jl Kembang Jepun becomes a huge street kitchen known as Kya Kya. Much of the food here is sourced nearby at **Pasar Pabean** and the **fish market** (pasar ikan; Jl Panggung; ⊙ from 8pm).

For accommodation some of the very cheapest, and roughest, hotels can be found near Kota train station, but it's best to spend a little extra. The **Hotel Kenongo** (✆ 031-531 0009; www.hotelkenongo.com; Jl Embong Kenongo 12; r 225,000-240,000Rp; ❋ 🛜) is probably the best base in town for backpackers. Offering good comfort levels for the price, this hotel has clean, light, airy rooms. It's also known as the Hotel 88 Kenobo. If that's full, the **Hotel Paviljoen** (✆ 031-534 3449; Jl Genteng Besar 94; r with fan/air-con from 110,000/165,000Rp; ❋) is a slightly shabby colonial villa that still has a twinkle of charm and grandeur. Rooms are plain but clean and have some lovely touches, including front porches with chairs.

Sinar Harapan   HOTEL $
(✆ 0335-701 0335; Jl Bengawan Solo 100; r 75,000-125,000Rp; ❋ 🛜) This new hotel has a contemporary feel and high comfort standards. Its three classes of rooms represent excellent value.

ℹ Information

However you approach Bromo, a 75,000Rp park fee is payable at one of the many PHKA (National Parks Office) checkpoints.

PHKA Post (✆ 0335-541038; ⊙ 8am-3pm Tue-Sun) The PHKA post in Cemoro Lawang is opposite Hotel Bromo Permai and has information about Bromo. Note that the Gunung Penanjakan viewpoint is outside the park and these fees are not applicable. The Sand Sea, though, is within the national park and you'll need to pay your fee at the park office on the edge of Cemoro Lawang. You won't, quite rightly, be able to talk your way out of paying by saying you're only going to the view point. Tickets are valid for the duration of your stay.

ℹ Getting There & Away

Probolinggo's bus station is 5km west of town on the road to Bromo; catch a yellow *angkot* from the main street or the train station for 4000Rp to 5000Rp.

Shop around before you purchase a ticket. Normal/air-con buses travel to Surabaya (17,000/27,000Rp, two hours), Banyuwangi (35,000/55,000Rp, five hours), Bondowoso (16,000/27,000Rp), Yogyakarta (70,000/175,000Rp, nine hours), Malang (17,000/27,000Rp) and Denpasar (100,000/150,000Rp, 11 hours).

Gunung Bromo minibuses leave from Probolinggo's Bayuangga bus terminal and from the main bus station, heading for Cemoro Lawang (30,000Rp, two hours) via Ngadisari (30,000Rp, 1½ hours) until around 4pm. The late-afternoon buses charge more to Cemoro Lawang, when fewer passengers travel beyond Ngadisari. Make sure it goes all the way to Cemoro Lawang before you board.

About 2km north of town, the train station is 6km from the bus terminal. Probolinggo is on the Surabaya–Banyuwangi line. Most services are *ekonomi* class. The *Mutiara Timur* leaves for Surabaya at 12.55pm (*bisnis/eksekutif* 55,000/75,000Rp, two hours) and Banyuwangi at 11.06am (*bisnis/eksekutif* 90,000/130,000Rp, five hours).

Bondowoso

📞 0332 / POP 70,000

Bondowoso is merely a transit point for near-by attractions such as Ijen, but it has banks with ATMs and internet facilities. Tours to Ijen can be organised here.

🛏 Sleeping & Eating

Hotel Anugerah HOMESTAY $
(📞0332-421870; Jl Sutoyo 12; r incl breakfast 125,000Rp, with air-con 175,000-200,000Rp, meals around 14,000Rp; ❄) More of a homestay than a hotel, this is a secure, friendly family-run place with a wide selection of clean, garishly coloured rooms. The English-speaking folk here offer inexpensive meals and trips to Ijen (200,000/600,000Rp return by *ojek*/4WD) can be arranged.

❶ Getting There & Away

There are many (cramped) minibuses to Sempol (35,000Rp, 2½ hours), the access village for Ijen; all leave before noon. From Seppol take an *ojek* (around 50,000Rp) to the park gates. Other destinations from Bondowoso include Probolinggo (normal/air-con 16,000/27,000Rp, 2½ hours) and Surabaya (34,0000/54,000Rp, five hours).

Ijen Plateau

The Ijen Plateau is a vast volcanic region dominated by the three cones of Ijen (2368m), Merapi (2800m) and Raung (3332m). A beautiful and thickly forested alpine area, these thinly populated highlands harbour coffee plantations and a few isolated settlements.

The highlight of a visit here is without doubt the descent into the crater of Kawah Ijen, with its steaming, evil sulphurous lake, where an army of miners dig sulphur out of the crater floor in conditions that can only be described as a medieval vision of hell.

Access roads to the plateau have recently improved and visitor numbers are rising fast as word gets out that Ijen hides one of the most extraordinary sights in Java.

◎ Sights & Activities

Kawah Ijen Hike HIKE
Bubbling and moody, the turquoise lake of Kawah Ijen lies at 2148m above sea level and is surrounded by sheer, and utterly sterile, crater walls. At the edge of the lake, noxious and sulphurous smoke billows from the volcano's

vent, and the lake bubbles and boils when activity increases.

Ijen is a major sulphur-gathering centre, and you'll pass the collectors as you hike up the trail. Most ask for a fee for photographs.

The starting point for the trek to the crater is the PHKA post at Pos Paltuding, which can be reached from Bondowoso or Banyuwangi. Sign in and pay the 150,000Rp entry fee here. The easy, but steep, 3km path up to the sulphur-weighing point takes just over an hour. From here it's a further 45 minutes to the crater rim.

From the crater, a steep, gravelly path leads down to the lake and the sulphur deposits. Due to the extreme conditions, many people choose not to descend down into the crater and content themselves with a peek over the crater rim. If you do continue down to the lake, make sure you are suitably equipped: the sulphur gases are highly noxious and it's absolutely essential that you have some kind of face mask (if only basic surgical face masks are available, wear several at the same time and soak them in water before putting them on). People with any kind of respiratory problems, or those travelling with children, should not descend into the base of the crater. Also bear in mind that photographic equipment doesn't like the gases either. Keep your camera wrapped up as much as possible. Most people start their walk around 6am, but you can also head up the mountain at 1am or 2am when you will get to witness the sulphur fire burning bright blue.

If you walk at dawn and are only going to the crater rim, then a guide is not really needed, but at night, or if you're going into the bottom of the crater, then a guide is near essential. There are a number of guides hanging around the Pos Paltuding PHKA post. We found Mr Sunandi very helpful.

🛏 Sleeping & Eating

You'll find a couple of store-*warung* at the PHKA post at Pos Paltuding, where you can get hot tea or a snack.

Kartimore GUESTHOUSE $
(📞0813 3619 9110, 0813 5799 9800; catimor_n12@yahoo.com; r 145,000-290,000Rp; ❄) This place boasts an excellent location in the Kebun Balawan coffee plantation, close to hot springs. Unfortunately the whole place is pretty creaky (especially inside the original wooden Dutch lodge, which dates back to 1894). There's a separate block of cheap, reasonably clean, if featureless, rooms in a long row.

Arabika GUESTHOUSE $

(✉ 081 1350 5881, 082 8330 1347; arabica.home stay@gmail.com; r incl breakfast from 150,000-280,000Rp, set dinner 50,000Rp; 🛜) This dated mountain lodge is managed by the Kebun Kalisat coffee plantation, which is a short walk away. It's not great but it's not going to make you recoil in fear either. All rooms have hot water. Meals are served. It's at Sempol, 13km before Pos Paltuding on the Bondowoso side.

🛈 Getting There & Away

It is possible to travel nearly all the way to Kawah Ijen by public transport, but most visitors charter transport.

FROM BONDOWOSO

From Wonosari, 8km from Bondowoso towards Situbondo, a partially resurfaced road runs via Sukosari and Sempol all the way to Pos Paltuding. Sign in at the coffee-plantation checkpoints (around 4500Rp) on the way. Several minibuses run from Bondowoso to Sempol (35,000Rp, 2½ hours), but only until noon. They will normally drop you at the Cartimore or Arabika guesthouses. You should be able to find someone in Sempol, or at either of the guesthouses, who will take you the 13km to Pos Paltuding by motorbike for around 50,000Rp one way.

FROM BANYUWANGI

The Banyuwangi–Ijen road is steep but has recently been resurfaced and is in good condition. Cars (600,000Rp per vehicle) can be organised through **Banyuwangi Tourist Office** (✉ 0333-424172; Jl Ahmad Yani 78; ⏱7am-4pm Mon-Thu, to 11am Fri). There's no public transport all the way from Banyuwangi to Pos Paltuding. It may be possible to DIY using a minibus and an *ojek* or two, but don't count on it. From Banyuwangi's Blambangan terminal, take a Lin 3 *angkot* to Sasak Perot (2000Rp) on the eastern outskirts of town and then a minibus to Jambu (8000Rp) at the turn-off to Kawah Ijen, a further 17km away. From Jambu, you might be able to persuade an *ojek* to take you via Sodong to Pos Paltuding for around 60,000Rp. If you're confident riding a scooter up steep mountains, hire one in Banyuwangi and head up yourself.

Banyuwangi

✉ 0333 / POP 110,000

The end of the line, Java's land's end is a pleasant enough town, but there's no reason to hang around here. Confusingly, the ferry terminus for Bali, bus terminal and train station are all some 8km north of town in the port of Ketapang, though all transport uses 'Banyuwangi' as a destination.

🍴 Sleeping & Eating

For cheap eats, there are *warung* on the corner of Jl MT Haryono and Jl Wahid Haysim.

Hotel Baru HOTEL $

(✉ 0333-421369; Jl MT Haryono 82-84; r with fan & mandi 50,000Rp, with air-con & shower 100,000Rp; ❄) On a quiet backstreet near the *alun alun*, this welcoming place has friendly staff, very cheap rooms and a cafe-restaurant.

🛈 Getting There & Away

BOAT

Ferries from Ketapang depart roughly every 30 minutes around the clock for Gilimanuk in Bali. The ferry costs 8000Rp for passengers, 18,000Rp for a motorcycle and 80,000Rp for a car. Through buses between Bali and Java include the fare in the bus ticket and are by far the easiest option (if going from Java to Bali there are often no buses at all waiting at Gilimanuk).

BUS

Banyuwangi has two bus terminals. The Sri Tanjung terminal is 3km north of the Bali ferry terminal at Ketapang, and 11km north of town. Buses from this terminal travel to northern destinations, such as Probolinggo (normal/air-con 35,000/55,000Rp, five hours) and Surabaya (42,000/69,000Rp, seven hours). Buses also go right through to Denpasar (from 40,000Rp, five hours including the ferry trip). Brawijaya terminal (also known as Karang Ente), 4km south of town, has most of the buses to the south.

TRAIN

The main Banyuwangi train station is just a few hundred metres north of the ferry terminal. The express *Mutiara Timur* leaves at 8.30am and 10pm for Probolinggo (4½ hours) and Surabaya (*bisnis/ eksekutif* 100,000/150,000Rp, 6½ hours).

BALI

Impossibly green rice terraces, pulsing surf, enchanting Hindu temple ceremonies, mesmerising dance performances, ribbons of beaches, charming people: there are as many images of Bali as there are flowers on the ubiquitous frangipani trees.

This small island – you can drive the entire coast in one day – looms large in any visit to Southeast Asia. No place is more visitor friendly. Hotels range from surfer dives where the fun never stops to hidden retreats in the lush mountains. You can dine on local foods bursting with flavours fresh from a market or snack on seafood from a beachside

Bali

20 km
12 miles

JAVA

Ketapang

Gunung
Prapat Agung
(310m)
Gilimanuk
Cekik
Labuhan
Lalang
Pulau Menjangan

Banyuwedang
Pemuteran
Celukanbawang

Gunung Musi
(1224m)

Taman Nasional
Bali Barat
Melaya

Gunung Merbuk
(1388m)

Negara
Mendoyo
Medewi
Perancak

BALI SEA

Sangsit
Singaraja
Sukasade
Lovina
Gitgit
Seririt
Mayong
Pupuan
Pujungan

Kubutambahan
Yeh Sanih
Jagaraga
Sawan
Gunung Penulisan
(1745m)
Gunung Catur
(2096m)
Danau Buyan
Danau Bratan
Pura Ulun Danau Bratan
Danau Tamblingan
Munduk
Pancasari
Candikuning
Bedugul
Gunung Batukau
(2276m)
Pura Luhur Batukau
Wangayagede

Tejakula
Sembirenteng
Tembok
Tianyar
Kubu
Tulamben
Culik
Amed
Aas

Gunung Seraya
(1175m)
Ujung

Penulisan
Kintamani
Batur
Gunung Batur
(1717m)
Danau Batur
Toya Bungkah
Songan
Kedisan
Penelokan
Pelaga
Petang
Pacung
Jatiluwih
Pujung

Gunung Agung
(3142m)
Tirta Gangga
Amlapura
Candidasa
Padangbai

Kayuanbua
Muncan
Rendang
Kayubihi
Bangli
Pampatan
Duda
Tenganan
Sideman
Semarapura
(Klungkung)
Kusamba
Nusa

Lombok Strait (25km)

Sampalan
Toyapakeh
Karangsari
Semaya
Nusa Penida
529m

Nusa Lembongan
Jungutbatu
Lembongan
Nusa Ceningan

Padang Strait

Bukit Jambul
Sidan
Bedulu
Lebih
Pura Masceti
Sidan
Gianyar
Pejeng
Ubud
Tampaksiring
Payangan
Marga
Tabanan
Kediri
Antosari

Pura Mas
Batuan
Sukawati
Ketewel
Celuk
Mengwi
Pura Taman Ayun
Sempidi
Batubulan
Canggu
Kerobokan
Seminyak
Legian
Kuta

Ketewel
Sanur
Denpasar
Pulau Serangan
Benoa
Pelabuhan Benoa
Tanjung Benoa
Nusa Dua

Ngurah Rai
International Airport
Jimbaran
Bingin
Padang Padang
Pecatu
Pura Luhur Ulu Watu
Bukit Peninsula

Pura Tanah Lot
Echo Beach

Lalang-Linggah
(Balian Beach)

INDIAN OCEAN

Bali Strait

Tanjung
Sembulungan

JAVA

Taman Nasional
Alas Purwo
Plengkung
Blambangan
Peninsula

Lombok (25km)

shack. From a cold Bintang at sunset to an epic night clubbing, your social whirl is limited only by your own fortitude. And when it comes time to relax, you can get a cheap beach massage or lose yourself in an all-day spa.

And small doesn't mean homogeneous. Manic Kuta segues into luxurious Seminyak. The artistic swirl of Ubud is a counterpoint to misty treks amid the volcanoes. Mellow beach towns like Amed, Lovina and Pemuteran are found right round the coast, and just offshore is the laid-back idyll of Nusa Lembongan.

As you stumble upon the exquisite little religious offerings that seem to materialise everywhere as if by magic, you'll see that their tiny tapestry of colours and textures is a metaphor for Bali itself.

History

Bali's first prehistoric tourists strolled out of the spume and onto the island's western beaches around 3000 BC. Perhaps distracted by primitive beach life, however, they got off to a relaxed start and it was only in the 9th century that an organised society began to develop around the cultivation of rice.

Hinduism followed hot on the heels of wider cultural development, and as Islam swept through neighbouring Java in the following centuries, the kings and courtiers of the embattled Hindu Majapahit kingdom began crossing the straits into Bali, making their final exodus in 1478. The priest Nirartha brought many of the complexities of the Balinese Hindu religion to the island.

In the 19th century the Dutch began to form alliances with local princes in northern Bali. A dispute over the ransacking of wrecked ships was the pretext for the 1906 Dutch invasion of the south, which climaxed in a suicidal *puputan* (fight to the death). The Denpasar nobility burnt their own palaces, dressed in their finest jewellery and, waving golden *kris* (traditional daggers) marched straight into the Dutch guns.

In later years Bali's rich and complex culture was actually encouraged by many Dutch officials. International interest was aroused and the first Western tourists arrived in the 1930s. The tourism boom, which started in the early 1970s, has brought many changes, and has helped pay for improvements in roads, telecommunications, education and health. Though tourism and Bali's sizzling economic development has had marked adverse environmental and social effects, Bali's

unique culture has proved to be remarkably resilient, even as visitor numbers approach four million per year.

Dangers & Annoyances

Persistent hawkers are the bane of most visitors to Bali. The best way to deal with them is to ignore them from the first instance. 'Temporary' tattoos in any colour may cause permanent damage due to the use of toxic chemicals, and *arak* (alcohol typically distilled from the sap of the coconut palm or from rice) should always be viewed with suspicion. And there is a rabies epidemic.

The beaches on the west side of the island, including Kuta and Seminyak, are subject to heavy surf and strong currents. The sea water near touristed areas is commonly contaminated by run-off from both built-up areas and surrounding farmland, especially after heavy rains. You can smell it.

Bali's economic and tourism boom means that traffic is now a huge problem across South Bali. It's also a menace: someone dies on Bali's choked roads every day, reason enough to wear a helmet while riding your motorbike.

ⓘ Getting There & Away

AIR

The only airport in Bali, Ngurah Rai International Airport (code DPS) is just south of Kuta; however, it is sometimes referred to on flight-booking sites as Denpasar or simply as Bali. A vast and flashy new terminal opened in 2014.

Bali is a hub for international flights. Domestic services in Bali seem to be in a constant state of flux. However, competition is fierce and you can usually find flights to a range of destinations for under US$100.

> ### ⓘ WRONG NUMBER?
> Bali's landline phone numbers (those with area codes that include ☎0361, across the south and Ubud) are being changed on an ongoing basis through 2015. To accommodate increased demand for lines, a digit is being added to the start of the existing six- or seven-digit phone number. So ☎0361-761 xxxx might become ☎0361-4761 xxxx. The schedule and plans for the new numbers change regularly but usually you'll hear a recording first in Bahasa Indonesia and then in English telling you what digit to add to the changed number.

194

Air Asia (www.airasia.com) Has a web of Indonesian domestic flights and regional international destinations.

Garuda Indonesia (www.garuda-indonesia.com) The national carrier serves numerous cities.

Lion Air/Wings Air (www.lionair.co.id) Has service across the archipelago.

Merpati Airlines (www.merpati.co.id) Serves many smaller Indonesian cities.

BOAT

Ferries operate between Gilimanuk in western Bali and Ketapang, Java.

Lombok is accessible by regular public ferries from Padangbai. Fast boats for tourists serve the Gili Islands.

Pelni ships sporadically link Bali to several other islands. You can inquire and book at the Pelni office (☑ 021-7918 0606, 0361-763963; www.pelni.co.id; Jl Raya Kuta 299; ◉ 8am-noon & 1-4pm Mon-Fri, 8am-1pm Sat) in Tuban.

BUS

Bali's main long-distance bus terminal is now 12km northwest of Denpasar in a large terminal near Mengwi, just off the main road to west Bali. Fares vary between operators; it's worth paying extra for a decent seat and air-con. Typical fares and travel times include 250,000R and 16 hours to Yogyakarta, and 350,000Rp and 24 hours to Jakarta. Lombok is 225,000Rp. You can also get buses from Singaraja in north Bali.

You can get bemos from the long-distance terminal to Denpasar's Batubulan terminal (20,000Rp) and on to Padangbai (50,000Rp) for the Lombok ferry. Taxis to Kerobokan cost 120,000Rp; Kuta is 140,000Rp. And note that in classic Balinese fashion, some buses still use the Ubung terminal in Denpasar.

TRAIN

The state railway company (Kerata API; ☑ 0361-227131; www.kereta-api.co.id; Jl Diponegoro 150/B4; ◉ 8.30am-6pm) has an office in Denpasar that sells combined tickets for buses linking to train services on Java. Fares and times are comparable to bus-only travel but the air-conditioned trains are more comfortable even in economy class. Note: on the website *Jadwal* means schedule.

ℹ Getting Around

Bali is a small island with good but traffic-clogged roads and myriad transport options.

TO/FROM THE AIRPORT

Fixed-price taxis are found at the airport. The rather high fees range from 80,000Rp for Seminyak to 250,000Rp for Ubud. Save money by ...g 300m northeast from the terminal across ...arking lot and busy access road to catch a ...ed Bluebird taxi just outside the airport exit.

BEMO & BUS

The main bemo hub is in Denpasar, but the proliferation of motorbikes and taxis means that the network is in decline. Bemos don't serve popular spots like Seminyak, and getting from Kuta to Ubud can be an all-day ordeal. Rides cost a minimum of 4000Rp.

Perama (www.peramatour.com) and a slew of others run tourist shuttle-bus services in Bali. Book at least one day before you want to travel and note that popular areas like Seminyak and the Bukit Peninsula are poorly served. Rates are about one-third of a taxi's rates.

Trans-Sarbagita (fare 3500Rp) runs large, air-con commuter buses like you find in major cities the world over. Routes include: Batubulan and along the bypass linking Sanur to Nusa Dua and another running from Denpasar to Jimbaran. The highly visible roadside bus stops have maps. The routes converge at a stop just east of Kuta in the large parking lot south of the Istana Kuta Galleria shopping centre.

BICYCLE

Ask at your accommodation about where you can rent a good bike; hotels often have their own. Generally, prices range from 20,000Rp to 30,000Rp per day.

BOAT

Boats of various sizes and speeds serve Nusa Lembongan and Nusa Penida from Benoa Harbour, Sanur and Padangbai.

CAR & MOTORCYCLE

A small Suzuki or Toyota jeep is the usual rental vehicle in Bali. Typical costs are 150,000Rp to 200,000Rp per day, including insurance and unlimited kilometres.

Motorbikes are a popular way to get around Bali, but can be dangerous. Typically you can expect to pay from around 30,000Rp to 50,000Rp a day. This includes a flimsy helmet, which is compulsory.

If you don't have an International Driving Permit, ask the renter to take you to the relevant police station in Denpasar, where you can buy a temporary licence (200,000Rp).

Hiring a car with driver will cost around 400,000Rp to 700,000Rp for an eight- to 10-hour day (includes fuel). You can arrange rentals from your accommodation or in tourist areas just by walking down the street. Offers will pour forth. This is the most common way for transferring from one part of the island to another.

A speedy new toll road links the Sanur bypass at Benoa with the airport and Nusa Dua.

TAXI

Metered taxis are common in South Bali. They are essential for getting around Kuta and Seminyak, where you can easily flag one down. But any driver who claims meter problems or who won't use it should be avoided.

The most reputable taxi agency is **Bluebird Taxi** (📞 0361-701111; www.bluebirdgroup.com), which uses blue vehicles with the words 'Bluebird Group' over the windshield (watch out for myriad fakes). Drivers speak reasonable English, won't offer you illicit opportunities and use the meter at all times.

Kuta, Legian, Seminyak & Kerabokan

📞 0361

The Kuta region is overwhelmingly Bali's largest tourist beach resort. Many budget visitors come here because it's close to the airport and has the greatest range of cheap hotels, bars, restaurants and tourist facilities. It's fashionable to disparage Kuta and its immediate neighbour to the north, Legian, for their tawdry vibe and crass commercialism, but the cosmopolitan mixture of beach-party hedonism (mushrooms are now sold everywhere) and glitzy new diversions like Beachwalk (Map p196; www.beachwalkbali.com; Jl Pantai Kuta; ⊙10am-midnight) give it a buzz. At its worst, Legian is the vulgar Oz ghetto not actually found in Australia.

Seminyak is immediately north of Kuta and Legian and in many respects it feels like another island. It's flash, brash and filled with hipsters and expats. Its beach is as deep and sandy as Kuta's, but less crowded. Kerobokan immediately north is more of the same.

Busy Jl Legian runs roughly parallel to the beach through Legian and Kuta. Jl Raya Seminyak is the continuation of Jl Legian and is lined with hip shops. Jl Laksmana and Jl Petitenget are the heart of trendy Bali.

Between Jl Legian and the beach is a tangle of narrow side streets, with an amazing hodgepodge of tiny hotels, souvenir stalls, *warung*, bars, construction sites and even a few remaining stands of coconut palms. A small lane or alley is known as a *gang*.

Sights

Much of your time in Kuta will centre on the famous beach, which stretches out of sight to the north and west. Hawkers will sell you sodas and beer, snacks and other treats, and you can rent lounge chairs and umbrellas (negotiable at 10,000Rp to 20,000Rp) or just crash on the sand.

Pura Petitenget TEMPLE
(Map p198; Jl Pantai Kaya Aya) In Seminyak, north of the string of hotels on Jl Kaya Aya,

Pura Petitenget is an important temple and a scene of many ceremonies. It is one of a string of sea temples that stretches from Pura Luhur Ulu Watu on the Bukit Peninsula north to Tanah Lot in western Bali.

Memorial Wall MONUMENT
(Map p196; Jl Legian; ⊙24hr) Reflecting the international scope of the 2002 bombings is the memorial wall, where people from many countries pay their respects. Listing the names of the 202 known victims, including 88 Australians and 35 Indonesians, it is starting to look just a touch faded. Across the street, a parking lot is all that is left of the Sari Club (Map p196).

🏄 Activities

Kuta's famed beach is a mighty fine place to catch a wave or learn to catch one. Stalls on the side streets hire out surfboards (for a negotiable 30,000Rp per day) and boogie boards, repair dings and sell new and used boards.

★Wave Hunter SURFING
(Map p196; www.supwavehunter.com; Jl Sunset 18X at Jl Imam Bonjol; rental per day 250,000Rp) Rents stand-up paddle boards, gives lessons and arranges great-value transport to and from whatever beaches have good conditions on a particular day.

Pro Surf School SURFING
(Map p196; www.prosurfschool.com; Jl Pantai Kuta; lessons from €45) Right along the classic stretch of Kuta Beach, this well-regarded school has been getting beginners standing for years. It has a fun cafe.

Rip Curl School of Surf SURFING
(Map p196; 📞 0361-735858; www.ripcurlschoolofsurf.com; Jl Arjana; lessons from 650,000Rp) Usually universities sell shirts with their logos; here it's the other way round: the beachwear company sponsors a school. You can learn to surf at popular Double Six Beach; there are special courses for kids.

Putri Bali SPA
(Map p196; 📞 0361-755987; Jl Padma Utara, Wisata Beach Inn; massages from 80,000Rp; ⊙10am-9pm) The cream bath here has set the hearts of many spa-o-philes a-flutter with delight. Located off the main street, it's a lovely spa and a big step up from the 60,000Rp massage offered everywhere.

INDONESIA KUTA, LEGIAN, SEMINYAK & KERABOKAN

Kuta & Legian

0 _____ 500 m
0 _____ 0.25 miles

INDONESIA

19
18
Jl Arjuna (Jl Double Six)
17
16
Kimia Pharma Legian
5 8
Jl Nakula
Jl Sunset
6
Double Six Beach
Gate
Jl Pura Bagus Taruna (Jl Werkudara)
Jl Legian
10
Sungai Mati
4 13
Jl Padma Utara
Jl Dewi Sri
Gate Jl Padma (Jl Yudistra)
Gate
LEGIAN
Jl Sahadewa
Legian Beach
Jl Pura Puseh
Gate Jl Melasti
Jl Majapahit
Trans-Sarbagita (300m)
Legian Medical Clinic
Teluk Kuta
Jl Benesari
Jl Lebak Bene
Jl Pantai Kuta (Kuta Beach Rd)
Jl Legian
Jl Majapahit
9
7
2 1
Poppies Gang II (Jl Batu Bolong)
20
21
KUTA
Gang Sorga
Gang Bedugul
Kuta Beach
3
11
12
Poppies Gang I
BEMO CORNER
BIMC (850m)
Kimia Pharma Kuta
Central Kuta Money Exchange
Beach Walkway
14
Jl Pantai Kuta
Kuta Sq
Jl Tengal Wangi
Jl Buni Sari
Jl Raya Kuta
Jl Blambangan
Jl Bakung Sari (Jl Singasari)
15
Kimia Pharma Tuban (400m);
Pelni Ticket Office (1km)

Kuta & Legian

🛏 Sleeping

Bali's tourist boom means that prices of even budget guesthouses have soared. Think US$20 per night as the median for a simple room on a *gang* a few minutes from the beach in Kuta or Seminyak.

🛏 Kuta & Legian

Many cheap places crowd the tiny alleys and *gang* between Jl Legian and the beach in central Kuta. You'll be close to the beach, shops, nightlife and scores of other budget travellers. In Legian, leave the main streets with the touts and gaudy shabbiness for quieter *gang* inland.

★ Hotel Ayu Lili Garden   HOTEL $
(Map p196; ☑ 0361-750557; ayuliligardenhotel@
yahoo.com; off Jl Lebak Bene; r with fan/air-con from
150,000/300,000Rp; ✳ ✙) In a *relatively* quiet area near the beach, this vintage family-run hotel has 22 bungalow-style rooms. Standards are high and for more dosh you can add amenties like a fridge.

Puri Agung Homestay   GUESTHOUSE $
(Map p196; ☑ 0361-750054; off Gang Bedugal; r with
fan/air-con from 120,000/200,000Rp) The budget
winner in Kuta. Hungover surfers will appreciate the 12 dark, cold-water-only rooms at this attractive little place that features a tiny grotto-like garden.

Bene Yasa I   HOTEL $
(Map p196; ☑ 0361-754180; Jl Lebak Bene; r with
fan/air-con from 110,000/250,000Rp; ✳ ✙) The
grounds at this 44-room hotel are large and open, with palms providing some shade.

Three-storey blocks overlook the pool area, and the plethora of patios encourages a lively social scene.

Sri Beach Inn   GUESTHOUSE $
(Map p196; ☑ 0361-755897; Gang Legian Tewngah;
r with fan/air-con from 150,000/300,000Rp; ✳ ☎)
Follow a series of paths into the heart of old Legian; when you hear the rustle of palms overhead, you're close to this homestay with five rooms. The gardens get lovelier by the year; agree to a monthly rate and watch them grow.

Mimpi Bungalows   HOTEL $
(Map p196; ☑ 0361-751848; kumimpi@yahoo.com.
sg; r 250,000-500,000Rp; ✳ ☎ ✙) The cheapest
of the 12 bungalow-style rooms here are the best value (and are fan-only). Private gardens boast orchids and shade, and the pool is a good size.

Blue Ocean   HOTEL $
(Map p196; ☑ 0361-730289; off Jl Pantai Arjuna; r
with fan/air-con from 250,000/400,000Rp; ✳ ✙)
Ideally located almost on the beach, the Blue Ocean is a basic place with hot water and pleasant outdoor bathrooms. Many of the 20 rooms have kitchens and there's action nearby day and night.

Island   HOTEL $
(Map p196; ☑ 0361-762722; www.theislandhotelbali.
com; Gang Abdi; dm 250,000Rp, r from 500,000Rp;
✳ @ ☎ ✙) A real find, literally. Hidden in the attractive maze of tiny lanes west of Jl Legian, this stylish hotel lies at the confluence of *gang* 19, 21 and Abdi. It has a deluxe dorm room with eight beds.

Seminyak & Kerobokan

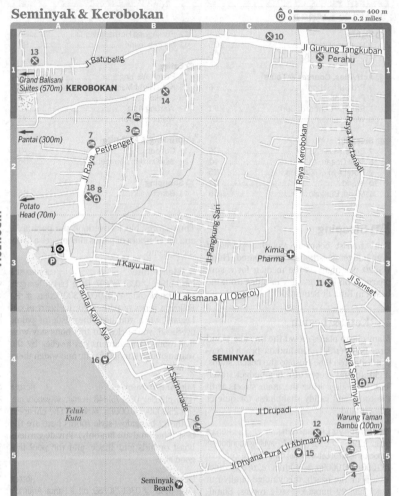

Seminyak & Kerobokan

Seminyak & Kerobokan

The stylish surrounds mean that it can be hard to find a cheap sleep in these rarefied climes, but persistence pays off.

★ Ned's Hide-Away GUESTHOUSE $
(Map p198; ☑0361-731270; nedshide@dps. centrin.net.id; Gang Bima 3; r with fan/air-con from 150,000/200,000Rp; ❈ 🛜) There are 16 good-value basic rooms behind Bintang Supermarket. A newish expansion includes both extra-cheap and more plush rooms.

Sarinande Beach Inn HOTEL $$
(Map p198; ☑0361-730383; www.sarinande hotel.com; Jl Sarinande 15; r 450,000-600,000Rp; ❈🛜🏊) Excellent value. The 26 rooms are in older two-storey blocks around a small pool; the decor is a bit dated but everything is well maintained. Amenities include fridges, satellite TV and a cafe. The beach is three minutes by foot.

Happy Day Hostel HOSTEL $
(Map p198; ☑0361-4780 2777; www.happy dayhostel.com; Jl Petitenget 100B; dm/r from 140,000/400,000; ❈@🛜) A hostel suitably stylish for its location, dorm rooms have 10 beds, private rooms share baths. It's all bright and cheery with white walls and clean lines. Rates include a breakfast toast buffet.

Guess House Hostel HOSTEL $
(Map p198; ☑0361-473 0185; www.guesshousehos tel.com; Jl Petitenget; dm from 200,000Rp; ❈@🛜) Right in the heart of Kerobokan's action, this newish hostel has rooms with four, six and 10 beds. There's a kitchen, shared baths, included breakfast, luggage storage and more.

Inada Losmen GUESTHOUSE $
(Map p198; ☑0361-732269; putuinada@hotmail. com; Gang Bima 9; s/d 130,000/150,000Rp) Bur-

---

---

ied in a *gang* behind Bintang Supermarket, this budget champ is a short walk from clubs, beach and other Seminyak joy. The 12 rooms are small and somewhat dark.

Taman Ayu Cottage HOTEL $$
(Map p198; ☑0361-730111; www.tamanayucottage. com; Jl Petitenget; r US$50-100; ❈@🛜🏊) In a popular part of Kerobokan sits this great-value hotel. Despite the name, most of the rooms are in two-storey blocks around a pool shaded by mature trees. Everything is a bit frayed around the edges, but all is forgotten when the bill comes.

✗ Eating

There's an incredible selection of restaurants in the Kuta area, from no-nonsense noodle bars to seriously swanky eateries in Seminyak. For excellent local fare, head north towards Kerobokan.

✗ Kuta & Legian

Busy Jl Pantai Kuta keeps beachside businesses to a minimum in Kuta. Beach vendors are pretty much limited to drinks. A clutch of cafes front popular Double Six beach at the end of Jl Arjuna.

★ Beach Warung BALINESE $
(Map p196; Kuta Beach; meals from 15,000Rp; ⊙8am-7pm) Simple stalls with shady tables right on Kuta Beach dish up some of the freshest local fare you'll find. Tops is a bowl of spicy *garang asem*, a tamarind-based soup with chicken or pork and many traditional seasonings. Enter the beach where Jl Pantai Kuta turns north and walk south 100m along the beach path.

Warung Murah INDONESIAN $
(Map p196; Jl Arjuna; meals from 30,000Rp; ⊙9am-5pm) Lunch goes swimmingly at this authentic *warung* specialising in seafood. An array of grilled fish awaits; if you prefer fowl over fin, the *satay ayam* is succulent *and* a bargain. Hugely popular at lunch; try to arrive right before noon.

Warung Asia ASIAN, CAFE $
(Map p196; off Jl Arjuna & Jl Pura Bagus Taruna; meals from 30,000Rp; ⊙8am-10pm; 🛜) Look down a little *gang* for this gem: traditional Thai and Indonesian dishes served in a stylish open-air cafe, an authentic Italian espresso machine and lots of newspapers to peruse.

Kuta Night Market
INDONESIAN $

(Map p196; Jl Blambangan; meals 15,000-25,000Rp; ☺6pm-midnight) This enclave of stalls and plastic chairs bustles with locals and tourism workers chowing down on hot-off-the-wok treats, grilled goods and other fresh foods.

Saleko
INDONESIAN $

(Map p196; Jl Nakula 4; meals from 15,000Rp; ☺8am-10pm) Just off the madness of Jl Legian, this modest open-front place draws the discerning for its simple Sumatran fare. Spicy grilled chicken and fish dare you to ladle on the volcanic sambal. Saleko is a perfect spot to start trying Indonesian fare that has not been utterly rethought for timid tourist palates. Everything is cooked halal.

✗ Seminyak & Kerobokan

Seminyak and Kerobokan have a great choice of inexpensive places alongside some of Asia's most remarkable restaurants.

★ Warung Sulawesi
INDONESIAN $

(Map p198; Jl Petitenget; meals from 30,000Rp; ☺10am-6pm) Find a table in a quiet family compound and enjoy fresh Balinese and Indonesian food served in classic *warung* style. Choose a rice, then pick from a captivating array of dishes that are always at their peak at noon. The long beans – yum!

Warung Mimpi
INDONESIAN $

(Map p198; ☎0361-732738; Jl Abimanyu; meals from 40,000Rp; ☺8am-10pm) A sweet little open-air shop-front *warung* in the midst of cacophonous nightlife. A dear husband-and-wife team cook Indo classics simply and well. It's all fresh and tasty.

Warung Taman Bambu
BALINESE $

(Jl Plawa 10; meals from 20,000Rp; ☺8am-10pm; 🖹) You'll be diverted from reaching the pretty garden out back by the array of lovely food out front. This classic *warung* may look simple from the street but the comfy tables are – like the many fresh and spicy dishes on offer – a cut above the norm.

Warung Sobat
SEAFOOD $

(Map p198; ☎0361-738922; Jl Batubelig 11; meals 50,000-150,000Rp; ☺5-10pm) Set in a sort of bungalow-style brick courtyard, this old-fashioned restaurant (with bargain prices) excels at fresh Balinese seafood with an Italian accent – lots of garlic!

Warung Ibu Made
INDONESIAN $

(Map p198; Jl Raya Seminyak; meals 15,000Rp; ☺7am-7pm) The woks roar almost from dawn to dusk amid the constant hubbub on this busy corner of Jl Raya Seminyak where several stalls cook food fresh under the shade of a huge banyan.

Fruit Market
MARKET $

(Map p198; cnr Jl Raya Kerobokan & Jl Gunung Tangkuban Perahu; ☺7am-7pm) Bali's numerous climate zones (hot and humid near the ocean, cool and dry up the volcano slopes) mean that pretty much any fruit or vegetable can be grown within the island's small confines.

★ Biku
FUSION $$

(Map p198; ☎0361-857 0888; www.bikubali.com; Jl Petitenget; meals 40,000-120,000Rp; ☺8am-10pm) Housed in an old shop that used to sell antiques, splurge-worthy Biku retains a timeless vibe. The menu combines Indonesian, other Asian and Western influences; book for lunch or dinner. Dishes, from the exquisite breakfasts and the elegant local choices to Bali's best burger, are artful and delicious.

🍷 Drinking & Nightlife

The distinction between drinking and clubbing is blurry at best, with one morphing into another as the night wears on (or the morning comes up). Most bars are free to enter. Savvy partiers follow drink specials from venue to venue and enjoy a massively discounted night out; look for cut-price drinks coupon fliers.

Bali's rowdiest clubs cluster in about a 300m radius of Sky Garden Lounge. You'll find many low-key boozers, amid their flashier brethren, along Jl Legian. In Seminyak numerous scenester spots line Jl Pantai Kaya Aya.

Sky Garden Lounge
BAR, CLUB

(Map p196; www.skygardenbali.com; Jl Legian 61; ⊗24hr) This multilevel palace of flash flirts with height restrictions from its rooftop bar where all of Kuta twinkles around you. Look for top DJs, a ground-level cafe and paparazzi-wannabes.

Potato Head
CLUB

(Jl Petitenget; ⊗8am-late; 🛜) Kerobokan's popular beach club is South Bali's grooviest. Wander up off the sand or follow a long drive off the main road and you'll discover a truly captivating creation on a grand scale.

Cocoon
CLUB

(Map p196; www.cocoon-beach.com; Jl Arjuna; ⊗10am-late) A huge pool with a view of Double Six Beach anchors this sort of high-concept club (alcohol-branded singlets not allowed!) which has parties and events around the clock. Beds, loungers and VIP areas surround the pool.

Bali Jo
BAR

(Map p198; Jl Abimanyu; ⊗8pm-3am) Simply fun – albeit with falsies. Drag queens rock the house, the crowd lining the street and the entire neighbourhood with songs amped to 11 nightly. Surprisingly intimate, it's a good place to lounge about for a few.

🛍 Shopping

Kuta has a vast concentration of cheap places, as well as huge, flashy surf-gear emporiums on Kuta Sq and Jl Legian.

Seminyak has absolutely fabulous shopping along Jl Raya Seminyak, Jl Laksmana, Jl Petitenget and adjoining lanes. There are lots of local designers, crafts you won't find elsewhere and more to be found just by wandering the main shopping streets to see what you can find.

★Ashitaba
HANDICRAFTS

(Map p198; Jl Raya Seminyak 6) Tenganan, the Aga village of east Bali, produces the intricate and beautiful rattan items sold here. Most fit right into a backpack.

Ganesha Bookshop
BOOKS

(Map p198; Jl Petitenget) In a corner of the fabulous Biku restaurant, this tiny branch of Bali's best bookshop up in Ubud has all manner of local and literary treats.

ℹ Information

You'll find tour-booking agencies every few metres along the main tourist streets of Kuta.

ATMs abound and can be found everywhere, including in the ubiquitous Circle K convenience stores (which have the best prices). Be very careful with 'authorised' money changers. Extra fees may apply or they may be adeptly short-changing customers.

Kimia Farma is a good chain of local pharmacies.

BIMC (☑0361-761263; www.bimcbali.com; Jl Ngurah Rai 100X; ⊗24hr) On the bypass road just east of Kuta near the Bali Galleria. It's a modern Australian-run clinic that can do tests, hotel visits and arrange medical evacuation. Visits can cost US$100 or more.

Legian Medical Clinic (Map p196; ☑0361-758503; Jl Benesari; ⊗on call 24hr) Has an

SUNSET BEERS ON A BUDGET

Bali sunsets regularly explode in stunning displays of reds, oranges and purples. Sipping a cold one while watching this free show to the beat of the surf is the top activity at 6pm. Try these spots:

Legian The best place for this is the strip of beach that starts north of Jl Padma. Along this car-free stretch of sand you'll find genial young local guys with simple chairs and cheap, cold beer (20,000Rp).

Seminyak At the beach end of Jl Abimanyu turn left for a purely Balinese experience. All manner of simple bars line the path along the sand. You'll discover mock-Moorish affairs with oodles of huge pillows for lounging and more. A bit north, skip over-hyped **Ku De Ta** (Map p198; Jl Laksmana; ⊗7am-1am) and grab a cheap beach beer (25,000Rp) from a vendor. Slouch in a lounger and enjoy the same views as the swells above you.

Kerobokan On Batubelig Beach, just north along the sand from the W Hotel, are a couple of open-air bamboo beach bars that have cheap drinks, simple views and fab views. The authorities regularly bulldoze **Pantai** (⊗11am-9pm) but the plucky owners always return.

ambulance and dental service. It's 600,000Rp for a consultation with an English-speaking Balinese doctor. Hotel room visits can be arranged.

Central Kuta Money Exchange (Map p196; ☑0361-762970; Jl Raya Kuta; ⊗8am-6pm) Trustworthy; deals in myriad currencies.

❶ Getting There & Away

Bemos regularly travel between Kuta and the Tegal terminal in Denpasar – the fare should be 8000Rp. The route goes from Jl Raya Kuta near Jl Pantai Kuta, looping past the beach and then on Jl Melasti and back past Bemo Corner for the trip back to Denpasar.

Tourist buses serve Sanur, Ubud, Padangbai and Lovina.

❶ Getting Around

Metered cabs from **Bluebird** (☑0361-701 111; www.bluebirdgroup.com) are easily hailed. A taxi to the heart of Kuta from Seminyak will be about 30,000Rp. You can beat the horrific traffic, save the ozone and have a good stroll by walking along the beach.

Canggu Area

Canggu adjoins Kerobokan to the north and, with its neighbour Umalas, is the next fast-developing area of the south. Look for great beaches and epic surf.

Just up the coast from Batubelig Beach, **Batu Bolong Beach** is a few kilometres along the sand northwest of Seminyak (but a long drive around). Just 500m northwest of Batu Bolong Beach along the sand, **Echo Beach** (Batu Mejan) has condos, trendy shops and beachside cafes. Both are popular with expats living in nearby villas.

🛏 Sleeping & Eating

Villa Serenity   GUESTHOUSE **$**
(www.balivillaserenity.com; Jl Nelayan; s/d from 170,000/350,000Rp; ❋🛜🏊) ∅ Funky in the best way, this hotel is an oasis among the sterility of walled villas. Rooms range from shared-bath singles to quite nice doubles with bathrooms. The grounds are appealingly eccentric; Nelayan beach is a five-minute walk. There is yoga and you can rent surfboards, bikes, cars and more.

Canggu Mart   GUESTHOUSE **$**
(☑0361-824 7183; Jl P Batu Mejan 88; r from 300,000Rp; ❋🛜) About 300m from Echo Beach this basic place has four simple yet comfy rooms (with terraces) behind a con-venience store, a key resource for cheap, cold beer.

Green Room   HOTEL **$$**
(☑0361-923 2215; www.thegreenroombali.com; Jl Subak Catur; r US$60-140; 🛜❋🏊) Popular with surfers, the Green Room exudes hippie chic. Lounge on the 2nd-floor veranda and check out the waves (and villa construction) in the distance. The 14 rooms are comfy and breezy with a bit of a flashpacker vibe.

Mandira Cafe   CAFE **$**
(Jl Pura Batu Mejan; meals 25,000-50,000Rp; ⊗8am-10pm; 🛜) Although Echo Beach has gone upscale, this classic surfers' dive has battered picnic tables with front-row seats for surfing action. The timeless menu includes jaffles, banana pancakes, club sandwiches and smoothies.

Bukit Peninsula

☑0361

Hot and arid, the southern peninsula is known as Bukit (*bukit* means 'hill'). It's the centre of much tourism in Bali; backpackers will be especially interested in the rugged west coast running down to the important temple of Ulu Watu. It fronts some of the best surfing in the world. Little beach coves anchor cool and groovy guesthouses and hotels at places such as Balangan and Bingin.

❶ Getting There & Away

Public transport is unheard of. Ride your rented motorbike or arrange for transport with your accommodation. Bluebird taxis from Kuta to Jimbaran cost about 80,000Rp; to the Bukit beaches and surf breaks will average 200,000Rp. Hire a car or scoot down on a (surfboard-rack-equipped) motorbike.

Jimbaran

Just south of Kuta and the airport, Teluk Jimbaran (Jimbaran Bay) is an alluring crescent of white sand and blue sea, fronted by a long string of popular **seafood warungs**. These open-sided affairs are right on the beach and perfect for enjoying sea breezes and sunsets. The usual deal is to select your seafood fresh from iced displays or tanks and to pay according to weight.

Balangan Beach

Balangan Beach is a long and low strand at the base of the cliffs, covered with palm trees and fronted by a ribbon of near-white sand, picturesquely dotted with sun umbrellas. Surfer bars (some with bare-bones sleeping rooms), cafes in shacks and even slightly more permanent guesthouses precariously line the shore where buffed first-world bods soak up rays amid third-world sanitation.

Balangan Beach is 6.5km off the main Ulu Watu road via Cenggiling.

🛏 Sleeping

Flower Bud Bungalows   GUESTHOUSE $
(☑ 0828 367 2772; www.flowerbudbalangan.com; r 350,000-600,000Rp; 🔊 ✉) On the knoll. Eight bamboo bungalows are set on spacious grounds near a classic kidney-shaped pool, with six more new ones nearby. There's a certain Crusoe-esque motif, and fans and sprightly pillows are among the 'luxuries'.

Bingin

Your best Bukit bet? Bingin comprises scores of funky lodgings scattered across the cliffs and on the strip of white sand below. A 1km paved road turns off the Ulu Watu road (look for the thicket of accommodation signs).

An elderly resident collects 5000Rp at a T-junction, which is near parking for the trail down to the gorgeous **beach**. The surf is often savage, but the sands are calm and the roaring breakers mesmerising.

🛏 Sleeping

More than twenty places to stay are scattered amid the trees and right up to the cliffs.

⭐ **Adi's Home Stay**   BUNGALOW $
(☑ 0816 297 106, 0815 5838 8524; Jl Pantai Bingin; r with fan/air-con from 250,000/400,000Rp; ❄ 🔊) Nine bungalow-style rooms facing a nice garden are new and comfy. It's down a very small lane, near the beach parking. It has a small cafe.

Bingin Garden   GUESTHOUSE $
(☑ 0816 472 2002; tommybarrell76@yahoo.com; r from 250,000Rp) Six basic rooms in bungalows are set around tidy grounds back from the cliffs and 300m north of the toll gate. Each unit sleeps two and has cold water and a fan.

Merta Sari Bungalows   GUESTHOUSE $
(☑ 0815 5805 8724; Jl Pantai Bingin; r 150,000-300,000Rp; ❄) Just before the toll gate, there are eight simple rooms here set in lush grounds. It's very quiet and you can expect good service from the affable manager, Ryan

(a name to trust!). The more expensive rooms have hot water and air-con.

Padang Padang Beach

Small but perfect, this little cove is near the main Ulu Watu road where a stream flows into the sea. Parking is easy and it is a short walk. Experienced surfers seeking tubes flock here.

🛏 Sleeping

Thomas Homestay   GUESTHOUSE $
(☑ 0813 3803 4354; r from 250,000Rp) Enjoy stunning views up and down this spectacular coast. Thirteen very simple rooms lie at the end of a very rough 400m track off the main road. You can take a long walk down stairs to the mostly deserted swath of Padang Padang Beach west of the river. The cafe is a secret find for its views.

Ulu Watu & Around

Ulu Watu has become the generic name for the southwestern tip of the Bukit Peninsula. It includes the much-revered temple and the nearby fabled surf breaks.

About 2km north of the temple there is a dramatic cliff which has steps that lead to the legendary Ulu Watu surf breaks. All manner of cafes and surf shops spill down the nearly sheer face to the water below. Views are stellar, new places open constantly, growth is out of control; it's quite the scene!

◉ Sights & Activities

⭐ **Pura Luhur Ulu Watu**   TEMPLE
(admission incl sarong & sash rental 20,000Rp; ⊙ 8am-7pm) Pura Luhur Ulu Watu is perched precipitously on the southwestern tip of the peninsula, atop sheer cliffs that drop straight into the pounding surf. Watch out for monkeys, who like to snatch sunglasses and anything else within reach. The sunset **Kecak dance** (admission 80,000Rp; ⊙ sunset) is one of the more delightful performances on the island.

🛏 Sleeping & Eating

The cliffs above the main Ulu Watu surf break are lined with a hodgepodge of cafes and guesthouses. Some cling to rocks over the waves. You can enter from the east (crowded) or from the south (a pretty walk).

Ulu Watu & Around

Ulu Watu & Around

◉ Top Sights
1 Pura Luhur Ulu Watu A3

✪ Activities, Courses & Tours
2 Bingin..B1
3 Ulu Watu...A2

🛏 Sleeping
4 Adi's Home Stay....................................B2
5 Bingin Garden.......................................B2
6 Flower Bud Bungalows C1
7 Gong..A3
8 Merta Sari Bungalows.........................B2
9 Thomas Homestay B2

✖ Eating
10 Delpi Rock Lounge...............................A2

✪ Entertainment
11 Kecak Dance..A3

Gong   GUESTHOUSE $
(📞 0361-769976; thegongacc@yahoo.com; Jl Pantai
Suluban; r from 200,000Rp; @ 🏊) Few stay away
long from the Gong. The 12 tidy rooms have
good ventilation and hot water and face a
small compound with a lovely pool; some
have distant ocean views. It is about 1km
south of the Ulu Watu cliffside cafes.

Putu Home Stay   GUESTHOUSE $
(📞 0361-769883; putu_accommodation@yahoo.
com; Jl Pantai Suluban; r from 300,000Rp; ❄ 🏊)
Just behind the Ulu Watu action, you can
hear the waves pound in the 13 modern
rooms.

★ Delpi Rock Lounge   CAFE $
(meals from 50,000Rp; ⏰ noon-9pm) At one
branch of the Delpi empire, you can nab a
sunbed on a platform atop a rock nearly surrounded by surf. Further up the cliff there is
a cafe which has three simple rooms for rent
(from 300,000Rp).

Nusa Dua & Tanjung Benoa

The Tanjung Benoa peninsula extends about
4km north from the gated resort area of
Nusa Dua to the fishing village of Benoa.
The area caters to top-end travellers and
package holidaymakers.

Denpasar

📞 0361 / POP 800,000
Sprawling, hectic and ever-growing, Bali's
capital is home to most Balinese and you can
sense the island's new-found wealth. Mostly
untrodden by tourists, Denpasar can seem a
little daunting and chaotic, but spend some

time on the tree-lined streets in the relatively affluent government and business district of Renon and you will discover a more genteel side to the city.

◉ Sights

★ **Museum Negeri Propinsi Bali**   MUSEUM
(☑0361-222680; adult/child 10,000/5000Rp; ⊗8am-12.30pm Fri, to 4pm Sat-Thu) Denpasar's most important attraction, the Museum Negeri Propinsi Bali showcases a range of Balinese crafts, antiquities and cultural objects. This museum is quite well set up and most displays are also labelled in English. Alongside the fine handspun textiles, you'll see some incredibly intricate drawings of the Ramayana, and startling *barong* costumes used for Balinese dance.

🛏 Sleeping & Eating

Beaches, smeaches. Stay in Denpasar and savour contemporary urban Balinese life.

It has the island's best range of Indonesian and Balinese food. Savvy locals and expats each have their own favourite *warung* and restaurants.

Nakula Familiar Inn   GUESTHOUSE $
(☑0361-226446; www.nakulafamiliarinn.com; Jl Nakula 4; r with fan/air-con from 150,000/200,000Rp;

Denpasar

◉ **Top Sights**
1 Museum Negeri Propinsi Bali B2

🛏 **Sleeping**
2 Nakula Familiar Inn A1

🍴 **Eating**
3 Ayam Goreng Kalasan D3
4 Cak Asm C4

🛍 **Shopping**
5 Pasar Badung A2

INDONESIA DENPASAR

Denpasar

❄ ☎) The eight rooms at this sprightly urban family compound, which has been a traveller favourite since before Seminyak existed, have small balconies. The traffic noise isn't too bad and there is a nice courtyard and cafe in the middle.

★ **Cak Asm**   BALINESE $
(Jl Tukad Gangga; meals from 25,000Rp; ☺8am-10pm) Join the government workers and students from the nearby university for superb dishes cooked to order in the bustling kitchen. Order the *cumi cumi* (calamari) with *telor asin* sauce (a heavenly mixture of eggs and garlic).

Ayam Goreng Kalasan   INDONESIAN $
(Jl Cok Agung Tresna 6; meals from 25,000Rp; ☺8am-10pm) The name here says it all: fried chicken *(ayam goreng)* named for a Javanese temple (Kalasan) in a region renowned for its fiery, crispy chicken. There are several other excellent little *warung* in this strip.

🔒 Shopping

A must-see destination: shoppers browse and bargain at the sprawling **Pasar Badung** (Jl Gajah Mada) morning to night. It's a retail adventure and you'll find produce and food from all over the island.

❶ Getting There & Around

Denpasar is *the* hub for the creaky bemo network around Bali. The city has several terminals – you'll often have to go via Denpasar and transfer from one terminal to another. Each terminal has regular bemo connections to the other terminals in Denpasar for 7000Rp. Key terminals include:

Batubulan Bus & Bemo Terminal Located an inconvenient 6km northeast of Denpasar on a road to Ubud, this terminal is for destinations in eastern and central Bali. This is where you get minibuses to the long-distance bus terminal in Mengwi (20,000Rp, one hour).

Tegal Bemo Terminal Bemos south, including Kuta and Jimbaran.

Ubung Bus & Bemo Terminal The west, including Mengwi and Gilimanuk, plus north to Singaraja. Many long-distance buses still use this terminal in addition to the new one in Mengwi.

Sanur

📋 0361

Sanur is a genteel alternative to Kuta. The white-sand beach is sheltered by a reef. The resulting low-key surf contributes to Sanur's nickname 'Snore', although this is also attrib-

utable to the area's status as a haven for expat retirees. The **beachfront walk** was the first in Bali and from day one has been delighting locals and visitors alike. Over 4km long, it follows the sand as it curves to the southwest. Oodles of cafes with tables in the sand give plenty of reason to pause.

🛏 Sleeping

Usually the best places to stay are right on the beach; however, beware of properties that have been coasting for decades.

Kesumasari   GUESTHOUSE $
(📋0361-287824; Jl Kesumasari 6; r with fan/air-con from 300,000/450,000Rp; ❄☎❄) The only thing between you and the beach is a small shrine. Beyond the lounging porches, the multihued carved Balinese doors don't prepare you for the riot of colour inside the 15 idiosyncratic rooms at this family-run homestay.

Keke Homestay   GUESTHOUSE $
(📋0361-287282; Jl Danau Tamblingan 100; r with fan/air-con from 150,000/250,000Rp; ❄) Set 150m down a *gang* from the noisy road, Keke welcomes backpackers to its genial family (often busy making offerings). The five quiet, clean rooms vary from fan-only to air-con cool.

🍴 Eating & Drinking

The beach path offers restaurants, *warung* and bars where you can catch a meal, a drink or a sea breeze.

★ **Manik Organik**   ORGANIC $
(www.manikorganikbali.com; Jl Danau Tamblingan 85; meals from 50,000Rp; ☺8am-10pm; ✈) Actual trees shade the serene terrace at this creative and healthful cafe. Vegetarians are well-cared for but there are also meaty dishes made with free-range chicken and the like. Smoothies include the fortifying 'immune tonic'.

Sari Bundo   INDONESIAN $
(📋0361-281389; Jl Danau Poso; ☺24hr) This spotless *padang*-style shopfront is one of several at the south end of Sanur. Choose from an array of fresh and very spicy food. The curry chicken is a fiery treat that will have your tongue alternatively loving and hating you.

Warung Pantai Indah   CAFE
(Beachfront Walk; ☺noon-11pm) Sit on benches in the sand under a tin roof at this uberauthentic old Sanur beach cafe. Just north of the Hotel Peneeda View and near some of Sanur's most expensive private beach villas, this outpost of good cheer has cheap beer and regular

specials on fresh-grilled seafood (100,000Rp). The views and owners are delightful.

ℹ Getting There & Around

Tourist bus destinations include Kuta (25,000Rp, 30 minutes), Ubud (40,000Rp, one hour) and Padangbai (60,000Rp, two hours). There's a **Perama** (☑ 0361-285592; Jl Hang Tuah 39; ⊙ 7am-10pm) office.

Bemos go up and down Jl Danau Tamblingan and Jl Danau Poso for 4000Rp.

Nusa Lembongan

☑ 0366

Laidback Nusa Lembongan is one of three islands (along with Nusa Penida and Nusa Ceningan) that comprise the Nusa Penida archipelago. It's the Bali many imagine but never find: rooms on the beach, cheap beers with incredible sunsets, days spent surfing and diving, and nights spent riffling through a favourite book or hanging with new friends.

◉ Sights

Jungutbatu Beach   BEACH
Jungutbatu beach, a fine swath of white sand with clear blue water, has superb views across to Gunung Agung in Bali. The village itself is pleasant, with quiet lanes, no cars and mellow locals harvesting and drying seaweed.

Mushroom Bay Beach   BEACH
This beautiful bay, unofficially named after the mushroom corals offshore, has a crescent of bright white beach. By day, the tranquility can be disturbed by banana-boat rides or parasailing.

The most interesting way to get here from Jungutbatu is to walk along the trail that starts from the southern end of the main beach and follows the coastline for a kilometre or so. Alternatively, get a boat from Jungutbatu.

🏃 Activities

Most places will rent bicycles for 30,000Rp per day, surfboards for 50,000Rp and motorbikes for 30,000Rp per hour. Good **snorkelling** can be had just off Mushroom Bay as well as in areas off the north coast of the island. The **diving** at Nusa Penida is legendary and challenging. **Surfing** just off Jungutbatu is a major draw.

World Diving   DIVING
(☑ 081 2390 0686; www.world-diving.com; 2 dives US$85) World Diving, based at the Pondok

Baruna location on Jungutbatu Beach, is well regarded. It offers a complete range of courses plus diving and snorkelling trips to dive sites all around the three islands.

🛏 Sleeping & Eating

Lembongan has become flashpacker central. The row of guesthouses (most with cafes) along Jungutbatu beach are continuously upgrading. As you follow the elevated coastal path west to Mushroom Bay, standards and prices generally elevate as well.

Pondok Baruna   GUESTHOUSE $
(☑ 0812 394 0992; www.pondokbaruna.com; r 250,000-700,000Rp; ❋ @ 🛜 ≋) This place offers four very simple rooms with terraces facing the ocean. They are an excellent budget option. Six plusher rooms with air-con surround a dive pool off the beach. Eight more rooms are located back in the palm trees around a large pool.

Morin Lembongan   GUESTHOUSE $
(☑ 0812 385 8396; wayman40@hotmail.com; r US$30-45; @) More lushly planted than many of the hillside places, Morin has woodsy rooms with views over the water from their verandas. This is a good choice if you want to feel close yet removed from Jungutbatu. Wayan, the owner, is a great surf guide.

Two Thousand Cafe & Bungalows   GUESTHOUSE $
(☑ 0812 381 2775; r 200,000-500,000Rp; ❋ 🛜 ≋) Grassy grounds surround 28 rooms in two-storey blocks; some have hot water and air-con. There's a fun cafe-bar right on the sand, with various sunset drink specials.

ℹ Information

It's vital that you bring sufficient cash for your stay, as the ATM can fail; there are few other services.

ℹ Getting There & Around

Boats anchor offshore, so be prepared to get your feet wet. And travel light – wheeled bags are comically inappropriate in the water and on the beach and dirt tracks. There are numerous ways of travelling between Nusa Lembongan and Sanur.

Public boats leave from the northern end of Sanur beach at 7.45am (60,000Rp, 1¾ to two hours). This is the boat used for supplies, so you may have to share space with a chicken.

Numerous fast boat companies haul tourists on a wild ride over the waves from Sanur (about US$55, 30 to 40 minutes). **Scoot**

INDONESIA

(☑ 0361-285522; www.scootcruise.com) runs several returns daily. There are also useful fast boat links between Nusa Lembongan and the Gilis.

The island is fairly small and you can easily walk most places. There are no cars. One-way rides on motorbikes or trucks cost 10,000Rp and up.

Ubud

☑ 0361

Perched on the gentle slopes leading up towards the central mountains, Ubud is the other half of Bali's tourism duopoly. Unlike South Bali, however, Ubud's focus remains on the remarkable Balinese culture in its myriad forms.

It's not surprising that many people come to Ubud for a day or two and end up staying longer, drawn in by the rich culture and many activities. Besides the popular dance-and-music shows, there are numerous courses that allow you to become fully immersed in Balinese culture.

Ubud is home to chilled-out restaurants and cafes, myriad yoga studios, plus artful and serene places to stay. Around Ubud are temples, ancient sites and whole villages producing handicrafts (albeit mostly

Ubud Area

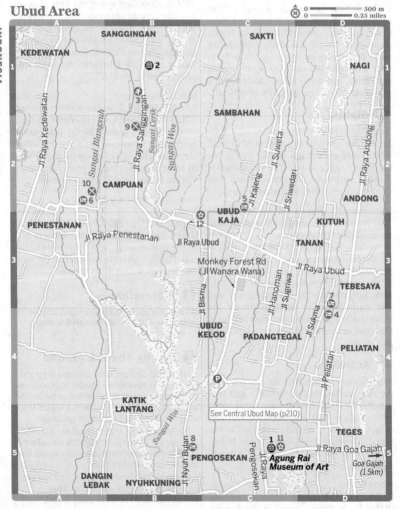

for visitors). Although the growth of Ubud has engulfed several neighbouring villages, leading to an urban sprawl, parts of the surrounding countryside remain unspoiled, with lush rice paddies and towering coconut trees.

◎ Sights

Spend time in the museums and walking the beautiful countryside. If you only visit for a brief time on a day trip you may wonder what the fuss is all about.

★ Agung Rai Museum of Art   GALLERY
(ARMA; Map p208; ☑0361-976659; www.arma museum.com; Jl Raya Pengosekan; admission 50,000Rp; ☺9am-6pm daily, Balinese dancing 3-5pm Mon-Fri, 10.30am-noon Sun) This museum, gallery and cultural centre is the only place in Bali at which to see works by the influential German artist Walter Spies.

It features work by 19th-century Javanese artist Raden Saleh. It exhibits classical Kamasan paintings, Batuan-style work from the 1930s and '40s, and works by Lempad, Affandi, Sadali, Hofker, Bonnet and Le Mayeur. The collection is well labelled in English.

It's fun to visit ARMA when local children practise Balinese dancing and during *gamelan* practice.

Ubud Area

Sacred Monkey Forest Sanctuary   WILDLIFE RESERVE
(Mandala Wisata Wanara Wana; Map p210; ☑0361-971304; Monkey Forest Rd; adult/child 20,000/10,000Rp; ☺8.30am-6pm) This cool and dense swath of jungle, officially called Mandala Wisata Wanara Wana, houses three holy temples. The sanctuary is inhabited by a band of grey-haired, greedy long-tailed Balinese macaques who are nothing like the innocent looking doe-eyed monkeys on the brochures.

Museum Puri Lukisan   MUSEUM
(Museum of Fine Arts; Map p210; ☑0361-975136; www.museumpurilukisan.com; off Jl Raya Ubud; adult/child 20,000Rp/free; ☺9am-5pm) On Jl Raya Ubud, this museum compound has displays in a beautiful garden setting excellent examples of all schools of Balinese art.

Neka Art Museum   GALLERY
(Map p208; ☑0361-975074; www.museumneka. com; Jl Raya Sanggingan; adult/child 50,000Rp/ free; ☺9am-5pm Mon-Sat, noon-5pm Sun) Quite distinct from Neka Gallery, the Neka Art Museum is the creation of Suteja Neka, a private collector and dealer in Balinese art. It has an excellent and diverse collection and is the best place to learn about the development of painting in Bali.

★ Activities

As well as visiting the museums and galleries, it is well worth exploring the natural beauty that inspires so much of it. There are wonderful walks around Ubud: east to Pejeng; across picturesque ravines south to Bedulu; north along the Campuan ridge; and west to Penestanan and Sayan, with views over the Sungai Ayung (Ayung River) gorge.

Ubud is a nexus of pampering: spas, yoga and myriad New Age activities are on offer. Check the bulletin board outside **Bali Buddha** (Map p210; Jl Jembawan 1; meals from 30,000Rp; ☑), a health-food cafe and shop, for listings. You can also find courses in Balinese arts.

★ Bali Botanica Day Spa   SPA
(Map p208; ☑0361-976739; www.balibotanica. com; Jl Raya Sanggingan; massage from 150,000Rp; ☺9am-8pm) Set beautifully on a lush hillside past little fields of rice and ducks, this splurge-worthy spa offers a range of

INDONESIA UBUD

Central Ubud

N 0 ———————— 200 m
0 ———————— 0.1 miles

**UBUD
KAJA**

1

Pura Dalem
Ubud (130m)

Jl Kajeng

Jl Suweta

23 20

26 Jl Sriwedari

Jl Sandat

13

TANAN

Ubud
Tourist
Information

24

Jl Anggada

Jl Arjuna

Market

Jl Raya Ubud

Jl Bisma

11

9

Jl Karna

Jl Maruti

8 Jl Goutama

25

Football
Field

19

Jl Dewi Sita

6

14

12

21

Jl Jembawan

5

16

Jl Sugriwa

Monkey Forest Rd (Jl Wanara Wana)

17

Jl Hanoman

PADANGTEGAL

22 18

**UBUD
KELOD**

15

7

10

4

Jl Sukma

6 P

2

3

Perama

Jl Raya Pengosekan

Central Ubud

INDONESIA UBUD

treatments including Ayurvedic ones. Like a good pesto, the herbal massage is popular. Will provide transport.

Yoga Barn YOGA
(Map p210; ☑0361-070992; www.balispirit.com; off Jl Raya Pengosekan; classes from 110,000Rp; ☺7am-8pm) The chakra for the yoga revolution in Ubud, the Yoga Barn sits in its own lotus position in a compound amid trees back near a river valley. The name exactly describes what you'll find. A huge range of classes in yoga, Pilates, dance and life-affirming offshoots are held through the week.

Herb Walks NATURE WALKS
(☑0361-975051; www.baliherbalwalk.com; walks US$20; ☺8.30am) Three-hour walks through lush Bali landscape; medicinal and cooking herbs and plants are identified and explained.

🛏 Sleeping

There are hundreds of places to stay. Choices range from simple little *losmen* to world-class luxurious retreats. Inexpensive family lodgings are very small and tend to operate in clusters, so you can easily look at a few before choosing.

There's no need to pay for air-con, as it's cool at night.

🛏 Central Ubud

Small streets east of Monkey Forest Rd, including Jl Karna and Jl Maruti, have numerous, family-style homestays, as does Jl Goutama. Don't settle for a room with road noise along Ubud's main drags.

★**Nirvana Pension & Gallery** GUESTHOUSE $
(Map p210; ☑0361-975415; www.nirvanaku.com; Jl Goutama 10; r 250,000-450,000Rp; ☜) There are *alang-alang* (thatched roofs), a plethora of paintings, ornate doorways and six rooms with modern bathrooms in a shady, secluded locale next to a large family temple. Batik courses are also held.

Padma Accommodation GUESTHOUSE $
(Map p208; ☑0361-977247; aswatama@hotmail. com; Jl Kajeng 13; r 250,000-250,000Rp; ☜) There are five bungalows in a tropical garden here (three are newish). Rooms are decorated with local crafts and the modern outdoor bathrooms have hot water. Nyoman Sudiarsa, a painter and family member, has a studio here and often shares his knowledge with guests.

Donald Homestay HOMESTAY $
(Map p210; ☑0361-977156; Jl Goutama; r 200,000-250,000Rp; ☜) The four rooms – some with hot water – are in a nice back corner of a compound that's home to four generations. The chickens running around here have a date with a bamboo skewer.

★**Oka Wati Hotel** HOTEL $$
(Map p210; ☑0361-973386; www.okawatihotel. com; off Monkey Forest Rd; r from US$55; ✳ ☜ ☜) Oka Wati (the owner) is a lovely lady who

grew up near the Ubud Palace. The 19 rooms have large verandahs where the delightful staff will deliver your choice of breakfast (do not miss the house-made yoghurt). Follow narrow footpaths to get here.

Sama's Cottages
GUESTHOUSE $$

(Map p210; ☑0361-973481; www.samas cottagesubud.com; Jl Bisma; r with fan/air-con from 430,000/580,000Rp; 🛜🛏) This lovely little hideaway is terraced down a hill. The nine bungalow-style rooms have lashings of Balinese style layered on absolute simplicity. The oval pool feels like a jungle oasis. Ask for low-season discounts.

Padangtegal & Tebesaya

East of central Ubud, but still conveniently located, Padangtegal has several budget lodgings along Jl Hanoman. In Tebesaya, Jl Sukma and the *gang* that runs parallel just to the east are excellent hunting grounds for budget stays.

★ Family Guest House
HOMESTAY $$

(Map p210; ☑0361-974054; familyhouse@telkom. net; Jl Sukma; r 200,000-350,000Rp; 🛜) There's a bit of bustle from the busy family at this charming homestay. The rooms have all had upgrades; some also include tubs. It's a perfect Balinese compound and it backs up to a valley and stream.

Suastika Lodge
GUESTHOUSE $

(Map p208; ☑0361-970215; suastika@hotmail.com; off Jl Sukma; r 150,000-200,000Rp; 🛜) On the lane east of Jl Sukma, you'll find four tidy rooms in a classic family compound. It's bungalow-style and you'll enjoy privacy and serenity.

SPLURGE

One of Ubud's most inventive and appealing places to stay is **Swasti Cottage** (Map p208; ☑0361-974079; www.baliswasti.com; Jl Nyuh Bulan; r 600,000-1,200,000Rp; @🛜🛏), just five minutes' walk from the south entrance to the Sacred Monkey Forest Sanctuary. Run by a French-Balinese couple, this guesthouse has large, manicured grounds. Some rooms are in simple two-storey blocks; others are in vintage traditional bungalows brought here from across Bali.

Pande Home Stay
GUESTHOUSE $

(Map p210; ☑0361-970421; pandehomestay@ gmail.com; Jl Sugriwa; r 150,000-200,000Rp; 🛜) One of Ubud's great family-compound home-stays, Pande is but one of many in a cluster here. It's close to the Yoga Barn and other highlights. The stone carvings are especially elaborate.

Artini Cottages 1
HOMESTAY $

(Map p210; ☑0361-975348; www.artinicottage. com; Jl Hanoman; r 250,000Rp; 🛜) The Artini family runs a small empire of good-value guesthouses on Jl Hanoman. This, the original, is in an ornate family compound with many flowers. The three bungalows have hot water and large bathtubs. The more upscale Artini 2, with rice-field views and a pool, is opposite.

Biangs
HOMESTAY $

(Map p210; ☑0361-976520; Jl Sukma 28; r 90,000-200,000Rp; 🛜) In a little garden, Biangs (meaning 'mama') has six well-maintained rooms with hot water. The best rooms have views of a small valley.

Aji Lodge
HOMESTAY $

(Map p208; ☑0361-973255; ajilodge11@yahoo. com; Tebesaya 11; r from 150,000Rp) One of a group of comfortable family compounds, it lines a footpath east of Jl Sukma. Get a room down the hill by the river for the full bed-time symphony of birds, bugs and critters.

Penestanan

Penestanan is west of Ubud but still in walking distance. Out here, you can hear water coursing through the surrounding rice fields.

★ Santra Putra
GUESTHOUSE $

(Map p208; ☑0361-977810; karjabali@yahoo. com; off Jl Raya Campuan; r US$25-40; 🛜) Run by internationally exhibited abstract artist I Wayan Karja (whose studio/gallery is also on site), this place has nine big, open, airy rooms with hot water. Enjoy paddy-field views from all vantage points. Painting and drawing classes are offered by the artist.

 Eating

Central Ubud

There are busy and tasty choices on Ubud's main street, Jl Raya Ubud.

★Coffee Studio Seniman   CAFE $
(Map p210; Jl Sriwedari; mains from 30,000Rp;
☺8am-7pm; 🕾) That 'coffee studio' moniker
isn't for show: you see the roasters as you
enter this temple of joe. Take a seat on the
large porch and choose from an array of
Bali-grown brews. Foods are organic and
creative.

Dewa Warung   INDONESIAN $
(Map p210; Jl Goutama; meals 15,000-20,000Rp)
When it rains, the tin roof sounds like a
tap-dance convention and the bare light-
bulbs sway in the breeze. A little garden
surrounds tables a few steps above the road
where diners tuck into plates of sizzling
fresh Indo fare.

Warung Ibu Oka   BALINESE $
(Map p210; Jl Suweta; meals from 50,000Rp;
☺11am-4pm) Opposite Ubud Palace, you'll
see touristy lunchtime crowds waiting for
one thing: the Balinese-style roast *babi
guling* (suckling pig). Order a *spesial* to get
the best cut. Get there early.

Tutmak Cafe   CAFE $
(Map p210; Jl Dewi Sita; meals 30,000-90,000Rp;
🕾) The breezy multilevel location here,
facing both Jl Dewi Sita and the football
field, is a popular place for a refreshing
drink or a meal. Local comers on the make
huddle around their laptops plotting their
next move.

★Three Monkeys   FUSION $$
(Map p210; Monkey Forest Rd; meals from
80,000Rp) Have a passionfruit-crush cock-
tail and settle back amid the rice field's
frog symphony. Add the glow of tiki torches
for a magical effect. By day there are sand-
wiches, salads and gelato. At night there's a
fusion menu of Asian classics.

Padangtegal & Tebesaya

★Sopa   VEGETARIAN $
(Map p210; Jl Sugriwa 36; meals 30,000-
60,000Rp; 🕾📶) Open air and oh so groovy,
this popular place captures the Ubud vibe
with creative and (more importantly) tasty
vegetarian fare with a Balinese twist. Look
for specials of the day on display.

Mama's Warung   INDONESIAN $
(Map p210; Jl Sukma; dishes 10,000-20,000Rp;
☺8am-10pm) A real budget find among the
bargain homestays of Tebesaya. Mama her-
self cooks up Indo classics that are spicy

and redolent with garlic (the avocado salad,
yum!). The freshly made peanut sauce for
the satay is silky smooth.

Kafe   CAFE $
(Map p210; 📞0361-970992; www.balispirit.com; Jl
Hanoman 44; dishes 15,000-40,000Rp) 🍴 Buzz-
ing Kafe has an organic menu great for
veggie grazing or just having a coffee, juice
or house-made natural soft drink. Break-
fasts are healthy while lunch meals feature
excellent salads and burritos, with many raw
items.

Sanggingan & Penestanan

The restaurants and cafes west of the cen-
tre are dotted among rice fields, lanes and
roads.

★Warung Pulau Kelapa   INDONESIAN $
(Map p208; Jl Raya Sanggingan; dishes 15,000-
30,000Rp) A popular place along the road
from Campuan to Sanggingan, Kelapa
has stylish takes on local classics. The sur-
rounds are stylish as well: plenty of white-
wash and antiques.

Yellow Flower Cafe   INDONESIAN $
(Map p208; 📞0361-889 9865; meals from
30,000Rp; 🕾) New Age Indonesian right up
in Penestanan along a little path through
the rice fields. Nearby views look out over
Ubud but you'll be happier concentrating
on organic mains, snacks and coffees.

🍷 Drinking & Nightlife

No one comes to Ubud for wild nightlife. A
few bars get lively around sunset and later
in the night, but the venues certainly don't
aspire to the club partying found in Kuta
and Seminyak.

Jazz Café   BAR
(Map p210; Jl Sukma 2; ☺5pm-midnight) Ubud's
most popular nightspot (and that's not
faint praise even though competition
might be lacking), Jazz Café offers a re-
laxed atmosphere in a charming garden.
The menu offers a range of good Asian fu-
sion food and you can listen to live music
from Tuesday to Saturday after 7.30pm.

Napi Orti   BAR
(Map p210; Monkey Forest Rd; drinks from
12,000Rp; ☺noon-late) This upstairs place
is your best bet for a late-night drink. Get
boozy under the hazy gaze of Jim Morrison
and Sid Vicious.

BALINESE DANCE & MUSIC

Enjoying a Balinese dance performance is for many a highlight of a visit to Bali. The haunting sounds, elaborate costumes, careful choreography and even light-hearted comic routines add up to great entertainment. Swept up in the spectacle, you'll soon understand why Balinese culture is among the world's most developed.

Balinese music is based around an ensemble known as a *gamelan*, also called a *gong*. This melodic, sometimes upbeat and sometimes haunting percussion that often accompanies traditional dance is one of the most lasting impressions for tourists to Bali.

You can choose amongst many quality dance performances virtually every night in Ubud.

There are more than a dozen different basic dances in Bali and myriad variations. The most important:

Kecak Probably the best-known dance for its spell-binding, hair-raising atmosphere, the *kecak* features a 'choir' of men and boys who sit in concentric circles and slip into a trance as they chant and sing the 'chak-a-chak-a-chak', imitating a troupe of monkeys.

Barong and Rangda Features the good, a mischievous and fun-loving shaggy dog-lion called a *barong*, battling the bad, an evil widow-witch called Rangda. One or more monkeys attend the *barong* and these characters often steal the show.

Legong Characterised by flashing eyes and quivering hands, this most graceful of Balinese dances is performed by young girls. Their talent is so revered that in old age, a classic dancer will be remembered as a 'great *legong*'.

Kekac Fire Dances These dances were developed to drive out evil spirits from a village. Two young girls dance a dream-like *legong* in perfect symmetry and a boy in a trance dances around and through a fire of coconut husks.

☆ Entertainment

Few travel experiences can be more magical than experiencing a Balinese dance performance, especially in Ubud. Cultural entertainment keeps people returning and sets Bali apart from other tropical destinations. Get there a little early and buy a beer from the old women selling them out of ice-filled buckets.

Ubud Tourist Information has performance information and sells tickets (usually about 80,000Rp). For performances outside Ubud, transport is often included in the price. Tickets are also sold at the venues. In a week in Ubud, you can see *kecak*, *legong* and *barong* dances, *wayang kulit* puppets, *gamelan* and more.

Arma Open Stage　　TRADITIONAL DANCE
(Map p208; ☏0361-976659; Jl Raya Pengosekan) Has among the best troupes.

Pura Dalem Ubud　　TRADITIONAL DANCE
(Map p208; Jl Raya Ubud) At the west end of Jl Raya Ubud, this open-air venue has a flamelit carved-stone backdrop and in many ways is the most evocative place to see a dance performance. Watch for the Semara Ratih troupe.

Pura Taman Saraswati　　TRADITIONAL DANCE
(Ubud Water Palace; Map p210; Jl Raya Ubud) The beauty of the setting may distract you from the dancers, although at night you can't see the lily pads and lotus flowers that are such an attraction by day.

Ubud Palace　　TRADITIONAL DANCE
(Map p210; Jl Raya Ubud) Performances are held here almost nightly against a beautiful backdrop in the palace compound, with the carvings highlighted by torches. You'll see lots of locals peeking over walls and around corners to see the shows.

🔒 Shopping

In Ubud, Jl Hanoman and Jl Dewi Sita should be your starting points. Surrounding villages are hotbeds for arts and crafts – as you'll have noticed on your drive to Ubud.

Ganesha Bookshop　　BOOKS
(Map p210; www.ganeshabooksbali.com; Jl Raya Ubud) Ubud's best bookshop has an amazing amount of stock jammed into a small space; an excellent selection of titles on Indonesian studies, travel, arts, music, fiction (including used titles) and maps. Good staff recommendations.

❶ Information

Along the main roads, you'll find most services you need. Ubud has numerous banks, ATMs and money changers along Jl Raya Ubud and Monkey Forest Rd.

Ubud Tourist Information (Yaysan Bina Wisata; Map p210; ☑ 0361-973285; Jl Raya Ubud; ⊙ 8am-8pm) The one really useful tourist office in Bali. It has a good range of information and a noticeboard listing current happenings and activities. Staff can answer most regional questions and have up-to-date information on ceremonies and traditional dances in the area; dance tickets are sold here.

❶ Getting There & Around

Transport between South Bali and Ubud costs about 250,000Rp whether you take a metered taxi or arrange it with a guy on the street. There are no local metered taxis, but the ubiquitous drivers and motorbike owners will take you around town for a negotiable 10,000Rp to 50,000Rp depending on distance.

Ubud is on two bemo routes. Orange bemos travel from Gianyar to Ubud (8000Rp) and larger brown bemos from Batubulan terminal in Denpasar to Ubud (8000Rp). Tourist buses run to Sanur (40,000Rp, one hour) and Kuta (50,000Rp, 90 minutes).

Shops renting bikes have their cycles on display along the main roads; your accommodation can always arrange bike rental.

Around Ubud

Two kilometres east of central Ubud, the cavern of Goa Gajah (Elephant Cave; adult/child 10,000/5000Rp, parking 2000Rp; ⊙ 8am-6pm) was discovered in the 1920s; the fountains and bathing pool were not unearthed until 1954. It is believed to have been a Buddhist hermitage.

In Tampaksiring, 18km northeast of Ubud, you'll find the most impressive ancient site in Bali, Gunung Kawi (adult/child 10,000/5000Rp, sarong 3000Rp, parking 2000Rp; ⊙ 7am-5pm). This astonishing group of stone *candi* (shrines) cut into cliffs on either side of the plunging Pakrisan River valley is being considered for Unesco Heritage status. They stand in awe-inspiring, 8m-high sheltered niches cut into the sheer cliff face. From the end of the access road, a steep, stone stairway leads down to the river, at one point making a cutting through an embankment of solid rock.

East Coast Beaches

The main road that runs east from Sanur passes many black-sand beaches. One good stop is Pura Masceti Beach, 15km east of Sanur. Pura Masceti, one of Bali's nine directional temples, is right on the beach. It's architecturally significant and enlivened with gaudy statuary.

Semarapura (Klungkung)

Once the centre of an important Balinese kingdom, Semarapura (also known as Klungkung) is the capital of Klungkung regency (a historical and present-day administrative area) and a great artistic and cultural focal point. Formerly the seat of the Dewa Agung dynasty, the Semara Pura Complex (adult/child 12,000/6000Rp, parking 2000Rp; ⊙ 7am-5pm) has now largely crumbled away, but history and architecture buffs will enjoy a wander past the Kertha Gosa (Hall of Justice) and Bale Kambang (Floating Pavilion). The nearby market is also worth a visit, it teams with goods.

Sidemen Road

Winding through one of Bali's most beautiful river valleys, the Sidemen road offers marvellous paddy-field scenery, a delightful rural character and extraordinary views of Gunung Agung (when the clouds permit). The region is getting more popular every year as a verdant escape, where a walk in any direction is a communion with nature.

Among the many mellow places scattered about the impossibly green rice fields, Pondok Wisata Lihat Sawah (☑ 0361-530 0516; www.lihatsawah.com; r from 300,000Rp; ▣) has 12 rooms with views of the valley and mountain (all have hot water, nice after a morning hike, and the best have lovely wooden verandahs).

Padangbai

☑ 0363

There's a real backpacker vibe about this little beach town, which is also the port for the main public ferry connecting Bali with Lombok.

Padangbai is on the upswing. It sits on a small bay and has a nice little curve of beach. It has a whole compact seaside travellers' scene with cheap places to stay and some funky and fun cafes. The pace is slow, but should ambition strike there's good snorkelling and diving, plus some easy walks and a couple of great beaches.

🛏 Sleeping & Eating

Accommodation in Padangbai – like the town itself – is pretty laid-back. Prices are fairly cheap; simple cafes and *warung* are common.

Topi Inn   GUESTHOUSE **$**
(📋 0363-41424; www.topiinn.com; Jl Silayukti; r from 150,000Rp; @ 🛜) Sitting at the east end of the strip in a serene location, Topi has five pleasant rooms, some of which share bathrooms. The cafe is excellent for breakfast.

Pondok Wisata Parta   GUESTHOUSE **$**
(📋 0817 975 2668, 0363-41475; off Gang Segara III; r 1500,000-350,000Rp; ❄🛜) The pick of the nine rooms in this hidden and snoozy spot is the 'honeymoon room', which has a harbour view and good breezes. The most expensive rooms have air-con and have a common terrace and views.

❶ Getting There & Away

Padangbai is 2km south of the main Semarapura–Amlapura road.

Among the tourist buses, **Perama** (📋 0363-41419; Café Dona, Jl Pelabuhan; ⊘7am-8pm) has a stop here for its services around the east coast; trips include Kuta (60,000Rp, three hours) and Ubud (50,000Rp, two hours).

Ferries run hourly, day and night, to Lembar on Lombok (adult/motorbike/car 40,000/112,000/687,000Rp, five to seven hours). There are also fast boats to the Gili Islands and Lombok.

Candidasa

Candidasa is slouching into middle age, no longer the tourism darling it once was. The main drawback is the lack of a beach, which, except for the far eastern stretch, has eroded away as fast as hotels were built. It's a favourite place for sedate travellers to be, well, sedate.

Tirta Gangga

📋 0363

Tirta Gangga (Water of the Ganges) is the site of a holy temple, some great water features and some of the best views of rice fields and the sea beyond in east Bali. High on a ridge, it is a relaxing place to stop for an hour or a longer period, which will allow for some treks through the surrounding terraced countryside, which ripples with coursing water.

◎ Sights & Activities

Taman Tirta Gangga   PALACE
(adult/child 10,000/5000Rp, parking 2000Rp; ⊘site 24hr, ticket office 6am-6pm) Amlapura's water-loving rajah, after completing his lost masterpiece at Ujung, had another go at building the water palace of his dreams. He succeeded at Taman Tirta Gangga, which has a stunning crescent of rice-terrace-lined hills for a backdrop. Today, it is an aquatic fantasy with several swimming pools and ornamental ponds.

Hiking in the surrounding hills is recommended. The rice terraces around Tirta Gangga are among the most beautiful in Bali. Back roads and walking paths take you to many picturesque traditional villages. Or you can ascend the side of Gunung Agung. Guides are a good idea. Ask at Homestay Rijasa, where the owner I Ketut Sarjana is an experienced guide.

Among the possible treks is a six-hour loop to Tenganan village, plus shorter ones across the local hills, which include visits to remote temples and all the stunning vistas you can handle. Rates average about 50,000Rp per hour for one or two people.

🛏 Sleeping & Eating

Most places to stay have cafes with mains under 20,000Rp.

Homestay Rijasa   HOMESTAY **$**
(📋 0813 5300 5080, 0363-21873; r 100,000-250,000Rp; 🛜) With elaborately planted grounds, this well-run, nine-room homestay is a recommended choice opposite the water palace entrance. Better rooms have hot water, good for the large soaking tubs.

Good Karma   HOMESTAY **$**
(📋 0363-22445; goodkarma.tirtagangga@gmail.com; r 200,000-250,000Rp; 🛜) A classic homestay, Good Karma has four very clean and simple bungalows and a good vibe derived from the surrounding pastoral rice field. The cafe's gazebos are the setting for some fine meals, including excellent tempey satay.

AMED & THE FAR EAST COAST

Stretching from Amed to Bali's far eastern tip, this once-remote stretch of semiarid coast draws visitors to a succession of small, scalloped, black-sand beaches and a relaxed atmosphere. The coast here is often called simply 'Amed', but this is a misnomer, as the coast is a series of seaside *dusun* (small villages) that start with the actual Amed in the north and then run southeast to Aas.

In nearby Tulamben (a 20-minute drive from Amed), the big attraction sank over 60 years ago. The WWII wreck of the US cargo ship *Liberty* is among the best and most popular dive sites in Bali, and this has given rise to an entire town based on scuba diving.

Snorkelling is excellent along the coast (in addition to the *Liberty*) and scuba diving is good. There are scores of dive operators in the area. **Euro Dive** (☑ 0363-23605; www.euro divebali.com; Lipah), in the heart of the Amed coast, and **Tauch Terminal** (☑ 0363-22911, 0363-774504; www.tauch-terminal.com), in Tulamben, are both recommended. Expect to pay about US$80 for a two-tank dive. Tauch also has an upscale hotel.

Every place to stay has at least a cafe. Driving the long road along the Amed coast you will find many options.

At chilled-out hideaway **Meditasi** (☑ 082 8372 2738; www.meditasibungalows.blog-spot.com; Aas; r 300,000-500,000Rp) you can take a break from the pressures of life. Meditation and yoga help you relax, and the four rooms are close to good swimming and snorkelling. Open-air baths allow you to count the colours of the bougainvillea and frangipani that grow in profusion.

Choose from a cold-water room with fan or something more posh (hot water) in a bungalow at **Sama Sama Bungalows** (☑ 0813 3738 2945; Jemeluk; r 150,000-400,000Rp), which is just across from the beach and has a good seafood cafe.

Alternatively, try the new **Amed Stop Inn** (☑ 081 7473 8059; im.stop@yahoo.co.id; r from 200,000Rp), which is right in Amed village and has two simple rooms that are close to the beach. There are numerous walks in the surrounding rice fields and into the temple-dotted hills. The owners are charmers and are experienced guides.

Most people drive to the Amed area via the main road from Tirta Gangga to Culik. Public-transport options are limited. Many hotels rent bicycles for about 35,000Rp per day. There are fast boats to/from the Gilis, which are just east on the horizon.

ⓘ Getting There & Away

It's easiest to visit this region with your own transport.

Gunung Batur Area

☑ 0366

Volcanic Gunung Batur (1717m) is a major tourist magnet, offering treks to its summit and spectacular views of Danau Batur (Lake Batur), at the bottom of a huge caldera. Annoying touts and tourist buses detract from the experience around the rim of the vast crater, but the crater lake and cone of Batur are well worth exploring. Entry to the area costs 10,000Rp per person.

On a clear day, the village of **Penelokan** has superb views across to Gunung Batur and down to the lake at the bottom of the crater. It has numerous huge tourist restaurants catering to busloads of day trippers; avoid these.

The villages of Batur and Kintamani now virtually run together. Kintamani is famed for its large and colourful **market**, which is held every three days. If you don't want to go on a trek, the sunrise view from the road here is pretty good.

ⓘ Getting There & Around

There are two main roads in the Gunung Batur area. The caldera-rim road links Penulisan and Penelokan, and from Penelokan you drop down onto the inner-rim road. The latter is rough in parts, especially the western side of the circuit, but drivable for all vehicles. This is a tough destination for public transport. Best to use – or arrange – your own transport. Day trips from south Bali and Ubud are popular.

WORTH A TRIP

GUNUNG BATUKAU AREA

Often overlooked, Gunung Batukau is Bali's second-highest mountain (2276m), the third of Bali's three major mountains and the holy peak of the island's western end. Enjoy a magical visit to one of the island's holiest and most underrated temples, **Pura Luhur Batukau** (donation 10,000Rp). It has a seven-roofed *meru* (multiroofed shrine) dedicated to Maha Dewa, the mountain's guardian spirit. Mountain streams tumble down around the site. At **Jatiluwih**, which means 'Truly Marvellous', you will be rewarded with vistas of centuries-old rice terraces that exhaust your ability to describe green. The locals will also be rewarded with your 'green', as there's a road toll for visitors (15,000Rp per person, plus 5000Rp per car). The terraces have acheived Unesco status. You'll understand why just viewing the panorama from the narrow, twisting 18km road, but get out for a **ricefield walk**.

All this serenity can be intoxicating and you can ponder your own karma at one of Bali's most unusual places to stay, the **Bali Silent Retreat** (☑ 0813 5348 6517; www.bali silentretreat.com; Penatahan; dm $15, r $40-120). Set in amidst gorgeous scenery, it's just what the name says: a place to meditate, practice yoga, go on nature walks and more – all in total silence. Note that the minimalist ethos stops at the food, which is organic and fabulous (per day US$25).

The only realistic way to explore the Gunung Batukau area is with your own transport.

Toya Bungkah

The main tourist centre is Toya Bungkah, which is scruffy but has a cute charm and a serene lakeside setting in the ancient caldera below the peaks.

The most popular local trek is from Toya Bungkah to the top of Gunung Batur for sunrise – a magnificent sight requiring a 4am start from the village. The **HPPGB** (Mt Batur Tour Guides Association; ☑ 0366-52362; ◷ 3am-noon) has a monopoly on guided climbs up Gunung Batur and charges about 450,000Rp for one to four people to hike Batur. Those attempting to trek Batur alone can expect hassle from the HPPGB.

With a lovely, quiet lakeside location opposite vegetable plots, **Under the Volcano III** (☑ 0813 3860 0081; r 200,000Rp) has six clean and pretty rooms. Other nearby inns are run by the same clan.

Danau Bratan Area

Approaching from the south, you gradually leave the rice terraces behind and ascend into the cool, often misty mountain country around Danau Bratan.

The name **Bedugul** is sometimes used to refer to the whole lakeside area but, strictly speaking, Bedugul is just the first place you reach at the top of the hill when coming up from South Bali. Candikuning and Munduk hold the star attractions in this area.

The big sight is **Pura Ulun Danau Bratan** (adult/child 15,000/10,000Rp, parking 5000Rp; ◷ tickets 7am-5pm, site 24hr), a graceful, very important Hindu-Buddhist lakeside temple. It dates to the 17th century.

ⓘ Getting There & Away

Danau Bratan is beside the main north–south road, so it's easy to reach from South Bali or Lovina using your own transport. Most minibuses running from Denpasar's Ubung terminal to Singaraja (for Lovina) will stop along the road near the temple.

Munduk

West from Danau Bratan, Munduk is a pretty, spread-out village perched high on a ridge. It's popular for its good trekking and hiking to oodles of waterfalls, coffee plantations, rice paddies and villages. Arrange a guide through your lodgings.

🛏 Sleeping

Puri Alam Bali   GUESTHOUSE $
(☑ 0812 465 9815; www.purialambali.com; r 250,000-500,000Rp; 🛜) Perched on a precipice at the east end of the village, the bungalow-style rooms (all with hot water and balconies) have better views the higher you go. The rooftop cafe is worth a visit for its views.

Think of the long concrete stairs down from the road as trekking practice.

Guru Ratna GUESTHOUSE $
(📞 0813 3719 4398; r 175,000-300,000Rp; 🛜) The cheapest place in the village has seven comfortable hot-water rooms in a colonial Dutch house (some share bathrooms). The best rooms have some style, carved wood details and nice porches. Ponder the distant north coast from the cafe.

Lovina & the North
📞 0362

Relaxed is how people most often describe Lovina, and they are correct. This low-key, low-rise beach resort is the polar opposite of Kuta. Days are slow and so are the nights.

Almost merging into Singaraja, the regional capital to the west, the town is really a string of coastal villages – Pemaron, Tukad Mungga, Anturan, Kalibukbuk (the main area), Kaliasem and Temukus – that have taken on this collective name.

Lovina is a convenient base for trips around the north coast or the central mountains. The beaches are made up of washed-out grey and black volcanic sand, and they are mostly clean near the hotel areas, but generally unspectacular. Reefs protect the shore, so the water is usually calm and clear.

🔘 Sights & Activities

Besides walking the modest beach path and not doing much of anything, the sights in Lovina are in the hills to the south, where waterfalls pour down into dense forest.

About 11km south of Singaraja, a well-signposted path goes 800m west from the main road to the touristy waterfall, **Air Terjun Gitgit** (adult/child 10,000/5000Rp). The path is lined with souvenir stalls and guides to nowhere. The 40m waterfalls pound away and the mists are more refreshing than any air-con.

⭐ **Komang Dodik** HIKING
(📞 0877 6291 5128; lovina.tracking@gmail.com) Komang Dodik leads hikes in the hills along the north coast. Trips start at 250,000Rp per person and can last from three to seven hours. The highlight of most is a series of waterfalls, over 20m high, in a jungle grotto. Routes can include coffee, clove and vanilla plantations.

🛏 Sleeping

Hotels are spread out along the many side roads running off Jl Raya Lovina to the beach. There are decent places to stay in every price range.

A little over 10km from Singaraja, Kalibukbuk is the 'centre' of Lovina, with the biggest concentration of hotels. Anturan has a narrow beach and charming fishing village vibe.

Harris Homestay HOMESTAY $
(📞 0362-41152; Gang Binaria; r 120,000-170,000Rp; 🛜) Sprightly and white, Harris avoids the weary look of some neighbouring cheapies. The charming family live in back; guests enjoy five bright, modern rooms up front.

Gede Home Stay Bungalows HOMESTAY $
(📞 0362-41526; gedehomestay@yahoo.com; Jl Kubu Gembong, Anturan; r 200,000-300,000Rp; ❄🛜) Don't forget to shake the sand off your feet as you enter this beachside eight-room homestay. Cheap rooms have cold water while better ones have hot water and air-con.

Sea Breeze Cabins GUESTHOUSE $
(📞 0362-41138; Jl Bina Ria; r 400,000Rp; ❄🏊) One of the best choices in the heart of Kalibukbuk and right off Jl Binaria, the Sea Breeze has seven bungalows by the pool and beach, some with sensational views from their verandahs.

Rini Hotel HOTEL $
(📞 0362-41386; www.rinihotel.com; Jl Mawar, Kalibukbuk; r 200,000-400,000Rp; ❄🛜🏊) This tidy 30-room place has a large pool. Cheaper rooms have fans and cold water but the more expensive ones are huge, with air-con and hot water.

🍴 Eating & Drinking

Lovina's modest social scene centres on Kalibukbuk. Cafes by the beach are popular at sunset.

Akar VEGETARIAN $
(📞 0817 972 4717; Jl Binaria; meals 30,000-50,000Rp; 🕗 8am-10pm; 📷) 🌿 The many shades of green at this cute-as-a-baby-frog cafe aren't just for show. They reflect the earth-friendly ethics of the owners. Enjoy organic smoothies, gelati and fresh and tasty noodle dishes. A tiny back porch overlooks the river.

INDONESIA LOVINA & THE NORTH

Khi Khi Restaurant
CHINESE $

(☑ 0362-41548; meals 15,000-100,000Rp; ⊙ noon-10pm) Well off Jl Raya Lovina and behind the night market, this barn of a place specialises in Chinese food and grilled seafood, including lobster. It's always popular in a rub-elbows-with-your-neighbour kind of way.

ℹ Information
There are ATMs and internet places.

ℹ Getting There & Around
From South Bali by public transport, take a mini-bus from Denpasar (Ubung terminal, 40,000Rp) via Bedugul to Singaraja, where you connect to a blue bemo to Kalibukbuk (about 10,000Rp).

Perama (☑ 0362-41161) links Lovina with Kuta (100,000Rp, four hours), Ubud (100,000Rp, three hours) and other destinations. The Lovina strip is *very* spread out, but you can easily travel back and forth on bemos (5000Rp). Bikes are easily rented around town for about 30,000Rp per day.

Southwest Bali
From the busy western road along the south coast, turn north to **Mengwi**, where there's the impressive **Pura Taman Ayun** (adult/child 15,000/7500Rp; ⊙ 8am-6pm) water palace and temple. A bit further west, and south of the main road, is **Pura Tanah Lot** (adult/child 30,000/15,000Rp, parking 5000Rp), a reconstructed temple and major tourist trap, especially at sunset.

West Bali

Balian Beach
Wild waves pounding an almost empty shore are driving the newfound popularity of this beach, which has a cool surfer's vibe and some funky guesthouses. It's 800m off the main road west at Lalang-Linggah.

🛏 Sleeping

★ **Surya Homestay**
GUESTHOUSE $

(☑ 0813 3868 5643; wayan.suratni@gmail.com; r 150,00-200,000Rp) There are five rooms here in bungalow-style units at this sweet little family-run place (Wayan and Putu are charmers) that is about 200m along a small lane. It's spotless and rooms have cold water and fans. Ask about long-term rates.

Pondok Pisces
GUESTHOUSE $$

(☑ 780 1735, 0813 3879 7722; www.pondokpisces bali.com; s/d from 420,000/560,000Rp; 🛜) You can hear the sea at this tropical fantasy of thatched cottages and flower-filled gardens. Of the 10 rooms, those on the upper floor have large terraces with surf views. In-house **Tom's Garden Cafe** has grilled seafood and surf views.

Gilimanuk
Charm-challenged Gilimanuk is the terminus for the ferries to/from Banyuwangi just across the turbulent channel on Java. Ferries from Gilimanuk depart roughly every 30 minutes around the clock. It costs 6000Rp for passengers, 16,000Rp for a motorcycle and 114,000Rp for a car. Through buses between Bali and Java include the fare in the bus ticket and are by far the easiest option.

Taman Nasional Bali Barat
Visitors to Bali's only national park, Taman Nasional Bali Barat (West Bali National Park), can hike through bird-filled forests, enjoy the island's best diving at Pulau Menjangan and explore coastal mangroves. The **park headquarters** (⊙ 7am-5pm) at Cekik displays a topographic model of the park and has some information about plants and wildlife. The **Labuhan Lalang visitors centre** (⊙ 7.30am-5pm) is in a hut located on the northern coast; snorkellers and dive boats launch here. At both places you can arrange for trekking guides.

Pemuteran
This oasis in the far northwest corner of Bali is on a little bay and is the place to come for a real beach getaway. Most people dive or snorkel the underwater wonders at nearby Pulau Menjangan while here. The bay and beach are great for swimming and strolling.

🏊 Activities

★ **Reef Seen**
DIVING

(☑ 0362-93001; www.reefseen.com) Right on the beach in a large compound, Reef Seen is active in local preservation efforts. It is a PADI dive centre and has a full complement of classes.

WORTH A TRIP

PULAU MENJANGAN

Bali's most-rewarding dive area, **Pulau Menjangan**, has a dozen superb dive sites. The diving is excellent – iconic tropical fish, soft corals, great visibility (usually), caves and a spectacular drop-off. Most of the sites are close to shore and suitable for snorkellers or diving novices. Some decent snorkelling spots are not far from the jetty – ask the boat-man where to go.

The most convenient place to stay for diving Menjangan is Pemuteran, where every hotel runs snorkelling trips and there are good dive shops. Day trips from other parts of Bali entail long, early-morning drives.

Sleeping & Eating

Pemuteran has many midrange hotel choices on the bay. Just behind them there is a growing collection of budget guesthouses and cafes along the main road, which is not overly busy.

Jubawa Homestay GUESTHOUSE $
(✆0362-94745; www.jubawa-pemuteran.com; r 375,000-550,000Rp; ❄❄❄❄) On the south (hill) side of the road, this is a rather plush budget choice. The 27 rooms are in expansive gardens around a pool. The cafe serves Balinese and Thai food and there is a popular bar.

Taruna GUESTHOUSE $
(✆0813 3853 6318; r fan/air-con from 300,000/450,000Rp; ❄❄❄) On the beach side of the main road and just a short walk from the sand, the nine rooms here are new and well-designed. It's a professionally run place.

Taman Sari Bali Cottages SPA RESORT $$
(✆0362-93264; www.tamansaribali.com; bungalows US$75-100; ❄@❄❄) With excellent green credentials and a beautiful site on the beach and bay, this is a good place to take a break from your travels. The 31 rooms are set in gorgeous bungalows that feature intricate carvings and traditional artwork inside and out.

Bali Re BALINESE $
(meals from 30,000Rp; ⊙8am-9pm) The staff is as sweet as the meat is succulent at this open-air *babi guling* cafe on the beach side of the main road. It even has tables in a small garden.

ℹ Getting There & Away

Pemuteran is served by any of the buses and bemos on the Gilimanuk–Lovina run. Labuhan Lalang and Taman Nasional Bali Barat are 12km west. It's at least a four-hour drive from South Bali, either over the hills or around the west coast.

NUSA TENGGARA

An arc of islands extending from Bali towards northern Australia, Nusa Tenggara is lush and jungle green in the north, more arid savannah in the south, and in between a land of pink-sand beaches, schooling sharks and rays, and the world's largest lizard: the swaggering, spellbinding komodo dragon.

The Gili Islands see the bulk of the tourism, but those with a hunger for adventure head further east to Flores, sail to the Komodo Islands and back, then keep going south and east where the *bule* (foreigner) crowds and creature comforts are thin on the ground.

ℹ Getting There & Away

Most visitors use Bali as the gateway to Nusa Tenggara. However, you can reach Lombok from Kuala Lumpur and Singapore and the main cities have flights to Jakarta.

ℹ Getting Around

The easiest and most popular way to explore Nusa Tenggara is to fly from Bali to Labuanbajo (Flores) or Kupang (West Timor) and island hop from there.

AIR

Airports dot NTT. Major airports include Lombok, Labuanbajo and Kupang.

BOAT

Regular vehicle/passenger ferries run Bali–Lombok, Lombok–Sumbawa, Sumbawa–Flores and Flores–Sumba. Tourist boats link Lombok with Flores.

BUS

Air-con coaches run across Lombok and Sumbawa, and from Kupang to Dili in Timor, but elsewhere small, slow minibuses are the norm.

CAR & MOTORCYCLE

A motorcycle is an ideal way to explore Nusa Tenggara, but hiring one is not always easy outside Lombok. You can rent one in Bali or Lombok and take it across by ferry. Bring an extra petrol can. For groups, cars with driver/guides are a great option. They cost 500,000Rp to 800,000Rp per day, depending upon the season.

Nusa Tenggara

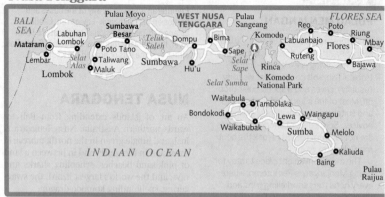

Lombok

Lombok is an easy hop from Bali, and is the most popular spot in Nusa Tenggara. It has a spectacular, mostly deserted coastline with palm coves, Balinese Hindu temples, looming cliffs and epic surf. The majestic and sacred Gunung Rinjani rises from its centre – a challenging and rewarding climb.

The Gilis, a carless collection of islands infused with a sun-drenched party vibe, are Lombok's biggest draw although the beautiful surf breaks and beaches of Kuta are fast gaining popularity.

ℹ Getting There & Away

AIR

Surrounded by rice fields and not far from the small village of Praya in South Lombok, the recently opened **Lombok International Airport** (LOP; www.lombok-airport.co.id) has completely replaced the old airport at Mataram. It's not huge, but is very modern and has a full range of services such as ATMs.

Thanks to new and improved roads, the airport is only 30 minutes from both Mataram and Kuta and is well-linked to the rest of the island by road. Taxis offer fixed-price transport to major destinations. Damri operates tourist buses, buy tickets in the arrivals area.

Intense competition keeps fares for the quick jaunt to Bali cheap. Airlines include the following:

Air Asia (www.airasia.com) Kuala Lumpur.

Garuda Indonesia (www.garuda-indonesia.com) Jakarta and Bali.

Lion Air/Wings Air (www.lionair.co.id) Bali, Jakarta and Surabaya.

Merpati (www.merpati.co.id) Bali.

Silk Air (www.silkair.com) Singapore.

Transnusa/Aviastar Airlines (www.transnusa.co.id) Nusa Tenggara destinations including Sumbawa and Bima, plus Bali.

BOAT

Large car ferries link Padangbai on Bali to Lembar as well as Labuhan Lombok and Poto Tano on Sumbawa. Small, fast tourist boats link Lombok and the Gilis with several Bali ports.

BUS

Long-distance public buses depart daily from Mataram's Mandalika terminal for major cities in Bali and Java in the west, and to Sumbawa in the east.

ℹ Getting Around

BICYCLE

Empty but well-maintained roads, spectacular vistas and plenty of flat stretches make cycling in Lombok a dream.

BUS & BEMO

Mandalika, Lombok's main bus/bemo terminal, is a hub for service. With greatly improved roads, you can reach most corners of Lombok in well under two hours. Tourist buses link Lembar, Mataram, Senggigi and Kuta.

CAR & MOTORCYCLE

Car rental is easy and fairly cheap in all tourist areas, think about 200,000Rp per day. Motorbikes can be had for 50,000Rp.

Lembar

📋 0370

Hassle-filled Lembar, Lombok's main port, is where Bali ferries and Pelni ships

dock. Ferries run hourly, day and night, to Padangbai on Bali (adult/motorbike/car 40,000/112,000/687,000Rp, five to seven hours).

Bus connections are abundant and bemos run regularly to the Mandalika bus/bemo terminal (15,000Rp), so there's no reason to linger. Taxis cost 80,000Rp to Mataram, and 150,000Rp to Senggigi.

Mataram

☑ 0370 / POP 410,000

Lombok's sprawling capital, actually a cluster of four towns – Ampenan (port), Mataram (administrative centre), Cakranegara (commercial centre) and Sweta (bus terminal) – has some allure.

There are large malls, decent restaurants and a few cultural sights, but few travellers spend any time here.

◉ Sights

Pura Meru TEMPLE
(Jl Selaparang; admission 10,000Rp; ⊙8am-5pm) Pura Meru is the largest and second most important Hindu temple on Lombok. Built in 1720, it's dedicated to the Hindu trinity of Brahma, Vishnu and Shiva. The inner court

has 33 small shrines and three thatched, teak-wood *meru* (multitiered shrines).

🛏 Sleeping & Eating

A handful of good budget options are hidden among the quiet streets off Jl Pejanggik/Selaparang, east of **Mataram Mall** (Jl Selaparang; ⊙7am-8pm). The latter is sprawling and offers a fascinating look at modern, consumer-driven Indonesia and it has good cafes and a superb supermarket.

Hotel Melati Viktor GUESTHOUSE $
(☑0370-633830; Jl Abimanyu 1; r 100,000-200,000Rp; ❋ 🛜) The high ceilings, 37 clean rooms and Balinese-style courtyard, complete with Hindu statues, make this one of the best values in town. The cheapest rooms have fans.

★Ikan Bakar 99 SEAFOOD $
(☑0370-643335, 0370-664 2819; Jl Subak III 10; mains 20,000-55,000Rp; ⊙11am-10pm) Think: squid, prawns, fish and crab brushed with chilli sauce and perfectly grilled or fried and drenched in spicy Padang or sticky sweet-and-sour sauce. You will munch and dine among Mataram families.

BUSES FROM MATARAM

DESTINATION	PRICE (RP)	DURATION
Denpasar	225,000	10-12hr
Labuhan Lombok	15,000	2hr
Lembar	15,000	30min
Sumbawa Besar	100,000	6hr

INDONESIA LOMBOK

Lombok

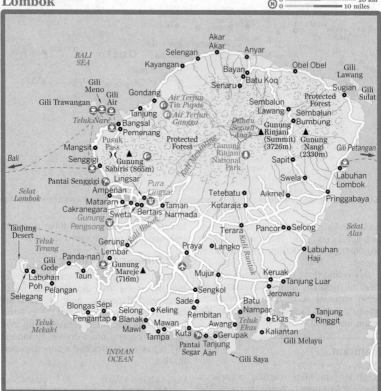

Mi Rasa   BAKERY $
(☎ 0370-633096; Jl AA Gede Ngurah 88; snacks from 5000Rp; ⏰ 6am-10pm) Cakra's middle-class families adore this modern bakery. They do doughnuts, cookies and cakes as well as local wontons stuffed with chicken.

ℹ Information

Banks on wide Jl Selaparang and Jl Pejanggik have ATMs. Most change foreign cash and travellers cheques.

Rumah Sakit Harapan Keluarga (☎ 0370-670000, 0370-617 7000; www.harapankeluarga.co.id/rshk; Jl Ahmad Yani 9 ; ⏰ 24hr) The best private hospital on Lombok is just east of downtown Mataram and has English-speaking doctors and modern facilities.

ℹ Getting There & Around

Mandalika Terminal is 6km from the centre and is a bus and bemo hub. It's surrounded by the city's chaotic main market. Use the official ticket office

to avoid touts. Yellow bemos shuttle to the centre (4000Rp).

Senggigi

☎ 0370

The beaches around Senggigi are hard to beat. Think: a series of sweeping bays with white-sand beaches, coconut palms, cliff and mountain backdrops, and blood-red sunset views of Bali's Gunung Agung. Lombok's original tourist area, it can be tatty along the main road. With the Gilis stealing all the cool, Senggigi is best used as a jumping off point to the rest of Lombok. Senggigi spans nearly 10km of coast. Hotels, shops, banks, ATMs and restaurants are clustered along a central strip starting 6km north of Ampenan.

⊙ Sights

Strolling the beach, especially at sunset, yields many lovely views.

Pura Batu Bolong
TEMPLE

(admission by donation; ☉ 7am-7pm) It's not the grandest, but Pura Batu Bolong is Lombok's sweetest Hindu temple, and particularly lovely at sunset. Join the ever-welcoming Balinese community as they leave offerings at the 14 altars and pagodas that tumble down a rocky volcanic outcropping about 2km south of central Senggigi. The rock underneath the temple has a natural hole, hence the name (*batu bolong* literally means 'rock with hole').

🏃 Activities

There's decent **snorkelling** off the rocky point that bisects Senggigi's sheltered bay in front of Windy Cottages; many hotels and restaurants in central Senggigi hire out mask-snorkel-fin sets for 25,000Rp per day. Diving trips from Senggigi normally visit the Gili Islands, so consider basing yourself there. Offers to climb Gunung Rinjani abound.

Blue Coral Diving
DIVING

(☑ 0370-693441; www.bluecoraldive.com; Jl Raya Senggigi; 2-tank dive 800,000Rp) Senggigi's biggest dive shop hits the same sites as the shops in the Gilis.

Blue Marlin
DIVING

(☑ 0370-693719; www.bluemarlindive.com; Holiday Resort Lombok, Jl Raya Senggigi; two-tank dive 800,000Rp) The local branch of a well-regarded Gili T dive shop.

Royal Spa
SPA

(☑ 0370-660 8777; Jl Raya Senggigi; treatments from 85,000Rp; ☉ 10am-9pm) A professional yet inexpensive spa with a tempting range of scrubs, massages and treatments. The *lulur* massage is a real treat and includes a body mask.

🛏 Sleeping

Senggigi has a lot of budget rooms, but beware of those south of the centre which may be rattled by the all-night blare of 'karaoke' joints.

★ Wira
GUESTHOUSE $

(☑ 0370-692153; www.thewira.com; Jl Raya Senggigi Km 8; dm 75,000Rp, r 250,000-350,000Rp; ※ 🛜) This boutique *losmen* is on the beach side of the main Senggigi strip. They have 11 simple, tasteful, sizeable rooms with bamboo furnishings and private porches out back. There is a 10-bed dorm room.

Hotel Elen
HOTEL $

(☑ 0370-693077; Jl Raya Senggigi; d from 110,000Rp; ❋) Elen is the long-time backpackers' choice. The 36 rooms are basic, but those facing the waterfall fountain and koi pond come with spacious tiled patios that catch the ocean breeze. It's down a narrow *gang* which limits road noise.

Sonya Homestay
HOMESTAY $

(☑ 0813 3989 9878; Jl Raya Senggigi; r 90,000-160,000Rp; ❋ 🛜) A shady family-run enclave of nine rooms with nice patios and bright-pink beds (the cheapest are fan-only). Nathan, the owner, offers driving tours of Mataram and the surrounding area. It's off the road amidst a small garden.

Central Inn
HOTEL $$

(☑ 0370-692006; Jl Raya Senggigi; r from 300,000Rp; ❋ 🛜 ≋) A new and growing hotel set in the centre of town. The 54 rooms have high ceilings, fresh tiles and a bamboo seating area out front with views of the surrounding hills. It's on the beach side of the main drag and away from noise.

🍴 Eating & Drinking

For authentic street food, head to the hillside *warung* on the route north to Mangsit where *sate* sizzles, pots of noodles bubble and corn roasts at dusk.

Avoid the influx of cavernous, windowless 'karaoke' bars with names like 'One Stop Entertainment' where cheaply done-up night maidens seek out red-nosed expats to ask the age-old question, 'You want maaaaassaaaage?'

★ Cafe Tenda
INDONESIAN $

(Jl Raya Senggigi; mains 12,000-15,000Rp; ☉ noon-11pm) Barely enclosed, this roadside *warung* wows the stool-sitting masses with hot-out-of-the-wok Indo classics. Get the *nasi goreng* made extra hot with extra garlic and you'll be crying *and* sweating.

★ Coco Beach
INDONESIAN $

(☑ 0817 578 0055; Pantai Kerandangan; mains from 25,000Rp; ☉ noon-10pm; 🖊) About 2km north of central Senggigi, this wonderful beachside restaurant features a healthy menu that includes lots of salads and choices for vegetarians. They have a full bar, blend authentic jamu tonics and offer tastefully secluded seating.

Senggigi

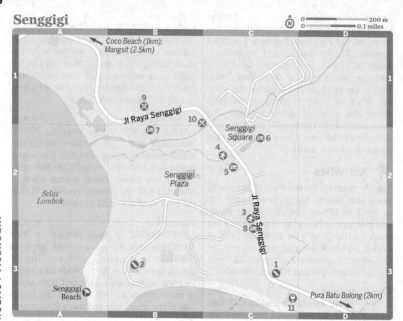

Senggigi map

Asmara
INTERNATIONAL $
(☎0370-693619; www.asmara-group.com; Jl Raya Senggigi; mains 18,000-75,000Rp; 🖰) An ideal family choice, this place spans the culinary globe from tuna carpaccio to Wiener schnitzel to Lombok's own *sate pusut* (minced-meat or fish *sate*). It also has a playground and kids' menu.

Hotel Lina
BAR
(☎0370-693237; Jl Raya Senggigi) The ancient Hotel Lina's seafront deck is a great spot for a sundowner. Happy hour starts at 4pm and ends an hour after dusk.

ⓘ Information
The main drag groans with ATMs.

ⓘ Getting There & Around
You can catch fast tourist boats to Bali (about 600,000Rp) from Teluk Nare 10km north of the centre. Look for offers around town.

Regular bemos travel between Senggigi and Ampenan's Kebon Roek terminal (4000Rp, 20 minutes, 10km), where you can connect to Mandalika Terminal in Mataram.

Damri runs buses to/from the airport (30,000Rp, 90 minutes). A taxi costs 190,000Rp.

Gunung Rinjani
Lombok's highest peak, and the second-highest volcano in Indonesia, Gunung Rinjani (3726m) supports a smattering of villages and is of great climatic importance to Lombok. The Balinese call it 'the seat of the Gods' and place it alongside Gunung Agung in spiritual lore. Lombok's Sasaks also revere it and make biannual pilgrim-

TREKKING GUNUNG RINJANI

Agencies in Senggigi arrange all-inclusive treks, but you can make your own, cheaper, arrangements. Seek out the **Rinjani Trekking Centre** (RTC; ☑ 0817 573 0415, 0370-693202; www.info2lombok.com; Jl Raya Senggigi Km 08) in Senggigi, which is based in Senaru. It has great maps, and rotates local guides and porters for trekking tours. June to August is the best trekking season. During the wet season (November to April), tracks can be slippery and dangerous.

A good Senaru outfitter is **John's Adventures** (☑ 0817 578 8018; www.rinjanimaster. com).

The most common trek is to climb from Senaru to Pos III (2300m) on the first day (about five hours of steep walking), camp there and climb to Pelawangan I, on the crater rim (2600m), for sunrise the next morning (about two hours). From the rim, descend into the crater and walk around to the **hot springs** (two hours) on a very exposed track. The hot springs, revered by locals for their healing properties, are a good place to relax and camp for the second night.

Or continue east from the hot springs and camp at Pelawangan II (about 2900m). From there a track branches off to the summit. It's a heroic climb (three or four hours) over loose footing to the top (3726m). Start at 3am so that you can glimpse the sunrise on the summit.

The most popular package is the three-day, two-night trek from Senaru to Sembalun Lawang via the summit. It includes food, equipment, guide, porters, park fee and transport back to Senaru. This costs about 2,500,000Rp per person.

Bring several layers of clothing, solid footwear, rain gear, extra water (do not depend on your guide for your water supply) and a torch (flashlight). Buy food and supplies in Mataram or Senggigi. People die every year on the mountain; it shouldn't be approached lightly.

INDONESIA LOMBOK

ages to honour the mountain spirit. It sure is one hell of a climb. Reach the summit and look down upon a 6km-wide caldera with a crescent-shaped cobalt lake, hot springs and smaller volcanic cones. The stunning sunrise view from the rim takes in north Lombok, Bali's Gunung Agung and the Indian Ocean, drenched in an unforgettable pink hue.

SENARU
☑ 0370

With sweeping views and an eternal spring climate, the mountain villages of Senaru and nearby **Batu Koq** are the best bases for Rinjani climbs. Be sure to make the 30-minute walk to the spectacular **Air Terjun Sendang Gila waterfalls** (5000Rp), and visit the traditional village, **Dusun Senaru**.

Many *losmen* along the main road have basic rooms with breakfast. **Gunung Baru Senaru** (☑ 0819 0741 1211; rinjaniadventure@gmail. com; r 100,000Rp) is a small family-run property with just five simple, tiled cottages with western toilets and *mandi* in a blooming garden.

Pondok Senaru & Restaurant (☑ 0818 0362 4129; pondoksenaru@yahoo.com; r 250,000-600,000Rp; ☎) is a class act, with 14 lovely little terracotta-tiled cottages and comfortable suites. Or just grab a table (dishes 20,000Rp

to 35,000Rp) and eat perched on the edge of a rice-terraced valley.

From Mandalika terminal in Mataram catch a bus to Bayan (40,000Rp, two hours), then a bemo to Senaru (12,000Rp). A tourist shuttle from Senggigi costs 120,000Rp.

Kuta
☑ 0370

They may share a name, but Lombok's Kuta is languid and stunningly gorgeous, with white-sand beaches, rugged hills and world-class surf. An ever-growing collection of fun and funky guesthouses cater to the ever-growing numbers of visitors. Don't be surprised if a goat nibbles on your pack while you lounge on the sand.

Kuta Bay has a wide golden beach with stunning headlands on both ends, and exposed turquoise shallows at low tide. Rollers crash on a reef 300m from shore. Seek out **Tanjung Aan**, an empty horseshoe bay with looming headlands. **Pantai Seeger** is likewise gorgeous.

The new highway linking the new Lombok International Airport to Mataram brings all of South Lombok close to Mataram and various Bali connections. This is especially true for the fab beaches at Kuta.

🏃 Activities

For surfing, stellar lefts and rights break on the reefs off Kuta Bay and east of Tanjung Aan. Boatmen will take you out for around 120,000Rp. Seven kilometres east of Kuta is the fishing village of **Gerupak**, where there's a series of reef breaks, both close to the shore and further out, but they require a boat, at a negotiable 300,000Rp per day. Wise surfers buzz past Gerupak, take the road to Awang, and hire a boat (350,000Rp for up to six people) to **Ekas**, where crowds are thin and surf is plentiful. West of Kuta you'll find **Mawan**, a stunning swimming beach (the first left after Astari), and **Mawi**, a popular surf paradise with world-class swells and a strong riptide.

Kimen Surf   SURFING
(📞0370-655064; www.kuta-lombok.net; board rental per day 50,000Rp, lessons per person 480,000Rp; ⏱9am-8pm) Swell forecasts, tips, kite-surfing, board rental, repairs and lessons. It runs guided excursions to breaks such as Gerupak (400,000Rp).

Scuba Froggy   DIVING
(📞0877 6510 6945; www.scubafroggy.com; per dive 375,000Rp; ⏱9am-8pm) Runs local trips to a dozen sites, most above 18m. From June to November they also run trips to the spectacular and challenging ocean pinnacles in Belongas Bay, famous for schooling hammerheads and mobula rays. Snorkelling trips are 150,000Rp.

🛏 Sleeping

Most accommodation is on or within walking distance of the beach. Simple guesthouses and cafes dominate. A dearth of street names makes navigation an adventure.

Hey Hey Homestay   HOMESTAY $
(📞0818 0522 8822; r 150,000Rp) An outstanding homestay with five clean, spacious rooms and sea views from private patios. If you get lucky, score the bamboo room on the top floor where the view is epic. Take the dirt road south from the intersection.

Kuta Baru   HOMESTAY $
(📞081 854 8357; Jl Pariswata Kuta; r with fan 180,000-250,000Rp, with air-con 370,000Rp; 🛜❄) One of Kuta's best homestays. There's a cute patio strung with the obligatory hammock, daily coffee service, sparkling tiles and an all-round good vibe. It's 110m east of the intersection.

GR Homestay   GUESTHOUSE $
(📞0819 0727 9797; r 220,000Rp; 🛜❄) A solid spot. Ten simple tiled rooms with pastel paint jobs and rain showerheads in otherwise simple baths. There's a nice pool out front.

★Yuli's Homestay   HOMESTAY $$
(📞0819 1710 0983; www.yulishomestay.com; r 375,000Rp; ❄🛜❄) The eight rooms are immaculately clean, extremely spacious and have big front terraces. There's a guest kitchen and a huge garden and pool to enjoy. It's about 600m from the beach, down a narrow *gang* off the Praya road.

🍴 Eating & Drinking

★Astari   VEGETARIAN $
(dishes 18,000-30,000Rp; ⏱7am-6.30pm; 🍴) Perched on a mountaintop 2km west of town on the road to Mawan, this breezy, Moroccan-themed vegetarian lounge-restaurant has spectacular vistas of pristine bays and rocky peninsulas that take turns spilling further out to sea.

Shore Beach Bar   CAFE $
(Jl Pariwisata; mains 30,000-50,000Rp; ⏱10am-late) Owned by Kimen, Kuta's original surf entrepreneur, the open dance-hall interior has a fantastic sound system, good for the live music Saturday nights. The beachside annexe has intoxicating views and drinks plus grilled seafood.

Solah Cafe   CAFE $
(mains 22,000-50,000Rp; ⏱9am-10pm; 🛜🍴) Right on the beach strip, they serve up an array of Western and Indonesian breakfasts in the morning (try the *bubur*, a sweet rice porridge with palm sugar). At lunch and dinner the menu diverges in many good directions. They also offer daily yoga at 8am.

Warung Bule   SEAFOOD $$
(📞0819 1799 6256; mains 40,000-140,000Rp; ⏱8am-10pm; 🛜) The skilled chef-owner delivers tropical seafood tastes at an affordable price. The grilled mahi (mild whitefish) is good, and so is the lobster Tom yam soup. He has other creative concoctions like a Sasak chicken wrap. Enjoy the views.

ℹ Information

Wi-fi is common and there are ATMs.

Reports of deals gone bad make it worthwhile to only rent a vehicle or motorbike from your accommodation.

As you drive up the coastal road west and east of Kuta, watch your back – especially after dark. There have been reports of muggings in the area.

ⓘ Getting There & Away

Most everything in Kuta is on a single road that parallels the beach and crosses the road from Praya. This intersection is a local landmark.

How many bemos does it take to get to Kuta? Three. Take one from Mataram's Mandalika terminal to Praya (10,000Rp), another to Sengkol (5000Rp) and a third to Kuta (5000Rp). Simpler are the daily tourist buses serving Mataram (125,000Rp) plus Senggigi and Lembar (both 150,000Rp). A fixed-price taxi from the airport costs 85,000Rp.

Labuhan Lombok

You're here to catch a Sumbawa-bound ferry. Frequent buses and bemos travel between Labuhan Lombok and Mandalika terminal (15,000Rp, two hours) in Mataram. Some buses drop you at the port entrance road. If they do, catch another bemo to the ferry terminal. It's too far to walk.

Ferries run every 45 minutes, 24 hours a day, to Poto Tano (22,000Rp, 1½ hours).

Gili Islands

🖉 0370

For decades, travellers have made the hop from Bali for a dip in the turquoise-tinted, bathtub-warm waters of the irresistible Gili Islands and stayed longer than anticipated. Perhaps it's the deepwater coral reefs teeming with sharks, rays and reasonably friendly turtles? Maybe it's the serenity that comes with no motorised traffic? Or it could be the beachfront bungalows, white sand, alluring cafes and friendly locals. Each of these pearls, located just off the northwestern tip of Lombok, has its own unique character.

Gili Air is the closest to the mainland, with plenty of stylish bungalows dotted among the palms. Mellow Gili Meno, the middle island, makes for a quiet retreat.

Gili Trawangan, the furthest out, has been tagged as the 'party island'. It gets the most crowds and parts are often both jammed and raucous.

🏊 Activities

Diving around the Gilis is great. Marine life is plentiful and varied. Turtles and black-

and white-tip reef sharks are common, and the macro life (small stuff) is excellent, with seahorses, pipefish and lots of crustaceans. Around full moon, large schools of bumphead parrot fish appear to feast on coral spawns, while at other times of year, mantas soar.

Safety standards are generally high in the Gilis despite the modest dive costs. Rates are fixed (no matter who you dive with) at about 400,000Rp a dive, with discounts for packages of five dives or more. A PADI open-water course costs 4,200,000Rp.

Snorkelling is fun and the fish are plentiful on all the beach reefs. Gear can be rented for 25,000Rp to 30,000Rp per day. You can get to good sites right off the beaches, no boat needed.

Walking and cycling are the best land activities. Bikes can be hired from 30,000Rp per day. On Trawangan, time your circumnavigation (2½ hours on foot) with the sunset, and watch it from the hill on the southwest corner where you'll have a tremendous view of Bali's Gunung Agung.

Beaches are deceiving as each island seems ringed by perfect white sand although you'll soon discover that many of the beaches have coral and rocks right up to the water's edge, making just getting in and out – not to mention swimming – a literal pain. However, each island has stretches of sand bordering open water where conditions are idyllic.

ⓘ Information

All islands have internet cafes and wi-fi is widespread. Gili T and Air have ATMs.

DANGERS & ANNOYANCES

There are seldom police on any of the Gilis (though this is changing). Report thefts to the island *kepala desa* (village head) immediately, who will deal with the issue; staff at the dive schools will direct you to him. On Gili Trawangan, contact Satgas, the community organisation that runs island affairs, via your hotel or dive centre.

Although it's rare, some women have experienced sexual harassment and even assault while on the Gilis – walk home in pairs to the quieter parts of the islands.

As tranquil as these seas do appear, currents are strong in the channels between the islands. Do not try to swim between Gili islands as it can be deadly.

The drug trade remains endemic to Trawangan. Tourists have been injured and killed by adulterated *arak* on the Gilis; skip it.

ⓘ Getting There & Away

PRIVATE BOATS

Fast boats advertise swift connections (about two hours) between Bali and Gili Trawangan. They leave from several departure points in Bali, including Benoa Harbour, Sanur, Padangbai and Amed. Some go via Nusa Lembongan. Many dock at Teluk Nare on Lombok north of Senggigi before continuing onto Air and Trawangan (you'll have to transfer for Meno). Note that with land connections and various stops, your Bali to the Gilis travel time may be much greater than advertised.

Two useful websites, **Gili Bookings** (www.gilibookings.com) and **Gili Fastboat** (www.gili-fastboat.com), present a range of fast-boat operations. Book well ahead in July and August. One-way fares (with transport to/from tourist areas of Bali) average about US$60.

Be warned that the sea between Bali and Lombok can get very rough (particularly during rainy season). Long-running operators include:

Gili Cat (☎ 0361-271 680; www.gilicat.com; adult/child 660,000/475,000Rp) Serves the Gilis from Padangbai.

Scoot (☎ 0370-612 3433; www.scootcruise.com) Links Sanur with Nusa Lembongan and the Gilis.

For more on travelling safely by boat, see p310.

PUBLIC BOATS

Coming from other parts of Lombok, you can travel via Senggigi, or via the public boats that leave from Bangsal harbour (the cheapest route), or charter your own boat from Bangsal (280,000Rp to 375,000Rp, carries up to 20 people).

Coming by public transport via Mataram, catch a bus or bemo to Pemenang, from where it's a 1.2km walk (5000Rp by *cidomo* (horse-drawn cart, or *ojek*) to Bangsal harbour. A metered taxi to/from Senggigi runs about 100,000Rp.

Boat tickets at Bangsal harbour are sold at the port's large ticket office which has posted prices and which is where you charter a boat. Buy a ticket elsewhere and you're getting played.

Public boats run to all three islands before 11am, after that you may only find one to Gili T. One-way fares are 10,000Rp to Gili Air, 12,000Rp to Gili Meno and 13,000Rp to Gili Trawangan. Boats may pull up on the beach when they get to their Gili, prepare to wade ashore.

GETTING AROUND

The Gilis are flat and easy enough to get around by foot or bicycle (although sand can bog down bikes). A torch (flashlight) is useful at night. Hiring a *cidomo* (from 10,000Rp) will shorten distances to far-flung accommodation – especially on Gili T – but note that many of the horses look to be in poor physical condition.

There's a twice-daily island-hopping boat service that loops between all three islands (25,000Rp to 30,000Rp). Check the latest timetable at each island's dock. You can also charter

Gili Air

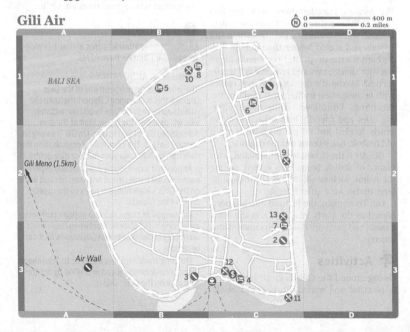

your own island-hopping boat (350,000Rp to 400,000Rp).

Gili Air

Closest to Lombok, for many Air is 'just right'. It has great eating and drinking options to rival Gili T, but lacks the frenetic crowds. The southern and eastern coasts have the best swimming beaches. Walking around the island takes about 90 minutes and you'll find little development along most of the north and west coasts.

🏃 Activities

Blue Marlin Dive Centre   DIVING
(✓0370-634387; www.bluemarlindive.com) The Air branch of the Gili's original dive franchise.

Manta Dive   DIVING
(✓0813 3778 9047; www.manta-dive.com) A long-running dive operation with excellent lodging available.

Oceans 5   DIVING
(✓0813 3877 7144; www.oceans5dive.com) The Gili's leading-edge dive centre has a 25m training pool and an in-house marine biologist.

🛏 Sleeping

Hotels and restaurants are mostly scattered along the southern and eastern coasts and cover all budgets.

★ Bintang Beach Bungalows   BUNGALOW $
(✓0877 6522 2554; r 150,000-300,000Rp; ✴) On quiet Gili Air's even quieter north coast, this sandy but tidy compound has 19 rooms and bungalows that range from budget-friendly fan-cooled to mildly snazzy. The bar area is a delight.

7 Seas   HOSTEL $
(✓0370-647   779;   www.facebook.com/7seas.international; hostel per person 80,000Rp; ☎❄)

Yes, they do have a range of rather splashy, spacious bungalows, but we like them for their bamboo, loft-like, four-bed hostel rooms.

Damai   GUESTHOUSE $$
(✓0878 6142 0416; damaihomestay.giliair@gmail.com; r 200,000-500,000Rp; @☎) It's worth finding this funky, thatched enclave. Rooms are basic yet tasteful and open onto a garden. The cosy dining patio is elegantly lit with paper lanterns. It's set exquisitely in the coco palms.

Pelangi Cottages   BUNGALOW $$
(✓0819 3316 8648; r from 400,000Rp; ✴) Set out on the north end, with a sweet slab of white sand out front, they have spacious but basic concrete and wood bungalows.

Gita Gili   BUNGALOW $$
(✓0878 6452 2124; bungalows with fan/air-con from 350,000/500,000Rp; ☎) A chilled-out bungalow property just north of the main action. The concrete and bamboo bungalows are fan-cooled, clean and decent value. Enjoy the hammocks.

🍴 Eating & Drinking

Most places on Gili Air offer an unbeatable setting for a meal, with tables right over the water facing Lombok's Gunung Rinjani. Almost every place closes by 10pm.

Warung Cika   CAFE
(meals from 15,000Rp; ☺8am-9pm) There are three tables on the sand at this basic thatch-sided cafe right on the harbour. The Indo classics are cheap and fresh.

Biba   ITALIAN $
(✓0819 1727 4648; www.bibabeach.com; mains 25,000-70,000Rp; ☺11.30am-10pm) Book a table on the sand for a memorable, romantic setting. Biba serves the best wood-oven pizza and foccacia on the islands. It also does authentic ravioli, gnocchi and tagliatelle.

Gili Air

Wiwin Café   INDONESIAN $
(meals 25,000-60,000Rp; ⊘7am-10pm) A great
choice for grilled fish in one of five homemade sauces. Service is attentive and there's
a nice bar area too.

Mirage   CAFE $
(snacks from 20,000; ⊘) Set on a sublime
stretch of beach with technicolour sunsets
nightly, there is no better place for a sundowner. The menu includes funky, veggie
options.

★**Scallywags**   INTERNATIONAL $$
(☑0370-645301; www.scallywagsresort.com; mains
45,000-95,000Rp; ⊘8am-10pm; 🛜) Set on Gili
Air's softest and widest beach, there's the ele-
gant decor, upscale comfort food, great grilled
seafood, homemade gelati, superb cocktails
and free wi-fi. But the best of them all is that
alluring beach dotted with lounges (although
the sambal bart is a secret weapon).

Gili Meno

While Trawangan continues to boom and Air
develops a buzz, Meno remains the humble
neighbour, content to whisper, unnoticed.
Compared to the other islands, services and
amenities are few. The east coast has the
widest and nicest beach. Inland you'll find
scattered homesteads, coconut plantations
and a salty lake.

🏃 Activities

Gili Meno Divers   DIVING
(☑0878 6409 5490; www.giliairdivers.com)
French and Indonesian owned and our fa-
vourite dive shop on Meno.

🛏 Sleeping

Jepun Bungalows   BUNGALOW $
(☑0819 1739 4736; www.jepunbungalows.com;
bungalow 250,000-600,000Rp; 🛜) Some 100m
from the main beach strip and harbour with
charming accommodation dotted around
a garden. Choose from lovely thatched
lumbung.

Tao Kombo   BUNGALOW $
(☑0812 372 2174; www.tao-kombo.com; r 200,000-
350,000Rp; 🛜) An innovatively designed
place with two open-sided backpackers' huts
that have bamboo screens for privacy, plus
eight *lumbung* cottages with thatched roofs.
It's home to the Jungle Bar, 200m inland
from the main strip.

Paul's Last Resort   BUNGALOW $
(☑0878 6569 2272; r from 200,000Rp) Choose
among woven open-sided bamboo shacks
on the beach that have electricity and share
a toilet and shower. And while they receive
delegations from the insect kingdom and
get inundated with Gili T's thumping bass, if
you bed down here you will also be privvy to
a starry night spectacular.

Adeng Adeng   BUNGALOW $$
(☑0818 0534 1019; www.adeng-adeng.com; r
300,000-650,000Rp; 🛜) 🌿 An understated
elegant resort set back in the trees from a

Gili Meno

⚐ 0 ▬▬▬▬▬ 400 m
0 ▬▬▬▬▬ 0.2 miles

fine stretch of sand. Its simple wooden bungalows have all the creature comforts and stylish outdoor terrazzo baths. The rambling property is sprinkled with artisinal accents.

✖ Eating & Drinking

Most accommodation has at least a simple cafe; nothing on Meno reaches the culinary heights found on the other Gilis.

Ya Ya Warung INDONESIAN $
(dishes 10,000-20,000Rp) Ramshackle *warung*-on-the-beach that serves up Indonesian faves, curries, pancakes and plenty of pasta.

Rust Warung SEAFOOD $
(☑0370-642324; mains 15,000-75,000Rp) Renowned for its grilled fish, but it also has pizza, espresso, a grocer and bungalows too. It also serves the only espresso on the island. Tables are perched over the water.

Diana Café BAR
(drinks 12,000-30,000Rp; ⊙8am-9pm) If by any remote chance you find the pace of life on Meno too busy, head to this little tiki bar par excellence.

Gili Trawangan

More party than pastoral, Gili T's main drag boasts a glittering roster of lounge bars, hip hotels and cosmopolitan restaurants, mini-marts and dive schools. And yet behind this glitzy facade, a bohemian character endures, with rickety *warung* and reggae joints surviving between the cocktail tables, even as massive 200-plus room hotels colonise the wild and ragged west coast.

Some detractors would call it Kuta East, but to the raving masses, that's the point.

🏃 Activities

There's fun **snorkelling** off the beach north of the boat landing – the coral isn't in the best shape here, but there are tons of fish. The

reef is in much better shape off the northwest coast but rocks and coral make access difficult.

Big Bubble DIVING
(☑0370-612 5020; www.bigbubblediving.com) The original engine behind the Gili Eco Trust (www.giliecotrust.com) which promotes local green initiatives.

Blue Marlin Dive Centre DIVING
(☑613 2424, 0813 3993 0190; www.bluemarlindive.com) Gili T's original dive shop, and one of the best tech diving schools in the world.

Dream Divers DIVING
(☑0370-613 4496; www.dreamdivers.com) One of the longest-tenured dive shops on Gili T.

Freedive Gili DIVING, YOGA
(☑0370-640503; www.freedivegili.com) The Gili's only free-diving centre. It also offers strenuous but stress-relieving yoga classes (per class 100,000Rp) in its sweet studio.

🛏 Sleeping

Cheap places are inland from the main strip and are actually some of the most serene choices on Gili T as the lanes back here are quiet and flower-lined.

★**Gili Hostel** HOSTEL $
(☑0877 6526 7037; www.gilihostel.com; dm from 150,000Rp; ❄⊚) The island's only dedicated hostel is a co-ed dorm complex with a shaggy Torajan-styled roof. Rooms sleep seven, have concrete floors, high ceilings and a sleeping loft. There's a rooftop bar.

Pondok Gili Gecko GUESTHOUSE $
(☑0818 0573 2814; r from 250,000-350,000Rp) An inviting village guesthouse with a charming gecko motif. Rooms are super clean and have ceiling fans and private tiled patios overlooking the garden.

Koi Gili GUESTHOUSE $
(☑0819 5995 760; s/d from 300,000/350,000Rp; ❄) The young and hip gravitate to this groovy village guesthouse with a daybed in the garden and a mod colour scheme on the facade.

Lumbung Cottages 2 BUNGALOW $
(☑0819 3679 6353; www.lumbungcottage.com; bungalows from 400,000Rp; ❄⊚) Thatched *lumbung*-style cottages, set deep in the village, tucked up against the hillside, surrounding a black-bottom pool.

Gili Trawangan

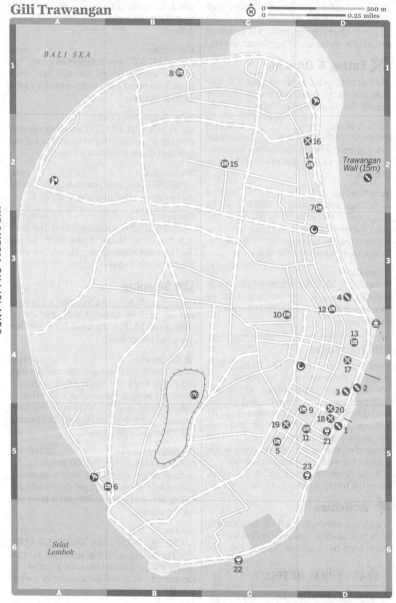

Oceane Paradise COTTAGE $
(☎0812 3779 3533; s/d from 250,000/300,000Rp)
Five wooden cottages with stylish outdoor
bathrooms sit quietly back in the village.

Exile BUNGALOW $
(☎0819 0707 7475; r 350,000-500,000Rp; @) A
thumping west-coast compound of woven
bamboo bungalows, with a jamming beach
bar and bamboo lounges on the sand. It's 15 to
20 minutes to the main strip on foot.

Gili Trawangan

Tanah Qita   BUNGALOW $

(☑ 0370-613 9159; bungalows with fan/air-con from 250,000/600,000Rp; ✳) Tanah Qita (Homeland) has large, immaculate *lumbung* (with four-poster beds) and smaller fan-cooled versions. The garden is a bucolic delight.

Black Sand   GUESTHOUSE $

(☑ 0812 372 0353; r 250,000-450,000Rp; ✳) Tucked away on the inland side of the village, this is archetypal flashpacker terrain. Offers superb value, well-presented two-storey bungalows and rooms – plus a great garden for lounging.

★**Woodstock**   BUNGALOW $$

(☑ 081 2396 7744; www.woodstockgili.com; r 350,000-700,000Rp; ✳🛜🏊) The hippest spot on Trawangan. Commune with the spirit of the dead, Baez and Hendrix in 11 super-clean rooms with tribal accents, private porches and outdoor baths, surrounding a fabulous pool area.

Sama Sama Bungalows   BUNGALOW $$

(☑ 0370-612 1106; r with fan/air-con from 200,000/500,000Rp; ✳) We like the six, fan-cooled backpacker rooms with high beamed ceilings, modern baths and a great price.

Karma Kayak   INN $$

(☑ 0818 0559 3710; www.karmakayak.com; r from 500,000Rp; ✳🛜🏊) Simplicity is the key here at this wonderful retreat where the fine rooms adopt a less-is-more uncluttered design, with generous balconies or verandahs. The beachside cafe has front-row seats at sunset.

✗ Eating

With more than one hundred places for a meal, you'll be spoiled for choice. There's few interesting choices in the west, so picnic as you perambulate.

Pasar Malam   NIGHT MARKET $

(mains 15,000-30,000Rp; ☺6pm-midnight) Blooming nightly in front of the art market, this market is the place to indulge in ample local eats.

Warung Indonesia   INDONESIAN $

(meals from 25,000Rp; ☺8am-9pm; 🛜) Tucked away at the rear of the village, this scores high marks for its tasty pick-and-mix bar, as well as a menu of Indo staples. Its lofted, thatched dining room is lit with vintage lanterns.

Warung Mamas   INDONESIAN $

(mains from 15,000Rp; ☺9am-9pm) A typical roofless, open-air, family-run *warung* found on the backstreets of the village. You can't get fresher – or much cheaper – fare on the island.

★**Blu da Mare**   ITALIAN $$

(☑ 0858 8866 2490; www.bludamare.it; mains 60,000-110,000Rp; ☺12.30-3pm & 6.30-10pm Sat-Thu) An authentic and intimate (few tables, limited seatings available) Italian-owned trattoria where the lady of the house bakes the bread, makes her own pasta and grills meat, fish and seafood to perfection.

Pesona   INDIAN $$

(☑ 0370-660 7233; www.pesonaresort.com; mains 60,000-80,000Rp; ☺7am-11pm; ✍) The Indian kitchen serves up an abundance of vegetarian options along with a menu of tandoori

INDONESIA GILI ISLANDS

classics. Once sated, lay back on the cushions and fire up a sheesha.

Drinking & Nightlife

Official party nights on Gili Trawangan are Monday, Wednesday and Friday – although given the number of cool beach bars to investigate, each and every night can be a party.

★ Tir na Nog   PUB
(☑ 0370-613 9463; ⏰ 7am-2am Thu-Tue, to 4am Wed; 🛜) Known simply as 'The Irish', this barnlike place has a sports-bar interior with big screens ideal for international football matches. Its shoreside bar is probably the busiest meeting spot in the island.

Surf Bar   BAR
(⏰ 8am-late) Opposite the break, this tiki bar has a sweet slab of beach, a rack of boards to rent, a pumping stereo and a young crowd.

Rudy's Pub   BAR
Rudy's hosts arguably the best party on the island (Fridays), with a good mix of locals and a huge dance floor at the rear.

Sumbawa

Beautifully contorted and sprawling, Sumbawa is all volcanic ridges, terraced rice fields, jungled peninsulas and sheltered bays. The southeast coast is the most accessible playground, which explains why Lakey Peak has become a year-round surf magnet.

Though well connected to Lombok, Sumbawa is a very different sort of place. It's far less developed, much poorer and conservatively Islamic. Transport connections off the cross-island road are infrequent and uncomfortable, and most overland travellers don't even get off the bus as they roll from Lombok to Flores. For now, it's the domain of surfers, miners and mullahs.

❶ Getting There & Away

Sumbawa's main highway is in good condition and runs from Taliwang (near the west coast) through Sumbawa Besar, Dompu and Bima to Sape (on the east coast). Long-distance buses, most of them air-conditioned, cruise to Bima, with some going as far as the ferry dock in Sape.

Car hire is possible through hotels in Sumbawa Besar and Bima, but prices are much higher than in Bali or Lombok at about 600,000Rp to 800,000Rp per day, including a driver. Plan on paying for your driver's meals and lodging as well.

Ferries link Labuhan Lombok and Poto Tano. In the east, Sape has ferries to Labuanbajo, Flores.

Poto Tano & Around

Poto Tano is the Lombok-bound ferry port; there's no reason to hang around. Most travellers pass straight through to Sumbawa Besar. You can also venture south of Taliwang to the superb surf at Maluk, a contemporary boomtown thanks to a nearby copper mine. Santai (☑ 0878 6393 5758; Senkongkang; r with shared/private bath from 100,000/180,000Rp; @) attracts surfers to its basic rooms. Fifteen kilometres further south is another gorgeous surf beach, Sengkongkang, where you can join the fun at eccentric and gregarious Yo Yo's (☑ 0819 3592 1777, 0819 3591 7888; Yoyos hotel@yahoo.co.id; Rantung; dm/standard/deluxe 150,000/400,000/600,000Rp; P ❋ @ 🛜).

❶ Getting There & Around

Ferries run every 45 minutes, 24 hours a day, between Labuhan Lombok and Poto Tano (22,000Rp, 1½ hours).

The through buses from Mataram to Bima include the ferry fare, but you'll move faster if you stay indie, and hop on one of the buses that meet the Poto Tano ferry and go to Taliwang (15,000Rp, one hour) and Sumbawa Besar (30,000Rp, three hours). Bemos link Taliwang to Maluk (20,000Rp, 30 minutes).

There is also a twice-daily fast ferry between Benete Harbour near Maluk and Kayangan Lombok near Labuhan Lombok (100,000Rp, 90 minutes), which is ideal for the surf set.

Sumbawa Besar
☑ 0371 / POP 57,000

Sumbawa Besar, nestled in a lush, sun-kissed breadbasket, is the main town on the western half of the island.

🛏 Sleeping & Eating

The best sleeping and eating options are clustered along Jl Hasanuddin. The nearby mosque provides free wake-up calls.

Hotel Suci   HOTEL $
(☑ 0371-21589; Jl Hasanuddin 57; r with fan/aircon from 150,000/200,000Rp; P ❋) Right next to the mosque, there's a range of rooms here, but the best are on the top floor of the newish building with high ceilings and aircon. The economy rooms aren't great.

Aneka Rasa Jaya CHINESE **$**

(📞0371-21291; Jl Hasanuddin 16; mains from 20,000Rp; ⊙8am-3pm & 6-10pm) Clean and popular, this Chinese seafood house plates tender fish fillets, shrimp, squid, crab and scallops in various sauces. The *soto kepiting* (crab soup) is particularly popular.

ⓘ Getting There & Away

Sumbawa Besar's main long-distance bus station is Terminal Sumur Payung, 5.5km northwest of town on the highway. You can book tickets at **Tiara Mas** (📞0371-21241; Jl Yos Sudarso). Service includes Bima (80,000Rp, seven hours) and Mataram (bus/minibus 100,000/150,000Rp, six hours).

Hu'u & Lakey Beach

Lakey Beach, a gentle crescent of golden sand 3km south of Hu'u, is where Sumbawa's tourist pulse beats year-round, thanks to seven world-class surf breaks that curl and crash in one massive bay. From August to October the wind gusts, which turns Pantai Lakey into Indonesia's best kite-surfing destination.

🛏 Sleeping & Eating

Blue Lagoon BUNGALOW **$**

(📞0813 3982 3018; r 200,000-250,000Rp; ❄) A vast complex of well-looked-after tiled rooms with private patios that stretches from the beach to the cell tower. All are spacious, but some are in better shape than others. The restaurant and bar draws a crowd.

Alamanda Bungalows BUNGALOW **$**

(📞0371-623519; Jl Raya Hu'u; r from 100,000Rp) The cheapest joint on the block is also one of the most charming. Crash on a bamboo bed in a stand-alone hexagonal *casita* that is quite spacious and set in a palm garden.

★**Aman Gati Hotel** RESORT **$$**

(📞0821 4473 4511, 0371-623031; www.lakeypeak amangati.com; Jl Raya Hu'u; s/d from US$40/50; ❄@🛜🏊) The most professional operation on the beach, this Balinese-run spot has modern rooms perfectly oriented to the break. Many prefer the cottages; the bar and restaurant have fine views.

ⓘ Information

Stop by an ATM for cash in Sumbawa Besar or Bima before you come to the beach.

ⓘ Getting There & Away

From Dompu (buses from Bima 20,000Rp, two hours) there are two daily (slow) buses as far as Hu'u (25,000Rp, 1½ hours), where you can hire an *ojek* (10,000Rp) to Pantai Lakey.

Try doing this with a surfboard and you'll see why so many people take a taxi from Bima airport (around 600,000Rp, four people). Leaving Hu'u, there's one early morning bus, but any of the hotels can arrange a taxi to Bima. *Ojeks* to Dompu cost 150,000Rp.

The *ojek* cartel is omnipresent in Lakey, but to minimise the haggle, they've issued a fixed price list for round-trip *ojek* transport to the surf breaks (25,000Rp to 80,000Rp).

Bima & Raba

📞0374 / POP 273,000

These twin cities – grubby but lively Bima and orderly but dull Raba – form Sumbawa's main port and commercial hot spot, but there's no good reason to nest here.

🛏 Sleeping & Eating

Most hotels are in central Bima, near the market.

Hotel Lila Graha HOTEL **$**

(📞0374-42740; Jl Lombok 20; r 165,000-370,000Rp; ❄🛜) One of two four-storey, block-long hotels, each with a wide range of rooms. Ground floor suite rooms are newest and nicest.

★**Rumah Makan Sabar Sabur** SEAFOOD **$**

(📞0374-646236; Jl Salahudin, Bandara; meals 20,000Rp; ⊙7am-7pm) The long wooden tables are always crowded with locals who come to munch *bandeng goreng* (a flash-fried tiny freshwater fish). Enjoy with their fiery crushed-tomato *sambal,* torn leaves of lemon basil and a bit of rice.

ⓘ Getting There & Away

Bima's airport (code BMU) is 17km out of town; 70,000Rp by taxi. Services include: **Lion Air/ Wings Air** (www.lionair.co.id) with services to Bali, and **Merpati** (www.merpati.co.id) and **Transnusa** (www.transnusa.co.id), for services to both Bali and Mataram.

Pelni (📞0374-42625; Jl Kesatria 2) sails twice monthly from Bima to Ende, Waingapu and Kupang and back to Benoa in Bali.

Buses to points west of Bima leave from the central bus station, south of town. Several companies offer express night service to Mataram (180,000Rp, 11 to 14 hours).

INDONESIA SUMBAWA

KOMODO DRAGONS

The Komodo dragon (*ora*) is a monitor lizard, albeit one on steroids. Growing up to 3m in length, they are an awesome sight and make a visit to Komodo National Park well worth the effort. Lounging about lethargically in the sun, these are actually as fearsome as their looks imply. Park rangers keep them from attacking tourists; random encounters are a bad idea. Some dragon details:

➡ They are omnivorous, and enjoy eating their young. Juvenile dragons live in trees to avoid becoming a meal for adults.

➡ *Ora* often rise up on their hind legs just before attacking, and the tail can deliver well-aimed blows that knock down their prey.

➡ Bacteria in the dragons' mouth are their secret weapon. One bite from a dragon leads to septic infections that inevitably kill the victim. The huge lizard lopes along after its victim waiting for it to die, which can take up to two weeks.

➡ Komodos will feed on mammals up to 100kg. They do this at one sitting and then retire for up to a month to digest the massive meal.

➡ There is no accepted reason the dragons are only found in this small area of Indonesia, although it's thought that their ancestors came from Australia four million years ago. There are about 4000 in the wild today.

➡ A recent discovery has biologists baffled: female dragons kept isolated from other dragons their entire lives have recently been observed in zoos giving birth to fertilized eggs.

Buses to Sape (20,000Rp, two hours) depart from Kumbe in Raba, a 20-minute bemo ride (2000Rp) east of Bima. Charter a car (300,000Rp, 1½ hours) to Sape to make the early ferry.

Sape

📞 0374

This tumbledown port town is not a place to linger. The docks, perfumed with the conspicuous scent of drying cuttlefish, are 3km from town.

Express buses with service to Lombok and Bali meet arriving ferries. There are twice-daily ferries to Labuanbajo (54,000Rp, eight to nine hours); always double-check the latest ferry schedules.

Komodo & Rinca

Parched, desolate, beautiful Komodo and Rinca rise from waters that churn with riptides and whirlpools and are patrolled by lizard royalty, the **komodo dragon**. Drawing ever-more visitors each year, the park is driving the booming popularity of Flores.

Komodo National Park (www.komodo-park. com) encompasses both islands and several neighbouring isles. The park entrance fee (20,000Rp) is collected on arrival. There's an additional camera fee of 50,000Rp. English-speaking park rangers offer various guided hikes.

The islands are easily reached from Labuanbajo on day trips which usually include stops for snorkelling and swimming at various idyllic little beaches on tiny islets in the beautiful waters west of Labuanbajo.

⊙ Sights & Activities

On **Rinca**, you have a choice of guided hikes (50,000Rp to 250,000Rp) from the pleasant ranger station close to the docks. The 90-minute 'medium' hike is literally just right as it includes the shady lowlands plus a trip up the hillside where the views across the arid landscape to palm-dotted ridges, achingly turquoise waters and pearly white specks of beach are spectacular. Besides dragons, you may see deer, snakes, monkeys, wild pigs and myriad birds. For many, Rinca, which can be reached from Labuanbajo in under an hour, is the best option for park visits as it packs a lot into a compact area.

Komodo rewards visitors willing to invest time. It's further from Labuanbajo (up to two hours by fast boat) and the best hikes (50,000Rp to 400,000Rp) go beyond the one favoured by most visitors: the 30-minute stroll from the docks and park office at **Loh Liang** to **Banu Nggulung**.

Spending a night on Komodo or on a tour boat offshore allows for longer hikes. The

Poreng Valley (5.5km, four to five hours return) is a good place to see dragons in wilder surrounds than the ones inevitably sunning themselves near the park offices and has a more out-in-the-wild feeling. The trail continues over Bukit Randolph, to Loh Sebita (9km, four hours). This is the best hike. It's challenging, the sea views are spectacular, you'll likely see a dragon or two, and you can organise your boat to pick you up in Loh Sebita, so you don't have to retrace your steps.

Diving   DIVING
(2-dive trips from 800,000Rp) Komodo National Park has some of the most exhilarating scuba diving in Indonesia. Mantas and whales are drawn here to feed on the plankton during their migration from the Indian Ocean to the South China Sea. Dolphins are also common in the waters between Komodo and Flores.

Among the several dozen dive sites mapped in the park are Batu Bolong, a split pinnacle with pristine coral and a relatively light current, and Crystal Bommie (aka Crystal Rock), with electric soft corals, turtles and schooling pelagics.

Dive shops abound in Labuanbajo and choices are myriad. Day trips (about 1.1 million rupiah with a park stop) can combine visits to either Rinca or Komodo islands or both. Multiday packages on live-aboard boats vary widely in price depending on comfort levels (five million rupiah for three days and two nights is average).

🛏 Sleeping

PHKA Camp   GUESTHOUSE $$
(per person per night 400,000Rp) Komodo's PHKA camp is an overpriced version of a basic Indonesian hotel. Most overnighters opt to sleep aboard their charterted or live-aboard boats.

ⓘ Getting There & Away

Organise your Komodo National Park visit from Labuanbajo where there are dozens of dive shops and agencies offering tours.

A typical day trip on a fast boat to Rinca (under one hour one-way) costs about 250,000Rp per person and includes beach and snorkelling stops. A simple lunch is usually included as well as snacks plus the use of snorkelling gear (but confirm this). Day trips to Komodo cost more as you'll be travelling longer (up to two hours one-way).

Chartering a boat for the day costs at least 950,000Rp but will allow you to fully customise your trip. Note that regular (slow) boats take double the times above to reach the islands. Shop around and compare the many offers.

SEVEN DAYS ON FLORES

You can take as long as you like exploring Flores, but a common trip for the visa-expiry-date-conscious using a hired car and driver goes like this:

➡ Three days in Labuanbajo and the surrounding park and waters

➡ One day driving to the hill town of Bajawa

➡ One day driving to the sweet mountain village of Moni via the Ngada village of Bena and the steamy port town of Ende

➡ One day exploring the area around Moni, including Kelimutu National Park

➡ One day driving to Maumere, with a stop at the beach in Paga

You can fly out of Maumere and you can do this trip in either direction, although it's easiest to find a driver you'll like in Labuanbajo. Add a couple of extra days to the schedule above if you're sticking to buses.

Flores

Flores, the island named 'flowers' by 16th-century Portuguese colonists, has become Indonesia's 'Next Big Thing'. In the far west, Labuanbajo is a booming tourist town that combines tropical beauty with nearby attractions like Komodo National Park, myriad superb dive spots and beach-dappled little islands.

The often lush interior is attracting an ever-greater river of travellers who in just a few days' journey overland encounter smoking volcanoes, spectacular rice fields and lakes, exotic cultures and hidden beaches. You'll even see plenty of steeples as most people away from the port towns are nominally Catholic.

The 670km serpentine, yet rapidly improving, Trans-Flores highway skirts knife-edge ridges that sheer into spectacular river canyons, brushes by dozens of traditional villages and always seems to have a perfectly conical volcano in view.

ℹ Information

Foriegn aid money has funded the creation of an excellent string of tourist offices in key towns across Flores. Their enthusiastic information is backed by an excellent website (www.flores tourism.com) and several publications well worth their modest prices: a huge and detailed map plus books covering activities and culture.

ℹ Getting There & Away

Labuanbajo is the main gateway to Flores and is well-served by flights from Bali. Maumere and Ende are also serviced by daily flights.

Daily ferries connect Labuanbajo with Sape, Sumbawa. From Larantuka, infrequent ferries go to Kupang (West Timor). From Ende and Aimere, boats will take you to Waingapu on Sumba.

ℹ Getting Around

Regular buses ply the Trans-Flores Hwy. They're cheap and cramped. Much more comfortable and only somewhat more expensive are public minibuses (often a Toyota Kijang) that link major towns in air-con comfort. Many hire a car and driver, which costs from 600,000Rp to 800,000Rp per day. If you have a group of six, this is a fair deal. Your accommodation will usually have details on all the above options.

Labuanbajo

☑ 0385 / POP 20,000

Ever more travellers are descending on this gorgeous, slightly ramshackle bay harbour, freckled with islands and blessed with surrealist sunsets. The main drag, Jl Soekarno-Hatta, is lined with cool cafes and modestly priced guesthouses. The waterfront is much spiffed up and what with the many beguiling islands just offshore, you may find Labuanbajo hard to leave.

SPLURGE

Set on its own 15-hectare island and linked to Labuanbajo by private boat, the **Angel Island Resort** (☑ 0385-41443; www.angelisleflores.com; d per person from €125, minimum 2-night stay; ❄ ☏) has 10 sweet villas scattered about the trees behind one of three white-sand beaches. All meals are included; the food and service is casual and superb. You can easily while away your days here on the deserted beaches or out snorkelling, diving and visiting the park.

🏃 Activities

The pristine reefs and preponderance of underwater life in Komodo National Park and the surrounding waters is one of the big draws to Labuanbajo. Prices tend to be uniform.

Blue Marlin   DIVING
(www.bluemarlindivekomodo.com; Jl Soekarno-Hatta) Runs live-aboards between the Gilis and Labuanbajo, and has *boucoup* experience in the Komodos.

CNDive   DIVING
(☑ 0385-41159; Jl Soekarno Pelabuhan; per person per day from US$120) Condo Subagyo, the proprietor of CNDive, is the area's original Indonesian dive operator with over 10,000 dives. He offers two- and three-day trips.

Reefseekers   DIVING
(☑ 0385-41443; www.reefseekers.net; Jl Soekarno-Hatta) One of the longest-tenured dive shops in town. If you want a special experience, consider their dive resort on Angel Island (p240).

🛏 Sleeping

July to August is peak season, be sure to book. Booming popularity means that deals are scant; skip the over-priced beach resorts south of the centre. New guesthouses are opening regularly and many of the dive shops offer a few simple rooms.

Bayview Gardens Hotel   INN $$
(☑ 0385-41549; www.bayview-gardens.com; Jl Ande Bole; r from 450,000Rp; ❄ ☏) A lovely seven-room inn notched onto the hillside above the town with epic sunset and harbour views. Breakfast on your own terrace is a treat. It books up so reserve in advance.

Bajo Beach Hotel   GUESTHOUSE $$
(☑ 0385-41008; Jl Soekarno-Hatta; r 250,000-400,000Rp; ❄) A shady near-budget option in the city centre with basic but spacious tiled rooms that are quite clean and well tended, each with private seating area out front.

Green Hill Hotel   GUESTHOUSE $$
(☑ 0385-41289; www.greenhillboutiquehotel.com; Jl Soekarno-Hatta; s/d from 400,000/450,000Rp; ❄ ☏) The communal terrace with its view of the town, bay and sunsets makes this an excellent choice. Rooms are a brief climb from the very centre of town and range from scruffy older to sprightly newer. Breakfasts are excellent.

BOAT TOURS BETWEEN LOMBOK & FLORES

Travelling by sea between Lombok and Labuanbajo is a popular way to get to Flores, as you'll glimpse more of the region's spectacular coastline and dodge painfully long bus journeys. Typical itineraries take in snorkelling at Pulau Satonda or Pulau Moyo off the coast of Sumbawa and a dragon-spotting hike on Komodo or Rinca.

But note, this is usually no luxury cruise – a lot depends on the boat, the crew and your fellow travellers. Some operators have reneged on 'all-inclusive' deals en route, and others operate decrepit old tugs without lifejackets or radio. And this crossing can be hazardous during the rainy season (October to January), when the seas are rough.

Most travellers enjoy the journey though, whether it involves bedding down on a mattress on deck or in a tiny cabin. Itineraries last from three to four days. The cost ranges about US$170 to US$200 per person and includes all meals, basic beverages and use of snorkelling gear.

Two long-running and reliable operators are **Kencana Adventure** (☑ 0370-693432; www. kencanaadventure.com; Jl Raya Senggigi, Senggigi, Lombok, Jl Soekarno-Hatta, Front of Gardena Hotel, Labuanbajo, Flores) and **Perama Tour** (☑ 0361-750808; www.peramatour.com; Jl Raya Legian, Kuta, Bali).

🍴 Eating & Drinking

Labuanbajo punches way above its weight in the food department. Look for market-fare and cheap stalls at the north end of the waterfront.

Bajo Bakery BAKERY $
(Jl Soekarno-Hatta; mains 20,000-40,000Rp, sweets 9000Rp; ⊘7am-7pm Mon-Sat) Expect good fresh breads, seductive banana muffins, tasty breakfasts, a few sandwiches and a quiche of the day.

Paradise Bar PUB $
(mains 22,000-45,000Rp; ⊘11am-2am) Set on a hilltop, Paradise satisfies all the requirements of a definitive tropical watering hole. There's ample deck space, a mesmerising sea view, a natural wood bar serving ice-cold beer, and live music. And the food's good.

★ Made In Italy ITALIAN $$
(☑ 0385-41366; www.miirestaurants.com; Jl Soekarno-Hatta; mains 50,000-80,000Rp, cruise per person 1,500,000Rp; ⊘11am-11pm; 🛜) A fun and stylish indoor–outdoor dining room known the island over for having fantastic pizza and pasta. In fact we'll just say it: it's some of the best pizza we've ever had anywhere; wafer thin and crunchy with perfectly delectable toppings. You'll dig the rattan lighting, custom wood furnishings, ceiling fans and long drinks menu.

Tree Top INDONESIAN $$
(Jl Soekarno-Hatta; mains 28,000-100,000Rp; ⊘9am-11pm; 🛜) This fun, triple-decker art cafe offers a pub vibe and billiards table downstairs, and harbour and island views from the split-level upstairs dining rooms where it serves tasty, spicy Indonesian seafood.

ⓘ Information

Banks, ATMs and shops line Jl Soekarno-Hatta.
Tourist Office (www.florestourism.com; Jl Soekarno Pelabuhan; ⊘8.30am-4.30pm Mon-Sat) This excellent new office has details on local activities, maps and books plus all the transport info – and tickets – you'll need.

ⓘ Getting There & Away

AIR
Labuanbajo's Komodo Airport has a new terminal and a recently lengthened runway. Flights – especially from Bali – are proliferating.
Garuda (www.garuda-indonesia.com) Bali.
Lion Air/Wings Air (www.lionair.co.id) Bali, Ende and Kupang.
Transnusa (www.transnusa.co.id) Bali and Ende.

BOAT
The ASDP ferry to Sape (54,000Rp, eight to nine hours) is scheduled to leave at 8am and 4pm daily, but is prone to cancellation when seas are rough. Tickets can be purchased at the harbour master's office (in front of the pier). The **Pelni agent** (☑ 0385-41106) is easy to miss, tucked away in a side street in the northeast of town. The *Tilongkabila* heads to Makassar and the east coast of Sulawesi.

Many travellers choose to take a boat trip between Flores and Lombok, stopping at Komodo and Sumbawa along the way for snorkelling and exploration. See the boxed text for more details.

RIUNG

Fans of laid-back coastal mangrove villages will love Riung, which has garnered a hearty traveller buzz. But the 21 offshore islands of the **Seventeen Islands Marine Park** (strangely named in honour of Indonesia's 17 August Independence Day), with luscious white-sand beaches and excellent snorkelling, are the real attraction. Guides are essential for their knowledge of underwater spots (**Al Itchan** (📱 0813 8759 0964) is good). A day trip costs 500,000Rp (for up to six), including boat charter, but not including park admission (per person 15,000Rp).

Pondok SVD (📱 0813 3934 1572; www.pondoksvdriung.com; r 170,000-330,000Rp; ❉) has spotless rooms with desks, reading lights and Western toilets, while **Rumah Makan Murah Muriah** (📱 0813 3717 2918; mains 25,000-45,000Rp; ⏱7am-10pm) serves delicious, fresh grilled fish and icy Bintang.

There's a daily bus to/from Bajawa over the rugged road (50,000Rp, at least four hours). A chartered 4WD with driver will cost at least 600,000Rp.

BUS

With no bus terminal in Labuanbajo, most people book their tickets through a hotel or agency, however the, tourist office has the best prices. All buses run via Ruteng (70,000Rp, four hours), with some continuing on to Bajawa (150,000Rp, eight hours). **Gunung Harta** (📱 0385-42068) runs a minibus to Bajawa (170,000Rp) and beyond.

Ruteng

📱0385

The greatest site locally is actually 20km west of town just off the Trans-Flores Hwy near the village of Cancar. The legendary **Spiderweb Rice Fields** are vast creations that are shaped exactly as their name implies. The surrounding region is beautifully lush with paddies.

Ruteng makes a fine lunch stop thanks to **Agape** (Jl Bhayangkara; meals 20,000-40,000Rp; ⏱8am-10pm; 📶), a great cafe that's popular with both locals and seemingly every traveller who drives past.

There are regular buses to Bajawa (70,000Rp, four hours).

Bajawa

📱0384

With a pleasant climate, and surrounded by forested volcanoes, Bajawa is a great base from which to explore dozens of traditional villages that are home to the Ngada people. Their fascinating architecture features *ngadhu* (carved poles supporting a conical thatched roof).

◉ Sights & Activities

Bajawa's top attractions are the traditional villages. Guides linger around hotels and arrange day trips for 250,000Rp per person with motorbike transport, village entry fees and lunch. Alternatively, the villages are easily reached if you're driving across Flores. **Bena**, 19km south of Bajawa on the flank of picture-perfect volcano Gunung Inerie (2245m), is the best village in the area with several megalith tombs and soaring thatched roofs. Women with betel-nut-stained grins sell elaborate *ikat* fabrics and macadamia nuts. **Nage** is likewise fascinating.

🛏 Sleeping & Eating

Edelweis HOTEL $
(📱0384-21345; Jl Ahmad Yani 76; r 150,000-300,000Rp; @📶) Bajawa's venerable choice offers a range of rooms including cheaper tiled jobs in the main building, older but still quaint garden rooms and sparkling newish ones with hot water.

★**Hotel Happy Happy** GUESTHOUSE $$
(📱0853 3370 4455, 0384-421763; www.hotelhappyhappy.com; Jl Sudirman; s/d from 300,000/350,000Rp; 📶) This simple yet classy guesthouse has six immaculate tiled rooms. It gets everything right, from the free water-bottle refills to the excellent included breakfast. It's a short walk from the main cluster of tourist businesses.

Dito's INDONESIAN $
(📱0384-21162; Jl Ahmad Yani; mains 25,000-50,000Rp; ⏱8am-10pm) Twinkling with Christmas lights, Dito's does a brisk business serving pork and chicken *sate*. The tamarillo juice is delish.

Camellia INDONESIAN $
(📱0384-21458; Jl Ahmad Yani 74; mains 20,000-35,000Rp; ⏱8am-10pm) The dining room is too

bright, but the food works. There are Western dishes, but try the chicken *sate*.

ℹ Information

Tourist Office (www.florestourism.com; Jl Ahmad Yani; ◷8.30am-4.30pm Mon-Sat) Small but highly useful; rents motorbikes for Ngada village explorations (per day 100,000Rp).

ℹ Getting There & Away

Hotels arrange bus tickets and pick-ups. Buses to Ende (60,000Rp, five hours) depart several times a day.

Ende

⏏ 0381 / POP 95,000

Muggy, dusty and crowded, this south-coast port's ultimate saving grace is its spectacular setting. The eye-catching cones of Gunung Meja and Gunung Iya loom over the city, while barrels roll in continuously from the Sawu Sea and crash over a coastline of black sand and blue stones.

◉ Sights

Musium Bung Karno   MUSEUM
(Jl Perwira; admission by donation; ◷7am-noon Mon-Sat) History buffs can visit the house where Sukarno was exiled in the 1930s. Most of the original period furnishings remain. This is where the beloved revolutionary penned the risable *Frankenstein* knock-off, *Doctor Satan*.

🛏 Sleeping & Eating

Accommodation is spread all over town, but frequent bemos make it easy to get around.

Guesthouse Alhidayah   GUESTHOUSE $
(☑0381-23707; Jl Yos Sudarso; s/d with fan 100,000/150,000Rp, air-con 150,000/250,000Rp; ❊) Relatively new, this spot offers sparkling but otherwise basic tiled rooms with a private porch area. The location isn't ideal, but it's still the best budget choice in Ende.

Hotel Safari   HOTEL $
(☑0381-21997; Jl Ahmad Yani 65; s/d with fan 100,000/125,000Rp, with air-con 200,000/250,000Rp; ❊🛜) Rooms aren't fabulous but are large, bright and reasonably clean.

★Roda Baru   PADANG $
(☑0381-24135; Jl Kelimutu; meals from 35,000Rp; ◷9am-midnight) This spotless pick-and-mix Padang diner serves fish, chicken and prawns fried or grilled and sauced five ways. The beef *rendang* is locally beloved; great sambal.

Rumah Makan Istana Bambu   SEAFOOD $
(☑0381-21921; Jl Kemakmuran 30A; mains 25,000-50,000Rp) Here's a classic, funkified Chinese fish house. It's old-fashioned and dark but the fresh fish, squid, prawns and lobster, and spicy *sambal* (which they bottle and sell) are all tops.

ℹ Information

The modern main drag to the airport, Jl Kelimutu, has banks and ATMs.

Tourism Office (www.florestourism.com; Jl Bakti; ◷8.30am-4.30pm Mon-Sat) The enthusiastic staff here dispense up-to-date transport information.

ℹ Getting There & Away

AIR
The airport (code ENE) is on the narrow isthmus just east of the centre.

Lion Air/Wings Air (www.lionair.co.id) and **Transnusa** (www.transnusa.co.id) serve Bali via Labuanbajo as well as Kupang.

BOAT
ASDP (☑0813 3948 9103) operates a weekly ferry to Waingapu (seven hours) on Sumba.
   Pelni (☑0381-21043; Jl Kathedral 2; ◷8am-noon & 2-4pm Mon-Sat) sails every two weeks

---

THE NGADA

Over 60,000 Ngada people inhabit the upland Bajawa plateau and the slopes around Gunung Inerie. Older animistic beliefs remain strong, and most Ngada practise a fusion of animism and Christianity. They worship Gae Dewa, a god who unites Dewa Zeta (the heavens) and Nitu Sale (the earth).

The most evident symbols of continuing Ngada tradition are pairs of *ngadhu* and *bhaga*. The *ngadhu* is a parasol-like structure about 3m high, consisting of a carved wooden pole and thatched 'roof', and the *bhaga* is a miniature thatched-roof house.

The *ngadhu* is 'male' and the *bhaga* is 'female', and each pair is associated with a particular family group within a village. Some were built over 100 years ago to commemorate ancestors killed in long-past battles.

west to Waingapu, Bima, Benoa and Surabaya, and east to Kupang.

BUS

It's about 5km from town to Wolowana terminal, where you catch eastbound buses for Moni (30,000Rp, two hours) and Maumere (60,000Rp, minibus 80,000Rp, five hours).

Westbound buses leave from the Ndao terminal, 2km north of town.

Kelimutu

Kelimutu National Park (☑0381-23405; Jl El Tari 16; per car/ojek 6000/3000Rp, per person 20,000Rp, camera 50,000Rp; ⊙4am–sunset) remains a Nusa Tenggara must: there aren't many better ways to wake up than to sip ginger coffee as the sun crests Mt Kelimutu's western rim, filtering through mist and revealing three deep volcanic lakes, each one a different, striking primary colour that seems the thickness of paint.

Most visitors glimpse them at dawn, leaving nearby Moni at 4am, but afternoons are usually empty and peaceful at the top of Mt Kelimutu, and when the sun is high the colours sparkle. The main viewspot is a mere 20-minute walk from the car park.

To get there, hire an *ojek* (50,000Rp one way) or car (400,000Rp return, maximum five people) from Moni. You can walk the 13.5km down through the forest and back to Moni in about 2½ hours. A *jalan potong* (short cut) leaves the road back to Moni 1km south of the PHKA gate and goes through Manukako village, then meanders back to the main road 750m uphill from Moni.

Moni

Moni, the gateway to Kelimutu, is a picturesque hillside village sprinkled with rice fields, ringed by soaring volcanic peaks, with distant sea views. The cool, comfortable climate invites long walks and a few extra days. Ask about routes to waterfalls and hot springs.

🛏 Sleeping & Eating

Moni has a cluster of budget guesthouses along the main – and only – road. Prices peak in July and August when it's wise to book ahead.

Watugana Bungalows   LOSMEN **$**
(Jl Trans Flores; r 150,000-350,000Rp) Downstairs rooms are older and kept reasonably clean though they are dark and the bathrooms are

a bit moist. The newish rooms upstairs are bright and have hot water.

Bintang Lodge   GUESTHOUSE **$$**
(☑0812 3761 6940, 0852 3790 6259; www.bintang-lodge.com; Jl Trans Flores km 54; r 150,000-350,000Rp; ❋@) Two floors of new rooms are clean and large plus there's hot water, which is nice on chilly mornings and evenings. The older bungalows have a cute homey feel.

Chenty Café   INDONESIAN **$**
(dishes 15,000-40,000Rp; ⊙8am-9pm) Long-running, popular place with a nice porch overlooking the rice fields. The special locally is the Moni cake, a starchy mashed potato pie topped with cheese.

❶ Information

Mobile (cell) signals are weak and there are no ATMs. But the new **Tourist Office** (www.flores tourism.com; ⊙9am-4pm Mon-Sat) is a great resource and right next to Chenty Café.

❶ Getting There & Away

Maumere is four hours east (bus/minibus 30,000/45,000Rp).

Paga

Halfway between Moni and Maumere, the village of Paga has a long, white-sand beach that's the stuff of fantasy. Right off the road and on the sand, **Restaurant Laryss** (☑0852 5334 2802; www.floresgids.com; Jl Raya Maumere-Ende; meals from 40,000; ⊙10am-4pm), a bamboo fish joint, serves ultra-fresh seafood with superbly prepared sides. The owner, Agustus Naban, is also a talented guide.

Maumere

☑ 0382 / POP 53,000

Maumere has the second-busiest airport on the island, and you'll likely need to spend a night here if you're doing the one-way, cross-Flores drive. Unfortunately the drab city centre holds little interest.

🛏 Sleeping & Eating

Maumere is ripe for tourist development, in the meantime accommodation is of a low standard – especially at various hostelries along the thin grey beaches near town.

Gardena Hotel   HOTEL **$**
(☑0382-22644; Jl Patirangga 28; r with fan/air-con 100,000/150,000Rp; ❋) Central and popular

ALOR

Alor, the final link in an island chain that extends east of Java, is as remote, rugged and beautiful as it gets. Thanks to impenetrable terrain, the 185,000 inhabitants of the Alor Archipelago are fractured into over 100 tribes with 52 dialects, and they were still taking heads into the 1950s. Alor is also famous for its strange, bronze *moko* drums.

Superb diving can be arranged through **La Petite Kepa** (☑ SMS only 0813 3910 2403; www.la-petite-kepa.com; bungalows incl meals per person 225,000-650,000Rp) on **Pulau Kepa**. **Alor Dive** (☑ 0813 3964 8148, 0386-222 2663; www.alor-dive.com; Jl Gatot Subroto 33, Kalabahi) also arranges trips.

Kalabahi, located on a sweeping, palm-fringed bay, is the main port. There are banks and ATMs. **Cantik Homestay** (☑ 0386-21030, 0813 3229 9336; Jl Dahlia 12; r 200,000Rp; ❄) has six simple rooms. The owner rents motorbikes, and the home cooking here is sensational.

The airport is 9km from town, and offers one of the most dramatic approaches in the country. Merpati (p247) and Transnusa (p247) fly to/from Kupang.

with backpackers. There's a common space, but rooms are musty and showing their age.

★ **Wailiti Hotel** HOTEL $$
(☑ 0382-23416; Jl Raya Don Silva; bungalows 250,000-400,000Rp; ❄@🛜🖥) Rooms at Maumere's most pleasant accommodation are in one-story blocks and bungalows. The flash-free vibe here extends to the spacious grounds, large pool and narrow black-sand beach with views of off-shore islands. The simple cafe serves superb seafood and some amazingly good eggplant fritters. It's 6.5km west of the centre; airport transport costs 100,000Rp and is reliable.

Restaurant Gazebo SEAFOOD $$
(☑ 0382-22212; Jl Yos Sudarso 73; meals 50,000-80,000Rp; ⊙ 9am-10pm Mon-Sat, 5-10pm Sun) A central and reasonably priced fish house. The spicy, *kuah asam* soup is delicious and the *ikan bakar* is nice too.

ℹ Information

The non-compact centre has banks and ATMs.

ℹ Getting There & Around

Maumere's Frans Seda Airport (code MOF) is 3km east of town. Services include: **Merpati** (www.merpati.co.id), for Kupang, Labuanbajo and Makassar; **Transnusa** (www.transnusa.co.id), for Kupang plus Labuanbajo via Ende; and **Lion Air/Wings Air** (www.lionair.co.id), for Bali plus Labuanbajo via Ende. Many key flights are early in the morning. Beware that prebooked transport (about 100,000Rp) may not show up at your accommodation, leaving you scrambling at dawn.

Hop on an *ojek* to/from the airport for 10,000Rp, avoiding the high fixed taxi fare.

Buses to Larantuka (60,000Rp, minibus 80,000Rp, four hours) leave from the Lokaria (or Timur) terminal, 3km east of town. Buses west to Moni leave from the Ende terminal 1.5km southwest of town.

Around Maumere

A small army of expert artisans lies in wait in the weaving village of **Sikka**, 26km south of Maumere. Along the north coast, east of Maumere, is where you'll find the best beaches and healthiest reefs.

The beaches of **Ahuwair** and **Waiterang**, 24km and 26km east of Maumere, ooze tranquillity. **Lena House 1 and 2** (☑ 0813 3940 7733; r 115,000Rp) offer five clean bamboo bungalows set on two pristine coves. Newer Lena 2 is more comfortable and secluded.

Ankermi (☑ 0812 466 9667; www.ankermi-happydive.com; r from 300,000Rp), located 29km from Maumere, has cute, tiled, thatched bungalows with private porches and stunning sea views. The dive shop is the best in the Maumere area, they grow their own organic rice and vegetables on site, and meals are delicious.

Larantuka

☑ 0383

A bustling little port of rusted tin roofs at the easternmost end of Flores, Larantuka rests against the base of Gunung Ili Mandiri (1510m), separated by a narrow strait from Pulau Solor and Pulau Adonara. It has a fun street-market vibe at dusk, but most visitors stay just one night on their way to Kupang or Alor.

🛏 Sleeping & Eating

★ Hotel Rulies
GUESTHOUSE $

(☑ 0383-21195; Jl Yos Sudarso 40; s/d/tr 75,000/120,000/150,000Rp) This funky spot near the harbour and across the street from the sea has clean rooms with concrete floors and private *mandis*. Management is on top of current transport schedules.

Rumah Makan Nirwana
INDONESIAN $

(Jl Yos Sudarso; meals 20,000-30,000Rp; ⊘ 7am-9pm) Still the one and only kitchen in town with edible food. Don't expect miracles, though the *soto ayam* (chicken soup) is tasty and the house *sambal* scintillating.

🛈 Getting There & Away

All boats depart from the main pier in the centre of town. Double-check departure times.

Pelni (☑ 0383-21155; Jl Diponegoro) runs twice monthly ships to Kupang and weekly ferries to Kalabahi (Alor). ASDP has twice-weekly ferries to Bolok near Kupang (15 hours).

The main bus station is 5km west of town (3000Rp by bemo).

West Timor

With rugged countryside and scores of traditional villages, West Timor is an undiscovered gem in the province of East Nusa Tenggara. Deep within its lontar palm–studded interior, animist traditions persist alongside 14 tribal dialects, while Kupang, its coastal capital and East Nusa Tenggara's top metropolis and

transport hub, buzzes to a typical Indonesian beat.

🛈 Getting There & Away

A good way to explore East Nusa Tenggara (also known as Nusa Tenggara Timur, NTT) is to fly directly from Bali to Kupang and island hop from there.

Regular car-and-passenger ferries link Bolok, 14km southwest of Kupang, to numerous East Nusa Tenggara destinations.

Pelni passenger ships serve various ports infrequently.

🛈 Getting Around

The good main highway is surfaced all the way from Kupang to East Timor, though the buses that ply it are of the crowded, thumping-disco variety. Away from the highway, roads are improving but can be impassable in the wet season. Note that assaults by *ojek* drivers on women have become an issue; choose carefully.

Kupang

☑ 0380 / POP 350,000

Kupang, the capital of East Nusa Tenggara, is noisy, energetic, scruffy, bustling with commerce and a fun place to hang around for a few days. Captain Bligh did, after his mutiny issues in 1789.

Kupang sprawls. You'll need to take a bemo (5000Rp) or *ojek* (10,000Rp) to get around. The waterfront district, which stretches along Jl Sumba and rambles inland with Jl Ahmad Yani, has the bulk of the budget lodging options. Jl Mohammad Hatta/Jl Sudirman to the south, is the commercial centre with a selection of hotels, restaurants and shops.

Kupang

GETTING TO TIMOR-LESTE: KUPANG TO DILI

From Kupang, bus connections (175,0000Rp to 250,000Rp one way, 10 to 11 hours) to Dili are operated by **Timor Tour & Travel** (☎0380-881543; 185,000Rp), **Paradise Tours & Travel** (☎0380-830414) and **Livau** (☎0380-821892; 185,000Rp). Call for a hotel pick-up. This is the easiest and most cost-effective way to cross the border, but before making the trek you will need to apply for a Timor-Leste (East Timor) visa ($30) at the Kupang consulate, which takes three business days.

Still, it's the cheapest way to renew your Indonesian visa from Nusa Tenggara. Once in East Timor, you can get another 30-day visa at the Indonesian embassy.

🍴 Sleeping & Eating

⭐**Hotel Maliana** GUESTHOUSE $
(☎0380-821879; Jl Sumatera 35; r with fan/air-con 130,000/200,000Rp; ❖❋❄✆) These 20 basic yet comfy rooms are a popular budget choice. Rooms are clean and have ocean views from the front porch that dangles with vines.

⭐**Pasar Malam** STREET MARKET $
(Jl Garuda; dishes from 10,000Rp; ◷6-10pm) This wonderful, lamp-lit market takes over Jl Garuda with hundreds of stalls serving seafood and a plethora of Indonesian dishes.

Rumah Makan Palembang CHINESE $
(☎0821 4796 6011; Jl Mohammad Hatta 2; dishes 20,000-85,000Rp; ◷10am-2:30pm & 6-11pm) This is first-rate Chinese Indonesian food, and among the best restaurants in NTT. Get the *ikan bakar rica rica* (grilled fish with chilli sauce).

Rumah Makan Wahyu Putra Solo PADANG $
(☎0380-821552; Jl Gunung Mutis 31; meals 10,000-25,000Rp; ◷8am-10pm; ✆) Kupang's best pick-and-mix *warung* includes many vegetarian options.

ℹ️ Information

Kupang has scores of banks, ATMs and services as befitting a regional capital.
Lavalon (☎0812 377 0533, 0380-832256; www.lavalontouristinfo.com; Jl Sumatera 44; ☎) Edwin Lerrick, the proprietor of this cafe, is a vital source for the latest transport information, as well as interesting cultural attractions throughout NTT. The website is loaded with good info.

ℹ️ Getting There & Around

AIR
Kupang's El Tari airport (code KOE) is 15km east of town and the most important hub in East Nusa Tenggara. Taxi fare into town is fixed at 70,000Rp.
Garuda Air (www.garuda-indonesia.com) Bali and Jakarta.

Lion Air/Wings Air (www.lionair.co.id) Surabaya and Jakarta plus Ende and Maumere on Flores and Sumba's Tambulaka.
Merpati (www.merpati.co.id) Bali, Waingapu, Tambolaka, Maumere and Ende.
Transnusa (www.transnusa.co.id) Flies to numerous airports in East Nusa Tenggara.

BOAT
ASDP (☎0380-890420) Ferries leave from Bolok, 14km southwest of Kupang, for Larantuka (15 hours, Sunday and Thursday), Waingapu (13 hours, Monday and Friday) and Kalabahi (17 hours, Tuesday and Saturday).
Pelni (☎0380-824357; Jl Pahlawan 3; ◷8.30am-3pm Mon-Sat, 9-11am Sun) Near the waterfront. Ships dock here with weekly departures for Waingapu, Bima, Ambon, Larantuka, Aimere, Ende, Makassar and Bali.

BUS
Long-distance buses depart from Oebobo terminal on the eastern side of town – catch bemo 10.

Soe

☎0368 / POP 31,000 / ELEV 800M
Traditional, beehive-like *lopo* (hut) villages and the indigenous Dawan people who live in them are the attraction of this market town 800m above sea level. The government has deemed the *lopo* a health hazard (they're smoky and lack ventilation) and is in the process of replacing them with cold concrete boxes, which the Dawan have deemed a health hazard. They've built new *ume kebubu* (beehive-shaped huts) behind the approved houses, and live there. Village tours are easily arranged in Soe.

The **tourist information centre** (☎0368-21149; Jl Diponegoro; ◷9am-3pm Mon-Fri) can arrange guides.

Air-con isn't needed here. **Hotel Jati Asih** (☎22407; Jl Tien Soeharto; economy/standard/VIP 150,000/190,000/225,000Rp; ❂) and **Hotel Bahagia II** (☎21095; Jl Gajah Mada 55; standard/VIP/deluxe 185,000/265,000/290,000Rp, cottages 300,000-725,000; @) both have large rooms.

The Haumeni bus terminal is 4km west of town (2000Rp by bemo). Regular buses go to Kupang (25,000Rp, three hours) and Oinlasi (20,000Rp, 1½ hours), while bemos serve Niki Niki (5000Rp).

Sumba

The island of Sumba is a dynamic mystery. With its rugged undulating savannah and low limestone hills knitted together with more maize and cassava than rice, physically it looks nothing like Indonesia's volcanic islands to the north. Sprinkled throughout the countryside are hilltop villages with thatched clan houses clustered around megalithic tombs, where villagers claim to be Protestant but still pay homage to their indigenous *marapu* with bloody sacrificial rites.

One of the poorest islands in Indonesia, an influx of welcome government investment has brought recent improvements in infrastructure – best seen in Tambolaka, the island's newest city. And change has trickled down to traditional villages where among modest improvements in living standards, locals expect large donations from visitors. Sumba is definitely, an adventurous, far-off-the-beaten path destination.

❶ Getting There & Away

Waingapu and Tambolaka are connected by flights to Bali and Kupang. The latter also has flights to Ende on Flores.

Waingapu has weekly ferries to Ende (and on to Kupang) and Aimere on Flores. Pelni has useful services from Waingapu to Ende, and beyond.

Waingapu

☏ 0387 / POP 55,000

Sumba's gateway town has grown up from a dusty trading post to an urbanising commercial centre. But just like in the old days, business revolves around dyewoods, timber and the island's prized horses. You're here to explore the surrounding villages, although be sure to have a decent meal before you set off into the eating-option-poor hinterlands.

Waingapu spreads from the harbour in the north, 1.5km southeast to the main market and bus station.

🛏 Sleeping & Eating

Most hotels are in the new part of Waingapu, near the bus station. The best dinner option is the *pasar malam* (night market) at the old wharf.

Hotel Merlin   HOTEL $
(☏ 61300; Jl Panjaitan 25; r 150,000-275,000Rp; ❋ 🖥) This long-standing travellers' favourite has 18 assorted rooms over three floors, with Flores views from the good rooftop restaurant. The top-floor fan rooms are nicer and cleaner than the VIP rooms on the 1st floor.

Hotel Sandle Wood   HOTEL $
(☏ 0387-61887; Jl Panjaitan 23; r with fan 99,000-143,000Rp; s/d with air-con 187,000/209,000Rp; ❋) Some 25 rooms are set around a bright courtyard on a quiet street. The cheapest have shared baths. Management can hook you up with cars (with drivers) and motorbikes for your Sumba adventures.

★ Warung Enjoy Aja   SEAFOOD $
(Pelabuhan; mains 15,000-40,000Rp; ☺6-10pm) Part of the harbour night market, this is the last *warung* before the pier on the eastside. The fish and squid are expertly grilled and

WORTH A TRIP

PASOLA FESTIVAL – SUMBA AT WAR

The thrilling, often gruesome mock battles between spear-hurling horsemen during Sumba's Pasola festival are a must for travellers passing through Nusa Tenggara in February or March. The high-energy pageant aims to placate the spirits and restore harmony with the spilling of blood. Happily, though, blunt spears have been used in recent decades to make the affair less lethal. The ritualistic war kicks off when a sea worm called *nyale* washes up on shore, a phenomenon that also starts the planting season. Call hotels in Waingapu or Waikabubak to find out the latest schedules. The festival is generally held in the Lamboya and Kodi districts in February, and at Wanokaka and Gaura in March.

served with three types of sambal and a sea salt garnish.

ⓘ Information

Choose from the many banks and ATMs and hit the markets and shops before heading off into the rest of Sumba.

ⓘ Getting There & Around

AIR

The airport is 6km south on the Melolo road. Hotels offer free pick-up and drop-off service for guests. **Merpati** (www.merpati.co.id) serves Kupang and Bali as does **Lion Air/Wings Air** (www.lionair.co.id).

BOAT

Waingapu is served by weekly **ASDP ferries** (📞0387-61533; Jl Wanggameti 3) departing for Aimere (10 hours) and Ende (seven hours) on Flores as well as Kupang. Confirm schedules carefully.

Pelni (📞0387-61665; www.pelni.co.id; Jl Hasanuddin) ships serve Ende, Benoa in Bali, and Surabaya from the Darmaga dock west of town. It's too far to walk. Bemos charge 5000Rp per person.

BUS

Eastbound buses to Melolo and Rende leave from the bus station near the market. Buses to Waikabubak (50,000Rp, five hours) leave from the West Sumba terminal, 5km west of town. Book at your hotel or through an agency opposite the bus station.

Around Waingapu

Several traditional villages in the southeast can be visited from Waingapu by bus and bemo. The stone tombs are impressive and the area produces some of Sumba's best *ikat*. Donations are expected.

Located about 7km away from unspectacular **Melolo** – accessible by bus from Waingapu (20,000Rp, 1½ hours) – is **Praiyawang**, the ceremonial centre of **Rende**, with its traditional Sumbanese compound and stone-slab tombs. The massive one belongs to a former raja.

There's epic surf at **Tarimbang**, a palm-draped cove south of Lewa. There's also some nearby snorkelling, and rustic accommodation at Marthen's Homestay and the *kepala desa*'s six-room place. Both charge about 100,000Rp per person including meals. Daily trucks to Tarimbang leave Waingapu in the morning (40,000Rp, five hours).

ⓘ GUIDES

Sumba is such a mystery that the services of a guide can make all the difference in fully appreciating the island and its multitude of cultures and practices, such as the Pasola. Two to consider:

Yuliana Ledatara (📞0852 3918 1410; Kampung Tarung, Waikabubak; per day 300,000Rp (maximum 4 people), horse tours per person 50,000-100,000Rp) Can organise tours of traditional villages throughout West Sumba where she sniffs out funerals and sacrifices, horse tours through rice fields, and can arrange village homestays too.

Sumba Adventure (📞0813 3710 7845, 0387-21727; www.sumbarentcar.com; Waikabubak, Tambolaka; chartered SUV per day from 600,000Rp, guide per day 250,000Rp) Philip Renggi is one of the best in West Sumba. He and his team of guides lead trips into seldom-explored villages north of Waikabubak, including his native Manukalada village and Wawarungu.

Waikabubak

📞0387 / POP 19,000

A conglomeration of thatched clan houses, ancient tombs, concrete office buildings and satellite dishes, Waikabubak is strange but appealing. Interesting traditional villages such as **Kampung Tarung**, up a path next to Tarung Wisata Hotel, are right within town. One of the spectacular attractions of West Sumba is the **Pasola**, the epic mock battle held near Waikabubak each February or March.

🛏 Sleeping & Eating

Warung congregate opposite the mosque on the main strip.

Karanu Hotel   GUESTHOUSE **$**
(📞0387-21645; Jl Sudirman 43; r 100,000-220,000Rp) A bright garden hotel east of the downtown swirl and within view of nearby rice fields.

★**Mona Lisa Cottages**   BUNGALOW **$$**
(📞0387-21364; www.monalisacottages-sumba.com; Jl Adhyaska 30; r 250,000-750,000Rp; ❄@🛜) You'll find the best night's sleep 2km northwest of town, across from the rice fields. It includes attractive, fan-cooled

budget rooms and a few higher-end cottages as well.

★ **Rumah Makan Gloria**   INDONESIAN $
(☑ 0387-21140; Jl Bhayangkara 46; meals 18,000-30,000Rp; ⊗ 9.30am-9pm; P) Cute and cheerful; good food including *soto ayam* (chicken soup), *ikan kuah assam* (tamarind fish soup) and, if you special order it, *ayam kafir*, a Sumba-style fire-roasted chicken, salted and served with a sublime, super spicy *sambal*.

ℹ Information

There are banks and ATMs. For a real selection of services, head to Tambolaka, 45km northwest.
Tourist Office (☑ 0387-21240; Jl Teratai 1; ⊗ 8am-3pm Mon-Sat) The staff here are well informed about forthcoming funerals and cultural events. It's on the outskirts of town.

ℹ Getting There & Away

Taxis to the new Tambolaka airport, 42km northwest, cost 200,000Rp. **Merpati** (www.merpati. co.id) and **Lion Air/Wings Air** (www.lionair. co.id) serve Kupang and Denpasar. **Transnusa** (www.transnusa.co.id) serves Ende on Flores.

Buses run to Waingapu (50,000Rp, five hours) throughout the day. Frequent bemos (5000Rp) rattle to Anakalang.

Around Waikabubak

Set in a lush valley 22km east of Waikabubak, **Anakalang** sports some of Sumba's most captivating megalith tombs. More interesting villages are south of town past the market. **Kabonduk** has Sumba's heaviest tomb. It took 2000 workers more than three years to carve it.

Located south of Waikabubak is Wanoka district, which is a centre for the Pasola festival. **Praigoli** is a somewhat isolated village and deeply traditional.

Our favourite place in West Sumba, **Oro Beach Houses & Restaurant** (☑ 0813 5378 9946, 0813 3911 0068; www.oro-beachbungalows. com; r 475,000Rp, bungalows 525,000Rp; P ⌂), is not far from **Tambolaka** along a mostly rutted dirt road. Think three wild beachfront acres featuring a simple, artful house. There are excellent seafood meals, local village tours and snorkelling just off shore.

SUMATRA

Lush, enormous and intriguing, Sumatra stretches for 2000km across the equator.

Happily, there is a payoff for every pothole along the Trans-Sumatran Hwy: steaming volcanoes brew and bluster while standing guard over lakes that sleepily lap the edges of craters created by Jurassic-era lava; orangutans swing through rainforests; and long, white beaches offer world-class surf breaks on the surface and stunning coral reefs below.

Besides natural beauty, the world's sixth-largest island boasts a wealth of resources, particularly oil, gas and timber. These earn Indonesia the bulk of its badly needed export dollars, even as their extraction devastates habitats.

When Mother Nature is this majestic and bountiful, there is usually a flip side, and Sumatra has seen more than its share of her fury. Eruptions, earthquakes, floods and tsunamis are regular headline grabbers and the steep cost of living in one of the richest ecosystems in the world.

ℹ Getting There & Away

The international airports at Medan, Padang, Banda Aceh and Pekanbaru are visa free, as are the seaports of Sekupang (Pulau Batam), Dumai, Padang and Sibolga.

AIR

Medan is Sumatra's primary international airport, with frequent flights to mainland Southeast Asian cities such as Singapore, Kuala Lumpur and Penang. In West Sumatra, Padang receives flights from Singapore and Kuala Lumpur.

You can also hop on a plane from Jakarta to every major Sumatran city aboard a range of airlines. Flights from Sumatra to other parts of Indonesia often connect through Jakarta.

BOAT

Ferries to southern Sumatra from Java leave from the small industrial town of Merak, three hours west of Jakarta. Buses to Merak cost 22,000Rp to 30,000Rp and leave from the Kalideres bus terminal. From Merak, fast ferries run every 30 minutes from 7am to 5pm (30,000Rp); the crossing takes 45 minutes. A slow ferry runs every 30 minutes, 24 hours a day and costs 11,500Rp for the two-hour trip. Damri buses sell a bus-boat-bus combination ticket from Jakarta to Bandarlampung (bisnis/eksekutif 120,000/160,000Rp, eight to 10 hours).

Despite cheap airfares, a handful of travellers still heed the call of the sea and enter Sumatra by ferry from Malaysia. The only ferry route commonly used by backpackers is the convenient Melaka (Malaysia) to Dumai (Indonesia) crossing. Dumai is on Sumatra's east coast and is a 10-hour bus ride from Bukittinggi. There are also several daily departures to Tanjung Pinang

Sumatra

INDONESIA

200 km
120 miles
0
0

ANDAMAN SEA

Pulau Weh Marine National Park
Pulau Weh
Pulau Breueh
Banda Aceh
Meulaboh
Gunung Leuser (3404m)
ACEH
Bireuen
Tangkahan
Langsa
Gunung Sinabung (2450m)
Pulau Penang
MALAYSIA
KUALA LUMPUR
Pulau Simeulue
Sinabang
Gunung Leuser National Park
Bukit Lawang
Berastagi
Gunung Sibayak (2094m)
Medan
Tebing-tinggi
Pulau Penang
Melaka
Tanjung Balai
Pulau Rupat
Dumai
Bengkalis
Pulau Rupat
Pulau Kalimun
Pulau Batam
SINGAPORE
Pulau Bintan
Kepulauan Banyak
Singkil
Pulau Nias
Gunung Sitoli
Teluk Dalam
Sibolga
Parapat
Rantauparapat
Danau Toba
NORTH SUMATRA
Trans-Sumatran Hwy
Strait of Melaka
Pulau Rangsang
Pulau Mendol
Pulau Kundur
Pulau Singkep
Pulau Galang
Pulau Lingga
LINGGA ISLANDS
Selat Berhala
Selat Berhala
RIAU
Pekanbaru
Bonjol
Bukittinggi
Sungaipenuh
Bukit Tigapuluh National Park
Muarabungo
Bangko
JAMBI
Jambi
Bukit Duabelas National Park
Sikabaluan
Pulau Siberut
Muara Siberut
Tuapejat
MENTAWAI ISLANDS
Pulau Sipora
Siobah
Sikakap
Pulau Pagai Utara
Pulau Pagai Selatan
Mukomuko
Solok
Danau Maninjau
Danau Singkarak
WEST SUMATRA
Sungaipagar
Padang
Gunung Kerinci (3805m)
Pegunungan Bukitbarisan
Lubuklinggau
Lahat
SOUTH SUMATRA
Palembang
Perabumulih
Batureja
Kotabumi
Bandarlampung
LAMPUNG
Way Kambas National Park
Merak
Pulau Seribu
Bakauheni
Sunda Strait
JAVA
Gunung Krakatau
Kota Krakatau
Gunung Agung
Krui
Bintuhan
Danau Ranau
Manna
Bengkulu
BENGKULU
Ipuh
Bukit Barisan Selatan National Park
Pulau Enggano
Belinyu
Mentok
Pulau Bangka
Pangkal Pinang
Pulau Belitung
Pulau Lingga
Tanjung Pandan

INDIAN OCEAN

Equator

SOUTHERN SUMATRA

Aside from Krakatau and the ferry crossing to Java, southern Sumatra is something of a blank on the backpacker map, but the region hides plenty of enticing little secrets. Chief among these are the wild forests and swamps of the **Way Kambas National Park** to the northeast of Bandarlampung. The highlight of a visit to this park is the elephant-back safari rides.

If sun, sand and surf is more your thing, the laid-back village of **Krui** has your name all over it. Five hours' drive from Bandarlampung, Krui has recently gained a serious name for itself among travelling surfers thanks to the coastline being littered with world-class spots (many of them *not* beginner-friendly). Backpackers are still a rare sight, but if the backpack trail ever takes off in South Sumatra, Krui, with its sublime beaches, will quite rightly become every beach bum's favourite hang-out.

The main city in these parts, and a place you're certain to transit, is **Bandarlampung**. There's nothing much to see here but if you need to stay try the **Hotel Andalas** (☑ 0721-263432; hotelandalas1@yahoo.co.id; Jl Raden Intan 89; s/d incl breakfast from 175,000/200,000Rp). You've got several bus options for getting from here to Java. The most convenient option is the **Damri** bus-boat-bus combination ticket to Jakarta (*bisnis/eksekutif* 120,000/160,000Rp, eight to 10 hours). Buses leave from Bandarlampung's train station at 10am, 9pm and 10pm. Damri's office is in front of Bandarlampung's train station. Heading north through Sumatra there are a number of buses to Padang, Medan or elsewhere, but needless to say this is one very long bus ride.

on Bintan (one-way 280,000Rp, 2½ hours) from Johor Bahru in Malaysia (on the Singapore–Malaysia border).

From Singapore, ferries make the quick hop to Pulau Batam and Bintan, the primary islands in the Riau archipelago.

From Batam, boats serve the following mainland Sumatran ports: Dumai, Palembang and Pekanbaru. Again, once you hit Indonesian soil it's a long old bus ride to any postcard-worthy spots.

Ferries cross the narrow Sunda Strait linking the southeastern tip of Sumatra at Bakauheni to Java's westernmost point of Merak. The sea crossing is a brief dip in a day-long voyage that requires several hours' worth of bus transport from both ports to Jakarta on the Java side and Bandarlampung on the Sumatran side.

❶ Getting Around

Most travellers bus around northern Sumatra and then hop on a plane to Java, largely avoiding the dreadful conditions of Sumatra's highway system. Most of the island is mountainous jungle and the poorly maintained roads form a twisted pile of spaghetti on the undulating landscape. Don't count on getting anywhere very quickly on Sumatra.

AIR

An hour on a plane is an attractive alternative to what may seem like an eternity on a bone-shaking bus. For long-distance travel, airfares are competitive with bus and ferry fares. Medan to Banda Aceh and Medan to Padang are two popular air hops.

BOAT

Most boat travel within Sumatra connects the main island with the many satellite islands lining the coast.

BUS

If you stick to the Trans-Sumatran Hwy and other major roads, the big air-con buses can make travel fairly comfortable – which is fortunate since you'll spend a lot of time on the road in Sumatra. The best ones have reclining seats, toilets and video but run at night to avoid the traffic, so you miss out on the scenery. The non-air-con buses are sweaty and cramped, but unforgettable. Numerous bus companies cover the main routes and prices vary greatly, depending on the comfort level. Buy tickets directly from the bus company. Agents usually charge 10% more.

Travel on the back roads is a different story. Progress can be grindingly slow and utterly exhausting.

TRAIN

Sumatra has a very limited rail network. The only useful service runs from Bandarlampung in the south to Palembang.

Padang

☑ 0751 / POP 834,000

Most backpackers fly into Padang only to catch the first bus to Bukittinggi. Big mis-

Padang

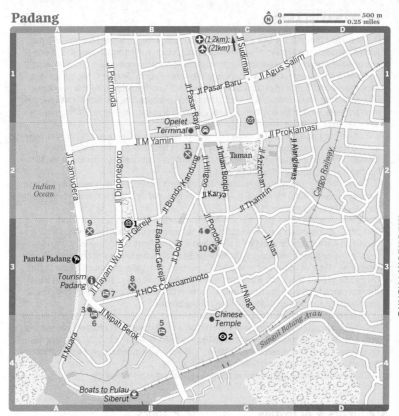

take. Despite a devastating earthquake in September 2009 that left around 5000 people dead and destroyed large sections of Padang, Sumatra's largest west-coast city has a gorgeous waterfront setting, with Minangkabau roofs soaring from modern public buildings and a leafy old quarter dominated by a narrow, brackish river harbour crowded with colourful fishing boats, yachts and luxe Bugis schooners. The coastline south of town is magnificent too, and the city beach is edged by a popular promenade, which is where you'll want to be when the sun drops.

The Teluk Bayur port is 8km east of the centre, the airport is located 20km to the north, and the Bengkuang bus terminal is inconveniently located in Aie Pacah, about 12km from town.

Padang

⊚ Sights
1 Adityawarman Museum	B3
2 Colonial Quarter	C4

⊙ Activities, Courses & Tours
3 East West Tour & Travel	A3
4 Sumatran Surfariis	C3

🛏 Sleeping
5 Brigitte's House	B4
6 Golden Homestay	A3
7 Spice Homestay	B3

⊗ Eating
8 Ikan Bakar Pak Agus	B3
9 Nelayan Restaurant	A3
10 Pagi Sore	C3
11 Simpang Raya	B2

MENTAWAI ISLANDS

It was surfing that put the Mentawais on the tourism radar; nowhere else on earth has such a dense concentration of world-class surf spots in such a small area. Today, dozens of wave-hunting live-aboards run from Padang harbour year-round and a growing number of dedicated surf camps populate the banner spots. Surfing is big business here year-round, but the season peaks between April and October. Like many Indonesian surf areas, the Mentawais are not suitable for learners. The waves, which break over shallow reefs, tend to be fast, hollow, heavy and unforgiving, and many of the spots are not even suitable for intermediate surfers.

But it's not just surfers who come out here; more and more ecotourists are also braving the rugged ocean crossing and muddy jungle of this remote archipelago to trek, glimpse traditional tribal culture and spot endemic primates. Many consider it the highlight of their trip through Southeast Asia.

The economic, and culturally responsible, choice for touring is to take a public boat to Siberut and seek out a Mentawai guide. You pay less and directly benefit the community you've come to experience.

As far as surfing tours go, the vast majority of surfers pre-arrange boat charters or surf camp accommodation with a surf travel company in their home country. These are ideal if all you want to do is get off a plane and surf your guts out. However, it's a real bubble-like existence and the only Indonesians you're actually likely to meet will be your boat crew. If you've got lots of time then it's perfectly possible, and much closer to the true spirit of old-school surf travel, to take the public ferry out to the islands and once there arrange local boat transport and accommodation in one of the cheap and simple *losmens* that can be found close to many of the breaks.

There is no longer a public speedboat to the islands and flights (from Padang) are unreliable and irregular so almost everyone not on a pre-booked surf charter boat use the public ferries to Mentawai. These charge between 85,000Rp and 150,000Rp depending on class of travel and speed of boat (slow!). The ferry schedules are changing constantly so always check what's available on arrival in Padang.

Tickets can be bought directly at the **port** (Jl Batang Arau) in Padang.

◉ Sights & Activities

Locals converge on the beach promenade at sunset for snacks, cool drinks and football games on the sand.

Colonial Quarter   NEIGHBOURHOOD
Although damaged in the 2009 earthquake, Padang's colonial quarter around Jl Batang Arau is still worth a lazy stroll. Old Dutch and Chinese warehouses back onto a river brimming with fishing boats. The beach along Jl Samudera is the best place to watch the sunset.

Adityawarman Museum   MUSEUM
(Jl Diponegoro; admission 1500Rp; ⊙ 8am-4pm Tue-Sun) Adityawarman Museum, built in the Minangkabau tradition, has pleasant grounds, though non–Bahasa Indonesia speakers may find the dusty collections detailing everyday Minangkabau life rather dry. The entrance is on Jl Gereja.

☞ Tours

Sumatran Surfariis   SURFING
(Bevys Sumatra; ☑ 0751-34878; www.sumatran surfariis.com; Komplek Pondok Indah B 12, Parak Gadang) Long-established Mentawai surf-boat charter company. It's also an excellent contact if you're keen to partake of West Sumatra's surprising golfing scene. The area's three spectacular courses – one designed by a dual winner of the British Open – are virtually empty on weekdays, and local animal spectators may include monkeys and wild pigs.

East West Tour & Travel   SURFING
(☑ 0751-36370; Jl Nipah Berok) Indonesian-run charter-boat company offering Mentawai surf trips.

🛏 Sleeping

The 2009 earthquake destroyed a lot of Padang's cheaper hotels, but since then a crop of midrange hotels has arisen. Of the budget places still running many have hoisted their prices by so much that price wise, if not quality wise, there's little to differentiate between budget and midrange digs. Therefore we'd recommend spending a little bit more in order to get a whole lot more.

Brigitte's House   HOMESTAY $

(☑0751-36099; http://brigittehouse.blogspot.com.au; Jl Kampung Sebalah 1/14; s 175,000Rp; d 200,000-300,000Rp; ❋🛜) Brigitte's has a relaxed and homely ambience, with good quality, well-maintained rooms. The surrounding residential neighbourhood is quiet and leafy, and Brigitte has plenty of information on buses, ferries and Mentawai adventures.

Golden Homestay   HOMESTAY $

(☑0751-32616; Jl Nipah Berok 1B; dm 125,000Rp; r 200,000-325,000Rp; ❋🛜) Spotless dorms and private rooms named after classic Sydney surf beaches. Grab a bed in the shared Bronte room, or splash out on the Bondi or Manly rooms with private bathrooms.

★Spice Homestay   HOMESTAY $$

(☑0751-25982; spicehomey@yahoo.com; Jl HOS Cokroaminoto 104; r incl breakfast 310,000-355,000Rp; ❋🛜) Relocated after the 2009 earthquake, this friendly and relaxed guesthouse is perfect for families and surfers. A compact Zen garden combines with colourful rooms and artwork, and the lovely Balinese owner Sri is the perfect contact for information on onward travel to the islands or Bukittinggi.

✗ Eating

The city is famous as the home of *nasi Padang* (Padang food), the spicy Minangkabau cooking that's found throughout Indonesia, and is served quicker than fast food. Try **Pagi Sore** (Jl Pondok 143; dishes 9000Rp) and **Simpang Raya** (Jl Bundo Kandung; dishes 8000Rp).

★Ikan Bakar Pak Agus   SEAFOOD $$

(Jl HOS Cokroaminoto 91; meals around 50,000Rp) Pak Agus flame-grills his dead sea creatures to perfection with a smoky sambal sauce. The fresh-every-afternoon marine selection includes shoals of different fish, squid and huge king prawns (around 110,000Rp for three). Fish is definitely more affordable, so grab a spot at the shared tables and tuck in for a quintessential Padang experience.

Nelayan Restaurant   SEAFOOD $$

(Jl Samudera; mains 30,000-50,000Rp) Great seafood the Chinese way, cold beers and one of the best views in town of a Padang sunset. Treat yourself to grilled prawns or crab, but definitely ask the price before you dig in. We're pretty partial to a chilled Bintang with the *cumi asam manis* (squid in a sweet and sour sauce).

ℹ Information

Padang has branches of all the major Indonesian banks. There are ATMs all over town, including a string on Jl Pondok.

Imigrasi Office (☑0751-444511; Jl Khatib Sulaiman) Visa extensions from 30 days to two months can be made at the Padang Imigrasi office. It's about 5km out of town by *ojek* or taxi.

Post Office (Jl Azizchan 7; per hr 6000Rp) Near the corner of Jl M Yamin and Jl Azizchan. Has internet access.

Rumah Sakit Yos Sudarso (☑0751-33230; Jl Situjuh 1) Privately owned hospital.

Tourism Padang (☑0751-34186; Dinas Kebudayaan Dan Pariwisata, Jl Samudera 1; ⊙7.30am-4pm Mon-Fri, 8am-4pm Sat & Sun) Maps and a range of English-language regional brochures.

ℹ Getting There & Away

AIR

Bandara Internasional Minangkabau (BIM; Jl Adinegoro) airport (code BIM) is 20km north, off Jl Adinegoro. All the main players (and a few small fry) fly in and out of Padang and the city has links with Jakarta, Medan and Kuala Lumpur among others. There is a 100,000Rp departure tax on international flights.

BOAT

Depending on the tide, boats to Siberut and other Mentawai islands will leave from either the river mouth (Sungai Muara) on Sungai Batang Arau, just south of Padang's city centre, or from Teluk Kabung port at Bungus, 20km (45 minutes) away. Check the boat's departure point with your travel agent on sailing day.

BUS

The days of heading 12km out of town to the Bengkuang terminal at Aie Pacah are over. Most locals prefer to take minibuses directly from Padang.

Buses and minibuses will often pick you up (or drop you off) outside your hotel of choice. Ask your hotel to call in advance to organise this.

Tranex (☑705 8577) has a depot 2km north of the Pangeran Beach Hotel, opposite the Indah

Theatre. Catch any white *opelet* (2000Rp) heading north on Jl Permuda and ask for 'Tranex'.

For Medan and Jakarta, it's cheaper and faster to fly.

ℹ️ Getting Around

Airport taxis start from 120,000Rp. Tranex buses (25,000Rp) are a cheaper alternative and loop through Padang. Tell the conductor your street and they'll drop you at the right stop. Heading to the airport, they pass by Bumiminang Hotel and Jl Pemuda/Veteran. From Bukittinggi alight at the motorway overpass and take an *ojek* to the terminal.

There are numerous *opelet* around town, operating out of the Pasar Raya terminal off Jl M Yamin. The standard fare is 3000Rp.

Bukittinggi

📞 0752 / POP 91,000 / ELEV 930M

Early on a bright clear morning, the market town of Bukittinggi sits high above the valley mists as three sentinels – fire-breathing Merapi, benign Singgalang and distant Sago – all look on impassively. Modern life seems far removed until 9am. Then the traffic starts up, and soon there's a mile-long jam around the bus terminal and the air turns the

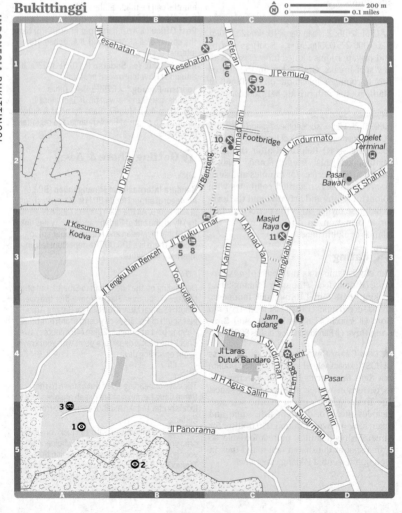

Bukittinggi

colour of diesel. The mosques counter the traffic by cranking their amps up to 11.

Such is the incongruity of modern Bukittinggi, blessed by nature, choked by mortals. Lush. Fertile. Busy. And at 930m above sea level, deliciously temperate all year round.

Bukittinggi was once a mainstay of the banana-pancake tourist trail, but recent years have seen the traveller tide reduced to a low ebb. Those who do make the effort of coming though will be rewarded with volcanic hikes, stinky flowers and idyllic crater lakes.

◉ Sights

Taman Panorama   LOOKOUT
(Panorama Park; Jl Panorama; admission 5000Rp) Taman Panorama, on the southern edge of town, overlooks the deep **Ngarai Sianok** (Sianok Canyon), where fruit bats swoop at sunset. Friendly guides will approach visitors – settle on a price (around 30,000Rp) before continuing – to lead you through **Gua Jepang** (Japanese Caves), wartime defensive tunnels built by Japanese slave labour.

🛏 Sleeping

Most hotels include a simple breakfast. On holidays, rooms fill quickly with Indonesian visitors. In Bukittinggi's temperate climate, hot water is more desirable than air-con.

Orchid Hotel   HOTEL $
(✎ 0752-32634; roni_orchid@hotmail.com; Jl Teuku Umar 11; r with cold/hot water 110,000/150,000Rp)

Bukittinggi

Roni runs this popular backpacker inn that features clean rooms and a friendly atmosphere. There's a good-value cafe and bar downstairs, and it's also ground zero for arranging tours and activities with **Roni's Tour & Travel** (✎ 0752-32634, 081 2675 0688; www.ronistours.com; Jl Teuku Umar).

Rajawali Homestay   HOMESTAY $
(✎ 0752-26113; ulrich.rudolph@web.de; Jl Ahmad Yani 152; r 70,000Rp) The rooms are basic but cosy in this tiny homestay right in the centre. The irrepressible Ulrich is a fount of local knowledge and has lots of information and advice on the area's attractions. The roof terrace is perfect for a few sunset beers as you watch the twilight squadrons of bats flying past.

Hotel Khartini   HOTEL $
(✎ 0752-22885; Jl Teuku Umar 6; r incl breakfast 150,000-250,000Rp) Clean, light-filled rooms, but it's very close to a mosque – it gets noisy with the call to prayer early each morning.

Hotel Asia   HOTEL $
(✎ 0752-625277; Jl Kesehatan 38; r incl breakfast 100,000-250,000Rp; ❄) Centrally located, the Asia offers spotless rooms for a bargain price. The airy common balconies evoke a Himalayan vibe.

✖ Eating & Drinking

Bukittinggi has always been the one place in West Sumatra that weary road-bums can give their poor chilli-nuked organs a chance to recover with lashings of boringly bland *makan Amerika*.

Jl Ahmad Yani comes alive at night with food stalls doing excellent satay and *nasi/ mie goreng*. For *nasi Padang*, try **Simpang Raya** (Jl Minangkabau), which all offer classic Indonesian dishes in a setting just one step up from a street food cart.

★**Waroeng Spesifik Sambal**   INDONESIAN $
(Jl Kesehatan; dishes 10,000-15,000Rp; 🌐) Fans of spicy dishes will love this shady garden *warung* specialising only in sambal dishes. Squid, prawns, chicken and eel are all cooked in a rich chilli sauce, and the 15 different dishes also include vegetarian spins on eggplant, tempeh and tofu.

Turret Café   CAFE $
(Jl Ahmad Yani 140-142; mains 20,000-35,000Rp) Good food, cold beer, relaxed outdoor lounges, internet access and the best guacamole in town. Sorted in Sumatra.

INDONESIA BUKITTINGGI

OUT & ABOUT IN BUKITTINGGI

A vast array of local tours can be arranged in Bukittinggi. Generally these fall into two categories: culture and nature. They can range from a half-day meander through neighbouring villages, a scour of the nearby jungles for the worlds largest (and smelliest) flowers *Rafflesia Arnoldii* and *Amorphophallus Titanium* or, for something more demanding, a three-day jungle trek to Danau Maninjau, or an overnight assault on Gunung Merapi.

Guides hang out in all the cafes. Be clear about what you want and what is and isn't included. If going solo, make sure somebody knows who's guiding you. Full day tours start at around 200,000Rp.

There's also a healthy climbing scene. A day on the cliffs costs around US$40, but if you can find some locals and avoid the entrepreneurs, it'll work out cheaper.

Bedudal Café   CAFE **$**
(Jl Ahmad Yani; mains 20,000-40,000Rp; 🛜) All your old backpacker favourites in a cosy, intimate atmosphere. The waiters break out the bongos and guitars for occasional jam sessions, and it's also the home base for organising activities and excursions with **Lite 'n' Easy Tours** (📲 0813 7453 7413; www. liteneasy.nl; Jl Ahmad Yani).

☆ Entertainment

Medan Nan Balinduang   DANCE
(Jl Lenggogeni; tickets 40,000Rp; ⊘ 8.30pm) Medan Nan Balinduang presents Minangkabau dance performances. Check with the tourist office for the latest schedule.

ℹ Information

Banks with ATMs, and money changers are clustered along Jl Ahmad Yani, home also to dozens of travel agents and many more services.
Tourist Office (Jl Sudirman; ⊘ 7am-4pm) Opposite the clock tower. Offers maps, tours and tickets to cultural events. Travel agencies line Jl Ahmad Yani for flight and bus bookings.

ℹ Getting There & Away

The chaos of the Aur Kuning bus terminal 2km south is easily reached by *opelet* (3000Rp). Ask for 'terminal'.

Minibuses run regularly to Padang (17,000Rp, two hours) and Solok (16,000Rp, two hours). A full-sized bus to Padang is 17,000Rp. Decrepit

buses make the Danau Maninjau run (15,000Rp, 1½ hours) while a taxi starts at 180,000Rp.

Trans-Sumatran buses also stop here, though only masochists sign up for the really long-haul trips (Jakarta, Medan etc). Still, if you get off on being bounced about for hour upon hour in a hot bus the table 'Buses from Bukittinggi' might be useful.

ℹ Getting Around

Opelet cost 2500Rp. *Bendi* start from 20,000Rp. An *ojek* from the bus terminal to the hotels costs 10,000Rp and a taxi costs 25,000Rp. Transfers direct to Padang airport can be arranged from any travel agent for 40,000Rp.

Danau Maninjau

📲 0752

Maninjau, 38km west of Bukittinggi, is one of Sumatra's most spectacularly peaceful crater lakes. The unforgettable final descent includes 44 hairpin turns that offer stunning views over the shimmering sky-blue lake (17km long, 8km wide) and the 600m crater walls. Maninjau is well set up for travellers (even if low numbers mean that locals have turned to fishing), and should be considered an alternative to Bukittinggi as a place to stay. Life travels slowly here, making it the ideal place to kick back and do nothing. On the other hand, the rainforests and waterfalls of the caldera are just waiting to be explored.

BUSES FROM BUKITTINGGI

DESTINATION	PRICE ECONOMY/AIR-CON (RP)	DURATION (HR)
Jakarta	270,000/350,000	30-35
Medan	130,000/180,000	20
Parapat	150,000/180,000	16
Sibolga	80,000/100,000	10-12

✦ Activities

The Lake
SWIMMING, BOATING

This is an outstanding swimming lake. Though it's 480m deep in some places, the water is warm, and outside town, the water becomes pure as liquid crystal. Some guesthouses rent dug-out canoes or truck inner tubes to float upon.

When relaxation becomes too much, many visitors tackle the 70km sealed road that circles the lake. It's about six hours by mountain bike or two and half hours by moped.

Sakura Hill
HIKING

There's a strenuous two-hour trek to Sakura Hill and the stunning lookout of **Puncak Lawang.** Catch a Bukittinggi-bound bus to Matur and climb 5km to the viewpoint; from there descend to the lake on foot.

🛏 Sleeping

🛏 Maninjau

Aquaculture has transformed the lake shore and the majority of accommodation options around the town now look out across these fish farms.

Muaro Beach Bungalows
BUNGALOW $

(☑ 61189, 0813 3924 0042; neni967@yahoo.com; Jl Muaro Pisang 53; r 80,000-100,000Rp) Down a maze of footpaths (about 300m northwest of the main intersection), these beachfront bungalows are the best value in Maninjau. The beach is (almost) free of aquaculture and fish farming, and there's a good restaurant that's also open to outside guests. Local tours and activities are on offer.

★House of Annisa
HISTORIC HOTEL $$

(☑ 0857 6604 1558; Jl H Udin Rahmani; r 250,000Rp) Located around 150m south of Maninjau's main intersection, this wonderful heritage Dutch villa has been lovingly restored by the great-grandchildren of the original owners. There are only three romantic rooms – one with a brass four-poster bed festooned with mirrors – and it's shared bathrooms only. There's a gorgeous balcony filled with antique benches and chairs.

🛏 Bayur

The following is beyond Bayur village and there are several similar places out here.

Beach Inn
BUNGALOW $

(☑ 081 3740 80485; 4km N; r 60,000-75,000Rp) Outstanding value for money is to be found at this rickety little place right on a private patch of beach. It offers accommodation in either rooms or private bungalows and it gets our vote as one of the friendliest places in the area. It's a 300m walk through the rice paddies from the road.

✗ Eating

Most of the guesthouses serve standards such as *nasi/mie goreng,* some Western favourites and freshly caught fish.

★Rama Café
INDONESIAN $

(Maninjau; mains 25,000-35,000Rp) Share a *martabak* (meat, egg and vegetable pancake-like dish) before hooking into a plate of *ikan panggang* (baked fish) while lazing on cushions amid kites and drums. The lovely owner/chef Anita is an excellent cook, and also a poignant and heartfelt singer who is always keen to pick up her guitar.

ⓘ Getting There & Around

Buses run hourly between Maninjau and Bukittinggi (15,000Rp, 1½ hours). Taxis from Bukittinggi start from 180,000Rp.

Several places rent out mountain bikes (per day 35,000Rp), motorcycles (80,000Rp) and canoes (25,000Rp).

Minibuses plod around the lake road during daylight hours (from 2500Rp). Alternatively, an *ojek* from the Maninjau intersection to Bayur will cost around 8000Rp.

Danau Toba

☑ 0625 / POP 550,000 / ELEV 905M

There's no denying the beauty of Danau Toba (Lake Toba), home of the fun-loving Christian Batak people. This 1707-sq-km, 450m-deep lake, set in the collapsed caldera of an extinct volcano, is surrounded by mountains ribboned with waterfalls and terraced with rice fields. Its pale-blue magnificence hits you on the bus ride into Parapat, when you'll also spot in the middle of the lake Pulau Samosir – a Singapore-sized island of blissful greenery and chilled-out vibes. When there's a touch of mist in the air, and the horizon is obscured, the water seems to blend perfectly with the sky. Combine the climate, scenery, sights and friendly locals with some great food and an impressive array of cheap accommodation

INDONESIA DANAU TOBA

and you'll see why Lake Toba is Sumatra's backpacker hang-out par excellence.

Parapat

 0625

The mainland departure point for Danau Toba, Parapat has everything a transiting tourist needs: transport, lodging and supplies.

The commercial sector of the town clumps together along the Trans-Sumatran Hwy (Jl SM Raja). Branching southwest towards the pier, Jl Pulau Samosir passes most of Parapat's hotels. After 1km, a right fork (Jl Haranggaol) leads to the pier, another 1km southwest. The bus terminal is 2km east of town, but most buses pick up and drop off passengers from ticket agents along the highway or at the pier.

❶ Getting There & Away

The **bus terminal** (Jl SM Raja) is about 2km east of town on the way to Bukittinggi, but is not frequently used (so say the travel agents). Prices are highly negotiable, so shop around at the different ticket agents.

Pulau Samosir

 0625 / POP 120,000 / ELEV 900M

Trek, swim, explore traditional Batak villages, soak in hot springs, party or just chill with cool local people in Pulau Samosir. Your bus-beaten body will begin to unwind on the slow, 8km ferry cruise over to this volcanic isle. (It's actually connected to the mainland by a narrow isthmus, but why quibble?) **Tuk Tuk**, the island's resort town, has low prices, high value and heaps of tranquillity.

◉ Sights

The main sights are located around Danau Toba.

Simanindo   VILLAGE

At the northern tip of the island, in Simanindo, there's a fine old traditional house that has been restored and now functions as a **museum** (admission 30,000Rp; ⊙10am-5pm). It was formerly the home of Raja Simalungun, a Batak king, and his 14 wives. Displays of traditional **Batak dancing** are performed at 10.30am from Monday to Saturday.

The village of Simanindo is 15km from Tuk Tuk and is accessible with a hired motorbike.

Pangururan   VILLAGE

The road that follows the northern rind of Samosir between Simanindo and the town of Pangururan is a scenic ride through the Bataks' embrace of life and death. Amid fertile rice fields are large **multistorey graves** decorated with the distinctive Batak-style house and a simple white cross. Typical Christian holidays, such as Christmas, dictate special attention to the graves. Crossing the island back to Tuk Tuk from here, you can dip into hill-top **hot springs** (admission 10,000Rp) and enjoy spectacular views.

King Sidabutar Grave   HISTORIC SITE

(admission by donation; ⊙dawn-dusk) The Batak king who adopted Christianity is buried in Tomok, a village 5km southeast of Tuk Tuk. The king's image is carved on his tombstone, along with those of his bodyguard and Anteng Melila Senega, the woman the king is said to have loved for many years without fulfilment. The tomb is also decorated with carvings of *singa*, mythical creatures with grotesque three-horned heads and bulging eyes.

Next to the king's tomb is the tomb of the missionary who converted the tribe and an older Batak royal tomb, which souvenir vendors say is used as a multilingual fertility shrine for childless couples.

The tombs are 500m up a narrow lane lined with souvenir stalls. Very close by are some well-preserved traditional Batak houses, which some might find more interesting.

Stone Chairs   HISTORIC SITE

(admission by donation, guides 20,000Rp; ⊙8am-6pm) Ambarita, about 5km north of the Tuk Tuk Peninsula, has a group of 300-year-old stone chairs where important matters were

BUSES FROM PARAPAT

DESTINATION	BUS	DURATION (HR)	TOURIST MINIBUS	DURATION (HR)
Berastagi	100,000Rp	4	N/A	N/A
Bukittinggi	150,000-180,000Rp	15	250,000Rp	15
Medan	22,000Rp	5	65,000Rp	4
Padang	190,000Rp	18	280,000Rp	18
Sibolga	60,000-75,000Rp	6	100,000-150,000Rp	6

discussed among village elders and wrong-doers were tried – then apparently led to a further group of stone furnishings where the accused were bound, blindfolded, sliced and rubbed with garlic and chilli before being beheaded.

🍲 Courses

Heddy's Cooking Class   COOKING COURSE
(☑0625-451217; 300,000Rp; ⊕1-4pm) Held at Ju-wita Café in Tuk Tuk, this class will teach you the tricks of the trade in order to cook up an Indonesian banquet to impress the folks back home. The three-hour course covers a veg-etarian, chicken and fish dish and a dessert of your choice. You need to reserve in person the day before.

🛏 Sleeping

The best sleeping options are along the north and south coasts, where little guesthouses are tucked in between village chores: washing the laundry on the rocks and collecting the news from neighbours.

Bagus Bay Homestay   GUESTHOUSE $
(☑0625-451287; www.bagus-bay.page.tl; Tuk Tuk; s/d without bathroom 30,000/40,000Rp, d 100,000-175,000Rp; @🛜) Rooms in traditional Batak houses overlook avocado trees, a children's playground and a volleyball court. The cheap-er rooms are fairly uninspiring, but the more expensive ones come with great bathrooms (complete with hot water – a rarity for a cheap hotel in these parts) and the pot plants add a nice green touch.

At night its restaurant, which has fre-quent film evenings and Batak dance shows (Wednesday and Saturday), is a lively spot for travellers to congregate.

Samosir Cottages   HOTEL $
(☑0625-451170; www.samosircottages.com; Tuk Tuk; r 70,000-500,000Rp; @🛜) A good choice for travellers who want to hang out with young like-minded folk and boisterous young staff. The rooms span a wide variety of prices and styles and range from dark, cell-like cheapies to quite plush rich-boy rooms. We didn't see any evidence of it, but some guests have com-plained that room cleanliness isn't always what it could be. It has every traveller service you can imagine – travel agency, tour guides, internet, sunloungers, children's playground and a busy restaurant. The swimming is pret-ty good too.

Tuk Tuk

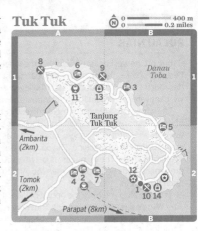

Merlyn Guesthouse   GUESTHOUSE $
(☑0813 6116 9130; http://merlynguesthouse.com; Tuk Tuk; r 60,000-70,000Rp) Situated right on the lake shore, this place receives consistently good feedback from readers. You can choose between sleeping in a traditional wooden Ba-tak house with dwarf-sized doors or a modern room in sunny colours with a hot-water bath-room. Whichever you opt for though the lake views will be as memorable as the rooms.

PULAU NIAS

Sitting off the west coast of Sumatra, the lonely island of Nias is home to one of the world's best surf spots – the legendary righthander of Lagundri Bay. For nonsurfers the island also has much to offer: the traditional hill villages, such as **Tundrumbaho** and **Bawomataluo**, will captivate even casual cultural tourists as well as ethno-architectural buffs.

The waves of Lagundri (or more correctly Pantai Sorake), on the southwest corner of the island, are best between April and October. On smaller days it's a fairly accessible wave for all but total beginners, but as soon as the swell starts to pick up, it becomes an experts-only barrel machine. The point here is lined by a string of very basic and almost identical *losmen*. The going rate is between 50,000Rp and 100,000Rp per night, but you are expected to eat at your *losmen* too. And that'll cost you. A plate of chicken or fish can fetch 50,000Rp.

To get to Nias you have the option of flying from Medan several times a day with **Lion Air/Wings Air** (www.lionair.co.id). The more romantic way of reaching the island is by ferry from the seedy mainland port of Sibolga. Ferries run every day except Sundays from Sibolga to Gunung Sitoli, the 'capital' of Nias, or, Teluk Dalam in the south of Nias and much closer to the surf.

Liberta Homestay   GUESTHOUSE $
(☑ 0625-451035;   liberta_homestay@yahoo.com. co.id; Tuk Tuk; r with bathroom 50,000-80,000Rp, r without bathroom 35,000Rp; ☎) This place may have only limited lake views, but a chilled universe is created here by a lazy-day garden and arty versions of traditional Batak houses. Crawling around the balconies and shortened doors of the rooms feels like being a deckhand on a Chinese junk. However, more attention could be given to cleanliness.

The owner, and ever popular, Mr Moon is a great source of travel information.

Harriara Guesthouse   GUESTHOUSE $
(☑ 0625-451183;   http://hariara-guesthouse.webs. com; Tuk Tuk; r 100,000Rp) This guesthouse has a top-notch lakeside setting, riotous tropical flower gardens and rooms that are so sparkling clean you'd never guess they were nearly 25 years old! If there's nobody at the reception enquire in the nearby restaurants.

SPLURGE

German-run, lakeside **Tabo Cottages** (☑ 0625-451318; www.tabocottages. com; Tuk Tuk; r 250,000-350,000, cottage 350,000-500,000Rp; @☎) has beautiful traditional-style Batak houses, which come with huge bathrooms and hammocks swinging lazily on the terrace. The home-made cakes are worthy of mention as well. A great place for a splurge.

✖ Eating & Drinking

The guesthouses tend to mix eating and entertainment in the evening. Most restaurants serve the Batak speciality of barbecued carp (most from fish farms). Magic or 'special' omelettes are commonly seen on restaurant menus. We probably don't need to warn you that the mushrooms contained in these are not the sort that you can buy at your local supermarket.

★ **Jenny's Restaurant**   INTERNATIONAL $
(Tuk Tuk; mains 20,000-50,000Rp) Although there are lots of different options on the menu at Jenny's, there's only really one thing to eat – grilled or fried lake fish with chips and salad. Follow it up with the fruit pancake, which is almost embarrassingly well proportioned.

Today's Cafe   INTERNATIONAL $
(Tuk Tuk; mains 20,000-40,000Rp) This little wooden shack has a laid-back vibe just in keeping with Tuk Tuk life. It's run by a couple of friendly ladies who whip up some fabulous Batak dishes such as *sak sang* (chopped pork with brown coconut sauce and cream and a wealth of spices).

Bamboo Restaurant & Bar   INTERNATIONAL $
(Tuk Tuk; mains 20,000-50,000Rp) With incredible lake views, Bamboo is a stylish place to watch the sun slink away, with cosy cushion seating, a down-tempo mood and a reliable menu. Mixes some good cocktails, too.

🍸 Drinking & Nightlife

On most nights, music and spirits fill the air with the kind of camaraderie that only grows in small villages. The parties are all local – celebrating a wedding, new addition on a house or the return of a Toba expat. Invitations are gladly given and should be cordially accepted. Bagus Bay Homestay (p261) and Samosir Cottages (p261) both have traditional Batak music and dance performances on Wednesday and Saturday evenings.

Brando's Blues Bar   BAR

(☑0625-451084; Tuk Tuk) There are a handful of foreigner-oriented bars, such as this one, in between the local jungle-juice cafes. Happy 'hour' is a civilised 6pm to 10pm.

☆ Entertainment

Roy's Pub   LIVE MUSIC

(Tuk Tuk; ☺9pm-1am) Has live music (normally local rock bands) several nights a week (Tuesday, Thursday and Saturday) in a graffiti-splattered building. Provides free transport back to your hotel if you're out late.

ℹ Information

There is a small police station. Load up on reading material in Toba, because the rest of Sumatra is a desert for the printed word. **Penny's Books** (Tuk Tuk) and **Gokhan Library** (Tuk Tuk) have both used and rental books.

Internet access (10,000Rp per hour) is available at many of the guesthouses and restaurants. Change your money before you get to Samosir. Exchange rates at the island's hotels and money changers are pretty awful. The only post office is in Ambarita.

ℹ Getting There & Away

BOAT

Ferries between Parapat and Tuk Tuk (7000Rp) operate about every hour from 7am to 7pm. The ferries stop near Bagus Bay Homestay (35 minutes); other stops are by request. When leaving for Parapat, stand on your hotel jetty and wave a ferry down.

Five ferries a day (passenger/car 5000/95,000Rp, 7am to 9pm) shuttle vehicles and people between Ajibata, just south of Parapat, and Tomok.

BUS

Parapat is the mainland transit point for bus travel to/from Danau Toba.

On Samosir, to get to Berastagi, you'll have to catch a bus from Tomok to Pangururan (15,000Rp, 45 minutes), from where you take an-other bus to Berastagi (35,000Rp to 40,000Rp, three hours). This bus goes via Sidikalang, and the price depends on demand and bus type.

ℹ Getting Around

Local buses serve the whole of Samosir except Tuk Tuk. You can rent motorcycles in Tuk Tuk for 70,000Rp to 80,000Rp a day, which includes petrol and helmet. Bicycle hire costs from 25,000Rp per day.

Minibuses run between Tomok and Ambarita (3000Rp), continuing to Simanindo (6000Rp) and Pangururan (15,000Rp). The road along the neck of the peninsula is a good spot to flag down these minibuses. Services dry up after 5pm.

Berastagi

☑ 0628 / POP 600,000 / ELEV 1300M

Escaping from the infernal heat of sea-level Medan, the colonial Dutch traders climbed high into the lush, cool volcanic hills, took one look at the stunningly verdant, undulating landscape and decided to set up camp and build a rural retreat where Berastagi (also called Brastagi) now stands.

Beyond the town are the green fields of the Karo Highlands, dominated by two volcanoes: Gunung Sinabung to the west and the smoking Gunung Sibayak to the north. Each is a day hike, making them two of Sumatra's most accessible volcanoes and the primary reason why tourists get off the bus in the first place.

◎ Sights & Activities

Gunung Sibayak   VOLCANO

(hot springs admission 3000-5000Rp) Jungle draped Gunung Sibayak (2094m) is probably one of the most accessible of Indonesia's volcanoes, and it's steamy, sulphurus heart one of north Sumatra's most memorable sights. The hike can be done in five hours return by any reasonably fit, and suitably equipped, person. You should set out as early as possible and it's best to hire a guide – people have died after getting lost on this mountain.

There are three ways to tackle the climb, depending on your energy level. The easiest way is to take the track that starts to the northwest of Berstagi, a 10-minute walk past the Sibayak Multinational Resthouse. Take the left-hand path beside the hut where you pay the entrance fee. From here, it's 7km (about three hours) to the top and fairly easy to follow, mostly along a road. Finding the path down is a little tricky. When you reach

Berastagi

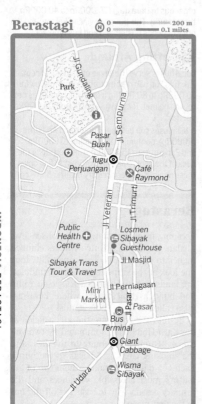

Park

Pasar
Buah

Tugu
Perjuangan

Café
Raymond

Jl Gundaling

Jl Sempurna

Jl Veteran

Jl Trimurti

Public
Health
Centre

Losmen
Sibayak
Guesthouse

Sibayak Trans
Tour & Travel

Jl Masjid

Mini
Market

Jl Perniagaan

Jl Pasar

Pasar

Bus
Terminal

Giant
Cabbage

Wisma
Sibayak

Jl Udara

the crater, turn 90 degrees to the right (anticlockwise), climb up to the rim and start looking for the stone steps down the other side of the mountain. If you can't find the steps, you can also go back the way you came.

Rather than trekking from Berastagi, you can catch a local bus (3000Rp) to Semangat Gunung at the base of the volcano, from where it's a two-hour climb to the summit. There are steps part of the way, but this track is narrower and in poorer condition than the one from Berastagi.

The longest option is to trek through the jungle from Air Terjun Panorama; this waterfall is on the Medan road, about 5km north of Berastagi. Allow at least five hours for the walk from here.

Rates for guides are 150,000Rp for the easy way along the road and 250,000Rp through the jungle. Before setting out, pick up a map from any of the guesthouses in Berastagi and peruse their guestbooks for comments and warnings about the hike.

Gunung Sinabung   VOLCANO
(admission 4000Rp) This peak, at 2450m, is considerably higher than that of nearby Gunung Sibayak, with even more stunning views from the top. Be warned, though, that the clouds love mingling with the summit and can often obscure the vista.

This mountain is much more bad tempered than Sibayak and you should take an experienced guide (350,000Rp), as hikers have gotten lost and died. The climb takes seven to eight hours depending on your skill and the descent route.

To reach the trailhead, take an *opelet* to Danau Kawar (8000Rp, 1½ hours). There is a scenic camp site surrounding Danau Kawar for those travelling with gear.

Note that at the time of going to press, Gunung Sinabung had started erupting and was closed to the public; check locally for updates.

🛏 Sleeping

In general Berastagi isn't blessed with the world's finest selection of backpacker hotels, but at least the welcome is normally warm!

Sibayak Multinational
Resthouse   GUESTHOUSE $
(☎ 0628-91031; Jl Pendidikan 93; r with/without bathroom 250,000/150,000Rp) Set in immaculate gardens, surrounded by nothing but peace and quiet, and with the perfect hill-country vibe, the vast, modern rooms here virtually sparkle. There's hot water in the bathrooms of the pricier rooms and breakfast is included.

The hotel is a short *opelet* ride north of town on the road to Gunung Sibayak.

Wisma Sibayak   GUESTHOUSE $
(☎ 0628-91104; Jl Udara 1; r without bathroom 50,000-60,000Rp, with bathroom 100,000-200,000Rp; @ 🖘) This is a travellers' institution, with tidy and spacious rooms, that are quiet and comfortable. Cheaper rooms have cold showers, pricier ones hot-water showers. There's lots of excellent travel information, a friendly family feel, a decent restaurant and a big smile from the owner. Book ahead in high season.

Losmen Sibayak Guesthouse   GUESTHOUSE $
(☎ 0628-91122; dicksonpelawi@yahoo.com; Jl Veteran 119; r with/without bathroom 85,000/50,000Rp; @ 🖘) Nice cheapies with a lot of Indonesian personality make this place feel more like

a homestay. However, the cheapest rooms directly overlook the main road and are very noisy. Wi-fi in the lobby.

✕ Eating

Café Raymond INTERNATIONAL $
(Jl Trimurti 49; mains 8000-20,000Rp; ⊘7am-midnight) Berastagi's local bohemians hang out at Café Raymond, which serves fruit juices, beer and Western food.

❶ Information

Berastagi is essentially a one-street town spread along Jl Veteran. Banks have ATMs.

Sibayak Trans Tour & Travel (☑0628-91122; dicksonpelawi@yahoo.com; Jl Veteran 119) Your first and only port of call for almost any onward travel advice as well as local tours.

Tourist information centre (☑0628-91084; Jl Gundaling 1; ⊘8am-5pm Mon-Sat) Has maps and can arrange guides. Opening hours are rather flexible.

❶ Getting There & Away

The **bus terminal** (Jl Veteran) is conveniently located near the centre of town. You can also catch buses to Padang Bulan in Medan (10,000Rp, 2½ hours) anywhere along the main street, Jl Veteran.

To reach Danau Toba without backtracking through Medan, catch an *opelet* to Kabanjahe (3000Rp, 15 minutes) and change to a bus for Pematangsiantar (20,000Rp, three hours), then connect with a Parapat-bound bus (10,000Rp, 1½ hours).

Medan

☑ 061 / POP 2.11 MILLION

Sumatra's major metropolis, and Indonesia's third-largest city, has a dubious legend in SE Asia travellers' circles, but question the detractors further and it normally turns out that few of them have actually spent much time here. So, while it's true that the pollution, poverty and persistent cat calls of 'Hello Mister!' can be an unnerving jolt of dirt-under-your-fingernails Asia, this is also a city with real gritty, Indonesian character – something that can be lacking in many of the popular North Sumatran tourist towns. The upshot of all this is that if you came to Indonesia merely because all the other backpackers were heading here then by all means skip Medan and head straight to Lake Toba. If on the other hand you came to Indonesia to experience Indonesia then devote some time

to Medan's markets and streets with their hint of crumbling Dutch colonial charm.

◉ Sights

Istana Maimoon PALACE
(Jl Katamso; admission 5000Rp; ⊘8am-5pm) Standing as grand as ever, the Maimoon Palace was built by the sultan of Deli in 1888. The 30-room palace features Malay, Mogul and Italian influences. Only the main room, which features the lavish inauguration throne, is open to the public.

Museum of North Sumatra MUSEUM
(Jl HM Joni 51; admission 1000Rp; ⊘9am-3pm Tue-Sun) The Museum of North Sumatra has a well-presented collection ranging from early North Sumatran civilisations to Hindu, Buddhist and Islamic periods to colonial and military history.

Mesjid Raya MOSQUE
(cnr Jl Mesjid Raya & SM Raja; admission by donation; ⊘9am-5pm, except prayer times) The impressive Grand Mosque was commissioned by the sultan in 1906. The Moroccan-style building has towering ceilings, ornate carvings, Italian marble and stained glass from China.

Tjong A Fie Mansion HISTORIC BUILDING
(www.tjongafieinstitute.com; Jl Ahmad Yani 105; admission incl guide 35,000Rp; ⊘9am-5pm) Tjong A Fie Mansion, the former residence of a famous Chinese merchant, mixes Victorian and Chinese styles. The exquisite hand-painted ceilings, Tjong's huge bedroom, interesting art pieces, an upstairs ballroom (which now exhibits work by local artists) and Taoist temples help to make it one of the most impressive historic buildings in town.

🛏 Sleeping

The majority of accommodation is on or near Jl SM Raja. Expect serious road and Mosque inspired noise, carbon monoxide inhalation and grubby rooms with cold showers. On the plus side though there are lots of other backpackers hanging around.

Wisma Hari Kota GUESTHOUSE $
(☑061-453 3113; Jl Lobak 14; r 80,000-170,000Rp; ❊🛜) We can't begin to tell you how much better value this place – located only 10 minutes from the airport in a quiet and peaceful area – is compared to most cheap options in Medan. Even the cheapest rooms are vast and have been polished until they sparkle; more expensive rooms feature hot-water showers.

Medan

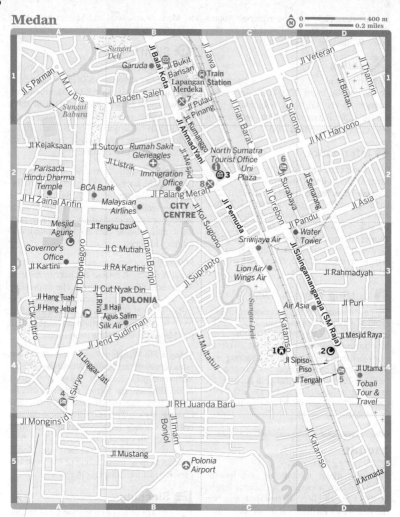

Medan

◉ Sights

🛏 Sleeping

⊗ Eating

Breakfast is included (except for the cheaper rooms).

JJ's Guesthouse   GUESTHOUSE **$**
(☎ 061-457 8411; www.guesthousemedan.com; Jl Suryo 18; s/d incl breakfast 150,000/180,000Rp; ❄) In an old Dutch villa, JJ's has tidy boarding-house-style rooms run by a mannerly Dutch-speaking Indonesian woman. It's opposite KFC; its lack of signage makes it tricky to find. Ask for the Hotel Pardede and JJ's is right behind it.

Ponduk Wisata Angel GUESTHOUSE **$**
(Hotel Angel; ☑ 061-732 0702; a_zelsy_travel@
yahoo.com; Jl SM Raja 70; s with fan 60,000Rp, d
with fan/air-con 100,000/130,000Rp; ❀ ☎) If you
must stay in and around the increasingly
down-beat Jl SM Raja backpacker area, then
this place, where the rooms are a swirl of
vivid blues and yellows, is probably about
the best bet – but that still doesn't make it
great!

✖ Eating

Medan has the most varied selection of cuisines in Sumatra, from basic Malay-style *mie*
(noodle) and *nasi* (rice) joints to top-class
hotel restaurants.

★ **Merdeka Walk** SOUTHEAST ASIAN **$**
(Lapangan Merdeka, Jl Balai Kota; dishes 10,000-
25,000Rp; ☺ 5-11pm; ☎) Inspired by Singapore's al fresco dining, this collection of
outdoor cafes in Lapangan Merdeka offers
both fast-food and proper restaurants.

You can burn off the calories on the
bizarre public exercise equipment at the adjoining sports ground or waste some money
in the amusement centre that sits at the
heart of it all.

Tip Top Restaurant INTERNATIONAL **$$**
(Jl Ahmad Yani 92; dishes 15,000-35,000Rp; ☎)
Only the prices have changed at this old co-
lonial relic, which dates back to 1934 and
is great for a drink to bygone imperialism.
Though it offers an array of Indonesian, Chi-
nese and Western dishes, you certainly don't
come here for the quality of the food. Instead,
just focus on the setting and atmosphere.

❶ Information

ATMs are everywhere, with a string on Jl Pemuda.
Jl Katamso is packed with travel agencies that
handle air tickets and ferry tickets. Visa exten-
sions can be processed at the **immigration
office** (Jl Mangkubumi; ☺ 8am-4pm Mon-Fri).
Technically it takes three days, costs US$25 (or
equivalent in rupiah) and cannot be processed

until a few days before your current visa expires;
the office you need is on the 2nd floor.
BCA Bank (Bank Central Asia; cnr Jl Diponegoro
& Jl H Zainal Arifin) Exchanges money.
Main Post Office (Jl Bukit Barisan; ☺ 8am-
6pm) Located in an old Dutch building on the
main square. Internet, fax and photocopying also
available.
North Sumatra Tourist Office (☑ 061-452
8436; Jl Ahmad Yani 107; ☺ 8am-3pm Mon-Fri)
Brochures, maps and basic information.
Rumah Sakit Gleneagles (☑ 061-456 6368;
Jl Listrik 6) The best hospital in the city, with a
24-hour walk-in clinic and pharmacy, as well as
English-speaking doctors and specialists.
Tobali Tour & Travel (☑ 061-732 4471; Jl SM
Raja 79C) For tourist buses to Danau Toba.

❶ Getting There & Away

AIR
Polonia Airport is close to the centre; a taxi
ride from the airport into Medan should cost
40,000Rp. There's a departure tax of 75,000Rp.

You can fly from Medan to most major Sumat-
ran cities and elsewhere in Indonesia (sometimes
via Jakarta), as well as to Malaysia, Singapore and
some other international destinations.

BUS
There are two main bus stations. Buses south
leave from the **Amplas bus terminal** (Jl SM

BUSES FROM MEDAN

DESTINATION	COST (RP)	DURATION (HR)	FREQUENCY
Banda Aceh	120,000-200,000	12-14	Several daily
Bukittinggi	150,000-245,000	22	Twice daily
Jambi	250,000-265,000	30	Twice daily
Palembang	280,000-290,000	40	Twice daily
Pekanbaru	140,000	13	Once daily

Raja), 6.5km south of downtown. Almost any *opelet* heading south on Jl SM Raja will get you to Amplas. A bemo from Amplas to the centre costs 5000Rp.

Buses to the north leave from **Pinang Baris bus terminal** (Jl Gatot Subroto), 10km west of the city centre. Get there by taxi (around 40,000Rp) or by *opelet* down Jl Gatot Subroto.

❶ Getting Around

Becak drivers fetch about 8000Rp for most destinations in town, and *opelets* (3000Rp) are omnipresent. *Opelets* run along colour-coded routes: the white line hits Kesawan Sq, Merdeka Walk and the train station; yellows will take you to Little India and Sun Plaza. They cost 2500Rp per ride. Bargain hard with taxi drivers.

Bukit Lawang

✔ 061 / POP 30,000

Lost in the depths of the Sumatran jungle is this sweet little tourist town built around an orang-utan viewing centre. While orang-utan spotting is easily the highlight of a visit to Bukit Lawang, the town has much more to offer beyond our red-haired cousins. It's very easy to while away a few days lounging in the many riverside hammocks, listening to the mating calls (mainly those of the orang-utans) over the gushing river and watching the jungle life swing and sing around you. The forests surrounding Bukit Lawang are part of the vast Gunung Leuser National Park, which is one of the richest tropical-forest ecosystems in the world. The park as a whole is home to eight species of primate plus tigers, rhinos, elephants and leopards.

However, aside from orang-utans and various other primates, you are very unlikely to see any other large mammals here (or elsewhere in the park for that matter). The forests immediately surrounding Bukit Lawang are absolutely not pristine jungle – palm-oil plantations extend right up to the edge of the village and at weekends, when foreign tourists are joined by masses of domestic visitors, Bukit Lawang can feel as much like Tarzan country as a busy afternoon in a supermarket. But don't let this put you off, because when you first come face to face with a tree-swinging gentle giant or spend the night under a tarp in the forest you'll quickly forget the tourist circus that accompanies a visit here.

The bus station is 1km east of the riverside tourist district. Minibuses may go a bit further to the small square at the end of the road, where a rickety hanging bridge crosses the river to the hotels.

◉ Sights & Activities

Orang-utan
Feeding Centre WILDLIFE RESERVE
Bukit Lawang's famous orang-utan centre was set up in 1973 to help primates readjust to the wild after captivity or displacement through land clearing. Many of the original duties of the centre have been moved to more remote locations, but twice-daily feedings are still provided to semi-dependent orang-utans.

There are two feeding times a day: 8.30am to 9.30am and 3pm to 4pm. These are the only times visitors are allowed to enter the national park without a guide.

The feeding platform is located on the west bank of Sungai Bohorok within the park boundaries, about a 20-minute walk from the village. The river crossing to the park office is made by dugout canoe. Permits are required to enter the park (20,000Rp). Technically these are only available from the Bukit Lawang Visitors Centre in the village proper, not the office at the foot of the trail to the platform. In reality it's often possible to buy a ticket from the park office and either way you'll need to show a ticket here in order to be allowed to continue to the feeding platform. If you have a camera or video camera you'll have to pay an additional 50,000Rp or 150,000Rp at the office, with no refunds if orang-utans don't come to the feeding platform – during peak fruit season they often don't.

Trekking GUIDED TOUR
Treks into the Gunung Leuser National Park is an absolute must. Most people opt for two days so that they can spend the night in the jungle, which increases the likelihood of seeing orang-utans in the wild. Guides are mandatory and prices are fixed at US$10 for a three-hour trek, US$25 for a day trek and US$45 for a two-day trek. Prices include basic meals, guide fees, camping equipment and the park permit.

Take your time in choosing a guide. If you've got serious flora or fauna curiosities, you should arrange a trek with one of the park rangers who often collaborate with foreign researchers.

If you just want a few souvenir pictures and stories, find a guide you like. People who trekked with guides from the village have mainly positive feedback, with the greatest kudos going to the nightly meals and campfire socials. Common complaints range from guides who don't know enough about the flora and fauna, bunching of treks together and feeding of the orang-utans.

🛏 Sleeping & Eating

The further up river you go, the more likely you are to spot the swinging monkeys and apes from your porch hammock. You won't find hot water or air-con at any of the guesthouses, but all serve food.

★ On The Rocks   BUNGALOW $
(📞 0812 6303 1119; www.ontherocksbl.com; r 120,000-200,000Rp; 🛜) More on the hill than on the rocks, the handful of 'tribal' huts here verge on being luxurious in a rustic kind of way. Each hut has a verandah and sunken bathroom, and all are shrouded in peace and beautiful views.

Back to Nature   GUESTHOUSE $
(📞 0813 7565 7004; www.backtonature-bukitlawang. com; r 100,000-150,000Rp) 🍴 A world away from the hustle of Bukit Lawang village, this place, which is set on a giant patch of private jungle, has comfortable wooden rooms raised off the ground on stilts and a long communal balcony on which many a happy hour can be spent chatting to other guests and relishing the forest views.

It's a half-hour walk from the river crossing for the feeding station.

Sam's Bungalows   GUESTHOUSE $
(📞 0813 7009 3597; samsbungalow@yahoo.com; r 100,000-300,000Rp) There's an excellent range of wooden tree houses here as well as more solidly built rooms painted in sunny Mediterranean colours with huge bathrooms and Italian rain showers.

Jungle Inn   GUESTHOUSE $
(📞 0821 6596 4000; www.jungleinnbukitlawang. com; d 50,000-450,000Rp) The last guesthouse along the strip near the park entrance, Jungle Inn is an old favourite of many a reader. One room overlooks a waterfall, while another incorporates the hill's rock face, and the bathroom sprouts a shower from living ferns.

Green Hill   GUESTHOUSE $
(📞 0813 7034 9124; www.greenhill-bukitlawang. com; r incl breakfast 60,000-250,000Rp) Run by an English conservation scientist and her Sumatran husband, Green Hill has lovely stilt-high rooms ideal for couples, with en suite bamboo-shoot showers that afford stunning jungle views while you wash.

ℹ Information

The **Bukit Lawang Visitors Centre** (⏰7am-3pm) has displays of flora and fauna found in Taman Nasional Gunung Leuser, plus a book of medicinal plants and their uses. Past visitors often record reviews of guides in the sign-in book.

A fee of 15,000Rp is charged for entrance to Bukit Lawang.

ℹ Getting There & Away

Buses leave from the edge of the village about a 30-minute walk from the feeding station. There are direct buses to Medan's Pinang Baris bus terminal every half-hour between 5.30am and 5pm (20,000Rp, four hours). Tourist minibuses depart daily for Medan (75,000Rp to 100,000Rp), Parapat (150,000Rp to 220,000Rp) and Berastagi (100,000Rp to 185,000Rp).

Tangkahan

Tangkahan is the new hot spot on the Sumatran backpacker trail. Having ticked off seeing the orang-utans in Bukit Lawang, in-the-know backpackers come here to see the jungle from an elephant's perspective. After a few days of riverside lounging and elephant-back safaris many find this still simple, low-key retreat has a magic to it that keeps them here far longer than expected.

🏃 Activities

Elephant Trekking   ECOTOUR
(⏰closed Mon & Thu) In a former life Tangkahan's population of domesticated elephants all worked in the logging industry dragging once grand jungle trees to nearby saw mills. Today, with the village's loggers having largely turned conservationists, many of the

---

JUNGLE TREKKING FEES

TREK DURATION	PER PERSON (UP TO 2 PEOPLE)	PER PERSON (3 OR MORE PEOPLE)
Half-day	200,000Rp	180,000Rp
1 day	360,000Rp	300,000Rp
2 days	720,000Rp	600,000Rp
3 days	1,200,000Rp	900,000Rp

elephants have been reincarnated as a lure to tourists: you can give them their daily **bath** (100,000Rp) or explore the jungle on a one-hour **elephant trek** (650,000Rp).

🛏 Sleeping & Eating

All accommodation options provide meals and nonguests are welcome to eat at these as well.

Jungle Lodge   GUESTHOUSE **$**
(☑ 0813 7633 4787; www.junglelodge.net; r 100,000-150,000Rp) The cottages at this popular place are scattered across the attractive gardens like fallen forest leaves. Some have fab river views. There's a large, thatched restaurant overlooking the bubbling river, and friendly staff.

Linnea Resort   GUESTHOUSE **$**
(☑ 0812 6046 3071; s/d 150,000/160,000Rp) This place has cottages scattered about a rock garden a little way back from the river. Although the rooms are arguably the best in the village it needs a little time for the gardens to really mature.

ⓘ Getting There & Away

There are two direct buses that depart daily to Medan's Pinang Baris terminal (25,000Rp, four hours). To get to Tangkahan from Bukit Lawang you can take one of the many buses to Binjai (12,000Rp to 14,000Rp, 2½ hours). If you time it well you'll be able to get on one of the twice-daily buses from here direct to Tangkahan (25,000Rp, 2½ hours), otherwise take one to Tittamangga (20,000Rp, two hours) and from there hop on the back of a motorbike to Tangkahan (50,000Rp to 60,000Rp). Alternatively, any of the local guides will take you direct from Bukit Lawang on a moped (200,000Rp to 250,000Rp, three hours) – be warned that the road is treacherous and this is a very bouncy ride. Or you can do as most people do and team up with other travellers to hire a 4WD (500,000Rp to 600,00Rp, three hours).

Banda Aceh

☑ 0651 / POP 210,000
Indonesian cities are rarely coupled with pleasant descriptions, but Banda Aceh breaks the mould. The sleepy provincial capital is a pleasant spot to spend a few days. The village-like atmosphere and dusty, unobtrusive streets make for an easy-to-explore and laid-back town filled with cheery faces. The proud folk rarely betray the tragedy experienced during the Boxing Day tsunami (which

killed 61,000 here), and it's impossible to correlate the reconstructed city with the distraught images of 2004.

Banda Aceh is a fiercely religious place, and the ornate mosques are at the centre of daily life. In this devoutly Muslim city, religion and respect are everything. The hassles are few and the people are easygoing and extremely hospitable to visitors.

◎ Sights

Tsunami Museum   MUSEUM
(Jl Iskandar Muda; ⊘ 9am-noon & 2-4.30pm Sat-Thu) 🆓 **FREE** It cost a whopping US$5.6 million to build, and today Banda Aceh's impressive Tsunami Museum is the highlight (in a very sad and depressing kind of way) of a trip to Banda Aceh. A visit opens with the sound of muffled and terrified voices, followed by a powerful set of images from the aftermath of the waves. Upstairs a very graphic short film is aired, followed by more pictures and models recreating the scenes of destruction.

Tsunami Sights   MONUMENT
Aside from the Tsunami Museum, the most famous of the tsunami sights are the **boat in the house** in Lampulo, and the 2500-tonne **power generator vessel** that was carried 4km inland by a wave.

Mesjid Raya Baiturrahman   MOSQUE
(admission by donation; ⊘ 7-11am & 1.30-4pm) With its brilliant white walls and liquorice-black domes, the Mesjid Raya Baiturrahman is a dazzling sight on a sunny day. The best time to visit the mosque is during Friday afternoon prayers, when the entire building and yard are filled with people. A headscarf is required for women.

Museum Negeri Banda Aceh   MUSEUM
(☑ 0651-23144; Jl Alauddin Mahmudsyah 12; admission 7500Rp; ⊘ 8.00am-noon & 2-5pm Tue-Sun) The Museum Negeri Banda Aceh has displays of Acehnese weaponry, household furnishings, ceremonial costumes, everyday clothing, gold jewellery, calligraphy and some magnificently carved *recong* (Acehnese daggers) and swords.

🛏 Sleeping

Backpackers have a hard time of it in Banda Aceh. There's no shortage of cheap places to stay but very few of them are willing to accept foreigners. Therefore most people end up spending more than normal here.

Hotel Medan HOTEL $
(☎0651-21501; www.hotel-medan.com; Jl Ahmad Yani 17; r with breakfast 235,000-420,000Rp; ❄@📶) This business-class hotel has comfortable and spotless rooms. It's probably the most popular hotel in town with both foreign and Indonesian visitors, and is certainly the best value.

Hotel Prapat HOTEL $
(☎0651-22159; Jl Ahmad Yani 19; d with fan/air-con 100,000/200,000Rp; ❄) One of the more affordable spots. From the outside Prapat has the feel of a cheap run-down motel, though rooms are fair value with Western toilets and clean sheets.

Hotel 61 HOTEL $$
(☎638 866; www.hotel61.co.id; Jl Panglima Polem 28; r incl breakfast 450,000-800,000Rp, ste incl breakfast 930,000Rp; ❄📶) Despite its bizarre location inside an amusement centre and fast-food restaurant, this is the best value top-end hotel in the city centre – that is assuming you get a room away from the noise and that they offer you a discount (which they will!). Rooms are comfortable and there's excellent internet reception, which is a real rarity.

Eating

The square at the junction of Jl Ahmad Yani and Jl Khairil Anwar is usually the setting for the Pasar Malam Rek, Banda Aceh's lively night food market. Many night food stalls are found on Jl SM Raja.

★**Restauran Bunda** INDONESIAN $
(☎0813 9680 8482; Jl Pante Pirak 7-9; mains 8,000-25,000Rp) Think bright lights, modern furnishings, a shiny canteen and uniformed waiters piling endless plates of sublime *masakan minang* (basically the same as Padang food) dishes onto your table and you get this fantastic 'posh *warung*' style restaurant.

Information

There are plenty of ATMs and internet cafes around town.

Getting There & Away

There are several flights a day from Banda Aceh to Medan with Garuda, Sriwiyaya and Lion Air. Air Asia flies daily to Kuala Lumpur, and Firefly to Penang in Malaysia.

South of the city centre you'll find the **Terminal Bus Bathoh** (Jl Mohammed Hasan), which has numerous buses to Medan. *Ekonomi* buses (175,000Rp, 14 hours) depart at 4pm, while *eksekutif* buses leave all day (230,000Rp, 12 hours).

Getting Around

Airport taxis charge a set rate of 70,000Rp for the 16km ride into town. A taxi from the airport to Uleh-leh port, 15km northwest of town, will cost 100,000Rp; from town to Uleh-leh is 50,000Rp.

Labi labi (minibuses) are the main form of transport around town and cost 2000Rp. For Uleh-leh (5000Rp, 30 minutes), take the blue *labi labi* signed 'Uleh-leh'.

From the bus station, a becak into town will cost around 15,000Rp. A becak around town should cost between 5000Rp and 10,000Rp.

Pulau Weh

☎0652 / POP 25,000

A tiny tropical rock off the tip of Sumatra, Weh is a little slice of peaceful living that rewards travellers who've journeyed up through the turbulent greater mainland below. After hiking around the jungles, volcanoes and lakes of the mainland, it's time to jump into the languid waters of the Indian Ocean. Snorkellers and divers bubble through the great walls of swaying sea fans, deep canyons and rock pinnacles, while marvelling at the prehistorically gargantuan fish. Both figuratively and geographically, Pulah Weh is the cherry on top for many visitors' trip to Sumatra.

Activities

Beaches BEACH
It's all about fun in the sun on this blessed island, and there are some mighty fine patches of sand on which to frolic, as well as even finer underwater landscapes to explore with a mask strapped to your face.

About a 2km walk from Sabang town, Pantai Kasih (Lover's Beach), is a palm-fringed crescent of white sand. Popular with a mixture of domestic and international tourists is Gapang Beach, which offers terrific swimming, with frequent turtle sightings. Just over the headland from Gapang Beach is Iboih Beach, which is saturated in a castaway vibe that makes it pretty much irresistible to backpackers.

Rubiah Tirta Divers DIVING
(☎0652-332 4555; www.rubiahdivers.com; intro dive/open-water course all inclusive €45/280) At Iboih, Rubiah Tirta Divers is the oldest of several dive operations on the island.

Lumba Lumba Diving Centre DIVING
(☎ 332 4133, 081 1682 787; www.lumbalumba.com;
intro dive/open-water course all inclusive €45/299)
At Gapang, Lumba Lumba Diving Centre is
the centre of activity.

🛏 Sleeping & Eating

Iboih, with its simple palm-thatch bungalows, many built on stilts and overhanging
crystal-clear water, is Pulau Weh's backpacker
hang-out par excellence. There are dozens of
different places to stay with almost nothing
whatsoever to differentiate them from each
other. In fact, it's often hard to know where
one place ends and another begins. Wherever
you choose to hang your flip-flops, if you stay
for several days, you can usually negotiate a
discount on the normal daily rates.

Rates and visitors double on weekends.

Yulia's HUT $
(☎ 0821 6856 4383; r with/without bathroom
250,000/100,000Rp; 🛜) A 500m trudge over
the cliffs rewards you with the best of Iboih's
huts, some excellent front-door snorkelling
and a good restaurant with shakes and light
fare.

Olala HUT $
(r 50,000-150,000Rp) Of the many places offering cheap and cheerful beach huts, Olala is
the current flavour of the month. And talking of flavours, its restaurant (open to all) receives an equal amount of praise.

Iboih Inn HUT $$
(☎ 0812 6904 8397; www.iboihinn.com; r with break-
fast 150,000-350,000Rp; ❄🛜) The top-dog
rooms here come with hot-water showers,
air-con and fab sea views and are aimed very
much at backpackers who are now too old to
backpack. Room price and quality then drops
downward until you get to simple wooden
shacks with thin partitioning walls ideal for
backpackers filled with youthful zeal.

ℹ Information

There are a couple of internet places in Iboih and
a bank or two (with ATMs) in Sabang.

ℹ Getting There & Away

Fast ferries to Pulau Weh (*ekonomi/eksekutif/*
VIP 55,000/65,000/85,000Rp, 45 minutes)
leave from Uleh-leh, 15km northwest of
Banda Aceh. Slow ferries (*ekonomi/eksekutif*
19,000/37,000Rp, two hours) also leave daily.
Check schedules at the port.

ℹ Getting Around

From the port, there are regular minibuses to
Gapang and Iboih (50,000Rp, 40 minutes). Allow
at least an hour to travel from the port to Iboih.

KALIMANTAN

With its dense jungles, hothouse biodiver-
sity and indigenous peoples, Kalimantan is
one of the world's last great wildernesses.
As mysterious as it is vast, it covers some
two thirds of Borneo and 30% of Indone-
sia's total landmass. Formerly headhunting
country, this is a land of longhouses and
superstitious Dayak villages where, despite
incursions of 21st-century technology, the
drum-roll of the shaman effortlessly coa-
lesces with the trill of mobile phones. Given
Kalimantan's ongoing environmental strug-
gles, particularly with palm-oil plantations,
there has never been a more vital time to
visit.

History & Culture

Kalimantan's riches drew Chinese and In-
dian traders as far back as AD 400. Dutch
and English imperialists began sparring over
Kalimantan in the early 17th century; Hol-
land won and England took Sarawak and
Sabah. Global industrialisation and expand-
ing wealth spurred demand for traditional

PALM OIL

Found in hundreds of products in
Western supermarkets, this high-yield
'miracle crop' is the single biggest
threat to Kalimantan's forests. Despite
the considerable local employment its
plantations create, the real loser is the
planet; huge swaths of rainforest have
been indiscriminately destroyed, criti-
cally endangering Kalimantan's unique
biodiversity.

A two-year moratorium, beginning
in 2011, on clearing forests has given
conservationists a chance to establish
the argument for 'REDD+ programs',
where standing, preserved forests can
be monetised with local people finan-
cially rewarded for preserving their vital
function as global carbon silos. Perhaps
then carbon sequestration can finally
compete economically with palm oil.

commodities and new ones: coal and oil. Petroleum drew Japan's attention during WWII. It also spelled the end of white man's rule, for the war's end brought independence to Indonesia. Over the past six decades, Kalimantan has struggled to find its place in Indonesia. Economic opportunity increasingly attracts outsiders; with a cast of crusading missionaries and imams, loggers, palm-oil planters and conservationists, government administrators and traditional leaders, the struggle for Kalimantan's soul continues.

ⓘ Getting There & Away

The only entry points to Kalimantan that issue visas on arrival are Balikpapan's Sepinggan Airport, Pontianak's Supadio Airport and the Tebedu–Entikong land crossing between Kuching (Sarawak) and Pontianak. All other entries from outside Indonesia – by land, sea and air – require a visa issued in advance.

AIR

Air Asia (p308) flies from Kuala Lumpur to Balikpapan. **Silk Air** (www.silkair.com) flies between Singapore and Balikpapan, but not inexpensively.

BOAT

Major ferry ports in Kalimantan include Balikpapan, Samarinda, Banjarmasin and Pontianak. **Pelni** (www.pelni.co.id) and other carriers connect to Jakarta, Semarang and Surabaya on Java, and Makassar, Pare Pare and others on Sulawesi. There are ferries from Tawau (Sabah) to Nunukan and Tarakan.

ⓘ Getting Around

As an alternative to riding infernally hot buses, *kijang*, Kalimantan's ubiquitous taxi, can be chartered between cities. Short journeys can be taken in a *colt*, a hop-on hop-off minibus, usually blue, green and orange, which operate on given routes.

Catching internal flights is often the only way to see Kalimantan's scattered highlights in a short space of time.

Klotoks (wooden boats with covered passenger cabins converted into accommodation) are best for exploring the jungle.

West & Central Kalimantan

Entering Kalimantan from Sarawak, your first destination will be Pontianak, which has plenty of accommodation and forward flights to the rest of the country (including Pangkalan Bun for Tanjung Puting National Park). We've focused on major highlights *outside* West Kalimantan.

Central Kalimantan (KalTeng) segues from coastal mangrove to peatland swamps and dipterocarp forest. Heavily Dayak, it's also home to Tanjung Puting National Park, inside which is Camp Leakey, the best place in the world for close encounters with semiwild orang-utans.

Pangkalan Bun

☎ 0532 / POP 43,000

Functional Pangkalan Bun has a handful of ATMs, hotels, tasty cafes and roadside *warung*. Serviced by a nearby airport, it's the easiest place to stay if you're en route to Tanjung Puting National Park to see orang-utans up close.

☞ Tours

The following tour operators will happily visit your hotel lobby to consult with you on your trip.

★**Borneo Wisata Permai Tours**   ADVENTURE
(☎ 081 2500 0508; www.borneowisata.com) The best tour company in the area. Diligent owner Harry Purwanto knows every *klotok*, captain and guide and can help you organise the best trip from all available choices.

Borneo Orangutan Adventure Tour   ADVENTURE
(☎ 0852 4930 9250; www.orangutantravel.com) Run by the excellent Ahmad Yani, the first official guide in the area.

🛏 Sleeping

Hotel Bahagia   HOTEL $
(☎ 0532-21226; Jl P Antasari 100; r 85,000-245,000Rp; ❋ 🛜) A fair option for Tanjung Puting backpackers if you can't find a closer

room in Kumai. Upper-floor economy rooms 201, 206 and 210 have streetside windows and a common porch.

Hotel Andika   HOTEL $
(☎ 0532-21218; Jl Hasanudin 20A; r incl breakfast 70,000-110,000Rp; ❋) Rooms here are more interesting than the usual concrete box – all have windows facing a verdant courtyard. Midway down Jl Hasanudin.

★**Yayorin Homestay**   HOMESTAY $$
(☎ 0532-29057; Jl Bhayangkara, Km 1; r incl breakfast 300,000Rp; ❋) A unique woodland setting with a working fishpond sets these charming cottage rooms apart. Yayorin is a local NGO working to preserve Kalimantan's forests. About 4km east of town.

✖ Eating

In addition to the eateries reviewed, you will find more *warung* on Jl Kasumayuda and Jl P Antasari.

★**Iduna Bakery & Café**   WESTERN $
(☎ 0532-24007; Jl Rangga Santrek 5; mains 15,000-32,000Rp; ⊙9am-9pm) A sophisticated surprise, uniting a warm and trendy cafe with a tasty bakery (closes at 5pm).

Pranaban Fish Restaurant   SEAFOOD $
(Jl Hasanudin; mains from 40,000Rp; ⊙8am-10pm) This semi-alfresco resto is a real gem renowned by locals and expats for its grilled and fried *bakar* (fish), chicken and duck.

ℹ Information

Post Office (Jl Kasumayuda 29)
RS Sultan Imanudin (Jln Sutlan Syahrir) Hospital.

ℹ Getting There & Away

There are no longer any flights connecting Pangkalan Bun and Palangka Raya. The best option is to fly from Pangkalan Bun to Sampit, then take a *Kijang* (pick-up truck; 75,000Rp, buy two front seats if possible) to Palangka Raya. Reserve your car ahead (☎ 0852 4920 5199, English shaky). Otherwise it is a brutal 15-hour bus trip, although you could get off in Sampit if you can't take any more.

ℹ Getting Around

Taxis to/from the airport (5km) cost 50,000Rp. *Opelet* (minibuses) around town cost 10,000Rp. Minibuses to Kumai (20,000Rp, 20 minutes) and *ojek* leave from the roundabout at the end of Jl Kasumayuda.

ℹ REGISTRATION & RULES IN TANJUNG PUTING NP

Visitors should register at Pangkalan Bun police station upon arrival. Bring photocopies of your passport and visa (airport taxi drivers know the steps). This can also be organised by your guide. Once in Kumai, the next stop is the PHKA Office (National Parks Office; fax 0532-23832; Jln HM Rafi'l Km 1.5; ⊙ 8am-2pm Mon-Thu, 8am-11am Fri, 8am-1pm Sat) located portside. Registration costs 120,000Rp per day per person, 50,000Rp per trip for a *klotok* parking permit (30,000Rp per speedboat) and 50,000Rp per trip for a camera licence. Provide a copy of your police letter from Pangkalan Bun and another photocopy of your passport. When the park office is closed, it may be possible to arrange entry at the first feeding station, Tanjung Harapan. Ask your boat captain or guide.

Many of the orang-utans are unafraid of humans, so under no circumstances approach them; they're semiwild and some are prone to biting visitors. If a female is with her baby, be especially vigilant. Resist the temptation to swim in rivers – large saltwater crocodiles still lurk; several years ago a British volunteer was killed just off the dock at Camp Leakey.

Kumai

☑ 0532 / POP 23,000

Kumai is the departure point for Tanjung Puting National Park; come here to choose your *klotok* and acquire a permit from the PHKA Office – situated next to your departure point. Note: there are no ATMs here, so stock up on cash in Pangkalan Bun, 20 minutes away.

ℹ Getting There & Away

Reach Kumai by minibus from Pangkalan Bun (20,00Rp, 20 minutes). Taxis from Pangkalan Bun airport to Kumai cost 150,000Rp, including all stops for visiting Tanjung Puting National Park.

Tanjung Puting National Park

Possibly *the* highlight of Borneo, this unforgettable adventure takes you puttering up Sungai (river) Sekonyer to Camp Leakey. Established in 1971 by eminent primatologist Dr Biruté Galdikas, a visit here almost guarantees you intimate encounters with orang-utans. En route you'll see macaques, pot-bellied proboscis monkeys, kingfishers, majestic hornbills and – if you're lucky – false gharial crocodiles. Around the camp you may also spot sun bears, porcupines, gibbons and Sambar deer.

◉ Sights & Activities

Part of the rehabilitation process here is the daily feeding of orang-utans at jungle platforms, where you'll go and view them. Rangers, armed with panniers of bananas whoop to empty trees and gradually our distant cousins appear.

Feedings take place at three camps: Tanjung Harapan at 3pm, Pondok Tangui at 9am and Camp Leakey at 2pm (check for schedule changes). Reaching feeding stations requires a short, sometimes slippery walk (about 15 minutes) from the dock. Bring rain protection and vats of insect repellent!

Two-tiered *klotoks* are the most romantic way to visit Tanjung Puting and serve as your restaurant, watchtower and home, accommodating up to four guests. Come twilight, moor up beside the jungle, your *klotok* aflicker with candlelight.

You usually bed down early – the upper deck transformed with mattress and mozzie net – then wake at dawn to the gibbon's mellow call and myriad animal sounds... Pure epiphany material.

Boat demand peaks in July and August. Daily rates fluctuate from 400,000Rp to 450,000Rp for a boat and captain, including fuel. Cooks and food generally costs 100,000Rp per person per day. It's considered normal to provide the crew's food. When you factor in permits and fees, the total cost for a three-day, two-night guided trip for two people is about 3,295,000Rp.

Book a *klotok* in advance with tour agencies in Pangkalan Bun and throughout Kalimantan.

Taking a guide is vital for facilitating a smooth trip: purchasing food, communicating with your *klotok* driver and getting you to the feeding platform at the right time, as well as taking you trekking. Guide fees range from 150,000Rp to 250,000Rp per day. We recommend the following licensed guides (it's worth emailing them in advance).

Erwin   GUIDE
(☑ 0858 6666 0159; erwinvanjava@gmail.com)

Ancis Banderas   GUIDE
(☑ 0813 4920 5251; ecotourism.820@gmail.com)

INDONESIA WEST & CENTRAL KALIMANTAN

Andy Arysad   GUIDE
(☎0813 5295 0891; andijaka01@gmail.com) The
park's most experienced guide.

🛏 Sleeping

Only visitors that absolutely must bed down
on terra firma should miss sleeping on a
klotok. Some alternate nights on water and
land.

Rimba Lodge   HOTEL $$$
(☎0532 671 0589; www.ecolodgesindonesia.com;
r incl breakfast 585,000-1,485,000Rp; ❄) This
riverside lodge set in the jungle has the
right ambiance, with comfortable en suite
cabanas, warm showers and traditional de-
cor. Book via an agent and get 20% off.

❶ Getting There & Away

Tanjung Puting is typically reached via a flight
to nearby Pangkalan Bun and a taxi to Kumai
(120,000Rp, 20 minutes).

Speedboats from Kumai cost 500,000Rp per
day, and take about two hours to reach Camp
Leakey, but this is pure transport, not wildlife-
spotting. Canoes are a quieter alternative for
exploring Sungai Sekonyer's shallow tributaries,
and can be rented at Sekonyer Village store for
50,000Rp per day.

East Kalimantan

East Kalimantan (KalTim) may have been
long exposed to logging and oil extraction,
but it can still boast vast unpenetrated
jungle, the mighty Mahakam River and
some of the best off-coast diving in Borneo.

Berau

☎ 0554 / POP 52,000

Riverbound Berau, your pit-stop before
paradisical Sangalaki Archipelago, comes
into its own by night, with a carnivalesque
atmosphere of fairy-lit *warung* on Jl Yani.

🛏 Sleeping

Hotel Kartika   HOTEL $
(☎0554-21379; Jl P Antasari; r 140,000-
200,000Rp; ❄) Cheap but rough: these con-
crete cubes are dark and badly need paint.

Hotel Sederhana   HOTEL $$
(☎0554-21353; Jl P Antasari 471; r incl breakfast
280,000-365,000Rp; ❄🖥) The deluxe rooms
here are the best in town, but nothing to
write home about.

✗ Eating & Drinking

Sari Ponti Restaurant   CHINESE $
(Jl Durian II, 35; mains from 20,000Rp; ⏰8am-
9pm) The local Chinese favourite: clean,
well-lit, attentive staff, reliable food.

❶ Information

Find ATMs along Jl P Antasari and Jl Maulana.

❶ Getting There & Away

AIR

Trigana (☎0554-202 7885; www.trigana-air.
com; Jl Tendean 572) flies from Berau to Balikpapan, **Kal-Star** (☎0554-21007; Jl Maulana 45)
to Samarinda, Nunukan and Tarakan, Trigana to
Balikpapan, Banjarmasin and Solo, and **Sriwijaya**
(☎0554-202 8777; Jl Pemuda 50) to Surabaya
and Balikpapan.

BUS

The **bus terminal** (Jln H Isa) is just south of the
market on *angkot* routes. Buses to Tanjung Batu
(50,000Rp, two hours) drop you off at the dock,
from where you pick up a speedboat to Derawan
Island.

Kijang gather across from the terminal and
demand a minimum of four passengers. Destinations include Tanjung Batu (60,000Rp, two
hours), Tanjung Selor (70,000Rp, 2½ hours) and
Samarinda (250,000Rp, 14 to 18 hours).

❶ Getting Around

Taxis to the airport (9km) cost 50,000Rp while
angkot cost 3000Rp.

Pulau Derawan

☎ 0551

Fringed by coral-blue water and powder-
fine beaches, this tear-shaped fishing island is a traveller's dream and one of the
richest dive spots in Southeast Asia. Where
else can you step off your *losmen* jetty and
be gliding with giant green turtles, clown
fish, scorpion fish, moray eel and parrot
fish a moment later? By night Derawan is a
sleepy affair, braziers glowing on street corners as the Celebes Sea incandesces with
fishing boats.

🏃 Activities

Pulau Derawan's underwater activities are
best conducted from upmarket **Derawan
Dive Lodge** (☎0878 4646 2413; www.derawan
divelodge.com). A full day diving Derawan

(up to three dives) is US$115; a dive trip to Maratua, Kakaban and Sangalaki is US$165. Village boats to dive sites cost around 700,000Rp per boat, exclusive of equipment.

🍽 Sleeping & Eating

Stilted *losmen* here are cosy and offer the sea as your back garden. Cafes along Main St serve up fresh seafood.

Lestari I   LOSMEN $
(✆0813 4722 9636; Pulau Derawan; r 75,000-150,000Rp; ❄) Imagine a longhouse on a pier and you have this pleasant *losmen*, with colourful verandahs, some with air-con. The owner will take you to neighbouring islands for 700,000Rp.

★ Pelangi Guesthouse   LOSMEN $$
(✆0813 4780 7078; r 200,000-300,000Rp; ❄) Derawan has many *losmen* built out on docks, but this is the best one, offering colourful en suite rooms with private verandahs over the sea, a basic cafe/restaurant, and sea turtles for free.

April's Restaurant   INDONESIAN $
(✆0813 5058 2483; mains 25,000Rp; ❀7am-8pm) Wedged between Danakan and Lestari 1, guacamole-green April's dishes up reliable Indonesian favourites.

❶ Getting There & Away

There is no regularly scheduled public transport in the Derawan Archipelago. Chartered speedboats for Pulau Derawan leave from the dock at Tanjung Batu, a coastal town two hours' drive from Berau. The 20-minute ride is 250,000Rp for the boat, which seats five. Ask to be dropped off near your hotel. Chartering to other islands is expensive for an individual traveller, but of course decreases when divided among a group. A four-hour return trip from Derawan to Sangalaki and Kakaban is 1,500,000Rp. From Tanjung Batu to Nabucco costs 3,250,000Rp return. Enquire about specifics at the speedboat dock, and take your driver's mobile phone number for future reference.

The cheapest, and slowest, way to get between islands is by *tok-tok*, a local open fishing boat with a noisy little engine. You can arrange this in any village, just be aware of the time involved, as you may be bobbing around in the sun for hours (eg Berau to Maratua is eight hours). Having said that, it is a fun way to get between nearby islands, like Nabucco and Maratua (50,000Rp).

SULAWESI

Looking like the remains of blanket shredded by a pack of mad jackals, Sulawesi is as wild in reality as it appears on a map. The massive island's many-limbed coastline is drawn with sandy beaches, fringing coral reefs and a mind-boggling variety of fish. Meanwhile the interior is shaded in with impenetrable mountains and jungles thick with wildlife, such as rare nocturnal tarsiers and flamboyantly colourful maleo birds. Just exploring this ink blot of an island can gobble up a 30-day visa before you know it, so be sure to leave time for the diving around Pulau Bunaken. It's reached by the legendary travellers' trail along Sulawesi's spine: from bustling Makassar to Tana Toraja, on to the chilled Togean Islands and finally Manado and Bunaken.

❶ Getting There & Away

AIR
The three transport hubs are Makassar and Manado, which are well connected with the rest of Indonesia, and Palu, which offers connections to Balikpapan in Kalimantan. SilkAir flies to Manado from Singapore while Air Asia flies to Makassar from Kuala Lumpur.

BOAT
Sulawesi is on several boat routes, with more than half Pelni's fleet calling at Makassar and Bitung (the seaport for Manado), as well as a few other towns.

Makassar (Ujung Padang)

✆ 0411 / POP 1.6 MILLION

Makassar – the long-time gateway to eastern Indonesia, and Sulawesi's most important city – can be unnerving, so most travellers immediately head for Tana Toraja. However, you're likely to spend at least one night here, so check out the busy harbour and the newly gentrified waterfront in the centre, where you can join the strolling and snacking masses. Shopping is good as are the seafood restaurants. Makassar played a key role in Indonesian history. The 16th-century Gowa empire was based here until the Dutch weighed in. Three centuries later, in the 1950s, the Makassarese and Bugis revolted unsuccessfully against the central government.

Sulawesi

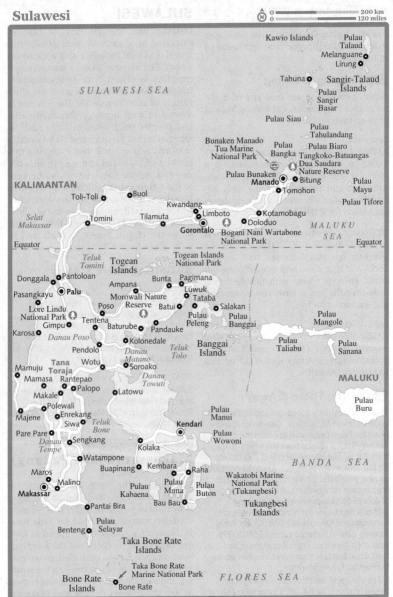

0 | 200 km
0 | 120 miles

◉ Sights

Most of the action takes place in the west, near the sea. The port is in the northwest; Fort Rotterdam is in the centre of the older, and walkable, commercial hub. Look for remnants of the old Kingdom of Gowa 7km southeast of the centre.

Fort Rotterdam   HISTORIC SITE

(Jl Pasar Ikan; museums admission 10,000Rp; ⊙8am-5pm) One of the best-preserved examples of Dutch architecture in Indonesia,

Fort Rotterdam dates back to 1545. The original fort was rebuilt in Dutch style after the Treaty of Bungaya in 1667. Inside its not as interesting as you might hope, although the **Museum Negeri La Galigo** (Jl Pasar Ikan, Fort Rotterdam; admission Rp2000; ☺ 8am-12:30pm Tue-Sun) has cultural displays.

Pelabuhan Paotere   NEIGHBOURHOOD
(Paotere Harbour; admission 500Rp)   FREE
Pelabuhan Paotere, a 15-minute becak ride north of the city centre, is where the Bugis sailing ships berth and is arguably the most atmospheric part of the city. There is usually lots of activity on the dock and in the busy **fish market** a few streets south.

🛏 Sleeping

Pondok Suada Indah   HOTEL **$**
(☎ 0411-317179; Jl Sultan Hasanuddin 12; r from 200,000Rp; ❀) Set in a spacious, old colonial-era house that feels far from the city's hubbub just out the front door. Rooms are huge and are decorated with a tatty mix of heavy antiques and cheap modern furniture. It's not pristine but it's a great deal in this price range.

Makassar (Ujung Padang)

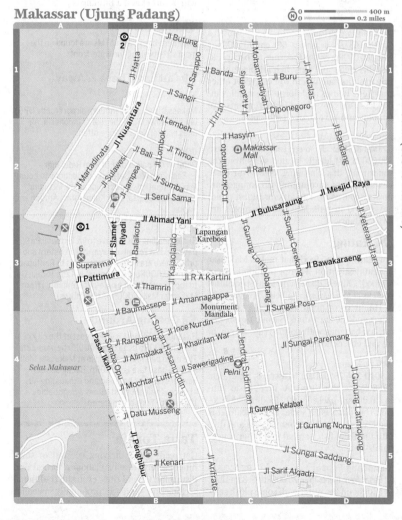

Makassar (Ujung Padang)

New Legends Hostel   HOSTEL $

(☏ 0411-313777; Jl Jampea 5G; dm 70,000Rp, r from 100,000Rp; ✳🛜) Catering to backpackers, this clean and very helpful place has a tiny upstairs cafe where you can meet other travellers. Rooms and dorms are small, windowless and box-like. Cheaper rooms are fan-only and have shared bathrooms.

Asoka Homestay   HOMESTAY $$

(☏ 0411-873476; Jl Yosep Latumahina; r from 300,000Rp; ✳) Ideally located steps from the waterfront, this charming family-run place has six rooms surrounding an immaculate flowery courtyard. The little breakfast tables are draped in pink lace and the rooms are large and airy.

✖ Eating

For many it's the food that makes Makassar a great destination. There's an abundance of seafood, Chinese dishes and local specialities such as *coto makassar* (a beefy, spicy soup).

Hundreds of night *warung* line Jl Penghibur and the surrounds. Savour *piseng epe* (grilled bananas with palm syrup) or any of myriad other choices.

★ Lae Lae   SEAFOOD $

(☏ 0411-334326; Jl Datu Musseng 8; meals from 20,000Rp; ⊙ noon-10pm) A very basic dining hall jam-packed with food-frenzied locals, this place is as social as the seafood is good. Wash up, roll up your sleeves and dive into the flaky fish, sambal and other sauces hands-first.

Kampoeng Popsa   FOOD COURT $

(Jl Pasar Ikan; meals from 25,000Rp; ⊙ 8am-11pm; 👪) Right on the water with some plush seat-ing, breezes, plenty of hip clientele and lots of choices from *mei titi* to Japanese food, pizza and ice cream.

Cafe Dapoer Sulawesi   CAFE $

(cnr Jl Pasar Ikan & Jl Supratman; meals from 20,000Rp; 🛜) Slightly stylish corner cafe has excellent coffees, a shady wrap-around terrace and good juices.

Kios Semarang   SEAFOOD $$

(Jl Penghibur; mains 15,000-40,000Rp; ⊙ noon-11pm) At the closest thing to a Makassar institution, climb the stairs to the 3rd floor where you will be rewarded with a rowdy expat crowd, good seafood and cheap beer. Start with a sunset and a Bintang.

ℹ Information

Countless banks with ATMs are found on the main streets along the waterfront.

ℹ Getting There & Away

AIR

Makassar's slick and modern airport (code UPG) is well connected to the rest of Indonesia. Airlines and services change often.

BOAT

Pelni (www.pelni.co.id; Jl Sam Ratulangi; ⊙ 8am-2pm Mon-Sat) has connections to countless destinations across Indonesia, including Surabaya, Jakarta, East Kalimantan, Ambon and Papua.

BUS

Buses heading north leave from Terminal Panaikang, aka Terminal Daya, in the eastern suburbs. There are numerous services to Rantepao (from 80,000Rp, eight hours) in Tana Toraja. Get to the terminal with a *pete-pete* (minibus) from Makassar Mall (3000Rp, 30 minutes).

ℹ Getting Around

Hasanuddin airport is 22km east of the city centre, 100,000Rp by taxi or 5000Rp by *pete-pete*. The main *pete-pete* station is at Makassar Mall, and the base fare is 2000Rp. Becak drivers/hawkers can be charming and exhausting all at once. Their shortest fare is a negotiable 10,000Rp. Taxis are metered.

Tana Toraja

Get ready for a dizzying cocktail of stunningly serene beauty, elaborate, brutal and disturbing funeral rites, exquisite traditional architecture and a profoundly peculiar fascination with the dead. It comes garnished with a pinch of Indiana Jones intrigue and is served by some of the warmest and toughest people you'll ever meet: the Torajans. Life for the Torajans revolves around death and their days are spent earning the money to send away their dead properly. During funeral season, in July and August, the tourist numbers swell and prices soar, but the rest of the year it's nearly empty, which means grateful hosts, good deals and a frontier-like appeal.

The capital, Makale, and Rantepao, the largest town and tourist magnet, are the main centres. Bemos link them to surrounding villages, where you'll find cultural hot spots tucked into spectacular countryside.

Rantepao

📋 0423 / POP 49,000

With a variety of lodgings, Rantepao is the best base for exploring Tana Toraja. There is one unforgettable sight: **Pasar Bolu**, the market 2km northeast of town. It peaks every six days, overflowing with livestock. The main market is a very big, social occasion that draws crowds from all over Tana Toraja.

🏃 Activities

Plan on spending your days exploring this captivating region. Guides charge 300,000Rp to 400,000Rp per day. In addition, motorbikes cost about 70,000Rp per day; a guide with a car for up to four people costs 600,000Rp per day. You'll get to some of the most interesting places by foot or motorbike, although improving roads have made much accessible by car.

Be sure to hire a Torajan guide, as interlopers won't have the same access and sensitivity to funerals and other cultural events. A good contact for guides is **Elda Tato** (📋 0813 5523 9856), who speaks excellent English. Guides will also inevitably find you.

To fully immerse yourself in Toraja land, trek off the main roads. Good footwear is vital and so is ample food, water, a torch (flashlight; some villages lack electricity) and rain gear. If you desire a professional trekking outfitter, contact **Indosella** (📋 0813 4250 5301, 0423-25210; www.sellatours.com; Jl Andi Mappanyukki 111), which also organises complex tours and white-water rafting trips (from 700,000Rp for two people).

For a brilliant day trek, take a morning bemo to Deri, then veer off-road and traverse the incredible cascading rice fields all the way to Tikala. Farmers and villagers will help point the way, but a guide would be a wise decision for this trek.

Another good day trek starts in the hills at Batutumonga and follows rice fields back to

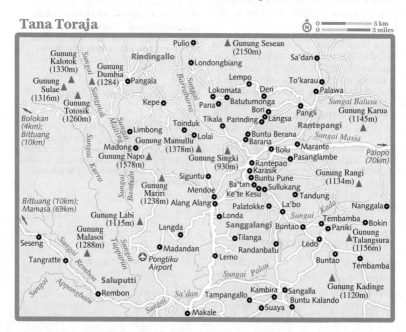

Tana Toraja

0 —— 5 km
0 —— 3 miles

Rantepao. Popular multiday treks include the following:

➡ Batumonga–Lokomata–Pangala–Baruppu–Pulu Pulu–Sapan; three days.

➡ Bittuang–Mamasa; three days.

➡ Pangala–Bolokan–Bittuang; two days on a well-marked trail.

🛏 Sleeping

Wisma Maria I   GUESTHOUSE $
(📋 0423-21165; adespasaka1@yahoo.com; Jl Sam Ratulangi 23; s/d from 130,000/160,000Rp) At our favourite rock-bottom cheapie in the town centre, rooms are plain but good-sized, bright and very clean. This place also rents out scooters and bicycles and they can suggest itineraries. It's all set around a large garden.

Wisma Imanuel   GUESTHOUSE $
(📋 0423-21416; Jl W Monginsidi 16; r 150,000-200,000Rp) Set in a large house backed by the river (but there's no access), the seven rooms here are a generous size and the more expensive include hot-water showers. Big balconies out front offer views over the garden and street action beyond.

Hotel Pison   HOTEL $
(📋 0423-21344; s/d 130,000/160,000Rp; 🖥) The bland but good-value Pison has 32 rooms, each with a clean bathroom and mini balcony with mountain views. All rooms come with hot water.

Hotel Indra Toraja   HOTEL $$
(📋 0423-21163; www.indratorajahotel.com; Jl Landorundun 63; r 250,000-700,000Rp; ❄🖥) Right in the centre of Rantepao, rooms here are in good shape and have terraces overlooking a common courtyard area. All are clean, have hot water and HBO, breakfasts are good and the service is stellar. It's a busy, happy place.

Wisma Monika   GUESTHOUSE $$
(📋 0423-21216; 36 Jl Sam Ratulangi; r 250,000-350,000Rp) A very friendly family-run central spot with 16 rooms in a modern cement building. Inspect a few to find a bright one.

🍴 Eating

The best-known dish is *pa'piong* (meat stuffed into bamboo tubes along with vegetables and coconut). Order in advance and enjoy it with black rice.

Gazebo   TORAJAN $
(Jl Abdul Gani; meals 20,000-40,000Rp; ⊙ 8am-10pm) The nicest setting for a meal in town is at this carved rice barn-style place with a front garden and a semi-outdoor eating area. The menu is mostly Indonesian with plenty of Torajan specialities that need to be ordered a few hours in advance.

Rimiko Restoran   WESTERN, INDONESIAN $
(📋 0423-25223; Jl Andi Mappanyukki; dishes from 20,000Rp; ⊙ 8am-10pm) A popular tourist-oriented restaurant, it has a few Torajan specialities on the menu that don't require ordering in advance. It's two doors down from the Indosella office.

Rumah Makan Saruran   INDONESIAN CHINESE $
(Jl Diponegoro 19; mains around 20,000Rp; ⊙ 8am-10pm) Indonesian-style Chinese food is served at this hopping restaurant that's popular with young travelling Indonesians. The atmosphere is basic but the food is good and cheap.

ℹ Information

Jl Diponegoro has banks, internet places and ATMs. Bring sunscreen, as none is sold locally.

Government Tourist Office (📋 0423-21277; Jl Ahmad Yani 62A; ⊙ 9am-2pm Mon-Sat) Staff provide accurate, independent information about local ceremonies, festivals and other activities and arrange guides.

ℹ Getting There & Away

BUS

Companies are clustered in the town centre along Jl Andi Mappanyukki. Numerous companies compete for business and note that higher fares get you more leg room and better suspension – which sounds trivial until you actually travel the local roads.

BUSES FROM RANTEPAO

DESTINATION	COST (RP)	DURATION (HR)
Makassar	80,000-150,000	8
Poso	130,000	12
Tentena	110,000Rp	10

TORAJA CULTURE

The local culture in Tana Toraja is among the world's most unique and distinctive. That the people are genuinely welcoming of visitors makes it unmissable.

Architecture

Traditional *tongkonan* houses – shaped like boats or buffalo horns, with the roof rearing up at the front and back – are the enduring image of Tana Toraja. They are similar to the Batak houses of Sumatra's Danau Toba and are always aligned north–south, with small rice barns facing them.

A number of villages are still composed entirely of these traditional houses, but most now have corrugated-iron roofs. The houses are painted and carved with animal motifs, and buffalo skulls often decorate the front, symbolising wealth and prestige.

Burial Customs

The Toraja generally have two funerals, one immediately after the death and a second, more elaborate, four-day ceremony after enough cash has been raised. Between the two ceremonies, the dead will live at home in the best room of the house and visitors will be obliged to sit, chat and have coffee with them. Regularly. This all ends once buffalo are sacrificed (one for a commoner, as many as 24 for a high-ranking figure) and the spirit soars to the afterlife.

The expenses associated with funerals are *the* major expense for locals. People keep careful track of who brings what to ceremonies (gifts are often announced to the funeral throngs over a loudspeaker) and an offering considered 'cheap' is cause for great shame. A run-of-the-mill buffalo costs 25 million rupiah, while the most prized animals (with white heads and perfect hides) cost 80 million rupiah – about the same as a new house.

To deter the plundering of generous burial offerings, the Toraja started to hide their dead in caves or on rocky cliff faces. You can often see *tau tau* – life-sized, carved wooden effigies of the dead – sitting in balconies on rock faces, guarding the coffins. Descendents are obliged to change and update their fake deceased relatives clothing regularly.

Funeral ceremonies are the region's main tourist attraction. Visitors are welcomed to the multiday affairs and are shown great hospitality, including tea and snacks. In return your guide will advise you on what modest gifts to bring (cigarettes and snacks in lieu of, say, a buffalo). The ritual slaughter of buffalo, pigs and other animals is grisly, often inhumane and is disturbing to many.

Ceremonies & Festivals

The end of the rice harvest, from around May onwards, is ceremony time in Tana Toraja. These festivities involve feasting and dancing, buffalo fights and *sisemba* kick-boxing. Guides will also take you to these ceremonies.

CAR

A car and driver between Makassar and Rantepao costs from 500,000Rp and takes six hours. Make arrangements with your accommodation at either end. Cars seat up to five, so this can be a good bus alternative.

ⓘ Getting Around

Kijangs leave for Makale (5000Rp, 30 minutes) constantly, and will drop you at the signs for Londa, Tilanga or Lemo to walk to the villages. From Terminal Bolu, 2km northeast of Rantepao, frequent vehicles go east to Palopo, and regular bemos and *kijangs* go to all the major villages, such as Lempo (near Batutumonga).

Motorbikes can be rented from hotels and tour agencies for 70,000Rp per day.

Around Rantepao

On day trips from Rantepao there's the beautiful – stunning panoramas, magical bamboo forests and rice terraces, shaped by natural boulders and fed by waterfalls, that drop for 2000m; there's the strange – *tau tau* (wooden effigies) of long-lost relatives guarding graves carved out of vertical limestone rock faces or hung from the roof of deep caves; and there's the intermingling of the two – incredibly festive and colourful four-day funerals where buffalo are slaughtered and stewed, palm wine is swilled from bamboo carafes and a spirit soars to the afterlife.

SOUTH OF RANTEPAO

Karasik (1km from Rantepao) is on the outskirts of town, just off the road leading to Makale. The traditional houses were erected years ago for a funeral.

Just off the main road, southeast of Rantepao, Ke'te Kesu (6km) is famed for its woodcarving. On the cliff face behind the village are cave graves and some very old hanging graves – the rotting coffins are suspended from an overhang.

Located about 2km off the Rantepao–Makale road, Londa (6km) is an extensive burial cave, one of the most interesting in the area. Above the cave is a line-up of *tau tau* that peer down, in fresh clothes, from their cliffside perch. Inside the dank darkness, coffins hang above dripping stalagmites. Others lie rotting on the stone floor, exposing skulls and bones.

Lemo (11km) is among the largest burial areas in Tana Toraja. The sheer rock face has dozens of balconies for *tau tau*. There would be even more *tau tau* if they weren't in such demand by unscrupulous antique dealers who deal in bad karma. A bemo from Rantepao will drop you off at the road leading up to the burial site, from where it's a 15-minute walk.

EAST OF RANTEPAO

Marante (6km) is a traditional village right by the road east to Palopo, near rice fields and stone and hanging graves guarded by *tau tau*. Further off the Palopo road, Nanggala (16km) has a grandiose traditional house with 14 rice barns. Charter a bemo from Rantepao, and you can be taken straight here, or take a public one, and walk 7km from the Palopo road.

NORTH & WEST OF RANTEPAO

This is where you'll find the finest scenery in Tana Toraja. Batutumonga (20km) has an ideal panoramic perch, sensational sunrise views and a few homestays. The best is Mentirotiku (☑ 081 342 579588; r from 300,000Rp). The views are even more stunning from the summit of Gunung Sesean, a 2150m peak towering above the village. Most bemos stop at Lempo, an easy walk from Batutumonga.

There are more cave graves and beautiful scenery at Lokomata (26km), just a few kilometres west past Batutumonga.

The return to Rantepao is an interesting and easy trek down the slopes through tiny villages to Pana, with its ancient hanging graves, and baby graves in the trees. The path ends at Tikala, where regular bemos go to Rantepao.

The three-day, 59km trek from Mamasa in the west to Bittuang is popular, and there are plenty of villages en route with food and accommodation (remember to bring gifts). Morning buses link Rantepao and Mamasa (150,000Rp), taking 12 hours because the roads are appalling. SUVs tackle the legs from Mamasa to Ponding (where you overnight) and then on to Bittuang. Each segment costs 150,000Rp and takes three hours.

MAKALE & AROUND

The Makale Market, held every six days, is one of the region's best.

One of the most stunning sights in Tana Toraja is the *tau tau* at Tampangallo, between Sangalla and Suaya, which is 6km east of Makale. The graves belong to the chiefs of Sangalla, descendants of the mythical divine being Tamborolangiq, who is believed to have introduced the caste system, death rituals and agricultural techniques into Torajan society. Take a *kijang* from Makale to Sangalla, get off about 1km after the turn-off to Suaya, and walk a short distance (less than a kilometre) through the rice fields to Tampangallo.

Tentena

☑ 0458 / POP 13,000

This lakeside town of white picket fences and churches is a good place to break your bus journey north from Rantepao. Surrounded by clove-covered hills, it's a peaceful and very easy-to-manage town.

The price is right, service is good and the 18 rooms are clean at the popular Hotel Victory (☑ 0458-21392; Jl Diponegoro 18; r 150,000-250,000Rp; ✳). Only the higher-end rooms have air-con. This is a good spot to meet guides. Buses make the run to Poso (40,000Rp, two hours) throughout the day.

Poso

☑ 0452 / POP 48,000

Poso is the main town, port and terminal for road transport on the northern coast of Central Sulawesi. It's a spread out, noisy place and there's little reason to stay besides to hit up an ATM, change money, shop or change buses. Services are few until Manado.

Losmen Alugoro (☑0452-324735; Jl P Sumatra 20; s/d 65,000/90,000Rp, d with air-con 130,000-200,000Rp; ❋) is a reliably decent yet simple place that's central to the bus offices.

Buses leave the terminal, 800m north of the post office, for Tentena (40,000Rp, two hours), Ampana (minibus 75,000Rp, five hours) and Rantepao (130,000Rp, 12 hours).

Ampana

☑0464

Ampana is the gateway to the Togeans. Given bus and ferry schedules, you will likely spend a night here.

Oasis Hotel (☑0464-21058; Jl Kartini; r with fan/air-con from 120,000/200,000Rp; ❋ 🛜) has 17 clean rooms and dorms, but don't expect to sleep till the karaoke shuts down at 11pm. The most expensive rooms include air-con and hot water. It's near the Togean Islands boat dock.

Minibuses travel each day to Luwuk (120,000Rp, seven hours) and Poso (minibus 75,000Rp, five hours).

Togean Islands

Yes, it does take some determination to get to the Togean Islands, but believe us, it takes much more determination to leave. Island hop from one forested golden-beach beauty to the next, where hammocks are plentiful, the fish is fresh and the welcome is homely. There are lost lagoons and forgotten coves, and arguably the best diving in Sulawesi (which ranks it near the top worldwide). Plunge into crystal-clear, bottomless seas to explore all three major reef systems – atoll, barrier and fringing. Colours absolutely pop. Fish are everywhere.

🛈 Getting There & Away

Getting boat information in advance of a trip to the Togeans can be a challenge. Your best option is to contact the place you intend to stay at and let them advise you. If you are travelling the length of Sulawesi, try to go from Ampana to the Togeans to Gorontolo (or the reverse), which will save you the endless land journey via Palu.

FROM THE SOUTH

Boats depart Saturday to Thursday from Ampana to Wakai, the Togeans' hub (about 50,000Rp, three hours) and usually make other stops in the islands.

FROM THE NORTH

Overnight boats from Gorontalo to Wakai cost 75,000Rp (cabins 350,000Rp), take 12 hours and run a couple of times per week.

🛈 Getting Around

Charters around the Togeans are easily arranged in Wakai, Bomba, Kadidiri and through your accommodation (about 300,000Rp).

Pulau Kadidiri

This is definitely the island if you're feeling social, but during the low season you could potentially wind up on your own here. Just a short boat trip from Wakai, the three lodging options (all right next to each other) are on a perfect strip of sand with OK snorkelling and swimming, and superb diving beyond.

🛏 Sleeping & Eating

Hotels usually provide transport from Wakai. Rates usually include all meals.

Pondok Lestari   GUESTHOUSE $
(☑0464-22304; www.lestari.ladz.de; cottages 125,000-175,000Rp) Stay with a charming Bajau family who take their guests on free daily snorkelling trips and fishing excursions where you can catch your own dinner. Both the older bamboo bungalows and newer wooden ones are pretty rustic but the setting is dreamy.

Kadidiri Paradise Resort   RESORT $$
(☑0464-21058; www.kadidiriparadise.com; r 200,000-300,000Rp) This resort on stunning planted grounds nearly surrounded by water is Kadidiri's poshest option. Rooms are huge and all have generous decks and big stone bathrooms. The dive centre is particularly well run.

Togean Island & Around

The main settlement on Togean Island is the very relaxed Katupat village, which has a small market and a couple of shops. Around the island there are magical beaches, and some decent hikes for anyone sick of swimming, snorkelling and diving.

🛏 Sleeping

Fadhila Cottages   GUESTHOUSE $
(☑0813 4117 9990; fadhilacottage@gmail.com; full board per person 250,000-300,000Rp) Clean wooden bungalows with terraces line a palm-shaded beach that faces Katupat Village. There's a good

dive centre here; take a free canoe to find snorkelling spots around the island.

Pulau Batu Daka

BOMBA

This tiny outpost at the southeastern end of Pulau Batu Daka has nearby reefs and exquisite beaches.

Island Retreat (✆ 0852 4115 8853, 0868 1101 7582; www.togian-island-retreat.com; Bomba; r per person US$25-28) is run by an expat Californian woman and her band of friendly dogs. Set on the beautiful beach at Pasir Putih, the 20 cottages are well cared for and the food is great. There's a dive centre here; staff are good at arranging transport from afar.

WAKAI

The Togeans' largest settlement is a departure point for ferries to Ampana and Gorontalo and for charters to Pulau Kadidiri and beyond. There are a few general stores if you need supplies, but there's no reason to stay the night.

Gorontalo

✆ 0435 / POP 155,000

The port of Gorontalo has the feel of an overgrown country town, where all the locals seem to know each other. The town features some of the best-preserved Dutch houses in Sulawesi; it offers the best services north of Poso.

★ **Melati Hotel** (✆ 0435-822934; avelberg@hotmail.com; Jl Gajah Mada 33; r 130,000-400,000Rp; ❄@🖥) is a longtime traveller favourite. It's based around a lovely home, built in the early 1900s. The 14 rooms in the original house are basic but atmospheric; the newer rooms are set around a pretty garden.

❶ Getting There & Away

Lion Air (www.lionair.co.id) has daily flights from Manado (40 minutes). Several carriers fly from Makassar (90 minutes).

The main bus terminal is 3km north of town. There are direct buses to Manado (from 80,000Rp, 10 hours); minibuses/minivans are more comfortable and cost from 150,000Rp.

Manado

✆ 0431 / POP 420,000

Once described by anthropologist Alfred Russel Wallace as 'one of the prettiest

[cities] in the East', Manado has sold its soul to commerce. However, it remains a necessary base for exploring North Sulawesi.

Along Jl Sam Ratulangi, the main north–south artery, you'll find restaurants, hotels and supermarkets. The flash shopping-mall blitz dominates parallel Jl Pierre Tendean (aka 'The Boulevard') and continues right to the waterfront.

🛏 Sleeping

Rex Hotel   HOTEL **$**
(✆ 0431-851136; Jl Sugiono 3; r 115,000-140,000Rp; ❄) These are the best budget rooms in town: all are clean but there is lots of noise via the road, other guests and thin walls. Shared-bathroom economy rooms are microscopic, but standards with private bathrooms are quite comfortable.

★ **Hotel Minahasa**   HOTEL **$$**
(✆ 0431-874871; www.hotelminahasa.com; Jl Sam Ratulangi 199; r with fan/air-con from 235,000/380,000Rp; ❄🖥🏊) Manado's answer to a boutique hotel has flower-filled grounds stretching up the hill to a luxurious pool and fitness centre with city views. Fan rooms are basic and you may be tempted to upgrade to a much more elegant, superior room with a terrace and a view.

Hotel Regina   HOTEL **$$**
(✆ 0431-850090; Jl Sugiono 1; r incl breakfast from 220,000Rp; ❄🖥) Some 33 bland but big rooms here are spotless and very plush for the price. The included Indonesian breakfasts make this a great deal and it's often full.

🍴 Eating

Adventurous Minahasan cuisine can be found around Manado. Get a taste for *rica-rica*, a spicy stir-fry made with *ayam* (chicken), *babi* (pork) or even *r.w.* (pronounced 'air weh' – dog!). *Bubur tinotuan* (corn porridge) and fresh seafood are local specialities worth looking out for.

Most malls have extensive food courts on their upper floors. The best ones are those at Mega Mall and Bahu Mall.

Singapura Bakery   JAVANESE **$**
(Jl Sam Ratulangi 22; snacks from 5000Rp) Has a mind-boggling array of baked goods, fresh juices and shakes, plus a popular cheap cafe next door serving Javanese fare.

❶ Information

You're never far from a bank and ATM.

❶ Getting There & Around

AIR

Mikrolets (minibuses) from Sam Ratulangi International Airport go to Terminal Paal 2 (4000Rp), where you can change to a *mikrolet* heading to Pasar 45 or elsewhere in the city for a flat fee of 2500Rp. Fixed-price taxis cost 100,000Rp for the trip from the airport to the city (13km).

Manado is well connected by air. Airlines have offices at the airport.

BOAT

Pelni (www.pelni.co.id) ships use the deep-water port of Bitung, 55km from Manado. Service includes Ternate, Ambon, Sorong, Luwuk and other ports along the southeastern coast.

BUS

Terminal Malalayang (far south of the city) has service to Gorontalo (from 80,000Rp, 10 hours); minibuses/minivans are more comfortable and cost from 150,000Rp.

PUBLIC TRANSPORT

There's no *mikrolet* shortage in Manado. Destinations are shown on a card in the front windscreen. There are various bus stations around town for destinations outside Manado; get to any of them from Pasar 45, the main traffic circle near the harbour. Bluebird taxis use their meters.

Pulau Bunaken

Pulau Bunaken is Sulawesi's top destination: 300 varieties of pristine coral and 3000 species of fish in **Bunaken Manado Tua Marine National Park** draw acolytes from around the globe. Tourist accommodation is spread out along two beaches and there is a delightful island vibe, thanks especially to the lovely locals. When not on the water, you can wander the lush paths alongside the mangroves.

🏃 Activities

Snorkellers are rewarded with rich reefs close to the surface; divers have a menu of choices from muck to drop-offs. The Bunaken park fee is 50,000Rp per day or 150,000Rp for an annual pass. Trips around Bunaken and nearby islands will cost from US$70 for two dives. Whole schools of dive operators are at the resorts and most people usually go with the outfit native to where they're staying. The **North Sulawesi Watersports Association** (NSWA; www.divenorthsulawesi.com) has info and promotes green initiatives.

🍽 Sleeping & Eating

Pantai Liang, to the west, is remote from the rest of the island and has a beautiful stretch of sand. Pantai Pangalisang, near Bunaken village, is the eco choice. There's no beach to lie on, but it overlooks an armada of stately mangrove trees closer to Bunaken village, and the nearby reef is ideal for snorkelling. Most hotels quote rates per person for full board. Stroll around for simple places under 200,000Rp per night.

🍽 Pantai Pangalisang

Lorenso's Beach Garden GUESTHOUSE $
(📞 0852 5697 3345; www.lorensobunaken.com; r & bungalows €16-35) Fun-filled Lorenso's has simple wood rooms and flashier, more private bungalows. Meals invariably involve lots of fresh fish, some of the island's best snorkelling is just through the mangroves.

Daniel's Homestay GUESTHOUSE $
(📞 0852 4086 1716; www.immanueldivers.com; bungalows from 170,000Rp; 🛜) This is a busy but relaxing place with plenty of mingling with locals and dive-tired backpackers. Wood cottages in a mature flower-filled garden are very basic but spacious.

★ Living Colours DIVE RESORT $$
(📞 0812 430 6401; www.livingcoloursdiving.fi; cottages from €50; @🛜) By far the most comfortable choice on this main strip of beach, this Finnish-run place has wooden bungalows with enormous terraces, stylish furniture clad in drapy white fabrics and spacious hot-water bathrooms. It's perched up on a little hill and both the food and service are fantastic.

🍽 Pantai Liang

Panorama GUESTHOUSE $
(📞 0813 4021 7306, 0813 4021 7027; www.bunakendiving.wordpress.com; cottages from 150,000Rp; 🛜) Tucked in corner up on a hillside, the basic wood bungalows with terraces and commanding views are one of the best budget deals on the island. It's a friendly, family-style place that now includes a second property nearby.

ℹ Getting There & Away

Every day between 2pm and 3pm (except Sunday), a public boat leaves Manado harbour, near Pasar Jengki fish market, for Bunaken village and Pulau Siladen (50,000Rp, one hour). A charter speedboat costs at least 250,000Rp to 400,000Rp one way (bargain hard). Many places to stay will also arrange transport.

Tomohon

Pleasantly cool and lush, this popular weekend escape from Manado rests at the foot of the regularly erupting Gunung Lokon in the Minahasa Highlands. It is renowned for its beauty and its market, which reaches its lurid peak on Saturdays when all manner of species are sold for food. *Mikrolets* travel frequently to Tomohon (7000Rp, 40 minutes) from Manado's Karombasan terminal.

MALUKU

Welcome to the original 'spice islands'. Back in the 16th century when nutmeg, cloves and mace were global commodities that grew nowhere else, Maluku was a place where money really did grow on trees. Today the spices have minimal economic clout and Maluku (formerly known as 'the Moluccas') has dropped out of global consciousness. The region is protected from mass tourism by distance, unpredictable transport and memories of a brief if tragically destructive period of ethnic conflict between 1999 and 2002 (with occasional ongoing echoes).

While transport can prove infuriatingly inconvenient, given flexibility and patience you can visit the amazing Bandas, with their beaches, nutmeg forests and ruined Dutch fortresses.

Maluku

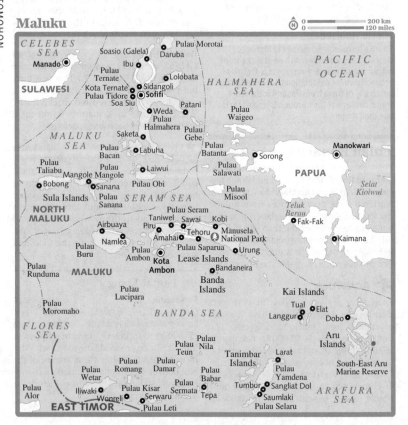

ⓘ Getting There & Around

Ambon is the region's air hub. There are flights daily to Jakarta and Makassar, which is a good place to transfer for other points on Sulawesi and Bali. There are also connections to Papua.

Ambon is a hub for Pelni services.

Pulau Ambon

Pulau Ambon is ribboned with villages, dressed in shimmering foliage and defined by two great bays. This is your launch pad to the Bandas, but also a charming retreat and diving base in its own right. Although at times a source of friction, the close proximity of Christian churches – often filled with hymn-singing parishioners – and mosques is an interesting study of Indonesian multiculturalism.

Kota Ambon

☑ 0911 / POP 335,000

By the region's dreamy tropical standards, Maluku's capital, commercial centre and transport hub is a busy, regional centre. Sights are minimal (although look for the odd mouldering colonial pile) but it does retain a languid charm. And its waterfront location can't be beaten.

🛏 Sleeping & Eating

Browse Jl Diponegoro and Jl Said Perintah for good eats. Accommodation clusters in the compact centre.

Penginapan Asri   GUESTHOUSE $
(☑ 0911-311217; Jl Baru 33; r 120,000-170,000Rp; ❄) Many rooms lack natural light, but the Asri is very central and much better kept than most other hotels in this price range. More expensive rooms have hot water and air-con. All have private baths.

Hotel Mutiara   HOTEL $$
(☑ 0911-353075; www.hotelmutiaraambon.com; Jl Pattimura 12; r 350,000-450,000Rp; ❄🌐) Behind a dainty curtain of tropical foliage, and a bit stodgier and more lived in than the upstart newbies nearby. Rooms have wooden floors, bathtubs, crown mouldings and framed *ikat* on the walls.

★**Sibu-Sibu**   CAFE
(☑ 0911-312525; Jl Said Perintah 47A; snacks from 3000Rp, breakfasts from 20,000Rp; ⊘7am-10pm; 🌐) Portraits of Ambon-born stars deck the walls of this sweet little coffee shop, which plays Malukan music and has tourist info.

It serves local snacks such as the wonderful *koyabu* (cassava cake), fried breadfruit that you'll dip into melted palm sugar, and rocket-fueled ginger coffee.

Ratu Gurih   SEAFOOD $$
(☑081343388883; Jl Diponegoro 26; meals 50,000-100,000Rp; ⊘10am-10pm; 🌐) It has fluorescent tiles and the atmosphere is simple, but the fish is perfectly grilled, smothered in chilli and served alongside tasty sambals. Try the lobster-like *Udang Net.*

ⓘ Information

Change or withdraw enough money in Kota Ambon for trips to outlying islands where there are no exchange facilities whatsoever.

Michael Erenst (☑0813 4302 8872; erenst_michael@yahoo.co.id) Highly helpful fixer, usually found working the info desk at the airport. Works with Banda guesthouses on transport logistics for guests. Can arrange very basic homestays near the airport (about 100,000Rp).

ⓘ Getting There & Away

Pattimura airport is 37km round the bay from central Kota Ambon. By road it can take an hour although a new bridge will drastically cut this when complete. An *ojek* costs about 5000Rp, a taxi 150,000Rp.

There is also an **airport bus** (per person 30,000Rp) that leaves from the Peace Gong in the city centre three times daily at 5am, 10am and 1pm. It runs to Ambon when the main jet flights arrive.

Garuda (www.garuda-indonesia.com) Daily flights to Surabaya and Jakarta.

Lion Air/Wings Air (www.lionair.co.id) Daily flights include Makassar and Jakarta.

Pelni (www.pelni.co.id) Has an office opposite the Pattimura Memorial. Boats depart for much of the region from Yos Sudarso harbour.

LEIHITU

The portion of land across the bay from Ambon, Leihitu is much more than just the location of the airport. It has beaches and historic places of genuine interest, especially if you are having transport challenges and need to kill time. Chartering a car and driver will cost about 350,000Rp for a half day's touring of Ambon's most picturesque and archetypal coastal villages. In **Hila** the 1649 **Benteng Amsterdam** (20,000Rp; ⊘8am-6pm) retains hefty ramparts and a three-storey keep.

Banda Islands

📞 0910 / POP 23,000

This tiny yet historically fascinating cluster of 10 picturesque islands is Maluku's most inviting travel destination: a gathering of epic tropical gems, with deserted stretches of white sand and crescent bays. In the 1990s they briefly blipped onto the backpacker radar and have now faded back into glorious anonymity. Which means you'll have the beaches and those stark undersea drop-offs draped in technicolour coral gardens to yourself.

The Dutch and the English wrestled for control of these islands for several centuries (beginning in the 1600s) all because of nutmeg, which is native to the islands and once commanded extravagant prices in Europe. The legacy of this era is everywhere, with ruined forts, evocative colonial buildings and still-thriving plantations.

Snorkelling – often from various deserted beaches – is richly rewarding. **Blue Motion Dive Center** (📞0812 4714 3922; www.dive-blue motion.com; Bandaneira; 2 dives from 800,000Rp; ☉Aug-May) is both good and the only option for exploring the fabled local dive sites.

ℹ Getting There & Around

The biggest problem when visiting the Bandas is transport. Fortunately the recommended guesthouses are adept at making arrangements.

AIR

Merpati flies from Ambon two to three times a week. However, the flights are prone to cancellation and you may have to wait a week for another chance. Tickets are obtained in advance through your Banda guesthouse but are quite cheap (300,000Rp, one hour); make certain you reconfirm your seats right up to departure.

BOAT

Pelni (📞 0910-21196; Jl Kujali; ticket from 100,000Rp; ☉8.30am-1pm & 4-6pm Mon-Sat) has various ships that pass through sporadically. The run to/from Ambon takes seven to 12 hours. Ships are usually overcrowded (try to reserve a cabin) and, in the case of the *Kelimutu*, quite dirty.

Passenger longboats buzz between Bandaneira and Pulau Banda Besar (5000Rp) and Pulau Ai (20,000Rp). Guesthouses can arrange tours and boat charters (from 600,000Rp for a journey with stops to/from Pulau Ai).

Bandaneira

The main port of the Banda Islands, situated on Pulau Neira, is a friendly, pleasantly sleepy town. It's streets are lined with a stunning array of colonial buildings.

Stop by the impressive **Benteng Belgica**, built on the hill above Bandaneira in 1611. The fort's upper reaches have incredible views of **Gunung Api**. Several historic Dutch houses have been restored. Down in the flats, **Benteng Nassau** is a moody ruin.

🛏 Sleeping & Eating

Most accommodation is here in the Banda's main town, where there is also a couple of cafes. Three guesthouses stand out.

★**Mutiara Guesthouse** GUESTHOUSE $
(📞0813 3034 3377, 0910-21344; www.banda-mutiara.com; r with fan/air-con from 150,000/200,000Rp; dinner 80,000Rp; ☒@) Superb-value rooms and sturdy, classically styled furniture highlight this homestay run by the fantastically helpful Abba. Fabulous and convivial buffet dinners feature local foods and attract smart diners from other guesthouses.

Delfika GUESTHOUSE $
(📞0910-21027; delfika1@yahoo.com; r with fan 100,000-150,000Rp, with air-con 175,000-250,000Rp; ☒@) There are two locations. For great bay views, the spacious upstairs rooms at the **Delfika 2** annexe are hard to beat. The original Delfika has an old-world charm, with an atmospheric garden courtyard and a range of rooms, mostly well renovated, on a street of colonial relics. It has internet (per hour 15,000Rp).

Vita Guesthouse GUESTHOUSE $
(Fita; 📞0812 4706 7099, 0910-21332; allandarman@gmail.com; Jl Pasar; d with fan/air-con from 110,000/150,000Rp; ☒) It has seven comfortable rooms set in a colonnaded L-shape around a waterfront palm garden. The wonderful wooden jetty area is an ideal perch from which to gaze at Gunung Api while sipping a cold beer.

Other Islands

Pulau Banda Besar is the largest of the Banda islands, and the most important historical source of nutmeg. You can explore nutmeg groves or the ruins of fort **Benteng Hollandia** (c 1624). **Spice tours** (📞0813 3034 3377; tour 200,000Rp) by Abba of the Mutiara Guesthouse should not be missed.

Pulau Hatta has crystal waters and a mind-expanding, coral-encrusted vertical drop-off near Lama village.

PULAU TERNATE & TIDORE

The perfect volcanic cone of Ternate is an unforgettable sight. Pulau Tidore, Ternate's age-old, next-door rival, is a laid-back island of charming villages and empty beaches.

The dramatic volcanic cone of 1721m Gamalama *is* Pulau Ternate. Settlements are sprinkled around its lower coastal slopes, with villages on the east coast coalescing into North Maluku's biggest town, Kota Ternate. The city makes a useful transport gateway for the region, and neighbouring volcano islands look particularly photogenic viewed from the few remaining stilt-house neighbourhoods, colourful boats in the harbour or hillside restaurant terraces. It has three 17th-century Dutch forts that have been over-restored.

Gently charming Tidore makes a refreshing day-trip escape from the bustle of Ternate, its neighbour and implacable historical enemy. An independent Islamic sultanate from 1109, Tidore's sultanate was abolished in the Soekarno era, but the 36th sultan was reinstated in 1999. The island's proud volcanic profile looks especially magnificent viewed from Bastiong on Ternate.

Ternate has places to stay for all budgets strung out along its encircling, volcano-hugging ring road. It can be reached with **Lion Air/Wings Air** (www.lionair.co.id) from Manado and Ambon or by various Pelni ships.

Pulau Ai is also blessed with rich coral walls and postcard beaches. It has a few very simple homestays, from which you can explore the perfectly empty white-sand beaches. Simple guesthouses near the dock have fine views or enjoy pure tropical fantasy at **CDS Bungalow** (r per person incl meals 175,000-200,000Rp), which has two secluded rooms perched over a nearly deserted beach; book through Mutiara Guesthouse in Bandaneira. Furthest west, **Pulau Run** is mostly notable as the island the Dutch received from the English in return for Manhattan – guess who got the better deal?

PAPUA (IRIAN JAYA)

Even a country as full of adventure travel as Indonesia has to have its final frontier, and here it is – Papua, half of the world's second-biggest island, New Guinea. A land where numberless rivers rush down from 5km-high mountains to snake across sweating jungles populated by rainbow-hued birds of paradise and kangaroos that climb trees. Peaks are frosted with glaciers and snow-fields, and slopes and valleys are home to an array of exotic cultures (250 and counting), like the gourd-wearing Dani, wood carving Asmat warriors and tree house–dwelling Korowai. The coast is more modern, and more Indonesian feeling, unless you venture to the Raja Ampats, a remote archipelago where you can find empty beaches and, according to experts, the world's richest reefs.

Papua's history is no slouch either. The battle for the Pacific was decided here – with memorials and WWII wrecks to prove it. Indonesia didn't inherit Papua until 1963, when they named it Irian Jaya and immediately began capitalising on its abundant resources. This did not sit well with the Papuans, whose Free Papua Organisation (OPM) remains active. Many Papuans want to be free of Indonesian rule, but their chances of that seem slim now that Papua is home to over one million non-Papuans.

ℹ Getting There & Around

Papua is well connected by air with the rest of Indonesia, and with so few viable roads, flying is the only way to travel once you're here. The transport centres are Sorong (the biggest city on the bird's head–shaped west coast), Biak and Jayapura.

Garuda (www.garuda-indonesia.com), **Lion Air/Wings Air** (www2.lionair.co.id), **Merpati** (www.merpati.co.id) and **Expressair** (www.expressair.biz) are the main carriers to, from and within Papua.

Several Pelni boat liners link Papuan ports with Maluku, Sulawesi and Java every two or four weeks.

Jayapura

♪ 0967 / ELEVATION 139M / POPULATION 149,000

Most residents are Indonesian and street life pulses to their rhythm, but the environment is all Papua. Dramatic jade hills cradle the city on three sides, while the gorgeous

Papua (Irian Jaya)

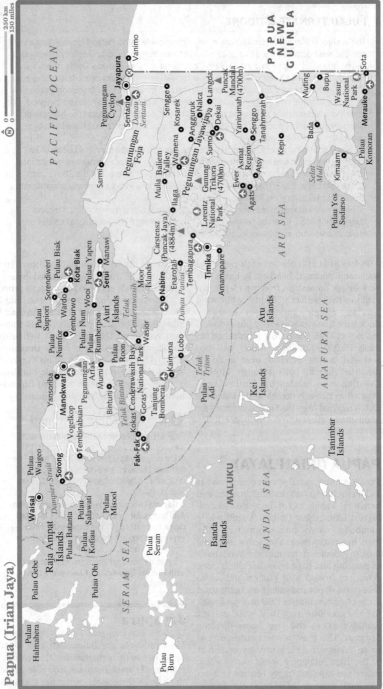

250 km
150 miles

PACIFIC OCEAN

PAPUA NEW GUINEA

Vanimo
Jayapura
Sentani
Danau Sentani
Pegunungan Cyclop
Sengge
Kosarek
Langda
Puncak Mandala (4700m)
Muting
Bupu
Sota
Merauke
Wasur National Park
Pegunungan Foja
Mulia
Baliem Valley
Wamena
Angguruk
Nalca
Dekai
Sumo
Yanirumah
Senggo
Tanahmerah
Kepi
Bada
Sarmi
Ilaga
Pegunungan Jayawijaya
Gunung Trikora (4700m)
Asmat Region
Ewer
Agats
Atsy
Pulau Komoran
Pulau Yos Sudarso
Selat Muli
Carstensz (Puncak Jaya) (4884m)
Lorentz National Park
Tembagapura
Timika
Amamapare
ARU SEA
Kimaam
Sorendiweri
Pulau Biak
Kota Biak
Pulau Yapen
Manawi
Serui
Pulau Num
Wooi
Nabire
Enarotali
Danau Paniai
ARAFURA SEA
Pulau Supiori
Wardo
Yemburwo
Auri Islands
Rumberpon
Moor Islands
Aru Islands
Pulau Numfor
Pulau
Wasior
Pulau Room
Teluk Cenderawasih
Aru Islands
Kaimana
Lobo
Teluk Triton
Pulau Adi
Kei Islands
Tanimbar Islands
Yansoriba
Manokwari
Mumi
Pegunungan Arfak
Bintuni
Teluk Bintuni
Tanjung Bomberai
Goras National Park
Kokas
Cenderawasih Bay
Fak-Fak
Sorong
Vogelkop
Tembinabuan
BANDA SEA
MALUKU
Pulau Seram
SERAM SEA
Banda Islands
Pulau Buru
Waisai
Raja Ampat Islands
Pulau Waigeo
Dampier Strait
Pulau Batanta
Pulau Kofiau
Pulau Salawati
Pulau Misool
Pulau Gebe
Pulau Obi
Pulau Halmahera

Teluk Yos Sudarso kisses the north coast. Unless you're headed to PNG, it's not necessary to stay here, as the airport is in nearby Sentani, which has all the services. But Jayapura has more soul.

◎ Sights

Museum Loka Budaya   MUSEUM
(Jl Abepura, Abepura; donation suggested; ⊙7.30am-4pm Mon-Fri) **FREE** Cenderawasih University's cultural museum contains a fascinating range of Papuan artefacts between 80 and 300 years old, including a superb collection of Asmat carvings and 'devil-dance' costumes, plus fine crafts from several other areas, historical photos and musical instruments. With luck you'll be guided round by an English-speaking staff member and learn a lot about Papuan culture. The museum is next to the large Auditorium Universitas Cenderawasih on the main road in Abepura.

⊨ Sleeping & Eating

Amabel Hotel   HOTEL $
(☑0967-522 102; Jl Tugu 100; s 198,000Rp, d 242,000-297,000Rp; ❄🛜) Easily the best budget option, the Amabel has neat little rooms with windows and its own inexpensive little restaurant. With 26 rooms, it often has vacancies when other budget places don't. It's signposted from Jl Sam Ratulangi about 100m past the Base G *taksi* stop.

Hotel Papua   HOTEL $$
(☑0967-531889; Jl Percetakan 78; s 280,000Rp, d 410,000-450,000Rp; ❄) This place goes the extra decorating mile with colourful, even tasteful, murals and photos. It's well kept and there's a reasonable restaurant.

★ Duta Cafe   SEAFOOD $$
(Duta Dji Cafe; Jl Pasifik Permai; whole fish 40,000-60,000Rp, vegetable dishes 15,000-25,000Rp; ⊙5pm-2am) Long lines of evening *warungs* open along Jl Pasifik Permai, cooking up all sorts of Indonesian goodies, including seafood galore. At the large, clean Duta Cafe, halfway along the street, an excellent *ikan bakar* comes with five types of sambal lined up on your table, and the juice drinks go down very nicely.

Don't confuse this with another Duta Cafe further along near the Swiss-belhotel.

❶ Information

You'll find everything you need on Jl Ahmad Yani and the parallel Jl Percetakan. Jl Sam Ratulangi and Jl Koti front the bay.

Immigration Office (☑0967-533647; Jl Percetakan 15; ⊙8am-4pm Mon-Fri) This office will issue one 30-day extension to a visa on arrival (VOA) for 250,000Rp: apply at least one week before your visa expires. Travellers with VOAs must come here for a (free) exit stamp before crossing the land border to Vanimo, Papua New Guinea.

Polresta (Polda; Jl Yani 11; ⊙9am-3pm Mon-Fri) Police elsewhere in Papua will often only issue a *surat jalan* for their own regencies, but here you can get one for everywhere you want to go in Papua (that's not off limits).

❶ Getting There & Away

Jayapura airport (p294) is actually located in Sentani 36km west.

Pelni (☑0967-533270; www.pelni.co.id; Jl Argapura 15) liners leave Jayapura every two weeks bound for Sorong via intermediate ports – including Biak, Serui and Manokwari – and then on to Maluku and/or Sulawesi.

INDONESIA JAYAPURA

GETTING TO PAPUA NEW GUINEA: JAYAPURA TO VANIMO

Getting to the border There are no flights between Papua and Papua New Guinea, and the only route across the border that is open to foreigners is between Jayapura (northeast Papua) and Vanimo (northwest PNG, about 65km from Jayapura).

At the border Most visitors to PNG need a visa; the standard 60-day tourist visa (225,000Rp) can be obtained (after a three-day wait) at the **Papua New Guinea Consulate** (☑0967-531250; congenpng_id@yahoo.com; Jl Raya Argapura; ⊙9am-noon & 1-3pm Mon-Thu, variable hr Fri), 3km south of downtown Jayapura. You can charter a *taksi* from the market at Abepura (called Pasar Abepura or Pasar Yotefa), 13km south of downtown Jayapura, to the border at Wutung (1½ hours) for 250,000Rp to 400,000Rp.

Moving on Cross the border itself on foot then hire a car to Vanimo for about 10 to 15 kina (US$3.50 to US$5). Air Niugini links Vanimo with Port Moresby three times weekly.

VISITOR PERMITS (SURAT JALAN)

If you plan on venturing into remote Papua, you must obtain a *surat jalan,* a permission to travel, from the local police station *(polres)*. They are easiest to get in Jayapura. Take your passport, two passport photos, and one photocopy each of the passport pages showing your personal details and your Indonesian visa. The procedure normally takes about an hour with no payment requested.

List every conceivable place you might want to visit, as it might be difficult to add them later. As you travel around Papua, you are supposed to have the document stamped in local police stations. It is worth keeping a few photocopies of the permit in case police or hotels ask for them.

At the time of writing, you could visit Jayapura, Sentani, Pulau Biak and Sorong without a *surat jalan*. Elsewhere, get your papers in order.

Sentani

☑ 0967 / ELEVATION 289M

Sentani, the growing airport town 36km west of Jayapura, is set between the forested Pegunungan Cyclop and beautiful Danau Sentani. It's quieter, cooler and more convenient than Jayapura.

Don't miss the soul-soothing views of Danau Sentani from Tugu MacArthur. Most facilities are on Jl Kemiri Sentani Kota.

🛏 Sleeping & Eating

Hotel Minang Jaya   HOTEL $
(☑ 0967-591919; Jl Bestour Post 2; r 150,000-230,000Rp; ❄) It's well past its prime, but this budget hotel is kept reasonably clean. Upstairs rooms are brighter. The cheapest rooms share *mandis*; the most expensive have air-con.

Rasen Hotel   HOTEL $$
(☑ 0967-594455; rasenhotel_papua@yahoo.com; Jl Penerangan; r incl breakfast 230,000-345,000Rp; ❄🛜) The best choice near the airport, the Rasen has good-sized, clean rooms with hot showers and large-screen TVs, plus a decent restaurant, free airport drop offs and even a small fish pond.

Warung Maduratna   INDONESIAN $
(Jl PLN; meals 25,000-40,000Rp) An unassuming spot that does excellent chicken *sate* and *gado gado*, and they're happy for you to bring in a beer from the shop next door.

❶ Getting There & Away

Jayapura airport (☑ 591 809) is actually at Sentani. Airlines, most with Jayapura offices, include the following:

Expressair (www.expressair.biz) Flies to Sorong, Makassar and Jakarta.

Garuda (www.garuda-indonesia.com) Flies to Biak, Denpasar, Makassar and Jakarta.

Lion Air/Wings Air (http://www2.lionair.co.id) To Makassar, Merauke and Jakarta.

Merpati (www.merpati.co.id) Flies to Biak, Merauke, Makassar, Jakarta and Manado.

Getting to Sentani from Jayapura via public transport demands three different bemos, and 90 minutes. Taxis are pricey (200,000Rp, half-price outside the airport) but more direct.

Baliem Valley

The Baliem Valley is the most accessible gateway to tribal Papua. It's a place where *koteka* (penis gourds) are not yet out of fashion, pigs can buy love, sex or both, and the hills bloom with flowers and deep-purple sweet-potato fields.

Unless you land here during the August high season, when Wamena and nearby villages host a festival with pig feasts, mock wars and traditional dancing to attract the tourism buck, you will be outnumbered by Christian missionaries (a constant presence since the valley's 'discovery' in 1938) and Javanese *transmigrasi* (migrants through a resettling program).

You may also be startled by evidence of Indonesia's neocolonisation of Papua, but mostly you will marvel at the mountain views, roaring rivers, tribal villages and at the tough but sweet spirit of the warm Dani people.

Wamena

☑ 0969 / ELEV 1550M / POP 25,000

The commercial centre in the Baliem Valley, Wamena is dusty and sprawling, but the air is cool, purple mountains peek through billowy white clouds and local markets are enthralling. It's also a base from which to

HIKING & TREKKING IN THE BALIEM VALLEY

Beyond the reach of roads you come closer to traditional Dani life. In one day you may climb narrow rainforest trails, stroll well-graded paths past terraces of purple-leafed sweet-potato plants, wend through villages of grass-roofed *honai* (circular thatched huts), cross rivers on wobbly hanging footbridges, and traverse hillsides where the only sounds are birds, wind and water far below.

The classic trekking area, offering up to a week of walking, is in the south of the valley (beyond Kali Yetni), along with branch valleys to the east and west. Dani life here is still relatively traditional, the scenery gorgeous and the walking varied.

Accommodation is available in nearly all villages. Some have dedicated guesthouses (sometimes in *honai*-style huts); elsewhere you can often stay in a teacher's house, the school or other houses. Either way you'll usually be asked 80,000Rp to 120,000Rp per person. You sleep on the floor, but it may be softened with dried grass and you may get a mat. Make sure you've been invited before entering any compound or hut.

Larger villages have kiosks selling basics such as biscuits, noodles and rice (the final reliable supplies are at Manda and Kimbim in the north and Kurima in the south) and you can obtain sweet potatoes, other vegetables and fruit here and there. But you need to take at least some food with you from Wamena. Villages can normally supply firewood for cooking, for 10,000Rp a load.

Guides & Porters

In the more frequented trekking areas it's possible to head off alone and ask the way as you go, or pick up a local porter-cum-guide for 80,000Rp to 100,000Rp a day if you need one. But for hiking anywhere off the major trails, a guide is an extremely good idea – not only for finding the way but also for smoothing the path with local people.

A good source of recommendations for reliable guides in Wamena is Papua.com (p296). It's worth seeking out one of the Baliem Valley's 20 or so officially licensed guides.

There are no fixed prices in the Baliem trekking world. Hard bargaining is the norm. Don't be put off by glum faces and do insist on clarifying any grey areas. No decent guide will agree to anything he's unhappy about. The guides' association requests 400,000Rp to 500,000Rp per day for a guide (and more for harder treks to, for example, the Yali or Korowai areas), but some decent, English-speaking guides will work for less. Dependable Wamena-based agencies and individual guides include the following:

➡ **Jonas Wenda** (✆0852 4422 0825; jonas.wenda@yahoo.com) Highly experienced and notably knowledgeable on flora and fauna.

➡ **Kosman Kogoya** (✆0852 4472 7810) A popular, reliable guide who will quote reasonable prices from the outset and won't waste your time bargaining.

➡ **Papua/Irian Jaya Adventure** (✆0813 4486 3958; justinusdaby@yahoo.com; Jl Gatot Subroto 15, Wamena) Run by Justinus Daby, a Baliem Valley native who has been guiding here since the year dot.

In addition to a guide, porters are a good idea and cost 70,000Rp to 120,000Rp each per day, depending partly on the toughness of the trek. A cook costs 100,000Rp to 150,000Rp per day, but guides or porters can cook if you're looking to cut costs. You'll have to provide enough food for the whole team (costing around 40,000Rp each per day), and probably cigarettes for them and your village hosts.

explore nearby tribal villages. It's expensive as a consequence of having to fly everything in from Jayapura.

Sleeping & Eating

⭐ **Hotel Rainbow Wamena** HOTEL $$
(Hotel Pelangi; Jl Irian 26; r incl breakfast 350,000-600,000Rp) This has excellent, clean, well-sized rooms with good hot-water bathrooms and nice touches such as shampoo, tissues, coffee and tea. Staff are friendly and helpful and Restaurant Pelangi is here too.

Baliem Pilamo Hotel HOTEL $$
(✆0969-31043; baliempilamohotel@yahoo.co.id; Jl Trikora 114; r incl breakfast 456,000-996,000Rp; ☏) The more expensive rooms at this efficiently

run hotel are tasteful, contemporary, brown-and-white affairs. Of the cheaper ones, the 'standards' are smallish and plain but acceptable, and the 'superiors' have a semi-luxury feel and quirky garden-style bathrooms.

Putri Dani Hotel
HOTEL $$
(☑0812 4825 1889; Jl Irian 40; s/d 440,000/495,000Rp) This small family-run place offers nine spotless, comfortable rooms with hot showers and endless tea and coffee. From December to July it's often home to Wamena's Persiwa football team, so may be booked out.

ⓘ Information
No banks exchange foreign cash or travellers cheques, but two ATMs accept international cards. *Wartel* (telephone offices) dot Jl Trikora.

Papua.com (☑0969-34488; fuj0627@yahoo.co.jp; Jl Ahmad Yani 49; per hr 12,000Rp; ⊘9am-8.30pm Mon-Sat, from 1pm Sun) This efficient internet cafe has fax and scanning services, and also functions as an informal tourist information centre. Its owner is a highly experienced Papua traveller and a willing mine of information.

Police Station (☑0969-31972; Jl Safri Darwin; ⊘7am-2pm) Come here to report within 24 hours of arrival, or to obtain a *surat jalan*.

ⓘ Getting There & Around
The main carriers between Jayapura (Sentani) and Wamena are **Trigana Air** (☑0969-31611; airport) and **Susi Air** (☑081 1212 3931; Jl Gatot Subroto). Between them there are around five flights a day.

Sorong
☑0951 / POP 144,000
Papua's second-biggest city, Sorong, sits at the northwest tip of the Vogelkop. It's a busy port and a base for oil and logging operations in the region. Few travellers stay longer than it takes to book passage to the epic Raja Ampat Islands.

🛏 Sleeping & Eating
The best rooms book up fast.

Hotel Tanjung
HOTEL $
(☑951-323782; Jl Yos Sudarso; s 201,000-230,000Rp, d 241,000-270,000Rp; ❀🛜) At the north end of the Tembok Berlin waterfront, the Tanjung has tired but acceptable rooms, all with air-con.

Royal Mamberamo Hotel
HOTEL $$
(☑0951-325666; www.royalmamberamo.com; Jl Sam Ratulangi 35; r incl breakfast 500,000-1,200,000Rp; ❀@🛜) A sparkling and popular place with a good 24-hour restaurant, in the Kampung Baru area, just inland from the Tembok Berlin waterfront.

★ Lido Kuring
SEAFOOD $
(Jl Yos Sudarso; mains 25,000-50,000Rp) Chinese Indonesian seafood doesn't get much better or less frilly than what you'll find in this plain, cavernous dining hall on the Lido pier next to Hotel Tanjung.

ⓘ Information
Raja Ampat Tourism Management Office (☑0951-328358; www.diverajaampat.org; Jl Basuki Rahmat Km7.5, JE Meridien Hotel; ⊘9am-4pm Mon-Fri, to noon Sat) This incredibly helpful office can tell you almost anything you need to know about the Raja Ampat Islands, and it's the best place to buy the tag permitting you to visit the islands.

ⓘ Getting There & Around
Official airport taxis charge 100,000Rp to hotels in town; out on the street you can charter a public *taksi* for half that.

Expressair (☑0951-328200; Jl Basuki Rahmat km 7, JE Meridien Hotel) flies to Ambon, Jakarta, Jayapura and Makassar among others. Wings Air and Merpati also link Sorong with the wider Indonesian world.

Pelni (Jl Yani 13), near the west end of Jl Yani, posts its schedule in front of this ticket office. Ships sail fairly frequently to Jayapura and west to Maluku, Sulawesi and Java.

The town sprawls, so taxis, *ojek* and chartered *angkot* are the best way to visit banks, airline offices, the main port or government offices.

Raja Ampat Islands
POP 40,000
This archipelago of approximately 1500 stunning, mostly uninhabited limestone islands off the coast of Sorong are sheltered by some of the world's richest and most diverse coral reefs. Though not geared to travellers on tight budgets, things are getting easier on the purse strings thanks to the opening of a number of homestays.

The four biggest islands are Waigeo in the north, with the fast-growing new regional capital, Waisai; Salawati, just southwest of Sorong; Batanta, off northern Salawati; and Misool to the southwest. The Dampier Strait between Waigeo and Batanta has many of the best dive sites.

Visitors to the islands must pay an entry fee (Indonesians/others 250,000/500,000Rp) at the Raja Ampat Tourism Office in Sorong.

🛏 Sleeping & Eating

There are several dive resorts and dozens of village homestays scattered among the islands.

★ Yenkoranu Homestay   HOMESTAY $$
(☑ 0852 5455 5526, 0821 9849 8519; yenko ranuhomestay@ymail.com; Pulau Kri; full board per person 250,000Rp) On a long, palm-fringed beach with a coral reef offshore, Yenkoranu is a near-perfect getaway. Run with care by a large and lovable family, it has just four simple rooms, an over-water hammock deck where you can watch fabulous sunsets and (with luck) walking sharks, and food that's as good and varied as you'll get in a homestay.

They'll take guests snorkelling and diving. Waisai transfers are free if you stay five nights, otherwise 350,000Rp round-trip per boat.

Raja Ampat Biodiversity   LODGE $$
(☑ 0821 8922 2577; www.rajaampatbiodiversity. com; Pantai Yenanas; 7 nights full board incl 12 dives €747-992) 🤿 Two kilometres east of Yenbeser village on Gam, Spanish-run Biodiversity is a great option for divers on relatively limited budgets. Accommodation is in simple but spacious and comfortable cabins, good Indonesian and Western food is served, the dive operation is of a high standard, and PADI and SSI diving courses are offered too.

Harapan Jaya Homestay   HOMESTAY $$
(☑ 0813 4435 3030; Harapan Jaya village; full board per person 400,000Rp) This superior-standard homestay is currently the only one on large, remote Pulau Misool (actually it's on a small offshore island). A great base, if you have funds, for exploring Misool's islands, beaches, caves and waterfalls.

ℹ Getting There & Around

Waisai's newly built airport was due to start operating in early 2014.

Fast Marina Express passenger boats (economy/VIP 120,000/150,000Rp, two hours) and a larger, slower boat (100,000Rp, three hours) depart for Waisai from Sorong's **Pelabuhan Feri** (Pelabuhan Rakyat; Jl Feri, off

Jl Sudirman) at 2pm daily. The boats head back from Waisai at 2pm Sunday to Friday, and noon Saturday.

To arrange transport around the islands once there, your best bet is to ask at your accommodation or Waisai's Tourism Information Centre. Prices depend on boat, distance and petrol price (9000Rp/L in Waisai at research time), and are usually negotiable.

UNDERSTAND INDONESIA

Indonesia Today

Indonesia is a land of good news and bad news. First the good.

Economically, Indonesia is booming with growth surpassing 5% a year. More than a decade after the first open elections, the consensus is that the nation has established itself as a workable democracy. And on the terrorism front there have been steady gains, although threats remain.

On the bad news front there are the ferry sinkings and plane crashes that emphasise the nation's decrepit infrastructure. Other challenges include corruption, the destruction of the environment, poverty and fundamentalism (protests over the 2013 Miss World pageant made headlines worldwide). Sectarian violence is never far from the surface, with isolated outbreaks from Java to Papua.

And the good news is often tempered by the bad. Even as Bali enjoys record tourism and growth that is spurring the creation of a new middle class, there are growing pollution and congestion woes that tarnish the island's shine.

History

Beginnings

Until the last few years it was widely believed that the first humanoids (*Homo erectus*) lived in Central Java around 500,000 years ago, having reached Indonesia across land bridges from Africa, before either dying off or being wiped out by the arrival of *Homo sapiens*.

But the discovery in 2003 of the remains of a tiny islander, dubbed the 'hobbit', seems to indicate that *Homo erectus* survived much longer than was previously thought, and that previously accepted timelines of Indonesia's evolutionary history need to be re-examined (though many scientists continue to challenge the hobbit theory).

Most Indonesians are descendents of Malay people who began migrating around 4000 BC from Cambodia, Vietnam and southern China. They steadily developed small kingdoms and by 700 BC these settlers had developed skilful rice-farming techniques.

Hinduism & Buddhism

The growing prosperity of these early kingdoms soon caught the attention of Indian and Chinese merchants, and along with silks and spices came the dawn of Hinduism and Buddhism in Indonesia.

These religions quickly gained a foothold in the archipelago and soon became central to the great kingdoms of the 1st millennium AD. The Buddhist Srivijaya empire held sway over the Malay peninsula and southern Sumatra, extracting wealth from its dominion over the strategic Straits of Melaka. The Hindu Mataram and Buddhist Sailendra kingdoms dominated Central Java, raising their grandiose monuments, Borobudur and Prambanan, over the fertile farmland that brought them their prosperity.

When Mataram slipped into mysterious decline around the 10th century AD, it was fast replaced with an even more powerful Hindu kingdom. Founded in 1294, the Majapahit empire made extensive territorial gains under its ruler, Hayam Wuruk, and prime minister, Gajah Mada, and while claims that they controlled much of Sulawesi, Sumatra and Borneo now seem fanciful, most of Java, Madura and Bali certainly fell within their realm.

But things would soon change. Despite the Majapahit empire's massive power and influence, greater fault lines were opening up across Indonesia, and Hinduism's golden age was swiftly drawing to a close.

Rise of Islam

With the arrival of Islam came the power, the reason and the will to oppose the hegemony of the Majapahits, and satellite kingdoms soon took up arms against the Hindu kings. In the 15th century the Majapahits fled to Bali, where Hindu culture continues to flourish, leaving Java to the increasingly powerful Islamic sultanates.

Meanwhile, the influential trading kingdoms of Melaka (on the Malay peninsula) and Makassar (in southern Sulawesi) were also embracing Islam, sowing the seeds that would later make modern Indonesia the most populous Muslim nation on earth.

European Expansion

Melaka fell to the Portuguese in 1511 and European eyes were soon settling on the archipelago's riches, prompting two centuries of unrest as the Portuguese, Spanish, Dutch and British wrestled for control. By 1700 the Dutch held most of the trump cards, with the Dutch East India Company (VOC) controlling the region's lucrative spice trade and becoming the world's first multinational company. Following the VOC's bankruptcy, however, the British governed Java under Sir Stamford Raffles between 1811 and 1816, only to relinquish control again to the Dutch after the end of the Napoleonic wars, who then held control of Indonesia until its independence 129 years later.

It was not, however, a trouble-free tenancy and the Dutch had to face numerous rebellions: Javan Prince Diponegoro's five-year guerrilla war was finally put down in 1830, costing the lives of 8000 Dutch troops.

Road to Independence

By the beginning of the 20th century, the Dutch had brought most of the archipelago under their control, but the revolutionary tradition of Diponegoro was never truly quashed, bubbling beneath the surface of Dutch rule and finding a voice in the young Soekarno. The debate was sidelined as the Japanese swept through Indonesia during WWII, but with their departure came the opportunity for Soekarno to declare Indonesian independence, which he did from his Jakarta home on 17 August 1945.

The Dutch, however, were unwilling to relinquish their hold over Indonesia and – supported by the British, who had entered Indonesia to accept the Japanese surrender – moved quickly to reassert their authority over the country. Resistance was stiff and for four bitter years the Indonesian resistance fought a guerrilla war. But American and UN opposition to the reimposition of colonialism and the mounting casualty toll eventually forced the Dutch to pack it in, and the Indonesian flag – the *sang merah putih* (red and white) – was finally hoisted over Jakarta's Istana Merdeka (Freedom Palace) on 27 December 1949.

Depression, Disunity & Dictatorship

Unity in war quickly became division in peace, as religious fundamentalists and nationalist separatists challenged the fledgling central government. After almost a decade of political impasse and economic depression, Soekarno made his move in 1957, declaring Guided Democracy (a euphemism for dictatorship) with army backing and leading Indonesia into nearly four decades of authoritarian rule.

Despite moves towards the one-party state, Indonesia's three million–strong Communist Party (Partai Komunis Indonesia; PKI) was the biggest in the world by 1965 and Soekarno had long realised the importance of winning its backing. But as the PKI's influence in government grew, so did tensions with the armed forces. Things came to a head on the night of 30 September 1965, when elements of the palace guard launched an attempted coup. Quickly put down by General Soeharto, the coup was blamed – perhaps unfairly – on the PKI and became the pretext for an army-led purge that left as many as 500,000 communist sympathisers dead. Strong evidence later emerged from declassified documents that both the US (opposed to communism) and the UK (seeking to protect its interests in Malaysia) aided and abetted Soeharto's purge by drawing up hit lists of communist agitators. By 1968 Soeharto had ousted Soekarno and was installed as president.

Soeharto brought unity through repression, annexing Irian Jaya (Papua) in 1969, and reacting to insurgency with an iron fist. In 1975 Portuguese Timor was invaded, leading to tens of thousands of deaths, and separatist ambitions in Aceh and Papua were also met with a ferocious military response. But despite endemic corruption, the 1980s and 1990s were Indonesia's boom years, with meteoric economic growth and a starburst of opulent building ventures transforming the face of the capital.

Soeharto's Fall

As Asia's economy went into freefall during the closing years of the 1990s, Soeharto's house of cards began to tumble. Indonesia went bankrupt overnight and the country found an obvious scapegoat in the cronyism and corruption endemic in the dictator's regime. Protests erupted across Indonesia in 1998, and the May riots in Jakarta left thousands, many of them Chinese, dead. After three decades of dictatorial rule, Soeharto resigned on 21 May 1998.

Passions cooled when Vice President BJ Habibie took power on a reform ticket, but ambitious promises were slow to materialise, and in November of the same year riots again rocked many Indonesian cities. Promises of forthcoming elections succeeded in closing the floodgates, but separatist groups took advantage of the weakened central government and violence erupted in Maluku, Irian Jaya, East Timor and Aceh. East Timor won its independence after a referendum in August 1999, but only after Indonesian-backed militias had destroyed its infrastructure and left thousands dead.

Democracy & Reform

Against this unsettled backdrop, the June 1999 legislative elections passed surprisingly smoothly, leaving Megawati Soekarnoputri (Soekarno's daughter) and her reformist Indonesian Democratic Party for Struggle (PDI-P) as the largest party with 33% of the vote. But months later the separate presidential election was narrowly won by Abdurrahman Wahid (Gus Dur), whose efforts to undo corruption met with stiff resistance. Megawati was eventually sworn in as president in 2001, but her term proved a disappointment for many Indonesians as corrupt infrastructures were left in place, the military's power remained intact, poverty levels remained high and there were high-profile terrorism attacks such as the 2002 Bali bombings.

Megawati lost the 2004 presidential elections to Susilo Bambang Yudhoyono (or 'SBY'), an ex-army officer who served in East Timor but who also has an MBA. Dubbed the 'thinking general', his successes have included cracking down on Islamic militants, pumping more money into education and health, and introducing basic social-security payments.

SBY's term has also been marked by a series of disasters, beginning with the 2004 Boxing Day tsunami that ravaged Aceh in northern Sumatra. In 2006, a quake shook Yogyakarta, killing 6800 people,

INDONESIA HISTORY

and in 2009 a quake devastated Padang in Sumatra.

Elections in 2009 were largely peaceful. SBY cruised to an easy re-election on a platform of continuing moderate policies. Extremist Islamic parties have fared poorly against more moderate parties.

People & Culture

The old Javanese saying '*bhinneka tunggal ika*' (they are many; they are one) is said to be Indonesia's national dictum, but with a population of more than 247 million, 300-plus languages and 17,000 islands it's not surprising that many from the outer islands resent Java, where power is centralised. Indonesia is loosely bound together by a single flag (which is increasingly flown with pride during national holidays) and a single language (Bahasa Indonesia), but in some ways can be compared to the EU – a richly diverse confederacy of peoples.

The world's most populous Muslim nation is no hardline Islamic state. Indonesians have traditionally practised a relaxed form of Islam, and though there's no desire to imitate the West, most see no conflict in catching a Hollywood movie in an American-style shopping mall after prayers at the mosque. The country is becoming more cosmopolitan; Facebook usage is epic. Millions of Indonesians now work overseas – mainly in the Gulf, Hong Kong and Malaysia – bringing back extraneous influences to their villages when they return. A boom in low-cost air travel has enabled a generation of Indonesians to travel internally and overseas conveniently and cheaply for the first time, while personal mobility is much easier today – it's possible to buy a motorbike on hire purchase with as little as a 500,000Rp deposit.

But not everyone has the cash or time for overseas jaunts and there remains a yawning gulf between the haves and the have-nots. Indonesia is much poorer than many of its Asian neighbours, with over 40% surviving on US$2 a day, and in many rural areas opportunities are few and far between.

Population

Indonesia's population is the fourth-biggest in the world, with over 247 million people. Over half this number live on the island of Java, one of the most crowded places on earth with a population density of over 945 people per square kilometre. But while Java (and Bali and Lombok) teem with people, large parts of the archipelago are very sparsely populated, particularly Papua (under 10 per square kilometre) and Kalimantan.

Birth rates have fallen considerably in recent years (from an average of 3.4 children per woman in 1987 to 2.2 today) thanks to successful family-planning campaigns and increasing prosperity levels.

Religion

If Indonesia has a soundtrack, it is the muezzin's call to prayer. Wake up to it once and it won't come as a surprise that Indonesia is the largest Islamic nation on earth, with over 213 million Muslims (86% of the total population).

But while Islam has a near monopoly on religious life, many of the country's most impressive historical monuments, such as the temples of Borobudur and Prambanan, hark back to when Hindu and Buddhist kingdoms dominated Java. These religions maintain important communities, with Hinduism (2% of the population) continuing to flourish in Bali, while Buddhists (1%) are scattered throughout the country.

Christians make up nearly 9% of the nation, forming the majority in Papua, on several islands of Nusa Tenggara and Maluku, and in parts of Sumatra. Animist traditions also survive below the surface in many rural areas.

Arts

DANCE

Indonesia has a rich heritage of traditional dances. In Yogyakarta there's the Ramayana ballet, a spectacular dance drama; Lombok has a mask dance called the *kayak sando* and war dances; Malaku's *lenso* is a handkerchief dance; while Bali has a multitude of elaborate dances, which are a major reason to visit the island.

MUSIC

Indonesia has a massive contemporary music scene that spans all genres. The popular *dangdut* is a melange of traditional and modern, Indonesian and foreign musical styles that features instruments such as electric guitars and Indian *tablas* (a type of drum), and rhythms ranging from Middle Eastern pop to reggae or salsa. Among the best performers and bands of late are Neonomora, Frau, Glovves and Banda Neira.

Gamelan is the best-known traditional Indonesian music: besides Bali, Java has orchestras composed mainly of percussion instruments, including drums, gongs and *angklung* (shake-drums), along with flutes and xylophones.

Environment

Indonesia has lost more tropical forest than anywhere else in the world, bar Brazil, in the last few decades. That said, some incredible national parks and landscapes remain virtually untouched, mainly in remote areas away from the main centres of population.

The Land

At 1.92 million sq km, Indonesia is an island colossus, incorporating 10% of the world's forest cover and 11,508 uninhabited islands (6000 more have human populations). From the low-lying coastal areas, the country rises through no fewer than 129 active volcanoes – more than any country in the world – to the snow-covered summit of Puncak Jaya (4884m) in Papua. Despite the incredible diversity of its landscapes, it is worth remembering that Indonesia is predominantly water; Indonesians refer to the country as Tanah Air Kita (literally 'Our Earth and Water').

Wildlife

In his classic study, *The Malay Archipelago,* British naturalist Alfred Russel Wallace divided Indonesia into two zones. To the west of the so-called Wallace Line (which runs between Kalimantan and Sulawesi and south through the straits between Bali and Lombok) the flora and fauna resemble that of the rest of Asia, while the species and environments to the east become increasingly like those of Australia. Scientists have since fine-tuned Wallace's findings, but while western Indonesia is known for its orang-utan, rhinos and tigers, as well as spectacular *Rafflesia* flowers, eastern Indonesia boasts fauna such as the komodo dragon and marsupials, including Papuan tree kangaroos.

National Parks

There are officially 50 *taman nasional* (national parks) in Indonesia. Most are in remote areas and have basic visitor facilities, but they are remarkable in their ecological diversity and wildlife. Some of the finest include Tanjung Puting in Kalimantan for its orang-utans and wetland birds, and Komodo and Rinca for their dragons and official coral reefs.

INDONESIA ENVIRONMENT

ORANG-UTANS

Orang-utans, the world's largest arboreal mammal, once swung through the forest canopy throughout all of Southeast Asia but are now found only in Sumatra and Borneo. Researchers fear that the few that do remain will not survive the continued loss of habitat to logging and agriculture.

While orang-utans are extremely intelligent animals, their way of life isn't compatible with a shrinking forest. Orang-utans are mostly vegetarians; they get big and strong (some males weigh up to 90kg) from a diet that would make a Californian hippie proud: fruit, shoots, leaves, nuts and tree bark, which they grind up with their powerful jaws and teeth. They occasionally also eat insects, eggs and small mammals.

The 'orang hutan' (a Malay word for 'person of the forest') has an extremely expressive face that has often suggested a very close kinship with the hairless ape (humans). But of all the great apes, the orang-utans are considered to be the most distantly related to humans.

Mothers rear their young for seven years – the longest nursery time in the animal kingdom. During this intensely intimate period, they teach them everything, for example how to climb through the canopy by brachiation (travelling from branch to branch), how to identify the medicinal qualities of plants and the poisonousness of certain nuts, and how to mentally map the forest. The rehabilitation of orphans involves as close an approximation of this as possible.

The two classic places to view orang-utans in Indonesia are Bukit Lawang on Sumatra and Tanjung Puting National Park on Kalimantan.

Environmental Issues

From the perspective of a Jakarta-based bureaucrat, Indonesia has full environmental responsibility credentials, with stringent land-use and environmental impact regulations, and large tracts of forest lands set aside for conservation. In the field, the picture is markedly different, as a wilful disregard of regulations – generally with the collusion of the newly empowered regional authorities – make official environmental policies mere words on paper.

Forest continues to be cleared at a horrific rate, both through illegal logging and conversion to palm-oil plantations. Greenpeace estimates that more than 50% of Indonesia's virgin rainforests have been cleared. Despite pledges to the contrary, the government continues to sanction official clearances on a huge scale. Furthermore, more than 70% of Indonesia's mangrove forests have been damaged according to the US-based Mangrove Action Project, through pollution and projects such as the new toll road on Bali.

The side effects of deforestation are felt across the nation and beyond: floods and landslides wash away valuable topsoil, rivers become sluggish and fetid, and haze from clearing fires blankets Malaysia and Singapore every dry season. The problems flow right through to Indonesia's coastline and seas, where over 80% of reef habitat is considered to be at risk by the UN.

The rampant consumerism of the burgeoning middle class is straining the nation's wholly inadequate infrastructure: private vehicles clog urban streets creating massive air pollution; waste removal services have difficulty coping with household and industrial garbage; and a total lack of sewerage-disposal systems makes water from most sources undrinkable without boiling, putting further pressure on kerosene and firewood supplies.

Food & Drink

By eating in Indonesia you savour the essence of the country, as few nations are so well represented by their cuisine. The abundance of rice reflects Indonesia's fertile landscape, the spices are reminiscent of a time of trade and invasion, and the fiery chilli echoes the passion of the people. Indonesian cuisine is really one big food swap. Chinese, Portuguese, colonists and traders have all influenced the ingredients that appear at the Indonesian table, and the cuisine has been shaped over time by the archipelago's diverse landscape, people and culture.

Coriander, cumin, chilli, lemongrass, coconut, soy sauce and palm sugar are all important flavourings; sambal is a crucial condiment. Fish is a favourite and seafood restaurants are common in this island nation. Indonesians traditionally eat with their fingers, hence the stickiness of the rice. Satay (skewered meat), *nasi goreng* (fried rice) and *gado gado* (vegetables with peanut sauce) are some of Indonesia's most famous dishes. *Nasi campur* (mixed rice) is the national dish and includes a sampling of dishes served in myriad variations.

Regional Variations

Popular dishes are not surprisingly diverse in this land of more than 300 languages.

JAVA

The cuisine of the Betawi (original inhabitants of the Jakarta region) is known for its richness. *Gado gado* is a Betawi original, as is *ketoprak* (noodles, bean sprouts and tofu with soy and peanut sauce). *Soto Betawi* (beef soup) is made creamy with coconut milk. There's also *nasi uduk* (rice cooked in coconut milk, served with meat, tofu and/or vegetables).

Central Javan food is sweet, even the curries, such as *gudeg* (jackfruit curry). Yogyakarta specialities include *ayam goreng* (fried chicken) and *kelepon* (green rice-flour balls with a palm-sugar filling).

BALI

High-quality *warung* popular with visitors can be found across Bali. *Babi guling* (spit-roast pig stuffed with chilli, turmeric, garlic and ginger) is widely sold as is *bebek betutu* (duck stuffed with spices, wrapped in banana leaves and coconut husks and cooked in embers). The local satay, *sate lilit,* is made with minced, spiced meat pressed onto skewers.

NUSA TENGGARA

In dry East Nusa Tenggara you'll eat less rice and more sago, corn, cassava and taro. Fish remains popular and one local dish is Sumbawa's *sepat* (shredded fish in coconut and mango sauce).

The Sasak people of Lombok like spicy *ayam Taliwang* (roasted chicken served with a peanut, tomato, chilli and lime dip) and *pelecing* (sauce made with chilli, shrimp paste and tomato). In fact, Lombok-style chicken is popular across the nation.

SUMATRA

In West Sumatra, beef is used in *rendang* (beef coconut curry). Padang food is famed for its rich, chilli-heavy sauces and is popular throughout Indonesia. It's usually delicious, though not cooked fresh – dishes are displayed for hours (days even) in the restaurant window. Padang restaurant *(masakan Padang)* food is served one of two ways: usually a bowl of rice is plonked in front of you, followed by a whole collection of small bowls of vegetables, meat and fish; or you approach the window display and pick a few dishes yourself.

KALIMANTAN

Dayak food varies, but you may sample *rembang,* a sour fruit that's made into *sayur asem rembang* (sour vegetable soup). The regional soup, *soto banjar,* is a chicken broth made creamy by mashing boiled eggs into the stock. Chicken also goes into *ayam masak habang,* cooked with large red chillies.

SULAWESI

South Sulawesi locals love seafood, especially *ikan bakar* (grilled fish). For sugar cravers, there's *es pallubutun* (coconut custard and banana in coconut milk and syrup). The Toraja people have their own distinct cuisine. The best-known dish is *pa'piong* (meat stuffed into bamboo tubes along with vegetables and coconut).

MALUKU

A typical Maluku meal is tuna and *dabu-dabu* (raw vegetables with a chilli and fish-paste sauce). Sometimes fish is made into *kohu-kohu* (fish salad with citrus fruit and chilli).

INDONESIA FOOD & DRINK

WHERE TO SURF

New surf spots are being discovered all the time in Indonesia, the choices simply never end.

Java

Batu Karas, with fine breaks, is one of the most enjoyable places to kick back in Java. **Pangandaran** is also popular.

Bali

It really is a surfer's paradise in Bali. Breaks are found right around the south side of the island and there's a large infrastructure of schools, board-rental places, cheap surfer dives and more that cater to the crowds.

Five famous spots you won't want to miss:

➡ **Kuta Beach** Where surfing came to Asia. This is a good place for beginners, with long, steady breaks.

➡ **Bingin** A white-sand beach backed by funky accommodation makes this a natural.

➡ **Ulu Watu** Some of the largest sets in Bali.

➡ **Medewi** Famous point break with a ride right into a river mouth.

➡ **Nusa Lembongan** The island is a mellow scene for surfers and nonsurfers. The breaks are right in front of the places to stay.

Nusa Tenggara

Lombok's **Kuta** has world-class waves and turquoise water. Sumbawa has superb surf at isolated **Maluk**.

Sumatra

Northern Sumatra's **Pulau Nias** is the most visited surfing destination in the province. The **Mentawai Islands** have good surf camps and draw charters.

PAPUA

In the highlands of Papua the sweet potato is king. Other plants, such as sago palms, are also cultivated. The locals eat the pith of the sago palm and also leave the plant to rot so that they can collect and eat beetle grubs. On special occasions, chickens and pigs are cooked in earth ovens.

Drink

Bottled water and soft drinks are available everywhere, and many hotels and restaurants provide *air putih* (boiled water) for guests. Iced juice drinks can be good, but take care that the water/ice has been purified or is bottled. (Ice in Jakarta and Bali is usually fine.)

Indonesian tea is fine and coffee can be excellent; for a strong local brew ask for *kopi java* or *kopi flores,* depending on where you are of course. Beer is quite good: Bintang is one of Asia's finest lagers and costs 15,000Rp to 30,000Rp for a large bottle in most places.

Bali Brem rice wine is really potent, and the more you drink the nicer it tastes. *Es buah,* or *es campur,* is a strange concoction of fruit salad, jelly cubes, syrup, crushed rice and condensed milk. And it tastes absolutely *enak* (delicious).

SURVIVAL GUIDE

ℹ Directory A–Z

ACCOMMODATION

Hotel, *losmen*, *penginapan* (simple lodging house), *wisma* (guesthouse): there are several words for somewhere to lay a weary head, and options to suit every budget in most Indonesian towns.

Cheap hotels are usually pretty basic, but a simple breakfast is often included. In-room, Western-style toilets are nearly standard in tourist areas. Traditional washing facilities consist of a usually private *mandi*, a large water tank from which you scoop cool water with a dipper. Climbing into the tank is very bad form! The air-con symbol (❄) denotes whether air-con rooms are available; otherwise rooms are assumed to come with a fan.

Accommodation prices in tourist areas peak in August, and during Easter and the Christmas period, though at the budget end of the market, price hikes are marginal. Elsewhere in the country, rates increase during Idul Fitri (the period following Ramadan).

Generally, budget rooms are plain and purely functional rooms. But along the main travelling trail, in Yogyakarta and in parts of Flores, Lombok and Sumatra, budget places can be very attractive and decorated with artistic touches, and often come with a verandah. Bali is in a league of its own in terms of quality: for 200,000Rp a night you can still find a fine room – often with a pool.

Price Ranges

Average prices are higher in Bali and Lombok's Gili Islands; in this chapter, our price indicators are separated into two price bands.

Note that the Indonesian government plans to redenominate the rupiah in the next year or two; see the boxed text.

Bali & Gili Islands
$ less than 450,000Rp (US$40)
$$ 450,000Rp to 1,400,000Rp (US$40 to US$120)
$$$ more than 1,400,000Rp (US$120)

Rest of Indonesia
$ less than 250,000Rp (US$20)
$$ 250,000R to 800,000Rp (US$20 to US$70)
$$$ more than 800,000Rp (US$70)

BOOKS

➜ Lonely Planet's *Bali & Lombok, Borneo* and *Indonesia* guides explore the country in great detail, while Lonely Planet's *Indonesian Phrasebook* is the perfect guide to the language.

➜ *Krakatoa – The Day the World Exploded* is Simon Winchester's highly readable account centred on the 1888 eruption of Krakatau – the world's biggest bang.

➜ *The Year of Living Dangerously,* by Christopher J Koch, is the harrowing tale of a journalist in Soekarno's Indonesia of 1965. Many have seen the movie with a young Mel Gibson and Linda Hunt. The book is more harrowing.

➜ *This Earth of Mankind,* by Pramoedya Ananta Toer, is the first book in the author's renowned Buru quartet, which he wrote while a political prisoner. The brutalities of the Dutch colonial era are the backdrop of the novel's coming-of-age tale.

➜ *Eat, Pray, Love,* by Elizabeth Gilbert, is the notorious bestseller (and less than successful movie). Fans of the lurid, self-absorbed prose flock to Ubud seeking inner discovery.

CUSTOMS REGULATIONS

Indonesia has the usual list of prohibited imports, including drugs, weapons, fresh fruit and anything remotely pornographic.

RELIABLE TRANSPORT INFO

In a country where accurate information for ferries, airlines and buses can at best be elusive, guesthouses, hotels and resorts are good sources of information, especially for more obscure destinations. They need you to reach them to stay in business and often can give you all the up-to-date details needed.

Items allowed include the following:
→ 200 cigarettes (or 50 cigars or 100g of tobacco)
→ a 'reasonable amount' of perfume
→ 1L of alcohol

EMBASSIES & CONSULATES
Bali
Australian Consulate (☎0361-241118; www. bali.indonesia.embassy.gov.au; Jl Tantular 32, Denpasar; ⊙8am-4pm Mon-Fri) The Australian consulate has a consular sharing agreement with Canada.

US Consulate (☎0361-233605; BaliConsular Agency@state.gov; Jl Hayam Wuruk 310, Renon, Denpasar; ⊙9am-noon & 1-3.30pm Mon-Fri)

Jakarta
Australian Embassy (☎021-2550 5555; www. indonesia.embassy.gov.au; Jl HR Rasuna Said Kav C 15-16)

Brunei Embassy (Map p156; ☎021-3190 6080; Jl Teuku Umar 9, Menteng)

Canadian Embassy (☎021-2550 7800; www.canadainternational.gc.ca/indonesia-indonesie/; World Trade Centre, 6th fl, Jl Jenderal Sudirman Kav 29-31)

French Embassy (Map p156; ☎021-2355 7600; www.ambafrance-id.org; Jl Thamrin 20)

German Embassy (Map p156; ☎021-3985 5000; www.jakarta.diplo.de; Jln MH Thamrin No 1)

Malaysian Embassy (Map p154; ☎021-522 4974; www.kln.gov.my/web/idn_jakarta/home; Jln HR Rasuna Said Kav X/6, No 1-3, Kuningan)

Netherlands Embassy (Map p154; ☎021-524 8200; http://indonesia.nlembassy.org; Jln HR Rasuna Said Kav S-3)

New Zealand Embassy (Map p154; ☎021-2995 5800; www.nzembassy.com; Jl Asia Afrika No 8, 10th fl, Sentral Senayan 2)

Papua New Guinea Embassy (Map p154; ☎021-725 1218; www.kundu-jakarta.com; Jl Jenderal Sudirman 1, 6th fl, Panin Bank Centre)

Singapore Embassy (Map p154; ☎021-2995 0400; www.mfa.sg/jkt; Jl HR Rasuna Said, Block X/4 Kav 2)

Thai Embassy (Map p156; ☎021-390 4052; www.thaiembassy.org/jakarta; Jl Imam Bonjol 74)

UK Embassy (Map p156; ☎021-2356 5200; http://ukinindonesia.fco.gov.uk; Jln MH Thamrin No 75)

US Embassy (Map p156; ☎021-3435 9000; http://jakarta.usembassy.gov; Jl Medan Merdeka Selatan, No 3-5)

Medan
Malaysian Consulate (☎061-453 1342; www.kln.gov.my/web/idn_medan; Jl Diponegoro 43)

FESTIVALS & EVENTS
Religious events and official holidays are a vital part of Indonesian life. There are many through the year and they're often cause for celebrations and festivals. With such a diversity of people in the archipelago, there are many local holidays, festivals and cultural events. This is especially true on Bali where religious events can easily occupy a third of the typical person's calendar.

The Muslim fasting month of Ramadan requires that Muslims abstain from food, drink, cigarettes and sex between sunrise and sunset. Many bars and restaurants close and it is important to avoid eating or drinking publicly in Muslim areas during this time. For the week before and after Lebaran (Idul Fitri), the festival to mark the end of the fast, transport is often fully booked and travelling becomes a nightmare – plan to stay put at this time. Ramadan, Idul Fitri and Idul Adha (Muslim day of sacrifice) move back 10 days or so every year, according to the Muslim calendar.

Although some public holidays have a fixed date, the dates for many events vary each year depending on Muslim, Buddhist or Hindu calendars.

January/February
New Year's Day Celebrated on 1 January.

Imlek (Chinese New Year) Special food is prepared, decorations adorn stores and homes, and *barongsai* (lion dances) are performed; held in January/February.

Muharram (Islamic New Year) The date varies each year, but is usually in late January.

Mohammed's Birthday Celebrated in January in 2014 and 2015; prayers are held in mosques throughout the country, and there are street parades in Solo and Yogyakarta.

A NOTE ON THE RUPIAH

Indonesia has plans to redenominate the rupiah by removing three digits from the currency sometime in 2014 or 2015. For example, the 20,000Rp note would become the 20Rp note. The exchange value of the new notes would remain the same. Changing the national currency is likely to be a very complex process, with many implications for travellers. These include:

➡ New notes will be introduced that are identical to the current ones, with the exception of the final three zeros missing. Long-term plans call for all-new designs.

➡ The government stresses that current banknotes will retain their value (eg the 100,000Rp note will be the same as the new 100Rp note), however, how this will play out is anyone's guess. In other nations, such as Russia, there has been widespread refusal to accept old notes, even after government guarantees of their value.

➡ It will likely take years for price lists and computer systems to be fully updated, so it will be up to customers to make certain that they are being charged – and paying – appropriately.

➡ Introduction of the new denominations is likely to occur with little notice to avoid financial upheavals.

March/April

Hindu New Year (Nyepi) Held in March/April; in Bali and other Hindu communities, villagers make as much noise as possible to scare away devils. Virtually all of Bali shuts down.

Good Friday Occurs in March or April.

April/May

Waisak (Buddha's Birthday) Mass prayers are said at the main Buddhist temples, including Borobudur.

May/June

Ascension of Christ Occurs in May/June.

Ascension of Mohammed Special prayers are held in mosques.

August

Independence Day Celebrated on 17 August with plenty of pomp and circumstance; government buildings are draped in huge red-and-white flags and banners, and there are endless marches.

Lebaran (Idul Fitri) Everyone returns to their home village for special prayers and gift giving, and it's a time for charity donations.

October

Idul Adha The end of the Haj is celebrated with animal sacrifices, the meat of which is given to the poor.

November/December

Christmas Day Marked by gift giving and special church services in Christian areas; the celebration falls on 25 December.

FOOD

Food is cheaper outside of the main tourist hubs of Bali and Lombok's Gili Islands. As such, our price indicators for a main course or meal are separated into two price bands.

Bali & Gili Islands

$ less than 60,000Rp (US$5)

$$ 60,000Rp to 250,000Rp (US$5 to US$20)

$$$ more than 250,000Rp (US$20)

Rest of Indonesia

$ less than 50,000Rp (US$4)

$$ 50,000Rp to 200,000Rp (US$4 to US$18)

$$$ more than 200,000Rp (US$18)

For an overview of Indonesian cuisine see p302.

GAY & LESBIAN TRAVELLERS

Gay travellers in Indonesia will experience few problems, especially in Bali. Physical contact between same-sex couples is acceptable (Indonesian boys and girls often hold hands or link arms in public). Homosexual behaviour is not illegal – the age of consent is 16. Immigration officials may restrict entry to people who reveal HIV-positive status. Gay men in Indonesia are referred to as *homo* or *gay*; lesbians are *lesbi*.

Indonesia's transvestite and transsexual *waria*, from *wanita* (woman) and *pria* (man), community has always had a public profile.

INTERNET ACCESS

Indonesia is somewhat wired, but speed varies from fast to painfully slow.

Wi-fi is widely available in hotels and cafes. It is often free but watch out for hotels that may charge ridiculous rates by the hour or by data use.

LEGAL MATTERS

The government takes the smuggling, using and selling of drugs very, *very* seriously. Once caught, you may have to wait for up to six months in jail before trial. Gambling is illegal (although it's common, especially at cock-fights), as is pornography.

Generally, you are unlikely to have any encounters with the police unless you are driving a rented car or motorcycle, in which case you may be stopped for a dubious reason and asked to pay an impromptu 'fine' of about 50,000Rp.

The age of consent is 18.

OPENING HOURS

Standard hours are as follows. Significant variations are noted in listings.

Banks 8am to 2pm Monday to Thursday, 8am to noon Friday, 8am to 11am Saturday.

Government offices 8am to 3pm Monday to Thursday, 8am to noon on Friday, but they are not standardised.

Post offices 8am to 2pm Monday to Friday; longer in tourist centres.

Restaurants and cafes 8am to 9pm daily.

Shops and services catering to visitors 9am to 8pm.

POST

The postal service in Indonesia is generally good.

PUBLIC HOLIDAYS

Official holidays and religious events are intertwined in the Indonesian calendar, with the result being a plethora of days when much of the nation shuts down or has the day off. See p305 for more details.

SAFE TRAVEL

If you've never been before, Indonesia might seem like one of the world's most dodgy nations: accident-prone and cursed by natural disasters and terrorist outrages.

But while transport safety standards are dodgy, earthquakes are frequent and there has been a number of highly publicised incidents of terrorism and sectarian violence, Indonesia is actually a very safe nation for travellers.

Personal safety, even in the big cities, is not usually a major concern. Keep your wits about you, yes, but violent crime is rare in Indonesia. Be mindful of your valuables and take the usual precautions and the chances of getting into trouble are small.

It *is* important to keep abreast of current political developments, however. At the time of writing, the country was peaceful.

Drug penalties can be severe. Be very wary of *arak*, the potent rice or palm alcohol that figures in many drinks aimed at tourists and locals alike; deaths and serious injuries occur constantly due to unscrupulous vendors using dangerous chemicals. And on Bali, beware of dogs, as there is a rabies epidemic.

But most importantly, go and enjoy yourself.

TELEPHONE

Cheap SIM cards (which should never cost more than 5000Rp than any included calling credit) and internet calling make it easy to stay in touch with home from Indonesia at reasonable prices.

In urban areas and Bali, 3G networks are common. **Telkomsel** (www.telkomsel.com) has the most widespread mobile service across the nation.

TIME

Indonesia has three time zones. Western Indonesia time (Sumatra, Java, West and Central Kalimantan) is seven hours ahead of GMT, Central Indonesia time (Bali, South and East Kalimantan, Sulawesi and Nusa Tenggara) is eight hours ahead, and East Indonesia time (Maluku and Irian Jaya) is nine hours ahead.

TOILETS

Public toilets are extremely rare except in bus and train stations. Expect to have to dive into restaurants and hotels.

Indonesian toilets are holes in the ground with footrests on either side (although Western toilets are common in tourist areas). To flush, reach for that plastic scooper, take water from the tank *(mandi)* and flush it away.

TRAVEL PERMITS

Technically, if you're heading to Papua you should obtain a *surat jalan* (visitor permit). See p294 for more information.

VISAS

Most visitors obtain a 30-day visa on arrival (VOA) at recognised entry points in Indonesia, which comprise 20 airports and 23 sea ports. These include ferry ports to/from Sumatra: Penang–Belawan, Melaka–Dumai and Singapore–Batam/Bintan. All major international airports are covered. For land border crossings other than at Etikong in West Kalimantan, you'll need a visa in advance.

At the time of writing, citizens of more than 60 countries were eligible for a VOA, including those from Australia, Canada, much – but not all – of the EU including Ireland, the Netherlands and the UK, plus New Zealand and the USA. The cost is US$25 and it is best to have exact change. It's possible to renew a 30-day VOA for another 30 days. To do so you must go to a local immigration office at least one week before your VOA expires. The process can be complex.

To get a much-prized 60-day visa you have to apply through an embassy or consulate before you arrive in Indonesia.

Your passport must be valid for six months following your date of arrival.

VOLUNTEERING

There are excellent opportunities for aspiring volunteers in Indonesia.

Bali is a hub for many charitable groups and NGOs.

Borneo Orangutan Survival Foundation (www.orangutan.or.id) Has rehabilitation and reforestation programs on Kalimantan.

East Bali Poverty Project (☑0361-410071; www.eastbalipovertyproject.org) Works to help children in the impoverished mountain villages of east Bali.

IDEP (Indonesian Development of Education & Permaculture; ☑0361-294993; www.idepfoundation.org) Bali-based, has projects across Indonesia; works on environmental projects, disaster planning and community improvement.

ProFauna (www.profauna.net) A large nonprofit animal-protection organisation operating across Indonesia; the Bali office has been aggressive in protecting sea turtles. Volunteers needed to help with hatchery releases and editing publications.

Smile Foundation of Bali (Yayasan Senyum; ☑0361-233758; www.senyumbali.org) Organises surgery to correct facial deformities; operates the **Smile Shop** (Map p210; ☑0361-233758; www.senyumbali.org; Jl Sriwedari) in Ubud to raise money.

SOS (Sumatran Orangutan Society; www.orangutans-sos.org) Works to save endangered species throughout Indonesia.

Volunteer in Java (www.volunteerinjava.com) Organises volunteers to teach English in the schools of West Java.

Yayasan Bumi Sehat (☑0361-970002; www.bumisehatbali.org) Operates an award-winning clinic and offers reproductive services to disadvantaged women in Ubud; accepts donated time from medical professionals and casual volunteers interested in teaching English.

Yayasan Rama Sesana (☑0361-247 363; www.yrsbali.org) Dedicated to improving reproductive health for women across Bali; accepts volunteers.

ⓘ Getting There & Away

The main bureaucratic consideration for entering Indonesia involves visas. See p307 for details.

AIR

Jakarta and Bali are the main hubs, but other useful international connections include Balikpapan (Kalimantan), Mataram (Lombok), Manado (Sulawesi), Medan (Sumatra), Palembang (Sumatra), Padang (Sumatra), Solo (Java) and Surabaya (Java).

The following are major airlines with services to/from and within Indonesia:

Air Asia (www.airasia.com) Serves large Indonesian cities, plus Bangkok, Kuala Lumpur and Singapore.

Emirates (www.emirates.com) Serves Jakarta from Dubai.

Eva Air (www.evaair.com) Serves Bali and Jakarta from Taipei, with good connections from North America.

Firefly (www.fireflyz.com.my) Serves major cities on Sumatra from Kuala Lumpur and Penang in Malaysia.

Garuda (www.garuda-indonesia.com) Indonesia's main national airline serves Bali and Jakarta from Australia, Asia and Amsterdam.

Jetstar/Qantas (www.qantas.com.au) Serves Bali, Lombok and Jakarta from Australia.

KLM (www.klm.com) Serves Jakarta and Bali from Amsterdam.

Lion Air (www.lionair.co.id) Fast-growing budget airline serves airports across Indonesia from major Asian cities and has a web of domestic flights.

Malaysia Airlines (www.mas.com.my) Serves Bali and Jakarta from Kuala Lumpur.

Merpati Airlines (www.merpati.co.id) Serves Dili in East Timor from Bali; also flies to more remote parts of the nation.

Qatar Airways (www.qatarairways.com) Serves Bali from Doha with connections to Europe.

SilkAir (www.silkair.com) Serves several Indonesian destinations from Singapore, including Balikpapan and Lombok.

Singapore Airlines (www.singaporeair.com) Numerous flights to Bali and Jakarta daily.

Thai Airways International (www.thaiair.com) Serves Bali and Jakarta from Bangkok.

Tiger Airways (www.tigerairways.com) Singapore-based budget carrier serving larger Indonesian cities.

Virgin Australia (www.virginaustralia.com) Serves Bali from several Australian cities.

LAND

There are three land links between Indonesia and neighbouring countries. Buses link Pontianak and Kuching on Borneo. And you can cross from Jayapura to Vanimo in Papua New Guinea.

ⓘ INTERNATIONAL DEPARTURE TAX

Indonesian airports charge a departure tax. This charge varies by airport – as high as 150,000Rp for international flights – and is payable in cash.

SEA

Malaysia and Singapore are linked to Sumatra by boats and ferries, although the links are inconvenient and most travellers fly. Boats make the Melaka (Malaysia) to Dumai (Indonesia) crossing. From Singapore, ferries make the quick hop to Pulau Batam and Bintan, the primary islands in the Riau archipelago.

There is a link on Borneo from Nunukan in East Kalimantan to Tawau in Malaysian Sabah. There is currently no sea travel between the Philippines and Indonesia.

ℹ️ Getting Around

AIR

The domestic-flight network in Indonesia continues to grow; schedules and rates are in a constant state of flux. Local carriers servicing small routes often operate cramped and dated aircrafts, whereas flights to Jakarta, Bali and other major destinations are usually on larger, newer crafts.

Depending on the size of the airlines and where they fly, timetables will vary from accurate, national schedules to hand-adjusted printouts of localised areas or provinces on specific islands. Website information is useful for the bigger carriers but nonexistent for the smaller ones. The best option is to check with local airline offices and travel agents to see what's available.

Tickets

The larger Indonesian-based carriers have websites listing fares; however, it may be hard if not impossible to purchase tickets online from outside Indonesia (Air Asia and Garuda are exceptions). You may have to call the airline in Indonesia – or better, if the option exists, an office outside Indonesia. Note that you may not reach anyone on the phone who speaks English.

Another option is to enlist the services of a travel agent. Sometimes the best way to get a ticket for travel within Indonesia is to simply go to the airport and compare prices at the various airline offices. Many airlines are strictly cash-based. Expect problems in the outer islands, where flights are limited, communications poor and booking procedures haphazard – you should reconfirm and reconfirm again.

BICYCLE

Bicycles can be hired in all major centres for 15,000Rp to 50,000Rp per day from hotels, travel agents and shops. The tropical heat, heavy traffic and poor road conditions make long-distance travel a challenge, but some hardy souls manage it.

ℹ️ DOMESTIC DEPARTURES TAX

Indonesian airports typically charge a departure tax. This charge varies by airport – it averages 40,000Rp for domestic flights and goes as high as 150,000Rp for international flights – and is payable in cash.

BOAT

Sumatra, Java, Bali and Nusa Tenggara are connected by ferries. Pelni, the national passenger line, covers the archipelago, albeit infrequently.

Pelni Ships

Pelni (www.pelni.co.id) has a fleet of large vessels linking all of Indonesia's major ports and the majority of the archipelago's outlying areas. Pelni's website is a good resource, showing arrivals and departures about a month in advance, although times can change right until the vessel leaves port.

Pelni ships have four cabin classes, plus *kelas ekonomi*. Class I has two beds per cabin (and is often more expensive than using a low-cost airline); Class IV has eight beds to a cabin. *Ekonomi* is extremely basic, with mattresses that can be rented. However, these designations are often meaningless on the many boats that are both filthy and overcrowded. By all means book the best class of service you can afford, noting that the bathroom may be unworkable, decks impassable with throngs of stoic passengers and food unpalatable.

You can book tickets up to two weeks ahead; it's best to book at least a few days in advance.

Other Boats

Sumatra, Java, Bali, Nusa Tenggara and Sulawesi are all connected by regular ferries, and you can use them to island hop all the way from Sumatra to Timor. These ferries run either daily or several times a week, so there's no need to spend days in sleepy little port towns. Check with shipping companies, the harbour office or travel agents for current schedules and fares.

However, schedules are often very vague, so be prepared to hang around until something turns up. Be warned that because vessels may be ancient and routinely overcrowded, safety standards are at times poor – though most people make it across the archipelago in one piece.

It's also possible to make some more unusual sea trips. Tourist boats travelling between Lombok and Flores with a stop on Komodo are popular.

TRAVELLING SAFELY BY BOAT

Boat safety is an important consideration across Indonesia, where boats that barely seem seaworthy may be your only option to visit that idyllic little island. In many cases these services are accidents waiting to happen, as safety regulation is not even spotty.

This is especially true on the busy routes linking Bali, Nusa Lembongan, Lombok and the Gilis. Each year there are accidents with the fast boats that kill and injure tourists. Even in the waters around Bali there are no emergency services to rescue you if problems arise.

Conditions are often rough in Indonesia's waters. Although the islands are in close proximity and are easily seen, the ocean between can get more turbulent than is safe for small speedboats zipping across the heavy seas.

With these facts in mind, it is essential that you take responsibility for your own safety, as no one else will. Consider the following points:

Bigger is better It may take you 30 minutes or more longer, but a larger boat will simply deal with the open ocean better than the over-powered small speedboats.

Check for safety equipment Make certain your boat has life preservers and that you know how to locate and use them. In an emergency, don't expect a panicked crew to hand them out. Also, check for life boats.

Avoid overcrowding Travellers report boats leaving with more people than seats and with aisles jammed with stacked luggage.

Look for exits Cabins may only have one narrow entrance making them death traps in an accident. Try to sit near an easy path into the water, although outboard motors are known to explode, injuring passengers sitting nearby.

Avoid fly-by-nighters Taking a fishing boat and jamming too many engines on the rear in order to cash in on booming tourism is a recipe for disaster.

BUS

Most Indonesians use buses to get around, so there is a huge variety of services, with everything from air-con deluxe buses with blaring TVs, toilets and karaoke that speed across the major islands, to *trek* (trucks) with wooden seats that rumble along remote dirt roads. Local buses are the cheapest; they leave when full and stop on request – on the outer islands this is often your only choice.

Look for 'public cars' or other permutations that are minivans with air-con which offer greater comfort and speed for about twice the rate of regular buses.

CAR & MOTORCYCLE

Self-drive mini-SUVs can be hired for as little as 80,000Rp to 150,000Rp a day with limited insurance in Bali, but become increasingly expensive and hard to come by the further you get from tourist areas. If you're not happy negotiating Indonesia's chaotic roads, a vehicle with driver can usually be hired for between 350,000Rp and 600,000Rp per day; the more remote areas tend to be the most expensive.

Motorcycles and scooters can be hired across Indonesia for 25,000Rp to 50,000Rp per day. Be sure to get a crash helmet, as wearing one is supposed to be compulsory.

LOCAL TRANSPORT

Public minibuses (most commonly called bemos, but also known as *colt, opelet, mikrolet, angkot, angkudes* and *pete-pete*) are everywhere. Bemos run standard routes (fares average 3000Rp to 5000Rp), but can also be chartered like a taxi.

Cycle rickshaws are called becak, while *bajaj* are Indonesian túk-túk: three-wheelers that carry two passengers (three at a squeeze) and are powered by rasping two-stroke engines. In quieter towns, you may find horse-drawn carts, variously called *dokar, cidomo, andong* and *ben hur*.

An extremely handy form of transport is the *ojek* (motorcycle taxi); expect to pay about 2500Rp to 10,000Rp for a short ride. Most towns have taxis, which require careful negotiations. In major cities (Jakarta, South Bali etc) look for Bluebird taxis, which are reliable and use their meters.

TRAIN

Java has a good railway service running the length of the island. There is also an extremely limited rail service in Sumatra.

Laos

⌥ 856 / POP 6.7 MILLION

Best for Regional Specialities

➡ Makphet (p321)

➡ Pho Dung (p321)

➡ Tamarind (p336)

Best Places for Cultural Connections

➡ Handicraft Night Market (p337)

➡ Minority villages (p334)

➡ Luang Prabang's temples (p330)

Why Go?

It's no accident that Laos appears as a favourite in many Southeast Asian odysseys, for this landlocked country lays claim to incredibly genuine people and the chance for your inner adventurer to let rip. The 'Land of a Million Elephants' oozes magic from the moment you spot a Hmong tribeswoman looming through the mist; trek through a glimmering rice paddy; or hear the sonorous call of one of the country's endangered gibbons. But it's also a place to luxuriate, whether by pampering yourself like a French colonial in a spa, or chilling under a wood-blade fan in a delicious Gallic restaurant. 'Old World' refinement is found in pockets across the country, especially in languid Vientiane and legendary Luang Prabang.

The country has also acquitted herself to green tourism, harnessing her forests with excellent treks and tribal homestays operated by eco-responsible outfits. Be it flying along jungle ziplines, elephant riding, exploring creepy subterranean river caves or motocross adventures, Laos will burn herself into your memory.

When to Go
Vientiane

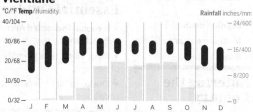

Jan Cool-season breezes and even the normally sweltering south is pleasantly bearable.

Oct Cool weather; locals celebrate the full moon and boat-racing festivals.

Nov & Dec Celebrations for Pha That in November. Cool weather but peak prices during December.

LAOS

⇒ **Currency** Kip

⇒ **Language** Lao

⇒ **Money** ATMs in major centres. Credit cards accepted in Luang Prabang and Vientiane.

⇒ **Visas** On arrival (valid for 30 days; US$30–42 depending on which passport you hold).

⇒ **Mobile phones** Prepaid SIMs available for as little as 10,000K. Decent connections.

Fast Facts

⇒ **Area** 236,000 sq km

⇒ **Capital** Vientiane

⇒ **Emergency** Police ☑191

Exchange Rates

Australia	A$1	7250K
Cambodia	1000r	2020K
Euro Zone	€1	11,020K
Thailand	10B	2470K
UK	£1	113,365K
US	US$1	8025K
Vietnam	10,000d	3805K

Set Your Budget

⇒ **Budget hotel room** US$10

⇒ **Evening meal** US$5

⇒ **Museum entrance** US$2

⇒ **Beer** US$1

Entering the Country

There are more than a dozen border crossings into Laos from Cambodia, China, Thailand and Vietnam. There are also frequent flights connecting Laos with neighbouring countries.

Don't Miss

There's no better way to discover the real Laos than by trying a homestay. Beyond the cities, 80% of the population lives in rural villages and, with minimal impact on the community and the environment, you can experience an evening with them. Given Laos' rich ethnicity and varied geography no two homestays will be the same, but you can rely on a few commonalities: you'll be woken by children and the local rooster, communally bathe and eat by the fire, and be guaranteed one of your most memorable nights in this country.

ITINERARIES

One Week

After spending a few days in riverside Vientiane sampling its Soviet-Franco architecture, sophisticated bars and Asian-fusion cuisine, travel north to the unforgettable ancient city of Luang Prabang to experience its temples, crumbling villas, pampering spas, elephant treks and Gallic cuisine.

Two Weeks

Fly to Vientiane, taking in its cafes, bars and cuisine for a few days, then head north to Vang Vieng for climbing, kayaking and tubing in serene karst scenery. Move on to enchanting Luang Prabang, bedecked with bakeries, temples, boutiques and restaurants. After a few days here take a two-day slowboat up the Mekong River to Huay Xai, having already booked yourself in for the memorable Gibbon Experience and the overnight stays in jungle treehouses.

If you've got time, head up to Luang Namtha for an ecoconscious trek in the wild Nam Ha National Protected Area. From here you can fly back to Vientiane to catch your flight out.

Essential Outdoor Activities

⇒ **National Protected Areas** Trek the dense forests of 20 national protected areas spread across Laos.

⇒ **Vang Vieng** Tube Vang Vieng's Nam Song River, a Lao rite of passage.

⇒ **The Loop** Hire a decent motocross bike and tackle 'The Loop'.

⇒ **Luang Prabang** Elephant ride through rivers in Luang Prabang.

⇒ **Gibbon Experience** Zipline through the jungle canopy with the Gibbon Experience or Treetop Explorer.

VIENTIANE

♪ 021 / POP 254,500

With its cosmo mix of Soviet-, Sino- and Franco-styled architecture, Vientiane (ວຽງຈັນ) is one of the most languid capital cities in Asia. Eminently walkable, its historic old quarter beguiles with tree-lined boulevards, glittering temples and colourful Buddhist monks. For the backpacker, Vientiane is wallet-friendly, with low-cost digs and delicious street food, as well as myriad cafes, bakeries and restaurants of almost every cuisine – particularly Gallic. Take a bicycle tour, practise yoga, sample a spa treatment, try a traditional herbal sauna, or shop for silk scarves and bespoke jewellery before watching the sunset over the Mekong River. Trust us, you'll like Vientiane more than you initially think.

The three main streets parallel to the Mekong – Th Fa Ngoum, Th Setthathirath and Th Samsènethai – form the central inner city of Vientiane and are where most of the budget guesthouses, bars and restaurants are located.

History

Vientiane was first settled as an early Lao fiefdom. Through 10 centuries of history it was variously controlled, ravaged and looted by the Vietnamese, Burmese, Siamese and Khmer. When Laos became a French protectorate at the end of the 19th century, it was renamed as the capital, was rebuilt and became one of the classic Indochinese cities, along with Phnom Penh and Saigon (Ho Chi Minh City). By the early 1960s and the onset of the war in Vietnam, the city teemed with CIA agents, madcap Ravens (maverick US Special Ops pilots) and Russian spies.

In 2009 the city hosted the Southeast Asian Games, a major illustration of the country's new profile. And while the newly constructed trainline from Thailand to within a few klicks of Laos is still largely useless, China's Kunming to Vientiane express route will be completed over the next few years at a massive cost to Laos. In 2012 Vientiane saw its first gay pride event, and in 2013 the capital enjoyed a visit from then US Secretary of State Hillary Clinton.

⊙ Sights

Pha That Luang   STUPA

(Great Sacred Reliquary, Great Stupa, ພະທາດຫລວງ; Th That Luang; admission 5000K; ⊙8am-noon & 1-4pm Tue-Sun) Svelte and gold-en Pha That Luang is the most important national monument in Laos; a symbol of Buddhist religion and Lao sovereignty. Legend has it that Ashokan missionaries from India erected a *tâht* (stupa) here to enclose a piece of Buddha's breastbone as early as the 3rd century BC.

Wat Si Saket   BUDDHIST TEMPLE

(ວັດສີສະເກດ; Map p318; cnr Th Lan Xang & Th Setthathirath; admission 5000K; ⊙8am-noon & 1-4pm, closed public holidays) Built between 1819 and 1824 by Chao Anou, Wat Si Saket is believed to be Vientiane's oldest surviving temple. And it shows; this beautiful temple turned national museum is in dire need of a face-lift.

Patuxai   MONUMENT

(Victory Monument, ປະຕູໄຊ; Map p316; Th Lan Xang; admission 5000K; ⊙8am-5pm) Vientiane's Arc de Triomphe replica is a slightly incongruous sight, dominating the commercial district around Th Lan Xang. Officially called 'Victory Monument' *and* commemorating the Lao who died in prerevolutionary wars, it was built in 1969 with cement donated by the USA intended for the construction of a new airport; hence expats refer to it as 'the vertical runway'. Climb to the summit for panoramic views over Vientiane.

Xieng Khuan   MUSEUM

(Suan Phut, Buddha Park, ຊຽງຂວັນ; admission 5000K, camera 3000K; ⊙8am-4.30pm) Twenty-five kilometres southeast of Vientiane, eccentric Xieng Khuan thrills with other-worldly Buddhist and Hindu sculptures, and was designed and built in 1958 by Luang Pu, a yogi-priest-shaman who merged Hindu and Buddhist philosophy, mythology and iconography into a cryptic whole.

Bus 14 (8000K, one hour, 24km) leaves the Talat Sao Bus Station every 15 or 20 minutes throughout the day and goes all the way to Xieng Khuan. Alternatively, charter a túk-túk (200,000K return).

DOS & DON'TS IN LAOS

➡ Always ask permission before taking photos.

➡ Don't prop your feet on chairs or tables while sitting.

➡ Refrain from touching people on the head.

➡ Remove your shoes before entering homes or temple buildings.

Laos Highlights

1 Experience **Luang Prabang** (p330), the ancient city of temples which has it all: royal history, Indochinese chic, colourful monks, waterfalls, elephant rides, stunning river views and world-class French cuisine

2 Take a boat ride through exhilarting yet spooky **Tham Kong Lo** (p353), a 7.5km cave that's home to fist-sized spiders and stalactite woods

3 Trek and zip across the forest by day at the **Gibbon Experience** (p351), guided by ex-poachers turned forest rangers, who lead you to your bed for the night in cosy treehouses

4 Trek through **Nam Ha National Protected Area** (p348) to some of the wildest, densest jungle in the country, home to tigers and a rich variety of ethnic tribes

5 Relax at **Si Phan Don** (p365), hammock capital of Laos; a steamy traveller's idyll where the Mekong turns turquoise and your pulse palpably drops

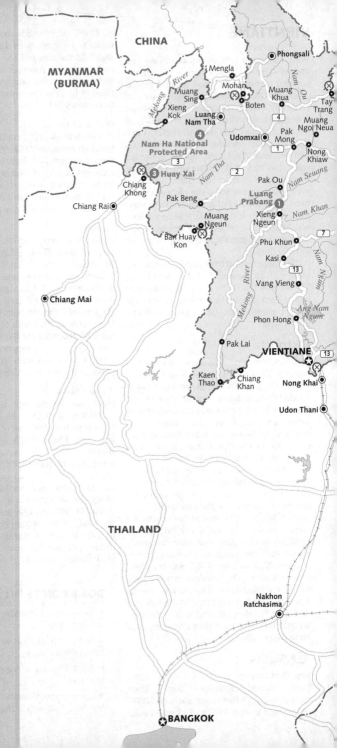

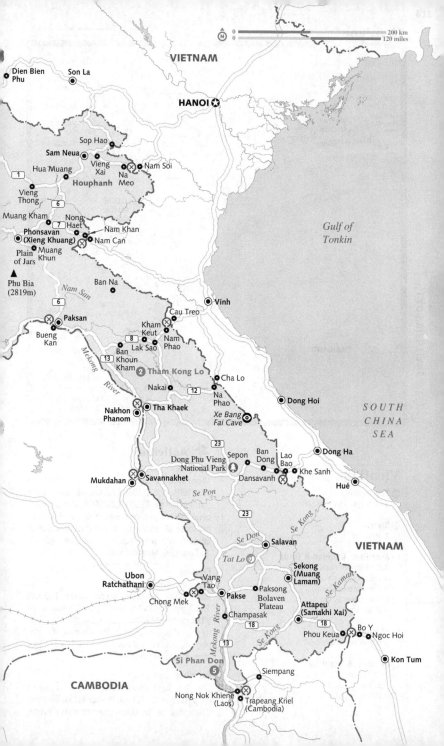

Vientiane

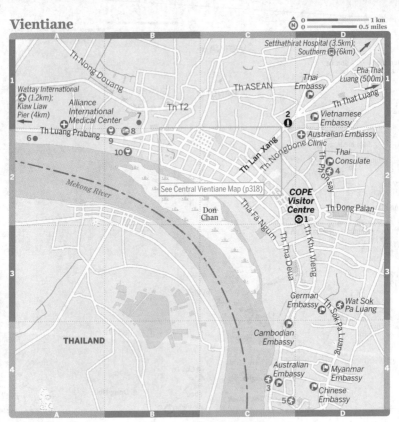

See Central Vientiane Map (p318)

LAOS VIENTIANE

Vientiane

🏃 Activities

Cycling

Vientiane By Cycle   CYCLING TOUR
(Map p316; ☑ 020 5581 2337; www.vientianebycycle.
com; full/half day 450,000/350,000K) Run by energetic Aline, this tour affords you the chance to
meander along Vientiane's riverfront, through
affluent and poor suburbs, and past schools
and temples. Starts at 8am.

Frisbee

Ultimate Frisbee   FRISBEE
(Map p316; American soccer pitch; 12,000K;
⊙6.30pm Mon) Every Monday at 6.30pm aerial
wizards meet at the American soccer pitch
to play Ultimate Frisbee (two teams of seven
players). Check out the Facebook page (Vientiane Ultimate Frisbee).

Bowling

Lao Bowling Centre   BOWLING
(Map p318; ☑ 021 218 661; Th Khun Bulom; per game
3 with shoe hire 16,000K; ⊙9am-midnight) Bright

lights, Beerlao and boisterous bowlers are what you'll find here.

Gym & Aerobics

Bee Bee Fitness   HEALTH & FITNESS

(Map p316; ☑ 021 315 877; opposite the Australian Embassy; 1-day membership 40,000K; ⊙ 6am-9pm Mon-Fri, 7am-9pm Sat & Sun) This roomy gym overlooks the Mekong and has decent rowing machines, spinning bikes and weightlifting apparatus, as well as regular Zumba and Pilates classes.

Massage & Herbal Saunas

Wat Sok Pa Luang   MASSAGE, SPA

(Map p316; Th Sok Pa Luang; ⊙ 1-7pm) In the leafy grounds of Wat Sok Pa Luang this Lao-style herbal sauna (20,000K) also offers traditional massage (40,000K) and meditation classes (free). It's 3km from the city centre. Avoid rush hour between 3pm and 6pm.

Oasis   MASSAGE

(Map p318; Th François Ngin; ⊙ 9am-9pm) Cool, clean and professional, this is an excellent central place to enjoy foot massage (50,000K), Lao-style body massage (60,000K) or a peppermint body scrub (200,000K), to name a few.

Swimming

The **Vientiane Swimming Pool** (Map p318; ☑ 020 5552 1002; Th Ki Huang; admission 15,000K; ⊙ 8am-7pm) is a 25m alfresco delight, but buy some goggles (15,000K) – there's enough chlorine in there to strip the barnacles off a shipwreck. The **Lao Plaza Hotel** (Map p318; ☑ 021 218 800; www.laoplazahotel.com; 63 Th Samsènethai) has a rooftop pool and plenty of loungers but will set you back 120,000K, and for Hollywood glamour sample the kidney-shaped pool at the **Settha Palace Hotel.** (Map p318; ☑ 021 217 581; 6 Th Pangkham; ⊙ 7am-8pm)

📚 Courses

Lao-language courses are held at the Centre Culturel et de Coopération Linguistique (p322).

Cooking

Villa Lao   COOKING COURSE

(Map p316; ☑ 021 242 292; www.villa-lao-guesthouse.com; off Th Nong Douang; half-day class 150,000K) As well as being a great place to stay, Villa Lao offers cooking courses at 9am and 2pm by appointment, involving a trip to the market, preparation of three dishes of your choice and sampling your creations. The price is per class, so the more people

involved the cheaper it will be per person; to give you an idea it should cost around 150,000K per person.

Meditation & Yoga

Foreigners are welcome at a regular Saturday afternoon sitting at Wat Sok Pa Luang (p316;). The session runs from 4pm until 5.30pm with an opportunity to ask questions afterwards.

Lemongrass Yoga   YOGA

(Map p316; ☑ 020 5887 2027; www.lemongrass yoga.com; per 90-min class 70,000K; ⊙ 6.30-8pm Thu, noon-1.30pm Sun) The city's best yoga instructor is based at her own traditional wooden Lao house (close to the Thai consulate) and teaches hatha yoga one-to-one or in small groups. The yoga house (number 6) is located in the middle of a *soi* (lane) just off of Th Boulichanh in Dongphalan Thong Village.

🎉 Festivals & Events

Pi Mai   LAO NEW YEAR

(⊙ Apr) Lao New Year is celebrated once more in mid-April at this mass water fight. Be warned – drunk driving and theft go through the roof at these times so remain vigilant.

COPE VISITOR CENTRE

Since the end of the Secret War in Laos more than 12,000 people have fallen victim to unexploded ordnance (UXO) – many of them children. A 10-minute bike ride from the city centre, the excellent **COPE Visitor Centre** (ສູນ ພື້ນ ฟู ถิบ ພິການ ແขຯ ຊาถ; Map p316; ☑ 021 88427; www.copelaos.org; Th Khu Vieng; ⊙ 9am-6pm) is an inspiring not-for-profit organisation dedicated to supporting victims, providing clinical mentoring and training programs for local staff in the manufacture of artificial limbs and related rehabilitation activities. COPE makes high-tech but low-cost artificial limbs, transforming the lives of people who've had to make do with their own improvised limbs. The UXO exhibition is fascinating, with photographs portraying the salvaged lives of victims, as well as 'the cave cinema', a bunker-style screening room showing a number of documentaries. Take a free tour around the centre accompanied by an English-speaking guide.

LAOS VIENTIANE

Central Vientiane

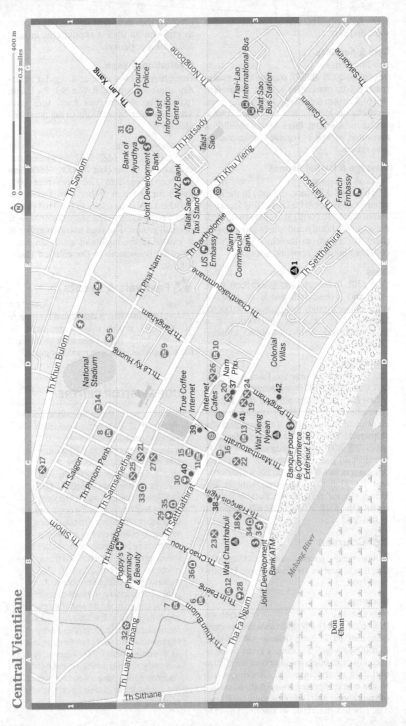

LAOS

Th Lan Xang
Tourist Police
Tourist Information Centre
Th Nongbone
Th Hatsady

31
Bank of Ayudhya
Joint Development Bank
ANZ Bank
Th Saylom

Talat Sao
Talat Sao Taxi Stand
Th Khu Vieng
Thai-Lao International Bus
Talat Sao Bus Station
Th Galiliani
Th Sakkarine

Th Bartholomie
US Embassy
Siam Commercial Bank
French Embassy
Th Mahasot

Th Setthathirat
4
Th Phai Nam
Th Pangkham
Th Chanthakoummane
1
Colonial Villas
Mekong River

2
5
6
Th Ky Huong
Th Khun Bulom

National Stadium

14
8
17
Th Salgon
Th Phnom Penh
Th Samsenethai
25 21 27
33

Nam Phu
26 10
20 37 24
19 41 42
13
16 22
Th Manthaturath
Wat Xieng Nyean
Banque pour le Commerce Extérieur Lao

True Coffee
Internet Cafes
39

30 40 11 15

29 35
38
Th Setthathirat
Th François Ngin
23
18 34 3
Th Chao Anou
36
Th Wat Chanthabuli

Poppy's Pharmacy & Beauty
Th Hengboun
Th Sihom

7 9
Th Khun Bulom
12 28
Th Pang
Th Tha Fa Ngum
Joint Development Bank ATM

32
Th Luang Prabang
Th Sithane

Don Chan

0 400 m
0 0.2 miles
N

Central Vientiane

⊙ Sights
1 Wat Si Saket E3

⊙ Activities, Courses & Tours
2 Lao Bowling Centre D1
3 Oasis...B3
4 Settha Palace Hotel.............................. E1
5 Vientiane Swimming Pool.....................D1

⊜ Sleeping
6 Auberge Sala Inpeng.............................B2
7 Hotel Khamvongsa.................................B2
8 Lao Heritage Hotel.................................C1
9 Lao Plaza Hotel D2
10 Mali Namphu Guest House...................D3
11 Mixok Guest House.................................C2
12 Phonethip Guesthouse B3
13 Saysouly Guest House...........................C3
14 Syri 1 Guest House..................................D1
15 Vayakorn House......................................C2
16 Vientiane Backpackers
   Hostel C3

⊗ Eating
17 Ban Anou Night Market.........................C1
18 Istanbul B3
19 JoMa Bakery Café..................................D3
20 Khop Chai Deu..D3
21 Lao Kitchen...C2
22 Le Banneton C3
23 Makphet B3

24 Phimphone Market................................D3
25 Pho Dung C2
26 Scandinavian Bakery D3
27 YuLaLa Cafe...C2

⊙ Drinking & Nightlife
28 Bor Pennyang B3
29 iBeam...B2
   Khop Chai Deu...........................(see 20)
30 Samlo Pub..C2

⊙ Entertainment
31 Centre Culturel et de
   Coopération Linguistique...................F2
32 Wind West A2

⊙ Shopping
33 Book Café...C2
34 Couleur d'Asie...B3
35 Indochina Handicrafts C2
36 T'Shop Lai Gallery B2

⊙ Information
37 Green Discovery D3
38 Lasi Ticketing C3
39 Maison du Cafe.......................................C2

⊙ Transport
40 Europcar...C2
41 Jules' Classic Rental C3
42 Lao Airlines..D3

Bun Nam BOAT RACE
(Bun Suang Héua; ⊙Oct) At the end of *pansăh* (the Buddhist rains retreat) in October, boat races are held on the Mekong River; the riverbank is lined with food stalls, temporary discos, carnival games and beer gardens for three days and nights.

Bun Pha That Luang CULTURE
(That Luang Festival; ⊙Nov) Bun Pha That Luang, usually in early November, is the largest temple fair in Laos. The festivities begin with a *wéean téean* (circumambulation) around Wat Si Muang, followed by a procession to Pha That Luang. The festival climaxes on the morning of the full moon with the *đák bàht* ceremony, during which several thousand monks from across the country receive alms.

🛏 Sleeping

The old days of shadowy flophouses are out the window. Shoestringers can expect clean, basic guesthouses for their money, or have the option of further stretching their cash by staying in a dorm. Accommodation here

is listed in order of price tier: budget (less than US$20, or 160,000K), midrange (US$20 to US$80, or 160,000K to 626,000K) and top end (more than US$80, or more than 626,000K).

Syri 1 Guest House GUESTHOUSE $
(Map p318; ☑ 021 212 682; Th Saigon; r 50,000-150,000K; ❄@☎) Syri sits on a quiet street and has been a traveller fave for many years with good reason: generously sized rooms (both air-con or fan, en suite or shared bathroom), a DVD lounge, bikes for rent, and tailored bike tours of the city. 100% friendly.

Phonethip Guesthouse GUESTHOUSE $
(Map p318; ☑ 021 217 239; 72 Th In Paeng; r with fan/air-con US$10/15; ❄☎) With its babbling water feature and shaded courtyard peppered with swing chairs and spots to relax, this place feels like an escape from the heat and crowds. There's a range of rooms, some with fridges and TVs, and a friendly owner.

Saysouly Guest House GUESTHOUSE $
(Map p318; ☑ 021 218 383, 021 218 384; www.saysouly.com; 23 Th Manthatourath; s/d without

bathroom 50,000/90,000K, r with air-con & bathroom 130,000K; ✳) Two minutes' walk from Nam Phu and popular with backpackers, this three-storey place offers basic but clean rooms, some with shared bathrooms. Service can't exactly be described as enthusiastic, but the atmosphere is social.

Vientiane Backpackers Hostel HOSTEL $

(Map p318; 📳020 974 84227; www.vientianebackpackerhostel.com; Th Nokèokoummane; @🛜) Great new hostel with three large, fan-cooled dorms. There's a cafe, free vodka after 9pm, laundry services, free wi-fi and bike (10,000K) and scooter (70,000K) rental. Bathrooms and showers are modern and clean, while self-catering facilities are more than adequate. Free breakfast, ticketing and visa services.

Mixok Guest House GUESTHOUSE $

(Map p318; 📳021 251 606; Th Setthathirath; r 130,000K; ✳🛜) Rooms here all enjoy air-con, TV, wi-fi, and include breakfast. There's also an attached internet cafe (6000K per hour) and bus-ticketing service, but sadly staff have taken charm-avoidance classes.

★Hotel Khamvongsa HOTEL $$

(Map p318; 📳021 218 415; www.hotelkhamvongsa.com; Th Khounboulom; s/d/tr incl breakfast US$35/50/60; ✳🛜🏿) This lovely French-era building has been reincarnated as a homely boutique hotel, with belle époque touches such as glass tear lightshades, chess-tiled floors, and exquisitely simple rooms, softly lit with wood floors and Indo-chic decor. Rooms on the 3rd and 4th floors have masterful views. There's also a restful courtyard and restaurant.

★Lao Heritage Hotel GUESTHOUSE $$

(Map p318; 📳021 265 093; Th Phnom Penh; r US$20-25; ✳@🛜) This quirky old Lao house hidden in vines is not far off being classed as a boutique hotel; it's undergoing a steady makeover under new management, with a great new tapas restaurant. Rooms have wood floors, bed runners, TVs, somewhat tired en suites, and fridges. There are plenty of nooks to chill out in, as well as in-room wi-fi. Rooms 1 and 2 are our favourites. Delightful staff.

Auberge Sala Inpeng GUESTHOUSE $$

(Map p318; 📳021 242 021; www.salalao.com; Th In Paeng; r incl breakfast US$25-40; ✳🛜🏿) This pretty complex of wood cabanas and a handsome traditional Laotian house is set in gardens spilling with champa flowers. The

grander rooms have a whiff of rustic chic, with en suites and air-con, while the cheaper cabanas burst with atmosphere.

Vayakorn House HOTEL $$

(Map p318; 📳021 241 911; www.vayakorn.biz; 91 Th Nokèokoummane; s/d/tr 140,000/200,000/260,000K; ✳🛜) This is a calm, clean and great-value spot to rest up. There's a welcoming lobby, with a pleasant breakfast area plus a chill-worthy verandah outside to watch life go by on the busy street. There are 21 pristine and stylishly spartan rooms with fresh linen, en suites, TV and air-con. Accepts credit cards.

Mali Namphu Guest House GUESTHOUSE $$

(Map p318; 📳021 215 093; www.malinamphu.com; 114 Th Pangkham; s/d/tr incl breakfast 210,000/260,000/350,000K; ✳@🛜) On the tailor's street, Mali Namphu's bright rooms, wrapped around a leafy courtyard, are fragrant and decked in Lao handicrafts. All have desks and enjoy impeccably clean bathrooms and air-con. There's also cable TV.

BAKERIES

Le Banneton (Map p318; Th Nokèokoummane; breakfast 45,000K; ⊙7am-9pm; ⊖✳) Le Banneton's Doisneau-spattered interior makes for a nice place to read a paper over a tart, salad, panini or tasty omelette, or you can sit outside on the small terrace. Hands-down the country's best croissants.

Scandinavian Bakery (Map p318; www.scandinavianbakerylaos.com; Nam Phu; mains 10,000-30,000K; ⊙7am-9pm; ⊖✳🛜🏿) Its wilting facade might look as if it's shipwrecked, but this bakery is a treasure trove of fresh subs, breakfasts, brownies, muffins, bagels and delicious coffees. Loads of comfy couches and alfresco tables upstairs and down.

JoMa Bakery Café (Map p318; Th Setthathirath; mains 29,000K; ⊙7am-9pm Mon-Sat; ⊖✳🛜🏿) This mocha-hued cafe is Vientiane's busiest thanks to its soothingly cool atmosphere and cornucopia of lush salads (25,000K) and bespoke bagels – choose from salami, ham, salmon, turkey, cheese and salad fillings. They also serve tacos, breakfast and soup.

✖ Eating

Few places in Southeast Asia boast such a dizzying array of global gastronomy, be it felafel from a Turkish restaurant, top-flight Parisien cuisine, Italian, Vietnamese, Korean, Japanese or Indian. Vientiane is also celebrated for its bakeries, while Lao food has enjoyed a recent 21st-century makeover.

✖ Around Th Setthathirath & Nam Phu

★ Makphet LAOTIAN $
(Map p318; Th Setthathirath; mains 40,000K; ☺11am-9pm Mon, Wed, Thu, Fri & Sat, 6-9pm Tue; ❋🏠) ✐ Managed by Friends International (www.friends-international.org), Makphet helps disadvantaged kids build a future as chefs and waiters. Guacamole-green walls and hardwood furnishings add style to delicious dishes such as spicy green papaya salad. It's located opposite Wat Ong Teu off Th Setthathirath.

Istanbul TURKISH $
(Map p318; ✐020 7797 8190; Th François Ngin; mains 20,000-90,000K; ☺9.30am-10.30pm; ❋🏠) This welcoming Turkish joint has a colourful menu of doner and shish kebabs as well as favourites such as meatballs, hummus and felafel. Try the Iskender kebab – grilled beef with pepper sauce, yoghurt and green chilli. The super-charged Turkish coffee will put a spring in your step.

Ban Anou Night Market LAOTIAN $
(Map p318; meals 10,000-15,000K; ☺5-10pm) Setting up on a small street off the north end of Th Chao Anou every evening, this atmospheric open-air market dishes up Lao cuisine, from grilled meats to chilli-based dips with vegetables and sticky rice.

Phimphone Market SELF-CATERING $
(Map p318; 94/6 Th Setthathirath; ☺7am-9pm Mon-Sat; 🏠) This self-catering oasis stocks everything from Western magazines, ice cream, imported French and German salami, bread, biscuits and chocolate, as well as Western toiletries. They also stock Hobo maps of the city.

Khop Chai Deu FUSION $$
(Map p318; ✐021 251 564; 54 Th Setthathirath; mains 25,000-60,000K; ☺8am-midnight; ❋🏠✐) Khop Chai Deu has been a travellers' favourite for years because of its range of well-prepared Lao, Thai, Indian and assorted European fare.

You can pick your live fish from the kitchen and see it a few minutes later on your plate.

✖ Th Samsènethai & Around

★ Lao Kitchen LAOTIAN $
(Map p318; ✐021 254 332; www.lao-kitchen.com; Th Hengboun; mains 30,000-40,000K; ☺11am-10pm; ⊜❋🏠✐) This superb new Lao restaurant is unfailingly creative in its execution of trad-Lao dishes. Colourful walls dotted with photography complement a menu spanning stews to Luang Prabang sausage (full of vim), *láhp* (spicy mint and shredded meat salad) variations, stir-fried morning glory, and various palate-friendly sorbets.

Pho Dung LAOTIAN $
(Map p318; ✐021 213 775; 158 Th Hengboun; noodle soup 12,000-15,000K; ☺6am-2pm) This excellent *fĕr* (rice noodle soup) diner is packed with a melting pot of locals and travellers. Choose from pork, beef or chicken noodle soup. Run by a friendly Vietnamese family, the gargantuan bowls here are served Lao-style, that is, with heaps of optional seasonings and immense plates of fresh veggies and herbs.

YuLaLa Cafe FUSION $$
(Map p318; Th Hengboun; mains 50,000K; ☺11.30am-2pm & 6-9.30pm Tue-Sun; ❋🏠) Piping classical music across its wood-floored space as travellers sit cross-legged on cushions (leave yer shoes outside!), YuLaLa offers dishes such as tofu dumplings, stewed eggplant and sautéed salt pork. A little bit of zen to take you away from the bustle of the city.

🍸 Drinking & Nightlife

The river plays host to a parade of American-style bars. For more chic refinement comb the backstreets radiating from Th Setthathirath. Conveniently, two of the better nightclubs are within walking distance of each other. **Echo** (Map p316; ✐021 213 570; Th Samsènethai; ☺8pm-1am), at the Mercure Hotel, is pretty cool and is popular with Vientiane's beautiful people. Just up the road, **At Home** (Map p316; Th Luang Prabang; ☺8pm-midnight) thumps with trance and house.

★ Khop Chai Deu BAR
(Map p318; ✐021 025 1564; www.inthira.com; Th Setthathirath) KCD is the city's original watering hole and these days has massively finessed its nocturnal offerings – think low-lit interiors and a sophisticated drinks list, plus

LAOS VIENTIANE

more activities than any other bar, such as speed dating and women's arm wrestling. Upstairs on the 3rd floor a new bar has opened, more South Beach Miami than Vientiane; it's slick urban, and very cool.

★ iBeam   BAR
(Map p318; 🖉 021 254 528; Th Setthathirath; ⊙ 11am-11pm; 🛜) The classiest new joint in town, with glass panel walls and interior flair; snack on tapas and work your way through an extensive wine list. Wednesday is ladies' night and nets you 50% off.

Spirit House   COCKTAIL BAR
(Map p316; 🖉 021 262 530; Th Fa Ngoum; cocktails 40,000K; ⊙ 7am-11pm; 🛜) This traditional Lao house facing the Mekong has a well-stocked bar with enough cocktails on the menu to keep any old boozer smiling. Chilled tunes complement the dark woods and comfy couches of its stylish interior.

Bor Pennyang   BAR
(Map p318; 🖉 020 787 3965; Th Fa Ngoum; ⊙ 10am-midnight) Way up in the gods, a cast of locals, expats, bar girls and travellers assemble at this tin-roofed, wood-raftered watering hole to gaze out at nearby Thailand over a sunset Beerlao. There are pool tables and a huge bar to drape yourself over, as well as sports on TV.

Samlo Pub   BAR
(Map p318; 🖉 021 222 308; Th Setthathirath; ⊙ 7pm-late) Sleazy and dimly lit, this joint feels like the lovechild of a Cockney East End pub and a Patpong good-time bar, and is perfect for an atmospheric drink. The person next to you could be a rogue, hooker, ladyboy, criminal, or your own reflection. Duck in for a quickie (drink) but don't hang around!

☆ Entertainment

By law, entertainment venues close at 11.30pm. Vientiane has movies, cultural shows, a circus and Lao boxing to keep you busy, as well as music concerts. By the time you read this a multiplex cinema may well have opened.

Centre Culturel et de
Coopération Linguistique   CINEMA
(French Cultural Centre; Map p318; 🖉 021 215 764; www.ambafrance-laos.org; Th Lan Xang; ⊙ 9.30am-6.30pm Mon-Fri, to noon Sat) FREE Dance, art exhibitions, literary discussions

and live music all take place in this hive of Gallic cultural activity. As well as cult French films (shown Saturdays at 7.30pm), the centre also offers French and Lao language lessons.

Wind West   LIVE MUSIC
(Map p318; 🖉 020 200 0777; Th Luang Prabang; ⊙ 5pm-1am) A US 'roadhouse'-style bar and restaurant, Wind West has live Lao and Western rock music most nights – the music usually starts about 9pm and finishes around 1pm.

🛍 Shopping

Numerous handicraft and souvenir boutiques are dotted around streets radiating from Nam Phu, particularly Th Pangkham and Th Setthathirath.

★ T'Shop Lai Gallery   BEAUTY, HOMEWARES
(Map p318; www.laococo.com/tshoplai.htm; off Th In Paeng; ⊙ 8am-8pm Mon-Sat, 10am-6pm Sun) 🍃 Easily Vientiane's finest shopping experience – step into this palace of the senses and the first thing you notice is the melange of aromas: coconut, aloe vera, honey, frangipani and magnolia; all of them emanate from the body oils, soaps, sprays, perfumes and lip balms that are made and beautifully packaged by self taught *parfumier*, Michel 'Mimi' Saada.

Next check out the tortoise-shell-inlaid furniture, and the cards, bangles, prints and fountain pens...these wonderful objets d'art and products are all made with sustainable, locally sourced products.

Indochina Handicrafts   HANDICRAFTS
(Map p318; 🖉 021 223 528; Th Setthathirath; ⊙ 10am-7pm) Laos' version of the Old Curiosity Shop, this enchanting den of Buddha statuary, antique Ho Chi Minh and Mao busts, Russian wristwatches and communist memorabilia, Matchbox cars, medals, snuff boxes and vintage serving trays is a stop that shouldn't be missed.

★ Couleur d'Asie   FASHION
(Map p318; 🖉 021 223 008; www.couleurdasie.net; 201 Th François Ngin; ⊙ 9am-5pm Mon-Sat) 🍃 This delightful boutique owned by a French-Vietnamese dress designer has a vivid range of ladies' dresses, men's linen shirts and boho chemises. They also sell lovely jewellery, bed runners and silk shawls. Upstairs you can have clothes fitted to order.

Book Café
BOOKS

(Map p318; Th Hengboun; ⊙8am-8pm Mon-Fri) Vientiane's best stocked secondhand bookshop sells loads of travel guides, thrillers and informative books on Lao culture and history.

ℹ️ Information

EMERGENCY
Ambulance (☑195)
Fire (☑190)
Police (☑191)
Tourist Police (Map p318; ☑021 251 128; Th Lan Xang)

INTERNET ACCESS
There are several internet cafes on Th Samsènethai and Th Setthathirath, open from 9am to 11pm and charging 6000K an hour. Wi-fi is often free and available at many of Vientiane's cafes.

True Coffee Internet (Map p318; Th Setthathirath; per hr 8000K; ⊙9am-9pm; 🛜 💻) This great cafe also sells Apple Mac accessories and has brownies, yoghurt and fresh juices. Enjoy a latte as you email, Skype, or use the free wi-fi on your own laptop.

MEDIA
Laos' only English-language newspaper is the hopelessly state-censored *Vientiane Times*. French-speakers should look for *Le Rénovateur*. Also worth keeping an eye on for listings of upcoming happenings is the Facebook page of Pasai.

MEDICAL SERVICES
Vientiane's medical facilities will do for broken bones and the diagnosis of dengue fever and malaria, but for anything more serious cross to Thailand for the nearby **Aek Udon International Hospital** (☑ in Thailand 0066 4234 2555; Th Phosri) which can dispatch an ambulance, or in critical situations an airlift, to take you to Udon Thani. The Friendship Bridge is closed between 10pm and 6am, but Thai/Lao immigration will open for ambulances.

Alliance International Medical Center (Map p316; ☑021 513 095; Th Luang Prabang) This brand new hospital is fresh, clean and treats broken bones and dispenses antibiotics. Behind the Honda Showroom near Wattay International Airport.

Australian Embassy Clinic (Map p316; ☑021 353 840; Th Thadeua; ⊙8.30am-5pm Mon-Fri) For nationals of Australia, Britain, Canada, Papua New Guinea and New Zealand only. This clinic's Australian doctor treats minor problems by appointment; it doesn't have emergency facilities. Accepts cash or credit cards. A block southeast of Patuxai.

Poppy's Pharmacy & Beauty (Map p318; ☑030 981 0108; Th Hengboun; ⊙8am-10pm) Bright and clean, this modern, well-stocked pharmacy is great for toiletries, cosmetics, sun cream, malaria pills (not Larium), and sleeping tablets for long bus journeys.

MONEY
Licensed money-changing booths can be found along Th Setthathirath. Banks listed here change cash and travellers cheques and issue cash advances (mostly in kip, but occasionally in US dollars and Thai baht) against Visa and/or

LAOS VIENTIANE

GETTING TO THAILAND: VIENTIANE TO NONG KHAI

Getting to the border The Thai–Lao Friendship Bridge at the Tha Na Long/Nong Khai border is 22km southeast of Vientiane. The easiest way to cross is on the comfortable Thai–Lao International bus (22,000K, 90 minutes), which leaves Vientiane's Talat Sao bus station for the border roughly every hour from 7.30am till 6pm. The VIP bus, which continues on to Bangkok (248,000K), leaves Talat Sao daily at 6pm. Alternatively, catch a taxi (300B) or jumbo (four-wheeled túk-túk, seating 12; 250B), or public bus 14 from Talat Sao (15,000K) between 6am and 6.30pm.

Since 2009, it's also possible to cross the bridge by train, as tracks have been extended from Nong Khai's train station 3.5km into Laos, terminating at Dongphasy Station, about 13km from central Vientiane. From Nong Khai there are two daily departures (9.30am and 4pm, fan/air-con 20/50B, 15 minutes) and border formalities are taken care of at the respective train stations.

At the border Travellers from most countries can travel visa-free to Thailand.

Moving on From the Thai border catch a túk-túk (20B) to Nong Khai train station where a sleeper train leaves for Bangkok at 6.20pm and costs US$23/37 for a 2nd-class/sleeper ticket.

MasterCard. Most now have 24-hour ATMs that work with foreign cards.

Bank of Ayudhya (Map p318; ☑ 021 214 575; 79/6 Th Lan Xang) Cash advances on Visa cards here carry a 1.5% commission.

Banque pour le Commerce Extérieur Lao (BCEL; Map p318; cnr Th Pangkham & Th Fa Ngoum; ⊙ 8.30am-7pm Mon-Fri, to 3pm Sat & Sun) Best rates; longest hours. Exchange booth on Th Fa Ngoum and three ATMs attached to the main building.

Joint Development Bank (Map p318; 75/1-5 Th Lan Xang) Usually charges the lowest commission on cash advances. Also has an ATM.

Siam Commercial Bank (Map p318; 117 Th Lan Xang) ATM and cash advances on Visa.

POST

Post, Telephone & Telegraph (PTT; Map p318; cnr Th Lan Xang & Th Khu Vieng; ⊙ 8am-5pm Mon-Fri, to noon Sat & Sun) Come here for poste restante and stamps.

TELEPHONE

International calls can be made from most internet cafes for about 5000K per minute, though it's better if you can Skype.

TOURIST INFORMATION

Tourist Information Centre (NTAL; Map p318; www.ecotourismlaos.com; Th Lan Xang; ⊙ 8.30am-noon & 1.30-4pm) Between Talat Sao and Patuxai and based in an easy-to-use room with descriptions of each province, the tourist information centre has English-speaking staff, free brochures and regional maps – worth a visit.

TRAVEL AGENCIES

Green Discovery (Map p318; ☑ 021 264 528; www.greendiscoverylaos.com; Th Setthathirath) Deservedly the country's most respected adventure tours specialist, as well as kayaking, cycling, ziplining and trekking trips; can also help with travel arrangements.

Lasi Ticketing (Map p318; ☑ 021 222 851; www.lasiglobal.com; Th François Ngin; ⊙ 8am-5pm Mon-Fri, 8.30am-noon Sat) With helpful English-speaking staff, Lasi sells air, VIP bus and train tickets, as well as arranging visas for Cambodia and Vietnam. Speak to Miss Pha.

Maison du Cafe (Map p318; ☑ 020 780 4842, 021 219 743; 119 Th Manthatourath; ⊙ 8am-10pm) This shop offers ticketing and visa services, and has a few computers for internet use (6000K per hour).

BUSES FROM VIENTIANE

Talat Sao Bus Station

DESTINATION	PRICE (K)	DURATION (HR)	DISTANCE (KM)
Nong Khai	17,000	1½	95
Udon Thani	22,000	2	76
Vang Vieng	30,000	4	153

Northern Bus Station

DESTINATION	PRICE (K)	DURATION (HR)	DISTANCE (KM)
Huay Xai	230,000	30-35	869
Kunming	635,000	30	781
Luang Namtha	180,000	18	676
Luang Prabang	110,000	11	384
Phonsavan	110,000-150,000	9-11	374
Sam Neua	170,000-190,000	15-17	612
Udomxai	170,000-190,000	13-15	578

Southern Bus Station

DESTINATION	PRICE (K)	DURATION (HR)	DISTANCE (KM)
Attapeu	140,000	22-24	812
Lak Sao	35,000	7-9	334
Pakse	110,000	14-16	677
Savannakhet	75,000	8-11	457
Tha Khaek	40,000	7	332

ⓘ Getting There & Away

AIR

Wattay International Airport is the main transport hub for the rest of the country. Beside it is the rickety domestic terminal. **Lao Air** (✈ 021 513 022; www.lao-air.com; Wattay Airport Domestic Terminal; ⊙8am-5pm) and **Lao Airlines** (Map p318; ✈ 021 212 051; www.laoairlines.com; Th Pangkham; ⊙8am-noon & 1-4pm Mon-Sat, to noon Sun) both fly from Vientiane to domestic destinations.

BOAT

Passenger boat services between Vientiane and Luang Prabang have become almost extinct, however a regular slow boat makes the trip from Vientiane to Pak Lai, 115km away. Boats leave Monday, Wednesday and Saturday at 8am (120,000K, about eight hours) from Kiaw Liaw Pier.

BUS & SŎRNGTǍAOU

Buses use three different stations in Vientiane.

For buses to China, contact **Tong Li Bus Company** (✈ 021 242 657) at the Northern Bus Station. For Vietnam, **S.D.T** (✈ 720 175) has buses leaving daily from the Southern Bus Station: for Hanoi (220,000K, 24 hours) via Vinh (180,000K, 16 hours), and for Danang (230,000K) via Hué (200,000K, 19 hours). On Mondays, Thursdays and Sundays they leave at 6pm. For Ho Chi Minh City change at Danang. Some buses to Vietnam also leave from the Northern Bus Station.

Northern Bus Station (Th Asiane) The Northern Bus Station is exactly 9km northwest of the centre, and serves all points north of Vang Vieng, including China and some buses to Vietnam. Destinations and the latest ticket prices are listed in English.

Southern Bus Station (Rte 13 South) The Southern Bus Station is commonly known as Dong Dok Bus Station or just *kéw lot lák ków* (Km 9 Bus Station). It is 9km out of town and serves everywhere south. Buses to Vietnam leave from here.

Talat Sao Bus Station (Map p318; ✈ 216 507; Th Khu Vieng) International buses to Thailand's Udon Thani (22,000K) leave here every hour. A VIP bus for Bangkok (248,000K) also leaves from here every day at 6pm.

ⓘ Getting Around

Central Vientiane is all accessible on foot.

TO/FROM THE AIRPORT

Wattay International Airport is about 4km northwest of the city centre. Fixed fare airport taxis cost US$10 into town. Alternatively, walk 500m to the airport gate where you can get a shared túk-túk for about 20,000K. Official túk-túk tariffs from the city centre list the airport as a 60,000K ride.

BICYCLE, MOTORCYCLE & CAR

Bicycles can be rented for 10,000K per day from tour agencies and guesthouses. Scooters can be hired on the west side of Th Nokèokoummane near the Douang Deuane Hotel. The place directly in front of the hotel rents 110cc bikes for 70,000K per day.

Europcar (Map p318; ✈ 021 223 867; www.europcarlaos.com; Th Setthathirath; ⊙8.30am-6.30pm Mon-Fri, 8.30am-1pm Sat & Sun) Hires quality cars (from US$55 per day). You can leave the car at your destination for a charge. Third-party insurance as standard.

Jules' Classic Rental (Map p318; ✈ 020 9728 2636; www.bike-rental-laos.com; Th Setthathirath; per day US$35, minimum rental 1 week) Regularly serviced scooters and, for the intrepid jungle seeker, heavy-duty 250cc and 450cc motocross bikes. Jules can even send your luggage on to your destination (for a charge), or if you're headed far afield and don't want to double back (say Luang Prabang), you can also leave the bike there for US$50.

TÚK-TÚK

Many túk-túk have a laminated list of vastly inflated tourist prices, and won't budge for less than the price already agreed upon with the other drivers. You can also flag down shared, fixed-route túk-túk (with passengers already in them), which cost around 20,000K, depending on your destination.

A FRESH START

Back in '99 Vang Vieng was a little-known affair where travellers came to float down the river on tractor inner tubes, smoke the odd spliff and explore its fantastical caves. Then the rumour was out – Vang Vieng was Southeast Asia's next hedonistic mecca. Lao locals were quick to erect more guesthouses, then the drugs got heavier, the party darker.

By 2009 makeshift rave platforms were spawning along the tubing route with many ignoring the natural environment in favour of reefer, methamphetamine and opium cocktails. By 2011 a staggering 20-odd tourists were dying each year from heart attacks, drowning and broken necks, plus there were frequent drug busts. In August 2012 most of the river bar owners were ordered by the government to shut down, thus ending a dark chapter in the town's history.

NORTHERN LAOS

Whether you're here to trek, ride an elephant, zipline, kayak, cycle or try a homestay, a visit to Laos' mountainous north is unforgettable. Bordered by China to the far north, Vietnam to the east and Myanmar (Burma) to the west, there's a fascinating cast of ethnic peoples here. Hidden amid this rugged simplicity is Southeast Asia's premier Shangri La, Luang Prabang, and, beyond it, unfettered, dense forests still home to a cornucopia of animals.

East of here, rugged Xieng Khuang Province holds the mysterious Plain of Jars and is still cratered by the heavy US bombing from the war in Vietnam (1964–73), while distant Hua Phan Province in the northeast is home to gothic karst scenery, serene mountains and the enigmatic Viengxai caves.

Vang Vieng ວັງວຽງ

🎵 023 / POP 33,000

Like a rural scene from an Oriental silk painting, Vang Vieng is surely one of the prettiest places in Laos. The city crouches low over the Song River with a backdrop of serene cliffs and a tapestry of vivid green paddy fields. Since 2012 the previously toxic party scene – which was renowned for thumping music, disrespectful teens and the misconception that anything goes – has been banished, with a widespread feeling of relief among the locals, who are recalibrating the town as an outdoor paradise with a raft of adrenalin-inducing and nature-based activities; nowadays a more chilled crowd are visiting to kayak, go caving and climb the karsts. Spend a few days here and prepare to manually close your jaw as you gape at one of Laos' most stunningly picturesque spots.

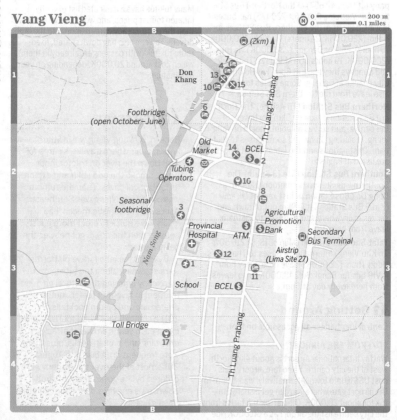

Vang Vieng

◉ Sights & Activities

There's a wealth of activities on offer from tubing, cycling and trekking, plus caving, kayaking and climbing.

Caves   CAVE

The stunning limestone karsts around Vang Vieng are honeycombed with tunnels and caverns, and, after tubing, caving has to be the town's main draw. You can buy a map and do the caves yourself, and it's also possible to go in an organised group. Check your guesthouse for info.

The most famous cave, **Tham Jang** (ຖ້ຳຈັງ; admission 17,000K), 1km south of town, was used as a hideout from marauding Yunnanese Chinese in the early 19th century. A set of stairs leads up to the main cavern entrance. There's also a cool spring at the foot of the cave.

Another popular cave is **Tham Phu Kham** (Blue Lagoon, ຖ້ຳພູຄຳ; admission 10,000K). To reach it, cross the **seasonal bamboo footbridge** (walking/cycling/scooter toll 4000/6000/10,000K) then walk or pedal 7km along a scenic, unsealed road to Ban Na Thong, from where you have to walk 1km to a hill on the northern side of the village. It's a tough final 200m climb but worth it for a dip in the blue stream afterwards.

Vang Vieng

◉ Activities, Courses & Tours

1 Adam's Rock Climbing School	B3
2 Green Discovery	C2
3 V.L.T.	B2
Vang Vieng Jeep Tour	(see 5)

🛏 Sleeping

4 Champa Lao	C1
5 Chez Mango	A4
6 Domon Guesthouse	C1
7 Easy Go Hostel	C1
8 Inthira Hotel	C2
9 Maylyn Guest House	A3
10 Nam Song Garden	C1
11 Pan's Place	C3

🍴 Eating

12 Le Café De Paris	C3
13 Living Room	C1
14 Luang Prabang Bakery	C2
15 Nam Song Garden	C1
The Kitchen	(see 8)

🍸 Drinking & Nightlife

16 Gary's Irish Bar	C2
17 Kangaroo Sunset Bar	B4

Tham Sang (admission 5000K), 13km north along Rte 13, is a small cavern containing a few Buddha images and a Buddha 'footprint', plus the elephant-shaped stalactite that gives the cave its name.

Kayaking   KAYAKING

(day trips per person 100,000K) Kayaking trips typically take you down a few rapids and stop at caves and villages. We recommend Green Discovery and V.L.T. Average prices are about US$15 per person, per day.

Tubing   ADVENTURE TOUR

(50,000K rental, 20,000K deposit, US$7 fine if not returned on time) Depending on the speed and level of the river, tubing the Nam Song can be a soporific crawl beneath the jungle-vined karsts, or a speedy glide downstream back to Vang Vieng. It's fantastic fun, but always wear a life jacket when the river runs fast – the currents are lethal even if you're not stoned, and the many stories of travellers who have drowned doesn't make for pleasant reading.

It's 55,000K to rent a tube plus a 60,000K refundable deposit. Life jackets are available and you can rent a dry bag for 20,000K. The fee includes transport to the tubing drop-off point (3.5km), but keep in mind that you must return the tube before 6pm, otherwise you'll have to pay a 20,000K late fee. If you lose your tube, you have to pay 60,000K. Enjoy!

👣 Tours

★ Green Discovery   ADVENTURE TOUR

(☑ 023 511 230; www.greendiscoverylaos.com; Th Luang Prabang; 1-day cycling tour per person US$37, half-/full-day rock climbing US$27/36, kayaking to Vientiane per person US$53) Green Discovery is Vang Vieng's most reliable operator, offering trekking, kayaking, rafting, rock climbing and caving. From here you can also head out with them to **Nam Lik Jungle Fly** (☑ 020 5662 2001; www.laosjunglefly.com). GD's equipment is up to date, plus they have a solid reputation to protect, so safety comes first.

Adam's Rock Climbing School   ADVENTURE TOUR

(☑ 020 5501 0832; www.laos-climbing.com; opposite the hospital; half-/full-day climbing 180,000/260,000K, 2-day course US$100; 👣) The only dedicated climbing outfit in town, with experienced, multilingual guides and sturdy kit.

LAOS VANG VIENG

SPLURGE

Best enjoyed first thing in the morning, hot-air ballooning is the perfect way to take in the jaw-dropping scenery. **Flights** (☑ 020 2220 2259; www.vang viengtour.com/ballooning; costs US$80) take place at 6.30am, 4pm & 4.30pm (admission US$80) and last approximately 40 minutes. Call to book a flight, or contact Mr Vone at V.L.T Tour (p327).

V.L.T ADVENTURE TOUR
(☑ 020 5520 8283, 023 511 369; www.vangvieng tour.com) V.L.T is well established and charges US$13 for one day's kayaking, US$22 for one-day mountain-bike trips and US$33 for one-day treks.

🛏 Sleeping

Increasingly, midrangers and boutique hotels are moving in as VV ditches its dreads in favour of a stylish coiffure. Avoid the ugly town and head downriver.

🛏 Over the River and Out Of Town

★**Phoudindaeng Organic Farm** GUESTHOUSE $
(☑ 023 511 220; www.laofarm.org; dm 30,000K, r 40,000-150,000K, deluxe cliff-facing bungalows 200,000K; P@🛜🛏) 🅟 Located a few kilometres out of town by the Nam Song River. Bungalows here front the soaring cliffs and are sparklingly clean, featuring mosquito nets, bedside lamps, en suites and verandahs. Up the hill are three eight-bed fan-cooled dorms. There's also a great restaurant – try the mulberry pancakes or mulberry mojitos!

If you have time, ask about volunteering for the permaculture program. There are also art classes for local kids at the weekend and stone painting if you want to lend a hand. Cooking classes here cost US$30.

Maylyn Guest House GUESTHOUSE $
(☑ 020 5560 4095; jophus_foley@hotmail.com; r 50,000-80,000K; P🌸🛜🛏) Run by gregarious Jo, Maylyn's cosy, well-spaced cabanas are set in lush gardens bursting with butterflies and lantana flowers, affording possibly the most dramatic views of the karsts. There's a new building with immaculate en suite rooms plus a cafe to read in. Over the bridge.

Chez Mango GUESTHOUSE $
(☑ 020 5443 5747; www.chezmango.com; r 50,000-70,000K; 🌸) Located over the bridge, Mango is friendly, scrupulously clean and has seven basic but colourful cabanas (some with bathrooms) in its flowery gardens. Run by a Frenchman, Noé, it makes for a soporific and restful spot. Breakfast is available. Noé also runs **Vang Vieng Jeep Tours** (☑ 020 5443 5747; noedouine@yahoo.fr; Chez Mango; minimum group of 4, per person 120,000K; 🛏) from here. Recommended.

🛏 In Town

★**Champa Lao** GUESTHOUSE $
(☑ 020 5823 4612; r without/with bath 70,000/100,000K, tr 130,000K; @🛜) This heavily wooded traditional stilted Lao house has basic fan rooms with mosquito nets. The ambient-lit garden restaurant casts off heavenly aromas, while there are also bungalows down the bank by the river. Great views.

Pan's Place GUESTHOUSE $
(☑ 023 511 484; Th Luang Prabang; r 30,000-70,000K, cabanas s/d 30,000/40,000K; @🛜) This old trusty has basic, cosy fan rooms with tiled floors and en suites. Out the back are cabanas in a leafy garden, plus a communal chilling area. There's also a natty little cafe (crêpes, fruit salads) and a cinema room upstairs with hundreds of DVDs to choose from.

Domon Guesthouse GUESTHOUSE $
(☑ 023 511 210, 020 9989 8678; r with fan & without view/with air-con & view 100,000/150,000K; 🌸🛜) On the banks of the Nam Song north of the old market, this place has large, clean rooms with powder-blue walls, quality furniture, TV, en suite and oodles of space. A sun deck and restaurant will have been built by the time you read this.

Nam Song Garden GUESTHOUSE $
(☑ 023 511 544; bungalows 50,000-70,000K, 4-bed dm 120,000K; 🛜) At the north end of the town this higgledy-piggledy hillside affair enjoys one of the best views in town from its leafy garden. There's a large room which sleeps four, and various bungalows with and without bathrooms and fine views. Food is available (mains 40,000K).

Easy Go Hostel HOSTEL $
(☑ 020 5536 6679; www.easygohostel.com; next to Champa Lao; dm/d without bathroom

25,000/40,000K) Crafted from bamboo and rattan, with its wooden walkways and maze of five cramped dorms, Easy Go smacks a little of *The Beach*. While the rooms themselves are nothing to get excited about, they're clean, and the friendly owners are proactive at keeping you busy with activities.

Inthira Hotel　　　　BOUTIQUE HOTEL $$
(☑023 511 070; www.inthirahotel.com; Th Luang Prabang; standard/superior/deluxe incl breakfast US$32/43/54; ☺✳@☎ⓘ) An oasis of oxblood rooms with views of the karsts, it has hardwood floors, upscale furniture, elegant art, bedside lamps and modern, spotless en suites. The restaurant is cool and leafy, and staff are professional.

✖ Eating

Vang Vieng sees contemporary Lao food mixing it up with Western, and a few affordable French cuisine options. Come evening there are pancake vendors opposite the hospital.

★Living Room　　　　ASIAN $
(☑020 5491 9169; next to Champa Lao Guesthouse; ☺3-11pm) Classy new cafe with a funky sundowner terrace enjoying amazing karst views and a Lao – wait for it – Austrian fusion menu. Fresh juices, shakes (10,000K), soups, tofu, pork schnitzel and really inventive dishes such as spaghetti Vang Vieng – a kind of bolognese with spicy *láhp* salad. Delicious.

★The Kitchen　　　INTERNATIONAL $
(www.inthira.com; Inthira Hotel, Th Luang Prabang; mains 30,000K; ☺7am-10pm; ✳☎ⓘ) This place strikes a fine balance between informality and style and is often packed to the gills; once you've tasted their coconut shrimp, *pàt tai,* spare ribs and steamed fish, you'll understand why.

Le Café De Paris　　　　FRENCH $
(mains 20,000-30,000K; ☺5.30-11.30pm) Le Café is celebrated for its steak tartare, boeuf bourguignon and hot dog Parisien. A number of red and white wines on the menu, plus the homely decor and friendly, low-lit ambience, make this a worthwhile haunt.

Nam Song Garden　　　　FUSION $
(☑023 511 544; ☺7am-11pm; ☎) This alfresco haunt makes for a romantic stop to gaze at the jagged karsts. The menu is pretty varied, spanning barbecued fish, chicken and meat dishes, breakfasts, *láhp* variations and sweet

and sour dishes. Pop in for a sunset cocktail (mojitos 30,000K).

Luang Prabang Bakery　　　　BAKERY $
(☑023 511 145; mains 25,000-60,000K; ☺7am-10.30pm; ☎) Never so chic, the LPB has upgraded her decor to wood lanterns and wicker chairs and tables. The real ace though is the treasure chest of choccy brownies, cookies, doughnuts, gateaux and danish – a treat for the munchies.

▾ Drinking

Vang Vieng has ditched all-night parties in favour of chilling.

Gary's Irish Bar　　　　IRISH PUB
(☑020 5825 5774; mains 35,000K; ☺9am-midnight) This is a cool, easy joint to while away an evening listening to indie tunes, playing pool or watching sports on the box. Great full breakfasts, homemade pies, and happy hour from 6pm to 10pm.

Fluid Bar　　　　BAR
(☑020 5929 5840; ☎) Within its riverside walls are original trippy art, mosaics, a relaxing balcony bar, pool table, cool tunes, great grub, a crazy golf course, and a vibrant garden with sun loungers and hammocks.

Kangaroo Sunset Bar　　　　BAR
(☑020 771 4291; mains 35,000K; ☺8am-11.30pm; ☎) Colourful lanterns and chilled rock and jazz complement a menu of Lao and Western cuisine. It's also well placed for meditative sunset beers by the river.

ⓘ Information

Agricultural Promotion Bank (Th Luang Prabang) Exchanges cash only.

Banque pour le Commerce Extérieur Lao (☺8.30am-3.30pm Mon-Sun) Thanon Luang Prabang (☑023 511 434; ☺8.30am-3.30pm); Old Market (☺8.30am-3.30pm) Does exchanges and cash advances and has a 24-hour ATM.

Post Office (☑023 511 009) Beside the old market.

Provincial Hospital (☑023 511 604) This modest hospital has X-ray facilities and is fine for broken bones, cuts and malaria. When we visited, the doctor spoke reasonable English.

DANGERS & ANNOYANCES

The Nam Song River is lethal when it runs high after the wet season: never hire a tube on your own, nor attempt to return after dark.

　Since the 2012 clean up, hard drugs are not so widespread, but dope is still around and local police are adept at sniffing out spliffs. If you're caught with a stash of marijuana (or anything else) the normal practice is for police to take your passport and fine you US$500.

🛈 Getting There & Away

From the **bus station** (Rte 13) 2km north of town, minibuses/VIP buses leave for Luang Prabang (110,000/130,00K, six to eight hours, 168km, several daily), Vientiane (fan/minibus/air-con 40,000/60,000/80,000K, three to 4½ hours, 156km, several daily) and Phonsavan (100,000K, minibus only, six to seven hours, 219km, daily at about 9.30am).

Alternatively, *sŏrngtăaou* (pick-up trucks; 30,000K, 3½ to 4½ hours) leave for Vientiane about every 20 minutes from 5.30am until 4.30pm, and as they're often not full the ride can be quite enjoyable.

Tickets for minibuses and VIP buses are sold at guesthouses, tour agencies and internet cafes in town.

🛈 Getting Around

The township is small enough to walk around with ease. Bicycles/mountain bikes can be rented for around 10,000/30,000K a day, while scooters rent for 50,000K per day (automatics cost 70,000K).

For cave sites out of town you can charter *sŏrngtăaou* near the old market site – expect to pay around US$10 per trip up to 20km north or south of town.

Luang Prabang
ຫລວງ ພະ ບາງ

📞 071 / POP 70,000

This Unesco-protected gem of 33 Buddhist temples is a traveller's dream, with affordable, top-class cuisine and French colonial buildings. There are few places in Southeast Asia that can compete with such a special mix of chic refinement and ancient charm as found on Luang Prabang's hallowed peninsula.

The good news is there are still bags of great-value digs and the best things are cheap or free: hiring a bike, chilling by the riverbank, temple-hopping, shopping in the night market, taking a spa or yoga class, and visiting the menthol-blue Kuang Si cascades. Spend a little more and you can ecotrek, elephant ride or take a cooking course – your choices are myriad.

The stamp of the French lives on as freshly baked croissants send out aromas from Gallic-style cafes; and old Indo-Chinese mansions have been reborn as boutique hotels. Prepare to relax and re-plot your itinerary. Luang Prabang will effortlessly seduce you.

◉ Sights

★ **Royal Palace Museum**　　　MUSEUM
(Ho Kham, ພະຣາຊະວັງຽງແກວ; 📞 071 212 470; Th Sisavangvong; admission 30,000K; ⊙ 8-11.30am & 1.30-4pm Wed-Mon, last entry 3.30pm) The former Royal Palace, built in 1904, was the main residence of King Sisavang Vong (r 1905–59) whose statue stands outside. Note that you must be 'appropriately dressed' to enter, which means no sleeveless shirts or short shorts.

The main palace building is approached from the south. Italian marble steps lead into an entry hall where the centrepiece is the gilded dais of the former Supreme Patriarch of Lao Buddhism. To the right, the king's reception room has walls covered in light-suffused Gauguinesque canvases of Lao life. A line of centuries-old Khamu metal drums leads back to the main throne room, whose golden trimmed walls are painted deep red and encrusted with a feast of mosaic-work in Japanese coloured mirror glass.

Behind the throne room are the former royal family's residential quarters, left as they were when King Savang Vatthana was forcibly evicted by the communist regime in 1975.

Beneath, but entered from the western side, is a series of exhibition halls used for temporary exhibits. Separate outbuildings display the **Floating Buddha collection** of meditation photographs and the five-piece **Royal Palace car collection**, including two 1960s Lincoln Continentals, a rare wing-edged 1958 Edsel Citation and a dilapidated Citroën DS.

No single treasure in Laos is more historically resonant than the **Pha Bang**, an 83cm-tall gold-alloy Buddha for which the whole city is named. Its arrival here in 1512 spiritually legitimised the Lan Xang royal dynasty as Buddhist rulers. The Siamese twice carried the Pha Bang off to Thailand (in 1779 and 1827) but it was finally restored to Laos by King Mongkut (Rama IV) in 1867. Nearing completion in the southeast corner of the palace gardens, **Wat Ho Pha Bang** (Royal Temple) is a soaring, multiroofed temple designed to eventually house the Pha Bang Buddha. For now, however, the Pha Bang lives in an easy-to-miss little room surrounded by engraved elephant tusks and three silk screens

Central Luang Prabang

LAOS

0 | 200 m
0 | 0.1 miles

Mekong River

Nam Khan

Labels and streets:

- Wat Xieng Thong
- Th Sakkarin
- Th Kingkitsarat
- Th Khem Khong
- Th Thugnaithao
- Th Sisavangvong
- Th Sisavang Vatthana
- Buddha Footprint
- Bamboo Footbridge (dry season only)
- Bamboo Bridge (dry season only)
- Longboat Office
- Boats to Pak Ou Caves & Nong Khiaw
- Navigation Office
- Slow Boat Landing
- Floating Buddha Photographs
- Royal Palace Car Collection
- BCEL
- Royal - Pha Bang
- Royal Palace Exhibition Halls
- Royal Palace Museum
- ATM
- Minipost Booth
- That Chomsi Ticket Booth
- Phu Si
- Phu Si
- That Chomsi
- That Chomsi Ticket Booth
- TAEC
- Dara Market
- Th Chao Phanya Kang
- Th Hoxieng
- Th Chao Fa Ngum
- Provincial Tourism Department
- Th Chao Sisuphon
- Th Kitsarat
- Th Phommatha
- Th Wisunarat
- Th Bunkhong
- Th Pha Mahapatsaman
- Provincial Hospital
- Fresh Produce Market
- Naluang Minibus (1.3km); Southern (1.3km); Northern (2.5km)

Numbers on map: 1, 2, 3, 4, 5, 6, 7, 8, 9, 10, 11, 12, 13, 14, 15, 16, 17, 18, 19, 20, 21, 22, 23, 24, 25, 26, 27, 28, 29, 30, 31, 32, 33, 34, 35, 36, 37, 38, 39, 40, 41, 42, 43, 44, 45, 46, 47, 48, 49, 50, 51, 52

Central Luang Prabang

embroidered by the former queen. To find it, walk east along the palace's exterior south terrace and peep in between the bars at the eastern end.

Footwear cannot be worn inside the museum, no photography is permitted and you must leave bags in a locker room to the left-hand side of the main entrance.

★ **Wat Xieng Thong** BUDDHIST TEMPLE
(ວັດຊຽງທອງ; off Th Sakkarin; admission 20,000K; ⏰8am-5pm) Luang Prabang's best-known monastery is centred on a 1560 *sĭm* (chapel). Its roofs sweep low to the ground and there's an idiosyncratic 'tree of life' mosaic set on its west exterior wall. Inside, gold stencil work includes dharma wheels on the ceiling and exploits from the life of legendary King Chanthaphanit on the walls.

Dotted around the *sĭm* are several stupas and three compact little chapel halls called *hăw*. **Hăw Tai**, shaped like a tall tomb,

was originally a 'library' but now houses a standing Buddha. The **Hăw Pa Maan** ('success' Buddha sanctuary) remains locked except during the week following Pi Mai. The **Hăw Tai Pha Sai-nyàat** (reclining Buddha sanctuary) was dubbed La Chapelle Rouge (Red Chapel) by the French. It contains an especially rare reclining Buddha that dates from the construction of the temple.

Fronted in especially lavish gilt work, the **Hóhng Kép Mîen** is a garage for a ceremonial carriage designed to carry the huge golden funeral urns of the Lao royalty. This glittering vehicle is festooned with seven red-tongued *naga* (mythical serpent-being).

Wat Wisunarat BUDDHIST TEMPLE
(Wat Visoun, ວັດວິຊຸນ; Th Wisunarat; admission 20,000K; ⏰8am-5pm) Though touted as one of Luang Prabang's oldest operating temples, this is actually an 1898 reconstruction of the

1513 original, which was destroyed following Black Flag raids. Peruse the collection of gilded 'Calling for Rain' Buddhas placed here, along with some medieval ordination stones, having been rescued from various abandoned or ravaged temples for their protection.

★ Phu Si   HILL

(ພູສີ; admission 20,000K; ⊙8am-6pm) Dominating the old city centre, the 100m-tall hill of Phu Si is crowned by a 24m gilded stupa called That Chomsi. Viewed from a distance, especially when floodlit at night, the structure seems to float in the hazy air. It's a favourite with sunset junkies thanks to its staggering views.

Ascending Phu Si from the north side (329 steps), stop at the decaying **Wat Pa Huak** (admission by donation). It has a splendid carved wood Buddha riding Airavata, the three-headed elephant from Hindu mythology, and original 19th-century murals in its interior.

Reaching That Chomsi is also possible from the south and east sides. Two such paths climb through large **Wat Siphout-thabat Thippharam** to a curious miniature shrine that protects a Buddha Footprint. Directly southwest of here a series of new gilded Buddhas are nestled into rocky clefts and niches around **Wat Thammothayalan**. The monastery is free to visit if you don't climb beyond to That Chomsi.

Other Temples   TEMPLE

In the Old Quarter, the ceiling of **Wat Xieng Muan** (ວັດຊຽງມວນ; ⊙8am-5pm) is painted with gold *naga* and the elaborate *háang thien* (candle rail) has *naga* at either end. With backing from Unesco and New Zealand, the monks' quarters have been restored

BIG BROTHER MOUSE

If you want to get involved in improving local literacy, seek out **Big Brother Mouse** (BBM; ☑ 071 254 937; www.bigbrothermouse.com; Th Sothikuman), a homegrown initiative that brings the delights of the written word to infants in remote villages who, for lack of materials, rarely get the chance to read. If a bunch of you sponsor a book party (US$350), you can go with the BBM staff and distribute books. Alternatively, hang out at the BBM office for a couple of hours and read to the kids who attend.

as a classroom for training young novices and monks in the artistic skills needed to maintain and preserve Luang Prabang's temples. Among these skills are woodcarving, painting and Buddha-casting, all of which came to a virtual halt after 1975.

★ TAEC   MUSEUM

(Traditional Arts & Ethnology Centre; ☑ 071 253 364; www.teaclaos.org; admission 20,000K; ⊙9am-6pm Tue-Sun) Visiting this three-room museum is a must to learn about northern Laos's various hill-tribe cultures, especially if planning a trek. TAEC is within a former French judge's mansion, which was among the city's most opulent buildings of the 1920s. There's also a cafe here.

🏃 Activities

The best way to explore the city is by bike, taking time to meander through the peninsula past scenes of monastic life and children playing. Basic/mountain bikes cost 15,000/30,000K per day and can be hired along Th Sisavangvong. For easier journeys, automatic one-gear scooters cost around US$20 per day. Motorcycle rental typically costs US$15 a day or US$20 for 24 hours. **KPTD** (☑ 071 253 447; Th Kitsarat) has a wide range of scooters as well as a Honda CRF (US$65) for motocross riders only.

Massage & Yoga

Luang Prabang is all about yoga and pampering to ease your soul and those trekked-out calves.

Hibiscus Massage   MASSAGE

(☑ 030 923 5079; Th Sakkarin; traditional massage from 60,000K; ⊙10am-10pm) Set in a former gallery in an old French building, Hibiscus wafts chilled tunes through its silk-draped walls while you get pummelled to perfection.

Spa Garden   MASSAGE, SPA

(☑ 071 212 325; massage 60,000-350,000K, sauna/manicure 30,000/60,000K) Attractive property set amid a flourishing garden, with various relaxation and detox packages.

Luang Prabang Yoga   YOGA

(☑ 020 2388 1771; www.luangprabangyoga.org; Utopia bar, off Th Phommatha; per hr 30,000K; ⊙7.30-8.30am Mon-Sat, 5.30-6.30pm Tue, Thu & Sat; 🛜 📶) Based in the lush riverside gardens of Utopia bar, there are daily sessions to clear your cocktail haze and sync your spirit with the city's Buddhist vibe.

SPLURGE

Learn to weave your own scarf and dye your own textiles with the excellent one-day course at **Ock Pop Tok** (☑071 212 597; www.ockpoptok.com; full-/half-day course US$72/42; ⊙8.45am-4pm Mon-Sat). Teachers are master craftspeople, you get to keep your handiwork, and lunch is included. Situated 2km past Phousy market, a free túk-túk will pick you up and bring you back.

🍜 Courses

Tamarind COOKING COURSE
(☑020 7777 0484; www.tamarindlaos.com; Ban Wat Nong; full-day course 270,000K; ⊙9am-3pm Mon-Sat) Join Tamarind at its lakeside pavilion for a day's tuition in the art of Lao cuisine, meeting first at its restaurant before heading to the market to buy ingredients for classic dishes such as *mok pa* (steamed fish in banana leaves). Evening classes are available from 4pm for 200,000K, but no market visit is included.

🎍 Tours

If you have a few days, whimsical Kuang Si waterfalls and Pak Ou Caves are well worth a visit. There's a plethora of tour companies down Th Sisavangvong. We recommend **All Lao Travel** (☑253 522; Th Sisavangvong; ⊙8am-10pm) as a one-stop shop for flights, boat and VIP bus tickets, and visa extensions.

Green Discovery OUTDOORS
(☑071 212 093; www.greendiscoverylaos.com; 44/3 Th Sisavangvong) The daddy of ecotourism in Laos. They offer kayaking, trekking, mountain biking, motorcycling and multiday trips north, including motorcycle tours.

White Elephant HIKING
(☑071 254 481; www.white-elephant-adventures-laos.com; Th Sisavangvong) 🌿 White Elephant has solid relationships with Hmong and Khamu villages, allowing you a deeper insight into ethnic life. You can do this on a trek or by cycle in two- and three-day tours. Look out for the BMW motorbike.

Tiger Trail HIKING
(☑071 252 655; www.laos-adventures.com; Th Sisavangvong; ⊙8.30am-9pm) 🌿 Focusing on socially responsible treks benefiting local people, Tiger Trail offers hikes through Hmong and Khamu villages. All tours can be tailored to include kayaking, elephant riding, rafting or mountain biking.

🎉 Festivals & Events

The two most important annual events in Luang Prabang are **Pi Mai** (Lao Lunar New Year) in April, when Luang Prabang is packed to the gills with locals armed with water pistols (book accommodation well in advance), and boat races during **Bun Awk Phansa** (Ok Watsa; ⊙Full Moon) in October.

🛏 Sleeping

The most memorable area to stay is on the historic peninsula. There are also decent guesthouses near the Mekong, a few blocks southwest of the Hmong handicraft night market.

🛏 Old Quarter

Nora Singh Guesthouse GUESTHOUSE $
(☑071 212 033; Th Sisavangvong; r 130,000K; ❄️🌐) Tucked away in the lower reaches of Phu Si, this is a likeable little wooden home with just seven guest rooms, which include air-con, hot water and free wi-fi. It feels quite secluded when compared to the main drag.

Namsok Guesthouse 1 GUESTHOUSE $
(☑071 212 251; www.namsok-hotel.com; Th Sisavang Vatthana; r 100,000-200,000K; ❄️🌐) The friendly and helpful Namsok has rooms spread over two buildings with cheaper fan digs in the old building. The new building includes mod cons like air-con, TV and a fridge.

Silichit Guest House GUESTHOUSE $
(☑071 212 758; Th Sisavang Vatthana; r 80,000-120,000K; ❄️🌐) A popular place with boxy, basic rooms finished in traditional Lao style, but it's the location that wins you over, in the heart of the old town near the Mekong. Try for rooms 4 or 6 upstairs.

Paphai Guest House GUESTHOUSE $
(☑071 212 752; Th Sisavang Vatthana; r without bathroom 50,000-60,000K; 🌐) Cheap and basic, rooms here are set in a traditional wooden house near the heart of Th Sisavangvong, are fan-cooled, rattan-walled and have padlocks on the doors.

Bou Pha Guesthouse GUESTHOUSE $
(☑071 252 405; Th Sisavangvong; r 60,000-100,000K; 🌐) This takes us back to 1990s Luang Prabang – an old house in the heart

of the city with rooms for less than a tenner. It's run by a lovely older couple and the cheapest rooms have shared bathrooms. Upstairs rooms at 100,000K include a street view.

Sackarinh Guest House GUESTHOUSE $
(☑071 254 412; Th Sisavangvong; r 120,000-150,000K; ❉ 🛜) Hidden down a side street that chokes on flowers, this is a colourful and central option while you get your bearings. Right in the centre of town. Rooms are basic but spacious.

★ Khoum Xiengthong Guesthouse GUESTHOUSE $$
(☑071 212 906; www.khoumxiengthong.com; Th Sisalernsak; r US$50-70; ❉ 🛜) This delightful guesthouse, with a strong whiff of Indochic, nestles around a pretty garden. Stone-floored, white-walled rooms enjoy golden tapestries and chrome fans: rooms 2 (lower floor) and 5 (upper floor) are vast and include four-poster beds.

Thanaboun Guesthouse GUESTHOUSE $$
(☑071 260 606; Th Sisavangvong; r 160,000-280,000K; ❉ @ 🛜) In the heart of town, Thanaboun excels with clean, tastefully finished rooms. Rooms out back, which back on to the temple grounds, are quieter. There's also an internet cafe.

Villa Senesouk HOTEL $$
(☑071 212 074; senesouk@laohotel.com; Th Sakkarin; r US$30-50; ❉ 🛜) The morning monks' procession passes right outside Senesouk's cheaper rooms. The upper ones are brighter and share a wat-view balcony. Tucked away across a garden courtyard, the 'new' block is designed to look like a traditional family home.

Around Luang Prabang

★ Xayana Guesthouse GUESTHOUSE $
(☑071 260 680; www.mylaohome.com; Th Hoxieng; dm 40,000K, r from 80,000K; 🛜) Also known as the X3 Capsule Hotel, this budget pad has immaculately clean dorms with three bathrooms to every eight beds. There's an inviting courtyard out front to hang, drink coffee and meet other travellers.

Souksavath Guesthouse GUESTHOUSE $
(☑071 212 043; Th Hoxieng; r 120,000-200,000K; ❉ 🛜) Souksavath has house-proud rooms with fresh paint, bureaux and wall-mounted flat-screen TVs. Good value.

Mano Guest House GUESTHOUSE $
(☑071 253 112; manosotsay@hotmail.com; Th Pha Mahapatsaman; r 80,000-120,000K; ❉ 🛜) Spacious and homey, Mano has all-wood rooms with large TVs, tiled bathrooms, iris-stemmed lights and wall hangings.

Lemon Laos Backpackers HOSTEL $
(☑071 212 500; www.spicylaosbackpacker.com; Th Noradet; dm 30,000K; 🛜) One of the cheapest crashpads in town; travellers aren't really here for the beds, but to avoid going to bed, as it rumbles on into the early hours. BBQs and cheap shots add up to a carnival atmosphere.

🍴 Eating

The city's bakeries and French restaurants could give Paris' Left Bank a run for its money. Quick, cheap eats are found at baguette stalls opposite the tourist office from early morning till sunset. After this the adjacent night market is packed with exotic barbecued food.

★ Le Banneton BAKERY $
(Th Sakkarin; meals 20,000-40,000K; ⏱6.30am-6pm; ❉ ❉) In the heart of the peninsula, this is the best place in Laos to breakfast– specifically for their melt-in-the-mouth pastry. Get here early; by 10am the golden-brown croissants have all gone. Also serves fruit shakes, sandwiches, quiches and homemade sorbets.

Café Toui FUSION $
(Th Sisavang Vatthana; mains 30,000-80,000K; ⏱7am-10pm; 🛜🍴) Candle-lit tunes harmonise with gold-stencilled oxblood walls at this chichi little eatery. The vegetarian-friendly menu is Asian fusion with standout dishes such as tofu *láhp*, plus an inviting sampler menu.

Big Tree Café KOREAN, INTERNATIONAL $
(www.bigtreecafe.com; Th Khem Khong; mains 25,000-50,000K; ⏱9am-9pm; 🛜) Eat in the cafe - which is full of Adri Berger's alluring Lao photography – or outside on the sun terrace overlooking the Mekong. There's also a choice of Western and Japanese dishes. Deliciously fresh.

Le Café Ban Vat Sene FRENCH $
(Th Sakkarin; mains 30,000K; ⏱7.30am-10pm; 🛜) Retro fans whir over an Indochinese scene of flower-shaded lights and stylish refinement. This is the place to work, sip an afternoon pastis and read a paper.

French wine, salads, quiche, pasta and pizza...*parfait!*

Saffron CAFE $
(Th Khem Khong; mains 20,000-35,000K; ⊙7am-9pm; 🛜) The perfect riverside stop for breakfasts, this stylish cafe hung with lush black-and-white photography turns out great pasta dishes, serves excellent coffee and has warm service. There's also a choice of interior and alfresco dining.

Xieng Thong Noodle-Shop LAOTIAN $
(Th Sakkarin; noodle soup 15,000K; ⊙from 6.30am) The best *kòw bʉeak sèn* (round rice noodles served in a broth with pieces of chicken or deep-fried crispy pork belly) in town is served from an entirely unexotic shopfront well up the peninsula. Stocks are usually finished by 2pm.

⭐**Tamarind** LAOTIAN $$
(📱071 213 128; www.tamarindlaos.com; Th King-kitsarat; mains 25,000-60,000K; set dinners 100,000-150,000K; ⊙11am-10pm; 🛜) On the banks of the Nam Khan, chic Tamarind's à la carte menu boasts delicious sampling platters which include bamboo dip, stuffed lemongrass and *meuyang* (DIY parcels of noodles, herbs, fish and chilli pastes, and vegetables).

Tangor FUSION $$
(📱071 260 761; www.letangor.com; Th Sisa-vangvong; mains 40,000-80,000K; ⊙11am-10pm; 🛜) A gastronomic addition to the Luang Prabang dining scene, Tangor serves beautifully crafted fusion food, blending the best of seasonal Lao produce with French flair.

🍷 Drinking

The following do their best to squeeze as much hedonistic juice as possible before the 11.30pm curfew.

⭐**Ikon Klub** BAR
(Th Sisavang Vatthana; ⊙5pm-late; 🛜) Ikon is bohemian, from its shadowy 1930s decor hung with objets d'art and prints of old Hollywood starlets, to the charming Hungarian poetess who runs it. The best mojitos are mixed here, the bloody Marys are full of vigour, and it makes for a great spot to meet others while listening to cool tunes.

Utopia BAR
(🛜) This vernal oasis with a Khmer twist is all recliner cushions, low-slung tables and

SPLURGE

If you're thinking of proposing, this is the place to do it. Get your glad rags on and head down the peninsula to **Auberge les 3 Nagas** (📱071 253 888; www.3-nagas.com; Th Sakkarin; r from US$200; ❋@🛜), Luang Prabang's original boutique hotel where Indo-chic was minted. The 100-year-old Lao-style building, shaded in mango trees, brims with old-world atmosphere and romance. Its classy restaurant features an exquisite Asian fusion menu – and perhaps the best *láhp* in the city – all served with French flair.

hookah pipes. Chill over a fruit shake, play a board game or volleyball, or practise yoga at dawn. By day it's the perfect spot to sink into your Kindle between admiring the bucolic river-life below, and come sunset it's lit by a sea of candles.

Hive Bar BAR
(Th Kingkitsarat; 🛜) The buzz is back at this stylish den of hidden coves. Out back in the garden there's a dance floor, projector wall and more tables. Check out the excellent ethnic fashion show every night at 7pm, which also features an amazing hip-hop crew (expect your palms to be raw with clapping). Tapas, happy hour and cocktails.

☆ Entertainment

Phrolak-Phralam Theatre TRADITIONAL DANCE
(Royal Palace Grounds; tickets 70,000-170,000K; ⊙shows 6pm or 6.30pm Mon, Wed, Fri & Sat) The misleadingly named Royal Lao Ballet puts on slow-moving traditional dances accompanied by a 10-piece Lao 'orchestra'. Performances last about 1¼ hours and include a Ramayana-based scene. It's well worth reading the typewritten notes provided at the entrance to have an idea of what's going on.

🛍 Shopping

Big Tree Gallery GALLERY
(📱071 212 262; Th Khem Khong; ⊙9am-10pm) Photographer Adri Berger's compositions of rural Lao are exquisite; nobody else captures Laos' honeyed afternoon light like him. His gallery-cum-restaurant has a range

of his work on the walls, with prints starting at an affordable US$100.

Handicraft Night Market
MARKET

(Th Sisavangvong; ☺5.30-10pm) Every evening this market assembles along Th Sisavangvong from the Royal Palace Museum to Th Kitsarat. Low-lit and quiet, it's devoid of hard selling with tens of dozens of traders selling silk scarves and wall hangings, Hmong appliqué blankets, T-shirts, clothing, shoes, paper, silver, bags, ceramics, bamboo lamps and more.

Ock Pop Tok
HANDICRAFTS, CLOTHING

(☑071 254 761; www.ockpoptok.com; 73/5 Ban Wat Nong; ☺8am-9pm) OckPopTok works with a wide range of different tribes to preserve their handicraft traditions. Fine silk and cotton scarves, chemises, dresses, wall hangings and cushion covers make perfect presents. Also has a branch on **Thanon Sisavangvong** (☑071 254 406; ☺8am-9pm).

L'Etranger Books & Tea
BOOKS

(Th Kingkitsarat; ☺8am-10pm Mon-Sat, 10am-10pm Sun) The cheapest spot for secondhand travel books and thrillers. Upstairs there's a comfy lounge-lizard cafe in which to read them. Films shown nightly.

ℹ Information

INTERNET ACCESS & TELEPHONE
Most internet cafes in Luang Prabang town have Skype and charge around 100K per minute, with a 20-minute minimum. For free wi-fi access try Le Café Ban Vat Sene (p335) and most hotel lobbies. Internet cafes are peppered along Th Sisavangvong.

MEDICAL SERVICES
Luang Prabang's **Provincial Hospital** (☑071 254 025; Ban Naxang; doctor's consultation 100,000K) is OK for minor problems but for any serious illnesses consider flying to Bangkok or returning to Vientiane for Aek Udon International Hospital (p323) just over the Thai border. Note the Provincial Hospital charges double for consultations on weekends or anytime after 4pm.

MONEY
BCEL (Th Sisavangvong; ☺8.30am-3.30pm Mon-Sat) Changes major currencies in cash or travellers cheques, has a 24-hour ATM and offers cash advances against Visa and MasterCard.

Minipost Booth (Th Sisavangvong; ☺7.45am-8.30pm, cash advances 9am-3pm) Changes most major currencies at fair rates and is

open daily. After 6pm it's easy to miss, hidden behind market stalls.

POST
Post Office (Th Chao Fa Ngum; ☺8.30am-3.30pm Mon-Fri, to noon Sat) Phone calls and Western Union facilities.

TOURIST INFORMATION
Provincial Tourism Department (www.tourismlaos.com; Th Sisavangvong; ☺8am-4pm Mon-Fri) General information stop on festivals and ethnic groups. Also offers some maps and leaflets, plus information on buses and boats.

ℹ Getting There & Away

AIR
Around 4km from the city centre, **Luang Prabang International Airport** (☑071 212 173) is decidedly modest, though big expansion plans are afoot. For Bangkok (from US$190, 100 minutes), **Bangkok Airways** (www.bangkokair.com) and **Lao Airlines** (☑071 212 172; www.laoairlines.com; Th Pha Mahapatsaman) both fly twice daily. Lao Airlines also serves Vientiane (US$101, several daily), Pakse (US$182, daily), Chiang Mai (US$150, daily), Hanoi (US$155, daily) and Siem Reap (US$195, daily). **Vietnam Airlines** (☑071 213 049; www.vietnamairlines.com) flies to both Siem Reap and Hanoi daily.

BOAT
Slow boats motor northwest daily to Huay Xai (220,000K), departing at 8am by the **Navigation Office** (☺8-11am & 2-4pm) located behind the Royal Palace. You can buy tickets direct from there or from a travel agent. The trip takes two days with an overnight stop in Pak Beng (110,000K, nine hours). From Pak Beng it's also possible to take the bus northeast to Udomxai.

White-knuckle speedboats up the Mekong leave from around 8.30am daily (when boats are full) from Ban Don pier, 7km north of the town centre (turn west off Rte 13 beside the Km 390 post, then head 300m down an unpaved road). Compared to the slow boat, they rocket to Pak Beng (250,000K, three hours) and Huay Xai

---

MEKONG COWBOYS

Beware Luang Prabang's boatmen scam, whereby they claim that they can't leave until the boat is full. You and the other *falang* (foreigners) end up clubbing together for the 'ghost' fare and then magically the last person appears stage left. Don't leave until you get the extra fare cash back.

(400,000K, six hours) in a fraction of the time but with 10 times the danger. Is it worth it?

BUS & SŎRNGTĂAOU

Most interprovincial buses and *sŏrngtăaou* (pick-up trucks) heading north depart from the northern bus station, while southbound vehicles use the southern bus station, 3km south of town. On all these routes the durations can vary wildly during monsoonal weather.

A better option is the **Naluang minibus station** (☏ 071 212 979; souknasing@hotmail.com; Rte 13, 800m past Km 382) – opposite the southern bus station – that runs minibuses to Nong Khiang, Vang Vieng, Phonsavan, Luang Namtha, Hanoi and Kunming. Although you can travel as one or two people and just turn up in the morning, for less than double the bus fare, a great option is to gather your own group and rent a comfortable six-seater minivan. Directly booked through the minibus station, prices are about 1,000,000K to Phonsavan or Vang Vieng and 500,000K to Nong Khiaw, including pick-up from the guesthouse.

Sainyabuli

Buses to Sainyabuli (60,000K, three hours) depart the southern bus station at 9am and 2pm. Travel to Sainyabuli for onward travel to Hongsa or Vientiane.

Nong Khiaw & Sam Neua

For Nong Khiaw (40,000K, four hours), 9am minibuses start from Naluang minibus station. Alternatively, from the northern bus station use *sŏrngtăaou* (40,000K) at 9am, 11am and 1pm or the 8.30am bus that continues to Sam Neua (140,000K, 17 hours) via Vieng Thong (110,000K, 10 hours). Another Sam Neua–bound bus (from Vientiane) should pull in sometime around 5.30pm.

Vientiane & Vang Vieng

From the southern bus station there are up to 10 daily Vientiane services (express/VIP 130,000/150,000K, nine to 12 hours) via Vang Vieng between 6.30am and 7.30pm. VIP buses leave at 9am. A plethora of morning minibuses to Vang Vieng (105,000K, seven hours) depart from the Naluang minibus station.

China, Udomxai, Luang Namtha & Phonsavan

The sleeper bus to Kunming, China (450,000K, 24 hours) departs from the southern bus station at 7am, sometimes earlier. From the northern bus station run buses to Udomxai (55,000K, five hours) at 9am, noon and 4pm, Luang Namtha (90,000K, nine hours) at 9am and Huay Xai (Borkeo; 120,000K, 15 hours) at 5.30pm and a VIP service at 7pm (145,000K).

For Phonsavan (10 hours) there's an 8.30am minibus (95,000K) from Naluang minibus station and an 8am bus (ordinary/express 85,000/105,000K, 10 hours) from the southern bus station.

❶ Getting Around

From the airport into town, 4km away, jumbos or minitrucks charge a uniform 50,000K per vehicle, and up to six can share the ride. In the reverse direction you can usually pay less. Most of the town is accessible on foot. Jumbos (motorised three-wheeled taxis) usually ask foreigners for 20,000K a ride. Scooters cost US$15 per day, mountain/ordinary bikes cost 50,000/20,000K per day.

Around Luang Prabang

◉ Sights

Pak Ou Caves   CAVE
(Tham Ting; admission 20,000K) Located about 25km upstream on the Mekong from Luang Prabang and at the mouth of the Nam Ou, the dramatic Pak Ou Caves are set into limestone cliffs and are crammed with hundreds of Buddha images; a kind of statues' graveyard where unwanted images are placed. Bring a torch.

Most boat trips stop at small villages along the way, especially Ban Xang Hai. Boatmen call this tourist-dominated place 'Whisky Village', as it's known for its free-flowing *lào-láo* (rice whisky).

Luang Prabang's longboat office sells return boat tickets to Pak Ou (per person/boat 60,000/400,000K return). The trip takes two hours upriver and one hour down, plus stops. Túk-túk make the trip for about half the price.

Tat Kuang Si   PARK
(admission 20,000K) This beguiling spot 32km south of town has a wide, many-tiered waterfall that tumbles over limestone formations into a series of cool, turquoise pools. The lower level of the falls has been turned into a well-maintained public park with shelters and picnic tables; some of the trees near the waterfall have been labelled. Just past the entrance are enclosures housing cuddly sun bears at the **Tat Kuang Si Bear Rescue Centre** (www.freethebears.org.au) **FREE**. All have been confiscated from poachers and are kept here in preference to releasing them to the same certain fate.

Túk-túk from Luang Prabang typically charge 200,000K for one person, from 300,000K for several.

Nong Khiaw   ບ້ານຫ້ວຍຂຽວ
☑ 071

Nestled along the cherry blossom riverbank of the Nam Ou and towered over by forest-clad karsts, pretty Nong Khiaw is a haven of cafes, guesthouses and, thanks to the arrival of Green Discovery and Tiger Trail, it now has plenty of activities to keep you busy. Eat at a couple of tasty restaurants or just chill by the river. Note: the opposite side of the river where most guesthouses are based is called Ban Sop Houn. There's now a BCEL ATM too.

◉ Sights & Activities

Head to the bridge at dusk when fabulous star shows turn the deep indigo sky into a pointillist canvas that subtly outlines the riverside massifs.

You can walk to **Tham Pha Tok**, an enormous cave of many levels where villagers hid out during the Second Indochina War. Head 2.5km east of the bridge then look for a clearly visible cave mouth in the limestone cliff on the right. It costs 5000K, and is open from 7.30am until 6.30pm.

Tiger Trail   HIKING, CYCLING
(☑ 071 252 655; www.laos-adventures.com; Delilah's Place) ⚑ This ecoconscious outfit has treks around the local area, including one-day trips to the '100 waterfalls' (350,000K per person, group of four). A two-day trek through Hmong villages, incorporating a homestay and school visit, costs 500,000K per person.

Green Discovery   HIKING, CYCLING
(☑ 071 810 018; www.greendiscoverylaos.com) GD has several treks and various kayaking options, including a three-day paddle-camping expedition to Luang Prabang (from 1,330,000K per person). A one-day trip starting with a longboat ride to Muang Ngoi Neua then paddling back costs 350,000K per person, assuming four participants in two-person kayaks.

🛏 Sleeping & Eating

Guesthouses in Nong Khiaw are near the bridge on the west side of the river, and in the more popular village of Ban Sop Houn, on the east side.

Amphai Guesthouse   GUESTHOUSE $
(☑ 020 5577 3637; Ban Sop Houn; r 60,000K; ☎) It lacks the riverfront location of some competitors, but the prices more than reflect this. Rooms are spacious and cool, with clean bathrooms and hot water. A new Indian restaurant has just opened in the downstairs courtyard.

Namhoun Guesthouse   GUESTHOUSE $
(☑ 071 810 039; bungalows 50,000-100,000K; ☎) Cheaper bungalows are set around a small garden behind the family house. Better are the riverside bungalows facing the Nam Ou, but they come at a premium 100,000K. All rooms have mosquito nets and balconies with the ubiquitous hammock.

Sengdao Chittavong Guesthouse   GUESTHOUSE $
(☑ 030 923 7089; r 80,000-100,000K; ☎) The only central riverfront place on the west bank, this place offers sizeable bungalows located in gardens of cherry blossom. En suite rooms are rattan-walled, with simple decoration, fresh flowers, clean linen and balconies, making it all-round good value. There's also a convivial fairy-lit restaurant with river-garden views.

★ Coco Home Bar & Restaurant   LAOTIAN, INTERNATIONAL $
(mains 15,000-45,000K; ☎) Located on the main drag on the west bank, this is the liveliest all-rounder in town, offering dining in an attractive garden setting above the boat dock. The menu includes Lao, Thai and international favourites. Movies are screened upstairs nightly.

Deen   INDIAN $
(Ban Sop Houn; mains 20,000-35,000K; ◷ 8.30am-10pm; ☎) A superb little Indian eatery with wood-fired naan bread, moreish tandoori dishes, zesty curries and a homely atmosphere; it's always packed. There's also a bank of computers (internet 15,000K per hour, wi-fi is free).

CT Restaurant and Bakery   INTERNATIONAL, LAOTIAN $
(Ban Sop Houn; mains 15,000-30,000K; ◷ 7am-10pm) Located in a commanding position at the end of the bridge, CT has a Western-friendly menu of pancakes, breakfasts, sandwiches and staple Lao dishes. It also offers takeaway sandwiches for trekking.

ℹ Getting There & Away

BOAT
In the high season, boats heading up the Nam Ou to Muang Ngoi Neua (one way 25,000K,

1¼ hours) leave at 11am and 2pm. Tickets are bought at an office at the bus station. The 11am boat continues to Muang Khua (120,000K, seven hours) for connections to Phongsali and Dien Bien Phu in Vietnam.

Public boats make the five- to eight-hour trip through striking karst scenery to Luang Prabang. With a minimum of 10 people tickets cost 110,000K per person. If this is not happening you can charter the boat for 1,500,000K.

BUS & SŎRNGTǍAOU

The journey to Luang Prabang takes three to four hours. Minibuses or *sŏrngtǎaou* (40,000K) start at around 9am and 11am, plus there's a minivan (50,000K) at 1pm. Tickets are sold at the bus stand but the 11am service starts at the boat office, filling up with folks arriving off the boat(s) from Muang Ngoi.

For Udomxai a direct minibus (50,000K, three hours) leaves at 11am. Alternatively take any westbound transport and change at Pak Mong (25,000K, 50 minutes).

The minibus to Sam Neua (130,000K, 12 hours) via Vieng Thong (100,000K, five hours) makes a quick lunch stop in Nong Khiaw around 11.30am, with another passing through at night.

Muang Ngoi Neua
ເມື່ອງງອຍເໜືອ

Street stalls fry up pancakes in the morning and mist hangs on the pyramid-shaped karsts as river life in Muang Ngoi Neua crackles to life. Chill in your hammock and take in the jaw-dropping views of the karsts, or ready yourself for trekking, caving and kayaking. While Nong Khiaw may offer finer digs, Muang Ngoi Neua is less vulnerable to 21st-century mores, and abounds in authentic rural life.

GETTING TO VIETNAM: NORTHERN BORDERS

Muang Khua to Dien Bien Phu

Getting to the border The Sop Hun/Tay Trang border in Phongsali Province has now opened as an international entry point to Tay Trang in Vietnam. There are daily buses bound for Dien Bien Phu leaving from the Lao village of Muang Khua (50,000K, 6.30am).

At the border This remote crossing sees a handful of travellers. Organise a Vietnamese visa in advance.

Moving on There are no facilities or waiting vehicles at either border posts, which are separated by about 4km of no-man's-land. From the Tay Trang side of the border, it is about 31km to Dien Bien Phu.

Phonsavan to Vinh

Getting to the border Direct buses to Vinh (on the Vietnamese side) leave Phonsavan four times per week, crossing at the lonely Nong Haet/Nam Can border (open 8am to noon and 1.30pm to 5pm).

At the border If entering Vietnam, you'll need to have organised a Vietnamese visa in advance.

Moving on The first town en route to Vinh, 403 km away, is Mu'òng Xén where there's a basic hotel. From here there's a 4pm bus to Vinh.

Sam Neua to Thanh Hoa

Getting to the border If you're crossing the Nam Soi/Na Meo border (open 7.30am to 11.30am and 1.30pm to 4.30pm), take the daily bus from Sam Neua's Nathong bus station bound for Thanh Hoa (180,000K, 11 hours, 8am). Buy your ticket at the bus station to avoid being overcharged on the bus.

At the border Heading into Vietnam you'll need to have prearranged a visa. There are no ATM facilities at this remote border crossing. On the Lao side there are a couple of restaurants.

Moving on There's a night train from Thanh Hoa to Hanoi departing at 11.30pm and arriving at 4am. Departing for Laos from Thanh Hoa is an 8am bus which should cost 200,000d, but you may be asked to pay more.

Tours

Lao Youth Travel KAYAKING
(☑ 030 514 0046; www.laoyouthtravel.com; ☺ 7.30-10.30am & 1.30-6pm)

🛏 Sleeping

Muang Ngoi Neua has 'budget' tattooed over its dip-and-pour, hammock-slung cabanas. Restaurants are generally tagged on to guesthouses.

★Ning Ning Guest House GUESTHOUSE $
(☑ 020 3386 3306; r incl breakfast US$17-20) Nestled around a peaceful garden, Ning Ning has immaculate wooden bungalows with mosquito nets, verandahs, en suite bathrooms and bed linen. There's a nice restaurant with riverfront views.

Bungalows Ecolodge GUESTHOUSE $
(r 80,000K) Decent-sized bungalows hidden down a side street have sliding shutters that allow you to lie in bed and gape at the karsts. Tasteful linen, solar-heated showers, mosquito nets and locally sourced food elevate it above the crowd.

Aloune Mai Guesthouse GUESTHOUSE $
(r 70,000K) This hidden gem, found down a dirt track and over a bridge, sits beside a meadow and has 10 fresh rooms in a handsome rattan building with heated showers. There's a little restaurant and stunning views of the cliffs on the other side, but no river views.

Rainbow Guest House GUESTHOUSE $
(☑ 020 2295 7880; r 60,000K) Close to the boat ramp, this newly constructed house has clean if charmless rooms, fragrant linen, large en suites, a communal verandah and a sunset-facing cafe.

✗ Eating

The best food is served by street-side vendors.

★Riverside Restaurant LAOTIAN $
(meals 15,000-35,000K; ☺ 7.30am-10pm) Shaded by a mature mango tree festooned with lanterns, this lively haunt has lovely views of the Nam Ou. The menu encompasses noodles, fried dishes and *láhp*.

Nang Phone Keo Restaurant LAOTIAN $
(mains 10,000-20,000K; ☺ 7.30am-9pm) This is a Main St house-restaurant on whose deck you can order Muang Ngoi's most exotic dessert, a flaming plate of fried bananas flambéed in *lào-láo*. Also imaginative is the

falang (foreigner) roll with peanut butter, banana, sticky rice and honey.

Phetdavanh Street Buffet LAOTIAN $
(per person 20,000K; ☺ 7pm) Phetdavanh runs a nightly buffet that sets up on the street around 7pm, and serves up barbecued pork, chicken, fish, sticky rice and vegetables.

ℹ Information

There is now electricity in the village and wi-fi too, but no bank so bring plenty of cash. A couple of pharmacies sell basic medicines; for anything serious get yourself back to Luang Prabang.

ℹ Getting There & Away

Boats to Nong Khiaw leave at 9am (or when full) and cost 25,000K. Heading north, a 9.30am boat goes most days to Muang Khua (minimum 10 persons, 120,000K, seven hours) for those headed for the Sop Hun–Tay Trang border crossing. Buy tickets at the boat office, halfway up the boat landing stairs next to Ning Ning Guesthouse. There's a boat to Nong Khiaw from Muang Khua that stops in Muang Ngoi Neua at 1.30pm.

A new road to Nong Khiaw is under construction, so make the most of the delicious isolation.

Phonsavan ໄຊບນສະຫວັນ
☑ 061 / POP 60,000

Phonsavan bears its cratered war scars like an acne-ridden pensioner, while stoic locals make the most of decommissioned unexploded ordnance (UXO), using it to decorate houses and hotel foyers. Touchingly, while other areas of Laos erupt in pockets of sophistication, Phonsavan, like some retro-leaning Muscovite, barely changes. Often mist-shrouded, this dusty old town (latterly known as Xieng Khuang) has a rugged charm if you look past its nondescript, Soviet facade – blame that on its hasty rebuild after it was decimated.

The town is inhabited by an intriguing cast of Chinese, Vietnamese, Lao and Hmong, and is well serviced by an airport, and a handful of guesthouses and restaurants.

◎ Sights

**Xieng Khouang UXO-Survivors'
Information Centre** MUSEUM
(www.laos.worlded.org; ☺ 8am-8pm) The insightful Xieng Khouang UXO-Survivors' Information Centre displays prosthetic limbs, wheelchairs and bomb parts and gives a harrowing insight into the UXO problem. See the boxed text p343 for more.

Mulberries FARM
(ບໍ່ສາ; ☎061 561 271; www.mulberries.org; ⊙8am-4pm Mon-Sat) This is a fair-trade silk farm that offers interesting free visits that include a complete introduction to the silk-weaving process from cocoon to colourful scarves. It's off Rte 7 just west of the main bus station.

☞ Tours

Amazing Lao Travel HIKING TOUR
(☎020 2234 0005; www.amazinglao.com; Rte 7) Runs treks to the jar sites and two-day treks in the mountains including a homestay in a Hmong village. As ever, the more the merrier, with prices falling for larger groups.

Sousath Travel GUIDED TOUR
(☎061 312 031; Rte 7) Sousath offers reliable tours to the Plain of Jars and the Ho Chi Minh Trail as well as homestays in Hmong villages. It also rents motorbikes (100,000K per day). Films are shown nightly at the little office-cum-cafe.

🛏 Sleeping

Kong Keo Guesthouse GUESTHOUSE $
(☎061 211 354; www.kongkeojar.com; r 50,000-80,000K; 🖥📶) A memorable backpacker haunt, Kong Keo has cabins with en suites, as well as a newer block of more comfortable rooms. There is a small bar-restaurant with an open-pit barbecue and occasional guitar strum-alongs. Charismatic owner Mr Keo runs excellent tours to the jars, as well as specialised trips.

Nice Guesthouse GUESTHOUSE $
(☎061 312 454; vuemany@hotmail.com; r 80,000-110,000K; 📶) With fresh and fragrant rooms, clean bathrooms and firm beds, Nice's Chinese lanterns cast ruby glows into the chilled night, and upstairs rooms include a bathtub.

White Orchid Guesthouse GUESTHOUSE $
(☎061 312 403; r incl breakfast 80,000-200,000K; 🖥📶) The menthol-green walls include clean en suite bathrooms and welcome blankets. The higher you ascend, the higher the price and better the views. The price includes a pick-up from the airport or bus station.

★**Auberge de la Plaine des Jarres** CABIN $$
(☎030 517 0282; www.plainedesjarres.com; r US$50-60; 🖥📶) Hillside elevation, Scotch pines and Swiss-style wooden interiors give these inviting all-wood cabins an incongruously alpine feel. There's a great French and Lao restaurant with a nightly fire and some panoramic vistas over the town. Rooms show signs of age, but there is oodles of charm. It's a 10-minute drive from town.

Anoulack Khen Lao Hotel HOTEL $$
(☎061 213 599; www.anoulackkhenlaohotel.com; r 200,000-300,000K; 🖥📶) Bright, clean and ample-sized 200,000K rooms are the best value here, with white linen, kettles, fridges, shower booths and breakfast included.

🍴 Eating & Drinking

Wild *matsutake* mushrooms *(hét wâi)* and fermented swallows *(nok qen dạwng)* are local specialities. Try the **fresh food market** (⊙6am-5pm) behind Rte 7. Several Vietnamese restaurants serve dog *(thit chó)* if you want to avoid an unpleasant surprise.

★**Bamboozle Restaurant & Bar** INTERNATIONAL $
(Rte 7; meals 15,000-52,000K; ⊙7-10.30am & 3.30-11pm; 📶) 🍴 The liveliest spot in town after dark, Bamboozle offers a decent range of comfort food, including pizzas, as well as the best of Lao cuisine. A percentage of profits go towards the **Lone Buffalo Foundation** (LBP; www.facebook.com/lonebuffalo), which supports the town's youth.

Nisha Restaurant INDIAN $
(Rte 7; meals 10,000-30,000K; ⊙7am-10pm; 📶) It doesn't look like much from the outside, but inside Nisha turns out to be one of the best Indian restaurants in northern Laos; with a wide range of vegetarian options, delicious dosa (flat bread), tikka masala and rogan josh.

Simmaly Restaurant LAOTIAN $
(Rte 7; meals 15,000-30,000K; ⊙6am-9pm) Dishes up a tasty line of rice dishes, noodles and spicy meats, including steaming *fĕr* (rice-noodle soup). The pork with ginger is lovely.

Craters Bar & Restaurant INTERNATIONAL $
(Rte 7; meals 20,000-50,000K; ⊙7am-10pm; 📶) An old-timer establishment popular with NGOs and travellers, Craters has CNN to watch on the tube as you munch through its toasties, soups, burgers, fried chicken, steaks and pizzas.

AN ENDURING LEGACY

Between 1964 and 1973, the USA conducted one of the largest sustained aerial bombardments in history, flying 580,344 missions over Laos and dropping two million tonnes of bombs, costing US$2.2 million a day. Around 30% of the bombs dropped on Laos failed to detonate, leaving the country littered with unexploded ordnance (UXO).

For people all over eastern Laos (the most contaminated provinces being Xieng Khuang, Salavan and Savannakhet), living with this appalling legacy has become an intrinsic part of daily life. Since the British **Mines Advisory Group** (MAG; www.mag.org. uk; Rte 7, Phonsavan; ⊙4-8pm) began clearance work in 1994, only a tiny percentage of the quarter of a million pieces in Xieng Khuang and Salavan has been removed. At the current rate of clearance it will take more than 100 years to make the country safe. Visit their **UXO Information Centre** (☑061 252 004; www.maginternational.org/laopdr; Phonsavan; ⊙8am-8pm) **FREE** to watch a number of late afternoon documentaries including *Bomb Harvest* (4.30pm), *Surviving the Peace* (5.50pm) and *Bombies* (6.30pm).

Barview BAR

(⊙8am-11pm) Try this simple shack for sunset beers over the rice-paddy fields. Locals gather here to play guitars and munch on barbecued meat.

❶ Information

Currency exchange is available at **Lao Development Bank** (☑061 312 188), at **BCEL** (☑061 213 291; Rte 7) and from several travel agents. There are two ATMs along Rte 7.

Don't underestimate the dangers of UXO (unexploded ordnance); keep to established paths.

Lao-Mongolian Friendship Hospital (☑061 312 166) Can assist with minor health concerns.

Post Office (⊙8am-4pm Mon-Fri, to noon Sat) Domestic phone service.

Provincial Tourist Office (☑061 312 217) Offers some regional treks and free maps and leaflets for Phonsavan and Xieng Khuang Province.

❶ Getting There & Away

AIR

Lao Airlines (☑061 212 027; www.laoairlines. com) has daily flights to/from Vientiane (US$101). Sometimes a weekly flight to/from Luang Prabang operates in peak season.

BUS

Longer-distance bus tickets presold by travel agencies typically cost around 40,000K more than standard fares but include a transfer to the bus station, around 4km west of the centre. From here Vietnam-bound buses depart to Vinh (180,000K, 11 hours) at 6.30am on Tuesday, Thursday, Friday and Sunday, continuing seasonally (generally from November to January) on Mondays to Hanoi (320,000K). For Vientiane (140,000K, 11 hours) there are air-con buses at 7am, 8am, 10.30am, 4.30pm, 6.30pm and a VIP bus (160,000K) at 8pm. These all pass through Vang Vieng, to where there's an additional 7.30am departure (95,000K). For Luang Prabang (10 hours) both minivans (95,000K) and VIP buses (120,000K) depart at 8.30am. There's an 8am bus to Sam Neua (110,000K, eight to 10 hours) plus two Vientiane–Sam Neua buses passing through. A 7.30am bus is timetabled to Paksan (130,000K) on the new road.

Plain of Jars ທົ່ງໄຫຫິນ

The Plain of Jars represents a huge area of Xieng Khuang Province, scattered with thousands of limestone jars of undetermined age. Thought to be funerary urns after bones were discovered within them, the jars have been divided into 160 sites, three of which represent the greatest concentration. These are the designated UXO-cleared tourist areas you should visit.

Site 1 (Thong Hai Hin; admission 10,000K), the biggest and most accessible site, is 15km southwest of Phonsavan and features 250 jars, most of which weigh from 600kg to 1 tonne each. The largest jar weighs as much as 6 tonnes and is said to have been the victory cup of mythical King Jeuam, and so is called Hai Jeuam. Two other jar sites are readily accessible by road from Phonsavan. **Site 2** (Hai Hin Phu Salato; admission 10,000K), about 25km south of town, features 90 jars spread across two adjacent hillsides. Vehicles can reach the base of the hills, then it's a short, steep walk to the jars.

More impressive is 150-jar **Site 3** (Hai Hin Lat Khai; admission 10,000K). It's about 10km south of Site 2 (or 35km from Phonsavan) on a scenic hilltop near the charming village of **Ban Xieng Di**, where there's a small

LAOS PLAIN OF JARS

monastery containing the remains of Buddha images damaged in the war. The site is a 2km hike through rice paddies and up a hill.

❶ Getting Around

Túk-túk cost from 10,000K for a short hop to about 20,000K to the airport. **Lao-Falang Restaurant** (☑ 020 2221 2456; Rte 7, Phonsavan; ⊘ 8am-6pm) rents bicycles (40,000K per day) and 100cc motorbikes (100,000K), ideal for reaching a selection of jar sites. They also have some Chinese quad bikes (160,000K) if you're feeling brave.

Chauffeured six-seater vans or 4WDs can be chartered through most guesthouses and hotels, but you're looking at US$150 to Sam Neua or US$120 to Luang Prabang.

It's possible to charter a jumbo to the jar sites for about 100,000K.

Sam Neua   ຊຳເໜືອ

☑ 064 / POP 16,000

Behind a shallow disguise of well-spaced concrete modernity, Sam Neua offers eye-widening produce markets (think dissected rats and a panoply of not-so-mouthwatering insects) and a colourful ethnic diversity. The town is a logical transit point for visiting nearby Vieng Xai or catching the daily bus to Vietnam, and remains one of Laos's least-visited provincial capitals. At an altitude of roughly 1200m, some warm clothes are advisable in the dry winter period, at least by night and until the thick morning fog burns off.

🛏 Sleeping & Eating

Sam Neua's digs are found beside the Nam Sam River. For cheap *fĕr*, samosas, spring rolls and fried sweet potato, the nearby **market** (⊘ 6am-6pm) is the place to go.

★ Xayphasouk Hotel   HOTEL $
(☑ 064 312 033; xayphasoukhotel@gmail.com; r 150,000-200,000K; ✳ 🛜) Currently the smartest hotel in Sam Neua with comfortable rooms featuring piping-hot showers, flat-screen TVs, tasteful furnishings and crisp linen. Free wi-fi.

Phonchalern Hotel   HOTEL $
(☑ 064 312 192; www.phonechalernhotel.com; r 100,000-120,000K; ✳ 🛜) The first place in Sam Neua to install a lift, this clean and comfortable hotel is a real deal, with rooms including a TV and fridge. Try to bag a front-facing room with a balcony overlooking the river.

Bounhome Guest House   GUESTHOUSE $
(☑ 064 312 223; r 60,000-100,000K; 🛜) Plenty of sunlight fills the fine little rooms upstairs in this guesthouse. Their neat interiors have firm, low-set beds, are fan-cooled and include hot-water showers.

Dan Nao Muang Xam Restaurant   LAOTIAN $
(mains 15,000-50,000K; ⊘ 7am-9.30pm) This hole-in-the-wall spot is hardly brimming with atmosphere, but it has the most foreigner-friendly menu in town in concise English. Breakfast includes cornflakes and a delicious *fĕr*. Dinner includes some excellent rice and soup combinations, plus a steak with al dente vegetables arranged starlike around the plate.

Chittavanh Restaurant   LAOTIAN $
(mains 20,000-40,000K; ⊘ 7am-9.30pm) It's worth braving the reverberant clatter of this cavernous hotel restaurant to savour a delicious Chinese fried tofu dish. Locals like to eat here as well – always a good sign.

❶ Information

Agricultural Promotion Bank (⊘ 8am-noon & 1.30-4pm Mon-Fri) Exchanges Thai baht and US dollars at fair rates.

Lao Development Bank (☑ 064 312 171; ⊘ 8am-4pm Mon-Fri) On the main road 400m north of the bus station on the left; exchanges cash and travellers cheques.

Post Office (⊘ 8am-4pm Mon-Fri) In a large building directly opposite the bus station. A telephone office at its rear offers international calls.

Provincial Tourist Office (☑ 064 312 567; ⊘ 8am-noon & 1.30-4pm Mon-Fri) An excellent tourist office with English-speaking staff eager to help.

❶ Getting There & Away

Lao Air (www.lao-air.com) flies to Vientiane on Monday, Wednesday and Friday (915,000K, 1½ hours). The airport is 3km from town.

Set on a hilltop, Sam Neua's main bus station is roughly 1.2km away (túk-túk 8500K) from town. There are three buses a day to Vientiane (170,000K, 22 hours) via Phonsavan (80,000K, eight to 10 hours) at 9am, noon and 2pm. It's a sinuous but beautiful hike through the mountains. An additional 8am bus to Vientiane goes via Nong Khiaw (130,000K, 12 hours, 8am) and continues to Luang Prabang (140,000K, 17 hours) and Vang Vieng. If you're heading for Udomxai, take this bus and change at Pak Mong.

GETTING TO THAILAND: NORTHERN BORDERS

Huay Xai to Chiang Rai

Since the completion of the Thai-Lao Friendship Bridge 4 at Huay Xai/Chiang Khong border in late 2013, the former boat crossing across the Mekong is only for locals.

Getting to the border Túk-túks cost about 80B per person to the immigration post.

At the border A bus (20B to 30 B) crosses the bridge. A 15-day Thai visa waiver is automatically granted when entering Thailand. Arriving in Chiang Khong, pay the 30B port fee and catch a 30B túk-túk to take you to the bus station. The nearest ATM on the Thai side is 2km south.

Moving on Many travellers leave Huay Xai bound for Chiang Rai (365B, 2½ hours) with buses typically departing from Chiang Khong's bus station every hour from 6am till 5pm. **Greenbus** (🗷 in Thailand 0066 5365 5732; www.greenbusthailand.com) has services to Chiang Mai at 6am, 9am and 11.40am. Several overnight buses for Bangkok (500 to 750B, 10 hours) leave at 3pm and 3.30pm.

Hongsa to Phrae

Getting to the border The Muang Ngeun/Ban Huay Kon border crossing (8am to 5pm) is around 2.5km west of Muang Ngeun junction. Several *sŏrngtăaou* make the run from Hongsa (40,000K, 1½ hours) to Muang Ngeun. Once the new bridge north of Pak Beng is open, there will also be a bus service.

Moving on From the Thai side, if you don't want to walk your bags across the 1km of no-man's-land you can pay 100B for a motorbike with luggage-carrying sidecar. The Thai border post, Ban Huay Kon, is not quite a village but does have simple noodle shops. The only public transport is a luxurious minibus (🗷 083-024 3675) to Phrae (160B, five hours) via Nan (100B, three hours) departing from the border post at 11.45am. Northbound it leaves the bus stations in Phrae at 6am, and Nan at 8am.

Pak Lai to Loei

Getting to the border The quiet rural Kaen Thao/Tha Li border crossing (8am to 6pm) is the home of yet another (small) Friendship Bridge, this time over the Nam Heuang. From Pak Lai, there are *sŏrngtăaou* to the border post at Kaen Thao at around 10am and noon (40,000K, 1¾ hours).

Moving on After walking across the bridge you'll have to take a short *sŏrngtăaou* ride (30B) 8km to Tha Li before transferring to another *sŏrngtăaou* (40B) the remaining 46km to Loei, from where there are regular connections to Bangkok and elsewhere.

Nathong bus station is 1km to the east of town, heading for Vieng Xai. *Sŏrngtăaou* run from here to Vieng Xai (15,000K, 50 minutes, 29km) at 8am, 10am, 11am, 2.30pm and 4pm; the scenery is among the most stunning in Laos. The 'Nameo' (actually the Nam Soi border post) bus leaves at 8am (30,000K, three hours), and the Sam Tai (Xamtay) bus at 9.30am (50,000K, five hours).

Vieng Xai ຢງໄຊ

🗷 064 / POP 10,000

Set amid valleys glistening with wet rice paddies and towered over by dramatic karsts, beautiful Vieng Xai seems an unlikely place to have suffered a decade's worth of American air assaults. Its 450 limestone caves provided sanctuary for more than 23,000 people during the Secret War (1964–73; Laos' clandestine conflict running parallel to the Vietnam War), playing host to bakeries, a hospital, school, a metalwork factory and, more importantly, the political headquarters of the communist Pathet Lao party. As the bombs fell near the virtually unassailable caves, President Kaysone Phomvihane plotted the transformation of his country in a dank grotto, undecorated but for a framed photo of Che Guevara and a few other keepsakes.

Six kilometres from Vieng Xai bus station heading towards Sam Neua, keep an eye out for **Tham Nok Ann** (Nok Ann Cave, ຖ້ຳນົກແອນ; admission 10,000K, twin kayak 30,000K; ⊘8am-

LAOS VIENG XAI

DEADWOOD: LAOS' ILLEGAL LOGGING TRADE

Laos has some of the largest remnant tracts of primary rainforest in mainland Southeast Asia and represents a vulnerable target for foreign companies. The Environmental Investigation Agency (EIA) claims that the furniture industry in Vietnam has grown tenfold since 2000, with Laos facilitating the flow of its timber to enable this. An estimated 500,000 cu metres of logs find their way over the border every year. While an outwardly hard-line approach has been taken against mass logging by the government, it's the self-funded military and local officials in remote areas who can fall prey to bribes.

Forest cover fell from 70% in the 1940s to less than 40% in the early 2000s. An estimated 30% of forest cover will remain in Laos by 2020.

5pm), a newly opened cave complex you can kayak through.

⊙ Sights & Activities

★ **Vieng Xai Caves**   CAVE
(ຖ້ຳວຽງໄຊ; www.visit-viengxay.com; admission incl audio tour 60,000K) Fringed with frangipani trees, the beautiful gardens that now adorn the caves can easily make you forget what their inhabitants had to endure. Perhaps the most atmospheric, as it housed the long-reigning president himself and hosted his politburo meetings, is Phomvihane's eponymous **Tham Than Kaysone**. The electricity is often out so you'll most likely be exploring by candlelight, your flame falling on his meagre library, a Russian oxygen machine poised for a chemical attack, and a bust of Lenin.

Tham Than Souphanouvong, named after the communist-leaning 'Red Prince', has a crater formed by a 230kg bomb near the entrance, while **Tham Than Khamtay**, where up to 3000 Pathet Lao hid, is the most spectacular of the caves.

The best way to visit the caves is by a **bicycle** (per tour/day 10,000/20,000K), available to rent from the **Vieng Xai Cave Tourist Office** (☑064 314 321; www.visit-viengxay.com; ⊙8-11.30am & 1-4.30pm), which allows you to see more caves in less time. There's also an excellent audio guide giving you historical context, and a moving yet balanced glimpse of how people survived in these caves during the war years. Two-hour tours leave the office between 9am and 11am and 1pm and 4pm, and take in three or four caves. At other times you will need to pay an additional fee of 50,000K per tour to cover staff costs. Getting to the tourist office involves a 2km walk from the bus station by the market.

🛏 Sleeping & Eating

By 9pm the town is in hibernation. Several *fĕr* shops in the market serve rice and cheap noodle dishes until around 5pm.

Naxay Guesthouse   GUESTHOUSE $
(☑064 314 330; r 60,000-80,000K) Opposite the caves office, Vieng Xai's most comfortable option offers bamboo-lined bungalows or concrete cubicles. Beds are comfy, hot water flows and the attached beach-style cafe pavilion occasionally serves up food.

❶ Getting There & Away

Sŏrngtăaou to Sam Neua (15,000K, 50 minutes) leave at 7am, 10am, 1pm, 2.30pm and 4pm from the market. Buses between Sam Neua and Sam Tai, Nam Soi or Thanh Hoa bypass Vieng Xai 1km to the north but will usually stop on request.

Udomxai   ອຸດົມໄຊ

☑081 / POP 25,000

Booming Udomxai is a Laos–China trade hub. The absence of a traveller vibe, not to mention a deterring cast of gruff Chinese truck drivers, prostitutes and ugly Soviet style buildings puts off many short-term visitors. That said, it takes minimal effort to find the 'real' Laos nearby; Udomxai Province is home to some of Laos' thickest forests and is a great place to visit Khmu and Hmong villages.

There's also a well-organised tourist office with paper-making and cooking courses (both from 100,000K per person), and some great treks and homestays to tempt you to stay longer. Meanwhile **Samlaan Cycling** (☑020 5560 9790; www.samlaancycling.com) runs recommended one-day/multiday cycling tours.

🛏 Sleeping & Eating

Most places are along – or just off – Rte 1.

Saylomen Guesthouse GUESTHOUSE $
(☑ 081 211 377; r with fan/air-con 60,000/100,000K; ❋) These simple, fair-sized fan rooms are better value than the average guesthouse around town. Air-con is a welcome investment in the hot season.

Xayxana Guest House GUESTHOUSE $
(☑ 020 5578 0429; off Rte 1; r 70,000-100,000K; ❋ ☎) Xayxana is cool and spacious, with immaculate white en suite rooms, tiled floors and very comfy beds.

★**Villa Keoseumsack** HOTEL $$
(☑ 081 312 170; Rte 1; r 120,000-200,000K; ❋ ☎) The town's best-value rooms, with varnished floors, en suites, TVs, Hmong-woven bed runners and freshly plumped pillows. Free wi-fi and a cool reading balcony finish it off.

Meuang Neua Restaurant LAOTIAN $
(mains 20,000-40,000K; ☺ 7am-10pm) The walls here are decorated with arabesques and there's an imaginative menu, from salads through to pumpkin soup, curry, fish and stir-fries.

★**Cafe Sinouk** LAOTIAN, INTERNATIONAL $$
(Charming Lao Hotel; mains 20,000-95,000K; ☎) Sinouk Coffee is stylish and cool. Meals include a wide range of Lao and international dishes, including some whole fish to share. Lunch (15,000K) and dinner (20,000K) specials are one-plate value.

❶ Information

BCEL (☑ 081 211 260; Rte 1) Has an ATM, changes several major currencies and accepts some travellers cheques (2% commission).
Tourist Office (Provincial Tourism Department of Oudomxay; ☑ 081 211 797; www.oudomxay. info; ☺ 7.30-11.30am & 1.30-6pm Mon-Fri Apr-Sep, 8am-noon & 1.30-4pm Mon-Fri Oct-Mar) The tourist office organises a selection of treks and tours and sells the GT-Rider Laos maps. The office sometimes opens on weekends, but the hours are irregular.

❶ Getting There & Away

Lao Airlines (☑ 081 312 047; www.laoairlines. com) flies to Vientiane (one way 695,000K) every Tuesday, Thursday and Saturday.

The **bus terminal** (☑ 081 212 218) at the southwestern edge of town has buses to Luang Prabang (all VIP buses, 55,000K, five hours, 9am, noon and 3pm daily), Nong Khiaw (45,000K, four hours, 9am daily), Pak Beng (40,000K, five hours, 8.30am and 10am daily), Pakmong (30,000K, 2pm and 4pm daily), Luang Namtha (40,000K, three hours, 8.30am, 11.30am and 3.30pm daily), Muang Khua (35,000K, four hours, 8.30am, 11.30am and 3pm daily), Boten (40,000K, four hours, 8am daily), Phongsali (75,000K, eight to 12 hours, 8.30am daily) and Vientiane (ordinary bus 150,000K, 16 hours, 11am; VIP bus 140,000K, 18 hours, 4pm and 6pm daily).

Luang Namtha ຫລວງນ້ຳທາ

☑ 086 / POP 21,000

Nowhere else in Laos offers a better range of outdoor activities and organised eco-adventures than this trekker's paradise. Thanks to its location next to the Nam Ha National Protected Area (NPA), Luang Namtha is one of the best bases in the country for jungle junkies. There are bags of cheap guesthouses, restaurants serving tasty food and a lively market, as well as a couple of banks, internet cafes and cycle-hire and scooter shops. Take a day to explore the valley's local waterfalls and temples before setting out into the wilds of Nam Ha.

LAOS LUANG NAMTHA

GETTING TO CHINA: LUANG NAMTHA TO MENGLA

Getting to the border The Lao immigration post at the Boten/Mohan border crossing is a few minutes' walk north of Boten market. Túk-túk shuttle across no-man's land to the Chinese immigration post in Mohan (Bohan) or it's an easy 10-minute walk. The border is open from 7.30am to 4.30pm Laos time, or 8.30am to 5.30pm Chinese time.

Alternatively, take one of the growing number of handy Laos–China through-bus connections such as Udomxai–Mengla, Luang Namtha–Jinghong and Luang Prabang–Kunming.

At the border It is necessary to have a Chinese visa in advance before attempting to enter the country.

Moving on From the Chinese immigration post it's a 15-minute walk up Mohan's main street to the stand where little buses depart for Mengla (RMB16, one hour) every 20 minutes or so till mid-afternoon. These arrive at Mengla's bus station No 2. Nip across that city to the northern bus station for Jinghong (RMB42, two hours, frequent till 6pm) or Kunming (mornings only).

◉ Sights & Activities

The dense jungle of the **Nam Ha National Protected Area** is home to clouded leopards, gaur and elephants (plus the odd tiger – we know, we met one!). Visiting the NPA involves going on a tour with an experienced guide. Guides also offer **rafting, canoeing** and **mountain biking** along the Nam Tha River, as well as **homestays**. The **Nam Ha Ecotourism Project** (www.unescobkk.org/culture/our-projects/sustainable-cultural-tourism-and-ecotourism/namha-ecotourism-project) tries to ensure tour operators and villagers work together to provide an authentic experience for trekkers with minimal impact on local communities and the environment.

Places of interest within easy cycling or motorbiking distance include **Wat Ban Vieng Tai** and **Wat Ban Luang Khon**, near the airfield; a hilltop stupa, **That Phum Phuk**, about 4km west of the airfield; a small **waterfall** about 6km northeast of town past **Ban Nam Dee**; plus a host of Khamu, Lanten, Thai Dam and Thai Lü villages dotted along dirt roads through rice fields. Pick up a map and brochures at the provincial tourism office before setting off.

Luang Nam Tha Museum   MUSEUM
(ພິພິດຕະພັນຫລວງນ້ຳທາ; admission 5000K; ⊙8.30-11.30am & 1.30-3.30pm Mon-Thu, 8.30-11.30am Fri) The Luang Nam Tha Museum contains a collection of local anthropological artefacts, such as ethnic clothing, Khamu bronze drums and ceramics. There is also a number of Buddha images.

☞ Tours

Nam Ha Ecoguide Service   ECOTOUR
(☏086 211 534; ⊙8am-noon & 1.30-8pm) ◢ A wing of the provincial tourism office. Retains the rights to some of the best trekking routes.

Green Discovery   ECOTOUR
(☏086 211 484; www.greendiscoverylaos.com; ⊙8am-9pm) ◢ Reliable Green Discovery offers different tours to those offered by the tourism office in order to eliminate direct competition and increase the spread of proceeds.

Namtha River Experience   KAYAKING, RAFTING
(☏086 212 047; www.namtha-river-experience-laos.com; ⊙8am-9pm) ◢ Specialises in kayaking and rafting trips through Khamu and Lanten villages. Also facilitates homestays.

⌑ Sleeping

In the high season (November to February) the town gets busy, so it's worth calling ahead to book a room.

★ Phou Iu III Guesthouse   GUESTHOUSE $
(☏030 571 0422; www.luangnamtha-oasis-resort.com; r from 100,000K) Bungalows are spacious and nicely fitted out with lumber-wood beds, fireplaces and inviting terraces. The garden is a work in progress, but at this price it's a steal. It's well-signposted from the centre of town.

Zuela Guesthouse   GUESTHOUSE $
(☏020 5588 6694; www.zuela-laos.com; r 60,000-120,000K; ✳❀☎) Located in a leafy courtyard, Zuela has a great restaurant serving 'power breakfasts', pancakes, shakes, salads and chilli-based Akha dishes. Spacious rooms have wooden floors, fans and fresh linen. Zuela also rents scooters and operates an air-con minivan service to Huay Xai.

Khamking Guesthouse   GUESTHOUSE $
(☏086 312 238; r 70,000-100,000K) Fresh and colourful with interior flourishes such as bedside lights and attractive curtains and bedcovers. Be warned though – you're in the chicken zone with a coop just behind you, so earplugs are essential!

Adounsiri Guest House   GUESTHOUSE $
(☏020 2299 1898; adounsiri@yahoo.com; r 60,000-100,000K; ☎) Located down a quiet street, this homely Lao villa has scrupulously clean rooms with white walls draped in handicrafts, fresh bed linen and tiled floors. There are TVs in every room, plus free wi-fi, tea and coffee.

Thoulasith Guesthouse   GUESTHOUSE $
(☏086 212 166; www.thoulasith-guesthouse.com; r 70,000-100,000K; ✳❀☎) This traveller-friendly spot on the main strip offers spotless rooms with bedside lamps, art on the walls and comfortable wi-fi-enabled balconies. It's set back from the road and is a peaceful spot to wind down before or after a trek.

✗ Eating

★ Forest Retreat Gourmet Cafe   INTERNATIONAL $
(www.forestretreatlaos.com; mains 20,000-50,000K, pizzas 50,000-90,000K) Forest Retreat feels like a home away from home, with sandwiches, pastas, woodfired pizzas, vegetarian risottos and homemade pancakes. Doubles as Bamboo Bar by night with cocktails aplenty.

BUSES FROM LUANG NAMTHA

DESTINATION	COST (K)	DURATION (HR)	STATION	DEPARTURES
Boten	35,000	2	district	6 daily 8am-3.30pm
Huay Xai ('Borkeo')	60,000	4	long distance	9am, 1.30pm bus, 8.30am minibus
Jinghong (China)	90,000	6	long distance	8.30am
Luang Prabang	90,000-100,000	8	long distance	9am bus, 8am minibus
Luang Sing	30,000	2	district	6 daily 8am-3.30pm
Mengla (China)	50,000	3½	long distance	8am
Muang Long	60,000	4	district	8.30am
Na Lae	40,000	3	district	9.30am, noon
Udomxai	40,000	4	long distance	8.30am, noon, 2.30pm
Vieng Phukha	35,000	1½	long distance	9.30am, noon
Vientiane	180,000-200,000	21-24	long distance	8.30am, 2.30pm

Minority Restaurant   LAOTIAN $
(mains 15,000-35,000K; ☉7am-10.30pm) This
inviting, wood-beamed restaurant hidden
down a little side alley offers the chance to
sample typically ethnic dishes from the Khamu, Thai Dam and Akha tribes. If the likes
of rattan shoots and banana-flower soup
don't appeal, there's also a range of stir-fries.

**Manychan Guesthouse
& Restaurant**   LAOTIAN, INTERNATIONAL $
(mains 15,000-40,000K; ☉6.30am-10.30pm; ☏)
An inviting all-wood interior that spills out
onto a fairy-lit street terrace keeps this place
among the most popular *falang* venues in
town. Wi-fi is free and the menu covers the
gamut of possibilities.

Boat Landing Restaurant   LAOTIAN $$
(meals 20,000-150,000K; ☉7am-8.30pm) The
relaxing riverside setting offers five-dish
menus for two or three people, to one-
plate meals, and the flavour combinations
are divine. Try snacking on a selection of
jqaou used as dipping sauces for balls of
sticky rice. Located about 7km from the
new town.

ⓘ Information

BCEL (☉8.30am-3.30pm Mon-Fri) Changes
major currencies (commission free), travellers
cheques (2% commission, minimum US$3) and
has a 24-hour ATM.
Provincial Tourism Office (☏086 211 534;
☉8am-noon & 2-5pm) Doubles as Nam Ha
Ecoguide Service.

ⓘ Getting There & Away

AIR
Lao Airlines (☏086 312 180; www.laoairlines.
com) flies to Vientiane (895,000K) daily.

BOAT
You can reach Huay Xai on a two-day longboat
odyssey down the Namtha, sleeping en route at a
roadless village. Luang Namtha agencies charge
around US$120 to US$300 per person depending
on exact numbers, including accommodation,
meals and a tour guide throughout. You might get
a better deal from the **boat station** (☏086 312
014) beside the Boat Landing Guest House. When
river levels are low (January to June), departures
are from Na Lae, with agencies providing túk-túk
transfers and prearranging a boat.

BUS
There are two bus stations. The district bus sta-
tion is walking distance from the traveller strip.
The main long-distance bus station is 10km
south of town. For Nong Khiaw take a Vientiane or
Luang Prabang bus and change at Pak Mong.

ⓘ Getting Around

Chartered túk-túk charge 10,000K per person
(minimum 40,000K) between the bus station
or airport and the town centre. Most agen-
cies and guesthouses sell ticket packages for
long-distance buses, which include a transfer
from the guesthouse and cost around 20,000K
above the usual fare. Cycling is the ideal way
to explore the wats, waterfalls, villages and
landscape surrounding Luang Namtha. There
are a couple of **bicycle shops** (bicycle per day
10,000-25,000K; motorcycle per day 30,000-
50,000K; ☉9am-6.30pm) in front of the Zuela
Guesthouse that also rent scooters.

Muang Sing ເມືອງສິງ

📞 081 / POP 10,000

At the heart of the infamous 'Golden Triangle' and rubbing shoulders with Myanmar and China, Muang Sing's wilting houses hark back to a simpler time. Although tribeswomen are likely to offer you a rock of opium – Hmong, Thai Lü, Akha, Thai Dam and Yao are all seen here in traditional dress – trekking has overtaken smuggling contraband. While the town feels torpid, your primary reason for visiting is to experience the vernal glory of the nearby Nam Ha National Protected Area.

◉ Sights & Activities

The main draw for Muang Sing is its proximity to tribal villages and trekking in Nam Ha National Protected Area. If you're just here to cycle, grab a map (such as Wolfgang Kom's excellent *Muang Sing Valley* map) from the tourist office, hire a bike and make your own explorations.

Tribal Museum   MUSEUM
(admission 5000K; ⊙ 8.30am-4.30pm Mon-Fri, 8-11am Sat) The most distinctive of the old Lao-French buildings is now home to the two-room Tribal Museum, which boasts costume displays downstairs and six cases of cultural artefacts upstairs. Watching a 40-minute video on the Akha people costs 5000K extra.

Phou Iu Travel   ADVENTURE TOUR
(📞 081 400 012; www.muangsingtravel.com; ⊙ 7am-7pm) The leading tour operator in Muang Sing, run out of the Phou Iu II Guesthouse, offers well-organised treks around Muang Sing. It also offers treks to the more remote Xieng Khaeng district towards Myanmar, but check www. adventure-trek-laos.com for details.

🛏 Sleeping & Eating

Most of Muang Sing's extremely basic guesthouses and attached restaurants are on the town's main strip.

★ Adima Guesthouse   GUESTHOUSE $
(📞 020 2239 3398; r 100,000K) Adima's sturdy brick-and-thatch bungalows include hot showers and bucket-flush toilets. Their appealing rustic restaurant overlooks fishponds. From Muang Sing take the Pang Hai road to the far edge of Ban Udomsin (500m

after Km7), turn right and Adima is 600m south. A túk-túk from town costs about 20,000K.

Thai Lü Guest House   GUESTHOUSE $
(📞 086 400 375; r 30,000-40,000K) Looking like a backdrop in an old Bruce Lee flick, this creaky wooden building has a certain charm, even if the rattan-walled, squat-loo rooms are uninspiring. The restaurant downstairs (meals 10,000K to 25,000K) serves Thai, Laotian and Western dishes..

Phou Iu II Guesthouse   GUESTHOUSE $$
(📞 086 400 012; www.muangsingtravel. com; bungalow small/medium/large 100,000/200,000/400,000K) Set around an expansive garden, all rooms here have comfortable beds, mosquito nets, fans and verandahs, plus there's an on-site herbal sauna (10,000K) and massage service (50,000K per hour). There is also a small restaurant.

Phunnar Restaurant   LAOTIAN $
(Panna Restaurant; mains 15,000-30,000K; ⊙ 7.30am-8pm) Located in a quiet backstreet, the Phunnar is an airy open-air place for inexpensive fried rice, noodles, *láhp* and soups.

ℹ Information

Lao Development Bank (⊙ 8am-noon & 2-3.30pm Mon-Fri) Exchanges US dollars, Thai baht and Chinese yuan but at less than favourable rates.

Post Office (⊙ 8am-4pm Mon-Fri) As tiny as the *petang* rectangle next to it.

Tourist Office (⊙ 8am-4pm Mon-Fri) Displays of fact scrolls are useful, but the office suffers from lacklustre staff.

ℹ Getting There & Around

From the bus station in the northwest corner of town, *sŏrngtăaou* depart for Muang Long

---

(40,000K, 1½ hours) at 8am, 11am and 1.30pm. To Luang Namtha (50,000K, two hours, 58km) minibuses leave at 8am, 9am, 11am, 12.30pm, 2pm and 3pm.

Kalao Motorcycle (per day 80,000K; ⊘ 8am-5pm), on the road to the main market, rents motorbikes. Bicycle rental (30,000K per day) is available from several main-street agencies and guesthouses.

Huay Xai   ຫ້ວຍຊາຍ
📍 084 / POP 17,800

A US heroin processing plant was allegedly based here during the Secret War, but these days the only things spirited through Huay Xai are travellers en route to Luang Prabang. Separated from Thailand by the cocoa-brown Mekong River, it is for many their first impression of Laos (don't worry, it gets better!).

By night its central drag dons fairy lights and roadside food vendors fire up their wares. There are some welcoming guesthouses and cafes, and Huay Xai is also the HQ of the fabled Gibbon Experience, Laos' most talked-about jungle adventure.

🛏 Sleeping & Eating

Budget sleeping and eating haunts are going strong, with a wealth of choice on the main street.

⭐ **Daauw Homestay**   HOMESTAY $
(📱 030 904 1296; www.projectkajsiablaos.org; r 60,000-80,000K) The Daauw Homestay offers a way to contribute something to women's empowerment and minority rights with an overnight stay in a bungalow. As well as accommodation, there is a restaurant-bar, plus a small handicrafts shop. One-week to one-month volunteering positions are available for 850,000K per week, including board and lodging.

Phonetip Guesthouse   GUESTHOUSE $
(📱 084 211 084; Th Saykhong; r 50,000-120,000K; ❄ 🌐) Simple, central and clean by budget standards. The cheapest options are just beds in boxes but there's a pleasant road-facing communal area upstairs.

Friendship Guesthouse   GUESTHOUSE $
(📱 084 211 219; s/d/tr/q from 70,000/80,000/160,000/200,000K; 🌐) Beds are creaky but the selling point here is the open roof with great views.

LAOS HUAY XAI

THE GIBBON EXPERIENCE

Essentially a series of navigable 'ziplines' criss-crossing the canopy of some of Laos' most pristine forest, the **Gibbon Experience** (📱 084 212 021; www.gibbonexperience.org; express 2-day US$190, 3-day classic or waterfall US$290) traverses the realm of tigers, clouded leopards, black bears and the eponymous black-crested gibbon.

A little over a decade ago poaching was threatening the extinction of the black-crested gibbon. Cue Animo – a conservation-based tour group – who convinced the hunters of Bokeo Nature Reserve to become the forest's guardians. As guides, they now make more money for their families than in their old predatory days.

You'll stay in fantastical tree houses complete with cooking facilities and running rainwater showers, 60m up in the trees, while in between scouting for wildlife, you'll be zipping. It's a heart-stopping, superhero experience.

Your day will also involve a serious amount of trekking. Bring a pair of hiking boots and long socks to deter the ever-persistent leeches, plus a torch and earplugs. The guides are helpful, though be vigilant with the knots in your harness.

There are three options to choose from: the 'Classic', which gives you more time to ponder the jungle and less time trekking; the 'Waterfall', with an increased amount of slog balanced by a wonderful dip in a cascade pool; and 'The Gibbon Spa', incorporating the best of the former but with gourmet food, improved lodgings and massages. Fees include transport to and from the park, plus all food and refreshments. Options are for two nights; however, a newer express version offers you the chance to stay for just one.

Payments can be made well in advance via Paypal. Turn up in Huay Xai the day before your trek and report to the **Gibbon Experience office** (Th Saykhong). Next door you can buy gloves, torches and stock up on treats.

BAP Guesthouse
LAOTIAN $

(Th Saykhong; mains 15,000-35,000K; ❄ 🍴) Run by English-speaking Mrs Changpeng, this wayfarer's fave has an inviting restaurant that dishes up snacks, vegetarian dishes and Lao staples. It's one of the closest spots to Lao immigration so it's good for some arrival or departure fodder.

Muang Ner Cafe
LAOTIAN, INTERNATIONAL $

(Gecko Bar; Th Saykhong; meals 20,000-40,000K; ⊙6.30am-11pm) With its worn turquoise walls adorned in animal horns, Muang Ner remains a popular choice. Mouthwatering *lâhp*, Western breakfasts and wood-fired pizzas all complement the welcoming vibe.

Daauw
LAOTIAN $

(mains 20,000-50,000K; 🍴) Reminiscent of a Thai island with its chill-out terrace, low cushions and open-pit fire, Daauw serves organic Hmong food, plenty of vegetarian options or whole barbecued Mekong fish or chicken. Linger for *laojitos* if there's a crowd, a mojito made with *lào-láo*.

🍸 Drinking

Bar How
BAR

(Th Saykhong; meals 20,000-40,000K; ⊙6.30am-11pm; 🛜) Funky Bar How is a little hole-in-the-wall serving food by day and plenty of drinks by night.

ℹ Information

BCEL (Th Saykhong; ⊙8.30am-4.30pm Mon-Fri) Has a 24-hour ATM, exchange facility and Western Union.

Lao Development Bank Exchange Booth (⊙8am-5pm) Handy booth right beside the pedestrian immigration window. Most major currencies are exchanged into kip. US-dollar bills must be dated 2006 or later.

Tourist Information Office (📞084 211 162; Th Saykhong; ⊙8am-4.30pm Mon-Fri) Has free tourist maps of the town and some suggestions for excursions around the province.

ℹ Getting There & Away

AIR

Huay Xai's airport is perched on a hillside 1.5km northwest of the bus station. **Lao Airlines** (📞084 211 026; www.laoairlines.com) flies daily to/from Vientiane for 895,000K.

BOAT

Slow boats headed down the Mekong River to Luang Prabang (200,000K per person, two days, not including overnight accommodation)

hold about 70 people, but captains try to cram in more than 100. Refuse en masse and a second boat will be drafted in. Boats leave from the boat landing at the north end of town at 11am and stop for one night in Pak Beng (100,000K, six to eight hours). Tickets are available from the boat landing the afternoon before you travel, or from guesthouses.

Speedboats to Pak Beng (160,000K, three hours) and Luang Prabang (360,000K, six hours) leave when full, from a landing about 2km south of town, from 8am daily. Buy your ticket at any one of the guesthouses or on arrival at the kiosk above the boat landing. Deaths are not uncommon given the recklessness of the drivers. If you do decide to make the journey, bring earplugs and close your eyes.

Slow boats also run to Luang Namtha (1,530,000K to 1,700,000K per boat split between passengers, plus 40,000K each for food and accommodation) via Ban Na Lae. Ask at BAP Guest House for more information.

For any journey take plenty of water, food supplies and padding for your back.

BUS

The bus station is 5km east of town. Buses to Luang Prabang (120,000K, 14 to 17 hours) via Luang Namtha and Udomxai depart at 9am, 11.30am, 1pm and 5pm. The 11.30am bus continues to Vientiane (230,000K, 25 hours); the 5pm Luang Prabang bus is a VIP service (135,000K). For Udomxai (85,000K, nine hours) there's also an 8.30am service. For Luang Namtha (60,000K, four hours) an additional bus departs at 9am.

Travel-agency minibuses to Luang Namtha leave from central Huay Xai at around 9am (100,000K).

CENTRAL & SOUTHERN LAOS

Steamy rice plains, gothic karst formations, vast forests, coffee-growing plantations and authentic riverine life: all of this beckons those en route to and from Cambodia. Ever since Tha Khaek opened her faded colonial petals a few years back, many have been using it as a picturesque springboard to access Tham Kong Lo, a vast 7.5km subterranea that can only be traversed by boat; and the ragged black karsts of Khammuane Province, home to the legendary Loop, a terrific three-day motorbike adventure. Further south, Savannakhet charms with its old French buildings and trekking options while close to the rural charms of turquoise-watered Four Thousand

GETTING TO THAILAND: CENTRAL BORDERS

Tha Khaek to Nakhon Phanom

Getting to the border A Friendship Bridge has opened here (the ferry boat that used to run is now closed to foreigners). The bridge is some 7km from Tha Khaek and a túk-túk carrying two people over the bridge will cost 20,000K per person from Tha Khaek's bus station (departing every half hour). The immigration office on the bridge opens at 7am and closes at 4pm.

At the border A free 15-day visa is granted on entry to Thailand. There's an exchange booth and 24-hour ATM.

Moving on From the bridge it's a 30B túk-túk ride to Thailand's Nakhon Phanom bus station, from where buses leave regularly for Udon Thani and also Bangkok (at 7.30am and from 7pm to 8pm).

Paksan to Bueng Kan

Getting to the border In Paksan follow a sign to the port and Lao border post (open 8am to noon and 1.30pm to 4.30pm). The boat across the Mekong to Bueng Kan takes a few minutes and costs 60B per person or charter for 480B.

At the border Fifteen-day Thai visas are granted on arrival but check in advance with the Thai Embassy in Vientiane as this is a remote spot seldom used by travellers.

Moving on Buses leave Bueng Kan in Thailand for Udon Thani and Bangkok.

Islands, you'll find sleepy Champasak with its beautiful Khmer ruins.

Route 8 to Lak Sao

Wind your way through a lost world of jungle and dreamlike rock formations in some of the country's trippiest landscape. The first major stop is **Ban Khoun Kham** (also known as Ban Na Hin), 41km east of Rte 13, in the lush Hin Bun valley. The village makes a base from which to explore Phu Hin Bun National Protected Area. You can also catch your forward bus to the extraordinary **Tham Kong Lo**. Community-based treks gear up at the **tourist information centre** (📞 020 5559 8412; Rte 8; ⏰ 8am-4pm) just south of the Tat Namsanam entrance.

◉ Sights

Tham Kong Lo   CAVE
(per boat 106,000K) If you were to realise the ancient Greek underworld (minus the spirits), you might end up with Tham Kong Lo. Situated in the 1580-sq-km wilderness of **Phu Hin Bun National Protected Area**, this 7.5km tunnel running beneath an immense limestone mountain is unearthly.

Puttering upriver (longtail boat is the only means to enter the subterranean caves) you witness the gaping, ragged mouth of the cave, your breath stolen before you've

even entered the eerie, black cavern. Passing into the church-high darkness (100m in some places) and watching the light of the cave mouth recede is a spooky experience. A section of the cave has now been atmospherically lit, and while your longtail docks in a rocky inlet and you explore a haunting stalactite wood, your imagination will likely be in overdrive; are they Gollum's eyes in the bat-black gloom or just another boatman?

Note that once you get to the other side of the cave and stop for refreshments in a nearby shelter, you still have to come back! Remember to bring a decent torch, plus rubber sandals (life-jackets are provided). It costs 105,000K per boat for the return trip (2½ hours, maximum four people). Spend the night near the cave in Kong Lo village (about 1km downstream of the cave mouth), where you'll find restaurants and plenty of guesthouses.

🛏 Sleeping & Eating

🏠 Ban Khoun Kham

Digs in Ban Khoun Kham are basic with warm showers and private bathrooms.

Xok Xai Guesthouse   GUESTHOUSE $
(📞 051 233 629; Rte 8; r 80,000K; 🅿 ❄) Lovely rooms in a traditional house set back off

Rte 8 (or 400m north from the market). Details include spotless varnished floors, thick duvets, TV, air-con, powder-blue curtains and hot-water en suites.

Sainamhai Resort RESORT $
(☎ 020 233 1683; www.sainamhairesort.com; r 130,000K; P ❄ 🛜) Riverside Sainamhai has a handsome longhouse restaurant (mains 25,000K) and 12 well-maintained rattan-walled cabanas with private balconies, en suites and clean linen. It's 3km east of Rte 8; follow the sign near the junction of Rte 8 and the road that borders the Theun Hin Bun dam housing compound at the east end of town.

Call ahead for a pick up from the bus station.

🛏 Kong Lo Village

Not as comfortable as Chantha Guest House perhaps, but definitely more memorable are the homestay options (per person including breakfast and dinner 50,000K) in Kong Lo village. Ask around and a family will take you in.

Chantha Guest House GUESTHOUSE $
(☎ 020 210 0002; Ban Kong Lo; r without/with aircon 60,000/100,000K; P ❄ @ 🛜) This Swiss-style accommodation has 15 cool and well-kept rooms with doubles and twins, plus a dorm which sleeps five people (180,000K). There's a DVD lounge and a small cafe, and the owners are friendly.

Mithuna Restaurant LAOTIAN $
(Ban Kong Lo; mains 20,000K; ⊙ 7am-8pm) Close to the entrance to Tham Kong Lo, this semi-alfresco, fan-cooled restaurant serves up noodles, fried rice and pork *láhp,* as well as Western breakfasts.

ℹ Getting There & Away

From Tha Khaek there's a daily 8am and 9am departure for Ban Khoun Kham (50,000K). Alternatively there's a direct daily bus to Kong Lo from Tha Khaek's Talat Phetmany at 7am (80,000K). All transport along Rte 8 stops at Ban Khoun Kham. If you're coming from

---

GETTING TO VIETNAM: CENTRAL BORDERS

Tha Khaek to Dong Hoi

Getting to the border The Na Phao/Cha Lo border (open 7am to 4pm) is so out of the way it might be better to opt for an easier crossing elsewhere. Transport on either side is slow and scarce, though there are two daily *sŏrngtǎaou* from Tha Khaek (50,000K, 3½ hours, 142km) at 8am and noon bound for Lang Khang, 18km short of the border. Catch the early *sŏrngtǎaou* as you'll need to organise your own forward transport to the border.

At the border This is a small, sleepy border post. On the Vietnamese side the nearest sizeable city is Dong Hoi. Remember to organise your Vietnamese visa in advance.

Moving on A direct bus from Tha Khaek to Dong Hoi (90,000K, 10 to 14 hours) leaves four times a week at 7pm, making this the easiest way to cross this border.

Lak Sao to Vinh

Getting to the border The Nam Phao/Cau Treo border crossing (open 7am to 4.30pm) is at the Kaew Neua Pass, 36km from Lak Sao. *Sŏrngtǎaou* (20,000K, 45 minutes) leave every hour or so from Lak Sao market and drop passengers at the border. Alternatively, direct buses from Lak Sao to Vinh, Vietnam (120,000K, five hours) leave several times a day between noon and 2pm (you may have to change buses at the border).

At the border You'll need to prearrange a visa if heading into Vietnam. There's an exchange booth on the Laos side with ungenerous rates and, inconveniently, the Vietnam border post is another 1km up the road.

Moving on On the Vietnamese side beware of an assortment of piranhas who'll offer to take you to Vinh by minibus for US$30 – it *should* cost US$5 per person. A metered taxi costs around US$40 while a motorbike fare is 200,000d. Hook up with other travellers to improve bargaining power. These woes can be avoided by taking the direct bus from Lak Sao to Vinh. Once in Vinh take the sleeper train, **Reunification Express** (www.vr.com.vn), direct to Hanoi.

Vientiane hop off at Vieng Kham and continue by *sŏrngtăaou* (25,000K, 7am to 7pm) to Ban Khoun Kham.

Buses for Vientiane (75,000K) usually stop between 7am and 10.30am. For Tha Khaek (75,000K, three hours, 143km), there are a couple of buses in the morning; for Lak Sao take any passing bus or *sŏrngtăaou* (25,000K).

From Ban Khoun Kham to Ban Kong Lo, it's a 20-minute journey by scooter or *sŏrngtăaou* (25,000K), which depart at 10am, 12.30pm and 3pm. Headed the other way from Ban Kong Lo to Ban Khoun Kham, *sŏrngtăaou* depart at 6.30am, 8am and 11am.

Tha Khaek ທາແຂວງ

📞 051 / POP 31,000

This ex Indochinese trading post is a pleasing melange of crumbling French villas and wilting Chinese merchant shopfronts, and, despite the new bridge over to nearby Thailand, it shows little signs of radical change. Catch a riverside sundowner or wander along its atmospheric streets as dusk's amber light kicks in and douses the old buildings in charm. With its dusty centrepiece fountain and tree-shaded boulevards glowing with braziers, Tha Khaek is reminiscent of Vientiane 15 years ago.

Tha Khaek is also a comfy base from which to visit Tham Kong Lo, or experience The Loop, the legendary three-day motorbike odyssey. And forget those rickety scooters for tackling either: Tha Khaek now has a proper motorbike rental outfit, Mad Monkey Motorbike (p356).

🗲 Tours

The Tourist Information Centre (p356) run by reliable **Mr Somkiad** (📞 030 530 0503, 020 5571 1797; somkiad@yahoo.com) runs various adventures, such as a two-day trek in the Phu Hin Bun National Protected Area for a group of four (650,000K per person). These treks typically involve a homestay. Ask him too about the 3km-long newly discovered river cave, **Tham Pa Seuam** (Fish Cave). Slated to open in late 2014, it's similar in scope to Tham Kong Lo, and, conveniently, it's only 15km away.

Green Discovery   ADVENTURE TOUR
(📞 051 251 390; Inthira Hotel, Th Chao Annou; ⊙ 8am-9pm) Has a desk at the Inthira Hotel and runs a range of treks and kayaking excursions in the lush Phu Hin Bun NPA,

including to Tham Kong Lo. Cycling, kayaking and a homestay can also be combined.

🛏 Sleeping

⭐ **Thakhek Travel Lodge**   GUESTHOUSE $
(📞 051 212 931; thakhektravellodge@gmail.com; Rte 13; dm 30,000K, r 40,000-180,000K; 🅿 ❄ @ 🛜) If only all guesthouses were as calm, inventive and homely as this travellers' oasis. Just five minutes in a túk-túk east of town, it excels, with a spectrum of bog-standard patchy rooms to elements of Indo-chic. The lodge's centrepiece is a leafy courtyard with a nightly firepit next to which you can swap stories of The Loop.

There's also a natty cafe serving up Lao fare such as *láhp*, Western salads, pork chops and various juices. Just finished when we passed were seven new rooms out the back with slate floors, flat-screen TVs and fridges.

Mekong Hotel   HOTEL $
(📞 051 250 777; Th Setthathirat; s/d 130,000/140,000K; 🅿 ❄ 🛜) Thanks to a re-paint, this blue, Soviet-inspired monolith is much improved, with decent rooms enjoying cable TV, air-con and fresh en suites. There's also a restaurant facing the Mekong.

Thipphachanh Guesthouse   GUESTHOUSE $
(📞 051 212 762; Rte 13; r with fan/air-con 60,000/80,000K; 🅿 ❄) Despite its dusty location, these digs, based around a courtyard, are fragrantly fresh with white walls, tiled floors, TVs and en suites. There are also clean sheets and blankets for cold nights (do they exist?).

🍴 Eating

Several *khào jìi* (baguette) vendors can be found on or near Fountain Sq in the morning, and the adjacent riverfront is good for a cheap meal any time.

Duc Restaurant   LAOTIAN $
(Th Setthathirat; meals 15,000K; ⊙ 6am-10pm; 🚲) On the riverfront just off Fountain Sq, this fan-cooled, family-run joint is fastidiously clean, has tables inside and out, and serves up delicious *fĕr hàang* (dry rice noodles served in a bowl with various herbs and seasonings but no broth).

Kesone Restaurant   FUSION $
(📞 051 212 563; Th Setthathirat; mains 25,000-35,000K; ⊙ 9.30am-11.30pm) With dining in the garden or indoors, this is a popular place

serving a mix of Thai, Thai-Chinese and Lao dishes. The ice cream is also pretty good.

★ **Inthira Restaurant** FUSION $$
(Th Chao Anou; mains 45,000K; ☺7am-10pm; ❄ 🛜 ✐) With its low-lit ambience and open-range kitchen, this is the place to stop for breakfast, lunch or dinner. An Asian fusion menu features delicious *steak au poivre*, tom yum soup, copious salads, curries, stir-fries and very competent burgers. Recommended.

ⓘ Information

BCEL (Th Vientiane) Changes major currencies and travellers cheques, and makes cash advances on Visa. Has three ATMs in town, including one in Fountain Sq, as well as one at the bus station.

Lao Development Bank (Th Vientiane) Cash only – no exchange or Visa advance.

Post Office (Th Kuvoravong) Also offers expensive international phone calls.

Tha Khaek Hospital (cnr Th Chao Anou & Th Champasak) Tha Khaek Hospital is fine for minor ailments or for malaria and dengue fever. Seek out English-speaking Dr Bounthavi.

Tourist Information Centre (✆030 530 0503, 020 5571 1797; www.khammuanetourism.com; Th Vientiane; ☺8.30am-5pm)

Tourist Police (✆051 250610; Fountain Sq) The police here know how to write insurance reports – if you can track down an officer.

ⓘ Getting There & Away

Tha Khaek's **bus station** (Rte 13) is about 3.5km from the centre of town. For Vientiane (70,000K, six hours, 332km), buses leave every hour or so between 5.30am and 9am; there's also a VIP departure at 9.15am (85,000K, six hours) and a sleeper VIP at 1am (85,000K). Any buses going north stop at Vieng Kham (Thang Beng; 30,000K, 90 minutes, 102km) and Paksan (40,000K, three to four hours, 193km). There are two daily services to Attapeu (85,000K, 10 hours, 3.30pm and 11pm), Salavan (85,000K, 11pm) and Sekong (75,000K, 10am and 3.30pm).

Southward buses to Savannakhet (30,000K) depart every half hour, and there's a VIP bus (70,000K, six hours) to Pakse that leaves at 9am, plus hourly local buses (70,000K). For travellers heading to Vietnam, buses for Hué (120,000K) leave Monday, Tuesday, Wednesday and Saturday at 8am; every Monday and Friday at 8pm for Danang (120,000K); 8pm on Tuesday and Saturday for Hanoi (160,000K, 17 hours), and every Monday and Friday for Dong Hoi (90,000K, 10 hours).

If you're headed direct to Don Khong (150,000K, 15 hours, 452km) in the Four Thousand Islands, a bus from Vientiane stops around 5.30pm.

Sǒrngtǎaou depart every hour or so from Talat Phetmany to Mahaxai Mai (35,000K, 1½ hours, 50km). One also goes direct to Ban Kong Lo (80,000K, four hours) at 7.30am.

Sook Som Boon Bus Terminal has buses that serve the Khammuane Province interior with *sǒrngtǎaou* leaving every hour between 7.30am and 9.30am for Gnommalath (45,000K, two to three hours, 63km), Nakai (45,000K, 2½ to 3½ hours, 80km) and an 8pm departure for Na Phao (for the Vietnam border; 80,000K, 3½ hours, 142km).

ⓘ Getting Around

It should cost about 20,000K to hire a jumbo (motorised three-wheeled taxi) to the bus terminal. Rides around town cost around 15,000K per person.

The one and only place to hire a tough, reliable motocross bike to tackle The Loop (scooters are just not built for it) and other adventures is **Mad Monkey Motorbike** (✆020 5993 9909, 020 2347 7799; dcn66@hotmail.com; Fountain Sq; 250cc bikes/automatic scooters per day US$38/28, day trips to Tham Kong Lo for a group of 4 per person 300,000K; ☺9am-8pm). If you break down you can phone the owner and for a price he'll come and get you. He can also take you to Tham Kong Lo and back in a day by bus, leaving at 8am and returning at 8pm (300,000K per person for a group of four).

Mr Ku's Motorbike Rental (✆020 220 6070; per day 100,000K; ☺7.30am-4.30pm), located at Thakhek Travel Lodge, has 110cc Korean bikes for getting around town or to the closer caves. **Phavilai Restaurant** (Fountain Sq; per day 60,000K; ☺6am-9pm) has a few scooters for hire, as does **Wangwang** (✆020 5697 8535; Fountain Sq; per day 50,000-60,000K; ☺8am-9pm) internet shop.

Around Tha Khaek

Travellers rave about the The Loop, a brilliant three-day motorbike trip through dense jungle and karst country passing via Nakai, Lak Sao, Khoun Kham (Na Hin) and Tham Kong Lo; for details look at the travellers' log at Thakhek Travel Lodge (p355). Meanwhile, buzz continues in anticipation of trips to the fantastic 9.5km subterranea of Xe Bang Fai cave, located at the edge of Hin Namno NPA. Also don't miss the myriad caves that can be swum and explored right on Tha Khaek's doorstep. Talk to English-speaking Mr Somkiad at Tha Khaek's Tourist Information Centre (p356).

Savannakhet ສະຫວັນນະເຂດ

☑ 041 / POP 139,000

Languid, time-trapped and ghostly quiet during the sweltering days that batter the old city's plasterwork, Savannakhet is a beguiling mix of yesteryear coupled with increasingly modern commerce.

The best it has to offer is the historic quarter with its staggering display of decaying early-20th-century architecture. These grand old villas from Indochina's heyday now lie unwanted like aged dames crying out for a makeover. There's little to do in town but amble the riverfront and plonk down in one of a clutch of stylish restaurants and bijou cafes.

That said there's loads to do nearby; Savannakhet has a dedicated tourist information centre and ecoguide unit, which has myriad trips to tempt into the nearby national protected areas (NPAs).

◉ Sights

Hire a bicycle and pedal through the cracked streets and along the riverfront, or take a trek in the neighbouring protected areas with Savannakhet's Eco Guide Unit.

Savannakhet Provincial Museum MUSEUM
(ພິພິດຕະພັນແຂວງຂະຫວັນນະເຂດ; Th Khanthabuli; admission 5000K; ⊙ 8-11.30am & 1-4pm Mon-Sat) The Savannakhet Provincial Museum is a good place to see war relics, artillery pieces and inactive examples of the deadly UXO that has claimed the lives of more than 12,000 Lao since the end of the Secret War (see the boxed text, p343).

Musée Des Dinosaures MUSEUM
(Dinosaur Museum, ຫໍພິພິດຕະພັນໄດໂນເສົາ; ☑ 041 212 597; Th Khanthabuli; admission 5000K; ⊙8am-noon & 1-4pm) In 1930 a major dig in a nearby village unearthed 200-million-year-old dinosaur fossils. This enthusiastically run museum is an interesting place to divert yourself for an hour or so. Savannakhet Province is home to five dinosaur sites.

🛏 Sleeping

Souannavong Guest House GUESTHOUSE $
(☑ 041 212 600; Th Saenna; r without/with aircon 70,000/100,000K; P❄🅿🅿) This little guesthouse, down a quiet street abloom in

Savannakhet

◉ Sights
1 Musée Des Dinosaures.................A2
2 Savannakhet Provincial Museum.......A4

🛏 Sleeping
3 Leena Guesthouse.....................B3
4 Salsavan Guesthouse..................A3
5 Souannavong Guest House..............B3

🍽 Eating
6 Café Chez Boune......................B2
7 Chai Dee.............................B3
8 Lin's Café...........................A3
9 Riverside Snack & Drink Vendors......A3
10 Xokxay Restaurant...................A3

bougainvillea, has unfailingly fresh en suite rooms, wi-fi and bikes to rent. A welcoming spot to stay.

Leena Guesthouse GUESTHOUSE $
(📋 041 212 404; leenaguesthuse@hotmail.com; Th Chaokeen; r 50,000-90,000K; P ✳ @ 🛜) Fairy-lit Leena is something of a motel with kitsch decor in comfortable peach-coloured rooms with hot-water showers, TVs and a pleasant breakfast area. The air-con rooms are bigger.

★ Salsavan Guesthouse GUESTHOUSE $$
(📋 041 212 371; Th Kuvoravong; s/d incl breakfast US$23/28; P ✳ 🛜) Rooms are large and atmospherically old-fashioned with wood floors and shuttered windows and balconies. That said, the en suites are unattractively Soviet and the place feels like it's in need of invigoration. Outside there's a delightful garden terrace.

🍴 Eating

With sidewalk cafes and a scattering of French restaurants, the cuisine on offer here is pretty varied. Opposite Wat Sainyaphum the **riverside snack and drink vendors** (⊙ 5-10pm) are great for sundowners and, as evening approaches, *seen dàat* (Korean-style barbecue) is also available.

★ Chai Dee JAPANESE, INTERNATIONAL $
(📋 020 5988 6767; Th Ratsavongseuk; mains 20,000K; ⊙ 8.30am-9pm; ✳ 🛜 📋) Run by friendly Moto, this Japanese cafe is a real traveller magnet; there are rattan mats to lounge on, books to exchange, cool T-shirts for sale and a wide menu of samosas, home-made yoghurt, Thai food and tofu.

★ Lin's Café INTERNATIONAL $
(Th Latsaphanith; mains 30,000K; ⊙ 8am-8pm; ✳ 🛜 📋) This chic cafe on a pretty side street is a mix of antique furniture, easy tunes and coffee with attitude. There are also fruit shakes, stir-fries, vegie dishes, breakfasts, fruit salads and *láhp* – they even make bacon sandwiches!

Xokxay Restaurant LAOTIAN $
(Th Si Muang; mains 15,000K; ⊙ 9am-9pm; 📋) A great hole in the wall on the square near the Catholic church, Xokxay is clean and popular, and dishes up tasty Laotian food, including noodle dishes, fried rice, salads and crispy fried shrimp.

Café Chez Boune FRENCH $$
(Th Ratsavongseuk; mains 75,000K; ⊙ 7am-10pm; ⊜ ✳ 🛜) Glacially cool Chez Boune has tasty steaks, pasta dishes, lasagne, pork chops and *filet mignon* – all of which are executed with élan.

ℹ️ Information

BCEL (Th Ratsavongseuk; ⊙ 8.30am-4pm) ATM, cash exchange and credit-card advances.

Eco Guide Unit (📋 041 214 203; www.savannakhet-trekking.com; Th Latsaphanith; ⊙ 8am-noon & 1-4.30pm Mon-Fri) The industrious ecoguide unit offers treks to Dong Natad PPA and Dong Phu Vieng NPA, bus times, accommodation and can advise where to get a decent massage or hire a motorbike.

Lao Development Bank (Th Udomsin; ⊙ 8.30-11.30am & 1.30-3.30pm) Changes cash and offers credit-card advances. Also has an ATM.

Post Office (📋 041 212 205; Th Khanthabuli) For calls, use an internet cafe instead.

Provincial Hospital (📋 041 212 717, 020 260 1993; Th Khanthabuli; ⊙ 8am-noon & 1-4pm) Ask for English-speaking Dr Outhon.

Provincial Tourism Office (📋 041 212 755; Th Muang Sing; ⊙ 8-11.30am & 1.30-4.30pm) Has helpful city maps and English-speaking staff with suggestions of things to do, from food to local sights.

Tourist Police (📋 041 260 173)

ℹ️ Getting There & Away

Savannakhet's airport fields daily flights to and from Vientiane (US$128), Pakse (US$75) and Bangkok (US$155). Buy tickets at the **Lao Airlines** (📋 041 212 140; Savannakhet Airport; ⊙ 6.30am-4.30pm) office.

Savannakhet's **bus terminal** (📋 041 212 143) is 2km north of town on Th Makkasavan. Buses leave for Vientiane (75,000K, nine hours, 470km) hourly from 6am to 11.30am. Thereafter you'll have to catch buses headed to Pakse that pass through Tha Khaek (30,000K, 2½ to four hours, 125km) until 10pm. A sleeper VIP bus to Vientiane (120,000K, six to seven hours) leaves at 9.30pm.

Heading south, at least 10 buses start here or pass through from Vientiane for Pakse (45,000K, five to six hours, 230km) and a daily bus to Don Khong (80,000K, six to eight hours) leaves at 7pm.

Buses for Dansavanh (60,000K, five to seven hours) on the Lao/Vietnamese border leave at 7am, 8.30am and 11am, stopping at Sepon (50,000K, four to six hours). A daily local bus heads to Hué (90,000K), while a VIP bus (110,000K) runs Monday to Friday at 10.30am. A bus to Danang (110,000K) leaves Tuesday,

GETTING TO VIETNAM: SOUTHERN BORDERS

Savannakhet to Dong Ha

Getting to the border Buses for the Dansavanh/Lao Bao border (open 8am to 5pm) leave from Savannakhet (60,000K, five to seven hours) at 7am, 8.30am and 11am, and stop en route at Sepon (50,000K).

At the border It's a 1km walk between the two border posts (hop on a motorbike taxi on the Vietnamese side for 10,000d). Formalities don't take long given that all Vietnamese visas must be issued prior to arrival. There is simple accommodation on both sides of the border.

Moving on A daily 8am bus runs from Savannakhet to Dong Ha (80,000K, about eight hours, 329km), while a daily local bus runs from Savannakhet to Hué (90,000K, 13 hours, 409km); a VIP bus (110,000K, eight hours, 409km) also runs from Savannakhet to Hué from Monday to Friday at 10.30am. A bus to Danang (110,000K) leaves Tuesday, Thursday and Saturday at 10pm, continuing to Hanoi (200,000K, 24 hours, 650km). No matter what you hear, you will have to change buses at the border.

Attapeu to Kon Tum

Getting to the border The Phou Keua/Bo Y border is in far southeastern Attapeu Province. It's 113km southeast of Attapeu town. **Mai Linh Express** (in Attapeu 030 539 0216, in Vietnam 0592-211 211) operates a daily minibus connecting Pakse with Kon Tum (Vietnam; 145,000K) leaving at 5.45am and reaching Attapeu five hours later. In Attapeu you can buy tickets to cross the border at the **Duc Loc Hotel** (020 9982 2334; Rte 18A; r 80,0000K; ✳ 🛜).

At the border Vietnamese visas *must* be arranged in advance. Thirty-day visas are granted on arrival in Laos and cost between US$30 and US$40 depending on your nationality. Bring a passport photo if you're headed into Laos, otherwise pay an extra 40B.

Moving on Once on the Vietnamese side minibuses continue to Ngoc Hoi, 18km away. There are places to stay here and morning departures for a wide range of destinations.

Thursday and Saturday at 10pm, continuing to Hanoi (200,000K, 24 hours, 650km).

ℹ️ Getting Around

A túk-túk to the bus terminal will cost about 20,000K; prices double after dark. The town is fairly sprawled out so it might be a good idea to rent a scooter (70,000K) from Souannavong Guest House (p357). Hire bikes (10,000K) along Th Ratsavongseuk.

Pakse   ປາກເຊ

031 / POP 75,000

Don't expect Luang Prabang from this dusty, ex Indochinese capital, but if you're moving north from the Four Thousand Islands or headed south to Cambodia, chances are you'll stay here a day or two and grow to like the place. Thanks to Green Discovery's Tree Top Explorer ziplining adventure and a more active 'eco' drive from the tourist office, the city is now worth staying in longer. Pakse is also close to the beguiling Khmer

ruins of Wat Phu in Champasak, and the Bolaven Plateau coffee-growing region with its Edenic waterfalls, where many head via rented scooter.

Central Pakse is bound by the Mekong to the south and by the Se Don River to the north and west. On and below Rte 13 towards the Mekong are most of Pakse's guesthouses, shops and restaurants. Heading west across Se Don takes you to the northern bus terminal. The southern bus terminal and market are 8km in the opposite direction.

◉ Sights & Activities

Wats   BUDDHIST TEMPLES

There are about 20 wats in Pakse, among which Wat Luang and Wat Tham Fai, both founded in 1935, are the largest. A monastic school at **Wat Luang** (ວັດຫຼວງ; Th 11) features ornate concrete pillars, carved wooden doors and murals. Behind the *sǐm* is a monks' school.

Wat Tham Fai (ວັດຖ້ຳໄຟ; Rte 13), near the Champasak Palace Hotel, is undistinguished

Pakse

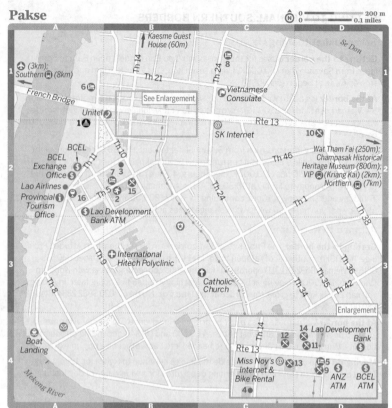

except for its spacious grounds, making it a prime site for temple festivals. It's also known as Wat Pha Bat because there is a small Buddha footprint shrine.

Champasak Historical Heritage Museum
MUSEUM
(ພິພິດທະພັນມໍລະດົກປະຫວັດສາດຈໍາປາສັກ; Rte 13; admission 10,000K; ⊙8-11.30am & 1-4pm Mon-Fri) This museum has a few interesting artefacts, including three very old Dong Son bronze drums, and a Siam-style sandstone Buddha head dating to the 7th century. Also on display are musical instruments, a scale model of Wat Phu Champasak, and some American UXOs and other weaponry.

Clinic Keo Ou Done
MASSAGE
(Traditional Medicine Hospice; ☑ 020 543 1115, 031 251 895; massage 30,000-70,000K, sauna 10,000K; ⊙9am-9pm, sauna 4-9pm) This professional and popular massage centre has an air-conditioned massage room and herbal sauna segregated by gender. To get here, head out of town on Rte 38 and turn right towards Pakse Golf, 1km east of Champasak Grand Hotel.

Dok Champa Massage
MASSAGE
(Th 5; massages from 35,000K, body scrub 200,000K; ⊙9am-10pm) This is the longest-running and still the best massage emporium in the centre of town. Prices are very reasonable for the stylish set-up.

☞ Tours

Most hotels and guesthouses can arrange day trips to the Bolaven Plateau, Wat Phu Champasak and Si Phan Don (Four Thousand Islands). The provincial tourism office (p362) also arranges community-based two- or three-day treks in Se Pian NPA and Phou Xieng Thong NPA, involving kayaking and camping combos, as well as homestays on Don Kho and Don Daeng.

Pakse

Green Discovery ADVENTURE TOUR
(☑031 252 908; www.greendiscoverylaos.com; Th 10; 2-day Tree Top Explorer tour 2-/4-person group per person US$300/200) Green Discovery's ace card is the Tree Top Explorer adventure in the nearby Dong Hua Sao NPA; think ziplining, canopy walks and jungle trekking. Green Discovery also offers kayaking and much more.

Xplore-Asia ADVENTURE TOUR
(☑031 251 983; www.xplore-laos.com; Th 14) Xplore-Asia specialises in multiday adventures, including a variety of options for Mekong River trips to Si Phan Don and on into Cambodia, using boats and/or kayaks. English-speaking guides are US$35 per day.

Sleeping

Affordable, traveller-magnet digs abound in Pakse.

★**Alisa Guesthouse** HOTEL $
(☑031 251 555; www.alisa-guesthouse.com; Rte 13; r 110,000K; ❉@⎙) Sleepy service aside, the centrally located Alisa is an exceptional deal, offering clean, stylish accommodation. Rooms have comfy, immaculately made

beds, working satellite TV and fridge. There's also a large fleet of motorbikes for hire.

Kaesme Guest House GUESTHOUSE $
(☑020 9948 1616; Se Don riverfront; r 30,000-70,000K; ❉⎙) The quiet location and wood deck over the Se Don are the main draws, but the simple rooms, which come with or without bathrooms and air-con, are a great deal. Towels and soap are a nice bonus.

Fang Sedone Guesthouse GUESTHOUSE $
(☑031 212 158; Th 11; r with fan/air-con 50,000/70,000K; ❉) Rooms here are as basic as it gets, but the riverside setting is quiet compared with budget hotels on the main drag. Air-con rooms include hot water.

Sabaidy 2 Guesthouse GUESTHOUSE $
(☑031 212 992; www.sabaidy2tour.com; Th 24; dm 30,000K, s/d/tr without bathroom 50,000/70,000/114,000K, d with bathroom 85,000-100,000K; @⎙) Sabaidy has a reputation as a backpacker magnet. It's often booked out if you walk in so try booking ahead. The en suite rooms out back are good value.

Eating

Chow down with locals at the **Lankham Noodle Shop** (under the Lankham Hotel, Rte 13; noodles 15,000-25,000K; ⊙7am-10pm; ⎙) and at the **Mengky Noodle Shop** (Rte 13; meals 8000-15,000K; ⊙7am-10pm). Rte 13 in the centre of town is scattered with baguette vendors, and by night the braziers light up, selling barbecued chicken and pork. Self-caterers can head to the **Friendship Minimart** (Rte 13; ⊙8am-8pm).

★**Bolaven Cafe** CAFE $
(www.bolavenfarms.com; Rte 13; mains 20,000-40,000K; ⊙7am-9.30pm Mon-Sat; ❉⎙) Great coffee-fuelled breakfasts and an extensive menu of Laotian and Thai food, as well as sandwiches.

Delta Coffee CAFE $
(Rte 13; mains 25,000-40,000K; ⊙7am-9pm; ⎙) Delta has a hearty selection of Italian and Thai dishes as well as lasagne, pastas and pizzas, while the coffee is from their plantation near Paksong.

Xuan Mai Restaurant LAOTIAN, VIETNAMESE $
(Th 5; mains 18,000-30,000K; ⊙6am-11.30pm) Vietnamese-run Xuan Mai serves freshly prepared *fĕr*, *năam néuang* (pork balls) *and kòw bûn* (white flour noodles with

LAOS PAKSE

SUPER FLY GUY

Pakse's Green Discovery (p360) runs excursions to the **Tree Top Explorer**, a series of 11 exhilarating ziplines in the Bolaven Plateau that rival the Gibbon Experience for its sheer adrenalin rush. The longest ride is 450m but the most dramatic cable is that which crosses directly in the spray of a huge waterfall. Trek through jungle and stay in eco-conscious 20m-high tree houses in the semi-evergreen forests of Don Hua Sao NPA on two-day, one-night excursions; a group of two costs US$187 per person. Thanks to safety-conscious guides and controlled visitor numbers, current reviews are excellent.

sweet-spicy sauce), while the house *láhp* is full of zing.

Jasmine Restaurant   INDIAN $
(Rte 13; mains 20,000-30,000K; ⊘8am-10pm) Delicious curries and Malaysian fare such as nasi goreng with mutton, plus sizzling chicken tikka masala so tasty you'll be wiping the bowl with the pillow-soft naan.

🍷 Drinking

Wander down the Mekong riverfront and stop at a terrace bar for a beer. Alternatively, nurse a bloody Mary on the Parisien-style rooftop Panorama Bar at the **Pakse Hotel** (✆ 031 212 131; www.pakehotel.com; Th 5).

Sinouk Coffee Shop   CAFE
(cnr Th 9 & Th 11; dishes 25,000-45,000K; ⊘6.30am-8.30pm; ❇🐕) A good breakfast or lunch stop, with sandwiches, salads, pasta, pastries, fresh bread and blasting air-con. Rich Arabica coffee from the Bolaven Plateau too.

ⓘ Information

ATMs are strung out along Rte 13, including an ANZ machine outside the Lankham Hotel on Rte 13. The Lankham also has a useful **currency exchange counter** (⊘7am-7pm) that offers decent rates and does cash advances on Visa cards.
BCEL (Th 11; ⊘8.30am-3.30pm Mon-Fri) Changes travellers cheques (1% commission) and gives cash advances on Visa and MasterCard (3%). Its exchange office (Th 11; ⊘8.30am-7pm Mon-Fri, to 3pm Sat & Sun) next door has longer hours. BCEL ATMs are across the city.

International Hitech Polyclinic (VIP Clinic; ✆031 214 712; ihpc_lao@yahoo.com; Th 46; ⊘24hr) Adjacent to the public hospital, with English-speaking staff and much higher standards of care, service and facilities, plus a pharmacy.
Lao Development Bank (Rte 13; ⊘8am-4pm Mon-Fri, to 3pm Sat & Sun) Changes cash and travellers cheques. Also houses a Western Union (which does money transfers on weekdays).
Main Post Office (cnr Th 8 & Th 1; ⊘8am-noon & 1-4pm Mon-Fri)
Miss Noy's Internet & Bike Rental (Rte 13; per hr 500K; ⊘7am-8pm) Also rents bicycles and motorbikes.
Police (✆031 212 145; Th 10)
Provincial Tourism Office (✆031 212 021; Th 11; ⊘8am-noon & 1.30-4pm)
SK Internet (Rte 13; per hr 5000K; ⊘7.30am-9pm) Fast connections.
Unitel (Rte 13; ⊘8am-5pm Mon-Fri, to noon Sat) A convenient stop for a local SIM card if you are just arriving in Laos. Staff can set your smart phone up with 3G internet.

ⓘ Getting There & Away

AIR

Lao Airlines flies daily between Pakse and Vientiane (one way US$147, 70 minutes), and also to Luang Prabang (US$184, one hour 40 minutes), as well as Savannakhet (US$75, 30 minutes). Internationally there are flights to Ho Chi Minh City (US$170, four weekly), Siem Reap (US$160, daily), and Bangkok (US$165, five weekly). A túk-túk to the airport from Pakse costs 50,000K.

The airport has a BCEL exchange office. Note: you can't buy tickets at the airport, so purchase them at the **Lao Airlines office** (✆031 212 252; Th 11; ⊘8am-noon & 1-5pm Mon-Fri, 8am-noon Sat).

BOAT

A tourist boat motors to Champasak (two hours away) most mornings at 8.30am, provided there are enough punters (one way per person 70,000K). The return trip from Champasak is at 1.30pm.

BUS & SŎRNGTĂAOU

Confusingly, Pakse has several bus and *sŏrngtăaou* terminals. 'Sleeper' VIP buses leave from the **VIP bus station** (✆031 212 428; Rte 13, Km2) off Rte 13, for Vientiane (170,000K, eight to 10 hours, 677km) every evening. The same bus passes through Tha Khaek (140,000K, 4½ hours) and Savannakhet (140,000K, three hours). The handy Thai–Lao International Bus, which heads to Bangkok (200B, 8.30am and

---

GETTING TO THAILAND: SOUTHERN BORDERS

Savannakhet to Mukdahan

Getting to the border Regular buses (15,000K, 45 minutes) leave Savannakhet's bus station and cross the new Friendship Bridge for Thailand's Mukdahan between 8.15am and 7pm. Buses leave Mukdahan's bus station (50B, 45 minutes) roughly every hour from 7.30am till 7pm.

At the border This is a well-organised, busy border (open 6am to 10pm). A free 15-day tourist visa is given on entering Thailand. Note that to obtain a 30-day Thai visa, you'll need to arrive in the country by air.

Moving on Onward from Mukdahan, there are five daily buses bound for Bangkok between 5.30pm and 8.15pm.

Pakse to Ubon Ratchathani

Getting to the border Heading to the busy Vang Tao/Chong Mek border (open 6am to 8pm) is straightforward if catching a *sŏrngtăaou* from Pakse (10,000K per person, 75 minutes, 37km). Alternatively take the 8.30am or 3.30pm Thai-Lao international bus (80,000K, three hours, 126km) to Ubon Ratchathani (Thailand) from Pakse's 2km bus terminal (also known as the VIP bus terminal and the Kriang Kai bus station).

At the border There are ATMs on the Thai side, a market and restaurants. You have to walk a bit between the two posts but in general it's hassle free. Free 15-day visa waivers are granted on arrival in Thailand.

Moving on The Thai-Lao international bus continues on to Bangkok (235,000K, 14 hours). From Chong Mek to Ubon (80km, 1½ hours) costs 50B by bus, while taxi drivers charge between 1000B and 1200B.

3.30pm) and Ubon (80,000K), also departs from here. It's also possible to buy a combo bus/sleeper train ticket to Bangkok (280,000K) from Pakse travel agents.

From the **northern bus terminal** (Rte 13) sometimes referred to as 'Km7 bus terminal', agonisingly sweltering local buses crawl north every 40 minutes or so between 6.30am and 4pm for Savannakhet (40,000K, four to five hours, 277km), Tha Khaek (70,000K, eight to nine hours) and, for those with a masochistic streak, Vientiane (110,000K, 16 to 18 hours). Fancier air-con buses also leave for Vientiane (140,000K, 10 to 12 hours) throughout the day from the **southern bus terminal** (Rte 13).

For buses or *sŏrngtăaou* anywhere south or east, head to the southern bus terminal, also known as 'Km8 bus terminal'. It costs 15,000K by túk-túk to get there. For Si Phan Don, transport departs for Muang Khong on Don Khong island (including ferry 40,000K, three hours, 120km) between 8.30am and 3pm, and for Ban Nakasang (for Don Det and Don Khon; 40,000K, three to four hours) hourly between 7.30am and 4pm. A *sŏrngtăaou* runs to Kiet Ngong (Xe Pian NPA) and Ban Phapho (25,000K, two to three hours) at 1pm.

To the Bolaven Plateau, transport leaves the southern bus terminal for Paksong (25,000K, 90 minutes) hourly between 7am and 4pm, stopping

at Tat Fan if you ask. For Tat Lo take the Salavan bus (25,000K, three to four hours, five daily).

Regular buses and *sŏrngtăaou* leave Talat Dao Heung (New Market) for Champasak (20,000K, one to two hours). Buses leave the southern bus terminal for Vietnam's Danang (180,000K, 18 hours) at 7pm, and Hué (160,000K, 15½ hours) at 6.30pm.

Mai Linh Express operates a daily minibus service from outside the Saigon Champasak Hotel to Lao Bao (140,000K, 6.30am) on the Vietnamese border. Ask about other Vietnam fares within the hotel.

ⓘ Getting Around

A jumbo to the airport, 3km northwest of town, should cost about 40,000K. Pakse's main attractions are accessible by foot. Bicycles/scooters (around 15,000/50,000K per day) can be hired from the Lankham Hotel which also has Honda Bajas for 240,000K a day – excellent for super-swift day trips to the Bolaven Plateau.

Bolaven Plateau

ພູພຽງບໍລະເວນ

Laos' principal coffee-growing region, the Bolaven Plateau (Phu Phieng Bolaven in

Lao) is home to dense jungles and celebrated by travellers for its handful of refreshing waterfalls and cooler climate. Surging 1500m above the Mekong valley, the claw-shaped plateau is home to several Mon-Khmer ethnic groups, including the Alak, Laven (Bolaven means 'land of the Laven'), Ta-oy, Suay and Katu. You're probably here for the rustic serenity of Tat Lo, which is an excellent place to hire a bike, take an elephant trek or explore the nearby waterfalls.

Tat Lo   ຕາດເລາະ
☑ 034

90km from Pakse, remote and sleepy Tat Lo is an oasis of menthol-green waterfalls with deliciously cool pools to swim in, and is well worth the effort to get here. There are decent digs at affordable prices and a couple of places to eat, but the real charm of the place is its paradiselike setting and chilled vibe.

The nearest cascade to the village is **Tat Hang**, which can be seen from the bridge, while **Tat Lo** itself is about 700m upriver via a path leading through Saise Guest House. The spectacular third cascade is **Tat Suong**, about 10km from town and best reached by motorbike or bicycle – get directions from Bah at Palamy Guesthouse. For **elephant treks** (leaving at 8am, 10am, 1pm and 3pm; 100,000K per person) head to Tad Lo Lodge.

🛏 Sleeping & Eating

The village is a one-street affair, with most accommodation either side of the bridge (budget places are concentrated on the east side).

★ Saise Guest House & Restaurant   LODGE $
(☑ 034 211 886; r with fan/air-con from 60,000/180,000K, mains 40,000-60,000K; 🗟) In lush gardens on the west bank of the river, rooms here range from cheap fan-cooled numbers to sophisticated air-conditioned bungalows. The restaurant is Tat Lo's best, and includes stir-fries, salads and various fish incarnations.

★ Fandee   GUESTHOUSE $
(r 50,000-60,000K; 🗟) The four raised-wood bungalows are sturdy, comfortable and airy and feature thatched roofs, private porches, and pebble-floor, cold-water bathrooms. A communal vibe reigns in the restaurant. It's opposite the tourist office.

Palamy Guesthouse   GUESTHOUSE $
(☑ 030 962 0192; r without/with bathroom from 40,000/60,000K; 🗟) Overlooking a pretty meadow, the better rooms have mosquito nets, terraces with tables and, in some cases, fridges and kitchens. The owner, Poh, is an excellent cook so it's well worth dropping in for a meal.

Champasak   ຈຳປາສັກ
☑ 031 / POP 14,000

Many eschew arid Pakse for the lush riverine charms of this southern Laos belle. Thanks to its silkscreen-style mountain, fringed by emerald rice paddies and the easy manner of its locals, you too may stay a little longer than planned. Among faded colonial villas there's a sprinkling of high-end style with a boutique hotel and a couple of upscale restaurants. Champasak's highpoint is the picturesque ruins of Wat Phu Champasak, and, although it won't wow you like Angkor, it's a serene spot to visit.

The town stirs once a year when pilgrims gravitate here for **Bun Wat Phu Champasak,** a three-day Buddhist festival (usually held in February) of praying, offerings, traditional music, Thai boxing, comedy shows and cockfights. Guesthouses are mainly found near the fountain south of Champasak's only roundabout.

⊙ Sights

Wat Phu Champasak   BUDDHIST TEMPLE
(admission 8am-4.30pm 30,000K, 6-8am & 4.30-6pm 40,000K; ⊙ 6am-6pm, museum 8am-4.30pm) The archaeological site itself is divided into six terraces on three main levels, joined by a long, stepped promenade flanked by statues of lions and *naga*.

🛏 Sleeping & Eating

Anouxa Guesthouse   GUESTHOUSE $
(☑ 031 511 006; r with fan 60,000K, with air-con 100,000-200,000K; ❈🗟) Pricier, balconied air-con rooms face the river and have clean bathrooms and decent linens, along with a tempting riverside restaurant which make it worth the splurge.

Thavisab Guesthouse   GUESTHOUSE $
(☑ 020 5535 4972; r without/with air-con 50,000/100,000K; ❈) Pleasant rooms with mint-coloured curtains and clean linen, in an airy old house set back from the river.

Inthira Hotel & Restaurant
SOUTHEAST ASIAN $

(mains 35,000K; 🛜) The belle of the river, Inthira's sumptuous low-lit restaurant gives you yet another reason to stay another day in Champasak. Based in a beautifully renovated Chinese shophouse.

Frice and Lujane Restaurant
ITALIAN $$

(mains 40,000-60,000K; ⊙5-9pm) The Italian founder has gone but his legacy, in the form of cuisine inspired by Italy's Friulian alpine region, lives on at this atmospheric restaurant based in a renovated villa. Gnocchi, marinated pork ribs, goulash and homemade sausage grace the menu.

ℹ Getting There & Around

Regular buses and *sŏrngtǎaou* run between Champasak and Pakse (20,000K, one hour) from about 6.30am until 1pm; early morning is busiest.

If you're heading south to Ban Nakasang (for Don Det) or Muang Khong (on Don Khong), get to Ban Lak 30 (on Rte 13), where you can flag down anything going south.

Bicycles (per day 15,000K) and scooters (per half/full day 50,000/80,000K) can be hired from guesthouses.

Si Phan Don (Four Thousand Islands)
ສີ່ພັນດອນ

📋 031

This beguiling archipelago of islets is the emerald jewel near the end of the Mekong's 4350km journey. The river passes around thousands of sandbars sprouting with sugar palms, its colour an electric peacock-green. At night the waters are dotted with the lights of fishing boats and fireflies, the soundtrack provided by braying buffalo and cicadas. Between tubing, kayaking and cycling around the three main islands – Don Khong, and sister islands Don Det and Don Khon – spotting the rare Irrawaddy dolphin or visiting waterfalls, there's little to do but hammock dwell.

Don Khong
ດອນໂຂງ

POP 13,000

Life moves slowly on Don Khong, an 18km-long, 8km-wide sleepy idyll where fishing nets dry in the sun, the turquoise Mekong slips by and locals barely look up from

their Beerlao to register your arrival. Its main settlement, Muang Khong, is a one-street affair with a couple of guesthouses and restaurants. Quiet and authentic, it's a nice place to take a sunset boat ride to Cambodian waters, to read by the river or to hire a bike to explore the island.

🛏 Sleeping

There are a few great-value oases at which to rest your bones; all of them are located in Muang Khong.

★Ratana Riverside Guesthouse
GUESTHOUSE $

(☑020 2220 1618, 031 213 673; vongdonekhong@hotmail.com; r 100,000K, mains 15,000-40,000K; ❄🛜) The four comfortable river-facing rooms here enjoy marble floors, balconies, Siberian air-con and handsome furnishings. Ground-floor rooms have enormous windows close to the road, so you might want to get one upstairs. The river-deck restaurant has about the best selection of Western food on the island.

Khong View Guesthouse
GUESTHOUSE $

(☑020 2244 6449; r with fan/air-con 80,000/100,000K; ❄🛜) Rooms are set around a breezy wood deck overlooking a big bend in the Mekong. Choose between dark woody riverfront rooms or bright tiled rooms at the back.

Villa Kang Khong
GUESTHOUSE $

(☑020 2240 3315; r 50,000-60,000K) The most romantic budget digs in town, this stalwart teak house creaks with uneven floors and nostalgic furnishings. Rooms are basic and fan-cooled and, with their colourful wood interiors, remind us vaguely of Roma caravans.

Pon's River Guesthouse & Restaurant
GUESTHOUSE $

(☑020 2227 0037; www.ponarenahotel.com; r 60,000-100,000K; ❄🛜) Pon's original guesthouse gets less TLC since he opened the swish Arena Hotel. The basic rooms, which come in fan and air-con flavours are OK, but the sprawling public balcony in view of the river is the place to hang.

ℹ Information

One road back from the river, 400m south of Wat Phuang Kaew, the **Agricultural Promotion Bank** (⊙8.30am-3.30pm Mon-Fri) exchanges travellers cheques and cash and has an ATM that works with Visa and MasterCard. There's also

LAOS SI PHAN DON (FOUR THOUSAND ISLANDS)

Si Phan Don

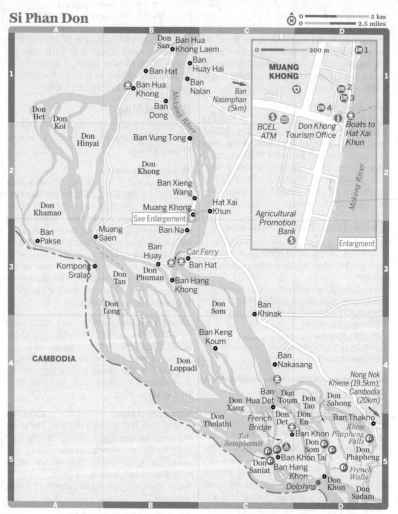

a BCEL ATM next to the post office. For medical complaints, the hospital is a little further south of the bank; ask for English- and French-speaking Dr Bounthavi.

Si Phan Don

The **Don Khong Tourism Office** (📱 020 9784 6464; panhjuki@yahoo.com; ⊙ 8.30am-4pm Mon-Fri) can organise boats to Don Khon and Don Det (250,000K). The **post office** (⊙ 8am-noon & 2-4pm Mon-Fri) is just south of the bridge.

❶ Getting There & Away

From Don Khong to Pakse, buses (60,000K incl ferry, 2½ to three hours, 128km) and *sŏrngtăaou* leave from Hat Xai Khun over the river on the mainland. Be there for 11am.

For those heading to Cambodia, there's usually a 9am connection to Stung Treng, Kratie, Ban Lung, Siem Reap and Phnom Penh.

There are regular boats between Hat Xai Khun and Don Khong's Muang Khong town – 15,000K per person.

Boats for Don Det and Don Khon (40,000K, 1½ hours, minimum six passengers) leave when you stump up the cash – boatmen are under the tree near the bridge.

ⓘ Getting Around

Bicycles/motorbikes (10,000/60,000K per day) can be hired from guesthouses and elsewhere along the main street.

Don Det & Don Khon
ດອນເດດ/ດອນຄອນ

While many choose to hammock-flop here, there are loads of inexpensive activities to busy yourself with, be it cycling, tubing and kayaking by day, or relaxing in the river bars come sunset. Expect to see fishermen in pirogues, doe-eyed buffalo in the shallows and villagers taking morning ablutions. By night, campfires burn on the beach and conversation flows.

A tropical yin and yang, Don Det is overcrowded with *falang* – particularly by the ferry point of **Ban Hua Det** (known as 'Sunrise' boulevard) – while sultry Don Khon is quieter, teems with rapids, and rare Irrawaddy dolphins swim off its southern tip.

◎ Sights

Most sights are on Don Khon and are accessed on a bicycle hired from just about any guesthouse for 10,000K per day. When you cross the French bridge to Don Khon, you will be asked to pay 25,000K. This covers the entrance fee to Li Phi Falls.

Tat Somphamit   WATERFALL
(Li Phi Falls, ຕາດສົມພະມິດ; admission 25,000K; ⊙ticket booth 8am-5pm) About 1.5km downriver from the French bridge on Don Khon is a raging set of rapids called Tat Somphamit, but referred to by just about everyone as Li Phi Falls. Li Phi means 'spirit trap' and locals believe the falls act as just that – a trap for bad spirits (of deceased people and animals) as they wash down the river.

You may notice local fishermen edging out onto the rocks to clear the enormous bamboo traps. During the early rains, a well-positioned trap can catch half a tonne of fish a day.

Dolphins   VIEWPOINT
A pod of rare Irrawaddy dolphins hangs out beneath the rapids in a wide pool known as Boong Pa Gooang, off the south tip of Don Khon. Boats are chartered (60,000K, maximum three people) for one-hour trips from the old French landing pier in Ban Hang Khon. Sightings are regular year-round, but the best viewing is from January to May. Try to go early evening or first thing in the morning, when sightings are more regular and the river is at its most scenic.

🏃 Activities

Full-day and half-day kayaking tours are widely offered. The full-day trips (180,000K per person) take in the dolphin pool and Khon Papaeng Falls; you pick up before the falls off Don Khon and you and your kayaks are transported overland to Ban Hang Khon. **Wonderful Tours** (☑ 020 5570 5173) is useful.

Renting a kayak to paddle around on your own costs 50,000K per day, but don't go past the French bridge or you'll hit the fast currents that feed into the lethal falls. The same rule applies to inner tubes, which cost 10,000K (avoid these during the monsoon when the river runs dangerously fast).

Guesthouses offer sunset boat cruises, full-day island hops, morning birdwatching trips and fishing trips. Prices vary, but figure on 50,000K to 75,000K per person provided you have a few people.

🛏 Sleeping

Don Det's 'Sunrise Boulevard' on the northern tip is claustrophobic and noisy, but if you want to keep the party going (at least till the 11pm curfew) head here. More upscale digs are further south and over on sedate

PARADISE RETAINED!

Thankfully, Don Det has distanced itself from its former stoner image by cultivating a range of activities such as cycling and kayaking; these days you're more likely to see travellers fishing with locals than buying joints off them. Villagers are grateful for your trade and there are a few things you can do to keep your impact positive. If partaking in a little spliff, be subtle. And a word to women travellers: the village chief has asked that you keep more than just a bikini on around the island; the Lao find it culturally offensive.

68

Don Khon. In low season expect prices 25% cheaper than those listed here.

Don Det

★ Sunset View
GUESTHOUSE $

(☏ 020 9788 2978; Sunset Blvd; r 120,000K; 🅿) More of a flashpacker option, the bathrooms are shinier, the living quarters roomier and beds thicker than anywhere else in the area. The riverfront rooms are in a wood house with a common sunset-facing deck practically hanging over the water.

★ Crazy Gecko
GUESTHOUSE $

(info@crazygecko.ch; r 150,000K; 🛜) Funky crazy Gecko's four rooms surround a balcony festooned with hammocks, sculptures and random furniture. Bathrooms are shared (for now) and rooms are fragrant and simple – just tidy spaces for beds, really. The riverside restaurant across the path is delightful.

★ River Garden
GUESTHOUSE $

(☏ 020 7770 1860; r 60,000-80,000K; 🛜) Gay-friendly River Garden has rooms set back from the river with a whiff of style: think tidy bathrooms and seductive maroon-stained walls. Opposite is a shaded terrace restaurant.

Sengthavan Guesthouse & Restaurant
GUESTHOUSE $

(☏ 020 5613 2696; Sunset Blvd; r 100,000K; 🛜) Probably the best the sunset side has to offer in the budget range, Sengthavan's en suite rooms are fastidiously clean and enjoy uncluttered balcony views of Cambodia. Its low-key cafe has recliner cushions, checked-cloth tables and a Lao menu.

Last Resort
RESORT $

(mrwatkinsonlives@googlemail.com; d/tr 50,000/60,000K) It would be hard to match the free-spiritedness of this teepee 'resort' in a field about a 15-minute walk south of the main Sunset Blvd strip. Aussie host Jon grows veggies, bakes bread and screens movies alfresco. The teepees are unique, and there's a kitchen for self-caterers.

Mr B's Sunset View
GUESTHOUSE $

(☏ 020 5418 1171; Sunset Blvd; r without/with bathroom from 30,000/50,000K; 🛜) English-speaking Mr B's has a variety of simple bungalows, including some with sunset views, for which you pay extra. The restaurant is the bigger draw; the pumpkin burger is the stuff of legend.

Dalom Guesthouse
GUESTHOUSE $

(☏ 020 5418 8898; Sunrise Blvd; r with fan/air-con 80,000/160,000K; ❄🛜) This is the best option if you want to be near the action in Ban Hua Det. If comfort is more important than being right on the river, you'll find good-value fan bungalows in the garden and spiffy air-con rooms in a two-storey concrete structure.

★ Little Eden Guesthouse
GUESTHOUSE $$

(☏ 030 534 6020; www.littleedenguesthouse-dondet.com; Ban Hua Det; standard/deluxe 250,000/320,000K; ❄@🛜) Little Eden is set in lush gardens of sugar palms and betel trees on the northern tip of the island. Fragrant rooms have cool, tiled floors and soft linens. The spacious deluxe rooms, with textile bed runners, white walls, snazzy bathrooms and dark-wood trim, are a substantial upgrade on the fairly basic standard rooms, so consider splurging.

Don Khon

Guesthouse Souksan
GUESTHOUSE $

(☏ 020 2233 7722; s/d from 20,000/30,000K; @🛜) Still the cheapest place on the Don Khon strip, Souksan has rooms set in a bungalow block with a shared river-view terrace, which is adjacent to a restaurant with cushion seating right over the water. Bathrooms have cold water. Mr Souksan's BBQ boat tours are popular and fun.

Pan's Guesthouse
GUESTHOUSE $$

(☏ 020 9797 8222; www.donkhone.com; garden/riverfront d 160,000/200,000K, tr 220,000K; ❄@🛜) A range of soporific bungalows finished in solid stained wood with creamy white rattan interiors, immaculate en suites and balconies slung with hammocks. Spring for a riverfront room.

🍴 Eating & Drinking

Establishments open for breakfast early, and close anytime around 11pm – some a little later.

★ Four Thousand Sunsets
FUSION $

(Don Khon; mains 30,000-40,000K; 🛜🍴) Auberge Sala Done Khone's floating restaurant is classy – think white tablecloths, wine glasses and an eclectic menu of European, Thai and other Asian fare. Nothing beats a sunset drink here, watching the light cast its amber net over the Mekong.

Getting to the border Many travellers from the Four Thousand Islands take a minibus and pass through the Nong Nok Khiene/Trapeang Kriel border to Cambodia. From Pakse catch the Sorya Penh Transport bus which leaves at 7.30am from the VIP (Km2) bus terminal (also known as the Kriang Kai bus station) and goes to Phnom Penh (US$27, 12 to 14 hours) via Stung Treng (US$15, 4½ hours) and Kratie (US$20, seven hours) in Cambodia.

At the border Thirty-day tourist visas for Cambodia are available at the border and cost around US$25. You'll also pay US$2 for a cursory medical inspection. Thirty-day tourist visas are granted in Laos on arrival and cost US$30 to US$40 depending on the passport you hold. Bring a passport photo if you're headed into Laos, otherwise pay an extra 40B.

Moving on If you're not on a direct bus, head to Stung Treng to catch a bus to Phnom Penh, Siem Reap and Ban Lung. Taxis from the border cost US$40.

Jasmine Restaurant   INDIAN $
(Sunrise Blvd; mains 20,000-35,000K) This fan-cooled eatery is hugely popular thanks to its central riverside location and excellent Malaysian and Indian grub.

★**Little Eden
Restaurant**   LAOTIAN, INTERNATIONAL $$
(Ban Hua Det, Don Det; mains 35,000-60,000K; ❄🛜) Little Eden is one of the best places to eat upmarket Laotian and Western cuisine. The eclectic menu features tender New Zealand beef steak, spaghetti Bolognese and fish *láhp,* to name a few. Warm up with a *lào-láo* mojito.

4000 Island Bar   BAR
(Sunrise Blvd, Don Det) Near the boat landing, this is the most happening place in town, filling up nightly with youthful travellers eager to munch happy snacks and get their freak on. While it officially closes before midnight, it's likely to stay open unofficially until 1am.

❶ Information

There is no bank, so take the ferry over to Ban Nakasang, which has a BCEL with an ATM. Little Eden Guesthouse (p368) on Don Det will do cash advances on your card for a 5% commission.

Ban Nakasang is also the place to go for medical and postal services.

❶ Getting There & Around

Boats regularly leave Don Det for Ban Nakasang (per person/boat 15,000/30,000K). You can charter a private boat to Don Khong from Paradise Bungalows for 75,000K per person with a minimum of two people.

For Pakse (70,000K, 2½ to three hours, 148km), buses or *sŏrngtăaou* leave Ban Nakasang at around 11am, with a second wave of departures early evening, while túk-túk (40,000K, 3½ hours) leave early morning up until 8am. Wonderful Tours (p367) organises daily VIP buses to Stung Treng, Ban Lung, Kratie, Phnom Penh and Siem Reap in Cambodia (which leave Ban Nakasang at about 9.30am), as well as buses to Vietnam's Hué and Danang.

UNDERSTAND LAOS

Laos Today

Up until early 2008 it was all going extremely well for Laos, with record figures of foreign visitors; newly built hydroelectric power dams; copper and gold mining concessions; and largely foreign investors keen to climb into bed with Laos' natural resources. Then the economic axe fell on the US and those subprime mortgages started impacting on every aspect of Laos' attempt, by 2020, to escape its status as one of the 20 poorest nations. Suddenly the foreign investors pulled out because of their own lack of liquidity, and mining concessions collapsed as the price of copper was slashed. Fewer travellers were arriving, too. Through no fault of its own, Laos looked to be heading back to the dark days of stagnation.

Times haven't been easy, but they certainly could have been worse: by 2011, despite global gloom, Laos' economy reported growth of 8%, one of the strongest growth rates in Asia. And now, as China flourishes, Laos is reaping the rewards of the two

LAOS LAOS TODAY

countries' close association. China, ever the opportunist, has moved in to grab what it can in return for improving Laos' transport infrastructure. Beijing's Southeast Asian rail network will eventually connect the red giant with countries as far afield as Pakistan, India and Singapore, and to achieve this the network will pass directly through Laos. Route 3, from Kunming to Vientiane, via Luang Prabang, should be ready in the next five years, and, in the next 10 years, it's predicted that travellers will be able to travel at speeds of up to 400km/h through this beautiful green country. How this will impact on this sleepy paradise is anyone's guess, but it's all the more reason for you to visit right now. As US relations begin to improve and the first rumblings of gay expression make themselves heard in the capital, Laos is on one hand embracing the 21st century, while holding fast to its old-guard hegemony.

History

The Kingdom of Lan Xang

Before the French, British, Chinese and Siamese drew a line around it, Laos was a collection of disparate principalities subject to an ever-revolving cycle of war, invasion, prosperity and decay. Laos' earliest brush with nationhood was in the 14th century, when Khmer-backed Lao warlord Fa Ngum conquered Wieng Chan (Vientiane). It was Fa Ngum who gave his kingdom the title still favoured by travel romantics and businesses – Lan Xang, or (Land of a) Million Elephants. He also made Theravada Buddhism the state religion and adopted the symbol of Lao sovereignty that remains in use today, the Pha Bang Buddha image, after which Luang Prabang is named. Lan Xang reached its peak in the 17th century, when it was the dominant force in Southeast Asia.

French Rule

By the 18th century the nation had crumbled, falling under the control of the Siamese, who coveted much of modern-day Laos as a buffer zone against the expansionist French. It was to no effect. Soon after taking over Annam and Tonkin (modern-day Vietnam), the French negotiated with

Siam to relinquish its territory east of the Mekong, and Laos was born.

The first nationalist movement, the Lao Issara (Free Lao), was created to prevent the country's return to French rule after the invading Japanese left at the end of WWII. In 1953, without any regard for the Lao Issara, sovereignty was granted to Laos by the French. Internecine struggles followed with the Pathet Lao (Country of the Lao) Army forming an alliance with the Vietnamese Viet Minh (which opposed French rule in their own country). Laos was set to become a chessboard on which the clash of communist ambition and US anxiety over the perceived Southeast Asian 'domino effect' played itself out.

The Secret War

In 1954 at the Geneva Conference Laos was declared a neutral nation – as such neither Vietnamese nor US forces could cross its borders. Thus began a game of cat and mouse as a multitude of CIA operatives secretly entered the country to train anticommunist Hmong fighters in the jungle. From 1964 to 1973, the US, in response to the Viet Minh funnelling massive amounts of war munitions down the Ho Chi Minh Trail, devastated eastern and northeastern Laos with nonstop carpet-bombing (reportedly a plane load of ordnance dropped every eight minutes). The intensive campaign exacerbated the war between the Pathet Lao and the Royal Lao armies and, if anything, increased domestic support for the communists.

The US withdrawal in 1973 saw Laos divided up between Pathet Lao and non-Pathet Lao, but within two years the communists had taken over and the Lao People's Democratic Republic (PDR) was created under the leadership of Kaysone Phomvihane. Around 10% of Laos' population fled, mostly to Thailand. The remaining opponents of the government – notably tribes of Hmong (highland dwellers) who had fought with and been funded by the CIA – were suppressed, often brutally, or sent to re-education camps for indeterminate periods.

A New Beginning

Laos entered the political family of Southeast Asian countries known as Asean in 1997, two years after Vietnam. In 2004 the US promoted Laos to Normal Trade Relations, cementing the end to a trade embargo in place since the communists took power in 1975. Politically, the Party remains firmly in control. And with neighbours like one-party China and Vietnam, there seems little incentive for Laos to move towards any meaningful form of democracy. While still heavily reliant on foreign aid, Laos has committed to income-generating projects in recent years in a bid to increase its prosperity. Ecotourism is flourishing and the country is enjoying more Western visitors every year. China has recently pulled the financial reins on its extensive high-speed rail network across Southeast Asia, with Laos now stepping in and picking up the cost in the form of a US$7.2 billion loan from China. It's a big gamble, but the hope is that it will improve trade, with the rail system passing through the likes of Luang Prabang and Vientiane.

In recent years, 2012 saw the international press starting to ask questions over the disappearance of Sombath Somphone, an award-winning civil-society activist and land-rights campaigner, with fingers directly pointed at the Lao government as the main culprit. In 2013, in an effort to counterbalance China's growing influence over the region, the US Obama administration sent then-Secretary of State Hillary Clinton to broker tighter relations with Laos.

People & Culture

National Psyche

Trying to homogenise the people and psyche of Laos is difficult, for the country is really a patchwork of different beliefs, ranging from animism to the prevailing presence of Thervada Bhuddism – and often both combined. But, certainly, there's a commonality in the laid-back attitude you'll encounter. Some of this can be ascribed to Buddhism, with its emphasis on controlling extreme emotions by keeping *jai yen* (cool heart), making merit and doing good in order to receive good. You'll rarely hear a heated argument, and can expect a level of kindness that you often don't see to the same extent in neighbouring countries.

Etiquette

Touching another person's head is taboo, as is pointing your feet at another person or at a Buddha image. Strong displays of emotion are also discouraged. The traditional greeting gesture is the *nop* or *wâi*, a prayerlike placing together of the palms in front of the face or chest, although in urban areas the handshake is becoming more commonplace.

For all temple visits, dress neatly.

Population

The government has been at pains to encourage national pride and a unifying 'Lao' identity, despite the fact that 132 ethnic groups make up the population of Laos. Around 60% of these are Lao Loum (lowland Lao), who have the most in common with their Thai neighbours, and it's their cultural beliefs and way of life that are known as 'Lao culture'. The remainder is labelled according to the altitude at which the groups live: Lao Theung (midlevel mountain group including Khamu, Lamet and Alak), Lao Thai (upland valleys), Lao Thoung (upland Lao) and Lao Soung (1000m or more above sea level, including Hmong, Mien and Akha).

SPIRITS, ARE YOU THERE?

The life of a Lao person involves a complex appeasement of spirits through a carousel of sacrifices and rituals designed to protect the supplicant. The *pěe héuan* (good spirits) represent both the guardian spirits of the house and ancestral spirits. In order to promote domestic happiness they're fed with Pepsi, and come crisis time it's their job to recalibrate the troubled household.

In the backyard or garden, you'll often see what look like miniature ornamental temples, the *pha phum* (spirits of the land). Their task is to protect the grounds from any malignant spirits – for in Laos the air is thick with them. Before anything is built within their grounds, offerings must be made and permission granted. The same goes for a tree that must be knocked down to make way for a bridge, a field before a harvest...and so on. It's an endless animistic communion between the seen and unseen, the prosaic and the spiritual.

Laos' strongest cultural and linguistic links are with Thailand; Thai music and TV are an almost ubiquitous presence in the country.

Religion

Most lowland Lao are Theravada Buddhists and many Lao males choose to be ordained temporarily as monks, typically spending anywhere from a month to three years at a wat (temple). Indeed, a young man is not considered 'ripe' until he has completed his spiritual term. After the 1975 communist victory, Buddhism was suppressed, but by 1992 the government had relented and it was back in full swing, with a few alterations. Monks are still forbidden to promote *phǐi* (spirit) worship, which has been officially banned in Laos along with *sǎiyasàht* (folk magic).

Despite the ban, *phǐi* worship remains the dominant non-Buddhist belief system. Even in Vientiane, Lao citizens openly perform the ceremony called *sukhwǎn* or *bạsǐi*, in which the 32 *kwǎn* (guardian spirits of the body) are bound to the guest of honour by white strings tied around the wrists (you'll see many Lao people wearing these).

Outside the Mekong River valley, the *phǐi* cult is particularly strong among tribal Thai, especially among the Thai Dam. The Khamu and Hmong-Mien tribes also practise animism.

Arts

The true expression of Lao art is found in its religious sculpture, temples, handicrafts and architecture. Distinctively Lao is the Calling for Rain Buddha, a standing image with hands held rigidly at his sides. Similarly widespread is the Contemplating the Bodhi Tree Buddha, with crossed hands at the front.

Wats in Luang Prabang feature *sǐm* (chapels), with steep, low roofs. The typical Lao *tâht* (stupa) is a four-sided, curvilinear, spirelike structure. There are also hints of classical architectural motifs entering modern architecture, as with Vientiane's Wattay International Airport. Many of the beautiful villas from the days of Indochina were torn down by the new regime in favour of harsh Soviet designs, though fortunately there are plenty of villas left, with their distinctive shuttered windows and classic French provincial style.

Upland crafts include gold- and silversmithing among the Hmong and Mien tribes, and tribal Thai weaving (especially among the Thai Dam and Thai Lü). Classical music and dance have all but evaporated, partly due to the vapid tentacles of Thai pop and the itinerant nature of Laos' young workforce.

Food & Drink

Food

The standard Lao breakfast is *fěr* (rice noodles), usually served in a broth with vegetables and meat of your choice. The trick is in the seasoning, and Lao people will stir in some fish sauce, lime juice, dried chillies, mint leaves or basil, testing it along the way. *Láhp* is the most distinctively Lao dish, a delicious spicy salad made from minced beef, pork, duck, fish or chicken, mixed with fish sauce, small shallots, mint leaves, lime juice, roasted ground rice and lots and lots of chillies. Another famous Lao speciality is *dạm màhk hung* (known as *som tam* in Thailand), a salad of shredded green papaya mixed with garlic, lime juice, fish sauce, sometimes tomatoes, palm sugar, land crab or dried prawns and, of course, chillies by the handful. In lowland Laos almost every dish is eaten with *khào nǐaw* (sticky rice), which is served in a small basket. Take a small amount of rice and, using one hand, work it into a walnut-sized ball before dipping it into the food.

Drink

Beerlao remains a firm favourite with 90% of the nation, and, although officially illegal, *lào-láo* (Lao liquor, or rice whisky) is a popular drink among lowland Lao. It's usually taken neat and offered in villages as a welcoming gesture. Water purified for drinking purposes is simply called *nâm deum* (drinking water), whether it's boiled or filtered. All water offered to customers in restaurants or hotels will be purified, and purified water is sold everywhere. Having said that, do be careful of the water you drink – there was an outbreak of E. coli in

2008, so check that the ice in your drink originated from a bottle.

Juice bars and cafes proliferate in cities. Lao coffee is usually served strong and sweet. Chinese-style green tea is the usual ingredient in *nâm sáh* or *sáh lôw* – the weak, refreshing tea traditionally served free in restaurants.

Environment

The Land

With a landmass of 236,800 sq km, Laos is a little larger than the UK and, thanks to its relatively small population and mountainous terrain, is one of the least altered environments in Southeast Asia. Unmanaged vegetation covers an estimated 85% of the country, and 10% of Laos is original-growth forest. A hundred years ago this last statistic was nearer 75%, which provides a clear idea of the detrimental effects of relentless logging and slash-and-burn farming. (See the boxed text, p346).

In 1993 the government set up 18 National Protected Areas (NPAs) comprising a total of 24,600 sq km, just over 10% of the land. An additional two were added in 1995 (taking the total coverage to 14% of Laos). International consulting agencies have also recommended another nine sites, but these have yet to materialise. Despite these conservation efforts, illegal timber felling and the smuggling of exotic wildlife are still significant threats to Laos' natural resources.

Wildlife

Laos is home to Asian elephants, jackals, Asiatic black bears, black-crested gibbons, langurs, leopards, tigers, pythons, king cobras, 437 kinds of bird and the rare Irrawaddy dolphin – to name a few! The illegal wildlife trade is flourishing, driven by neighbours – particularly China – who seek body parts of endangered animals for traditional medicine and aphrodisiac purposes. Compared with Vietnam and Thailand though – much of which are now deforested, urbanised and farmed – Laos is an enviable hothouse of biodiversity.

Almost two-thirds of Lao people live in rural areas and rely on wildlife as a source of protein to supplement their diet.

SURVIVAL GUIDE

 Directory A–Z

ACCOMMODATION

Budget digs – usually a room with a fan and sometimes private bathroom – are getting better every year. Even though guesthouse prices are rising, particularly in the cities, they're still unbeatable value when compared with the West. At less than US$10 (80,000K) a night, who can argue?

Homestays

For more than 75% of Laotians, the 'real Laos' is life in a village. Minority people in villages across the country now welcome travellers into their homes to experience life Lao-style. This means sleeping, eating and washing as they do. It's not luxury – the mattress will be on the floor and you'll 'shower' by pouring water over yourself from a 170L (44-gallon) drum while standing in the middle of the yard (men and women should take a sarong). But it's exactly this level of immersion that makes a homestay so worthwhile. It's also good to know that the 50,000K you'll pay for bed, dinner and breakfast is going directly to those who need it most.

Price Ranges

Accommodation prices listed are for the high season.

$ less than 160,000K (US$20)
$$ 160,000K to 640,000K (US$20 to US$80)
$$$ more than 640,000K (US$80)

ACTIVITIES
Cycling

Laos' uncluttered, peaceful roads are a haven for cyclists with a head for heights and a decent set of gears. Many roads are now sealed, though if you're visiting straight after the monsoon you'll find them potholed or, in the case of the Bolaven Plateau, mired in mud. In Vientiane be careful about leaving bags in the front basket, as passing motorcyclists have been known to lift them. Laos' main towns all have bicycle-rental shops. Several companies offer mountain-bike tours, particularly from Luang Namtha, Nong Khiaw and Luang Prabang.

Kayaking & Rafting

Laos has several world-class rapids, as well as lots of beautiful, less challenging waterways. The industry remains dangerously unregulated, however, and you should not go out on rapids during the wet season unless you are completely confident about your guides and equipment. Vang Vieng has the most options. **Green Discovery** (www.greendiscoverylaos.com) has a good reputation.

LAOS DIRECTORY A–Z

Rock Climbing

Organised rock-climbing operations are run by Green Discovery (www.greendiscoverylaos.com) and Adam's Rock Climbing School (p327) in the karst cliffs around Vang Vieng, while Green Discovery is the only real operator in Nong Khiaw. Vang Vieng has the most established scene, with dozens of climbs ranging from beginner to expert.

Trekking

Where else can you wander through forests past ethnic hill tribes and rare wildlife with a triple canopy towering above you? Several environmentally and culturally sustainable tours allow you to enter these pristine areas and experience the lives of the indigenous people without exploiting them. These treks are available in several provinces and are detailed on www.ecotourismlaos.com. You can trek from Luang Nam Tha, Muang Sing, Udomxai, Luang Prabang, Vientiane, Tha Khaek, Savannakhet and Pakse. Treks organised through the provincial tourism offices are the cheapest, while companies such as Green Discovery (www.greendiscoverylaos.com) offer more expensive and professional operations.

Tubing

Tubing involves inserting yourself into an enormous tractor inner tube and floating down a river. Vang Vieng, Muang Ngoi Neua and Si Phan Don are all hot spots to do this. Just keep an eye on reefer intake and how much you drink; the two combined can be lethal, especially in the dark if you take a tumble in a rogue current.

BOOKS

Lonely Planet's *Laos* has all the information you'll need for extended travel in Laos, with more detailed descriptions of sights and wider coverage to help get you off the beaten track. The following offer further insights:

➡ *A Dragon Apparent* (1951) Follows Norman Lewis' travels through the twilight of French Indochina.

➡ *The Lao* (2008) Robert Cooper's locally published book (available in Vientiane) offers a penetrating insight into Lao culture and its psyche.

➡ *The Ravens: Pilots of the Secret War of Laos* (1987) Christopher Robbins' page-turning account of the 'Secret War' and the role of American pilots and the Hmong is an excellent read.

COURSES

There are no formal opportunities to study in Laos, although short courses in cooking are available in the capital and Luang Prabang, and informal Lao-language lessons are advertised in Vientiane.

CUSTOMS REGULATIONS

You can expect borders to be fairly sleepy affairs, and customs officers are equally chilled – so long as you're not carrying more than 500 cigarettes and 1L of spirits, or any drugs, knives or guns on your person.

EMBASSIES & CONSULATES

Australian Embassy (Map p316; 021 353 800; www.laos.embassy.gov.au; Th Tha Deua, Ban Wat Nak, Vientiane; 8.30am-5pm Mon-Fri) Also represents nationals of Canada and New Zealand; Brits should use this embassy or contact their British embassy in Bangkok.

Cambodian Embassy (Map p316; 021 314 952; Th Tha Deua, Km3, Ban That Khao, Vientiane) Issues visas for US$20.

Chinese Embassy (Map p316; 021 315 105; http://la.china-embassy.org/eng; Th Wat Nak Nyai, Ban Wat Nak, Vientiane; 8-11.30am Mon-Fri) Issues visas in four working days.

French Embassy (Map p318; 021 215 258; www.ambafrance-laos.org; Th Setthathirath, Ban Si Saket, Vientiane; 9am-12.30pm & 2-5.30pm Mon-Fri)

German Embassy (Map p316; 021 312 110; www.vientiane.diplo.de; Th Sok Pa Luang, Vientiane; 9am-noon Mon-Fri)

Myanmar Embassy (Map p316; 021 314 910; Th Sok Pa Luang, Vientiane) Issues tourist visas in three days for US$20.

Thai Embassy (Map p316; 021 214 581; www.thaiembassy.org/vientiane; Th Kaysone Phomvihane, Vientiane; 8.30am-noon & 1-3.30pm Mon-Fri)

Thai Consulate (Map p316; 021 214 581; 15 Th Bourichane, Vientiane; 8am-noon & 1-4.30pm) Come here for visa renewals, extensions etc.

Thai Consulate (041 212 373; cnr Th Tha He & Th Chaimeuang, Savannakhet) Tourist and nonimmigrant visas (1000B) issued the same day.

US Embassy (Map p318; 021 267 000; http://laos.usembassy.gov; Th Bartholomie, Vientiane)

Vietnamese Embassy (Map p316; 021 413 400; www.mofa.gov.vn/vnemb.la; Th That Luang, Vientiane; 8.30am-5.30pm Mon-Fri) Issues tourist visas in three working days for US$45, or in one day for US$60.

Vietnamese Consulate (Th Naviengkham, Luang Prabang) Issues tourist visas within a few minutes for US$60 or for US$45 if you wait three days.

Vietnamese Consulate (031 214 199; www.vietnamconsulate-pakse.org; Th 21, Pakse; 7.30-11.30am & 2-4.30pm Mon-Fri) This consulate issues same-day visas for US$60.

Vietnamese Consulate (☎041 212 418; Th Sisavangvong, Savannakhet) A one-month tourist visa costs US$60.

FOOD

The following prices refer to the cost of a main course.

$ less than 40,000K (US$5)

$$ 40,000K to 80,000K (US$5 to US$10)

$$$ more than 80,000K (US$10)

GAY & LESBIAN TRAVELLERS

Laos has a liberal attitude towards homosexuality, but a very conservative attitude towards public displays of affection. Gay couples are unlikely to be given frosty treatment anywhere. Laos doesn't have an obvious gay scene, though Luang Prabang has Laos' first openly gay bar, Khob Chai (opposite Hive Bar; p336), and has the rainbow-coloured gay pride flag flying in a few places around town.

Lesbians won't be bothered, but do expect some strange looks from Lao men.

LEGAL MATTERS

There is virtually nothing in the way of legal services in Laos. If you get yourself in legal strife, contact your embassy in Vientiane, though the assistance it can provide may be limited.

It's against the law for foreigners and Lao to have sexual relations unless they're married. Be aware that a holiday romance could result in being arrested and deported.

MAPS

The best all-purpose country map available is *Laos* by **GT-Rider** (http://gt-rider.com), a sturdy laminated affair with several city maps. Look for editions dated from 2005 onwards.

Hobo Maps has produced a series of decent maps for Vientiane, Luang Prabang and Vang Vieng. These maps are widely available in the relevant destinations.

MEDIA

The government-run *Vientiane Times* is a bland, censored sketch of improving Sino–Lao relations and reveals very little. The *Bangkok Post, Economist, Newsweek* and *Time* can be found in minimarts and bookshops. BBC and CNN are widely available on satellite TV.

MONEY

The official national currency in Laos is the Lao kip (K). Although only kip is legally negotiable in everyday transactions, in reality three currencies are used for commerce: kip, Thai baht (B) and US dollars (US$).

Bargaining

With the exception of túk-túk drivers in Vientiane (who are a law unto themselves), most Lao are not looking to rip you off. Take your time when haggling: start lower and gradually meet in the middle. And always keep in perspective that you're a comparatively rich person in a very poor country – is it really that important to screw them for that precious 50 cents?

Exchanging Money & Travellers Cheques

US dollars and Thai baht can be exchanged all over the country. Banks in Vientiane and Luang Prabang change UK pounds, euro, Thai baht, Japanese yen, and Canadian, US and Australian dollars. The best overall exchange rate is usually offered by BCL. Banks in all provincial centres will exchange US-dollar travellers cheques. If you are changing cheques into kip, there is usually no commission, but changing into dollars attracts a minimum 2% charge.

OPENING HOURS

Government offices are typically open from 8am to noon and 1pm to 4pm Monday to Friday. Banking hours are generally 8.30am to 4pm Monday to Friday. Shops have longer hours and are often open on weekends. Restaurants typically close by 10pm and bars stay open until around 11.30pm, sometimes later.

POST

Postal services from Vientiane are painfully slow but generally reliable; the provinces less so. If you have valuable items or presents to post home, there is a **Federal Express** (☎021 223 278; ◷8am-noon & 1-5pm Mon-Fri, 9am-noon Sat) office inside the main post office compound in Vientiane.

PUBLIC HOLIDAYS

Aside from government offices, banks and post offices, many Lao businesses do not trouble themselves with weekends and public holidays. Most Chinese- and Vietnamese-run businesses close for three days during Vietnamese Tet and Chinese New Year in January/February. International Women's Day is a holiday for women only.

International New Year 1 January

Army Day 20 January

International Women's Day 8 March

Lao New Year 14 to 16 April

International Labour Day 1 May

International Children's Day 1 June

Lao National Day 2 December

SAFE TRAVEL

Urban Laos is generally very safe thanks to the gentle, nonconfrontational nature of its people. You should still exercise vigilance at night in Vientiane (due to more widespread drug taking and bag snatching), while Vang Vieng suffers from theft – usually in budget accommodation – as well as 'soft' muggings after dark.

Since the 1975 revolution, there have been very occasional shootings by Hmong guerrillas on Rte 13 between Vang Vieng and Luang Prabang. Given that their numbers are now depleted, their insurrection is unlikely to reignite. Finally, in the eastern provinces, particularly Xieng Khuang, Salavan and Savannakhet, UXO (unexploded ordnance) is a hazard. *Never* walk off well-used paths.

TELEPHONE

Laos' country code is ✆ 856. To dial out of the country press ✆ 00 first. As a guide, all mobile phone numbers have the prefix ✆ 020, while the newer WIN phones (fixed phones without a landline) begin with ✆ 030.

TOILETS

Unlike Thailand, the hole-in-the-floor toilet is not common in Laos. The exception is if you're visiting destinations such as hill-tribe villages.

TOURIST INFORMATION

The Lao National Tourism Administration (NTAL) and provincial tourism authorities have offices throughout Laos. The offices in Tha Khaek, Savannakhet, Pakse, Luang Nam Tha, Sainyabouli, Phongsali and Sam Neua are excellent, with well-trained staff and plenty of brochures.

NTAL also has three good websites:

Central Laos Trekking (www.trekkingcentral-laos.com)

Ecotourism Laos (www.ecotourismlaos.com) Focusing on trekking, the environment and eco-activities.

Lao National Tourism Administration (www.tourismlaos.org)

TRAVELLERS WITH DISABILITIES

Laos is woefully unprepared for people with special physical needs; however, its main cities such as Vientiane, Savannakhet and Luang Prabang have decent pavements (generally) and disabled toilets in most international hotels. Transport is a no-no with cramped conditions on most buses. Contact hotels in advance to see what facilities they have.

VOLUNTEERING

It's not easy to find short-term volunteer work in Laos. Phoudindaeng Organic Farm (p328) in Vang Vieng needs volunteers occasionally, as does Big Brother Mouse (p333). If you're an orthopaedic surgeon, physio or an IT and graphic designer, you may be able to work at the COPE Visitor Centre (see boxed text, p317).

WOMEN TRAVELLERS

Stories of women being hassled are few. Much of the time any attention will be no more than curiosity, as Western women are generally so physically different to Lao women.

Remember, you're in a strictly Buddhist country so the revealing of flesh, despite the heat, is seen as cheap and disrespectful. Sarongs and long-sleeved T-shirts are a good idea – in Lao peoples' eyes, wearing a bikini is no different to wandering around in your underwear.

WORK

English teaching is the most common first job for foreigners working in Laos, and schools in Vientiane are often hiring. There are also an inordinate number of development organisations – see www.directoryofngos.org for a full list – where foreigners with technical skills and volunteer experience can look for employment. Ask around.

ⓘ Getting There & Away

AIR

With over a dozen border crossings into Laos, visiting the country has never been easier. Also, the newly improved Lao Airlines, with a fleet of 10 new planes, is servicing most corners of the country and neighbouring countries with frequent flights.

Bangkok Airways (www.bangkokair.com) Connects Luang Prabang, Vientiane and Pakse to Bangkok, plus Luang Prabang to Chiang Mai.

China Eastern Airlines (www.ce-air.com) Flies daily to Kunming and Nanning from Vientiane.

Lao Airlines (www.laoairlines.com) National carrier. The extensive international flight network includes Vientiane to Bangkok, Chiang Mai, Danan, Guangzhou, Hanoi, Ho Chi Minh City, Kunming, Phnom Penh, Siem Reap and Singapore; Luang Prabang to Bangkok, Chiang Mai, Hanoi and Siem Reap; Pakse to Bangkok, Danang, Ho Chi Minh City and Siem Reap; and Savannakhet to Bangkok and Danang.

Thai Airways International (www.thaiairways.com) Vientiane to Bangkok connections twice daily.

Vietnam Airlines (www.vietnamairlines.com) Connects Vientiane with Ho Chi Minh City, Hanoi and Phnom Penh, plus Luang Prabang with Hanoi and Siem Reap.

LAND

Laos has open land borders with Cambodia, China, Thailand and Vietnam, but not Myanmar. Under current rules, 30-day tourist visas are available on arrival at several (but not all) international checkpoints. We also recommend checking the **Thorn Tree** (lonelyplanet.com/thorntree) for other travellers' accounts, as things change frequently.

ℹ Getting Around

AIR

Lao Airlines (☏ 021 512 028; Wattay Airport International Terminal; ⊙ 4am-8pm) handles all domestic flights in Laos, including between Vientiane and Huay Xai (US$128, four weekly), Luang Prabang (US$103, 40 minutes, three daily), Luang Nam Tha (US$128, six times weekly), Pakse (US$147, four times weekly), Phonsavan (Xieng Khuang; US$103, daily), Savannakhet (US$128, four times weekly) and Udomxai (US$128, four times weekly). Fortunately, its revamped new fleet has slick MA60s, with the airline rapidly improving its safety record. Check the Lao calendar for public festivals before you fly, as it can be difficult getting a seat. In provincial Lao Airlines offices you'll be expected to pay in cash.

Lao Air (www.lao-air.com), formerly Lao Capricorn Air, flies small planes from Vientiane to Phongsali (US$126, twice per week), Sainyabuli (US$91, three times per week) and Sam Neua (US$116, three times per week).

Always reconfirm your flights a day before departing, as undersubscribed flights may be cancelled or you could get bumped off the passenger list.

BICYCLE

The light and relatively slow traffic in most Lao towns makes for favourable cycling conditions. Bicycles are available for rent in major tourist destinations, costing around 10,000K per day for a cheap Thai or Chinese model.

BOAT

Given Laos' much improved trade roads, the days of mass river transport are almost over. The most popular river trip in Laos – the slow boat between Huay Xai and Luang Prabang – remains a daily event. Other popular journeys – between Pakse and Si Phan Don, or between Nong Khiaw and Luang Prabang – are all recommended if you have time.

River ferries are basic affairs and passengers usually sit, eat and sleep on the wooden decks; it's worth bringing some padding. The toilet (if there is one) is an enclosed hole in the deck at the back of the boat. For shorter river trips, such as Luang Prabang to the Pak Ou Caves, you can easily hire a river taxi.

Between Luang Prabang and Huay Xai and between Xieng Kok and Huay Xai, deafeningly loud and painfully uncomfortable speedboats operate, covering the same distance in six hours as that of a river ferry in two days. Be warned that passengers are killed and injured every year when the boats disintegrate on contact with floating debris, or flip when they hit a standing wave.

BUS & SŎRNGTĂAOU

Long-distance public transport in Laos is either by bus or *sŏrngtăaou* (literally 'two rows'), which are converted trucks or pick-ups with benches down either side. Buses are more frequent and go further than ever. Privately run VIP buses operate on some busier routes, but slow, simple standard buses (occasionally with air-con) remain the norm.

Sŏrngtăaou usually service shorter routes within a given province. Most decent-sized villages have at least one *sŏrngtăaou*, which will run to the provincial capital daily except Sunday, stopping wherever you want.

CAR & MOTORCYCLE

Scooters can be rented for 50,000K to 90,000K a day in Vientiane, Tha Khaek, Savannakhet, Pakse and Luang Nam Tha. In Vientiane, Luang Prabang, Tha Khaek and Pakse it's also possible to rent dirt bikes for around US$35 per day. Jules' Classic Rental (p325) and Mad Monkey Motorbike (p356) have a range of performance dirt bikes and the former offers the option to rent in Vientiane and drop off in Luang Prabang or Pakse for an additional charge.

Car rental in Laos is a great if relatively costly way of reaching remote places. Europcar (p325) offers vehicles from US$55 per day, charging US$20 extra for an optional driver.

HITCHING

Hitching is possible in Laos, if not common. It's never entirely safe and not recommended, especially for women, as the act of standing beside a road and waving at cars might be misinterpreted.

LAOS GETTING AROUND

Malaysia

Includes ➡

Best for Regional Specialities

➡ Laksa asam, Penang (p405)

➡ Satay celup, Melaka (p393)

➡ Sarawak laksa, Kuching (p450)

➡ Ikan bakar, Kuantan (p420)

➡ Tea, Cameron Highlands (p400)

➡ Dim Sum, Ipoh (p403)

Best Places for Culture

➡ Batu Caves (p383)

➡ Khoo Kongsi (p406)

➡ Gelanggang Seni (p427)

➡ Rumah John Ramba (p462)

Why Go?

Malaysia is like two countries in one, cleaved in half by the South China Sea. The multicultural peninsula flaunts Malay, Chinese and Indian influences, while Borneo hosts a wild jungle of orang-utans, granite peaks and remote tribes. Throughout these two regions is an impressive variety of microcosms ranging from the space-age high-rises of Kuala Lumpur to the smiling longhouse villages of Sarawak. And then there's the food. Malaysia (particularly along the peninsular west coast) has one of the best assortments of cuisines in the world. Start with Chinese-Malay 'Nonya' fare, move on to Indian curries, Chinese buffets, Malay food stalls and even impressive Western food. Yet despite all the pockets of ethnicities, religions, landscapes and the sometimes-great distances between them, the beauty of Malaysia lies in the fusion of it all into a country that is one of the safest, most stable and manageable in Southeast Asia.

When to Go
Kuala Lumpur

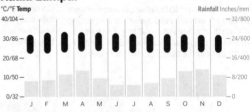

Dec–Feb High season: school holidays and Chinese New Year. Prices rise; bookings essential.

Nov–Mar Monsoon season sees many east-coast peninsular islands shut; Cherating fills with surfers.

Jul–Aug Many restaurants close during the day for Ramadan. Food bazaars open at night.

Don't Miss

You'll find excellent food markets and hawkers all around the country but the west coast, and in particular Kuala Lumpur and Penang, has a thriving street food scene that offers up some of the best eats in Southeast Asia. Hit up Jalan Alor or the Imbi Market in KL or try any on our list of hawker centres in Penang. Every place has a speciality but follow your nose, appetite and instincts to choose your favourite noodles, rice dishes, salads, grilled meats and icy desserts. Go for busy stalls, where the wok is kept hot and you'll avoid tummy troubles too.

ITINERARIES

One Week

Gorge on endless street food in Penang then cool off in the Cameron Highlands by exploring mossy forests and tea plantations. Hop over to the Perhentian Islands for snorkelling, diving and beachside revelry.

Two Weeks

Follow the one-week itinerary backwards then catch a flight to Kota Kinabalu and spend the next week trekking the wild jungles of Borneo, perhaps ascending Mt Kinabalu, one of the highest mountains in Southeast Asia.

Essential Food & Drink

➡ **Breakfast** *Nasi lemak* (coconut rice served with a variety of accompaniments), *roti canai* (Indian flat bread), *won ton mee* (egg noodles and wontons), dim sum or rice congee (savoury rice porridge).

➡ **Barbecue** Fish, lobster, prawns, squid, cockles and stingray. Point to it then watch it get slathered in sambal and grilled in a banana leaf.

➡ **Noodles** Fried or in soup. The best include *char kway teow* (fried noodles with egg, soy sauce, chilli and a variety of additions), laksa, *curry mee* (curry noodles), *Hokkein mee* (fried noodles with chicken, pork and other additions) and *won ton mee*.

➡ **Rice** *Nasi campur* is a lunch favourite of rice and a buffet of toppings.

➡ **Dessert** Malaysians *drink* their sweets via sugared fruit juices, sweetened condensed milk in hot beverages and scary looking icy concoctions such as *cendol* and ABC (shaved ice covered in coconut cream, jellies, beans and other crazy stuff).

AT A GLANCE

➡ **Currency** Malaysian ringitt (RM)

➡ **Language** Bahasa Malaysia, Chinese (Hakka & Hokkien), Tamil, English

➡ **Money** ATMs in large towns

➡ **Visas** Most nationalities get a 30- to 90-day visa on arrival

➡ **Mobile phones** SIMs start at RM10, calls are 15 sen per minute, data 4G plans are RM7 per week

Fast Facts

➡ **Area** 328,600 sq km

➡ **Capital** Kuala Lumpur

➡ **Emergency** ☎ 999

MALAYSIA

Exchange Rates

Australia	A$1	RM2.95
Euro Zone	C$1	RM4.50
Indonesia	10,000 Rp	RM4.54
Singapore	S$1	RM2.60
Thailand	10B	RM1.00
UK	UK£1	RM5.45
USA	US$1	RM3.30

Set Your Budget

➡ **Guesthouse room** RM45

➡ **Meal (hawker stall)** RM6

➡ **Beer** RM8

➡ **Snorkelling** RM35

Entering the Country

Kuala Lumpur is the main flight hub on the peninsula while Kota Kinabalu receives most Sabah flights and Kuching Sarawak flights.

Malaysia Highlights

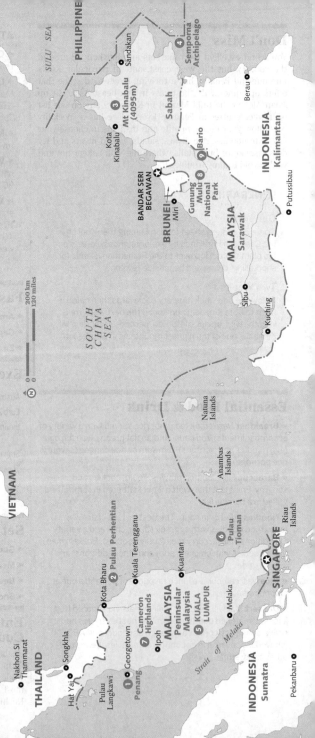

1 Gorge on hawker food, breathe incense and explore Georgetown's alleyways on **Penang** (p405)

2 Swim, lie on the beach, snorkel, eat and snooze on **Pulau Perhentian** (p425)

3 Hoof it over pitcher plants and moonscapes for sunrise atop the granite spire of **Mt Kinabalu** (p440)

4 Smile in your scuba mask as you pass turtles, sharks and technicolour coral in the **Semporna Archipelago** (p447)

5 Admire the view from the Petronas Towers over the modern sprawl of **Kuala Lumpur** (p381)

6 Hop between perfect beach villages, diving reefs and wrecks, and spotting monkeys on **Pulau Tioman** (p418)

7 Trek through mossy forests to verdant, rolling tea plantations for a cuppa in the **Cameron Highlands** (p400)

8 Climb the crags of the Pinnacles at **Gunung Mulu National Park** (p466)

9 Sip wild teas at a wobbly longhouse in **Bario** (p468)

KUALA LUMPUR

📍 03 / POP 1.5 MILLION

One hundred and fifty years since tin miners hacked a base out of the jungle, KL has evolved into an affluent 21st-century metropolis remarkable for its cultural diversity. Ethnic Malays, Chinese prospectors, Indian immigrants and British colonials all helped shape the city, and each group has left its indelible physical mark as well as a fascinating assortment of cultural traditions. Historic temples and mosques rub shoulders with space-age towers and shopping malls; traders' stalls are piled high with pungent durians and counterfeit handbags; monorail cars zip by lush jungle foliage; and locals sip cappuccinos in wi-fi–enabled cafes or feast on delicious streetside hawker food.

Merdeka Sq is the traditional heart of KL. Southeast across the river, the banking district merges into Chinatown, popular with travellers for its budget accommodation and lively night market.

To the east of Pudu Sentral bus station, around Jln Sultan Ismail, the Golden Triangle is the modern, upmarket heart of the new KL.

⊙ Sights

Six-lane highways and flyovers may slice up the city but the best way to get a feel for KL's atmosphere is to walk.

⊙ Chinatown & Merdeka Square

Circuitous streets and cramped chaos create a pressure cooker of sights and sounds in Chinatown. **Jln Petaling** is a bustling street market selling souvenirs, such as 'authentic' Levis and cheap Crocs; it opens around 10am and shuts late at night. Chinatown is reached on the Putra LRT to Pasar Seni station or on the KL Monorail to Maharajalela station. Chinese coffee shops are along Jalan Panggong and Jalan Balai Polis .

Merdeka Square   SQUARE
(Dataran Merdeka; Map p384; 🚇 Masjid Jamek) The huge open square where Malaysian independence was declared in 1957 is ringed by heritage buildings and dominated by an enormous flagpole and fluttering Malaysian flag. In the British era, the square was used as a cricket pitch.

Masjid Negara   MOSQUE
(National Mosque; Map p384; www.masjidnegara. gov.my/v2/; Jln Lembah Perdana; ⊙ 9am-noon,

3-4pm & 5.30-6.30pm, closed Fri morning; 🚇 Kuala Lumpur) **FREE** This gigantic mosque, inspired by Mecca's Grand Mosque, is able to accommodate 15,000 worshippers. Rising above the mosque, a 74m-high minaret issues the call to prayer, which can be heard across Chinatown. Non-Muslims are welcome to visit outside prayer times; robes are available for those who are not dressed appropriately.

Sri Mahamariamman Temple   TEMPLE
(Map p384; www.batucavesmuruga.org; 163 Jln Tun HS Lee; ⊙ 6am-8.30pm; 🚇 Pasar Seni) **FREE** The oldest Hindu shrine in Malaysia was founded by migrant workers from the Indian state of Tamil Nadu in 1873. Flower-garland vendors crowd the entrance and the temple is crowned by a huge *gopuram* (temple tower). Non-Hindus are welcome to visit, but leave your shoes at the entrance.

Sze Ya Temple   TEMPLE
(Map p384; Jln Tun HS Lee; ⊙ 7am-5pm; 🚇 Pasar Seni) **FREE** This Taoist temple is one of the most atmospheric in Chinatown. You can enter the temple through the stucco gatehouse on Jln Tun HS Lee or the back gate on the next alley west.

KL Train Station   HISTORIC BUILDING
(Map p384; Jln Sultan Hishamuddin; 🚇 Kuala Lumpur) South is the old railway station, a fanciful castle of Islamic arches and spires.

⊙ Little India & Around

Little India has the feel of a bazaar. The sari shops and the women shopping along **Jalan Masjid India**, the district's main street, are swathed in vibrant sherbets, turquoise and vermilions. Meanwhile Indian pop blasts through tinny speakers, and musky incense and delicious spices flavour the air. The district swings into a full spectacle during the Saturday *pasar malam* (night market). On the first and third weekends of every month **CapSquare** (Map p382; www.capsquare.com.my; cnr Jln Munshi Abdullah & Jln Dang Wangi; 🚇 Dang Wangi) hosts a bazaar that features food and fashion as well as some interesting knick-knacks.

Little India is best reached on the Star or Putra LRT to Masjid Jamek station.

Masjid Jamek   MOSQUE
(Friday Mosque; Map p384; off Jln Tun Perak; ⊙ 8.30am-12.30pm & 2.30-4pm Sat-Thu, 8.30-11am & 2.30-4pm Fri; 🚇 Masjid Jamek) **FREE**

Kuala Lumpur

N

| 0 | | 1 km |
| 0 | | 0.5 miles |

Sentul Park

Jln Sentul

Sungai Batu

Sungai Gombak

Jln Pahang

Lake Titiwangsa

Titiwangsa Lake Gardens

Sungai Bunus

Sentul LRT

Jln Ipoh

Titiwangsa LRT

National Visual Arts Gallery

Jln Tun Razak

TITIWANGSA

Pekeliling Bus Station

Hospital Kuala Lumpur

National Survey & Mapping Department

Jalan Kuching

Sungai Baru

Putra Bus Station

Jln Ipoh

Chow Kit MRT

Jln Raja Muda Abdul Aziz

PWTC LRT

Jln Putra

CHOW KIT

Putra KTM

Bazaar Baru Chow Kit

KAMPUNG BARU

Kampung Baru LRT

Ampang Elevated Hwy

Sultan Ismail LRT

Jln Raja Laut

Medan Tuanku MRT

Jln Raja Abdullah

Jln Yap Kwan Seng

KLCC LRT

Bank Negara Malaysia Museum & Art Gallery

Bandaraya LRT

Jln Dang Wangi

Dang Wangi LRT

Bukit Nanas MRT

Kuala Lumpur City Centre (KLCC) Park

Jln Sultan Salahuddin

Bank Negara KTM

Capital Café

Immigration Office

CapSquare

Masjid India Pasar Malam

LITTLE INDIA

Jln Ampang

Bukit Nanas Forest Reserve

Jln Raja Chulan

Raja Chulan MRT

Jln Parlimen

Jln Kuching

Masjid Jamek LRT

MERDEKA SQUARE

GOLDEN TRIANGLE

COLONIAL DISTRICT

Jln Cheng Lock

Jln Pudu

Bukit Bintang MRT

Jln Imbi

KL Bird Park

CHINATOWN

Pasar Seni LRT

Plaza Rakyat LRT

Imbi MRT

Tasik Perdana

Kuala Lumpur

Hang Tuah MRT

Hang Tuah LRT

National Museum

See Chinatown, Merdeka Square & Little India Map (p384)

See Golden Triangle Map (p388)

PUDU

Jln Travers

BRICKFIELDS

Jln Istana

Pudu LRT

Jln Pasar

KL Sentral

Jln San Peng

Pudu Market

Jln Tun Sambanthan

Tun Sambanthan MRT

Jln Syed Putra

Jln Lapangan Terbang

Jln Loke Yew

Jln Sungai Besi

Chan Sow Lin LRT

Sungai Klang

RAIL SYSTEMS	
KTM	
LRT	
MRT	

MALAYSIA

Constructed in 1907 at the confluence of the Klang and Gombak rivers, the mosque is an island of serenity, with airy open pavilions shaded by palm trees. Visitors are welcome outside prayer times, but please dress appropriately and remove your shoes before entering the mosque.

Bank Negara Malaysia Museum & Art Gallery   MUSEUM, ART GALLERY
(Map p382; www.museum.bnm.gov.my; 2 Jln Dato Onn; ☉10am-6pm; ⓡBank Negara) FREE The national bank's conservatively chosen but attractive art collection is housed in a futuristic, metal-clad complex (designed by top Malaysian architect Hijjas Kasturi) uphill from Bank Negara train station in a leafy area.

⊙ Golden Triangle

A forest of high-rises, the Golden Triangle is central KL's business, shopping and entertainment district. To get here, take the Putra LRT to KLCC station.

★**Petronas Towers**   NOTABLE BUILDING
(Map p388; www.petronastwintowers.com.my; Jln Ampang; adult/child RM80/30; ☉9am-9pm Tue-Sun; ⓡKLCC) The epitomy of contemporary KL are these stainless-steel-clad towers, the headquarters of the national oil and gas company Petronas. Opened in 1998, the 88-storey twin towers are nearly 452m tall, making them the tallest twin structures in the world. Designed by Argentinian architect Cesar Pelli, the twin towers' floor plan is based on an eight-sided star that echoes arabesque patterns. Islamic influences are also evident in each tower's five tiers – representing the five pillars of Islam – and in the 63m masts that crown them, calling to mind the minarets of a mosque and the Star of Islam.

Menara Kuala Lumpur   TOWER
(KL Tower; Map p388; ☑03-2020 5448; www.menarakl.com.my; 2 Jln Punchak; admission RM47; ☉9am-10pm, last tickets up 9.30pm; ⓡKL Tower) Sitting on a forested hill, Menara Kuala Lumpur easily trumps the Petronas Towers when it comes to the view. The tower's bulbous pinnacle is inspired by a Malaysian spinning top and the 276m-high **viewing deck** is over 100m higher than the Petronas Towers' Skybridge.

A free **shuttle bus** (☉9am-9.30pm, every 15 min) runs to the tower from the gate on Jln Punchak opposite the PanGlobal building.

⊙ Lake Gardens & Around

Escape from the heat and concrete to this inner-city garden district at the western edge of central KL. It's a 20-minute walk from Masjid Jamek or taxi drivers tend to charge an exorbitant RM15 to RM20 for the short distance back to the city centre.

National Museum   MUSEUM
(Muzium Negara; Map p382; ☑03-2282 6255; www.muziumnegara.gov.my; Jln Damansara; adult/child RM5/2; ☉9am-6pm; ⓡHop-On-Hop-Off Bus Tour, ⓡKL Sentral, then taxi) Housed in a building with a distinctive Minangkabau-style roof, this museum is one of the city's best. Galleries include Early History, Colonial Era and Malaysia Today. Outside, find a regularly changing exhibition (extra charge) and a couple of small free galleries including the **Orang Asli Craft Museum.**

MALAYSIA KUALA LUMPUR

BATU CAVES

Get closer to KL's Indian culture by visiting the **Batu Caves** (☑03-6189 6284; www.batucavesmuruga.org; Temple Cave free, other caves admission charges apply; ☉7am-9pm; ⓡBatu Caves), a system of three caves 13km northwest of the capital. The most famous is **Temple Cave**, because it contains a Hindu shrine reached by a straight flight of 272 steps, guarded by a 43m-high Murga statue, the highest in the world. **Dark Cave** (www.darkcavemalaysia.com; adult/child RM35/25; ☉10am-5pm Tue-Fri, 10.30am-5.30pm Sat & Sun, tours every 20min) ✐ lets you explore some limestone passageways via guided tour, and **Cave Villa** (☑03-6154 2307; www.cavevilla.com.my; adult/child RM15/7; ☉9am-6.30pm; ⓡBatu Caves) has Hindu paintings and a dance show every half-hour. About a million pilgrims visit the Batu Caves every year during Thaipusam (January/February) to engage in or watch the spectacularly masochistic feats of the devotees.

To get here take bus U6 (RM2.50, 45 minutes) from Medan Pasar in KL. Alternatively the KTM Komuter Train runs from KL Sentral to Batu Caves Station (RM1.30, 25 minutes) every 30 minutes. A taxi costs around RM20.

Chinatown, Merdeka Square & Little India

LITTLE INDIA

Jln Sultan Salahuddin

Jln Kuching

Sungai Gombak

Jln Raja Laut

Jln Gombak

Lg Gombak

Jln Tunku Abdul Rahman (TAR)

Lg Tuanku Abdul Rahman

Jln Masjid India

Jln Tun Perak

Jln Parlimen

Jln Tangsi

Jln Raja

Jln Raja

Jln Melaka

Royal Selangor Club

Masjid Jamek LRT

⊙5

●3

Jln Makhamah Persekutuan

MERDEKA SQUARE

Lebuh Ampang

12 🏧

Jln Kinabalu

Jln Raja

Jln Raja

Medan Pasar

Central Market Annexe

COLONIAL DISTRICT

Jln Cenderasari

Jln Sultan Hishamuddin

Central Market

Lebuh Pudu

7 🍴

9 🏧

Kompleks Dayabumi

13 🏧

15

Jln Lembah Perdana

Sungai Klang

CHINATOWN

Jln Hang Kasturi

6 ⛩

✉

Pasar Seni LRT

Islamic Arts Museum 🏛1

Jln Panggong

●4

Jln Tun HS Lee

Jln Tun Tan Cheng Lock

Jln Tun Sambanthan

Jln Lembah Perdana

Jln Tun

Jln Kinabalu

Tun Abdul Razak Heritage Park

2 🏛

Kuala Lumpur

MALAYSIA

Time your visit to coincide with one of the free **tours** given by enthusiastic volunteer guides. Although the museum is very close to KL Sentral station, it's surrounded by a snarl of highways – the easiest way to get here is by taxi or via the walkway over the highway south of the Lake Gardens.

KL Bird Park AVIARY
(Map p382; ☎03-2272 1010; www.klbirdpark.com; Jln Cenderawasih; adult/child RM48/38; ⊙9am-6pm; 🔊; 🚉Kuala Lumpur) This fabulous aviary brings together some 200 species of (mostly) Asian birds flying free beneath an enormous canopy. It's worth getting to the park for feeding times (hornbills 11.30am, eagles 2.30pm) or the bird shows (12.30pm and 3.30pm), which feature plenty of parrot tricks to keep youngsters amused. The park's Hornbill Restaurant is also good.

★**Islamic Arts Museum** MUSEUM
(Muzium Kesenian Islam Malaysia; Map p384; ☎03-2274 2020; www.iamm.org.my; Jln Lembah Perdana; adult/child RM10/5, with special exhibitions RM12/6; ⊙10am-6pm, restaurant closed Mon; 🚉Kuala Lumpur) This outstanding museum is home to one of best collections of Islamic decorative arts in the world. Aside from the quality of the exhibits, the building itself is a stunner, with beautifully decorated domes and glazed tilework. There's a good Middle Eastern restaurant and one of KL's best museum gift shops stocking beautiful products from around the Islamic world.

◎ Northern KL

National Visual Arts Gallery ART GALLERY
(Balai Seni Lukis Negara; Map p382; ☎03-4026 7000; www.artgallery.gov.my; 2 Jln Temerloh; ⊙10am-6pm; monorail Titiwangsa) **FREE** Occupying a pyramid-shaped block, the NVAG showcases modern and contemporary Malaysian art. There are often interesting temporary shows of local and regional artists, as well as pieces from the gallery's permanent collection of 4000 works. Overall though, the gallery lacks a wow factor.

🏃 Activities

There's a concentration of Chinese massage and reflexology places along the Jln Bukit Bintang, south of BB Plaza in the Golden Triangle. The going price is usually RM75 for a one-hour full-body massage. Expect to pay about RM30 for 30 minutes of foot reflexology.

MALAYSIA KUALA LUMPUR

Chinatown, Merdeka Square & Little India

Alternatively, fish spas are the hip, new thing: live fish nibble the dead skin off your feet for up to 30 minutes for around RM30.

Reborn   SPA
(Map p388; ☎ 03-2144 1288; www.reborn.com.my; 18 Jln Bukit Bintang; ⊙ 11am-3am; monorail Bukit Bintang) One of the more pleasantly designed places on the strip, offering spa treatments as well as massages and a fish spa.

🛏 Sleeping

Vibrant Chinatown is your best hunting ground for rock-bottom crash pads and is an easy walk from the Pudu Sentral bus station. The Golden Triangle area's budget options are pricier but cleaner and in a more low-key (and arguably less exciting) neighbourhood. Unless otherwise noted, all of the options listed share bathrooms.

🛏 Chinatown & Little India

If you're arriving from the airport or a long-distance bus station other than Pudu Sentral, these guesthouses can be reached via the Star LRT to Plaza Rakyat, Putra LRT to Pasar Seni or the KL Monorail to Maharajalela station.

Explorers Guesthouse   HOSTEL $
(Map p384; ☎ 03-2022 2928; www.theexplorers-guesthouse.com; 128-130 Jln Tun HS Lee; dm/s/d from RM30/68/88; ❄@🛜; 🚇Pasar Seni) Explorers follows up a comfy, spacious lobby with clean, airy rooms, a roof terrace, colourfully painted walls and a few arty touches.

Hotel Chinatown (2)   HOTEL $
(Map p384; ☎ 03-2072 9933; www.hotelchina-town2.com; 70-72 Jln Petaling; s/d from RM69/90; ❄@🛜; 🚇Pasar Seni) The cheapest rooms have no windows but are away from the

noisy main street. The lobby offers a comfy lounge area, water feature, book exchange and piano.

Wheelers Guest House   HOSTEL $
(Map p384; ☎ 03-2070 1386; www.backpackerskl.com/wheelers.htm; Level 2, 131-133 Jln Tun HS Lee; dm/r with shared bathroom from RM13/25, r with private bathroom RM50; ❄@; 🚇Pasar Seni) Prisonlike rooms, but this hostel does have a mini-aquarium, gay-friendly staff, a great rooftop terrace where free Friday-night dinners are hosted, and homemade yoghurt and muesli for breakfast.

★ BackHome   HOSTEL $$
(Map p384; ☎ 03-2022 0788; www.backhome.com.my; 30 Jln Tun HS Lee; dm/d/tr with breakfast from RM42/110/150; ❄@🛜; 🚇Masjid Jamek) This chic pit stop for flashpackers offers polished concrete finishes, Zen simple decoration, fab rain showers and a blissful central courtyard sprouting spindly trees. It can be noisy on the street outside, but they offer earplugs for light sleepers. Also check out its cool cafe LOKL (mains RM14 to RM20).

★ Reggae Mansion   HOSTEL $$
(Map p384; ☎ 03-2072 6877; www.reggaehotels malaysia.com/mansion; 49-59 Jln Tun HS Lee; dm/d from RM35/120; ❄@🛜; 🚇Masjid Jamek) Grooving to a more superior beat than most backpacker places, including its own guesthouses in the heart of Chinatown, this is one cool operation. The decor is whitewashed faux colonial with contemporary touches including a flash cafe-bar, rooftop bar and mini cinema (RM7 including popcorn and a drink).

Grid 19   HOSTEL $$
(Map p384; ☎ 03-9226 2629; www.grid9hotels.com; 9 Jln Maharajalela; dm/s/d from RM40/109/129;

✻ @ ☎; monorail Maharajalela) Steps from the monorail, this new flashpackers softens its concrete and steel industrial look with bold splashes of paint and equally colourful bean-bags. Guests also get a free ticket to top club Zouk.

🛏 Golden Triangle

These guesthouses can be reached via the KL Monorail to Bukit Bintang station.

Red Palm   HOSTEL $
(Map p388; ☑ 03-2143 1279; www.redpalm-kl.com; 5 Tengkat Tong Shin; dm/s/d/tr incl breakfast RM30/55/75/105; @ ☎; monorail Imbi) Cosy shophouse hostel offering small, thin-walled rooms with shared bathrooms. The communal areas are great and the owners are charming.

Classic Inn   HOSTEL $$
(Map p388; ☑ 03-2148 8648; www.classicinn.com.my; 52 Lg 1/77A, Changkat Thambi D-ollah; dm RM45, s/d from RM98/128; ✻ @ ☎; monorail Imbi) Occupying a smartly renovated, yellow-painted shophouse on the southern edge of the Golden Triangle, this is a retro-charming choice with dorms and private rooms, a small grassy garden and welcoming staff. A second, more upmarket branch along the street, **Classic Inn Premium**, opened in late 2013.

Rainforest Bed & Breakfast   HOSTEL $$
(Map p388; ☑ 03-2145 3525; www.rainforestbnbhotel.com; 27 Jln Mesui; dm/d/tw with breakfast RM39/115/140; ✻ @ ☎; monorail Raja Chulan) The lush foliage sprouting around and tumbling off the tiered balconies of this high-quality guesthouse is eye-catching and apt

for its name. Rooms have bright red walls with timber lining (some have no windows).

🍴 Eating

All the food groups – including Indian, Chinese, Malay and Western fast food – abound in the Malaysian capital.

🍴 Chinatown & Little India

In the morning, grab a marble-topped table in one of the neighbourhood's *kedai kopi* (coffee shops) for a jolt of coffee spiked with condensed milk. The midday meal can be slurped down at the stalls that line Jln Sultan serving all the you-name-it noodles, from prawn or *won ton mee* (Chinese-style egg noodles served with stuffed wontons) to *laksa lemak* (white rounded noodles served with coconut milk, also called curry laksa). Jln Petaling market is closed to traffic in the evenings and Chinese restaurants set up tables beside all the action.

Little India is your best hunting ground for a slap-up Indian curry sopped up with flaky *roti canai* (Indian-style flaky flat bread, also known as 'flying dough').

★ Madras Lane Hawkers   HAWKER $
(Map p384; Madras Lane; noodles RM5; ⊘ 8am-4pm Tue-Sun; 🚇 Pasar Seni) Weave your way through Chinatown Wet Market to find this alley of hawker stalls. It's best visited for breakfast or lunch, with standout operators including the one offering 10 types of *yong tau fu* (tofu pockets stuffed with a fish and pork paste) in a fish broth (9.30am to 3.30pm) and, at the far end of the strip, the stall serving *asam* (tamarind) and curry laksa (8am to 2pm).

FORESTRY RESEARCH INSTITUTE OF MALAYSIA (FRIM)

Birdsong and wall-to-wall greenery replaces the drone of traffic and air-conditioning at the **Forestry Research Institute of Malaysia** (FRIM; ☑ 03-6279 7575; www.frim.gov.my; Selangor Darul Ehsan; admission RM5, Canopy Walkway adult/child RM10/1; ⊘ information centre 8am-5pm Mon-Fri, 9am-4pm Sat & Sun, museum 9am-4pm Tue-Sun; 🚇 KTM Komuter to Kepong, then taxi) 🚶, 16km northwest of KL. The highlight of this 600-hectare jungle park is its 200m-long, 30m-high **Canopy Walkway** (admission RM10; ⊘ 9.30am-2.30pm Tue-Thu, Sat & Sun).

The walkway is reached by a steep trail from FRIM's information centre. Heading down from the walkway the trail picks its way through the jungle to a shady picnic area where you can cool off in a series of shallow waterfalls. The return hike incorporating the walkway takes around two hours.

Take a KTM Komuter train to Kepong (RM1.10) and then a taxi (RM5); arrange for the taxi to pick you up again later.

Golden Triangle

16

Petronas Towers ⊙1

⊛19

18

ℹ Malaysian Tourism Centre

Twin Towers Medical Centre KLCC ✚

Jln Ampang

⊙ Dang Wangi LRT

⊙ Bukit Nanas MRT

Jln Perak

Jln Punchak

New Zealand Embassy

Jln Perak

Sungai Klang

Jln Pinang

⊛17

Jln P Ramlee

Jln Sultan Ismail

Lg P Ramlee

Kenanga

❶2

Jln Punchak

Shuttle Bus Stop to Menara KL

Jln Tengah

⊙ Raja Chulan MRT

Bukit Nanas Forest Reserve

Jln Raja Chulan

Changkat Raja Chulan

Lg Cyclon

Jln Bukit Ceylon

Jln Mesui

Jln Nagasari

Jln Ceylon

13 🛏 5 ⊗10

Jln Berangan

Jln Angsoka

Jln Bedara

Jln Beremi

Pesiaran Raja Chulan

Changkat Bukit Bintang

14 🍴11

Jln Sahabat

Tengkat Tong Shin

Jln Bukit Bintang

Tung Shin ✚ Hospital

Jln Tong Shin

Jln Alor

Bukit Bintang MRT

Jln Pudu

🛏6

Plaza Rakyat LRT

1 ⊗

3 ✈

Jln Bulan

Jln Bulan 1

Jln 1/77

⊗20

Jln Imbi

Imbi MRT ⊙

Berjaya Times Square

Compass Coaches

Jln Hang Jebat

Hang Tuah MRT

Jln Hang Tuah

15 🛒 🍴4

Jln Kampung Dollah

Stadium Negara

Jln Stadium

Hang Tuah LRT

Jln Changkat Thambi Dollah

MALAYSIA

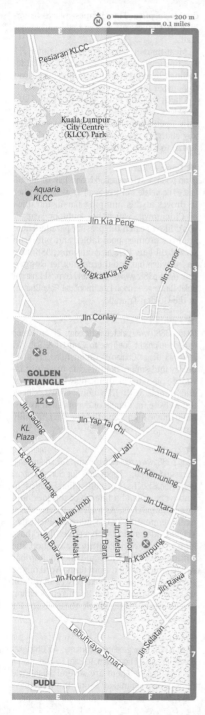

★ **Masjid India Pasar Malam**   MARKET
(Night Market; Map p382; Lg TAR; ⊙3pm-midnight Sat; ⓜMasjid Jamek) If you're in town on Saturday, don't miss the *pasar malam* that runs the length of Lg Tuanku Abdul Rahman, the alley between the Jln TAR and Masjid India, from around 3pm until late. There are plenty of stalls serving excellent Malay, Indian and Chinese snacks and drinks.

Capital Café   MALAYSIAN $
(Map p382; 213 Jln TAR; dishes RM3.50-5; ⊙7am-8.30pm Mon-Sat; ⓜBandaraya) Since it opened in 1956 this truly Malaysian cafe has had Chinese, Malays and Indians all working together in the same space. Try their excellent *mee goreng* or *rojak* or satay (only available in the evenings).

✕ Golden Triangle & KLCC

Jln Nagansari, off Changkat Bukit Bintang, is lined with Malay food stalls and open-air restaurants. Jln Alor, two streets northwest of Jln Bukit Bintang, has a carnival-like night market of Chinese hawker stalls. When it's hot outside, head to central KL's air-con shopping centres for international and local food. Take the KL Monorail to Bukit Bintang to reach this area.

★ **Imbi Market**   HAWKER $
(Pasar Baru Bukit Bintang; Map p388; Jln Kampung; meal RM10; ⊙6.30am-12.30pm Tue-Sun; monorail Bukit Bintang) Breakfast is like a party here with all the friendly and curious locals happily recommending their favourite stalls. We like **Sisters Crispy Popiah**; **Teluk Intan Chee Cheung Fun**, where Amy Ong serves a lovely oyster-and-peanut *congee* and egg puddings; and **Bunn Choon** for the creamy mini egg tarts.

The market is slated to move as the area is developed into the Tun Razak Exchange financial district over the next few years.

Blue Boy Vegetarian Food Centre   CHINESE, MALAYSIAN $
(Map p388; ☎03-2144 9011; Jln Tong Shin; mains RM3-10; ⊙8am-6pm; ⚲; monorail Imbi) It's hard to believe that everything prepared at this spotless hawker-style cafe at the base of a backstreet apartment block is vegetarian, but it's true – in fact, if you bypass the stall using egg, it's all vegan. The *char kway teow* (broad noodles fried in chilli and black-bean sauce) is highly recommended.

Golden Triangle

Restoran Nagansari
Curry House   MALAYSIAN, INDIAN $

(Map p388; Jln Nagansari; meals RM5-10; ⊙7am-midnight; monorail Raja Chulan) This simple hawker-style restaurant serves a good selection of Malay dishes – soup *mee, tom yam* and so on – with a few Indian favourites thrown in for good measure. Fans blow moist air around the dining hall to keep diners cool.

Food Republic   FOOD COURT $$

(Map p388; Level 1, Pavilion KL, 168 Jln Bukit Bintang; meals RM10-20; ⊙10am-10pm; monorail Bukit Bintang) Outstanding choice and slick design make this probably the best shopping mall food court in KL. It's also surrounded by scores of proper restaurants.

🍸 Drinking & Nightlife

Drinking in Malaysia is definitely no budget activity and drinks at 'proper' bars are nearly double in price. The cheapest places to imbibe are Chinese eateries or open-air hawker stalls.

Meat-market bars congregate along Jln P Ramlee while sophisticates and the indie-inclined heat up at nearby CapSquare. Head to Bangsar for classy expat bars and cafes.

Check out the latest club news in **KLue** (www.klue.com.my; RM5). Clubs are typically open Wednesday to Sunday and usually charge a cover (including one drink) of RM20 to RM40 Thursday to Saturday.

★**Reggae Bar**   BAR

(Map p384; www.reggaebarkl.com; 158 Jln Tun HS Lee; ⊙noon-late; 🚇Pasar Seni) Travellers gather in droves at this pumping bar in the thick of Chinatown, which has outdoor seats if you'd like to catch the passing parade. There are beer promos, pool tables and pub grub served till late. Reggae Mansion (p386) also has a stylish bar and there's another **Reggae Bar** (Map p388; www.reggaebarkl.com; 31 Changat Bukit Bintang; ⊙noon-late; monorail Raja Chulan) in the Golden Triangle.

★**Palate Palette**   CAFE

(Map p388; www.palatepalette.com; 21 Jln Mesui; ⊙noon-midnight Tue-Thu, to 2am Fri & Sat; 🚇; monorail Raja Chulan) Colourful, creative, quirky and super cool this cafe-bar is our favourite place to eat, drink, play board games, and mingle with KL's boho crowd. Check the website for details of events such as free indie movie nights and the queer community party.

★**Zouk**   NIGHTCLUB

(Map p388; www.zoukclub.com.my; 113 Jln Ampang; admission RM60; ⊙9pm-3am Tue-Sun; monorail Bukit Nanas) KL's top club offers spaces to suit everyone and a line-up of top local and international DJs. As well as the two-level main venue, there's the more sophisticated Velvet Underground with a dance floor that's glitter-ball heaven, Phuture for hip hop, the cutting-edge Bar Sonic and the rooftop bar Aristo which is open from 6pm. Word on the street at the time of research was that Zouk will have to move out of its current location in the near future; check the website for updates.

Green Man   PUB

(Map p388; www.greenman.com.my; 40 Changkat Bukit Bintang; ⊙noon-1am, to 2am Fri-Sun; monorail Raja Chulan) There are several Irish-style pubs along Changkat Bukit Bintang these days, but this is the original one and has a

MALAYSIA KUALA LUMPUR

very loyal crowd. It's calmer indoors than on the busy terrace. Join in the regular Thursday night quiz at 8pm for RM15.

Sixty Nine Bistro   CAFE
(Map p388; 14 Jln Kampung Dollah; ☺5pm-1.30am; monorail Imbi) A very funky youth venue that has a junk-shop chic vibe to its decor, a fun menu of bubble teas and the like, and resident fortune tellers.

Luk Yu Tea House   TEAHOUSE
(Map p388; ☑03-2782 3850; Feast fl, Starhill Gallery, 181 Jln Bukit Bintang; ☺10am-1am; monorail Bukit Bintang) Enjoy a premium brew inside a charming traditional Chinese teahouse along with dim sum and other dainty snacks.

☆ Entertainment

KL Live   LIVE MUSIC
(Map p388; www.kl-live.com.my; 1st fl, Life Centre, 20 Jln Sultan Ismail; monorail Raja Chulan) One of the best things to happen to KL's live-music scene in a while has been the opening of this spacious venue, which has been packing in rock and pop fans with an impressive line-up of overseas and local big-name artists and DJs.

Malaysian Tourism Centre   TRADITIONAL DANCE
(MaTiC; Map p388; ☑03-9235 4900; www.matic. gov.my; 109 Jln Ampang; admission RM5) Traditional Malaysian dances and music; there are good shows at 3pm Tuesday to Thursday and 8.30pm Saturday. There's also a changing list of events from car boot sales to free dance instructions so check the website for what's on.

TGV Cineplex   CINEMA
(Map p388; ☑03-7492 2929; www.tgv.com.my; Level 3, Suria KLCC) Take your pick from the mainstream offerings at this 12-screen multiplex. Book in advance or be prepared to queue, particularly at weekends.

🛍 Shopping

Pudu Market   MARKET
(Map p382; Jln Pasar Baharu; ☺4am-2pm; 🚇Pudu) Arrive early to experience KL's largest wet (produce) market at its most frantic. Here you can get every imaginable type of fruit, vegetable, fish and meat – from the foot of a chicken slaughtered and butchered on the spot to a stingray fillet or a pig's penis.

Petaling Street Market   MARKET
(Map p384; Jln Petaling; ☺noon-11pm; 🚇Kota Raya) The commercial heart of Chinatown is one of the most colourful and busiest shopping parades in KL, particularly at night when stalls cram the covered street. It offers everything from fresh fruit and cheap clothes and shoes to copies of brand-name watches and handbags, and pirated CDs and DVDs. Be prepared to bargain hard.

Bazaar Baru Chow Kit   MARKET
(Chow Kit Market; Map p382; 469-473 Jln TAR; ☺6am-8pm) It's sensory overload at this lively market, where tightly jammed stalls sell clothes, toys, buckets, stationery, noodles, spices, fresh meat and live, flapping fish, as well as a staggering array of weird and wonderful tropical fruit. Shops in the lanes around the market, particularly Jln Haji Hussein, specialise in made-to-order *songkok*, the traditional Malay-style fez.

Plaza Low Yat   ELECTRONICS
(Map p388; www.plazalowyat.com; 7 Jln Bintang; ☺10am-10pm; monorail Imbi) Come here for all your digital and electronic needs.

ℹ Information

IMMIGRATION OFFICES
Immigration Office (Map p382; ☑03-6205 7400; Jalan Sri Hartamas 1, off Jalan Duta; ☺7.30am-1pm & 2-5.30pm Mon-Fri) Handles visa extensions; about 8km northwest from the city centre.

INTERNET ACCESS
Internet cafes are everywhere; the going rate per hour is RM3. Wi-fi is free at hundreds of restaurants, bars and more around the city.

DON'T MISS

JALAN ALOR

The collection of roadside restaurants and stalls lining Jln Alor is the great common denominator of KL's food scene, hauling in everyone from sequined society babes to penny-strapped backpackers. From around 5pm till late every evening, the street transforms into a continuous open-air dining space with hundreds of plastic tables and chairs and rival caterers shouting out to passers-by to drum up business. Most places serve alcohol and you can sample pretty much every Malay Chinese dish imaginable, from grilled fish and satay to *kai-lan* (Chinese greens) in oyster sauce and fried noodles with frogs' legs.

MALAYSIA KUALA LUMPUR

MEDICAL SERVICES

Hospital Kuala Lumpur (Map p382; ☑03-2615 5555; www.hkl.gov.my; Jln Pahang) North of the centre.

Twin Towers Medical Centre KLCC (Map p388; ☑03-2382 3500; www.ttmcklcc.com.my; Level 4, Suria KLCC, Jln Ampang; ⊗8.30am-6pm Mon-Sat)

MONEY

You'll seldom be far from a bank or ATM. Money changers offer better rates than banks for changing cash and (at times) travellers cheques; they are usually open later hours and on weekends and are found in shopping malls.

POST

Main Post Office (Map p384; Jln Raja Laut; ⊗8.30am-6pm Mon-Sat, closed 1st Sat of month) Across the river from the Central Market. Has poste restante and packaging is available for reasonable rates at the post-office store.

TOURIST INFORMATION

Malaysian Tourism Centre (MaTic; Map p388; ☑03-9235 4900; www.matic.gov.my; 109 Jln Ampang; ⊗8am-10pm; monorail Bukit Nanas) Housed in a mansion built in 1935 for rubber and tin tycoon Eu Tong Sen, this is KL's most useful tourist office. Also hosts good cultural performances.

ⓘ Getting There & Away

Kuala Lumpur is Malaysia's principal international arrival gateway and it forms the crossroads for domestic bus, train and taxi travel.

AIR

Kuala Lumpur International Airport (KLIA; ☑03-8777 8888; www.klia.com.my) is the main airport, 75km south of the city centre at Sepang. **AirAsia** (☑03-8775 4000; www.airasia.com) flights arrive and depart from the nearby **Low Cost Carrier Terminal** (LCCT; ☑03-8777 8888; http://lcct.klia.com.my/), and a new, nearby Low Cost Carrier Terminal scheduled to open in 2014. **Firefly** (☑03-7845 4543; www.fireflyz.com.my) and **Berjaya Air** (☑03-2119 6616; www.berjaya-air.com) flights use the **SkyPark Subang Airport** (Sultan Abdul Aziz Shah Airport; ☑03-7845 1717; www.subangskypark.com), about 20km west of the city centre.

BUS

KL's main bus station is **Pudu Sentral** (Map p384; left luggage per day per bag RM3; ⊗6am-midnight) just east of Chinatown. The only long-distance destinations that Pudu Sentral doesn't handle are Kuala Lipis and Jerantut (for access to Taman Negara) – buses to these places leave from **Pekeliling bus station** (Map p382; ☑03-4042 7256) next to Titiwangsa LRT and monorail stations, just off Jln Tun Razak – and Kota Bharu and Kuala Terengganu, buses for which leave from **Putra bus station** (Map p382; ☑03-4042 9530; Jln Putra).

TAXI

Shared-taxi fares from the depot on the 2nd floor of Pudu Sentral (p392) include Melaka (RM150), Penang (RM500) and Johor Bahru (RM380). Toll charges are normally included.

TRAIN

KL Sentral station is the national hub of the **KTM** (Keretapi Tanah Melayu Berhad; ☑1300 88 5862; www.ktmb.com.my; ⊗info office 9am-9pm, ticket office 7am-10pm) railway system. There are daily departures for Butterworth, Wakaf Baharu (for Kota Bharu and Jerantut), Johor Bahru, Thailand and Singapore; fares are cheap, especially if you opt for a seat rather than a berth (for which there are extra charges), but journey times are slow.

Not to be confused with the intercity long-distance line is the KTM Komuter, which runs from KL Sentral, linking central KL with the Klang Valley and Seremban.

BUSES FROM KUALA LUMPUR

DESTINATION	PRICE (RM)	DURATION (HR)
Alor Setar	40	5
Butterworth	31.20	5
Cameron Highlands	30	4
Ipoh	18.80	2½
Johor Bahru	31.10	5
Kuantan	22	4
Melaka	12.30	2
Penang	35	5
Singapore	47	5½

ℹ️ Getting Around

TO/FROM THE AIRPORT

Kuala Lumpur International Airport (KLIA)

The efficient KLIA Ekspres (adult one way/return RM35/70, 28 minutes, every 15 to 20 minutes from 5am to 1am) spirits you to/from the international airport (KLIA) to the KL City Air Terminal, located in KL Sentral train station. This is without doubt the easiest way to travel to/from the airport.

If you have more time than money, catch the **Airport Coach** (www.airportcoach.com.my; one way/return RM10/18) to KL Sentral (one hour); it can also take you onwards to any central KL hotel from KLIA and pick up for the return journey for a round-trip total of RM18. The bus stand is clearly signposted inside the terminal.

Taxis from KLIA operate on a fixed-fare coupon system. Purchase a coupon from a counter at the arrival hall and use it to pay the driver. Standard taxis cost RM65.

Low Cost Carrier Terminal (LCCT)

Skybus (www.skybus.com.my; one way RM9) and **Aerobus** (www.aerobus.my; one way RM8) depart every 15 minutes from 4.30am to 12.45am and take an hour. From LCCT, prepaid taxis charge RM70 to Chinatown or Jln Bukit Bintang (50% more from midnight to 6am). Buy your coupon at the desk near the arrivals hall exit. A taxi from the city to LCCT will cost around RM65.

SkyPark Subang Airport

The only transport option to SkyPark Subang Airport is a taxi; expect to pay RM40.

BUS

Most buses in KL are provided by either **Rapid KL** (📞 03-7885 2585; www.myrapid.com.my) or **Metrobus** (📞 03-5635 3070). Local buses leave from many of the bus terminals around the city, including Pudu Sentral (p392) bus station, near Plaza Rakyat LRT station. The fare is RM2 to RM4; have the correct change ready when you board.

TAXI

KL's taxis are cheap, starting at RM3 for the first two minutes, with an additional 20 sen for each 45 seconds. From midnight to 6am there's a surcharge of 50% on the metered fare, and extra passengers (more than two) are charged 20 sen each. Luggage placed in the boot is an extra RM1 and there's a RM12 surcharge for taxis to KLIA.

Although required to use the meter by law, taxi drivers often don't, and tend to overcharge tourists. It should cost no more than RM10 to go right across the central city area, even in moderate traffic.

TRAIN

The user-friendly **Light Rail Transit** (LRT; 📞 03-7885 2585; www.myrapid.com.my; RM1-2.80; ⏱ every 6-10min, 6am-11.45pm, to 11.30pm Sun & holidays) system is composed of the Ampang/Sentul Timur, Sri Petaling/Sentul Timur and Kelana Jaya/Terminal Putra lines.

KL's zippy **monorail** (www.klmonorail.com.my; RM1.20-2.50; ⏱ 6am-midnight) runs between KL Sentral in the south to Titiwangsa in the north. It's a handy service linking up many of the city's sightseeing areas and providing a cheap air-con tour as you go.

KTM Komuter (📞 1300 88 5862; www.ktmkomuter.com.my; ⏱ every 15-20min, 6am-11.45pm) not to be confused with the long-distance KTM service, links Kuala Lumpur with outlying suburbs and the historic railway station. Tickets start from RM1 for one stop.

KL Sentral station, in the Brickfields area, is the central transit station for all train travel in KL.

PENINSULAR MALAYSIA – WEST COAST

Malaysia's multiculturalism is best viewed along the west coast. Nestled against the Strait of Melaka, the convenient shipping route has, over the centuries, created a cosmopolitan populace, well schooled in English. Besides Pulau Langkawi, the islands of this coast don't compare to those in the east or in Thailand, but they are always host to great seafood and an array of cultural adventures.

Melaka

📞 06 / POP 759,000

Melaka has all the advantages of a metropolis: seemingly hundreds of cheap, fantastic places to eat and stay; artistic and tolerant locals; diverse entertainment; and nightlife and a colourful history. Yet it's a small, manageable place that exudes a calm that's only a notch more stressful than a tropical beach. Melt into the daily grind of dim-sum breakfasts, the call to prayer followed by church bells, laksa lunches, rides in crazy and gaudy trishaws, tandoori dinners and late-night drinks at balmy bars. It's hard not to like this town.

Melaka was founded in the 14th century by Parameswara, a Hindu prince from Sumatra, became protected by the Chinese in 1405, then dominated by the Portuguese in 1511, then the Dutch in 1641 and then finally

MALAYSIA MELAKA

Peninsular Malaysia

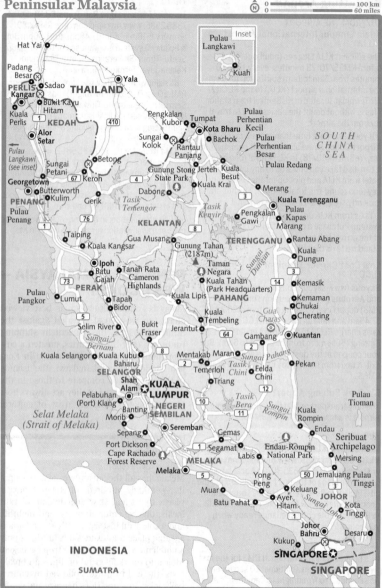

0 100 km
0 60 miles

MALAYSIA MELAKA

ceded to the British in 1795. The intermingling of peoples created the Peranakan people (also called Baba Nonya), who are descended from Chinese settlers; the Chitties, who are of mixed Indian and Malay heritage; and Eurasians born of Malay and Portuguese love affairs.

Chinatown is Melaka's most interesting and scenic area. Town Sq, also known as Dutch Sq, is the centre of a well-preserved museum district. Further northeast is Melaka's tiny Little India. Backpacker guesthouses are found in Chinatown and around the nearby, less scenic Jln Taman Melaka Raya.

◉ Sights & Activities

◉ Town Square & Bukit St Paul

Stadthuys HISTORIC BUILDING
(☑06-282 6526; Town Sq; adult/child RM5/2; ⊗9am-5.30pm Sat-Thu, 9am-12.15pm & 2.45-5.30pm Fri) Melaka's most unmistakable landmark and favourite trishaw pick-up spot is the Stadthuys, the imposing salmon-pink town hall and governor's residence. It's believed to be the oldest Dutch building in the East, built shortly after Melaka was captured by the Dutch in 1641, and is a reproduction of the former Stadhuis (town hall) of the Frisian town of Hoorn in the Netherlands.

Admission to the **History & Ethnography Museum** (⊗guided tours 10.30am & 2.30pm Sat & Sun) and **Literature Museum** (as well as the **Governor's House** and the **Democratic Government Museum**) is included in the admission price to Stadthuys.

St Paul's Church RUIN
(Jln Kota) From Stadthuys, steps lead up Bukit St Paul, which is a hill topped by the breezy ruins of St Paul's Church, built in 1521 by a Portuguese sea captain, and overlooking the Strait of Melaka.

Menara Taming Sari TOWER
(Jln Merdeka; adult/child RM20/10; ⊗10am-10pm) Take a ride upwards in this 80m revolving tower that's considered an eyesore by many. Waits can be long and it's all a bit tourist-tacky but it is a good way to get your bearings and enjoy great views.

Porta de Santiago RUIN
(A'Famosa; Jln Bandar Hilir) A quick photo stop at this fort is a must. Porta de Santiago was built by the Portuguese as a fortress in 1511.

Melaka River Cruise BOAT TOUR
(☑06-281 4322, 06-286 5468; www.melakarivercruise.com; adult/child RM15/7; ⊗9am-11.30pm) Riverboat cruises along Sungai Melaka (Melaka River) leave from two locations: one from the 'Spice Garden' on the corner of Jln Tun Mutahii and Jln Tun Sri Lanang in the north of town, and one at the quay (RM15) behind the Maritime Museum. Cruises go 9km upriver past Kampung Morten

> ### BIKE MELAKA'S COUNTRYSIDE
> Alias leads three-hour **eco bike tours** (☑019 652 5029; www.melakaonbike.com; 117 Jln Tiang Dua; per person RM100, min 2 people) through 20km of oil-palm and rubber-tree plantations and delightful *kampung* (village) communities surrounding town. Escort to and from your hotel is included and the tour can leave at 8.30am, 3pm or 7pm for night cycling any day of the week.

and old *godown* (river warehouses) and there's a recorded narration explaining the riverfront's history.

◉ Chinatown

Chinatown is the heart of Melaka. Stroll along **Jalan Tun Tan Cheng Lock**, formerly called Heeren St, which was the preferred address for wealthy Baba (Straits-born Chinese) traders who were most active during the early 20th century. The centre street of Chinatown is **Jalan Hang Jebat**, formerly known as Jonker St (or Junk St), which was once famed for its antique shops but is now more of a collection of clothing and craft outlets and restaurants. On Friday, Saturday and Sunday nights the street is transformed into the **Jonker's Walk Night Market**, a lively market of food and trinket stalls. The northern section of quiet **Jalan Tokong** (also known as Harmony St) has a handful of authentic Chinese shops.

Baba-Nonya Heritage Museum MUSEUM
(☑06-283 1273; 48-50 Jln Tun Tan Cheng Lock; adult/child RM15/7; ⊗10am-12.30pm & 2-4.30pm Wed-Mon) This captivating museum in a beautiful heritage building is arranged to look like a typical 19th-century Baba-Nonya residence. The highlight is the tour guides, who tell tales of the past with a distinctly Peranakan sense of humour.

Cheng Hoon Teng Temple BUDDHIST TEMPLE
(Qing Yun Ting or Green Clouds Temple; 25 Jln Tokong Emas; ⊗7am-7pm) **FREE** Malaysia's oldest traditional Chinese temple (dating from 1646) remains a central place of worship for the Buddhist community in Melaka. Notable for its carved woodwork, the temple is dedicated to Kuan Yin, the

Melaka

Jln Peng kalan

Jln Graha Maju

Jln Tan Chay Yan

Jln Hang Tuah

🏛9   11

Immigration
Office

Jln Kubu

Jln Munshi Abdullah

Jln Kampung Hulu

Jln Kee Ann

🏛15

Jln Masjid

Jln Portugis

Jln Bunga Raya

Jln Bendahara

Jln Tokong Emas

Jln Hang Jebat

LITTLE
INDIA

🏛16

Jln Kampung Pantai

Jln Bukit China

25   🍴22

Bukit China
(500m)

2

14

21   🍴17

26

🍴24

4   Jln Tokong Besi

Public
Bank

Jln Bukit China

Jln Temenggong

CHINATOWN

Jln Hang Lekir

Jln Hang Lekiu

🍴28   🍴19

Lg Hang Jebat

1

Jln Hang Kasturi

31

18

Jln Laksamana

Jln Gereja

Jln Banda Kaba

20

Jln Tun Tan Cheng Lock

🍴23

Jln Kota Laksamana

Christ
Church

Tourism
Melaka 🛈

Town
Square

🍴13

12

8 🏛   🏛3

BUKIT
ST PAUL

Sungai Melaka

Democratic
Government
Museum

Jln Kota

⚽7

Jln Chan Koon Cheng

Jln Quayside

Naval
Museum

6

Jln Bandar Hilir

Ferries
to Dumai

5

🛈 Tourism
Malaysia

Tunas Rupat
Follow Me Express

Jln PM2

Jln Merdeka

29

Jln PM8

Jln PM3

Fenix
Internet
Centre

Jln PM4

Jln PM5

30

Jln Melaka Raya 1

Jln Melaka Raya 3

MAHKOTA
MELAKA

32

Mahkota
Medical
Centre

10

Jln Syed Abdul Aziz

27   Airport
Buses

Melaka

Goddess of mercy. Across the street from the main temple is a **traditional opera theatre**.

Masjid Kampung Kling   MOSQUE
FREE This hoary mosque has a multitiered meru roof (a stacked form similar to that seen in Balinese Hindu architecture) that owes its inspiration to Hindu temples, and a Moorish watchtower minaret typical of early mosques in Sumatra.

⊙ Elsewhere

Villa Sentosa   HISTORIC BUILDING
(Peaceful Villa; ☑ 06-282 3988; Jln Kampung Morten; entry by donation; ⊙ flexible but around 9am-6pm) A member of the family will show you around this 1920s Malay house and its collection of objects. Most of all, it's an opportunity to wander through a genuine *kampung* house and chat with your charming host.

Bukit China   CEMETERY
(Jln Puteri Hang Li Poh) More than 12,500 graves, including about 20 Muslim tombs, cover the 25 grassy hectares of this serene hill. **Poh San Teng Temple** sits at the base of the hill and was built in 1795. To the right of the temple is the **King's Well**, a 15th-century well built by Sultan Mansur Shah.

🛏 Sleeping

🛏 Jalan Taman Melaka Raya & Around

A clutch of guesthouses congregate along charmless Jln Taman Melaka Raya (Jln TMR) about a five- to 10-minute walk from Chinatown, while a few other guesthouses have opened up around town closer to the river and Chinatown.

★ **Apa Kaba Home & Stay**   GUESTHOUSE $
(☑ 06-283 8196; www.apakaba.hostel.com; 28 Kg Banda Kaba; r incl breakfast RM40-90; ❀ 🛜) Nestled in a quiet and authentic Malay *kampung* that seems to magically float in a bubble in the heart of town, this homestay-style guesthouse is in a simple yet beautiful old Malay house complete with creaky wood floors, louvred shutters and bright paint.

🛏 Chinatown & Around

Chinatown, Melaka's most scenic area, is a really fun place to stay. Because of preservation restrictions, however, most places only have shared bathrooms. Take town bus 17 (RM1.40) from Melaka Sentral to Town Sq.

★ **River View Guesthouse**   GUESTHOUSE $
(☑ 012 327 7746; riverviewguesthouse@yahoo.com; 94 & 96 Jln Kampung Pantai; dm RM20, r RM45-70;

MALAYSIA MELAKA

❈ 🛜) Bordering the riverfront promenade, this immaculate guesthouse is housed in a large heritage building. There's a big shared kitchen and common area and the hosts begin your stay with a handy map of town and directions to sights and restaurants. The overflow property, **Rooftop Guesthouse** (📞06-327 7746; 39 Jln Kampung Pantai) is almost as nice.

Jalan Jalan Guesthouse   GUESTHOUSE **$**
(📞06-283 3937; www.jalanjalanguesthouse.com; 8 Jln Tokong Emas; dm/s/d RM15/30/50; @🛜) A lovely hostel in a restored shophouse painted periwinkle blue. Fan-cooled rooms with one shared bathroom are spread out over a tranquil inner garden-courtyard. As with some other older places, though, expect noise from your neighbours. Bike rental available.

Ringo's Foyer   GUESTHOUSE **$**
(📞016 354 2223; 46A Jln Portugis; r RM60-90; ❈🛜) Just far enough from central Chinatown to be quiet, but close enough to be convenient, Ringo's is plain and clean, and has friendly staff and a relaxing rooftop chill-out area that plays host to impromptu barbecues.

Tidur Tidur   GUESTHOUSE **$**
(📞014 928 3817; tidurtidurgh@yahoo.com; 92 Lg Hang Jebat; weekdays/weekends per person RM15/20) Rooms with bunk beds are small and boxy and sleep four to five people, but the hip vibe (it's at the back of the owner's unique T-shirt shop) and riverside hang-out area make this a great place to stay.

Voyage Guest House   GUESTHOUSE **$**
(📞06-281 5216; www.voyagetogether.com; Jln Tokong Besi; dm RM15) Clean, industrial-sized dorm rooms and common areas are decorated with a nouveau heritage Chinatown jazz-lounge look. It's run by Voyager Travellers Lounge and you get free bike rental too.

✖ Eating

Melaka's most famous cuisine is Nonya food. Also in the mix is the legacy of the Portuguese, who might have wreaked havoc on civic order, but also built up a tradition for cakes and seafood, which is most obvious in the Eurasian dish of devil's curry. Then there are the immigrant contributions of Indian curries and the ever-versatile Chinese noodle dishes.

★Pak Putra Restaurant   PAKISTANI **$**
(56 Jln Kota Laksmana; tandoori from RM8; ☺dinner, closed every other Mon) This fabulous

DON'T LEAVE MELAKA WITHOUT TRYING…

Cendol Shaved-ice treat with jellies, coconut milk and Melaka's famous cane syrup.

Laksa The regional version is distinguished by its coconut milk and lemongrass-infused broth.

Nonya pineapple tarts Buttery pastries with a chewy pineapple-jam filling.

Popiah An uber-springroll stuffed with shredded carrots, prawns, chilli, garlic, palm sugar and much, much more.

Satay celup Like fondue but better; dunk tofu, prawns and more into bubbling soup to cook it to your liking.

Pakistani place cooks up a variety of meats and seafood in clay tandoori ovens perched on the footpath. Apart from the tandoori try the *taw* prawns (cooked with onion, yoghurt and coriander; RM11) or mutton rogan josh (in onion gravy with spices and chilli oil; RM9).

★Capitol Satay   MELAKAN **$**
(📞06-283 5508; 41 Lg Bukit China; meals around RM8) Famous for its *satay celup* (a Melaka adaptation of satay steamboat), this place is usually packed and is one of the cheapest outfits in town. Stainless-steel tables have bubbling vats of soup in the middle where you dunk skewers of okra stuffed with tofu, sausages, chicken, prawns and bok choy.

★Selvam   INDIAN **$**
(📞06-281 9223; 3 Jln Temenggong; meals around RM8; ✎) ✦ This is a classic banana-leaf restaurant always busy with its loyal band of local patrons ordering tasty and cheap curries, roti and tandoori chicken sets. Even devout carnivores will second-guess their food preferences after trying the Friday-afternoon vegetarian special with 10 varieties of veg.

Hainan Food Street   HAWKER **$**
(Jln Hang Lekir; dishes from RM3; ☺6pm-midnight Fri, Sat & Sun) About a dozen very good food stalls, serving everything from Hainan chicken pie and Nonya laksa to Japanese barbecue, open with the Jonker's Walk Night Market on weekends.

Low Yong Mow   CHINESE $
(🖉06-282 1235; Jln Tokong Emas; dim sum RM1-8; ☺5am-noon, closed Tue) This place is China-town's biggest breakfast treat. With high ceilings, plenty of fans running and a view of Masjid Kampung Kling, the atmosphere oozes all the charms of Chinatown. It's great for early-bus-departure breakfasts and is usually packed with talkative, newspaper-reading locals by around 7am.

Vegetarian Restaurant   VEGETARIAN $
(43 Jln Hang Lekiu; mains around RM3; ☺7.30am-2.30pm Mon-Sat; 🖉) Every Chinatown needs its basic vegetarian cafe and this is Melaka's. All the local specialities from laksa and *won-ton mee* to 'fish balls' are here but, although they taste as good as the real thing, are com-pletely meat-free.

🍸 Drinking & Nightlife

During the weekend night market on Jonker St, the happening bar strip on Jln Hang Le-kir turns into a street party closed off to traf-fic. The alleys in the backpacker area off Jln TMR have lots of watering troughs.

Geographér Cafe   BAR
(🖉06-281 6813; www.geographer.com.my; 83 Jln Hang Jebat; ☺10am-1am Wed-Sun) This venti-lated, breezy bar with outside seating and late hours, in a prewar corner shophouse, is touristy yet still oozes charm. Seat yourself with a beer and applaud long-time musi-cian Mr Burns as he eases through gnarled classics. A tasty choice of local and Western dishes and laid-back but professional serv-ice rounds it all off.

Mixx   NIGHTCLUB
(2nd fl, Mahkota Arcade, Jln Syed Abdul Aziz; ad-mission RM10; ☺10pm-late Tue-Sat) Melaka's hottest club has two parts: Paradox, a laser-lit warehouse-style venue where interna-tional DJs spin techno and electronic beats; and Arris, which has a garden area and live bands. Cover is charged on Friday and Saturday nights only (when the place gets VERY crowded) and includes one drink.

Shantaram   BAR
(9 Jln Tokong Emas; ☺9pm-2am) 'Give piss a chance' is the mantra of this relaxed bar run by famed Melaka hippy artist Soon. If you like Soon's trademark cut-out collage art you can find more of his crazy creations at the used bookshop he runs on Jln Kampung Pantai.

🛍 Shopping

A wander through Chinatown, with its qual-ity assortment of clothing, trinket and an-tique shops, will have you wishing for more room in your pack. **Dataran Pahlawan** (Jln Merdeka), **Hatten Square** (Jln Merdeka) and **Mahkota Parade Shopping Complex** (🖉06-282 6151; Lot B02, Jln Merdeka) are Mela-ka's megamalls, the first two being the more fashion-conscious and the latter being better for practical needs such as a pharmacy or camera shop.

Jonker's Walk Night Market (Jln Hang Jebat; ☺6-11pm Fri-Sun) is Melaka's weekly shopping extravaganza and keeps the shops along Jln Hang Jebat open late while trinket sellers, food hawkers and the occasional for-tune teller close the street to traffic.

ℹ Information

Money changers are scattered about town, especially near the guesthouses off Jln TMR and Chinatown.
Fenix Internet Centre (156 Jln Taman Melaka Raya, Fenix Inn; per hr RM2.5) Also has fax and full business services.
Immigration Office (🖉06-282 4958; 2nd fl, Wisma Persekutuan, Jln Hang Tuah)
Mahkota Medical Centre (🖉06-284 8222, 06-281 3333; Lg Taman Aman) A private hospital offering a full range of services.
Post Office (Jln Laksamana; ☺8.30am-5pm Mon-Sat) Off Town Sq.
Tourism Malaysia (🖉06-283 6220; Jln Mer-deka; ☺9am-10pm) At the Menara Taming Sari tower; has very knowledgeable, helpful staff.

GETTING TO INDONESIA: MELAKA TO BUKITTINGI

Getting to the border High-speed ferries (one-way/return RM110/170, 1¾ hours) make the trip from Melaka to Dumai in Sumatra, Indonesia, daily at 10am. The quay is walking distance or a short túk-túk ride from most hotels and guesthouses and tickets are available at the **Tunas Rupat Follow Me Ex-press** (🖉06-283 2505; G-29 Jln PM10).

At the border Most visitors can obtain a 30-day visa on arrival (VOA) in Indo-nesia, depending on nationality.

Moving on Dumai is on Sumatra's east coast and is a 10-hour bus ride from Bukittinggi.

BUSES FROM MELAKA

DESTINATION	FARE (RM)	DURATION (HR)
Jerantut	25	5
Johor Bahru	21	3
Kota Bharu	53	10
Kuala Lumpur	17.50	2
Mersing	26	4½
Singapore	25	4½

Tourism Melaka (☑ 06-281 4803, 1800 889 483; www.melaka.gov.my; Jln Kota; ⊙ 9am-1pm & 2-5.30pm)

Tourist Police (☑ 06-281 4803; Jln Kota; ⊙ 8am-11pm)

❶ Getting There & Away

Melaka is 144km southeast of KL.

Melaka's local bus station, express bus station and taxi station are all combined into the massive **Melaka Sentral** (Jln Panglima Awang), roughly 5km north of Town Sq. Because Melaka is a popular weekend destination, make advance bus reservations for Singapore and Kuala Lumpur.

Transnational airport buses (RM22; 2¾ hours, departs 5am, 8am, 12.30pm and 2.30pm) run to the KL International Airport and LCCT from Melaka Sentral. Check schedules at the Tourism Malaysia office near the Menara Taming Sari.

❶ Getting Around

Bus 17 runs frequently from Melaka Sentral bus station to Town Sq, Mahkota Parade Shopping Complex and Jln Taman Melaka Raya (RM1.60).

Melaka is a walking city. Bicycles can be hired at some guesthouses and hotels for around RM10 a day.

Taking to Melaka's streets by trishaw is a fun option; they should cost about RM40 per hour, but you'll have to bargain.

Taxis should cost around RM15 for a trip anywhere around town with a 50% surcharge between 1am and 6am.

Cameron Highlands

☑ 05

If you've been sweating through jungles and beaches for weeks and another sticky day will make your clothes unwearable, we grant you a reprieve: the Cameron Highlands. This alpine-scape of blue peaks, cloud forests, fuzzy tea plantations and white waterfalls has a temperature that rarely drops below 10°C or climbs above 21°C. Trekking, tea tasting and visiting local agritourism sites are all on the to-do list. Unfortunately, development, erosion and poorly planned agriculture have taken their toll on the highlands, and landslips and floods have been the environmental by-product.

The Cameron Highlands stretches along the road from the town of Ringlet, through to the main highland towns of Tanah Rata, Brinchang and beyond to smaller villages in the northeast. There are a handful of ATMs in the tourist centre at Tanah Rata.

◉ Sights & Activities

There are over a dozen numbered trekking trails in the hills surrounding Tanah Rata and maps are available at most guesthouses, tour offices and online at www.cameron-highlands.com/jungle-trekking/. Ask about trail conditions before you set out as not all routes are maintained, and people occasionally get lost. At the highest elevations on Gunung Brinchang (take the main road or the steep and challenging trail 1 uphill), you'll be in the unique mossy forest environment that's like a *Lord of The Rings* world of orchids and green fuzz.

There are also strawberry, honey and butterfly farms to visit and produce markets to peruse.

Sungai Palas Boh Tea Estate TEA ESTATE (Gunung Brinchang Rd, Brinchang; ⊙ 9am-4.30pm Tue-Sun) FREE Sungai Palas Boh Tea Estate is the easiest plantation to visit on your own. Tours are free and the tea rooms out the back offer grand vistas. Hitch or take the local bus north from the main (Tanah Rata) bus station, past Brinchang towards Kampung Raja. In between is a tourist strip of strawberry and butterfly farms; hop off the bus at the roadside vegetable stalls and follow the intersecting road.

Sam Poh Temple   BUDDHIST TEMPLE
(Brinchang) `FREE` As unexpected sights in the hills go, a temple dedicated to a Chinese eunuch and naval officer just about tops the list. This temple, just below Brinchang about 1km off the main road, is a brilliant pastiche of imperial Chinese regalia, statuary dedicated to medieval admiral and eunuch Zheng Ho and, allegedly, the fourth-largest Buddha in Malaysia.

Tours

Tour operators in Tanah Rata offer a variety of day trips that include visits to a tea plantation, strawberry farm, flower and cactus nursery, honey farm and butterfly farm for around RM25 per person. Jungle treks to see the *Rafflesia* (the world's biggest flower) start at RM60. The best operators are **Cameron Secrets Tours & Travel** (☑ 016 566 1111; www.fathers.cameronhighlands.com) out of Fathers Guesthouse and **Hill Top Travel & Tours** (☑ 017 594 1192; www.hilltop.my; 24 Main Rd, Tanah Rata).

Sleeping

Book early during peak holiday periods (April, August and December) and weekends. Most guesthouses have a mix of dorms and rooms with shared and private bathrooms,

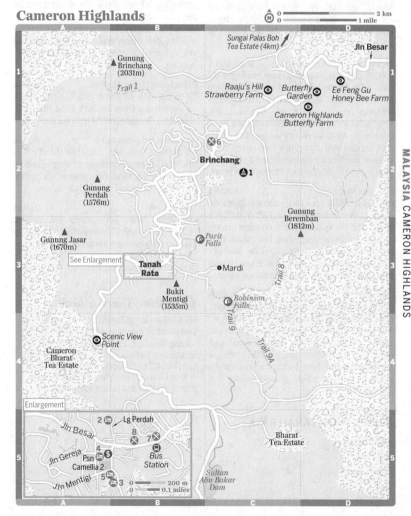

Cameron Highlands

MALAYSIA CAMERON HIGHLANDS

Cameron Highlands

◎ **Sights**

◔ **Sleeping**

◔ **Eating**

and all have hot water. Many also have libraries, video lounges, laundry, internet access and trekking information. All the following are in Tanah Rata.

★**Fathers Guest House**   GUESTHOUSE $
(☑016 566 1111; www.fathers.cameronhighlands. com; 4 Jln Mentigi, Tanah Rata; dm/s/d/tr from RM20/60/70/90; @🛜🖥) The backpacker's stalwart for over 20 years, Fathers has a new, quiet location a few minutes' walk from town with spotless, cheery rooms. The excellent service and amenities (top-notch mattresses, great outdoor lounge area etc) have kept it righteously famous through the years.

Daniel's Lodge   HOSTEL $
(☑05-491 5823; www.daniels.cameronhighlands. com; 9 Lg Perdah, Tanah Rata; dm RM15, r RM25-60; @🛜) The backpacker force remains strong at this long-standing, fun but basic hostel, also known as Kang's. On-site facilities range from a bar to a movie room, cheap tours and lots of inviting communal areas.

Twin Pines   HOSTEL $
(☑05-491 2169; www.twinpines.cameronhighlands. com; 2 Jln Mentigi, Tanah Rata; r RM20-60; 🛜🖥) The social vibe here mingles nicely with the peace and quiet of the flowery front garden. The attic rooms are closetlike with a mattress on the floor, but are a steal; walls are thin but the whole place is clean and friendly.

★**Orchid Lodge**   GUESTHOUSE $$
(☑010 395 1247; www.orchidlodge.cameronhighlands.com; 82D Persiaran Camelia 4, Tanah Rata; dm RM30, r RM90-150; 🛜) Your ever-smiling, orchid-loving, curry-making host Eawaisan gets guests cooking, chatting and dressing up in Bengali 'pyjamas' on a nightly basis. Rooms are colourfully painted, have small balconies and cosy, thick comforters. It's in an apartment above Gossip Corner Restaurant and a little tricky to find.

🍴 Eating

Tanah Rata has some great food and the cheapest places are the mainly **Malay food stalls** stretching down Jln Besar towards the bus and taxi stations – for a splurge in the same area try the steamboat (a Chinese-style fondue where you cook your meat and veg in bubbling vats of soup; RM32 for two people).

Brinchang Night Market   MARKET $
(☑05-491 5188; Brinchang; ⊙6.30-10pm) Snack on everything from savoury fried tidbits to chocolate-dipped strawberries on skewers.

Restoran Sri Brinchang   INDIAN $
(25 Jln Besar, Tanah Rata; mains RM4-20; 🍴) This bright place serves a range of simple Indian fare, including tandoori chicken set meals, fish-head curry and vegetarian dishes.

Lord's Cafe   CAFE $
(Jln Besar, Tanah Rata; mains RM2.50-4.90; ⊙10am-9pm Mon-Fri, 10am-6pm Sat) This cosy cafe serves what are allegedly the Cameron Highlands' best scones – in addition to a variety of teas and no shortage of Christian scripture.

ℹ Getting There & Around

Book tickets at the Tanah Rata bus station. For east-coast destinations, connect through Ipoh.

Kang Tours (☑05-491 5828; 47 Jln Besar) sells tickets for daily minibuses to Pulau Perhentian (RM140, eight hours), including the boat, or Kuala Tahan (Taman Negara; RM95, eight hours). You can also take these minibuses

BUSES FROM TANAH RATA

DESTINATION	PRICE (RM)	DURATION (HR)	FREQUENCY
Butterworth	35	6	2 daily
Kuala Lumpur	30	4	5 daily
Ipoh	18	2	4 daily
Singapore	125	10	10am

partway and get off at Gua Musang to catch the Jungle Railway.

Local buses run from Tanah Rata to Brinchang (RM1.50, every 1½ hours from 6.30am to 6.30pm) and less frequently on to Kampung Raja (RM4), passing butterfly attractions and the turn-off to Sungai Palas Boh.

Taxi services from Tanah Rata include Ringlet (RM20) and Brinchang (RM9).

While we never recommend hitchhiking, many travellers do so here to get between Tanah Rata and Brinchang and the tea plantations beyond.

Ipoh

🚗 05 / POP 704,572

Ipoh (ee-po) is a frenetic city of faded tropical mansions, a lively central *padang* (field) and food so good folks from Penang rave about it. The mellow Old Town showcases elegant colonial architecture and the magnificent train station (known locally as the 'Taj Mahal'). Traffic-clogged, charmless New Town east of the river is home to most of the hotels and restaurants.

The city is a transport hub to many travellers on their way to the Cameron Highlands or Pulau Pangkor. There's a tourist information centre (🚗 05-241 2959, 05-529 0894; Jln Tun Sambathan; ⊙ 8am-5pm Mon-Fri) near the *padang*.

🛏 Sleeping & Eating

Ipoh's culinary specialities include *ayam tauge* (chicken with beansprouts and rice cooked in broth) – look for it at restaurants on Jln Dato Onn Jaafar around the Tengkar Pasar intersection – and Ipoh white coffee, made with palm-oil margarine and served with condensed milk, and served all around town. Many Penang specialities are found here and, some say, are done better.

Steer clear of some of the city's cheap dingy 'hotels' that are actually brothels.

YMCA HOSTEL $
(🚗 05-254 0809; www.ymca-ipoh.com; 211 Jln Raja Musa Aziz; dm RM18, r RM60-80; ❄ 🖥) Ostensibly Ipoh's only real backpacker accommodation, the YMCA features cheap-n-tidy dorm beds and institutional-but-clean budget rooms. It's located about 1km north of the centre of Ipoh; follow Jln Raja Musa Aziz until you reach the northern end of the large park.

Medan Selera Dato' Tawhil Azar MALAYSIAN $
(Jln Raja Musa Aziz; mains RM2-8; ⊙ dinner) Better-known as the Children's Playground, this large food centre has mostly Malay stalls arranged around a small square filled with slides and swings.

★ **Nasi Lemak Ayam Kampung** MALAYSIAN $$
(43-45 Jln Ali Pitchay; mains RM5.50-30; ⊙ 4.30pm-2.30am) This popular restaurant is the place to come for fancy-pants (and delicious) *nasi lemak* (rice boiled in coconut milk, served with fried *ikan bilis* – dried sardines or anchovies – peanuts and a curry dish).

❶ Getting There & Away

Buses run to most destinations on the peninsula. The long-distance bus station called Terminal Amanjaya is 16km north of the train station and the city centre; shuttle buses to the local bus station cost RM2.50 but can take up to an hour. A taxi into town should cost around RM20.

The local bus station is near Old Town about 400m from the train station. Local buses depart from here for outlying regions close to Ipoh, such as Kuala Kangsar (RM6.50) and Tanah Rata in the Cameron Highlands (RM18).

Ipoh's train station (Jln Panglima Bukit Gantang Wahab) is on the main Singapore–Butterworth line. There are daily trains to both KL (RM22 to RM40, 4½ hours) and Butterworth (RM22 to RM36, five hours), the latter continuing to Hat Yai in Thailand (RM35 to RM87, 10 hours).

MALAYSIA IPOH

BUSES FROM IPOH

DESTINATION	PRICE (RM)	DURATION (HR)
Alor Setar	26	4
Butterworth	20	3
Kota Bharu	40	7
Kuala Lumpur	20	3
Lumut	10	2
Melaka	35	5
Tanah Rata	18	2

Lumut

☎05

Lumut is the departure point for Pulau Pangkor. **Tourism Malaysia** (☎05-83 4057; Jln Sultan Idris Shah; ⊙9am-5pm Mon-Fri, 9am-1.45pm Sat) is midway between the jetty and the bus station. Next door you'll find a money changer offering better rates than on Pulau Pangkor, and Maybank further down the street.

Direct buses run to/from KL (RM28, four hours, eight daily), Butterworth (RM18, five hours, three daily) and Melaka (RM42, six hours, two daily). There are no direct buses from Lumut to the Cameron Highlands; take a bus to Ipoh (RM10, two hours, hourly), then transfer to Tanah Rata.

The Pulau Pangkor pier is an easy walk from the bus station. Boats run every 30 to 45 minutes and cost RM10 return.

Pulau Pangkor

☎05 / POP 25,000

Pulau Pangkor is more of a girl-next-door island as opposed to the supermodels of the east coast and Langkawi. That said, it feels good to get away from the glitz and settle into an honest *kampung* with a lazy island atmosphere. The jungle is swarming with monkeys and hornbills, the beaches are dazzling and you can dine nightly on fresh fish while watching the sunset.

Ferries from Lumut first stop on the eastern side of the island at Sungai Pinang Kecil (SPK) and then go to Pangkor Town, where you'll find banks, restaurants and shops.

Sights & Activities

Snorkel gear and boats can be hired at hotels or on the beach. The main beaches are on the west coast. **Teluk Nipah** is a nice white-sand beach near most backpacker accommodation, but walk five minutes north over a headland to find the isle's prettiest beach, **Coral Bay**. Travellers, especially women, should take care on empty stretches at the island's northeastern side and south of Pangkor Town.

There's also good **walking** here; most guesthouses have lots of information and can organise a guide.

Sunset Guesthouse in Teluk Nipah has **hornbill feedings** at 6.30pm nightly when flocks of the birds dart out of the sky to eat tossed bread.

Sleeping & Eating

All these options are in Teluk Nipah on roads running inland from the beach. There are several restaurants along the main road and most serve alcohol.

Budget Beach Resort HOTEL $
(☎05-685 3529; www.budgetbeachresort.com; r RM75-120; ❄📶) The somewhat self-deprecating name doesn't do justice to the pretty, wood chalets here, all equipped with air-con and TV. Service is friendly and professional.

Nipah Bay Villa GUESTHOUSE $
(☎05-685 2198; www.nipahbay.com; s/d from RM30/80; ❄📶) Rooms are in good nick, and the clean and inviting compound has a cafe/restaurant and super-friendly service. The cheapest single is a fan room but all other options have air-conditioning.

Nazri Nipah Camp GUESTHOUSE $
(☎012 585 4511; dm RM15, r RM30-80; ❄📶) Teluk Nipah's long-running backpacker nest has a chilled-out reggae theme including a dreadlocked host. Accommodation ranges from simple A-frames to more comfortable chalets with bathrooms. It also has a social beer garden, communal kitchen and a TV lounge.

Getting There & Around

In the high season, ferries run to and from Lumut and Pangkor Town (return RM10, 30 minutes, departing every 30 to 45 minutes from 6.30am to 8.30pm).

There are no public buses, but pink minibus taxis operate between 6.30am and 9pm. Fares are set for the entire vehicle to/from the jetty in Pangkor Town and go to Teluk Nipah (RM15) and around the island (RM50).

Motorcycles (RM35) and bicycles (RM15) can be rented in Pangkor Town and at main beaches.

Butterworth

This mainland town is a major transport hub for Penang, and it's not a place worth lingering in. The Butterworth–Penang ferry jetty (RM1.20, every 15 to 20 minutes from 5.30am to 12.30am) is conveniently located next to the train and bus stations. Fares for the ferry are charged only for the journey from Butterworth to Georgetown (on Penang); returning to Butterworth is free. Buses run to most destinations on the peninsula.

There are three daily trains to KL (from RM36) from the **train station** (☎04-323

BUSES FROM BUTTERWORTH

DESTINATION	PRICE (RM)	DURATION (HR)
Ipoh	20	3
Johor Bahru	55	12
Kota Bharu	41	7
Kuala Lumpur	35	5
Melaka	45	12
Singapore	60	9

7962). Heading north, there are three daily trains to Hat Yai, Thailand (economy/berth RM34/108); the afternoon service continues to Bangkok, arriving the next day.

Penang

'Pearl of the Orient' conjures romantic images of trishaws pedalling past Chinese shophouses, blue joss smoke and a sting of chilli in the air. Or maybe it's ornate Chinese temples around the corner from grand white mosques sending a call to the midday prayer. But really, whatever you're imagining, chances are that Penang *is* that reality. Add some slick cafes, shopping malls, jungle and a few (mediocre) beaches and you'll have an even clearer picture.

Historically, Penang was the waterway between Asia's two halves and the outlet to the markets of Europe and the Middle East. Today the culture of this region, forged over

Penang Island

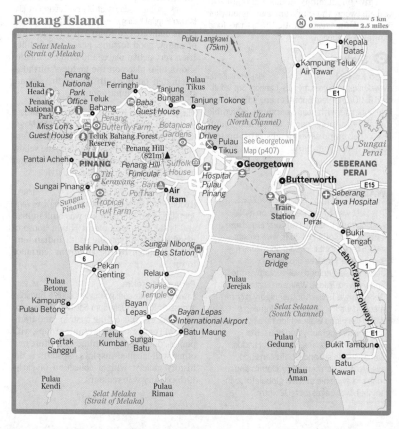

decades of colonialism, commercial activity and hosting tourists, is one of Malaysia's most tolerant, cosmopolitan and exciting – particularly when it comes to the food.

Georgetown

📍 04 / POP 740,200

It's full of car exhaust and has a marked lack of sidewalks, but Georgetown is able to woo even the most acute cityphobe with its explosive cultural mishmash. Dodge traffic while strolling past Chinese shophouses where people might be roasting coffee over a fire or sculpting giant incense sticks for a ceremony. Trishaws, pedalling tourists and the occasional local cruise around the maze of chaotic streets and narrow lanes, past British Raj–era architecture, strings of paper lanterns and retro-chic pubs, boutiques and cafes. Outside the historic centre, soaring skyscrapers and massive shopping complexes gleam high above.

Arrive on an empty stomach and graze at will. Between the city's outrageous hawker food and fine restaurants, this is the food capital of Malaysia.

⊙ Sights

Khoo Kongsi   HISTORIC BUILDING
(www.khookongsi.com.my; 18 Cannon Sq; adult/ child RM10/1; ⊙9am-6pm) Penang's finest clan house is rife with stone carvings, incredible murals, enormous paper lamps and countless other impressive details. The present *kongsi* dates from 1906.

Pinang Peranakan Mansion   MUSEUM
(www.pinangperanakanmansion.com.my; 29 Lebuh Gereja; adult/child RM10/5; ⊙9.30am-5.30pm Mon-Sat) Every door, wall and archway is carved and often painted in gold leaf; the grand rooms are furnished with majestic wood furniture with intricate mother-of-pearl inlay; and bright-coloured paintings and fascinating black and white photos of the family in regal Chinese dress grace the walls.

Cheong Fatt Tze Mansion   HISTORIC BUILDING
(www.cheongfatttzemansion.com; 14 Lebuh Leith; admission RM12; ⊙tours 11am, 1.30pm & 3pm Mon-Sat) This magnificent periwinkle-blue mansion was commissioned by Cheong Fatt Tze, a Hakka merchant-trader known as 'Rockefeller of the East'. Hour-long guided tours give you a glimpse of the beautiful interior, or stay the night at the luxury B&B (rooms from RM420).

Kuan Yin Teng   BUDDHIST TEMPLE
(Temple of the Goddess of Mercy; Lebuh Pitt (Jln Masjid Kapital Keling); ⊙24hr) FREE This temple is dedicated to Kuan Yin – the goddess of mercy, good fortune, peace and fertility. It's a very active place, and Chinese theatre shows take place on the goddess' birthday, celebrated on the 19th day of the second, sixth and ninth lunar months.

Masjid Kapitan Keling   MOSQUE
(cnr Lebuh Buckingham & Lebuh Pitt (Jln Masjid Kapitan Keling); ⊙7am-7pm) FREE Built by Penang's first Indian-Muslim settlers, the yellow Kapitan Keling mosque has a single minaret in an Indian-influenced Islamic style.

Sri Mariamman Temple   TEMPLE
(Lebuh Pitt (Jln Masjid Kapitan Keling); ⊙7am-7pm) FREE Sri Mariamman was built in 1883 and is Georgetown's oldest Hindu house of worship. It is a typically south Indian temple, dominated by the *gopuram* (entrance tower).

Penang Museum   MUSEUM
(www.penangmuseum.gov.my; Lebuh Farquhar; admission RM1; ⊙9am-5pm Sat-Thu) There are engaging exhibits on the customs and traditions of Penang's various ethnic groups, with photos, documents, costumes, furniture and other well-labelled displays. Upstairs is the history gallery, with a collection of early-19th-century watercolours.

Georgetown

MALAYSIA

200 m
0.1 miles

N

Selat Utara (North Channel)

Selat Selatan (South Channel)

Jetty Swettenham

Tourism Malaysia
Victoria Memorial Clock Tower
AirAsia
Langkawi Ferry Service
Immigration Office
HSBC Bank
Standard Chartered Bank
Penang Heritage Trust
Pesara King Edward
Tanjong City Marina
Pengkalan Weld Bus Stop

World War I Memorial
Padang
Lebuh Light
COLONIAL DISTRICT

Jln Tun Syed Sheh Barakbah
Lebuh Duke
Lebuh Leith
Green Hall
Lebuh Bishop
Lebuh Gereja
Lebuh Farquhar
Gat Lebuh Gereja
Gat Lebuh China
Lebuh China
Pengkalan Weld
Lebuh Victoria

Lebuh King
Lebuh Queen
Lebuh Pasar
Lebuh Penang
Lebuh Pantai
Lebuh Ah Quee
Lebuh Armenian
Cannon Square
Lebuh Acheh
Lebuh Buckingham
George Town Festival Office

LITTLE INDIA
LEBUH Pitt (Jln Masjid Kapitan Keling)
Lebuh Muntri
Love La
Lg Stewart
Lg Chulia
Lg Pasar

CHINATOWN
Lebuh Carnarvon
Lebuh Chulia
Lebuh Campbell
Lebuh Cintra
Lebuh Kimberley
Kuala Kangsar
Jln Pintal Tali
Market
Lg Carnarvon
Lebuh Carnarvon

Jln Penang
Jln Leith
Jln Sultan Ahmad Shah
Jln Transfer
Lg Hutton
Lebuh Phee Choon
Lebuh Dickens
Jln Kampung Malabar
Chowrasta Bazaar
Jln Sri Bahari
Jln Datok Koya
Jln Kedah
Lg Argyll
Jln Hutton
Jln Burma
Lg Madras
Lg Kuna
Lg Macalister
Jln Macalister
Jln Dr Lim Chwee Leong
Lebuh Tek Soon
Jln Gladstone
Lebuh Gladstone

Rope Walk
Lebuh 58 Hujong
Local Bus Station

Citibank
Cathay Pacific
Malaysia Airlines
Lg Swanton

1 2 3 4 5 6 7 8 9 10 11 12 13 14 15 16 17 18 20 21 22 23 24 25 26 27 28 29

Georgetown

⊙ Sights

⊟ Sleeping

⊗ Eating

⊕ Drinking & Nightlife

Fort Cornwallis   HISTORIC SITE

(Lebuh Light; adult/child RM2/1; ⊙ 9am-7pm) For all its size, this fort isn't particularly impressive; only the outer walls stand, enclosing a rather aged and spare park within. The fort is named for Charles Cornwallis, perhaps best known for surrendering at the Battle of Yorktown to George Washington, effectively ending the American Revolution.

⊟ Sleeping

Georgetown has plenty of cheap accommodation, mainly clustered in Chinatown along bustling Lebuh Chulia and quieter Love Lane. During holidays, most notably Chinese New Year (January/February), hotels fill up very quickly and prices soar. Cheaper rooms have shared bathrooms.

Roommates   HOSTEL $

(☑ 04-261 1567; www.roommatespenang.com; 178 Lg Chulia; dm incl breakfast RM28-30; ✳ @ 🛜) This new hostel – allegedly the island's smallest – boasts a young, communal, chummy vibe. There are 16 podlike dorm beds and a living roomlike communal area, but the real highlight is Yen, the friendly owner, who leads guests on free pub crawls, eating tours and other activities.

Red Inn   HOSTEL $

(☑ 261 3931; www.redinnpenang.com; 55 Love Lane; dm incl breakfast RM30-34, r incl breakfast RM80-90; ✳ 🛜) The heritage house and communal areas here – including elevated lounge area – are attractive and inviting, but the private rooms can feel like little more than beds in a closet. Dorms range from two to four beds and, although they're a little cramped, they're clean and have good mattresses.

Reggae Penang   HOSTEL $

(☑ 04-262 6772; www.reggaehostelsmalaysia.com; 57 Love Lane; dm incl breakfast RM28-30; ✳ @ 🛜) Another brick in Malaysia's Reggae empire, this expansive heritage building has several four- to 12-bed dorm rooms. Beds are double-decker pod style, and have individual lights, power point and free wi-fi. The lobby, outfitted with pool table and coffee shop,

---

STREET ART

For the 2012 George Town Festival, imaginative murals were commissioned from the young Lithuanian artist Ernest Zacharevic, who combines objects such as a bicycle (on Lebuh Armenian) and a chair (on Lebuh Pitt) with his figurative paintings. The street art has been a smash hit, with visitors constantly lining up to be photographed. For the 2013 George Town Festival many other pieces of street art and installations were created including the series 101 Lost Kittens (www.facebook.com/101lostkittens).

Pick up a free map pinpointing the various art sites from George Town Festival's **office** (www.georgetownfestival.com; 90 Lebuh Armenian) and look at www.penang-travel-tips.com (scroll down and click on George Town Street Art) for up-to-date details of the various public artworks around town.

feels more like a bar than a hostel. Perfect for the social traveller.

★ New Asia Heritage Hotel   HOTEL $$
(☑04-262 6171; www.newasiahotel.com; 71 Lebuh Kimberley; r RM88-158; ❊☎) The 24 rooms in this clean, well-run, comfortable midranger are equipped with TV, air-con and relatively attractive and functional furniture, although some rooms are slightly larger and have huge balconies. If you favour value rather than style, this would be your best option in Georgetown.

Ryokan   HOSTEL $$
(☑04-250 0287; www.myryokan.com; 62 Lebuh Muntri; dm incl breakfast RM35-38, r RM136; ❊@☎) As the name suggests, this new flashpackers has a minimalist – if not particularly Japanese – feel. The dorms, which range from four to six beds, are almost entirely white, and the bunk-style beds include a private light and power point. The similarly white rooms with en suite bathrooms are comfortable yet overpriced, and lack windows.

Moon Tree 47   HOTEL $$
(☑04-264 4021; 47 Lebuh Muntri; r RM80-120; ❊☎) In an antique shophouse, this place has a funky, retro vibe and friendly service, making it perfect for young couples or solo travellers; older travellers or families might be put off by some of the hotel's rather rustic amenities and features.

✕ Eating
Penang cuisine is legendary: Indian, Chinese and Malay purveyors jostle with one another for affection from a constantly snacking populace. Along with Melaka, Penang boasts the indigenous fusion of Baba Nonya cuisine. Lebuh Cintra is lined with bustling Chinese noodle and dim-sum joints. Lg Baru, just off Jln Macalister, has a row of food stalls whipping up satay; however, things don't start sizzling until nightfall. Little India is replete with cheap eating places, especially along Lebuh Pasar and Lebuh Penang, serving up curries, roti, tandoori and biryani.

Tho Yuen Restaurant   CHINESE $
(92 Lebuh Campbell; dim sum RM1-5; ⊙6am-3pm Wed-Mon) Our favourite place for dim sum. It's packed with newspaper-reading loners and chattering groups of locals all morning long, but you can usually squeeze in somewhere – as long as you arrive early. Servers speak minimal English but do their best to explain the contents of their carts.

Joo Hooi   HAWKER $
(cnr Jln Penang & Lebuh Keng Kwee; mains from RM3; ⊙11am-6pm) The hawker centre equivalent of one-stop shopping, this cafe-style joint has all of Penang's best dishes in one location: laksa, *rojak, char kway teow, lor bak* (deep-fried meats served with dipping sauces), *cendol* and fresh fruit juices.

Madras New Woodlands Restaurant   INDIAN, VEGETARIAN $
(60 Lebuh Penang; mains from RM1.50; ⊙8.30am-10pm; ☑) Tasty banana-leaf meals and north Indian specialities are the mainstays, as well as the thickest mango lassi in town. The daily set lunch for RM5.50 might be Penang's greatest food bargain.

Quay Café   SOUTHEAST ASIAN, VEGETARIAN $
(2 Gat Lebuh Gereja; mains RM5-15; ⊙10am-3pm Mon-Sat; ☑) Slick cafeteria serving Asian-style meat-free dishes. Expect set meals, an

PENANG MUST EATS
Penang is known as the hawker capital of Malaysia and most of the city's specialities – claiming mixed Malay and Chinese extraction – are best fetched from a portable cart or food centre. Don't leave without trying:

Cendol Garishly coloured green strands (made from sweetened pea flour) are layered with crushed ice, coconut milk and brown-sugar syrup.

Char kway teow Medium-width rice noodles are stir-fried with egg, vegetables, shrimp and Chinese sausage in a dark soy sauce.

Laksa asam Also known as Penang laksa, this is a fish-broth soup spiked with a sour tang from tamarind paste (*asam*) and a mint garnish; it's served with thick, white rice noodles (laksa).

Rojak A fruit-and-vegetable salad tossed in a sweet tamarind and palm sugar sauce and garnished with crushed peanuts, sesame seeds and chillies.

HAWKER-STALL HEAVEN

Not eating at a stall in Penang is like missing the Louvre in Paris – you simply have to do it. Prices are cheap and most serve beer as well.

Gurney Drive (Persiaran Gurney; ⊙dinner) Penang's most famous food area sits amid modern high-rises bordered by the sea. Try Laksa stall 11.

Lorong Baru (New Lane, cnr Jln Macalister & Lg Baru; ⊙dinner) You'll find all the standard faves along with a few more adventurous choices like the Chee Chong Chook stall, which serves 'pig spare parts porridge'.

Esplanade Food Centre (Jln Tun Syed Sheh Barakbah; ⊙dinner) You can't beat the seaside setting of this food centre, nestled right in the heart of Penang's colonial district.

New World Park Food Court (Lg Swatow; ⊙11am-7pm) Every stall serves something different at this ultramodern, covered food court with mist-blowing fans and shiny industrial decor.

Red Garden Food Paradise & Night Market (Lebuh Leith; ⊙lunch & dinner) Excellent location in the heart of Chinatown with a wide selection including most local specialities, dim sum, pizza and even sushi.

emphasis on noodle dishes, and fresh juices and herbal teas.

Kheng Pin
HAWKER $

(80 Jln Penang; mains from RM4; ⊙7am-3pm Tue-Sun) Locals swear by the specialities at this aged hawker joint, most famously *lor bak* and Hainan chicken rice (steamed chicken with broth and rice), one of the great fast foods of East Asia.

Sky Hotel
CHINESE $

(Lebuh Chulia; mains from RM6; ⊙10am-3pm) It's incredible that this gem sits in the middle of the greatest concentration of travellers in Georgetown, yet is somehow almost exclusively patronised (in enthusiastic numbers) by locals. It is incumbent on you to try the *char siew* (barbecued pork), *siew bak* (pork belly), *siew cheong* (honey-sweetened pork) and roast duck.

Restoran Sup Hameed
MALAYSIAN $

(☑04-261 8007; 48 Jln Penang; mains from RM3; ⊙24hr) With tables sprawling well beyond the actual restaurant like a trail of busy, dining ants down the sidewalk, this ultrapopular smorgasbord at the north end of Jln Penang has everything from spicy *sup* (soup!) and *nasi kandar* (rice served with a variety of curries and side dishes) to *roti canai*. Curried squid is the house speciality.

🍺 Drinking & Nightlife

The cheapest beer is found at the hawker stalls.

★ B@92
BAR

(92 Lebuh Gereja; ⊙noon-late) Food, an eclectic music selection and friendly regulars make B@92 the kind of bar you wish you could throw in your backpack and carry with you across Southeast Asia. Ask about the origin of Aleks' skull ring, and you might just get a discount.

★ Canteen
BAR

(www.chinahouse.com.my; China House, 183B Lebuh Victoria; ⊙5pm-midnight) This is about as close as Georgetown comes to a hipster bar – minus the pretension. Canteen has an inviting artsy/warehouse vibe, there's live music from Thursday to Sunday, and great bar snacks available every night.

Behind 50 Love Lane
BAR

(Lebuh Muntri; ⊙6pm-1am Wed-Mon) Pocket-sized, retro-themed bar that draws a largely local following, despite being close to the backpacker strip. There's a classic rock soundtrack and a short menu of Western-style comfort dishes (RM15 to RM19).

Upper Jalan Penang Bars
BAR

(Jln Penang; ⊙8pm-2am) This strip of road at the far northern end of Jln Penang is Georgetown's commercial-feeling entertainment strip. There's a row of about 10 open-air and air-con bars, but most flock to the mega-clubs: **Slippery Senoritas** offers live music shows that are as corny as the bar's name, although it's popular and all in good fun; **Voodoo** offers a slightly more sophisticated package.

ⓘ Information

Branches of major banks and 24-hour ATMs are concentrated around Kompleks Komtar and around Lebuh Pantai and Lebuh Downing. Almost every guesthouse has internet access, and it's easy to pick up on a wi-fi signal around town. You can stock up on reading supplies at a host of secondhand bookshops.

The monthly *Penang Tourist Newspaper* (RM3) has comprehensive listings of shops, tourist attractions and hotel promotions, as well as detailed pull-out maps. It's usually available free from tourist offices and some hotels.

Hospital Pulau Pinang (🖉 04-229 3333; www.hpp.moh.gov.my; Jln Hospital)

Immigration Office (🖉 04-261 5122; 29A Lebuh Pantai; ⊙ 7.30am-3.45pm Mon-Fri)

Tourism Malaysia (🖉 04-262 0066; www.tourism.gov.my; 10 Jln Tun Syed Sheh Barakbah; ⊙ 8am-5pm Mon-Fri) Georgetown's main tourist information office gives out maps and bus schedules.

ⓘ Getting There & Away

AIR

Airlines with services to Penang:

AirAsia (🖉 04-644 8701; www.airasia.com; Ground fl, Kompleks Komtar)

Cathay Pacific (🖉 04-226 0411; www.cathaypacific.com; 39 Jln Sultan Ahmad Shah, Menara Boustead)

Firefly (🖉 03-7845 4543; www.fireflyz.com.my; Bayan Lepas International Airport; ⊙ 6am-10pm)

Jetstar (🖉 1800 81 3090; www.jetstar.com; Bayan Lepas International Airport)

Malaysia Airlines (🖉 04-262 0011; www.malaysiaairlines.com; Jln Sultan Ahmad Shah, Menara KWSP)

Thai Airways International (🖉 04-226 6000; www.thaiair.com; Wisma Central, 41 Jln Macalister)

BOAT

There are daily ferries from Georgetown to Langkawi (one way/return RM63.50/120, 2½ hours). Boats leave at 8.15am and 8.30am, returning from Langkawi at 2.30pm and 5.15pm. Check the times the day before, as schedules vary.

BUS

Buses to all major towns on the southern peninsula leave from Komtar or Penang's main long-distance bus station in Sungai Nibong. Bus 401 (RM3) will take you to central Georgetown or a taxi will run you for RM25.

There are also bus and minibus services to Thailand: Ko Phi-Phi (RM90, 12 hours), Ko Samui (RM80, 12 hours) and Bangkok (RM115, 17 hours). The minibuses usually don't go directly to some destinations so there are significant waiting times. The train from Butterworth is usually quicker and more comfortable.

ⓘ Getting Around

Penang has a good public transport system that connects Georgetown with the rest of the island.

TO/FROM THE AIRPORT & FERRY TERMINAL

Penang's **Bayan Lepas International Airport** (🖉 04-643 4411) is 18km south of Georgetown.

Taxis take about 45 minutes from the centre of town, while the bus takes at least an hour. Bus 401 runs to and from the airport (RM3) every half-hour between 6am and 11pm daily and stops at Komtar and Weld Quay. A taxi is RM45.

If arriving via the Butterworth–Penang ferry, exit towards Pengkalan Weld and catch the MPPP Free Shuttle or any Kompleks Komtar–bound bus (RM1.50, 15 minutes) to reach accommodation in Chinatown.

BUS

There are several local bus stops in Georgetown. Kompleks Komtar and Pengkalan Weld, in front of the Butterworth–Penang jetty, are two of the largest stops. Most of the buses also have stops along Lebuh Chulia. Fares within Georgetown are RM1.50 to RM4; points beyond are RM1 to RM4 depending on the destination (exact change required).

MOTORCYCLE & BICYCLE

You can hire bicycles from shops at Lebuh Chulia, Batu Ferringhi (13km northwest of Georgetown) and some guesthouses. Bicycles cost RM10, and motorcycles start at RM40 per day. Remember that if you don't have a motorcycle licence, your travel insurance probably won't cover you in the case of an accident.

MALAYSIA PENANG

BUSES FROM PENANG

DESTINATION	PRICE (RM)	DURATION (HR)
Cameron Highlands	35	6
Ipoh	22	2½
Johor Bahru	55	9½
Kuala Lumpur	35	5
Melaka	45	7

TAXI

Penang's taxis all have meters, which many drivers flatly refuse to use, so negotiate the fare before you set off. Typical fares around town cost around RM12.

TRISHAW

Bicycle rickshaws are an ideal way to negotiate Georgetown's backstreets and cost around RM40 per hour but, as with taxis, agree on the fare before departure.

Penang Hill & Around

Once a fashionable retreat for the city's elite, Penang Hill (821m) provides cool temperatures and spectacular views. There are pretty gardens, an old-fashioned kiosk, a restaurant and a hotel, as well as a lavishly decorated Hindu temple and a mosque at the top.

From Kompleks Komtar or at Lebuh Chulia in Georgetown, you can catch one of the frequent local buses (204) to the funicular railway (RM30, every 15 to 30 minutes from 6.30am to 9.30pm). Those who feel energetic can get to the top by an interesting three-hour trek, starting from the Moon Gate at the Botanical Gardens.

Kek Lok Si Temple (⊙9am-6pm) FREE, the largest Buddhist temple in Malaysia, stands on a hilltop at Air Itam. To reach the entrance, walk through the souvenir stalls until you reach the seven-tier, 30m-high **Ban Po Thar** (Ten Thousand Buddhas Pagoda; admission RM2). There are several other temples here, as well as shops and a food court, while a **cable-car** (one way/return RM4/2) whisks you to the highest level, presided over by an awesome 36.5m-high bronze statue of **Kuan Yin**.

Batu Ferringhi
☑04

Following the coastal road east will lead you to Batu Ferringhi, Penang's best beach area, which is lined with resorts at one end and guesthouses at the other. While it doesn't compare with Malaysia's east-coast beaches or those on Langkawi, the sleepy village ambience at the eastern end of the beach is a lovely respite.

Low-key guesthouses are clustered together opposite the beach, and most will give discounts for multiday stays.

Baba Guest House (☑04-881 1686; baba-guesthouse2000@yahoo.com; 52 Batu Ferringhi;

r RM50-95; ✱) is a large Chinese family home with plain rooms (most of which have shared bathrooms) while **Lazy Boys** (☑04-881 2486; www.lazyboystravelodge.net; off Jln Batu Ferringhi; dm RM18, r RM35-150; ✱) is reminiscent of a university dorm hall and run by a Malaysian rocker.

Bus 101 or 102 from Kompleks Komtar takes around 40 minutes to reach Batu Ferringhi and costs RM4.

Teluk Bahang
☑04

There's not enough beach at the sleepy fishing village of Teluk Bahang for any resorts to crop up, so the main thing to do here is tool around the 23-sq-km **Penang National Park** (Taman Negara Pulau Pinang; admission free, canopy walkway adult/child RM7/5; ⊙ canopy walkway 10am-1pm & 2-4pm Sat-Thu).

The area encompasses white, sparkling beaches that are devoid of humans but popular with monkeys, and has some challenging trails through the jungle. Start at the **Penang National Park Office** (☑04-881 3500; ⊙8am-6pm) for maps and suggestions.

If you want to stay the night, stop at **Miss Loh's Guest House** (☑04-885 1227; r RM30-40), a ramshackle throwback to the good ol' days of long-term backpacking. To find the guesthouse, look for a store on Teluk Bahang's main street that says 'GH Information'.

Bus 101 (RM4) runs from Georgetown every half-hour all the way along the north coast of the island to just beyond the roundabout in Teluk Bahang.

Alor Setar
☑04

Most travellers use strongly Islamic Alor Setar as a hopping-off point to Thailand, Langkawi or southern Malaysia. The city's long association with Thailand is evident in Thai temples scattered around town, while its small Chinese population lives in an atmospheric, compact Chinatown.

Comfort Motel (☑04-734 4866; 2C Jln Kampung Perak; r RM28-50; ✱) is a good-value Chinese-style hotel located in a renovated wooden house across from the mosque.

To reach Langkawi from Alor Setar, take one of the frequent local Kuala Kedah buses (RM11, one hour) from the local bus station on Jln Langgar or a taxi (RM20) to the ferry

GETTING TO THAILAND

Alor Setar to Hat Yai

Getting to the border The Bukit Kayu Hitam/Sadao border, 48km north of Alor Setar, is the main road crossing between Malaysia and Thailand for those driving their own cars but there are no taxis or local buses at this border.

At the border The Malaysian border post is open every day from 6am to midnight. All passengers must disembark to clear customs and immigration (both Thai and Malaysian) before reboarding.

Moving on The only way you'll pass through here by public transport is if your bus or minivan, booked from various towns, goes all the way to Hat Yai.

Kangar to Hat Yai

Getting to the border There are regular buses from Kangar (RM4.20), stopping at an unmarked bus stop near BSN bank, about 500m from the Padang Besar border. The taxi stand is on the left before you reach the bus stop. Fares are posted for destinations, including Kangar (RM36) and Alor Setar (RM80).

At the border The Malaysian border post is open every day from 6am to 10pm. All passengers must disembark to clear customs and immigration (both Thai and Malaysian) before reboarding. Very few people, if any, walk the more than 2km of no-man's land between the Thai and Malaysian sides of the border. Motorcyclists shuttle pedestrian travellers back and forth for about RM2 each way.

Moving on There is one daily train connection between Padang Besar and Hat Yai (RM6 to RM13, 50 minutes).

jetty. The main long-distance bus terminal, called Shahab Perdana, is 4km away; a taxi between the two bus stations will cost RM10. Between April and October, from about 7am to 7pm, ferries operate roughly every half-hour in either direction between Kuala Kedah and Kuah on Langkawi (RM23, 1½ hours).

Buses from Alor Setar include Ipoh (RM25, four hours, three daily), Kota Bharu (RM35, six hours, two daily) and Kuala Lumpur (RM40, six hours, hourly).

The **train station** (Jln Stesyen) is a 15-minute walk southeast of town. There is one daily northbound train to Hat Yai, Thailand (from RM9, three hours), and one southbound to KL (seat/berth from RM22/108, 11½ hours).

Kangar

☎04

Kangar, the capital of the state of Perlis, is an extremely laid-back yet pious jumping-off point for the town of Kuala Perlis, about 10km to the southwest, from where there are ferries to Pulau Langkawi. Should you end up here for the night, the basic Chinese-style **Hotel Ban Cheong** (☎04-976 1184; 79 Jln Kangar; r RM60-160; ❄📶) is your best budget option.

Ferries (RM23) depart from the port in Kuala Perlis for Kuah, on Pulau Langkawi, every hour between 7am and 7pm.

To get from Kangar to the pier take a frequent bus (RM2) from the local bus station on Jln Tun Abdul Razak or a taxi for RM14. There are also infrequent buses that run to/from Kuala Perlis to destinations such as Butterworth and KL.

Pulau Langkawi

☎04

Ah, Langkawi. The main island of a string of 99 tropical dots is dominated by knife-edged peaks floating in dark vegetation. Surrounded by ocean blues, this island is an undisputed tropical paradise, despite the resort build-up. Just a little way off the main (quite lovely) beaches is idyllic rural Malaysia, all *kampungs* and oil lamps.

Plus Langkawi is fun – the district's been duty-free since 1986, so is one of the few places in Malaysia you can drink cheaply. You'll also see all sorts of wholesome Malaysian revelry going on.

The Langkawi archipelago sits 30km off the coast from Kuala Perlis and 45km from the border town of Satun. In the southeast corner of Langkawi is **Kuah**, the major town and the arrival point for ferries. On the west coast are **Pantai Cenang** (cha-*nang*), a lively beach strip with shops and restaurants, and adjacent **Pantai Tengah**, which is a bit quieter and a short walk to Pantai Cenang.

🛏 Sleeping

During peak tourist times (November to February) Langkawi's rooms fill quickly but at other times of the year supply far outstrips demand.

Pantai Cenang

The gorgeous 2km-long strip of sand at Pantai Cenang has the biggest concentration of hotels, jet skis and banana boats and is popular with everyone from 20-something backpackers to package tourists. The water is good for swimming, but jellyfish are common.

Lots of backpacker places are found along the small roads running inland away from the beach, so it's easy to shop around.

GETTING TO THAILAND: PULAU LANGKAWI TO SATUN & KO LIPE

Getting to the border There are five daily ferries from Kuah on Pulau Langkawi to Satun (one way RM30, 1¼ hours) on the Thai mainland. From October to May **Tigerline** (www.tigerlinetravel.com) and **Telaga Harbour** (www.telagaharbour.com/Lipeshuttle) run two ferries apiece each way between Langkawi and Ko Lipe (one way RM118, 1½ hours) in Thailand.

At the border You'll get stamped out of Malaysia at immigration at the ferry terminal then get stamped into Thailand when you arrive at the ferry terminal in Satun. Most visitors will get a 30-day Thai visa on arrival.

Moving on From Satun there are more bus and boat connections. From Ko Lipe there are onward services available to as far as Ko Lanta.

Delta Motel   HOTEL **$**
(🖉 04-955 1307; www.facebook.com/deltamotel; r RM60-140, bungalows RM70-100; 🕸 🛜) Tall trees and A-frame bungalows give this – the cheapest beachfront place you'll find on Langkawi – a distinct campground vibe. The aged interiors of the A-frames don't live up to their renovated exteriors, and you're better off staying in one of the new rooms.

Gecko Guesthouse   GUESTHOUSE **$**
(🖉 019 428 3801; rebeccafiott@hotmail.com; dm RM15, r RM35-60; 🕸 🛜) You'll find here a jungly collection of bungalows, chalets and dorms, lots of dreadlocked folk in the common area and very good chocolate milkshakes behind the bar.

Rainbow Lodge   HOTEL **$**
(🖉 04-955 8103; www.rainbowlangkawi.com; dm RM18, r RM50-150; 🕸 @ 🛜) Set a little way back from the beach, this is a suitable option for those needing a cheap place to rest in between eating, drinking, hangover and more drinking.

Pantai Tengah

Pantai Tengah is less built-up and is popular with Malay families. Its main drag is stuffed with upscale eateries and bars.

Zackry Guest House   GUESTHOUSE **$**
(www.zackryguesthouse.langkawinetworks.com; r RM35-90; 🕸 @ 🛜) This messy, friendly, rambling, family-run guesthouse has basic, yet clean and cosy rooms, and lots of ramshackle communal areas. Note that there's a two-night minimum, no phone bookings and only about half of the rooms have attached bathroom.

🍴 Eating

There's a roving *pasar malam* (6pm to 10pm) which is held north of Pantai Cenang Thursdays, in Kuah on Wednesdays and Saturdays and other locations the rest of the week; it's a good place to get authentic Malay food on the cheap. Otherwise, there's a number of cheap *nasi kandar* shops scattered through town with dishes around RM6.

Tomato   MALAYSIAN, INDIAN **$**
(🖉 04-955 5853; Pantai Cenang; mains from RM4; ⊙ 24hr) This busy cluster of stalls under one restaurant name serves good rotis as well as yummy tandoori and an Indian/Malay menu at all hours.

English Tea Room
CAFE **$**

(Pantai Cenang; mains RM6-15; ⊗8am-5pm) Come to this closet-sized cafe for good-quality sandwiches, sausage rolls, pies, scones and cakes. A great choice if you're growing weary of hotel breakfasts.

Palm View
SEAFOOD **$$**

(Pantai Cenang; mains RM7-32; ⊗noon-3pm & 6-11pm) The island has plenty of Chinese seafood places but this is one of the tastiest and is also much cheaper than its competitors. Try the butter fish or steamboat.

🍸 Drinking

Langkawi is arguably the best (and cheapest) spot for a drink in Malaysia. Most bars open around 5pm and close late.

Little Lylia's Chill Out Bar
BAR

(Pantai Cenang; ⊗9am-4am) This longstanding, chummy bar spills out on to Pantai Cenang until the late hours. The chairs and tables may be practically falling apart, but friendly service and a chilled-out vibe hold the place together.

Yellow Café
BAR

(Pantai Cenang; ⊗1pm-1am Tue-Sun) A fun, breezy place with tables right on the beach and a few imported beers. Come between 4pm and 6pm when beers are buy one, get one free.

Sunba Retro Bar
BAR

(www.sungroup-langkawi.com; Pantai Tengah; ⊗7pm-late) A cover band, DJ and, yes, duty-free alcohol, form the fuel that propels parties late into the night here.

ℹ Information

The only banks are at Kuah, although there are ATMs at the airport, Underwater World and Telaga Harbour Park and moneychangers tucked into and around duty-free shops and at Pantai Cenang.

Tourism Malaysia (✆04-966 7789; Jln Persiaran Putra, Kuah; ⊗9am-5pm) Located at the jetty in Kuah, this office offers comprehensive information on the whole island. There's another branch at Langkawi's airport.

ℹ Getting There & Away

AIR

Check prices online – during low season and promotions flying can cost the same as the ferry. **Malaysia Airlines** (✆1 300 88 3000; www. malaysiaairlines.com), **AirAsia** (✆600 85 8888; www.airasia.com) and **Firefly** (✆03-7845 4543;

www.firefly.com.my) all have two or three flights daily between Langkawi and KL. Malaysia Airlines and Firefly fly to Penang and **SilkAir** (✆04-955 9771; www.silkair.com) flies to Singapore.

BOAT

All passenger ferries to/from Langkawi operate out of Kuah. From about 8am to 6.30pm, ferries operate roughly every hour to/from the mainland port of Kuala Perlis (RM18, one hour) and every 30 minutes to/from Kuala Kedah (RM23, 1½ hours).

Langkawi Ferry Services (LFS; ✆04-966 9439; www.langkawi-ferry.com) operates daily ferries between Kuah and Georgetown on Penang (one-way/return RM63.50/120, 2½ hours). Boats depart from Georgetown at 8.15am and 8.30am and leave Kuah at 2.30pm and 5.15pm.

ℹ Getting Around

There is no public transport. Car hire is excellent value starting at RM60 per day, or RM35 for a motorbike. A few places also rent mountain bikes for RM15 per day.

Otherwise, taxis are the main way of getting around. Fixed fares for the entire vehicle (which can be split between passengers) include the following from the Kuah jetty: Kuah town (RM6), Pantai Cenang (RM24) and Pantai Tengah (RM24).

PENINSULAR MALAYSIA – EAST COAST

Refreshingly Malay, the peninsula's east coast is an entirely different experience from the more Westernised, traffic-clogged west coast. Headscarves, skullcaps and the hauntingly melodious call to prayer are as ubiquitous here as the white-sand beaches that fringe the sunrise-drenched coasts and jewel-like islands.

Johor Bahru

✆07

The frenetic border town of Johor Bahru (known as JB) is connected to Singapore by the 1038m-long Causeway bridge. Over the last few years the city has been cleaned up and has quietly broken out of its old mould as a dodgy, lacklustre border town to become a really decent place to hang out. Indian women hawk gold bracelets on the sidewalk as incense wafts from Chinese shops, giving the walkable heritage downtown area an exotic vibe. To check it out, walk west from the Customs, Immigration and Quarantine complex but keep alert for motorcycle snatch thieves – crime here is still higher than in most Malaysian towns.

◉ Sights

Heritage District NEIGHBOURHOOD
Wandering around the heritage area between Jln Ibrahim and Jln Ungku Puan is a real highlight of JB. Walk past colourful, old shophouses filled with sari shops, barbers, Ayurvedic salons, gorgeous temples and old-style eateries.

Royal Abu Bakar Museum MUSEUM
(☑ 07-223 0555; Jln Ibrahim; adult/child US$7/3; ◷ 9am-5pm Sat-Thu, ticket counter closes 4pm) The marvellous Istana Besar, once the Johor royal family's principal palace, was built in Victorian style by Anglophile sultan Abu Bakar in 1866. It was opened as a museum to the public in 1990 and displays the incredible wealth of the sultans. It's now the finest museum of its kind in Malaysia, and the 53-hectare palace grounds (free entry) are beautifully manicured.

▭ Sleeping & Eating

JB has some of the priciest rooms in Malaysia, but they are much cheaper than anything you'll find in Singapore. Most budget hotels ask for a room deposit of around RM30 that's returned to you when you check out. The food here, however, is great-value, tasty and you can get your drink on for cheap at the ZON (☑ 07-221 9999; Zon Ferry Terminal) duty-free clutch of bars at the ferry terminal.

Meldrum Hotel HOTEL $
(☑ 07-227 8988; www.meldrumhotel.com; 1 Jln Siu Nam; dm RM40, s/d with shared bathroom RM70/80, r with bathroom from RM90; ❄ ☎) All options here are air-conditioned, clean, spacious and freshly painted, and the rooms have TVs, free drinking water and kettles. It's worth upgrading to a RM100 superior room with attached bathrooms and free wi-fi – these are downright plush. Dorms are cramped, air-conditioned and filled mostly with local men.

JB Hotel HOTEL $
(☑ 07-223 4989; 80A Jln Wong Ah Fook; r RM70; ❄) Small air-con rooms come with TV, tiled floor and sinks, but bathrooms are shared. It's family-run, helpful and very clean.

Medan Selera Meldrum Walk STREET FOOD $
(Medan Selera Meldrum; meals from RM3; ◷ dinner) Every late afternoon, the little food stalls crammed along this alley (parallel to Jln Meldrum) start frying up everything from *ikan bakar* (barbecued fish) to the local curry laksa. Wash down your meal with fresh sugar-cane juice or a Chinese herbal jelly drink. Nothing here is excellent but it's all good.

ⓘ Information

There's a **Tourism Malaysia** (◷ 8am-4.30pm Mon-Thu, 8am-12.15pm & 2.45-4.30pm Fri, 8am-12.45pm Sat) in the Customs, Immigration and Quarantine complex just as you clear Singapore immigration that has some handy maps.

GETTING TO INDONESIA: JOHOR BAHRU TO RIAU ISLANDS

Getting to the border There are several daily departures to Batam (one way RM69, 1½ hours) and Tanjung Pinang on Bintan (one way RM86, 2½ hours), both islands (part of Indonesia's Riau Islands) with connections to Sumatra, Indonesia. Ferries depart from the ZON Ferry Terminal (for schedule details see www.zon.com.my/ferry.html) that's serviced by buses 10A, SS, 22, 123 and 507A from downtown Johor Bahru.

Additional boats depart from Kukup, southwest of JB, to Tanjung Balai on Karimun (RM130; three times daily) and to Sekupang, Batam (RM165; twice daily) also in Indonesia; see www.ferrytuah.comoj.com for schedules and reservations. Buses travel to Kukup from Johor Bahru (RM7, 1½ hours) and KL (RM28, 3½ hours). A taxi from JB to Kukup is RM80.

At the border From JB there's a RM10 seaport tax as you're stamped out of Malaysia; port fees at Kukup are RM25 per person.

Moving on From Batam, boats serve the mainland Sumatran ports of Dumai, Palembang and Pekanbaru, which are serviced by buses. From Bintan and Karimun ferries run via Batam to go onward to Sumatra. Thirty-day visas on arrival are available at all these ports and cost US$25.

BUSES FROM JOHOR BAHRU

DESTINATION	PRICE (RM)	DURATION (HR)
Butterworth	69	12
Ipoh	30	7
Kota Bharu	51	10
Kuala Lumpur	34	4
Kuala Terengganu	35	9
Kuantan	22	5
Melaka	21	3
Mersing	13	3

❶ Getting There & Away

AIR

JB is served by **Malaysia Airlines** (☑ 07-334 1011; www.malaysiaairlines.com.my), **Firefly** (☑ 03-7845 4543; www.firefly.com.my) and **AirAsia** (☑ 1300 889 933; www.airasia.com; Tune Hotel). Most domestic flights connect through KL, a four-hour bus ride away. Larkin bus station is 2.5km north of the city centre.

JB's airport is 32km northwest of town at Senai.

BOAT

Ferries leave Johor Bahru for islands in Indonesia.

BUS & TAXI

Most people travel from Johor Bahru to Singapore by bus. Johor Bahru's long-distance bus station is Larkin station, located 5km north of the centre. Buses run to and from Larkin to most parts of the country.

Long-distance taxis also leave from Larkin (there's a price list at the stand). A local taxi from central JB to the bus station should cost RM8. Metered taxis are found just beyond the bus station gate past berth 33.

TRAIN

Daily express trains depart Johor Bahru three times per day for Kuala Lumpur (from RM56). It is also possible to change at Gemas (from RM30) and hop aboard the Jungle Railway for connections to Jerantut (if you're headed for Taman Negara) and Kota Bharu.

Mersing

☑ 07

The jumping-off point for Pulau Tioman, Mersing is busy and compact, and has everything that travellers might need: wi-fi, good sleeping options, grocery stores, cold beer and a pharmacy. The river is clogged with colourful fishing boats but beyond the riverfront there's not much to explore.

MALAYSIA MERSING

GETTING TO SINGAPORE: JOHOR BAHRU TO SINGAPORE

Getting to the border There are frequent buses between JB's Larkin bus station, 5km north of the city, and Singapore's Queen St bus station. Most convenient is the Causeway Link (www.causewaylink.com.my; from JB/Singapore RM2.50/S$2.40; ⊙ 6.30am-midnight, every 10 minutes). Alternatively, there's the slower city bus 170 (RM2). The Trans Star Cross Border Coach (www.transtar.travel/crossborder/; from JB/Singapore RM7/S$7; ⊙ 5am-9pm) runs hourly between Kotaraya 2 Terminal in Johor Bahru and Singapore's Changi Airport – if you don't want to go all the way out to Kotaraya 2, hop off at Malaysian customs where Causeway Link buses depart to Larkin from the basement level.

At the border All buses stop at Malaysian immigration. Disembark from the bus with your luggage and go through immigration then reboard your bus (keep your ticket). The bus then brings you to Singapore immigration where you get off the bus with your luggage once more, clear Singapore customs then get back on your bus (again keep your ticket), which will take you to Singapore's Queen St bus station.

Moving on After clearing Singapore immigration, there are buses from Queen St, taxis and an MRT station that can take you anywhere you need to go in the city. There are ATMs at Singapore immigration and at the Queen St bus station if you need Singapore dollars.

BUSES FROM MERSING

DESTINATION	PRICE (RM)	DURATION (HR)	FREQUENCY
Johor Bahru	12.70	3	2 daily
Kuala Lumpur	41.50	6	5 daily
Kuala Terengganu	39	9	2 daily
Kuantan	19	5	2 daily
Singapore	20	3	2 daily

🛏 Sleeping & Eating

There are several places around town for *roti canai* and *kopi* (coffee) and seafood stalls open up nightly along Jln Endau by the river.

Hotel Embassy HOTEL $
(☏ 07-799 3545; 2 Jln Ismail; d/tr/q RM45/55/65; ❄ 🛜) This is a fabulous choice compared with the other cheapies in town, and is a great place to clean up and get back to reality after bumming it on island beaches. All rooms are huge, bright, have cable TV, air-con and attached bathrooms.

Omar's Backpackers' Hostel HOSTEL $
(☏ 019 774 4268, 07-799 5096; Jln Abu Bakar; dm/d RM15/30; 🛜) At this tiny, social backpackers pad very near the jetty, your experience will depend on Omar's variable mood. Reservations are recommended during the peak season.

ℹ Information

There are a few ATMs in the main part of town.
Mersing Tourist Information Centre (Jln Abu Bakar; ⏰ 8am-5pm, Mon-Sat) is on the road to the pier; this place is helpful and has all the bus schedules.

ℹ Getting There & Away

Most buses depart from the station near the bridge on the river although a few leave from bus company offices near the pier (which can be convenient if it's brutally hot or raining). Some buses will also drop you at the pier – it pays to ask. There are ferries to/from Pulau Tioman.

Pulau Tioman

☏ 09

From late nights at Salang bars to days of trekking through the wild jungles, surfing the beaches at Juara or diving the reefs and wrecks off the coast, Tioman has as much action or nonaction as anyone could hope for. The proximity to Singapore and the availability of upscale digs has made Tioman particularly popular with Singaporean and domestic tourists but the island is so big and the locals are so mellow that the weekend crowds are absorbed without affecting the island's laid-back vibe.

During the east-coast monsoon, from about November to March, boat services to the island are infrequent or suspended and most guesthouses and restaurants close – although something will always be open. If you plan to visit Tioman during this time be prepared to get stuck in Mersing or on the island overnight or longer.

Most budget accommodation is clustered in Air Batang (ABC) and Salang on the northern end of the west coast. Salang has wider stretches of sand and the mood is decidedly 'spring break', while ABC has a more Malay, chill-out-with-your-friends kind of vibe. On the east coast of the island, Juara has a stunning beach, surfing during the monsoon and affordable accommodation. Other small beaches reachable only by boat run south along the west coast.

⊙ Sights & Activities
Diving

Most places rent snorkelling gear (RM10 per day) and you can join day trips to Pulau Tulai, better known as Coral Island, where you can swim with fish and sometimes sharks.

Open-water dive courses cost from RM850, and fun dives are around RM100. There are nearly as many dive shops as accommodation options, so shop around for the best deal.

Hiking

There's a fantastic 7km hike that crosses the island's waist from Tekek to Juara (carry plenty of water). It takes around 2½ hours, is steep in parts and starts near the jetty in Tekek. Over the hill on the Juara side there's a small, hidden waterfall (look for a trail next to an abandoned cement house off the paved jeep road), and the jungle is awesome.

There are also several other trails on the island connecting beaches and climbing to more waterfalls.

🛏 Sleeping & Eating

In late July through August, accommodation becomes tight on weekends. Either side of these months it's a buyer's market. Budget digs around the island are nearly identical and are of low standard – think old mattresses and saggy floors – but most do have private bathrooms, fans and mosquito nets.

Restaurants, with similar menus, are usually attached to chalet operations. ABC, Tekek and Salang all have small convenience stores.

🛏 Air Batang (ABC)

The far northern and southern ends of the beach here have the best sand while some in-between areas are rocky and marshy. At night the whole beach ends up drinking at **Sunset Corner** at the southern end of the beach.

★ ABC Chalet   CHALET $
(📞 09-419 1154; d chalets RM50-150; ❄ 🛜)
Accommodation is spread over pleasant, well-tended grounds, with a couple of chalets almost on the beach. The large, pricier chalets come with hot water, air-con, sea views, hot showers, a freezer, and tea- and coffee-making facilities.

Mokhtar's Place   CHALET $
(d RM35-55; ❄ @) There's a very mellow family vibe going on at this quiet spot on the south end of ABC. Cheaper bungalows are set back from the beach under pleasant shady trees and all rooms are spacious and clean. Internet is (sporadically) available for RM10 per hour.

Johan's Resort   CHALET $
(📞 09-419 1359; dm/chalets/f RM20/40/100) A friendly, welcoming place offering tonnes of information. The two four-bed dorms up the hillside are decent value; the chalets are pretty much the same as other cheapies on the beach.

🛏 Salang

The small bay to the south of Salang has a beautiful beach and swimming area backed by a murky river that's teeming with giant monitor lizards.

Ella's Place   CHALET $
(📞 09-419 5004; chalets RM60-120; ❄) There's usually a lounge-able patch of sand at this cute-as-a-button family-run place at the quiet northern end of the beach. There are 10 clean chalets (some with air-con) and a small cafe.

Salang Indah Resort   RESORT $$
(📞 09-419 5015; chalets from RM60-185; ❄ @) An expanse of chalets seemingly sprawls forever at this resort complex. Most rooms aren't in tip-top condition, but if you look at several you'll probably find one to your liking.

🛏 Juara

There's little to do in Juara except swim, surf (between November and April), snooze under the swaying palms (but beware of sand flies) or take a wander into the jungle. It's actually two connected beaches and both are wide and white.

★ Beach Hut   HOSTEL $
(📞 012 696 1093; timstormsurf@yahoo.au; camp sites with 2-person tent RM15, dm/chalets from RM15/35; 🛜) Now in two locations a few hundred metres down the beach from each other, the bohemian-style decorated, eco-friendly buildings range from A-frames to dorm rooms and a more luxurious

Pulau Tioman Ⓝ 0 ———— 4 km / 0 ———— 2 miles

MALAYSIA PULAU TIOMAN

two-storey house with two suites. Beachside tent and sleeping-bag accommodation is available, as are surf lessons (RM60 per hour) with surf legend Tim Brent.

★ **Bushman** CHALET **$**
(☎ 09-419 3109; matbushman@hotmail.com; chalets with fan/air-con RM50/80; ❄ 🛜) Nabbing one of Bushman's five new varnished wood chalets, with their inviting wicker-furnished terraces, is like winning the Juara lottery – reserve in advance! The location is right up against the boulder outcrop and a small river that marks the end of the northern beach.

ⓘ Information

You'll be charged a RM5 Department of Marine Parks, Malaysia conservation fee and a RM20 Johor National Park Corporation fee before you board the ferry in Mersing.

Connected to ABC by a footpath over a rocky headland, Tekek is the island's main village, where you'll find a bank, the island's only ATM, telephones and a post office. The duty-free shop at the airport in town sells cheap beer and chocolate.

ⓘ Getting There & Away

Berjaya Air (☎ in KL 03-7846 8228, in Singapore 02-6481 6302; www.berjaya-air.com) has daily flights to/from KL and Singapore.

Mersing is the ferry port for Tioman (RM35, two to three hours). There are usually two to six ferry departures throughout the day between 7am and 5pm, but specific departure times vary with the tides. Ferries drop off passengers in south-to-north order on the island.

ⓘ Getting Around

You can walk from ABC to Tekek in about five minutes. But you'll need to charter a boat through a guesthouse or restaurant to travel between ABC and Salang (RM30).

To get to Juara hire a 4WD taxi (RM25 to RM40 for up to four people) in Tekek – better is to book your room in advance so your host can pick you up at the Tekek pier. Alternatively, you can walk through the jungle to Juara from Tekek (7km).

Kuantan
☎ 09

Many travellers find themselves on an overnight stopover in Kuantan, the pious and functional state capital, as it's the main transit point between Taman Negara and Pulau Tioman. Kuantan's star attraction is **Masjid Negeri**, one of the east coast's most impressive mosques. At night it's a magical sight with its spires and lit turrets.

🛏 Sleeping & Eating

The **food stalls** near the old long-distance bus terminal in town are your best bet for cheap eats.

Kuantan Backpackers HOSTEL **$**
(39 Jln Tun Ismail; dm RM28-35; 🛜) This new, very friendly, clean hostel is the most geared towards foreigners in town and gets excellent reviews from travellers. There's a women-only dorm, fan and air-con dorms, a kitchen and hot-water showers – the central location can't be beat.

★ **Ana Ikan Bakar Petai** SEAFOOD **$$**
(Tanjong Lumpur; ⊙ lunch & dinner) If it's authentic you're after, look no further than this huge open-air seafood restaurant across the river on the island of Tanjong Lumpur. An extraordinary selection of freshly caught fish, crab and shrimp is priced by weight.

ⓘ Information

Banks are clustered at Jln Bank and there are plenty of ATMs around Jln Haji Abdul Aziz (the continuation of Jln Mahkota).

Tourist Information Centre (☎ 09-516 1007; Jln Mahkota; ⊙ 8am-1pm & 2-5pm Mon-Thu, 8am-12.45pm & 2.45-5pm Fri) Has particularly helpful staff and a range of useful leaflets.

ⓘ Getting There & Away

AIR

Kuantan airport (☎ 09-538 2923; Lapangan Terbang Sultan Ahmad Shah) is 15km from the city centre; take a taxi (RM30). **Malaysia Airlines** (☎ 09-531 2123; www.malaysiaairlines.com.my) has direct flights to KL (three daily), and **Firefly** (☎ 03-7845 4543; www.firefly.com.my) also has two daily flights to/from KL's Subang Airport.

BUS & TAXI

All long-distance buses arrive and depart from the new **Terminal Sentral Kuantan** (Indera Mahkota) 11km from Kuantan. Rapidkuantan bus 303 (RM2) shuttles between the station and **Hentian Bandar** (City Bus Station; Jln Stadium) every 20 minutes between 6am and midnight.

There are two long-distance taxi stands in town – one on Jln Stadium near Hentian Bandar, and the other on Jln Mahkota. Destinations and costs (per car) include Mersing (RM220), Cherating (RM80) and Jerantut (RM200).

Kuantan

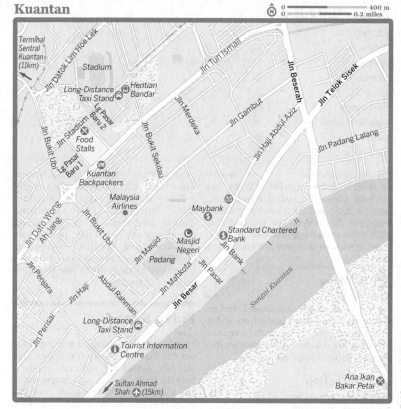

0 ————— 400 m
0 ————— 0.2 miles

Cherating

📍09

Back when there were no direct transport links between Taman Negara and the Perhentian Islands, Cherating was a major backpacker stop. Nowadays only dedicated wanderers, surfers and a few intrepid backpackers make it out this way, but most who do find that there's something special about this place.

The village itself is just a strip of guesthouses and shops with more monkeys, monitor lizards and cats walking around than humans, but between the cracks are a resident band of hipster Malay surfers, artists and *kampung* folk who genuinely want to hang out over a beer and share in the holiday spirit.

🏃 Activities

There's an exceptional amount to do in Cherating: try surfing from November to March – surf lessons and board rentals are

available with **Satu Saku** (Main Rd; ⊙ Nov-Mar), go on snorkelling tours (RM50), firefly viewing tours (RM20), try batik making (from RM25) or go check out the **Turtle Sanctuary** (entry by donation; ⊙ 9am-5pm Tue-Sun) to see the baby and rehabilitating turtles. The guesthouses can set you up with operators.

🍴 Sleeping & Eating

Cherating has a 'strip' where most of the restaurants and guesthouses congregate. Book in advance during the monsoon surf season from November through January.

Maznah's Guest House   CHALET **$**
(📞 09-581 9072; chalets incl breakfast RM30-35) Spirited kids happily chase chickens around the collection of sturdy wooden bungalows here. The owners speak little English and *nasi lemak* is served for breakfast, making this a great, friendly place to go local.

BUSES FROM KUANTAN

DESTINATION	PRICE (RM)	DURATION (HR)
Butterworth	53	8
Cherating	5	1½
Jerantut	18	3½
Kota Bharu	31	7
Kuala Lumpur	26	4½
Kuala Terengganu	18	3
Kota Bharu	32	7
Marang	15	3

Payung Guesthouse CHALET $
(☑ 09-581 9658; d/q chalets RM50/70; ☎) This excellent, friendly main-drag choice backs onto the river, with neat rows of ordinary chalets in the garden. The attached tour office offers everything from bike and surfboard rentals to mangrove or snorkelling tours.

 Drinking

Don't Tell Mama BAR
(☺ till late) Don't Tell Mama, located right on the beach, is the hippest bar in town and is a great place to stop by day or night to make friends over a cold beer. Impromptu barbecues and parties are the norm.

ℹ Information

There are no banks in Cherating.
Travelpost (☑ 09-581 9796; ☺ 9am-11pm) Can organise bus tickets to just about anywhere (takes a commission). There's also a book exchange, bike hire (per hour RM3), internet access (per hour RM4) and tourist information.

ℹ Getting There & Away

Cherating doesn't have a bus station, but any Kuantan–Terengganu bus will drop off passengers at the turn-off to the village road, which will involve a short stroll. To go south from Cherating you'll need to wave down the local bus bound for Kuantan that runs every 30 minutes (RM5, 1¼ hours); for Kuala Terengganu book long-distance bus tickets (RM17, three hours, frequent) through Payung Guesthouse or Travelpost.

Marang

Marang is the jump-off point for ferries to Pulau Kapas and a quiet fishing town, a little overbuilt by the highway but still pleasant in a rural way. If you're around on Sunday,

check out the excellent **Sunday Market**, which starts at 3pm near the town's jetties.

There are regular local buses to/from Kuala Terengganu (RM3). Buy long-distance bus tickets at the Kapas boat agents near the pier. There are buses to/from Kuala Lumpur (RM35, two daily, eight hours), Johor Bahru (RM36, two daily, nine hours), and Kuantan (RM15, four hours, five daily) via Cherating.

Pulau Kapas

☑ 09

There's not much action on tiny Pulau Kapas, but that's the beauty of the place. Outside July, August and weekends, expect to have the white beaches, aquamarine waters and wild jungle trails to yourself. Note that accommodation on the island shuts down during monsoon season (November to March).

All accommodation, the few restaurants and handful of dive shops are clustered together on two small beaches on the west coast, but you can walk around the headlands to quieter beaches. The diving, run by **Dive Kapas** (☑ 019 983 5879, 019 379 6808; www.divekapas.com; two dives RM180, PADI open-water courses RM1100), is excellent, with prices similar to those in the Perhentian Islands.

The most chilled-out option on Kapas is **Capt's Longhouse** (☑ 012 377 0241; www.captslonghouse.blogspot.com; dm/d RM30/60), a rustic but lovely elevated jungle longhouse with oil paintings by the owner, hammocks and mellow tunes on the sound system. Otherwise the Dutch-run **Kapas Beach Chalet** (KBC; ☑ 019 343 5606; dm RM15-20, r RM40-70; ☎), with accommodation choices from dorms to A-frames and with a good restaurant, is a social choice.

Six kilometres offshore from Marang, Kapas is reached by boats in 15 minutes from Marang's main jetty. Tickets (RM40 return) can be purchased from any of the agents nearby and boats depart when four or more people show up. Be sure to arrange a pick-up time when you purchase your ticket. You can usually count on morning departures from 8am.

Kuala Terengganu

☑ 09

A microcosm of Malaysia's economic boom: fishing village finds oil, money flows in, modernity ensues. Here and there you'll find an old *kampung* house seemingly hiding among the high-rises, and these glimpses, plus a seafood-heavy local cuisine and a slew of beautiful mosques, make Kuala Terengganu worth a day or two of exploration.

Note that Kuala Terengganu is very, very Islamic and official business is closed on Friday and Saturday.

◉ Sights

Central Market   MARKET
(cnr Jln Kampung Cina & Jln Banggol; ⊙8am-5pm Sat-Thu) The central market is a lively place to graze on exotic snacks, and the floor above the fish section has a wide collection of batik and *kain songket* (handwoven fabric). Across from the market is a flight of stairs leading up to **Bukit Puteri** (Princess Hill), a 200m hill with city vistas and the remains of a fort.

Chinatown   NEIGHBOURHOOD
Tiny Chinatown centred on Jln Kampung Cina (also known as Jln Bandar) is KT's most interesting area to explore.

Kompleks Muzium Negeri Terengganu   MUSEUM
(Terengganu State Museum; ☑ 09-622 1433; http://museum.terengganu.gov.my; adult/child RM15/10; ⊙9am-5pm Sat-Thu) On 26 hectares of land, exhibits here range from historical and slightly bizzare to an exhibit touting the goodness of the oil industry. To get here, take minibus 10 (RM1), marked 'Muzium/Losong', from Kuala Terengganu's main bus station. A taxi from Kuala Terengganu will cost RM20.

Pulau Duyung Besar   ISLAND
In the middle of Sungai Terengganu, Pulau Duyung Besar carries on the ancient boat-building tradition handed down for generations. Take the local ferry (60 sen) from the jetty near the Immigration Office across from Bukit Puteri.

Kuala Terengganu

Kuala Terengganu

⊙ Sights
  1 Central Market B1
  2 Chinatown B1

🛏 Sleeping
  3 Ping Anchorage Travellers' Inn B1

🍴 Eating
  4 Hawker Centre B2
  5 T. Homemade Cafe B2

ℹ Information
  6 Tourist Information Office B1

ℹ Transport
  7 Express Bus Station C1
  8 Main Bus Station B1
  9 Main Taxi Stand B2

🛏 Sleeping & Eating

Ping Anchorage
Travellers' Inn   HOTEL $
(☑ 09-626 2020; www.pinganchorage.com.my; 77A Jln Sultan Sulaiman; r RM25-65; 🛜) Spread over two floors above the travel agency of the same name, Ping's is central, clean and tidy. The inn's antique-filled rooftop cafe, which serves beer and food, has a spectacular view of the city.

T. Homemade Cafe   CHINESE, MALAYSIAN $
(Jln Kampung Cina; mains from RM5; ⊙ lunch & dinner) Right next to the Chinatown gate, this place is a conglomeration of a few Chinese and Malay food stalls in a shared space that serve everything from noodles and claypot to fresh juices. There's also a great homestay upstairs with doubles from RM50.

Hawker Centre   HAWKER $
(off Jln Kampung Cina) Chinatown's outdoor hawker centre is divided into Chinese and Malay sections and sizzles with cooking and socialising at night.

ℹ Information

Jln Sultan Ismail is the commercial hub and home to most banks, which are open 9.30am to 3.30pm, except Friday.

Tourist Information Office (☑ 09-622 1553; www.tourism.terengganu.gov.my; Jln Sultan Zainal Abidin; ⊙ 9am-5pm Sat-Thu) Brochures on Terengganu.

ℹ Getting There & Away

AIR

Malaysia Airlines (☑ 09-662 6600; www.malaysiaairlines.com) and **AirAsia** (☑ 600 85 8888; www.airasia.com) have direct flights to KL, and **Firefly** (☑ 03-7845 4543; www.firefly.com.my; airport) has flights to/from Singapore four times per week.

BUS & TAXI

The **main bus station** (Jln Masjid Abidin) is for local buses. Some long-distance buses depart from here as well, but most use the **express bus station** (Jln Sultan Zainal Abidin), in the north of town. The main taxi stand is at Jln Masjid Abidin across from the main bus station.

Kuala Besut

The primary jetty town for boats to Pulau Perhentian is Kuala Besut (bee-su), south of Kota Bharu. It's a sleepy fishing village with a mini-mall of collaborating boat-company tour offices.

There are direct buses from Kota Bharu (RM6) but the trip takes two hours so it makes more sense to take a minibus (RM35 per person) or share a taxi (RM80 for the whole taxi). From the south, you can go to/from Kuala Terengganu by bus (RM11) or taxi (RM100 per car). There are also two daily buses to/from KL (RM42, nine hours).

The agents at Kuala Besut's jetty also sell minibus tickets to the Cameron Highlands (RM70, six hours) and Taman Negara (RM65, eight hours).

BUSES FROM KUALA TERENGGANU

DESTINATION	STATION	PRICE (RM)	DURATION (HR)	FREQUENCY
Kota Bharu	Express	15	3	7 daily
Kuala Besut	Express	11	2½	5 daily
Kuala Lumpur	Express	40	7	frequent
Marang	Main	2	30 min	every ½hr, 6.30am-6.30pm
Melaka	Express	44	9	1 daily
Mersing	Express	34	7	2 daily

MALAYSIA KUALA BESUT

Pulau Perhentian

☑ 09

Long Beach on Pulau Kecil of the Perhentian Islands is not only one of Malaysia's most popular backpacker spots, it's also one of the cheapest places on the planet to get your PADI open-water dive certification (from around RM1000) – and the diving is spectacular. The near-perfect crescent of white sand is clogged with guesthouses (but no cars!), but the jungle backdrop, hypnotically fun vibe and turquoise water are all utterly sublime. This isn't a full-moon party – there are only two real bars on the sand – although you can stay out all night watching fire shows and swilling (expensive) whisky. Coral Beach, also on Kecil, is a touch classier and quieter than Long Beach, while the digs on Pulau Besar verge on the resortlike and everyone's in bed by 11pm. A taxi boat between the two islands costs RM20 for the whole boat.

The best time to visit is from March to mid-November. The Perhentians close for the monsoon season – some places don't bother opening till April or later – although some hotels remain open for hardier tourists. Some diving outfits stay open year-round but in the low season there's often poor visibility and rough seas.

There are no banks on the Perhentians although in an emergency you can get cash advances on your Visa or MasterCard at the Tropicana Backpacker Inn. Generators are the source of power and are run during limited hours. There are no public phones but mobile phones work and most accommodation has wi-fi.

🏃 Activities

A four-day open-water course costs RM850 to RM1100 and fun dives cost between RM80 and RM130. For the surface skimmers, guesthouses arrange excellent snorkelling trips around the island (around RM40).

🛏 Sleeping & Eating

On Pulau Kecil (Small Island), Long Beach has the biggest range of budget chalets and 'nightlife'. In the high season (usually from late May to early September), finding accommodation here can be tough, so book ahead or arrive early. Accommodation on Pulau Besar (Big Island) is more upmarket and usually includes air-con and a private bathroom.

Alcohol is available in a few bars and hotel restaurants on both islands. The best hunting grounds for a beer are the more popular Long Beach cafes and Watercolours Resort on Pulau Besar. For dinner, the restaurants at Coral Bay on Pulau Kecil have the best prices for *ikan bakar* with choices of several types of fish and seafood, and sauces in which to slather them.

🛏 PULAU KECIL

A trail over the narrow waist of the island leads from Long Beach to smaller Coral Bay (sometimes known as Aur Bay) on the western side of the island. It's a five- to 10-minute walk along a footpath through the quickly developing jungle interior.

🛏 LONG BEACH

The surf can get big on Long Beach and several places along the beach rent boogie boards and old clunky surfboards. Take care when swimming here as there have been several near tragedies.

Lemon Grass   CHALET $
(☑ 019 981 8393; chalets from RM40) At the southern tip of Long Beach, Lemon Grass has friendly management and 16 no-frills fan huts with shared bathrooms. There are great views from the verandah at reception and nice secluded spots to sit and gaze out to sea.

Panorama Chalets   GUESTHOUSE $
(☑ 09-691 1590; www.panoramaperhentianisland. com; chalets RM35-150) If you're diving and on a budget, this is the place to rest your fins. It's ultra-relaxed with a range of ageing but adequate rooms, good restaurant and some of the best deals on dive packages.

Matahari Chalets   GUESTHOUSE $
(☑ 019 956 5756; www.mataharichalets.com; chalets RM30-130; ❀) Rickety longhouse rooms and A-frame huts ramble around a well-kept but shadeless garden off the beach. All have attached bathrooms except the cheapest A-frame huts and there's an attached dive centre that offers good accommodation package deals.

🛏 CORAL BAY

Coral Bay faces the west for brilliant sunsets and calm swimming. Seafood barbecue on the beach offers a nightly feast and many people head over here from Long Beach for better deals on meals.

Butterfly Chalets GUESTHOUSE $
(r RM45-60) Ageing huts look out over Coral Bay, picking up sea breezes, and are tucked in by hibiscus flowers. They are nearly always full.

Aur Bay Chalet GUESTHOUSE $
(☑013 995 0817; Coral Bay; r RM30) Small but comfortable rooms with double beds, fans, cold showers and mosquito netting set in a longhouse structure just south of the Coral Bay Jetty.

Tropicana Backpacker Inn CHALET $
(☑09-6911 380; Coral Bay; dm RM15, r RM40-80; ☎) Forty bungalows in various condition are spread out over a hillside here, equidistant between Coral Bay and Long Beach.

OTHER BEACHES

There are also a number of small bays around the island, each with one set of chalets, and often only accessible by boat.

★**D'Lagoon Chalets** CHALET $
(☑019 985 7089; Teluk Kerma; camp site RM10, dm RM20, chalet RM60, tr RM150) Accommodation at this isolated, dreamy location ranges from a longhouse with dorm beds to simple chalets on stilts to a honeymoon treehouse. Get the boat captain to drop you here – otherwise it's an hour's hike from the Long Beach jetty. There's an on-site restaurant serving decent Western and Malay food.

PULAU BESAR

Pulau Besar has a busy main beach facing Pulau Kecil that offers skinny but shady stretches of white sand – you can camp at **Teluk Ke Ke Camp Site** (camp site per per-

son RM10), a 10-minute walk to the south. Teluk Dalam (also called Flora Bay), over the hill, is a silken secluded bay with good snorkelling and more peace and quiet. An easily missed track leads from behind the second jetty over the hill to Teluk Dalam (a 40-minute walk), or a five-minute taxi boat to Teluk Dalam costs RM15.

MAIN BEACH

All the following have good attached restaurants.

Watercolours Paradise Resort CHALET $
(☑09-691 1850; www.watercoloursworld.com; r RM70-130; ❇) This friendly resort has clean chalets operated under the same management as the attached Watercolours dive centre, and is about the best value on Besar.

D'Ayumni House CHALET $$
(☑019 436 4463, 09-691 1680; http://d-ayumnihouse.blogspot.com; dm RM55, r RM80-200; ❇@☎) A pretty wooden house rises over a series of low-slung, teak-chic chalets and bungalows. Popular with divers and those seeking a bit of budget backpacker vibe in Besar.

TELUK DALAM

Mandalica Beach Resort CAMPGROUND $
(☑019 983 7690; camping per site RM50) This lovely stretch of white sand on Teluk Dalam's western end has covered camp sites with showers and toilets plus a fantastic restaurant. The family arranges pick-up from all over the Perhentians, fishing trips and just about anything else.

JUNGLE RAILWAY

The name 'Jungle Railway' conjures images of forest people hunting tigers with blow pipes, but you're not going to find any of that here. Nowadays this clean, air-conditioned train trundles through the mountainous, oil palm–clad interior, stopping at *kampung*, letting on a few schoolchildren and headscarfed women lugging oversized bundles of produce. Enjoy views of misty jungle, cave-studded karst cliff faces and a few brightly painted railside Indian temples. It's not super adventurous, but this is one of the more pleasant ways to get from Pulau Perhentian to Taman Negara.

The northern terminus is Tumpat, but most travellers start/end at Wakaf Baharu, the closest station to the transport hub of Kota Bharu. The train departs from Wakaf Baharu on its southbound journey around 7am and it reaches Jerantut, the jumping-off point for Taman Negara, around eight hours later (RM25). The journey continues south to Gemas (RM34), meeting the Singapore–KL train line.

There are also express trains that travel at night, but that would defeat the purpose of seeing the jungle. The train's schedule changes every six months, so it pays to double-check departure times locally.

Samudra Beach Chalet CHALET **$**
(🖉 09-691 1677; www.samudrabeachchalet.com; r RM50-140) Samudra has traditional Malaysian A-frame chalets. Slightly dark on the inside, cheaper ones have fans; the air-conditioned family room with two double beds is a decent deal.

❶ Getting There & Around

Speedboats (RM70 return, 35 minutes) run several times a day from Kuala Besut to the Perhentians from 8.30am to 5.30pm. The boats will drop you off at any of the beaches. In the other direction, speedboats depart from the islands daily at around 8am, noon and 4pm. You'll pay a RM5 park entry fee when you buy your ferry ticket.

When the waves are high on Long Beach, you'll be dropped off or picked up on the other side of the island at Coral Bay. Also, guesthouse operators on Long Beach charge RM3 per person for ferry pick-ups and drop-offs.

The easiest way to island (or beach) hop is by boat (RM10 to RM25). Posted fares and boat operators usually camp out under a shady coconut tree. From island to island, the trip costs RM10 per boat.

Kota Bharu
🖉 09
Very Islamic but supremely mellow Kota Bharu has the energy of a midsized city, the compact feel and friendly vibe of a small town, superb food and a good spread of accommodation. It's the logical overnight stop between Thailand and the Perhentians, but you'd be wise to give Kota Bharu more time than a pit stop.

⊙ Sights

Gelanggang Seni CULTURAL CENTRE
(Cultural Centre; 🖉 03-744 3124; Jln Mahmud) If you want to see *gasing uri* (top-spinning), *silat* (a Malay form of martial arts), kitemaking, drumming, shadow-puppet shows and the like, the Gelanggang Seni is the place to go. Check with the tourist information centre (p428), or your hotel's owners, who should have a full timetable of events.

Central Market MARKET
(Pasar Besar Siti Khadijah; Jln Hulu; ⊙ 6am-6pm) One of the most colourful and active markets in Malaysia, the central market is at its busiest first thing in the morning, and has usually packed up by early afternoon.

Istana Jahar MUSEUM
(Royal Ceremonies Museum; Jln Istana; adult/child RM3/1.50; ⊙ 8.30am-4.45pm Sat-Thu) In an achingly beautiful 1887 building, the displays focus on Kelatanese ritual and crafts, from detailed descriptions of batik-weaving to circumcision and wedding nights.

Muzium Negeri Kelanta MUSEUM
(State Museum; 🖉 09-748 2266; Jln Hospital; adult/child RM2/1; ⊙ 8.30am-4.45pm Sat-Thu) This museum, next to the tourist information centre, is the official state museum. The exhibits on Kelantan's history and culture are interesting, but the accompanying signage is poor.

🛏 Sleeping

The backpacker places listed here are all great, and have shared-bathroom and private-bathroom (read: pricier) options.

★**Zeck's Traveller's Inn** HOMESTAY **$**
(🖉 09-743 1613; 7088-G Jln Sri Cemerlang; dm/s/d from RM10/15/25, r with air-con RM45-60; ✳ @ 🛜) Friendly and social, this family-owned and family-run place is a great way to get a feel for genuine Malaysian *kampung* life in the heart of Kota Bharu. The Zaki family are a mine of information and Zeck also helps to arrange tours into Taman Negara through the park's far-less trammelled Kelantan entrance.

KB Backpackers Lodge HOSTEL **$**
(🖉 019 944 5222, 09-748 8841; www.kb-backpackers.com.my; 1872-D Jln Padang Garong; dm/r from RM8/20; ✳ @) KB's rooms are only so-so but owner Pawi is so helpful and a wealth of information, and the vibe at his hostel is so internationally chill in the way that made us love backpacking in the first place, that it more than makes up for it. Bike rental available.

🍴 Eating

★**Night Market** MARKET **$**
(Jln Parit Dalam) Look for the yellow arch reading 'Medan Selera MPKB'. Specialities include *ayam percik* (marinated chicken on bamboo skewers) and *nasi kerabu* (rice with coconut, fish and spices), blue rice, squid-on-a-stick and *murtabak* (filled pan-fried flat bread). During evening prayers Muslims and non-Muslims must vacate the premises.

MALAYSIA KOTA BHARU

Kota Bharu

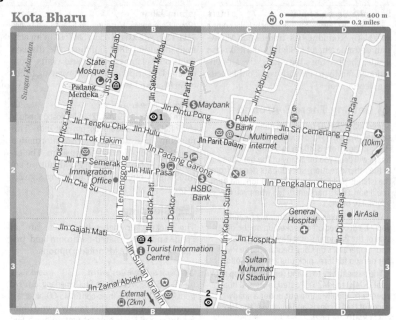

Kota Bharu

⊙ Sights

1 Central Market	B1
2 Gelanggang Seni	C3
3 Istana Jahar	B1
4 Muzium Negeri Kelanta	B3

🛏 Sleeping

5 KB Backpackers Lodge	B2
6 Zeck's Traveller's Inn	C1

✕ Eating

7 Night Market	B1
8 Sri Devi Restaurant	C2

ⓘ Transport

9 Central Bus Station	B2
Taxi Stand	(see 9)

Sri Devi Restaurant   MALAYSIAN **$**
(4213-F Jln Kebun Sultan; mains from RM4; ⊙ lunch
& dinner Sat-Thu) As popular with locals as it is
with tourists, this is a great place for an authentic banana-leaf curry and a mango lassi.

ⓘ Information

Banks and ATMs are scattered around town;
Maybank (Jln Pintu Pong), near the night market, is usually open till 7pm. Internet shops can
be found in the alleys around Jln Doktor and Jln
Kebun Sultan.

Tourist Information Centre (☑09-748 5534;
Jln Sultan Ibrahim; ⊙8am-1pm & 2-4.30pm
Sun-Thu) One of the best and most helpful in
Malaysia.

ⓘ Getting There & Away

AIR

AirAsia (☑09-746 1671; www.airasia.com;
Airport), **Malaysia Airlines** (☑09-771 4703;
www.malaysiaairlines.com; Jln Gajah Mati) and
Firefly (☑03-7845 4543; www.fireflyz.com.my;
airport) have direct daily flights to KL.

BUS

There are three bus stations in Kota Bharu.
Local buses depart from the **central bus station** (☑09-747 5971, 09-747 4330; Jln Padang
Garong), also known as the state-run SKMK bus
station. Most long-distance buses will drop off
passengers near here, but do not depart from
here. When buying your ticket, verify which
long-distance terminal the bus departs from.
Most Transnacional long-distance buses depart
from **Langgar bus station** (Jln Pasir Puteh), in
the south of the city. All the other long-distance
bus companies operate from the **external bus
station** (Jln Hamzah).

A few handy local buses include the ones to Pasir
Puteh (RM5.10) and Kuala Besut (RM7) – for the
ferry to the Perhentians, Kota Bharu airport (RM2,
every 20 minutes) and Wakaf Baharu (RM1.50).

Long-distance destinations from here include Butterworth (RM35, seven hours, one daily), Kuala Lumpur (RM40, 10 hours, hourly), Kuala Terengganu (RM15, three hours, two daily) and Kuantan (RM32, seven hours, five daily).

TAXI

The taxi stand is on the southern side of the central bus station. Destinations and costs per car (which can be split between four passengers) include Wakaf Baharu (RM45), Kuala Besut (RM80) and Kota Bharu Airport (RM42). Taxi drivers in Kota Bharu are uncharacteristically aggressive; do your homework on fares. Most guesthouses arrange shared taxis, especially for early morning departures.

TRAIN

The nearest **train station** (☑ 09-719 6986) to Kota Bharu is at Wakaf Baharu, on the Jungle Railway line. A line also runs to Bangkok, although services have been suspended for some time due to violence in southern Thailand.

PENINSULAR INTERIOR

A thick band of jungle buffers the two peninsular coasts from one another. Within the middle is Taman Negara, the peninsula's most famous national park, and the Jungle Railway, an engineering feat.

Jerantut

☑ 09

Jerantut is the first of several stepping stones to Taman Negara. It's a dingy yet easy town, where you can pick up supplies, change money or stay overnight to break up your trip.

There are two ATMs, both near the bus station, where you can cash up before heading to the jungle.

🍴 Sleeping & Eating

A food court specialising in *tom yam* (spicy Thai-style) seafood is on Jln Pasar Besar. Chinese liquor stores line up along Jln Diwangsa hoping you'll want to stock up on booze before heading to dry Kuala Tahan. There are lots of budget sleeping choices but a few stand out as favourites.

Greenleaf Traveller's Inn   HOTEL $
(☑ 09-267 2131; 3 Jln Diwangsa; dm RM10, d RM20-30; ❄ 🌐) A quiet choice with simple, clean rooms and dorms, owned by a sweet lady and her family. Ms Teh also runs a travel agency and can help you plan your trip to Taman Negara.

Chong Heng Hotel   HOTEL $
(☑ 09-266 3693; 24 Jln Besar; s/d/tr RM20/20/28; @) This clean budget hotel is located in a lovely renovated shophouse on Jerantut's prettier east side. Fan-cooled rooms are clean, comfortable and have shared bathrooms with hot-water showers. The ground floor is taken up by a small, colourful shop.

ℹ Getting There & Away

BOAT
Motor-run canoes (RM35 one way) make the scenic journey between Kuala Tembeling and Kuala Tahan – usually twice or more per day although services can be suspended in the rainy season (November to February). Buy tickets with agents in Jerantut or at the jetty.

BUS & TAXI
The bus station and taxi stand are in the centre of town.

Most people arriving in Jerantut want to head directly to the Kuala Tembeling jetty (where boats leave for Taman Negara). To do this, follow the NKS representative, who meets arriving buses and trains and organises minibus transfers (RM5) from Jerantut to Kuala Tembeling.

You can also skip the boat journey and hop on a Kuala Tahan–bound bus (signed as 'Latif'; RM7, one to two hours, four daily); Kuala Tahan is the base-camp village for Taman Negara. NKS minibuses ply the same route for RM25 twice a day. You save money by doing this, although many travellers cite the voyage upriver from Kuala Tembeling as a highlight of visiting Taman Negara.

Alternatively, you can hire a taxi to Kuala Tembeling (RM24 for the entire car) or to Kuala Tahan (RM70).

When you are ready to get the hell out of Jerantut, there are several daily buses to/from KL's Pekeliling bus station (RM20, three hours) – the last bus to/from Jerantut is at 5/4pm. Three daily buses run to/from Kuantan (RM18, 3½ hours).

NKS arranges minibuses and buses to a variety of destinations, including KL (RM40), Perhentian Islands jetty (RM65), Kota Bharu (RM60) and Cameron Highlands (RM65), all of which leave from the NKS cafe.

Long-distance taxis go to Temerloh (RM50), KL (RM200) and Kuantan (RM180).

TRAIN

Jerantut is on the Jungle Railway (Tumpat–Gemas line). The train station is off Jln Besar, just behind Hotel Sri Emas. For the jungle view, catch the northbound local train at around 12.30pm to Wakaf Baharu. If you opt to skip the view, two daily northbound express trains leave Jerantut in the middle of the night (four hours).

Two express trains run daily to Singapore (2am and 12.30pm), via Johor Bahru. For KL Sentral, take the 12.30am express. For an up-to-date timetable and list of fares, consult **KTM** (www.ktmb.com.my).

Taman Negara

📞 09

Taman Negara blankets 4343 sq km in shadowy, damp, impenetrable jungle. Inside this tangle, trees with gargantuan buttressed root systems dwarf luminescent fungi and orchids. Trudge along muggy trails in search of elusive wildlife (tigers, elephants and rhinos can hide much better than you'd think), balance on the creaky canopy walk or spend the night in a 'hide' where jungle sounds make you feel like you've gone back to the caveman days.

The best time to visit the park is in the dry season between February and September. During the wet season, or even after one good rainfall, leeches come out in force and everything will be very muddy.

Kuala Tahan is the base camp for Taman Negara and has accommodation, minimarkets and floating-barge restaurants. It's a scruffy place and standards are low but it's pleasant enough. Directly opposite Kuala Tahan, across Sungai Tembeling, is the entrance to the national park, Mutiara Taman Negara Resort and the park headquarters located at the Wildlife Department.

Most people purchase permits (park entrance/camera RM1/5) when they buy their bus and/or boat tickets to Kuala Tahan in Jerantut – there are rumours that this fee will be raised in the coming years. Otherwise you'll need to get your permits at the **Wildlife Department** (📞 09-266 1122; ☉ 8am-10pm Sat-Thu, 8am-noon & 3-10pm Fri). The reception desk also provides basic maps, guide services and advice.

🏃 Activities

There are treks to suit all levels of motivation, from a half-hour jaunt to a steep nine-day tussle up and down Gunung Tahan (2187m).

Park headquarters and tourist offices around town have info on the plethora of hikes available. Popular do-it-yourself treks, from one to five hours, include the following.

Canopy Walkway   HIKING
(admission RM5; ☉ 10am-3.30pm Sat-Thu, 9am-noon Fri) This hanging rope bridge constructed of wooden planks and ladders is elevated 45m above the ground; come early to avoid long waits in line. A trail (count on one hour return) behind the walkway leads up steep Bukit Teresik to a viewpoint. The short trail to popular swimming hole Lubok Simpon also leads from the walkway.

Kuala Trenggan   DAY HIKE
The well-marked main trail along the bank of Sungai Tembeling leads 9km to Kuala Trenggan. Allow five hours. From here, boats go back to Kampung Kuala Tahan, or it's a further 2km walk to Bumbun Kumbang. An alternative longer trail leads inland, back across Sungai Trenggan from Bumbun Kumbang to the camp site at Lubok Lesong on Sungai Tahan, then back to park headquarters (six hours). This trail is flat most of the way and crosses small streams. Check with park headquarters for river levels.

PLANNING FOR TAMAN NEGARA

Stock up on essentials in Jerantut. If it's been raining, leeches will be unavoidable. Tobacco, salt, toothpaste and soap can be used to deter them, with varying degrees of success. A liberal coating of insect spray over shoes and socks works best. Tuck pant legs into socks; long sleeves and long pants will protect you from insects and brambles. Even on short walks, take more water than you think you'll ever need, and on longer walks take water-purifying tablets.

Camping, hiking and fishing gear can be hired at the Mutiara Taman Negara Resort shop or at several shops and guesthouses on the Kampung Kuala Tahan side. Asking prices per day are around RM8 for a sleeping bag, RM10 for a rucksack, RM25 for a tent, RM20 for a fishing rod, RM5 for a sleeping pad, RM8 for a stove and RM8 for boots. Prices can be negotiated and it's good to shop around for bargains as well as quality.

Gunung Tahan   HIKING

Gunung Tahan, 55km from the park headquarters, is Peninsular Malaysia's highest peak (2187m). The return trek takes nine days at a steady pace, although it can be done in seven. Guides are compulsory (RM550 per person for nine days if there are four people; prices vary depending on how many are in the group). Try to organise this trek in advance through the Wildlife Department.

☞ Tours

Trekking

You really don't need a guide or tour for day trips – or even overnight trips – to the hides if you're prepared to organise your own gear, food and water. You'll need one for longer treks, however, and the going rate is RM180 per day (one guide can lead up to 12 people), plus a RM100 fee for each night spent out on the trail. Guides who are licensed by the Wildlife Department have completed coursework in forest flora, fauna and safety and are registered with the department. Often the Kuala Tahan tour operators offer cheaper prices than the Wildlife Department, although there is no guarantee that the guide is licensed.

Wildlife & Rapids

Everyone in Kuala Tahan wants to take you on a wildlife or boat tour (from RM35) where you motor down the rapids. There are popular night tours (from RM35) on foot or by 4WD. You're more likely to see animals (such as slow loris, snakes, civets and flying squirrels) on the drives, which go through palm-oil plantations outside the park, but even these don't guarantee sightings.

Orang Asli

Many travellers sign up for tours to an Orang Asli settlement where you'll be shown how to use a long blowpipe and start a fire. While local guides insist that these tours provide essential income for the Orang Asli, most of your tour money will go to the tour company. A small handicraft purchase in the village will help spread the wealth.

🛏 Sleeping & Eating

Arrive early in the day or book in advance (although many places never answer their phones) since the better places fill up quickly and there's invariably a nightly collection of lost souls searching for rooms in the rain.

Kuala Tahan is no culinary centre – unexciting Malaysian and Western fare can be found at a collection of floating restaurants on the river. The town is also dry and the only places that sell beer are the Mutiara Taman Negara Resort (for a hefty RM20) or Rainforest Resort (for a less shocking RM10).

Tahan Guesthouse   GUESTHOUSE $
(☑ 09-266 7752; dm/d RM10/50) Far enough from 'town' to feel away from it all but close enough to be convenient, Tahan Guesthouse has excellent four-bed dorms and even better, colourfully painted bright rooms upstairs. The whole place feels like a happy preschool with giant murals of insects and flowers all over the place.

Durian Chalet   CHALET $
(☑ 09-266 8940; www.durian-chalet.blogspot.tw; dm/d/f RM10/40/50) About 800m outside of the village (beyond the Teresek View Motel) in a flowery garden between rubber and durian plantations. This family-run forest hideaway has rustic, miniscule A-frames and larger double and family rooms.

HIDES & SALT LICKS

Animal-observation hides (*bumbun*) are built overlooking salt licks and grassy clearings, which attract feeding nocturnal animals. You'll need to spend the night in order to see any real action but staying in the heart of the jungle is what the Taman Negara experience is all about. There are several hides close to Kuala Tahan and Kuala Trenggan that are too close to human habitation to attract the shy animals, but even if you don't see any wildlife, the jungle sounds are well worth it – the 'symphony' is best at dusk and dawn.

Hides (per person per night RM5) need to be reserved at the Wildlife Department and they are very rustic with pit toilets. Some travellers hike independently in the day to the hides, then camp overnight and return the next day, while others go to more far-flung hides that require some form of transport and a guide; the Wildlife Department can steer you in the right direction. For overnight trips you'll need food, water and a sleeping bag. Rats on the hunt for tucker are problematic, so hang food high out of reach.

Popular hides include **Bumbun Blau** and **Bumbun Yong** on Sungai Yong, 3.1km from park headquarters; **Bumbun Kumbang**, a roughly five hours' walk from headquarters or a 45-minute walk from Kuala Trenggan, accessible by riverbus service from Kuala Tahan (four-person boat RM90, 35 minutes); and **Tabing Hide**, about 1½ hours' walk (3.1km) from park headquarters, or accessible by the riverbus service (it's near the river).

Tembeling Riverview Lodge　　LODGE **$**
(☑ 09-266 6766; www.trvtamannegara.blogspot.com; dm RM10, d/tr RM50/60) Straddling the thoroughfare footpath, this place has fan-cooled rooms with cold showers and mosquito netting and pleasant communal areas overlooking the river.

ⓘ Information

Internet access is unreliable and slow at the best of times and costs RM6 per hour. There are a handful of terminals at Agoh Chalets and a few more at an unnamed shop across from Teresek View Motel. There are no banks in Taman Negara.

ⓘ Getting There & Away

Most people reach Taman Negara by taking a bus from Jerantut to the jetty at Kuala Tembeling then a river boat from there to the park, but there are also popular private minibus services that go directly to/from several tourist destinations around Malaysia directly to/from Kampung Kuala Tahan. You can also take a bus from Jerantut direct to Kampung Kuala Tahan, but by doing this you miss the scenic boat trip.

BOAT

The river jetty for Taman Negara–bound boats is in Kuala Tembeling, 18km north of Jerantut.

Boats (one way RM35) depart Kuala Tembeling daily at 9am and 2pm (9am and 2.30pm on Friday). On the return journey, boats leave Kuala Tahan at 9am and 2pm (and 2.30pm on Friday). The journey takes three hours upstream and two

hours downstream. Note that the boat service is irregular during the November-to-February wet season.

BUS & TAXI

There are buses and taxis from Jerantut to Kuala Tembeling. A public bus from Kampung Kuala Tahan goes to KL (RM29) every day at 8am via Jerantut. **NKS** (☑ 03-2072 0336) and **Banana Travel & Tours** (☑ 017 902 5952; Information Centre, Kampung Kuala Tahan) run several useful private services including daily buses to KL (RM35) and minibuses to Penang (RM120), the Perhentian Islands (RM165 including boat) and the Cameron Highlands (RM95). These minibuses can also drop you off en route anywhere in between.

ⓘ Getting Around

There is a frequent cross-river ferry (RM1) that shuttles passengers across the river from Kuala Tahan to the park entrance and Mutiara Taman Negara Resort.

Nusa Camp's floating information centre in Kuala Tahan runs scheduled riverboat (also called riverbus) services along the river to Bumbun Blau/Bumbun Yong (one-way RM5, three daily), the Canopy Walkway (one-way RM15, two daily), Gua Telinga (one-way RM15, four daily) and Kuala Tembeling (one-way RM30, one daily). Check with the information desk for times and prices, as these services may be dropped entirely during the wet season. You can arrange for the boats to pick you up again for the return trip on their schedule, and there's a slight discount for a round-trip fare.

MALAYSIAN BORNEO – SABAH

Most visitors come to Sabah to experience nature in all its riotous equatorial glory. Especially popular destinations include the ancient rainforests and dramatic granite flanks of Mt Kinabalu; the jungle-clad banks of Sungai Kinabatangan, teeming with monkeys, hornbills and other exotic creatures; Sepilok, one of the only places in the world where you can see semi-wild orang-utans in their native habitat; and the spectacular reefs of Sipadan and the rest of the Semporna Archipelago. Sabah's cities are not as pretty as their counterparts in Sarawak but dynamic, cosmopolitan Kota Kinabalu (universally known as KK) can grow on you.

Kota Kinabalu

📞 088 / POP 453,000

Kota Kinabalu is probably not going to be the sleeper hit of your Southeast Asian odyssey, but as midsized Malaysian provincial capitals go, it's pretty cool. The centre is compact and walkable, there's a colourful waterfront packed with atmospheric markets, and you'll find some damn fine food. Few travellers come to Sabah for the urban scene, but you've gotta book permits somewhere, you've gotta hang out somewhere while recovering from Mt Kinabalu, and you need some place to connect to onward travel. KK is a good place (sometimes the only place) to do all of the above.

⊙ Sights

Sabah Museum MUSEUM
(Kompleks Muzium Sabah; 📞 088-253199; www.museum.sabah.gov.my; Jln Muzium; admission RM15; ⊙ 9am-5pm Sat-Thu; 🅿) A very worthwhile introduction to Sabah's ethnic groups, history and ecology. The admission ticket is also valid for the Agnes Keith House in Sandakan. Situated about 4km south of central KK. From Terminal Wawasan, take minibus 13A or 19A; a taxi from the city centre costs RM15.

Sunday Market MARKET
(Jln Gaya; ⊙ 6am-about noon Sun) A lively market completely takes over Jalan Gaya every Sunday morning, selling everything from tropical fruit to souvenirs to pets in cages.

Kota Kinabalu Wetland Centre OUTDOORS
(📞 088-246955; www.sabahwetlands.org; Jln Bukit Bendera Upper, Likas District; admission RM15; ⊙ 8.30am-5.30pm Tue-Sun; 🅿) 🏖 Once, much of what's now KK was mangrove forest; these 24 hectares, accessible by wooden walkways, are all that's left. It provides an excellent introduction to Borneo's wetland ecology and bird life; signage is excellent. From Terminal Wawasan, take any minibus heading to Likas and get off at the Likas Square shopping mall; a cab from the city centre costs RM15.

Tunku Abdul Rahman National Park PARK
(adult/child RM10/6) Just off the Kota Kinabalu coast, this 49-sq-km park consists of the islands of Manukan, Sapi, Mamutik, Sulug and Gaya (the largest) – and the reefs in between them. It has a number of nice beaches (equipped with bathrooms and changing facilities) and some fine snorkelling spots, though parts get crowded on weekends. Mamutik, Sapi and Gaya have official camping sites (RM5). To head out to the islands for a day trip, take a speedboat (RM30 return, 20 minutes) from Jesselton Point Ferry Terminal.

☞ Tours

Some of Sabah's outdoor activities (eg trekking and rafting) require logistical support that only a tour company can supply. And if you haven't made advance reservations for Sipadan or Mt Kinabalu, to which access is limited by a permit system, KK's tour outfits may be able to help. In either case, the best place to head is the city centre office building known as **Wisma Sabah** (cnr Jln Haji Saman & Jln Tun Fuad Stephens), which is chock-a-block with operators.

★**Adventure Alternative Borneo** ADVENTURE TOUR
(📞 019 802 0549; www.aaborneo.com; 1st fl, 97 Jln Gaya) 🏖 Specialises in getting visitors off the beaten path – an excellent resource for independent travellers interested in sustainable, responsible tourism.

GogoSabah TOUR
(📞 088-317385; www.gogosabah.com; Lot G4, ground fl, Wisma Sabah, Jln Haji Saman; ⊙ 9am-6pm Mon-Sat) Does a great job of booking just about anything, anywhere in Sabah. Especially excellent for motorbike rentals (per

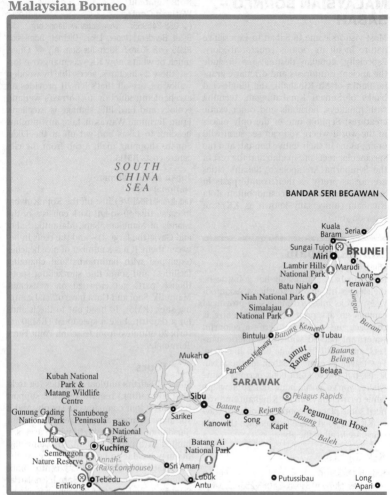

SOUTH CHINA SEA

BANDAR SERI BEGAWAN

Kuala Baram   Seria
Sungai Tujoh ⊗   BRUNEI
Miri
Lambir Hills   Marudi
National Park   Long
Batu Niah   Terawan
Niah National Park
Simalajau
National Park
Bintulu   *Batang Kemena*   Tubau
Batang Belaga
Mukah   Pan Borneo Highway   *Lumut Range*   Belaga
SARAWAK
Sibu   *Batang*   *Pelagus Rapids*
Rejang   *Pegunungan Hose*
Sarikei   Song   *Batang*
Kanowit   Kapit
Kubah National   *Baleh*
Park &
Matang Wildlife
Centre
Gunung Gading   Santubong   Batang Ai
National Park   Peninsula   Bako   National Park
National
Lundu   Park
Semenggoh   Kuching
Nature Reserve   *Annah*
(Rais Longhouse)   Sri Aman
Tebedu   Lubuk   Putussibau   Long
Entikong   Antu   Apari

day/week/month RM45/240/600, including
helmet).

Riverbug   RAFTING
(☎ 088-260501; www.riverbug.asia; Lot 227-229,
2nd fl, Wisma Sabah, Jln Haji Saman) Sabah's premier white-water-rafting operator.

Scuba Junkie   DIVING
(☎ 088-255816; www.scubajunkiekk.com; G23,
Wisma Sabah, Jln Haji Saman) Semporna's
most popular diving operator. Also runs
scuba trips to nearby Tunku Abdul Rahman
National Park.

★ Sticky Rice   TOUR
(☎ 088-251654; www.stickyricetravel.com; 3rd fl,
58 Jln Pantai) 🖉 The Sticky Rice guys are
extremely helpful, knowledgable about
Borneo, and committed to independent
travel and community engagement.

Sutera Sanctuary Lodges   TOUR
(☎ Wisma Sabah 088-287887, main office 088-
308914; www.suteraharbour.com; Lot G15, ground fl,
Wisma Sabah, Jln Haji Saman; ⊙ 9am-6pm Mon-Fri,
to 4pm Sat) The place to come for the least
expensive Mt Kinabalu summit packages. If
you didn't book ahead, drop by to check last-
minute availability.

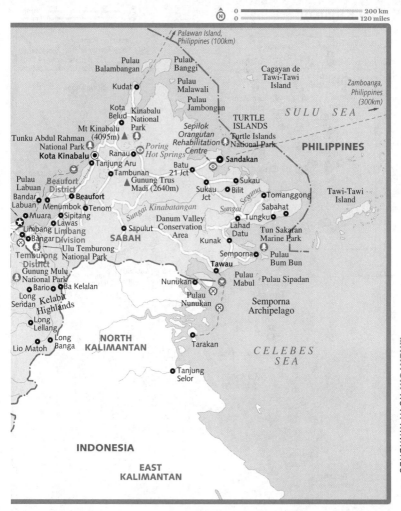

🛏 Sleeping

Almost all of KK's budget backpacker digs are on or near Jln Gaya, in the lively commercial area sandwiched between Jln Pantai (to the west) and Lg Dewan (to the east) – the latter is also known as Australia Pl because there was an Aussie army camp here in 1945. Hostel rooms usually have shared bathroom, and prices include a toast-and-jam breakfast.

A group of hostel and budget-hotel owners have banded together to form the Sabah Backpacker Operators Association (SBA; www.sabahbackpackers.com). Their website includes a list of reputable accommodation options around Sabah.

Stay-In Lodge
GUESTHOUSE $

(☎ 088-272986; www.stayinlodge.com; 1st fl, Lot 121, Jln Gaya; dm/d/tr/q RM20/45/65/90, with aircon RM25/55/80/120; ✸@☎) The big, breezy lounge makes this a friendly spot for meeting fellow travellers, and staff are helpful and knowledgable. The 17 simply furnished rooms include dorms with six beds.

Akinabalu Youth Hostel
HOSTEL $

(☎ 088-272188; www.akinabaluyh.com; 1st fl, Lot 133, Jln Gaya; dm/r incl breakfast from RM25/65;

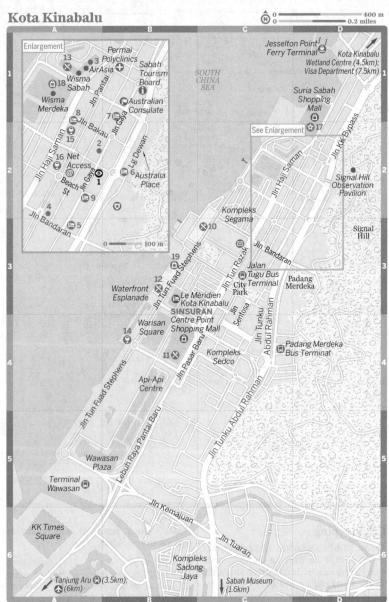

※ @ 🛜) Welcoming staff, a nice chill-out lobby and trickling Zen fountains make this an excellent option. The 12 rooms, many with hallway windows, are basic but clean; dorm rooms have five beds.

Lai Lai Hotel   HOTEL **$**

(📞 088-249533, 088-248533; lailaihotel09@gmail.com; 30 Jln Haji Saman; s/d RM72/105; ※) One of KK's best budget hotel deals. The 33 spotless, tourist-class-quality rooms all come with fast cable internet.

Kota Kinabalu

◉ Sights
1 Sunday Market A2

◉ Activities, Courses & Tours
2 Adventure Alternative Borneo A2
3 GogoSabah A1
   Riverbug ....(see 3)
   Scuba Junkie ....(see 3)
4 Sticky Rice A2
   Sutera Sanctuary Lodges ....(see 3)

◉ Sleeping
5 Akinabalu Youth Hostel A3
6 Borneo Backpackers B2
7 Borneo Gaya Lodge B1
8 Lai Lai Hotel A1
9 Stay-In Lodge A2

◉ Eating
10 Central Market C3
11 Centre Point Food Court B4
12 Night Market B3
13 Vege Garden A1

◉ Drinking & Nightlife
14 Bed B4
15 El Centro A2
16 Milimewa Superstore A2

◉ Entertainment
17 Golden Screen Cinemas D2

◉ Shopping
18 Borneo Books A1
19 Handicraft Market B3

Borneo Gaya Lodge   HOSTEL $
(☑088-242477; www.borneogayalodge.com; 1st fl, 78 Jln Gaya; dm incl breakfast from RM25, d/q with bathroom RM85/119; ❄@☎) Known for its friendly staff, living roomlike lounge and plentiful information on excursions and tours. Dorms have six or 10 beds.

Borneo Backpackers   HOSTEL $
(☑088-234009; www.borneobackpackers.com; 24 Lg Dewan, Australia Pl; dm/s/d incl breakfast from RM25/40/60; ❄☎) On the scene long enough to have become 'a KK institution', this 60-bed hostel has cosy public areas for meeting other backpackers.

✖ Eating

KK's cuisine scene isn't as sophisticated as Kuching's, but there's more than enough variety to keep your palate from getting bored.

Local specialities include *sayur manis* (a jungle fern) and *hinava* (raw fish pickled with fresh lime juice, chilli, sliced shallots and grated ginger).

Central Market   HAWKER $
(Pasar Besar Kota Kinabalu; Jln Tun Fuad Stephens; mains RM3-5; ⊙5am-4.30pm or 5pm) The upstairs food court has cheap, tasty food. Open during Ramadan.

Night Market   HAWKER $
(Jln Tun Fuad Stephens; fish/prawn per 100g from RM4/15, satay RM1; ⊙5-11pm) The most atmospheric place in KK for Malay- or Filipino-style broiled fish and seafood. To avoid food poisoning, don't order half-cooked fish that's been sitting around – instead, select something fresh (on ice) and ask the barbe-

cue guy to prepare it from scratch. Situated across the street from Le Méridien Hotel.

Centre Point Food Court   FOOD COURT $
(basement, Centre Point Shopping Mall, Jln Raya Pantai Baru; mains from RM3; ⊙9am-9.30pm; ☑) Your ringgit will go a long way at this hugely popular food court, whose offerings include Malay and Indian. Liew Chai Vegetarian (open until 7pm), three shops away from KFC, is vegetarian.

Vege Garden   VEGETARIAN $
(G17 Wisma Sabah, Jln Haji Saman; mains RM5.50-8; ⊙7am-6.30pm Mon-Sat, to 4pm Sun; ☑) Serves vegetarian versions of Chinese and Malay favourites.

Milimewa Superstore   SUPERMARKET $
(Jln Haji Saman; ⊙9.30am-9.30pm) Picnic supplies, toiletries and wine.

🍷 Drinking & Nightlife

If you're up for a quiet drink, your best bet may be to grab a beer in a Chinese *kopitiam* (cafe) – there are quite a few on the streets around Jln Gaya.

Pedestrianised **Beach Street**, which intersects Jln Gaya, has live music nightly from 9pm to 11.30pm.

For upscale, Western-style pubs, head to the Waterfront Esplanade on Jln Tun Fuad Stephens, just south of Le Méridien Hotel.

El Centro   PUB
(☑019-893 5499; www.elcentro.my; 32 Jln Haji Saman; ⊙11am-midnight, closed Mon; ☎) KK's premier travellers' hang-out – and great source of information on sustainable, culturally sensitive eco-tourism. It serves mainly

Western grub, including pasta, burgers, pizza, tacos and vegie options (RM10 to RM18).

Bed NIGHTCLUB
(☎ 088-251901; Waterfront Esplanade; admission Fri & Sat incl drink RM20, beer from RM21; ☺7pm-2am, until 3am Fri & Sat) Awash with hip locals in slinky/shiny/skimpy outfits, this old-fashioned discotheque has a live band from 9pm to 1am. Gets going after 10pm or 11pm.

☆ Entertainment

Two city-centre cinemas screen English-language films.

Golden Screen Cinemas CINEMA
(www.gsc.com.my; 8th fl, Suria Sabah Shopping Mall, Jln Haji Saman; RM11-17; ☺films begin 11.30am to midnight) Eight screens.

Growball Cinemax CINEMA
(www.growball.com; 8th fl, northern end, Centre Point Shopping Mall, Jln Raya Pantai Baru; RM7-15; ☺films begin 11.30am to midnight) Seven screens, with a 28-lane bowling alley (game RM6; open 9am to 12.30am) nearby.

🛍 Shopping

Handicraft Market MARKET
(Filipino Market; Jln Tun Fuad Stephens; ☺8am-9pm) Inexpensive souvenirs, some from the Philippines. Bargaining is a must!

Borneo Books BOOKS
(☎ 088-241050; www.borneobooks.com; shop 26, ground fl, Wisma Merdeka Phase 2, Jln Haji Saman; ☺10am-8pm Mon-Sat, 10am-5.30pm Sun) The best place in the world to shop for books on Borneo. Plenty of Lonely Planet guides, too.

ℹ Information

EMERGENCY
Police, Ambulance & Fire (☎999)

INTERNET ACCESS
Every sleeping spot we list has wi-fi, at least in the lobby, as do many cafes. Many guesthouses also have computers with internet access.
Net Access (Lot 44, Jln Pantai; per hr RM3; ☺9am-midnight) Inside Teleplus Telecommunication, a DiGi phone shop.

MEDICAL SERVICES
Hospital Queen Elizabeth II (☎088-324600; http://hqe2.moh.gov.my; Jln Damai, Luyang; ☺emergency 24hr) Sabah's largest public hospital. The new campus is 6km (by road) southeast of the city centre. A taxi from the centre costs RM20.

Permai Polyclinics (☎088-232100; www.permaipolyclinics.com; 4 Jln Pantai; consultation weekday RM60, Sat & Sun RM80; ☺doctors on duty 8am-6pm, emergency 24hr) A conveniently central outpatient clinic – great for minor ailments.

MONEY
There's a cluster of banks with 24-hour ATMs around the northern section of Jln Gaya. Several moneychangers in Wisma Merdeka on Jln Tun Razak offer better rates for cash than the banks.

POST
Main Post Office (Jln Tun Razak; ☺8am-5pm Mon-Sat)

TOURIST INFORMATION
Both airport terminals have information counters (open 8am to 11pm) run by Tourism Malaysia.
Sabah Tourism Board (☎088-212121; www.sabahtourism.com; 51 Jln Gaya; ☺8am-5pm Mon-Fri, 9am-4pm Sat, Sun & holidays) Helpful staff and a wide range of brochures. Ask about their homestay program.
Visa Department (☎088-488700; www.imi.gov.my; Kompleks Persekutuan Pentadbiran Kerajaan, Jln UMS; ☺8am-1pm & 2-5pm Mon-Thu, 8-11.30am & 2-5pm Fri) For visa extensions. Situated 7km northeast of the city centre.

ℹ Getting There & Away

AIR
Budget carrier **AirAsia** (www.airasia.com; ground fl, Wisma Sabah, Jln Haji Saman; ☺8.30am-5.30pm Mon-Fri, 8.30am-3pm Sat) has nonstop flights to Singapore, Jakarta, Bali, Manila, Cebu, Hong Kong, Taipei and China. Within Malaysia, it flies to Sandakan and Tawau (Sabah); Miri and Kuching (Sarawak); and KL, Penang, Johor Bahru and Kota Bharu (Peninsular Malaysia).

Destinations served by direct **Malaysia Airlines** (☎1300 883 000; www.malaysiaairlines.com) flights include Kuching, KL, Hong Kong, Taipei, Shanghai and Tokyo.

MASwings (☎1300 88 3000; www.maswings.com.my) serves Bornean destinations such as Bandar Seri Begawan (Brunei), Sandakan, Tawau and Labuan; and, in Sarawak, Miri, Sibu and Mulu National Park.

Other airlines have direct flights to Hong Kong and cities in China, Korea, Indonesia and the Philippines.

Most airlines operate out of newer, larger Terminal 1, while AirAsia and a few companies serving the Philippines and Indonesia use Terminal 2.

MALAYSIA KOTA KINABALU

BUSES FROM KOTA KINABALU

DESTINATION	TERMINAL	PRICE (RM)	DURATION (HR)
Bandar Seri Begawan (Brunei)	Jalan Tugu	100	8
Kinabalu National Park	Inanam	20	2
Kinabalu National Park	Padang Merdeka	minibus 20, share taxi 25	2
Menumbok (ferry to Labuan)	Padang Merdeka	30	2½
Menumbok (ferry to Labuan)	Jalan Tugu	18	2½
Miri (Sarawak)	Jalan Tugu	90	3
Sandakan/Sepilok	Inanam	43	6
Semporna	Inanam	73	8-9
Tawau	Inanam	70	9

BOAT

Passenger ferries connect **Jesselton Point Ferry Terminal** (Jln Haji Saman, 500m northeast of Wisma Sabah) with Pulau Labuan (economy/business RM40/45, 3¼ hours, departures at 8am and 1.30pm). If you take the morning boat, you can catch the 1.30pm ferry from Labuan to Brunei. Drop by to book – phone reservations are not accepted.

Speedboats link Jesselton Point with the five islands of Tunku Abdul Rahman National Park (RM30 return). Most people head out in the morning (the first departures are at 8.30am or 9am); the last boats back leave the park at about 5pm. Open-jaws travel to more than one island costs an extra RM10.

BUS & MINIVAN

KK has three bus terminals for inter-city travel. Reservations for many destinations can be made by phoning the bus company (your guesthouse can help) or online at www.busonlineticket.com. Same-day bookings are usually fine, although weekends can be busy and holidays even busier.

Inanam Bus Terminal (Terminal Bas Bandaraya – Utara; ⊘departures 6am-8.30pm) Buses heading to Sabah's east coast use Inanam Bus Terminal, KK's main long-haul station, which is 7.5km northeast of the city centre. Of the 20 or so companies here, two of the largest are Tung Ma Express (☏KK 088-381190, Sandakan 089-418904; www.tung-maexpress.com.my), which has almost hourly departures to Sandakan from 7am to 8pm; and Dyana Express (☏KK 088-389997, Semporna 089-784494), which sends buses to Semporna at 7.30am, 8.30am, 2pm and 7.30pm.

Inanam is linked to Terminal Wawasan, in the city centre, by blue-and-white minibuses 4A and 5A (RM1.80). A taxi from downtown costs RM25.

Padang Merdeka Bus Terminal (Jln Tunku Abdul Rahman) Conveniently situated 350m south of Australia Pl, Padang Merdeka is used by minibuses, share taxis and a few buses heading to destinations in western Sabah.

The most convenient way to get from KK to Kinabalu National Park is to take a minibus or share taxi heading towards Ranau; there are departures about hourly from 7am to 5pm. To get back to KK, take your driver's mobile number and call him to coordinate pick-up.

Jalan Tugu Bus Terminal (City Park Bus Terminal; Jln Tugu) A few blocks south of the Jln Gaya tourist area, the Jalan Tugu Bus Terminal serves Brunei, Sarawak and other places southwest of KK. Companies with offices here include Bintang Jaya (☏013 816 2178), which has a daily bus to Miri at 7.30am, and Jesselton Express (☏012 622 9722, 016 836 0009; www.sipitangexpress.com.my; ⊘Jln Tugu office 6am-6pm), which goes to Bandar Seri Begawan daily at 8am; by the time you read this, there may be a second departure at 10am.

ⓘ Getting Around

TO/FROM THE AIPORT

The airport is 7km southwest of the city centre. Taxis to the city operate on a voucher system (RM30). Taxis heading from the city centre *to* the airport cost RM25.

A public bus now links both airport terminals with the city centre's Padang Merdeka Bus Terminal (RM5, hourly until about 8pm).

BUS & MINIBUS

Minibuses serving destinations in greater KK use **Terminal Wawasan** (cnr Jln Kemajuan & Jln Tun Fuad Stephens), a big parking lot 2km southwest of Wisma Sabah. The vehicles, which run from about 7am to 9pm and depart when full, are colour-coded and have destinations painted on the side. There's no information office so if you have a question head to the rain shelter and ask one of the men shouting out destinations.

Terminal Wawasan is linked to the city centre and Jesselton Point Ferry Terminal (RM0.50, every 30 minutes from 6am to 9pm) by the slow, full-size buses of the City Bus line, painted red, green and yellow.

TAXI

A cab ride within the city centre should cost RM10. Few drivers use meters, so always agree on a fare before getting in. Prices rise by 50% from midnight to 6am. There's no central dispatch number, so to order a cab by phone (RM2), you'll need a particular driver's mobile number (available at hotels and guesthouses).

Mt Kinabalu & Kinabalu National Park

Climbing the great Kinabalu (4095m) – the highest peak between the Himalayas and New Guinea and a Unesco World Heritage Site – is a heart-pounding adventure that will take you through gorgeous rainforest habitats to breath-taking panoramas.

After checking in at park headquarters (elevation 1563m) around 9am, trekkers ride or walk the 4.5km to the Timpohon Gate trailhead (elevation 1866m) and then ascend for four to seven hours to Laban Rata (3270m), where they spend the night. Climbers usually hit the trail again at 3am or so in order to reach the summit (one to two hours) in time for sunrise. This is the only time of day when the view from the summit is reliably clear. Note that certain parts of the trail are impassable in heavy rain.

The ascent of Kinabalu is unrelenting as almost every step you take will be uphill – or downhill. You'll have to negotiate a variety of obstacles along the way, including slippery rocks, blinding fog and frigid winds. For details, see www.suteraharbour.com (click Sutera Sanctuary Lodges, then Mt Kinabalu) or, for one amateur's perspective, www.climbingmtkinabalu.com.

⊙ Sights & Activities

Climbing Mt Kinabalu

Only a limited number of beds are available at Laban Rata (elevation 3270m; dorm bed RM470), predawn launch point for the summit, and virtually all of them are controlled by Sutera Sanctuary Lodges. As a result, the only way to get to the top (unless you do a one-day climb) is to book a package. If you're shooting for a specific date, especially one that falls in July or August or around Christmas, it's *highly* recommended that you make reservations two or more months ahead.

Almost any tour operator in Sabah – including those with offices in the downtown KK office building known as Wisma Sabah – can organise a trip to the mountain. Many charge RM1100 to RM1400, but it's cheaper to book directly through Sutera Sanctuary Lodges (p434), the private company that has a monopoly on accommodation within the national park. If you don't have your reservations squared away before arriving in KK, drop by their office to check last-minute options. The more lead time you allow and the more flexible your travel itinerary, the better the chance that a window will open up.

Through Sutera, a three-day, two-night summit package, including dorm beds at park headquarters and Laban Rata and seven meals (vegie available – inform park headquarters when you arrive), costs RM671. Additional fees that have to be paid (cash only) at the Sabah Parks Visitor Centre:

→ **Park entry fee** (adult/child RM15/10 per day)

→ **Climbing permit** (RM100)

→ **Guide fee** (RM128 for up to three people, RM150 for three to six people)

→ **Insurance** (RM7)

For a group of three climbing together, the total per-person cost comes to RM835, not including transport to/from the park.

A two-day, one-night, five-meal version (without an overnight at park headquarters) costs about RM180 less per person but is available on a limited basis: either more

EQUIPMENT & CLOTHING

No special equipment is required to summit Mt Kinabalu. However, rubber-soled shoes will improve your traction on slippery granite and a headlamp is strongly advised for the predawn jaunt to the top – you'll need your hands free to negotiate the ropes on the summit massif. Expect freezing temperatures near the top, not to mention strong winds and the occasional rainstorm, so it's a good idea to bring along a quick-drying fleece jacket and a waterproof shell to go over it. Don't forget a water bottle, which can be refilled en route.

than a month ahead or (if available) at the very last minute, ie one day ahead.

You can also try your luck and just show up at the park to see if there's a last-minute cancellation – spaces at Laban Rata do open up. Do not attempt an 'unofficial' climb – permits are scrupulously checked at three points along the trail.

One-Day Climb

The only way to get around the Laban Rata bottleneck – and some of the associated expenses – is to do a one-day climb. Be warned: climbing up 2500 vertical metres and then back down again in a single day is *extremely* demanding, and by the time you reach the summit the view is likely to be obscured by clouds. Only four people a day (two per guide) are allowed to attempt a single-day ascent, and then only after park staff assess their fitness. Reservations are not possible – this option is strictly walk-in.

Other Hiking Trails

If you're not up for an ascent to the summit, can't afford an expensive package and/or didn't reserve ahead for the dates you need, it's still well worth coming here to explore the nine interconnected nature trails that wend their way through the beautiful jungles around the base of Mt Kinabalu. A climbing permit and a guide are required if you go above Tempohon Gate.

⛺ Sleeping

Privately run guesthouses – offering much better value than the Sutera-run lodges inside the park – are strung out along the highway that runs by the park.

Camping is not allowed in the park.

J Residence   GUESTHOUSE **$**
(☑ 012 869 6969; www.jresidence.com; d Mon-Fri RM88, Sat & Sun RM138; ☏) The most romantic guesthouse in the area, with seven very attractive rooms set in a hillside garden. Situated 400m towards KK from the park entrance, down a steep driveway.

Mountain Guest House   GUESTHOUSE **$**
(☑ 016 837 4040, 088-888632; dm/s/d/q incl breakfast from RM30/60/70/80) This old wooden house has basic but clean rooms and an old-time local vibe – a good choice if you're on a tight budget. Situated on a vine-drenched hillside 300m towards Ranau from the park entrance.

> ### VIA FERRATA
>
> The *via ferrata* ('iron road' in Italian) is a permanent network of mountaineering cables, rungs and rails attached to Mt Kinabalu's dramatic granite walls. After ascending the mountain in the usual way, climbers can use the *via ferrata*, managed by **Mountain Torq** (☑ 088-268126; www.mountaintorq.com), to return from 3776m to the Laban Rata rest camp. The **Low's Peak Circuit** (2-day summit climb RM1000-1500; minimum age 17) is a four- to five-hour scramble along Mt Kinabalu's sheer flanks. Prices are as high as the mountain (tour companies charge at least RM1200), and Mountain Torq does not offer refunds if the climb is cancelled for any reason, including weather.

D'Villa Rina Ria Lodge   LODGE **$$**
(☑ 088-889282; www.dvillalodge.com.my; dm/d/q RM30/120/180; @☏) This welcoming lodge has 17 cosy rooms – including a spartan 12-bed dorm – and a dining area with lovely mountain views. Situated 500m towards Ranau from the park entrance.

ℹ Getting There & Away

Park headquarters is 88km by road northeast of KK. All buses from KK's Inanam Bus Terminal to east coast destinations, including Sandakan, pass by the park (RM20, two hours), but if you're staying in central KK it's much more convenient to take a minibus from Padang Merdeka Bus Terminal (RM20, two hours). In order to check in by 9am, you'll need to leave KK by 7am – or consider spending the night somewhere near the mountain.

To get from the park to KK or Sandakan, you can flag down a bus right outside park headquarters. During holiday periods, though, every bus is likely to be full, in which case a taxi (RM150 to KK) may be your only option. If you know ahead of time when you'll be travelling, you can buy an onward bus ticket at Inanam. You could also try making a reservation by phone – the bus company, if amenable, will give you the approximate arrival time and the licence plate number of your bus.

Around Mt Kinabalu

Several places near Kinabalu National Park are well worth exploring.

Kundasang War Memorial

At the **Kundasang War Memorial** (admission RM10; ☉8.30am-5pm), flowery gardens commemorate the 1787 Australian and 641 British POWs who died in 1945 on the Sandakan Death Marches. Situated 10km east of park headquarters, a few hundred metres off the KK–Sandakan highway behind a market complex.

Poring Hot Springs

Steaming, sulphurous water is channelled into tile pools and tubs at **Poring Hot Springs** (adult/child incl Kinabalu National Park RM15/10; ☉entrance gate 7am-5pm, park until 8pm, Butterfly Garden & Canopy Walk closed Mon), a great spot to relax your aching muscles after conquering Mt Kinabalu. The site feels less like a national park than a budget tropical spa but it's still fun. Changing rooms are available, as are lockers (RM2, open until 4.30pm). Don't forget a swimsuit and a towel.

Other attractions here include **walking trails**, the **Butterfly Farm** (RM4) and the **Canopy Walkway** (per person RM5, camera RM5; last admission 4pm), a series of bouncy ropeways up to 40m high that take you from tree to tree.

Giant **Rafflesia flowers** often bloom on private land a few hundred metres down the hill from the entrance to Poring Hot Springs – keep an eye out for signs or ask locals. Admission is usually RM20.

🛏 Sleeping

There are a few small, basic guesthouses across the street from the entrance to the hot springs.

★**Lupa Masa**   LODGE **$**
(☎012 845 1987, 016 806 8194; www.facebook. com/lupa.masa; per person incl meals 1st/subsequent nights RM100/85) It doesn't get any more jungle-rustic than this incredible ecolodge, staffed by super-welcoming local staff. Reserve ahead. Situated 40 minutes on foot from Poring Hot Springs.

Round Inn   GUESTHOUSE **$**
(☎088-879584; hongkongmoi@hotmail.com; d RM78; ☎) Has 10 basic but serviceable rooms and a popular restaurant. Situated 50m down the hill from the park entrance.

ⓘ Getting There & Around

The gateway to Poring is the town of Ranau, 20km towards Sandakan from Kinabalu National Park headquarters, which is served by frequent buses to/from the park, KK (RM20) and Sandakan (RM30). Inter-city buses stop underneath the pedestrian bridge over the highway. A minibus (RM5) occasionally links Ranau with Poring (18km), but chances are you'll have to take a taxi (RM40). At Poring, the Bambu Borneo Shop, facing the hot springs' gate, can arrange a taxi to Ranau.

Sandakan

📖 089 / POP 396,000

Sabah's second city has long been a major trading port, but these days the grubby city centre feels provincial compared to KK. The main draw here is not the city itself but the nature sites of nearby Sepilok.

⊙ Sights

History buffs might be interested in the *Sandakan Heritage Trail* brochure available at the tourist office.

Agnes Keith House   MUSEUM
(☎089-221140; www.museum.sabah.gov.my; Jln Istana; admission RM15; ☉9am-5pm) The home of Agnes Keith, American author of *Land Below the Wind*, has been turned into a museum filled with furniture and photos evocative of the 1930s. To get there, walk up Tangga Seribu, the staircase diagonally across the square from the tourist office.

Sandakan Memorial Park   HISTORIC SITE
(☉9am-5pm) Marks the site of the Japanese POW camp where the infamous WWII 'death marches' to Ranau began. Of the approximately 2500 Australian and British troops imprisoned here, the only survivors by July 1945 were six Australian escapees.

From Terminal Bas Sandakan, take any bus or minibus to Batu 8 (Mile 8); get off at the 'Taman Rimba' signpost and walk down Jln Rimba. A taxi from downtown costs RM20 to RM25 one way.

🛏 Sleeping

If you've come to this part of Sabah to see wildlife, you're probably better off staying out at Sepilok. The places listed below are all right in the city centre, a short walk from Terminal Bas Sandakan.

Harbourside Backpackers   HOSTEL $

(✆089-217072; www.harboursidebackpackers.com; 1st fl, Lot 43, Block HS-4, Harbour Square; dm/s/d/tr/q RM25/55/70/105/120, d with shared bathroom RM60; ✴ 🅰) This new hostel has garnered enthusiastic reviews for its 11 clean, airy rooms and buzzing vibe. The four dorm rooms have six beds (bunks) each.

Sandakan Backpackers   HOSTEL $

(✆089-221104; www.sandakanbackpackers.com; Lot 107, Block SH-11, Harbour Square; dm/s/d/tr RM25/50/60/90; ✴ @ 🅰) A spartan but clean, well-lit place to meet other citizens of Backpackistan.

Sea View Sandakan   HOSTEL $

(✆089-221221; www.seaviewsandakan.com; 1st fl, Lot 126, Jln Dua, Harbour Square 14; dm RM19-26, d/tr/q RM67/93/110; ✴ 🅰) A fine, friendly little hostel with clean (if plain) rooms, a top-floor lounge and helpful staff. Situated across the street from Sandakan Central Market.

🍴 Eating

There's a row of restaurants along the waterfront, west of the new Harbour Mall.

Sandakan Central Market   MARKET $

(Jln Dua; mains RM1-8; ⊙3am-11pm) The upstairs food stalls – Malay, Chinese, Indonesian and Filipino – serve the city centre's cheapest eats. Stall 21 (open 5am to 3pm) is vegetarian.

English Tea House & Restaurant   TEAHOUSE $$

(✆089-222544; www.englishteahouse.org; Jln Istana; mains RM15.50-55, cocktails RM16.80-20;

⊙10am-11pm) Play croquet on the manicured lawn after taking your afternoon tea – with scones, of course. Alas, the food is not as nice as the panoramic view of KK and the Sulu Sea. Situated next to the Agnes Keith Museum.

🍷 Drinking & Nightlife

Much of Sandakan's dining and nightlife takes place in the suburb of Bandar Indah Jaya, 7km towards Sepilok at Batu 4 (Mile 4). To get there, take a bus or minibus (RM1.20) from Terminal Bas Sandakan.

★ Ba Lin Roof Garden   BAR

(Balin; ✆089-272988; www.nakhotel.com; 18th fl, Nak Hotel, Jln Pelabuhan Lama; mains RM14-26, cocktails RM16-25; ⊙7.30am-1am, happy hour 2-8pm; 🅰) The chill-out couches, wood-slat tables and oblique sea views bring a certain LA sexiness to Sandakan.

ⓘ Information

There's a cluster of banks around the intersection of Lebuh Tiga and Jln Pelabuhan Lama.

Duchess of Kent Hospital (✆089-248600; http://hdok.moh.gov.my/; Batu 2 (Mile 2), Jln Utara) Sabah's second-largest government hospital, with 400 beds.

TiN Internet (Lot 66, Harbour Square; per hr RM2.50; ⊙10am-midnight)

Tourist Information Centre (✆089-229751; Wisma Warisan, Lebuh Tiga; ⊙8am-4pm Mon-Fri, closed public holidays) Has details on regional attractions, including the Sandakan Heritage Trail. Situated up the stairs from Lebuh Tiga, very near city hall (the MPS), Muzium Warisan Sandakan (the Sandakan Heritage Museum) and the Sandakan Liberation Monument.

GETTING TO THE PHILIPPINES: SANDAKAN TO ZAMBOANGA

Getting to the border Weesam Express (✆089-212872; www.zimnet.com/weesam/php/booking.php; ground fl, Hotel New Sabah Bldg, Block 42-18, Jln Singapura) links Sandakan with Zamboanga (2nd/1st class RM260/280), on the Philippine island of Mindanao. Ferries depart Sandakan harbour at 6am on Tuesday and Friday, arriving in Zamboanga at 7.30pm the same day.

At the border Because of lawlessness (including kidnappings) and an Islamist insurgency, Western embassies warn against travel to or through Zamboanga, so check local conditions before taking this ferry. Travellers we spoke to said you don't need an onward ticket to enter the Philippines, but the Filipino government says otherwise; it may be wise to have one just in case.

Alternative route At press time there were plans to inaugurate car ferry services between Kudat, at the northern tip of Sabah, and Brooke's Point on the Philippine island of Palawan. MASwings (✆1300 88 3000; www.maswings.com) has announced plans to fly from KK to Puerto Princesa, Palawan.

ⓘ Getting There & Away

AIR

AirAsia (www.airasia.com) and **Malaysia Airlines** (www.malaysiaairlines.com) both have flights to KK and KL, while **MASwings** (📞1300 88 3000; www.maswings.com) flies to KK, Kudat and Tawau.

BUS

Sandakan's long-distance bus station is at Batu 2.5 (Mile 2.5), 4km north of the city centre. It is linked to Terminal Bas Sandakan, in the city centre, by minibuses (RM1, until 9pm or 10pm) that stop along the main road. A taxi to town should cost RM13.

Companies with services to KK include **Sida Express** (089-224990). All buses to/from KK pass by Kinabalu National Park but won't stop to pick up passengers if they're full – this can be a problem during holiday periods.

The best bet to Semporna is **Dyana Express** (📞089-784494). To get to Semporna, you can also head to Lahad Datu and then take a minibus.

ⓘ Getting Around

TO/FROM THE AIRPORT

The airport is 13km northwest of the city centre. The Batu 7 Airport bus (RM2) stops on the main road about 500m from the terminal.

A coupon taxi to the town centre costs RM30; going the other way, expect to pay about RM25.

BUS & MINIBUS

Terminal Bas Sandakan (Sandakan Bus Terminal; Jln Coastal), in the city centre, is a chaotic parking lot behind the downmarket Centre Point Plaza shopping mall. Most buses head north out of the centre along Jln Utara. Each is marked with a sign indicating how far it goes – to Batu 2.5 (Mile 2.5, ie the long-distance bus station; RM1), for instance, or Batu 14 (the turn-off to Sepilok; RM2.70).

The end of the line is Batu 32 (RM5), on the KK–Semporna highway.

Sepilok

📄 089

Sepilok's Orang-Utan Rehabilitation Centre is one of the only places in the world where you can see Asia's great ginger ape in its natural rainforest habitat. It's well worth sticking around to do some jungle hiking and mellow out in one of Sepilok's attractive, good-value guesthouses.

⊙ Sights & Activities

Sepilok Orang-Utan Rehabilitation Centre   ANIMAL SANCTUARY

(SORC; 📞089-531189, emergency 089-531180; sorc64@gmail.com; Jln Sepilok; adult/child RM30/15, camera fee RM10; ⊗ticket counter 9-11am & 2-3.30pm) 🦧 Orphaned and injured orang-utans are brought to Sepilok's primary rainforest for rehabilitation before being reintroduced to rainforest life. While this long process is under way, the semi-wild simians are offered food twice a day, at 10am and 3pm, to supplement their natural diet of forest fruits. Tickets are valid for the whole day, so if the orang-utans don't show in the morning you can come back in the afternoon, when there are fewer tour groups.

Orang-utans have been known to snatch visitors' possessions in search of food, so backpacks, handbags, food, drinks and insect repellent (which could poison the animals if they drink it) must be placed in secure lockers (no charge) at park headquarters.

Several lovely walking trails lead into the forest; register at the visitor reception centre before heading out.

Rainforest Discovery Centre   PARK

(RDC; 📞089-533780; www.forest.sabah.gov.my/rdc; adult/child RM17/5; ⊗ticket counter 8am-5pm, park until 8pm) The orang-utan centre's botanical counterpart, this densely forested park features a well-marked botanical garden, night walks and a **canopy walkway** whose eight towers give you a bird's-eye view of the

---

BUSES FROM SANKADAN

DESTINATION	PRICE (RM)	DURATION (HR)	FREQUENCY
Kinabalu National Park	35	4-5	frequently, 6.30am-8pm
Kota Kinabalu (Inanam Bus Terminal)	43	6-7	frequently, 6.30am-8pm
Lahad Datu	22	2½	N/A
Semporna	44	5½	7.30am, 2pm
Tawau	42	6	6.30-10am

tree tops. To get there from the SORC, head 1.4km north (towards Batu 14) and then 600m west.

🛌 Sleeping

The Sepilok area offers much more attractive and atmospheric accommodation options than Sandakan.

Sepilok B&B   B&B $
(📞089-534050; www.sepilokbednbreakfast.com.my; Jln Fabia; dm/d with fan RM31/68, d with aircon RM150) Surrounded by peaceful gardens, this relaxing place has an open-air verandah that's great for socialising. Rooms are simple but cosy; dorms have six beds. Situated 200m towards the Rainforest Discovery Centre from the Batu 14–Sepilok road.

Uncle Tan Guesthouse   GUESTHOUSE $
(📞016 824 4749; www.uncletan.com; Jln Batu 14; dm/d/tr incl meals RM48/100/150; ❀@🛜) You're assured of a warm welcome at this sprawling, basic place, run by a company known for its tours of the Kinabatangan area (RM420 for three days). Situated 400m towards Sepilok from Batu 14 junction – very convenient if you're arriving by bus. Offers free transport to Sepilok's sights.

★Sepilok Forest Edge Resort   RESORT $$
(📞013 869 5069, 089-533190; www.sepilokforestedgeresort.com; Jln Rambutan; dm RM40, chalets RM220-550; ❀🛜🏊) The 15 romantic chalets offer rustic luxury, but even travellers who stay in the four simple dorm rooms, with two or three beds each, can enjoy the gorgeous gardens, 5m pool and superb open-air restaurant. Rates include breakfast. Family-friendly.

★Paganakan Dii
Tropical Retreat   BOUTIQUE HOTEL $$
(📞089-532005; www.paganakandii.com; dm/chalet RM30/150; ❀🛜) Deep within a deer preserve, Taman Jalal Alip, this quiet and very welcoming retreat sports wooden chalets, chic design details made from recycled materials, and crisp white linens. Great value for money – book early! Offers free transport to/from the Sepilok sights and Batu 14, 2.5km to the southeast.

ℹ Getting There & Away

Sepilok is about 25km west of Sandakan. The area's main sights are 2km to 3km south of Sepilok Junction, aka Batu 14 (Mile 14), so named because it's 14 miles (23km) from Sandakan (towards KK).

If you're coming by bus from KK or Semporna, ask the driver to let you off at Batu 14 – look for a roundabout with a lichen-darkened statue of an orang-utan in the middle. From there, catch a 'pirate' taxi – one is usually waiting.

If you're coming from Sandakan, go to Terminal Bas Sandakan and take the bus marked 'Batu 14 Sepilok' (RM5, 45 minutes, departures at 8am, 9am, 10.30am, 11.30am, 1pm and 2pm), which has stops at the SORC and the RDC. Departures from Sepilok are at 9am, 10am, 11.30am, 12.30pm, 2pm and 4pm. You can also take any bus or minibus that passes by Batu 14 (RM2.70) and then catch a 'pirate' taxi.

A taxi from Sandakan or the airport costs RM40.

Sungai Kinabatangan

The 560km-long Kinabatangan River, Sabah's longest waterway, is one of the best places in Southeast Asia to see jungle wildlife in its native habitat. The reason, tragically, is that creatures such as orang-utans, proboscis monkeys (the C is silent), macaques, hornbills (all eight species) and blue-eared kingfishers have been pushed to the banks of the Kinabatangan by encroaching oil palm plantations.

The cathedral-like Gomantong Caves, Sabah's most famous source of swiftlet nests, are about midway between Kampung Sukau and Sukau Junction.

To explore the Kinabatangan, you can book a tour with a KK- or Sandakan-based agency (expect to pay about RM420 for three days and two nights) – but contrary to what you might hear, you can also come on your own and book boat trips à la carte.

However, you do need to arrange accommodation in advance, if only to coordinate transport from Sandakan or Sukau Junction.

🏃 Activities

The best way to see wild rainforest creatures is to take guided river cruises run by local guesthouses (and tour agencies). Most take place early in the morning and around sunset, when the animals are most active, and cost RM40 per person in an eight- to 12-person fibreglass motorboat. Some outfits also offer short jungle treks (RM20). Bring binoculars and, for photos, a telephoto lens.

MALAYSIA SUNGAI KINABATANGAN

Night cruises, with their bright lights and camera flashes, can be intrusive – ask your guide how you and your group can avoid disturbing the animals.

🛌 Sleeping

The places listed below are all in Kampung Sukau (population 3000). Board costs RM10 to RM20 per meal. Bilit has quite a few homestays (http://bilithomestay.wordpress.com).

Sukau Greenview B&B   B&B **$**
(☑ 013 869 6922, 089-565266; http://sukaugreenviewbnb.zxq.net; r with fan/air-con per person RM35/45) Basic but quite comfy for the price, with very friendly staff. Meals are served in a riverside pavilion.

Sukau Evergreen Lodge   GUESTHOUSE **$**
(☑ 017 831 3832; www.sukauevergreen.com; per person with fan/air-con incl breakfast RM35/55) A family-run guesthouse with a great verandah and 10 big, spacious, spotless rooms.

Barefoot Sukau Lodge   LODGE **$**
(☑ 089-237525; www.barefootsukau.com; r per person incl breakfast RM40; 🛜) In a lovely riverfront spot, this friendly, wood-built place has 10 decent, simple rooms with fan and attached hot-water bathroom.

Sukau B&B   B&B **$**
(☑ 014 559 3181, 019 583 5580; bnbsukau2013@yahoo.com; dm/s/tw incl breakfast RM20/40/40) As budget as the Kinabatangan gets, with eight spartan, wood-panelled, fan-equipped rooms. Situated 2km past Sukau village, at the end of the road (literally).

ℹ Information

In the centre of Kampung Sukau, **Pusat Internet 1 Malaysia** (per hr RM1.50; ⏲ 8am-5pm; 🛜) has satellite internet access and free 24hr wi-fi.

ℹ Getting There & Away

To get to Sukau, take any bus travelling from KK or Sandakan to Lahad Datu or Semporna (or vice versa) and get off at Sukau Junction (Simpang Sukau); minibuses to Sukau (42km; RM20 per person, minimum two) stop next to the tin-roofed rain shelter. Prearrange pick-up with your guesthouse.

Semporna

☑ 089 / POP 134,000

The mainland town of Semporna is ugly, chaotic and has, shall we say, rubbish dispos-al issues, but it's the only gateway to some of the world's most stunning scuba diving, off legendary Sipadan and around other islands of the storied Semporna Archipelago. There are no beaches on the mainland.

🏃 Activities

A variety of scuba operators have offices around the Semporna seafront complex and/or in KK.

Scuba Junkie   DIVING
(☑ 089-785372; www.scuba-junkie.com; Lot 36, Block B, Semporna seafront; diving/snorkelling day trips incl lunch RM300/110; ⏲ 9am-6pm) Hugely popular with backpackers, Semporna's largest operator runs a very attractive resort on Mabul. Boats to Mabul leave at 8am and 2.30pm.

Big John Scuba   DIVING
(BJ Scuba; ☑ 089-785399; www.smiffystravels.com/BJSUBA2.htm; Jln Kastam; 3-dive day trip RM280, snorkelling day trip RM150-180) 'Big John' is a local guy with almost 20 years of diving experience – and PADI instructor certification – who loves Sabah, Semporna and diving. Divers lodge on Mabul at Arung Hayat Guesthouse. Has a Facebook page.

Seahorse Sipadan   DIVING
(☑ 012 279 7657, 089-782289; www.seahorsesipadanscuba.com) Backpacker-oriented company that runs a hostel on Mabul.

Billabong Scuba   DIVING
(☑ 089-781866; www.billabongscuba.com; Lot 28, Block E, Semporna seafront) Known for low prices, this outfit has its own basic guesthouse on Mabul.

🛌 Sleeping

If you have to overnight in Semporna (likely given the bus and boat schedules), your options are limited – but not dire. Most of the dorm beds are in places owned by scuba companies.

Scuba Junkie Dive Lodge   HOSTEL **$**
(☑ 089-785372; www.scuba-junkie.com; Lot 36, Block B, Semporna seafront; dm/d RM50/130, d with bathroom RM160; ❄ @) A clean and sociable spot, with a very popular bar-restaurant. The dorms, spacious and well-ventilated, have six to 10 solid wooden beds. Scuba Junkie divers get 50% off. Breakfast not included.

Borneo Global Sipadan
BackPackers   HOSTEL **$**
(☏ 089-785088; www.borneotourstravel.com; Jln Causeway; dm/tr/f incl breakfast RM25/90/120; ❄ @ ☎) Cheap and cheerful, this simply furnished establishment has triples, family rooms and an eight-bed dorm room, all with air-con and attached bathroom. Situated across the street from the six-storey Seafest Hotel.

Sipadan Inn   HOTEL **$**
(☏ 089-781766; www.sipadaninn-hotel.com; Block D, Lot 19-24, Semporna seafront; d from RM86; ❄ @ ☎) Rooms are white, smallish, practical and clean.

Dragon Inn   HOTEL **$**
(Rumah Rehat Naga; ☏ 089-781088; www.dragoninnfloating.com.my; 1 Jln Kastam, Semporna Ocean Tourism Centre; dm RM25, r incl breakfast from RM80; ❄ @ ☎) Built over the water facing the Semporna seafront, this all-wood, Bajaustyle 'floating resort' has 62 rooms, including three basic dorm rooms with 22 beds each. Has space when other places don't.

ℹ Information

Semporna has several ATMs, including one in the outside wall of the Giant Supermarket.

ℹ Getting There & Away

AIR

From Tawau Airport (situated 70km from Semporna, 30km from Tawau and about 2.5km off the main highway), **AirAsia** (www.airasia.com) and **Malaysia Airlines** (☏ 1300 88 3000; www.malaysiaairlines.com) have flights to KK and KL. **MASwings** (☏ 1300 88 3000; www.maswings.com.my) links Semporna with Tawau, KK and the North Kalimantan (Indonesia) island of Tarakan.

From Semporna's bus station, a minibus to Tawau Airport (to the terminal) costs RM20; departures are most frequent in the morning. A taxi costs RM90.

Remember that flying less than 24 hours after scuba diving can be dangerous.

BUS

Semporna's bus terminal, with a row of ticket counters representing half-a-dozen companies, is near the waterfront 200m northwest of the big, light green mosque (past the mosque if you're coming from the Semporna seafront).

To KK, reliable companies include **Manis Liner** (6am and 7.30pm), **Sabariah Express** (7.30am) and **Madsahirun** (7.30am). Manis Express is often unreliable but it is the only one with buses to Tawau.

Perhaps the most reliable bus company is **Dyana Express** (☏ 089-784494; Jln Hospital), whose stop is a few hundred metres south of (inland from) the bus terminal.

Buses to KK and Sandakan leave at 7.30am and 2pm (the latter is the slightly more expensive VIP class), and there's an overnight bus to KK at 7.30pm.

Right around the bus terminal, minibuses head to Lahad Datu, where you can catch a bus to Sandakan (RM22).

Another option to Sandakan: take a KK-bound bus and get off at Batu 32 (Mile 32) Junction, where you can catch a bus or minibus into the city.

Semporna Archipelago

Take the word 'blue' and mentally turn it over through all of its possibilities, from the deepest, richest shades to the robin-egg tones of the sky at noon: this is the rippled waterscape of the Semporna Archipelago, accented with brightly painted boats, swaying palms and white sand. But no one comes this way just for the island beaches – it's the ocean and everything in it that has brought fame to these islands as one of the most spectacular diving destinations in the world.

🏃 Activities

Sipadan (Pulau Sipadan; www.sabahparks.org.my; three-day, two-night package RM1690), 40km from Semporna, is the shining star in the archipelago's constellation of shimmering islands. Volcanic in origin, it rises 600m from the seabed.

The macro-diving around **Mabul** (Pulau Mabul) is world-famous. Dive sites around **Kapalai** (a large sandbar) and the islands of **Mataking** (fantastic for snorkelling; onshore there's an ultra-luxury resort) and

BUSES FROM SEMPORNA

DESTINATION	PRICE (RM)	DURATION	DEPARTURES
Kota Kinabalu	75	9½hr	6am, 7.30am, 2pm, 7.30pm
Sandakan	45	5½hr	7.30am, 2pm
Tawau	20	80min	7.30am, 1.30pm, 3.30pm

GETTING TO INDONESIA: TAWAU TO TARAKAN & NUNUKAN

Getting to the border The port of Tawau, 100km southwest of Semporna, has an Indonesian consulate (☑089-752969, 089-772052; Jln Sinn Onn, Wisma Fuji; ☺8am-noon & 1pm or 2-4pm Mon-Fri, closed Indonesian and Malaysian public holidays) known for being fast and efficient – many travellers are in and out in an hour. A 60-day tourist visa costs RM170 and requires two passport photos. The consulate, 4km from the city centre, is served by two buses an hour from the central bus station.

At the border Ferries link Tawau with two islands in North Kalimantan: Tarakan (RM140, three to four hours, late-morning departures daily, except Sunday); and Nunukan (RM65, one hour, 10am and 3pm daily, except Sunday). MASwings (☑1300 88 3000; www.maswings.com.my) flies from Tawau to Tarakan.

Moving on Speedboats link Tarakan with Tanjung Selor, on the mainland. From Nunukan and Tarakan, Pelni (www.pelni.co.id) has ferries to Balikpapan (East Kalimantan) and the Sulawesi ports of Toli-Toli, Pare-Pare and Makassar (one to three days). Various airlines link Tarakan and Nunukan with cities on the Kalimantan mainland, on Sulawesi and elsewhere in Indonesia.

Sibuan are also exceptional. The northern islands of the archipelago, which has many of the area's nicest beaches, are protected as Tun Sakaran Marine Park (101 sq km).

If Sipadan is your dream dive, make reservations *at least two months ahead* (more for July and August and from mid-December to mid-January) – only 120 diving permits, divided among a dozen operators, are issued each day. These can be arranged through companies based in Semporna (p446) and/or KK (p433). If you have time to hang out in Semporna, Sipadan spots sometimes do open up at the last minute.

To dive elsewhere in the archipelago (as 80% of visitors do – and have a great time!) or take a PADI course (three-day Open Water certification costs about RM975), advance reservations are a very good idea. Weather rarely, if ever, affects diving here.

The cheapest way to dive is to stay in the town of Semporna and take day trips (diving RM300 to RM350, snorkelling RM110) but you'll miss out on post-dive chill sessions on the sand and some impossibly romantic equatorial sunsets.

🛏 Sleeping

The archipelago's only relatively inexpensive (ie non-luxury) accommodation is on Mabul (population 2000), 26km southeast of Semporna and 14km north of Sipadan (where sleepovers are completely banned). All the places listed below are affiliated with dive operators.

Mabul is endowed with a nice white-sand beach, fantastically blue waters, a marine police base and two small, impoverished settlements: on the northeast coast, a hamlet of Bajau sea gypsies, known for their colourful, pointy-prowed boats called *jonkong*; on the southwest coast, a Suluk and Malay stilt village is home to several guesthouses.

You can walk all the way around the island, which measures 800m by about 450m, in about 45 minutes. Little shops sell seashells, corals or shark's teeth but please don't buy them – collecting them is terrible for the reefs.

Accommodation rates include meals. Prices rise and places fill fast in July and August.

Scuba Junkie Mabul
Beach Resort   RESORT $$
(☑089-785372; www.scuba-junkie.com; dm RM130, d with fan/air-con RM320/430; ❊🗢) Surrounded by lovely gardens, this flowery place has wooden chalets with porches and two spacious, 10-bed dorm rooms. Runs a turtle conservation program. Divers (but not snorkellers) who book with Scuba Junkie get a 25% discount.

Arung Hayat Guesthouse   LODGE $$
(☑Mabul 013 559 4678, Mabul 017 896 6875, Semporna 089-782846; arunghayatsemporna@gmail.com; dm/d RM70/180) This friendly guesthouse, on stilts over the water, is a great place to meet people. Has 22 private rooms, plus two dorm rooms with six and 10 beds. Big John Scuba has eight rooms here.

Billabong Scuba

Backpackers   GUESTHOUSE **$$**
(☑089-781866; www.billabongscuba.com; d with fan/air-con RM140/240) Built on stilts over the water, this 23-room guesthouse is a fine spot to chill with fisherfolk and watch sunsets. All rooms have attached bathroom.

Seahorse Sipadan

Scuba Lodge   GUESTHOUSE **$$**
(☑Semporna 089-782289; www.seahorse-sipadan-scuba.com; dm/d from RM80/200) The 11 rooms, with overhead fans and colourful contact-paper floors, are basic but serviceable.

❶ Getting There & Around

Transport from Semporna to the archipelago is handled by dive operators and guesthouse owners – ask for details when you book. From Semporna, getting to Mabul costs RM50 one-way (50 to 60 minutes), plus a RM10 jetty fee.

Departures from Semporna are either from the Public Jetty (Jeti Umum), just east of the Semporna seafront, or the tourist jetty, 1km to the northwest, where the marine police check passenger manifests.

Pulau Labuan

☑087 / POP 85,000
The Federal Territory of Labuan (www.labuantourism.my) has been a duty-free port since the late 1840s when it became a British crown colony. These days, Malaysians, Bruneians and expat oil workers flock to the island for duty-free shopping, remarkably cheap alcohol (a six-pack of Carlsberg beer costs just RM13) and various fleshly pleasures. The main town, Bandar Labuan, is much cleaner and better organised than its counterparts in Sabah and is linked by ferry with Kota Kinabalu and Brunei. WWII buffs will find several sights of interest, including the Australian and British Labuan War Cemetery, 2km northwest of the city centre.

🛏 Sleeping

Mariner Hotel   HOTEL **$$**
(☑087-418822; mhlabuan@streamyx.com; U0468 Jln Tanjung Purun; s/d RM110/130; ❉@🛜) A good-value business hotel with 60 clean, well-kept rooms. Situated five long blocks east of the ferry terminal.

❶ Getting There & Away

Daily passenger ferries link KK's Jesselton Point Ferry Terminal with Bandar Labuan (economy/

GETTING TO BRUNEI: PULAU LABUAN TO BANDAR SERI BEGAWAN

Getting to the border Ferries from Bandar Labuan to the Bruneian port of Muara (RM35, 1¼ hours) generally depart at 9am, 1.30pm, 3.30pm and 4pm.

At the border Most travellers to Brunei are issued on-arrival visas valid for 14 or 30 days.

Moving on Ferries from Bandar Labuan dock at Terminal Feri Serasa in Muara, 20km northeast of Bandar Seri Begawan. To get to the city centre, take bus 37 or 39 (B$1, one hour) or the Express Bus Service (B$2, 30 minutes). A taxi should cost R$30.

business RM39/44, 3¼ hours, departures at 8am and 1.30pm). In the other direction, boats depart from Bandar Labuan at 8am and 1pm.

Passenger ferries to the Bruneian port of Muara (RM35, 1¼ hours), 20km northeast of Bandar Seri Begawan, generally leave Bandar Labuan at 9am, 1.30pm and 3.30pm. A car ferry departs at 4pm (☑013-868 7705; www.pkljaya.com; RM35, 1½ hours). Be at the terminal at least a half-hour before departure.

If you're travelling from KK to Brunei and don't want to overnight on Pulau Labuan, take the 8am boat from KK and then an afternoon ferry to Muara.

MALAYSIAN BORNEO – SARAWAK

Sarawak makes access to Borneo's natural wonders and cultural riches a breeze. From Kuching, the island's most sophisticated and dynamic city, pristine rainforests – where you can spot orang-utans, proboscis monkeys and the world's largest flower, the *Rafflesia* – can be visited on day trips, with plenty of time in the evening for a delicious meal and a drink in a chic bar.

More adventurous travellers can take a 'flying coffin' riverboat up the Batang Rejang, 'the Amazon of Borneo', to seek out remote longhouses, or fly to the spectacular caves and extraordinary rock formations of Gunung Mulu National Park, a Unesco World Heritage Site.

MALAYSIA PULAU LABUAN

Everywhere you go, you'll encounter the warmth, unforced friendliness and sense of humour that make the people of Malaysia's most culturally diverse state such delightful hosts.

Kuching

📍 082 / POP 594,000

The capital of Sarawak brings together a kaleidoscope of cultures, cuisines and crafts. The bustling streets – some very modern, others with a colonial vibe – amply reward visitors with a penchant for aimless ambling. Chinese temples decorated with dragons abut shophouses from the time of the White Rajahs, a South Indian mosque is a five-minute walk from stalls selling half-a-dozen Asian cuisines, and a landscaped riverfront park attracts families out for a stroll and a quick bite.

⦿ Sights

The main attraction here is the city itself. Leave plenty of time to wander aimlessly and soak up the relaxed vibe and charming cityscapes of areas such as Jln Carpenter (Old Chinatown), Jln India, Jln Padungan (New Chinatown) and the Waterfront Promenade.

Sarawak's excellent museums are free.

Waterfront Promenade   WATERFRONT
(along Main Bazaar & Jln Gambier; river cruises RM20) The walkways and flowerbeds along Sungai Sarawak are a fine place for a romantic stroll any time a cool breeze blows off the river, especially at sunset. In the evening the waterfront is ablaze with colourful fairy lights and full of couples and families eating snacks as *tambang* (small passenger ferries) glide past with their glowing lanterns.

The promenade affords great views across the river to the white, crenellated towers and manicured gardens of the **Astana** (official residence of the rajahs and governors of Sarawak since 1869); hilltop Fort Margherita; and, between the two, the **Sarawak State Assembly**, with its golden pointy roof.

Old Chinatown   NEIGHBOURHOOD
(Jln Carpenter) Lined with evocative, colonial-era shophouses and home to several vibrantly coloured Chinese temples, Jln Carpenter stretches from ornamental **Harmony Arch** (cnr Jln Tun Abang Haji Openg & Jln Carpenter) eastward to **Hong San Si Temple** (cnr Jln Wayang

& Jln Carpenter; ⊙ 6am-6pm) **FREE**, also known by its Hokkien name, Say Ong Kong.

India Street   STREET
(Jln India) Turn off this exuberant commercial thoroughfare (between Nos 37 and 39A) onto tiny **Indian Mosque Lane** (Jln Sempit) and you enter another world, anchored by Kuching's oldest **mosque** (Indian Mosque Lane; ⊙ 6am-8.30pm except during prayers) **FREE**, built in 1863 by Muslim traders from Tamil Nadu. Also accessible from Jln Gambier (between Nos 24 and 25A).

Sarawak Museum   MUSEUM
(www.museum.sarawak.gov.my; Jln Tun Abang Haji Openg; ⊙ 9am-4.45pm Mon-Fri, 10am-4pm Sat, Sun & holidays) **FREE** Sarawak's premier museum, extensively renovated in 2012 and 2013, has a first-rate collection of cultural artefacts and is a must-see for anyone interested in Borneo's peoples and habitats. In the **Ethnology Museum** (Old Building), on the top of the hill, the upstairs section has excellent (though recently bowdlerised) exhibits on Dayak crafts, customs and longhouses. Downstairs is an old-fashioned **natural history museum** whose highlight, some say, is a hairball attached to a 'human dental plate' that was found in the stomach of a man-eating crocodile. Across the street (and linked by a footbridge), **Dewan Tun Abdul Razak** (New Building) has exhibits on Sarawakian history and archaeology. The cafe has wi-fi.

Chinese History Museum   MUSEUM
(cnr Main Bazaar & Jln Wayang; ⊙ 9am-4.45pm Mon-Fri, 10am-4pm Sat, Sun & holidays) **FREE** An excellent introduction to the nine Chinese communities – each with its own dialect, cuisine and temples – who began settling in Sarawak around 1830. The entrance is on the river side of the building.

Fort Margherita   FORT
(Kampung Boyan; ⊙ 9am-4.30pm) **FREE** Inspired by an English Renaissance castle, whitewashed Fort Margherita (1879) manages to feel both medieval-European and tropical. At research time the interior was closed. To get there, take a *tambang* (boat; 50 sen) from the Waterfront Promenade to **Kampung Boyan** (graced by a new riverfront promenade) and follow the signs for 500m.

New Chinatown   NEIHHBOURHOOD
(Jln Padungan) Built starting in the 1920s, Kuching's liveliest commercial

Kuching

MALAYSIA

0   200 m
0   0.1 miles

KAMPUNG BOYAN

PADUNGAN

BUKIT MATA

Sungai Sarawak

Astana (200m)

Terminal One Club (200m);

Beds (200m); Great Cat of Kuching (250m)

Jln Padungan
Jln Abell
Jln Chan Chin Ann
Jln Song Thian Cheok
Jln Padungan
Jln Bukit Mata Kuching
Jln Matang
Jln Tabuan
Jln Ban Hock
Jln Ban Hock
Persiaran Ban Hock
Jln Tunku Abdul Rahman
Jln Brooke
Jln Borneo
Jln Padungan
Jln Green Hill
Jln Temple
Jln Wayang
Jln Bishopsgate
Main Bazaar
Jln McDougall
Jln Reservoir
Jln Tun Abang Haji Openg
Jln Tun Haji Openg
Jln Satok
Jln Pearl
Jln Barrack
Jln India
Jln Gambier
Indian Mosque Lane
Jln Market
Jln Khoo Hun Yeang
Jln P Banive
Jln Mosque (Jln Masjid)

Mohamed Yahia & Sons
Sarawak Plaza
Cat Fountain
Tun Jugah Shopping Centre
Cat Column
Malaysia Airlines
Sri Srinivasagar Kaliamman Hindu Temple
Riverside Shopping Complex
Cyber City
Pullman Kuching
Bukit Mata
An Hui Motor
Tua Pek Kong Temple
Klinik Chan
Visitors Sarawak Information Tourism Centre
National Park Booking Office
Square Tower
Hiang Thian Siang Temple
Bishop's House
Old Anglican Cemetery
St Thomas's Cathedral
Merdeka Plaza Mall
Padang Merdeka
Bishop's House
Dewan Tun Abdul Razak
Ethnology Museum
Museum Heroes Garden Monument
Islamic Museum
Kuching Mosque
Saujana Bus Station
Bus to Bako Bazaar
Sikh Temple
Sarawak General Hospital (1.2km)
Visa Department (2.5km)

1 2 3 4 5 6 7 8 9 10 11 12 13 14 15 16 17 18 19 20 21 22 23 24 25 26 28 29 30 31 32 33 34 35 36 37

Kuching

thoroughfare – pronounced pah-*doong*-ahn – is lined with Chinese-owned businesses, noodle shops and trendy cafes. It stretches for 1.5km from Jln Tunku Abdul Rahman to the **Great Cat of Kuching** (Jln Padungan).

◉ Tours

Lots of Kuching-based tour companies offer trips to places you can't easily visit on your own. Guesthouses are a good source of recommendations for itineraries and operators.

Adventure Alternative Borneo　　　　ADVENTURE TOUR
(☏ 012 845 1987; www.aaborneo.com; Lot 37, Jln Tabuan) Offers reasonably priced, sustainable trips to off-the-beaten-path destinations.

◉ Sleeping

Most guesthouse rooms have shared bathrooms; prices almost always include a toast-and-jam breakfast. Rates at some places rise in July (especially during the Rainforest World Music Festival), or from June to September. Beware: some guesthouses (not those we list) rent out musty, windowless cells.

★Threehouse B&B　　　　GUESTHOUSE $
(☏ 082-423499; www.threehousebnb.com; 51 Upper China St; dm RM20, d from RM60; @ 🛜) A spotless, family-friendly guesthouse in a great Old Chinatown location, with a warm and hugely welcoming vibe – everything a guesthouse should be!

★Singgahsana Lodge　　　　GUESTHOUSE $
(☏ 082-429277; www.singgahsana.com; 1 Jln Temple; dm RM30, d with shared/private bathroom RM88/108; ❄ @ 🛜) Decked out with stylish Dayak crafts, this hugely popular, 110-bed guesthouse has an unbeatable location, spacious rooms (all with windows) and Kuching's best chill-out lobby.

SPLURGE

A superb location, classy design and super-friendly staff make the **Batik Boutique Hotel** (☏ 082-422845; www.batikboutiquehotel.com; 38 Jln Padungan; d incl breakfast RM250; ❄ 🛜) a very romantic choice. The 15 spacious rooms, six with balconies, are sleek and elegant, and even come with i-Pod docks.

453

Lodge 121
GUESTHOUSE $

(☑082-428121; www.lodge121.com; Lot 121, 1st fl, Jln Tabuan; d/tr RM77/100, dm/s/d/tr/q with shared bathroom RM20/49/57/74/99; ▣@⊚) Polished concrete abounds at this mod charmer, a sleek, spotless, low-key hang-out for flashpackers. The carpeted dorm room, with 10 mattresses on the floor, is in the garret.

Nomad Borneo B&B
GUESTHOUSE $

(☑082-237831; www.borneobnb.com; Jln Green Hill 7; d RM75, dm/s/d/f with shared bathroom RM20/50/70/100; ▣@⊚) There's a buzzing backpacker vibe at this Iban-run favourite. Ten of the 17 rooms have windows; the others make do with exhaust fans. Dorm rooms have either four or eight beds.

Fairview Guesthouse
GUESTHOUSE $

(☑082-240017, Annie 013 816 4560; www.thefairview.com.my; 6 Jln Taman Budaya; s/d/f RM50/70/125; ▣@) Housed in a mid-20th-century villa, this hugely welcoming guesthouse is ideal if you're in the mood for a peaceful garden setting.

B&B Inn
GUESTHOUSE $

(☑082-237366; bnbswk@streamyx.com; 30-I Jln Tabuan; dm RM16, s/d/tr with shared bathroom RM30/40/54, d RM70; ▣@⊚) Clean and low-key, the B&B Inn has a lived-in, old-fashioned feel and a dozen of the cheapest decent rooms in town. Air-con costs RM5 extra a day. If the street door is padlocked, ring the bell.

Beds
GUESTHOUSE $

(☑082-424229; www.bedsguesthouse.com; 229 Jln Padungan; dm/s/d RM20/40/55; ▣@⊚) In the heart of Kuching's New Chinatown, this guesthouse gets great reviews thanks to its friendly vibe, spacious chill-out lobby and 12 spotless rooms, eight with windows.

Wo Jia Lodge
GUESTHOUSE $

(☑082-251776; www.wojialodge.com; 17 Main Bazaar; dm/s/d/tr with air-con RM20/40/52/90, s/d with fan RM35/48; ▣@⊚) The 18 spotless rooms (five with windows, the rest with effective exhaust fans) contain beds and nothing else. On the waterfront in an old Chinese shophouse.

Kapit Hotel
HOTEL $

(☑082-244179; kapithotelkuching@hotmail.com; 59 Jln Padungan; d/tr/q/f RM58/80/90/110; ▣⊚) Opened in 1974, this old-time cheapie has 16 clean, practical rooms with an early '80s vibe. Superbly central location; solid value.

John's Place
GUESTHOUSE $

(☑082-258329; 5 Jln Green Hill; d/tr/f RM72/105/125; ▣@⊚) A clean, welcoming spot to grab some Zs. Most of the 26 unexciting rooms have windows. The lively restaurant downstairs is a great place to meet other travellers.

Mandarin Hotel
HOTEL $

(☑082-418269; Jln Green Hill 3; d/tr from RM55/80; ▣⊚) This old-time Chinese hotel is head-and-shoulders above half-a-dozen similarly priced joints nearby. The 22 small, spotless, no-frills rooms were renovated in 2013; all have windows.

🍴 Eating

Kuching is the best place in Malaysian Borneo to work your way through the entire range of Sarawak-style cooking. At hawker centres, you can pick and choose from a variety of Chinese and Malay stalls, each specialising in a particular culinary tradition or dish. Jln Padungan is home to some of the city's best noodle houses.

Chong Choon Cafe
MALAYSIAN $

(Lot 121, Section 3, Jln Abell; mains RM4-5; ⊙7-11.30am or noon, closed Tue) You'd never guess it from the picnic tables, cooled by a fleet of overhead helicopter fans, but this unassuming cafe serves some of Kuching's most famously excellent Sarawak laksa.

Open-Air Market
MALAYSIAN $

(Tower Market; Jln Khoo Hun Yeang; mains from RM3-5; ⊙6am-9pm, a few stalls until midnight) Cheap, tasty local favourites include Sarawak laksa (available all day), Chinese-style *mee sapi* (beef noodle soup; from 6pm to midnight at Stall 32), red *kolo mee* (noodles with sweet barbecue sauce), tomato *kueh tiaw* (another fried rice-noodle dish) and shaved ice desserts (ask for 'ABC' at stall 17). An ideal spot for breakfast before boarding the bus to Bako National Park. Questions? Ask Gerard in Stall 10-11.

Yang Choon Tai Hawker Centre
CHINESE $

(23 Jln Carpenter; mains RM3.50-8; ⊙24hr except 1-4am) Six food stalls, run by members of the Teochew and Hainanese Chinese communities, serve up an eclectic assortment of dishes, including laksa (7am to about 5pm), rice porridge with pork (4am to 9am), *kolo mee* (5am to 3pm) and super fish soup (3pm to 10pm).

MALAYSIA KUCHING

LAKSA LUCK

Borneo's luckiest visitors start the day with a breakfast of Sarawak laksa, noodle soup made with coconut milk, lemon grass, sour tamarind and fiery *sambal belacan* (shrimp paste sauce), with fresh calamansi lime juice squeezed on top. Unbelievably *lazat* ('delicious' in Bahasa Malaysia)!

Green Hill Corner STREET FOOD $
(cnr Jln Temple & Jln Green Hill; meals RM3-6; ☉7am-10.30pm Mon-Sat, 7am-12.30pm Sun) Hugely popular with locals. Half-a-dozen stalls here crank out laska and porridge (morning only) as well as chicken rice and noodle dishes. The stall run by twin brothers serves superb beef noodle soup (RM4.50).

Kampung Boyan
Hawker Centres HAWKER $
(Kampung Boyan; mains RM3-6; ☉11.30am-11pm or midnight) Reached by *tambang* (RM0.50) from the Waterfront Promenade, Kampung Boyan's two tent-roofed hawker centres offer cheap, tasty Malay dishes and romantic views of the city centre.

Zhen Xiang Zhai
Vegetarian Cafe VEGETARIAN $
(139 Jln Padungan; mains RM2.80-8; ☉7am-7.30pm Mon-Sat; 🖉) Run by a Taoist family, this modest eatery serves vegetarian versions of local favourites, including laksa and delicious dishes made with shrimpless *sambal belacan* sauce.

Zhun San Yen Vegetarian
Food Centre VEGETARIAN $
(Lot 165, Jln Chan Chin Ann; mains RM3.50-5; ☉8am-6pm Mon-Sat; 🖉) Run by Buddhists, this place serves Taiwanese- and Malaysian-Chinese-style vegie meals (eg curries) that are as healthy as they are delicious. Buffet style from 8am to 2pm.

★ Tribal Stove DAYAK $$
(Block H, Jln Borneo; mains RM9-16, buffet lunch RM18; ☉11.30am-10.30pm Mon-Sat; 🖉🖉) A delicious slice of the Kelabit Highlands right in downtown Kuching. Specialities include *labo senutuq* (shredded beef cooked with wild ginger and dried chilli), *ab'eng* (shredded river fish) and *tuak* (rice wine; RM5). No MSG used. Situated directly opposite the main entrance to the Hilton.

★ Top Spot Food Court SEAFOOD $$
(Jln Padungan; fish per kg RM30-70, vegetable dishes RM8-12; ☉noon-11pm) A perennial favourite among local foodies, this neon-lit courtyard and its half-dozen humming seafooderies sits, rather improbably, on the roof of a concrete parking garage – look for the giant, backlit lobster sign. Ling Loong Seafood and the Bukit Mata Seafood Centre are particularly good. Stall K3 (open 8pm to 10pm) sells traditional Iban dishes.

Ting & Ting SUPERMARKET $
(30A Jln Tabuan; ☉9am-9pm, closed Sun & holidays) For self-catering, wine and toiletries.

🍷 Drinking & Nightlife

Cosmopolitan Kuching has plent of spirited drinking spots, including a clutch of attractive pubs and cafes along Jln Padungan Just for the record, Fort Margherita does not serve cocktails.

Ruai BAR
(7F Jln Ban Hock; ☉6pm-2.30am) This Iban-owned bar – a *ruai* is the covered verandah of an Iban longhouse – has a laid-back, cool and welcoming spirit all its own. A great place to meet people. Specialises in top-quality *tuak*. Starts to pick up after about 11pm or midnight.

Terminal One Club NIGHTCLUB
(Jln Padungan Utara, river end; admission free except special events; ☉5pm-2.30am) A genuine, thumping disco, complete with live Filipino cover bands, DJs and batteries of flashing lights. Things really get going after 10pm and hit their peak after midnight.

☆ Entertainment

Star Cineplex CINEMA
(www.starcineplex.com.my; 9th fl, multicoloured parking garage, Jln Temple; tickets 2D RM5-9, 3D RM9-14; ☉1st/last screenings at about 11.15am/11.15pm) Ideal for a rainy day. Most films are English; the rest have English subtitles. The elevator/lift is directly across Jln Temple from the Wong Eye Clinic & Surgery.

🛍 Shopping

Kuching is the best place in Malaysian Borneo to purchase the island's traditional arts and crafts, including hand-woven textiles and baskets, masks, drums, beaded headdresses, painted shields and Bruneian miniature cannons. Don't be afraid to negotiate a bit – there's plenty to choose from, and the quality varies as much as the price. Overpricing and dubiously 'aged' items are common, so be sure to spend some time browsing to familiarise yourself with the selection and prices.

Main Bazaar   HANDICRAFTS
(Main Bazaar; ⊘some shops closed Sun) The row of old shophouses facing the Waterfront Promenade houses crafts shops that range from upscale art galleries to chaotic establishments with a 'garage sale' appeal.

Mohamed Yahia & Sons   BOOKS
(🖊082-416928; Basement, Sarawak Plaza, Jln Tunku Abdul Rahman; ⊘10am-9pm) Specialises in English-language books about Borneo.

ℹ Information

EMERGENCY
Police, Ambulance & Fire (🖊999)

INTERNET ACCESS
Cyber City (Ground fl, Block D, Taman Sri Sarawak; 1st/2nd hr RM4/3; ⊘10am-11pm Mon-Sat, 11am-11pm Sun & holidays) To get there, exit the Riverside Shopping Complex (Jln Tunku Abdul Rahman) on the '2nd floor' and walk along the alley to the seventh shop on the right.

MEDICAL SERVICES
Klinik Chan (🖊082-240307; 98 Main Bazaar; ⊘8am-noon & 2-5pm Mon-Fri, 9am-noon Sat, Sun & holidays) Conveniently central. A consultation for a minor ailment costs RM30 to RM35.
Normah Medical Specialist Centre (🖊082-440055, emergency 082-311999; www.normah.com.my; Jln Tun Abdul Rahman, Petra Jaya; ⊘emergency 24hr, clinics 8.30am-4.30pm Mon-Fri, to 1pm Sat) Considered Kuching's best private hospital by many expats. Situated north of the river, about 6km by road from the centre.
Sarawak General Hospital (Hospital Umum Sarawak; 🖊082-276666; http://hus.moh.gov. my/v3; Jln Hospital; ⊘24hr) A large public hospital with modern facilities and reasonable rates; often overcrowded. Situated about 2km south of the centre; served by buses 2, B2, K6, K8 and K18 from Saujana Bus Station.

MONEY
Many of Kuching's banks and ATMs are clustered around the Cat Fountain on Jln Tunku Abdul Rahman.
Mohamed Yahia & Sons (Basement, Sarawak Plaza, Jln Tunku Abdul Rahman; ⊘10am-9pm) No commission, good rates and accepts over 30 currencies and travellers cheques.

TOURIST INFORMATION
National Park Booking Office (🖊082-248088; www.sarawakforestry.com; Jln Tun Abang Haji Openg, Sarawak Tourism Complex; ⊘8am-5pm Mon-Fri, closed public holidays) Helpful staff supply information on Sarawak's national parks, including news flashes on *Rafflesia* sightings (posted in the window when closed). Telephone enquiries are not only welcomed but patiently answered. Bookings for accommodation at Bako, Gunung Gading and Kubah National Parks and the Matang Wildlife Centre can be made in person, by phone or via http://ebooking.com.my. Situated next door to the Visitors Information Centre.
Visitors Information Centre (🖊082-410942, 082-410944; www.sarawaktourism.com; Jln Tun Abang Haji Openg, Sarawak Tourism Complex; ⊘8am-5pm Mon-Fri, closed public holidays) Located in the atmospheric Old Courthouse complex, this office has helpful and well-informed staff, lots of brochures and oodles of practical information (eg bus schedules), much of it on bulletin boards.

VISA EXTENSIONS
Visa Department (Bahagian Visa; 🖊082-245661; www.imi.gov.my; 2nd fl, Bangunan Sultan Iskandar, Kompleks Pejabat Persekutuan, cnr Jln Tun Razak & Jln Simpang Tiga; ⊘8am-5pm Mon-Thu, 8-11.45am & 2.15-5pm Fri) In a 17-storey federal office building about 3km south of the centre (along Jln Tabuan).

ℹ Getting There & Away

AIR
Kuching is linked by budget carrier **AirAsia** (www.airasia.com) with Kuala Lumpur, Johor Bahru, Penang and Singapore; and, within Borneo, Bintulu, Sibu, Miri and Kota Kinabalu. **Malaysia Airlines** (🖊1300 88 3000; www.malaysiaairlines.com) has direct flights to Singapore, Kota Kinabalu and Kuala Lumpur.
MASwings (🖊1300 88 3000; www.maswings. com.my) flies to Bandar Seri Begawan, Pontianak and 22 destinations in Sarawak and Sabah.

GETTING TO INDONESIA: KUCHING TO PONTIANAK

Getting to the border A variety of bus companies ply the route between Kuching's Kuching Sentral bus terminal (and other cities along the Sarawak coast) and the West Kalimantan city of Pontianak (economy RM45 to RM60, 1st class RM80, nine hours), crossing to the Tebedu/Entikong border.

At the border Travellers from 64 countries can get a one-month Indonesian 'visa on arrival' at the road crossing between Tebedu (Malaysia) and Entikong (Indonesia), 80km south of Kuching, the only official land border between Sarawak and Kalimantan.

Moving on Pontianak is linked to other parts of Indonesia and to Singapore by air.

BOAT

Much faster and a lot more fun than the bus, ferries to Sibu (economy/1st class RM45/55, 4¾ hours, daily at 8.30am), run by **Ekspress Bahagia** (☑ 016-800 5891, 016-889 3013, in Kuching 082-412 246, in Sibu 084-319-228), depart from the Express Wharf, 6km east of the centre. A taxi from town costs RM25.

BUS

Buses for many destinations can be booked online via www.busonlineticket.com.

Kuching Sentral (cnr Jln Penrissen & Jln Airport) This massive bus terminal-cum-shopping mall handles almost all of Kuching's long-haul bus services and some medium-haul lines too. Situated near the airport about 10km south of the city centre (hardly 'sentral'!), it is also known as Six-and-a-Half-Mile Bus Station. A

dozen companies send (usually over-airconditioned) buses along the Pan Borneo Highway to destinations such as Sibu, Bintulu and Miri from 6.30am to 10.30pm.

Kuching Sentral is linked to the Saujana Bus Station in central Kuching by local buses such as B2, K3, K6 and K10 (all RM1, departures from 6am to about 5pm). At taxi to/from the city centre costs RM33/30.

Saujana Bus Station (Jln Masjid & Jln P Ramlee) Kuching's chaotic local bus station, situated a few blocks from the western end of the Waterfront Promenade, handles services to a few destinations outside greater Kuching, including three national parks. Some buses have stops at the end of Jln Masjid, others around the corner on Jln P Ramlee (under the pedestrian bridge).

ⓘ Getting Around

TO/FROM THE AIRPORT

Kuching International Airport is 12km south of the centre. The price of a red-and-yellow taxi into Kuching is RM26, though this may soon rise.

The airport is a walkable 1.5km from Kuching Sentral bus station.

BOAT

Bow-steered wooden boats known as *tambang*, powered by an outboard motor, shuttle passengers back and forth across Sungai Sarawak, linking jetties along the Waterfront Promenade with Kampung Boyan and the Astana. The fare for Sarawak's cheapest cruise is 50 sen (more if you cross on the diagonal); pay as you disembark.

MOTORCYCLE

An Hui Motor (☑ 016 886 3328, 082-240508; 29 Jln Tabuan; ⊙8am-6pm Mon-Sat, 8.30-11am Sun & public holidays) Charges RM30 to RM40 per day for a motorbike (including helmet), plus a RM100 deposit. Insurance covers the bike but not the driver and is valid only within an 80km radius of Kuching.

BUSES FROM KUCHING

DESTINATION	STATION	PRICE (RM)	DURATION (HR)	FREQUENCY
Batu Niah Junction, for Niah NP	Kuching Sentral	80	12-14	hourly
Bintulu	Kuching Sentral	70	11-13	hourly
Kubah National Park	Saujana	4	1	4 per day
Lambir Hills NP	Kuching Sentral	80	13-15	hourly
Lundu, for Gunung Gading NP	Kuching Sentral	12	2-3	8 per day
Matang Wildlife Sanctuary	Saujana	4	1	4 per day
Miri	Kuching Sentral	80	13-15	hourly
Semenggoh Wildlife Centre	Saujana	3	1	6 per day
Sibu	Kuching Sentral	50	7-8	hourly

TAXI

Kuching taxis are required to use meters; over-charging is rare. Flag fall is RM10; note that this may soon change. Fares are 50% higher from midnight to 6am. To order a cab, call **ABC Radio Call Service** (☏ 016 861 1611, 082-611611) or **Kuching City Radio Taxi** (☏ 082-348898, 082-480000).

Around Kuching

Western Sarawak offers a dazzling array of natural sights and indigenous cultures, most within day-trip distance of Kuching.

Bako National Park

Occupying a jagged peninsula jutting out into the South China Sea, **Bako National Park** (☏ Bako Bazaar 082-431336, park HQ 082-478011; www.sarawakforestry.com; adult RM20; ☉ park office 8am-5pm) is just 37km northeast of downtown Kuching but feels like worlds and eons away. Many visitors cite this park – one of the best places in Sarawak to see rainforest animals – as one of their favourite Borneo experiences.

The coast of the 27-sq-km peninsula has lovely pocket beaches tucked into secret bays interspersed with wind-sculpted cliffs, forested bluffs and stretches of brilliant mangrove swamp. The interior of the park is home to streams, waterfalls and a range of distinct ecosystems, including classic low-land rainforest (mixed dipterocarp forest) and *kerangas* (heath forest).

Bako provides protected habitat for in-credible natural diversity. Scientists estimate that the park is home to about 200 kinds of bird, 24 reptile species and 37 species of mammal. Surprisingly, the area around park headquarters is one of the best places to spot wildlife, including reddish-brown proboscis monkeys, the males' pendulous noses flop-ping as they chew on tender young leaves.

Payment at the park is cash-only.

☉ Sights & Activities

Bako's 17 hiking trails – colour-coded and clearly marked with stripes of paint – are suitable for all levels of fitness and motiva-tion, with routes ranging from short nature strolls to strenuous all-day treks (at research time, all the trails in Bako's eastern reaches were closed pending repair). The ranger-led night walk (RM10, 1½ to two hours) gets great reviews.

At park headquarters it's possible to hire a boat to one of the more distant beaches and then hike back, or to hike to one of the beaches and arrange for a boat to meet you there.

🛏 Sleeping

In-park accommodation (110 beds) often fills up, especially from June to August, so if you'd like to stay over – highly recom-mended! – it's a good idea to book ahead on-line via http://ebooking.com.my, in person at the National Park Booking Office (p455) in Kuching, or by phoning the park. Space sometimes opens up at the last minute – ask at the Registration Counter.

In addition to several basic lodges, such as that old standby, the **Forest Lodge Type 6** (d RM53, 2-room chalet RM80) and **camping** (per person RM5), there are two hostels. Bring your own towel.

New Forest Hostel   HOSTEL **$**
(q RM64) Opened in 2013, the park's newest budget accommodation (32 beds), built of concrete, features spacious quads with non-bunk beds and attached bathroom.

Forest Hostel   HOSTEL **$**
(dm RM16, q RM43) Built of wood, the old hos-tel is scuffed and dented but perfectly serv-iceable. Rooms have fridges, wall-mounted fans and four single-storey beds lined up in a row.

❶ Getting There & Away

Getting from Kuching to Bako National Park is a cinch. Bright-red bus 1, run by **Rapid Kuching** (☏ 082-429418), starts its run to Bako Bazaar (RM3.50, 50 minutes) at 5 Jln Khoo Hun Yeang, in front of a buffet restaurant called Toko Minu-man Jumbo (and across the street from a bril-liant hawker centre that's perfect for breakfast). There are departures from Kuching every hour on the hour from 7am to 5pm, and from Bako Bazaar every hour on the half-hour from 6.30am to 4.30pm (and, often, 5.30pm too). Note: mid-day buses often depart early.

Hiring a five-passenger motorboat to park headquarters from **Bako Bazaar Dock** (Kam-pung Bako Terminal Jetty; ☏ 082-431068; ☉ 7.30am-4pm), where the park entry fee is collected, costs RM94 return. Visitors have to travel both ways with the same boatman – this is the boat cooperative's clumsy and wasteful way of maximising income for its 32 members. On the trip to the park, you'll be given a slip of paper with your boatman's name and mobile number; call him when you want to be picked up (placing a call from the park's Registration Counter costs RM0.50).

Not only does this system mean that lots of boats travel half-full, but if you assemble a group of five travellers in order to share costs and the cooperative finds out that some of you might return separately, they may try to force you to buy an extra return voucher (RM47). If you don't manage to link up with other travellers for the trip back, you can always summon a boat and pay cash. Unused vouchers cannot be reimbursed.

A cab from Kuching to Bako Bazaar (45 minutes), or hiring a private car in the other direction, costs RM45 to RM50.

Santubong Peninsula

The Santubong Peninsula (also known as Damai) is a 10km-long finger of land jutting out into the South China Sea. The main drawcards are the Sarawak Cultural Village, some of Malaysian Borneo's best beaches and **Gunung Santubong** (880m), which can be climbed from a point about 1km south of the Sarawak Cultural Village. Santubong is the best place in Sarawak for a lazy, pampered beach holiday.

◉ Sights & Activities

Access to **Damai Central Beach** (showers and lockers available), across the parking lot from the Sarawak Cultural Village, is free. For a small fee, nonguests can hang out on the sand and in the waves at **Damai Beach Resort** (RM2) and **Permai Rainforest Resort** (RM5).

Sarawak Cultural Village   MUSEUM
(SCV; ☑082-846411; www.scv.com.my; adult/child 6-12yr RM60/30; ⊙9am-5.15pm, last entry 4pm) This living eco-museum, centred on seven traditional dwellings (including three longhouses) housing crafts demonstrations, is a great introduction to the traditions of Sarawak's diverse peoples. Twice a day (at 11.30am and 4pm), an energetic, 45-minute cultural performance showcases traditional music and dance. It may sound hokey but the SCV is held in high esteem by local Dayak for its important role in keeping their cultures and traditions alive.

🛏 Sleeping & Eating

Damai Central has several inexpensive eateries.

BB Bunkers   HOSTEL $
(☑082-846835; www.bbbunkers.com; Damai Central; dm or s RM50, d/f RM80/120; ❄🔊) With the

Sarawak Cultural Village on one side and lovely Damai Central Beach on the other, this chic, sleek hostel has the peninsula's only dorm beds. The hangarlike space is subdivided by curtains, creating cosy sleeping spaces.

Santubong Homestay   HOMESTAY $
(☑082-846773, Mariah 011 1989 3575; niesa0619@gmail.com; House 207, Kampung Santubong; per person RM40, with lunch RM50, with lunch & dinner RM60) Sauji and Mariah rent out three rooms in their home, one with attached bathroom – homey and tranquil. Situated in Kampung Santubong, about 5km towards Kuching from the Sarawak Cultural Village.

❶ Getting There & Away

Two minibuses (45 minutes) and one bus line link Kuching with the Santubong Peninsula.

Damai Beach Resort Minibus (☑082-380970, 082-846999) Has departures from Kuching's Grand Margherita Hotel and Riverside Majestic Hotel four times a day between 9am and 6.15pm; if possible, book a day ahead. The last run back to Kuching leaves at about 5.15pm.

Setia Kawan Minibus (☑019 825 1619; adult/child under 12yr RM12/6) Has departures from hotels along Kuching's waterfront every two hours or so from about 9am to 6pm. Stops include the Singgahsana Lodge (p452), which can take bookings. The last van back leaves at 7.20pm.

Semenggoh Nature Reserve

One of the best places in the world to see semi-wild orang-utans in their natural habitat, the **Semenggoh Wildlife Centre** (☑082-618325; www.sarawakforestry.com; adult RM10; ⊙8am-5pm) can be visited on a half-day trip from Kuching or combined with a visit to Annah Rais Longhouse. Hour-long feedings of our ginger-haired cousins, all of them either rescued from captivity or born here, begin daily at 9am and 3pm. The animals often turn up later at park headquarters, so don't rush off straightaway even if everything seems quiet.

❶ Getting There & Away

Two bus companies provide reliable public transport from Kuching's Saujana Bus Station to the park gate, situated 1.3km down the hill from park headquarters:

City Public Link Bus K6 (RM3, one hour) departs from Kuching at 7.20am, 9.50am, 1pm and 3pm, and from Semenggoh (spelled 'Semenggok' on bus schedules) at approximately

8.20am, 11.15am, 2.05pm and 4.05pm. Buses have been known to leave *before* their scheduled departure time, so get there early.

Sarawak Transport Company Bus 6 (RM2, one hour) has Kuching departures at 7.20am and 1.20pm; buses back pass by Semenggoh at about 9.45am and 3.45pm.

Tours to Semenggoh are organised by Kuching guesthouses and tour agencies. A taxi from Kuching costs RM50 to RM60 one way.

Annah Rais Longhouse

Although this 97-door **Bidayuh longhouse** (adult/student RM8/4) has been on the tourist circuit for decades, it's still an excellent place to get a sense of what a longhouse is and what longhouse life is like.

The 500 residents of Annah Rais are as keen as the rest of us to enjoy the comforts of modern life – they do love their mobile phones and 3G internet access – but they've made a conscious decision to preserve their traditional architecture and the social interactions it engenders. They've also decided that welcoming tourists is a good way to earn a living without moving to the city, something most young people end up doing.

Once you pay your entry fee (in a pavilion next to the parking lot), you're free to explore Annah Rais' three longhouses with a guide or on your own. The most important feature is the *awah*, a long, covered common verandah with a springy bamboo floor, used for economic activities, socialising and celebrations. A dozen smoke-blackened human skulls still have pride of place – suspended over an 18th-century Dutch cannon – in the headhouse.

🛏 Sleeping

Half-a-dozen families run homestays with shared bathrooms, either in one of the three longhouses or in an adjacent detached house. Standard overnight rates are RM98 per person for accommodation and delicious Bidayuh board, and RM298 per person for a package that includes activities such as trekking, rafting, fishing, (mock) blowgun hunting, soaking in a natural hot spring and a dance performance.

Emily & John Ahwang   HOMESTAY **$$**
(☑Emily 010 977 8114, John 016 855 2195; http://22.com.my/homestay) Emily and John, both of whom speak fluent English, love to welcome guests to their spotless, modern, two-storey home, built right into the longhouse.

Akam Ganja   HOMESTAY **$$**
(☑010 984 3821; winniejagig@gmail.com) It's a pleasure to be hosted by Akam, a retired forestry official, and his wife Winnie, an English teacher, at their comfortable detached house on the riverbank.

❶ Getting There & Away

Annah Rais, 60km south of Kuching, is not served by public transport. A taxi from Kuching costs RM90 one-way.

In Kuching, a variety of guesthouses and tour agencies offer half-day tours to Annah Rais for about RM85 per person (RM140 including Semenggoh Nature Reserve).

Kubah National Park & Matang Wildlife Centre

If you've dreamed of being enveloped by the wild fecundity of Borneo's ancient rainforests, 22-sq-km **Kubah National Park** (☑082-845033; www.sarawakforestry.com; admission incl Matang Wildlife Centre RM20; ⊙8am-5pm) makes an ideal day trip (or overnight) from Kuching. The park's three mountains are a haven for mixed dipterocarp forest, among the lushest and most threatened habitats in Borneo.

When you pay your entry fee, you'll receive a hand-coloured schematic map of the park's four interconnected trails (two other trails were closed at the time of research). They're well marked, so a guide isn't necessary.

A 15km drive beyond Kubah National Park, the **Matang Wildlife Centre** (☑082-374869; www.sarawakforestry.com; admission incl Kubah National Park RM20; ⊙8am-5pm, last entry 3.30pm) has had remarkable success rehabilitating jungle animals rescued from captivity, especially orang-utans and sun bears. The highly professional staff do their best to provide their abused charges with natural living conditions with limited funds, but there's no denying that the centre looks like a low-budget zoo plopped down in the jungle. Because of the centre's unique role, there are endangered animals here that you cannot see anywhere else in Sarawak.

It is no longer possible to walk between the Kubah National Park and Matang Wildlife Centre because the area's semi-wild orang-utans can be aggressive.

🛏 Sleeping & Eating

Kubah and Matang's attractive, inexpensive accommodation, including Kubah's **Forest Hostel** (dm RM15), can be booked by phone, online via http://ebooking.com.my, or at the National Park Booking Office in Kuching.

Cooking is allowed in the chalets, which have fully equipped kitchens, but there's nowhere to buy food, so bring everything you'll need.

❶ Getting There & Away

Kubah National Park is 25km northwest of Kuching. A taxi from Kuching costs RM50.

From Kuching's Saujana Bus Station, bus K21 to 'Politeknik' stops on the main road 400m from park headquarters (RM4, one hour), next to the Kubah Family Park. Departures from Kuching are at 8am, 11am, 2pm and 4.30pm, and from the Politeknik – 2km beyond (ie north) of Kubah – at 6.30am, 9.30am, 12.30pm and 3.30pm.

Gunung Gading National Park

The best place in Sarawak to see the world's largest flower, the renowned *Rafflesia*, 41-sq-km **Gunung Gading National Park** (☎082-735144; www.sarawakforestry.com; adult RM20; ☺8am-5pm) makes a fine day trip from Kuching. Its old-growth rainforest covers the slopes of four mountains (*gunung*) – Gading, Lundu, Perigi and Sebuloh – traversed by well-marked walking trails that are great for day hikes. To find out if a *Rafflesia* is in bloom – something that happens here only about 25 times a year – and how long it will stay that way (never more than five days), call the park or the National Park Booking Office in Kuching (p455).

🛏 Sleeping & Eating

The park has a **hostel** (dm/r RM15/40) with four fan rooms and two three-bedroom **forest lodges** (RM150; ✳) that can sleep up to six people. **Camping** (per person RM5) is possible at park headquarters. Cooking is permitted in park accommodation.

❶ Getting There & Away

Gunung Gading National Park is 85km northwest of Kuching. Eight buses a day, run by the Sarawak Transport Company and City Public Link, connect Kuching Sentral long-distance bus station with Lundu (RM12). From there, you'll either have to walk north 2.5km to the park, or hire an unofficial taxi (about RM5 per person).

Sibu

☎084 / POP 240,000

Gateway to the Batang Rejang, Sibu has been a busy centre for trade with upriver hinterlands since the time of James Brooke. These days, it's a major transit point for travellers, and while the 'swan city' – Borneo's most Chinese urban centre – is no rival to Kuching in terms of charm, it's a fine place to spend a day or two before or after a waterborne trip to the interior.

◉ Sights

Tua Pek Kong Temple　　　BUDDHIST TEMPLE
(Jln Temple; ☺6.30am-8pm) FREE A colourful Buddhist and Taoist temple established in the early 1870s. For a brilliant view up and down the muddy Batang Rejang, climb the seven-storey Kuan Yin Pagoda; ask for a key at the ground-floor desk.

Sibu Heritage Centre　　　MUSEUM
(Jln Central; ☺9am-5pm, closed Mon & public holidays) FREE The well-presented exhibits, rich in evocative photographs, explore the captivating history of Sarawak and Sibu. Don't miss the shot of a 1940s street dentist – it's painful just to look at.

🛏 Sleeping

Sibu has dozens of hotels. Some of the ultrabudget 'hotels' (with rooms for RM35 or less) situated north of the Central Market (towards Jln Market) are of a very low standard and double as brothels.

★**Li Hua Hotel**　　　HOTEL $
(☎084-324000; www.lihua.com.my; cnr Jln Maju & Lg Lanang 2; s/d/ste from RM50/75/150; ✳@☞) Sibu's best-value hotel has 68 spotless, tile-floor rooms, all with wi-fi. Very convenient if you're arriving or leaving by boat.

River Park Hotel　　　HOTEL $
(☎016 578 2820; siewling1983@hotmail.com; 51-53 Jln Maju; d/tr/q from RM68/95/110; ✳☞) A well-run place with 30 rooms, across the park from the ferry terminal.

New Hai Ping Hotel　　　HOTEL $
(☎084-333 214; 1st fl, 13 Jln Maju; s/d RM30/45) Very basic fan rooms across the park from the ferry terminal.

✗ Eating

Sibu is a great spot for street food, especially Foochow-style Chinese. Try the city's signature dish, *kam pua mee* (thin round noodles soaked in pork fat and served with a side of roast pork).

BUSES FROM SIBU

DESTINATION	PRICE (RM)	DURATION (HR)	FREQUENCY
Bintulu	25	3¼	roughly hourly 6am-3.30am
Kuching	50	7-8	6.15am-4am
Miri	50	6½	roughly hourly 6am-3.30am

★ **Sibu Central Market**   MARKET $
(Pasar Sentral Sibu, PSS; Jln Channel; RM3-5; ⊙food stalls 3am-midnight) Malaysia's largest fruit and vegie market has more than 1000 stalls. Upstairs, food stalls serve up local specialities, inluding *kam pua mee* (eg at evening-only Stall 102) and *kompia* (sesame-flaked mini-bagels; check out Stall 17 and Stall FL12, facing Stall 91). Got questions? Head to Stall 98 and ask for Noriza.

Night Market   MARKET $
(Pasar Malam; Jln Market; ⊙5-11pm or midnight) Chinese stalls (selling pork and rice, steamed buns etc) are at the western end of the lot, while Malay stalls (with superb satay and scrumptious barbecue chicken) are to the northeast.

Roots Food Court   HAWKER $
(Jln Central; RM3.50-5; ⊙7am-3pm; 🍴) The small hawker centre on the ground floor of the Sibu Heritage Centre has two vegetarian food stalls.

ℹ️ Information

Email Centre (ground fl, Sarawak House Complex, cnr Jln Central & Jln Kampung Nyabor; per hr RM4; ⊙9.30am-9pm Mon-Sat, to 3pm Sun) Internet access. The entrance is on the building's northern side.

Rejang Medical Centre (☑084-323333; www. rejang.com.my; 29 Jln Pedada; ⊙emergency 24hr) Used by most expats. Situated about 1km northeast of the Sibu Gateway.

Visitors Information Centre (☑084-340980; www.sarawaktourism.com; 32 Jln Tukang Besi; ⊙8am-5pm Mon-Fri, closed public holidays) Well worth a stop. Has a friendly and informative staff (ask for Jessie), plenty of maps, and bus and ferry schedules.

ℹ️ Getting There & Around

BOAT

Unless you fly, the quickest way to get from Sibu to Kuching is by boat. **Ekspress Bahagia** (☑016-8893013, 016-8005891, in Kuching 082-429242, in Sibu 084-319228; ⊙from Sibu 11.30am, from Kuching 8.30am) runs a daily express ferry from Sibu's **express ferry terminal** (Terminal Penumpang Sibu; Jln Kho Peng Long; 📞) to Kuching's Express Wharf (economy/1st class RM45/55, 4¾ hours, departure at 11.30am).

'Flying coffin' express boats run by half-a-dozen companies head up the Batang Rejang to Kapit (140km; economy/business/1st class RM20/25/30, 2½ to three hours) once or twice an hour from 5.45am to 2.30pm. It can be hard to find a seat on Sunday.

One boat a day, departing at 5.45am, goes all the way to Belaga (295km; RM60, 11 hours) – unless the Bakun Dam is closed for scheduled maintenance.

For all ferries, be on board at least 15 minutes before departure.

BUS

Sibu's **long-distance bus station** (Jln Pahlawan), which has departures almost 24 hours a day, is about 3.5km northeast of the centre (along Jln Pedada).

ℹ️ Getting Around

To get from the local bus station (in front of the Express Ferry Terminal) to the long-distance bus station, take Lanang Bus 20 or 21 (RM1.20, 15 minutes, once or twice an hour 6.30am to 5pm).

Batang Rejang

A trip up the tan, churning waters of the Batang Rejang (Rejang River) – the 'Amazon of Borneo' – is one of Southeast Asia's great river journeys. Though the area is no longer the jungle-lined wilderness it was in the days before Malaysian independence, it still retains a frontier, *ulu-ulu* (upriver, ie back-of-the-beyond) vibe, especially in towns and longhouses accessible only by boat.

To avoid backtracking, you can travel from Sibu to Kapit and Belaga by river boat, and then from Belaga to Bintulu (on the coast) by 4WD, or vice versa.

Kapit

☑ 084 / POP 19,500
The main upriver settlement on the Batang Rejang, Kapit is a bustling trading and transport centre dating back to the days

UPRIVER TRAVEL PERMITS

An outdated permit system is in place for tourists travelling from Kapit to Belaga, or up the Batang Baleh. Although the **Resident's Office** (📋084-796230; www.kapitro.sarawak.gov.my; 9th fl, Kompleks Kerajaan Negeri Bahagian Kapit, Jln Bleteh; ⊘8am-1pm & 2-5pm Mon-Thu, 8-11.45am & 2.15-5pm Fri), linked to Pasar Teresang by minibus (RM2), continues to issue permits (which are free), we've never heard of any authority actually checking if travellers have them. Strangely, a permit is not required for travel to Belaga from Bintulu.

of the White Rajahs. Its lively markets, including **Pasar Teresang** (⊘5.30am-6pm), are important commercial hubs for nearby longhouse communities.

⊙ Sights & Activities

Fort Sylvia   MUSEUM
(Jln Kubu; ⊘10am-noon & 2-5pm, closed Mon & public holidays) Built of ironwood by Rajah Charles Brooke in 1880. Exhibits present the traditional lifestyles of the Batang Rejang Dayak.

Longhouse Visits   LONGHOUSES
Quite a few longhouses, many of them quite modern, are situated along Kapit-area rivers; some are accessible by road.

Lión Anak Lading (📋011-2510 2322, 019-818 6635), an English-speaking, Iban former primary school teacher (he now drives a licensed minivan), does a great job taking visitors to Iban longhouses, including nearby **Rumah John Ramba** (per van RM20 one-way; all-day tour RM50 per group), where he lives; and **Rumah Jandok** (per van RM60 one-way), about 35km from town, where lots of local folk speak English. Staying overnight costs RM50 per person, plus RM50 per group.

We've heard reports that a local minibus cooperative is demanding outrageous prices for transport to longhouses, and that one local guide whose licence was revoked is still approaching travellers.

🛏 Sleeping & Eating

New Rejang Inn   HOTEL $
(📋084-796600; 104 Jln Teo Chow Beng; d RM78; ❄🔊) A welcoming, superbly run hotel whose 15 spotless rooms come with comfort-

able mattresses and wi-fi. Often full, so call ahead.

Hiap Chiong Hotel   HOTEL $
(📋084-796314; 33 Jln Temenggong Jugah; s/d RM40/45; 🔊) The 15 rooms have dinged-up, outdated furniture but are clean and have wi-fi.

Night Market   MARKET $
(Taman Selera Empurau; mains RM2.50-5; ⊘5-11pm or midnight) An excellent place for satay, barbecue chicken and Malay-style rice and noodle dishes. Situated a block up the slope from Kapit Town Sq.

ⓘ Information

Kapit has several banks with ATMs.
Good Time Cyber Centre (1st fl, 354 Jln Yong Moo Chai; per hr RM3; ⊘8.30am-10.30pm) Internet access upstairs facing the library. Has 42 computers.

ⓘ Getting There & Away

'Flying coffin' fast ferries run by six companies link the **Kapit Passenger Terminal** (Jln Panglima Balang; 🔊) with Sibu (economy/business/first class RM20/25/30, 2½ to three hours) once or twice an hour from 6.40am to 3.15pm. Boats fill up fast on Friday.

Unless the Bakun Dam is undergoing maintenance, a boat sets out on the exciting ride to Belaga (RM45, five hours upriver) daily at about 9.30am from **Belaga Wharf** (Kapit Town Sq).

Boats sometimes depart a few minutes early, so be on board at least 15 minutes before departure time.

Belaga

📋 086 / POP 2500

There's not much to do in Belaga except soak up the frontier outpost vibe, but nearby rivers are home to quite a few Kayan/Kenyah and Orang Ulu longhouses.

ⓖ Tours

The main reason travellers visit Belaga is to venture into the jungle in search of remote longhouses and hidden waterfalls. But before you can share stories with smiling locals, you need to find a guide. Fortunately, guesthouse owner **Daniel Levoh** (📋013 848 6351, 086-461997; daniellevoh@hotmail.com; Jln Teh Ah Kiong) can help out – he offers day trips (RM85 per person, including lunch) and three-day, two-night longhouse visits (RM600 to RM750 for a group of three).

🛏 Sleeping

Belaga has several cheap, shabby hotels.

Daniel Levoh's Guesthouse   GUESTHOUSE $
(📱 013 848 6351, 086-461997; daniellevoh@
hotmail.com; Jln Teh Ah Kiong; dm RM20, d/tr
RM30/40; 🛜) Daniel, a retired school head-
master now serving on the Kapit District
Council, loves meeting travellers and sharing stories of Kayan longhouse life. The four
simple rooms, a chill-out balcony and bathrooms are on the 2nd floor.

ℹ Information

Belaga's BSN bank branch has an ATM and also
does cash advances at the counter.

ℹ Getting There & Away

Unless the Bakun Dam is closed for maintenance, an icily air-conditioned boat departs for
Kapit (155km; RM45, four hours downriver) and
Sibu (RM60, 10 hours) – via the infamous Pelagus Rapids – daily at about 7.45am. An overloaded ferry capsized 40 minutes downstream from
Belaga in June 2013, so legal limits on passenger
capacity are now strictly enforced.

There are 4WDs that link Belaga's Main Bazaar
with Bintulu (RM60 per person, four hours)
pretty much daily, with departures at about
7.30am. If you're heading towards Miri, ask to be
dropped off at Bakun Junction (Simpang Bakun),
53km northeast of Bintulu and 159km southwest
of Miri, where you can flag down a passing bus.

A paved road linking Belaga with Bakun Junction (four hours) via the Bakun Dam opened in
late 2013.

Bintulu

📱 086 / POP 184,000

Roughly midway between Sibu and Miri
(about 200km from each), the gritty port of
Bintulu owes its existence to vast offshore
natural gas fields. There's no reason to overnight here unless you're heading overland to
Belaga.

🛏 Sleeping

Bintulu has plenty of ultrabudget lodgings
(eg on or near Jln Keppel, Jln Abang Galau
and Jln Masjid) but some are definitely
dodgy.

Kintown Inn   HOTEL $
(📱 086-333666; ktowninn@ymail.com; 93 Jln Keppel; s/d RM87/92; ❄🛜) The 50 clean, tourist-
class rooms offer fast in-room cable internet

and wi-fi. The best value for your buck in
town.

ℹ Getting There & Away

Bintulu's long-distance bus terminal is 5km
northeast of the centre (aka Bintulu Town)
at Medan Jaya; a taxi to/from the city centre
costs RM15. A dozen companies run buses approximately hourly to Kuching (RM60, 10 hours,
departures 6am to 12.30am) and Miri (RM23,
3½ hours, departures from 6.15am to at least
9.45pm).

Buses to Kuching go via Sibu (RM20, four
hours); buses to Miri stop at Niah Junction
(RM12 to RM20, two hours).

To arrange a 4WD inland to Belaga (per person RM60, four hours), contact **Daniel Levoh**
(📱 086-461997, 013 848 6351; daniellevoh@
hotmail.com). Departures are generally between
noon and 2pm.

Niah National Park

Near the coast about 115km south of Miri,
31-sq-km **Niah National Park** (📱 085-737450,
085-737454; www.sarawakforestry.com; admission
RM20; ⏰ park office 8am-5pm) is home to one
of Borneo's gems, the Niah Caves. In addition to lots of bats and swiftlets, they shelter
some of the oldest evidence of human habitation in Southeast Asia.

◎ Sights

★**Great Cave**   CAVE
A vast cavern approximately 2km long, up to
250m across and up to 60m high. Reached
along a 3.1km plankwalk through the
rainforest.

🛏 Sleeping

Bookings for the **hostel** (r RM42, towel rental
RM7) and **forest lodges** (1/2 rooms with fan
RM106/159, with air-con RM159/239) can be
made at park headquarters or through one
of the **National Park Booking Offices** (📱 in
Kuching 082-248088, in Miri 085-434184). **Camping** (per person RM5) is permitted near the
park headquarters.

The Iban longhouse of Rumah Patrick Li-
bau, near the Great Cave (3km on foot from
park headquarters), has a **homestay** (📱 019
805 2415; per person incl dinner & breakfast RM70)
program.

ℹ Getting There & Away

Park headquarters is 122km northeast of Bintulu
and 115km southwest of Miri, not right on the

main (inland) Miri–Bintulu highway but rather 15km north of the highway's lively Batu Niah Junction. The good news is that all the long-haul buses that link Miri with Bintulu, Sibu and Kuching pass by here. The bad news is that the only way to get from the junction to the park is to hire a private car (RM30, for four people RM40) – to find one, ask around outside Ngu's Garden Food Park. National park staff (or, after hours, park security personnel) can help arrange a car back to the junction.

Guesthouses in Miri offer day trips to Niah.

Lambir Hills National Park

The 69-sq-km **Lambir Hills National Park** (☑ 085-471609; www.sarawakforestry.com; admission RM20; ☺ park office 8am-5pm, last entry 4pm) offers jungle waterfalls, cool pools where you can take a dip, and a bunch of great, colour-coded **walking trails** that branch off four primary routes and lead to 14 destinations. Rangers can supply you with a map and are happy to make suggestions. A guided **nightwalk** starts at 7pm.

🛏 Sleeping

The park's 12 reasonably comfortable **chalets** (1/2 rooms with fan RM50/75, with air-con RM100/150) have two bedrooms that can be rented separately, each with two beds (three in air-con rooms). **Camping** (per person RM5) is permitted near the park headquarters. To book, call or email the park, or contact Miri's National Park Booking Office (p465).

❶ Getting There & Away

Park headquarters is 32km south of Miri on the inland (old) Miri–Bintulu highway. All the buses linking Miri's Pujut Bus Terminal with Bintulu pass right by here (RM10 from Miri).

Miri

☑ 085 / POP 295,000

The dynamic oil town of Miri is busy and modern – not much about it is Borneo – but there's plenty of money sloshing around so the eating is good and the broad avenues are brightly lit. The population is about 40% Dayak (mainly Iban), 30% Chinese and 18% Malay. The city's friendly guesthouses are a great place to meet other travellers.

Miri is a major transport hub, so if you're travelling to/from Brunei, Sabah, the Kelabit Highlands or the national parks of Gunung Mulu, Niah or Lambir Hills, chances are you'll pass this way.

◉ Sights

Miri City Fan PARK
(Jln Kipas; ☺ 24hr) Decked out in coloured lights at night, this 10.4-hectare park's Chinese- and Malay-style gardens and ponds are great for a romantic stroll. Also boasts a beautiful **library** and an Olympic-sized **swimming pool** (RM1).

🛏 Sleeping

Miri has some excellent backpacker guesthouses. Some establishments with 'guesthouse' signs out front do short-term business for Miri's many dodgy massage parlours.

★ **Dillenia Guesthouse** GUESTHOUSE $
(☑ 085-434204; https://sites.google.com/site/dilleniaguesthouse; 1st fl, 846 Jln Sida; dm/s/d/q incl breakfast RM30/50/80/110; ❋ @ ☎) This super-welcoming hostel has 11 rooms and lots of nice little touches (eg plants in the bathrooms). Mrs Lee is an artesian well of useful travel information and tips – and leech socks. All rooms have shared bathrooms.

Cocottage Guesthouse GUESTHOUSE $
(Minda Guesthouse; ☑ 085-411422; www.cocottage.com.my; 1st & 2nd fl, Lot 637, Jln North Yu Seng; dm per person incl breakfast RM20, d RM50-60; ❋ @ ☎) In the heart of Miri's dining and drinking district, this popular establishment has 12 colourful rooms and a great rooftop sundeck. Dorms are pretty packed, with eight or 12 beds. Street-facing rooms are noisy until 2am.

Highlands Backpacker Lodge GUESTHOUSE $
(☑ 085-422327; www.highlandsmiri.com; 2nd fl, Lot 839, Jln Merpati; dm with fan RM18, dm/s/d with air-con RM22/40/50; ❋ @ ☎) Miri's original backpacker guesthouse offers 13 rooms, all but four with windows. Dorms have eight to 13 beds but don't feel cramped. The affable owner, a Twin Otter pilot from New Zealand everyone calls Captain David, sometimes drops by.

✕ Eating

Restaurants of all sorts line Jln North Yu Seng from the landmark Mega Hotel north to the Imperial Mall, with lots more cheap, popular places south of the Mega Hotel along pedestrians-only Persiaran Kabor. A number of informal but excellent seafooderies serve critters plucked live from tanks – but beware of the prices, which are per 100g.

★ **Summit Café**   DAYAK $

(☎ 019 885 3920; Lot 1245, Centre Point Commercial Centre, Jln Melayu; mains RM2.50-7; ☺ 7am-4pm Mon-Sat; ⚡) If you've never tried Kelabit or Kenyah/Kayan cuisine, this place will be a revelation! Try the colourful array of 'jungle food', such as fern tips, *terong asam* (local eggplant), *dure'* (fried jungle leaf) and minced tapioca leaves. For the best selection, come around 11.30am. Situated just a few blocks from the tourist office, two short blocks behind the Maybank branch on Jln Melayu.

Miri Central Market   HAWKER $

(Jln Brooke, Pasar Pusat Miri; mains RM2.50-4; ☺ 4am-midnight or 2am) The cheapest meals (mainly Chinese) in central Miri. Stall 5 serves up chicken curry rice from 7am to 1pm or 2pm, while Stall 6 is known for its chicken porridge (available from 7.30pm to 11pm or later).

Puma Sera   BUFFET $

(Persiaran Kabor; RM3-5; ☺ 24hr; ⚡) Hugely popular at all hours, with two dozen freshly cooked Malay and Indian buffet dishes. Many are spicy; a quarter are vegie. Prices depend on how much you take. Situated on a corner facing the south side of the landmark Mega Hotel.

Ming Café   ASIAN, WESTERN $$

(www.mingcafe.com.my; cnr Jln North Yu Seng & Jln Merbau; mains RM5-25; ☺ 10am-2am, hot food to 11.30pm) Take your pick of Chinese, Mamak (Indian-Malay fusion) and Western food at this hugely popular corner establishment. Bar offerings include six beers on tap (from RM11), including Guinness. Happy hang-out of the Hash House Harriers.

ℹ Information

ATMs can be found at Miri airport and are sprinkled all over the city centre.

EcoLaundry (☎ 016 878 9908, 085-414266; 638 Jln North Yu Seng; per kg RM5; ☺ 7am-7pm Mon-Sat, to 5pm Sun) Friendly, efficient service, with free pick-up and drop-off at guesthouses.

Internet Shop (Ground fl, Shop G-02, Soon Hup Tower, cnr Jln Bendahara & Jln Merbau; per hr RM2; ☺ 8am-8pm) Hang-out of zombified teenage gamers.

Miri City Medical Centre (☎ 085-426622; www.mcmcmiri.com; 916-920 Jln Hokkien; ☺ emergency 24hr) Conveniently situated in the city centre. Accepts direct payment for in-patient care from certain insurance companies.

National Park Booking Office (☎ 085-434184; www.sarawakforestry.com; 452 Jln Melayu; ☺ 8am-5pm Mon-Fri) Inside the Visitors Information Centre, at the desk to the left. Has details on Sarawak's national parks and can book beds and rooms at Niah and Lambir Hills (but not at Gunung Mulu or Similajau). Not always staffed.

Visitors Information Centre (☎ 085-434181; www.sarawaktourism.com; 452 Jln Melayu; ☺ 8am-5pm Mon-Fri, 9am-3pm Sat, Sun & public holidays) The helpful staff can provide city maps and brochures on Sarawak.

ℹ Getting There & Away

Miri is 212km northeast of Bintulu and 36km southwest of the Brunei border.

AIR

Miri is the main hub of the Malaysia Airlines subsidiary **MASwings** (☎ 1300 88 3000; www.maswings.com.my), whose 22 destinations around Malaysian Borneo include Bario (Kelabit Highlands), Gunung Mulu National Park (Mulu), Pulau Labuan, Kota Kinabalu, Kuching and Sibu.

AirAsia (www.airasia.com) can get you to Kuching, Kota Kinabalu, Kuala Lumpur, Johor Bahru, Singapore and Manila, while **Malaysia Airlines** (☎ 1300 88 3000; www.malaysiaairlines.com) has direct flights to KL.

MALAYSIA MIRI

BUSES FROM MIRI

DESTINATION	PRICE	DURATION (HR)
Bandar Seri Begawan (Brunei)	RM40 from Miri, B$18 from BSB	3½
Batu Niah Junction (for Niah NP)	RM10 -12	1½
Bintulu	RM25	3½
Kota Kinabalu	RM90	10
Kuching	RM80-90	13-15
Sibu	RM50	7-8

GETTING TO BRUNEI: MIRI TO BANDAR SERI BEGAWAN

Getting to the border The only company that's allowed to take passengers from Miri to destinations inside Brunei is **PHLS Express** (✉ Danny Hardini in Brunei +673-880 1180, Danny Hardini via SMS in Malaysia 016 585 9814, in BSB +673-714 5734), which has two buses a day from Miri's Pujut Bus Terminal to Bandar Seri Begawan (RM40, 3½ hours, 8.15am and 3.45pm). All services also run from BSB to Miri (see p63).

Another option is to take a **private van** (✉ from 7-9am & 5-7pm in Miri 013-833 2231, from noon-1pm in BSB +673-878 2521) run by Mr Foo (RM60 per person, 2½ hours); reservations can be made through Miri's Dillenia Guesthouse (p464). Other vans to BSB leave from Miri's Pujut Bus Terminal. All services also run from BSB to Miri.

At the border Border formalities (open 6am to 10pm) are usually quick, and for most nationalities (but not Australians!) Bruneian visas are free. If you'll be continuing on to Sabah, make sure you have enough pages in your passport for no fewer than 10 chops (stamps)!

Moving on The bus from Miri stops very near the centre of BSB.

BUS

Long-distance buses use the **Pujut Bus Terminal**, about 4km northeast of the centre. It's linked to the city centre's **local bus terminal** (next to the tourist office) by MTC buses 20 and 33A (RM1.60 or RM2.60), which run about every 90 minutes from 6.30am to 6.20pm. A taxi costs RM15.

A bunch of companies send frequent buses southwestward to destinations such as Bintulu, Sibu and Kuching from 6.30am to 10pm; all pass by Lambir Hills National Park. Taking a spacious 'VIP bus', with just three seats across, is like flying 1st class!

PHLS Express sends buses to Brunei, including Bandar Seri Begawan and Bangar, at about 8.15am and 3.45pm. Tickets are sold at the **Bintang Jaya** (✉ Kuching 082-250178, Miri 085-432178; www.bintangjayaexpress.com) counter.

Borneo Bus has a service to Kota Kinabalu (KK) every day at 7.45am, while Bintang Jaya's daily KK bus leaves at 8.30am. The new road bridge over Sungai Pandaruan, opened in December 2013, should make the trip a bit faster.

Seats for many routes can be booked via www.busonlineticket.com.

Gunung Mulu National Park

Few national parks anywhere in the world pack so many natural marvels into such a small area. From caves of mind-boggling proportions to other-worldly geological phenomena such as the Pinnacles to brilliant old-growth rainforest, 529-sq-km **Gunung Mulu National Park** (Gunung Mulu World Heritage Area; ✉ 085-792300; www.mulupark.com; for five calendar days RM30) – declared a Unesco World Heritage Site in 2002 – is truly one of our planet's wonders.

◉ Sights & Activities

When you register, helpful park staff will give you a placemat-sized schematic map of the park on which you can plan out your daily itineraries.

You can take several excellent jungle trails unaccompanied as long as you inform the park office (or, when it's closed, someone in the Park Security building) – great options include the 8km **Paku Valley Loop**, opened in 2013.

Mulu's '**show caves**' (caves that can be visited without special training or equipment) are the parks' most popular attractions and for good reason: they are truly awe-inspiring. Cave routes that require special equipment and a degree of caving experience are known as '**adventure caves**'. For both, bring a torch/flashlight.

The park also offers some of the best and most accessible jungle trekking in Borneo.

Nightwalk   WALKING
(Night Shift; per person RM15; ◷ 7pm or 7.30pm except if raining) The ideal first-night introduction to the park's fauna. Creatures you're likely to see – but, at least at first, only after the guide points them out – include tiny tree frogs, enormous spiders, vine snakes and stick insects (phasmids) up to 30cm long. If you bring your torch up to the level of your eyes and shine it into the foliage, the eyes of hidden creatures will reflect brightly back.

★ **Deer Cave & Lang's Cave**   CAVING
(per person RM25; ⊙ departures at 2pm & 2.30pm)
Over 2km in length and 174m in height,
breathtaking Deer Cave is the world's largest cave passage open to the public. Every
evening around dusk (unless it's raining), millions of bats (see www.mulubat-
batcams.com) fly off in search of insects
in spiralling, twirling clouds – an awe-
inspiring sight! Their corkscrew trajectories
are designed to foil the dinner plans of bat
hawks perched nearby on the cliffs.

★ **Wind Cave**   CAVING
(per person incl boat ride RM65; ⊙ departures
8.45am & 9.15am) Named for its deliciously
cool breezes, Wind Cave has chambers filled
with phantasmagorical forests of stalactites
and stalagmites.

Fast Lane   CAVING
(per person incl boat RM60; ⊙ 2pm) This route
through Lagang Cave gets rave reviews
thanks to its extraordinary stalactites and
stalagmites.

Mulu Canopy Skywalk   WALKING
(per person RM35; ⊙ departures every 1 or 2 hours
7am-2pm) Climbing up into the forest canopy
is the only way to see what a tropical rainforest is all about, since most flora and fauna
do their thing high above the ground.

The Pinnacles   HIKING
(per person RM350) The Pinnacles are an
incredible formation of 45m-high stone
spires protruding from the forested flanks
of Gunung Api. Getting there involves two
overnights at Camp 5 and an intense, un-
relentingly steep 2.4km ascent. The final
section – much tougher than anything on
Mt Kinabalu – involves serious clambering
and some rope and ladder work.

Gunung Mulu Summit   HIKING
(per person RM460) If you're looking for real
adventure and are *very* fit, the 24km, four-
day climb from park headquarters (elevation 50m) to the summit of Gunung Mulu
(2376m) – gruelling but exhilarating – may
be for you. Only 30 or 40 people attempt this
ascent each year.

Headhunters' Trail   HIKING
Linking the park with Limbang, this physically undemanding, overnight route is
named after the Kayan war parties that used
to make their way up Sungai Melinau. To
make arrangements, contact a tour agency

such as Limbang-based **Borneo Touch Eco-
tour** (☑ 013 844 3861; www.walk2mulu.com), run
by the irrepressible Mr Lim.

🛏 Sleeping

Options at park headquarters – a truly lovely spot – include a **hostel** (dm incl breakfast
RM43) that has 20 beds in a clean, spacious
dormitory-style room (lockers available),
as well as **longhouse rooms** (s/d/tr/q incl
breakfast RM190/220/250/280; ❄), **chalets**
(d/tr/q incl breakfast RM230/288/346; ❄) and
garden bungalows (s/d/tr incl breakfast
RM222/262/302; ❄). Book well in advance,
especially from June to September – just
call ☑ 085-792300 or visit www.mulupark.
com. Space sometimes opens up at the last
minute.

Several budget places, unaffiliated with
the park, can be found across the bridge
from park headquarters, along the banks of
Sungai Melinau. There are plenty of beds, so
if you don't mind very basic digs, you can
fly up without worrying about room availability.

★ **D'Cave Guesthouse**   GUESTHOUSE $
(☑ for Dina 012 872 9752, for Robert 014 771 4098;
beckhamjunior40@yahoo.com; dm/d incl breakfast
RM25/70) Garners rave reviews for its homey
atmosphere, warm welcome (both Robert
and Dina speak fluent English) and great location midway between the airport and park
headquarters (about 500m from each). Book
ahead – the 12 dorm beds and five private
rooms fill fast.

GUIDES, FEES & RESERVATIONS

All of the caves and some of the rainforest treks require a certified guide.
Advance reservations are a must, especially if you've got your heart set on
'adventure' caving, or on trekking to the
Pinnacles or up to the summit of Gunung Mulu. July, August and September
are the park's busiest months (some
dates are booked out months ahead),
but even then spots do open up at the
last minute if you're able to hang out at
the park for a few days. Tour agencies
charge more than the park itself but
may be able to find a guide on short
notice.

Mulu River Lodge HOSTEL **$**
(Edward Nyipa Homestay; ☑ 012 850 4431, 012 852 7471; dm/d/q incl breakfast RM35/70/140) Has 30 beds, most in a giant, nonbunk dorm room equipped with clean shower and toilet facilities at one end. Electricity flows from 5pm to 11.30pm. Has a restaurant.

Melinau Homestay GUESTHOUSE **$**
(MC; ☑ 019 861 4062, for Diang 012 871 1372; dm RM20) Has nine extremely basic rooms, river-water bucket showers and flickering electricity from 6pm to 10pm or later. Diang meets all incoming flights (she runs the airport van). To get there from the bridge, walk along the river bank behind Mulu River Lodge.

Eating

At park headquarters, the convivial **Café Mulu** (mains RM7-17; ⊙ 7.30am-9.30pm, last orders 9pm) serves tasty meals for double what you'd pay on the coast. Inexpensive curries, fried rice (RM5 to RM8) and noodle dishes are available at several places across the bridge from park headquarters. Cooking is not allowed in park accommodation.

ℹ Information

Park headquarters accepts credit cards and does credit card cash advances. The shop (open 8am to 7pm) next to Café Mulu sells access to 24-hour satellite wi-fi (RM5 a day) that's fast enough for email but not necessarily to book air tickets.

ℹ Getting There & Away

Unless you walk the Headhunters' Trail, pretty much the only way to get to Mulu is by air. **MASwings** (☑ 1300 88 3000; www.maswings.com. my) flies 68-seat ATR-72 turboprops from/to Miri (20 minutes) and Kuching (1½ hours, three times a week), with onward flights to KK (daily) and other destinations. Park headquarters is a walkable 1km from the airport; taking a van costs RM5.

Tickets can be purchased at Mulu Airport, ideal if you're not sure how long you'd like to stay (eg to wait for space on a trek), but some discounts are available only online.

Kelabit Highlands

Nestled in Sarawak's northeastern corner, the upland rainforests of the Kelabit (keh-*lah*-bit) Highlands are sandwiched between Gunung Mulu National Park and the Indonesian frontier. The main activity here,

other than enjoying the clean, cool air, is trekking from longhouse to longhouse on mountain trails.

The area is home to the Kelabits (see www.kelabit.net and www.unimas.my/ebario/community.html), a particularly well-educated Dayak group who number only about 6500; and the Penan, a seminomadic group whose members have fared much less well in modern Malaysia.

Bario

The 'capital' of the highlands, Bario consists of about a dozen 'villages' spread over a beautiful valley, much of it given over to rice growing. Some of the appeal lies in the mountain climate (the valley is 1500m above sea level) and splendid isolation (the only access is by air and torturous 4WD track), but above all it's the unforced hospitality of the Kelabit people that will quickly win you over.

Bario's annual **Slow Food Festival**, held each July, will celebrate its 10th anniversary in 2015.

⊙ Sights & Activities

The temperate Kelabit Highlands offer some of the best jungle trekking in Borneo, taking in primary rainforest, rugged peaks and remote Kenyah, Penan and Kelabit settlements. Treks from Bario range from easy overnight trips to nearby longhouses to week-long slogs into the wilds of Kalimantan. Be prepared to encounter leeches – many trails are literally crawling with them.

Bario Asal Longhouse LONGHOUSE
This all-wood, 22-door longhouse has the traditional Kelabit layout: each family has a hearth on the *dapur* (enclosed front verandah), while on the other side of the family units is the *tawa'*, a wide back verandah used for weddings, funerals and celebrations and decorated with historic family photos. A few of the older residents still have earlobes that hang almost down to their shoulders, created by a lifetime of wearing heavy brass earrings.

Junglebluesdream Art Gallery ART GALLERY
(http://junglebluesdream.weebly.com; ⊙ daylight hours) Many of artist Stephen Baya's paintings have traditional Kelabit motifs.

Prayer Mountain HIKING
From Bario Asal Longhouse (where you can ask for directions), it's a steep, slippery

TREKKING GUIDES

With very few exceptions, the only way to explore the Kelabit Highlands is to hire a local guide. Fortunately this could hardly be easier. Any of the guesthouses in Bario can organise a variety of short walks and longer treks led by guides they know and rely on.

The going rate for guides is RM100 per day for either a Bario-based day trip or a longer trek. If your route requires that you camp in the forest, expect to pay approximately RM120 per night, and you may be asked to supply food. If you're trekking in one direction only (eg Bario to Ba Kelalan), you have to pay your guide for the time it takes for him to walk home.

If you are connecting the dots between rural longhouses, expect to pay RM70 for a night's sleep plus three meals (you can opt out of lunch and save RM10 or RM15).

ascent (45 minutes) to the cross (erected 1973) at the summit. The views of the Bario Valley are amazing.

Megalith Trails HIKING
(boat ride up to 4 people RM250) Hidden deep in the jungle around Bario are scores of mysterious megaliths and other 'cultural sites'. Short-haul options (guides can suggest more) include the **Pa' Umur Route** (1½ hours), which passes a salt spring, and the **Pa' Lungan Route** (3½ or four hours from Bario to Pa' Lungan, where you'll find longhouse homestays). Trails for megalith treks lasting two, three and five days are being marked.

Bario to Ba Kelalan HIKING
The three-day trek from Bario to Ba Kelalan covers a variety of mostly gentle terrain – some of it inside Indonesia – and gives a good overview of the geography and flora of the Kelabit Highlands.

🛌 Sleeping & Eating

Laid-back Bario offers several cosy options, most offering bed-and-board deals that include delicious Kelabit cuisine. Very few guesthouses offer private bathrooms.

No need to book ahead – available rooms outstrip the space on flights. Some guesthouse owners meet incoming flights at the airport. Just a few of the options are listed below.

Bario Asal Lembaa' Longhouse HOMESTAY $
(📱 Jenette 014 590 7500; www.dayangsworld. blogspot.com; bed RM30, per person incl 3 meals RM65; 🛜) A fantastic way to experience traditional longhouse living. Four families let out rooms, while others prepare delicious Kelabit food. Transport from the airport costs RM20 per vehicle one-way.

Junglebluesdream GUESTHOUSE $
(📱 019 884 9892; http://junglebluesdream.weebly. com; per person incl board RM90; 🛜) Owned by artist and one-time guide Stephen Baya and his friendly Danish wife Tine, this super-welcoming lodge (and art gallery) has four mural-decorated rooms and fantastic Kelabit food. Guests can use bicycles and go kayaking. The wi-fi doesn't always work.

Tarawe Lodge GUESTHOUSE $
(📱 019 438 1777; john.tarawe@gmail.com; per person RM20; 🛜) Run by John Tarawe, Bario's most prominent civic leader, this pleasant place, surrounded by fields, has six bright, airy rooms, each with three beds. Meals are available 200m down the road at the commercial centre.

Labang Guesthouse GUESTHOUSE $
(📱 019 815 5453; lucysrb@yahoo.com; per person incl meals RM110) David and Lucy warmly welcome guests to their 15-room, longhouse-style guesthouse, decorated with Orang Ulu designs and historic B&W photographs. A dorm room is planned for 2014. Prices include airport transport.

❶ Information

There are no banks, ATMs or credit-card facilities anywhere in the Kelabit Highlands, so bring plenty of small-denomination banknotes, plus extra cash in case you get stranded.

There's free wi-fi at the airport and 24 hours a day around 'downtown' Bario's eBario Telecentre. Several guesthouses offer wi-fi, at least in theory.

The best Malaysian cellphone service to have up here is Celcom.

eBario Telecentre (www.ebario.org; ⊙ approximately 9am-noon & 2-5pm, closed Sat afternoon & Sun; 🛜) Solar-powered internet access.

ⓘ Getting There & Away

Bario Airport (✆ Joanna 013 835 9009; 📶) is linked with Miri two or three times a day by 19-seat Twin Otters operated by **MASwings** (✆ 1300 88 3000; www.maswings.com.my); checked baggage is limited to 10kg. Weather sometimes causes delays and even cancellations. Demand for seats often outstrips supply, especially for flights to Bario, so book ahead.

The people of Bario treat the air link to Miri like their own private airline and absolutely love dropping by the airport terminal, which is a 30-minute walk from the 'centre of town', insofar as there is one. Some guesthouse prices include airport transport.

The overland trip between Bario and Miri, on very rough logging roads, is possible only by 4WD (per person RM150, 12 to 15 hours or more).

When the new road from Bario to Ba Kelalan opens (hopefully sometime in 2014), it will be easy to drive to Lawas (five hours), from where there are bus links to Kota Kinabalu (RM20, three hours) and Brunei.

UNDERSTAND MALAYSIA

Malaysia Today

Malaysia has been ruled by the same coalition of major political parties (called the BN: National Front) since the 1970s and, from the time of the country's independence in 1956, the country has been ruled by the same interest groups under different titles. Opposition parties have claimed for years that the BN have manipulated elections and that there have been restrictions put on opposing parties. The BN maintains that it has created a stable government that rightfully retains its popularity. Meanwhile Malaysia was ranked 145th out of 196 countries in the 2013 Freedom of the Press survey and has consistently ranked lower each year.

In 2007, 2011 and 2012 Bersih (Coalition for Clean and Fair Elections), a group of nongovernment organisations, staged huge rallies in KL demanding that the electoral committee clean up the electoral list, reform absentee voting, use indelible ink, allow all parties free access to the media and put an end to electoral fraud. Despite this, elections went on as usual in 2013 with widespread reports from voters of the same shenanigans. Although the BN were victorious in winning the majority of parliament seats, it

was their worst victory since 1969. The next elections will be scheduled before 2018.

The BN is primarily supported by Malays and not Malaysia's other ethnicities and is thus veering with the Malay populace towards more conservative Islamic rule. Prime Minister Najib's three-pronged strategy since the last elections has been a closer embrace of Islamic Sharia laws, a stronger *bumiputra* agenda that essentially acts as affirmative action for Malays while trying to mastermind how his political party can woo the six million new, young voters who will vote in the next elections.

History

Early Influences

The earliest evidence of human life in the region is a 40,000-year-old skull found in Sarawak's Niah Caves. But it was only around 10,000 years ago that the aboriginal Malays, the Orang Asli, began moving down the peninsula from a probable starting point in southwestern China.

By the 2nd century AD, Europeans were familiar with Malaya, and Indian traders had made regular visits in their search for gold, tin and jungle woods. Within the next century Malaya was ruled by the Funan empire, centred in what's now Cambodia, but more significant was the domination of the Sumatra-based Srivijayan empire between the 7th and 13th centuries.

In 1405 Chinese admiral Cheng Ho arrived in Melaka with promises to the locals of protection from the Siamese encroaching from the north. With Chinese support, the power of Melaka extended to include most of the Malay Peninsula. Islam arrived in Melaka around this time and soon spread through Malaya.

European Influence

Melaka's wealth and prosperity attracted European interest and it was taken over by the Portuguese in 1511, then the Dutch in 1641 and the British in 1795.

In 1838 James Brooke, a British adventurer, arrived to find the Brunei sultanate fending off rebellion from inland tribes. Brooke quashed the rebellion and in reward was granted power over part of Sarawak. Appointing himself Raja Brooke, he founded a dynasty that lasted 100 years. By 1881 Sabah was controlled by the British government, which eventually acquired Sarawak after WWII when the third Raja Brooke realised he couldn't afford the area's upkeep. In the early 20th century the British brought in Chinese and Indians, which radically changed the country's racial make-up.

Independence to the Current Day

Malaya achieved *merdeka* (independence) in 1957, but it was followed by a period of instability due to an internal Communist uprising and an external confrontation with neighbouring Indonesia. In 1963 the north Borneo states of Sabah and Sarawak, along with Singapore, joined Malaya to create Malaysia. In 1969 violent interracial riots broke out, particularly in Kuala Lumpur, and hundreds of people were killed. The government moved to dissipate the tensions, which existed mainly between the Malays and the Chinese. Present-day Malaysian society is relatively peaceful and cooperative.

Led from 1981 by outspoken Prime Minister Dr Mahathir Mohamad, Malaysia's economy grew at a rate of over 8% per year until mid-1997, when a currency crisis in neighbouring Thailand plunged the whole of Southeast Asia into recession. After 22 momentous years, Dr Mahathir Mohamad retired on 31 October 2003. He handed power to his anointed successor, Abdullah bin Ahmad Badawi, who went on to convincingly win a general election in March 2004. Since this win, the prime minister has increasingly been criticised by Mahathir for scrapping many of the former prime minister's projects.

People & Culture

The National Psyche

From the ashes of the interracial riots of 1969, the country has forged a more tolerant multicultural society, exemplified by the coexistence in many cities and towns of mosques, Christian churches and Chinese temples. Though ethnic loyalties remain strong and there are undeniable tensions, the concept of a much-discussed single 'Malaysian' identity is gaining credence and for the most part everyone coexists harmoniously. The friendliness and hospitality of Malaysians is what most visitors see and experience.

Moving from the cities to the more rural parts of the country, the laid-back ethos becomes stronger and Islamic culture comes more to the fore, particularly on the peninsula's east coast. In Malaysian Borneo you'll be fascinated by the communal lifestyle of the tribes who still live in jungle longhouses (enormous wooden structures on stilts that house tribal communities under one roof). In longhouses, hospitality is a key part of the social framework.

Lifestyle

The *kampung* (village) is at the heart of the Malay world and operates according to a system of *adat* (customary law) that emphasises collective rather than individual responsibility. Devout worship of Islam and older spiritual beliefs go hand in hand with this. However, despite the mutually supportive nature of the *kampung* environment, and growing Westernisation across Malaysia, some very conservative interpretations of Islam continue in certain areas, particularly along the peninsula's east coast.

The rapid modernisation of Malaysian life has led to some incongruous scenes. In Sarawak, some ramshackle longhouses and huts sport satellite dishes and have recent-vintage cars parked on the rutted driveways out front. And almost everywhere you go people incessantly finger mobile phones as if they're simply unable to switch them off.

Population

Malaysians come from a number of different ethnic groups: Malays, Chinese, Indians, the indigenous Orang Asli (literally, 'Original People') of the peninsula, and the various tribes of Sarawak and Sabah in Malaysian Borneo. The mixing of these groups has created the colourful cultures and delicious cuisine that makes Malaysia such a fabulous destination.

TRAVEL HINTS

➡ Malaysia is a Muslim country so dress appropriately by covering everything to the knees and over the shoulders.

➡ Airfares can be so cheap around Borneo that flying is sometimes cheaper than bussing.

MALAYSIA PEOPLE & CULTURE

It's reasonable to generalise that the Malays control the government while the Chinese dominate the economy. Approximately 85% of the country's population of nearly 30 million people lives in Peninsular Malaysia and the other 15% in Sabah and Sarawak on Borneo.

There are still small, scattered groups of Orang Asli in Peninsular Malaysia. Although most of these people have given up their nomadic or shifting-agriculture techniques and have been absorbed into modern Malay society, a few such groups still live in the forests.

Dayak is the term used for the non-Muslim people of Borneo. It is estimated there are more than 200 Dayak tribes in Borneo, including the Iban and Bidayuh in Sarawak and the Kadazan in Sabah. Smaller groups include the Kenyah, Kayan and Penan, whose way of life and traditional lands are rapidly disappearing.

Religion

The Malays are almost all Muslims. But despite Islam being the state religion, freedom of religion is guaranteed. The Chinese are predominantly followers of Taoism and Buddhism, though some are Christians. The majority of the region's Indian population comes from the south of India and are Hindu and Christian, although a sizeable percentage are Muslim.

While Christianity has made no great inroads into Peninsular Malaysia, it has had a much greater impact in Malaysian Borneo, where many indigenous people have been converted and carry Christian as well as traditional names. Others still follow animist traditions.

Arts

It's along the predominantly Malay east coast of Peninsular Malaysia that you'll find Malay arts and crafts, culture and games at their liveliest. Malaysian Borneo is replete with the arts and crafts of the country's indigenous peoples.

ARTS & CRAFTS

A famous Malaysian Bornean art is *pua kumbu*, a colourful weaving technique used to produce both everyday and ceremonial items.

The most skilled woodcarvers are generally held to be the Kenyah and Kayan peoples, who used to carve enormous, finely detailed *kelirieng* (burial columns) from tree trunks.

Originally an Indonesian craft, the production of batik cloth is popular in Malaysia and has its home in Kelantan. A speciality of Kelantan and Terengganu, *kain songket* is a handwoven fabric with gold and silver threads through the material. *Mengkuang* is a far more prosaic form of weaving using pandanus leaves and strips of bamboo to make baskets, bags and mats.

DANCE

Menora is a dance-drama of Thai origin performed by an all-male cast in grotesque masks; *mak yong* is the female version. The upbeat *joget* (better known around Melaka as *chakuncha*) is Malaysia's most popular traditional dance, often performed at Malay weddings by professional dancers.

Rebana kercing is a dance performed by young men to the accompaniment of tambourines. The *rodat* is a dance from Terengganu and is accompanied by the *tar* drum.

THE PERANAKANS

One of Peninsular Malaysia's most celebrated cultures is that of the Peranakans, descendants of Chinese immigrants who, from the 16th century onwards, settled in Singapore, Melaka and Penang. While these arrivals often married Malay women, others imported their wives from China; all of them like to refer to themselves as Straits-born or Straits Chinese to distinguish themselves from later arrivals from China. Another name you may hear for these people is Baba-Nonyas, after the Peranakan words for males (baba) and females (nonya).

The Peranakans took the religion of the Chinese, but the customs, language and dress of the Malays. The Peranakans were often wealthy traders who could afford to indulge their passion for sumptuous furnishings, jewellery and brocades. Today they are most famous for their delicious fusion cooking that's best experienced in Melaka.

MUSIC

Traditional Malay music is based largely on the *gendang* (drum), of which there are more than a dozen types. Other percussion instruments include the gong, *cerucap* (made of shells), *raurau* (coconut shells), *kertuk* and *pertuang* (both made from bamboo), and the wooden *celampang*.

Wind instruments include a number of types of flute (such as the *seruling* and *serunai*) and the trumpetlike *nafiri*, while stringed instruments include the *biola*, *gambus* and *sundatang*.

The *gamelan*, a traditional Indonesian gong-orchestra, is also found in the state of Kelantan, where a typical ensemble will comprise four different gongs, two xylophones and a large drum.

Food & Drink

Food

Meal time in Malaysia is a highly social event and the food strongly reflects the country's Malay, Chinese and Indian influences.

There are fewer culinary choices outside the cities, where staple meals of *mee goreng* (fried noodles) and *nasi goreng* (fried rice) predominate. Vegetarian dishes are usually available at both Malay and Indian cafes, but are hardly sighted at *kedai kopi* (coffee shops). You can also find an excellent selection of fruit and vegetables at markets.

Roti canai (flaky flat bread dipped in a small amount of dhal and potato curry) is probably the cheapest meal (around RM1.50) in Malaysia. But really everything, from seafood laksa to the freshly caught and cooked wild cat or mouse deer you may be offered at a longhouse, is good and often cheap.

Halfway between a drink and a dessert is *ais kacang*, something similar to an old-fashioned snow-cone, except that the shaved ice is topped with syrups and condensed milk, and it's all piled on top of a foundation of beans and jellies (sometimes corn kernels). It sounds and looks gross but tastes terrific.

Drink

Tap water is safe to drink in many big cities, but check with locals if you're unsure.

With the aid of a blender and crushed ice, simple and delicious juice concoctions are whipped up in seconds. Lurid soybean drinks are sold at street stalls and soybean milk is also available in soft-drink bottles. Medicinal teas are a big hit with the health-conscious Chinese.

Alcohol isn't popular with the Muslim population and incurs incredibly high taxes. A mug of beer at a *kedai kopi* will cost around RM7, and around RM12 to RM15 at bars and clubs. Anchor and Tiger beers are popular, as are locally brewed Carlsberg and Guinness. Indigenous people have a soft spot for *tuak* (rice wine), which tends to revolt first-timers but is apparently an acquired taste. Another rural favourite is the dark-coloured spirit *arak*, which is smooth and potent.

Environment

The Land

Malaysia covers 329,758 sq km and consists of two distinct regions. Peninsular Malaysia is the long finger of land extending south from Asia and through the mountainous northern half has some dense jungle coverage, though unprotected forests are getting cut down at an alarming rate, mostly to create palm-oil plantations. The peninsula's western side has a large fertile plain running to the sea, while the eastern side is fringed with sandy beaches. Malaysian Borneo consists of Sarawak and Sabah; both states are covered in thick jungle and have extensive river systems. Sabah is crowned by Mt Kinabalu (4095m), the highest mountain between the Himalaya and New Guinea.

Wildlife

Malaysia's ancient rainforests are endowed with a cornucopia of life forms. In Peninsular Malaysia alone there are more than 8000 species of flowering plants, including the world's tallest tropical tree species, the *tualang*. In Malaysian Borneo, where hundreds of new species have been discovered since the 1990s, you'll find the world's largest flower, the *Rafflesia*, measuring up to 1m across, as well as the world's biggest cockroach. Mammals include elephants, rhinos (extremely rare), tapirs, tigers, leopards, honey bears, *tempadau* (forest cattle), gibbons and monkeys (including, in Borneo, the bizarre proboscis monkey), orangutans and pangolins (scaly anteaters). Bird species include spectacular pheasants, sacred hornbills and many groups of colourful birds such as kingfishers, sunbirds, woodpeckers and barbets. Snakes include cobras, vipers and pythons. Once a favourite nesting ground for leatherback turtles, recorded landings now hover at around 10 per year.

National Parks

Malaysia's 23 national parks cover barely 5% of the country's landmass. The country's major national park is Taman Negara, on the peninsula, while Gunung Mulu and Kinabalu are the two main parks in Sarawak and Sabah, respectively. Especially on Borneo, the rarity and uniqueness of local flora and fauna is such that scientists – from dragonfly experts to palm-tree specialists – are regular visitors and vocal proponents of new parks and reserves both on land and in the surrounding waters. There are also 13 marine parks in Malaysia, notably around Pulau Perhentian, Tioman and Sipadan, although enforcement of protection measures is very loose.

Environmental Issues

When it comes to environmental faux pas, Malaysia has done it all. Logging is believed to have destroyed more than 60% of the country's rainforests and generates some US$4.5 billion per year for big business. Another growing phenomenon is palm-tree plantations, where vast swathes of land are razed and planted with trees that yield lucrative palm oil. But the crown of eco and social irresponsibility goes to Bakun Dam in Sarawak, which flooded some 690 sq km of some of the world's most diverse rainforest in late 2010 and forced up to 10,000 indigenous peoples from their homes. The dam has been criticised as being corrupt, ill-planned and unnecessary, but the state already has plans to build 12 more dams in the region.

Responsible ecotourism is the traveller's best antidote to these trends.

SURVIVAL GUIDE

 Directory A–Z

ACCOMMODATION
The following prices refer to a double room.

$ less than RM100 (US$30)
$$ RM100 to RM400 (US$30 to US$120)
$$$ more than RM400 (US$120)

CUSTOMS REGULATIONS
When arriving in Malaysia, note that you are legally entitled to carry 1L of alcohol and 200 cigarettes. Cameras, portable radios, perfume, cosmetics and watches do not incur duty. Trafficking of illegal substances can result in the death penalty – don't do it.

EMBASSIES & CONSULATES
Unless otherwise specified, all the following foreign embassies are in Kuala Lumpur and are generally open 8am to 12.30pm and 1.30pm to 4.30pm Monday to Friday. A full list of embassies and consulates in Malaysia can be found at www.mycen.com.my/malaysia/embassy.html.

Australian High Commission (☎03-2146 5555; www.australia.org.my; 6 Jln Yap Kwan Seng)

Canadian High Commission (☎03-2718 3333; Level 18, Menara Tan & Tan, 207 Jln Tun Razak)

French Embassy (☎03-2053 5500; 196 Jln Ampang)

German Embassy (☎03-2142 9666; www.kuala-lumpur.diplo.de; Level 26, Menara Tan & Tan, 207 Jln Tun Razak)

Irish Embassy (☎03-2161 2963; Ireland House, the Amp Walk, 218 Jln Ampang)

Netherlands Embassy (☎03-2168 6200; www.netherlands.org.my; 7th fl, the Amp Walk, 218 Jln Ampang)

New Zealand High Commission (☎03-2078 2533; Level 21, Menara IMC, 8 Jln Sultan Ismail)

UK High Commission (☎03-2148 2122; www.britain.org.my; 185 Jln Ampang)

US Embassy (☎03-2168 5000; http://malaysia.usembassy.gov; 376 Jln Tun Razak)

FESTIVALS & EVENTS
There are many cultures and religions coexisting in Malaysia, which means there are many occasions for celebration throughout the year.

Ramadan is the major annual Muslim event, connected with the 30 days during which Muslims cannot eat, drink, smoke or have sex from sunrise to sunset. The dates of Ramadan change every year; in 2014 it begins on 28 June, and in 2015 it begins on 18 June.

Chinese New Year (January/February) The most important celebration for the Chinese community is marked with dragon dances and street parades.

Thaipusam (January/February) One of the most dramatic Hindu festivals, in which devotees honour Lord Subramaniam with acts of amazing physical resilience. Self-mutilating worshippers make the procession to the Batu Caves outside KL.

Malaysian Grand Prix (March/April) Formula One's big outing in Southeast Asia is held at the Sepang International Circuit in Selangor either at the end of March or early April.

Gawai Dayak (late May/early June) Festival of the Dayaks in Sarawak, marking the end of the rice season. War dances, cock fights and blowpipe events take place.

Festa de San Pedro (June) Christian celebration on 29 June in honour of the patron saint of the fishing community; notably celebrated by the Eurasian-Portuguese community of Melaka.

Dragon Boat Festival (June to August) Celebrated in Penang.

Rainforest World Music Festival (July/August) Held for three days at the Sarawak Cultural Village, this music and arts festival features musicians from around the world and highlights indigenous music from Borneo.

National Day (Hari Kebangsaan) (August) Malaysia celebrates its independence on 31 August with events all over the country, but particularly in KL where there are parades and a variety of performances in the Lake Gardens.

Moon Cake Festival (September) Chinese festival celebrating the overthrow of Mongol warlords in ancient China with the eating of moon cakes and the lighting of colourful paper lanterns.

Festival of the Nine Emperor Gods (October) Involves nine days of Chinese operas, processions and other events honouring the nine emperor gods.

Deepavali (November) The Festival of Lights, in which tiny oil lamps are lit outside Hindu homes; celebrates Rama's victory over the demon King Ravana.

FOOD

The following refers to the price of a main dish.

$ less than RM10 (US$3)
$$ RM10 to RM20 (US$3 to US$6)
$$$ more than RM10 (US$6)

GAY & LESBIAN TRAVELLERS

Conservative political parties and religious groups make a regular habit of denouncing gays and lesbians in Malaysia, a country where Muslim homosexuality is punishable by imprisonment and caning. Fortunately, these groups remain on the fringe and outright persecution of gays and lesbians in the country is rare. Nonetheless, while in Malaysia, gay and lesbian travellers (particularly the former) should avoid any behaviour that attracts unwanted attention. Visit www.utopia-asia.com or www.fridae.com, both of which provide good coverage of gay and lesbian events and activities right across Southeast Asia.

INTERNET ACCESS

Internet access is widespread and available at numerous internet cafes, backpacker hang-outs and shopping malls, generally on fast broadband connections. In cities, rates range from RM2 to

RM4 per hour; on islands and in remote areas, rates skyrocket (and speed plummets) to around RM6 to RM20 per hour. Wi-fi is easily found in cities, sparingly in medium-sized towns but less in the countryside.

LEGAL MATTERS

In any of your dealings with the local police it pays to be deferential. Minor misdemeanours may be overlooked, but don't count on it and don't offer anyone a bribe.

It's simply not worth having anything to do with drugs in Malaysia: drug trafficking carries a mandatory death penalty, and even the possession of tiny amounts of drugs for personal use can bring about a lengthy jail sentence and a beating with the *rotan* (cane).

MAPS

Periplus (peripluspublishinggroup.com) has maps covering Malaysia, Peninsular Malaysia and KL. Tourism Malaysia's free *Map of Malaysia* has useful distance charts, facts about the country and inset maps of many of the major cities.

For accurate maps of rural areas contact the **National Survey & Mapping Department** (Ibu Pejabat Ukur & Pemetaan Malaysia; Map p382; ☑ 03-2617 0800; www.jupem.gov.my; Jln Semarak, Kuala Lumpur; ☼7.30am-5.30pm Mon-Fri).

MONEY

Bargaining is not usually required for everyday goods in Malaysia, but feel free to bargain when purchasing souvenirs, antiques and other tourist items, even when the prices are displayed. Transport prices are generally fixed, but negotiation is required for trishaws and taxis around town or for charter.

Tipping is not common in Malaysia.

OPENING HOURS

Exceptions to these hours are noted in individual reviews.

Banks 10am to 3pm Monday to Friday, 9.30am to 11.30am Saturday

Government offices 8am to 12.45pm and 2pm to 4.15pm Monday to Thursday; 8am to 12.15pm and 2.45pm to 4.15pm Friday

Shopping malls 10am to 9pm

Shops 9am to 6pm Monday to Saturday

In the more Islamic-minded states of Kedah, Perlis, Kelantan and Terengganu, government offices, banks and many shops close on Friday and on Saturday afternoon.

POST

There are poste restante services at all major post offices, which are open from 8am to 5pm daily except Sundays and public holidays (also closed on Fridays in Kedah, Kelantan and Terengganu districts).

Aerograms and postcards cost 50 sen to send to any destination. Letters weighing 20g or less cost 90 sen to Asia, RM1.40 to Australia or New Zealand, RM1.50 to the UK and Europe, and RM1.80 to North America.

You can send parcels from any major post office, although the rates are fairly high (from RM20 to RM60 for a 1kg parcel, depending on the destination).

PUBLIC HOLIDAYS

Although some public holidays have a fixed annual date, Hindus, Muslims and Chinese follow a lunar calendar, which means the dates for many events vary each year.

The major holiday of the Muslim calendar, Hari Raya Puasa, marks the end of the month-long fast of Ramadan with three days of joyful celebration. During Hari Raya Puasa and Chinese New Year, accommodation may be difficult to obtain. At these times, many businesses may also be closed and transport can be fully booked.

In addition to national public holidays, each state has its own holidays, usually associated with the sultan's birthday or a Muslim celebration.

National holidays:

New Year's Day 1 January

Chinese New Year January/February

Birth of the Prophet March

Wesak Day April/May

Labour Day 1 May

Agong's (King's) Birthday 1st Saturday in June

National Day 31 August

Hari Raya Puasa September/October

Deepavali November

Hari Raya Haji December

Awal Muharam December

Christmas Day 25 December

SAFE TRAVEL

In general Malaysia is very safe, with violent attacks being uncommon. However, the usual travel precautions apply, such as restraining your urge to go wandering around seedy areas alone late at night. The snatching of bags by thieves on motorcycles is a recurring crime in KL, Johor Bahru, Melaka and Penang's Georgetown, so keep bags away from the roadside in these areas.

Credit-card fraud is a growing problem, so only use your cards at established businesses and guard your credit-card numbers.

Rabies is an ever-present problem in Malaysia – you should treat any animal bite very seriously. Leeches can be a nuisance after heavy rain on jungle walks.

TELEPHONE

If you have your mobile phone with you, once you've sorted out a local SIM (buy one for RM10) you should have no problem dialling overseas. If you're sticking to Peninsular Malaysia any of the major mobile phone service providers are fine, but if you're heading into the remoter parts of Malaysian Borneo then get **Celcom** (🗘 013 or 🗘 019 numbers; www.celcom.com.my), which has the largest coverage. Rates for a local call are around 15 sen per minute, an SMS is around 6 sen and 4G data service costs around RM7 per week. Top-up cards for prepaid SIM cards are available at all 7-Elevens.

The access code for making international calls to most countries is 🗘 00. For information on international calls, dial 🗘 103.

To call Malaysia from outside the country, dial 🗘 60, drop the 0 before the Malaysian area code, then dial the number you want.

TOILETS

Although there are still some places with Asian squat-style toilets in Malaysia, you'll most often find Western-style ones these days. At public facilities toilet paper is not usually provided. Instead, you will find a hose which you are supposed to use as a bidet or, in cheaper places, a bucket of water and a tap.

Public toilets in shopping malls and at transport depots are usually staffed by attendants and cost 10 sen to 30 sen to use; an extra 10 sen often gets you a dozen sheets of toilet paper.

TOURIST INFORMATION

Tourism Malaysia (www.tourismmalaysia.gov.my) has a network of overseas offices, which are useful for predeparture planning. Its domestic offices range from extremely helpful to hardly ever open, depending on the region. All stock some decent brochures as well as the excellent *Map of Malaysia*.

TRAVELLERS WITH DISABILITIES

For the mobility impaired, Malaysia can be a nightmare. In most cities and towns there are often no footpaths, kerbs are very high and pedestrian crossings are few and far between. Budget hotels almost never have lifts. On the upside, KL's modern urban railway lines are reasonably wheelchair-accessible.

Malaysia Airlines and Keretapi Tanah Melayu (the national railway service) offer 50% discounts for travellers with disabilities.

VISAS

Visitors must have a passport valid for at least six months beyond the date of entry into Malaysia. Nationals of most countries are given a 30- to 90-day visa on arrival. As a general rule you'll be given 60 days if arriving by air, although if you arrive overland you may be given 30 days unless you ask for a 60-day permit. Full details of visa regulations are available on the website www.kln.gov.my.

Citizens of Israel can only enter Malaysia under special circumstances.

Sarawak and Sabah are semi-autonomous. If you travel from Peninsular Malaysia or Sabah into Sarawak, your passport will be checked on arrival and a new stay-permit issued, usually for the period left on your original Malaysian visa. Travelling from either Sabah or Sarawak back to Peninsular Malaysia there are no formalities and you do not start a new entry period, so your permit from Sabah or Sarawak remains valid.

VOLUNTEERING

Great Orangutan Project (www.orangutan-project.com) Places paying volunteers at the Matang Wildlife Centre in Sarawak.

LASSie (www.langkawilassie.org.my) Dog and cat lovers can help out at the Langkawi Animal Shelter & Sanctuary Foundation, next to Bon Ton Resort.

Malaysian AIDS Council (www.mac.org.my) Seeks volunteers and interns to assist in its campaigning work.

Miso Walai Homestay Program (www.miso walaihomestay.com) Gets travellers involved with local wetlands restoration projects.

Nur Salaam (www.rumahnursalam.blogspot. com) This charity works with street kids in the Chow Kit area of KL.

Regional Environmental Awareness Cameron Highlands (Reach; www.reach.org.my) Take part in reforestation and recycling programs in the Cameron Highlands.

Sepilok Orang-Utan Rehabilitation Centre (☏089 531180; soutan@po.jaring.my; Sepilok, Sabah) Has one of the best established volunteer centres.

Wild Asia (www.wildasia.org) A variety of volunteer options generally connected with the environment and sustainable tourism in the region.

WOMEN TRAVELLERS

Foreign women travelling in Malaysia can expect some attention, though most of it will just involve stares from locals unfamiliar with (or curious about) Westerners. It helps, and is much more respectful of the culture, if you dress conservatively by wearing long pants or skirts and loose tops that cover the shoulders. Western women are not expected to cover their heads with scarves (outside mosques, that is). In resort areas you can wear shorts, sleeveless tops and swimwear, but it isn't appropriate anywhere in the country to sunbathe topless. On more remote beaches you're better off doing like the locals do and swimming fully clothed. Keep

a watch out for sleazy local beach boys in Langkawi, Cherating and the Perhentians.

Tampons and pads are widely available, especially in big cities, and over-the-counter medications are also fairly easy to find.

ⓘ Getting There & Away

AIR

The gateway to Peninsular Malaysia is the city of Kuala Lumpur, although Penang and Johor Bahru (JB) also have international connections. Singapore is a handy arrival/departure point, since it's just a short trip across the Causeway from JB. Malaysia Airlines is the country's main airline carrier, although AirAsia flights are much cheaper.

AirAsia (☏03-8775 4000; www.airasia.com) Flies to Brunei, Cambodia, Indonesia, the Philippines, Singapore, Thailand and Vietnam.

Berjaya Air (☏03-7847 8228; www.berjaya-air. com)

Cathay Pacific Airways (☏03-2035 2788; www.cathaypacific.com)

Emirates (www.emirates.com)

Eva Air (www.evaair.com)

Jetstar (www.jetstar.com)

Malaysia Airlines (MH; ☏03-2161 0555, 1300 883 000; www.malaysiaairlines.com) Flies to Brunei, Cambodia, the Philippines, Singapore and Vietnam.

Royal Brunei Airlines (☏03-2070 7166; www. bruneiair.com)

Silk Air (www.silkair.com)

Singapore Airlines (☏03-2692 3122; www. singaporeair.com) Serves Singapore.

Thai Airways International (☏03-2031 2900; www.thaiairways.com) Flies to Thailand.

LAND
Brunei
Border crossings are possible from Sarawak and Sabah.

Indonesia
Frequent buses link Pontianak in Kalimantan with Kuching and Miri in Sarawak, and Kota Kinabalu in Sabah. The buses cross at the Tebedu/ Entikong border.

Singapore
At the southern tip of Peninsular Malaysia you can cross into Singapore via Johor Bahru by bus.

Thailand
From western Peninsular Malaysia, you can travel by car or private bus from Alor Setar to the border crossing at Bukit Kayu Hitam and on to the transit town of Hat Yai in Thailand, via Sadao.

There are trains passing through Alor Setar to Padang Besar and then continuing north into Thailand.

Though there is a border crossing at Rantau Panjang on the eastern peninsula that is geographically convenient to Kota Bharu, all travel through this section of southern Thailand should be avoided until the security situation vastly improves.

There is also a border crossing between Keroh (Malaysia) and Betong (Thailand), but at the time of writing it was inadvisable to travel here due to the violence in Yala Province, Thailand.

SEA
Indonesia

The following are the main ferry routes between Indonesia and Malaysia:

➡ Pulau Bengkalis, Sumatra to Melaka

➡ Dumai, Sumatra to Melaka

➡ Pekanbaru, Sumatra to Melaka

➡ Tanjung Pinang on Pulau Bintan (Riau Islands) to JB

➡ Pulau Batam (Riau Islands) to JB

➡ Tarakan, Kalimantan to Tawau

Philippines

Boats link Sandakan with Zamboanga on the Philippine island of Mindanao, but at the time of writing, travel through Zamboanga was not advised because of lawlessness and an Islamist insurgency.

Thailand

Regular ferries run between Pulau Langkawi and Satun in Thailand and to Ko Lipe in Thailand with onward service as far as Ko Lanta.

❶ Getting Around

AIR

The main domestic operators are **Malaysia Airlines** (MAS; ☏ 03-2161 0555, outside Malaysia 1300 883 000; www.malaysia-airlines.com.my), MAS subsidiary **Firefly** (☏ 03-7845 4543; www.fireflyz.com.my) and **AirAsia** (☏ 03-8660 4343, outside Malaysia 1300 889 933; www.airasia.com).

Berjaya Air (☏ 03-7847 8228; www.berjaya-air.com) flies between KL (Subang), Pulau Tioman and Pulau Redang, as well as Singapore and Ko Samui in Thailand.

In Malaysian Borneo, **MASwings** (☏ 03-7843 3000, outside Malaysia 1300 883 000; www.maswings.com.my) offers domestic flights within and between Sarawak and Sabah. These services often book up during school holidays.

BICYCLE

The main road system in Malaysia has good surfaces, making the country good for bike touring, but the secondary road system is limited. Mountain bikes are recommended for forays off the beaten track.

KL Bike Hash (www.klmbh.org) has a whole load of useful information and links to other cycling-connected sites in Malaysia. Also see **Bicycle Touring Malaysia** (www.bicycletouring-malaysia.com).

BOAT

There are no ferry services between Malaysian Borneo and the peninsula. On a local level, there are boats and ferries between the peninsula and offshore islands, and along the rivers of Sabah and Sarawak. If a boat looks overloaded or otherwise unsafe, do not board it.

BUS

Peninsular Malaysia has an excellent bus system. In larger towns there may be several bus stations. Local and regional buses often operate from one station and long-distance buses from another; in other cases, KL for example, bus stations are differentiated by the destinations they serve.

On major runs you can usually just turn up and get on the next bus. On many routes there are air-conditioned buses – but take your arctic gear, the air-con is usually pumped up to the max! *Ekspres*, in the Malaysian context, often means indeterminate stops.

In Sabah, frequent buses, minivans and share taxis follow the asphalt arc of the Pan Borneo Highway from Beaufort to Kota Kinabalu to Tawau, passing by (or near) most of the state's tourism hot spots, including Mt Kinabalu, Sandakan and Semporna. For some destinations, such as the top of Mt Kinabalu and Sipadan, there's no real way to avoid booking a package.

In Sarawak, the Pan Borneo Highway from Kuching to Sabah via Miri and Brunei is in great shape, especially since the last ferry, across Sungai Pandaruan (near Limbang), was replaced by a bridge in December 2013. Express buses ply the Kuching–Miri route many times a day. For travel between Kuching and Sibu, though, the ferry is faster, and boats (or aeroplanes) are the only way to get to some parts of the interior. Bus transport to/from Brunei, and from Miri through Brunei to KK, is limited to just a few buses a day.

CAR & MOTORCYCLE

Roads in Malaysia are generally high quality and driving standards aren't too hair-raising. Road rules are basically the same as in Britain and Australia. Driving in KL and some of the bigger cities can be a nightmare, however, and you'll always have to keep an eye out for motorcyclists and animals. Cars are right-hand drive and you drive on the left side of the road. The speed limit is officially 110km per hour.

Unlimited-distance car-rental costs from around RM190/1320 per day/week, including insurance and collision-damage waiver. A valid overseas driving licence is required for vehicle rental. Be aware that insurance companies will most likely wash their hands of you if you injure yourself driving a motorcycle without a licence.

HITCHING

Malaysia has long had a reputation for being an excellent place to hitchhike but, with the ease of bus travel, most travellers don't bother. On the west coast hitching is quite easy but it's not possible on the main *lebuhraya* (highway). On the east coast traffic is lighter and there may be long waits between rides. Of course hitching is never entirely safe and you do so at your own risk.

LOCAL TRANSPORT

Local transport varies but almost always includes local buses and taxis. In a few Peninsular Malaysia towns there are also bicycle rickshaws but in general these are dying out. The best towns for rickshaws are Georgetown and Melaka.

In the cities and larger towns of Malaysian Borneo you'll find taxis, buses and minibuses. Once you're out in the villages, though, you can either walk or find someone to give you a ride. If you're upriver or in the boondocks your alternatives are riverboats, aeroplanes or lengthy jungle treks.

TAXI

Drivers are legally required to use meters if they exist – you can try insisting that they do so, but more often than not you'll just have to negotiate the fare before you get in.

Compared to buses, long-distance (or share) taxis are expensive. The taxis work on fixed fares for the entire car and between major towns

you'll have a reasonable chance of finding other passengers without having to wait around too long; otherwise, you'll probably have to charter a whole taxi.

TRAIN

There are two main types of rail services: express and local trains. Express trains are air-conditioned and have 'premier' (1st class), 'superior' (2nd class) and sometimes 'economy' seats (3rd class). Similarly on overnight trains you'll find 'premier night deluxe' cabins, 'premier night standard' cabins and 'standard night' cabins. Local trains are usually economy class only, but some have superior seats. Express trains stop only at main stations, while local services stop everywhere, including the middle of the jungle.

Peninsular Malaysia

Malaysia's privatised national railway company is **Keretapi Tanah Melayu** (KTM; ☎ 03-2267 1200; www.ktmb.com.my). It runs a modern, comfortable and economical railway service, although for the most part services are slow.

One line runs up the west coast from Singapore, through KL, Butterworth and on into Thailand. The other branches off from this line at Gemas and runs through Kuala Lipis up to the northeastern corner of the country near Kota Bharu in Kelantan. Often referred to as the 'Jungle Railway', this line is properly known as the 'East Coast Railway'.

Malaysian Borneo

In Sabah, the **Sabah State Railway** (www.sabah. gov.my/railway/indexeng.html) runs Borneo's only train line. Inaugurated in 1896, it stretches for 134km from Tanjung Aru, near KK, southwest to Beaufort and then southeast to Tenom.

Myanmar (Burma)

✔ 95 / POP 66.2 MILLION

Why Go?

Now is the moment to visit this extraordinary land, scattered with gilded pagodas, where the traditional ways of Asia endure and previously off-limits areas are opening up. As the country makes tentative steps towards democracy, sanctions have been dropped and the world is rushing to do business here. Thankfully, the pace of change is not overwhelming,

Travelling in Myanmar remains a chance to swap the hubbub and electronic demands of modern life for the spirituality of sacred temples and hushed monasteries. Enjoy slowly unfolding journeys through serene landscapes, including meandering rivers, lush jungles, ethnic minority villages and pristine palm-fringed beaches. Best of all, you'll encounter locals who are gentle, humorous, engaging, considerate, inquisitive and passionate.

Best Places to Eat

➡ Aung Thukha (p486)

➡ Daw Yee (p501)

➡ Starbeam Bistro (p528)

➡ Lin Htett Myanmar Traditional Food (p505)

Best Places for Cultural Connections

➡ Hsipaw (p521)

➡ Kyaingtong (p509)

➡ Mrauk U (p534)

➡ Mawlamyine (p500)

When to Go

Yangon

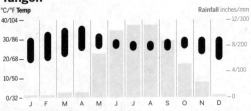

Jan Independence Day (4 January), celebrating the end of British rule, is marked by nationwide fairs.

Apr The Water Festival (Thingyan) is fun, but it's one of the hottest times of year.

Dec Peak season with many visitors heading here over the Christmas–New Year break.

Don't Miss

Myanmar is one of the most devout Buddhist countries in the world. Yangon's Shwedagon Paya, Mandalay's Mahamuni Paya and Bagan's plain of temples are all must-see locations, but there are many other Buddhist sites that will impress you with their beauty and spirituality. A 10-storey-tall seated Buddha watches over Pyay's hill-top Shwesandaw Paya providing sweeping views of the town. The old Rakhine capital of Mrauk U is dotted with ruined and functioning temples and monasteries, while in Mt Kyaiktiyo you can join the pilgrims.

ITINERARIES

One Week

In Yangon, visit the Shwedagon Paya and shop for handicrafts at Bogyoke Aung San Market. Overnight on a bus to Mandalay, climb Mandalay Hill, see the famed Mahamuni Paya and beautiful teak monastery Shwe In Bin Kyaung. Take a morning boat to Mingun, home to a giant earthquake-cracked stupa, following up with a sunset boat ride past U Bein's Bridge at Amarapura. Connect by bus or boat to Bagan, allowing a couple of days to explore the temples there.

Three Weeks

In addition to the above, venture east to beautiful Inle Lake; consider trekking there from Kalaw (minimum two days). From Bago head to Mt Kyaiktiyo to view the amazing Golden Rock, then to Mawlamyine for a taste of tropical Myanmar. Use the Kayin State capital, Hpa-an, as a base for exploring lush countryside peppered with sacred caves and limestone mountains. Return to Yangon then fly to Sittwe, where you can take another boat to the amazing temple ruins of Mrauk U (minimum five days).

Essential Food & Drink

➡ **Äthouq** Light, tart and spicy salads made with raw vegetables or fruit tossed with lime juice, onions, peanuts, roasted chickpea powder and chillies. A common one is *leq-p'eq thouq*, which includes fermented tea leaves.

➡ **Mohinga ('moun-hinga')** A popular breakfast dish of rice noodles served with fish soup and as many other ingredients as there are cooks.

➡ **Shan khauk-swe** Shan-style noodle soup; thin wheat noodles in a light broth with meat or tofu, available across the country but most common in Mandalay and Shan State.

➡ **Htamin chin** Literally 'sour rice', this turmeric-coloured rice salad also hails from Shan State.

➡ **Black tea** Brewed in the Indian style with lots of milk and sugar.

AT A GLANCE

➡ **Currency** Burmese kyat (K)

➡ **Language** Burmese

➡ **Money** Cash mainly.

➡ **Visas** 28 days, extendable.

➡ **Mobile phones** International roaming available. Limited availability of prepaid SIMs for local phones.

MYANMAR (BURMA)

Fast Facts

➡ **Area** 676,578 sq km

➡ **Capital** Nay Pyi Taw

➡ **Emergency** Police (Yangon) ☑ 199

Exchange Rates

Australia	A$1	K8890
Euro Zone	€1	K1350
Laos	10,000K	K1225
Thailand	10B	K300
UK	UK£1	K1640
USA	US$1	K985

Set Your Budget

➡ **Guesthouse** US$10–30

➡ **Street-stall meal** US$2–5

➡ **Large beer** US$1.50

Entering the Country

The main land border crossings are from Mae Sai, Ranong and Mae Sot in Thailand, and Ruili in China.

Myanmar (Burma) Highlights

❶ Witness the beauty of a misty dawn breaking over 4000 Buddhist temples on the plains of **Bagan** (p522) from the upper terraces of one of the paya (temples)

❷ Spend longer than you planned at gorgeous **Inle Lake** (p503), a mythical landscape of floating villages, stilted monasteries and aquatic gardens

❸ Use **Mandalay** (p509) as the base for visiting the intriguing old cities of Amarapura, with its famed teak bridge, and some stupa-pendous views from Sagaing

❹ Be dazzled by **Shwedagon Paya** (p483), the country's most important Buddhist temple, and the buzz of political and economic reconstruction in Yangon

❺ Trek through forested hills, fields and fascinating, friendly minority villages between Inle Lake and **Kalaw** (p507)

❻ Test your mettle by making the full 7-mile uphill pilgrimage to the sacred and gravity-defying **Kyaiktiyo** (p499), the Golden Rock

❼ Lose yourself amid the hundreds of ruined temples and fortifications in timeless **Mrauk U** (p534), former grand capital of Rakhine.

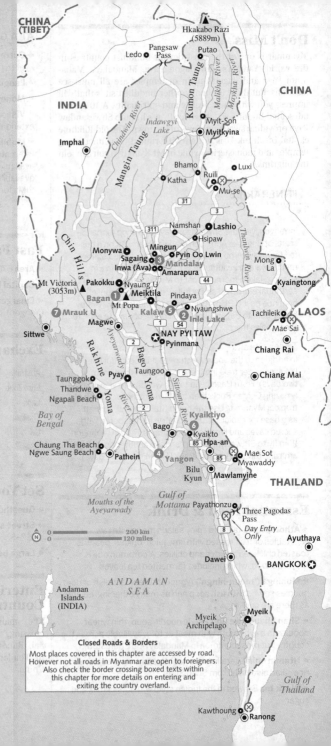

Closed Roads & Borders

Most places covered in this chapter are accessed by road. However not all roads in Myanmar are open to foreigners. Also check the border crossing boxed texts within this chapter for more details on entering and exiting the country overland.

YANGON

♪ 01 / POP 4.35 MILLION

The former capital, during colonial times known as Rangoon, is emerging from bloody and neglectful military rule into an era of glittering possibilities. Exiles are returning and foreign investors and adventurers are flooding in, triggering a blossoming of new restaurants, bars, shops, building sites and traffic jams.

Yangon's awe-inspiring Buddhist monument Shwedagon Paya is the one sight in Myanmar not to miss. Vibrant streets lined with food vendors, colourful open-air markets, evocative colonial architecture – some of the most impressive you'll find in Southeast Asia – are other reasons for lingering.

◉ Sights

★ **Shwedagon Paya**   BUDDHIST TEMPLE
(ရွှေတိဂုံဘုရား; Map p490; www.shwedagon pagoda.com; Singuttara Hill, Dagon; admission US$8/K8000; ☺4am-10pm) Visible from almost anywhere in Yangon, this is one of Buddhism's most sacred sites. The 325ft *zedi* (religious monument), adorned with 27 metric tons of gold leaf and thousands of diamonds and other gems, is believed to enshrine eight hairs of the Gautama Buddha as well as relics of three former Buddhas.

Four long, graceful entrance stairways lead to the main terrace which, depending on the time of day you visit, can be quiet and contemplative or bustling and raucous. If you prefer the former, visit in the cool of dawn. Otherwise, pay your respects when the golden stupa flames crimson and burnt orange in the setting sun.

★ **Botataung Paya**   BUDDHIST TEMPLE
(ဗိုလ်တထောင်ဘုရား; Map p486; Strand Rd, Botataung; admission US$3/K3000, camera US$1/

K1000; ☺6am-9.30pm) Botataung's spacious riverfront location and lack of crowds give it a more down-to-earth spiritual feeling than Shwedagon or Sule Paya. Its most original feature is the dazzling zig-zag corridor, gilded from floor to ceiling, that snakes its way around the hollow interior of the 131ft golden *zedi*. Also look out for a bronze Buddha that once resided in the royal palace in Mandalay, and a large pond full of hundreds of terrapin turtles.

The nearby **Botataung Jetty** provides a good view of activity on the Yangon River.

Sule Paya   BUDDHIST STUPA
(ဆူးလေဘုရား; Map p486; cnr Sule Paya Rd & Mahabandoola Rd, Pabedan; admission US$2/ K2000; ☺5am-9pm) It's not every city where the primary traffic circle is occupied by a 2000-year-old golden temple. This 50yd *zedi,* said to be older than Shwedagon Paya, is an example of modern Asian business life melding with ancient Burmese tradition.

National Museum   MUSEUM
(အမျိုးသားပြတိုက်; Map p488; 66/74 Pyay Rd, Dagon; admission US$5/K5000; ☺9.30am-4.30pm Tue-Sun) Even though the museum's collection is appallingly labelled and lit, the treasures that lie within this cavernous building deserve a viewing.

The highlight is the spectacular 26ft-high, jewel-encrusted **Sihasana** (Lion Throne), which belonged to King Thibaw Min, the last king of Myanmar.

Mahabandoola Garden   PARK
(မဟာဗန္ဓုလပန်းခြံ; Map p486; Mahabandoola Garden St, Kyauktada; ☺6am-6pm) FREE This recently revamped park offers pleasant strolling in the heart of the downtown area and views of surrounding heritage buildings including **City Hall**, the **High Court** and the old **Rowe & Co** department store.

DON'T MISS

RIDING THE CIRCLE LINE

The nearly 31-mile Yangon Circle Line (US$1/K1000) is a slow-moving, three-hour train trip around Yangon and the neighbouring countryside. The ancient carriages shake at times like washing machines on full spin cycle. However, hopping on the line is a great way to experience commuter life, interact with passengers and vendors on the trains, and see off-the-beaten-track areas of the city.

Trains leave at 6.10am, 8.20am, 8.35am, 10.10am, 10.45am, 11.30am, 11.50am, 1.05pm, 1.40pm, 2.25pm, 4.40pm and 5.10pm from platform 6/7 at the Yangon train station, accessed off Pandsodan St; tickets are bought on the platform. Trains go in either direction and some don't always do the full circuit. The train is least crowded after 10am and before 4pm, and at weekends.

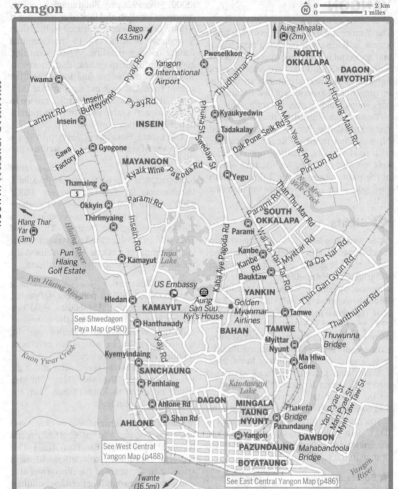

The park's most notable feature is the **Independence Monument**, a 165ft white obelisk surrounded by two concentric circles of *chinthe* (half-lion, half-dragon deity). There's also a good childrens' playground.

Musmeah Yeshua Synagogue   SYNAGOGUE
(Map p488; 85 26th St, Pabedan; ⊙10am-noon & 4-6pm) Watched over by trustee Moses Samuels, a member of Yangon's now tiny community of Jews, the lovingly maintained interior of this 1896 building contains a *bimah* (platform holding the reading table for the Torah) in the centre of the main sanctuary, and a

women's balcony upstairs. The wooden ceiling features the original blue-and-white Star of David motif.

★**Chaukhtatgyi Paya**   BUDDHIST TEMPLE
(ခြောက်ထပ်ကြီးဘုရား; Map p490; Shwegondine Rd, Tamwe; ⊙6am-8pm) Housed in a large metal-roofed shed, this beautiful 70yd-long reclining Buddha has a placid face, topped by a crown encrusted with diamonds and other precious stones.

★**Ngahtatgyi Paya**   BUDDHIST TEMPLE
(ငါးထပ်ကြီးဘုရား; Map p490; Shwegondine Rd, Tamwe; admission US$2/K2000; ⊙6am-8pm)

The gorgeous 46ft-tall image is one of the most impressive sitting buddhas in southern Myanmar. In fact, it's worth going to see for its carved wooden backdrop alone.

Kandawgyi Lake
LAKE
(ကန်တော်ကြီး; Map p490; Kan Yeik Thar Rd, Dagon; admission K2000) Also known as Royal Lake, this artificial lake, built by the British as a reservoir, is most attractive at sunset, when the glittering Shwedagon is reflected in its calm waters. The boardwalk, which runs mainly along the southern and western sides of the lake, is also an ideal place for an early-morning jog or stroll.

🛏 Sleeping

Central Yangon is by far the liveliest part of the city and staying here will save you a small fortune in taxi fares. All prices include breakfast.

★ Mother Land Inn 2
BUDGET HOTEL $
(Map p486; 01-291 343; www.myanmarmotherlandinn.com; 433 Lower Pazundaung Rd, Pazundaung; s/d US$25/30, dm/s/d with shared bathroom US$10/24/28; ❄@🤶) It's often fully booked and is a long walk or a short taxi ride from the core of downtown, but the Motherland remains a backpacker favourite for its professional service, cleanliness, well-proportioned rooms, travel advice and services.

Three Seasons Hotel
GUESTHOUSE $
(Map p486; 01-297 946; phyuaung@mptmail.net.mm; 83-85 52nd St, Pazundaung; s/d/tr US$30/35/45; ❄@🤶) The nine rooms in this homey guesthouse are large, spotless and well endowed with everything that would make your granny smile. The outdoor terrace, with tree shade, is a nice place to sit and watch the world cruise by.

Ocean Pearl Inn
HOTEL $
(Map p486; 01-297 007; www.oceanpearlinn.com; 215 Botataung Pagoda Rd, Pazundaung; s/d/tr US$25/30/38; ❄🤶) Freshly painted rooms washed and polished by a team of cleaning addicts make the Ocean Pearl one of the tidiest choices in the budget range. Another perk is free airport pick-up.

Beautyland Hotel II
HOTEL $
(Map p486; 01-240 054; www.goldenlandpages.com/beauty; 188-192 33rd St, Kyauktada; s/d US$20/25, with air-con from US$28/38; ❄🤶) Exceedingly tidy rooms with friendly and confident service make this one of the better budget choices in central Yangon. The cheapest rooms don't have windows while the more expensive front-side rooms boast heaps of natural light.

May Fair Inn
GUESTHOUSE $
(Map p486; 01-253 454; maytinmg@gmail.com; 57 38th St, Kyauktada; s/d/tr US$15/24/30; ❄🤶) Family-run, and ever reliable, this old-fashioned place is best for the traveller looking for tranquillity rather than a party.

Hninn Si Budget Inn
GUESTHOUSE $
(Map p486; 01-299 941; www.hninnsibudgetinn.com; 213-215 Botataung Pagoda St, Pazundaung; s/d with shared bathroom US$23/30; ❄🤶) Sparkling-clean new backpacker guesthouse with 15 mostly windowless rooms with sparse decoration.

🍴 Eating

Yangon has Myanmar's best range of restaurants. Central Yangon is packed with streetside stalls selling a dizzying array of cheap snacks, and many inexpensive Burmese, Shan, Chinese and Indian restaurants. Smarter places are found in the more affluent, expat-occupied north. While most restaurants are open from about 7am until 9pm daily, it can be hard to find a meal anywhere after 9pm.

Yangon's numerous teashops are not just places to have cups of milk tea and coffee or tiny pots of Chinese tea. They're also places to hang out with locals, grab a snack or a better breakfast than that provided at your guesthouse.

Along Anawrahta Rd, west of Sule Paya Rd, there are many super-cheap Indian biryani shops (*keyettha dan bauk* in Burmese). All-you-can-eat *thali* meals or biryani cost from about K800.

DON'T MISS

PANSODAN GALLERY

There's a free drinks party every Tuesday night from 7pm at Pansodan Gallery (Map p486; 1st fl, 286 Pansodan St; 10am-6pm). It's an immensely friendly scene with gallery owner Aung Soe Min and his expat wife helping the crowd connect with local culture and art. The couple also runs Pansodan Scene (Map p486; www.pansodan.com; 144 Pansodan St, Kyauktada), a community art space with a cafe further down Pansodan St – it's possible the party will have moved here by the time you read this.

East Central Yangon

MYANMAR (BURMA)

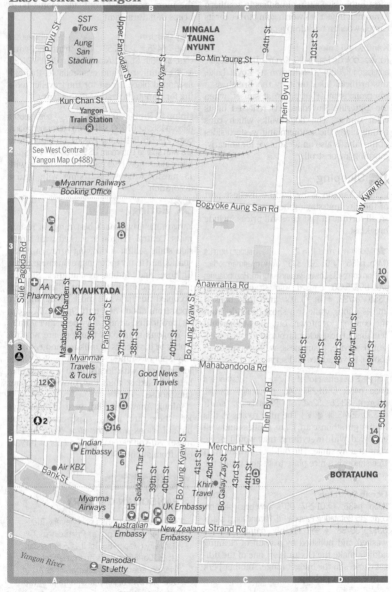

★**Aung Thukha**   BURMESE **$**
(Map p490; ☎ 01-525 194; 17A 1st St, Bahan; meals from K2000; ☻ 9am-9pm) This longstanding institution is a great place to sample Myanmar food – everything from rich, meaty curries to light, freshly made salads. The fla-vours are more subtle here than elsewhere, emphasising herbs rather than oil and spice. It's almost constantly busy, but manages to maintain gentle, friendly service and a pal-pable old-school atmosphere, making the experience akin to eating at someone's home.

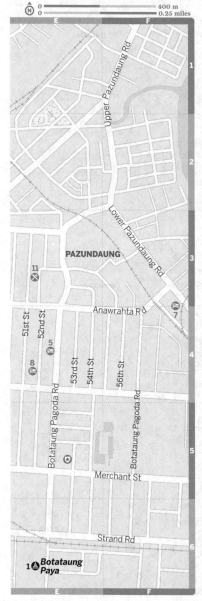

N
0 — 400 m
0 — 0.25 miles

E
F

Upper Pazundaung Rd

Lower Pazundaung Rd

PAZUNDAUNG

Anawrahta Rd

51st St
52nd St
53rd St
54th St
56th St

Botataung Pagoda Rd
Botataung Pagoda Rd

Merchant St

Strand Rd

1 Botataung Paya

MYANMAR (BURMA) YANGON

standing, as are most other Burmese-style noodle dishes.

Shwe We Htun   TEAHOUSE **$**
(Map p486; 81 37th St, Kyauktada; snacks from K300; ⊙6am-6pm, to noon Sun) A buzzing old-school teashop that serves better quality food than most. There's no English sign, but you'll know it by the crowds.

Nilar Biryani & Cold Drink   INDIAN **$**
(Map p488; 216 Anawrahta Rd, Pabedan; meals from K800; ⊙4am-10pm) Giant cauldrons full of spices, broths and rice bubble away at the front of this bright and brash Indian joint. It's never less than packed, and with good reason: the biryanis are probably among the best your lips will meet.

999 Shan Noodle Shop   SHAN **$**
(Map p486; 130/B 34th St, Kyauktada; noodle dishes from K500; ⊙6am-7pm) A handful of tables are crammed into this tiny, brightly coloured eatery behind City Hall. The menu

★**Lucky Seven**   TEAHOUSE **$**
(Map p486; 49th St, Pazundaung; snacks from K300; ⊙6am-5.30pm Mon-Sat, to noon Sun) Tidy, lively and with excellent food. The *mohinga* (soup of thin rice noodles and fish broth) is out-

West Central Yangon

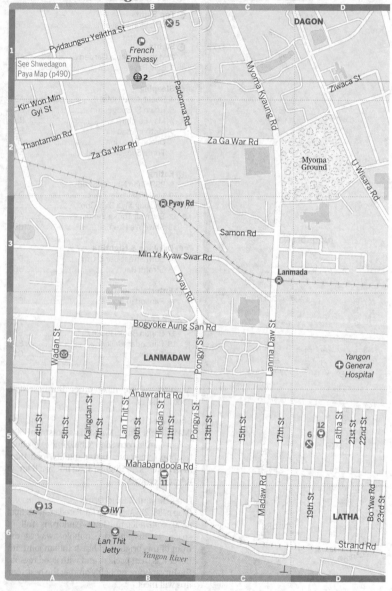

includes noodles such as *Shàn k'auq swèh* (thin rice noodles in a slightly spicy chicken broth) and *myi shay* (Mandalay-style noodle soup) and tasty non-noodle dishes such as Shan tofu (actually made from chickpea flour) and the delicious Shan yellow rice with tomato.

New Delhi
INDIAN $

(Map p488; 274 Anawrahta Rd, Pabedan; mains from K500; ⊙5.30am-9.30pm) This grubby

West Central Yangon

Thone Pan Hla   TEAHOUSE **$**
(Map p488; 454 Mahabandoola Rd, Pabedan; snacks K400-600; ⊙6am-7.30pm) Centrally located and has an English-language menu.

★**Feel Myanmar Food**   BURMESE **$$**
(Map p488; ☎01-511 6872; www.feelrestaurant.com; 124 Pyidaungsu Yeiktha St, Dagon; meals from K3000; ⊙6am-8.30pm) This long-running operation is a superb place to get your fingers dirty experimenting with the huge range of tasty Burmese dishes, which are laid out in little trays that you can just point to. It's very popular at lunchtime with local businesspeople and foreign embassy staff.

Danuphyu Daw Saw Yee
Myanma Restaurant   BURMESE **$$**
(Map p488; 175-177 29th St, Pabedan; meals from K2000; ⊙9am-9pm) Ask locals where to eat Burmese food in central Yangon and they'll most likely point you in the direction of this longstanding shophouse restaurant. All dishes are served with sides of soup du jour (the sour vegetable soup is particularly good) and *ngapi ye,* a pungent dip served with par-boiled vegies and fresh herbs.

Aung Mingalar Shan Noodle
Restaurant   SHAN **$$**
(Map p488; Bo Yar Nyunt St, Dagon; mains from K1500; ⊙7am-9pm) Aung Mingalar is an

place serves tasty Muslim-influenced South Indian dishes such as a rich mutton curry, as well as meat-free options including *puris* (puffy breads), *idli* (rice balls), various *dosai* (savoury pancakes) and banana-leaf *thalis* (meals; K1000).

Shwedagon Paya

See West Central
Yangon Map (p488)

excellent place to indulge simultaneously in people-watching and noodle-sipping. It's a simple and fun restaurant with trendy city-cafe overtones.

🍷 Drinking & Nightlife

Places that fit the Western concept of a bar or a club are becoming slightly more common. However, most places close by 10pm and locals prefer hanging out in a teahouse or air-conditioned cafe as much as one of the ubiquitous beer stations and beer gardens – the last two being favourite places to catch satellite TV broadcasts of soccer matches.

Myanmore (www.myanmore.com) publish a weekly free pamphlet guide to Yangon's nightlife scene, available in several bars, cafes and restaurants around town.

★ Bar Boon   CAFE-BAR
(Map p488; FMI Centre, 380 Bogyoke Aung San Rd, Pabedan; ⊙ 8.30am-9pm; 🛜) Recharge and

relax at this contemporary-styled cafe serving excellent coffee, iced tea and Dutch beer along with tasty snacks and pastries. The outdoor terrace offers brilliant people-watching near Bogyoke Aung San Market.

Kosan   BAR
(Map p488; 108 19th St, Latha; ⊙ 6pm-2am; 🛜) A reasonably decent mojito for K800? No wonder this Japanese-owned bar with seats spilling onto buzzing 19th St is popular with partying locals and expats. The next-door grilled-food joint Kaung Myat is where Anthony Bourdain ate when he was in town.

50th Street Bar & Grill   BAR
(Map p486; ☎ 01-397 060; www.50thstreetyangon; 9-13 50th St, Botataung; ⊙ 11am-midnight; 🛜) One of Yangon's longest established Western-style bars, in a handsomely restored colonial building, continues to draw in the crowds with its mix of event nights (US$6 pizzas and jazz on Wednesday, salsa every second

Shwedagon Paya

◉ Top Sights
1 Chaukhtatgyi Paya E2
2 Ngahtatgyi Paya...................................E2
3 Shwedagon Paya C3

◉ Sights
4 Kandawgyi Lake E4

✖ Eating
5 Aung Thukha C2
6 Myaung Mya Daw Cho D3

Tuesday, live music on Friday), free pool table and all-day happy hour on Sunday.

Coffee Club CAFE

(Map p488; http://coffeeclub.com.mm; cnr 11th St & Mahabandoola Rd, Latha; ⊙9am-7pm; 🛜) Above a mobile-phone shop is this hip cafe hang-out where you can get a soy latte or extra-strong espresso fix with a side order of gourmet sandwich, pie or cake (courtesy of Yangon Bakehouse). Slip back in time by leafing through the stock of vintage news magazines.

Zero Zone Rock Restaurant BAR

(Map p488; 4th fl, 2 Theingyi Zei Market, Latha) This rooftop bar is more fun than the unintentionally self-deprecating name suggests. Live music starts at 7pm, there's a 'fashion show' of parading girls, the draught beer is cheap and the cool breezes are free.

Wadan Jetty Beer Station BAR

(Map p488; Wadan Jetty, Lanmadaw; ⊙6am-9pm) Entering the docks from the main road, turn right at the waterfront to find this small beer station with a cluster of outdoor seating. It's a great spot for sunset drinks when you can also watch (or join in) with locals playing football or the Burmese sport of *chinlon*.

Strand Bar BAR

(Map p486; Strand Hotel, 92 Strand Rd, Kyauktada; ⊙to 11pm; 🛜) Primarily an expat scene, this classic bar inside the Strand Hotel has any foreign liquors you may be craving behind its polished wooden bar. It gets packed on Friday nights (5pm to 11pm), as all drinks are half-price.

🛍 Shopping

★ Bogyoke Aung San Market MARKET

(Map p488; Bogyoke Aung San Rd, Dagon; ⊙10am-5pm Tue-Sun) Half a day could easily be spent wandering around this sprawling covered market, sometimes called by its old British name, Scott Market. It has more than 2000 shops and the largest selection of Myanmar handicrafts and souvenirs you'll find under several roofs, from lacquerware and Shan shoulder bags to puppets and jewellery.

Theingyi Zei MARKET

(Map p488; Shwedagon Pagoda Rd, Pabedan) Most of the merchandise at downtown Yangon's largest market is ordinary housewares and textiles, but it's also renowned for its large selection of traditional herbs and medicines, which can be found on the ground floor of the easternmost building.

★ Pomelo HANDICRAFTS

(Map p486; www.pomeloyangon.com; 89 Thein Pyu Rd, Botataung; ⊙10am-9pm) The best selection of contemporary handicrafts in Yangon, and all produced by projects supporting

YANGON'S STREET EATS

Yangon's street-food options can be both overwhelming and challenging (pork offal on a skewer, anyone?). Some of our favourites and the best places to eat them:

Samusa thoke During the day a line of **vendors** (Map p486; Mahabandoola Garden St, Kyauktada; samosas K500) near Mahabandoola Garden sell this 'salad' of sliced samosas served with a thin lentil gravy.

Bein moun & moun pyar thalet These delicious 'Burmese pancakes' (K200), served sweet *(bein moun)* or savoury *(moun pyar thalet)*, can be found at most Yangon corners day and night.

Dosai At night along Anawratha St, several street-side vendors sell this thin southern Indian crepe (from K500), known in Burmese as *to-shay*.

Mohinga This breakfast soup of thin rice noodles and fish broth is just about everywhere but our favourite is from **Myaung Mya Daw Cho** (Map p486; 149 51st St, Pazuntaung; noodles from K500; ☺4.30-9am). There's no English sign here; look for the green sign near some trees. There is a more formal branch near **Shwedagon Paya** (Map p490; ☑01-559 663; 118A Yay Tar Shay Old St, Bahan; noodles K500; ☺5-11am).

Grilled food Every night, the strip of 19th St between Mahabandoola and Anawrahta Rds hosts dozens of stalls and open-air restaurants serving **grilled snacks** (Map p488; 19th St, Latha; meals from K5000; ☺5-11pm) and draught beer.

disadvantaged groups in Myanmar. Fall in love with the colourful papier mâché dogs and bags featuring bold graphic images, as well as the exquisite Chin weavings and jewellery made from recycled materials.

Bagan Book House BOOKS
(Map p486; ☑01-377 227; 100 37th St, Kyauktada; ☺9am-6.30pm) This Yangon institution has the most complete selection of English-language books on Myanmar and Southeast Asia, and owner U Htay Aung really knows his stock, which includes tomes dating back to the 19th century.

ℹ Information

EMERGENCY
Your embassy (p541) may also be able to assist in an emergency.
Ambulance (☑192)
Fire (☑191)
Police (Map p486; ☑199)
Red Cross (☑01-383 680)

INTERNET ACCESS
Nearly all hotels and many restaurants, cafes and bars offer free wi-fi access; there's even free wi-fi at Shwedagon Paya! There are also plenty of internet shops around town. Server speeds have improved, but still tend to be frustratingly slow in comparison to almost any other country.

MEDICAL SERVICES
AA Pharmacy (Map p486; 142-146 Sule Paya Rd, Kyauktada; ☺9am-10pm) Just north of Sule Paya.
International SOS Clinic (☑01-667 871; www.internationalsos.com; Inya Lake Hotel, 37 Kaba Aye Pagoda Rd, Mayangone) Your best bet in Yangon for emergencies, this clinic claims to be able to work with just about any international health insurance and has a 24-hour emergency centre with an expat doctor.

MONEY
You'll get the best rates for changing money at the airport and at official bank exchange counters in places such as Bogyoke Aung San Market and Shwedagon Paya.

There are also many ATMs dotted around Yangon that accept international Visa and Mastercards; there's a K5000 charge for using these ATMs.

POST
Central Post Office (Map p486; cnr Strand Rd & Bo Aung Kyaw St, Kyauktada; ☺7.30am-6pm Mon-Fri)
DHL (Map p488; ☑01-215 516; www.dhl.com; 58 Wadan St, Lanmadaw; ☺8am-6pm Mon-Fri, 8am-2pm Sat)

TOURIST INFORMATION
Myanmar Travels & Tours (MTT; Map p486; ☑01-374 281; www.myanmartravelsandtours.com; 118 Mahabandoola Garden St; ☺8.30am-5pm) The people at this government-run information centre are quite friendly and helpful, although their resources are very limited. This is

the place to go to arrange the necessary paperwork and guides for areas of the country that still require travel permits. It can also arrange local sightseeing tours to a variety of locations.

TRAVEL AGENCIES

Yangon's privately run travel agencies are the best place in the country for hiring a car or guide, booking an air ticket and checking on the latest travel restrictions.

Good News Travels (Map p486; ☑ 09 511 6256, 01-375 050; www.myanmargoodnewstravel.com; Room 1101, 11th floor, Olympic Tower, cnr Bo Aung Kyaw St & Mahabandoola Rd, Kyauktada) The owner, William Myatwunna, is extremely personable and knowledgeable, and can help arrange visits to remote parts of Myanmar. Also has an office in Bagan.

Khiri Travel (Map p486; ☑ 09 7313 4924, 01-375 577; http://khiri.com; 1st floor, 5/9 Bo Galay Zay St, Botataung) Biking and kayak trips, walking tours of markets and meetings with fortune tellers are some of its offerings.

Oway (Map p490; ☑ 01-230 4201; www.oway. com.mm; 2nd floor, Bldg 6 Junction Square, Pyay Rd, Kamayut) Offers online bookings for a wide range of hotels and all domestic flights. It also arranges visas online which can be picked up at international airports.

SST Tours (Map p486; ☑ 01-255 536; www. sstmyanmar.com; Rm S-6, 2nd floor, Aung San Stadium, Mingalar Taung Nyunt) A specialist for ecotours. The managers have excellent contacts in the country's national parks and reserves and can arrange trips that will delight nature lovers.

❶ Getting There & Away

AIR

Yangon International Airport (Map p484; ☑ 01-533 031; www.ygnia.com; Mingalardon; ☑) is Myanmar's main international gateway as well as the hub for domestic flights.

BOAT

Pansodan Street Jetty (Map p486) is the jumping-off base for daytime river-crossing boats to Dalah (return K4000, 10 minutes), which leave roughly every 20 minutes between 5.30am and 9pm.

Lan Thit Jetty (Map p488) is where **IWT** (Inland Water Transport; ☑ 01-380 764, 01-381 912;

TRANSPORT TO/FROM YANGON

DESTINATION	BUS	TRAIN	AIR/FERRY
Bago	2½hr; K1500	3hr; US$2-4	N/A
Chaung Tha Beach	7hr; K10,000	N/A	N/A
Dawei	16hr; K13,000	N/A	flight 70min; US$126
Heho (for Inle Lake & Kalaw)	N/A	N/A	flight 1-3hr; US$102-112
Hpa-an	7-8hr; K5000-8600	N/A	N/A
Hsipaw	15hr; K14,500-16,500	N/A	N/A
Kalaw	10-12hr; K10,000-16,500	N/A	N/A
Kyaikto	5hr; K8000	4-5hr; US$3-10	N/A
Mandalay	9hr; K10,500	15 ½hr; US$11-33	flight 1hr; US$75-135
Mawlamyine	7hr; K5000-10,000	9-11hr; US$5-14	N/A
Myitkyina	N/A	N/A	flight 2hr; US$180
Ngwe Saung Beach	6-7hr; K9000	N/A	N/A
Nyaung U (for Bagan)	10hr; K13,000-18,000	16hr; US$20-40	flight 70min; US$100-110
Pathein	4hr; K3600	N/A	ferry 17hr; US$8 deck, US$40 cabin
Pyay	6hr; K5500	7-8hr; US$5-13	N/A
Sittwe	N/A	N/A	flight 1hr 15min; US$120-146
Taunggyi (for Inle Lake)	12hr; K15,000	N/A	N/A
Taungoo	6hr; K4300-5000	7hr; US$5-13	N/A
Thandwe (for Ngapali)	14hr; K14,000	N/A	flight 55min; US$100-120

MYANMAR (BURMA) YANGON

runs ferries to Pathein Monday and Friday at 5pm (deck class/private cabin US$8/40, 17 hours). Foreigners must buy tickets from the deputy division manager's office next to Building 63 on Lan Thit Jetty.

BUS

Guesthouses can assist with purchasing tickets for a small additional fee. Several larger companies have convenient bus-ticket offices opposite Yangon train station.

Aung Mingalar Bus Station This is the only official bus terminal for all 150 bus lines leaving for the northern part of Myanmar, as well as for Kyaiktiyo (Golden Rock), Mawlamyine and destinations to the south. A taxi here costs K7000 and takes 45 minutes to an hour driving north of downtown Yangon.

Hlaing Thar Yar Bus Station This terminal is for travel to the delta region (officially called Ayeyarwady Region) and to destinations west of Yangon. It's 45 minutes to an hour away by taxi (K7000) west of the city centre.

TRAIN

Yangon's train station (☎ 01-202 178; ☉ 6am-4pm) is located a short walk north of Sule Paya, although advance tickets must be purchased at the adjacent **Myanmar Railways Booking Office** (Map p486; Bogyoke Aung San Rd; ☉ 7am-3pm).

Major destinations that can be reached by daily departures from Yangon include Bagan, Bago, Kyaikto, Mandalay, Mawlamyine, Nay Pyi Taw, Pyay, Taungoo and Thazi. There's a chance that in 2014 a new service to Pathein will commence.

❶ Getting Around

TO/FROM THE AIRPORT

Taxi drivers will approach you before you exit the airport terminal. The fare for a ride from the air-port to downtown Yangon is around K8000 and will take an hour (more if traffic is heavy). **JTB Polestar** (☎ 01-382 528; www.jtb-pst.com) offers coach transfers to major hotels for US$10.

BUS

With taxis in Yangon being such a fantastic deal, you'd really have to be pinching pennies to rely on buses. They're impossibly crowded, the conductors rarely have change, the routes are confusing and there's virtually no English, spoken or written.

If you're determined, the typical fare within central Yangon is K100 (use small bills – bus conductors don't tend to have change). Prices often double at night, but they're still cheap and still crowded.

TAXI

Yangon taxis are one of the best deals in Asia, despite not using a meter. Most drivers speak at least some English (although it's advisable to have someone write out your destination in Burmese) and are almost universally honest and courteous.

All licensed taxis have a visible taxi sign on the roof, but many other drivers will give you ride for a negotiated fare. If you'd prefer to book a taxi, a service we've had recommendations for is **Golden Harp** (☎ 09 4500 19186, 09 4281 17348), run by ex political prisoners.

The following should give you an idea of what to pay: a short hop (say from the Strand to Bogyoke Market) will be K1000; double this distance will be K2000; from downtown to Shwedagon Paya and the southern half of Bahan township will be K3000 depending on the state of traffic.

You can also hire a taxi for about K5000 an hour. For the entire day, you should expect to pay US$60 to US$80, depending on the quality of the vehicle and your negotiating skills.

OFF THE BEATEN TRACK

DALAH & TWANTE

One of the easiest and most enjoyable short trips out of Yangon is to board a double-decker ferry (return K4000, every 15 minutes) that shuttles between Pansodan St Jetty and **Dalah** (ဒလမြို့) across the Yangon River. As well as the breezy views provided on the 15-minute journey, there's a lively scene on board as hawkers jostle to sell everything from sunhats and *paan* (areca nut and/or tobacco wrapped in a betel leaf and chewed as a mild stimulant) to bags of speckled eggs. Tip: take the ferry around 5.30pm for a cheap sunset cruise back and forth across the river.

Dalah, which is one of Yangon's townships, is no great shakes; the main aim is to continue on to **Twante**, a pleasant town 30 to 45 minutes' drive west into the delta where you can visit **Shwesandaw Paya** (ရွှေဆံတော်ဘုရား; camera fee K200; ☉ 6am-9pm), an ancient temple, and the **Oh-Bo Pottery Sheds** (အိုးဘို အိုးလုပ်ငန်း). Chances are you'll be approached on the ferry by someone offering their services as a motorbike taxi; the going rate is around K10,000 return including stops at the various sights. Regular taxis charge around K30,000, while a squashed seat in a pick-up van to Twante is K1000.

Fares usually leap by 30% or so after sunset and on weekends. After 11pm or so, day rates tend to double as there are fewer taxis on the streets.

TRISHAW

In Myanmar, trishaw passengers ride with the driver, but back-to-back (one facing forward, one backward). These contraptions are called *saiq-ka* (as in side-car) and to ride one costs about K1000 for short journeys. Given the heaviness of downtown Yangon's traffic during the day, you may find trishaw pedallers reluctant to make a long journey across town at this time.

THE DELTA, WEST COAST BEACHES & NORTH OF YANGON

Unlike the teeming beaches in neighbouring Thailand, Myanmar's are virtually empty except on weekends. Ngapali Beach in the south of Rakhine State is the finest, but the long and/or expensive trip and lack of budget accommodation mean most shoestringers skip it; for details see Lonely Planet's *Myanmar (Burma)* guide. Instead, head from Yangon through the Ayeyarwady Delta to sleepy Pathein and on to Ngwe Saung or Chaung Tha beaches.

North of Yangon the main roads pass through a few interesting towns that are worth a look or stopover en route to Bagan, Mandalay and Inle Lake.

Pathein   ပုသိမ်

🖉 042 / POP 300,000

A good staging post on the way to Chaung Tha or Ngwe Saung beaches, Pathein, 112 miles west of Yangon, is Myanmar's fourth-largest city. Despite being the commercial and administrative heart of the Ayeyarwady Delta, Pathein has a languid, easy-going ambience. It's known primarily for its parasol industry and fragrant rice, and can be reached either by road or ferry from Yangon.

◉ Sights

Shwe Sar Umbrella Workshop   HANDICRAFTS

(🖉 042-25127; 653 Tawya Kyaung Rd; ⊘8am-5pm) Sun shades are made in workshops scattered across the northern part of the city, particularly around the Twenty-Eight Paya, off Mahabandoola Rd. It's fun to wander the area, sticking your head into a workshop here

and there to see how they're made. They're cheap, and the saffron-coloured ones, made for monks, are actually waterproof. This workshop is particularly welcoming.

Shwemokhtaw Paya   BUDDHIST STUPA

(ရွှေမုဋ္ဌောဘုရား; Shwezedi Rd; ⊘6am-8pm) **FREE** Looming with grace over Pathein is the golden bell of the Shwemokhtaw Paya.

The *hti* (decorated top of a stupa) consists of a topmost layer made from 14lb of solid gold, a middle tier of pure silver and a bottom tier of bronze; all three tiers are gilded and reportedly embedded with a total of 829 diamond fragments, 843 rubies and 1588 semiprecious stones.

Settayaw Paya   BUDDHIST TEMPLE

(စက်တော်ရာဘုရား) **FREE** This charming *paya*, spread across a green hilly setting, is dedicated to a mythical Buddha footprint left by the Enlightened One during his legendary perambulations through Southeast Asia. The footprint symbol itself is an oblong, 3ft-long impression.

🛏 Sleeping & Eating

Day to Day Motel   HOTEL $

(🖉 042-23368; Jail St; r from US$10; ❋ 🛜) This new guesthouse has high-standard rooms in a quieter part of town, opposite the Sikh Temple dating from 1938. A big roof terrace provides a pleasant place to sit and take in the surrounding leafy view.

Taan Taan Ta Guest House   HOTEL $

(🖉 042-22290; 7 Merchant St; s/d from US$10/15; ❋) This popular budget guesthouse is often full, even though it's very much no-frills. If you're not on a shoestring, check out the more expensive double rooms on the top floor, which feature air-conditioning, TV and fridge.

★ Shwe Ayar   BURMESE MUSLIM $

(32-35 Mingalar Rd; mains K1500) It doesn't look like much but this place offers high-quality biryani which you can supplement with chicken or mutton. The lentil and bean soup is so delicious you'll want a second helping. Find it opposite Zaw Optical.

ℹ Getting There & Away

BOAT

To Yangon (deck/cabin US$8/40), boats leave Wednesday and Sunday at 2pm, arriving in Yangon the next day at 11am. Tickets must be bought with dollars only at the **Inland Water Transport Office** (Mahabandoola Rd;

MYANMAR (BURMA) PATHEIN

WORTH A TRIP

CHAUNG THA BEACH & NGWE SAUNG BEACH

If you're in search of a sea breeze and soft sand while visiting Myanmar, either **Chaung Tha Beach** (ချောင်းသာကမ်းခြေ) or **Ngwe Saung Beach** (ငွေဆောင်ကမ်းခြေ) do the trick.

A motorbike taxi trip between the two resort areas (K18,000 oneway or return) is highly recommended. The route involves three river crossings on small wooden boats and passes deserted beaches and rustic villages amid palm groves.

Of the two resorts, Ngwe Saung, 28 miles west of Pathein, is the nicer with miles of white-sand beach, but it has limited budget accommodation; try **Shwe Hin Tha Hotel** (☑ 042-40340; bungalows US$25-50; ✴) or **Silver Coast Beach Hotel** (☑ 042-40324; htoo.maw@mptmail.net.mm; r US$25-60; ✴). For eats and drinks, **Royal Flower** (Myoma St; mains K4000; ☺ 6-10pm) distinguishes itself from the same-same crowd of restaurants with nightly concerts by a mellow guitar-playing duo.

Chaung Tha, 25 miles west of Pathein, offers as much of a beach-party vibe as you're going to get in Myanmar and is popular with locals. The best places to crash here are **Hill Garden Hotel** (☑ 09 4957 6072; www.hillgardenhotel.com; r US$25; ☎), a 20-minute walk north of the main resort area, or the centrally located **Shwe Ya Min Guesthouse & Restaurant** (☑ 042-42127; Main Rd; s/d US$15/20; ✴☎) which is also the best spot for a meal.

Connect between Chaung Tha and Pathein by minibus (K4000, 2½ hours, 7am, 9am, 11am and 1pm) or motorbike taxi (K12,000, two hours). The 9.30am departure by Asia Dragon to Yangon is the most comfortable bus service and terminates conveniently at Aung San Stadium.

From Ngwe Saung there are also minibuses to Pathein (K3000, two hours, five daily) and buses to Yangon (K9000, six hours, 6.30am and 8am).

☺10am-noon), located in a wooden colonial-era building near the jetty.

BUS

If you're bound for Yangon (four hours), head to the informal **bus company offices** (Shwezedi Rd) located directly east of Shwe Zin Yaw restaurant. The cheapest air-con service is offered six times a day by **Ayer Shwe Zin** (☑ 09 4974 5191) for K3600; other operators charge K6000.

Insanely uncomfortable minibuses ply the route from Pathein to Chaung Tha Beach (K3000, 2½ hours, 36 miles) every two hours between 8am and 4pm, departing from an informal **bus station** (Yadayagone St) a couple of blocks northeast of the clock tower.

To Ngwe Saung Beach (K4000, two hours, 29 miles), buses leave from yet another **bus station** (Strand Rd) at 9am, 11am and 3pm.

Bago   ပဲခူး

☑ 052 / POP 200,000

Founded in AD 573 by the Mon, this one-time capital probably contains a greater density of blissed-out buddhas and treasure-filled temples than any other similar-sized town in southern Myanmar. All this makes Bago a superb and simple day trip from Yan-

gon, or the ideal first stop when you leave the city behind.

☉ Sights & Activities

Many of Bago's monuments are actually centuries old, but don't look it, due to extensive restorations. This is an excellent place to explore by bicycle, as most attractions are near each other. Bikes are available for rent at **Bago Star Hotel** (☑ 052-30066; http://bago starhotel.googlepages.com; 11-21 Kyaikpon Pagoda Rd; s/d US$35/40; ✴☎); it also has a basic map of the town you can follow.

To gain access to Bago's main sites, including Shwemawdaw Paya, foreigners must buy the **Bago Archaeological Zone ticket** (US$10/K10,000). Nearly all of the sights charge an additional K300 for cameras and K500 for videocameras.

Shwethalyaung Buddha   BUDDHIST TEMPLE
(ရွှေသာလျောင်းဘုရား;   ☺5am-8pm)   **FREE**
Legend has it that this gorgeous reclining Buddha was built by the Mon king Mgadeikpa in the 10th century. Measuring 180ft long and 53ft high, the monument's little finger alone extends 10ft.

Following the destruction of Bago in 1757, the huge Buddha was overgrown by jungle and not rediscovered until 1881 when a contractor unearthed it while building the Yangon–Bago railway line.

Shwemawdaw Paya
BUDDHIST STUPA

(ရွှေမော်တောဘုရား; Shwemawdaw Paya Rd; ⊙5am-8pm) A pyramid of washed-out gold in the midday haze and glittering perfection in the evening, the 376ft-high Shwemawdaw Paya stands tall and proud over the town. The stupa reaches 46ft higher than the Shwedagon in Yangon.

At the northeastern corner of the stupa is a huge section of the *hti* toppled by an earthquake in 1917. The Shwemawdaw Paya is a particularly good destination during Bago's annual pagoda festival, in March/April.

Hintha Gon Paya
BUDDHIST STUPA

(ဟင်္သာ်ကုန်း) This shrine was once the one point in this whole vast area that rose above sea level and so was the natural place for the *hamsa* to land. Images of this mythical bird decorate the stupa built by U Khanti, the hermit monk who was the architect of Mandalay Hill.

Kyaik Pun Paya
MONUMENT

(ကျိုက်ပွန်ဘုရား) Built in 1476 by King Dhammazedi, the Kyaik Pun Paya consists of four 100ft-high sitting buddhas (Guatama Buddha and his three predecessors) placed back to back around a huge, square pillar, about a mile south of Bago just off the Yangon road.

🛏 Sleeping & Eating

Bago has some good-value rooms, but few travellers spend the night. Main Rd is deafeningly noisy – ask for a room at the back.

Emperor Motel
HOTEL **$**

(☑052-21349; 8 Main Rd; r US$5-10; 🕸🛜) The pick of the downtown budget selection – which is not saying much. Musty rooms are painted pink; the more expensive ones have a bit of light and space. The rooftop offers great views of the surroundings.

San Francisco Guest House
HOTEL **$**

(☑052-22265; 14 Main Rd; s/d US$10/15; 🕸) The rooms are rough and ready and there's a curfew from 10pm to 5am. The guys who run it offers motorbike tours (K8000) of Bago's sights.

Hanthawaddy
CHINESE, BURMESE **$$**

(192 Hintha St; mains K2000-8000; ⊙8am-11pm) The food here isn't amazing, but it's the only restaurant in central Bago with a bit of atmosphere. The open-air upper level is breezy and offers great views of Shwemawdaw Paya.

Hadaya Café
TEAHOUSE **$**

(14 Main Rd; ⊙2am-midnight) This popular, central teahouse, keeping very long hours, has a good selection of pastries and good-quality tea and coffee.

ℹ Getting There & Away

BUSES

Buses to Yangon depart approximately every 30 minutes from 6.30am to 5.30pm.

Going south, buses to Kinpun, the starting point for Mt Kyaiktiyo (Golden Rock), leave every hour or so during the day. During the rainy season (May to October), buses go only as far as Kyaikto, 10 miles from Kinpun.

Heading north, for Mandalay, Taungoo and Inle Lake, apart from a handful of direct services from Bago, it's also possible to hop on services coming from Yangon – book ahead with a local agent, such as **Sea Sar** (☑09 530 0987; seasar. tickets918@gmail.com), or ask your hotel to help.

TAXI

Some travellers make a day trip out of Bago with a hired car from Yangon. It costs around US$80, but it does give you the advantage of having transport between sites once you get to Bago and saves traipsing all the way out to the bus station in Yangon. One-way taxis back from Bago straight to your hotel in Yangon cost about K40,000.

A guide and driver to Mt Kyaiktiyo can be hired for around US$55 return. For any of these

TRANSPORT FROM BAGO

DESTINATION	BUS	TRAIN
Kyaikto	1½hr; K3500	3hr; US$2-4
Mandalay	9hr; K14,000	14hr; US$10-27
Mawlamyine	6hr; K7000	7hr; US$4-8
Taungoo	6hr; K6000	5hr; US$3-6
Yangon	2hr; K2000	2hr; US$2-4

options, you can inquire at the town's **taxi stand** (Yangon-Mandalay Rd) or through any of the central Bago hotels.

TRAIN

Bago is connected by train with Yangon and Mawlamyine and stops north towards Mandalay.

ℹ Getting Around

Trishaw is the main form of local transport. A one-way trip in the central area should cost no more than K500. Hiring a trishaw or motorcycle for the day should cost about K7000.

Taungoo   တောင်ငူ

📞 054 / POP 120,000

It's hard to imagine Taungoo, lying just under halfway from Yangon to Mandalay, was once the nerve centre of a powerful kingdom. Today it's a sleepy place that most people see from a bus or train window. However, it gets the 'real-deal experience' thumbs up from those who do stop, and is home to one of Myanmar's more memorable guesthouses.

On the town's west side, **Shwesandaw Paya** (built 1597) is the main pilgrimage site. Nearby, pretty **Kandawgyi Lake** is pleasant to stroll or cycle around.

At the south end of town **Myanmar Beauty Guest House II, III & IV** (📞 054-23270; four doctors@mptmail.net.mm; Pauk Hla Gyi St; s US$15-40, d US$20-50, tr US$40-60; 🌬) consists of three teak houses with four-poster beds, hot showers and wide-open views of the rice paddies and hills that loom beyond. Rates include a gut-busting local breakfast.

Heading north or south on air-con buses, you'll pay the full Mandalay–Yangon fare. Most stop near the hospital in the town centre. Local buses to Yangon (K4300 to K5000, six hours) leave at 7am and 7pm. Mandalay buses (K7500 to K9000, nine hours) pass about 6.30pm.

Trains between Yangon (ordinary/upper US$5/13, seven hours) and Mandalay (US$7/17, nine hours) stop here too.

Pyay   ပြည်

📞 053 / POP 95,000

With a breezy location on the Ayeyarwady, Pyay is the most interesting stop on the Yangon–Bagan Hwy. Soak up its lively atmosphere along the riverfront and the roundabout, at the centre of which is a gilded equestrian statue of Aung San.

◉ Sights

The city's glory days date back to the ancient Pyu capital of **Thayekhittaya** (သရေခေတ္တရာ; admission US$5, incl museum US$10; ⊙ 8am-5pm), the partially excavated remains of which lay 5 miles east of Pyay's main attraction: the dazzling **Shwesandaw Paya**. Perched atop a central hill, this temple is 3ft taller than Yangon's Shwedagon Paya and apparently dates from 589 BC. Facing the *paya* from the east is **Sehtatgyi Paya** (Big Ten Storey), a giant seated Buddha.

Follow Strand Rd north during the morning to catch all the action at the lively and colourful **central market**, which spreads over several blocks.

About 8½ miles south of Pyay, **Shwemyetman Paya** is home to a large, white-faced, seated Buddha – sporting a pair of giant gold-plated glasses! Hop on a local Yangon-bound bus or southbound pick-up, and get off in Shwedaung town.

🛏 Sleeping & Eating

The **night market** on Mya Zay Tann St between the Aung San statue and the river is well worth browsing for cheap eats.

Myat Lodging House   HOTEL $
(📞 053-25695; 222 Bazaar St; r with fan US$5-15, with air-con US$20-25; 🌬) This small backstreet guesthouse has simple rooms a block from the Pyay 'action'. The US$5 rooms are a cell with a fan and shared bathroom. Higher-priced rooms come with a private bathroom and are set at the back of the maze of buildings. Friendly English-speaking staff give out maps of Pyay and Thayekhittaya.

Smile Motel   HOTEL $
(📞 053-22523; 10-11 Bogyoke Rd; r US$24-35; 🌬) Shabby and reminiscent of *The Shining,* but it's all pretty clean and the staff are nice, if a bit surprised at your existence. The US$35 rooms are essentially triples if three's not a crowd.

ℹ Getting There & Away

The **IWT office** (📞 053-24503; Strand Rd; ⊙ 9am-5pm Mon-Fri) is helpful on ever-changing times for slow-going government ferries. At research time, a cargo ferry left around 3am in the middle of Tuesday night for Yangon (deck/cabin US$12/24, about three days).

The highway bus station, 1 mile east of the town centre, sends frequent buses to Yangon (K4500, seven hours). No direct buses go to Bagan; either jump on a Yangon–Bagan bus (for full fare) or take the 8.30am bus to Magwe (K4100, six hours), from where there are departures the next morning for Bagan.

A daily train leaves Pyay's central train station at 11.30pm for Yangon (sleeper/upper/1st/ordinary class US$14/13/10/5, nine hours). From Shwethekar station, 3 miles east of the city, you can also board the Bagan–Yangon train as it makes a three-minute pause at 10pm (sleeper/upper/1st class US$28/26/23); Yangon departures are at 2.30am.

SOUTHEASTERN MYANMAR

Teetering on a cliff edge, the Golden Rock of Kyaiktiyo draws a few visitors off the main trail for a tough but rewarding pilgrimage. Further south, Mawlamyine offers glimpses of old Burma while way-off-the-beaten-track Hpa-an is the way-welcoming capital of Kayin (Karen) State.

Mt Kyaiktiyo (Golden Rock)
ကျိုက်ထီးရိုးတောင်

🎵 057

The gravity-defying golden rock Kyaiktiyo (Golden Rock; US$6, ticket valid for 30 days) is one of Myanmar's most enigmatic and intriguing sights. Perched on the very edge of a cliff on Mt Kyaiktiyo, this giant, gold-leaf-covered boulder is topped by a stupa containing a Buddha hair donated by a hermit in the 11th century. Apparently, the hair was salvaged from the bottom of the sea and brought here by boat. The boat subsequently turned to stone and is visible a few hundred metres away.

Kyaiktiyo has a mystical aura; it's a place of miracles, not least of which is how the boulder has managed to hang on, withstanding several earthquakes, for all these years. Pilgrims come in their thousands and the experience is more interesting because of them. That said, on weekends especially the mountaintop can feel like a theme park.

Since the rock is especially beautiful illuminated in the evening, plan on spending a night in the 'base camp' of Kinpun, a collection of restaurants and guesthouses 7 miles from the summit of Mt Kyaiktiyo. Kyaikto, where trains and long-distance buses stop, has several guesthouses, none of them very appealing, and there really is no reason to stay here rather than in Kinpun.

🏃 Activities

There are two ways to the rock: hiking 7 miles uphill from Kinpun (four to six hours one way), or trucking (K2500 to K3000, 45 minutes, 6am to 6pm). Walking down to Kinpun takes three to four hours and should not be attempted in the dark, even with a torch; it's too easy to stumble.

There is a K6000 government entrance fee, payable at the checkpoint near the top, just after the Mountain Top Hotel. Men shouldn't wear shorts at the shrine and women should wear long skirts only – no trousers, miniskirts or skimpy tops.

🛏 Sleeping & Eating

There is a veritable food court of restaurants at the summit.

Bawga Theiddhi Hotel HOTEL $
(no roman-script sign; 🖊 094 92 99899; r incl breakfast US$20-80; ❋ 🛜) Kinpun's newest – and flashiest – hotel has rooms that are clean, spacious and equipped with TV, fridge and free wi-fi, making them good value.

Sea Sar Hotel HOTEL $
(🖊 09 872 3288; r incl breakfast US$10-35; ❋ ❋ 🛜) The rooms of this operation in the heart of Kinpun cover a lot of ground, some good, some not so good. The best are the various air-con bungalows out back, some of which are relatively new and attractive.

★ Golden Sunrise Hotel HOTEL $$
(🖊 09 872 3301, in Yangon 01-701 027; www.golden sunrisehotel.com; s/d incl breakfast US$45/58; ❋)

TRANSPORT TO/FROM KYAIKTO

DESTINATION	BUS	TRAIN
Bago	K5000; 3hr; frequent 8am-4pm	N/A
Hpa-an	K5000; 3hr; frequent 11am-4pm	N/A
Mawlamyine	K7000; 4hr; frequent 11am-4pm	US$3-6; 4hr; daily noon & 11.30pm
Yangon	K5000; 5hr; frequent 8am-4pm	US$3-8; 5hr; daily noon & midnight

A few minutes' walk outside Kinpun village in the direction of the highway, the low-slung, semi-detached rooms here are undisturbed by noise, decked out with attractive wood furniture, immaculately clean, and have private verandas overlooking the secluded gardens.

Mountain Top Hotel
HOTEL $$

(☑ 09 871 8392, in Yangon 01-502 479; grtt@goldenrock.com.mm; r incl breakfast US$100-120; ❄ ☎) Grossly overpriced rooms, but they're clean and well maintained, with good service. They're also situated right on the summit of the mountain only a couple of moments' stroll to the shrine complex – an unbeatable position. The more expensive 'deluxe' rooms have air-con, a TV, a minibar and great views.

🛈 Getting There & Away

The major transport hub at Mt Kyaiktiyo is Kyaikto. This is where the train station is, and the town's main street is where you'll board (or disembark from) buses.

BUS & PICK-UPS

Tickets for relatively comfortable Win Express buses can be purchased in Kinpun across from Sea Sar Hotel. The ticket price includes truck fare to Kyaikto.

Frequent pick-ups cruise the road between Kyaikto's train station and Kinpun from 7am to 4pm (K500, 20 minutes).

TRAIN

In addition to regular daily trains between Yangon and Mawlamyine that stop at Kyaikto, every Saturday a service using air-conditioned carriages departs Yangon for Kyaikto at 6.25am (US$10, 4½ hours); it returns on Sunday at noon arriving in Yangon, in theory, at 4.25pm.

The air-conditioned carriages are eventually destined to be used on the Yangon Circle Line, once station platforms on that route have been upgraded.

Mawlamyine မော်လမြိုင်

☑ 057 / POP 300,000

With a ridge of stupa-capped hills on one side, the sea on the other, and a centre filled with mosques and crumbling colonial-era buildings, Mawlamyine is a unique combination of landscape, beauty and melancholy. Indeed, the setting inspired two of history's finest writers of the English language – George Orwell and Rudyard Kipling.

Formerly known as Moulmein, the city and its surrounds have enough attractions, ranging from beaches to caves, to keep a visitor happy for several days.

⊙ Sights

About 8½ miles south of Mawlamyine is **Pa-Auk-Taw-Ya Monastery** (ဖားအောက်တောရသုခန်းကြီးကျောင်း; ☑ 057-22853; www.paaukforestmonastery.org) FREE, one of the largest meditation centres in Myanmar. Foreigners can stay the night or several days; sleeping and eating is gratis.

★ Kyaikthanlan Paya
BUDDHIST TEMPLE

(ကျိုက်သံလန်ဘုရား; Kyaik Than Lan Phayar St; ⊙ daylight hours) FREE The 'Moulmein Pagoda' cited in the poem 'Mandalay' was most likely **Kyaikthanlan Paya**, the city's tallest and most visible stupa.

The best way to approach the temple complex, a favoured spot for watching the sunset, is via the long covered walkway that extends from Kyaik Than Lan Phayar St.

Mon Cultural Museum
MUSEUM

(မွန်ယဉ်ကျေးမှုပြတိုက်; cnr Baho & Dawei Jetty Rds; admission K2000; ⊙ 10am-4.30pm Tue-Sun) Recently renovated, and well worth a visit, Mawlamyine's museum is dedicated to the Mon history of the region. Most of the displayed items are accompanied by English-language descriptions.

Gaungse Kyun (Shampoo Island)
ISLAND

(ခေါင်းဆေးကျွန်း; ⊙ daylight hours) FREE This picturesque, peaceful isle just off Mawlamyine's northern end is so named because, during the Ava period, the yearly royal hair-washing ceremony customarily used water taken from a spring on the island.

You can hire a boat out here from the pier at the north end of town, not far from the former Mawlamyine Hotel, for around K2000 return.

🛏 Sleeping & Eating

Most of Mawlamyine's accommodation is a K2000 motorcycle-taxi ride from the train station, bus station or boat pier.

★ Cinderella Hotel
HOTEL $

(☑ 057-24411; www.cinderellahotel.com; 21 Baho Rd; r incl breakfast US$25-65; ❄ @ ☎) Where else could you afford to stay in the nicest place in town? This shockingly purple structure has numerous and capable staff who look after huge rooms with heaps of amenities: 24-hour

TRANSPORT TO/FROM MAWLAMYINE

DESTINATION	BUS	TRAIN
Bago	K5100-10,000; 5hr; daily 8am, 9am, 1pm, 2pm, 7pm, 9pm, 8.30pm & midnight	US$4-12; 7hr; daily 8am, 7.30pm & 9pm
Dawei	K8000-10,000; 10hr; 7pm	US$6-15; 16hr; daily 4.30am & 7.20am
Hpa-an	K1050; 2hr; hourly 6am-4pm	N/A
Kyaikto (for Mt Kyaiktiyo)	K5100-10,000; 4hr; daily 8am, 9am, 1pm, 2pm, 7pm, 9pm, 8.30pm & midnight	US$3-7; 4hr; daily 8am, 7.30pm & 9pm
Mandalay	K15,000; 13hr; daily 5pm & 6pm	N/A
Yangon	K5100-10,000; 7hr; daily 8am, 9am, 1pm, 2pm, 7pm, 9pm, 8.30pm & midnight	US$5-16; 10hr; daily 8am, 7.30pm & 9pm

electricity, TV, air-con, wi-fi and huge fridges positively stuffed with junk food.

Breeze Guest House HOTEL $
(☑ 057-21450; breeze.guesthouse@gmail.com; 6 Strand Rd; r incl breakfast US$7-25; ❋ 🛜) The rooms aren't much but the staff at this colonial-style villa on Strand Rd are an endless source of information, pleasant conversation and superb guiding skills.

★ **Daw Yee** BURMESE $
(no roman-script sign; off Strand Rd; meals from K2000; ⏲ 9am-10pm) This place serves some of the best Burmese food we've come across in the country. Highlights of our meal included an insanely fatty prawn curry and a deliciously tart soup of young tamarind leaves and tiny shrimp. The only downside is locating it; continue south along Strand Rd until you see Beer Garden 2 then start asking the locals for Daw Yee – everybody knows it.

Mi Cho Restaurant MUSLIM-BURMESE $
(no roman-script sign; North Bogyoke Rd; meals from K1500; ⏲ 10am-9pm) This busy hole-in-the-wall serves excellent Muslim-style Burmese cuisine, in particular a rich biryani and a delicious dhal soup. There's no English-language sign here; look for the green awning.

❶ Getting There & Away

AIR

At press time, **Myanma Airways** (☑ 09 871 8220, 21500; ⏲ 9am-3pm) was the only domestic airline flying out of Mawlamyine, while Thai airline **Nok Air** (☑ in Yangon 01-533 030, international call centre +662 900 9955; www.nokair.com) operates a route between Mawlamyine and Mae Sot, in Thailand.

BUS & TRAIN

There are bus and train services from Mawlamyine. Share taxis run to Myawaddy (K8000 to K10,000, four to six hours, frequent daily between 5am and 10am).

Bilu Kyun ဘီလူးကျွန်း

Fascinating Bilu Kyun (Ogre Island), east of Mawlamyine, is peppered with villages involved in the production of coconut-fibre mats and even coconut-inspired and created cutlery and teapots.

There's public transportation to Bilu Kyun, but the boats run a confusing schedule from a variety of piers. The local authorities also require notice to visit Bilu Kyun, so the best way to approach the island is via a day tour with Mr Antony or Mr Khaing at Breeze Guest House in Mawlamyine. They charge US$30 per person for the tour, which typically runs from 9am to 5pm, circling the island, stopping in at various craft workshops and even tacking on a swim stop. The fee covers transport and lunch.

Hpa-An ဘားအံ
☑ 058

Kayin State's scruffy riverside capital, isn't going to inspire many postcards home. But the city is the logical base from which to explore the Buddhist caves, sacred mountains and cloud-scraping islands of the surrounding countryside.

◉ Sights & Activities

Take a boat across the Thanlwin River from Hpa-an (K500, every half-hour from 7am to 5pm) to reach **Hpan Pu Mountain**, a craggy pagoda-topped peak that can be scaled in one sweaty morning.

Another demanding two-hour climb is up **Mt Zwegabin** (2372ft), 7 miles south of town,

MYANMAR (BURMA) BILU KYUN

for gods'-eye views, an 11am monkey-feeding session and a free monastery lunch at noon.

Around 17 miles southeast of Hpa-an, vast **Saddan Cave** (သဒ္ဒန်; ☉ daylight hours) **FREE**, aka the Gates of Hell, is full of Buddhist iconography and stalagmites, but can only be traversed during the dry season (November to April).

🛏 Sleeping & Eating

★ Soe Brothers Guesthouse
BACKPACKER HOTEL **$**

(☑ 058-21372, 09 497 71823; soebrothers 05821372@gmail.com; 2/146 Thitsar St; r US$6-25; ✳) A classic backpackers crash pad the rooms here are correspondingly basic, but the family that runs the place is lovely and highly tuned in to travellers' needs. Three 'luxury' rooms have a bit more space, air-con and no queues for the toilet. There are lots of welcoming communal areas to relax or chat, and hassle-free excursions, boat hire and bus tickets can be arranged here.

Parami Motel
HOTEL **$**

(☑ 058-21647; cnr Ohn Taw & Paya Sts; incl breakfast s US$33-38, d US$35-40; ✳ 🛜) Large and comfortable – if not entirely new-feeling – rooms that come with satellite TV and hot-water bathrooms make this a distinctly midrange-feeling budget stop.

★ San Ma Tau Myanmar Restaurant
BURMESE **$**

(1/290 Bo Gyoke St; meals from K2000; ☉ 11am-9pm) This friendly and popular place serves a vast selection of rich curries, hearty soups and tart salads, all accompanied by platters of fresh vegies and herbs and an overwhelming 10 types of local-style dips to eat them with.

GETTING TO THAILAND

The following information is liable to change, so be sure to check the situation locally before you travel.

Hpa-an to Mae Sot
The Myawaddy–Mae Sot border crossing is 93 miles southeast of Hpa-an.

Getting to the border 'Vans' (share taxis) and buses terminate a short walk from the Friendship Bridge.

At the border The **Myanmar immigration office** (☑ 058-50100; AH1, Myawaddy; ☉ 6am-6pm) is at the foot of the Friendship Bridge. After walking across the 460yd bridge, if you don't already have a visa, the **Thai immigration office** (☑ 055 56 3004; AH1, Mae Sot; ☉ 6.30am-6.30pm) will grant you permission to stay in Thailand up to 15 days.

Moving on Mae Sot's bus station is 2 miles east of the border and has good connections to destinations in northern Thailand and Bangkok. Mae Sot's airport is 2 miles east of the border, offering connections to Bangkok, Chiang Mai and Yangon. Both the bus station and airport can be reached by frequent *sŏrngtăaou* (pick-ups) that run between the Friendship Bridge and Mae Sot from 6am to 6pm (20B).

Kawthoung to Ranong
Kawthoung (also known as Victoria Point) is at the far southern end of Tanintharyi Region.

Getting to the border The bright green **Myanmar border post** (Strand Rd; ☉ 7am-4pm) is located a few steps from Kawthoung's jetty.

At the border If you've arrived in Kawthoung from elsewhere in Myanmar, you're free to exit the country here. After clearing Myanmar immigration, you'll be herded to a boat (per person from 50B) for the 20-minute ride to Ranong. On the Thai side, the authorities will issue you permission to stay in Thailand up to 15 days, or you can enter with a Thai visa obtained overseas.

Moving on Ranong is a 60B motorcycle-taxi ride or 20B *sŏrngtăaou* from Saphan Pla Pier. There are daily flights between Ranong and Bangkok (from 2000B, 1½ to 1¾ hours, four to six departures daily), while major bus destinations include Bangkok (240B to 680B, 10 hours), Hat Yai (410B, five hours) and Phuket (240B, five to six hours).

For more information on making this trip in the opposite direction, see p760.

TRANSPORT TO/FROM HPA-AN

DESTINATION	BUS
Bago	K5000; 6hr; 4 departures 7am-7pm
Kyaikto	K5000; 4hr; 4 departures 7am-7pm
Mawlamyine	K1000; 2hr; hourly 6am-4pm
Yangon	K5000; 7-8hr; 4 departures 7am-7pm

❶ Getting There & Away

It's possible to charter a **private boat** between Hpa-an and Mawlamyine seating about 10 people, taking approximately two hours to reach Mawlamyine (K60,000). This can be arranged at Soe Brothers Guesthouse.

Hpa-an's bus station is inconveniently located about 4 miles east of town but tickets can be bought and buses boarded at a few centrally located **ticket stalls** (at the clock tower). Staff at Soe Brothers can also arrange tickets.

'Vans' (share taxis) to Myawaddy (K8000 to K10,000, four to six hours, daily 6am and 7am) depart, on odd-numbered days only, from a stall near the clock-tower intersection.

Dawei ထားဝယ်

The doorway to Myanmar's little-visited deep south, known as **Tanintharyi Region** (တနင်္သာရီတိုင်း), is its administrative capital **Dawei**. This sleepy, tropical seaside town, with plenty of interesting architecture, can be used a base for visiting the 243ft-long, 69ft-high **Shwethalyaung Daw Mu**, the largest reclining Buddha in Myanmar, located a few miles outside of Dawei.

Spotless rooms are available in Dawei at the **Garden Hotel** (☑059-22116; 88 Ye Rd; r US$10-40; ❋ ☁). A good place to eat is **Hla Hla Hnan** (no roman-script sign, Neik Ban St; dishes from K300; ☉noon-9pm).

The coastline south of Dawei consists of bridal-white beaches fronting a vast archipelago of more than 800 largely uninhabited islands, nearly all of which have only recently opened to general tourism. The most accessible beach is **Maungmagan**, where places to stay include the delightful Burmese/French-run **Coconut Guesthouse & Restaurant** (☑ 09 737 00052; Phaw Taw Oo St, Maungmagan; s/d US$20/25; @).

At the time of research, foreigner tourists were not allowed to connect between Mawlamyine and Dawei by train (this may change). To continue southward from Dawei to Myeik and the bordertown of Kawthoung, you'll need to take a boat or fly.

INLE LAKE & SHAN STATE

Slicing the crystal, placid waters of Inle Lake in a boat; trekking among Pa-O and Danu villages outside Kalaw; feeling like you've travelled back in time at a remote hill-tribe market. What do some of Myanmar's most emblematic experiences have in common? They can all be tackled in the country's east in Shan State.

Trekking is hugely popular around here and Kalaw is the affordable base for adventure. Homestays are possible and the Shan are some of the friendliest folk in the country.

Inle Lake & Nyaungshwe ညောင်ရွှေ

☑ 081 / POP 10,000

A wonderful watery world of floating gardens, stilted villages and crumbling stupas, Inle Lake is one of those few places that are a tonic for the soul. While away the days canoeing, cycling and walking through the lush countryside.

TRANSPORT TO/FROM DAWEI

DESTINATION	AIR	BOAT	BUS
Kawthoung	US$111; 80min; 2 daily	US$80; 12hr; 4.30am	N/A
Mawlamyine	N/A	N/A	K9000-11,000; 9-12hr; 5am
Myeik	US$71; 35min; 2 daily	US$35; 4hr; 4.30am	N/A
Yangon	US$126; 70min; 2 daily	N/A	K13,000; around 16hr; 4pm

In September and October the **Phaung Daw U festival** runs for nearly three weeks, and is followed by the **Thadingyut festival**. Always cooler than the rest of the country, Inle gets downright chilly at night in January and February – bring warm clothes.

The village of Nyaungshwe, at the lake's north end, is home to all the budget accommodation and traveller services and is easily navigated by foot or bicycle.

There is a compulsory US$10 fee to enter the Inle Lake area, which you must pay on arrival at the **permit booth** (⊙6am-9pm) by the bridge at the entrance to Nyaungshwe.

◎ Sights & Activities

Yadana Man Aung Paya   BUDDHIST TEMPLE
(ရတနာမာန်အောင်ဘုရား; Phoung Taw Site St; ⊙daylight hours) **FREE** The oldest and most important Buddhist shrine in Nyaungshwe, this handsome gilded stupa is hidden away inside a square compound south of the Mingala Market. The stepped stupa is unique in Myanmar, and the surrounding pavilion contains a museum of treasures amassed by the monks over the centuries, including carvings, lacquerware and dance costumes.

Cultural Museum   MUSEUM
(ဗုဒ္ဓပြတိုက်; Museum Rd (Haw St); admission US$2/K2000; ⊙10am-4pm Tue-Sun) This equal parts imposing and crumbling structure is the former *haw* (palace) of the last Shan *sao pha* (sky lord), Sao Shwe Thaike, who briefly served as the first president of independent Burma. Today, the mostly empty building holds a few dusty displays and is worth visiting more for the stately brick-and-teak structure itself than any educational summary of Shan culture or history.

Mingala Market   MARKET
(မင်္ဂလာဈေး; Yone Gyi Rd; ⊙5am-2pm) This busy market at the entrance to town is flooded with locals every morning, when traders from the lake bring in fresh fish and produce from the floating gardens. The market doubles in size when it hosts the five-day rotating market.

Motorboat Trips   BOAT TOUR
Every hotel in town can arrange boat trips around the lake, and freelance boat drivers will approach you in the street. A whole-day trip around the lake costs between K18,000 and K20,000 if you include a stop at Inthein, where the weather-beaten pagodas on the hilltop are incredibly atmospheric despite the crowds.

Other popular stops include the monastery **Nga Phe Kyaung**, on the eastern side of the lake, which is famous for its cats trained by the monks to leap through hoops; **floating gardens**, where Intha farmers raise flowers, fruit and vegetables on long wooden trellises supported on floating mats of vegetation; and **village markets** and **artisans' shops**, where weaving, blacksmithing and jewellery-making go on. There's no obligation to buy anything.

🛏 Sleeping

Nyaungshwe is teeming with good budget rooms, so if the below options are all full there are plenty of decent alternatives. All include breakfast and most rent out bicycles.

May Guest House   GUESTHOUSE $
(☑081-209 417; 85 Mya Wa Ti St; r US$20-30; @🛜) Minor bathroom issues (low water pressure, tiny towels) and rather thin walls aside, we love this homey, neat and friendly guesthouse. Room are basic, but clean and cool, there's an inviting garden area and free wi-fi. Thoughtful, pressure-free staff can arrange boat trips and other travel needs.

Inle Inn   HOTEL $
(☑081-209 016; inleinns@gmail.com; Yone Gyi Rd; r US$30-40; 🛜) Potted plants, inviting trellises, and bamboo rooms result in a pleasing cocoon of vegetation at this budget place. Superior rooms are slightly larger and tack on a desk.

DON'T MISS

BIKE RIDE TO HOT SPRINGS

Rent a bike and pedal through beautiful countryside to **Kaung Daing**, a quiet Intha village on Inle's northwestern shore, about 5 miles from Nyaungshwe. Here take a dip in the **hot springs** (swimming pool US$8, private bath US$5, mixed hot pool US$8; ⊙6am-6pm), which are also the start or end point of several trekking routes between Kalaw and Inle Lake. If you don't feel like pedalling all the way back, load your bike onto a boat and motor across to Maing Thauk (K5000) before cycling home, starting on a long wooden bridge.

Nyaungshwe

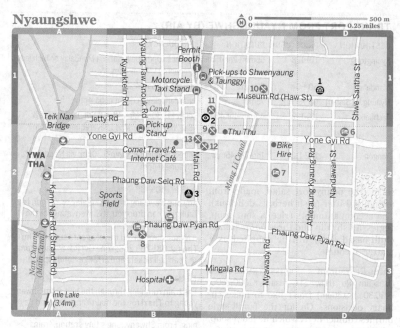

Golden Empress Hotel   GUESTHOUSE $
(☑ 081-209 037; www.facebook.com/golden empresshotel; 19 Phaung Daw Pyan Rd; r US$35-70; ❋@🛜) An expansive house looked after by friendly owners. The 13 rooms at this new place, attractively decked out with blond-wood panelling, are reminiscent of a ski lodge. All should be equipped with air-con by the time you read this.

Aquarius Inn   GUESTHOUSE $
(☑ 081-209 352; aquarius352@gmail.com; 2 Phaung Daw Pyan Rd; r US$18-40; ❋@🛜) The cheapest rooms here are pretty standard for this price range, and the real highlights are the family atmosphere, friendly service and the communal garden. Ten new air-con rooms should by finished by the time you read this.

🍴 Eating

The food situation in Nyaungshwe is pretty uninspiring. For cheap local eats, check out the **food stalls** (Yone Gyi Rd; meals K1000; ⊙6-9am) in Mingala Market. Local specialities include *shàn k'auq-swèh* (Shan-style noodle soup) and *to·p'ù thouq* (Shan tofu salad), prepared using yellow chickpea tofu, chilli, coriander and chilli oil.

Every evening a very basic **night market** (⊙5-9pm) unfolds just off Yone Gyi Rd.

★**Lin Htett Myanmar Traditional Food**   BURMESE $
(Yone Gyi Rd; meals from K2500; ⊙9am-9pm) Hands down, our favourite place to eat in Nyaungshwe. Choose a curry or two (refer to the pictures or, better yet, have a look behind the counter) and perhaps a

TRANSPORT FROM NYAUNGSHWE (BY AIR)

DESTINATION	PRICE (US$)	DURATION	FREQUENCY
Kyaingtong	119-128	55min–2hr 45min	direct 1.10pm Tue & Sat; via Mandalay or Tachileik frequent 11.30am-4pm.
Mandalay	50-60	30min	frequent noon-4pm
Nyaung U (Bagan)	68-79	75min	via Mandalay frequent noon-4pm
Tachileik	119-129	45min–1hr 45min	direct 11.30am Mon, Wed & Sat, 1.50pm Tue & Sat; via Lashio or Mandalay frequent 11.30am-4pm
Yangon	102-112	1hr–2hr 45min	direct frequent 8.30am-5.30pm; via Mandalay & Nyaung U 4pm

salad (the pennywort salad, made from a slightly bitter fresh herb, is delicious). The accompaniments (rice, a sour soup, vegies, a fishy dip and three *balachaung*, chilli-based dips) will be supplied as a matter of course.

Lotus Restaurant　INTERNATIONAL, BURMESE **$**
(Museum Rd (Haw St); mains K1000-3500; ⊙10.30am-9.30pm) Don't like to make culinary decisions? Go for the family-style Burmese dinner here, which includes soup, salad, curry and a generous fruit plate for only K3500.

Thukha Caffee　TEAHOUSE **$**
(cnr Lan Ma Taw St & Yone Gyi Rd; snacks from K200; ⊙5am-4pm; ✍) Ostensibly Nyaungshwe's only Muslim teashop, this tidy place serves good tea and, in the mornings, tasty *pakoda* (deep-fried vegetable dumplings) and other teashop snacks.

Everest Nepali Food Centre 2　NEPALI **$**
(Kyaung Taw Anouk Rd; mains K1500-3500, set meals K3500; ⊙6.30am-9pm; ✍) A branch of the longstanding Kalaw-based Nepali restaurant. The Nyaungshwe outlet does hearty set meals spanning rice, chapatti, curries and sides.

ⓘ Getting There & Away

AIR
The region's main airport is at Heho, 25 miles northwest of Nyaungshwe on the way to Kalaw. Hotels and private travel agents in Nyaungshwe can make bookings.

Either take a taxi from the airport to Nyaungshwe (K25,000, one hour) or hike half a mile to the highway and wait for a pick-up or bus bound for Taunggyi (K2000, 1½ hours); ask to be let off at **Shwenyaung**, from where you can change for Nyaungshwe (K6000) 7 miles away. Bear in mind that you might face a long wait.

BUS & PICK-UP
Any bus travelling from Mandalay or Yangon to Taunggyi can drop you at Shwenyaung for the full Taunggyi fare.

Nyaunshwe-based travel agents such as **Thu Thu** (☑081-209 258; Yone Gyi Rd; ⊙6am-9pm; 🛜) can sell tickets and arrange hotel pick-up.

TRAIN
The train rumbling through the hills from Shwenyaung to **Thazi** (on the main Yangon–Mandalay route) is slow but the scenery en route is stunning. From Shwenyaung's tiny station, trains depart at 9.30am and 10.30am, arriving in Kalaw after three hours (US$3) and reaching Thazi at least another six hours later (US$5).

ⓘ Getting Around

Several shops on Yone Gyi Rd and Phaung Daw Pyan Rd rent out clunky Chinese bicycles for K1500 per day. Motorcycle taxis at the **stand** (Lan Ma Taw St) near the market go to Shwenyaung for around K6000.

Pindaya

The **Shwe Oo Min Natural Cave Pagoda** (ရွှေဥမင်သဘာဝဂူဘုရား; Shwe U Min Pagoda Rd; admission US$3 or K3000, camera fee K300; ⊙6am-6pm) at Pindaya is a popular stop on the Shan State circuit. More than 8700 Buddha images form a labyrinth throughout the chambers of the caves.

Pleasant rooms, a great location on the steps of the caves and helpful staff make **Golden Cave Hotel** (☑081-66166; www.goldencavehotel.com; Shwe U Min Pagoda Rd; r US$35-40; @🛜) worth the money.

From Kalaw, take a bus or pick-up to Aungban (K1000, 20 minutes), There, you'll find two daily pick-ups (K1000 to K2000, 1½ hours, 8am and 11am), as well as waiting motorcycles (K6000 one way, K10,000 return) and taxis (K30,000 one way, K50,000 return).

Kalaw ကလော

♪ 081 / POP ABOUT 25,000

Welcome to Myanmar's trekking heartland, combining cool mountain climbs and a chilled vibe beloved by backpackers. Located at 4330ft on the rolling, pine-clad hills of the Shan Plateau, Kalaw is the beginning point for treks heading west to Inle Lake (about 28 miles), over mountains dotted with Palaung, Pa-O, Intha and Shan villages.

Kalaw is easy to navigate on foot. **Cyber World Internet Café** (Aung Chan Thar St; per hr K1000; ☻8am-11pm) is just uphill from **Aung Chan Thar Zedi** (အောင်ချမ်းသာ စေတီ; Aung Chan Thar St; ☻daylight hours) **FREE**, a glittery stupa covered in gold- and silver-coloured glass mosaics.

🏃 Activities

Trekking

During high season (November to February) it can get pretty busy on the more popular routes, while in the wet season paths get miserably muddy and few tourists head this way.

The most popular trek is the two- to four-day trek to Inle Lake. A less common route is the multiday trek to Pindaya, via Taung Ni. It's worth requesting a route via the villages of several different ethnic groups. Have good shoes and warm clothing for the cool evenings. Guesthouses can transport your unneeded bags for a small charge.

Trekking without a guide is not recommended – the trails are confusing, the terrain challenging and few people in the hills speak English. The going rate for a day hike is around K8000 to K9000 per person, overnight treks between K10,000 and K15,000 per person, per day, in groups of two or more.

Recommended guiding outfits include **Ever Smile** (♪081-50683; Yuzana St; ☻8am-8pm), **Rural Development Society** (RDS; ♪081-50747, 09 528 0974; sdr1992@gmail.com; Min St), **Sam's Trekking Guide** (♪081-50377; Union Hwy (NH 4); ☻7am-7pm) and **JP Barua** (♪081-50549).

🛏 Sleeping

Electricity is especially temperamental here, but you won't need air-con (or even a fan) to sleep. All rates include breakfast.

★**Dream Villa Hotel Kalaw** HOTEL $
(♪081-50144; dreamvilla@myanmar.com.mm; 5 Za Ti' La St; r US$40-45; ☎) A cut above your average Myanmar hotel, the Dream Villa is a spotless, three-storey home with 24 tasteful, wood-panelled rooms attractively decorated with a few local design touches. All rooms have TV and fridge, while the more expensive ones have a bit more legroom and bathtubs.

Eastern Paradise Motel HOTEL $
(♪081-50315; 5 Thiri Min Ga Lar St; r US$25-40; ☎) A central location, large, homey and well-equipped rooms, and gracious service make this one of the best deals in town.

Pine Breeze Hotel HOTEL $
(♪081-50459; pinebreezehotel@gmail.com; 174 Thittaw St; r US$25-45; ✳☎) Located just west of 'downtown' Kalaw, this baby-blue hilltop structure has four floors of new, neat rooms equipped with TV, fridge, balconies and great views over the town.

Honey Pine Hotel HOTEL $
(♪081-50728; honeypinehotelkalaw@gmail.com; 44 Za Ti' La St; r US$20-45; ✳☎) The budget-priced rooms at this new-feeling hotel include midrange amenities such as TV and fridge, although some of the single rooms lack windows and feel a bit tight.

🍴 Eating & Drinking

★**Thu Maung Restaurant** BURMESE $
(Myanmar Restaurant; Union Hwy (NH4); meals from K2500; ☻11am-9pm) One of our fave Burmese curry restaurants serves rich, meaty chicken, pork, mutton and fish curries coupled with exceptionally delicious dips, sides, salads, pickles and trimmings. The tomato salad, made from crunchy green tomatoes, is a work of art. It's located adjacent to the steps that lead to Thein Taung Paya; the English-language sign says 'Myanmar Restaurant'.

Ma Hnin Si Cafe TEAHOUSE
(Bu Tar St; mains from K200; ☻6am-6pm) There's a tiny English-language sign here, but a better locator is the crowd of locals enjoying plates of *pakoda* and other tasty deep-fried snacks, and excellent noodle dishes.

Pyae Pyae Shan Noodle SHAN $
(Union Hwy (NH4); mains from K500; ☻7am-8pm) This cosy, friendly shop sells delicious bowls

Kalaw

Kalaw

◎ Sights
1 Aung Chan Tha Zedi C2

⊕ Activities, Courses & Tours
2 Ever Smile C2
3 Rural Development Society C2
4 Sam's Trekking Guide C2

▢ Sleeping
5 Dream Villa Hotel Kalaw B2
6 Eastern Paradise Motel B2
7 Honey Pine Hotel B2
8 Pine Breeze Hotel A2

⊗ Eating
9 Everest Nepali Food Centre C3
10 Pyae Pyae Shan Noodl A1
11 Thu Maung Restaurant C2

◉ Drinking & Nightlife
12 Hi Snack & Drink C2
13 Ma Hnin Si Cafe C2

of the eponymous noodle, and has an English-language menu of other one-plate dishes.

Everest Nepali Food Centre NEPALI $
(Aung Chan Thar St; set meals K2500-3000; ⊙9am-9pm; 🛜) Relive memories of trekking in Nepal with a plate of *dhal baht* (rice served with lentils and other side dishes) at this convivial eatery run by a Nepali family.

Hi Snack & Drink BAR
(Kone Thai St; ⊙5-10pm) Hi is the size of a closet and boasts a fun, speakeasy feel; if you haven't had a rum here, you haven't been to Kalaw.

❶ Getting There & Away

AIR
Kalaw is about 16 miles from Heho airport (p506) and a taxi there costs K20,000. Coming from Heho by taxi, it's hard to find people to share with, as most passengers head to Inle Lake. Consider negotiating to Heho village and boarding a pick-up (K3000) from there.

BUS
Several **bus ticket offices** across from the market book seats on the long-distance buses between Yangon and Mandalay. These buses stop on the main road, in front of the market.

Buses, minivans and pick-ups bound for Thazi (K2500, four hours) stop periodically on the highway and will drop you in Shwenyaung (Inle Lake; two hours) for the same fare.

TRAIN
A single daily train departs from either end of the winding line that links Thazi and Shwenyaung.

TRANSPORT TO/FROM KALAW

DESTINATION	BUS	MINIBUS	PICK-UP	TRAIN
Aungban (for Pindaya)	N/A	K500; 20 min; daily 6.30am, 7am & 7.30am	K500; 4-5hr; frequent 7am-6pm	N/A
Heho (airport)	N/A	K2500; 3hr; daily 6.30am, 7am & 7.30am	N/A	N/A
Mandalay	K7000-10,000; 7-8hr; frequent 8-10pm	N/A	N/A	N/A
Nyaung U (Bagan)	K7000; 7-8hr; daily 9am & frequent 8-9pm	N/A	N/A	N/A
Shwenyaung (for Inle Lake)	N/A	K2500; 3hr; daily 6.30am, 7am & 7.30am	N/A	US$1-3; 3hr; daily 10.15am & 12.30pm
Thazi	N/A	K5000; 4hr; frequent 7am-noon	K3000; 4hr; frequent 7am-6pm	US$2-5; 7hr; daily 2pm
Yangon	K10,000-16,500; 10-12hr; frequent 5-8pm	N/A	N/A	N/A

Kyaingtong   ကျိုင်းတုံ

☑ 084 / POP 20,000

Also known as Kengtung or sometimes Chiang Tung, Kyaingtong is one of Myanmar's most attractive towns. The vast majority of its residents belong to one of several Tai ethnic groups. It's packed with Buddhist monasteries such as **Wat Jong Kham** (ဝတ်ကျင်ခန်း; off Mine Yen Rd; ☉ daylight hours) and among other attractions are an atmospheric **Central Market** (ြ မေဈး; Zeigyi Rd; mains from K500; ☉ 5am-1pm) and the Buddhist temple **Yat Taw Mu** (ရပ်တော်မူ; off Tachileik-Taunggyi Rd (Main Rd); ☉ daylight hours) , home to the landmark 60ft-high standing Buddha statue.

Kyaintong's accommodation will inspire few postcards home; the best budget sleeps are **Sam Yweat Hotel** (☑ 084-21235; www.samywethotel.blogspot.com; cnr Kyaing Lan 1 Rd & Kyaing Lan 4 Rd; r US$30-35; ✳) and **Private Hotel** (☑ 084-21438; www.privatehotelmyanmar.com; 5 Airport Rd; r US$35-42; ✳ @).

Shwe Myo Taw Express (☑ 084-23145; Tachileik Rd) and **Thet Nay Wun** (Kyain Nyan Rd) run air-con buses to Tachileik. 'Vans' (share taxis) bound for Tachileik depart from Kyaingtong's bus station, west of town.

Several airlines connect Kyaingtong and other destinations in northern Myanmar via a confusing, web-like flight map. Note that several flights aren't direct, with many – including flights to Yangon – involving sometimes as many as two stops. Be sure to double-check before buying your ticket. Taxis charge K5000 and *thoun bein* (auto rickshaws) K3000 for the 2-mile trip to/from Kyaingtong's airport.

MANDALAY & AROUND

Myanmar's second biggest city – economically booming and culturally vibrant – is worth a stop if only to use as a base for visiting the surrounding former royal capitals. Escape the sweltering flatlands in the surreal hill station of Pyin Oo Lwin, home to brilliant old colonial buildings, horse-drawn carriage taxis and good restaurants catering for an influx of Myanmar's nouveau riche. Further north, charming little Hsipaw makes a great alternative base for easy treks into fascinating minority villages.

Mandalay   မန္တလေး

☑ 02 / POP 950,000

For those who haven't been – and that includes *The Road to Mandalay* author Rudyard Kipling – the mention of 'Mandalay' typically conjures up images of Asia at its most traditional and timeless. The reality is instead a sprawling city where dusty streets teem with traffic and there's a construction project on every block. In spite of this, it's

GETTING TO THAILAND: KYAINTONG TO MAE SAI

The following information is liable to change, so be sure to check the situation locally before you travel.

Getting to the border The border is a short walk from 'downtown' Tachileik, or 1 mile and a 20B truck ride or a K1500/50B motorcycle-taxi ride from the town's bus station.

At the border If you've arrived in Kyaingtong or Tachileik via air from elsewhere in Myanmar, you can freely exit the country at Tachileik. The Myanmar border post is open from 6am to 6pm, and upon crossing to Thailand, the Thai authorities will issue you permission to stay in Thailand up to 15 days, or you can enter with a Thai visa obtained overseas.

Moving on Mae Sai's bus station is 1 mile from the border; pick-ups ply the route between the bus station and Soi 2, Th Phahonyothin (15B, five minutes, 6am to 9pm). Alternatively, it's a 50B motorcycle-taxi ride to/from the stand at the corner of Th Phahonyothin and Soi 4. From Mae Sai, major bus destinations include Bangkok, Chiang Mai and Chiang Rai.

impossible not to be impressed by the golden Buddha of Mahamuni Paya, or the sunset views across the flat landscape from stupa-studded Mandalay Hill. Mandalay is also the nation's cultural capital and a fine place to delve into many Burmese arts.

Mandalay became the capital of the Burmese empire in 1861, an entity that by 1885 had been exiled into history by the British. Prior to Mandalay, several other places within a short distance also served as capitals, and it's these ancient cities that are the real attractions.

◉ Sights

Several of Mandalay's top attractions are covered by a K10,000 Archaeological Zone ('combo') ticket valid one week from first purchase. Currently the ticket is only checked (and sold) at Mandalay Palace and Shwenandaw Kyaung, two sites at Inwa (Ava) and one minor one in Amarapura.

★**Mandalay Hill**　　LANDMARK
(မန္တလေးတောင်; Map p511; camera fee K1000) To get a sense of Mandalay's pancake-flat sprawl, climb the 760ft hill that breaks it. The barefooted walk up covered stairways on the hill's southern slope is a major part of the experience, passing through and around a colourful succession of prayer and shopping opportunities. The climb takes a good 30 minutes, but allow much longer for stops en route. The summit viewpoint is especially popular at sunset when young monks converge on foreigners for language practice.

It's also possible to drive most of the way up Mandalay Hill. From the upper car park

both a lift and an escalator tower should whisk you up to the hilltop. However, as both are often broken you'll probably need to walk the last five minutes by stairways. From 10th St at 68th St, shared pick-up route 16 (per person K1000) shuttles to the car park. Motorcycle taxis typically charge K3000 up, K2000 down (even though the down route is much further due to a long one-way loop).

★**Mahamuni Paya**　　BUDDHIST TEMPLE
(မဟာမုနိဘုရား; 83rd St; ⊙ complex 24hr, museum sections 8am-5pm) **FREE** Every day, thousands of colourfully dressed faithful venerate Mahamuni's 13ft-tall **seated Buddha**, a nationally celebrated image that's popularly believed to be some 2000 years old. Centuries of votary gold leaf applied by male devotees (women may only watch) has left the figure knobbly with a 6-inch layer of pure gold... except on his radiantly gleaming face, which is ceremonially polished daily at 4am.

★**Shwe In Bin Kyaung**　　BUDDHIST MONASTERY
(ရွှေအင်ပင်ကျောင်း; Map p514; 89th St, 37/38) If you want a place for quiet meditation in Mandalay, you couldn't find a better spot than this beautifully carved teak monastery. Commissioned in 1895 by a pair of wealthy Chinese jade merchants, the central building stands on tree-trunk poles and the interior has a soaring dark majesty. Balustrades and roof cornices are covered in detailed engravings, a few of them mildly humorous.

Shwenandaw Kyaung　　BUDDHIST MONASTERY
(ရွှေနန်းတော်ကျောင်း; Golden Palace Monastery; Map p511; combo ticket K10,000) Lavished in

carved panels, this fine teak monastery-temple is noted for its carvings, particularly the interior gilded Jataka scenes (past-life stories of Buddha). The building once stood within the Mandalay Palace complex as the royal apartment of King Mindon, who died inside it in 1878.

Mandalay Palace   PALACE
(မန္တလေးနန်းတော်; Map p511; combo ticket K10,000; ⏰7.30am-4.30pm) The glittering 1990s reconstruction of Mandalay's royal palace complex is impressive for its scale, with more than 40 timber buildings constructed to resemble the 1850s originals. Climb the

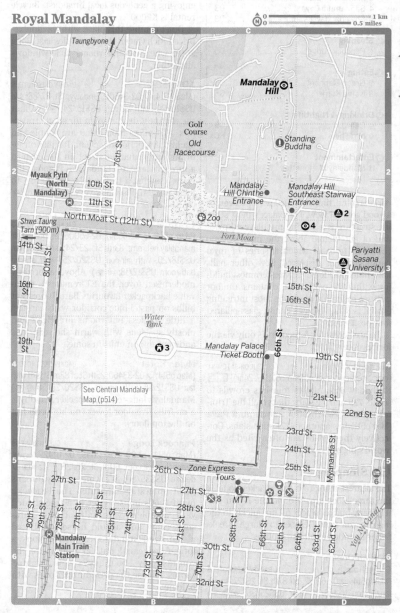

Royal Mandalay

0 —————— 1 km
0 —————— 0.5 miles

Taungbyone

Mandalay Hill ⦿1

Golf Course
Old Racecourse

Standing Buddha

Myauk Pyin (North Mandalay)
10th St
11th St
North Moat St (12th St)

Mandalay Hill Chinthe Entrance

Mandalay Hill Southeast Stairway Entrance ▲2

Shwe Taung Tarn (900m)
14th St

⦿Zoo

⦿4

Fort Moat

Pariyatti Sasana University ▲5

16th St
80th St

14th St
15th St
16th St

Water Tank

19th St

🚩3

Mandalay Palace Ticket Booth

66th St

19th St

60th St

See Central Mandalay Map (p514)

21st St

22nd St

23rd St
24th St

25th St

Myananda St

26th St Zone Express Tours
27th St
27th St
28th St

⦿8 ℹMTT 🌸7
9
11

10

80th St
79th St
78th St
77th St
76th St
75th St
74th St
73rd St
72nd St
71st St
70th St
68th St
66th St
65th St
64th St
63rd St
62nd St

Mandalay Main Train Station

30th St

32nd St

Yay Nyi Canal

curious spiral, timber-walled **watchtower** for a good general view. The palace's most striking structure is a soaring multilayered pyramid of gilt filigree above the main **throne room**, in front of which a series of royal paraphenalia is displayed. Few other halls have much inside but the westernmost building within the palace oval contains a minor **culture museum** where the most intriguing exhibit is King Thibaw's dainty, glass-pillared four-poster bed.

Palace access for foreigners is only via the fortress's east gate.

Kuthodaw Paya   BUDDHIST TEMPLE
(ကုသိုလ်တော်ဘုရား; Map p511; ⊙24hr) FREE
Kuthodaw Paya draws tour-bus crowds to see its 729 marble slabs that retell the Tripitaka canon. Nearby, the **Sandamuni Paya** (Map p511) has another 1774 such slabs. Collectively these slabs are often cited as the 'world's biggest book'.

🛏 Sleeping

The nearest thing to a 'backpacker zone' is the three-block area around the Nylon Hotel. Many budget places fill up quickly in the high season from October to March. Breakfast is included at all listed places.

★**Rich Queen
Guesthouse**   BACKPACKER HOTEL **$**
(Map p514; ☎02-60172; off 87th St, 26/27; s with fan/air-con US$15/20, d/tr US$25/35; ❄@☎)

This friendly new hotel is one of Mandalay's best-value retreats, especially if you score a front-corner room with giant windows, fridge, high ceilings and piping-hot showers. Avoid the few dark box-rooms at the back. It's near the market on a quiet narrow alley along which monks often pass while you're enjoying a generous local breakfast. Bicycle rental is K2000.

Don't confuse this place with the double-priced Rich Queen Hotel 1¾ miles east along 26th, where several rooms lack windows altogether.

AD1 Hotel   BACKPACKER HOTEL **$**
(Map p514; ☎02-34505; Eindawya St, 87/88; s/d US$10/20, with air-con US$15/24; ❄) About the cheapest deal in town for single travellers, AD1 offers rooms that are simple and ageing, if functionally clean. It's just off vibrant 'onion market street' in the eastern approach lane to Eindawya Pagoda. Beware if asking a taxi to take you here – to local ears 'AD1' sounds very much like '81' (ie 81st St).

ET Hotel   BACKPACKER HOTEL **$**
(Map p514; ☎02-66547, 02-65006; ethotelmdy@mandalay.net.mm; 83rd St, 23/24; s/d with fan US$18/20, with air-con US$20/25, with shared bathroom US$12/18; ❄☎) Above a brightly modernised foyer, the ET remains a good-value backpacker favourite. Bare fluorescent bulbs on pastel-blue corridor walls can feel a little soulless but rooms are clean and mostly spacious with warm showers, fans and new air-con units in some.

Nylon Hotel   BACKPACKER HOTEL **$**
(Map p514; ☎02-33460; 25th St at 83rd St; s/d with fan US$12/15, with air-con US$20/25; ❄@☎) Mandalay's long-term backpacker standby is a no-frills five-floor tower (no lift, breakfast on the top floor).

Peacock Lodge   GUESTHOUSE **$$**
(Map p511; ☎09 204 2059, 02-61429; www.peacocklodge.com; 60th St, 25/26; r standard/deluxe US$35/50; ❄) One of Myanmar's great homestay-style inns. The Peacock's main 1960s house is set in a tree-shaded yard complete with fairy lights, parasol seating and an old horsecart. Dated if fair-sized standard rooms overlook a lotus-filled canal but far better are the contrastingly boutiquey new 'deluxe' rooms: choose the prized upper ones with balcony.

✖ Eating & Drinking

Mandalay has plenty of inexpensive Asian restaurants. However, there is definitely not a lively night scene.

Cafes with wide-ranging international menus include comfortably hip **Cafe JJ** (Map p511; www.cafejj.com; 26th St at 65th St; coffee K1000-2300, cocktails K2900-6100; ⊙9am-10.30pm; 🛜); good value, cutesy **V Cafe** (Map p514; 🖊02-24688; 25th St at 80th St; mains/burgers K5000/2000, espresso/draught beer/cocktails K800/1000/3000; ⊙9am-10.30pm; 🛜); and loungey **Koffie Korner** (Map p511; 🖊02-68648; 27th St at 70th St; mains K3500-7500; ⊙9am-11pm; 🅿🛜). Each mix cocktails, but for a drink with a sunset view it's hard to beat the rooftop bar of the **Ayarwaddy River View Hotel** (Map p514; 🖊02-64946, 02-72373; www.ayarwaddyriverviewhotel.com; Strand Rd, 22/23).

There are many beer stations. Some lack English signs but are easy to spot from the Myanmar or Dagon Beer awnings. If you can't find your own, handy examples in the backpacker zone include **Pyi Taw Win** (Map p514; 81st St, 24/25; barbecue items K200-1800; ⊙8am-10.30pm) and part-restaurant **Rainbow** (Map p514; 83rd St at 23rd St; beer K600, barbecue/mains from K500/2000; ⊙10am-11pm).

Ruby   NEPALI, VEGETARIAN $
(Map p514; 28th St, 81/82; thali K1500; ⊙7am-9pm; 🖊) Organic vegetarian Indian/Nepali meals served up in a small shop-room box-restaurant by a friendly family from Mogok. Nearby **Nepali Food** (NVC; Map p514; 81st St, 26/27; thali K2000; ⊙8am-9pm) is similar.

Lashio Lay   SHAN $
(Map p514; 23rd St, 83/84; per plate K500-1300; ⊙10am-9.30pm) Simple long-running shop-restaurant for consistently excellent pre-cooked Shan food. Point and pick, pay per dish. Two dishes plus rice make an ideal meal.

STREET DINING

Along with beer-station barbecues, the best-value dining is usually at street stalls. Certain corners or street sections have culinary specialities, but knowing which takes some insider knowledge.

Morning Only

➡ Baosi dumplings – **Yong Xing** (Map p514; 83rd St, 30/31; baosi K350; ⊙5am-7.15am).

➡ Shan noodles with *dofubyo* (bean paste) – 29th St, 80/81 before 10am.

➡ *Mohinga* – Mandalay's best breakfast three-wheel street-trolley stall at 32nd St at 81st St, from 6.30am to 9.30am only.

Daytime

➡ Point-and-pick multi-curries are offered at several inexpensive family snack outlets dotted along an unnamed lane between 74th and 75th Sts. Our favourite is the furthest east – unsigned, super-cheap **Mtay Myint Thar** (Map p514; 74th-75th link-lane 28/29; meal K500; ⊙10am-7.30pm), a traditional wooden shack-house decked with contorted roots and plants.

➡ Burmese sweets to take away from near 85th St at 27th St in Zeigyo Market.

➡ Sweet tea and fresh *nanbya* (tandoor bread) from **Min Thiha** (Map p511; 28th St at 72nd St; tea/nanbya K300/250; ⊙5am-5pm) or **Unison Teahouse** (Map p514; 38th St at 88th St; tea K300; ⊙5am-1am).

Nighttime Only

➡ Indian chapatti and curry – 28th St at 82nd St or **Nay** (Map p514; 27th St at 82nd St; curry/chapatti K1200/150; ⊙5pm-11pm).

➡ Indian/savoury 'pancakes' and biryanis – **Karaweik** (Map p514; 26th St at 83rd St; ⊙5.30pm-midnight).

➡ Chinese food stalls – 34th St at 76th St, with a night market (vegetables) stretching along 34th St.

Central Mandalay

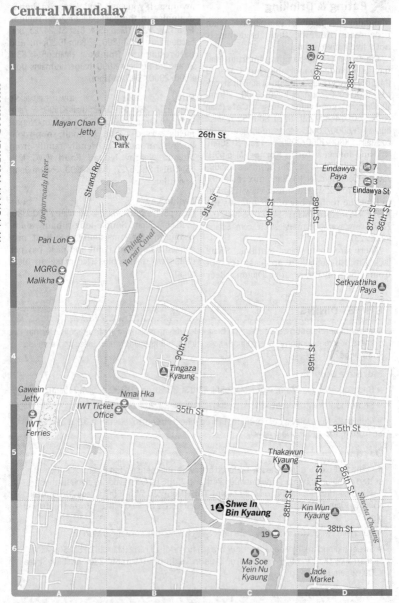

★ **Green Elephant** BURMESE $$
(Map p511; 02-61237; www.greenelephant-restaurants.com; 27th St, 64/65; mains K5000-8000, set menus K8000-10,000, service tax 15%; 11am-2pm & 6-9pm;) It's hard to do better for Burmese cuisine than with Green

Elephant's attractively presented multi-dish set menus. While these are aimed at tour groups, individuals can usually get a slightly adapted version on request. Ours featured six dishes including tasty roast-aubergine salad and a scrumptiously tangy

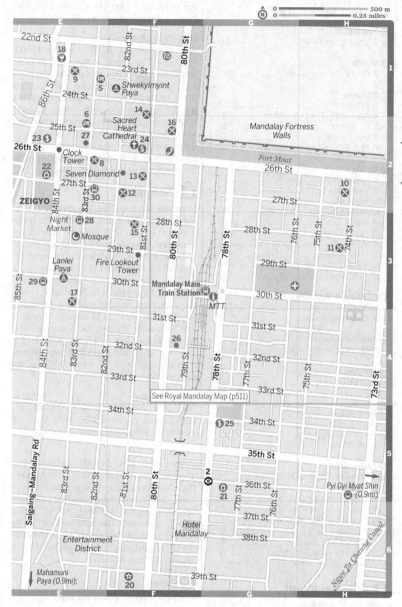

mango-pork curry – one of our best meals in Myanmar.

Marie-Min VEGETARIAN **$$**
(Map p514; off 27th St, 74/75; mains K1500-2500; ◷9am-10pm, closed Jun; ✐) An all-vegetarian menu fits the owners' stated principle: 'Be kind to animals by not eating them.' Highlights include tofu curry, a meal-sized aubergine 'dip' and avocado milkshakes (K1500) that are as 'fabulous' as promised.

Central Mandalay

☆ Entertainment

Mandalay Marionettes   PUPPET SHOW
(Map p511; www.mandalaymarionettes.com; 66th St at 27th St; admission K10,000; ⊙ 8.30pm) On a tiny stage, colourful marionettes expressively recreate snippets of traditional tales. Occasionally a sub-curtain is lifted so that you can briefly admire the deft hand movements of the puppeteers (one an octogenarian) who have performed internationally.

Moustache Brothers   COMEDY
(Map p514; 39th St, 80/81; admission K8000; ⊙ 8.30pm) This classic *a-nyeint* (a form of vaudeville folk opera with dance, music, jokes and silly walks) group became world-famous in the 1990s for their jokes and rants against the Myanmar government, which brought them a string of prison sentences, as well as a name-check from Hugh Grant's character in the movie *About a Boy*. The show, now entirely in English, doesn't please everyone but it remains a classic Mandalay must-see.

🛍 Shopping

Mandalay is a major crafts centre, and probably the best place in the country for traditional puppets and hand-woven embroidered tapestries. Virtually nothing you see will be 'antique'; items are often scuffed up or weathered to look much older than they are.

There are numerous **silk workshop-shops** and a couple more handicraft emporia along main Sagaing road in Amarapura. Puppets are sold at Moustache Brothers and Mandalay Marionettes. There are also several interesting shops on 36th St beside the **gold-leaf-pounding workshops** (Map p514; 36th St, 77/79), where you can buy square gold-leaf sheets.

Shwe Pathein   SOUVENIRS
(Map p514; 141 36th St, 77/78; ⊙ 8am-5pm) Pathein-style parasols. Next door there's a leather workshop and a gold-leaf shop.

Zegyo   MARKET
(Zaycho; Map p514; 84/86th, 26/28th) The 25-storey tower that brutally overpowers the Mandalay skyline balances atop one of three horrendous, neighbouring concrete 'malls', stiflingly crammed full of fabric sellers. However, the surrounding older market areas are fascinating places to wander amid piles of dried fish, sacks of chilli and giant arms of bananas.

ℹ Orientation

Mandalay city streets are laid out on a grid system and numbered from east to west (up to 49th) and from north to south (over 50th). A street address that reads 66th, 26/27 means the place is located on 66th St between 26th and 27th Sts. Corner addresses are given in the form 26th at 82nd St. Some of the longer east–west streets can also take names once they cross the Shweta Chaung (Shweta Canal) heading west.

The 'downtown' area runs roughly from 21st to 35th Sts between 80th and 88th Sts. Major east–west thoroughfares include 26th and 35th Sts, plus 19th St east of the moat.

ℹ Information

INTERNET ACCESS

Wi-fi is available in better cafe-bars and in the lobbies of most foreigner-licensed accommodation. Internet cafes are dotted every two or three blocks throughout the city centre.

MONEY

Pristine euro, US dollar and Singapore dollar banknotes can be changed for excellent rates at Mandalay Airport, at downtown money-changers, including **Faith** (Map p514; 26th St, 81/82; ⊙9am-6pm), and at several branches of **KBZ Bank** (Map p514; 34th St at 78th St; ⊙9.30am-3pm Mon-Fri) and **CB Bank** (Map p514; 26th St, 84/86; ⊙9.30am-3pm Mon-Fri). Both banks have 24-hour ATMs. **Zone Express** (Map p511; www.myanmarzonetravel.com; 68th St, 26/27; ⊙8am-8pm) has good rates for US dollars and euros, bearable rates for Thai baht and, if you're desperate, will change UK pounds.

POST

Main Post Office (Map p514; 22nd St, 80/81; ⊙10.30am-4pm Mon-Fri)

TELEPHONE

Local/national calls cost K100/200 per minute from PCO street stands. Mobile-phone SIM cards are available from ever-multiplying phone shops.

TOURIST INFORMATION & TRAVEL AGENCIES

Seven Diamond (Map p514; ☎02-30128, 02-72868; www.sevendiamondtravel.com; 82nd St, 26/27; ⊙8.30am-6pm) Helpful, major agency that can pre-book flights and hotels by email request and organise airport-bound shared taxis.

MTT (Myanmar Travels & Tours; Map p511; ☎02-60356; www.myanmartravelsandtours.com; 68th St at 27th St; ⊙9.30am-4.30pm) The government-run travel company doubles as a tourist office, giving away multi-city maps as well as selling transport tickets and permit-needing tours.

ℹ Getting There & Away

AIR

Mandalay International Airport (www.mandalayairport.com), just over 20 miles south of the city, has both domestic and international connections.

BOAT

Taking a boat on the Ayeyarwady River is one of Mandalay's delights. Flits to Mingun or all-day rides to Bagan are most popular, though the new afternoon return service to Inwa is a great alternative. Pre-booking one day ahead is usually fine for Bagan or Bhamo; bring plenty of drinking water. For Mingun and Inwa just show up 30 minutes before departure. Passort required.

IWT Ferries (Map p514; ☎02-36035; www.mot.gov.mm/iwt; Gawein Jetty) Slow boats to Bhamo and Bagan plus the more picturesque *Hantharwaddy* Bagan-bound cruiser depart from Gawein Jetty.

Malikha (Map p514; ☎02-72279; www.malikha-rivercruises.com) Three Malikha boats do the Bagan run; Malikha 3 is the most elegant. Buy tickets through hotels or agencies.

MGRG (Map p514; ☎09 505 7685; http://mgrgexpress.com; Strand Rd) Bagan express ferries (October to March). Tickets from a booth at the jetty.

Nmai Hka (Map p514; ☎09 4027 00072; www.nmaihka.com; A-15, 2nd fl, train station) Shwei Keinnery ferries to Bagan (tourist season) and Bhamo (summer) plus seasonal *Tharlarwaddy* to Mingun and Inwa. Ticket office is 100yd east of IWT. Departures from Gawein Jetty.

TRANSPORT TO/FROM MANDALAY

DESTINATION	AIR	BOAT	BUS	TRAIN
Bagan	30min, US$60-68	10-14hr, US$15-45	9hr, US$10	8hr, US$4-10
Bhamo	1hr, US$58-134	34-72hr, US$9-100	N/A	N/A
Hsipaw	N/A	N/A	5-6hr, US$4-5	11hr, US$4-9
Inle Lake	30min, US$75 via Heho +1hr taxi	N/A	11-13hr, US$12-25	N/A
Katha	N/A	1-2 days, US$36-80	US$80	13½hr to Naba +1hr bus, US$10-25
Yangon	85min, US$79-150	N/A	9-10hr, US$12-20	15½-16½hr, US$11-33

Pan Lon (Map p514; Strand Rd; ⊘ticket office 5am-6pm) Express boats to Katha.

BUS & SHARED TAXI

Thiri Mandalar bus station (Map p514; 89th St, 21/22) is relatively central. Buses for Monywa, Shwebo and Bhamo leave from here (though foreigners currently may not take Bhamo services). **Pyi Gyi Myat Shin bus station** is 2 miles east of the centre and has buses for Hsipaw and Lashio. **Kwe Se Kan Highway bus station** is 6 miles south of centre, and it can take 45 minutes for the K3000/6000 motorbike/taxi ride from central Mandalay, even more by pick-up. Allow plenty of time once you're there to find the right bus in the mayhem.

Pre-booking bus tickets for longer-distance routes is wise. Booking through backpacker hotels will usually incur a commission but that's rarely more than the motorbike-taxi fare you'd incur when buying your own. Alternatively use a city-centre ticket agency. There are many, especially on 32nd St where Ko Htay/Shwe Mann Thu has a particularly wide choice of destinations and offers several transfer buses ('ferries') to the main bus station, most costing K1000 per person.

Long-distance shared taxis, where available, are worth considering as most offer door-to-door service, saving potentially long trips to/from bus stations at either end of your journey.

TRAIN

Mandalay's gargantuan, butt-ugly **train station** (30th St, 78/79) is in the city centre. The **MTT sub-office** (Myanmar Travel & Tours; Map p514; train station, near south door; ⊘9.30am-6pm) here can sell tickets (with commission) if the queues upstairs look too daunting.

❶ Getting Around

GETTING TO/FROM THE AIRPORT

From Mandalay airport there are free shuttle buses for AirAsia customers (and leaving for the airport from 9am from 79th St, 26/28) and Golden Myanmar customers (5.30am from Sedona Hotel, picking up at Hotel Mandalay 5.45am). Otherwise there's no airport bus.

Several taxi companies with booths in the arrivals area offer shared taxis at K12,000/4000 per vehicle/seat. These include **Shwe Myanmar** (✏02-72325; 34th St, 79/80) and **Great Taxi**

(✏02-32534). Even if you choose the K4000 'shared' option you'll still be collected/dropped at your hotel as long as it's reasonably central. Coming from town, book one day ahead if possible.

BICYCLE & MOTORCYCLE

Several rental agents in the central backpacker area charge K1500/10,000 per day for bicycles/motorbikes, including long-established **Mr Jerry** (Map p514; 83rd St, 25/26; ⊘8am-8pm). Several hotels rent bicycles too. Cyclists are advised to carry a head-torch at night.

To go further afield, expat-run **Mandalay Motorcycle** (Map p514; ✏09 4440 22182; www.mandalaymotorbike.com; 32nd St, 79/80; city/trail bike per day K12,000/40,000) has 125cc and 150cc trail bikes. The office is only manned by appointment and supply is limited so call ahead to book a bike.

TAXI

Motorcycle taxis lurk near hotels and on many a city corner. Expect to pay K1000 for a short hop, K1500 across the centre, and K10,000 for all-day hire within Mandalay (or K15,000 including Amarapura, Inwa and Sagaing). Guesthouses can help you find a reliable taxi or motorcycle driver.

TRISHAW

Traditionally the main form of city transport, pedal trishaws are now relatively rare except around the markets. Fares include city centre to base of Mandalay Hill for K4000 return and all-day hire from around K10,000.

English-speaking drivers include eloquent **Ko Re** (koore6070@gmail.com; often waits 27th/83rd) and **Mr 'Take it Easy'** (myintshin15@gmail.com; 27th St, 80/81).

Around Mandalay

From Mandalay it's easy to day-trip to four old cities nearby. Entry to Inwa's two main sites and Amarapura's Bagaya Kyaung are included in Mandalay's K10,000 'combo' ticket. A separate K3000 ticket for Mingun and Sagaing is patchily enforced. No one checks for tickets at the other sites.

A popular option is to combine Amarapura, Sagaing and Inwa into a full-day trip by motorcycle taxi (K15,000) or taxi (K30,000 to K50,000).

BUS & PICK-UP

DESTINATION	PRICE	DURATION	FREQUENCY
Inle Lake	K10,000-16,000	11hr	7.30pm & 8pm
Nyaung U (Bagan)	K10,000-11,000	10hr	7am & 7pm
Yangon	K13,000-22,000	12hr	frequent 5.30pm-7pm

Motorbike taxis typically add around K2000 to drive around the Inwa ruins (if you insist). Add another K5000 more to include Mingun too. Beware that doing the whole lot in one very long day will feel very rushed. Ideally, make two or three more modest day trips.

Amarapura   အမရပူရ

The 'City of Immortality', a short-lived capital 7 miles south of Mandalay, is famed for **U Bein's Bridge**, the world's longest teak bridge at 1300yd. At 200 years old, the bridge sees lots of life along its 1086 teak posts, with monks and fishers commuting to and fro. It leads to **Kyauktawgyi Paya** and small **Taungthaman** village, with tea and toddy shops. A popular sunset activity is renting a **boat** (about K5000) to drift along as the skies turn orange, or watching life go by from a waterside beer station.

Just west is the monastery **Maha Ganayon Kyaung**, where hundreds of monks breakfast at 10.30am. Resist the temptation to thrust a camera in their faces, as some travellers do.

It's possible to cycle here from Mandalay in about 45 minutes.

Inwa   အင်းဝ

Cut off by rivers and canals, Inwa (called Ava by the British) served as the Burmese capital for nearly four centuries. **Horse carts** (one-/two-hour tours K6000/9000 for up to two people) make a loop around Inwa's beaten track; if you're lucky you may get them to stop at other crumbling sights sans vendors, or to allow you to rest your butt.

The finest sights are the atmospheric **Bagaya Kyaung** (တံးကရာကျောင်း; combo ticket required), an 1834 teak monastery supported by 267 posts; the **Maha Aungmye Bonzan** (aka Ok Kyaung), which is a brick-and-stucco monastery dating from 1822; and the 88ft **Nanmyin** watchtower, which leans precariously.

Sagaing   စစ်ကိုင်း

Across the Ava Bridge from the Inwa junction and 11 miles from Mandalay, the stupa-studded hilltops of Sagaing are where Burmese Buddhists come to relax and meditate. Sagaing is also known for **silver shops** and **guitars**.

Sagaing Hill is the big attraction. Trees hang over stone steps leading past monas-teries to the top. There are great views, and pathways lead all the way to the water for the adventurer. The hill is half a mile north of the market.

Sagaing is spread out. Take a motorbike taxi here from Mandalay, then rent a trishaw for the day.

Mingun   မင်းကွန်း

Home to a trio of unique pagodas, Mingun is a compact riverside village site that's a great half-day excursion from Mandalay. The journey is part of the attraction, whether puttering up the wide Ayeyarwady or roller-coasting from Sagaing along a rural lane through timeless hamlets of bamboo-weave homes.

The **Mingun Paya** is actually the remains of a planned 492ft stupa, surely a candidate for the world's largest pile of bricks. It is still possible to climb up. Just to the north is the **Mingun Bell**, which holds the record for the world's largest uncracked bell. Press on to the white, wavy-terraced **Hsinbyume Paya**.

Mingun is a pleasant 35-minute drive from Sagaing, but it's more popular to go by boat (one hour out, 40 minutes back, passport required). From Mandalay's 26th St 'tourist jetty' (Mayan Chan), boats depart at 9am (foreigner/bicycle K5000/500 return) returning at 1pm. Alternatively, Nmai Hka's *Tharlarwaddy* (US$6 return, bicycles free) departs 8.30am from Gawein Jetty, returning 11.30am. For US$8 extra, the latter boat continues to Inwa.

Pyin Oo Lwin   ပြင်ဦးလွင်
☑ 085 / POP 80,000

Set in the foothills of northern Shan State, this colonial hill station was established by British Captain May as a retreat from the stifling heat of Mandalay, and was subsequently named Maymyo for him (*myo* means town). Under the British it served as a summer capital and domestic tourists still flock here during the hottest months (March to May).

The main activity is cycling through history, passing faded English-style country mansions and cute pony-led miniature wagons, straight out of the Wells Fargo stagecoach days of the American West (actually India, 1914, as one driver told us), that serve as local transport. You will no doubt also notice a lot of green uniforms around here as Pyin Oo Lwin is home to the Defence Services Academy.

Pyin Oo Lwin is very spread out. The Mandalay–Lashio Rd doubles as the main road. Bicycle is the best way to get around.

◉ Sights

Most of Pyin Oo Lwin's trademark colonial-era buildings are dotted amid the southeastern woodland suburbs on and off Circular Rd. Check out the splendid **former Croxton Hotel** (Gandamar Myaing Hotel; Circular Rd), as well as the **Number 4 High School** (Circular Rd) and the **Survey Training Centre** (Multi-Office Rd).

★ National Kandawgyi Gardens   PARK
(အမျိုးသားကန်တော်ကြီးဥယျာဉ်; Nandan Rd; adult/child under 12yr/camera US$5/3/1; ⊙7am-6pm, aviary 8am-5pm, orchid garden & butterfly museum 8.30am-5pm, Nan Myint Tower lift operates to 5pm) Founded in 1915, this lovingly maintained 435-acre botanical garden features more than 480 species of flowers, shrubs and trees. For casual visitors, its most appealing aspect is the way flowers and overhanging branches frame views of Kandawgyi Lake's wooden bridges and small gilded pagoda. Admission includes the swimming pool, visits to the **aviary**, **orchid garden** and **butterfly museum** and the bizarre **Nan Myint Tower**.

National Landmarks Garden   MUSEUM
(adult/child US$4/2; ⊙8am-6pm) This extensive hilly park is dotted with representations of famous landmarks from around Myanmar. Some are pretty tacky. There is also an **amusement park** just to the north; one ticket gets you into both sites.

Central Market   MARKET
(Zeigyo Rd; ⊙6.30am-5.30pm) Sample Pyin Oo Lwin's famous (if seasonal) strawberries and other fruit – fresh, dried, or as jams and wine. Also has cheap Western clothes and *longyi* (Burmese-style sarong). There are tailors on the 1st floor if you need alterations or something knocked up.

Purcell Tower   LANDMARK
Marking the town centre, this 1936 clock tower thinks it's Big Ben, judging by its hourly chimes.

⌁ Sleeping & Eating

Many of Pin Oo Lwin's cheaper hotels aren't licensed to accommodate foreigners. Those listed here are all in, or within walking distance of the town centre, and

WORTH A TRIP

ANISAKAN FALLS

About 1½ miles north of Anisakan village (5½ miles south of Pyin Oo Lwin), the plateau disappears into an impressively deep wooded amphitheatre, its sides ribboned with the Anisakan Falls (အနီ္စခန်းရေတံခွန်).

To get here from Pyin Oo Lwin, take the main Mandalay highway. In Anisakan town take the second asphalted turn right (signposted) and keep right past the first large pagoda. At the end of this road a pair of basic shack-restaurants mark the start of a forest trail along which the falls' base is reached by a 45-minute trek. Sales-kids act as guide (K1000) and can prove helpful, especially if taking the 'alternative' route back (very steep, almost a climb).

include breakfast. Decent Shan, Burmese, Chinese and Indian food is available on or just off the main road; eat early or miss out.

Ruby Hotel   HOTEL $
(☎085-21909; rubyhotel@gmail.com; Block 4, 32/B Mingalar St; r US$30; ❋ 🛜) Tucked down a quiet side street, but close to the centre of town, this Muslim-owned newcomer has nice, bright, well-kept rooms with decent bathrooms. Prices drop out of season.

Grace Hotel 2   GUESTHOUSE $
(☎085-22081; 46/48 Mandalay-Lashio Rd; r US$5-20) For the money, the best deal in town. Compact rooms (the cheapest without windows and bathrooms) but the doubles with shower are acceptable.

Grace Hotel 1   GUESTHOUSE $
(☎085-21230; 114A Nan Myaing Rd; s/d/tr US$15/25/36) The high-ceilinged rooms with solid wooden furniture mirror Pyin Oo Lwin's retro colonial vibe. Comfortable beds, obliging staff and a pleasant garden with fading sun-loungers. Bike hire is K2500 a day.

★ Aung Padamyar   INDIAN $
(44, Block 28 Thumingalar; curries K3500; ⊙11am-7pm) The finest Indian in town: a secluded, friendly, family-run joint with a range of curries, all of which come with side dishes

to create a veritable feast. To find it, take the first right off Circular Rd after the Shan Market and then the first left down a small alley. Look for the red sign.

Family Restaurant　　　BURMESE, THAI **$**
(off Mandalay-Lashio Rd; curries from K2800; ⊙9.30am-9pm) The decor is bland and there's no alcohol served, but the delicious curry spread comes with complimentary veggie side dishes, salad, rice, soup, pappadams and chutneys and dips.

❶ Getting There & Away

Yangon buses leave from the inconvenient main bus station Thiri Mandala, 2 miles east of the Shan Market.

All other buses leave from behind the San Pya Restaurant, a quarter of a mile south of the bus station, as do some shared taxis and pick-ups to Mandalay.

Pick-ups to Mandalay leave from near the gas station at the roundabout at the entrance to town, as well as less frequently from outside the train station – north of the town centre.

Shared taxis to Mandalay leave from 4th St.

Trains to Mandalay are much slower and rarely run to schedule.

❶ Getting Around

BICYCLE
Crown Bicycle Rental (Mandalay-Lashio Rd; ⊙7.30am-7pm) rents bicycles (K3000 for 24 hours) and motorbikes (K10,000 for 24 hours).

MOTORCYCLE TAXIS
Easy to find close to the Central Market and the Bravo Hotel. Expect to pay K1500 to National Kandawgyi Gardens. For longer hires, consider engaging English-speaking **Jeffrey** (✆09 4025 10483), who acts as a guide and motorcycle driver. Rates are US$20 for a full day.

THREE-WHEEL PICK-UPS
These congregate outside the market; it costs around K2000 to Kandawgyi Gardens.

WAGON
Pyin Oo Lwin's signature horse-drawn buggies can be found near the Central Market. Reckon on K1500 to K2000 for a short trip across town, K15,000 for an all-day tour.

Hsipaw　　　သီပေါ
✒ 082 / POP 54,000

Travellers come to this laid-back highland town for a couple of days, and before they know it a week has passed. Trekking is the main draw, but Hsipaw is not without charms, including a bustling riverside market, good food and, in season, lively guesthouses.

Guesthouses can arrange guides (K10,000 to K20,000 per day) to take you on fascinating treks into the hills above town, visiting Shan, Palaung and Lisu villages. Mr Charles Guest House is especially well organised.

◉ Sights

Produce Market　　　MARKET
(⊙4.30am-1pm) Most interesting before dawn when the road outside is jammed with hill-villagers selling their wares; all will have cleared away by 7am, though the market continues until 1pm.

Mahamyatmuni Paya　　　BUDDHIST TEMPLE
(Namtu Rd) South of the central area, Mahamyatmuni Paya is the biggest and grandest pagoda in the main town. The large brass-faced Buddha image here was inspired by the famous Mahamuni Buddha in Mandalay. He's now backed by an acid-trip halo of pulsating coloured lights that would seem better suited to a casino.

Myauk Myo　　　NEIGHBOURHOOD
In the north of town Hsipaw's oldest neighbourhood has a village-like atmosphere, two delightful old teak monasteries and a collection of ancient brick stupas known locally as **Little Bagan**. The multifaceted wooden

MYANMAR (BURMA) HSIPAW

TRANSPORT TO/FROM PYIN OO LWIN

DESTINATION	BUS	SHARED TAXI	PICK-UP TRUCKS	TRAIN
Mandalay	K2000, 7am & 8am, 2hr	back/front seat K6000/7000, frequent, 2hr	K2000, frequent to 6pm, 2-3hr	ordinary/1st/upper class US$4/8/9, 1 daily 5.40pm, 6hr
Hsipaw	K5000, air-con 7.30am & 4pm, 3hr	N/A	N/A	US$3/5/6, daily at 8.22am, 7hr
Yangon	K11500, frequent 5.30am-6pm, 11hr	N/A	N/A	N/A

TRANSPORT TO/FROM HSIPAW

DESTINATION	BUS	MINIBUS	SHARED TAXI	TRAIN
Mandalay	K4500-6000, 5.30am, 7am, 8am, 10am, 7pm & 8pm daily, 5½hr	K8000, 7am & 9am daily, 5hr	back/front seat K12000/14000, whole car K50000	ordinary/1st/upper class US$4/8/9, 9.40am daily, 13hr
Pyin Oo Lwin	K5000, 7pm & 8pm daily, 3hr	N/A	N/A	US$3/5/6, 9.40am daily, 7hr
Yangon	K14,500-16,500, 7 daily, 15hr	N/A	N/A	N/A
Taungyi	K15000, 3.30pm daily, 12hr	N/A	N/A	N/A

Madahya Monastery looks especially impressive when viewed from across the palm-shaded pond of the Bamboo Buddha Monastery (Maha Nanda Kantha).

Sunset Hill   VIEWPOINT
For sweeping views across the river and Hsipaw, climb to Thein Daung Pagoda, also known as Five Buddha Hill or, most popularly, Sunset Hill. It's part of a steep ridge that rises directly behind the Lashio road, around 1½ miles south of Hsipaw.

🛏 Sleeping & Eating

The market stalls offer Hsipaw's best cheap eats.

★ Mr Charles Guest House   HOTEL $
(📞 082-80105; www.mrcharleshotel.com; 105 Auba St; dm US$7, r US$9-55; ❄ 🛜) Still the most efficient, comfortable and traveller-friendly guesthouse in town, the ever-expanding Mr Charles operation encompasses everything from simple mattresses on the floor in the dorms, to swish suites with heating and air-con. Expect to pay US$16 to US$22 for a room with its own bathroom, but book ahead in peak periods.

Lily Guesthouse   GUESTHOUSE $
(📞 082-80318; namkhaemaoguesthouse@gmail.com; 108 Aung Tha Pyay Rd; s/d with shared bathroom US$10/15, d US$30-35; ❄ @ 🛜) Rooms here are bright, spacious and clean and the staff obliging. Treks can be organised and there's bike hire (K2000 per day).

San   SHAN, CHINESE $
(Namtu Rd; mains from K1500, barbecue from K200; ⏲ 8am-11pm) With its retro interior and small terrace, San is popular with travellers who come for the many barbecue options and the Chinese-style mains. Dali beer from China is K800.

Law Chun   CHINESE $
(Mr Food; Namtu Rd; mains from K1000; ⏲ 7am-9pm) With Chinese dishes for Burmese and Western palates (so light on the spices), 'Mr Food' stands out from the pack thanks to its bright and breezy interior. There's Dagon beer on tap.

ⓘ Information

A remarkable source of local information is Ko Zaw Tun (aka Mr Book), who runs a small bookstall (Namtu Rd; ⏲ 7am-8.15pm) opposite the entrance to the Central Pagoda.
City Net (Auba St; per hr K500; ⏲ 8.30am-11pm) The only reliable internet cafe in town. The connection is best in the morning.

ⓘ Getting There & Away

Buses and minibuses leave from a variety of locations: the two Khaing Dhabyay bus stands on the Mandalay–Lashio road close to Mr Kid's Guesthouse, from the Yee Shin Guesthouse and the Duhtawadi Cafe on Lammataw St opposite the market.
    Hsipaw's tiny train station is across the tracks from the end of Thirimingalar St.

BAGAN & AROUND

Bagan   ပုဂံ
📞 061
The Bagan Archaeological Zone stretches 26 sq miles across central Myanmar. Despite centuries of neglect, looting, erosion, regular earthquakes (including a massive one in 1975) not to mention dodgy restoration, this temple-studded plain remains a remarkably impressive and unforgettable vision.

In a 230-year building frenzy up until 1287 and the Mongol invasions, Bagan's kings commissioned more than 4000 Buddhist temples. These brick-and-stucco religious structures are all that remain of their grand city, since the wooden 11th- to 13th-century buildings have long gone.

Many restoration projects have resulted in a compromised archaeological site that can barely be described as ruined. Still, Bagan remains a wonder. Working temples such as Ananda Pahto give a sense of what the place was like at its zenith, while others conceal colourful murals and hidden stairways that lead to exterior platforms and jaw-dropping views across the plain.

◉ Sights

Plan your daily temple viewing around a dawn/dusk visit, building in a leisurely lunch/siesta/poolside-lounging period from around 12.30pm to 4pm. Temperatures at dawn/dusk will be more pleasant and the light is better for photographs.

All foreign visitors to the Bagan Archaeological Zone are required to pay a US$15 entrance fee. If you arrive by boat or air, the fee will be collected at the river jetty or airport. Visitors are issued with a credit-card-sized plastic ticket embossed with a number and it is necessary to show this when checking into a hotel or guesthouse. The fee covers a one-week visit, but it's unlikely you'll be asked to pay again if you stay longer.

TOP TEMPLES
. . . .

Ananda Pahto One of the best-preserved and most revered of all the Bagan temples.

Dhammayangyi Pahto An absolute colossus, this red-brick temple is visible from all over Bagan.

Sulamani Pahto This late-period beauty is known as Crowning Jewel, and with good reason.

Pyathada Paya Super sunset (or sunrise) spot and typically less crowded.

Thatbyinnyu Pahto Named for omniscience, this is Bagan's highest temple.

◉ Old Bagan ပုဂံမြို့ဟောင်း

At just over 1 mile, this circuit within the old city walls is manageable on foot or by bicycle.

North of the **Archaeological Museum** (ကျောက်စာသမိုင်းပြတိုက်; Map p524; Bagan-Nyaung U Rd; admission K5000, child under 10yr free; ◉9am-4.30pm Tue-Sun), the 197ft-tall **Gawdawpalin Pahto** (ဂေါ်တော်ပလ္လင်ပုထိုး; Map p524) ᴿᴱᴱ is one of Bagan's most imposing temples. About 220yd north of here, a dirt road leads past **Mimalaung Kyaung** (မီးမလောင်ကျောင်း; Map p524) – note the *chinthe,* a half-lion, half-guardian deity – and the only remaining Hindu temple at Bagan, **Nathlaung Kyaung** (နတ်လှောင်ကျောင်း; Map p524) to the 207ft-tall **Thatbyinnyu Pahto** (သဗ္ဗညုပုထိုး; Map p524). Built in 1144, it has a square base, surrounded by diminishing terraces, rimmed with spires.

Another 220yd north of Thatbyinnyu is **Shwegugyi** (ရွှေဂူကြီး; Map p524), a temple dating from 1131 with lotus *sikhara* (Indian-style temple finial) atop and stucco carvings inside. Back on the main Nyaung U–Old Bagan Rd continue to the 9th-century **Tharabar Gate** (သရဖါတံခါး; Map p524), the former eastern entry to the walled city.

◉ North Plain

Roughly 490yd east of Thatbyinnyu, the 170ft-high **Ananda Pahto** (အာနန္ဒာပုထိုး; Map p524), with its golden *sikhara* top and gilded spires, is probably Bagan's top draw. Finished in 1105, the temple has giant teak Buddha images facing each of the four entranceways. On the full moon of the month of Pyatho (between mid-December and mid-January), a three-day *paya* festival attracts thousands of pilgrims.

Just northwest is **Ananda Ok Kyaung** (အာနန္ဒာအုတ်ကျောင်း; Map p524), with colourful murals detailing 18th-century life, some showing Portuguese traders. No photos allowed.

Midway between Old Bagan and Nyaung U, **Upali Thein** (ဥပါလိသိမ်; Map p524) features large, brightly painted murals from the early 18th century. Across the road, the location for the terraced 490ft-high **Htilominlo Pahto** (ထီးလိုမင်းလိုပုထိုး; Map p524) was picked in 1218 by King Nantaungmya. Just south of Anawrahta Rd, **Buledi** (ဗူးလယ်သိုး; Map p524) is a good sunrise/sunset viewing spot and useful for getting your bearings.

Bagan

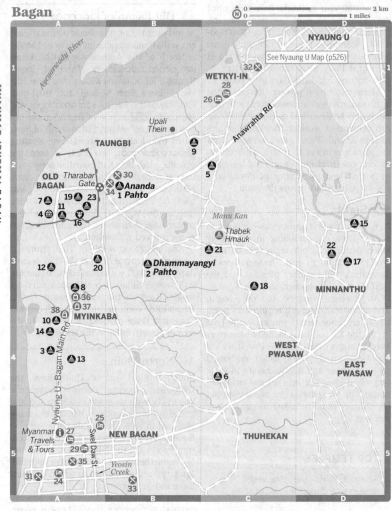

See Nyaung U Map (p526)

NYAUNG U

WETKYI-IN

TAUNGBI

Upali Thein

OLD BAGAN

Tharabar Gate

Ananda Pahto

Anawrahta Rd

Manu Kan

Thabek Hmauk

Dhammayangyi Pahto

MINNANTHU

MYINKABA

Nyaung U–Bagan Main Rd

WEST PWASAW

EAST PWASAW

Myanmar Travels & Tours

Swe Daw St

NEW BAGAN

THUHEKAN

Yeosin Creek

Central Plain

South of Anawrahta Rd, the 11th-century, five-terraced **Shwesandaw Paya** (ရွှေဆံတော်ဘုရား; Map p524) is a graceful white pyramid-style pagoda with 360-degree views of Bagan's temples. It's packed for sunset, but pretty empty during the day. Note the original *hti* (decorated top of a stupa) lying to the south – it was toppled by a 1975 earthquake.

About 550yd east, monumental **Dhammayangyi Pahto** (ဓမ္မရံကြီးပုထိုး; Map p524) has two encircling passageways, the inner one of which has been intentionally filled. It's said that King Narathu, who commissioned the temple, was so cruel that the workers ruined it after his assassination in 1170.

About 880yd east, the broad two-storeyed 1181 **Sulamani Pahto** (စူဠာမဏိပုထိုး; Map p524) is one of the area's prettiest temples, with lush grounds and carved stucco. Just 165yd east, **Thabeik Hmauk** (သပိတ်မှောက်) looks like a mini Sulamani, but without the hawkers – *and* you can climb to the top. And at sunset, don't miss the broad viewing platform at **Pyathada Paya** (ပြဿဒါးဘုရား; Map p524), about half a mile southeast.

Bagan

◎ Around Myinkaba

Just north of Myinkaba, the 1274 **Mingalazedi Paya** (မင်္ဂလာစေတီဘုရား; Map p524) has three receding terraces lined with 561 glazed tiles and tasty views of the nearby river and temples.

On the north edge of town, the 1113 **Gubyaukgyi** (ဂူပြောက်ကြီး; Map p524) sees a lot of visitors thanks to its richly coloured interior paintings. In the village, the modern-looking 1059 **Manuha Paya** (မနူဟာဘုရား; Map p524) was named for the Mon king who was held captive here. Note the four giant Buddha images that are seemingly too large for the enclosure, symbolic of Manuha's discontent with his prison life. Stairs at the rear lead above the reclining Buddha.

Just south, **Nan Paya** (နန်းဘုရား; Map p524), from the same era, is a cave-style shrine; Nan Paya was possibly once Hindu, as suggested by the three-faced Brahma situated on the pillars.

About 550yd south of Myinkaba, the 11th-century **Abeyadana Pahto** (အပါယ်ရတနာပုထိုး; Map p524) was likely to have been commissioned by King Kyanzittha's Bengali wife and features original frescoes. Across the road, **Nagayon** (နဂါးရုံ; Map p524) has some tight stairs leading up to the roof. Its corncob *sikhara* (finial) was possibly a prototype for Ananda.

◎ South Plain

About 1¾ miles east of New Bagan, the 1196 **Dhammayazika Paya** (ဓမ္မရာဇိကဘုရား; Map p524) is unusual for its five-sided design. It's very well tended with lush grounds and lavish attention from worshippers. A dirt road leads a mile north to Dhammayangyi.

An excellent cluster of sites is about 2 miles east. North of the road, **Tayok Pye Paya** (တရုတ်ပြေးဘုရား; Map p524) has good westward views of Bagan. To the south, 13th-century **Payathonzu** (ဘုရားသုံးဆူ; Map p524), a small complex of three interconnected shrines, draws visitors to its murals.

About 220yd north, **Nandamannya Pahto** (နန္ဒပညာပုထိုး; Map p524), from the same period, features the 'temptation of Mura' murals – in the form of topless women reaping no response from a meditating Buddha. It's often locked; ask at Payathonzu for the 'key master'. Just behind, **Kyat Kan Kyaung** (Map p524) has been a cave-style monastery for nearly 1000 years.

Nyaung U

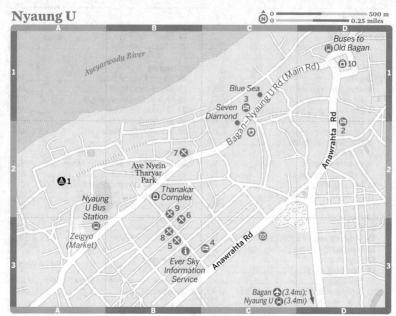

⊙ Nyaung U ညောင်ဦး

The gilded bell of the 1102 **Shwezigon Paya** (ရွှေစည်းခုံဘုရား; Map p526) is considered by many to be the prototype for many Burmese pagodas. A yellow compound on the east side (called '37 Nats' in English) features figures of each of the animist spirits.

🛏 Sleeping

Bagan accommodation can be loosely categorised as: Nyaung U for budget travellers; New Bagan for good-value midrange rooms; and Old Bagan's for top-end hotels for bigger wallets.

🛏 Nyaung U ညောင်ဦး

★**New Wave Guesthouse**   GUESTHOUSE **$**
(Map p524; ☑ 061-60731; Bagan–Nyaung U Rd, Wetkyi-in; r US$25-50; ✳ 🛜) Opened in 2013, and it is to be hoped this place sparks a new wave of smarter guesthouses around Bagan. The attractive rooms include hotel-like touches such as hairdryer and kettle, plus hand-crafted wooden beds. Highly recommended but watch out for rapidly rising prices, as it was very new during our visit.

New Park Hotel   HOTEL **$**
(Map p526; ☑ 061-60322; www.newparkmyan-mar.com; 4 Thiripyitsaya; s US$20-40, d US$25-45; ✳ @ 🛜) One of the best all-round budget hotels. The older rooms, with bungalow-style front decks, are comfortable, wood-floor set-ups, with spic-and-span bathrooms. Rooms in the newer wing bring more space, a fridge, TV and even a rain shower.

Eden Motel   GUESTHOUSE **$**
(Map p526; ☑ 061-60812; Anawrahta Rd; r US$15-25; ✳ 🛜) Spread over three buildings and split in two by the busy road to the airport, Eden isn't exactly paradise. The best rooms are found in the newest Eden Motel III and include flat-screen TV and a well-appointed bathroom with a bathtub. The young staff are quite attuned to backpacker needs.

May Kha Lar Guest House   GUESTHOUSE **$**
(Map p526; ☑ 061-60907; Nyaung U–Bagan Main Rd; s US$13-20, d US$18-28; ✳ 🛜) One of the more appealing budget options on the main road. The reception includes lots of handy traveller info and a shrine room. On the ground floor, the cheap, gaudily tiled rooms are compact, with air-conditioning,

Nyaung U

◎ Sights
1 Shwezigon Paya.....................................A2

🛏 Sleeping
2 Eden Motel..D2
3 May Kha Lar Guest House C1
4 New Park Hotel C3

🍴 Eating
5 Aroma 2..B3
6 Black Bamboo B3
7 San Kabar Restaurant & Pub B2
8 Shwe Ya Su...B3
9 Weather Spoon's Bagan B2

🛍 Shopping
10 Mani-Sithu Market...............................D1

ceiling fan and attached bathroom. Nicer upstairs options have wooden floors and TV. The cheapest singles and doubles share the bathroom.

Winner Guest House   GUESTHOUSE **$**
(Map p524; ☎061-61069; Nyaung U–Bagan Main Rd, Wetkyi-in; s US$9-20, d US$15-23; ❋ 🛜) This little family-run guesthouse on the road to Old Bagan is one of the old-school cheapies. Bargain-basement rooms share the common bathroom. A new wing at the rear includes air-con and private bathrooms. Another advantage is that it is somewhat nearer the temples than the average Nyaung U address.

🏙 New Bagan ပုဂံမြို့သစ်

Yun Myo Thu Motel   GUESTHOUSE **$**
(Map p524; ☎061-65276; 3 Khat Tar St; s/d US$20/30; ❋) Translating rather romantically as 'the lady of lacquer city', this is a typical Burmese guesthouse that sees few foreigners and is consequently pretty good value for money. The well-tended rooms include flat-screen TV, air-con and hot water, but there is little English spoken.

Bagan Central Hotel   HOTEL **$**
(Map p524; ☎061-65057; Khaye St (Main Rd); s/d US$35/40; ❋ 🛜) These stone-clad chalets have an original look compared with other 'budget' places around Bagan. The interior switches to bamboo and the clean rooms include a wooden floor and recently renovated bathrooms. All rooms are set around a tree-shaded courtyard where breakfast is served.

Thiri Marlar Hotel   HOTEL **$**
(Map p524; ☎061-65050; thirimarlar@mptmail. net.mm; r US$35-50; ❋ 🛜) The teak walkways leading to the 15 lovely rooms are wrapped around a small pagoda-style dining room, though most guests eat breakfast on the roof deck with temple views. Spotless standard rooms are rather compact but inviting, with shiny wood floors and small rugs. Superior rooms are much more spacious and worth the extra bucks.

⭐ Kumudara Hotel   HOTEL **$$**
(Map p524; ☎061-65142; www.kumudara-bagan. com; superior s/d US$38/44, junior ste s/d

WORTH A TRIP

MT POPA
....
Considered the spiritual HQ to Myanmar's infamous '37 *nat*', Mt Popa (ပုပ္ပားတောင်) is the premier venue for worship of these pre-Buddhist spirits (see p538) and an easy day trip from Bagan.

A gilded Buddhist temple accessed by 777 steps teeters atop a towerlike 2418ft volcanic plug. The 20-minute climb up goes past devout pilgrims, cheeky monkeys and, occasionally, slow-stepping hermit monks called *yeti*. From the temple there are mammoth views back towards the Myingyan Plain and beyond.

At the foot of the complex, the **Mother Spirit of Popa Nat Shrine** features a display of the 37 *nat*. If you have more time, and a guide, there are tracks up the nearby 4980ft extinct volcano called **Taung Ma-gyi** (Mother Mountain), covered in lush forests protected within the Popa Mountain Park.

A **pick-up** (K3000, two hours) leaves Nyaung U bus station at 8.30am, and returns at 1pm. Far easier is a slot in a **share taxi** (K35,000 to K45,000, split between four passengers). Ask the driver to point out remnants of the petrified forest along the way, and to pause at toddy palm plantations where you can sample the homemade alcohol and jaggery (palm sugar).

US$50/56; P✳@🛜🏊) No hotel boasts better balcony views of the mighty sprawl of red-brick temples than Kumudara. Opt for the chic junior suites and suites in a green geometrical building that fits well with the arid, desert-like setting. Inside, rooms have a mix of wood panelling, modern art and retro-style safe boxes. Kumudara also has a pool and a restaurant.

✖ Eating & Drinking

🍴 Nyaung U ညောင်ဦး

Nyaung U's Yarkinnthar Hotel Rd (aka Restaurant Row) is touristy, but easily the hub(bub) of Bagan action. Many of the restaurants are copycats, with similar 'everything goes' menus (Chinese, Burmese, Thai, Indian, pizza and 'Western' options).

★ Myo Myo Myanmar
Rice Food   BURMESE $
(Map p524; Bagan–Nyaung U Rd; meals K2000-4000; ⊙7am-6pm) Deservedly popular place where the owners specialise in the personalised tabletop buffets that characterise the national cuisine. However, here they really go to town, with 25 dishes or more appearing at the table, including seasonal specials like asparagus.

Aroma 2   INDIAN $
(Map p526; Yarkinnthar Hotel Rd; dishes K2000-8000; ⊙11am-10pm; 🛜) 'No good, no pay' is the mantra of this justifiably confident operation serving delicious veggie and meat curries on banana leaves (or plates) with an endless stream of hot chapattis and five dollops of condiments (including tamarind and mint sauces). With some advance notice, the chef can also whip up various biryani rice dishes.

Weather Spoon's Bagan   INTERNATIONAL $
(Map p526; Yarkinnthar Hotel Rd; mains K2000-5000; ⊙7am-10pm; 🛜) Brits abroad may be familiar with the name, borrowed from one of the UK's discount pub chains. Owner Winton studied balloon piloting in Bristol and clearly spent some time in the local boozers. But Bagan benefits from his experience and he offers the best burger in town, as well as some Asian and international favourites. Lively drinking spot by night.

San Kabar Restaurant & Pub   ITALIAN $
(Map p526; Nyaung U–Bagan Main Rd; pizza K4000-6000, mains K2500-5500; ⊙7am-10pm; 🛜)

Famous as the birthplace of Bagan pizza, the San Kabar's street-side candlelit courtyard is all about its thin-crust pies and well-prepared salads. There is so much variety on offer here that staff present diners with not one, but three menus.

Shwe Ya Su   BEER STATION $
(Map p526; Yarkinnthar Hotel Rd; dishes K1500-4000; ⊙7am-10.30pm) Thanks to the barrels of draught Myanmar Beer, this place has become quite the local hang-out. It's a lively spot to revive with twinkling fairy lights hanging from the trees and tasty barbecued snacks.

★ Black Bamboo   EUROPEAN $$
(Map p526; ☑061-60782; off Yarkinnthar Hotel Rd; dishes K3500-7000; ⊙9am-10pm; 🛜) Run by a French woman and her Burmese husband, this garden cafe and restaurant is something of an oasis. It's a lovely place to relax over a decent steak-frites, a well-made espresso or a delicious homemade ice cream. Service is friendly but leisurely.

🍴 Old Bagan ပုဂံမြို့ဟောင်း

Save yourself the schlep back to Nyaung U by having lunch in Old Bagan.

★ Starbeam Bistro   INTERNATIONAL $
(Map p524; mains K3500-7000; ⊙7am-10pm) Located close to Ananda Pahto, this garden bistro was set up by chef Tin Myint who spent several years working with the Orient-Express hotel group. Dishes include Rakhine fish curry, market-fresh specials, traditional salads like avocado or tea leaf, and classic baguettes and sandwiches. Best washed down with a healthy blend of fresh juice.

Be Kind to Animals the Moon   VEGETARIAN $
(Map p524; off Bagan–Nyaung U Rd; mains K1500-4000; ⊙7am-10pm; ☑) The original among the couple of vegetarian restaurants clustered near Tharabar Gate, this place offers a friendly welcome and delicious food including pumpkin and ginger soup, aubergine curry and a lime and ginger tea that the owners claim is good for stomach upsets.

Sarahba III/Gyi Gyi's   VEGETARIAN, BURMESE $
(Map p524; off Bagan–Nyaung U Rd; mains K500-2000; ⊙6am-6pm) Join the crowds under a shady tree near Tharabar Gate squatting on low chairs at green-painted tables and tucking into some of Bagan's best tucker, all freshly prepared and supremely tasty.

There's no sign and the name refers to what locals jokingly call the place (after owner Gyi Gyi).

Scoopy's ICE CREAM $

(Map p524; off Bagan–Nyaung U Rd; mains from K500-2500; ⊙11am-6pm) Run by the French-Burmese owners of the Black Bamboo in Nyaung U, this relaxed cafe and ice-cream parlour is something of a godsend. Toasted sandwiches, homemade muffins and treats such as Western chocolate bars are available, all great for picnic snacks while touring the temples.

✕ New Bagan ပုဂံမြို့သစ်

Naratheinkha Restaurant FRENCH, INTERNATIONAL $

(Map p524; ✆09-5242420; New Bagan; K1500-5500) Blink and you'll miss this tiny little shopfront restauran, it is well-regarded thanks to the chef-owner's extensive experience at Le Planteur Restaurant in Yangon. The menu is predominantly French influenced or Asian fusion and includes a delicious pan-fried fish with lemon butter sauce.

Mother's House BURMESE $

(Map p524; Chauk Rd; K500-1500; ⊙7am-9pm) A tiny place on the Chauk Rd, this is the place to come and sample a traditional Burmese breakfast before exploring the temples, or after catching sunrise somewhere near New Bagan. Try Shan noodles or deep-fried doughnuts.

Silver House BURMESE, ASIAN $

(Map p524; Khaye St (Main Rd); mains K2000-6000; ⊙7am-10pm) A welcoming family-run restaurant that offers large, tasty portions of dishes such as traditional Myanmar chicken curry and tomato salad.

OFF THE BEATEN TRACK

CRUISING THE UPPER AYEYARWADY

Drifting down the Ayeyarwady, past friendly villagers for whom the river and its traffic are a lifeline to the outside world, is a memorable experience but one you will need to set aside a chunk of time for – the journey is quicker travelling downstream.

SInce 2012, foreign travellers have been banned from arriving or leaving the Kachin State capital of **Myitkyina** by boat – you can fly there or take the train; for more details see Lonely Planet's *Myanmar (Burma)* guide.

An alternative start point is **Bhamo**, which has a bustling daily market, drawing Lisu, Kachin and Shan folk from surrounding villages. Worth searching out is the awesome **bamboo bridge** (return toll with bicycle K300), near the **Shwe Kyina Pagoda**, 3 miles north of Bhamo, that allows you to make your precarious way across the wide Tapin River. Bhamo's **Friendship Hotel** (✆074-50095, in China 0086-692 687 6670; Letwet Thondaya Rd; s/d/tr US$25/30/40, with shared bathroom US$10/20/30; ❄@) is one of the better provincial pads, with good-value rooms and an English-speaking manager.

IWT ferries leave from a jetty 2½ miles south of Bhamo. Fast boats leave from a pier on the central riverfront. The airport is a 10-minute ride from the centre of town.

Between Bhamo and **Shwegu**, the scenery reaches a modest climax in the short second defile where the Ayeyarwady passes through a wooded valley with a rocky cliff face at one section (often described misleadingly as a gorge).

The next major stop is the sleepy town of **Katha**, where fans of George Orwell's *Burmese Days* will enjoy foraging around. Eric Blair (Orwell's real name) was stationed here in 1926–27 and based his novel on this setting. Several Orwell-related buildings that featured in the book are still standing but none are marked as such and none are commercialised tourist attractions, so ask politely before trying to barge in.

The best of Katha's three accommodation options is **Eden Guesthouse** (✆074-25429; Shwe Phone Shein St; r US$20; ❄🠶) which is the only spot in town with wi-fi.

IWT ferry tickets are only available an hour before departure and can be bought from opposite the main jetty. Buy tickets for the Katha–Mandalay express boat a day before departure from the office on the riverfront.

At **Naba**, 16 miles west of Katha, there's a train station on the Mandalay–Myitkyina line. A daily train connects Katha and Naba (US$2, 2pm), while there are two afternoon buses to Naba (K1000, 2pm and 5pm).

Shopping

Bagan is the lacquerware capital of Myanmar. Head to Myinkaba, where several family-run workshops produce high-quality traditional pieces – look for earthy colours.

Art Gallery of Bagan LACQUERWARE
(Map p524) English-speaking Maung Aung Myin has two rooms and a busy workshop on the road 200yd north of Mahamuni. Apart from the full range of lacquerware, including some beautiful and pricey cabinets and casks, there are also antique and new puppets (US$20 to US$150).

Family Lacquerware Workshop LACQUERWARE
(Map p524) At this smaller workshop off the east side of the road, there are some contemporary styles using alternative colours such as blue and yellow with fewer layers of lacquer.

Golden Cuckoo LACQUERWARE
(Map p524) Just behind the Manuha Paya, this family-run workshop spans four generations and focuses on 'traditional' designs, which are applied to some unusual objects, including a motorbike helmet (US$250) and a guitar (US$500).

Mani-Sithu Market MARKET
(Map p526; ⊙ 6am-5pm Mon-Sat) Near the roundabout at the east end of the main road, this market offers a colourful display of fruit, vegetables, flowers, fish and textiles and is best visited early in the day to see it at its liveliest. There are plenty of traveller-oriented goods (woodcarvings, T-shirts, lacquerware) at its northern end.

❶ Orientation

Bounded by the Ayeyarwady on its northern and western flanks, Bagan is a vast plain dotted with settlements. Most independent travellers stay in Nyaung U, home to the bus station and 3 miles northwest of the airport and train station. Old Bagan, about 2½ miles southwest and atmospherically located amid the bulk of the temples, is an enclave of expensive hotels. Between here and New Bagan, about 2 miles further south, is the village of Myinkaba. Well-paved roads connect these centres, crisscrossed by dirt trails leading to the temples.

In Nyaung U, 'Main Rd' is used (locally and in text) to refer to the main strip, which runs along the north–south Bagan–Nyaung U Rd, and along the Anawrahta Rd from the market to the Sapada Paya. Just east of the bus station is Yarkinnthar

Hotel Rd, more popularly known as 'restaurant row', with lots of eating options.

❶ Information

Nyaung U is home to most traveller life-support systems, including a post office, several internet cafes and pricey international calls.

Ever Sky Information Service (Map p526; ☑ 061-60895; Yarkinnthar Hotel Rd; ⊙ 7.30am-9.30pm) On the restaurant strip, this friendly place has travel and transport information and a secondhand bookshop. Staff can get share taxis (to Mt Popa, Kalaw, Salay, around Bagan) for the best available rates.

Internet (Thanakar Complex, Yarkinnthar Hotel Rd; ⊙ 9am-9pm)

❶ Getting There & Away

Most travel services operate from Nyaung U. Ask at Ever Sky Information Service or your guesthouse about air tickets or hiring a share taxi. A charter to Inle Lake is about US$170, Mandalay US$80.

AIR

Nyaung U Airport is about 2 miles southeast of the market. Travel agencies sometimes have cheaper tickets than the airline offices. Try **Seven Diamond** (Map p526; ☑ 061-60883; on Nyaung U–Bagan Main Rd.

BOAT

Boats to Mandalay go from either Nyaung U or Old Bagan, depending on water levels. The Nyaung U jetty is about half a mile northeast of the market.

The government-run IWT ferry (aka 'slow boat') heads to Mandalay on Monday and Thursday at 5am (US$15, two days) and overnights near Pakokku. At the time of writing there were no southbound passenger ferries operating to Magwe or Pyay. If open (unlikely!), the IWT office, about 275yd inland from the jetty, sells tickets. Alternatively book a ticket through your hotel or one of the travel agencies listed earlier, which can also secure tickets for the faster **Malikha 2** (US$35, 11 hours) or **N Mai Hka** (Shwe Keinerry; US$35, 12 hours) boats to Mandalay.

BUS

Bagan's main bus station is on the main road in Nyaung U. During peak season, it's wise to book bus tickets for Mandalay, Taunggyi (for Inle Lake) and Yangon a couple of days in advance.

TRAIN

The Bagan train station is about 2½ miles southeast of Nyaung U. The shop **Blue Sea** (Map p526; ☑ 061-60949; Main Rd) sells tickets for a K20,000 commission.

TRANSPORT TO/FROM BAGAN

TO/FROM YANGON	COST	DURATION	FREQUENCY
Air	US$100-110	70min	frequent
Bus	K13,000-18,000	10hr	frequent
Car	K150,000	9hr	charter
Train	US$30-50	16hr	daily

TO/FROM MANDALAY	COST	DURATION	FREQUENCY
Air	US$50-55	30min	frequent
Boat (slow)	US$15	2 days	2 weekly
Boat (fast)	US$35	11hr	daily in high season
Bus	K7500-9000	7hr	frequent
Car	K130,000	6hr	charter
Train	US$4-10	8hr	daily

❶ Getting Around

BICYCLES
Daily rental ranges from K2000 to K5000 depending on the condition of the bike. Carry water when you cycle though, as some temples don't have vendors.

HORSE CART
Uncomfortable and slow but you do get some shade from the canopy and the drivers do know the temples. It's K15,000 to K20,000 for the whole day, but there is only really sufficient space for two people.

PICK-UP
Between Nyaung U, Old Bagan and New Bagan, pick-ups (K500, hourly 7am to 3pm) run along the main street, starting from the roundabout outside the Nyaung U market.

TAXI
Costs about US$35 for the day. Taxis between Nyaung U and New Bagan cost about K7000, or K15,000 return. From the airport to Nyaung U/New Bagan is K5000/7000.

Monywa

🗸 071 / POP 180,000

With a pleasant Chindwin riverside setting, this engaging town is a sensible stopping point if you're looping between Mandalay and Bagan. The main sights are out of town.

About 6 miles south, **Thanboddhay Paya** (admission US$3; ⊙6am-5pm) bursts with carnival shades of pink, orange, yellow and blue. Inside are more than half a million Buddhas filling nooks and crannies.

About 5 miles east of the *paya* is **Bodhi Tataung**, a Buddha frenzy in the foothills,

including **Laykyun Setkyar**, at 424ft, the world's second-tallest standing Buddha. The easiest way to visit is by taxi.

Across the Chindwin River and 15 miles west, the 492 **Hpo Win Daung Caves** (admission US$2) were carved into a limestone hillside between the 14th and 18th centuries. Many of the 'caves' are just big enough for a single Buddha image but a few of the best (notably caves 478 and 480) have retained some colourfully well-executed murals. To get here, rent a chauffeured motorbike in Monywa for the day (around K10,000) and catch a boat from the Monywa jetty (one way K3000 for up to five people).

🛏 Sleeping & Eating

Shwe Taung Tarn　　　　　GUESTHOUSE $
(🗹071-21478; 70 Station Rd; s US$13-20, d US$20-27; ✸) The facade looks unkempt, but better rooms behind a pair of newer two-storey buildings amid an unexpectedly pleasant little garden area. While rooms were once relatively stylish, many now suffer seriously scuffed floors and gob-stained walls. There's also a restaurant, with a chic rooftop dining area, serving Chinese food.

Monywa Hotel　　　　　　HOTEL $
(🗹071-21581; monywahotel@goldenland.com.mm; Bogyoke Rd; s US$30-35, d US$35-40; ✸) Set well back from the busy street amid birdsong and creeper-draped trees, are these well-maintained, good-value series of multiroom cabins. Interiors are definitely dated and the colour schemes are hideous, but even the cheaper rooms are fair-sized with effective air-conditioning, desk,

GETTING TO CHINA: MU-SE TO RUILI

The Mu-se/Ruili (Shweli) border crossing between is nominally open to travellers. However, getting to Mu-se requires a permit that will take at least two weeks to be issued and even then is only available if you book a package including car, driver and guide through Myanmar Travels & Tours (MTT) in Yangon or Mandalay. This will cost around US$200 from Lashio where your guide will collect you at a pre-designated hotel.

You'll need to have your Chinese visa already. In reverse you'll need to organise things through a travel agency in Kunming where there's also a Myanmar consulate.

Permits are also required for the appallingly rough Mu-se–Namhkam–Bhamo road. MTT Mandalay can fix things and provide a Lashio–Bhamo vehicle for US$350/370/390 (one/two/three passengers) but again you'll need at least two weeks prep time. It might take much longer.

fridge, piping-hot showers, satellite TV and comfy beds.

❶ Getting There & Away

The bus station is just over a mile southeast of the clock tower down Bogyoke St.

Several companies operate hourly buses 5am to 4pm to **Mandalay** (K2000/3000 without/with air-con, three hours). There are also regular buses to **Pakokku** (K2500, three hours) with onward connections to Bagan available there, taking an extra hour. Aung Gabar Express operates a direct service to Bagan (K3500) departing at 7.30am.

The **train** to Mandalay departs at 6am (US$3, six hours), but it takes twice as long as the bus in an uncomfortable box car.

WESTERN MYANMAR

Even as more of Myanmar's remote areas become 'open' and tourist numbers increase, Rakhine State remains staunchly untouristed.

Adventurous travellers should aim for the scrappy, atmospheric capital Sittwe and the old capital of Mrauk U, an amazing archaeological site, studded with hundreds of temples.

Sittwe စစ်တွေ

♩ 043 / POP 200,000

For most people, a trip to Mrauk U will include a stay in Sittwe, a port town where the wide Kaladan River meets the Bay of Bengal. The British moved the regional capital here from Mrauk U in the 1820s and called it Aykab.

Sittwe has seen better days and sectarian violence in 2012 means that most visitors are not encouraged to linger. When we were in town, Sittwe's former Muslim quarter, virtually empty, was strictly off limits, and like the town's oldest mosque, was protected by armed guards. A loosely enforced 10pm to 5am curfew was also in place. This said, there are a few sights of note.

◉ Sights

Central Market   MARKET

(မြို့ ဈေး; Strand Rd; ⊙6am-6pm) Focussed on the 1956 municipal market building, there's lots going on here from dawn to noon and beyond – it's well worth popping by before your boat or plane leaves. Head straight past *longyi* (sarong), fishing net and vegetable stands to the fish and meat area, where stingrays and gutted eels and drying sharks make quite a scene. In the bay, small boats jostle for space to unload their catch.

View Point   LANDMARK

(စစ်တွေ ချူးပွိုင့်; Strand Rd) FREE The riverside Strand Rd leads about 1½ miles south to a smashing location called the View Point, where you can sip on a beer or eat at the somewhat overpriced **Point Restaurant** (Strand Rd; mains K1000-6000; ⊙9am-9pm) as the sun sets over the Bay of Bengal. Just west, in front of a closed naval base, is **Sittwe Beach**, a broad, grey-brown strip of sand.

It would make a long but pleasant walk, otherwise auto rickshaws, known locally as *thoun bein*, will take you there and back for 5000K, taxis for 10,000K.

Lokananda Paya   BUDDHIST TEMPLE

(လောကနန္ဒာဘုရား; May Yu St; ⊙daylight hours) You can't miss this big golden pagoda between the airport and the centre. Its gilded, cavernous worship hall held aloft by decorated pillars is pretty spectacular.

Rakhine State Cultural Museum   MUSEUM
(ရခိုင်ပြည်နယ်ယဉ်ကျေးမှုပြတိုက်; Main Rd; admission K2000; ⊙9.30am-4.30pm Tue-Sat) This museum features two floors of Rakhine cultural goodies that benefit from just barely enough English subtitles.

🛏 Sleeping & Eating

Mya Guest House   HOTEL $
(☑043-23315, 043-22358; 51/6 Bowdhi Rd; s/d US$20/30) Tucked just off Sittwe's busy main road, this basic cement building has simple, spacious rooms with fans and private bathrooms (no hot water).

Prince Guest House   GUESTHOUSE $
(☑043-22539; 27 Main Rd; r with shared bathroom US$7-15) Rather dingy rooms (small, with a fan and a mosquito net and coil) with shared bathrooms. Check a few rooms before choosing – some are better than others.

★Aung   BURMESE $
(no roman-script sign; off Thar Bar St; mains from K2500; ⊙10am-9pm) Located on a small street directly behind the museum, this place does Burmese-style set meals with an emphasis on Rakhine-style spice and tartness. You could work from the English-language menu, but pointing to whatever looks tastiest is a better strategy.

Móun·di Stand   BURMESE $
(May Yu St; mains K200; ⊙6am-6pm) *Móun·di*, thin rice noodles in a peppery, fish-based broth, is Rakhine State's signature noodle dish. Many claim Sittwe's best is served at this stall (look for the green awning) facing the city hall.

Mya Teahouse   TEAHOUSE $
(51/6 Bowdhi Rd; mains from K200; ⊙6am-5pm) Sit on bright-blue plastic chairs under shady trees amid the potted plants and flowers at this delightful teahouse. Good for a breakfast of fried rice or *mohinga,* too.

ℹ Information

KISS (Main Rd; per hr K500; ⊙noon-9pm) Internet cafe with plenty of terminals.

ℹ Getting There & Away

Overland routes between Sittwe, Yangon and Mrauk U are closed to foreigners. The airport is about 1½ miles southwest of the town centre; the main boat jetty is about 1¾ miles north.

Note that schedules change from season to season and from year to year, so double-check everything well in advance.

AIR

In peak season flights connect Sittwe with Yangon (US$120 to US$146, one hour 15 minutes) and Thandwe (US$80 to US$110, 45 minutes). During the rainy season (from July to October), schedules can drop to one or two times a week.

The airport is about 1½ miles southwest of the centre. *Thoun bein* (K3000 to K4000) and taxis (K6000 to K7000) await flights.

BOAT

For Mrauk U slow **IWT ferries** depart Sittwe Tuesday and Friday at 8am, and return on Wednesday and Saturday at 8am (US$5, four to seven hours). There's also a private ferry service leaving Sittwe on Monday, Thursday and Sunday at 7am, and returning on Tuesday, Friday and Sunday at 7am (US$15, four to seven hours).

Slightly faster is a chartered **private boat** (K150,000, four to seven hours). Generally a boat can fit four to six people, with a driver who will wait with the boat for two or three nights.

By far the fastest option are the 'speedboats' run by **Shwe Pyi Tan** (no roman-script sign; ☑09 4959 2709; cnr Main Rd & U Ottama St;

SITTWE BY LAND & SEA

It is possible to access Sittwe without flying by using the following route. From **Pyay** catch the 5pm minibus for **Taunggok** (K11,000, 11 hours). Here connect with boats run by either **Shwe Pyi Tan** (☑043-65130, in Taunggok 043-60704) with departures at 6.30am on Monday, Tuesday and Friday (US$35, 10 to 11 hours); or **Malikha Travels** (☑in Taunggok 043-60127), leaving at 6.30am on Monday, Wednesday and Saturday (US$30, 10 to 11 hours).

Leaving from Sittwe, Shwe Pyi Tan has departures on Tuesday, Wednesday, Saturday and Sunday at 6am; Malikha Travels on Monday, Thursday and Saturday at 6am.

Should you need to sleep over in Taunggok, **Royal Guest House** (no roman-script sign; ☑043-61088; r US$7-20), near the bus station, is licensed for foreigners.

MYANMAR (BURMA) SITTWE

⏲7am-9pm), leaving Sittwe on Wednesday and Sunday at 7am, and from Mrauk U on Monday and Thursday at 7am (US$20, two hours).

Mrauk U မြောက်ဦး

☎ 043 / POP 50,000

'Little Bagan'? Not by a long shot. Mrauk U (pronounced 'mraw-oo') was the Rakhine capital from 1430 to 1826, during which time hundreds of temples were built. Unlike in Bagan, goat shepherds and vegetable farmers live around the ruins and still-functioning temples sited amid gorgeous lush scenery of rounded hillocks. Think laid-back smiles, no hassle, almost no motorised transport and very few tourists.

Internet is available at the Mrauk U Princess hotel (US$4 per hour).

Sights

The original site of Mrauk U is spread over 17½ sq miles, though the town today and the bulk of the 700 or so temples to visit cover a 2.7-sq-mile area. With a bike, a packed lunch and the heart for exploration, you could take any path for DIY adventures.

The sights are not always marked so an experienced guide can come in handy. Not only do many of the guides in the **Regional Guides Society – Mrauk U** (☎ 09 4217 20168, 09 4217 20296; www.facebook.com/rgs.mrauku; per day US$20) speak English well and have a good grasp on local history and culture, but they're also locally based, work independently and are dedicated to the principles of community-based tourism.

For foreign visitors to Mrauk U there's an archaeological site 'entry fee' of K500; this is usually collected at the Shittaung Paya or at the boat jetty; on the government ferry you'll be asked to show proof of payment before leaving.

★Shittaung Paya BUDDHIST TEMPLE
(ရှစ်သောင်းဘုရား; admission K5000; ⏲7am-5pm) The usual starting point is at this, Mrauk U's most complex temple. Shittaung means 'Shrine of the 80,000 Images', a reference to the number of holy images inside. King Minbin, the most powerful of Rakhine's kings, built Shittaung in 1535. It's a frenzy of stupas of various sizes; some 26 surround a central stupa. Thick walls, with windows and nooks, surround the two-tiered structure, which has been highly reconstructed over the centuries – in some places, rather clumsily.

Just north is the sublime 16th-century **Andaw Paya** (အံ့တော်ဘုရား; ⏲daylight hours) FREE and beyond is the **Ratanabon Paya** (ရတနာပုံဘုရား; ⏲daylight hours) FREE, a stupa dating from 1612 that survived a WWII bomb.

★Dukkanthein Paya BUDDHIST TEMPLE
(ထုက္ခံသိမ်ဘုရား; ⏲daylight hours) FREE Dating from 1571, this bunker-like pagoda features an interior of spiralling cloisters lined with images of Buddhas and common people (such as landlords, governors, officials and their spouses) sporting all of Mrauk U's 64 traditional hairstyles. The passageway nearly encircles the centre three times before reaching the sun-drenched Buddha image.

★Mahabodhi Shwegu BUDDHIST TEMPLE
(မဟာဗောဓိရွှေဂူ; ⏲daylight hours) FREE The highlight of this squat, little-visited temple is its passageway with bas-relief illustrations of the *tribumi* – Buddhist visions of heaven, earth and hell – including acrobats, worshippers and animals. At the end there's a 6ft central Buddha and four Buddhas in niches; the throne of the former includes some erotic carvings.

OFF THE BEATEN TRACK

CHIN VILLAGES

Day boat excursions along the Lemro River to traditional Chin villages can be arranged in Mrauk U. It's a long day, but we found the Chin villagers a hoot – let's just say that having a web pattern tattooed on their faces (a dying cultural practice) has done nothing to diminish the sense of humour of these old ducks.

Typical trips, which the Regional Guides Society – Mrauk U or your hotel can help arrange, include a half-hour car transfer to the jetty, an approximately two-hour boat trip upstream, and an hour or so at a couple of villages. Car transfer will run about K38,000 and the boat another K48,000. You'll also need a guide – about US$20. There's not much in the way of food or drink to buy in the Chin villages so pack any food and water you'll need.

Mrauk U

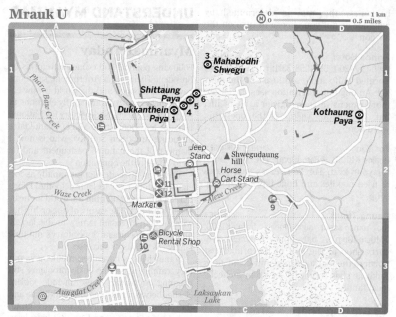

★ **Kothaung Paya** BUDDHIST TEMPLE

(ကိုးေသာင်းဘုရား; ⊘ daylight hours) FREE
Mrauk U's largest temple was built in 1553 by King Minbin's son, King Mintaikkha, to outdo his pop's Shittaung by 10,000 images ('Kothaung' means 'Shrine of 90,000 Images'). It's located a mile or so east of the palace; follow the road directly north of the market, veering left on the much smaller road before the bridge.

Stairways lead up to a top terrace, once dotted with 108 stupas.

🛏 Sleeping & Eating

Golden Star

Guest House BACKPACKER GUESTHOUSE **$**

(☑ 09 4967 4472; r US$8-18) Mrauk U's long-standing backpacker crash pad offers 13 fan-cooled rooms, some with en suite, all needing a fair bit of TLC.

★ **Royal City Guest House** HOTEL **$**

(☑ 043-24200, 09 850 2400; r US$25, bungalows s/d US$35/40; ✴) Clean, comfortable, attractive fan-cooled rooms in the main building for the budget set, and new, air-con (available from 5pm to 11pm) bungalows across the road for those who can afford a bit more, all in a homey atmos-

Mrauk U

⊙ **Top Sights**
1 Dukkanthein Paya	B1
2 Kothaung Paya	D1
3 Mahabodhi Shwegu	C1
4 Shittaung Paya	B1

⊙ **Sights**
5 Andaw Paya	B1
6 Ratanabon Paya	B1
Shittaung Pillar	(see 4)

🛏 **Sleeping**
7 Golden Star Guest House	B2
8 Mrauk U Palace	A2
9 Prince Hotel	C2
10 Royal City Guest House	B3

🍴 **Eating**
11 For You	B2
12 Kaung Thant	B2

phere looked after by a team of charming, friendly staff.

Mrauk U Palace HOTEL **$**

(☑ 09 4217 51498; www.mraukupalaceresort. com; r US$30-40; ✴) The town's newest accommodation takes the form of 18 identical yellow duplex bungalows equipped with fridge, hot-water showers and small balconies; the rate is determined by whether or not you choose to turn on the air-con.

Prince Hotel GUESTHOUSE **$**
(📞 043-24200, 09 4958 3311; r US$25-45; ❄️) Located half a mile southeast of the market. An ongoing renovation sees the larger, more expensive rooms given a bit of life, but, in general, 'rustic' is the operating word here.

For You CHINESE, BURMESE **$**
(mains K1000; ⏰ 8am-10pm) The best bang for your kyat, For You serves vast plates of fried noodles and huge bowls of noodle soup.

Kaung Thant BURMESE **$**
(no roman-script sign; meals from K1500; ⏰ 10am-10pm) A bare-bones Burmese-style curry shop at the foot of the bridge just north of the market, 'Good and Clean' does Rakhine-style set meals served by a cheeky local family.

ℹ️ Getting There & Around

Mrauk U's jetty is about half a mile south of the market. Go here, or to the adjacent Hay Mar teashop, where Aung Zan can assist in buying tickets.

Foreigners are allegedly banned from riding on Mrauk U's *thoun bein* due to an accident involving a foreign tourist in 2011. This may have changed by the time you're in town.

Aged 4WDs can be hired for day (about K38,000) from the **stand** on the north side of the palace site. A horse-cart around the temples is around K15,000 per day. Bicycles can be hired from the **shop** (per day K2000; ⏰ 7am-5pm) south of the bridge leading to the central market.

UNDERSTAND MYANMAR

Myanmar Today

Following political and economic reforms by President Thein Sein's government, sanctions have been dropped and the world is now eager to engage with Myanmar. By-elections in April 2012 saw a landslide victory for National League for Democracy (NLD) candidates including Aung San Suu Kyi, who is now a member of the national parliament and de facto leader of the opposition.

The economy is developing rapidly as foreign investors rush to gain a foothold in a market largely cut off from the world for nearly half a century. The easing of censorship has witnessed an explosion in new media, largely unafraid to document the country's multiple failings as well as its successes.

Some changes have been momentous but they cannot mask the toxic problems still plaguing Myanmar. These include violent clashes between Muslims and Buddhists, and the plight of the Rohingya minority group in Rakhine State (around 125,000 have been forced into squalid camps guarded by troops). Human rights abuses remain prolific and deeply worrying. The flawed constitution, if it remains unamended, also diminishes the chances of a democratic result to the 2015 general election.

History

Long before the British took control of Burma in three successive wars in the 19th century, the area was ruled over by several major ethnic groups, with the Bamar only coming into prominence in the 11th century. Britain managed the mountainous border regions separately from the fertile plains and delta

---

BURMA OR MYANMAR?

What to call the Republic of the Union of Myanmar (the country's official name as of 2011) has, since 1989, been a political flashpoint. That was the year in which the military junta dumped Burma, the name commonly used since the mid-19th century, into the rubbish bin, along with a slew of other British colonial-era place names such as Rangoon, Pagan, Bassein and Arakan.

The UN recognises Myanmar as the nation's official name; Myanmar is more inclusive than Burma for a population that isn't by any means 100% Burman. However, nearly all opposition groups (including the NLD), many ethnic groups and several key nations including the USA and UK continue to refer to it as Burma.

We go with Myanmar, with Burma used for periods before 1989. 'Burmese' refers to the Bamar people, the food and the language.

of central and lower Burma, building on a cultural rift between the lowland Bamar and highland ethnic groups that lingers today. Civil war erupted between minority groups after independence in 1948, and in pockets of the country continues still.

General Ne Win wrested control from the elected government in 1962 and began the world's longest-running military dictatorship, which pursued xenophobic policies leading Burma to full isolation. State socialism ruined the economy, necessitating several major currency devaluations, the last of which sparked massive, yet peaceful, street protests in 1988.

The prodemocracy marches saw Aung San Suu Kyi, daughter of independence hero General Aung San, emerge as the leader of the NLD. The military used violence to stop the marches, but allowed a national election in 1990 in which the NLD won 82% of the assembly seats. The military simply refused to transfer power and threw many elected politicians into jail.

Trade with its neighbours (particularly Thailand and China) and Myanmar's membership of Asean enabled the junta to withstand increased international scorn and Western sanctions. The military's brutal reaction to the 2007 protests (the failed 'Saffron Revolution') and its shameful response to Cyclone Nargis in 2008, the worst natural disaster ever to befall the nation, caused it to become even more despised and feared.

An election in October 2010 brought in a quasi-civilian government to replace the military junta. It was the first time Myanmar citizens had been able to vote for a government in 20 years but the UN called the election 'deeply flawed'. Former general and old prime minister Thein Sein was 'chosen' by the elected reps to take over from Senior General Than Shwe, Myanmar's supreme ruler for the past two decades.

Aung San Suu Kyi, who had spent 15 of the 21 years since 1989 shut away either in her home or Insein jail as a prisoner of conscience, was released in November 2010. The fear that this would be a temporary state of affairs soon evaporated when less than a year later she held talks with Thein Sein, followed by meetings with world leaders.

People & Culture

Myanmar people are as proud of their country and culture as any nationality on earth. Locals gush over ancient kings, *pwe* (festi-

vals), *mohinga* (noodles with chicken or fish) breakfasts, great temples and their religion. A typical Burmese Buddhist values meditation, gives alms freely and sees his or her lot as the consequence of sin or merit in a past life. The social ideal for most Burmese is a standard of behaviour commonly termed *bamahsan chin* (Burmese-ness). The hallmarks of *bamahsan chin* include showing respect for elders, acquaintance with Buddhist scriptures, and discretion in behaviour towards the opposite sex. Most importantly, *bamahsan chin* values the quiet, subtle and indirect over the loud, obvious and direct.

Lifestyle

About three-quarters of Myanmar's population are rural-dwellers, so much of local life revolves around villages and farming the countryside. Here, national politics or dreams of wealth can pale in comparison to the season, the crop or the level of the river (used for bathing, washing and drinking water). Everywhere, people are known for helping each other when in need, and call each other 'brother' and 'sister' affectionately.

Families tend to be large; you might find three or four generations of one family living in a two- or three-room house. The birth of a child is a big occasion. Girls are as equally welcomed as boys, if not more so, as they're expected to look after parents later in life. Some thatched huts in the countryside have generators, powering electric bulbs and pumping life into the TV a couple of hours a night; many don't. Running water outside the cities and bigger towns is rare.

Life is much more 21st century in Yangon and Mandalay but even these big cities suffer

---

DOS & DON'TS

➡ Don't touch anyone's head, as it's considered the spiritual pinnacle of the body.

➡ Don't point feet at people if you can help it, and avoid stepping over people.

➡ Hand things – food, gifts, money – with your right hand, tucking your left under your right elbow.

➡ Dress modestly when visiting religious sites – avoid above-the-knee shorts, tight clothes or sleeveless shirts.

➡ Take off your shoes when entering temple precincts, usually including the long steps up to a hilltop pagoda.

power outages. The extremes of Myanmar's wealth and poverty are very apparent too in the urban centres.

Population

Statistics relating to Myanmar's population have been vague for decades. Between 30 March and 10 April 2014, a national census was carried out under the auspices of the United Nations Fund for Population Activities (myanmar.unfpa.org) – the results were not available at the time of writing. In a country with more than 135 ethnic groups, at least 19 major languages and areas where armed conflicts could still be in progress, undertaking such a survey is no simple exercise. The census results should be ready by August 2014.

Under the 2008 constitution Myanmar is divided into seven regions (they used to be called divisions; these are where the Bamar are in the majority) and seven states (minority regions, namely Chin, Kachin, Kayah, Kayin, Mon, Rakhine and Shan States). In addition there are six ethnic enclaves (Danu, Kokang, Naga, Palaung, Pa-O and Wa) with a degree of self-governance.

The relatively large numbers of Indians and Chinese you'll encounter in Myanmar are a legacy of colonial times and ongoing economic cooperation.

Religion

Freedom of religion is guaranteed under the country's constitution. However, around 87% of Myanmar's citizens are Theravada Buddhists and the religion is given special status.

Myanmar's ethnic patchwork of people also embraces a variety of other faiths, among which Islam and Christianity are the most popular. There is also a strong belief in *nat* (guardian spirit beings).

BUDDHISM

For the average Burmese Buddhist much of life revolves around the merit (*kutho*, from the Pali *kusala*, meaning 'wholesome') that is accumulated through rituals and good deeds. One of the more common rituals performed by individuals visiting a stupa is to pour water over the Buddha image at their astrological post (determined by the day of the week they were born) – one glassful for every year of their current age plus one extra to ensure a long life.

Every Burmese male is expected to take up temporary monastic residence twice in his life: once as a *samanera* (novice monk), between the ages of five and 15, and again as a *pongyi* (fully ordained monk), some time after the age of 20. Almost all men or boys under 20 years of age participate in the *shinpyu* (initiation ceremony), through which their family earns great merit.

While there is little social expectation that they should do so, a number of women live monastic lives as *dasasila* ('ten-precept' nuns). Burmese nuns shave their heads, wear pink robes and take vows in an ordination procedure similar to that undertaken by monks.

NAT WORSHIP

Buddhism in Myanmar has overtaken, but never entirely replaced, the pre-Buddhist practice of *nat* worship. The 37 *nat* figures are often found side by side with Buddhist images. The Burmese *nat* are spirits that can inhabit natural features, trees or even people. They can be mischievous or beneficent.

The *nat* cult is strong. Mt Popa is an important centre. The Burmese divide their devotions and offerings according to the sphere of influence: Buddha for future lives, and the *nat* – both Hindu and Bamar – for problems in this life. A misdeed might be redressed with offerings to the *nat* Thagyamin, who annually records the names of those who perform good deeds in a book made of gold leaves. Those who commit evil are recorded in a book made of dog skin.

Arts

For centuries the arts in Myanmar were sponsored by the royal courts, mainly through the construction of major religious buildings that required the skills of architects, sculptors, painters and a variety of craftspeople. Such patronage was cut short during British colonial rule and has not been a priority since independence. This said, there are plenty of examples of traditional art to be viewed in Myanmar, mainly in the temples that are an ever-present feature of town and countryside. There's also a growing contemporary art scene, particularly in Yangon.

MARIONETTE THEATRE

Yok-thei pwe (Burmese marionette theatre) was the forerunner of Burmese classical dance. Marionette theatre declined following

WWII and is now mostly confined to tourist venues in Yangon, Mandalay and Bagan.

MUSIC

Traditional Burmese music relies heavily on rhythm and is short on harmony, at least to the Western ear. Younger Burmese listen to heavily Western-influenced sounds – you will often hear Burmese-language covers of classic oldies, usually sappy love or pop tunes. A number of Burmese rock musicians, such as Lay Phyu of the band Iron Cross, produce serious songs of their own. Current darlings of the local pop scene are the Me N Ma Girls, a toned down Spice Girls–style troupe.

PWE

The *pwe* (show) is everyday Burmese theatre. A religious festival, wedding, funeral, celebration, fair, sporting event – almost any gathering – is a good excuse for a *pwe*. Once underway, a *pwe* traditionally goes on all night. If an audience member is flaking at some point during the performance, they simply fall asleep. To experience one, ask a trishaw driver if a *pwe* is on nearby.

Myanmar's truly indigenous dance forms are those that pay homage to the *nat*. In a special *nat pwe*, one or more *nat* are invited to possess the body and mind of a medium. Sometimes members of the audience seem to be possessed instead, an event greatly feared by most Burmese.

Environment

Myanmar covers an area of 261,000 sq miles, which is roughly the size of Texas or France.

From the snowcapped Himalaya in the north to the coral-fringed Myeik (Mergui) Archipelago in the south, Myanmar's length of 1250 miles crosses three distinct ecological regions, producing what is probably the richest biodiversity in Southeast Asia.

Unfortunately, that wildlife – which includes a third of the world's Asiatic elephants and the largest tiger reserve on the planet – is threatened by habitat loss. Rampant deforestation by the timber industry, which occurs in order to feed demand in Thailand and China, is a primary cause. Optimistically, about 7% of the country is protected in national parks and other protected areas, but most of these are just lines on maps. Wildlife laws in Myanmar are seldom enforced, due to a desperate lack of funding, and in recent years some wildlife reserves that date back to the colonial era have been un-reserved to allow logging.

For travellers, seeing wildlife will be more a matter of luck than design. And without some serious cash, forget about visiting national parks.

Food & Drink

Food

Mainstream Burmese cuisine represents a blend of Bamar, Mon, Indian and Chinese influences. A typical meal has *htamin* (rice) as its core, eaten with a choice of *hin* (curry dishes), most commonly fish, chicken, pork, prawns or mutton. Soup is always served, along with a table full of condiments (including pickled vegies as spicy dipping sauces).

'MOUTH-WATERING SNACKS'

Fancy yourself as an adventurous eater? Seek out *tha yei za* (mouth-watering snacks) at night markets in Yangon and street stalls around the country. Desserts are common, and come in the form of multicoloured sticky-rice sweets, poppyseed cakes, banana puddings and the like. Others test local claims that 'anything that walks on the ground can be eaten' – not to mention any claims you might have to 'hardcore traveller' status – and are definitely in the unidentified frying object category:

Wek thaa douk htoe (barbecue stands) Footpath stalls selling graphic, sliced-up pig.

Pa-yit kyaw (fried cricket) Sold on skewers or in a 10-pack for about K500.

Bi-laar (beetle) Prepared like crickets; locals suggest 'suck the stomach out, then chew the head part'.

Thin baun poe (larva) Insect larvae, culled from bamboo, are lightly grilled and served still wriggling.

Most Burmese food is pretty mild on the chilli front, with cooks favouring a simple masala of turmeric, ginger, garlic, salt and onions, plus plenty (and we mean loads!) of peanut oil and shrimp paste. *Balachaung* (chillies, tamarind and dried shrimp pounded together) or the pungent *ngapi kyaw* (spicy shrimp paste with garlic) is always nearby to add some kick. Almost everything savoury in Burmese cooking is flavoured with *ngapi* (a salty paste concocted from dried and fermented shrimp or fish).

Noodle dishes are often eaten for breakfast or as light snacks between meals. The seafood served along the coasts is some of the best and cheapest you'll find in the entire region.

Drink

NON-ALCOHOLIC DRINKS

Teashops, a national institution, are good places to meet people over a drink and inexpensive snacks such as *nam-bya* and *palata* (flatbreads) or Chinese fried pastries. Burmese tea (about K250 a cup), brewed Indian-style with lots of condensed milk and sugar, is the national drink. Ask for *lahpeq ye* (tea with a dollop of condensed milk); *cho*

DRINKING WATER

Only drink purified water. Be wary of ice in remote areas, though it is usually factory-produced in towns and cities. Bottled water costs from K300 a litre and is widely available. Consider sterilising your water, and saving dozens of PET bottles, by using a UV sterilising wand.

bouk is less sweet, and *kyauk padaung* is very sweet. Most restaurants will provide as much free Chinese tea as you can handle. Real coffee is limited to a handful of modern, Western-style cafes in Yangon and other large cities. Sugarcane juice is a very popular street-side drink.

ALCOHOL

Myanmar Beer is a bit lighter in flavour and alcohol than other Southeast Asian beers. A more watery beer is Mandalay Beer. Mandalay Brewery, in Yangon, also produces the New Mandalay Export label, which is the best-tasting local beer.

Very popular in Shan State is an orange brandy called *shwe leinmaw*, a pleasant-tasting liqueur that packs quite a punch. There's a couple of vineyards making wine, and in Pyin Oo Lwin there are several sweet strawberry-based wines.

There are also a variety of stronger liquors, including rum in Mandalay, and the fermented palm juice known as toddy.

SURVIVAL GUIDE

ℹ Directory A–Z

ACCOMMODATION

The cheapest places are very plain; think concrete floors, squashed mosquitoes on the walls, a fan (usually) and a shared bathroom down the hall, with a basic breakfast if you're lucky. For a few dollars more you get air-con, hot water and even TV. These, however, will be of limited value unless your lodging has a generator, because electricity supplies are sketchy right across

Myanmar. Unless stated otherwise, prices include private bathroom.

Nearly all hotels and guesthouses quote prices in US dollars. Most accept kyat. Prices listed in reviews are for peak season, roughly October to March. Discounts may be available in the low season; don't be afraid to haggle gently if planning a longer stay. Passport and visa details are required at check-in, but hotels don't need to hold your passport.

All accommodation supposedly must be licensed to accept foreign guests, meaning the cheapest places are usually off limits. In out-of-the-way towns, some unlicensed guesthouses will accept weary travellers.

Price Ranges

The following price ranges are for a double room. Note that most hotels charge one price for foreigners and another for locals.

$ less than K48,600 (US$50)

$$ K48,600 to K145,800 (US$50 to US$150)

$$$ more than K145,800 (US$150)

CUSTOMS REGULATIONS

Any foreign currency in excess of US$2000 is supposed to be declared upon entry (we, and other travellers we've met, have failed to declare larger amounts and have not had problems). Genuine antiques cannot be taken out of the country.

ELECTRICITY

Connect (when it's working) to the electricity supply (230V, 50Hz AC). Many hotels have generators (some run at night only). Local power sources in many towns are scheduled for night hours only.

EMBASSIES & CONSULATES

Most foreign embassies and consulates are in Yangon. Check the government's **Ministry of Foreign Affairs** (www.mofa.gov.mm) for more information.

Australian Embassy (Map p486; ☎01-251 810; www.burma.embassy.gov.au; 88 Strand Rd, Kyauktada)

Bangladeshi Embassy (Map p490; ☎01-515 275; 11B Than Lwin Rd, Kamayut)

Chinese Embassy (Map p490; ☎01-221 281; http://mm.china-embassy.org/eng; 1 Pyidaungsu Yeiktha Rd, Dagon)

French Embassy (Map p488; ☎01-212 520; www.ambafrance-mm.org; 102 Pyidaungsu Yeiktha Rd, Dagon)

German Embassy (Map p490; ☎01-548 951; www.rangun.diplo.de; 9 Bogyoke Aung San Museum Rd, Bahan)

Indian Embassy (Map p486; ☎01-243 972; www.indiaembassyyangon.net; 545-547 Merchant St, Kyauktada)

ⓘ MEASUREMENTS

Petrol is sold by the gallon; distances are in miles, not kilometres; 1 Burmese viss or 100 tical = 3.5lb (1.5kg); 1 gaig = 36in (91cm).

Japanese Embassy (Map p490; ☎01-549 644; http://www.mm.emb-japan.go.jp; 100 Nat Mauk Rd, Bahan)

New Zealand Embassy (Map p486; ☎01-230 5805; 43 Inya Myiang Rd, Bahan)

Thai Embassy (Map p490; ☎01-226 721; www.thaiembassy.org/yangon/en; 94 Pyay Rd, Dagon)

UK Embassy (Map p486; ☎01-256 438, 01-370 863; www.gov.uk/government/world/burma; 80 Strand Rd, Kyauktada)

US Embassy (Map p484; ☎01-535 756, 01-536 509; http://burma.usembassy.gov; 110 University Ave, Kamayut)

FESTIVAL & EVENTS

Myanmar follows a 12-month lunar calendar, and most festivals are on the full moon of the Burmese month in which they occur – hence shifting dates. The build-up to festivals can go on for days.

February/March

Shwedagon Festival Myanmar's largest *paya* festival takes place in Yangon.

March/April

Full-Moon Festival Biggest event of the year at Shwemawdaw Paya in Bago.

April/May

Buddha's Birthday The full moon also marks the day of Buddha's enlightenment and his entry to nirvana. One of the best places to observe this ceremony is at Yangon's Shwedagon Paya.

Thingyan (Water Festival) The Burmese New Year is the biggest holiday of the year, celebrated with a raucous nationwide water fight. It is impossible to go outside without getting drenched, so just join the fun. Businesses close and some transport – especially buses – stops running for around a week.

June/July

Buddhist Lent Start of the Buddhist Rains Retreat. Laypeople present monasteries with new robes, because during the three-month Lent period monks are restricted to their monasteries.

July/August

Wagaung Festival Nationwide exercise in alms-giving.

September/October

Thadingyut Celebrates Buddha's return from a period of preaching.

October/November

Tazaungdaing The biggest 'festival of lights' sees all Myanmar lit by oil lamps, fire balloons, candles and even mundane electric lamps.

Kathein A one-month period at the end of Buddhist Lent during which new monastic robes and requisites are offered to the monastic community.

December/January

Kayin New Year Karen communities throughout Myanmar celebrate by wearing their traditional dress and by hosting folk-dancing and singing performances. Big celebrations are held in the Karen suburb of Insein, just north of Yangon, and in Hpa-an.

Ananda Festival Held at the Ananda Pahto in Bagan at the full moon.

FOOD

The following price ranges refer to main dishes.

$ less than 4900K (US$5)

$$ 4900K to 14,700K (US$5 to US$15)

$$$ more than 14,700K (US$15)

GAY & LESBIAN TRAVELLERS

Gay and transgendered people in Myanmar are rarely 'out', except for 'third sex' spirit mediums who channel the energies of *nat* spirits. As elsewhere, it can be seen as a bit of a cultural taboo, though most of Myanmar's ethnic groups are known to be tolerant of homosexuality, both male and female. A local woman walking with a foreign man will raise more eyebrows than two same-sex travellers sharing a room. Public displays of affection, whether heterosexual or homosexual, are frowned upon. **Utopia-Asia** (www.utopia-asia. com) has some Yangon scene reports.

INTERNET ACCESS

Online access has improved, with wi-fi becoming the norm in big cities – most hotels, guesthouses, restaurants and cafes will have this and it's usually free. We even found internet access in relatively remote locations such as Mrauk U.

However, with tightly squeezed bandwidth and power outages it can often be a frustrating exercise to send and receive emails or check the internet, particularly in rural areas. Forget about streaming or big downloads.

LEGAL MATTERS

If you are arrested, you would most likely be permitted to contact your consular agent in Myanmar for possible assistance.

If you purchase gems or jewellery from persons or shops that are not licensed by the government, you run the risk of having them confiscated if customs officials find them in your baggage when you're exiting the country.

Forming public assemblies of more than two people without the prior permission of the authorities is illegal. Drug-trafficking crimes are punishable by death.

MAPS

Periplus Editions (scale 1:2,000,000), ITMB (1:1,350,000) and Nelles (1:1,500,000) all make dedicated maps of Myanmar.

Design Printing Services (DPS; www.dpsmap. com) prints useful tourist maps of Myanmar, Yangon, Mandalay and Bagan; sometimes these maps are sold locally for about K1000 or given away by tour agencies, at hotels and international gateway airports.

MEDIA

Read the daily English-language newspaper **Myanma Freedom** (www.mmfreedom-daily. com), the weekly **Myanmar Times** (www.mm-times.com) and the online news sites **Democratic Voice of Burma** (www.dvb.no), **Irrawaddy** (www.irrawaddy.org) and **Mizzima** (www. mizzima.com).

MONEY

Prices listed alternate between kyat (K) and US dollars (US$), depending on the currency in which prices are quoted.

Banks & ATMs

The most useful of the local banks (which are open 9.30am to 3pm Monday to Friday) are CB and KBZ, both of which now issue and accept Mastercard and Visa cards and have ATMs in which you can use overseas-issued cards for a K5000 charge per transaction. You'll find these ATMs all across Yangon and in other major cities and tourist spots.

Credit Cards & Travellers Cheques

Credit cards and travellers cheques remain largely useless. However, the situation is rapidly changing and in Yangon and other major tourist spots you'll increasingly find credit cards accepted by top-end hotels, restaurants and some shops.

Moneychangers

You'll find official bank and private licensed exchange booths at places such as Yangon and Mandalay airports, Bogyoke Aung San Market and Shwedagon Paya in Yangon.

Never hand over your money until you've received the kyat and counted them. Honest moneychangers will expect you to do this. Considering that K10,000 is the highest denomination, you'll get a lot of notes. Money-changers give readymade, rubber-banded stacks of a hundred K1000 bills. It's a good idea to check each note individually. Often you'll find one or two (or more) with a cut corner or taped tears, neither of which anyone will accept.

Many travellers do the bulk of their exchanging in Yangon, then carry the stacks of kyat around the country. Considering the relative safety from theft, it's not a bad idea, but you can exchange

> ### ⓘ BRING NEW BILLS!
>
> We cannot stress enough the need to bring pristine 'new' US dollar bills to Myanmar – that means no folds, creases, tears or pen or other marks on the notes, and they should be the ones with the larger full-frame heads. Anything else risks being rejected by moneychangers, hotels, restaurants, shops and museums.

money elsewhere and the spreading of ATMs is making such a strategy increasingly unnecessary.

Tipping
Tipping is not customary, though little extra 'presents' are sometimes expected (even if they're not asked for) in exchange for a service (such as unlocking a locked temple at Bagan, helping move a bag at the airport or showing you around the 'sights' of a village).

Have small notes (K50, K100, K200) handy when visiting a temple or monastery for donations.

OPENING HOURS
We spell out opening hours where they differ from those below.

➡ **Government offices** (including post offices and telephone centres) 9.30am to 4.30pm Monday to Friday

➡ **Shops** 9.30am to 6pm or later Monday to Saturday

➡ **Restaurants** 8am to 9pm

➡ **Internet cafes** noon to 10pm

PHOTOGRAPHY & VIDEO
Most internet cafes can burn digital photos onto a CD for about K1000. Some sights, including some pagodas, charge small camera fees. Avoid taking photos of military facilities, uniformed individuals, and strategic locations such as bridges.

POST
Most mail out of Myanmar gets to its destination quite efficiently. International-postage rates are a bargain: a postcard is K500, a 1kg package to Australia/UK/US is K16,200/18,900/20,700.

Post offices are supposed to be open from 9.30am to 4.30pm Monday to Friday, but you may find some keep shorter hours.

In Yangon, DHL (p492) is a more reliable but expensive way of sending out bigger packages.

PUBLIC HOLIDAYS
Major public holidays include:
Independence Day (4 January)
Union Day (12 February)
Peasants' Day (2 March)
Armed Forces Day (27 March)
Workers' Day (1 May)
Martyrs' Day (19 July)
National Day (27 November)
Christmas Day (25 December)

SAFE TRAVEL
Theft remains quite rare and usually the only time a local will be running with your money or belongings is if they're chasing you down the road with something you've dropped!

However, don't tempt fate in this poor country by flashing valuables or leaving them unguarded. The only real scams are dodgy moneychangers shortchanging you, and drivers or guides getting a commission for purchases at any shops you visit.

Areas around the Myanmar–Thai border, home to the country's notorious drug trade, can be dangerous (and off limits) to explore.

Power outages are highly annoying and commonplace everywhere except the surreal capital, Nay Pyi Taw. Many businesses have their own generators, but check with your guesthouse whether the power will be on all night, especially in the hot season.

The poor state of road and rail infrastructure, plus lax safety standards and procedures for flights and boats, means that travelling can sometimes be dangerous.

TELEPHONE
Local Calls
Most business cards purposely list a couple of phone numbers, and often a mobile (cell) phone number, as lines frequently go dead and calls just don't get through.

Local call stands – as part of a shop, or sometimes just a table with a phone or two on a pavement – can be found all over Myanmar. A local call should be K100 per minute.

To dial long distance within Myanmar, dial the area code (including the '0') and the number.

International Calls
Internet cafes using Skype and other VOI protocols, official telephone (call) centres and top-end hotels are sometimes the only way to call overseas, though sometimes this can be done on the street through vendors offering use of their mobile phones.

Generally, it costs about US$5 per minute to call Australia or Europe and US$6 per minute to phone North America.

To call Myanmar from abroad, dial your country's international access code, then ☑ 95 (Myanmar's country code), the area code (minus the '0') and the five- or six-digit number.

Mobile Phones
Mobile-phone numbers begin with ☑ 09.

RESPONSIBLE TRAVEL

➡ Travel independently or in small groups rather than in a big tour group.

➡ Support small independent businesses and those that have charitable and sustainable tourism programs in place.

➡ Spread your money around, ie buy souvenirs across the country and hire different guides at each destination.

➡ Talk to locals but take their lead on the substance of the conversation.

➡ Contribute to local charitable causes.

➡ Be environmentally conscious in your travel choices, ie opt for buses, trains and river cruises over flights, avoid using air-conditioning.

➡ Be sensitive to, and respectful of, local customs and behaviour, ie dress and act appropriately when visiting religious sites and rural villages.

➡ Read up about Myanmar's history, culture and current situation.

➡ Check out Dos & Don'ts For Tourists (www.dosanddontsfortourists.com).

In June 2013 the government awarded two companies concessions to create new mobile-phone networks. These are expected to come online before the end of 2014, expanding the range and quality of mobile communications in the country as well as impacting the cost of SIMs and calls.

At the time of research, international roaming for mobile phones was limited to a handful of Asian networks. Temporary local SIM cards costing K20,000 and lasting one month before expiring had been in circulation during 2013 but were sold out by August of that year. Permanent SIM cards costing K1700 had also been available via lottery. Top-up cards for calls come in amounts of K5000 and K10,000.

The only easy option we found for visitors was rental of a SIM or a SIM and handset at Yangon Airport from Yatanarpon. The cost, starting at US$60 for five days not including call charges, was prohibitive.

TIME

The local Myanmar Standard Time (MST) is 6½ hours ahead of Greenwich Mean Time (GMT/UTC). When coming in from Thailand, turn your watch back half an hour; coming in from India, put your watch forward an hour.

TOILETS

In many out-of-the-way places, Burmese toilets are often squat jobs, generally in a cobweb-filled outhouse that is reached by a dirt path behind a restaurant. In guesthouses and hotels you will usually find Western-style thrones. Toilet paper is widely available but as Confucius might have said: 'The wise traveller carries an emergency TP stash, the unwise traveller uses this page.' Either way, don't flush it.

TOURIST INFORMATION

Myanmar Travels & Tours, part of the Ministry of Hotels & Tourism, is the main 'tourist information' service with offices in Yangon (p492),

Mandalay (p517), **New Bagan** (MTT; Map p524; ☑061-65040; ⊘8.30am-4.30pm) and Inle Lake. Other than at Yangon, these offices are pretty quiet, and often the staff have sketchy knowledge on restricted areas.

Travellers who want to arrange a driver, or have hotel reservations awaiting them, would do well to arrange a trip with the help of private travel agents in Yangon and other major cities. Many Myanmar 'travel agents' outside Yangon only sell air tickets.

TRAVELLERS WITH DISABILITIES

Myanmar is a tricky country for mobility-impaired travellers. Wheelchair ramps are virtually unheard of and public transport is crowded and can be difficult, even for the fully ambulatory.

VISAS

Everyone requires a visa to visit Mynamar. If you're applying for a tourist visa (US$22, valid 28 days) at home, you should start the process no later than three weeks before your trip, or a month before to be safe.

If you're already travelling, it's possible to get a tourist visa at short notice from the **Myanmar embassy** in Bangkok (☑66-2233 7250; www.myanmarembassybkk.com; 132 Sathorn Nua Rd; application 9am-noon, collection ⊘3.30-4.30pm); the cost is 1260B for same day processing, 1035B for the next day.

Visa on Arrival?

At the time of our research, a visa on arrival was available at Yangon, Mandalay and Nay Pyi Taw international airports for business visas and only if you arrive with a letter of invitation from a sponsoring company and proof of your company registration or business.

Tourist visas on arrival are available only if you've made prior arrangements with a travel agency qualified to apply for visas, such as Oway (p493). You will need to apply at least 10 working days before your flight and bring two passport photos and the visa approval letter issued by the agent with you for the visa to be fully processed on arrival.

Applications

All visas are valid for up to three months from the date of issue and most embassies and consulates need at least a week to process an application.

Postal applications are usually OK, but it's best to check first with your nearest embassy about their specific application rules.

There is no need for you to conceal your profession on the visa application form.

Visa Extensions & Overstaying

Tourist visas can be extended for two weeks for US$36 and for a month for US$72. Business visas can also be extended.

You may have difficulties with some hotels and domestic airport officials if you've overstayed your visa and not officially extended it. If you do overstay, it's wise to stick with land routes and places within easy access of Yangon, as there have been cases in the past of tourists being instructed to leave the country immediately when discovered by the authorities.

If you haven't extended your visa, you will have to pay a fine of US$3 per day, plus a US$3 registration fee, at the airport or land border as you exit the country. The fine can be paid in kyat if you don't have dollars.

VOLUNTEERING

Official opportunities to volunteer are limited. A list of NGOs that may have volunteering opportunities can be found at www.ngoinmyanmar. org, although mostly the postings are for specific experienced workers (often in medicine). Also browse the links at **Burma Volunteer Program** (http://burmavolunteers.org).

Everyone in Myanmar wants to learn English, and few can afford to. Ask in towns or villages to sit in at an English class.

WEBSITES

7 Days in Myanmar (http://7daysinmyanmar. com) Multimedia showcase for the country crafted by 30 internationally renowned photographers in April 2013.

Go-Myanmar.com (www.go-myanmar.com) Plenty of up-to-date travel-related information and advice.

Myanmar Image Gallery (www.myanmar-image. com) Pictures and text on myriad Myanmar-related subjects.

Online Burma/Myanmar Library (www. burmalibrary.org) Database of books and past articles on Myanmar.

WOMEN TRAVELLERS

Women travelling alone are more likely to be helped than harassed. In some areas you'll be regarded with friendly curiosity – and asked, with sad-eyed sympathy, 'Are you only one?' – because Burmese women tend to prefer to travel en masse.

At remote religious sites, a single foreign woman may be 'adopted' by a Burmese woman, who will take you and show you the highlights. At some sites, such as Mandalay's Mahamuni Paya and Golden Rock, 'ladies' are not permitted to the central shrine; signs will indicate if this is the case.

ⓘ Getting There & Away

AIR

International flights arrive at Yangon (Rangoon; RGN), Mandalay (MDL) and Nay Pyi Taw (NPT) airports. The most common route is via Bangkok, though there are regular direct flights with several other regional cities including Singapore and Kuala Lumpur. Good deals are often available on budget airlines such as AirAsia and Silk Air.

ⓘ Getting Around

Unless you fly, all travel in Myanmar takes time. Often lots of time. Large areas of the country are off limits, or accessible only with permission. Securing such permission:

➡ Takes time – a minimum of at least two weeks but more commonly around a month.

➡ Requires the help of an experienced travel agency.

➡ Always involves paying fees to the government, usually via the government-owned travel agency MTT, even if you're dealing with another agency.

➡ Usually means dancing to MTT's tune when it comes to how you visit the area in question and who you go with.

Sometimes areas that were possible to visit with or without a permit suddenly become off limits: that's how it is in Myanmar.

Exiting Myanmar by a land border (only three possible) will require permits and 'guide' fees and plenty of advanced notice.

AIR

Travel agents sell flight tickets at a slightly discounted rate, so it usually makes little sense to buy directly from the airlines. Online booking and e-ticketing is currently offered by Air Bagan and Oway (p493) for all airlines.

One-way fares are half a return fare, and can bought between six months and a day in advance. It's sometimes difficult to buy a ticket that departs from a town other than the one you are in. There is no domestic departure tax. The following are domestic airlines, with addresses in Yangon.

Air Bagan (Map p490; ☑01-504 888; www. airbagan.com; 56 Shwe Taung Gyar St (Golden Valley Rd), Bahan) Has five planes.

Air KBZ (Map p486; ☎01-372 977; www.airkbz. com; 33-49 Bank St, cnr of Mahabandoola Garden St, Kyauktada) Owned by the same Kanbawza Bank tycoon who owns Myanmar Airways International; has three planes.

Air Mandalay (Map p490; ☎01-525 488; www. airmandalay.com; 146 Dhamma Zedi Rd, Bahan) A Singapore–Malaysia joint venture with three planes.

Asian Wings (Map p490; ☎01-516 654; www. asianwingsairways.com; 34 Shwe Taung Gyar St (Golden Valley Rd), Bahan) Its fleet has four planes.

Golden Myanmar Airlines (Map p484; ☎01-533 272; www.gmairlines.com; Sayar San Plaza, New University Avenue Rd, Bahan) Has two planes flying routes between Yangon, Mandalay and Singapore

Myanma Airways (Map p486; ☎01-373 828, 01-374 874; www.mot.gov.mm/ma; 104 Strand Rd, Kyauktada) Government airline.

Yangon Airways (Map p490; ☎01-652 533; www.yangonair.com; 166, Level 5, MMB Tower, Upper Pansodan Rd, Mingalar Taung Nyunt)

BOAT

There are 5000 miles of navigable river in Myanmar and, unlike elsewhere in Asia, slow boats remain a vital transport link here. Even in the dry season, boats can travel on the Ayeyarwady (Irrawaddy) from the delta to Bhamo, with small boats continuing to Myitkyina. Other important rivers include the Twante Canal, which links the Ayeyarwady to Yangon, and the Chindwin, which joins the Ayeyarwady a little north of Bagan. Most ferries are operated by the government's **Inland Water Transport** (IWT; www.iwt. gov.mm).

The Mandalay–Bagan service is popular among travellers. A government ferry runs at least twice a week, and in season there's also the faster, more comfortable private service *Malikha 2;* buy tickets from travel agencies.

BUS

Almost always faster and cheaper than trains, Myanmar buses range from luxury air-con express buses, less luxurious but nice buses (without air-con), local buses and mini 32-seaters.

Breakdowns are frequent and roads are so bad in most places that two vehicles travelling in opposite directions can't pass without pulling off the road. On the other hand, bus travel is cheap and reasonably frequent, and it's easy to meet local people during the regular food stops.

Buying tickets in advance is recommended, lest you get stuck sitting on a sack in the aisle. On minibuses, beware of the back seat – on Myanmar's rough roads you'll be bouncing around like popcorn. Keep some warm clothing handy for air-con or trips through mountains.

You can pay kyat for all bus fares. Note, foreigners will pay more than locals – and on occasion the price is 'set' on the spot.

CAR & MOTORCYCLE

There are no car-rental agencies per se, but most travel agencies in Yangon, Mandalay and Bagan – as well as guesthouses and hotels elsewhere – can arrange cars and drivers. Rates range between US$60 and US$80 per day.

Many locals remain reluctant to rent motorcycles to foreigners, but it is possible in some places, including Mandalay and Myitkyina, for around K10,000 per day.

LOCAL TRANSPORT

In most places, horse-carts *(myint hlei),* vintage taxis *(taxi),* tiny four-wheeled Mazdas *(lei bein,* meaning 'four wheels', or blue taxi) and bicycle rickshaws or trishaws *(saiq-ka* – that's pidgin for sidecar) double as public transport. We indicate sample rates, but prices are usually negotiable.

Larger cities – including Yangon, Mandalay, Pathein and Mawlamyine – have dirt-cheap public buses that ply the main streets.

Bicycles are widely available to hire for K500 to K3000 per day.

PICK-UP

You can get almost anywhere in Myanmar on the ubiquitous trucks with bench seats known variously as pick-ups (also called *kaa), lain-ka* (linecar) or *hi-lux.* They leave when full and stop pretty much everywhere. Sitting up the back is cheaper than a bus, while a seat at the front costs double for little more room. Journey times are wildly elastic.

TRAIN

Myanmar Railways is government owned and operated. Foreigners pay up to 10 times the local rate, always in US dollars. Services often run late, though as one local said: 'It's not as bad as some people say, not as good as you hope.'

Upper class offers reclining seats and (in theory) air-con, 1st class is hard-backed seats with some cushioning, and ordinary class involves stiff wooden seats. The Pyin Oo Lwin–Hsipaw line is the most scenic, particularly around the Gokteik Gorge.

Reservations and ticketing can be done at train stations. Smaller stations sometimes require some perseverance to get a ticket, as agents aren't used to foreigners climbing on.

Note that express trains are much more comfortable than the average Burmese train. Reserve sleepers (ie anything that contains sleeping berths, including some day trains) several days in advance.

Philippines

🕿 63 / POP 106 MILLION

Best Beaches

➡ Boracay (p576)

➡ Malapascua (p590)

➡ Sabang (p573)

➡ Sipalay (p582)

➡ Alona Beach (p593)

Best Places for Cultural Connections

➡ Bontoc (p567)

➡ Vigan (p568)

➡ Quiapo (p561)

➡ Banaue (p567)

➡ Siquijor (p583)

Why Go?

Just when you thought you had Asia figured out, you get to the Philippines. Instead of monks you have priests; instead of túk-túk you have tricycles; instead of *pho* (soup) you have *adobo*. At first glance the Philippines will disarm you more than charm you, but peel back the country's skin and there are treasures to be found – aplenty. For starters, you can swim with whale sharks, scale volcanoes, explore desert islands, gawk at ancient rice terraces, submerge at world-class dive sites and venture into rainforests to visit remote hill tribes.

Beyond its obvious physical assets, the Philippines possesses a quirky streak that takes a bit longer to appreciate. There are secret potions and healing lotions, guys named Bong and girls named Bing, grinning hustlers, deafening cock farms, wheezing *bangkas* (outrigger boats), crooked politicians, fuzzy *carabao* (water buffalo), graffiti-splashed jeepneys and cheap beer to enjoy as you take it all in.

When to Go
Manila

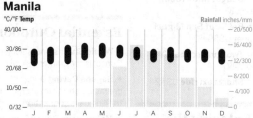

Jan–Feb Cool, pleasant weather and the height of the festival season.

Apr Easter festivals and the best time for whale-shark spotting.

Sep Typhoons are a surfer's delight; big low-season discounts on beaches.

AT A GLANCE

➡ **Currency** Peso (P)

➡ **Languages** Tagalog (Filipino), English

➡ **Money** ATMs abound in cities, scarce in remote areas

➡ **Visas** Visa waivers on arrival (30 days) the norm

➡ **Mobile phones** Prepaid SIM cards are cheap and easy to get

Fast Facts

➡ **Area** 300,000 sq km

➡ **Capital** Manila

➡ **Emergency** ☎ 117

Exchange Rates

Australia	A$1	P40
Euro Zone	€1	P60
Malaysia	RM1	P15
Thailand	10B	P15
UK	UK£1	P75
USA	US$1	P45

Set Your Budget

➡ **Budget hotel room** US$10

➡ **Bottle of San Miguel beer** US$0.60

➡ **Two-tank scuba dive** US$50

➡ **Short taxi ride** US$2

Entering the Country

Entering the country is straightforward and usually done by air through Manila, Cebu or Clark Airport.

Don't Miss

Filipino revel in colourful fiestas, and it's worth scheduling your travels around one. The granddaddy of them all is the Ati-Atihan festival in Kalibo. At Bacolod's MassKara festival, mischievous masked men stir the masses into a dancing frenzy every October. The Easter crucifixion ceremony in San Fernando, north of Manila, produces a more macabre tableau, with Catholic devotees being physically nailed to crosses. Every little town holds a fiesta, so your odds of seeing one are pretty good.

The Filipino joie de vivre manifests itself in other ways – namely, singing. A karaoke night out in Manila is essential. Or pay homage to Filipino cover bands worldwide with some live music. Cover-band shows in Malate can be lively, or head up to Quezon City or Makati for more original fare.

ITINERARIES

One Week

Beach bums and divers should select a Visayan island and just fly there. Popular, easy-to-reach picks include Bohol, with its mix of marine and terrestrial attractions; well-rounded southern Negros; and Cebu island, which has a little of everything. Kitesurfers and hedonists should plot a course towards Boracay. If mountains are your thing, do the spectacular North Luzon overland loop from Baguio to Sagada to Banaue and back to Manila.

Two Weeks

Spend a day exploring Manila, then complete the North Luzon loop. Fly from Manila to Coron in northern Palawan for some island-hopping, then make the eight-hour sea voyage to El Nido, gateway to cliff-addled Bacuit Bay. Travel overland to Puerto Princesa, taking maximum time to linger on lonely beaches along Palawan's west coast.

Essential Outdoor Activities

➡ **Whale Sharks** Snorkelling with the gentle *butanding* of Donsol is the quintessential Philippine adventure.

➡ **Sagada Caving** Dodge stalactites, slither through crevasses and swim in crisp underground pools on the thrilling cave connection.

➡ **Malapascua Diving** Drop onto Monad Shoal to view thresher sharks by morning and manta rays by day.

➡ **Boracay Kitesurfing** Bulabog Beach's shallow lagoon is perfect for learning, while stiff winds from December to March challenge experts.

➡ **Siargao Surfing** Tackle the Philippines' ultimate wave, Cloud Nine.

MANILA

📍 02 / POP 11.85 MILLION

Manila's moniker, the 'Pearl of the Orient', couldn't be more apt – its cantankerous shell reveals its jewel only to those resolute enough to pry. The city has endured every disaster both humans and nature could throw at it, and yet today the chaotic 600-sq-km metropolis thrives as a true Asian megacity. Skyscrapers pierce the hazy sky, mushrooming from the grinding poverty of expansive shanty towns, while gleaming malls foreshadow Manila's brave new air-conditioned world.

The determined will discover Manila's tender soul, perhaps among the leafy courtyards and cobbled streets of serene Intramuros, where little has changed since the Spanish left. Or it may be in the eddy of repose arising from the generosity of one of the city's 12 million residents.

History

The Spanish brushed aside a Muslim fort here in 1571 and founded the modern city as the capital of their realm. Spanish residents were concentrated around the walled city of Intramuros until 1898, when the Spanish governor surrendered to the Filipino at San Agustin Church. After being razed to the ground during WWII, the city grew exponentially during the postwar years as migrants left the countryside in search of new opportunities.

◉ Sights

The main sights are downtown in the old walled city of Intramuros, which lies just south of the Pasig River, and south of Intramuros around Rizal Park (Luneta). You can walk to both of these easily enough from Malate and Ermita.

★ Intramuros   HISTORIC SITE

A spacious borough of wide streets, leafy plazas and lovely colonial houses, the old walled city of Intramuros was the centrepiece of Spanish Manila. The Spanish replaced the original wooden fort with stone in 1590, and these walls stand much as they were 400 years ago. They're still studded with bastions and pierced with gates *(puertas)*.

At the mouth of the Pasig River you'll find Manila's premier tourist attraction, Fort Santiago (Map p556; Santa Clara St; adult/student P75/50; ⊙ 8am-6pm), fronted by a pretty lily pond and the Intramuros Visitors Center

(Map p556; 📞 02-527 2961; ⊙ 8am-5pm), which hands out a free guide to Intramuros. During WWII the fort was used as a prisoner-of-war camp by the Japanese. Within the fort grounds you'll find the Rizal Shrine (Map p556; admission free; ⊙ 9.30am-5pm) in the building where national hero José Rizal was incarcerated as he awaited execution. It contains Rizal's personal effects and an original copy of his last poem, 'Mi Ultimo Adios' (My Last Farewell).

The most interesting building to survive the Battle of Manila is the church and monastery of San Agustin (Map p556; 📞 02-527 4060; General Luna St). The interior is truly opulent and the ceiling, painted in 3D relief, will make you question your vision. You can visit during a Mass, or access it through the interesting San Agustin Museum (Map p556; adult/student P100/50; ⊙ 8am-noon & 1-6pm).

Opposite the church, Casa Manila (Map p556; 📞 02-527 4084; Plaza Luis Complex, General Luna St; adult/student P75/50; ⊙ 9am-6pm Tue-Sun) is a beautiful reproduction of a three-storey Spanish colonial mansion, filled with priceless antiques.

Rizal Park   PARK

(Map p556) One of the precious few bits of green in Manila, the 60-hectare Rizal Park (also known as Luneta) offers urbanites a place to decelerate among ornamental gardens and a whole pantheon of Filipino heroes. Located at the bay end of the park are the Rizal Monument (Map p556) and the moving site of Rizal's execution (Map p556; admission P20; ⊙ 7am-5pm Wed-Sun).

★ National Museum of the
Filipino People   MUSEUM

(Map p556; www.nationalmuseum.gov.ph; T Valencia Circle, Rizal Park; admission P150, free Sun; ⊙ 10am-5pm Tue-Sun) This splendid museum

ℹ Getting around

Metro Manila is composed of 17 cities. From a tourist perspective, the important ones are the City of Manila ('downtown'), Makati and Quezon City. Gritty downtown Manila includes the touristy districts of Malate, Ermita and Intramuros. Business hub Makati and its extension, Fort Bonifacio ('the Fort'), are cleaner, more organised and generally regarded as safer. The best restaurants and nightlife are all up here, as this is where a large chunk of Manila's expat community lives. Pleasant, youthful Quezon City is the country's most populous city with almost three million residents.

Philippines Highlights

1 Drift among the limestone cathedrals and azure lagoons of the Bacuit Archipelago around **El Nido** (p599)

2 Trek through the skyscraping **rice terraces** (p567) around Banaue and Bontoc in North Luzon's Cordillera Mountains

3 Have a night out in **Manila** (p549), a city that never sleeps

4 Explore sunken WWII wrecks and kayak amid myriad islands around **Coron** (p600)

5 Enjoy sun, sea sports and dancing till dawn on the stunning beaches of **Boracay** (p576)

6 Hop from natural spring to volcano to coral reef to waterfall around lush

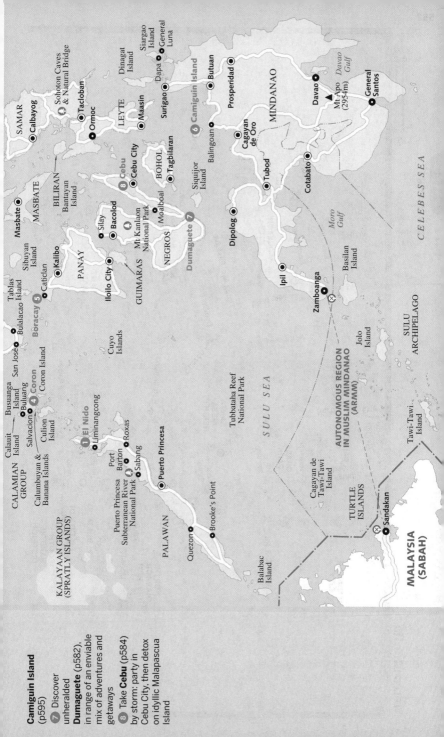

PHILIPPINES

Metro Manila

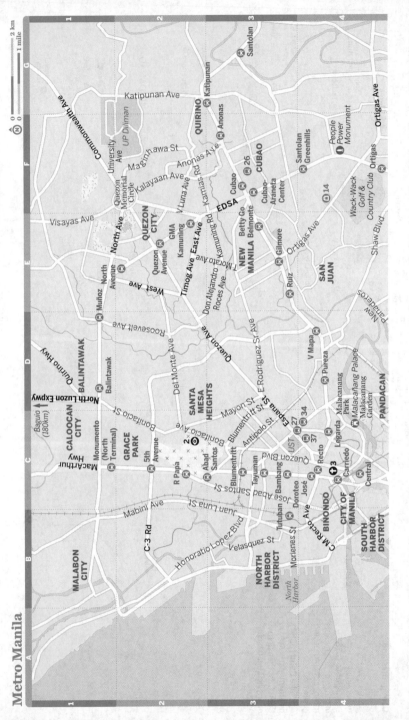

2 km
1 mile

N

North Luzon Expwy
Baguio
(180km)

Quirino Hwy

Commonwealth Ave

Katipunan Ave

QUIRINO

UP Diliman

University
Ave

Quezon
Memorial
Circle

Magrinhawa St

Anonas Ave

Kalayaan Ave

V Luna Ave

Kamias Rd

Katipunan

Anonas

CUBAO

26

Cubao

Cubao-
Araneta
Center

Santolan
Santol

Santolan
Greenhills

People
Power
Monument

Ortigas Ave

14

Wack-Wack
Golf &
Country Club

Shaw Blvd

Ortigas

Ortigas Ave

EDSA

Visayas Ave

North Ave

North
Avenue

Muñoz

North
Avenue

West Ave

QUEZON
CITY

Quezon
Avenue

GMA

Kamuning

Timog Ave

T Morato Ave

East Ave

Kamuning Rd

NEW
MANILA

Betty Go
Belmonte

Gilmore

Ortigas Ave

Ruiz

SAN
JUAN

New Panaderos

Roosevelt Ave

Don Alejandro
Roces Ave

Quezon Ave

E Rodriguez Sr Ave

V Mapa

Pureza

PANDACAN

Malacañang Palace
Malacanang
Malacañang
Garden

MacArthur Hwy

Del Monte Ave

SANTA
MESA
HEIGHTS

Mayon St

Blumentritt St

E España St

Bonifacio Ave

34

España

37

27

Legarda

Antipolo St

UST

Carriedo

Ortigas

CALOOCAN
CITY

Monumento
(North
Terminal)

GRACE
PARK

5th
Avenue

Bonifacio St

2

Abad
Santos

R Papa

Blumentritt

Tayuman

Doroteo
Jose

Quezon Blvd

3

Recto

Central

BALINTAWAK

Balintawak

MALABON
CITY

C-3 Rd

Mabini Ave

Juan Luna St

Jose Abad Santos St

CM Recto

Tutuban

Bambang

CITY OF
MANILA

BINONDO

Honoratio Lopez Blvd

Velasquez St

Morienes St

NORTH
HARBOR
DISTRICT

North
Harbor

SOUTH
HARBOR
DISTRICT

PHILIPPINES

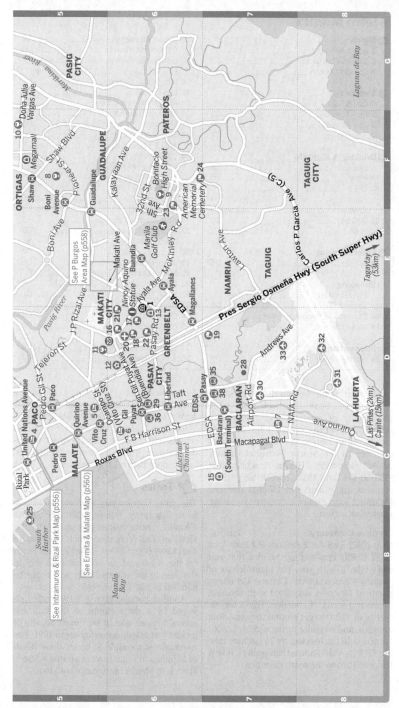

PASIG CITY

Marikina River

Doña Julia Vargas Ave

10

Megamall

Shaw Blvd

Pioneer St

8

ORTIGAS

Shaw

Boni Avenue

Boni Ave

PATEROS

GUADALUPE

Guadalupe

Kalayaan Ave

32nd St

Bonifacio High Street

5th Ave

23

9

American Memorial Cemetery

24

TAGUIG CITY

Laguna de Bay

Makati Ave

Manila Golf Club

McKinley Rd

Lawton Ave

NAMRIA

TAGUIG

Carlos P Garcia Ave (C-5)

See P Burgos Area Map (p558)

JP Rizal Ave

MAKATI CITY

Ninoy Aquino Statue

Ayala Ave

Buendia

Ayala

Magallanes

EDSA

GREENBELT

Pasay Rd

1

13

TAGUIG

Pres Sergio Osmeña Hwy (South Super Hwy)

Tagaytay (53km)

Pasig River

Teleron St

Pedro Gil St

PACO

Paco

United Nations Avenue

11

12

16

21

20

17

18

22

19

Sen Gil Puyat Ave

PASAY CITY

Libertad

Taft Ave

EDSA

35

Pasay

38

Andrews Ave

33

32

31

LA HUERTA

25

Rizal Park

Pedro Gil

Quirino Avenue

Vito Cruz

5

Ocampo St (Nto Cruz St)

6

Puyat

Sen Gil Puyat Ave

29

36

F B Harrison St

EDSA

Baclaran (South Terminal)

BACLARAN

28

30

Airport Rd

7

NAIA Rd

Macapagal Blvd

Quirino Ave

Las Piñas (2km); Cavite (15km)

See Ermita & Malate Map (p560)

See Intramuros & Rizal Park Map (p556)

South Harbor

Roxas Blvd

Libertad Channel

Manila Bay

MALATE

Quirino Avenue

PASIG CITY

Boni Avenue

Metro Manila

has interesting displays on the wreck of the *San Diego*, a Spanish galleon from 1600, plus plenty of artefacts and comprehensive exhibits on the various Filipino ethnic groups. Admission to the museum includes entrance to the nearby **National Gallery of Art** (Map p556; P Burgos St; adult/student P150/50, free Sun; ☺10am-5pm Tue-Sun), which contains many works of Filipino masters, including Juan Luna's impressive signature work, *Spoliarium*.

Chinese Cemetery   CEMETERY
(Map p552; Rizal Ave Extension; ☺7.30am-7pm)
FREE Boldly challenging the idea that you can't take it with you, the mausoleums of wealthy Chinese in the Chinese Cemetery, north of Binondo, are fitted with flushing toilets and crystal chandeliers. Hire a bicycle (per hour P100) to get around the sprawling grounds, and consider hiring a guide (P350) for access to the best tombs. To get here take the LRT to Abad Santos then walk or take a tricycle (P25) to the south entrance.

Ayala Museum   MUSEUM
(Map p552; www.ayalamuseum.org; Greenbelt 4, Ayala Centre, Makati; adult/student P300/425; ☺9am-6pm Tue-Fri) Here brilliant dioramas tell the story of the Filipino quest for independence. It also houses the Philippines' best contemporary art collection.

⌖ Tours

The most popular day tour out of Manila is to **Tagaytay**, 60km south. The town's 15km-long ridge road serves up spectacular views of **Taal Volcano**, which rises out of **Taal Lake** 600m below. Tours include lunch on the ridge and an optional boat trip to the base of the volcano itself, which can be climbed in just 45 minutes.

Another popular tour is a 4WD ride (followed by a short climb) to the stunning emerald crater lake of **Mt Pinatubo**, site of a cataclysmic volcanic eruption in 1991. The mountain is a couple of hours' drive north of Manila and tours leave at around 4.30am. Hostels in Manila can arrange both tours.

Carlos Celdran WALKING TOUR
(✆0920 909 2021; www.carlosceldran.com; adult
P1000-1100, student P600) If you're in Manila
over a weekend, don't miss out on the flamboyant tours of Intramuros and other destinations by Carlos Celdran.

Old Manila Walks WALKING TOUR
(✆0918 962 6452, 02-711 3823; www.oldmanila
walks.com; tours P650-1100) Tour leader Ivan
Man Dy has a deep knowledge of Manila
and its history and culture.

Sun Cruises BOAT TOUR
(✆02-831 8140; www.corregidorphilippines.com;
CCP Complex jetty, Pasay; excursion incl lunch weekday/weekend P2300/2500) Sun Cruises has
the market cornered for trips to infamous
Corregidor Island, the last bastion of
American resistance during the Japanese
invasion of Luzon in 1941. It loads up 100
to 200 passengers every morning at 7.30am;
you return to Manila by 3.45pm.

🛏 Sleeping

The best hostels have followed the best
bars and restaurants up to Makati, specifically to the P Burgos area. Of course Makati
hostels cost more, and the P Burgos area
is hardly sleaze-free, but if you want to escape Malate's squalor look no further. If you
need to be close to the airport, hone in on
Pasay.

🛏 Malate & Pasay

⭐**Pink Manila** HOSTEL $
(Map p552; ✆02-484 3145; www.pinkmanilahostel.
com; cnr Bautista & San Pedro Sts; dm P450-570,
d P1600; ❄) The formula for a good hostel
is elusive, but Floridian owner Crissy gets
it right. Nice mix of dorm rooms with beds
swathed in trademark pink linen? Check.
Open-air bar area with pool table, swimming pool and rocking monthly parties?
Check. Hammock-strewn roof deck? Check.
Its somewhat random location near Vito
Cruz LRT stop is equally convenient to both
Malate and Makati.

Chill-Out Guesthouse HOSTEL $
(Map p560; ✆0939 517 7019; chillout@manille
hotel.com; 612 Remedios St; dm P350, d P700-1500;
❄@�) Just off Malate's central Remedios
Circle, cosy Chill-Out delivers a kitchen, free
coffee and warm private rooms to complement a single eight-bed dormitory.

Pension Natividad HOSTEL $
(Map p560; ✆02-521 0524; 1690 MH del Pilar
St; dm with fan P400, d P1000-1500; ❄�) Set
around a private courtyard, this popular
Peace Corps–volunteer roost features low-
priced munchies and large single-sex dorms.
Stay elsewhere if you want to party.

Where 2 Next HOSTEL $
(Map p560; ✆02-354 3533; www.where2next
hostel.com; 1776 Adriatico St; dm P495, r P950-
1800; ❄�) This is a solid all-round hostel
with a few private fan rooms and plenty-
comfy air-con dorms. It lacks a killer bar but
organises bar crawls.

The Buoy HOSTEL $
(Map p552; ✆02-516 0561; https://thebuoy.ph;
640 Ocampo St; dm P395-450, d P2000; ❄) A
somewhat impersonal hostel a bit south of
the Malate tourist belt, hence closer to the
airport. It has 12 dorms and a single private
room. The hang-out area is, effectively, the
attached Buoy bar and restaurant.

Townhouse INN $
(Map p552; ✆02-854 3826; bill_lorna@yahoo.
com; 31 Bayview Dr; dm P180, s/d from P300/400;
❄@�) Woeful, yet undeniably cheap and
in a quiet location pretty close to the airport.
We've ended up here more than a few times.

⭐**Oasis Paco Park** HOTEL $$
(Map p552; ✆02-521 2371; www.oasispark.com;
1032-34 Belen St; r from P2000; ❄❄@��)
Well removed from the hustle and bustle of
Malate and Ermita, this friendly neighbour-
hood hotel is the rare Manila midranger
with a pool – and a good one at that. Cheap-
est rooms are windowless; ask for promo
rates on the fancier rooms.

Casa Bocobo HOTEL $$
(Map p556; ✆02-526 3783; www.casabocobo.
com.ph; Bocobo St; r incl breakfast P1600-3000;
❄❄@�) This is a solid if unspectacular
midrange hotel near Rizal Park. The standard rooms are cramped but the superior
rooms are downright flash. Discounts if you
walk in after 6pm.

🛏 Makati & Quezon City

⭐**Manila Boutique Hostel** HOSTEL $
(Map p558; ✆0917 858 5519; www.mnlboutique
hostel.com; cnr B Valdez & Santiago St; dm P480-
680, r P1400; ❄@�) Owner Gonz is an
artist, and his hostel is infused with both
his creative spirit and his art. The air-con

PHILIPPINES MANILA

Intramuros & Rizal Park

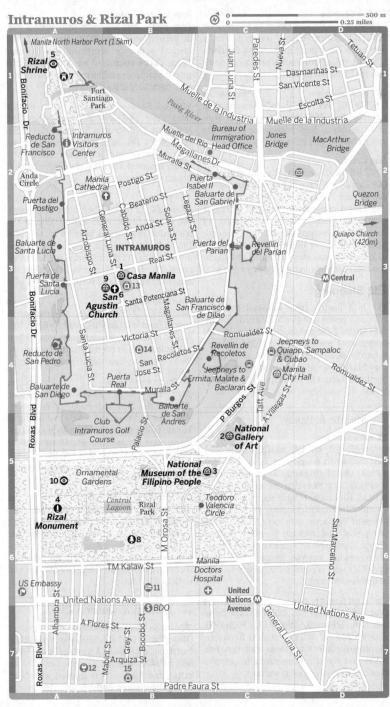

N

0 —————————— 500 m
0 —————————— 0.25 miles

PHILIPPINES

Manila North Harbor Port (1.5km)

5 Rizal Shrine
7

Fort Santiago Park

Bonifacio Dr

Reducto de San Francisco

Intramuros Visitors Center

Pasig River

Muelle de la Industria

Juan Luna St

Paredes St

Nueva St

Dasmariñas St
San Vicente St

Escolta St

Tetuan St

Muelle de la Industria

Jones Bridge

MacArthur Bridge

Anda Cirele

Puerta del Postigo

Manila Cathedral

Postigo St

Muelle del Rio

Magallanes Dr

Muralla St

Bureau of Immigration Head Office

Cabildo St

Beaterio St

Puerta Isabel II

Baluarte de San Gabriel

Quezon Bridge

Baluarte de Santa Lucia

General Luna St

Arzobispo St

Anda St

Solana St

Legazpi St

Puerta del Parian

Revellin del Parian

Quiapo Church (420m)

INTRAMUROS

Real St

Puerta de Santa Lucia

Bonifacio Dr

1 Casa Manila
9
6 San Agustin Church
13

Santa Potenciana St

Baluarte de San Francisco de Dilao

M Central

Victoria St

14

San Jose St

Magallanes St

Recoletos St

Revellin de Recoletos

Romualdez St

Jeepneys to Quiapo, Sampaloc & Cubao

Manila City Hall

Reducto de San Pedro

Santa Lucia St

Puerta Real

Muralla St

Jeepneys to Ermita, Malate & Baclaran

Tatt Ave

A Villegas St

Romualdez St

Baluarte de San Diego

Palacio St

Baluarte de San Andres

P Burgos St

National Gallery of Art
2

Club Intramuros Golf Course

National Museum of the Filipino People
3

San Marcelino St

10

Ornamental Gardens

Central Lagoon

Rizal Park

Teodoro Valencia Circle

4 Rizal Monument

M Orosa St

8

TM Kalaw St

Manila Doctors Hospital

US Embassy

11

United Nations Ave

BDO

United Nations Avenue M

United Nations Ave

Alhambra St

A Flores St

Mabini St

Grey St

Bocobo St

Arquiza St

General Luna St

12

15

Padre Faura St

Roxas Blvd

Roxas Blvd

Intramuros & Rizal Park

dorm rooms are far from huge (a problem at all Makati hostels), and some are windowless. But the beds are quality, towels are free (rare for Manila), unsavoury smells are absent, and the street-level locale makes for a robust Filipino-style happy hour.

Hilik Hostel HOSTEL $
(Map p558; ☑02-519 5821; hilikboutiquehostel@gmail.com; Mavenue Bldg, 7844 Makati Ave; dm P500-800, s/d from P750/1500; ❋ 🛜) Downstairs from Our Melting Pot, the dorms at Hilik ('snore' in Tagalog) are cramped but do have air-con, and the entire hostel is immaculate. Unfortunately it lacks a good common/kitchen area, although they plan to build one.

Our Melting Pot HOSTEL $
(Map p558; ☑02-659 5443; www.ourmeltingpotmakati.com; 4th fl, Mavenue Bldg, 7844 Makati Ave; dm incl breakfast P750-850, r incl breakfast P1000-1600; ⊕❋@☎) A large kitchen/common area gives recently relocated OMP a communal vibe, although the dorms (blessedly air-conditioned) and rooms are on the small side. Ask for dorm discounts midweek.

Hotel Durban HOTEL $$
(Map p558; ☑02-897 1866; www.hoteldurban.net; 4875 Durban St, Makati; s/d from P1450/1550;

❋🛜) Makati's best midrange value is a tightly run ship. The immaculate rooms, with faux-wood panelling, are more than adequate for the price. It's popular so book ahead.

🍴 Eating

Food courts in malls such as **Robinsons Place** (Map p560; Pedro Gil St; ⊙10am-9pm) in Ermita are always a good bet for affordable sustenance. For vegetarian food try the dozens of Korean and Chinese restaurants in Malate and Quiapo.

🍴 Malate & Ermita

★**Shawarma Snack Center** MIDDLE EASTERN $
(Map p560; 485 R Salas St; shawarma P55, meals P100-250; ⊙24hr) With freshly grilled kebabs and delectable appetisers such as falafel, *mutabal* (eggplant dip) and hummus, this street-side eatery is a gastronomic delight. Hookah pipes round out the effect.

Suzhou Dim Sum CHINESE $$
(Map p560; cnr Mabini & Alonzo Sts; mains P150-250; ⊙24hr) Suzhou has some of the best dim sum in Malate, plus large and wildly affordable noodle dishes.

Cafe Adriatico INTERNATIONAL $$
(Map p560; 1790 Adriatico St; mains P200-400; ⊙7am-5am; 🛜) A corner bistro where you can tuck into original Spanish fare with English, American and Italian effects, to the pleasant hum of robust conversation and dishware in motion. A true neighbourhood hang-out since 1979.

Hap Chan Tea House CHINESE $$
(Map p560; 561 General Malvar St; mains P200-400; ⊙11am-3am) Serves delicious, steaming platters of Hong Kong specialities; it's popular for a reason.

🍴 Makati & Quezon City

El Chupacabra TEX-MEX $
(Map p558; JVR Bldg, Felipe St; tacos P80-100; ⊙4pm-1am) Delicious 'street tacos' are the name of the game here, often with a Filipino twist, plus margaritas and P45 San Miguel. The street out front sometimes closes on weekends and becomes a party.

Greens VEGETARIAN $
(92 Scout Castor St, Quezon City; mains P120-200; ⊙11am-10pm Mon-Sat, noon-9pm Sun; ⊕🚭) It's almost worth the long slog up to Quezon

P Burgos Area

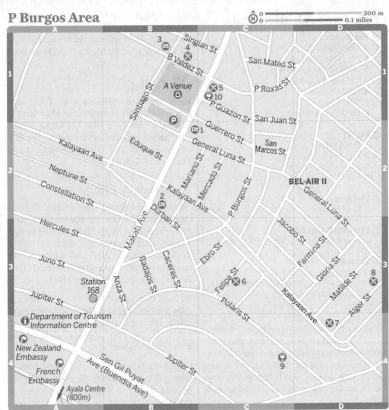

City just to sample the wonderful vego fare here. Try the 'beef' and broccoli.

Beni's Falafel MIDDLE EASTERN **$$**
(Map p558; 4364 B Valdez St; dishes P135-250; ⊙10am-midnight) There are only eight things on the menu at this unassuming Yemeni-owned hole-in-the-wall, all done well. The *shakshuka* (eggs poached in a spicy tomato sauce) and Beni's falafel are our faves.

Chihuahua MEXICAN **$$**
(Map p558; 7838 Makati Ave; mains P295-345; ⊙11am-late; 🛜) The burritos here are legendary, or try the yummy 'burrito bowls', a Chihuahua original.

Som's Noodle House THAI **$$**
(Map p558; 5921 A Alger St; mains P150-220; ⊙10.30am-10pm) Filipino generally struggle with Thai food but not Som's, which spices staples like red curry and *tom yam* to your liking.

Grilla Bar & Grill FILIPINO **$$**
(Map p558; 📋02-899 8775; cnr Kalayaan Ave & Rockwell Dr; mains P150-300; ⊙11am-2.30pm & 5pm-1am, to 3am Fri & Sat) Classic Filipino 'restobar' a short walk from P Burgos St along Kalayaan Ave.

🍷 Drinking & Entertainment

You name it, it's there. That about sums up Manila nightlife. As a rule, Malate has cover bands and karaoke bars; Makati and the Fort are where the nightclubs are; and Quezon City has the best original live music. The traditional gay-and-lesbian nexus is at the corner of J Nakpil St and M Orosa St in Malate, although the best gay clubs have migrated to Ortigas, Quezon City.

Movies (mostly imported blockbusters in English; tickets P120 to P170) are in the malls. Theatres and performing arts troupes are scattered all over the metropolis.

P Burgos Area

 Sleeping
1	Hilik Hostel	B2
2	Hotel Durban	B2
3	Manila Boutique Hostel	B1
	Our Melting Pot	(see 1)

 Eating
4	Beni's Falafel	B1
5	Chihuahua	C1
6	El Chupacabra	C3
7	Grilla Bar & Grill	D4
8	Som's Noodle House	D3

Drinking & Nightlife
9	Handlebar	C4
10	Time	C1

See www.clickthecity.com for extensive movie and entertainment listings.

Malate

Drinking opportunities abound down here. You can quaff cheap suds kerbside just west of Remedios Circle on Remedios St. On this same street are a couple of uni clubs that get going later in the evening.

★1951
CAFE
(Penguin Cafe; Map p560; 1951 Adriatico St; ☺from 6pm Tue-Sat) This legendary bar-cum-gallery is a magnet for bohemian types. On Fridays and Saturdays it squeezes in some of the finest musical talent in the Philippines, including, on occasion, Kalayo (see p605).

Erra's Place
BAR
(Map p560; Adriatico St; ☺24hr) Cheap snacks and P33 San Miguel in a perfectly located open-air setting make Erra's a logical warm-up – or warm-down – spot.

Hobbit House
BAR
(Map p556; www.hobbithousemanila.com; 1212 MH del Pilar St; admission P125-150; ☺5pm-2am) Often forgotten amid the vertically challenged waiters is that Hobbit House consistently draws Manila's best live blues acts.

The Library
COMEDY
(Map p560; ☑02-522 2484; www.thelibrary.com.ph; 1139 M Orosa St; shows P100-500; ☺shows from 9pm) In the heart of Malate's gay district, the Library has nightly comedy shows.

Makati & Quezon City

There are several worthy sports bars around P Burgos St, including the fantastic biker bar **Handlebar** (Map p558; www.handlebar.com.ph; 31 Polaris St; ☺3pm-3am). The club scene changes often. You'll find a gaggle of upscale clubs, all with strict dress codes and P300 to P500 cover charges, near the Fort Strip complex in the Fort. These include **Hyve** (Map p552; W Global Centre, The Fort; ☺10pm-5am Wed-Sat), **Urbn** (Map p552; Fort Pointe II Bldg; ☺from 6pm) and **Prive** (Map p552; www.priveluxuryclub.com; Fort Strip; ☺from 10pm Wed-Sat). Over in Makati, **Time** (Map p558; http://timeinmanila.com; 7840 Makati Ave; ☺from 5pm Tue-Sat) and **Palladium** (Map p552; New World Hotel, Esperanza St; admission incl drink P500; ☺Wed-Sat) are a bit more down-to-earth.

Bed
NIGHTCLUB
(Map p552; www.bed.com.ph; Mayflower St, Ortigas; admission incl some drinks P350; ☺6pm-2am Sun-Thu, to 5am Fri & Sat) A top gay club in Manila for years, Bed has a new home in Ortigas. Its infamous parties last until the wee hours.

O Bar
NIGHTCLUB
(Map p552; Ortigas Home Depot, Julia Vargas Ave, Ortigas; admission incl 3 beers P300-400; ☺10pm-6am Wed-Sun) O Bar expanded from gay bar to gay club upon its move to Ortigas from J Nakpil St in Malate.

SaGuijo
NIGHTCLUB
(Map p552; ☑02-897 8629; www.saguijo.com; 7612 Guijo St, Makati; admission after 10pm P150; ☺6pm-2am) A diminutive indie-rock club with superb and often very loud original live music. Hidden in a quiet Makati neighbourhood away from Makati's central business district, it's well worth seeking out.

B-Side
LIVE MUSIC
(Map p552; The Collective, Malugay St; ☺varies) Bands play most nights outside B-Side in the open-air courtyard of 'the Collective', a conglomeration of arty-farty shops and bars. Reggae bands kick off at 4.20pm on Sundays.

Shopping

With a hulking shopping centre seemingly around every corner, Manila is a mall-rat's fantasy. **Robinsons Place** (Map p560; Pedro Gil St; ☺10am-9pm) and the mammoth **Mall of Asia** (Map p552; Manila Bay; ☺10am-10pm) are the closest to the tourist belt in Malate. **Greenbelt** (Map p552; Ayala Centre) is an oasis of calm in the centre of Makati.

Ermita & Malate

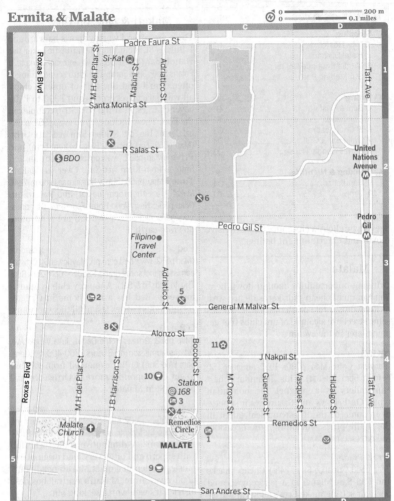

PHILIPPINES MANILA

Away from these air-conditioned temples, the masses shop in vast flea markets such as **Greenhills** (Map p552; Ortigas Ave, San Juan; ⊙9am-10pm) in Ortigas, or on the frenzied streets of Quiapo.

Worthy souvenir items include wood-carved Ifugao *bulol* (rice guards), *barong* (traditional Filipino shirts), lacquered coconut-shell trinkets and indigenous textiles.

Silahis Arts & Artifacts Center   SOUVENIRS
(Map p556; www.silahis.com; 744 General Luna St, Intramuros; ⊙10am-7pm) It's almost more

cultural centre than store here. Intricately woven baskets, *bulol* and textiles from North Luzon and Mindanao are some of the specialities.

La Monja Loca   SOUVENIRS
(Map p556; General Luna St, Intramuros; ⊙9am-6pm Tue-Sun) Great selection of creative souvenirs at 'the Crazy Nun', run by celebrated tour guide Carlos Celdran.

Fully Booked   BOOKS
(Map p552; Mall of Asia, Pasay; ⊙10am-9pm) Comprehensive bookstore with outstanding travel section.

Ermita & Malate

Solidaridad Bookshop   BOOKS
(Map p556; 531 P Faura St, Ermita; ⊙9am-6pm Mon-Sat) Leftie bookshop particularly good for books and documentaries on local history and politics.

ℹ Information

DANGERS & ANNOYANCES

Manila is probably no more dangerous than the next megacity, but it can still be dodgy, especially after dark. The district of Tondo, particularly around the north ports, is one area to avoid walking around solo after dark. The sheltered malls of Makati are pretty darn safe, as is most of Makati's CBD. The tourist belts in Malate and especially Ermita are rife with street-dwellers and destitution. Exercise caution walking around at night, especially south of Remedios Circle.

Manila is notorious for scams that target tourists. The most common scam involves confidence tricksters posing as a group of friends or a family and befriending (usually solo) travellers. They eventually invite them home or on a short excursion. The situation ends with the traveller being drugged, robbed or scammed out of some money – often through a too-good-to-be-true gambling game. If you feel that a stranger is acting overly friendly, walk away. Also, beware of people who claim to have met you before or claim to be staying in your hotel.

Be wary of the money-changers along HM del Pilar and Mabini Sts in Ermita. Some have been known to use amateur-magician card tricks to cheat people.

Traffic is the big annoyance in Manila; you'll probably spend half your time either stuck in it or talking about it. Leave extra time to get to airports, bus stations and dinner dates.

Pickpocketing is rampant on the MRT, and on major bar strips, where drunk tourists present easy prey.

INTERNET ACCESS

Malls such as Robinsons Place have internet cafes, and there are a few along Adriatico St in Malate, and along Makati Ave near the corner of Jupiter St. Rates vary from P30 to P60 per hour.

MEDICAL SERVICES

Makati Medical Center (Map p552; ☎02-888 8999; www.makatimed.net.ph; 2 Amorsolo St, Makati)
Manila Doctors Hospital (Map p556; ☎02-524 3011; www.maniladoctors.com.ph; 667 United Nations Ave, Ermita)

MONEY

Malate, Ermita and Makati are littered with ATMs. Popular banks are BDO, BPI and Metrobank, but all charge P200 for ATM withdrawals. Along Mabini and Adriatico Sts, you'll find numerous money-changers but, as always, be careful when using these services.
HSBC (Map p552; 6766 Ayala Ave, Makati) Allows P40,000 ATM withdrawals with no fees.

POST

Manila Central Post Office (Map p556; Magallanes Dr, Intramuros; ⊙6am-6.30pm Mon-Fri, 8am-noon Sat) A landmark; offers full services.

TOURIST INFORMATION

Department of Tourism Information Centre (DOT; Map p558; ☎02-524 2384; www.visit myphilippines.com; JB Bldg, 351 Sen Gil Puyat Ave, Makati; ⊙7am-6pm Mon-Sat) Recently transplanted from Rizal Park downtown. Hands out maps and dispenses advice. There are also smaller DOT offices at the various Ninoy Aquino International Airport terminals.

PHILIPPINES MANILA

WORTH A TRIP

BINONDO & QUIAPO MARKETS
....
Lovers of markets and utter chaos are advised to make DIY trips over the Pasig River to **Binondo** (Manila's old Chinatown) and **Quiapo**, where every manner of product is sold to a throng of humanity. Around **Quiapo Church** (Map p552; Quezon Blvd) look for the apothecary vendors. They sell herbal potions, folk medicines and amulets that are said to ward off evil spirits. Take the LRT-1 to the Carriedo stop to get to the heart of the action.

TRAVEL AGENCIES

Malate and Ermita are filled with travel agencies that can help with domestic air tickets (for a fee). **Filipino Travel Center** (Map p560; ☎02-528 4507; www.filipinotravel.com.ph; cnr Adriatico & Pedro Gil Sts, Malate; ⊗8am-6pm Mon-Fri, 9am-5pm Sat) Catering to foreign tourists, this agency organises a wide variety of tours; can buy Banaue bus tickets.

ℹ Getting There & Away

AIR

Ninoy Aquino International Airport (NAIA; p609) is about 6km south of Malate, in Parañaque. It has four separate terminals. See the boxed text on p610 for information on which terminal to use. See p610 and p611 later in this chapter for details on international and domestic routes and airlines flying in and out of NAIA. Airlines have offices at the terminal where they are based, and some also have satellite offices in Makati.

BOAT

Manila's port is divided into two sections: South Harbor and the flashy new **Manila North Harbor Port** (http://www.mnhport.com.ph; Piers 4 & 6, Tondo). The latter is a beacon of modernity in the capital's hardscrabble Tondo District. At the time of research it remained unclear which companies might use the new port.

2GO Travel (Map p552; ☎02-528 7000; http://travel.2go.com.ph; Pier 15, South Harbor) This is the main line operating long-haul ferries out of Manila to most major cities in the Visayas, Mindanao and Palawan. Full schedules are on the website. Also has a ticket office on Level 1 of Robinsons Place Mall in Ermita.

BUS

Confusingly there's no single long-distance bus station in Manila. The terminals are mainly strung along Epifanio de los Santos Ave (EDSA), with a cluster near the intersection of Taft Ave in Pasay City to the south, and in Cubao (part of Quezon City) to the north. Another cluster is north of Quiapo in Sampaloc. If you're confused, just tell a taxi driver which station you want in which city (eg 'the Victory Liner terminal in Cubao'), and they should know where it is. Buses heading into Manila will usually just have 'Cubao', 'Pasay' or 'Sampaloc' on the signboard.

North Luzon

Comfortable 27-seat 'deluxe' express buses are well worth the extra coin to Baguio and Vigan. It's recommended to book these, and the direct night buses to Banaue, a day or more ahead.

Mindoro

For Puerto Galera on Mindoro, **Si-Kat** (Map p560; ☎02-708 9628; Citystate Tower Hotel, 1315 Mabini St, Ermita) runs a bus-boat service, leaving around 8am from Ermita. These take about four hours and cost P700 – roughly P350 more than taking a public bus to Batangas pier and catching a public boat there.

BUSES FROM MANILA

DESTINATION	DURATION (HR)	PRICE (P)	COMPANY	FREQUENCY
Baguio	4½-6½	air-con–deluxe 450–715	Genesis, Victory Liner	frequent
Banaue	7-8	450	Florida, Ohayami	2-4 night buses
Batangas	1½	165	Jam Transit, RRCG	every 20min
Bontoc	11½	650	Florida	7pm
Clark Airport	3	450	Philtranco	6.30am, 11.30am, 8.30pm
Legazpi	10-11	air-con–deluxe 850–1000	Cagsawa, Isarog, Philtranco	frequent
Naga	8-9	air-con–deluxe 750–900	Cagsawa, Isarog, Philtranco	frequent
Solano (for Banaue)	8	375	Florida, Victory Liner	frequent
Tagaytay	2	77	San Agustin	hourly
Vigan	7-9	air-con–deluxe 680–825	Florida, Partas	hourly

Southeast Luzon

The main hub for Bicol-bound buses is the **Araneta Bus Terminal** (Map p552; btwn Times Sq & Gen Romulo Aves, Cubao). Isarog runs several deluxe sleeper buses to Legazpi via Naga every night. Cagsawa has two convenient night buses straight from Ermita. To save money, take one of myriad 'ordinary' (non-air-con) buses that leave from the Araneta Bus Terminal.

Clark Airport

For Clark Airport, take the Philtranco shuttle, which stops to pick up passengers at Megamall in Ortigas on the way out of town. Or just take any northbound bus to the Malabacat terminal in Dau (near Angeles), a short taxi ride from Clark.

Useful Bus Companies

Cagsawa

Florida Bus Lines (Map p552; cnr Extremadura & Earnshaw Sts, Sampaloc)

Genesis (www.genesistransport.com.ph)

Isarog Bus Lines (Map p552; ☑02-925 6835; Araneta Bus Terminal)

Jam Transit (Map p552; ☑02-831 0465; www.jam.com.ph; cnr Taft & Sen Gil Puyat Aves, Pasay; ☜)

Ohayami (Map p552; ☑0927 649 3055; cnr Loyola & Cayco Sts, Sampaloc)

Partas

Philtranco (Map p552; ☑02-851 8077/9; cnr EDSA & Apelo Cruz St)

RRCG (Map p552; cnr Taft & Sen Gil Puyat Aves, Pasay)

San Agustin (Map p552; Pasay Rotunda, cnr Taft Ave & EDSA)

Victory Liner (www.victoryliner.com)

❶ Getting Around

Epifanio de los Santos Ave (EDSA) is the main artery that links downtown Manila with Makati, Ortigas and Quezon City. The MRT line conveniently runs right along EDSA, and links with the LRT at Taft Ave.

TO/FROM THE AIRPORT, BUS TERMINALS & FERRY PORTS

Manila's airport situation is a mess. Since there are no direct public-transport routes from any of the four terminals to the tourist belt in Malate, bite the bullet and take a taxi, especially if you have a lot of luggage. Avoid the white, prepaid 'coupon' taxis that charge set rates of more than P400, and look for the yellow airport metered taxis. These have a flag fall of P70 (taxis on the street have a P40 flag fall). Your total bill to Malate should be about P250. To save a few pesos you can walk upstairs to the arrivals area of any of the terminals and angle for a regular metered taxi on a drop-off run.

If you arrive in Manila by boat, you're also better off catching a taxi into town, as the harbour is a pretty rough area and public-transport routes are complicated.

With the number of different bus stations in Manila, if you arrive by bus you could end up pretty much anywhere. Luckily, most terminals are located on or near Manila's major artery, Epifanio de los Santos Ave (EDSA), linked to the tourist belt in Malate by MRT and LRT.

JEEPNEY

Heading south from Ermita/Malate along MH del Pilar St, 'Baclaran' jeepneys end up on EDSA just west of the Pasay bus terminals and just east of Mall of Asia. Going north from Ermita/Malate along Mabini St, jeepneys go to Rizal Park before heading off in various directions: 'Santa Cruz' and 'Monumento' jeepneys take the MacArthur Bridge, passing the main post office, while 'Cubao' and 'Espana' jeepneys traverse the Quezon Bridge to Quiapo church before peeling off to, respectively, the Cubao and Sampaloc bus terminals.

TRAIN

There are three elevated railway lines in Manila known as LRT-1, LRT-2 and MRT-3. The most useful, if you are staying in Malate/Ermita, is the LRT-1, which runs south along Taft Ave to the MRT interchange at EDSA near the Pasay bus terminals, and north to Quiapo. From the EDSA interchange, the MRT runs north to Makati and Cubao. You'll need a separate ticket for each line. Prices start from P12, and trains run between 4am and midnight. During rush hour, these trains can get mosh-pit crowded.

NORTH LUZON

Luzon's north is a vast expanse of misty mountains, sprawling plains and endless coastline. The region's trophy piece is the central mountainous area known as the Cordillera, where the Ifugao built their world-famous rice terraces in and around Banaue more than 2000 years ago. Elsewhere, historic Vigan boasts a colonial hub that is the country's best-preserved vestige of its Spanish heritage. Explorers can continue north of Vigan to Luzon's wild northern tip, where remote white-sand beaches embrace the coastline and rarely-visited islands lurk offshore.

The Cordillera

Most who venture into North Luzon set their sights squarely on the Cordillera, a river-sliced hinterland of lush green forests covering hectare after hectare of jagged earth. The amazing rice terraces near Banaue are perhaps the Philippines' most iconic site. Lesser-known but no less spectacular terraces exist throughout the Cordillera, most notably around Bontoc. Hippie-esque Sagada has a few terraces of its own, although the main attractions there are caving, hiking and the laid-back ambience.

The tribespeople of the Cordillera, collectively known as the Igorot, are as compelling as the landscape, and it's worth studying their culture if you're heading up this way. In remote areas you may observe *cañao* (sacrificial ceremonies) and see elders wearing indigenous garb such as G-strings (loin cloths).

Throw a poncho in your bag, as the Cordillera can get chilly at night. Fog and rain are often part of the equation too – the rainy season starts earlier and ends later in the mountains. There are no functioning ATMs outside of Baguio so bring cash.

❶ Getting There & Around

The usual way into the Cordillera is via Baguio or Banaue, although more obscure routes exist. Rainy-season landslides often close the roads, so pack patience. The Halsema 'highway' linking Banaue with Bontoc is sealed nowadays. A real engineering feat when it was built in the 1920s, the Halsema snakes along a narrow ridge at altitudes up to 2255m, offering great views of precipitous valleys, green rice terraces and Luzon's highest peak, Mt Pulag (2922m).

OFF THE BEATEN TRACK

THE MUMMIES OF KABAYAN

A road heading north out of Baguio for 50 winding kilometres leads to picturesque Kabayan, the site of several caves containing eerie mummies entombed centuries ago by the Ibaloi people. Some of these caves can be visited, while others are known only to Ibaloi elders. After exploring Kabayan for a day or two, you can walk back to the Halsema Hwy (about five hours, straight uphill) via the Timbac Caves (admission P100), the spot where the best-preserved mummies lurk. The keys are with a caretaker who lives up the hill from the caves. From the caves, it's about a 45-minute walk out to the Halsema Hwy.

Baguio

📞 074 / POP 319,000 / ELEV 1450M

Vibrant, woodsy and cool by Philippine standards, Baguio (*bah*-gee-oh) is the Cordillera's nerve centre. The Philippines' 'summer capital' was founded as a hill station for the US military in the early 1900s. A university town, Baguio is known for live music, faith healers and funky restaurants. Unfortunately, even without tricycles (which can't climb the hills), Baguio has major air- and noise-pollution. The city's charm lies well outside the centre, in pine-forested parks such as Camp John Hay.

◉ Sights & Activities

Tam-Awan Village　　　　CULTURAL BUILDING
(📞 0917 553 4078, 074-446 2949; www.tam-awan village.com; Long-Long Rd, Pinsao; admission P50, workshops P450) 🌿 Eight traditional Igorot homes were taken apart and then reassembled on the side of a hill at the artist colony Tam-Awan Village. Spending the night in one of these huts is a rare treat. You can participate in art workshops, learn dream-catcher or bead making and see indigenous music and dance demonstrations. On clear days there are wonderful views of the South China Sea. To get here, take a Quezon Hill–Tam-Awan or Tam-Awan–Long-Long jeepney from the corner of Kayang and Shagem Sts (P8).

BenCab Museum　　　　MUSEUM
(www.bencabmuseum.org; Km 6, Asin Rd, Tadiangan; adult/student P100/80; ⊙9am-6pm Tue-Sun) The museum dedicated to the work of Benedicto Reyes Cabrera (aka 'BenCab') is well worth the short jeepney ride out of town. Filipino crafts and modern art are displayed in an ultra-modern space that, paradoxically, is partly modelled after a traditional rice terrace. Look for the saucy erotic art section. Stick around for a Cordillera-inspired meal at **Cafe Sabel**. Asin Rd jeepneys get you here from Abanao St near City Hall.

Markets　　　　MARKETS
Baguio is a shopping mecca where you can find all manner of handicrafts, including basketwork, textiles, Ifugao woodcarvings and jewellery (silver is a local speciality). Bargain hunters might check out the lively **City Market** (Magsaysay Ave), which sells everything from knock-off handicrafts to Cordillera coffee to fresh-grilled chicken foetus. Didn't realise Baguio was so cold

and wet? Buy a cheap hoodie or raincoat at the **Night Market** (Harrison Rd) along the northeast edge of Burnham Park.

Spa de la Fleur MASSAGE
(☑074-424 1230; ES Clemente Bldg, Shanum St; 1hr massage P250; ⊙10am-9pm) Quality pampering four storeys up, near the Benguet Pine Tourist Inn.

🛌 Sleeping

The most unique choice is **Tam-Awan Village** (☑0917 553 4078, 074-446 2949; www.tam-awan village.com; Long-Long Rd, Pinsao; per person P500; 🛜), but it's at least a 15-minute ride from the centre. For barflies, the well-appointed basement doubles (P800) at the Red Lion pub are good value.

Baguio Village Inn GUESTHOUSE $
(☑074-442 3901; 355 Magsaysay Ave; s/d from P350/700; 🛜) This warm and inviting backpacker special is reminiscent of the cosy pinewood guesthouses in Sagada. Only the noisy location, beyond the Slaughterhouse bus terminal, spoils the illusion.

Upstairs Bed & Bath HOSTEL $
(☑074-446 4687; upstairsbedandbath@gmail.com; GSP Bldg, Leonard Wood Rd; dm P299, d P800-1200; @🛜) At last, a true hostel in Baguio, with 90 beds spread over spotless two- to 25-bed dorm rooms. The outdoor common area could use improvement. It's a five-minute walk southeast of SM Mall.

YMCA Hostel HOSTEL $
(☑074-442 4766; Post Office Loop; dm/d P375/1300) The 'Y' boasts huge, bright dorm rooms and tidy, colourful private rooms with soft beds and flat-screen TVs – it's pretty good value. It's just off Session Rd, opposite SM Mall.

🍴 Eating

Baguio has some truly unique eateries that are worthy of a few extra pesos – think funky, earthy and often vegetarian.

★ Cafe by the Ruins FUSION $$
(25 Chuntug St; mains P200-300; ⊙7am-9pm; 🛜✍) The 'ruins' in this case are merely the former residence of an ex-governor, but the effect is still sublime, and the organic, Cordillera-inspired Filipino food is as original as the ambience.

Oh My Gulay VEGETARIAN $$
(La Azotea Bldg, Session Rd; mains P120-150; ⊙11am-8.30pm; ✍) Baguio's most creative

SPLURGE

If you don't mind being out of the centre – and in Baguio you shouldn't – the woodsy **Villa Cordillera** (☑074-442 6036; www.villacordillera.com; 6 Outlook Dr; d/tr/q P1600/2400/3200; 🛜), overlooking Baguio Country Club, is so quiet you'll hardly realise you're in Baguio. Rooms are spiffy with wood floors and tightly made single beds.

interior is five storeys up under a vast atrium. The mercifully compact all-vegetarian menu is equally creative. No booze.

Volante Pizza ITALIAN $$
(82 Session Rd; 6/10in pizza P85/220; ⊙24hr) The pan pizza here is tops in town, and it's not a bad place for a beer either, especially after everything else has closed.

🍷 Drinking & Entertainment

★18 BC BAR
(16 Legarda Rd; ⊙6.30pm-late) Don't be fooled by the roguish interior: this dive consistently features Baguio's best original live music, from jazz and blues to reggae. It's opposite Prince Plaza Hotel.

Red Lion Pub/Inn PUB
(☑074-304 3078; 92 Upper General Luna Rd; ⊙24hr; 🛜) You can find a drinking buddy or billiards partner any time of day at this expat fave. Good steaks and ribs too.

Rumours BAR
(56 Session Rd) Peace Corps volunteer hang-out.

Nevada Square BAR, NIGHTCLUB
(Loakan Rd, off Military Circle) Collection of bars and clubs with a raucous, fraternity-party atmosphere on weekends.

ℹ Information

Session Rd hosts several internet cafes and banks. **Cordillera Regional Tourist Office** (☑074-442 6708; Governor Pack Rd; ⊙8am-5pm Mon-Fri) arranges guides (P1000 to P1500 per day) and tours throughout the Cordillera.

ℹ Getting There & Away

Victory Liner (☑074-619 0000; Upper Session Rd) and neighboring **Genesis** (☑074-444 9989; Upper Session Rd) run a few nonstop deluxe buses to/from Manila along the

Subic–Clark–Tarlac Expressway (4½ hours, five daily; P685 to P715). Otherwise, regular air-con trips depart every 30 minutes (P450, 6½ hours). Other companies operate air-con and ordinary buses (P350) to Manila from Governor Pack Rd, where you'll also find **Partas** buses to Vigan.

GL Lizardo (☑ 074-304 5994) has hourly buses until 1pm to Sagada (P222, 5½ hours) and until 2.30pm to Bontoc (P212, 5½ hours) from the **Dangwa Terminal** (Magsaysay Ave), a five-minute walk north of Session Rd. **D'Rising Sun** (☑ 0910 709 9102) buses to Bontoc leave hourly until 4pm from the **Slaughterhouse Terminal** (Magsaysay Ave), five minutes by jeepney beyond the Dangwa Terminal. These routes follow the spectacular Halsema Hwy. Also from the Slaughterhouse Terminal, **NA Liner** has two or three morning buses to Kabayan (P135, 4½ hours).

KMS and **Ohayami** have several buses to Banaue (P415, 8½ hours) each day. Their terminals are near each other on Shanum St, west of Burnham Park.

Sagada

POP 1550 / ELEV 1547M

The epitome of mountain cool, Sagada (1477m) is the place to escape from civilisation for a few days – or months. Caves, peaks, waterfalls and hanging coffins beckon the active traveller, while more sedate types can just kick back with a hot drink and a book and revel in Sagada's delightfully earthy ambience. Try to time your visit for a *begnas* (traditional community celebration), when the hearty Kankanay locals gather in *dap-ay* (outdoor meeting places) to bang gongs, smoke pipes, swill brandy and sacrifice chickens.

Take a guide for any trekking or caving you do around here or you'll almost surely get lost; grab one at the tourist information centre in the old Municipal Hall, or at the Sagada Genuine Guides Association, down the hill a little past Yoghurt House. Our favourite excursion is the thrilling half-day cave connection (P400 per person).

Raft Sagada (☑ 0919 698 8361; www.luzonoutdoors.com) runs rafting trips on the upper Chico River and is the authority on mountain biking and other adventures in the region.

🛏 Sleeping

Sagada's basic but charming guesthouses, swathed in pinewood and cosy linen, are a delight. Knock P50 per person off prices in the low season.

Sagada Homestay   GUESTHOUSE $

(☑ 0919 702 8380; sagadahomestay@yahoo.com.ph; s/d from P300/600; @ 🛜) Flush with success born of rustic rooms and friendly service, this beloved guesthouse on the hill overlooking the town centre has added an attractive restaurant and an annex with a few en-suite rooms in addition to its original 'homestay'.

Misty Lodge & Cafe   LODGE $

(☑ 0928 332 7817; sigrid07@yahoo.com.ph; r without bathroom per person P300; @ 🛜) It's worth the 15-minute walk east out of town to stay (or just hang out) at this gem. The rooms are sizeable and swathed in radiant blonde wood, while a fireplace warms the cafe when needed.

Residential Lodge   GUESTHOUSE $

(☑ 0910 709 2631; s/d from P250/500; 🛜) The 16 rooms in this big sky-blue building down the hill past (and opposite) Yoghurt House lack the woody charm of some others, but are generously appointed for the price.

✕ Eating

Yoghurt House   FUSION $

(breakfast P60-140, mains P85-160; ⊘ 7am-8.30pm) Fuel up here with mountain coffee and the trademark yoghurt muesli breakfasts before a long day of hiking or caving. It's about 300m south of the central Municipal Hall.

Gaia Cafe   VEGETARIAN $

(mains P100-120; ⊘ 11am-7pm; ☑) Hidden in the woods, 1.8km south of the centre, Gaia Cafe serves locally sourced vegetarian fare enjoyed with rice-terrace views. There are books to browse and a little shop packed with stuff that hippies like. A pig devours the leftovers.

★ Log Cabin   FUSION $$

(☑ 0920 520 0463; mains P150-250; ⊘ 6-9pm) The fireplace dining here hits the spot on those chilly Sagada evenings. On Saturdays there's a wonderful buffet (P390, prepaid reservations only).

ℹ Getting There & Away

Jeepneys to Bontoc depart at least every hour until 1pm (P45, 45 minutes). The last bus to Baguio leaves at 1pm. For Manila, transfer in Baguio, Bontoc or Banaue.

Bontoc

☑ 074 / POP 3030

This Wild West frontier town is the central Cordillera's transport and market hub. You can still see tribal elders with full-body tattoos and G-strings strolling the streets, especially on Sunday when people descend from the surrounding villages to sell their wares at Bontoc's bustling market. Make a point of visiting the **Bontoc Museum** (admission P60; ☺ 8am-noon & 1-5pm), which has fascinating exhibits on each of the region's main tribes. Check out the grisly photos of head-hunters and their booty.

There's some mint trekking to be done around Bontoc, most notably to the stone-walled **rice terraces of Maligcong**, which rival those in Batad. Secure a guide (P1200 per day) and map at the handy **Tourism Information Center** (☑ 0907 489 7663; Town Plaza; ☺ 8am-5pm Mon-Fri) – ask for French- and German-speaking **Kinad** (☑ 0929 384 1745; kinad139@yahoo.com) or seek out veteran guide **Pike** (☑ 0910 425 7504).

To really get off the beaten track, head even further north into Kalinga province, where you can hike to remote villages and meet aged former head-hunters. **Francis Pa-In** (☑ 0915 769 0843) guides treks in Kalinga province.

If you are staying a night, **Churya-a Hotel & Restaurant** (☑ 0906 430 0853; darwin_churyaa@yahoo.com; s/d P250/500; ☜) has clean if unspectacular rooms, and a pleasant balcony over Bontoc's main street.

Florida has a bus to/from Manila, leaving Bontoc daily at 3pm (P650, 11½ hours) and leaving Manila nightly at 7pm. It goes via Banaue (P120, 1¾ hours) – a truly stunning drive. Also to Banaue there is a jeepney around noon and several morning buses. Jeepneys to Sagada (P45, 45 minutes) leave hourly until 5.30pm.

Banaue & the Rice Terraces

☑ 074 / POP 2600

Banaue is synonymous with the Unesco World Heritage–listed Ifugao rice terraces, hewn out of the hillsides using primitive tools and an ingenious irrigation system some 2000 years ago. Legend has it that the god Kabunyan used the steps to visit his people on earth.

The Ifugao by no means had a monopoly on rice terraces in the Cordillera, but they were arguably the best sculptors, as the mesmerising display above Banaue suggests. Banaue proper – a ragged collection of tin-roofed edifices along a ridge – isn't pretty but you can't argue with the setting.

Two kilometres north of town you can ogle rice terraces to your heart's content at the **viewpoint**; a tricycle there and back costs P200. If your heart's still not content, there are similarly impressive specimens lurking in nearby Bangaan, Hapao, Kiangan and, of course, Batad.

🛏 Sleeping & Eating

A 2012 fire that claimed the Halfway Lodge (now rebuilt) means most Banaue rooms now lack electrical sockets, so prepare to do battle for use of public power outlets.

Brookside Inn   GUESTHOUSE $
(d & tw per person P200; ☜) Walk down the hill from the tourist office for 300m and look for this simple but appealing new guesthouse on the right.

People's Lodge   GUESTHOUSE $
(☑ 074-386 4014; s/d from P250/500; @ ☜) This centrally located spot has a variety of basic accommodation, including some en-suite rooms. The popular if ugly restaurant has rice-terrace views and a balcony that its rivals lack.

Uyami's Greenview Lodge   GUESTHOUSE $
(☑ 074-386 4021; www.ugreenview.wordpress.com; s P250, d P500-1500; ☜) Right next to People's Lodge, the rooms here are cosy and clean, with shiny parquet floors, and there's a rustic restaurant downstairs. Unfortunately, it charges P20 for extras such as device charging and towels.

Sanafe Lodge & Restaurant   GUESTHOUSE $$
(☑ 0918 947 7226; www.sanafelodge.com; s/d/ste P800/1000/1600; ☜) Has the best-looking rooms in the centre and the best terrace views, while higher prices mean it's mellower than popular People's Lodge and Greenview.

ℹ Information

Pay your environmental fee (P20) at the **Tourist Information Centre** (☑ 0917 577 2010; ☺ 6.30am-7pm), adjacent to the plaza, which also arranges accredited guides (full day P1200), sells maps (P25) and posts a list of prices for private transport. You can change dollars at poor rates at Greenview or People's Lodge.

PHILIPPINES THE CORDILLERA

❶ Getting There & Away

Ohayami and Florida each run one overnight trip (more in the high season) to/from Manila (P450, seven to eight hours).

If you prefer daytime travel, get to Solano by jeepney (P110, 2½ hours with a transfer in Lagawe) and flag down a frequent Manila-bound bus (P375, eight hours).

Buses to Baguio ply the lowland route via Solano. To take the scenic highland route (ie via Bontoc and the Halsema Hwy), you must transfer in Bontoc. There's an early morning jeepney to Bontoc (P150, 1¾ hours), and a handful of Bontoc-bound buses (P120) pass through Banaue throughout the day.

Batad

POP 1025

To really see the **Ifugao rice terraces** in all their glory, you'll need to trek to Batad (1100m), which sits at the foot of a truly mesmerising amphitheatre of rice fields. Most of the inhabitants still practise traditional tribal customs in what must be one of the most serene, picture-perfect villages to grace the earth.

A slippery 40-minute walk beyond the village itself is the 30m-high **Tappiya Waterfall** and swimming hole. To escape tourists altogether, hike 1½ hours to the remote village of **Cambulo**, which has several simple guesthouses. Guides are available through the Batad Environmental Tour Guides Association (P900 to P1200 per day).

Most guesthouses are up on the 'viewpoint' overlooking Batad village and the amphitheatre, near where you enter the area and pay your heritage fee (P50). Hillside Inn, Batad Pension, Rita's, Simon's Inn and Ramon's all have restaurants and rooms for about P200 per head. They're all simple, clean and rustic, but Hillside wins our hearts with its good food and all-round charm.

From Banaue, it's 12km to Batad junction, where a mostly sealed road leads 3km up to the 'saddle' high above Batad. From the saddle it's a 45-minute hike to Batad.

A daily jeepney from Banaue to the saddle departs at 3pm (P150, 1¼ hours); the return to Banaue is the next morning. Alternatively, you can hire a jeepney (return P2800) or motorbike taxi (return P1000) to the saddle. Tricycles can get you as far as the junction (return P800).

Consider exiting Batad via the beautiful two-hour hike down to scenic **Bangaan**, where you can flag down morning jeepneys to Banaue.

Vigan

☑ 077 / POP 49,747

Spanish-era mansions, cobblestone streets and *kalesa* (two-wheeled horse carriages) are the hallmarks of Unesco World Heritage Site Vigan. Miraculously spared bombing in WWII, the city is considered the finest surviving example of a Spanish colonial town. Two of Vigan's finer mansions are the **Crisologo Museum** (Liberation Blvd; ⊙8.30-11.30am & 1.30-4.30pm) **FREE** and the **Syquia Mansion Museum** (Quirino Blvd; admission P20; ⊙9am-noon & 1.30-5pm Wed-Mon).

🛏 Sleeping & Eating

It's worth paying a little extra to stay in one of Vigan's charismatic colonial homes.

Hem Apartelle   GUESTHOUSE $
(☑077-722 2173; 32 Gov A Reyes St; d P600; ❋ 🛜) No heritage-style lodging here: the Hem is just an air-conditioned guesthouse that's the cleanest budget option in town.

Henady Inn   HOTEL $
(☑077-722 8001; National Hwy; dm P250, d P750-1250; ❋) Out on the highway right where Laoag-bound buses drop you off, the four-bed dorms here will please penny-pinchers or early-morning arrivals looking for a few extra hours of shut-eye.

Vigan Hotel   GUESTHOUSE $
(☑077-644 0169; Burgos St; s/d from P395/495; ❋🛜) Basic but cheap rooms in a rambling complex near the historic centre.

Leila's Cafe   CAFE $
(Gen Luna St; mains P80-150; ⊙10am-10pm; 🛜) This cosy cafe offers eclectic takes on regional Ilocano specialities such as *bagnet* (Ilocano crispy pork belly) and *sisig* (crispy fried pork ears and jowl), plus Western dishes such as fish and chips, an extensive coffee selection and tasty baked treats.

> ### SPLURGE
> A magnificent 130-year-old mansion, **Villa Angela** (☑077-722 2914; www.villangela.com; 26 Quirino Blvd; d/q incl breakfast from P1500/2800; ❋🛜) has a giant *sala* (living room) festooned with fabulous antique furniture and four huge bedrooms looking much as they would have in the 18th century. One of the Philippines' true gems.

Cafe Uno
FUSION **$**

(1 Bonifacio St; mains P80-130; ⊗ 9am-11.30pm; ☎) Attached to the respected Felicitas Cafe of neighbouring Grandpa's Inn, the impressive variety of food here is of the same high standard.

Street Stalls
STREET FOOD **$**

(Plaza Burgos; snacks P50) Evening street stalls peddle delicious local snacks such as *empanadas* (deep-fried tortillas with shrimp, cabbage and egg) and *okoy* (shrimp omelettes).

ⓘ Getting There & Away

Many bus companies serve Manila (ordinary/air-con/deluxe P450/680/825, seven to 10 hours). **Partas** (☎ 077-722 3369; Alcantara St) and **Dominion** (☎ 077-722 2084; cnr Liberation Blvd & Quezon Ave) have stations near the public market, 1km southwest of the historic centre. Florida buses drop you off on the national highway, 500m north of the historic centre.

Partas has about 10 daily air-con trips to Baguio (P350, five hours) via San Juan (P225, three hours).

SOUTHEAST LUZON

Fiery food, fierce typhoons and furious volcanoes characterise the adventure wonderland known as Bicol. The region's most famous peak, Mt Mayon, may just be the world's most perfect volcano. And it's no sleeping beauty, either. A steady stream of noxious fumes leaks out of its maw, and minor eruptions are frequent. Underwater, Bicol is home to one of the Philippines' top attractions: the gentle, graceful *butanding* (whale sharks) of Donsol.

Be sure to sample the spicy Bicolano cuisine. Must-try dishes include *pinangat* (taro leaves wrapped around minced fish or pork), 'Bicol *exprés*' (spicy minced pork dish), *ginataang pusit* (squid cooked in coconut milk), *laing* (a leafy green vegetable) and *pili* nuts mixed with miniscule, red-hot *sili* peppers.

You'll want to pay extra attention to the news before heading to Bicol, lest you waltz into one of the region's patented typhoons. The Pan-Philippine or Maharlika Hwy runs right through Bicol down to Matnog, where ferries cross to Samar.

Naga
☎ 054 / POP 160,516

Naga, the capital of Camarines Sur (CamSur) province has a vibrant student population and a burgeoning reputation as an adventure-sports mecca. The city centres on a pleasant double plaza that often hosts large concerts or festivals after sundown. In September the immensely popular **Peñafrancia Festival** kicks off, packing hotels to the gills.

🏃 Activities

Mt Isarog National Park HIKING

(admission P100) Superb hiking is available in this national park, 20km east of Naga. You can launch a two-day assault on **Mt Isarog** (1966m) or embark on shorter hikes through the jungle lower down. Hiking permits cost P450 per day and must be secured in advance through the visitor centre in Naga or a tour company. You'll also need a guide. You don't need a permit to visit the popular **Malabsay Falls** (admission P20), a short walk from the park entrance.

Access the national park from Panicuason, where you'll find guides as well as the **Mt Isarog Hot Springs** (admission P200; ⊗ 7am-6pm) and the Panicuason Hot Springs Adventure Park, with a high-tension jump (akin to a bungee jump), an obstacle course and more. Infrequent jeepneys to Panicuason (P22, 30 minutes) depart from just off Caceres St, near the Naga City Market. Alternatively, take a frequent jeepney to nearby Carolina and transfer to a tricycle.

CamSur Watersports
Complex WATER SPORTS

(☎ 054-477 3344; www.cwcwake.com; ⊗ 8.30am-7pm Mon-Thu, to 9pm Fri-Sun; ☎) The CamSur Watersports Complex, 12km south of Naga in the town of Pili, is an impressively modern cable-wakeboarding centre, complete with surfer-dude music, restaurants, wi-fi and a range of accommodation.

Kadlagan Outdoor Shop &
Climbing Wall ROCK CLIMBING

(☎ 0919 800 6299; kadlagan@yahoo.com; 16 Dimasalang St; ⊗ shop 9am-7pm, climbing wall by appointment) Hires out tents and other camping gear, and guides day and overnight excursions on Mt Isarog and camping safaris in the sublime Caramoan Peninsula. Jojo Villareal knows all the local rocks and routes and is usually here in the evenings. Guides cost P550 to P900 per day, excluding meals and equipment.

🛏 Sleeping

Sampaguita Tourist Inn HOTEL $
(☑054-472 2413; Panganiban Dr; s/d/tr from P300/400/700; ❇ 🛜) Flanking the river, this is an unexciting but functional budget option with 100 en-suite rooms of all shapes and sizes. Several other cheap hotels are nearby.

CBD Plaza Hotel HOTEL $$
(☑054-472 0318; www.cbdplazahotel.com; Ninoy & Cory Ave; s/d incl breakfast from P600/1000; ❇ 🛜) Opposite the bus station, this colourful place has tidy economy singles plus a huge selection of larger twin and matrimonial rooms.

🍴 Eating & Drinking

'Magsaysay' jeepneys along Peñafrancia Ave lead to bar- and restaurant-loaded Avenue Sq. Beyond this mall you'll find plenty of restobars with live music along Magsaysay Ave.

San Francisco Food Court STREET FOOD $
(Peñafrancia Ave; small dishes P10-20; ⊙24hr) To keep it real with the locals, head to this alley of food stalls next to San Francisco Church and fill up on genuine Bicol fare for less than P40.

Beanbag Coffee CAFE
(Magsaysay Ave; large/small latte P60/50; ⊙8am-11pm; 🛜) Does a great imitation of Seattle's best, only much cheaper. The cakes are delicious.

Bob Marlin BAR
(Magsaysay Ave; mains P150-300; ⊙11am-11pm) A Bob Marley–inspired seafood restobar, this is also your best bet for freshly prepared Bicol food, washed down with buckets of beer.

ℹ Getting There & Away

Cebu Pacific and PAL Express have frequent flights to/from Manila.

The bus station is over Panganiban Bridge next to SM Mall. **RSL** (☑054-472 6885) and **Cagsawa** (☑054-811 2541) go directly to Ermita in Manila, while several others go to Cubao. The deluxe sleeper buses fill up fast, so book those a few days ahead.

The fastest way to Legazpi is by minivan (P140, two hours) from the Naga Coliseum, opposite SM Mall. They leave when full, usually every 30 minutes, until 7pm. Air-con buses to Legazpi take much longer and cost P120, while ordinary (non-air-con) buses sometimes take six hours!

Legazpi

☑ 052 / POP 179,481

Charm is in short supply in the city of Legazpi, but with the towering cone of Mt Mayon hogging the horizon no one seems to notice. The city is divided into Albay District, where the provincial government offices and airport are located, and commercial Legazpi City. A steady stream of jeepneys connects the two districts along Rizal St. Make the vigorous 30-minute climb up Liñgon Hill, north of the city near the airport, for the best views of Mt Mayon. The **Magayon Festival** in Albay District lasts the entire month of April, packing all hotels.

🛏 Sleeping

⭐ **Mayon Backpackers Hostel** HOSTEL $
(☑052-480 0365; Diego Silang St; dm P250-350, d/q P1000/1200) Legazpi's clear top budget choice, with comfy six- and four-bed dorm rooms (albeit with narrow bunks), two lovely private rooms, a common kitchen and a rooftop with hammocks and views to Mt Mayon. It's in Albay District near St Gregory's Cathedral.

Catalina's Lodging House GUESTHOUSE $
(☑052-742 0351; 96 Peñaranda Ext; s/d from P180/250) This creaky old wooden standby in the middle of Legazpi City is cheap, basic and noisy, but who's complaining at these prices? Angle for a room at the back.

Sampaguita Tourist Inn HOTEL $
(☑052-480 6258; Rizal St, Legazpi City; s/d from P300/375; ❇ 🛜) There are heaps of rooms here in case everything else is booked out. Even the simplest rooms are bright and en suite, if nothing else.

Airport Hotel HOTEL $$
(☑052-481 0232; Airport Compound; r incl breakfast from P1000; ❇ 🛜) The best value – and closest to the airport – of the many midrange hotels in Albay District. Rooms are simple but functional.

🍴 Eating & Drinking

Try the nightly street stalls along Quezon Ave near the Trylon Monument in Legazpi City for budget Bicolano fare. For drinking head to **the Boulevard**, a long stretch of seafront restobars beyond the Embarcadero Mall (behind Sleeping Lion Hill).

Seadog Diner
FUSION $

(The Boulevard; mains P50-150; ⊙6am-midnight; ☎) Good pizzas and Bicol-accented Italian fare. Great spot for a drink too.

★ Small Talk
FUSION $$

(Doña Aurora St near National Hwy, Albay District; mains P95-250; ⊙11am-10pm) This delightful little eatery adds Bicol touches to its Italian fare. Try the pasta *pinangat* or 'Bicol *exprés*' pasta.

Sibid-Sibid
FILIPINO $$

(328 Peñaranda Ext; mains P150-200; ⊙10am-9pm; ⊜☎) A wonderful open-air restaurant 1km north of Legazpi City, Sibid-Sibid specialises in highly original, Bicol-inspired seafood concoctions like fish Bicol *exprés*. Has the best *pinangat* we've had.

ⓘ Information

The **Provincial Tourism Office** (☑052-820 6314; http://tourism.albay.gov.ph; Astrodome Complex, Aquende Dr, Albay District) hands out a map of the city for free.

ⓘ Getting There & Away

Cebu Pacific and PAL Express fly several times daily to/from Manila, and Cebu Pacific adds flights to Cebu.

The main bus terminal is at the Satellite Market, just west of Pacific Mall in Legazpi City. Cagsawa and RSL bus lines have night buses that go directly to Ermita in Manila, while several others go to Cubao.

Air-con minivans zip to Donsol (P100, 1¼ hours) roughly hourly until 5pm or so, and to Sorsogon (P90, 1¼ hours, frequent), where you can pick up a jeepney to Matnog, gateway to Samar.

Around Legazpi

Mt Mayon

Bicolanos sure hit the nail on the head when they named this monolith – *magayon* is the local word for 'beautiful'. The impossibly perfect cone rises to a height of 2462m above sea level and emits a constant plume of smoke.

Climbing Mt Mayon is possible but don't take it lightly: it's a difficult, dangerous and hot climb – you have to contend with both the searing sun and heat bubbling up from under the surface of the steep and slippery lahar slopes.

Frequent eruptions on Mt Mayon wreak havoc. Shortly after lava flows subsided in 2006, a biblical typhoon triggered mudslides that killed more than 1000 people. In 2013 Mayon belched boulders that killed four European climbers and a guide near the summit. Because of that accident, the volcano's summit was closed at the time of research.

For most people Mayon – when it's open – is a 1½-day climb with an overnight at 'Camp 2' (1600m), but fit climbers can do it in a day. Guides are mandatory. The 1½-day trek costs about P7000 per person for a group of two, including camping equipment, porters, permits, guides, food etc.

The best time of year to climb Mt Mayon is February to April. From May to August it's unbearably hot; from September to January it's wet. The following organise Mt Mayon climbs: **Bicol Adventure** (☑0918 910 2185, 052-480 2266; www.bicoladventure.com; V&O Bldg, Quezon Ave, Legazpi City) and **Mayon Outdoor Guides Association** (☑0915 422 4508; pinangat2001@yahoo.com). **ATV tours** (P600 to P3000) run by Bicol Adventure and **Your Brother Travel & Tours** (☑052-742 9871; http://mayonatvtour.com) are also popular.

Donsol
POP 4200

Every year, between December and early June, whale sharks *(butanding)* frolic in the waters off this sleepy fishing village about 50km from Legazpi. It's truly an exhilarating experience swimming along with these silver-spotted leviathans, which can reach 14m in length.

Worryingly, after two decades of near-guaranteed sightings during the peak months of January to May, 2012 and especially 2013 were down years. We highly recommend contacting the **regional tourism office** (☑0927 233 0364, 052-482 0712) in Legazpi or the Donsol Visitors Centre before you visit to see if the whale sharks are in town.

One possible culprit for the decline in whale-shark numbers around Donsol is global warming affecting the plankton supply. The hope is that the decline is cyclical and large numbers of *butanding* will return. If you miss the whale sharks, the **manta bowl** off nearby Ticao Island is a backup option, albeit one for advanced scuba divers only.

When you arrive in town, head to the **Donsol Visitors Centre** (☑0906 504 9287, 0927 483 6735; www.donsolwhalesharkecotour.

com; ⊙ 7am-5pm) to pay your registration fee (P300) and arrange a boat (P3500 for up to six people) for your three-hour tour. Each boat has a spotter and a *butanding* interaction officer on board – tip them a couple of hundred pesos, especially if you've had a good day. Snorkelling equipment is available for hire (P300). Scuba diving is prohibited.

🛏 Sleeping & Eating

Vitton & Woodland Resort   HOTEL **$**
(☑ 0927 912 6313; vittonandwoodlandresorts@ gmail.com; dm P500, d from P1800; ✳ ✳) Twin resorts a couple of hundred metres away from each other north of the visitors centre. The seven dorm rooms – all of the three-bed variety – are at Woodland. Each resort has a pool and a lovely garden, plus clean accommodation and friendly service.

Santiago Lodging House   HOMESTAY **$**
(☑ 0939 310 8758; Main Rd, town proper; d/tr P500/700) Basically a homestay with three good, clean rooms in a beaten-up wooden house.

Hernandez Guesthouse   GUESTHOUSE **$**
(☑ 0927 452 9405; Main Rd, town proper; r with fan/air-con from P500/1200; ✳) Opposite Santiago, it has a handful of simple rooms.

Amor Farm Beach Resort   RESORT **$$**
(☑ 0909 518 1150; r with fan/air-con from P1000/2000; ✳) A peaceful resort with cottages scattered around a garden. The cold-water-only fan rooms are the best value in the visitors centre area and can fit three.

❶ Getting There & Away

Air-con minivans (P100, 1¼ hours) and jeepneys (P80, two hours) leave hourly to Legazpi until 4pm.

MINDORO

There are two sides to this large island just south of Luzon: Puerto Galera, and the rest of Mindoro.

Puerto Galera is a dive mecca that lies at the heart of the Verde Island Passage – one of the world's most biologically diverse underwater environments. It's essentially an extension of Luzon.

The rest of Mindoro is an untamed hinterland of virtually impenetrable mountains populated by one of Asia's most primitive tribes, the Mangyan. Those who like to get

way off the beaten track need look no further. Off the west coast, accessible from the towns of Calintaan and Sablayan, underwater wonderland **Apo Reef** is populated by sharks and stingrays.

❶ Getting There & Away

From Batangas, you'll find frequent 'ROROs' (roll-on-roll-off, or car ferries; P192, 2½ hours) and speedy 'fastcraft' boats (P320, one hour) to Calapan in northern Mindoro, along with ferries to Abra de Ilog (P280, 2½ hours), gateway to Sablayan and Apo Reef.

Regular car ferries to Caticlan (for Boracay) depart from Roxas in southern Mindoro.

Puerto Galera

☑ 043 / POP 28,035

It lacks the beautiful beach, classy resorts and hip nightlife of Boracay, but this diving hot spot on the northern tip of Mindoro is conveniently located just a hop, skip and *bangka* ride from Manila. The name Puerto Galera (PG) typically refers to the town of Puerto Galera and the resort areas surrounding it – namely Sabang, 7km to the east, and White Beach, 7km to the west. The town proper has a breathtakingly beautiful harbour, but otherwise is of little interest.

Puerto Galera finally has ATMs – an Allied Bank in PG town, and a Max Bank in Sabang.

❶ Getting There & Around

Speedy *bangka* ferries to Puerto Galera town, Sabang Beach and White Beach leave regularly throughout the day from Batangas pier until about 4.30pm or 5pm (P310 including port and environmental fees, 1½ hours). The last trip back to Batangas from Sabang (P230) leaves at 1pm or 2pm (on Sundays and in peak periods there's a later boat); from White Beach it's 3pm, and from Puerto Galera town it's 3.30pm. Be prepared for a rough crossing.

To reach Roxas, where ferries depart for Caticlan (Boracay), take a jeepney (P80) or van (P100) to Calapan from the Petron station in PG town (1¼ hours, every 45 minutes), then transfer to a Roxas-bound van (P200, three hours).

Regular jeepneys connect Sabang and PG town during daylight hours (P20, 20 minutes); a tricycle between the two costs P100 (more at night) and from Sabang to Talipanan a tricycle costs P300. Motorcycle taxis are cheaper.

Sabang & Around

Sabang is where most of the hotels, restaurants and bars are concentrated. Drinking and underwater pursuits are the activities of choice, with plenty of establishments offering variations on these themes.

Sabang's 'beach' is a narrow sliver of brown sand traversed by rivulets of sewage, and its late-night entertainment scene is less than wholesome to say the least. To escape, walk around the headland to cleaner, more laid-back **Small La Laguna Beach**, where several resorts front a brown strip of sand. Beyond that is **Big La Laguna Beach**.

🏃 Activities

Dive prices vary wildly, so shop around. **Dive VIP** (P1200 per dive including equipment), **Blue Ribbon** (P1100 excluding equipment) and **Capt'n Gregg's** (P1400 including equipment) are reliable. An open-water course will set you back P15,000 to P20,000, with Blue Ribbon and Dive VIP offering the best rates.

🛏 Sleeping

Expect big discounts off these prices in the June-to-October low season. You'll find some great value down at the far eastern end of Sabang Beach.

★ **Reynaldo's Upstairs**   GUESTHOUSE $
(☎0917 489 5609; rey_purie@yahoo.com; r P650-1300; ❋🌐) Run by a nice family, Reynaldo's has a splendid mix of more-than-passable budget fan rooms and large 'view' rooms with kitchenettes and private balconies. It's on a hillside at the east end of Sabang Beach.

Dive VIP   INN $
(☎043-287 3140; www.divevip.com; Sabang; r P500-1000) The four rooms here are basic but in fine shape, with patios, hot water and TVs.

Big Apple Dive Resort   RESORT $
(☎043-287 3134; www.divebigapple.com; r P500-2000; ❋🌐🏊) In the middle of Sabang Beach, this is party central, with some noisy and tatty fan rooms to go with swankier digs around the pool out back.

Capt'n Gregg's Dive Resort   LODGE $$
(☎043-287 3070; www.captngreggs.com; r P800-1900; ❋🌐) This Sabang institution recently expanded after 24 years in business. The compact but cosy wood-lined 'old' fan rooms, right over the water, still have the most charm.

Cataquis   BUNGALOW $$
(☎0916 297 8455; Big La Laguna Beach; r P1000-2000; ❋) Stand-alone concrete cottages in two separate clusters near where you enter placid Big La Laguna Beach. The cheap fan cottages are flush with the water.

🍴 Eating & Drinking

Restaurants in Sabang are, in a word, expensive.

Tina's   GERMAN, FILIPINO $$
(mains P150-300; ⊙8am-10pm) Tina's has some of the best food on the beachfront, although prices have gone up recently. Do try the schnitzel.

Teo's Native Sizzling House   FILIPINO $$
(mains P150-300; ⊙24hr) Low-key place with a comprehensive menu of sizzling dishes, Filipino classics and steaks.

★ **Full Moon**   PUB $$$
(Small La Laguna Beach; mains P230-500; 🌐) It's worth a walk down here from Sabang just for the chilli con carne – it's the real McCoy. You can also get steaks, tacos, burgers, fish and chips, Indian curries and giant breakfasts.

★ **Point Bar**   BAR
(El Galleon Resort) With a plum spot on the point between Sabang and Small La Laguna Beach, this is the best spot for a sundowner. The music collection is as colourful as the cocktails.

Puerto Galera Town

The town proper boasts a row of restaurants that front the gorgeous harbour at Muelle Pier. **Bahay Pilipino** (☎0906 465 1652; r P420), near the public market, is the cheapest place to stay. Quarters are simple clapboard affairs with shared bathrooms. At Muelle Pier, **Hangout Bar** (mains P150-250; 🌐) has pub grub and computers with internet access, while the **Rusty Anchor Bar** has good views and a few simple fan rooms upstairs (P1200).

PHILIPPINES

Puerto Galera & Around

Puerto Galera & Around

West Beaches

About 7km west of Puerto Galera are three neighbouring beaches. First up is **White Beach**. It has a much better beach than Sabang, but accommodation is tacky and overpriced and it fills up with mobs of Manileños on weekends. During weekdays, it can be quiet and pleasant.

Next up is mellow, clean **Aninuan Beach**, but to escape the girlie bars of Sabang, a better option is attractive **Talipanan Beach**, at the end of the road in the shadow of Mt Malasimbo (860m). **Luca's Cucina Italiana & Lodge** (☑ 0916 417 5125; info@lucaphilippines. com; mains P250-400; ☎) is ideally positioned at the isolated west end of the beach. The food is delicious, especially the pizzas, which are cooked in an outdoor brick oven.

There are a few places to stay in Talipanan, but none with doubles for under P1000 in the high season. The best are Luca's (rooms from P1500) and, down the beach, **Mountain Beach Resort** (☑ 0906 362 5406; www.mountainbeachresort.com; s/d from P800/1000; ✴ @ ☎), which has a wide variety of bamboo-infused accommodation.

Roxas

☑ 043 / POP 10,000

Roxas is a dusty little spot with ferry connections to Caticlan. **Roxas Villa Hotel & Restaurant** (☑ 043-289 2026; roxasvillahotel@ yahoo.com; Administration St; s/d from P350/450; ✴ @) has basic rooms in the town centre,

and there are several hotels at Dangay pier, about 3km from the centre.

If you are heading to Caticlan (P400, four hours), call the **Ports Authority** (☑ 043-289 2813) at Dangay pier to check the schedule, as departures are infrequent during the day. At the time of research, **Montenegro Lines** (☑ 0932 461 9096) had a noon departure, a 4pm departure and several night trips; other companies had night trips only.

Vans to Calapan (P200, three hours) leave straight from Dangay pier.

THE VISAYAS

If it's white sand, rum and coconuts you're after, look no further than the jigsaw puzzle of central islands known as the Visayas. From party-mad Boracay and Cebu to mountainous Negros, to dreamy Siquijor and Malapascua, the Visayas have about everything an island nut could ask for. Hopping among paradisiacal, palm-fringed isles, you'll inevitably wonder why you can't go on doing this forever.

Indeed, many foreigners *do* give it all up and live out their years managing this resort or that dive centre on some exquisite patch of white sand. Others merely end up extending their trip for weeks – or months. This is one area of the country where you can dispense with advanced planning. Just board that first ferry and follow your nose.

❶ Getting There & Around

All the major cities in the Visayas are well connected to Manila by both air and sea. Cebu City has air connections to Palawan, Mindanao and Southeast Luzon.

To get to the Visayas overland from Luzon, head to Matnog on the southern tip of southeast Luzon, which is just a short ferry hop from Allen in northern Samar. Alternatively, make your way to Roxas, Mindoro, and take a ferry to Caticlan, Panay.

Cebu City is the Visayas' main ferry hub, and is linked to all major and minor Visayan ports by a veritable armada of zippy fastcraft and slower RORO ferries.

Panay

The large, triangular island of Panay is where you'll enter the Visayas if taking the ferry from Mindoro. To most travellers, mainland Panay is just a large planet around

The Visayas

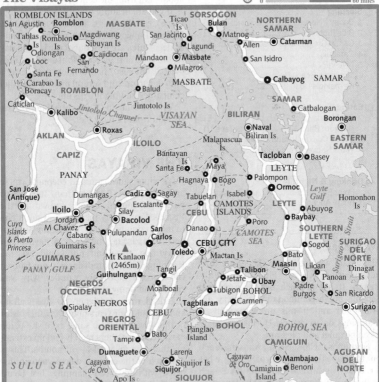

which orbits the diminutive party satellite Boracay island. Yet Panay proper has plenty to offer plucky independent travellers, including decaying forts, Spanish churches, remote thatch-hut fishing villages and the mother of all Philippine fiestas, Kalibo's Mardi Gras–like Ati-Atihan, which peaks in the third week of January. Panay's capital and gateway to the rest of the Visayas is Iloilo, a six-hour bus ride south of Boracay.

Boracay

036 / POP 9800

With a postcard-perfect, 3km-long white beach and the country's best island nightlife, it's not hard to figure out why Boracay is the country's top tourist draw. Overdevelopment has made some old-timers long for the halcyon days of no electricity, but the debate about whether it's better now or was better then won't worry you too much when you're

digging your feet into the sand on White Beach and taking in the Philippines' most famous sunset.

Parasails, seabirds, frisbees and *paraw* (small *bangka* sailboats) cut across the Technicolor horizon, while palm trees whisper in the breeze and reggae wafts through the air. Oh yeah, and you're in a beachfront bar that's generously serving two-for-one cocktails. Yes, even 'developed' Boracay remains a master mixologist of that mellow island vibe.

Activities

On Boracay you can try your hand at a stupendous array of sporting pursuits, including paraw rides (per hour P600), diving, windsurfing and parasailing. Daily games of football, volleyball and ultimate frisbee kick off in the late afternoon on White Beach.

PHILIPPINES PANAY

Kitesurfing

From December to March, consistent winds, shallow water and rapidly inflating but still decent prices (about US$450 for a 12-hour certification course) make **Bulabog Beach** on the east side of the island the perfect place to learn kitesurfing. The action shifts to White Beach during the less consistent May-to-October southwest monsoon.

Operators include **Hangin** (☑036-288 3766; www.kite-asia.com), **Islakite** (☑036-288 5352; www.islakite.com) and **Habagat** (☑036-288 5787; www.kiteboracay.com).

🛏 Sleeping

Rates everywhere drop 20% to 50% in the low season (June to October). Walking in often nets a discount, and bargaining might bear fruit at any time of year.

ANGOL

Walk-in guests are advised to venture south of Station 3 to a cluster of about 10 resorts located up a path behind Arwana Resort. The best deal is **Ocean Breeze Inn** (☑036-288 1680; www.oceanbreezeinn.info; r P990-1590; ✳🖥), where a couple of elegant rattan-swathed garden cottages complement air-conditioned concrete rooms. Cheapest (and furthest from the beach) is **Bora Bora Inn** (☑036-288 3186; r P900-1800; ✳), while *nipa* (traditional thatched Filipino hut) colony **Melinda's Garden** (☑036-288 3021; www.melindasgarden.com; d P1600-2500; ✳🖥) has the most charm. Other good options here are **Orchids** (☑036-288 3313; www.orchidsboracay.com; r P915-2000; ✳🖥) and **Escurel** (☑036-288 3611; bert_escurel@yahoo.com; s/d from P1300/1500; ✳@🖥). Haggle hard at all of the above.

White Beach Divers Hostel   HOSTEL $
(☑036-288 3809; www.whitebeachdivers.com; d/tr P650/1000; 🖥) A stellar deal, especially if you get the spacious bamboo loft at the back, which sleeps three. Other rooms are more basic and share bathrooms. The owner

is a receptacle of knowledge about tours in the area.

Tree House Da Mario   RESORT $
(☑036-288 3601; littlecornerofitaly@yahoo.com; dm P250-300, d P1000-3500; ✳🖥) The private rooms are nothing special but the four-bed dorms, spread across two complexes, are the island's cheapest crash pads.

NORTH OF STATION 3

Trafalgar Garden Cottages   BUNGALOW $
(☑036-288 3711; trafalgarboracay@hotmail.com; Original D'Talipapa; r P550-1700; ✳) It's close to the main road yet seals off the noise well, and the P550 stand-alone budget cottages, with small hammocks out front, are super value.

Frendz Resort   RESORT $$
(☑036-288 3803; frendzresort@hotmail.com; Station 1; dm P700, r P2800-3800; ✳@🖥) New management and friendlier prices have quickly turned Frendz into Boracay's backpacker HQ. Live music and cheap cocktails enliven the bar. The cosy dorms are single-sex.

Backpacker Meeting Place   GUESTHOUSE $$
(☑036-288 2607; Diniwid Beach; dm/s/d incl breakfast P1000/1700/2800; ✳🖥) Yes, the dorms (three-bed and six-bed varieties) are expensive, but you're paying for the location on dreamy Diniwid Beach. A good choice for solo travellers looking to get away from it all.

Jung's House Resort   HOTEL $$
(☑036-288 5420; Station 2; r with fan/air-con P900/1100; ✳) The Korean owner offers up the island's cheapest air-con rooms at this tidy spot about 150m in from the beach.

🍴 Eating

You'll find the best deals on Filipino food along the main road. Of course, it's worth paying a bit more for the ambience of White Beach –

just stroll along until you see something that takes your fancy. Self-caterers can shop at the Tourist Centre (p579) or at two supermarkets in D'Mall adjacent to the main road.

Smoke
FILIPINO $

(mains P100-150; ⊘24hr) Smoke is Boracay's best value, with freshly cooked Filipino food, appetising coconut-milk curries and a P80 Filipino breakfast. A second D'Mall branch (⊘7am-10pm) is closer to the main road.

Niu Chana
FILIPINO $

(Station 1; dishes P75-100; ⊘9am-midnight) Cheap Filipino faves like *sisig* (crispy fried

pork ears and jowl) right on the beachfront north of Station 1.

★ Plato D'Boracay
SEAFOOD $$

(D'Talipapa Market; seafood per kg P100-150; ⊘8am-9pm) The lobster, prawns and other shellfish at this family-style seafood grill come straight from the adjoining market; prices reflect the reduced transport costs.

Shibaya
JAPANESE $$

(Station 1; dishes P180-220; ⊘11am-1am) This Japanese teppanyaki joint, hidden down an alley behind the bakery Real Coffee, is superb and eminently affordable. Noodle

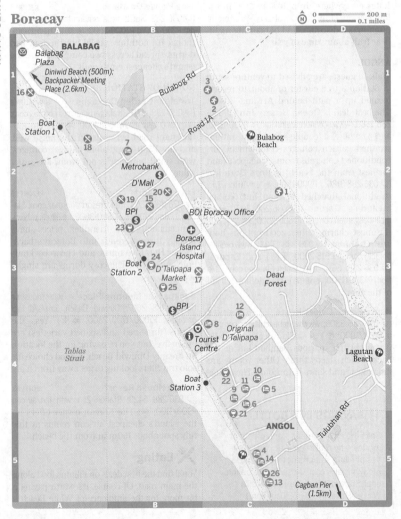

Boracay

dishes such as *oyakodon* and *yakisoba* are the speciality.

Drinking & Nightlife

Bars range from peaceful, beachfront cocktail affairs, where you can sip a mai tai while watching the sun set, to throbbing discos on the sand.

Follow thumping beats to find the discos; about five or six of them carry momentum into the wee hours, even in the low season. **Summer Place** (Station 2) is rowdiest, **Epic** (D'Mall) is most chichi, and gay-friendly **Juice** (Station 2) is the smallest and most down-to-earth.

★**Red Pirates**   PUB
(Angol) Way down at the south end of White Beach, this supremely mellow bar throws funky driftwood furniture onto the sand and best captures the spirit of 'old Boracay'.

Nigi Nigi Nu Noos   BAR
(Station 2; ☺ happy hour 5-7pm) The legendary mason jars of Long Island iced tea (P365), they're two-for-one during happy hour, more than capably kick-start any evening.

Arwana   BAR
(Angol; ☺ happy hour 1-10pm) All-day happy hour means White Beach's cheapest San Miguel (P25) on demand.

ⓘ Orientation

Most of the action is on White Beach, where three out-of-service 'boat stations' orient visitors. The area south of Station 3, known as Angol, most resembles the less-developed 'old Boracay' and is where most of the budget accommodation is located. The stretch

between Station 1 and Station 3 is busy and commercial. Most top-end accommodation is well north of Station 1 on an incredible stretch of beach.

North of White Beach, you can find relative solitude on sleepy **Diniwid Beach**, while explorers looking for genuine solitude should seek out **Ilig-Iligan Beach** near Boracay's northeast tip.

ⓘ Information

BPI (D'Mall) and **Metrobank** (D'Mall) have ATMs, and there are a few others along White Beach and the main road.

Tourist Centre (Station 3; ☺ 8am-midnight) Offers a range of services, including internet access, postal services and money-changing facilities (including Amex travellers cheques). Also sells plane tickets and posts ferry schedules.

ⓘ Getting There & Away

To get to Boracay, you must first travel to Caticlan. From Caticlan, small *bangka* ferries shuttle you to Boracay's Cagban pier (P205 including terminal and environmental fee, 15 minutes). Tricycles from Cagban pier cost P150 per tricycle, or P25 per person, for central White Beach destinations.

PHILIPPINES PANAY

Boracay

AIR

Cebu Pacific and PAL Express have multiple flights per day from both Manila and Cebu to Caticlan until 4.30pm or so. Caticlan airport to Caticlan pier is a five-minute walk or a one-minute tricycle ride (P50).

Flights to nearby Kalibo are a cheaper alternative to flying to Caticlan. Cebu Pacific and PAL Express both fly there from Manila, while Tigerair flies from Clark. For international flights to Kalibo, see Kalibo International Airport (p610).

Air-con vans meet flights in Kalibo and run to Caticlan pier (P180, 1½ hours).

BOAT

Caticlan is well connected by ferry to Roxas, Mindoro.

BUS

Ceres Lines has hourly buses to Iloilo (P350, six hours) via Kalibo (P107, 1½ hours) from Caticlan pier; the last one departs at 4pm.

ⓘ Getting Around

To get from one end of White Beach to the other, either walk or flag down a tricycle along the main road. These cost only P10 provided you steer clear of the disingenuously named 'special trips' offered by stationary tricycles, which cost a not-so-special P50 to P100.

Iloilo

☏ 033 / POP 419,000

Panay's bustling capital offers doses of culture and nightlife, and is a pleasant enough stopover on the Boracay–Negros route. For ideas try the informative **tourist office** (☏ 033-337 5411; Bonifacio Dr; ⊙ 8am-5pm Mon-Fri) next to Museo Iloilo.

◉ Sights

Museo Iloilo   MUSEUM
(Bonifacio Dr; admission P25; ⊙ 9am-5pm Mon-Sat) It has a worthwhile display on Panay's indigenous *ati* (Negrito) people and a collection of old *piña* (pineapple fibre) weavings, for which the area is famous.

☞ Tours

Panay Adventures   ADVENTURE TOUR
(☏ 0917 717 1348, 033-856 0558; panay_adventures@yahoo.com.ph) Anthropologist Daisy organises eco-cultural tours to visit tribal groups around Panay, mountain-bike trips on nearby Guimaras Island, and climbing and caving in Bulabog Puti-An National Park.

🛏 Sleeping

Family Pension House   GUESTHOUSE $
(☏ 033-335 0070; familypension@yahoo.com; General Luna St; s/d from P325/450; ❀) This old backpacker fave in a lovely art deco building is creaky but cheap and popular.

Ong Bun Pension   HOTEL $
(☏ 033-335 1271; cnr Ledesma St & Quezon St; s/d from P150/285; ❀🛜) In the noisy centre, the flash lobby and passably clean rooms belie the dirt-cheap rates.

Highway 21   HOTEL $$
(☏ 033-335 1839; General Luna St; s/d from P750/900; � ❀🛜) Terrific midrange deal.

🍴 Eating & Drinking

Butot Balat   FILIPINO $$
(Solis St; mains P150-250; ⊙ 10.30am-11pm) Centrally located Butot Balat is a great place to try local Ilonggo specialities like *tira-un* (chicken in banana leaves).

Smallville Complex   BAR, NIGHTCLUB
(Diversion Rd) No reason to look any further for bars and nightlife; most of the action is here. **Flow** (weekends/weekdays P150/free) is the king of the clubs.

ⓘ Getting There & Around

The **Travellers Lounge** (⊙ 5.30am-9pm) at SM City Mall north of Smallville on Diversion Rd offers ferry-booking and left-luggage (P30) services, and showers.

There are frequent flights to Manila and Cebu with Cebu Pacific, PAL Express, AirAsia Zest and Tigerair.

The airport is 15km north of town in Santa Barbara. Take a shuttle van (P70, 25 minutes) two hours before your flight from SM City Mall's north parking lot.

From Iloilo's central Muelle Pier, fastcraft ferry operators Oceanjet, Weesam Express and 2GO Travel take on the rough crossing between Iloilo and Bacolod (P340, one hour, 20 daily). There's no need to book ahead for these.

From the Lapuz Norte Pier, **Montenegro Lines** (www.montenegrolines.com.ph; P1220, 26 hours, 8am Saturday) and less seaworthy **Milagrosa Shipping** (☏ 033-337 8627; P950, 36 hours, 7pm Monday and Thursday) sail from Iloilo to Puerto Princesa, Palawan, via the Cuyo Islands.

From the Fort San Pedro Pier, **2GO Travel** (☏ 033-338 4502) has ferries to Manila (from P1000, 20 hours, five weekly). You'll also find Cebu-bound ferries here.

Ceres buses to Caticlan (P350, six hours) leave every 30 minutes until 4pm from the Tagbac Bus Terminal, about 7km north of the centre.

Negros

If any Visayan island can boast to have it all, it is surely Negros. Here you'll find one of the country's top dive spots (Apo Island), one of the top remote beaches (Sipalay) and one of the top treks (volcanic Mt Kanlaon). The heavily forested interior, besides being a major biodiversity hotbed, provides a stunning backdrop for drives around the island. Along the west coast, vast, bright-green sugarcane fields abut the shimmering waters of the Sulu Sea. Laid-back Dumaguete and hip Bacolod make fine bases for exploring it all.

Bacolod

🗹 034 / POP 500,000

Bacolod is a large, buzzing provincial capital with a budding arts scene and a fine reputation among Filipino foodies. The city boomed in the 19th century when Iloilo's clothing industry collapsed and the textile barons migrated across the Panay Gulf to try their luck at sugar. Locals masquerade in grinning masks for October's **MassKara Festival**.

🏃 Activities

In Bacolod you can secure permits for the protected areas around Negros. The trophy attraction is **Mt Kanlaon Natural Park** where the Visayas' highest peak (2465m) looms. Permits (Filipino/foreigner P300/500) can be obtained through Angelo Bibar at the **Office of the Park Superintendent** (🗹 0917 301 1410; angelobibar@gmail.com; cnr Porras & Abad-Santos Sts, behind Plaza Hotel; ⊙ 8am-5pm Mon-Fri). Access to the mountain is tightly controlled and guides (P700 per day) are mandatory, so reserve ahead. There are three routes to the top, one of which can be done by fit climbers in a day. The climbing seasons are March to May and October to December.

The trekking is at least as good in birdinfested **Northern Negros Natural Park**, accessible from Patag, a small town 32km east of Silay. The **Silay Tourist Office** (🗹 034-495 5553) can help you get a guide and a permit (required). In Bacolod the **Negros Forests & Ecological Foundation** (www.negrosforests.org; South Capitol Rd; admission by donation; ⊙ 9am-5pm Mon-Fri) has information

on the natural park, and also runs a small zoo with critically endangered species such as the Negros bleeding-heart pigeon.

🛏 Sleeping

Pension Bacolod GUESTHOUSE $
(🗹 034-433 3377; 27 11th St; s/d from P150/250; ❄ 🛜) This is a professionally run bargain, with a diverse array of rooms on a quiet side street and a decent cafe for breakfast.

Ong Bun Pension House HOTEL $
(🗹 034-709 8128; Luzuriaga St; r from P200; ❄ 🛜) Opposite the central market, it's a tidy clone of the Ong Bun in Iloilo.

Suites at Calle Nueva BOUTIQUE HOTEL $$
(🗹 034-708 8000; www.thesuitesatcallenueva.com; 15 Nueva St; s/d incl breakfast from P1000/1500; ❄ 🛜) For something flashier, this centrally located midranger may be the best deal in the country, with flat-screen TVs, gorgeous beds and bathrooms, and ample furniture.

🍴 Eating & Drinking

Cafe Bob's CAFE $$
(cnr Lacson Ave & 21st St; sandwiches P100-150; ⊙ 8am-midnight; 🛜) Bob's is a bright and bustling deli/coffee shop in the University District, 1.5km north of the city plaza. Sandwiches, pizza, Italian ice cream and wi-fi.

Art District BAR, CAFE
(Lacson St, Mandalagan) A complex of arty-farty bars, restaurants and galleries 3km north of the city plaza. Expats flock to eat tapas and down mojitos at **Txacho** (tapas P100-150; ⊙ 5.30pm-8am), students smoke sheeshas at **Gypsy Bar Tea Room** (⊙ 2pm-2am), hipsters smoke Dunhills at **Bar Aje**, while creative types prefer open-air **Café Joint** (⊙ 4pm-late) for original live jazz and blues.

ℹ Getting There & Away

PAL Express and Cebu Pacific have frequent flights to both Cebu City and Manila. AirAsia Zest and Tigerair fly just to Manila.

Frequent Iloilo-bound fastcraft ferries call in at the Bredco Port, near SM Mall about 1km west of the centre, while 2GO Travel's long-haul ferries to Manila (six weekly) depart from Banago Wharf, 7km north of central Bacolod.

From the **Ceres north bus terminal** (🗹 0917 771 1213; Lacson St), 1.5km north of Art District, frequent buses depart to San Carlos (P165, 3½ hours), where car ferries depart for Toledo, Cebu. Night and morning buses to Cebu City (air-con/deluxe P320/420, seven hours) also take this ferry.

From the **Ceres south bus terminal** (☏ 034-434 2387; cnr Lopez Jaena & San Sebastian Sts), buses run every 30 minutes until 7pm to Sipalay (P185, 5½ hours) and Dumaguete (ordinary/air-con P260/315, six hours) via Kabankalan.

Sipalay

☏ 034 / POP 11,275

You could get stuck for days – make that months – in this remote fishing town on Negros' southwest edge. At delicious Sugar Beach a small outcrop of resorts caters to those looking to achieve the full Robinson Crusoe effect. It really fills up in the high season these days, so book ahead. Divers should head 6km south of Sipalay to the pricier resorts of *barangay* (village) Punta Ballo.

🛏 Sleeping & Eating

★**Driftwood Village** RESORT $
(☏ 0920 900 3663; www.driftwood-village.com; Sugar Beach; dm P250-300, d from P450; 🛜) Hosts Daisy and Peter (he's Swiss) are a lot of fun, and so is their resort, which features a dozen cosy *nipa* huts, good Thai food and a marvellous pirate pub with a range of bar sports under a thatch canopy. Ask about treks in the area.

Sulu Sunset RESORT $
(☏ 0919 716 7182; www.sulusunset.com; Sugar Beach; r P550-1200) The rooms here range from comfy A-frame cottages to roomy open-front beachfront bungalows; all are superb value. The restaurant serves delicious wood-fired pizza and German specialities. It's at the far end of the beach.

🍷 Drinking

Sugar Rock BAR
(☏ 0908 429 8413) Perched atop a rocky outcrop at the far end of Sugar Beach, this bar ramps up at sunset and sometimes continues into the night. The owners were building rooms (P600) when we dropped by.

ℹ Getting There & Away

Ceres buses to/from Bacolod's south bus terminal (P185, 5½ hours) leave every half-hour until the evening.

Getting to Dumaguete requires three separate Ceres buses: Sipalay to Hinoba-an (P30, 45 minutes), Hinoba-an to Bayawan (P80, 1½ hours) and Bayawan to Dumaguete (P100, two hours). Connections are easy.

Sugar Beach is about 5km north of Sipalay proper, across two rivers. Arrange a boat transfer to your resort from Sipalay proper (P350, 15 minutes), or disembark from the Bacolod–Sipalay bus in *barangay* Montilla and take a tricycle to *barangay* Nauhang (P100, 15 minutes), where small paddle boats bring you across the river to Sugar Beach for P15.

Dumaguete

☏ 035 / POP 116,000

Dumaguete (doo-ma-*get*-ay) is a perfect base for exploring all that the southern Visayas offer. A huge college campus engulfs much of its centre, saturating the city with youthful energy and attitude. The location – in the shadow of twin-peaked Cuernos de Negros (1903m) and just a few clicks from some marvellous hiking, beaches and diving – takes care of the rest.

Most dining, drinking and strolling happens on and around the attractive waterfront promenade flanking Rizal Blvd.

🏃 Activities

The Dumaguete area boasts top-notch adventures, including **diving**. Nearby Apo Island is the big draw for underwater breathers. Operators include Harold's Mansion and, in the same building, **Scuba Ventures** (☏ 035-225 7716; www.dumaguetedive.com; Hibbard Ave).

Many tour operators offer trips to snorkel with **whale sharks** in nearby Tan-awan (a *barangay* of Oslob), Cebu. We do not endorse these as they are essentially captive whale sharks, kept there and disrupted from their normal migratory patterns because locals feed them.

Back on terra firma you'll find **caving**, **rock climbing** and **trekking** on Cuernos de Negros and around the **Twin Lakes**, north of Dumaguete near Bais.

🛏 Sleeping

★**Harold's Mansion** HOSTEL $
(☏ 035-225 8000; www.haroldsmansion.com; 205 Hibbard Ave; dm/s/d from P250/350/500; ❋ @ 🛜) With free coffee, a roomy six-bed dorm and a down-to-earth owner who runs cool tours, Harold's deserves its popularity among independent travellers.

OK Pensionne House GUESTHOUSE $
(☏ 035-225 5702; Santa Rosa St; d from P275; ❋ 🛜) Two blocks south of the central plaza, this place is indeed OK. It has an enormous

variety of rooms, the pricier ones being a huge step up in quality.

★ **Island's Leisure Hotel**   BOUTIQUE HOTEL **$$**
(☑035-994 9291; www.islandsleisurehotel.com; Hibbard Ave; d incl breakfast P1000-1400; ❀ 🖃) This alluring property combines Zen modernism with indigenous Philippine elements. Think woven lamps, contemporary art, stone love seats and plasma TVs. It doubles as a spa and is 1km north of Harold's Mansion.

✕ Eating & Drinking

Qyosko   FILIPINO **$**
(cnr Santa Rosa & Perdices Sts; mains P60-100; ⊙24hr; 🖃) A budget traveller's dream, this spot serves up hot Filipino dishes and delicious shakes and coffee from its adjoining coffee shop.

Mamia's   CAFE **$**
(San Jose St; snacks P50-100; ⊙6.30am-11pm; 🖃) A half-block in from the waterfront, Mamia's is a proper cafe with the essentials: affordable coffee, breakfasts, wi-fi and air-con.

Casablanca   EUROPEAN **$$**
(cnr Rizal Blvd & Noblefranca St; mains P185-575; 🖃) Go ahead, treat yourself to a decent meal; you deserve it. Casablanca is run by a charismatic Austrian. Choose an exotic beer to wash down your Wiener schnitzel or roast-beef sandwich.

Hayahay   FILIPINO **$$**
(Flores St; mains P100-250; ⊙4pm-late) In a cluster of bars and restaurants on the waterfront 1km north of the pier, Hayahay is known for delicious fresh seafood and rockin' reggae Wednesdays.

❶ Getting There & Away

Cebu Pacific and PAL Express each have two daily flights to Manila. Cebu Pacific flies to Cebu twice daily.

Oceanjet (☑0923 725 3734) fastcraft go to Cebu (P950, 4½ hours, 3.30pm) via Tagbilaran (P680, two hours) on Bohol. There are also RORO ferries to Cebu.

From the nearby port of Sibulan, frequent fastcraft (P62) and *bangka* (P45) alternate trips to Lilo-an on Cebu island (25 minutes), from where there are buses to Cebu City via Oslob. For Moalboal, cross from Tampi, Negros, to Bato, Cebu, by frequent RORO and pick up a north-bound Ceres bus there.

Ceres Bus Lines (Perdices St) connects Dumaguete and Bacolod (ordinary/air-con P260/315, six hours, hourly to 7pm).

Apo Island
☑035 / POP 745

For a taste of small-village life on an isolated island, it's hard to beat this coral-fringed charmer, one of the Philippines' best snorkelling and dive spots.

Most people visit on day trips from Dauin or Dumaguete (diving/snorkelling trips about P2900/1600 per person including two dives), but thrifty souls will fare better staying on the island. **Liberty's Lodge & Dive** (☑0920 912 4513; www.apoisland.com; dm/s/d incl full board from P800/1300/1950; @ 🖃) has appealingly rustic rooms and a laid-back atmosphere, and transfers guests to the island for P300 per person.

Behind Liberty's, **Mario Scuba** (☑0906 361 7254; marspascobello@hotmail.com; dm P300, d P600-1000) has a six-bed dorm and some large, en-suite private rooms with polished floors and private balconies.

Around the point from Liberty's, **Apo Island Beach Resort** (☑0917 701 7150; www.apoislandresort.com; dm P800, d from P2700) has a lovely secret cove all to itself, but Liberty's and Mario are better run and better value. There are also **homestays** available on the island for P500 (ask around).

A couple of *bangka* depart the island for Malatapay, 18km south of Dumaguete (P20, 40 minutes by bus or jeepney), around 6.30am and return around 3pm (P300, 45 minutes). Chartering a five-passenger *bangka* costs P1300 to P1700 one-way (negotiate).

Siquijor
☑035 / POP 87,700

Spooky Siquijor is renowned for its witches and healers, but don't be scared away. It's also a backpacker paradise with lovely scenery and the best-value beachfront accommodation in the Philippines. With your own motorbike you can travel around the island's 72km coastal ring road in a day and explore **beaches, colonial relics, waterfalls, caves** and charming **villages**. Rent a motorbike at the pier when you arrive (P250).

Sandugan, 15km northeast of Siquijor town, has an end-of-the-earth feel, but the beaches are nicer in **Solangon**, 9km southwest of Siquijor town.

🛏 Sleeping

★ **JJ's Backpackers Village & Cafe** HOSTEL **$**
(📞 0918 670 0310; jiesa26@yahoo.com; Solangon; tent/dm P150/300, d P500-700; @) JJ's has a prime patch of beach, well-maintained dorms, spacious private rooms, a camping option, and cheap, tasty food – basically everything a backpacker needs.

Kiwi Dive Resort RESORT **$**
(📞 0908 889 2283; www.kiwidiveresort.com; Sandugan; r P450-1090; ✳ @ 🛜) Kiwi has a truly remote feel, a dive centre (dives P1300 including equipment) and a nice range of rooms.

Casa Miranda GUESTHOUSE **$**
(📞 0917 910 6995; Solangon; d from P250) Perhaps the cheapest beachfront accommodation in the Philippines. The no-frills rooms occupy a rickety structure fronting a decent stretch of sand just southeast of JJ's.

Guiwanon Spring Park Resort BUNGALOW **$**
(📞 0935 121 6279; cottages P250-350) 🍃 The three cottages here are over-water tree houses on the edge of a mangrove reserve; staying here helps to preserve the reserve. The cottages are basic but face the sea. Look for the hard-to-spot sign on the left about 5km east of Siquijor town.

Luisa & Sons GUESTHOUSE **$**
(📞 0947 270 8826; Larena; s/d P200/300) Simple place at the sometimes noisy pier in Larena; convenient if you're leaving early the next morning.

Coral Cay Resort RESORT **$$**
(📞 019 269 1269; www.coralcayresort.com; d P950-2650; ✳ 🛜 ▣) This fine resort has lavish rooms on a perfect stretch of white-sand beach at Solangon. The roomy beachfront cottage suites are practically lapped by waves and at P1650 are a steal.

ⓘ Getting There & Around

The vast majority of visitors arrive at the pier in Siquijor town via fastcraft from Dumaguete. **Delta** (P120), **Oceanjet** (P200) and **GL Shipping** (📞 035-480 5534; P120) ply the route (1¼ hours, about eight total trips daily, fewer on Saturdays when GL doesn't operate). **Montenegro Lines** and **Aleson Lines** follow with a few slower ROROs (P100) to both Siquijor town and Larena, 9km northeast of Siquijor town.

At the pier in Larena, you'll find RORO ferries to Cebu (from P350, 8½ hours) most nights, sometimes via Tagbilaran (from P220, 3½ hours).

From the pier in Siquijor town, a tricycle costs about P120 to Solangon or Larena, and P170 to Sandugan.

Cebu

Surrounded on all sides by the Philippine isles and dotted with tranquil fishing villages, Cebu is the island heart of the Visayas. Cebuanos are proud of their heritage – it is here that Magellan sowed the seed of Christianity and was pruned for his efforts at the hands of the mighty Chief Lapu-Lapu. The island's booming metropolis, Cebu City, is a transport hub to pretty much anywhere. Pescador Island, near the laid-back town of Moalboal, placed Philippine diving on the world map, while the Malapascua marine scene boasts close encounters of the thresher-shark kind.

Cebu City

📞 032 / POP 866,000

The island capital is much more laid-back than Manila as a place to arrive in or leave the Philippines. One of the first stops on Spain's conquest agenda, Cebu lays claim to everything old – including the oldest street (Colon St), the oldest university and the oldest fort. By night Cebu turns decidedly hedonistic.

Cebu's Downtown District is its mercantile nucleus. Most of the sights are here, but you must wade through exhaust fumes, beggars, prostitutes and block after block of downmarket retail madness to get to them. Uptown is much more pleasant and has better accommodation, mostly near the central Fuente Osmeña roundabout. **Mactan Island**, where Magellan came a distant second in a fight with Chief Lapu-Lapu, is now the site of Cebu's airport.

⊙ Sights

★ **Fort San Pedro** FORT
(Map p585; S Osmeña Blvd; P20/30 student/adult; ⊙8am-8pm) This gently crumbling ruin, built by Miguel Legazpi in 1565, is the oldest Spanish fort in the country.

★ **Basilica Minore del Santo Niño** CHURCH
(Map p585; Pres Osmeña Blvd) Built in 1740, Cebu's holiest church houses a revered Flemish statuette of the Christ child (Santo Niño), which dates to Magellan's time. The church's belfry came toppling down in the October 2013 earthquake.

Downtown Cebu City

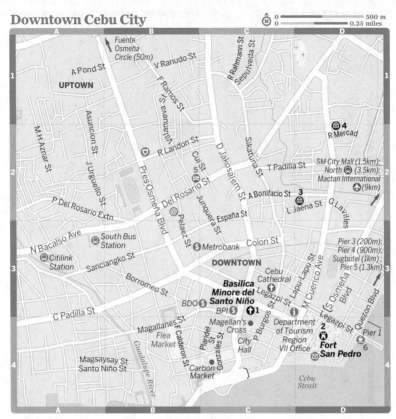

N 0 ——————— 500 m
0 ——————— 0.25 miles

Downtown Cebu City

◎ Top Sights
1 Basilica Minore del Santo Niño C3
2 Fort San Pedro D4

◎ Sights
3 Casa Gorordo Museum........................D2
4 Museo Sugbo D2

🛏 Sleeping
5 Elicon House..B2

ⓘ Transport
6 Cokaliong Shipping..............................D4
Lite Shipping Corporation ....(see 6)
Oceanjet..(see 6)

Museo Sugbo   MUSEUM
(Map p585; M Cuenco Ave; adult/child P75/50; ⊙9am-5.30pm Mon-Sat) On the site of a former jail, the three museums in this complex are oriented towards Cebu's fascinating history.

Casa Gorordo Museum   MUSEUM
(Map p585; 35 L Jaena St; admission P70; ⊙9am-5pm Tue-Sun) North of the church, the Casa Gorordo Museum, in an astonishingly beautiful ancestral house, offers a glimpse into upper-class life in Cebu in the 19th century.

Tops Lookout   VIEWPOINT
(admission P100) Make your way to JY Square Mall, where motorcycle taxis depart for the thrilling 30-minute ride (return P300) to Tops Lookout, 600m above Cebu.

🛏 Sleeping

It's worth spending extra to be uptown.

Elicon House   HOTEL $
(Map p585; ☎032-255 0300; www.elicon-house.com; cnr Del Rosario & Junquera Sts; s/d/tr/q P550/800/1050/1300; ✲◎☂) ✎ The downtown version of its sister Mayflower Inn. Same idea here – no-nonsense and clean rooms, delightful common spaces loaded

PHILIPPINES

Uptown Cebu City

0 — 400 m
0 — 0.2 miles

HIPPODROMO

HSBC Bank $
Luzon Ave

M Cuenco Ave

Cemetery †

8 ✕

Asiatown IT Park (1.2km);
Banilad Town Centre (1.3km);
Tonyo's Bar & Restaurant (1.5km)

Gen Maxilom Ave Extension

McCrew Ville Rd

9 ✕

Cardinal Rosales Ave

Gorordo Ave

Bohol St

Archbishop Reyes Ave

Gen Maxilom Ave

San Jose St

R Rahmann St

J Singson St

Tojong St
Acacia St

12 🏠
BPI $

6 ✕

Gorordo Ave

F Scotto Dr

D Jakosalem St

Gen Maxilom Ave (Mango Ave)

13 🏠

JY Square Mall (1km);
Outpost (1.3km);
Tops Lookout (12km)

N Escario St

UPTOWN

M Cristina St

R Aboitiz St

Metrobank $

10 ✕
14 🏠

F Ramos St

Downtown (1km)

@

J Osmeña St

Fuente
Osmeña
Circle

P Clavano St

J Avila St

E Capitol Rd
Villalon Dr

3 🏠

Cebu Doctors Hospital

P Osmeña Blvd

$ BDO

7 ✕🏠

5 🏠

Chong Hua Hospital

B Rodriguez St

M Soza St

Capitol Building

1 🏠

BPI $

2 🏠

Jasmine St

Orchid St

J Llorente St

DG Garcia St

M Cui St

J Avila St

P Rodriguez St

11 ✕

Guadalupe River

Canadian Consulate

Bataan St

M Velez St

4 ✕

V Rama Ave

Uptown Cebu City

😴 Sleeping

1 Cebu R Hotel	B2
2 Gran Tierra Suites	B3
3 Mayflower Inn	B2
4 Tr3ats	A3
5 Travelbee Pension	B3

🍴 Eating

6 Ayala Center	F1
7 Joven's Grill	B3
8 Laguna Garden Cafe	G1
9 Neoneo Grill House	E1
10 Persian Palate	D4
11 STK ta Bay! Sa Paolito's Seafood House	B3

🍷 Drinking & Nightlife

12 Koa	E1
13 Kukuk's Nest	E1
14 Mango Square	D4

with games, a vego-friendly cafe and slogans on permaculture philosophy plastered on the brightly painted walls.

Tr3ats HOSTEL $
(Map p586; ☎ 032-422 8881; www.tr3ats.com; 785 V Rama Ave; dm/d/q P350/850/1600; ❇ 🛜) Cebu's only true hostel has three cramped eight-bed air-con dorms and a few tidy en-suite private rooms. However, the location isn't perfect and there's not much of a common area; chill in the tiny rooftop bar.

Sugbutel HOTEL $
(☎ 032-232 8888; www.sugbutel.com; Osmeña Blvd nr Rd East; dm P250-300, d from P1200; ❇ 🛜) A new concept in Cebu lodging, the Sugbu-tel is a full-service hotel with compact, functional private rooms and three *giant* (we're talking 100-bed) air-con dorms. It's near Pier 5 and SM City Mall.

Travelbee Pension GUESTHOUSE $
(Map p586; ☎ 032-253 1005; reservations@travelbee. ph; 294 DG Garcia St; s/d from P400/600; ❇ 🛜) No-frills option with mostly windowless rooms.

★ Mayflower Inn HOTEL $$
(Map p586; ☎ 032-255 2800; www.mayflower-inn. com; Villalon Dr; s/d/tr/q P850/1150/1400/1750; ❇ 🛜) 🐾 The Mayflower bills itself as a 'per-maculture hotel' – don't laugh, the green credentials are legit. Besides tidy, meticulously painted rooms you get a feng-shui-friendly garden-cafe and a hang-out lounge/library with ping pong, foosball, stacks of *National Geographic* mags and board games.

Gran Tierra Suites HOTEL $$
(Map p586; ☎ 032-353 3575; www.grantierrasuites. com; 207 M Cui St; s/d P789/989; 🛜) Cebu City has some terrific value in the midrange price category, and this is a prime example. Bordering on boutique, rooms are equipped with canvas prints, small plasma TVs and ample desk space.

Cebu R Hotel HOTEL $$
Map p586; (☎ 032-505 7188; www.ceburhotel.com; 101 M Cui St; s/d incl breakfast from P950/1250; ❇ @ 🛜) Everything is tasteful here, from the smartly uniformed staff to the lime and dark-wood colour scheme. Rooms are kitted out with desks and flat-screen TVs.

🍴 Eating

The following are all uptown. Quality eating options are limited downtown – the cafe at Elicon House is your best bet.

Neoneo Grill House FILIPINO, CHINESE $
(Map p586; Acacia St; dishes P28-150; ⊙ 10am-2am) A classic Pinoy grill near the Ayala Center, Neoneo serves sizzling Filipino and Chinese dishes, plus discount tuna sashimi and sushi.

Ayala Center FOOD COURT $
(Map p586; Lahug District) As is the case in Ma-nila, many of the best restaurants are in the malls, particularly the Ayala Center. There is a **food court** on the 3rd floor for budget meals. For finer dining, consider one of the eateries at the **Terraces** on the north side of the mall, such as local fave **Laguna Garden Cafe** (mains P150-300; ⊙ 10am-10pm; 🛜).

★ STK ta Bay! Sa Paolito's Seafood House SEAFOOD $$
(Map p586; ☎ 032-256 2700; 6 Orchid St; meals P95-300; ⊙ 10am-2.30pm & 5-10pm; 🛜) Ask a Ce-buano where to dine and those in the know will point you to this large ancestral home turned restaurant. Don't miss the hot 'n' spicy *calamares* (squid).

Persian Palate MIDDLE EASTERN $$
(Map p586; Mango Sq Mall, J Osmeña St; dishes P75-300; ⊙ 10am-9pm; 🛜 🍴) The flagship res-taurant of this popular franchise is tucked away behind National Bookstore in Mango Sq. Middle Eastern mains like spinach hum-mus are complemented by too-mild South Asian and Thai fare.

Joven's Grill FILIPINO $$
(Map p586; cnr Pres Osmeña Blvd & Jasmine St; all-you-can-eat buffet P199; ⊙ 11am-9pm) A Cebu

PHILIPPINES CEBU

institution, its all-day buffet is pure gold after an extended boat journey.

🍷 Drinking & Nightlife

Two hot spots for clubs are **Banilad Town Centre** (M Cuenco Ave, Banilad) and **Asiatown IT Park** (Salinas Dr, Lahug), both about a five-minute cab ride northeast of Ayala Center.

★Outpost BAR
(976 Veterans Dr, Lahug; ⊗6pm-2am Tue-Sun) Live music in a rambling old wooden house? Works for us. Try to catch Cuarenta, an adrenalin-fuelled blues-rock band. Pub grub and good cocktails to boot. For sleaze-free good times look no further.

Tonyo's Bar & Restaurant BAR
(The Hangar, Salinas Dr, Lahug; ⊗24hr) Roughly opposite Asiatown IT Park, Tonyo's delivers 3L tubes of beer to your table (P225) while live bands thrash it out on stage.

Kukuk's Nest BAR
(Map p586; 124 Gorordo Ave; ⊗24hr) Cebu's prime bohemian hang-out is artist-owned and inspired. A convenient place to finish up after all the other bars close.

Koa BAR
(Map p586; 157 Gorordo Ave; ⊗9.30am-2.30am; 🛜) Located in the old Kukuk's space and opposite the new Kukuk's, Koa has good bar food (cheap too) and live music from hump night on.

Mango Square BAR, NIGHTCLUB
(Map p586; Gen Maxilom Ave; admission per club P50-100) This gaggle of clubs and bars in one central location attracts all types. The clubs here go in and out of fashion with the season. Among their number is usually at least one gay club.

ℹ️ Information

There are plenty of internet cafes and ATMs around Fuente Osmeña Circle.

Cebu Doctors Hospital (☎032-255 5555; Pres Osmeña Blvd; ⊗24hr)

Central Post Office (Quezon Blvd)

Department of Tourism Region VII Office (☎032-254 2811; LDM Bldg, Legaspi St; ⊗7am-5pm Mon-Fri) Informative office has maps of Cebu City and other Visayan locales.

HSBC Bank (Cardinal Rosales Ave; ⊗9am-4pm Mon-Fri) Cashes travellers cheques and allows

PHILIPPINES CEBU

FERRIES FROM CEBU CITY

DESTINATION	DURATION (HR)	PRICE (P)	COMPANY	FREQUENCY
Cagayan de Oro	8-10	650-980	2GO Travel, Trans Asia, Super Shuttle Ferry	at least daily
Calbayog, Samar	11	690	Cokaliong	3 weekly
Camiguin	11	880	Super Shuttle Ferry	8pm Fri
Dumaguete (fastcraft)	4½	950	Oceanjet	8am
Dumaguete (RORO)	6	300	Cokaliong, George & Peter Lines	at least nightly
Iloilo	11	700-800	Cokaliong, Trans Asia	4 weekly
Larena, Siquijor	8½	350	Lite Shipping	3 weekly
Maasin, Leyte	5	320	Cokaliong	almost daily, 7pm
Manila	23	850-1600	2GO Travel, Super Shuttle Ferry	3 weekly
Ormoc (fastcraft)	2¾	600	Supercat, Weesam	5 daily
Ormoc (RORO)	5	400	Lite Shipping, Super Shuttle Ferry	almost daily
Surigao City	11-13	550-700	2GO Travel, Cokaliong	almost daily, 7pm
Tagbilaran (fastcraft)	2¼	500-800	Oceanjet, Weesam, Supercat	12 daily
Tagbilaran (RORO)	4½	220	Lite Shipping, Trans Asia	most days
Tubigon	2	150	Lite Shipping	3 daily

fee-free P40,000 withdrawals at a 24-hour ATM.

Travellers Lounge (☎032-232 0293; ⏰6am-8.30pm) Located just outside SM City Mall, this handy lounge has a bag-drop servie (P50, same-day pickup only) and showers (P50). Also sells certain ferry tickets.

Getting There & Away

AIR

PAL Express, Cebu Pacific, PAL, Tigerair and AirAsia Zest have regular connections to Manila and scores of regional and international destinations.

BOAT

There's rarely a need to purchase tickets ahead for the popular fastcrafts to Tagbilaran (Bohol), Ormoc (Leyte) and Dumaguete. The *Sun Star* daily newspaper runs up-to-date schedules. Buy tickets at the piers.

2GO Travel (☎032-233 7000; http://travel.2go.com.ph; Pier 4)

Cokaliong Shipping (Map p585; ☎032-232 7211; Pier 1)

George & Peter Lines (☎032-254 5154; Pier 2)

Lite Shipping Corporation (Map p585; ☎032-416 6462; www.lite-shipping.com; Pier 1)

Oceanjet (Map p585; ☎032-255 7560; www.oceanjet.net; Pier 1)

Super Shuttle Ferry (☎032-345 5581; www.supershuttleferry.com; Pier 8)

Supercat (☎032-233 7000; www.supercat.com.ph; Pier 4)

Trans Asia Shipping Lines (☎032-254 6491; www.transasiashipping.com; Pier 5)

Weesam Express (☎032-412 9562; www.weesamexpressph.net; Pier 4)

BUS

There are two bus stations in Cebu. **Ceres Bus Lines** services southern and central destinations, such as Bato (P170, four hours, frequent) via Moalboal (P115, three hours) or via Oslob/Tan-awan (P155, 3½ hours), from the **South Bus Station** (Bacalso Ave). Quicker air-con vans ('V-hires') leave for Moalboal (P100) from the **Citilink Station** (Bacalso Ave), near the South Bus Station.

The **North Bus Station** (M Logarta Ave) is beyond SM City Mall. From here Ceres has buses to Hagnaya (P132, 3½ hours, hourly) for Bantayan Island, and to Maya for Malapascua Island.

Getting Around

Airport taxis at Mactan International Airport have a slightly inflated P70 flag fall and cost about P300 to the city centre, or you can walk upstairs to the arrivals area and grab a regular metered taxi (P40 flag fall). Taking public transport is complicated but possible; ask the tourist desk in the arrivals hall for directions.

To get uptown from the ports, catch one of the jeepneys that pass by the piers to Pres Osmeña Blvd, then transfer to a jeepney going uptown.

Moalboal

☎032 / POP 27,400

The Philippines' original diving hotbed, Moalboal remains a throwback to the days when diving came cheap and minus the attitude. **Panagsama Beach**, where the resorts are, meanders lazily along a sea wall within rock-skipping distance of a stunning diving wall (which can also be snorkelled). While the beach itself is hardly worthy of the name, non-divers can still find things to do here, including mountain biking and treks to nearby waterfalls.

Sights & Activities

Divers can paddle out to the coral-studded wall off Panagsama Beach, or take a 10-minute *bangka* ride to **Pescador Island**, which swarms with marine life. A single-tank dive shouldn't exceed US$25.

Beach lovers can take a tricycle (P150) 5km north to lovely **White Beach**.

Tours

Planet Action ADVENTURE TOUR
(☎032-474 3016; www.action-philippines.com) Run by the wry and affable Jochen, Planet Action runs mountain-biking, caving, canyoning and other mountain tours, including day trips that take in waterfalls. Reason alone to come to Moalboal.

Sleeping

Cora's Palm Resort GUESTHOUSE $
(☎032-474 3220; cora _abarquez@yahoo.com; d P400-1500; ❄📶) The original Panagsama guesthouse, Cora's is still going strong. Shoot for the cosy and cheap fan rooms. It's right in the centre of the village.

Moalboal Backpacker Lodge HOSTEL $
(☎0905 227 8096; www.moalboal-backpackerlodge.com; dm/s/d/cottage P275/350/480/750; 📶) This hostel has an airy dorm, and a couple of semiprivate rooms over a coffee shop, plus two fabulous two-floor cottages that are a steal.

✖ Eating & Drinking

Drinking is the national sport of the Moalboal Republic, and there are plenty of eateries where you can secure food to soak up the deluge of beer.

Chilli Bar RESTAURANT, BAR **$**
(mains P150-210; ⊙9.30am-last customer) A Panagsama institution known for big pizzas, chilli con carne, Swedish meatballs and a lethal cocktail menu. 'The liver is evil and it must be punished', proclaims a big board by the pool table.

Last Filling Station INTERNATIONAL **$$**
(meals from P180; ⊙7am-10pm; 🛜📶) Associated with Planet Action. Fuel up here for your trek with protein-heavy shakes and big breakfasts.

ℹ Getting There & Around

Frequent Ceres buses pass through town heading south to Bato (for Tampi and Dumaguete; P70, two hours) and north to Cebu's South Bus Station (P110, three hours). To Cebu, there are also air-con vans driven by sadistic drivers (P120, two hours).

Motorbike taxis to Panagsama Beach from Moalboal town cost about P40, tricycles double that.

Malapascua Island

POP 3500

A picturesque little island off the northeast tip of Cebu, Malapascua is the best place in the Philippines to view **thresher sharks**. Divers head out at 5am to **Monad Shoal**, where they park on the seabed at 35m hoping to catch a glimpse of these critters. The chances are pretty good – about 75%. By day Monad Shoal attracts manta rays. Once your dive is over you can relax on signature white-sand **Bounty Beach**, where a string of resorts offer seaside seating in the sand.

In November 2013, the eye of super-typhoon Yolanda (Haiyan) passed right over Malapascua, snapping trees like matchsticks and blowing off virtually every roof on the island. But the little island staged a remarkable recovery, with most resorts reopening within a couple of months.

🛏 Sleeping

Mike & Diose's Aabana
Waterfront Resort RESORT **$**
(📞0905 263 2914; www.aabana.de; d incl breakfast P500-2200; 🕸🛜) Lavish deluxe suites, smart

budget rooms – no matter what you choose, you're in for a treat. Easily Malapascua's best value. It's next to Exotic Island Dive Resort at the far east end of Bounty Beach.

Villa Sandra HOSTEL **$**
(📞0917 865 0958; jonjonmalapascua@gmail.com; s/d P300/500; @🛜) Very much a backpacker pad next to the elementary school in Logan village, with simple shared doubles, a kitchen, a hang-out patio and dudes in dreads hanging about.

White Sand Bungalows BUNGALOW **$$**
(📞0927 318 7471; www.whitesand.dk; r/bungalow P900/1200; 🛜) The rambling *nipa* huts are equipped with lofts and gorgeous balconies fronting scenic Poblacion Beach, away from the crowds near the boat landing in Logan. Marvellous spot if you can get a room (there are only four).

Exotic Island Dive Resort RESORT **$$**
(📞0999 997 6601; www.malapascua.net; s/d from P800/1000, with air-con from P1000/1300; 🕸🛜) A relatively fancy full-service dive resort, Exotic has a dozen economy rooms set away from the resort proper. Knock P300 off the price if you're diving with them.

✖ Eating & Drinking

Expect anything on Bounty Beach to cost more than you want to pay. **Hilty's Hideout** runs a floating bar in the high season that's plenty of fun. Otherwise be sure to hit **Oscar's** on Bounty Beach for a drink.

Ging-Ging's Flower Garden FILIPINO **$**
(mains P60-100; ⊙7am-10pm; 🍴) Inland from the beach, Ging-Ging's serves tasty, cheap, filling vegetarian food and curries.

Kiwi Bakhaw FILIPINO **$$**
(meals P100-220; ⊙7am-10pm) This place is well worth sniffing out. It's hidden in the maze-like village behind Exotic island, so ask a local to point the way. Gorgeous cordon-bleu home cooking, including curries. Expect to wait up to an hour, and bring bug spray.

ℹ Getting There & Away

Bangka from Maya (P80, 30 minutes) to Malapascua leave when full, roughly every hour until 5.30pm or so (until 2pm from Malapascua). If you miss the last boat, you'll have to charter a *bangka* for P800 to P2000. At low tide you must pay a barge operator P20 to shuttle you to/from the *bangka*.

Ceres buses depart Maya pier for Cebu (ordinary/air-con P163/180, 4½ hours) every 30 minutes until mid-evening.

Bohol

It's difficult to reconcile Bohol's bloody history with the relaxed isle of today. It's here that Francisco Dagohoy led the longest revolt in the country against the Spaniards, from 1744 to 1829. These days Bohol is a tourist magnet, with endearing little primates, coral cathedrals off Panglao Island and lush jungle, ripe for exploration. A powerful earthquake rocked the island in October 2013, destroying several centuries-old Spanish churches and causing erosion that turned the iconic Chocolate Hills an ugly shade of vanilla. Hopefully the hills will regain their lustre.

⊙ Getting There & Away

Tagbilaran is the main gateway, but ferries to Camiguin leave from Jagna, about 1½ hours east of Tagbilaran. Oceanjet has a daily 1.30pm fastcraft from Jagna to Benoni, Camiguin (P600, two hours), that continues to Cagayan de Oro (P900, five hours). Super Shuttle Ferry has a RORO to Balbagon, Camiguin, on Mondays, Wednesdays and Fridays at 1pm (P400, 3½ hours).

Additional ferries link Cebu and Tubigon in northwest Bohol, and Bato (Leyte) and Ubay in northeast Bohol.

Tagbilaran

⊙ 038 / POP 97,000

There's no reason to waste much time in traffic-snarled Tagbilaran. Your first port of call should be the **tourist office** (⊙8am-6pm) at the ferry dock, which can help with transport arrangements.

If you do need to stay the night, your best bet is homey **Nisa Travellers Hotel** (⊙ 038-411 3731; www.nisatravellershotel.com; CPG Ave; s/d incl breakfast from P500/600; ☀@☎) on the main drag. It has simple rooms and great common areas in a maze-like house. Directly opposite is bright and basic **Ellen's Bed & Bath** (⊙ 038-501 9341; CPG Ave; s/d from P350/400; ☀☎). Both are susceptible to street noise, so request rooms at the back. Eat, cool off and escape the tricycle madness at the food court in BQ Mall, opposite Nisa's.

The main domestic airlines all serve Tagbilaran from Manila.

Various fastcraft and slowcraft head to Cebu. Oceanjet operates a daily fastcraft to Dumaguete (P680, two hours) that continues to Siquijor town. A few weekly ferries serve Larena, Siquijor. Trans Asia has three trips weekly to/from Cagayan de Oro (P655, 10 hours).

The main bus terminal is next to Island City Mall in Dao, 3km north of the centre. Here you'll find air-con minivans to Jagna (P100, 1½ hours, hourly) and frequent buses to Carmen for the Chocolate Hills (P60, 2½ hours).

To avoid expensive van rides and slow public transport, consider hiring your own motorbike in Tagbilaran (P500 to P600 per day) to explore the rest of Bohol.

Around Tagbilaran

It's just a short drive north of Tagbilaran to two of the Philippines' signature attractions – the Chocolate Hills and that lovable palm-sized primate, the tarsier.

You can visit both on an excursion from Tagbilaran, but you're much better off basing yourself in Loboc at **Nuts Huts** (⊙0920 846 1559; walterken@hotmail.com; dm/s P300/400, d P600-1000), a backpacker Shangri-La in the middle of the jungle. With a sublime location overlooking the emerald-tinged Loboc River, Nuts Huts provides at least as much reason to visit inland Bohol as brown loam lumps or miniature monkeys. The Belgian hosts can tell you everything you need to know about exploring the area, and you can **hike** and **mountain bike** on a network of trails in the immediate vicinity.

To get to Nuts Huts from Tagbilaran, catch a Carmen-bound bus and get off at the Nuts Huts sign. It's a 15-minute walk from the road. Alternatively, take a bus to Loboc and then a *habal-habal* (motorcycle taxi; P50) or shuttle boat up the river from the Sarimanok landing (per person P200).

SAMAR & LEYTE: TYPHOON YOLANDA

Tragically, the eastern Visayan islands of Samar and Leyte, separated from each other by a narrow strait near Leyte's capital Tacloban, were devastated by super-typhoon Yolanda (Haiyan) in November 2013. The incredible images of death and destruction captured the attention of the world. While the death toll wasn't on the level of the Indian Ocean tsunami of 2004, some say the damage wrought by Yolanda was worse. The storm affected more than 16 million people and displaced more than four million. The vast majority of Yolanda's 6200-plus victims were from Tacloban, a major regional centre of 250,000. Parts of southeastern Samar, near where Yolanda made landfall, were also obliterated.

Recovery in both Tacloban and Samar was proceeding extremely slowly as we went to press. The devastation was simply too great, the affected area simply too wide, and the Philippines – no stranger to natural disasters – simply not prepared for a catastrophe of this magnitude. In early 2014, Tacloban remained a post-apocalyptic war zone. Electricity was nowhere close to being restored and corpses were still being dragged out of the rubble on a daily basis. More than 1700 people remained unaccounted for.

For the foreseeable future, the only visitors to Tacloban and southeastern Samar will be aid workers. Elsewhere, things should return to normal relatively swiftly. The island provinces could certainly use your tourist dollars. Both islands are quite rugged and receive few tourists, which is part of their appeal.

If you decide to head this way, two experiences to hone in on are **spelunking** around Catbalogan, Samar, and **diving** – with whale sharks if you're lucky – in southern Leyte's **Sogod Bay**. The spelunking tour of the **Jiabong Caves** is one of the Visayas' top one-day adventures. Tours are run out of Catbalogan by **Trexplore** (☎ 055-251 2301; www.bonifaciojoni.blogspot.com). The whale-shark season around Pintuyan, on the east side of Sogod Bay, is November to May. Sightings are sporadic, so get the low-down before you go from **Moncher Bardos** (☎ 0916 952 3354; moncher64bardos@yahoo.com), who assists with a community-based tourism project to snorkel with the tiki-tiki. On the west side of Sogod Bay, **Padre Burgos** has great diving and several resorts run trips across the bay to dive with the whale sharks when they are around.

The main ports of entry to the region are Allen in North Samar, which is served by regular ferries from Sorsogon in South Luzon (P120, 1¼ hours); Ormoc in northeast Leyte, served by various slow and fast boats from Cebu; and San Ricardo in southern Leyte, where regular ROROs chug to the Mindanao port of Lipata, near Surigao City (P120, 1½ hours).

Near Nuts Huts is the **Loboc Ecotourism Adventure Park**, with an exciting head-first 500m zipline (P350) running over the Loboc River gorge.

You are unlikely to spot the nocturnal tarsier in the wild, so head to the **Philippine Tarsier Sanctuary** (www.tarsierfoundation.org; admission P50; ☺9am-4pm) in *barangay* Canapnapan, between the towns of Corella and Sikatuna. About 10 saucer-eyed tarsiers hang out in the immediate vicinity of the centre – the guides will bring you right to them. This is a much more humane and ecofriendly way to appreciate the tarsier than visiting the animals kept in cages by tourist operators in Loboc.

From Nuts Huts the sanctuary is a 30- to 45-minute motorbike ride, or take a jeepney from Loboc (P25, 45 minutes). From Tagbilaran catch a jeepney to Sikatuna (P20, one hour) from the Dao terminal and ask to be dropped off at the sanctuary.

An interesting quirk of nature, the **Chocolate Hills** consist of more than 1200 conical hills, up to 120m high. They were supposedly formed over time by the uplift of coral deposits and the effects of rainwater and erosion. Since this explanation cannot be confirmed, the local belief that they are the tears of a heartbroken giant may one day prove to be correct.

From Nuts Huts, the Chocolate Hills are a 45-minute motorbike ride; alternatively, flag down a bus bound for Carmen (4km north of the Chocolate Hills) and hop off at one of the Chocolate Hills viewpoints.

A more invigorating method of seeing the hills is to take a *habal-habal* in and around the hills; a one-hour ride costs P250.

Panglao Island

♫ 038

Linked by two bridges to Bohol, Panglao is where divers head to take advantage of the spectacular coral formations and teeming marine life on the nearby islands of Balicasag and Pamilacan. Ground zero for divers is Alona Beach, an agreeable stretch of white sand in range of good snorkelling. Alona Beach has gone upscale in recent years, but determined deal-hunters can still find bargains on diving and accommodation.

🏃 Activities

Diving & Snorkelling

Dive prices average P1200 per dive, not including equipment. Rates vary wildly so shop around. Most dive trips go to Balicasag Island.

Dolphin-Watching

You can arrange early-morning dolphin-watching tours near Pamilacan Island through most resorts and dive centres. Figure on paying P1500 for a four-person boat.

🛏 Sleeping & Eating

Beachfront dining opportunities on Alona Beach are ample but come at a price. Most affordable eateries and bars are off the beach on the road to Tagbilaran.

Casa-Nova Garden   GUESTHOUSE $
(☑ 038-502 9101; s P300, d P500-700; ❀ 🛜) True shoestring accommodation survives in Alona thanks to this spot. The pricier en-suite doubles are a substantial upgrade on the leaky budget rooms. It's 700m west of town; access is easiest from the highway.

Bohol Divers Resort   RESORT $$
(☑ 038-502 9005; www.boholdiversresortph.com; s P500, d P600-4000; ❀ 🛜 ⛱) This sprawling complex is one of the few beachfront places still offering budget rooms. Accommodation runs the gamut from basic fan rooms to upscale villas.

Trudi's Place   FILIPINO $
(mains P150-200; ⊙ 6.30am-10.30pm; 🛜) Trudi's qualifies as budget eating on Alona Beach proper. Bonus: P40 San Miguel.

❶ Getting There & Around

From Tagbilaran, buses with 'Tawala Alona' signboards head to Alona Beach roughly hourly until 3pm from the corner of Hontanosas and F Rocha Sts (P25, 45 minutes). An easier option is to hire a *habal-habal* (P150), tricycle (P200) or taxi (P350).

MINDANAO

Sprawling Mindanao, the world's 19th-largest island, is known for dazzling scenery, primitive hill tribes and an almost complete lack of tourists because of political unrest and occasional fighting between the government and Muslim separatists. What most don't realise is that the lovely coastal stretch of northern Mindanao between Cagayan de Oro and Siargao Island is Catholic, Cebuano (Visayan) speaking – and quite safe. The area is known for first-rate surfing on Siargao and activities galore on dramatic, dynamic Camiguin. Mainland Mindanao offers up plenty of cherries for the intrepid traveller, including the Philippines' highest mountain, Mt Apo (2954m), accessible from Davao in southern Mindanao. Exercise caution if you are heading south or west of Cagayan de Oro.

❶ Getting There & Away

Popular jumping-off points for ferries from the Visayas include Dumaguete, Cebu City and Jagna (Bohol). The shortest crossing is from southern Leyte, where five daily ROROs connect the town of San Ricardo with the port of Lipata near Surigao City.

Siargao

♫ 086 / POP 70,000

It's best known for having one of the world's great surf breaks, but the island of Siargao is no one-trick pony. Surrounded by idyllic islands and sprinkled with coves and quaint fishing villages, it has plenty to offer non-surfers too.

❶ Getting There & Away

Cebu Pacific flies from Cebu to Siargao almost daily in the peak season (August to October), less frequently in the low season.

The other way to Siargao is by boat from Surigao City on mainland Mindanao. Speedy *bangka* ferries head to Dapa on Siargao from in front of Surigao's Tavern Hotel (P250, 2¼ hours,

6am and 11am). In bad weather, opt for the daily RORO (P150, 3¼ hours, noon) from Surigao's **main pier** (Borromeo St). *Bangka* from Dapa to Surigao City depart at 5.45am and 10.45am; the RORO is at noon.

To get to Surigao City, either fly in from Cebu or Manila, sail in from southern Leyte, or bus in from Butuan or Cagayan de Oro.

ⓘ Getting Around

Siargao's small airport is in Del Carmen on the west side of the island. An airport van shuttles passengers to/from the resorts around Cloud Nine (P300, 45 minutes).

From the pier in Dapa, a *habal-habal* costs a negotiable P200 to Cloud Nine (30 minutes). *Habal-habal* drivers in Cloud Nine ask double for the reverse trip. Tricycles cost the same but are much slower.

Sporadic jeepneys run from Dapa to General Luna ('GL') and points north. To explore the island, you're better off hiring a motorcycle (per day P500).

Cloud Nine & General Luna

The legendary **Cloud Nine** break off Tuazon Point is what put Siargao on the map. Board rental in the sleepy village of Cloud Nine, a bumpy 10-minute *habal-habal* ride north of GL, is P500 per day or P200 per hour. There are plenty of moderate swells around for beginners; lessons cost P500 per hour including board rental. Peak sea-

RIVER RAFTING IN CAGAYAN DE ORO

If you're travelling between Siargao and Camiguin, consider detouring to Cagayan de Oro (CDO) to take on the Class III and IV rapids of the Cagayan River. This is the only place in the country that offers year-round whitewater rafting. Tours cost P800 to P1500 per person depending on the length of the trip. Reputable rafting companies in CDO include **Kagay CDO Rafting** (☏ 088-310 4402; www. kagaycagayandeororafting.com) and long-running **Rafting Adventure Philippines** (☏ 088-856 3514; www. raftingadventurephilippines.com). CDO is a 2½-hour fastcraft ride from Camiguin.

son for waves is late August to November. Cloud Nine gets overrun in October for the **Siargao International Surfing Cup**.

Hippie's Surf Shop (www.surfshopsiargao.com; ☉6am-6pm), just before the Ocean 101 Beach Resort, rents boards and holds thrice-weekly yoga classes (P200). Resorts can organise boat transport to offshore surf breaks or **island-hopping** trips, often with a snorkelling or surfing option.

🛏 Sleeping

Prices mushroom and rooms fill up fast in the high season. Some resorts shut down during the rainiest months (December to March in these parts).

Ocean 101 Beach Resort HOTEL $
(☏0910 848 0893; www.ocean101cloud9.com; d with fan P500-1300, with air-con P1400-2500; ❄@🛜) This is surfing HQ, with a mix of well-maintained budget rooms and pricier beachfront quarters distributed among two ugly blue concrete edifices.

Kermit Surf Resort RESORT $
(☏0915 606 4227; www.kermitsiargao.com; dm/d incl breakfast from P350/600; ❄🛜) This newish place between Cloud Nine and GL gets rave reviews for its nice mix of affordable accommodation and welcoming atmosphere.

Point 303 HOTEL $
(☏0910 989 0725; r with fan P500-750, with air-con P1400-1800; ❄🛜) Ocean 101's sister property, opposite fancier Sagana Beach Resort, has 16 rooms; the cheapest share bathrooms but are big and clean.

Boardwalk at Cloud 9 HOTEL $$
(☏0939 164 1268; www.surfingsiargao.com; r incl breakfast P750-2750; ❄🛜) It stares straight at Cloud Nine and offers a mix of basic rooms and downright elegant beachfront cottages. Better than Kesa Cloud 9 in the same courtyard.

🍴 Eating & Drinking

In GL you'll find cheap eateries and a couple of bars frequented by local surfer dudes and chicks.

Arsenia FILIPINO $$
(meals P150; ☉6am-10pm) In an unsigned shack, 150m beyond Ocean 101, this place is worth finding for the chicken mango curry and other delights, many of which feed two.

Sagana Beach Resort INTERNATIONAL $$
(mains P150-450) Centrally located Sagana has tremendous food; do try the ceviche.

Nine Bar BAR
Located between Cloud Nine and GL, Nine Bar is where you go to swill beer and swap swell tales.

Camiguin

📍 088 / POP 84,000

With seven volcanoes, various waterfalls, hot springs, cold springs, deserted islands offshore and underwater diversions aplenty, Camiguin is a top adventure-tourism destination. The dramatic landscape makes it a great place to strike out on your own and explore, preferably by motorbike (per day P300 to P500) or mountain bike (per day P250).

Adventure lovers should head to **Camiguin Action Geckos** or **Johnny's Dive N' Fun** (📞088-387 9588; www.johnnysdive.com; Caves Dive Resort, Agoho). They both offer a range of trekking, rappelling, mountain-biking and diving tours, and are happy to dispense advice to do-it-yourselfers. Don't miss world-class diving at splendid **Mantigue Island**, snorkelling at the **Sunken Cemetery**, or the easy **Stations of the Cross** hike for great views. **White Island**, a marooned slick of sand 1km off Agoho, is best visited early in the morning before the crowds arrive; boats cost P400 to P450.

ℹ Getting There & Around

Cebu Pacific has daily flights from Cebu to Camiguin's airport just west of Mambajao.

Oceanjet fastcraft run from Camiguin's Benoni port, 17km southeast of Mambajao, to Jagna, Bohol (P600, two hours, 11am) and Cagayan de Oro (P600, 2½ hours, 4pm).

From the Balbagon pier 2km east of Mambajao, **Super Shuttle Ferry** (📞0909 236 1790) ROROs serve Jagna (P400, 3½ hours, three weekly) and Cebu (P880, 11 hours, 8pm Sunday).

From Benoni, there are hourly ferries until 5.30pm to Balingoan on mainland Mindanao (P170, 1½ hours), where Bachelor buses serve Surigao (ordinary/air-con P300/400, seven hours with a transfer in Butuan) and Cagayan de Oro (ordinary/air-con P90/150, two hours) all day and night.

Multicabs (mini-jeepneys) circle the island mostly counterclockwise, passing any given point roughly every hour until about 5pm. A special trip in a tricycle from Benoni to Mambajao/Agoho costs P200/350.

Around Mambajao

Most of Camiguin's resorts are on the black-sand beaches of *barangays* Bug-Ong, Agoho and Yumbing, 5km to 8km west of Mambajao. A tricycle to this area costs P75 to P100 from Mambajao. Several nondescript beach resorts in Yumbing proper rent out rooms from P700, although they raise their rates at the first sign of a crowd. The best is **Marianita's Cottages** (📞0926 451 9216; National Hwy, Yumbing; r from P700).

🛏 Sleeping & Eating

Enigmata Treehouse Ecolodge HOSTEL $
(📞088-387 0273; http://camiguinecolodge.com; Balbagon; dm/ste P300/1050; 📶) This hippie-esque artist hang-out in the woods is more a way of life than a resort. The two suites and one six-bed dorm are in a fantastic house built around a towering hardwood tree. To get here turn off the National Hwy at the Tarzan statue, about 2km east of Mambajao.

Seascape RESORT $
(📞0910 920 6152; Bug-Ong; cottage/r P600/700; 📶) The bungalows at this often eerily quiet resort are barren but boast big balconies with hammocks and prime ocean views. Cheaper rooms are concrete with inlaid bamboo.

★**Camiguin Action Geckos Resort** RESORT $$
(📞088-387 9146; www.camiguin.ph; Agoho; s/d without bathroom P700/900, cottages P2000-2900; ❄📶) The exceptional beachfront cottages here define rustic sophistication, while the cosy budget 'travellers' rooms' flank an exquisite chill-out deck above the restaurant. It sits on one of the widest stretches of charcoal beach in the area west of Mambajao.

Agohay Villa Forte RESORT $$
(📞088-387 9543; contact@agohovillaforte.com; Agoho; d P1000-1750, six-person r P2780; ❄📶) Solid all-round choice situated right on the beach offering a variety of garden- and

sea-facing rooms, including a large dorm-style room that's perfect for a group of backpackers.

Luna Ristorante ITALIAN $$
(National Hwy, Yumbing; mains P200; ⊘7am-midnight; 🔊) This is easily the best restaurant on the island, with the brick-oven pizza being the highlight.

PALAWAN

Drifting on the Philippines' western edge, Palawan is one of the country's last ecological frontiers. The Amazonian interior of the main island is barely connected by a few snaking roads that will make your teeth-filling jingle, and the convoluted coast comprises one breathtaking bay after another leading up to the limestone cliffs of El Nido and Bacuit Bay in the north. Eight hours north of mainland Palawan, the Calamian group of islands offers beaches, unbeatable wreck diving and a number of El Nido–esque cliffs of their own.

❶ Getting There & Around

Puerto Princesa and Coron receive plenty of flights and ships from both Manila and Cebu. The only option to El Nido from Manila is with pricey ITI; shoestringers fly to Puerto Princesa and travel to El Nido by bus or van.

Sporadic flights link Puerto and Coron. The only way from Coron to mainland El Nido is by almost-daily *bangka* ferries (about eight hours).

Puerto Princesa

📞 048 / POP 223,000
If only all Philippine cities could be a little more like earthy Puerto Princesa. Strictly enforced fines for littering (P200) keep the streets clean (we're not kidding!), while the municipal government actively promotes the city as an eco- and adventure-tourism hub. Yes, there's the usual stream of tricycles down the main commercial drag, Rizal Ave. But even the tricycles seem quieter than in most other provincial centres. In short, 'Puerto' makes a great launching pad for checking out the myriad natural attractions in the surrounding area.

❍ Sights & Activities

Dolphin-watching and **island-hopping** tours in scenic Honda Bay are the big draws.

Many pay a premium for day trips to the Subterranean River; instead, stay in idyllic Sabang and launch your trip there.

Pasyar Developmental Tourism ADVENTURE TOUR
(☑048-434 2113; www.pasyarpalawan.tripod.com; Manolo Ext, cnr Gabinete Rd) 🏄 Genuinely dedicated to conservation and community-based tourism, Pasyar is a great choice for day tours like Honda Bay and dolphin watching, as well as longer adventures. Also runs an **Environmental Enforcement Museum** (admission P20; ⊘8am-5pm), which displays confiscated chainsaws, boats, dynamite and (sometimes) animals such as civets.

🛏 Sleeping

⭐ **Banwa Art House** HOSTEL $
(☑048-434 8963; www.banwa.com; Liwanag St; dm P350, d from P600; @🔊) This backpacker oasis oozes charm from every artisan craft adorning its walls. The groovy lounge has cool tunes wafting from the house CD player, and the food is affordable and tasty.

Ancieto's Pension GUESTHOUSE $
(☑048-434 6667; arc_tess@yahoo.com.ph; cnr Mabini & Roxas Sts; s/d from P300/450; ❄🔊) Near Banwa Art House, this homey place has several cosy sitting areas and a rooftop with a garden and an open-air kitchen. The simple rooms are susceptible to some street noise.

Dallas Lodge HOSTEL $
(☑048-434 2086; www.dallasinnpalawan.com; 11 Carandang St; dm/d P300/600; 🔊) A tiny, friendly backpacker crash pad with four graffiti-splashed private rooms and a six-bed dorm, all clad in warm rattan.

Pagdayon Traveler's Inn GUESTHOUSE $$
(☑048-434 9102; Pagdayon Rd; r P950-1300; ❄🔊) Central but quiet, Pagdayon has six well-kept air-con rooms, each with individual verandahs, set around a delightful open-air common/dining area. It's 100m off Rizal Ave (turn south near Ugong Rock restobar).

🍽 Eating & Drinking

Vietnamese *chaolong* restaurants along Rizal Ave serve a Filipino version of *pho* (spicy noodle soup) for just P50. **Pham Chaolong** (Rizal Ave, btwn Valencia & Burgos Sts) is a good and central choice.

Ima's Vegetarian
VEGETARIAN $

(Fernandez St; dishes P80-130; ⊙11am-9pm Sun-Thu, 11am-3pm Fri, 6.30-9pm Sat; 🖉) A decidedly healthy and delicious option run by Seventh-Day Adventists. Try the spicy black-bean burger or vegan-cheese pizza for *merienda* (a daytime snack).

Neva's Place
PIZZERIA $

(Taft St; mains P100-215; ⊙8am-11pm) Budget Filipino food, Thai food and delicious wood-fired pizzas, all served in a blissful garden.

★Kalui Restaurant
FILIPINO $$

(🖉048-433 2580; 369 Rizal Ave; mains P180-350; ⊙11am-2pm & 6-11pm) This seafood specialist in a funky *nipa* complex thoroughly deserves its reputation as one of the finest restaurants in the country. Reservations are recommended, especially for dinner.

Cafe Itoy's
CAFE

(Rizal Ave; ⊙6am-11pm; 🖎) Starbucks-style coffee joint with light bites.

Kinabuch Grill & Bar
BAR

(Rizal Ave; mains P100-500; ⊙4pm-1am; 🖎) Outdoor 'KGB' has two pool tables, and is popular both for drinks and heaping portions of *lechon* (suckling pig) and other Filipino favourites.

Tiki Restobar
BAR

(cnr Rizal Ave & National Hwy; ⊙7pm-2am) A huge place in the middle of town, Tiki features bar games, beer buckets and – often – revellers shimmying on the dance floor to live music 'til the wee hours.

ℹ Information

Internet cafes line busy Rizal Ave. **Metrobank**, **BDO** and **BPI**, all on Rizal Ave, have mainland Palawan's only working ATMs.

Tourist Information & Assistance Counter
(🖉048-434 4211; Airport; ⊙8am-5pm Mon-Sat) Distributes a city map and can help with hotel bookings.

Subterranean River National Park Office
(🖉048-723 0904; www.puerto-underground river.com; City Coliseum, National Hwy; ⊙8am-4pm) Issues Subterranean River permits. It's about 2km north of the centre.

ℹ Getting There & Away

AIR
Cebu Pacific has daily flights to Puerto Princesa from both Manila and Cebu, while PAL Express, Tigerair and AirAsia Zest fly from Manila only.

BOAT
2GO Travel (🖉048-434 9344; Rizal Ave; P1200, 28 hours) has two weekly vessels to Puerto Princesa from Manila via Coron. **Milagrosa Shipping** (🖉048-433 4806; Rizal Ave; P950, 36 hours, two weekly) and **Montenegro Lines** (🖉048-434 9344; www.montenegrolines.com. ph; Puerto Princesa Pier; P1220, 26 hours) make the epic trip between Puerto Princesa and Iloilo via the Cuyo Islands.

BUS
The main bus terminal is at the San Jose market 6km north of town. To get there grab a multicab (mini-jeepney; P15) from the corner of Rizal Ave and the National Hwy.

Buses/jeepneys and/or vans serve Sabang, Port Barton and El Nido. To avoid waiting hours for a van to fill up, steer clear of the touts and take the scheduled vans to El Nido run from the bus station by **Eulen Joy** and **Fortwally**.

ℹ Getting Around

The airport is on Rizal Ave just east of the centre. Airport tricycles cost P50 or walk out and take a public trike for P8.

You can rent motorbikes (from P350) along Rizal Ave east of the National Hwy junction.

Sabang
🖉 048

Tiny Sabang has an indescribably beautiful beach, huge tracts of pristine jungle and the navigable **Puerto Princesa Subterranean River National Park** (admission P250, plus P40 environmental fee; ⊙8.30am-3.30pm), which winds through a spectacular cave before emptying into the sea. Tourist paddle boats are allowed to go 1.5km upstream into the cave (45 minutes return). It's possible to proceed 4.3km upstream with a permit from the national park office in Puerto Princesa (P1000, four hours return).

Book a boat (P700 for up to six people, 15 minutes) to the river mouth through the **Sabang Information Office** (🖉048-723 0904; ⊙8am-4pm) at the pier, or walk 5km through the jungle. Important note: if you are *not* sleeping in Sabang, you must secure your permit from the national park office in Puerto Princesa (or be forced to pay a lot more in Sabang).

Other activities in Sabang include **ziplines, stand-up paddle-boarding** and **body-surfing** (when there's swell). Seek out 'Jungle George' for all-day rainforest walks taking in indigenous Batak villages (P500 per person).

🛏 Sleeping & Eating

Most places have electricity only from 6pm to 10pm or 11pm. Two high-end beach resorts have 24-hour electricity and wi-fi.

Dab Dab Resort   BUNGALOW $
(📞0949 469 9421; cottage without/with bathroom from P500/900; 🛜) Dab Dab has tasteful dark-wood and bamboo cottages scattered around a lush garden, and a glorious common area under a soaring octagonal canopy. The catch: it fronts a rocky strip of shoreline 200m south of Sabang Beach.

Mary's Cottages   BUNGALOW $
(📞0928 832 8328; d P600-700, q P1000) Mary's occupies the peaceful north end of Sabang Beach. The four bungalows are exceedingly basic but have lovely balconies facing the ocean (all you need, really).

Tribal Beach Resort   GUESTHOUSE $
(📞0917 646 8700; kainansatribosabang@yahoo. com; d/q P700/1500) The six basic rooms here have a prime location next to Mary's, but lack beach-facing balconies. Mickey Mouse greets you.

Bambua Nature Park Resort   HOSTEL $
(📞0927 420 9686; www.bambua-palawan.com; s/d from P325/460, cottage P1250) Get up close and personal with Sabang's magnificent rainforest in this jungle lodge about a 15-minute walk south of town along the main road. There's a variety of rooms to choose from, many with stunning views.

ℹ Getting There & Away

Lexus vans depart to Puerto Princesa (P200, 1½ hours) at 7.30am, 2pm and 4pm; trips from Puerto are at 7.30am, 8.30am, 10am, 3pm and 4.30pm. Jumbo jeepneys (P150, 2½ hours) make four daily trips as well. If you're heading to Port Barton or El Nido, backtrack by road to Salvacion and flag down a northbound bus from the highway.

High-season *bangka* chug up to El Nido (P1800, seven hours) when there's enough demand, with drop-offs, but not pickups, in Port Barton (P1200, 3½ hours).

Port Barton

📞 048 / POP 4400

People find themselves unable to leave Port Barton, and only partly because of the town's poor transport links. Set on a small, attractive cove, the area has some fine islands in the bay and good snorkelling. Island-hopping excursions (up to 4 people P1500), sea kayaking and diving can be easily arranged.

🛏 Sleeping & Eating

Budget-friendly resorts on offshore islands include **Coconut Garden** (📞0918 370 2395; www.coconutgarden.palawan.net; Cacnipa Island; r P800-970, cottage P1250-1500) and **Blue Cove** (📞0908 562 0879; www.bluecoveresort. com; Albaguen Island; r from P1200; 🛜). Expect to pay a few hundred pesos per head for the boat transfer.

Thelma & Toby's Island Camping Adventure (📞048-434 8687; http://palawan camping.com; per person incl full board P1300) draws rave reviews.

Deep Moon Resort   RESORT $
(📞0917 449 9212; www.deepgoldresorts.com; cottages P400-1600; ❄🛜) Formerly Ysobelle's, the native-style cottages here are the nicest in Port Barton and come in many flavours, from simple cold-water shacks to prime beachfront affairs with private decks. Fine Japanese food is available.

El Dorado Sunset Resort   BUNGALOW $
(📞0920 329 9049; d P300-1000; 🛜) Up towards the northern end of the beach, El Dorado has very basic concrete cottages at the back and larger ones fronting the beach.

Summer Homes Beach Resort   RESORT $$
(📞0946 995 7608; www.portbarton.info/ summerhomes; r/cottage from P750/1250; ❄@🛜) Summer Homes spurns the native look with well-kept concrete cottages set on a manicured lawn.

★ **Jambalaya**   CAJUN $$
(mains P200-300; ⊙7am-9pm) The outspoken Irish-Filipina owners fire up Cajun food in a tree-fort-like bungalow with two gigantic chairs perched on the sand out front. Board games are available in a pillowy hang-out area, and Palawan's frostiest San Miguel cools 24/7 in the gas fridge.

ℹ Information

Jambalaya has a handy booklet with accommodation and other info; you can leave your bag there while you prowl the beach looking for a bed.

Summer Homes and Jambalaya have computers with internet access (when the power's on).

❶ Getting There & Away

There's an 8.30am jumbo jeepney to Roxas (P100, 1½ hours, reverse trip at 11am) and a 9am trip in either direction to Puerto Princesa (P250, 4½ hours). Change in Roxas for El Nido. You can also take a motorcycle taxi 22km out to the highway (P500, one hour) and flag down south- or north-bound buses. This road gets very muddy in the wet season.

The Port Barton boatmen's association bans the high-season Sabang–El Nido *bangka* from picking up passengers in Port Barton. Hiring a private three-passenger boat costs P6000 to El Nido, P3500 to Sabang.

El Nido

♪ 048 / POP 5600

El Nido is the primary base for exploring Palawan's star attraction, the stunning **Bacuit Archipelago**. Tiny swiftlets build edible nests out of saliva in the immense limestone cliffs that surround the ramshackle town – hence the name, El Nido (nest in Spanish). The town feels touristy by Philippine standards, but sporadic electricity (it cuts off from 6am to 2pm each day), crap wi-fi and rugged access roads are firm reminders that you are still in Palawan.

🏃 Activities

To escape the crowds, consider hiring a motorbike and tackling the rough road 20km north to isolated **Calitan Beach**. A few kilometres south of town is narrow but pretty **Corong-Corong Beach**. Or you could light out in a **sea kayak** (widely available for P500 to P800 per day) and paddle to **Cadlao Island**, which looms just west of El Nido. There are several **scuba-diving** operators in town, plus a range of terrestrial tours offered by myriad tour operators – Art Café's cliff-climbing and waterfall treks are recommended.

THE PERFECT BEACH

There's a rumour that the island described in Alex Garland's backpacker classic *The Beach* was somewhere in the Calamian Group. Garland set the book in Thailand, but admits that the real island was somewhere in the Philippines. He lived in the Philippines for a spell and set his second novel, *The Tesseract*, in Manila.

Island Hopping   BOAT TOUR

All-day or overnight island-hopping trips in the Bacuit Archipelago are ubiquitously available and cost P1200 to P1400 per person, including lunch (four-person minimum). Miniloc Island's **Big Lagoon** and **Small Lagoon** are not to be missed; for full effect get there at dawn when you'll have them to yourself.

🛏 Sleeping

El Nido's budget accommodation is generally substandard (don't expect toilet seats), so consider splashing out on the midrange hotels that line El Nido's beach west of the pier. Head south a couple of kilometres to Corong-Corong to escape the bustle of El Nido. Prices drop by as much as 60% in the low season.

El Nido Sands Inn   GUESTHOUSE $

(♪ 0999 452 5843; Serena St; dm/d without bathroom P300/600; 🛜) The simple clapboard rooms are arguably El Nido's best budget deal. Beds in the lone three-bed dorm are first-come, first-served. Nice wood floor, 24-hour electricity and public balcony with views. It's near the pier.

Cliffside Cottages   BUNGALOW $

(♪ 0910 956 7957; cliffsidecottages@yahoo.com; Rizal St; d/tr from P700/1050; 🛜) This place lies at the base of the dramatic cliffs that loom over El Nido south of the centre. Pluses: relative quiet, morning shade and private bamboo verandahs. Fusses: substandard beds and bathrooms.

Ogie's Beach Pension   HOTEL $

(♪ 0916 707 0393; ogspensionne@yahoo.com; cnr Hama & Del Pilar Sts; s/d/tr from P550/600/1000; ❄🛜) Has enough rooms (15) for there to be a good chance of something being available. The highlight is the common area with million-dollar views. The cheapest fan rooms are extremely basic and share grubby bathrooms.

Kape Pukka Pension   HOSTEL $

(♪ 0908 488 8832; Hama St; d P800-900) Associated with wildly popular Pukka Bar, this backpacker pad has five diminutive rooms with colourful walls, hammock-strewn private porches and basic shared bathrooms.

Bulskamp Inn   GUESTHOUSE $$

(♪ 0906 552 4624; www.bulskamp-inn.webs.com; Osmeña St; r from P1200; ❄🛜) Named after the owner's home town in Belgium, this place gets props for friendly service and a cosy ambience. Rooms have small beds but are spotless.

Rico's Beach Cottages GUESTHOUSE **$$**
(☎0929 467 1632; ricomfernandez@yahoo.com; Hama St; r from P1500; ❋☎) Most rooms in this two-storey wooden complex are beachfront. They are simple cold-water affairs but are roomy enough and have private verandahs. The rooms at the back have less appeal.

🍴 Eating & Drinking

★**Corner Beach Restaurant** INTERNATIONAL **$$**
(mains P150-500; ⊙8am-10pm) Seafood is the speciality, but the steaks, burgers and curries are all excellent. It's at the quiet northern end of the beach.

Lonesome Carabao MEXICAN **$$**
(Hama St; mains P200-300; ⊙7am-10pm) The best Mexican food in El Nido, if not Palawan, if not the entire southern Philippines!

Altrove ITALIAN **$$$**
(Hama St; pizzas P220-450; ⊙5-10.30pm) The Slovenian manager apparently crossed the border into Italy a few times to learn how to cook pizza – it's easily the best in town.

★**Pukka Bar** BAR
(mains P80-150) The most happening bar in El Nido features live reggae, buckets of Red Horse beer and bands of drunken backpackers spilling onto the beach.

Waterhole BAR
(Hama St; ⊙3pm-3am) The name says it all. Often gets going before happy hour, then peaks again late at night after Pukka Bar winds down.

ℹ Information

All visitors to El Nido must pay a P200 'eco-tourism development fee', good for 10 days, payable to your hotel or tour operator. There are no ATMs so bring cash. Internet cafes line Hama St; **Singh Internet Cafe** (cnr Hama & Del Pilar Sts; per hr P50; ⊙2-10.30pm), next to Ogie's Beach Pension, is faster (but pricier) than others.

El Nido Boutique & Art Café (☎0920 902 6317; www.elnidoboutiqueandartcafe.com; Serena St; ⊙6.30am-11pm; ☎) Near the wharf and run like clockwork by the Swiss owner, this is a repository for information about El Nido. You can buy plane tickets here,

---

OFF THE BEATEN TRACK

THE CORON LOOP

Looking to get off the beaten track? Hire a boat or sea kayak and wade around the untouched beaches and islands off the west coast of Busuanga. Or tackle the rough coastal road to Busuanga's northwest tip by motorcycle (P500 to P700), taking pit stops at beaches along the way (some off-road experience is advised if you do this).

Off the northwest tip is **Calauit Island**, home to the **Calauit Safari Park** (admission P400), where the descendents of giraffes, zebras and gazelles brought over from Kenya by Ferdinand Marcos in the 1970s roam. Boats to Calauit (P350, 10 minutes) leave from Macalachao, 7km north of Buluang.

---

check boat and bus schedules, change money, browse the library, buy clothes, rent kayaks, eat good food, drink real coffee and listen to live music most nights. It's also as good a place as any to arrange island-hopping trips into Bacuit Bay.

ℹ Getting There & Around

ITI flies from El Nido to Manila (P6750, three daily). The only way to the airport is by tricycle for P200.

Frequent vans (P600, 5½ hours) and Cherry buses (ordinary/air-con P280/465, 8½ hours, every two hours from 5am to 9pm) depart to Puerto Princesa from the bus station, about 2km south of town along Rizal St. For Port Barton, take a 7am or earlier van to Roxas (P450, 3½ hours) and catch the 11am jumbo jeepney.

High-season *bangka* wade down to Sabang (P2000, seven hours) when there's demand (roughly every other day), stopping in Port Barton (P1500, four hours) by request. For boats to Coron, see p600.

Coron

☑048 / POP 10,000

Divers know it as a wreck-diving hot spot, but the area known as Coron also has untouched beaches, crystal-clear lagoons and brooding limestone cliffs to tempt non divers. Coron itself is actually just the sleepy main town of Busuanga Island – not to be confused with Coron Island to the south. Both Busuanga Island and Coron Island are part of the Calamian Group.

Coron took a direct hit from Typhoon Yolanda in 2013, but the island recovered quickly and things should have returned to normal by the time you read this.

Activities

Wreck Diving
DIVING

Fifteen Japanese ships sunk by US fighter planes roost on the floor of Coron Bay around Busuanga. Getting to the wrecks from Coron town involves a one- to four-hour boat ride, but diving is still affordable, averaging about P2200 for a two-tank dive. Most of the wrecks are for advanced divers, although there are a few in less than 25m that are suitable for beginners.

Island Hopping
BOAT TOUR

Coron town lacks a beach, but you can join an island-hopping tour (from P650 per person) or hire a boat from the **Calamian Tourist Boat Association** at the pier. Prices to various destinations are clearly posted. **Coron Island**, with its towering spires of stratified limestone, is the star attraction. You can paddle around on a bamboo raft and swim in Coron Island's unspoiled **Lake Cayangan** (admission P250), or go diving in **Barracuda Lake** (admission P100), where the clear water gets scorching hot as you descend. A four-/eight-person boat to Coron Island costs P1500/2000. Other island highlights include world-class snorkelling on **Calumbuyan Island** and **Banana Island**. Paddling around the islands by **sea kayak** is a fantastic option; contact **Tribal Adventures** (✆0917 819 3049; www.tribaladventures.com; National Hwy; kayaks from P500).

Sleeping

The following are in Coron town.

Krystal Lodge
BUNGALOW $

(✆0949 333 0429; www.krystallodge.blogspot. com; r P400-800, cottage P1200; 🌐) Like much of Coron, this bamboo complex is built on stilts over the water. It's a maze of shady walkways ending in rooms that range from passable boxes to utterly unique overwater 'apartments'.

Coron Backpacker Guesthouse
HOSTEL $

(✆0919 388 6028; coronbackpacker@gmail. com; d P500; 🌐) This place has nine basic doubles in a shack over the water near the centre of town. The common area is pleasantly rustic, with a kitchen and lots of reading material.

Marley's Guesthouse
HOSTEL $

(✆0929 772 5559; r P500; 🌐) Newly opened hostel on the main road near the centre, with simple rooms and a decent common/kitchen area.

Eating & Drinking

★ Bistro Coron
FRENCH $$$

(Coron town; mains P200-500; ⊙8am-midnight) A mouth-watering French bistro on one of the Philippines' most isolated islands? Works for us. The tiger prawns are one of the best meals we've had in the Philippines, and the huge pizzas are top-notch.

Helldivers
BAR

(Coron town) Attached to the popular and central Seadive resort, Helldivers is a great place to spend sunset and beyond (often well beyond).

Getting There & Away

Cebu Pacific, PAL Express and AirAsia Zest have frequent flights daily between Manila and Coron. Coron's YKR airport is a smooth 30-minute ride north of Coron town; vans (P150) meet the flights.

2GO Travel has weekly ferries to Manila (P1200, 12 hours) and Puerto Princesa (P1200, 12 hours). Atienza Shipping Lines runs a weekly cargo boat from Manila with space for 80 to 100 passengers (P1000, 22 hours).

For El Nido, 15-passenger *bangka* depart most mornings at 8am (P1800, seven to nine hours). This route can get hairy in bad weather and there have been accidents, so check the forecast.

SPLURGE

If you really want to treat yourself – and be much closer to the wrecks – the superb **Sangat Island Dive Resort** (✆0920 954 4328; www.sangat.com. ph; cottage per person incl 3 meals from P4000) is on its own island, about a 45-minute boat ride from Coron (free transfers for guests). Perfect for R&R or action.

UNDERSTAND PHILIPPINES

Philippines Today

Philippines currently hums to the tune of President Benigno Aquino III, the squeaky-clean son of Corazon Aquino, hero of the 'People Power' revolution in 1986.

After he was elected in a landslide in 2010, Aquino's first three years in office were a smashing success as he faced down interest groups, tackled corruption and overcame a decade of staunch opposition by the Catholic Church to sign the Reproductive Health (RH) Act, a national family-planning program that could stem the country's explosive population growth.

But things soured around the midpoint of Aquino's six-year term. First, the Catholic Church indefinitely delayed implementation of the RH Act by challenging its constitutionality in court. Next, an explosive scandal erupted over revelations that congressmen had been collaborating with fake NGOs to steal billions of pesos in government 'pork-barrel' funds. In the ensuing investigation, Aquino was criticised for unfairly targeting the opposition.

Then in September 2013 a landmark Mindanao peace deal brokered by Aquino collapsed when a faction of the Moro National Liberation Front (MNLF) seized the southern port of Zamboanga, igniting two weeks of urban warfare that saw almost 200 people killed and tens of thousands displaced.

But thanks to a humming economy, Aquino is still popular. Whether he remains that way may depend on how he handles the various crises – especially the pork-barrel

scandal, which has infuriated Filipino and sparked massive street protests.

History

In a Nutshell

Ancient Filipino stuck to their own islands and social groups until the 16th century, when Ferdinand Magellan claimed the islands for Spain and began the bloody process of Christianisation. Filipino's waning acceptance of Spanish rule evaporated after the Spaniards executed national hero José Rizal in 1896. They revolted and won, only to have the Americans take over, whereupon they revolted again and lost.

WWII brought much bloodshed, but out of the war's ashes rose an independent republic, albeit one that would soon elect hardliner Ferdinand Marcos as president. Marcos' declaration of martial law in 1972 and the 1986 'People Power' revolution that led to his overthrow are the two defining moments of modern Filipino history.

After People Power, the country's fortunes didn't improve much under a string of leaders who did little to eradicate the paralysing corruption and cronyism of the Marcos years. Only with the election of Benigno Aquino III has the country finally begun to shed its reputation as the 'Sick Man of Asia'.

Spanish Colonialists

In the early 16th century all signs pointed to the archipelago universally adopting Islam, but in 1521 Portuguese explorer Ferdinand Magellan changed the course of Filipino history by landing at Samar and claiming the islands for Spain. Magellan set

---

VIEWING LIST

➡ *Give Up Tomorrow* (2011) Critically acclaimed documentary about a Cebu man wrongfully convicted of a high-profile rape and murder.

➡ *Serbis (2008)* Top actress Gina Pareño stars in Brillante Mendoza's film about a family-run, porn movie house in the Philippines' prostitution capital, Angeles.

* *Imelda* (2004) Filipina American Ramona Diaz directs this fascinating look into the psyche of Imelda Marcos.

➡ *Bwakaw* (2012) Touching story about an ageing gay man's relationship with a stray dog who falls terminally ill.

➡ *Don't Stop Believing* (2013) Inspiring documentary about Journey frontman Arnel Pineda's rise from Manila's streets to rock-and-roll stardom.

about converting the islanders to Catholicism and winning over various tribal chiefs before he was killed by Chief Lapu-Lapu on Mactan Island near Cebu City.

In 1565 Miguel de Legazpi returned to the Philippines and, after conquering the local tribes one by one, declared Manila the capital of the new Spanish colony. But outside Manila real power rested with the Catholic friars – the notoriously unenlightened *friarocracia* (friarocracy), who acted as sole rulers over what were essentially rural fiefdoms.

The Philippine Revolution

At the end of the 19th century, as Spain grew weaker and as the friars grew ever more repressive, the Filipino started to resist. The Spanish sealed their fate in 1896 by executing Rizal for inciting revolution. A brilliant scholar and poet, Rizal had worked for independence by peaceful means. His death galvanised the revolutionary movement.

With aid from the USA, already at war with Spain over Cuba, General Emilio Aguinaldo's revolutionary army drove the Spanish back to Manila. American warships defeated the Spanish fleet in Manila Bay in May 1898, and independence was declared on 12 June 1898.

American Rule

Alas, the Americans had other ideas. They acquired the islands from Spain and made the Philippines an American colony. War inevitably broke out in February 1899. But the expected swift American victory didn't materialise, and as the Philippine–American War dragged on, public opposition mounted in the US. The character of the American home-front debate, and the ensuing drawn-out guerrilla war, would have parallels to the Vietnam and Iraq wars many decades later.

It was only on 4 July 1902 that the US finally declared victory in the campaign.

The Americans quickly set about healing the significant wounds their victory had wrought, instituting reforms aimed at improving Filipino's lot and promising eventual independence. The first Philippine national government was formed in 1935 with full independence pencilled in for 10 years later.

RIZAL'S TOWER OF BABEL

The Philippines' answer to Gandhi and Mandela, writer and gentle revolutionary Dr José Rizal could read and write at the age of two. He grew up to speak more than 20 languages. He was also a doctor of medicine, and a poet, novelist, sculptor, painter, linguist, naturalist and fencing enthusiast. His last words were *consummatum est!* (it is done!).

This schedule was set aside when Japan invaded the islands in WWII. For three years the country endured a brutal Japanese military regime before the Americans defeated the Japanese in the Battle for Manila in February 1945.

The battle destroyed a city that had been one of the finest in Asia and resulted in the deaths of more than 100,000 civilians.

People Power

The 1983 assassination of Ferdinand Marcos' opponent Benigno 'Ninoy' Aquino pushed opposition to Marcos to new heights. Marcos called elections for early 1986 and the opposition united to support Aquino's widow, Corazon 'Cory' Aquino.

Both Marcos and Aquino claimed to have won the election, but 'people power' rallied behind Cory Aquino, and within days Ferdinand and his profligate wife, Imelda, were packed off by the Americans to Hawaii, where the former dictator later died.

Cory Aquino failed to win the backing of the army but managed to hang on through numerous coup attempts. She was followed by Fidel Ramos, Ferdinand Marcos' second cousin. In 1998 Ramos was replaced by B-grade movie actor Joseph 'Erap' Estrada, who promised to redirect government funding towards rural and poor Filipino. Estrada lasted only 2½ years in office before being ousted over corruption allegations in a second 'people power' revolt and replaced by his diminutive vice-president, Gloria Macapagal Arroyo, who would somehow serve nine years, battling her own corruption allegations and threats of a third 'people power' revolt.

Among the first acts of her successor, Benigno Aquino III, was to arrest Arroyo on charges of rigging elections during her presidency.

The Moro Problem

Muslim dissent emanating out of Mindanao has been the one constant in the Philippines' roughly 450 years of history as a loosely united territory. The country's largest separatist Muslim group, the Moro Islamic Liberation Front (MILF), has fought the government from its base in the Autonomous Region in Muslim Mindanao (ARMM) since the 1980s, conducting periodic bombings and abductions.

In October 2012, the MILF and the government signed the Bangsamoro Framework Agreement (BFA), a preliminary peace deal meant to hand the MILF more autonomy and end decades of conflict and poverty in Mindanao.

But the BFA, which had not been ratified at the time of writing, excluded the MILF's main rivals, the MNLF. One year later, the MNLF-orchestrated Zamboanga siege occurred, and peace in Mindanao once again seemed a tenuous proposition.

People & Culture

Lifestyle

It's impossible to deny it: Filipino have a zest for life that may be unrivalled on our planet. The national symbol, the jeepney, is an apt metaphor for the nation. Splashed with colour, laden with religious icons and festooned with sanguine scribblings, the jeepney flaunts the fact that, at heart, it's a dilapidated pile of scrap metal.

Like the jeepney, Filipino face their often dim prospects in life with a laugh and a wink. Whatever happens... 'so be it'. This

COCKSURE GAMBLERS

Heavy male drinking and bonding occur over gambling – on anything from *sabong* (cockfights) to horse racing. But *sabong* are what Filipino men get most excited about. All over the country, every Sunday and public holiday, irritable and expensive fighting birds are let loose on one another. The cockpits are full to bursting and the audience is high with excitement – as much as P100,000 may be wagered on a big fight. The loser usually ends up in the next batch of chicken soup.

fatalism has a name: *bahala na,* a phrase that expresses the idea that all things shall pass and in the meantime life is to be lived.

For centuries the two most important influences on the lives of Filipino have been family and religion. The Filipino family unit extends to distant cousins, multiple godparents and one's *barkada* (gang of friends). Filipino families, especially poor ones, tend to be large. It's not uncommon for a dozen family members to live together in a tiny apartment, shanty or *nipa* hut.

Filipino are a superstitious lot. In the hinterland, a villager might be possessed by a wandering spirit, causing them to commit strange acts. In urban areas, faith healers, psychics, fortune tellers, tribal shamans, self-help books and evangelical crusaders can all help cast away ill-fortune.

Another vital thread in the fabric of Filipino society is the Overseas Filipino Worker (OFW) – the nurse in Canada, the construction worker in Qatar, the entertainer in Japan, the cleaner in Singapore. Combined, they send home billions of dollars a year.

Population

A journey from the northern tip of Luzon to the southern tip of the Sulu islands reveals a range of ethnic groups speaking some 170 different dialects. Filipino are mainly of the Malay race, although there's a sizeable and economically dominant Chinese minority and a fair number of *mestizos* (Filipino of mixed descent).

The country's population is thought to be about 106 million and expanding at a rapid clip of almost 2% per year – one of the fastest growth rates in Asia. The median age is only 23.3 and almost a quarter of the population lives in or around metro Manila.

Arts

CINEMA

The Philippines has historically been Southeast Asia's most prolific film-making nation. The movie industry's 'golden age' was the 1950s, when Filipino films won countless awards.

In the 1980s and '90s the industry surged again thanks to a genre called 'bold' – think sex, violence and dudes with great hair in romantic roles. Today the mainstream studios are in decline, but the quality of films is improving with the proliferation of independent films such as Jeffrey Jeturian's *Kubrador* (2006) and *Ekstra* (2013), and the international success of indie directors such as Brillante Mendoza, who won Best Director at the 2009 Cannes Film Festival for his graphic, controversial film *Kinatay* (Slaughtered).

MUSIC

Filipino are best known for their ubiquitous cover bands and their love of karaoke, but 'OPM' is wildly popular too. Original Pinoy Music ('Pinoy' is what Filipino call themselves) encompasses a wide spectrum of rock, folk and New Age genres – plus a subset that includes all three.

Embodying the latter subset is the band Kalayo, which performs a sometimes frantic fusion of tribal styles and modern jam-band rock. The 11-piece band uses bamboo-reed pipes, flutes and percussion instruments and sings in languages as diverse as Visayan, French and Bicol.

The big three of Pinoy rock are slightly grungy eponymous band Bamboo, agreeable trio Rivermaya (formerly fronted by Bamboo), and sometimes sweet, sometimes surly diva Kitchie Nadal, who regularly tours internationally. Alternative-rock fans should give quintet Taken by Cars a listen.

Food & Drink

Kain na tayo – 'let's eat'. It's the Filipino invitation to eat, and if you travel here, you will hear it over and over again. The phrase reveals two essential aspects of Filipino people: one, that they are hospitable, and two, that they love to, well, eat. Three meals a day isn't enough, so they've added two *merienda*. The term means 'snack', but don't let that fool you – the afternoon *merienda* can include filling *goto* (Filipino congee) or *bibingka* (fluffy rice cakes topped with cheese).

Other favourite Filipino snacks and dishes:

Adobo Chicken, pork or fish in a dark tangy sauce.

Balut Half-developed duck embryo, boiled in the shell.

Crispy pata Deep-fried pork hock or knuckles.

CULTURE HINTS

➡ Don't lose your temper – Filipino will think you're *loco loco* (crazy).

➡ When engaged in karaoke (and trust us, you will be), don't insult the guy who sounds like a chicken getting strangled, lest it be taken the wrong way.

➡ Abstain from grabbing that last morsel on the communal food platter – your hosts might think you're a pauper.

Halo-halo A tall, cold glass of milky crushed ice with fresh fruit and ice cream.

Kare-kare Meat (usually oxtail) cooked in peanut sauce.

Kinilaw Delicious Filipino-style ceviche.

Lumpia Spring rolls filled with meat or vegetables.

Mami Noodle soup, similar to *mee* soup in Malaysia or Indonesia.

Pancit Stir-fried *bihon* (white) or *canton* (yellow) noodles with meat and vegetables.

Pinakbet Vegetables with shrimp paste, garlic, onions and ginger.

The national brew, San Miguel, is very palatable and, despite being a monopolist, eminently affordable at around P22 (P30 to P55 in bars). Tanduay rum is the national drink and is usually served with Coke. Popular nonalcoholic drinks include *buko* juice (young coconut juice with floating pieces of jelly-like flesh) and sweetened *calamansi* (small local lime) juice.

Environment

An assemblage of 7107 tropical isles scattered about like pieces of a giant jigsaw puzzle, the Philippines stubbornly defies geographic generalisation. The typical island boasts a jungle-clad, critter-infested interior and a sandy coastline flanked by aquamarine waters and the requisite coral reef. About 25% of the Philippines is forested, but only a small percentage of that is primary tropical rainforest.

Endangered animal species include the mouse deer, the tamaraw (a species of dwarf buffalo) of Mindoro, the Philippine crocodile of Northeast Luzon, the Palawan bearcat and the flying lemur. As for the country's national bird, there are thought to be about 500 pairs of *haribon*, or

PHILIPPINES FOOD & DRINK

Philippine eagles, remaining in the rainforests of Mindanao, Luzon, Samar and Leyte.

There's an unbelievable array of fish, shells and corals, as well as dwindling numbers of the *duyong* (dugong, or sea cow). If your timing's right, you can spot wild whale sharks in Donsol and southern Leyte.

National Parks

The Philippines' national parks, natural parks and other protected areas comprise about 10% of the country's total area, but most lack services such as park offices, huts, trail maps and sometimes even trails. The most popular national park is surely Palawan's Subterranean River National Park. See p597 for more details.

Environmental Issues

The Philippines has strict environmental laws on its books, but they just aren't enforced. Only 1% of the reefs is in a pristine state, according to the World Bank, while more than 50% is unhealthy.

The biggest culprit of reef damage is silt, which is washed down from hills and valleys indiscriminately – and often illegally – cleared of their original forest cover. Deforestation also exacerbates flooding and causes deadly landslides during frequent typhoons and earthquakes.

Some lip service is given to the issue by the government, but little is done to combat illegal logging. Incredibly shortsighted techniques for making a few extra bucks include dynamite and cyanide fishing.

SURVIVAL GUIDE

 **Directory A–Z**

ACCOMMODATION

Rooms in the P200 to P450 range are generally fan-cooled with a shared bathroom, and rooms in the P500 to P700 range usually have fan and private bathroom. Anything higher should have air-conditioning. Prices are higher in Manila and in trendy resort areas such as Boracay and Alona Beach, although Manila now has plenty of hostels with affordable dorm beds.

We list high-season (November to May) rates. Prices in tourist hot spots go down by up to 50% in the low season, but may triple or even quadruple during Holy Week (Easter) and around New Year.

Price Ranges

In our listings a hotel qualifies as 'budget' if it has double rooms for P1000 or less and/or dorm rooms for no more than P400 per bed.

$ less than P1000 (US$22)

$$ P1000 to P3000 (US$22 to US$67)

$$$ more than P3000 (US$67)

ACTIVITIES

Popular outdoor activities:

Cycling & Mountain Biking See www.bugoybikers.com.

Diving The best dive hot spots include Puerto Galera (Mindoro), Apo Island (Negros), Panglao Island (Bohol), and Moalboal and Malapascua Island (Cebu). Generally, it costs certified divers US$25 to US$30 for a single-tank dive with equipment. PADI open-water certification courses vary widely from resort to resort and can cost from US$300 to US$450.

Kayaking & Whitewater Rafting There's year-round rafting in Cagayan de Oro, Mindanao, and seasonal (July to December) whitewater on the upper Chico River around Bontoc.

Rock Climbing See www.climbphilippines.com.

Surfing The top surfing destination in the Philippines is Siargao Island. Other good breaks can be found all along the Philippines' eastern border, although many of the best breaks are virtually inaccessible and must be reached by boat. The season on the east coast generally coincides with typhoon season, roughly August to November. There is smaller but more consistent surf to be had from November to early March in San Juan, near San Fernando (La Union) on the west coast of Luzon.

Trekking See the wonderful website www.pinoymountaineer.com for comprehensive profiles of all the major peaks.

BOOKS

➡ *PacMan: Behind the Scenes with Manny Pacquiao, the Greatest Pound-for-Pound Fighter in the World* (2010) is Gary Andrew Poole's captivating look at the Filipino boxing icon's rags-to-riches story.

➡ *Altar of Secrets: Sex, Politics and Money in the Philippine Catholic Church* (2013), by Aries C Rufo, explores the far-reaching influence of the Catholic Church on life and politics in the Philippines.

» Playing with Water: Passion and Solitude on a Philippine Island (1998) is James Hamilton-Paterson's timeless account of life on a remote islet. It sheds light on many aspects of Philippine culture.

CLIMATE

» Hot throughout the year, with brief respites possible from December to February.

» Typhoons are common from June to early December. Use the website of **PAGASA** (www.pagasa.dost.gov.ph) or www.typhoon2000.ph to avoid meteorological trouble spots.

» For most of the country, the dry season is during the *amihan* (northeast monsoon), roughly November to May. Rains start once the *habagat* (southwest monsoon) arrives in June, peak in August, and taper off in October.

» On the country's eastern seaboard, the seasons are flipped. Siargao, Bicol, eastern Samar etc are rainy from December to February and, unless there's a typhoon stirring up trouble, relatively dry when the rest of the country is sopping.

EMBASSIES & CONSULATES

The **Philippines Department of Foreign Affairs** (DFA; www.dfa.gov.ph) website lists all Philippine embassies and consulates abroad, and all foreign embassies and consulates in the Philippines.

The following are located in Manila:

Australian Embassy (Map p552; ☏02-757 8100; 23rd fl, Tower 2, RCBC Plaza, 6819 Ayala Ave)

Brunei Embassy (Map p552; ☏02-816 2836; 11th fl, BPI Bldg, cnr Ayala Ave & Paseo de Roxas)

Canadian Embassy (Map p552; ☏02-857 9000; Levels 6-8, Tower 2, RCBC Plaza, 6819 Ayala Ave)

French Embassy (Map p558; ☏02-857 6900; 16th fl, Pacific Star Bldg, cnr Gil Puyat & Makati Aves)

German Embassy (Map p552; ☏02-702 3000; 25/F Tower 2, RCBC Plaza, 6819 Ayala Ave)

Indonesian Embassy (Map p552; ☏02-892 5061; 185 Salcedo St)

Lao Embassy (Map p552; ☏02-852 5759; 34 Lapu-Lapu Ave, Magallanes)

Malaysian Embassy (Map p552; ☏02-662 8200; 107 Tordesillas St, Salcedo Village, Makati)

Myanmar Embassy (Map p552; ☏02-893 1944; Gervasia Bldg, 152 Amorsolo St)

New Zealand Embassy (Map p558; ☏02-891 5353; 23rd fl, BPI Buendia Centre, Sen Gil Puyat Ave)

PROSTITUTION

Prostitution and its most insidious form, child prostitution, is unfortunately prevalent in the Philippines. **ECPAT Philippines** (☏02-920 8151; ecpatphil@gmail.com) in Quezon City works to promote child-safe tourism and end the commercial sexual exploitation of children. To report an incident, contact ECPAT, the **Philippine National Police Women & Children's Division** (☏0919 777 7377) or the **Human Trafficking Action Line** (☏02-1343).

Singaporean Embassy (Map p552; ☏02-856 9922; 505 Rizal Dr, Fort Bonifacio)

Thai Embassy (Map p552; ☏02-815 4220; 107 Rada St)

UK Embassy (Map p552; ☏02-858 2200; 120 Upper McKinley Rd, McKinley Hill)

US Embassy (Map p556; ☏02-301 2000; 1201 Roxas Blvd)

Vietnamese Embassy (Map p552; ☏02-521 6843; 670 Pablo Ocampo St)

FOOD

The following price ranges refer to the average price of a main course.

$ less than P120 (US$2.60)
$$ P120 to P250 (US$2.60 to US$5.50)
$$$ more than P250 (US$5.50)

GAY & LESBIAN TRAVELLERS

Bakla (gay men) and *binalaki* or *tomboy* (lesbians) are almost universally accepted in the Philippines. There are well-established gay centres in major cities, but foreigners should be wary of hustlers and police harassment.

The **Metro Manila Pride March** takes place in December, usually in Makati. Online resources include **Utopia Asian Gay & Lesbian Resources** (www.utopia-asia.com).

INTERNET ACCESS

» Speedy connections are readily available in all cities for P25 to P60 per hour.

» Wi-fi is the rule rather than the exception in hotels and coffee shops in large cities and touristy areas.

MAPS

E-Z Maps and **Accu-Map** produce excellent maps covering most major islands, large cities and tourist areas. They are widely available at hotels, airports, bookshops and petrol stations for P99 to P150.

MONEY
ATMs
➤ Prevalent in any decent-sized provincial city; dispense pesos.

➤ Banco de Oro (BDO), Bank of the Philippine Islands (BPI) and Metrobank are common, functional ATMs.

➤ Standard ATM charge is P200 per withdrawal. Exception: fee-free HSBC ATMs in Manila and Cebu.

➤ Standard withdrawal limit per transaction at ATMs: P10,000.

Cash
➤ Emergency cash in US dollars is a good thing to have in case you get stuck in an area with no working ATM. Other currencies, such as the euro or UK pound, are more difficult to change outside bigger cities.

➤ 'Sorry, no change' becomes a very familiar line. Stock up on P20, P50 and P100 notes at every opportunity.

Credit Cards
➤ Major credit cards are accepted by many hotels, restaurants and businesses.

➤ Outide major cities, many places still charge a bit extra (about 4%) for credit-card transactions.

➤ Most Philippine banks will let you take a cash advance on your card.

OPENING HOURS
Banks 9am to 4pm Monday to Friday

Bars 6pm to late

Restaurants 7am or 8am to 10pm or 11pm

Shopping malls 10am to 9.30pm

Supermarkets 9am to 7pm or 8pm

PUBLIC HOLIDAYS
Offices and banks are closed on public holidays, although shops and department stores stay open. Maundy Thursday and Good Friday are the only days when the entire country closes down – even most public transport and some airlines stop running.

New Year's Day 1 January

People Power Day 25 February

Maundy Thursday, Good Friday & Easter Sunday March/April

Araw ng Kagitingan (Bataan Day) 9 April

Labour Day 1 May

Independence Day 12 June

Ninoy Aquino Day 21 August

National Heroes' Day Last Sunday in August

All Saints' Day 1 November

End of Ramadan Varies; depends on Islamic calendar

Bonifacio Day (National Heroes' Day) 30 November

Christmas Day 25 December

Rizal Day 30 December

New Year's Eve 31 December

SAFE TRAVEL
The Philippines certainly has more than its share of dangers. Typhoons, earthquakes, volcano eruptions, landslides and other natural disasters can wreak havoc with your travel plans – or worse if you happen to be in the wrong place at the wrong time. Keep an eye on the news and be prepared to alter travel plans to avoid weather trouble spots.

Mindanao (the central and southwest regions in particular) and the Sulu Archipelago are the scenes of clashes between the army on one side and Muslim separatist groups on the other. See p604 in the History section for more information.

Most embassies strongly warn tourists against travelling to potential conflict zones such as Maguindanao province (and its notoriously violent capital, Cotabato) and Zamboanga on Mindanao, and the entire Sulu Archipelago. While embassies tend to be a bit alarmist, it pays to exercise considerable caution when travelling to these areas. Check local news sources to make sure your destination and travel route are safe.

TELEPHONE
The **Philippine Long-Distance Telephone Company** (PLDT) operates the Philippines' fixed-line network. International calls can be made from any PLDT office for US$0.40 per minute.

Dialling Codes
For domestic long-distance calls or calls to mobile numbers, dial 0 followed by the city code (or three-digit mobile prefix) then the seven-digit number.

The international dialing code is ✆ 00. To get an international operator, dial ✆ 108 from any land line, for a domestic operator dial ✆ 109.

Mobile Phones
Mobile phones are ubiquitous, and half the country spends much of its time furiously texting the other half.

➤ Prepaid SIM cards cost as little as P40 and come preloaded with about the same amount of text credits.

➤ The two companies with the best national coverage are **Globe** (www.globe.com.ph) and **Smart** (www.smart.com.ph).

➤ Text messages on all mobile networks cost P1 to P2 per message; local calls cost P7.50 per minute (less if calling within a mobile network). International text messages cost P15, and international calls cost US$0.40 per minute.

→ All Philippine mobile-phone numbers start with ⌨ 09 and take the following format: ⌨ 09XX XXX XXXX.

Phonecards

Use the PLDT 'budget' card to call the US for only P3 per minute (other international destinations cost slightly more). These cards are available at phone kiosks in malls.

TOILETS

Toilets are commonly called a 'CR', an abbreviation of the delightfully euphemistic 'comfort room'. Public toilets are virtually nonexistent, so aim for one of the ubiquitous fast-food restaurants should you need a room of comfort.

TRAVELLERS WITH DISABILITIES

Steps up to hotels, tiny cramped toilets and narrow doors are the norm apart from at four-star hotels in Manila, Cebu and a handful of larger provincial cities. Elevators are often out of order, and boarding any form of rural transport is likely to be fraught with difficulty. On the other hand, most Filipino are more than willing to lend a helping hand, and the cost of hiring a taxi for a day, and possibly an assistant as well, is not excessive.

VISAS

Citizens of nearly all countries do not need a visa to enter the Philippines for stays of less than 31 days. When you arrive, you'll receive a 30-day visa-waiver free of charge. If you overstay your waiver, you face fines, and airport immigration officials may not let you pass through immigration.

Avoid this inconvenience by extending your 30-day waiver to 59 days before it expires. Extensions cost P3030 and are a breeze at most provincial Bureau of Immigration (BOI) offices. The process is infinitely more painful at the **BOI head office** (BOI; Map p556; ⌨ 02-527 4536; Magallanes Dr, Intramuros; ⊙7.30am-5pm Mon-Fri) in Manila.

Another option is to secure a three-month visa before you arrive in the Philippines. These cost US$30 to US$45 depending on where you apply.

For a full list of provincial immigration offices, hit the 'BI-Subport Offices' link at http://immigration.gov.ph. Useful provincial offices include the following:

BOI Baguio Office (⌨ 074-447 0805; 38 Military Cut Off Rd)

BOI Boracay Office (⌨ 036-288 5267; Main Rd, next to Nirvana Resort; ⊙8am-5pm Mon-Wed, to noon Thu)

INSECT ALERT

Minuscule, stinging sandflies (aptly named *nik-niks*) delight in biting exposed skin and can be a curse on some western beaches. Malaria is an issue only in certain remote areas well off the tourist trail.

BOI Cebu Office (⌨ 032-345 6442; P Burgos St, Mandaue)

BOI Puerto Galera Office (⌨ 043-288 2245; 2nd fl, Public Market; ⊙8.30am-noon Mon-Wed, to 5pm Thu-Fri)

BOI Puerto Princesa Office (⌨ 048-433 2248; 2nd fl, Servando Bldg, Rizal Ave; ⊙8am-5pm Mon-Fri)

Onward Tickets

Be prepared to show the airline at your point of departure to the Philippines a ticket for onward travel. If you don't have one, most airlines make you buy one on the spot. BOI offices also sometimes ask to see onward tickets before they process visa extensions.

VOLUNTEERING

As might be expected in an overwhelmingly Christian country, the Philippines has loads of voluntourism opportunities.

Gawad Kalinga (www.gk1world.com/ph) GK's mission is building entire communities for the poor and homeless. Volunteers can build houses, teach children or get involved in a host of other activities.

Habitat for Humanity (⌨ 02-846 2177; www.habitat.org.ph) Builds houses for the poor all over the country, concentrating on disaster-affected areas.

Hands On Manila (⌨ 02-386 6521) This organisation is always looking for eager volunteers to help with disaster assistance and other projects.

Volunteer for the Visayas (⌨ 053-325 2462; www.visayans.org) Runs various volunteer programs around Tacloban, Leyte.

ⓘ Getting There & Away

Most people enter the Philippines via one of the three main international airports: Manila, Cebu or Clark. A handful of international flights also go straight to Davao, Mindanao, to Kalibo near Boracay, and to Iloilo on the island of Panay.

Flights, tours and train tickets can be booked online at www.lonelyplanet.com/bookings.

AIR

International departure tax is P550 at all airports.

Airports

Ninoy Aquino International Airport (NAIA; ☑ 02-877 1109; www.manila-airport.net) All flights into and out of Manila use one of the four terminals of Ninoy Aquino International Airport. See the boxed text, p610, for important information on navigating this diabolical airport. Shoestring travellers should hone in on the cheap flights offered by budget carriers AirAsia, Tigerair, Jetstar Asia and Manila-based Cebu Pacific.

Cities served by Asian budget carriers out of NAIA include the following: Bangkok (Cebu Pacific), Brisbane (AirAsia), Ho Chi Minh City (Cebu Pacific), Jakarta (Cebu Pacific), Kota Kinabalu (AirAsia, Cebu Pacific), Kuala Lumpur (AirAsia, Cebu Pacific), Phuket (Cebu Pacific), Seoul (AirAsia, Cebu Pacific), Siem Reap (Cebu Pacific), Singapore (Cebu Pacific, Jetstar Asia, Tigerair) and Shanghai (AirAsia, Cebu Pacific).

Diosdado Macapagal International Airport (Clark Airport, DMIA; www.clarkairport.com) Clark Airport is near Angeles, a two-hour bus ride north of downtown Manila. It's become a hot destination for Asian low-cost airlines, which serve the following cities, among others: Bangkok (Tigerair), Hong Kong (Cebu Pacific, Tigerair) and Singapore (Cebu Pacific, Tigerair).

Mactan International Airport (CEB; ☑ 032-340 2486; www.mactan-cebuairport.com. ph) If you're heading to the Visayas, consider flying into Cebu City, which is connected by direct flights to the following cities, among others: Bangkok (Cebu Pacific), Hong Kong (Cathay Pacific, Cebu Pacific, PAL), Kuala Lumpur (AirAsia), Singapore (Cebu Pacific, Silkair, Singapore), Seoul (AirAsia, Asiana, Cebu Pacific) and Tokyo (PAL).

Kalibo International Airport Useful direct flights to Kalibo, near Boracay: Beijing (AirAsia), Kunming (AirAsia), Hong Kong (Cebu Pacific), Seoul (AirAsia), Shanghai (AirAsia) and Singapore (Tigerair).

Airlines

The following are the main airlines servicing Southeast Asia from the Philippines.

AirAsia (AK; www.airasia.com)

Cathay Pacific (CX; ☑ 02-757 0888; www.cathaypacific.com)

Cebu Pacific (5J; ☑ 02-702 0888; www.cebupacificair.com)

Jetstar (3K; ☑ 1-800 1611 0280; www.jetstar.com)

Malaysia Airlines (MH; ☑ 02-887 3215; www.malaysiaairlines.com)

Philippine Airlines (PR; ☑ 02-855 8888; www.philippineairlines.com; NAIA Terminal 2)

Silk Air (MI; ☑ 032-239 2871; www.silkair.com)

Singapore Airlines (SQ; ☑ 02-756 8888; www.singaporeairlines.com)

Thai Airways (TG; ☑ 02-580 8424; www.thaiair.com)

Tigerair (DG; ☑ 02-798 4488; www.tigerair.com)

Vietnam Airlines (VN; ☑ 02-830 2335; www.vietnamairlines.com)

SEA

Although there are plenty of shipping routes within the Philippines, international services are scarce. The only route open to foreigners, as of this writing, was Zamboanga to Sandakan in the Malaysian state of Sabah. **Aleson Shipping Lines** (☑ 062-991 2687; Veterans Ave, Zamboanga) leaves Zamboanga on Monday

---

TERMINAL CHAOS

Navigating Manila's convoluted Ninoy Aquino International Airport (NAIA) is a nightmare. NAIA's four terminals share runways, but they are not particularly close to each other and are linked only by busy public roads. A shuttle bus links the four terminals, but it is slow and sporadic, so take a taxi between terminals if you're in a hurry.

Pay close attention to which terminal your airline uses and allow plenty of time between connecting flights if you have to switch terminals. Most international flights use dismal, antiquated Terminal 1 (T1). However, all Cebu Pacific flights – both domestic and international – use newish Terminal 3 (T3). All international carriers are expected to move to T3, which was built to replace T1, eventually. However, as of this writing only Cathay Pacific, Emirates Air, Delta and ANA were at T3 with Cebu Pacific.

Meanwhile, all Philippine Airlines (PAL) and most PAL Express flights use yet another terminal, the Centennial Terminal 2 (T2). But some PAL Express flights use T3, so check your ticket carefully.

Lastly, Tigerair Philippines and AirAsia Zest domestic flights use the ancient Manila Domestic Terminal (T4), located near T3.

and Thursday, and departs Sandakan on Tuesday and Friday (economy/cabin P2900/3300, 20 hours). However, travel in the Zamboanga region is considered risky.

ⓘ Getting Around

AIR

The main domestic carriers are Philippine Airlines (PAL) and low-cost carrier Cebu Pacific. Together they serve most main cities out of Manila and/or Cebu.

PAL's budget subsidiary, PAL Express (formerly Airphil Express), competes with rapidly expanding Cebu Pacific in the low-cost domestic market. Tigerair Philippines and AirAsia Zest are also popular. One-way flights cost P1000 to P3000 (including taxes) on most routes, provided you book in advance.

Flight times range from 45 minutes for short hops such as Manila to Caticlan, to 1½ hours for flights from Manila to southern Mindanao.

AirAsia Zest (Z2; Map p552; ☑02-855 3333; www.airasia.com; cnr Domestic Rd & Andrews Ave, Pasay City) AirAsia's domestic affiliate.

ITI (Map p552; ☑02-815 5674; www.island transvoyager.com; Andrews Ave, Pasay City) Serves El Nido from Manila.

PAL Express (2P; ☑02-855 9000; www.flypalexpress.com; NAIA Terminals 2 & 3)

Tigerair Philippines/Seair (DG; ☑02-798 4488; www.flyseair.com; 2nd fl, La'O Centre, A Arnaiz Ave, Makati)

BOAT

If boats are your thing, this is the place for you. The islands of the Philippines are linked by an incredible network of ferry routes and prices are generally affordable. Ferries usually take the form of motorised outriggers (known locally as *bangka*, also called pumpboats), speedy 'fastcraft' vessels, car ferries (dubbed RORO, or 'roll-on-roll-off' ferries) and, for long-haul journeys, vast multidecked ships. Fastcraft services are passenger-only and are popular on shorter routes. They can cut travel times by half but usually cost twice as much as slower RORO ferries. Some shipping lines give 20% to 30% off for students.

Bangka are also available for hire for diving, island-hopping or getting around. The engines on these boats can be deafeningly loud, and they aren't the most stable in rough seas, but on islands with poor inland infrastructure the *bangka* can be preferable to travelling overland.

Booking ahead is essential for long-haul liners and can be done at ticket offices or travel agents in most cities. For fastcraft and *bangka* ferries, tickets can usually be bought at the pier before departure.

MOVING ON FROM CLARK AIRPORT

Philtranco has direct buses from Clark to Manila (P450, three hours) at 11.30am, 5pm and 2am. Alternatively take the airport shuttle van (P45) or a fixed-rate taxi (P500) to Angeles' Dau (Mabalacat) bus terminal, where myriad buses serve Manila.

For points north of Clark, get to the Dau terminal, where you'll find plenty of buses going to Baguio, Vigan and elsewhere.

Getting to Banaue is trickier. If you're comfortable changing buses, the recommended route is Dau–Cabanatuan–Solano–Lagawe–Banaue. The alternative is to backtrack to Manila and get the direct night bus to Banaue.

For the most part, ferries are an easy, enjoyable way to island hop, but accidents are not unknown. In May 2008 a Sulpicio Lines ferry went down off Romblon in Typhoon Frank; fewer than 60 passengers survived and more than 800 perished. In May 2009 an overloaded *bangka* sank en route to Puerto Galera from Batangas. Twelve of the 60 passengers drowned. A large 2GO Ferry vessel collided with a cargo ship off Cebu in August 2013, resulting in more than 100 deaths.

BUS & VAN

Philippine buses come in all shapes and sizes, from rusty boxes on wheels to luxury air-con coaches. Depots are dotted throughout towns and the countryside, and most buses will stop if you wave them down.

Most buses follow a fixed schedule but may leave early if they're full. Night services are common between Manila and major provincial hubs in Luzon. Remote villages may be serviced by only one or two daily buses; generally these leave the village in the morning bound for the regional centre, and return early afternoon.

Speedier but cramped air-con minivans shadow bus routes in many parts of the Philippines and in some cases have replaced buses altogether. However, you may have to play a waiting game until the vehicles are full.

LOCAL TRANSPORT
Jeepney

The first jeepneys were modified army jeeps left behind by the Americans after WWII. They have been customised with Filipino touches such as chrome horses, banks of coloured headlights and neon paintings of everything from the Virgin Mary to scenes from action comic books.

Jeepneys form the main urban transport in most cities and complement the bus services between regional centres. Within towns, the starting fare is usually P8, rising modestly for trips outside of town. Routes are clearly written on the side of the jeepney.

Taxi

Metered taxis are common in Manila and most major provincial hubs. Flag fall is a mere P40, and a 15-minute trip rarely costs more than P150.

Most taxi drivers will turn on the meter; if they don't, politely request that they do. If the meter is 'broken' or your taxi driver says the fare is 'up to you', the best strategy is to get out and find another cab (or offer a low-ball price).

Tricycle

Found in most cities and towns, the tricycle is the Philippine rickshaw – a little, roofed sidecar bolted to a motorcycle. The standard fare for

local trips in most provincial towns is P8. Tricycles that wait around in front of malls, restaurants and hotels will attempt to charge five to 10 times that for a 'special trip'. Avoid these by standing roadside and flagging down a passing P8 tricycle. You can also charter tricycles for about P300 per hour or P150 per 10km if you're heading out of town.

Many towns also have nonmotorised push tricycles, alternately known as pedicabs, *put-put* or *podyak*, for shorter trips.

Habal-Habal

Common in many Visayan islands and northern Mindanao, these are simply motorcycle taxis with extended seats (literally translated as 'pigs copulating', after the level of intimacy attained when sharing a seat with four people). *Habal-habal* function like tricycles, only they are a little bit cheaper. Outside of the Visayas (and in the north Visayas) they're known as 'motorcycle taxis' or 'singles'.

Singapore

🛈 65 / POP 5.3 MILLION

Best for Regional Specialities

➡ Gluttons Bay (p631)

➡ Singapore Food Trail (p631)

➡ Ya Kun Kaya Toast (p631)

Best Places for Cultural Connections

➡ Peranakan Museum (p615)

➡ Asian Civilisations Museum (p615)

➡ Little India (p621)

Why Go?

One of Asia's success stories is tiny little Singapore, whose GDP consistently ranks it as one of the wealthiest countries in the world. Along with that wealth comes a rich culture borne of a multiracial population. Get lost in the mad swirl of skyscrapers in the central business district (CBD), be transfixed by the Bolly beats in the streets of ramshackle Little India, hike a dense patch of rainforest in Bukit Timah, or just give yourself up to the air-conditioned retail mayhem of Orchard Rd. There's something for everyone here.

It's affluent, high-tech and occasionally a little snobbish, but Singapore's great leveller is the hawker centre, the ubiquitous and raucous food markets where everyone mucks in together to indulge the local mania for cheap eating and drinking. In short, Singapore makes for a perfect pit stop to recover from the rough-and-tumble of the rest of Southeast Asia.

When to Go
Singapore

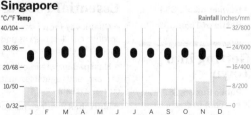

| Jan–Feb Chinese New Year and Chingay are the events to catch. | Apr–May Lots of events, and just before the local school holidays start. | Dec The northeast monsoons bring lashing rains, but they also cool Singapore down. |

SINGAPORE

Fast Facts

➡ **Area** 694 sq km

➡ **Emergency** ☎ 999

Exchange Rates

Australia	A$1	S$1.15
Euro Zone	€1	S$1.75
Indonesia	10,000 Rp	S$1.10
Malaysia	RM10	S$3.85
UK	UK£1	S$2.15
USA	US$1	S$1.25

Set Your Budget

➡ **Dorm bed** US$16-40

➡ **Hawker meal** US$4

➡ **Bottle of Tiger** US$5

Getting into Town

➡ **Public Bus** 36; S$2, every 10min 6am-midnight

➡ **MRT (Metro)** S$2.70, every 7min 6am-11.45pm, change at Tanah Merah

➡ **Taxi** S$25-35 approx, S$3-5 surcharge applies

➡ **Airport Shuttle** S$9, every 15-30min, 24 hours

Don't Miss

The Colonial District and Marina Bay are the heart of Singapore and the former seat of British power. Today the cityscape here is evidence of Singapore's ambitions, with gleaming architecture sitting cheek by jowl with preserved heritage buildings and a retro-futuristic conservatory garden. Get to a rooftop bar or up on the Singapore Flyer (an observation wheel) for a bird's-eye view of the entire area.

Of course, Singapore is famous for its cuisine. Find a hawker centre or food court (there's one in every mall) and follow your nose or join the longest queues for gastronomic delights.

ITINERARIES

Day One

Start in the Colonial District. Take in the architectural glory and wander along the Singapore River through the Quays towards Marina Bay. The area's museums are perfect for dodging the searing humidity while taking in some culture. Visit the impressive Gardens by the Bay before dining at Gluttons Bay. Cap the day off with drinks and dancing at Clarke Quay.

Day Two

Start the morning with a stroll in the Botanic Gardens before indulging in retail therapy along Orchard Rd. If malls aren't your thing, get to Little India for a slice of grubby, authentic Singapore. Finish the night with food, drinks and *sheesha* (water pipes) in Kampong Glam.

Day Three

Spend the day either checking out the zoo and Night Safari or out on an island. Pick Sentosa for beaches and kitschy theme parks or Pulau Ubin for a rustic getaway. If you have energy left, head to any neighbourhood in eastern Singapore for dinner and Tiger beer.

Essential Food & Drink

➡ **Char kway teow** Flat rice noodles wok-fried with bean sprouts, cockles, prawns and Chinese sausage in dark soy sauce and chilli sauce.

➡ **Nasi padang** Steamed white rice served with your choice of meats and vegetables; just choose and point. Lots of curries available.

➡ **Murtabak** Pan-fried pancake stuffed with spiced mince meat (chicken, beef or mutton), garlic, egg and onion.

➡ **Hainanese chicken rice** Tender poached chicken served on a bed of fragrant rice (cooked in chicken stock) with accompanying garlic chilli sauce.

➡ **Tiger beer** While not the national drink, Singapore's local brew is a pale lager that goes down a treat.

◉ Sights

◎ Colonial District

The Colonial District is where you'll find many imposing remnants of British rule, including the **Victoria Concert Hall & Theatre**, **Old Parliament House** (now an arts centre), **St Andrew's Cathedral**, **City Hall** and the **Old Supreme Court**, which are arranged around the **Padang**, a cricket pitch. Rising above them is the spaceship of the Norman Foster–designed **Supreme Court** building.

★**Asian Civilisations Museum**   MUSEUM
(Map p618; ✆ 6332 7798; www.acm.org.sg; 1 Empress Pl; adult/child S$8/4, half-price after 7pm Fri; ◷ 10am-7pm Sat-Thu, to 9pm Fri; Ⓜ Raffles Place) Features 10 richly thematic galleries that explore different aspects of Asian culture, from the Islamic world to the history of the Singapore River. Get a joint ticket with the Peranakan Museum to save some bucks.

★**Peranakan Museum**   MUSEUM
(Map p618; ✆ 6332 7591; www.peranakanmuseum.sg; 39 Armenian St; adult/child S$6/3, half-price 7-9pm Fri; ◷ 10am-7pm Sat-Thu, to 9pm Fri; Ⓜ City Hall) A testament to the Peranakan (Straits-born locals) cultural revival in the Lion City. Housed in a beautiful colonial-era school, it has thematic galleries and a variety of multimedia exhibits designed to introduce visitors to historical and contemporary Peranakan culture.

National Museum of Singapore   MUSEUM
(Map p618; www.nationalmuseum.sg; 93 Stamford Rd; adult/child S$10/5; ◷ history gallery 10am-6pm, living galleries 10am-8pm; Ⓜ Dhoby Ghaut) The sparkling white Victorian splendour of the National Museum of Singapore, with its architecturally brilliant modern annex and interactive historical displays on Singapore's history, food and film, is well worth a look.

Fort Canning Park   PARK
(Map p618; www.nparks.gov.sg; Ⓜ Dhoby Ghaut) `FREE` Pop out the back of the National Museum into Fort Canning Park, the former seat of colonial power, today a wonderfully peaceful, leafy retreat from the broiling masses below.

Singapore Art Museum   MUSEUM
(SAM; Map p618; ✆ 6332 3222; www.singaporeartmuseum.sg; 71 Bras Basah Rd; adult/student & senior S$10/5, admission free 6-9pm Fri; ◷ 10am-7pm Sat-Thu, to 9pm Fri; Ⓜ Bras Basah) Three blocks west of Raffles Hotel, the Singapore Art Museum showcases local and Southeast Asian art. Check out **8Q SAM** (Map p618; www.singaporeartmuseum.sg; 8 Queen St; admission free with SAM ticket; ◷ 10am-7pm Sat-Thu, 10am-9pm Fri; Ⓜ City Hall or Bras Basah), the experimental wing across the road.

Raffles Hotel   HISTORIC BUILDING
(Map p618; www.rafflhotel.com; 1 Beach Rd; Ⓜ City Hall) Birthplace of the Singapore Sling cocktail and inspiration for writers Joseph Conrad and Somerset Maugham, the grand Raffles Hotel is worth walking through for its colonial vibe. There's a variety of interesting shops and galleries in the shopping arcade. No flip-flops or shorts if you want to access the main hotel lobby though. Snobs!

◎ Marina Bay & the Quays

South of the Colonial District lies Marina Bay, Singapore's glittering new financial district and home to the now-iconic Marina Bay Sands and Gardens by the Bay.

★**Gardens by the Bay**   PARK
(Map p618; www.gardensbythebay.org.sg; 18 Marina Gardens Dr; admission free, conservatories adult/child S$28/15, skyway S$5/3 ; ◷ 5am-2am, conservatories & skyway 9am-9pm; last ticket sales conservatories 8pm, skyway 8pm Mon-Fri,

---

SINGAPORE ON THE CHEAP

➡ Always eat at hawker centres or food courts.

➡ Each neighbourhood tends to radiate out from a mall and a food centre or two – great places to people-watch, have cheap meals and order large S$6 bottles of Tiger beer.

➡ If you drink at a bar, go during happy hours (for discounted booze or one-for-one specials).

➡ Visit the museums for free (or cheap) after 6pm Friday, and catch free concerts at the Esplanade or Singapore Botanic Gardens.

➡ Pack a picnic and spend a day at the beach in East Coast Park or Sentosa.

➡ Hike in Bukit Timah Nature Reserve, around the MacRitchie Reservoir or along the Southern Ridges.

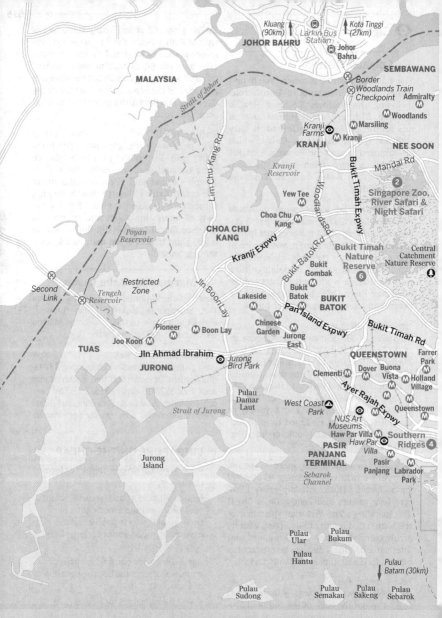

Singapore Highlights

① Navigate **Little India** (p621), a jumble of gold, textiles, temples and cheap eats

② Experience the animal magnetism of **Singapore**

Zoo (p623), the **River Safari** (p623) and the **Night Safari** (p624), three outstanding open-concept zoos

③ Book the detailed tour through **Baba House**

(p620), a gorgeous restored Peranakan house

④ Pack lots of water and walk along **Southern Ridges** (p625), Singapore's best urban trail

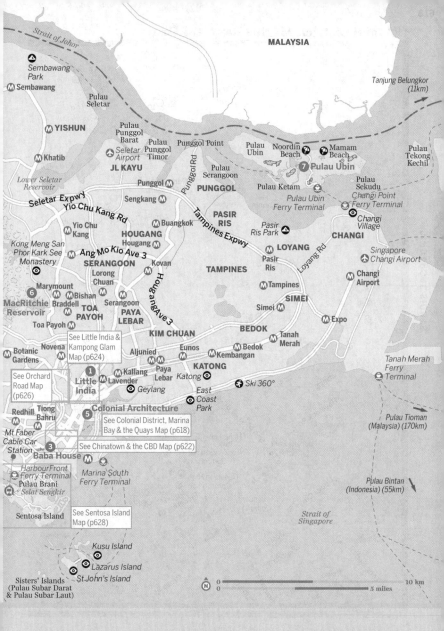

MALAYSIA

Strait of Johor

Ⓜ Sembawang Park

Ⓜ Sembawang

Ⓜ YISHUN

Ⓜ Khatib

Lower Seletar Reservoir

Pulau Seletar

Pulau Punggol Barat

Ⓜ Punggol

JL KAYU

Ⓢ Seletar Airport

Pulau Punggol Timor

Punggol Point

Ⓜ Sengkang

PUNGGOL

Pulau Serangoon

Pulau Ubin

Noordin Beach Ⓜ

Mamam Beach

Ⓜ Pulau Ubin

Pulau Tekong Kechil

Tanjung Belungkor (11km)

Pulau Ketam

Pulau Ubin Ferry Terminal

Pulau Sekudu

Changi Point Ferry Terminal

Ⓜ Changi Village

Seletar Expwy

Yio Chu Kang Rd

Ⓜ Yio Chu Kang

Ⓜ Buangkok

PASIR RIS

Tampines Expwy

Pasir Ris Park

CHANGI

Ⓢ Singapore Changi Airport

Kong Meng San Phor Kark See Monastery

HOUGANG

Ⓜ Hougang

Pasir Ris

LOYANG

Loyang Rd

Ang Mo Kio Ave 3

SERANGOON

Lorong Chuan

Kovan Ⓜ

TAMPINES

Pasir Ris

Ⓜ Tampines

Ⓜ Changi Airport

Ⓜ Marymount

Ⓜ Bishan

Braddell

Serangoon

Ⓜ Simei

SIMEI

Ⓜ Simei

Ⓜ⑥ MacRitchie Reservoir

TOA PAYOH

PAYA LEBAR

Ⓜ Toa Payoh

KIM CHUAN

BEDOK

Ⓜ Bedok

Tanah Merah

Ⓜ Expo

Tanah Merah Ferry Terminal

Ⓜ Botanic Gardens

Novena

See Little India & Kampong Glam Map (p624)

Aljunied

Eunos

Ⓜ Kembangan

Ⓜ Tanah Merah

See Orchard Road Map (p626)

①

Ⓜ Little India

Ⓜ Lavender

Kallang

Paya Lebar

Ⓜ Geylang

KATONG

Katong Ⓜ

Ski 360° Ⓢ

Pulau Tioman (Malaysia) (170km)

Tiong Bahru

Redhill

Colonial Architecture

⑤

See Colonial District, Marina Bay & the Quays Map (p618)

East Coast Park

Pulau Bintan (Indonesia) (55km)

Mt Faber Cable Car Station

③ Baba House Ⓜ

See Chinatown & the CBD Map (p622)

Strait of Singapore

HarbourFront Ferry Terminal

Pulau Brani

Selat Sengkir

Marina South Ferry Terminal

Sentosa Island

See Sentosa Island Map (p628)

Kusu Island

Lazarus Island

St John's Island

Sisters' Islands (Pulau Subar Darat & Pulau Subar Laut)

Ⓝ 0 ——————— 10 km
0 ——————— 5 miles

⑤ Hark back to the days of the empire as you stroll through the **colonial architecture** (p615) in the Colonial District

⑥ Hike through one of the world's only patches of urban primary rainforest at **Bukit Timah** (p627), or over a treetop walk at **MacRitchie Reservoir** (p627)

⑦ Time travel back to a Singapore stuck in the dusty, slow-paced village days at **Pulau Ubin** (p627)

Colonial District, Marina Bay & the Quays

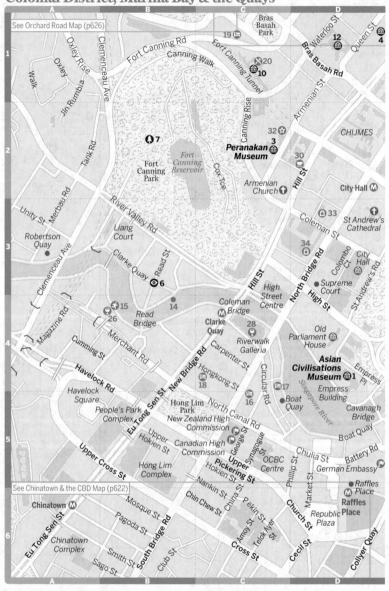

See Orchard Road Map (p626)

Bras
Basah
Park

19

20
10

7

32

3
Peranakan
Museum

30

CHIJMES

Armenian
Church

City Hall

33

St Andrew's
Cathedral

Robertson
Quay

Liang
Court

34

City
Hall

Supreme
Court

Colombo
Ct

Clarke Quay

6

14

Read
Bridge

15
26

Coleman
Bridge

Clarke
Quay

28

High
Street
Centre

Old
Parliament
House

Asian
Civilisations
Museum 1

Empress
Pl

Havelock Rd

Havelock
Square

People's Park
Complex

Hong Lim
Park

New Zealand High
Commission

Riverwalk
Galleria

Hongkong St

18

16

17

Boat
Quay

Empress
Building

Cavanagh
Bridge

Boat Quay

Canadian High
Commission

Hong Lim
Complex

Upper
Hokien St

Upper
Pickering St

OCBC
Centre

Chulia St

German Embassy

Battery Rd

See Chinatown & the CBD Map (p622)

Nankin St

Chin Chew St

Raffles
Place

Raffles
Place

Chinatown

Chinatown
Complex

Mosque St

Pagoda St

South Bridge Rd

Smith St

Club St

Sago St

Cross St

Republic
Plaza

Cecil St

Collyer Quay

7pm Sat & Sun; M Bayfront) Catapulting nature into the future, Gardens by the Bay is the latest blockbuster attraction at Marina Bay.

Highlights here include striking, sci-fi 'supertrees' and slinky, state-of-the-art conservatories housing plants from endangered habitats. The Heritage Gardens are also fascinating, inspired by Singapore's multicultural DNA.

Marina Bay Sands NOTABLE BUILDING
(Map p618; www.marinabaysands.com; 1 Bayfront Ave; M Bayfront) Across Marina Bay is the large 'fish slapped on top of three towers'

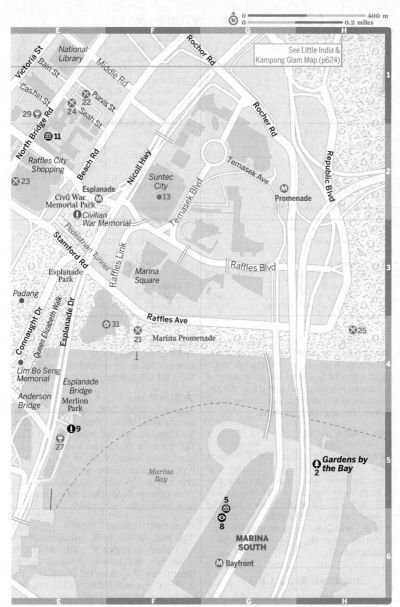

See Little India & Kampong Glam Map (p624)

SINGAPORE SIGHTS

building that is the Marina Bay Sands integrated resort. It houses a casino, loads of top-end shops and the **Artscience Museum** (adult/child S$28/16), which has interesting rotating exhibitions such as props from the Harry Potter films.

Merlion   MONUMENT

(Map p618; 1 Fullerton Rd; M Raffles Place) At the river mouth is the freakish Merlion statue, a water-spouting, hybrid lion/fish creature cooked up in the 1960s as a tourism icon for the Singapore Tourism Board. And you thought they'd banned drugs.

Colonial District, Marina Bay & the Quays

Clarke Quay   NEIGHBOURHOOD

(Map p618; www.clarkequay.com.sg; Ⓜ Clarke Quay) A darling among Singapore's fickle night-trippers is Clarke Quay, a strip of former warehouses dating back to the river's days as a trading hub and now home to bars, restaurants and clubs.

Boat Quay &
Robertson Quay   NEIGHBOURHOOD

(Ⓜ Raffles Place) Boat Quay and Robertson Quay are known for their eateries and bars, the latter being quiet and sans restaurant touts and home to the excellent **STPI Gallery** (☑ 6336 3663; www.stpi.com.sg; 41 Robertson Quay; ⊙ 10am-6pm Tue-Sat; 🚌 54 from Ⓜ Clarke Quay). Both areas offer great examples of early colonial-meets-Asian architecture.

⊙ Chinatown & the CBD

Bustling Chinatown is crammed with small shops, eateries and tradition, though some of the tradition has disappeared behind a wave of renovation, some of it good (the restored shophouses), some of it not so good (the Pagoda St tourist market). The CBD is Singapore's financial hub and sits beside Chinatown. The hive of activity during the weekdays stands in stark contrast to the weekends, when it's a proverbial ghost town. Architecture aficionados will enjoy the restored shophouses around the area (Ann Siang Rd and Hill are good places to start).

★ Baba House   MUSEUM

(Map p622; ☑ 6227 5731; http://nus.edu.sg/museum/baba; 157 Neil Rd; ⊙ tours 2pm Mon, 6.30pm Tue, 10am Thu, 11am Sat; Ⓜ Outram Park) **FREE** The one-hour free guided tour of this pre-war terrace house, built in the elaborate Peranakan style, is top-notch. Knowledgeable tour guides weave tales of Peranakan life with every detail. Open for guided tours only; book online or by phone.

Chinatown Heritage Centre   MUSEUM

(Map p622; ☑ 6221 9556; www.chinatownheritagecentre.sg; 48 Pagoda St; adult/child S$10/6; ⊙ 9am-8pm; Ⓜ Chinatown) Housed across three floors of a converted shophouse, the moving Chinatown Heritage Centre focuses on the squalid living conditions that early Chinese immigrants once endured.

Buddha Tooth Relic
Temple   BUDDHIST TEMPLE

(Map p622; www.btrts.org.sg; 288 South Bridge Rd; ⊙ 7am-7pm, relic viewing 9am-6pm; Ⓜ Chinatown) ✐ The main draw-card of this huge, eye-catching, five-storey, southern Chinese–style temple is what is believed to be a sacred tooth of Buddha (dental experts have expressed doubts over its authenticity).

Sri Mariamman Temple HINDU TEMPLE
(Map p622; 244 South Bridge Rd; ⏲7am-noon, 6-9pm; Ⓜ Chinatown) Chinatown's most recognised and photographed icon, ironically, is the colourful Sri Mariamman Temple, Singapore's oldest Hindu house of worship.

Thian Hock Keng Temple HINDU TEMPLE
(Map p622; www.thianhockkeng.com.sg; 158 Telok Ayer St; ⏲7.30am-5.30pm; Ⓜ Chinatown, Tanjong Pagar, Raffles Place) Singapore's oldest Hokkien building, with elaborately carved and painted beams and panels.

Little India & Kampong Glam

Disorderly and pungent, Little India is a world away from the rest of Singapore. Weekends are truly an eye-opener for locals and tourists alike. Produce, spices and trinkets spill onto the streets and crowd the five-foot ways (covered pedestrian walkways). Many businesses operate late into the night (some run 24 hours) and traffic slows to a messy crawl. Southeast of Little India is Kampong Glam, Singapore's Muslim quarter. Here you'll find shops selling clothing, raw cloth and dry goods.

The Little India riot in December 2013 has resulted in alcohol curbs and restrictions in the area so check with your hostel on the latest rulings to avoid getting on the wrong side of the law.

Malay Heritage Centre MUSEUM
(Map p624; ☎6391 0450; www.malayheritage.org.sg; 85 Sultan Gate; adult/under 6yr S$4/free; ⏲10am-6pm Tue-Sun; Ⓟ; Ⓜ Bugis) Istana Kampong Glam is the former palace of the last Sultan of Singapore, restored and turned into the Malay Heritage Centre. Permanent exhibits touch on the Malay community in Singapore; look also for travelling exhibitions.

Sultan Mosque MOSQUE
(Map p624; www.sultanmosque.org.sg; 3 Muscat St; ⏲9am-noon & 2-4pm Sat-Thu, 2.30-4pm Fri; Ⓜ Bugis) This golden-domed structure is the biggest and most active mosque in Singapore.

Sri Veeramakaliamman Temple HINDU TEMPLE
(Map p624; 141 Serangoon Rd; ⏲5.15am-12.15pm & 4-9.15pm; Ⓜ Little India) For temple hounds there is the Sri Veeramakaliamman Temple, dedicated to the goddess Kali.

Sakya Muni Buddha Gaya Temple BUDDHIST TEMPLE
(Map p624; 366 Race Course Rd; ⏲8am-4.45pm; Ⓜ Farrer Park) Further out is this Thai Buddhist temple, popularly known as the Temple of 1000 Lights. It houses a 15m-high seated Buddha.

Orchard Road

No one visits Orchard Rd for the sights alone, though the Christmas-light displays are breathtaking. The only major historical site is the President's digs, the **Istana** (Map p626; www.istana.gov.sg; Ⓜ Dhoby Ghaut), but it's only open on select public holidays; check the website for details.

★ **Singapore Botanic Gardens** GARDENS
(Map p626; ☎6471 7361; www.sbg.org.sg; 1 Cluny Rd; garden admission free, National Orchid Garden adult/senior/child S$5/1/free; ⏲5am-midnight, National Orchid Garden 8.30am-7pm, last entry 6pm; 🚌7, 105, 123, Ⓜ Botanic Gardens) When you're about to lose your mind from retail overload, the expansive, serene Singapore Botanic Gardens is a beautiful spot to rest and revive. The gardens host free open-air music concerts on the last Sunday of the month at the Shaw Foundation Symphony Stage – check the website for details.

HARRY LEE KUAN YEW'S HUMBLE ABODE

If you're planning a jaunt down Orchard Rd, make a short detour and head along Oxley Rd. The house of the father of modern Singapore, Harry Lee Kuan Yew, is on this street. Lee Kuan Yew was the leader of the People's Action Party in Singapore, and it was under his leadership that Singapore transformed itself into one of the most prosperous nations in Asia. In order to keep out the plebs and crazies, car gantries are installed at either end of the road. Pedestrians are free to walk through, but expect to be hurried along by heavily armed Gurkhas. Go on, walk on the side of the guards for a closer look – we dare you.

Chinatown & the CBD

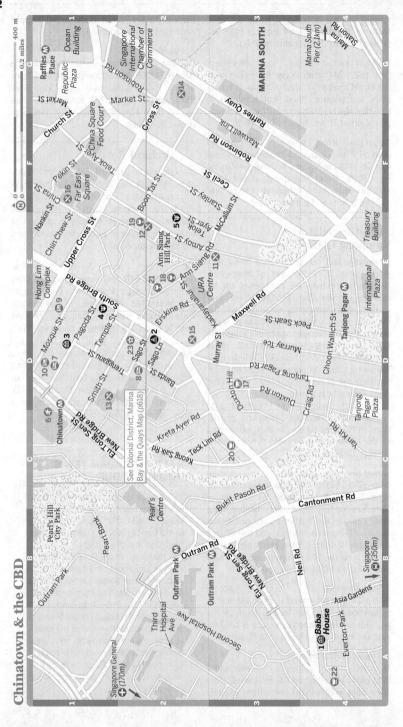

400 m
0.2 miles

Pearl's Hill City Park

Outram Park

Pearl Bank

Singapore General (170m)

Third Hospital Ave

Second Hospital Ave

Outram Park M

Outram Park

Eu Tong Sen St

New Bridge Rd

Outram Rd

Neil Rd

Cantonment Rd

Bukit Pasoh Rd

Pearl's Centre

Kreta Ayer Rd

Keong Saik Rd

Teck Lim Rd

20

Baba House 1

Everton Park

Asia Gardens

Singapore (350m)

22

Yan Kit Rd

Tanjong Pagar Plaza

Craig Rd

Duxton Hill

Tanjong Pagar Rd

Duxton Rd

Murray St

Murray Tce

Peck Seah St

Choon Wallich St

Tanjong Pagar M

International Plaza

Treasury Building

Maxwell Rd

Kadayanallur St

Erskine Rd

15

URA Centre

Ann Siang Rd

Ann Siang Hill Park

11

18

21

Sago Ln

Sago St

2

Banda St

23

8

Temple St

Pagoda St

Trengganu St

Smith St

13

Mosque St

10

7

3

9

6

Chinatown M

Eu Tong Sen Rd

New Bridge Rd

South Bridge Rd

Upper Cross St

Chin Chew St

Nankin St

China St

Pekin St

Far East Square

16

Hong Lim Complex

Telok Ayer St

China Square Food Court

Church St

Market St

Market St

Cross St

Robinson Rd

Cecil St

Stanley St

Boon Tat St

Telok Ayer St

Amoy St

McCallum St

12

19

5

4

See Colonial District, Marina Bay & the Quays Map (p618)

Raffles Place M

Ocean Building

Republic Plaza

Singapore International Chamber of Commerce

14

Raffles Quay

Maxwell Link

Robinson Rd

MARINA SOUTH

Marina South Pier (2.1km)

Marina Station Rd

Chinatown & the CBD

Emerald Hill Road   NEIGHBOURHOOD
(Map p626; M Somerset) Take some time out to wander through the pedestrianised Peranakan Pl (and its gauntlet of bars) to residential Emerald Hill Rd, where original Peranakan terrace houses totter between glamorous decay and immaculate restoration.

Cathay Gallery   MUSEUM
(Map p626; www.thecathaygallery.com.sg; 2nd fl, The Cathay, 2 Handy Rd; ⊙11am-7pm Mon-Sat; M Dhoby Ghaut) FREE Film buffs will go ga-ga at the Cathay Gallery, chock-a-block with local movie memorabilia and housed in Singapore's first high-rise building (circa 1935).

⊙ **Eastern Singapore**

Geylang   NEIGHBOURHOOD
Nowhere else is Singapore's mishmash of food, commerce, religion, culture and sleaze more at ease than in the Geylang area. Come

nightfall, you might see a crowd spill out onto the streets from evening prayer at a mosque, rubbing shoulders with prostitutes. Join hordes of people sweating over plates of local food. To get here, take the MRT to Kallang or Aljunied, then cross the road and head south towards all the action.

Katong   NEIGHBOURHOOD
This former Peranakan enclave is rife with food outlets, bars and beautiful shophouse architecture. Take bus 12 or 32 from North Bridge Rd and get off along East Coast Rd.

East Coast Park   PARK
Stretching for 15km along East Coast Parkway, East Coast Park is where Singaporeans come to take a dip in the soupy Strait of Singapore, windsurf, cable-ski, camp, eat, cycle, in-line skate, and chill out on the sand. Bus 401 runs here from Bedok MRT station on weekends, or take bus 197 and walk through the underpass from Marine Parade Rd.

Changi Village   NEIGHBOURHOOD
(M Tanah Merah then 🚌2) On the northeastern coast, Changi has a village atmosphere, with the lively and renowned hawker centre next to the bus terminus being a focal point. Across from the bus terminal is **Changi Beach**, where thousands of Singaporean civilians were executed during WWII. Changi Village is the jumping-off point for the rural retreat of Pulau Ubin (p627).

⊙ **Northern & Central Singapore**

★ **Singapore Zoo**   ZOO
(📞6269 3411; www.zoo.com.sg; 80 Mandai Lake Rd; adult/child S$22/12; ⊙8.30am-6pm; M Ang Mo Kio then 🚌138) Set on a peninsula jutting into the Upper Seletar Reservoir, the Singapore Zoo is world class. Its 28 landscaped hectares and open concept (no cages) are a far cry from the sad concrete confines some zoos retain. Energetic (but humane) animal shows and a playful polar bear make this a deservedly popular attraction. Save money by buying a combined pass to all three animal parks.

★ **River Safari**   WILDLIFE RESERVE
(www.riversafari.com.sg; 80 Mandai Lake Rd; adult/child S$35/23; ⊙8am-6pm; M Ang Mo Kio, then 🚌138) The River Safari was mostly built to house its new giant panda stars KaiKai and JiaJia. They might be the star attraction, but this river-themed

SINGAPORE SIGHTS

Little India & Kampong Glam

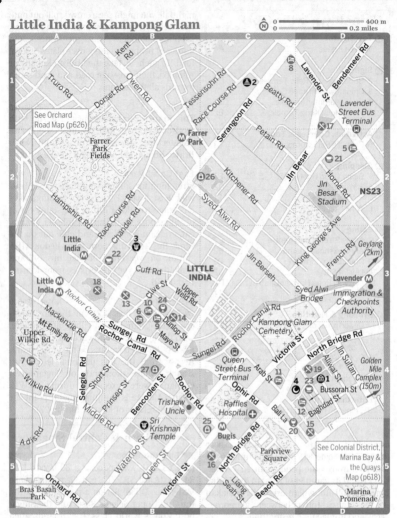

See Orchard
Road Map (p626)

See Colonial District,
Marina Bay &
the Quays
Map (p618)

park is also home to a delightful menagerie of wildlife. From gharials to manatees to red pandas, this park dazzles and delights. Next to the zoo and Night Safari.

★ **Night Safari**   WILDLIFE RESERVE
(www.nightsafari.com.sg; 80 Mandai Lake Rd; adult/child S$35/23; ⊙ 7.30pm-midnight, restaurants and shops from 5.30pm; M Ang Mo Kio then ☐ 138) Next door to the zoo is the Night Safari, a 40-hectare forested park where you can view nocturnal animals, including tigers, lions and leopards. The tram ride takes visitors close to the animal action and is a must.

Kong Meng San Phor Kark See Monastery   MONASTERY
(☑ 6453 5300; www.kmspks.org; 88 Bright Hill Rd; ⊙ gates 6am-10pm, halls 8am-4pm; M Bishan, then ☐ 52 or 410 white plate) **FREE** Singapore's largest and most stunning monastery has 12 buildings.

Expect dragon-topped pagodas, shrines, plazas and lawns linked by Escher-like staircases. Finish your visit by reflecting under a bodhi tree.

Little India & Kampong Glam

◉ Southern & Western Singapore

For a beautiful view, walk up 116m **Mt Faber**, then catch the **cable car** (www.mountfaber.com.sg; adult one-way/return $24/26, child one-way/return $14/15; ⊙8.30am-9.30pm) to the HarbourFront Centre or across to Sentosa Island. Mt Faber is connected to Kent Ridge Park via Telok Blangah Park and HortPark in a 9km-long chain known as the **Southern Ridges**, arguably Singapore's best walking trail. The walk takes visitors along shady forested paths and across amazing bridges that pass through forest canopy.

NUS Museum   MUSEUM
(www.nus.edu.sg/museum; University Cultural Centre, 50 Kent Ridge Cres; ⊙10am-7.30pm Tue-Sat, to 6pm Sun; Ⓜ Kent Ridge then 🚌 A2 university shuttle bus) **FREE** The South and Southeast Asian collection and the art museums on the National University of Singapore (NUS) campus are top-notch and worth a look.

Haw Par Villa   MUSEUM
(🖉6872 2780; 262 Pasir Panjang Rd; ⊙9am-7pm; Ⓜ Haw Par Villa) **FREE** 'That which is derived from society should be returned to society,' said Aw Boon Haw, creator of the Tiger Balm miracle salve. A million dollars later, what he returned was the Haw Par Villa, an unbelievably weird and undoubtedly kitsch theme park showcasing Chinese culture.

Jurong Bird Park   WILDLIFE RESERVE
(www.birdpark.com.sg; 2 Jurong Hill; adult/child S$20/13; ⊙8.30am-6pm; Ⓜ Boon Lay, then 🚌 194 or

251) Offers impressive enclosures and beautifully landscaped gardens for more than 8000 birds, from flamingos to penguins (all enveloped in the inescapable scent of bird poop).

◉ Sentosa Island

Epitomised by its star attraction, Universal Studios, Sentosa is essentially a giant theme park. The island itself is packed with rides, activities and shows, most of which cost extra. The beaches, of course, are completely free and very popular with locals and tourists alike.

Get to VivoCity (HarbourFront MRT) and walk across (S$1) or take the Sentosa Express monorail (return S$4). For a more spectacular ride, take the **cable car** (one-way S$24) from the HarbourFront Centre. All Sentosa-crossing options are signposted at the MRT station.

Universal Studios   AMUSEMENT PARK
(Map p628; www.rwsentosa.com; Resorts World; adult/child/senior S$74/54/36; ⊙10am-7pm; monorail Waterfront) Universal Studios is the top-draw attraction in Resorts World. Shops, shows, restaurants, rides and roller coasters are all neatly packaged into fantasy-world themes based on your favourite Hollywood films.

One of the highlights is the pair of 'duelling roller coasters' said to be the tallest of their kind in the world.

Fort Siloso   MUSEUM
(Map p628; www.sentosa.com.sg; Siloso Point; adult/child S$8/5; ⊙10am-6pm, free guided tours

Orchard Road

SINGAPORE

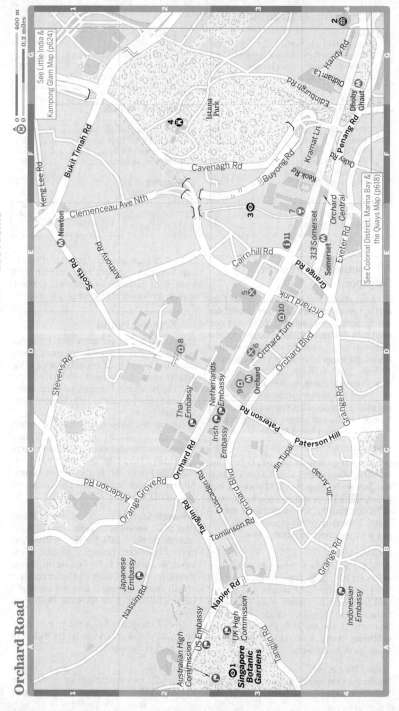

See Little India & Kampong Glam Map (p624)

See Colonial District, Marina Bay & the Quays Map (p618)

N
0   400 m
0   0.2 miles

Keng Lee Rd
Bukit Timah Rd
Clemenceau Ave Nth
Scotts Rd
Anthony Rd
Newton
Cairnhill Rd
Grange Rd
Orchard Link
Orchard Turn
Orchard Blvd
Paterson Rd
Paterson Hill
Stevens Rd
Orange Grove Rd
Anderson Rd
Orchard Rd
Tanglin Rd
Cuscaden Rd
Orchard Blvd
Jln Tupai
Jln Arnap
Grange Rd
Tomlinson Rd
Napier Rd
Nassim Rd
Tanglin Rd
Grange Rd

Cavenagh Rd
Istana Park
Buyong Rd
Kramat Ln
Keok Rd
Oxley Rd
Edinburgh Rd
Oldham La
Handy Rd
Penang Rd
Dhoby Ghaut
313 Somerset
Somerset
Exeter Rd
Orchard Central
Orchard

Japanese Embassy
Australian High Commission
US Embassy
UK High Commission
Singapore Botanic Gardens
Indonesian Embassy
Thai Embassy
Netherlands Embassy
Irish Embassy

1
2
3
4
5
6
7
8
9
10
11

Orchard Road

◎ Top Sights
   1 Singapore Botanic Gardens A3

◎ Sights
   2 Cathay Gallery G4
   3 Emerald Hill Road E3
   4 Istana...F2

⊗ Eating
   5 Din Tai Fung...E3
   6 Food Republic D3

◎ Drinking & Nightlife
   7 Emerald Hill Bars E3

◎ Entertainment
   Sistic ....(see 6)

◎ Shopping
   8 Far East Plaza......................................D2
   9 Ion Orchard Mall D3
  10 Ngee Ann City.....................................D3

ⓘ Information
   Ion Orchard Post Office ....(see 9)
   Singapore Visitors Centre @ Ion
     Orchard ....(see 9)
  11 Singapore Visitors Centre @
     Orchard E3

12.30pm & 3.30pm Fri-Sun; cable car Sentosa) A former military base, Fort Siloso re-creates the Japanese invasion and occupation.

◎ Singapore's Other Islands

★ Pulau Ubin   ISLAND
(www.pulauubin.com.sg; 🛶from Changi Village) **FREE** A rural, unkempt expanse of jungle full of fast-moving lizards, strange shrines and cacophonic birdlife. Tin-roofed buildings bake in the sun, chickens squawk and panting dogs slump in the dust, while in the forest, families of wild pigs run for cover as visitors pedal past on squeaky rented bicycles. Get to Tanah Merah MRT, then take bus 2 to Changi Village Ferry Terminal. There boats depart for the island (one way S$2.50, 10 minutes, 6am to 8pm) whenever there are 12 people aboard.

Southern Islands   ISLANDS
Three other islands popular with castaway-fantasising locals are **St John's**, **Lazarus** and **Kusu**. They're quiet and great for fishing, swimming, picnics and guzzling BYO six-packs. The islands have changing rooms and toilets. You can camp for free. Kusu Island is culturally interesting; devotees come to pray

for health, wealth and fertility at its Taoist temple and Malay *kramat* (shrine). There's nowhere to buy food or drink on any of the islands, so come prepared.

Catch a ferry from the **Marina South Pier** (🖉 6534 9339; www.islandcruise.com.sg; 31 Marina Coastal Dr; Southern Islands return S$18; ⊙ 10am & 2pm Mon-Fri, 9am, noon & 3pm Sat, 9am, 11am, 1pm, 3pm & 5pm Sun; Ⓜ Marina Bay, then 🚌 402).

🏃 Activities

Though the national pastimes are probably shopping and eating, there are opportunities for outdoorsy types. The best spot for **cycling** is definitely East Coast Park (p623). Pulau Ubin has dedicated mountain-biking trails. For **swimming** there are reasonable beaches on Sentosa, the Southern Islands and East Coast Park.

Massages are cheap and readily available, with reflexology a major trade. For a good foot-rub check out **People's Park Complex** (Map p622; Eu Tong Sen St; reflexology from S$18; Ⓜ Chinatown). Most malls have at least one reflexology place.

★ Bukit Timah Nature Reserve   OUTDOORS
(🖉 1800-471 7300; www.nparks.gov.sg; ⊙ 8.30am-6pm; 🚼) There are good trails in Bukit Timah Nature Reserve, the only large area of primary rainforest left in Singapore. Hike one of four trails including the one to the peak – at 163m, it's the highest natural point in Singapore. Look out for **Rock Path**, which will leave you clambering on your hands and knees in places, over rocks and tree roots; it all adds to the adventure. Watch out for troops of monkeys (long-tailed macaques)! Catch bus 171 from Orchard MRT station. Get off at Bukit Timah Shopping Centre and follow the road till you see Hindehede Dr to your right.

★ MacRitchie Reservoir Park   OUTDOORS
(🖉 1800-471 7300; www.nparks.gov.sg; Lornie Rd; ⊙ 8.30am-6pm; 🚌 157, Ⓜ Toa Payoh) MacRitchie Reservoir has a hiking trail up to a fantastic

---

SINGAPORE: AN (ART)WORK IN PROGRESS

The old Supreme Court and City Hall along St Andrew's Rd are being converted into Singapore's next major gallery, the **National Art Gallery** (www.nationalartgallery.sg), due to open in 2015. The collection will focus on 19th- and 20th-century Southeast Asian art.

Sentosa Island

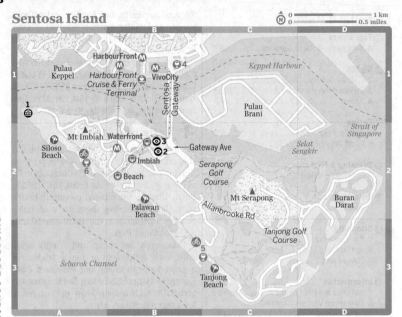

Sentosa Island

treetop walk, a 250m-long suspension bridge perched 25m up in the forest canopy. Trails then continue through the forest and around the reservoir, sometimes on dirt tracks, sometimes on wooden boardwalks.

Ski360°   WATER SPORTS
(www.ski360degree.com; 1206A East Coast Parkway; first hr weekdays/weekends S$38/50, each subsequent hr S$16/22; ⊙10am-7pm Mon-Fri, 9am-10pm Sat & Sun) Wakeboarders and waterskiers should check out the tethered Ski360° circuit at East Coast Park Lagoon.

🎓 Courses

Cookery Magic   COOKING COURSE
(📞6348 9667; www.cookerymagic.com; 117 Fidelio St; 3hr classes from S$100; Ⓜ Eunos then 🚌28)

Ruqxana conducts standout Asian cooking classes in her own home. She also conducts classes on an eco-farm (harvest your own veggies before cooking!) and on Pulau Ubin (in an old *kampong* home).

🔗 Tours

Original Singapore Walks   WALKING TOUR
(📞6325 1631; www.singaporewalks.com; adult S$35-55, child S$15) Conducts insightful tours of Chinatown, Little India, Kampong Glam, the Colonial District and Singapore's battlefields.

Duck Tours   TOUR
(Map p618; 📞6338 6877; www.ducktours.com.sg; 01-330, Suntec Shopping Mall, 3 Temasek Blvd; adult/child S$33/23; Ⓜ Esplanade) This city tour in a WWII amphibious vehicle is loud, garish and cheesy but oh-so-fun, especially when it splashes out into Marina Bay. Popular regular bus tours (from S$20) also on offer.

Singapore River Cruise   BOAT TOUR
(Map p618; 📞6336 6111; www.rivercruise.com.sg; adult/child from S$20/10; Ⓜ Clarke Quay) Jump on a bumboat along the Singapore River for a pleasant tour along the Quays into Marina Bay and back. Commentary ensures that you know what you're looking at.

Singapore Explorer BOAT TOUR
(Map p618; ☑ 6339 6833; www.riverexplorer.sg) Offers trips up and down the river in a glass-top boat (S$20, unlimited day pass) or traditional bumboat (adult/child S$18/9, 40 minutes). The audio commentary makes it easy to identify sights.

★☆ Festivals & Events

Singapore's multicultural population celebrates an amazing number of festivals and events. For a calendar, check out www.your singapore.com.

Chinese New Year is the major festival, held in January/February. Look out for parades throughout Chinatown and festive foods in shops. During the Great Singapore Sale in June and July, merchants drop prices to boost Singapore's image as a shopping destination.

🛏 Sleeping

Once, budget-room-hunters in Singapore were limited to flea-bitten flophouses (they still exist!), but thankfully these days there are good hostels and guesthouses even in the more expensive parts of the city. Most have female-only dorms. Unless otherwise stated, prices are for shared bathrooms and include breakfast.

🛏 Colonial District

Five Stones Hostel HOSTEL $
(Map p618; ☑ 6535 5607; www.fivestoneshostel. com; 61 South Bridge Rd; dm S$31-38, r S$108-113; ❄ @ 🛜; Ⓜ Clarke Quay) Perks at this upbeat hostel include comfy orthopaedic mattresses in both the dorms and private rooms, modern bathrooms, free breakfast and wi-fi, and an enviable location within walking distance of the Quays, Chinatown, the CBD and the Colonial District.

Prince of Wales HOSTEL $
(Map p618; ☑ 6536 9697; www.pow.sg; 51 Boat Quay; dm S$24-28, d S$70; ❄ @ 🛜; Ⓜ Clark Quay) A better-located spin-off from its Little India branch, Prince of Wales overlooks the Singapore River, and offers basic rooms plus lots of live music and pints at its bar downstairs.

River City Inn HOSTEL $
(Map p618; ☑ 6532 6091; www.rivercityinn.com; 33 Hong Kong St; dm S$25-35; ❄ 🛜; Ⓜ Clark Quay) Its location, on the 4th floor of a shophouse, hasn't deterred backpackers from booking beds en masse. The communal

areas are well done but the 26-bed dorms get just a bit too cosy...

YMCA International House HOSTEL $
(Map p618; ☑ 6336 6000; www.ymcaih.com.sg; 1 Orchard Rd; dm/d/f incl breakfast S$40/180/260; ❄ @ 🛜 ❄; Ⓜ Dhoby Ghaut) Even after you add on the S$3 temporary membership, the Y's roomy, modern two-bed dorms (with attached bathroom) are good value. It has a pool, it's centrally located, and hotel-quality rooms can be had cheaply online.

🛏 Chinatown

Wink Hostel HOSTEL $
(Map p622; ☑ 6222 2940; www.winkhostel.com; 8 Mosque St; s/d pod S$50/90; ❄ @ 🛜; Ⓜ Chinatown) This flashpacker favourite features private, sound-proof 'pods', each with comfortable mattress, coloured mood lighting, adjacent locker and enough room to sit up in. Communal bathrooms feature rainforest showerheads, while the in-house kitchenette, laundry and lounge areas crank up the homely factor.

Beary Good Hostel HOSTEL $
(Map p622; ☑ 6222 4955; www.abearygoodhostel. com; 66 Pagoda St; dm S$27-30; Ⓜ Chinatown) So popular it has spawned two branches: the Beary Nice Hostel and the Beary Best, both a stone's throw away at 46 Smith St and 16 Upper Cross St. All are fun, brightly

---

CAMPING IT UP

The National Parks Board (☑ 6391 4488; www.nparks.gov.sg) maintains four camping grounds around Singapore: Changi Beach, East Coast Park, West Coast Park and Pasir Ris Park. You need a S$1 permit to camp during the week, obtainable online (www.axs.com.sg) or from several AXS (ATM-like) machines in most malls. There's a small fee to use the barbecue pits and shower facilities. On Pulau Ubin you can camp at Noordin or Maman Beaches on the north coast. The sites are free, but very basic. There's no drinking water, so bring your own. You can also camp on the Southern Islands (Kusu, Lazarus and St John's) for free. BYO drinking water.

painted affairs, and have separate bathrooms for boys and girls – a beary nice touch.

Pillows & Toast
HOSTEL $

(Map p622; ☑ 6220 4653; www.pillowsntoast. com; 40 Mosque St; dm S$28-45; ❄ @ 🛜; Ⓜ Chinatown) Bright, clean and friendly with comfortable wood-framed bunk beds and well-looked-after common areas.

Fernloft
HOSTEL $

(Map p622; ☑ 6323 3221; www.fernloft.com; Unit 92, 2nd fl, 5 Banda St; dm S$22, r from S$65; ❄ @ 🛜; Ⓜ Chinatown) Fernloft is set in a traditional Singapore housing-development block and offers visitors a chance to live like a local. Limited beds and only two large (windowless) private air-con rooms, so book in advance. There's only one shower.

Little India

InnCrowd
HOSTEL $

(Map p624; ☑ 6296 9169; www.the-inncrowd.com; 73 Dunlop St; dm/d/tr S$20/59/79; ❄ @ 🛜; Ⓜ Little India) Ground Zero for Singapore's backpackers. Clean accommodation, living areas where travellers like to hang, and saccharine-sweet staff. The atmosphere's decidedly convivial, with free lockers and internet, discounted tickets to sights, laundry and cheap Tiger draught beer on tap.

At the Little Red Dot
HOSTEL $

(Map p624; ☑ 6294 7098; www.atthelittlereddot. com; 125 Lavender St; dm S$20-22; ❄ @ 🛜; Ⓜ Lavender) Located in Singapore's next up-and-coming neighbourhood, the Lavender hipster enclave, the Little Red Dot has plain but comfortable rooms, friendly staff and good communal areas, including an outdoor deck.

Hive
HOSTEL $

(Map p624; ☑ 6341 5041; www.thehiveback packers.com; 269A Lavender St; dm S$24-26; ❄ @ 🛜; Ⓜ Boon Keng) The Hive's friendliness and cleanliness go a long way towards making up for its slightly inconvenient location away from all the action. Dorms are fairly standard, but communal areas are lively.

hangout@mt.emily
HOSTEL $

(Map p624; ☑ 6438 5588; www.hangouthotels. com; 10A Upper Wilkie Rd; dm/d from S$35/120; ❄ @ 🛜 ♿; Ⓜ Little India, Dhoby Ghaut) Prices for the comfy seven-bed (not bunk) dorms at this flashpacker joint are a relative bargain considering its location within walking distance to Orchard Rd, the Colonial District and Little India (though it's quite a hike up to the hostel itself). Lovely rooftop terrace with a 'standing pool', a library, a cafe and cosy lounge areas. Book online for cheaper rates.

Checkers Inn
HOSTEL $

(Map p624; ☑ 6392 0693; www.checkersinn.com. sg; 46-50 Campbell Lane; dm $25-36; @ 🛜; Ⓜ Little India) Bright, spacious and fabulously funky, with freebies such as use of washing machines, dryers and shower gel. Female-only dorms also available.

Prince of Wales
HOSTEL $

(Map p624; ☑ 6299 0130; www.pow.com.sg; 101 Dunlop St; dm/d S$20/60; ❄ @ 🛜; Ⓜ Little India) The POW features a spit-and-sawdust live-music pub downstairs and clean, brightly painted dorms and private rooms upstairs. The noise won't suit everyone, but it's a fun place to stay. Free breakfast includes fresh coffee and fruit, as well as the usual buttered toast.

Kampong Glam

Shophouse the Social Hostel
HOSTEL $

(Map p624; ☑ 6298 8721; www.shophousehostel. com; 48 Arab St; dm S$20-24; ❄ @ 🛜; Ⓜ Bugis) A well-located, well-designed hostel with a fantastic rooftop lounge and terrace (great views!). Rooms feature dark-wood bunk beds and industrial elements such as raw concrete floors. Friendly staff complete the package.

The Sleepy Kiwi
HOSTEL $

(Map p624; www.sleepykiwi.com.sg; 55 Bussorah St; dm S$22-27, d S$89; ❄ @ 🛜; Ⓜ Bugis) This budget mainstay has rebranded and improved under new management. Its central location on a pedestrianised street is enhanced by a laid-back ambience, pier-and-beam ceilings, a book-filled common area/cafe and well-furnished dorm rooms.

SPLURGE

It's a compulsory and costly cliché to sink a Singapore Sling (S$30) in the **Long Bar** (open 11am to 12.30am) at the Raffles Hotel (p615). For a less touristy experience, head for the century-old snooker tables at the hotel's **Bar & Billiard Room** (open 11.30am to 12.30am), where you can almost hear Somerset Maugham clacking away on his typewriter in the courtyard.

Eating

Singaporean life is best epitomised by the ubiquitous (but wholly unique) hawker centre. Grab a seat, order a super-sweet coffee or a S$6 Tiger beer, join the queue for a local meal and listen to people talk about politics, English Premier League, Hollywood diets and maids. Dishes rarely cost more than S$5 (unless you're eating seafood), and each centre has a huge variety of cuisines, including Malay, South Indian, Cantonese, Hokkien, Teochew and Indonesian. There are also countless excellent restaurants, though costs are going to spiral up to at least S$12 per plate.

Colonial District

★ **Singapore Food Trail** HAWKER $
(Map p618; www.singaporefoodtrail.com.sg; Singapore Flyer, 30 Raffles Ave; dishes S$5-15; ⊙10.30am-10.30pm Sun-Thu, to 11.30pm Fri & Sat; ⓜPromenade) Retro-inspired re-creation of the hawker stalls from 1960s Singapore, except with air-conditioning. A good alternative to Gluttons Bay.

★ **Gluttons Bay** HAWKER $$
(Map p618; 01-15 Esplanade Mall; mains $8-20; ⊙6pm-3am; ⓜEsplanade) Food celebrity KF Seetoh took the hard work out of finding great hawker food by inviting the best ones here, beside the Esplanade Mall. You can't go wrong with dishes such as oyster omelette, satay and barbecued stingray. You have to try the divine *kaya* (coconut jam) fondue.

Seah Street
Food Outlets INTERNATIONAL $$
(Map p618; Seah St; dishes S$5-20; ⓜCity Hall) This street next to the impeccable Raffles Hotel has a few good eating options. Standouts include **Hock Lam Beef Noodles** (piquant thick sauce coats strips of beef and rice noodles) and chicken rice at **Sin Swee Kee** and **Swee Kee** (no relation to each other). Good burgers can be found at **Third & Sixth Bistro**.

Purvis Street
Food Outlets INTERNATIONAL $$
(Map p618; Purvis St; dishes S$5-25; ⓜCity Hall) Purvis St packs in a whole heap of restaurants. The chicken rice at old-school, 50-odd-year-old **Yet Con** is superb, and you can shovel Thai food at **Jai Thai** or get cheap traditional French at **Saveur**.

If you're in the area for brekkie, drop by **Killiney Koptiam** or **YY Kafei Dian** for some *kaya* (coconut jam) toast and thick coffee that'll knock your socks off.

Food for Thought FUSION $$
(Map p618; ☑6338 9887; www.foodforthought.com; National Museum, 93 Stamford Rd; mains from S$10; ⊙10am-10pm Mon-Sat, 10am-9pm Sun; ⓜBras Basah, Dhoby Gaut) We admire the philosophy behind this restaurant – a portion of the proceeds goes to aid projects. The food itself is a mix of familiar favourites: pastas, grilled meats and sandwiches... with a twist. The chicken chop is coated in a lightly curried batter, for example. It's popular, so expect to wait during peak times.

Raffles City INTERNATIONAL $$
(Map p618; www.rafflescity.com.sg; 252 North Bridge Rd; dishes from S$10; ⓜCity Hall) Get Vietnamese favourites *pho* or *bahn mi* at **Namnam**, yummy (but somewhat small) burgers at **Handburger**, divine *xiao long pao* (steamed pork dumplings) at **Din Tai Fung** or gourmet-topped pizzas made with flat cracker bread at **Skinny Pizza**. Check out the deli counters at the basement **Marketplace** supermarket for a picnic basket.

CBD & the Quays

★ **Ya Kun Kaya Toast** CAFÉ $
(Map p622; www.yakun.com; 01-01 Far East Sq, 18 China St; kaya toast set S$4; ⊙7.30am-6.30pm Mon-Fri, 8.30am-5pm Sat & Sun; ⓜChinatown, Raffles Place) Though a chain of outlets has mushroomed across Singapore, this outlet most closely matches the original 1940s stall, selling strong coffee, runny eggs and the *kaya* toast that so many Singaporeans love.

Amoy Street Food Centre HAWKER $
(Map p622; cnr Amoy & Telok Ayer St; dishes S$4-10; ⊙9.30am-7.30pm; ⓜTanjong Pagar) A fabulous cornucopia of local treats awaits diners at this decidedly local hawker centre. The range is truly mindboggling: try the 'local' ramen at **Noodle Story** (01-39) and anywhere else with a queue. Gets packed between noon and 1.30pm.

Lau Pa Sat HAWKER $
(Map p622; 18 Raffles Quay; dishes from S$5; ⓜRaffles Place) This Victorian market building (currently under renovation) will be chock-a-block with food. The street hawkers still operate come dinner time, perfect for that beer-and-satay fix!

Chinatown

★ Maxwell Road
Hawker Centre
HAWKER $

(Map p622; cnr Maxwell & South Bridge Rds; dishes from S$3; ⊙ individual stalls vary; 📷; Ⓜ Chinatown) Esteemed as one of Singapore's best hawker centres, this is in an open-sided food barn with more than 100 stalls under its roof. **Tian Tian Chicken Rice** (01-10) is hands down Singapore's best.

Annalakshmi Janatha
INDIAN $

(Map p622; www.annalakshmi.com.sg; 104 Amoy St; prices vary; ⊙ 11am-3pm Mon-Sat; 📷; Ⓜ Tanjong Pagar) A real gem, serving up Indian vegetarian buffets on a pay-what-you-feel basis (S$5 to S$10 per head is acceptable). It's run by volunteers and profits help support various charities.

Chinatown Complex
HAWKER $

(Map p622; 11 New Bridge Rd; dishes from S$2.50; ⊙ individual stalls vary; Ⓜ Chinatown) Join the locals for some Hainanese chicken rice (and a range of other local goodies) at this no-nonsense hawker centre smack bang in the middle of Chinatown. Find craft beers at the **Good Beer Company** stall (02-58).

Little India

★ Bismillah Biryani
INDIAN $

(Map p624; 50 Dunlop St; kebabs from S$4, biryani from S$6; ⊙ noon-8pm; Ⓜ Little India) A banner proclaims that Google lists this place as selling the 'best biryani in Singapore'. We have to agree. The mutton biryani is special, as is the mutton shish kebab, which is melt-in-your-mouth good. Most of the best dishes are long gone before 8pm.

Ananda Bhavan
INDIAN $

(Map p624; Serangoon Rd; set meals S$6-8, dishes S$3-5; ⊙ 7am-10pm; 📷; Ⓜ Little India) There are several branches of this superlative South Indian vegetarian eatery, which serves up excellent *idli* (rice dumplings), *thali, dosa* and lots of Indian sweets.

Tekka Centre
HAWKER $

(Map p624; cnr Serangoon & Buffalo Rds; dishes S$3-5; ⊙ 7am-11pm; 📷; Ⓜ Little India) Serves almost everything but with a focus on Indian food. Look out for **Al-Rahman Royal Prata** (01-248) for its divine *murtabak* (stuffed pancake).

Lavender Food Square
HAWKER $

(Map p624; cnr Jln Besar & Foch Rd; dishes from S$3; ⊙ 24hr; Ⓜ Lavender) People queue for ages to get the wonton noodles, but there's something for everyone here.

Kampong Glam

★ Warong Nasi
Pariaman
MALAYSIAN, INDONESIAN $

(Map p624; ✆ 6292 2374; 738 North Bridge Rd; dishes S$3-5; ⊙ 7.30am-2.30pm Mon-Sat; Ⓜ Bugis) You'll smell the food before you see the crowd waiting to order the *nasi padang* dishes at this corner coffee shop. The *beef rendang* (dry beef curry) and *sambal goreng* (long beans, tempeh and fried bean curd) are yummy.

Zam Zam
MALAYSIAN $

(Map p624; 699 North Bridge Rd; dishes S$5-8; ⊙ 8am-11pm; Ⓜ Bugis) These guys have been here since 1908, so we figure they know what they're doing. Longevity hasn't bred complacency though – the touts try to herd passers-by through the door as frenetic chefs whip up *murtabak*.

Golden Mile Food Centre
HAWKER $

(505 Beach Rd; dishes from S$3; ⊙ 10am-10pm) The famous *tulang* (bone marrow) soup from basement stalls is messily good. Also try the excellent *ah balling* (glutinous rice balls with sweet fillings) and *char kway teow* on the 2nd floor.

Golden Mile Complex
THAI $

(5001 Beach Rd; dishes from S$3.50; ⊙ 10am-10pm; Ⓜ Little India Lavender, Bugis) Here at 'Little Thailand', you'll find cheap Thai food stalls sitting next to travel agents and seedy discos.

Cold Storage
SUPERMARKET $

(Map p624; www.coldstorage.com.sg; B1-16, Bugis Junction, 200 Victoria St; Ⓜ Bugis) This supermarket is great for picking up make-your-own lunch items.

> ### SPLURGE
>
> With a perfectly poised location in a central but quiet part of the Colonial District, **Soho Coffee** (Map p618; 36 Armenian St; dishes from S$12; ⊙ 8am-6pm Mon-Fri, to 8pm Sat; Ⓜ City Hall) does delish burgers and superb coffee. Lunch sets (from S$15) offer good value.

Café Le Caire
MIDDLE EASTERN **$$**

(Map p624; www.cafelecaire.com; 33 Arab St; dishes S$4-22; ⊙10am-3.30am; 🍴; Ⓜ Bugis) This casual Egyptian hole-in-the-wall comes to life at night and attracts a multinational crowd. For a filling budget meal, you can't go past the meze platter, washed down with an iced mint tea and a relaxing puff on a water pipe.

✖ Orchard Road

Food Republic
FOOD COURT **$**

(Map p626; Level 4, Wisma Atria Shopping Centre, 435 Orchard Rd; dishes from S$5; ⊙8am-10pm Mon-Thu, to 11pm Fri-Sun; Ⓜ Orchard) Slightly upmarket food court, with views along Orchard Rd to match the yummy local dishes.

Din Tai Fung
TAIWANESE **$$**

(Map p626; www.dintaifung.com.sg; B1-03/06, Paragon Shopping Centre, 290 Orchard Rd; buns from S$3.80, dumplings from S$7; Ⓜ Somerset) While waiting, watch chefs at work through 'fishbowl' windows; they painstakingly make 18 folds in the dough used for the *xiao long pao* (steamed pork dumplings). Delicate dumplings are served steaming in bamboo baskets and explode with flavour in your mouth. There are branches all over town.

🍷 Drinking & Nightlife

Drinking in Singapore is expensive. The cheapest way to drink is to park yourself in a hawker centre, where beers cost S$6 to S$8 for a large bottle. If you're hitting the bars and clubs, start early: happy hours generally finish at 9pm. The main drinking places include Clarke and Boat Quays, and Emerald Hill Rd off Orchard Rd. Most bars open from 5pm daily until at least midnight Sunday to Thursday, and until 2am on Friday and Saturday.

🍷 Colonial District

Loof
BAR

(Map p618; www.loof.com.sg; 03-07 Odeon Towers Bldg, 331 North Bridge Rd; ⊙5pm-late Mon-Sat; Ⓜ City Hall) This breezy bar is situated on the 'loof'top of a building across from Raffles Hotel. Chilled-out vibes, comfy couches and good happy-hour specials make it stand out.

MINT Bar
BAR

(Map p618; www.emint.com; 26 Seah St; ⊙6pm-2am Mon-Thu, 6pm-3am Fri & Sat; Ⓜ City Hall) It might be incongruous to attach a bar to a toy museum, but who's complaining when the pints are cheap? Grab a seat outdoors or up at the rooftop bar.

ART DECO HIP: TIONG BAHRU

Hipsters (beards optional!) have been drawn to the heritage Tiong Bahru neighbourhood for its unique low-rise art deco flats and cluster of bars, cafes and boutiques. Hit new-school cool **Yong Siak Street** for indie bookstores and boutiques before heading to the **Tiong Bahru Market & Food Centre** for cheap local eats. Take the MRT to Tiong Bahru station, walk east along Tiong Bahru Rd for 350m, then turn right onto Kim Pong Rd.

🍷 CBD & the Quays

Clarke Quay is a popular (though very gaudy) nightspot in Singapore. If you don't mind mingling with off-work suits, bars around the CBD area (Raffles Place) are cheap after 5pm.

Brewerkz
BREWERY

(Map p618; www.brewerkz.com; 01-05 Riverside Point Centre, 30 Merchant Rd; ⊙noon-midnight Sun-Thu, to 1am Fri & Sat; Ⓜ Clarke Quay) Across the river from Clarke Quay, this large microbrewery (the irony doesn't escape us) brews eight beers on-site. Happy hours run from opening to 9pm, with prices escalating throughout the day (pints S$4 to S$15, jugs S$10 to S$37).

Boat Quay
NEIGHBOURHOOD

Boat Quay is a popular boozing haunt for expat city workers. The British-style **Penny Black** gets very busy, as does **Harry's Bar** next door. Get local microbrews from **Red Dot Brewhouse**.

Home Club
NIGHTCLUB

(Map p618; www.homeclub.com.sg; B1-1/06 The Riverwalk, 20 Upper Circular Rd; ⊙7pm-3am Tue-Fri, to 4am Sat; Ⓜ Clarke Quay) Set right by the Singapore River in between Boat and Clarke Quays, this thumping venue features DJs spinning house, dubstep, and drum and bass, and a wide variety of live rock and pop bands. Comedy nights on Tuesdays are a hoot!

Butter Factory
NIGHTCLUB

(Map p618; www.thebutterfactory.com; 02-02 One Fullerton, 1 Fullerton Rd; ⊙11pm-4am Wed, to 6am Fri & Sat; Ⓜ Clarke Quay) The 8000-sq-ft Butter Factory is slick as hell. Street art on the walls of Bump, the hip-hop and R&B room, appeals to the younger crowd.

GET YOUR (HIPSTER) CAFFEINE FIX

Singaporeans' tastes are heavily driven by 'flavour of the moment' and that flavour has recently been artisanal coffee. A clutch of cafes now channels the very best of Melbourne, Seattle and London. If you're in need of a latte or pourover fix and fancy cafe grub, head to these places.

Chye Seng Huat Hardware (Map p624; www.cshhcoffee.com; 150 Tyrwhitt Rd; ⊘9am-7pm Tue-Fri, to 10pm Sat & Sun; MLavender)

Maison Ikkoku (Map p624; www.maison-ikkoku.net; 20 Kandahar St; ⊘cafe 9am-9pm Mon-Thu, to 11pm Fri & Sat, to 7pm Sun, bar 6pm-late Mon-Sat; ☎; MBugis)

Common Man Coffee (www.commonmancoffeeroasters.com; 22 Martin Rd, Robertson Quay; ⊘8am-7pm; MRaffles Place)

Department of Caffeine (DOC; Map p622; ✎6223 3426; www.deptofcaffeine.com; 15 Duxton Rd; ⊘10.30am-7.30pm Mon-Fri, 9.30am-7.30pm Sat & Sun; MTanjong Pagar)

Stranger's Reunion (Map p622; ✎6222 4869; www.facebook.com/StrangersReunion; 33, 35, 37 Kampong Bahru Rd; ⊘9am-10pm; MOutram Park)

Oriole Coffee Roasters (Map p622; www.oriolecoffee.com; 10/10A Jiak Chuan Rd; ⊘10am-6pm Mon-Fri; ☎; MOutram Park)

Chinatown

Tanjong Pagar Rd has an active gay and lesbian bar scene but welcomes drinkers regardless of their sexuality. The sophisticated bars of **Club St** and **Ann Siang Hill** are housed in attractive, restored shophouses (many are closed Sunday). Bars come and go; the hippest ones at the time of writing include **Oxwell & Co** (Map p622; 5 Ann Siang Rd; ⊘8am-midnight Tue-Sun), **Ding Dong** (Map p622; 23 Ann Siang Rd; ⊘noon-3pm & 6pm-midnight Mon-Fri, 6pm-midnight Sat) and **Jigger & Pony** (Map p622; 101 Amoy St; ⊘6pm-1am Mon-Thu, 6pm-3am Fri & Sat).

Little India & Kampong Glam

Zsofi Tapas Bar
BAR

(Map p624; www.tapasbar.com.sg; 68 Dunlop St; ⊘5pm-late; MLittle India) Inspired by their travels through Spain, two mates decided to open a tapas bar named after a travelling companion. All drinks come with a tapas of choice. Now that's choice!

Kerbau Road Beer Garden
CAFE

(Map p624; Kerbau Rd; beer from S$4; ⊘10am-11pm; MLittle India) Little more than a couple of drinks stalls with plastic tables and chairs, this 'beer garden' is packed every night with Indian drinkers who come for the Bollywood movies shown on the small TV as much as for the cheap booze.

BluJaz Cafe
PUB

(Map p624; www.blujaz.net; 11 Bali Lane; ⊘noon-1am Mon-Thu, noon-2am Fri, 4pm-2am Sat; ☎; MBugis) This ultrabusy bar-restaurant is as close as you'll get to a bohemian hang-out in Singapore. There's live music (not always jazz) on weekends. If it's too packed, hit its sister joint **Piedra Negra** next door.

Orchard Road Area

Emerald Hill Bars
BAR

(Map p626; Emerald Hill Rd) Emerald Hill has a collection of bars in the renovated shophouses just off Orchard Rd, including the cool **Alley Bar** (No 2) and even cooler **No 5** (No 5). At the end of the strip, **Ice Cold Beer** (No 9) is a raucous spot with indie/rock music at high decibels.

Zouk
NIGHTCLUB

(www.zoukclub.com; 17 Jiak Kim St; entry fee incl 2 drinks S$25-30; ⊘Zouk 11am-late Wed, Fri & Sat, Phuture & Velvet Underground 9pm-late Wed, Fri & Sat, Wine Bar 6pm-late Tue-Sat) This stayer of the Singaporean club scene still nabs top-name DJs. It's actually three clubs in one, plus a wine bar, so go the whole hog and pay the full entrance. It's just northeast of Chinatown; taxi is the easiest way there.

Sentosa Island

Tanjong Beach Club
BAR

(Map p628; www.tanjongbeachclub.com; Tanjong Beach; ⊘11am-11pm Tue-Thu, 10am-11pm Fri & Sat)

The beautiful people flock here to sip cocktails and stretch out on deck chairs. If you don't fancy swimming in the beach, there's a pool for a dip.

Wave House BAR
(Map p628; www.wavehousesentosa.com; 36 Siloso Beach Walk; ⊙10am-11pm) Surfer-friendly beach bar with its own ordinary pool as well as two 'flowriders': wave pools that you can pay to surf in.

St James Power Station NIGHTCLUB
(Map p628; www.stjamespowerstation.com; 3 Sentosa Gateway; ⊙hours vary, generally 6pm-late Wed-Sun; Ⓜ HarbourFront) An entertainment complex housed in a 1920s coal-fired power station subdivided into a variety of bars and clubs. There's even a karaoke section! Minimum age is 21 for women and 23 for men at most outlets. If you get tired and hungry, the outdoor **Food Republic** serves some excellent hawker fare.

☆ Entertainment

Singaporeans love the cinema (a cheap way to dodge the tropical heat; tickets cost S$10 or so). The *Straits Times, I-S Magazine* and *Time Out* have listings for movies, theatre and music. Tickets for most events are available through **Sistic** (Map p626; ✆6348 5555; www.sistic.com.sg).

Chinese Theatre Circle OPERA
(Map p622; ✆6323 4862; www.ctcopera.com; 5 Smith St; show & dinner S$40, show & snacks S$25; Ⓜ Chinatown) Get into Chinese opera at a teahouse session organised by this nonprofit company. Friday and Saturday shows start at 7pm with a brief talk (in English) on Chinese opera, followed by an excerpt from a Cantonese opera (with English subtitles).

Timbrè@The Substation LIVE MUSIC
(Map p618; www.timbre.com.sg; 45 Armenian St; ⊙4pm-late Mon-Thu, from 5pm Fri & Sat; Ⓜ City Hall) At night, groups of art-school types hang out and bob heads to live alt-rock sets while downing pints of Erdinger, hands oily from one too many buffalo wings. Check the website for two other locations around Singapore.

🛍 Shopping

Once renowned as a bargain paradise, Singapore has been overtaken by other cities in the region, but there are still bargains to be had on items such as clothing, electronics, IT gear and books. Major high-street brands such as Uniqlo and H&M often run sales. Prices are usually fixed, except at markets and in smaller non-chain stores (don't start bargaining if you don't have any real interest in purchasing).

🏬 Orchard Road

Singapore's premier shopping strip; you would need the best part of a week to explore every floor of every mall in the Orchard Rd area.

Ngee Ann City MALL
(Map p626; www.ngeeanncity.com.sg; 391 Orchard Rd; Ⓜ Orchard) Packed with high-end brands and **Kinokuniya**, the best bookshop in the city.

Ion Orchard Mall MALL
(Map p626; www.ionorchard.com; 430 Orchard Rd; observation deck ticket counter level 4; observation deck adult/child S$16/8; Ⓜ Orchard) The Ion Orchard has a shimmery 21st-century media wall, an art space and a wide range of stores such as H&M and **Uniqlo**.

Far East Plaza MALL
(Map p626; www.fareast-plaza.com; 14 Scotts Rd; ⊙10am-10pm; Ⓜ Orchard) Great for cheap clothes and shoes, and getting inked.

🏬 Colonial District

Funan DigitaLife Mall ELECTRONICS
(Map p618; www.funan.com.sg; 109 North Bridge Rd; Ⓜ City Hall) IT greenhorns rejoice! Computers, software, camera gear and MP3 players are priced and labelled. Family-run **John 3:16** (04-27) is a popular camera shop; **Challenger** (06-01) supplies all your tech needs.

Cathay Photo ELECTRONICS
(Map p618; www.cathayphoto.com.sg; 01-11 Peninsula Plaza; ⊙10am-7pm Mon-Sat) All the pros (and

SINGAPORE ENTERTAINMENT

FREE CONCERTS

The **Esplanade: Theatres on the Bay** (Map p618; ✆6828 8377; www.esplanade.com; 1 Esplanade Dr; ⊙10am-6pm; Ⓜ Esplanade, City Hall) has free live performances on Friday, Saturday and Sunday that kick off around 7pm. The **Singapore Symphony Orchestra** (Map p618; ✆6348 5555; www.sso.org.sg; Ⓜ Esplanade) performs free at the Singapore Botanic Gardens monthly. Check the websites for details.

TOTO, WE'RE NOT IN ORCHARD RD ANYMORE

Farm owners in Kranji have formed **Kranji Countryside Association** (www.kranjicountry-side.com), to promote awareness of their existence. So far the collective has done a great job considering it doesn't have the multimillion-dollar advertising budgets of retail heavies, and hey, anyone who makes a living selling goats' milk deserves special mention.

The **Kranji Express** (Kranji MRT Station; tickets adult/child S$3/1; ☉9am-5.45pm, 8 buses daily), a daily minibus service, does a loop to and from Kranji MRT Station visiting the best farms en route. Look for organic vegies and fruit, pottery, frogs, wheatgrass, cafes and restaurants. And sample some goats' milk too. The bus also passes the under-rated **Sungei Buloh Wetland Reserve** (☑6794 1401; www.sbwr.org.sg; 301 Neo Tiew Cres; admission free; ☉7.30am-7pm Mon-Sat, 7am-7pm Sun; ☐925 to Kranji Reservoir, ⓜKranji).

wannabes) shop at the extensively stocked Cathay Photo. **Peninsula Shopping Centre** across the road has several good secondhand camera stores.

Little India & Kampong Glam

Little India bursts with handicrafts, gold, saris, incense, Bollywood music and DVDs. In Kampong Glam, for handicrafts, raw cloth and tourist trinkets, wander along **Bussorah Street** and **Arab Street**. **Haji Lane** has a series of stores selling up-to-the-minute fashion...assuming they haven't shut down because of soaring rent.

Mustafa Centre   DEPARTMENT STORE
(Map p624; www.mustafa.com.sg; 145 Syed Alwi Rd; ☉24hr; ⓜFarrer Park) Has all manner of goods (electronics, jewellery, household items, toys, shoes etc). An extension houses a supermarket with a wide range of food, and a rooftop Indian restaurant.

Bugis Village   MALL
(Map p624; Victoria St; ⓜBugis) This warren, opposite Bugis Junction, is a good hunting ground for cheap clothes, shoes and accessories.

Sim Lim Square   ELECTRONICS, MALL
(Map p624; www.simlimsquare.com.sg; 1 Rochor Canal Rd; ☉11am-8pm; ⓜBugis) This is a geek paradise, overflowing with cheap IT gear and electronics. We'd only advise going if you know your stuff, however, because novices can be fleeced.

❶ Orientation

The Singapore River cuts the city in two: south is the CBD and Chinatown, and to the north is the Colonial District. The trendy Clarke and

Robertson Quays, and the popular Boat Quay dining areas, hug the riverbanks.

Further north from the Colonial District are Little India and Kampong Glam, the Muslim quarter. Northwest of the Colonial District is Orchard Rd, Singapore's premier shopping strip.

To the west of the island, the predominantly industrial area of Jurong contains a number of tourist attractions. Heading south you'll find the recreational islands of Sentosa, Kusu and St John's.

Eastern Singapore has some historical (and sleazy) suburbs such as Geylang and Katong, and East Coast Park and Changi Airport. The central north of the island has much of Singapore's remaining forest and the zoo.

❶ Information

EMERGENCY
Ambulance/Fire (☑995)
Police (☑999)
SOS Helpline (☑1800-221 4444)

INTERNET ACCESS
Hostels offer free internet via PCs or wi-fi. Travellers with wi-fi enabled devices should sign up for free wireless internet, Wireless@SG, available in most malls and many public buildings. You need a mobile phone with a working SIM (local or global roaming) to register.

MEDIA
Free publications with events information, such as *Juice* and *I-S Magazine,* are available at tourist offices, most major hotels and several restaurants, cafes and bars. The international listings magazine *Time Out* has a Singapore edition. English daily newspapers include the progovernment broadsheet the *Straits Times,* the *Business Times* and the tabloid-style *New Paper. Straits Times* has decent coverage of Asia. *New Paper* is best for a flavour of 'real life' Singapore and sports. *Today* and *Mypaper* are freebie tabloids that you can pick up at MRT stations.

SINGAPORE SINGAPORE TODAY

MEDICAL SERVICES

Raffles Hospital (Map p624; ☑ 6311 1111; www.raffleshospital.com; 585 North Bridge Rd; ⊙ 24hr; Ⓜ Bugis)

Singapore General Hospital (☑ 6222 3322; www.sgh.com.sg; Level 2, Block 1, Outram Rd; ⊙ 24hr; Ⓜ Outram Park)

POST

Tourist information centres sell stamps and post letters. Changi Airport Terminal 2 has a post-office counter.

Ion Orchard Post Office (Map p626; B2-62 Ion Orchard, 2 Orchard Turn; Ⓜ Orchard)

TOURIST INFORMATION

Singapore Tourism Board (STB; www.visitsingapore.com) Most STB offices provide a range of services, including tour bookings and event tickets.

Singapore Visitors Centre @ Ion Orchard (Map p626; Level 1, Ion Orchard Mall, 2 Orchard Turn; ⊙ 10am-10pm; Ⓜ Orchard)

Singapore Visitors Centre @ Orchard (Map p626; ☑ 1800-736 2000; cnr Orchard & Cairnhill Rds; ⊙ 9.30am-10.30pm; Ⓜ Somerset) Brochures, maps, information about Singapore, helpful staff.

UNDERSTAND SINGAPORE

Singapore Today

Singapore is undergoing a development boom, gearing up to boost its population to 6.5 million and to position itself as a centre for everything from biomedical research to tourism. Large casino resorts on Sentosa Island and at Marina South were completed in 2011, while the entire Marina Bay area around the Esplanade theatre has been turned into an upmarket commercial, residential, leisure, botanic gardens and watersports centre (talk about a Swiss army knife of civic planning!). New subway lines are being installed, which, when completed, will rival London's Tube.

As of 2012, Singapore had the third-highest GDP in the world with over US$200 billion in reserve. While the incumbent People's Action Party (PAP) might have recently faced its greatest political election loss since independence, they've at least set the foundation stone for Singapore's continued prosperity. Current Singaporean concerns include the soaring cost of living, overpopulation and the influx of foreign workers.

History

Lion City

Singapore was originally a tiny sea town squeezed between powerful neighbours Sumatra and Melaka. According to Malay legend, a Sumatran prince spotted a lion while visiting the island of Temasek, and on the basis of this good omen he founded a city there called Singapura (Lion City).

Raffles

Sir Thomas Stamford Raffles arrived in 1819 to secure a strategic base for the British Empire in the Strait of Melaka. He decided to transform the sparsely populated, swampy island into a free-trade port. The layout of central Singapore is still as Raffles drew it.

World War II

The glory days of the empire came to an abrupt end on 15 February 1942, when the Japanese invaded Singapore. For the rest of WWII the Japanese ruled the island harshly, jailing Allied prisoners of war (POWs) at Changi Prison and killing thousands of locals. Although the British were welcomed back after the war, their days in the region were numbered.

Foundation for the Future

The socialist People's Action Party was founded in 1954, with Lee Kuan Yew as its secretary general. Lee led the PAP to victory in elections held in 1959, and hung onto power for more than 30 years. Singapore was kicked out of the Malay Federation in 1965, but Lee pushed through an ambitious, strict and successful industrialisation program.

His successor in 1990 was Goh Chok Tong, who loosened things up a little, but maintained Singapore on the path Lee had forged. In 2004 Goh stepped down to make way for Lee's son, Lee Hsien Loong.

Lee the Younger faces the huge challenge of positioning Singapore to succeed in the modern, globalised economy. As manufacturing bleeds away to cheaper competitors, the government is focused on boosting its population, attracting more 'foreign talent' and developing industries such as tourism, financial services, digital media and biomedical research.

People & Culture

The National Psyche

Affluent Singaporeans live in an apparently constant state of transition, continuously urged by their ever-present government to upgrade, improve and reinvent. On the surface, these are thoroughly modernised people, but many lives are still ruled by old beliefs and customs. There is also a sharp divide between the older generation, who experienced the huge upheavals and relentless graft that built modern Singapore, and the pampered younger generation, who enjoy the fruits of that labour.

Lifestyle

While family and tradition are important, many young people live their lives outside of home, working long hours and staying out late after work.

The majority of the population lives in Housing Development Board flats (you can't miss them). These flats are heavily subsidised by the government (which even dictates the ratio of races living in each block). These subsidies favour married couples, while singles and gay and lesbian couples have to tough it out on the private real-estate market.

Women have equal access to education and employment. Likewise, despite the oft-touted anti-homosexual stance of the government, gay men and lesbians are a visible part of everyday life in Singapore.

Population

The majority of the 5.31 million people are Chinese (74.2% of the population). Next come the Malays (13.2%), Indians (9.2%) and Eurasians and 'others' (3.4%). Western expats are a very visible group. Also visible is the large population of domestic maids and foreign labourers. Contrary to popular belief, English is the first language of Singapore. Many Singaporeans speak a second language or dialect (usually Mandarin, Malay or Tamil).

Religion

The Chinese majority are usually Buddhists or Taoists, and Chinese customs, superstitions and festivals dominate social life.

The Malays embrace Islam as a religion and a way of life. *Adat* (customary law) guides important ceremonies and events, including birth, circumcision and marriage.

More than half the Indians are Hindus and worship the pantheon of gods in various temples across Singapore.

Christianity, including Catholicism, is also popular in Singapore, with both Chinese and Indians pledging their faith to this religion.

Environment

Singapore's chief environmental issue is rubbish disposal. The government has recognised the need to encourage recycling, both industrial and domestic. However, massive government effort doesn't necessarily translate to environmental awareness on the ground level. Locals still love their plastic bags when shopping, and get domestic helpers to wash their cars daily. Singaporeans are encouraged to recycle but aren't provided with easy means to do so (all waste in public flats still goes into one central bin).

Air quality is much better than in most large Southeast Asian metropolises, but the annual haze that descends on the island around September and October, generated by slash-and-burn fires in Indonesia, is a serious concern.

Much of Singapore's fresh water is imported from Malaysia but, with large reservoirs, desalination plants and a huge waste-water recycling project called Newater, Singapore hopes to become self-sufficient within the next few decades. Tap water is safe to drink.

Singapore has a proud and well-deserved reputation as a garden city. Parks, often beautifully landscaped, are abundant and the entire centre of the island is a green oasis.

SURVIVAL GUIDE

ⓘ Directory A–Z

ACCOMMODATION

Hostels offer competitive prices (S$20 to S$40 for a dorm bed) and facilities such as free internet, breakfast and laundry use. Cheaper en-suite hotel rooms (S$50 to S$100) are cramped and often windowless. Most places offer air-con rooms. Establishments usually quote net prices, which include all taxes. If you see ++ after a price, you'll need to add a 10% service charge and 7% GST.

The following price ranges refer to a double room without bathroom in high season. Room prices quoted include all taxes.

$ less than S$100 (US$80)

$$ S$100 to S$250 (US$80 to US$200)

$$$ more than S$250 (US$200)

CLIMATE

There are no seasons in Singapore. The weather is uniformly hot and humid all year round. November to January are considered slightly wetter months, though rain is common throughout.

CUSTOMS REGULATIONS

You can bring in 1L each of wine, beer and spirits duty-free. Cigarettes are dutiable except for a personal opened pack. Electronic goods, cosmetics, watches, cameras, jewellery, footwear, toys, arts and crafts are not dutiable. Duty-free concessions are not available if you are arriving from Malaysia or if you've been out of Singapore for less than 48 hours.

EMBASSIES & CONSULATES

For a full list of foreign embassies and consulates in Singapore, check out the **Ministry of Foreign Affairs** (www.mfa.gov.sg) website.

Australian High Commission (Map p626; ☑ 6836 4100; www.australia.org.sg; 25 Napier Rd)

Canadian High Commission (Map p618; ☑ 6854 5900; www.singapore.gc.ca; #11-01, 1 George St)

French Embassy (☑ 6880 7800; www.amba france-sg.org; 101-103 Cluny Park Rd)

German Embassy (Map p618; ☑ 6533 6002; www.singapur.diplo.de; #12-00 Singapore Land Tower, 50 Raffles Pl)

Indonesian Embassy (Map p626; ☑ 6737 7422; www.kemlu.go.id/singapore; 7 Chatsworth Rd)

Irish Embassy (Map p626; ☑ 6238 7616; www.embassyofireland.sg; #08-00 Liat Towers, 541 Orchard Rd)

Italian Embassy (☑ 6250 6022; www.amb singapore.esteri.it; 27-02 United Sq, 101 Thomson Rd)

Japanese Embassy (Map p626; ☑ 6235 8855; www.sg.emb-japan.go.jp; 16 Nassim Rd)

Netherlands Embassy (Map p626; ☑ 6737 1155; www.mfa.nl/sin; #13-01 Liat Towers, 541 Orchard Rd)

New Zealand High Commission (Map p618; ☑ 6235 9966; www.nzembassy.com/singapore; 21-04, 1 George St)

Thai Embassy (Map p626; ☑ 6737 2158; www.thaiembassy.sg; 370 Orchard Rd)

UK High Commission (Map p626; ☑ 6424 4200; http://ukinsingapore.fco.gov.uk; 100 Tanglin Rd)

US Embassy (Map p626; ☑ 6476 9100; http://singapore.usembassy.gov; 27 Napier Rd)

FOOD

The following price ranges refer to a main course. Unless otherwise stated, tax is included in the price.

$ less than S$10 (US$8)

$$ S$10 to S$30 (US$8 to US$24)

$$$ more than S$30 (US$24)

GAY & LESBIAN TRAVELLERS

Male homosexuality is still technically illegal, but laws have not prevented the emergence of a thriving gay scene. Check out www.utopia-asia.com and www.fridae.asia for coverage of venues and events.

LEGAL MATTERS

The law is extremely tough in Singapore, but also relatively free from corruption. Possession and trafficking of drugs is punishable by death. Smoking in all public places, including bars, restaurants and hawker centres, is banned unless there's an official smoking 'area'.

MAPS

The Official Map of Singapore, available free from the STB, the airport and hotels, is excellent.

MONEY

The Singaporean dollar is made up of 100 cents. Singapore uses 5c, 10c, 20c, 50c and S$1 coins, while notes come in denominations of S$2, S$5, S$10, S$50, S$100, S$500 and S$1000.

Banks and ATMs are everywhere; Cirrus-enabled ATMs are commonly found at MRT stations and in malls. Money-changers are easily found in most malls and busy locations; you don't get charged any fees and you can haggle a little if you're changing a large-ish quantity.

Contact details for credit-card companies in Singapore:

American Express (☑ 6396 6000, local calls only 1800-299 1997; www.americanexpress.com/sg)

MasterCard (☑ 1800-110 0113; www.master card.com)

Visa (☑ 1800-448 1250; www.visa.com.sg)

OPENING HOURS

Banks 8.30am to 5pm Monday to Friday (some branches close at 6pm), 8.30am to 1pm Saturday.

Government & post offices Between 8am and 9.30am to between 4pm and 6pm Monday to Friday, between 8am and 9.30am to between 11.30am and 2pm Saturday.

Restaurants & bars Top restaurants generally open between noon and 2pm for lunch and between 6pm and 10pm for dinner. Casual restaurants and food courts open all day (some 24 hours). Bars usually open from 5pm to midnight, later on weekends.

SINGAPORE DIRECTORY A–Z

Shops 10am to 6pm daily (malls and larger shops open until 9.30pm or 10pm). Some smaller shops in Chinatown and Arab St close on Sunday.

POST

Post in Singapore is among the most reliable in Southeast Asia. Postcards cost S$0.50 to anywhere in the world, and a letter costs S$1.10 to S$2.50 depending on where it's going. Call ☑1605 to find the nearest post-office branch, or check www.singpost.com.sg. Letters addressed to 'Poste Restante' are held at the **Singapore Post Centre** (☑6841 2000; 10 Eunos Rd), next to the Paya Lebar MRT station.

PUBLIC HOLIDAYS

Many of the following public holidays are based on the lunar calendar, and their dates vary.

New Year's Day 1 January
Chinese New Year January/February (three days)
Good Friday March/April
Vesak Day May
Labour Day 1 May
Hari Raya Puasa July
National Day 9 August
Deepavali October
Hari Raya Haji October/November
Christmas Day 25 December

RESPONSIBLE TRAVEL

Modern and cosmopolitan though it appears, Singapore is a little sensitive when it comes to brash behaviour by foreigners – quiet, polite behaviour will win you more respect. Public transport is efficient and you can even call hybrid-fuel taxis.

SAFE TRAVEL

Short-term visitors are unlikely to be troubled by Singapore's notoriously tough laws, which have turned the city into one of the safest in Asia. Street crime is minimal, though pickpockets have been known to operate in Chinatown, Little India and other tourist areas.

TELEPHONE

There are no area codes in Singapore; landline telephone numbers are eight digits unless you are calling toll-free (1800).

Mobile-phone numbers in Singapore start with 8 or 9. If you have global roaming, your GSM phone will lock into one of Singapore's three networks: M1-GSM, ST-GSM or Starhub.

You can buy a SIM card (usually S$18) with data or a 'disposable' mobile from most post offices and 7-Eleven stores, though you need to show your passport.

TOILETS

Toilets in Singapore are clean and well maintained, though they might vary between the sit-down and rarer squatting types. In some hawker centres you may have to pay S$0.10. You can find toilets in malls, fast-food outlets and large hotels.

TRAVELLERS WITH DISABILITIES

Travellers using wheelchairs can find Singapore difficult, though a massive accessibility project to improve life for the elderly and those with disabilities has seen things improve. The pavements in the city are nearly all immaculate, MRT stations all have lifts and some buses and taxis have wheelchair-friendly equipment.

The **Disabled People's Association** (☑6899 1220; www.dpa.org.sg) has an online accessibility guide to the country.

VISAS

Citizens of most countries are granted 30-day visas upon arrival in Singapore whether by air or overland. The exceptions are citizens of the Commonwealth of Independent States (former Soviet republics), India, Myanmar, China and most Middle Eastern countries who need to apply for one prior. Visitors must have a passport valid for at least six months beyond the date of entry into Singapore. Extensions can be applied

---

GETTING TO INDONESIA: SINGAPORE TO THE RIAU ARCHIPELAGO

Getting to the borders Ferries and speedboats run between Singapore and the Riau archipelago islands (including Pulau Batam, Pulau Bintan, Tanjung Balai and Tanjung Batu) in Indonesia. The ferries are modern, fast and air-conditioned. Expect to pay around S$24 for a one-way ticket to Batam, and S$45 to Bintan, Balai or Batu. Ferries to Batam Centre, Sekupang and Waterfront City (all on Batam) depart from the HarbourFront ferry terminal. Ferries to Nongsapura (also Batam) depart from the Tanah Merah terminal.

At the borders The border post at Batam ferry terminal is open during ferry operational hours and immigration on both sides is straightforward. You'll have to purchase an Indonesian visa (US$25 for 30 days) upon arrival at any of the islands.

Moving on From Pulau Batam, you can find ferries on to Tanjung Buton on the Sumatran mainland, from where it's a three-hour bus ride to Palembang.

for at the **Immigration & Checkpoints Authority** (Map p624; ☑ 6391 6100; www.ica.gov.sg; 10 Kallang Rd; Ⓜ Lavender) or online. Applications take at least a day to process.

VOLUNTEERING

The **National Volunteer & Philanthropy Centre** (www.nvpc.org.sg) coordinates a number of community groups, including grassroots projects in areas such as education, the environment and multiculturalism.

WOMEN TRAVELLERS

There are few problems for women travelling in Singapore. In Kampong Glam and Little India, skimpy clothing may attract unwanted stares. Tampons and pads are widely available across the island, as are over-the-counter medications.

Getting There & Away

AIR

Singapore is a great hub for any Southeast Asian journey. The budget air-travel boom connects Changi Airport cheaply with all major (and many minor) Southeast Asian destinations. Budget airlines operating out of Changi include the following:

Air Asia (☑ 6307 7688; www.airasia.com)

Berjaya Air (☑ 6542 4563; www.berjaya-air.com) Daily flights to Tioman and Redang islands in Malaysia.

Cebu Pacific (☑ 3158 0808; www.cebupacificair.com)

Jetstar (☑ 6499 9702; www.jetstar.com)

Scoot (☑ 3158 3388; www.flyscoot.com)

Tiger Airways (☑ 3157 6434; www.tigerairways.com)

BUS

Arriving from Malaysia, you'll be dropped either at the **Lavender St Bus Terminal** (Map p624; cnr Lavender St & Kallang Bahru), a 500m walk north of Lavender MRT station, or outside the **Golden Mile Complex** (5001 Beach Rd).

Numerous private companies run comfortable bus services to many destinations in Malaysia, including Melaka and Kuala Lumpur. The buses depart from various points in Singapore. If you're stumped, head to the Golden Mile Complex, where there are many bus agencies selling tickets. You can also book online at www.busonlineticket.com.

The main terminal for buses to and from Thailand is at the Golden Mile Complex.

First Coach (☑ 6820 2211; www.firstcoach.com.my; The Plaza, 7500A Beach Rd) Daily buses to Kuala Lumpur departing from the Plaza.

Grassland Express (☑ 6292 1166; www.grassland.com.sg; 01-24 Golden Mile Complex,

(Map p624)

ⓘ TRANSPORT MADE EZ

If you're going to be using the MRT and buses a lot, it's cheaper and more convenient to buy a S$15 Ez-Link card from any MRT station (S$5 nonrefundable deposit and S$10 credit). Fares using this card are 20% cheaper than cash fares.

Alternatively, a **Singapore Tourist Pass** (www.thesingaporetouristpass.com.sg) offers unlimited train and bus travel for S$10 daily plus a S$10 refundable deposit.

5001 Beach Rd) Daily buses to Kuala Lumpur, Penang, Melaka, Perak and numerous other destinations including Hat Yai, Thailand.

Phya Travel (☑ 6294 5415; www.phyatravel.com; 01-19 Golden Mile Complex, 5001 Beach Rd) Buses to Hat Yai, Thailand, from where travellers can catch onward buses.

Transtar Travel (☑ 6299 9009; www.transtar.travel; 01-12 Golden Mile Complex, 5001 Beach Rd) Luxury coaches to Kuala Lumpur, Genting, Ipoh and Penang.

TRAIN

Malaysian company **Keretapi Tanah Melayu Berhad** (KTM; www.ktmb.com.my) operates three air-con express trains daily (1st/2nd class S$68/34) for the seven-hour run from Singapore to Kuala Lumpur, with connections on to Thailand. Trains depart from the **Woodlands Train Checkpoint** (11 Woodlands Crossing; ☒ 170, Causeway Link from Queen St); you can book tickets at the station or via the dreadful KTM website.

SEA

There are several main ferry terminals with services to Malaysia and Indonesia:

Changi Point Ferry Terminal (☑ 6546 8518; 51 Lorong Bekukong; Ⓜ Tanah Merah then ☒ 2) Located 200m north of the Changi Bus Terminal.

HarbourFront Cruise & Ferry Terminal (Map p628; ☑ 6513 2200; www.singaporecruise.com; Ⓜ HarbourFront)

Tanah Merah Ferry Terminal (☑ 6513 2200; www.singaporecruise.com; Ⓜ Tanah Merah then ☒ 35) The same companies that operate ferries from Batam also have several ferries a day from Tanah Merah Ferry Terminal to Tanjung Pinang, the main city on Bintan, or Teluk Sebong on the island's north coast, as well as to Nongsapura on Batam (Indonesia). The 45km journey takes about an hour and costs between S$38 and S$48 return; ferries depart from 9am to 8pm.

These are the main ferry operators that travel to Indonesia:

GETTING TO MALAYSIA: SINGAPORE TO JOHOR BAHRU OR TANJUNG KUPANG

While you can enter Malaysia via Tanjung Belungkor by boat, the following options provide better onward transport connections.

Getting to the borders The 1km-long Causeway bridge in the north, at Woodlands, connects Singapore with Johor Bahru (JB). To the west, the Second Link bridge connects Tuas to Tanjung Kupang. If you take the train, you'll pass the border at Woodlands.

For JB, the Causeway Express air-con buses (S$2.40) and the public SBS bus 170 (S$1.80) depart every 15 minutes between 6am and 11.45pm from the Queen St bus terminal (Map p624; cnr Queen & Arab Sts). Share taxis (S$12) to JB also leave from the Queen St terminal. To cross at Tuas/Tanjung Kupang, take bus CW4 or CW4S from the Jurong East bus interchange (S$4) to Gelang Patah interchange in Johor Bahru from where there are onward buses. For more details about the train crossing, see the Train section below.

At the borders The buses stop at the Malaysia checkpoint; keep your ticket and hop on the next bus that comes along after you've cleared immigration. Immigration procedures on both sides of the bridges are straightforward; you'll be granted a visa on arrival at no cost. The border is open 24 hours.

Moving on Your Malaysia-bound bus will stop at a bus terminus from where you can easily find local taxis or onward buses. For those heading beyond Johor Bahru, bus companies head to popular destinations such as Kuala Lumpur, Penang and more. Buses also go to Hat Yai, Thailand, where you can get onward buses to other parts of Thailand; most leave at around 6pm and travel overnight.

BatamFast (☑ 6270 0311; www.batamfast.com) Ferries to Batam Centre, Sekupang, Waterfront City and Nongsapura in Indonesia.

Berlian Ferries (☑ 6272 0501; www.wave master.com.sg) Ferries to Batam, Sekupang and Nongsapura.

Bintan Resort Ferries (☑ 6542 4369; www.brf. com.sg) Ferries to Bandar Bintan Telani depart from Tanah Merah Ferry Terminal.

Indo Falcon (☑ 6542 6786; www.indofalcon. com.sg) Ferries to Batam Centre, Sekupang, Waterfront City and Nongsapura.

❶ Getting Around

BICYCLE

There is an ever-expanding network of bike paths connecting Singapore's many parks. Search 'Park Connectors' on the website of the **National Parks Board** (www.nparks.gov.sg) for a map of the bike paths.

The 12km bike path along East Coast Park makes for a good ride; hire a decent mountain bike from S$6 at one of the numerous booths here. You can also get in-line skates.

BUS

Public buses run between 6am and midnight. Each bus stop has information on bus numbers and routes. Fares cost S$1 to S$2.10. When you board the bus, tell the driver where you're going, drop the exact money into the fare box (no change given) and collect your ticket. Use Ez-Link cards on all buses for discounted fares. You'll need to tap the card on the card-reader when boarding the bus and again when leaving.

TAXI

The major cab companies are **City Cab** (☑ 6552 1111) and **Comfort** (☑ 6552 1111). Fares start from S$2.80 to S$3.50 for the first kilometre, then 20c for each additional 385m. There are a raft of surcharges, ie late-night services (50%), peak-hour charges (30%), restricted-zone charges, airport pick-ups and bookings. All taxis are metered. Extra charges are always shown on the meter except for going into a restricted zone during peak hours. You can flag down a taxi any time or use a taxi rank outside hotels and malls.

TRAIN

The Mass Rapid Transit (MRT) subway system is the easiest, quickest and most comfortable way to get around. The system operates from 6am to midnight, with trains at peak times running every three minutes, and off-peak every six minutes. Single-trip tickets cost S$1.10 to S$2.70, with a S$1 refundable deposit for every ticket.

TRISHAW

Bicycle trishaws congregate at popular tourist places, such as Raffles Hotel and outside Chinatown Complex. Agree on the fare beforehand. Expect to pay around S$40 for half an hour. There's also a fixed-price trishaw tour system at **Trishaw Uncle** (Map p624; ☑ 6337 7111; www. trishawuncle.com.sg; Queen St btwn Fu Lu Shou Complex & Albert Centre Market; rides from S$39; Ⓜ Bugis).

Thailand

♪ 66 / POP 67.5 MILLION

Best for Regional Specialities

➡ nahm (p665)

➡ Kow Soy Siri Soy (p694)

➡ Larp Khom Huay Poo (p708)

➡ Ging Pagarang (p745)

Best Places for Cultural Connections

➡ Meditation Retreats in Chiang Mai (p691)

➡ Elephant Study Centre (p724)

➡ Ban Kham Pia (p718)

➡ Mae Hong Son (p708)

Why Go?

Lustrous Thailand radiates a hospitality that makes it one of the most accessibly exotic destinations on earth. Its natural landscape is part of the allure: the blonde beaches are lapped at by cerulean seas, while the northern mountains cascade into the misty horizon. In between are emerald-coloured rice fields and busy, prosperous cities built around sacred temples. It is a bountiful land where the markets are piled high with pyramids of colourful fruits and the *rót khĕn* (vendor cart) is an integral piece of a city's infrastructure.

You'll suffer few travelling hardships, save for a few pushy touts, in this land of comfort and convenience. Bangkok reigns as an Asian superstar, Chiang Mai excels in liveability and the tropical islands are up all night to party. It is relatively cheap to hop around by plane and the kingdom provides a gateway to everywhere else in the region – though the fiery curries and simple stir-fries might delay your departure.

When To Go?
Bangkok

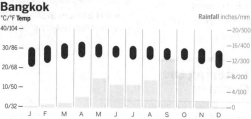

Nov–Feb Cool and dry season; peak tourist season is December to January.

Mar–Jun Hot season is hot but a good shoulder season for the beaches.

Jul–Oct Wet season begins with a drizzle and ends with a downpour; July to August is a mini high season.

⇒ **Currency** Baht (B)

⇒ **Language** Thai

⇒ **Money** ATMs widespread; 150B fee on foreign accounts

⇒ **Visas** 30-day free visa for air arrivals; 30- or 15-day free visa (depending on nationality) for land arrivals; pre-arrange 60-day tourist visas

⇒ **Mobile phones** Pre-pay SIMs from 150B

Fast Facts

⇒ **Area** 513,000 sq km

⇒ **Capital** Bangkok

⇒ **Emergency** ☑191

Exchange Rates

Australia	A$1	29B
Cambodia	10,000r	80B
Euro Zone	€1	45B
Laos	10,000K	41B
Malaysia	RM10	99B
UK	UK£1	54B
US	US$1	33B

Set Your Budget

⇒ **Basic room** US$10–25

⇒ **Market meals** US$1.50–2

⇒ **Beer** US$3

Entering the Country

Fly to Bangkok's Suvarnabhumi Airport, Bangkok. Popular land crossings include Poipet/Aranya Prathet (Cambodia), Huay Xai/ Chiang Khong (Laos) and Ko Lipe/Langkawi (Malaysia).

Don't Miss

Seeing the early-morning alms route – when barefoot, orange-robed monks walk the streets collecting food from the faithful – is one of the great highlights (made easy when suffering from jet-lag) in Thailand. The silent procession transforms Thailand's otherwise deafening cities into calm, meditative spaces.

ITINERARIES

One Week
Get tussled about by Bangkok's chaos, then cruise up to Sukhothai to tour the quiet old ruins. Continue north to Chiang Mai, an easygoing cultural city. Climb up the mountain range to Pai for mountain scenery and bluesy late-nighters.

Two Weeks
From Bangkok, head south to the Samui islands (Ko Samui, Ko Pha-Ngan, Ko Tao) to become a certified beachaholic and diver. Then hop the peninsula to the Andaman beaches of Krabi/Railay, Ko Phi-Phi and Ko Lanta.

Essential Food

⇒ **Pàt gàprow gài** Fiery stir-fry of chopped chicken, chillies, garlic and fresh basil.

⇒ **Kôw pàt** Fried rice, you never knew it could be so good; garnish it with ground chillies, sugar, fish sauce and a squirt of lime.

⇒ **Pàt prík tai krà-thiam gài/mŏo** Stir-fried chicken or pork with black pepper and garlic.

⇒ **Pàt tai** Thailand's oh-so-famous dish of rice noodles fried with egg and prawns garnished with bean sprouts, peanuts and chillies; eaten with chopsticks.

⇒ **Pàt pàk kanáh** Stir-fried Chinese greens, often fried with a meat (upon request), served over rice; simple but delicious.

BANGKOK

POP 8.3 MILLION

Bored in Bangkok? You've got to be kidding. This high-energy city loves neon and noise, chaos and concrete, fashion and the future. But look beyond the modern behemoth and you'll find an old-fashioned village napping in the shade of a narrow *soi* (lane). It's an urban connoisseur's dream: a city where the past, present and future are jammed into a humid pressure cooker.

You'll probably pass through Bangkok en route to some place else as it is a convenient transport hub. At first you'll be confounded, then relieved and pampered when you return, and slightly sentimental when you depart for the last time.

⊙ Sights

The country's most historic and holy sites are found in Ko Ratanakosin, the former royal district. To soak up Bangkok's urban atmosphere, wander around Chinatown. And to escape the heat and congestion, explore Mae Nam Chao Phraya.

⊙ Ko Ratanakosin & Around

With its royal and religious affiliations, this area hosts many Thai Buddhist pilgrims as well as foreign sightseers.

The temples with royal connections enforce a strict dress code – clothes should cover to the elbows and knees and foreigners should not wear open-toed shoes. Behave respectfully and remove shoes when instructed. Do your touring early in the morning to avoid the heat and the crowds. And ignore anyone who says that the sight is closed.

★**Wat Phra Kaew &**
Grand Palace   BUDDHIST TEMPLE, HISTORIC SITE
(วัดพระแก้ว, พระบรมมหาราชวัง; Th Na Phra Lan; admission 500B; ⊙8.30am-4pm; 🚤Tha Chang) Also known as the Temple of the Emerald Buddha, Wat Phra Kaew is Thailand's most important temple representing religion and the mon-

archy and is a pilgrimage site for and nationalists. Attached to the plex is the Grand Palace, the residence.

This ground was consec the first year of Bangkok rule hectare grounds encompass more than 100 buildings that represent 200 years of royal history and architectural experimentation. The resident Buddha is the famous and revered Emerald Buddha, housed in fantastically decorated *bòht* (chapel).

The buildings of the Grand Palace are used only for ceremonial purposes. The largest of the palace buildings is the Chakri Mahaprasat, the Grand Palace Hall. Thai kings housed their huge harems in the inner palace area, which was guarded by combat-trained female sentries.

Admission for the complex includes sameday entrance to Dusit Palace Park. See p652 for our illustrated highlight of the palace.

★**Wat Pho**   BUDDHIST TEMPLE
(วัดโพธิ์ (วัดพระเชตุพน), Wat Phra Chetuphon; Map p656; Th Sanam Chai; admission 100B; ⊙8.30am-6.30pm; 🚤Tha Tien) Wat Pho is a delightful temple to spend a few hours strolling around. The compound incorporates a host of superlatives: the city's largest reclining Buddha, the largest collection of Buddha images in Thailand and the country's earliest centre for public education.

Almost too big for its shelter, the genuinely impressive **Reclining Buddha**, 46m long and 15m high, illustrates the passing of the Buddha into nirvana (ie the Buddha's death). The figure is modelled out of plaster around a brick core and finished in gold leaf. Mother-of-pearl inlay ornaments the feet, displaying 108 different auspicious *lák·sà·nà* (characteristics of a Buddha).

Dating back to Rama III, the temple taught Thai massage and herbal medicine, a tradition that continues today. There are **massage pavilions** (Map p656; Thai massage per hr 420B; ⊙8.30am-6.30pm; 🚤Tha Tien) on the temple grounds and additional facilities at the off-site training centre.

Museum of Siam   MUSEUM
(สถาบันพิพิธภัณฑ์การเรียนรู้แห่งชาติ; Map p656; www.museumsiam.com; Th Maha Rat; admission 300B; ⊙10am-6pm Tue-Sun; 🚤Tha Tien) This fun museum explores the origins of the Thai people and their culture. Housed in a European-style 19th-century building that was once the Ministry of Commerce, the

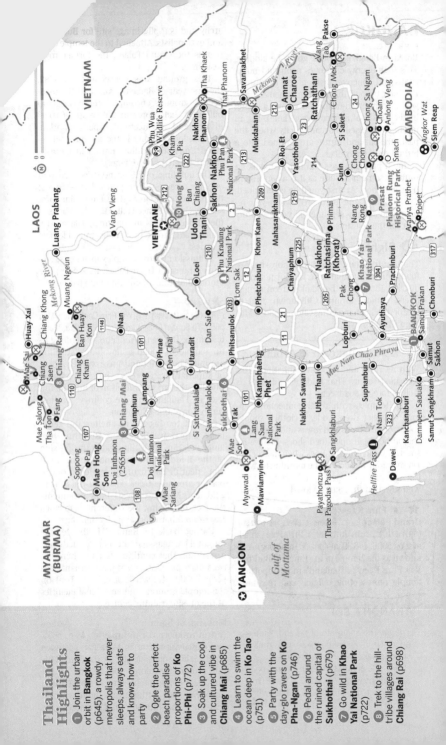

Thailand Highlights

1 Join the urban orbit in **Bangkok** (p645), a rowdy metropolis that never sleeps, always eats and knows how to party

2 Ogle the perfect beach paradise proportions of **Ko Phi-Phi** (p772)

3 Soak up the cool and cultured vibe in **Chiang Mai** (p685)

4 Learn to swim the ocean deep in **Ko Tao** (p751)

5 Party with the day-glo ravers on **Ko Pha-Ngan** (p746)

6 Pedal around the ruined capital of **Sukhothai** (p679)

7 Go wild in **Khao Yai National Park** (p722)

8 Trek to the hill-tribe villages around **Chiang Rai** (p698)

VIETNAM

PHNOM PENH

Psar Pruhm
Pailin
Cham Yeam
Krong Koh Kong
Sihanoukville

Hat Lek
Ko Kut

Pong
Nam Ron
Chanthaburi
Ban Phe
Laem Ngop
Ko Chang National Marine Park

Trat
3

Rayong
Ko Samet

Sattahip

Bang Saphan Yai

Thap Sakae

Prachuap Khiri Khan

Hua Hin

Cha-am
4

Mergui

Gulf of Thailand

Ko Tao
4

5 Ko Pha-Ngan

Ko Samui

Don Sak

Nakhon Si Thammarat

Hua Sai

Ranot
408

Chaiya

Ang Thong Marine National Park

Chumphon

Isthmus of Kra

Ranong

401

Surat Thani
41

Khao Sok National Park

Phang-Nga
Krabi
Ko Yao
Lam Ru National Park

Takua Pa
Khao Lak

Kawthoung

Ko Chang

Laem Son National Park

Surin Islands Marine National Park

Similan Islands Marine National Park

Khao Lak / Lam Ru National Park

Phuket
Ko Phi Phi
Ko Phi Phi Marine National Park

Phang-Nga

Ko Lanta
Ko Muk

Trang
Kuantungku

Phattalung

Songkhla

Hat Yai

Pattani

Kangar
42
Yala
Narathiwat

Sungai Kolok

Satun

Ko Tarutao Marine National Park

Pulau Langkawi

Alor Setar
Kuala Perlis
Padang Besar

Bukit Kayu Hitam
Sadao
4

Betong
Keroh

MALAYSIA

Rantau Panjang
Kota Bharu

Sungai Petani

ANDAMAN SEA

INDIAN OCEAN

Central Bangkok

A

Tha Saphan Krung Thon
Mae Nam
Chao Phraya
Th Khao
Soi 13
Wat Ratchathiwat
Tha Thewet
THEWET
19
National Library
Tha Samphraya
11
Th Phitsanulok
Th Krung Kasem
See Banglamphu Map (p656)

Th Ratchadamnoen Klang

PHAHURAT
Th Charoen Krung
Sampeng Lane
Tha Saphan Phut (Memorial Bridge)
27
CHINATOWN
3
Saphan Phra Phuttha Yot Fa (Memorial Bridge)
Tha Ratchawong
28
Th Somdet Chao Phraya
14
Th Itsaraphap
Tha Marine Department
KHLONG SAN
Tha Si Phraya
Tha Meuang Khae
13
51
Tha Oriental
23
Krung Thonburi
Saphan Taksin
Saphan Taksin
Th Charoen Nakhon
Tha Sathon (Central Pier)

B

SI YAN
Th Nakhon Chaisi
Th Sukhothai
Th Ratchawithi
2
Amphon Park
Dusit Zoo
DUSIT
Wat Benchamabophit
Chitlada Park
Royal Turf Club
Th Nakhon Sawan
Th Lan Luang
Th Bamrung Meuang
Th Luang
Th Mangkon
Th Krung Kasem
Th Charat Muang
Hua Lamphong Train Station
Wat Traimit
1
Hua Lamphong
5 7
TALAT NOI
Th Charoen Krung
Th Maha Nakhon
Th Phra Ram IV
Th Phayathai – Bangkok Expwy
Th Surasak
Surasak
Soi St Louis 3

C

Th Nakhon Chaisi
Samsen
Khlong Prem Pradaphak
Th Phra Ram V
Chitlada Palace
Th Sawankalok
Khlong Samsen
Th Si Ayuthaya
Th Phra Ram VI
Phaya Thai
Ratchaprarop
Ratchathewi
Th Phetchaburi
BAAN KRUA
Sra Pathum Palace
National Stadium
Siam
Th Chulalongkorn
PATHUMWAN
See Siam Square & Pratunam Map (p660)
Sam Yan
BANGRAK
61
Sri Mariamman Temple
66
12
17
Th Silom
73
80
79
22
21
59
65

D

PHAYATHAI
Th Ratchawithi
Victory Monument
Victory Monument
RATCHATHEWI
Th Yothi
Th Si Ayuthaya
Ratchadamri
SILOM
68 78 Si Lom
43 34 55
45
30
10
Sala Daeng
48 76
46
Chong Nonsi
44 58 24
62
SATHON
Th Sathon Tai (South)
Soi Suan Phlui
Soi Ngam Duphli

1
2
3
4
5
6
7

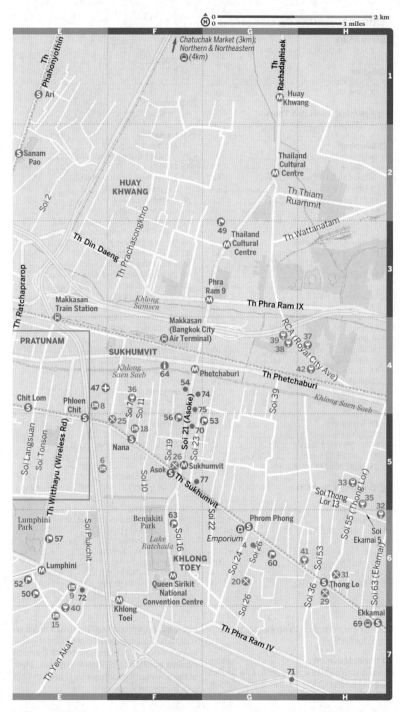

N
0 ——————— 2 km
0 ——————— 1 miles

Chatuchak Market (3km);
Northern & Northeastern
M (4km)

THAILAND

Th Phahonyothin

S Ari

Th Rachadaphisek

M Huay Khwang

S Sanam Pao

Soi 2

HUAY KHWANG

Thailand Cultural Centre

Th Thiam Ruammit

Th Prachasongkhro

Th Din Daeng

49

Thailand Cultural Centre

Th Wattanatam

Phra Ram 9 M

Th Ratchaprarop

Makkasan Train Station

Khlong Samsen

Th Phra Ram IX

RCA (Royal City Ave)

Makkasan (Bangkok City Air Terminal)

37
39 38

PRATUNAM

SUKHUMVIT

64 i

42

Khlong Saen Saeb

M Phetchaburi

Th Phetchaburi

Chit Lom S

Phloen Chit

47

36

54

74

Khlong Saen Saeb

S 8

Soi 7

Soi 11

Soi 39

25

18

56

75
53

Nana

Soi 21 (Asoke)

70

Soi Langsuan

Soi Tonson

Th Witthayu (Wireless Rd)

6

Soi 19

Soi 23

26

Asok S M Sukhumvit

33

35
32

77

Soi 10

Th Sukhumvit

Soi Thong Lor 13

Lumphini Park

57

Soi Phlukchit

Benjakiti Park

63

Phrom Phong

Soi 55 (Thong Lor)

Soi Ekamai 5

Lake Ratchada

Soi 16

Soi 22

Emporium

4

41

53

31

Soi 63 (Ekamai)

M Lumphini

KHLONG TOEY

Soi 24

Soi 26

60

Thong Lo

52

50

9 72

Queen Sirikit National Convention Centre

20

Soi 36

29

40

15

M Khlong Toei

Soi 26

Ekkamai

69

Th Yen Akat

Th Phra Ram IV

71

Central Bangkok

exhibits are presented in an engaging, interactive format.

National Museum MUSEUM
(พิพิธภัณฑสถานแห่งชาติ; Map p656; 4 Th Na Phra That; admission 200B; ☺9am-4pm Wed-Sun; ⓦTha Chang) Thailand's National Museum is home to an impressive collection of religious sculpture, best appreciated on one of the museum's twice-weekly guided **tours** (free with museum admission; ☺9.30am Wed & Thu). Most of the museum's structures were built in 1782 as a minor royal palace.

The history wing contains a succinct chronology of prehistoric, Sukhothai-, Ayuthaya- and Bangkok-era events and figures. Gems include King Ramkamhaeng's inscribed stone pillar, said to be the oldest record of Thai writing; King Taksin's throne; the Rama V section; and the screening of a movie about Rama VII, *The Magic Ring*.

★ Wat Arun BUDDHIST TEMPLE

(วัดอรุณฯ; Map p656; www.watarun.net; off Th Arun Amarin; admission 50B; ⊙ 8am-6pm; ☷ cross-river ferry from Tha Tien) Striking Wat Arun commands a martial pose as the third point in the holy trinity (along with Wat Phra Kaew and Wat Pho) of Bangkok's early history. After the fall of Ayuthaya, King Taksin ceremoniously clinched control here on the site of a local shrine (formerly known as Wat Jaeng) and established a royal palace and a temple to house the Emerald Buddha. The temple was renamed after the Indian god of dawn (Aruna) and in honour of the literal and symbolic founding of a new Ayuthaya.

It wasn't until the capital and the Emerald Buddha were moved to Bangkok that Wat Arun received its most prominent characteristic: the 82m-high *prang* (Khmer-style tower). Ornate floral mosaics made from broken Chinese porcelain decorate the facade.

Cross-river ferries from Tha Tien run over to Wat Arun every few minutes from 6am to 8pm (3B).

Democracy Monument MONUMENT

(อนุสาวรีย์ประชาธิปไตย; Map p656; Th Ratchadamnoen Klang; ⊙ 24hr; ☷ klorng boat to Tha Phan Fah) **FREE** The Democracy Monument is the focal point of the grand, European-style boulevard of Th Ratchadamnoen Klang. It was erected to commemorate Thailand's transformation from absolute to constitutional monarchy. The monument has long been the gathering place for political rallies and protests starting during the military dictatorship era, in 1973 and 1992, and again in the past decade leading up to the 2006 coup and its aftermath. If there is a political gathering at the monument, it is advised to avoid the area as demonstrations can turn violent.

◉ Chinatown & Phahurat

Cramped and crowded Chinatown is a beehive of commercial activity. The main thoroughfare is lined with gleaming gold shops, towering neon signs bearing Chinese characters and bisected by serpentine lanes with shopfronts spilling out onto the [...] The neighbourhood's energy is a [...] hilarating and exhausting. Th Ya[...] fun to explore at night when it is li[...] Christmas tree and filled with food[...]

Talat Mai MARKET

(ตลาดใหม่; Map p648; Soi 6 (Trok Itsaranuphap), Th Yaowarat; ⊙ 6am-6pm; ☷ Tha Ratchawong, Ⓜ Hua Lamphong exit 1 & taxi) With nearly two centuries of commerce under its belt, 'New Market' is no longer an entirely accurate name. Mostly Chinese goods are sold here, and the dried foodstuff, spices and sauces will be familiar to anyone who's ever lived on the mainland. The hectic atmosphere produces a surreal sensory experience. The section north of Th Charoen Krung (equivalent to Soi 21, Th Charoen Krung) is known for selling incense, paper effigies and ceremonial sweets – the essential elements of a traditional Chinese funeral.

★ Wat Traimit BUDDHIST TEMPLE

(วัด ไตรมิตร, Temple of the Golden Buddha; Map p648; Th Mitthaphap (Th Traimit); admission 40B; ⊙ 8am-5pm; ☷ Tha Ratchawong, Ⓜ Hua Lamphong exit 1) The attraction at Wat Traimit is undoubtedly the impressive 3m-tall, 5.5-tonne, solid-gold **Buddha image**, which gleams like, well, gold. Sculpted in the graceful Sukhothai style, the image was 'discovered' some 40 years ago beneath a stucco or plaster exterior, when it fell from a crane while being moved to a new building within the temple compound. It has been theorised that the covering was added to protect it from marauding hordes, either during the late Sukhothai period or later in the Ayuthaya period when the city was under siege by the Burmese. The temple itself is said to date from the early 13th century but recent donations have built an opulent marble structure.

◉ Other Areas

Dusit Palace Park MUSEUM, HISTORIC SITE

(วังสวนดุสิต; Map p648; bounded by Th Ratchawithi, Th U Thong Nai & Th Ratchasima; adult/child 100/20B or free with Grand Palace ticket; ⊙ 9.30am-3.15pm Tue-Sun; ☷ Tha Thewet, Ⓢ Phaya Thai exit 2 & taxi) Following Rama V's first European tour in 1897, he returned home with visions of European castles and Victorian mansions swimming in his head and set about transforming these styles into a uniquely Thai expression that would become the modern (for the time) residence of the monarchy.

t Phra Kaew & Grand Palace

XPLORE BANGKOK'S PREMIER MONUMENTS TO RELIGION AND REGENCY

This tour can be covered in a couple of hours. The first area tourists enter is the Buddhist temple compound generally referred to as Wat Phra Kaew. A covered walkway surrounds the area, the inner walls of which are decorated with the **murals of the *Ramakian* ❶** and **❷**. Originally painted during the reign of Rama I (r 1782-1809), the murals, which depict the Hindu epic the *Ramayana*, span 178 panels that describe the struggles of Rama to rescue his kidnapped wife, Sita.

After taking in the story, pass through one of the gateways guarded by *yaksha* ❸ to the inner compound. The most important structure here is the *bòht*, or ordination hall ❹, which houses the eponymous **Emerald Buddha** ❺.

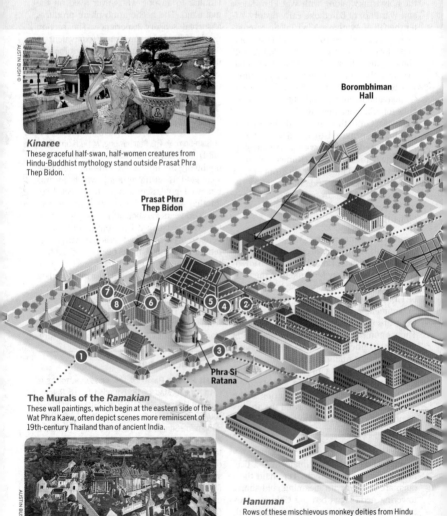

Kinaree
These graceful half-swan, half-women creatures from Hindu-Buddhist mythology stand outside Prasat Phra Thep Bidon.

Borombhiman Hall

Prasat Phra Thep Bidon

Phra Sí Ratana

The Murals of the *Ramakian*
These wall paintings, which begin at the eastern side of the Wat Phra Kaew, often depict scenes more reminiscent of 19th-century Thailand than of ancient India.

Hanuman
Rows of these mischievous monkey deities from Hindu mythology appear to support the lower levels of two small *chedi* near Prasat Phra Thep Bidon.

Head east to the so-called Upper Terrace, an elevated area home to the **spires of the three primary** *chedi* ⑥. The middle structure, Phra Mondop, is used to house Buddhist manuscripts. This area is also home to several of Wat Phra Kaew's noteworthy mythical beings, including beckoning *kinaree* ⑦ and several grimacing **Hanuman** ⑧.

Proceed through the western gate to the compound known as the Grand Palace. Few of the buildings here are open to the public. The most noteworthy structure is **Chakri Mahaprasat** ⑨. Built in 1882, the exterior of the hall is a unique blend of western and traditional Thai architecture.

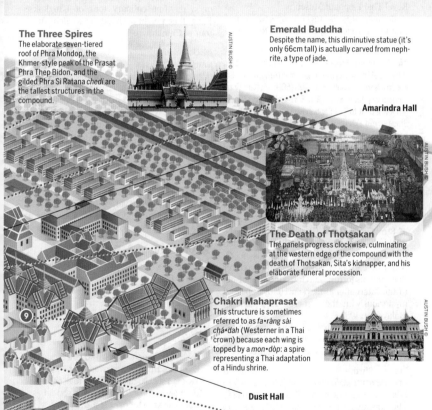

The Three Spires
The elaborate seven-tiered roof of Phra Mondop, the Khmer-style peak of the Prasat Phra Thep Bidon, and the gilded Phra Si Ratana *chedi* are the tallest structures in the compound.

Emerald Buddha
Despite the name, this diminutive statue (it's only 66cm tall) is actually carved from neph-rite, a type of jade.

Amarindra Hall

The Death of Thotsakan
The panels progress clockwise, culminating at the western edge of the compound with the death of Thotsakan, Sita's kidnapper, and his elaborate funeral procession.

Chakri Mahaprasat
This structure is sometimes referred to as *fa·ràng sài chá·dah* (Westerner in a Thai crown) because each wing is topped by a *mon·dòp*: a spire representing a Thai adaptation of a Hindu shrine.

Dusit Hall

Bòht (Ordination Hall)
This structure is an early example of the Ratanakosin school of architecture, which combines traditional stylistic holdovers from Ayuthaya along with more modern touches from China and the West.

Yaksha
Each entrance to the Wat Phra Kaew compound is watched over by a pair of vigilant and enormous *yaksha*, ogres or giants from Hindu mythology.

Today this complex holds a house museum and other cultural collections and the current royal residence has relocated.

Vimanmek Teak Mansion is said to be the world's largest golden-teak building, allegedly built without the use of a single nail. The mansion served as Rama V's residence in the early 1900s. The interior of the mansion contains various personal effects of the king and a treasure trove of early Ratanakosin art objects and antiques. Compulsory tours (in English) leave every half-hour between 9.45am and 3.15pm, and last about an hour.

Other collections include the Ancient Cloth Museum, Abhisek Dusit Throne Hall and the Royal Thai Elephant Museum.

Because this is royal property, visitors should wear clothing that covers to their elbows and knees.

★**Jim Thompson House**   HISTORICAL BUILDING
(Map p660; www.jimthompsonhouse.com; 6 Soi Kasem San 2; adult/child 100/50B; ⊙9am-5pm, compulsory tours in English & French every 20min; 🚤klorng boat to Tha Saphan Hua Chang, 🚇National Stadium exit 1) This tropically landscaped compound is the former home of the eponymous American silk entrepreneur. Six traditional wooden homes – that were rescued from derelict status from the old royal capital of Ayuthaya and from the traditional silk-weaving village across the canal – contain his personal collection of art that will invoke house-envy.

Thompson briefly served in the US Office of Strategic Services (the forerunner to the CIA) in Thailand during WWII. He remained in Bangkok and discovered that his neighbours were expert silk-weavers, an encounter that built his fortune and introduced Thai silk to the international market. He disappeared mysteriously in the Cameron Highlands in Malaysia in 1967.

Beware of well-dressed touts near the entrance who will tell you it is closed and then try to take you on a dodgy buying spree.

Erawan Shrine   MONUMENT
(ศาลพระพรหม; Map p660; cnr Th Ratchadamri & Th Ploenchit; ⊙6am-11pm; 🚇Chit Lom exit 8) FREE
The Erawan Shrine was built in 1956 as something of a last-ditch effort to end a string of misfortunes that occurred during the construction of the hotel, at that time known as the Erawan Hotel. After several incidents, ranging from injured construction workers to the sinking of a ship carrying marble for the hotel, a Brahmin priest was consulted. Since the hotel was to be named after the elephant escort of Indra in Hindu mythology, the priest determined that Erawan required a passenger, and suggested it be that of Lord Brahma. A statue was built, and lo and behold, the misfortunes miraculously ended.

Since then the shrine has become a prominent feature among Bangkok's mystical shrines, granting wishes to the faithful. Classical shrine dances are sometimes commissioned by successful recipients.

👉 Tours

Bangkok Food Tours   WALKING TOUR
(⌨08 9126 3657; www.bangkokfoodtours.com; tours from 850B) Figure out what to eat where on a daytime culinary tour of Bangkok's Bang Rak neighbourhood or a night-time tour of Chinatown.

ABC Amazing Bangkok Cyclists   BICYCLE TOUR
(Map p648; ⌨0 2665 6364; www.realasia.net; 10/5-7 Soi Aree, Soi 26, Th Sukhumvit; tours from 1300B; ⊙daily tours at 8am, 10am, 1pm & 6pm; 🚇Phrom Phong exit 4) A long-running operation offering bike tours of Bangkok and its suburbs.

Grasshopper Adventures   BICYCLE TOUR
(Map p656; ⌨0 2280 0832; www.grasshopperadventures.com; 57 Th Ratchadamnoen Klang; half-day tours from 1100B, full-day tours from 1600B; ⊙9am-6pm; 🚤klorng boat to Tha Phan Fah) This lauded outfit runs a variety of unique bicycle tours in and around Bangkok, including a night tour and a tour of the city's green zones.

🎊 Festivals & Events

Chinese New Year   NEW YEAR
(⊙Jan or Feb) Thai-Chinese celebrate the lunar New Year with a week of housecleaning,

---

BANGKOK BY WATER

You can observe remnants of urban river life by boarding a **Chao Phraya Express boat** at any riverside pier. Women should take care not to accidentally bump into a monk and should not sit next to them or stand in the same area of the boat.

You can also charter a longtail boat to explore **Khlong Bangkok Noi** and other scenic canals in Thonburi. Longtail boats can be arranged from any river pier, including Tha Chang. Just remember to negotiate a price before departure.

lion dances and fireworks. Most festivities centre on Chinatown. Dates vary.

Songkran
NEW YEAR

(☺mid-Apr) The celebration of the Thai New Year has morphed into a water war with high-powered water guns and water balloons being launched at suspecting and un-suspecting participants. The most intense battles take place on Th Khao San. Held in mid-April.

Royal Ploughing Ceremony
PLANTING CEREMONY

(☺May) The Crown Prince commences rice-planting season with a ceremony at Sanam Luang. Held in May; dates vary.

Vegetarian Festival
FOOD

(☺Sep or Oct) A 10-day Chinese-Buddhist festival wheels out yellow-bannered streetside vendors serving meatless meals. The greatest concentration of vendors is found in Chinatown. Dates vary.

Loi Krathong
FULL MOON

(www.loikrathong.net/en; ☺early Nov) A beautiful festival where, on the night of the full moon, small lotus-shaped boats made of banana leaf and containing a lit candle are set adrift on Mae Nam Chao Phraya. Held in early November.

Krating Daeng Fat Fest
MUSIC

(www.facebook.com/fatradio; ☺early Nov) Sponsored by FAT 104.5FM radio, Bangkok's indie-est indie bands gather for an annual fest. Held in early November.

🛏 Sleeping

Because the city has legendary traffic jams, narrow your search first by the geographic area that best suits your needs. If you're in the city for a layover, stay as close to your next mode of transport as possible.

🛏 Th Khao San, Banglamphu & Thewet

If you're returning to 'civilisation' and need traveller amenities, then the backpacker ghetto of Th Khao San and surrounding Banglamphu is cheap and convenient. The area is packed with guesthouses and hostels. Quieter and more charming enclaves are on Th Ram Buttri and on the numbered *soi* off Th Samsen. Th Si Ayuthaya, in Thewet, the district north of Banglamphu near the National Library, is a pleasant backpacker enclave, particularly popular with families and the over-30 crowd.

NapPark Hostel
HOSTEL $

(Map p656; ☑0 2282 2324; www.nappark.com; 5 Th Tani; dm 570-750B; ❄@🛜; 🚤Tha Phra Athit (Banglamphu)) This well-run hostel features dorm rooms of various sizes, all of which boast podlike beds outfitted with power points, mini-TV, reading lamp and wi-fi. Hyper-social communal areas ensure personal, not device, connections.

Fortville Guesthouse
HOTEL $

(Map p656; ☑0 2282 3932; www.fortvilleguesthouse.com; 9 Th Phra Sumen; r 790-1120B; ❄@🛜; 🚤Tha Phra Athit (Banglamphu)) The rooms here are stylishly minimal, and the more expensive ones include perks such as fridge, balcony and five hours of free wi-fi.

Wild Orchid Villa
HOTEL $

(Map p656; ☑0 2629 4378; www.wildorchidvilla.com; 8 Soi Chana Songkhram; r 600-1500B; ❄🛜; 🚤Tha Phra Athit (Banglamphu)) The cheapies here are some of the tiniest we've seen anywhere, but all rooms are clean and neat, and come in a bright, friendly package. Wild Orchid is popular, so it's best to book ahead.

Khaosan Baan Thai
GUESTHOUSE $

(Map p648; ☑0 2628 5559; www.khaosanbaanthai.com; 11/1 Soi 3, Th Samsen; r incl breakfast 390-730B; ❄@🛜; 🚤Tha Phra Athit (Banglamphu)) This cutesy wooden house holds 10 simple rooms decked out in bright pastels and hand-painted bunny pictures. Half of the rooms are fan-cooled, and all have little more than a mattress on the floor. But it has an authentic homey vibe.

Suneta Hostel Khaosan
HOSTEL $

(Map p656; ☑0 2629 0150; www.sunetahostel.com; 209-211 Th Kraisi; incl breakfast dm 440-590B, r 900-1090B; ❄@🛜; 🚤Tha Phra Athit (Banglamphu)) This hostel gets rave reviews for its retro-themed design, comfy and thoughtful dorms and friendly service.

Taewez Guesthouse
HOTEL $

(Map p648; ☑0 2280 8856; www.taewez.com; 23/12 Th Si Ayuthaya; r 390-820B; ❄@🛜; 🚤Tha Thewet) Popular with French travellers, the cheapest rooms here are plain and share bathrooms, but are good value.

Rambuttri Village Inn
HOSTEL $$

(Map p656; ☑0 2282 9162; www.rambuttrivillage.com; 95 Soi Ram Buttri; r incl breakfast 1030-1600B; ❄🛜❄; 🚤Tha Phra Athit (Banglamphu)) If you're

Banglamphu

Santichaiprakan
Park

Tha Phra Athit
(Banglamphu)

Th Phra Athit

Tha Saphan
Phra Pin Klao

Saphan Phra
Pin Klao

18

16
Soi Ram Buttri

Bangkok
Information
Center

Th Chao Fa

Th Somdet Phra Pin Klao

Th Rongmai

Bangkok Noi
Train Station

Khlong
Bangkok Noi

Tha Rot
Fai

Mae Nam Chao Phraya

THONBURI

29

Siriraj
Hospital

6

Tha Phra
Chan

Thammasat
University

Th Na Phra That

Sanam
Luang

Th
Phrannok

Tha Wang
Lang (Siriraj)

Th Phra Chan

Th Ratchadamnoen Nai

Tha
Maharaj

Soi Tambon
Wanglang 1

9

Th Maha Rat

BANGKOK
NOI

Tha Wat
Rakhang

Silpakorn
University

Tha
Chang

Th Na Phra Lan

4

Th Lak
Meuang

Th Sanam Chai

Mae Nam Chao Phraya

Th Maha Rat

KO RATANAKOSIN

Saranrom
Royal
Garden

Khlong Mon

Th Arun Amarin

Th Thai Wang

2

8

Wat Pho

Tha Tien

Soi Pratu
Nokyung

21

Th Chetuphon

Tha Wat
Arun

Soi Phen
Phat

5

1

Wat Arun

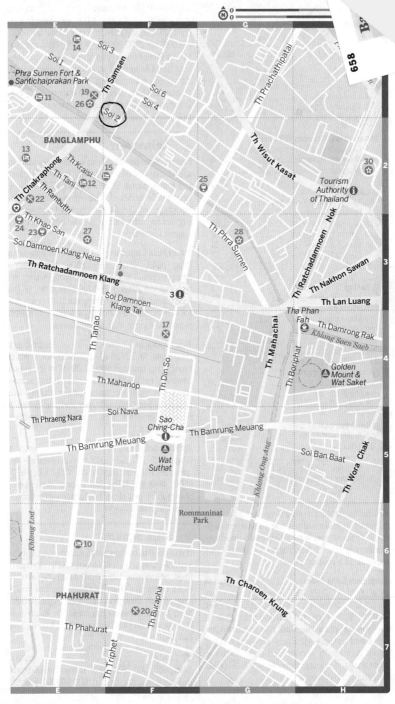

willing to subject yourself to the relentless gauntlet of tailors along the path approaching it ('Excuse me, suit?'), this plain and busy midranger has an abundance of good-value rooms and a rooftop pool.

Sam Sen Sam Place　　　　GUESTHOUSE $$
(Map p656; ☑0 2628 7067; www.samsensam.com; 48 Soi 3, Th Samsen; r incl breakfast 590-2500B; ❋ @ 🛜; ⊜ Tha Phra Athit (Banglamphu)) One of the homiest places around, this colourful, refurbished antique villa gets glowing reports about its friendly service and quiet location. Note that the cheapest rooms are fan-cooled and share a bathroom.

Feung Nakorn Balcony　　　　HOTEL $$
(Map p656; ☑0 2622 1100; www.feungnakorn. com; 125 Th Fuang Nakhon; incl breakfast dm 600B, r 1650B, ste 2000-3000B; ❋ @ 🛜; ⊜ klorng boat to Tha Phan Fah) A charming place to stay, this hotel is located in a former school with 42 rooms surrounding a garden courtyard. Rooms are large, bright and cheery, if slightly institutional. It has a quiet and secluded location away from the strip.

⌂ Chinatown

Hotels near the Hualamphong train station are cheap but not especially interesting and the traffic along Th Phra Ram IV has to be heard to be believed. The surrounding neighbourhood of Chinatown makes for fascinating urban adventures but is not especially geared for tourists.

Baan Hua Lampong　　　　GUESTHOUSE $
(Map p648; ☑08 3323 6806; www.baanhua lampong.com; 336/20-21 Trok Chalong Krung; incl breakfast dm 220B, r 290-700B; ❋ @ 🛜; ⊜ Tha Ratchawong, Ⓜ Hua Lamphong exit 1) Repeat visitors rave about the homey setting and warm, personal service at this guesthouse.

Siam Classic　　　　GUESTHOUSE $
(Map p648; ☑0 2639 6363; 336/10 Trok Chalong Krung; r incl breakfast 500-1200B; ❋ @ 🛜; Ⓜ Hua Lamphong exit 1) This homey place is just across the street from the train station. Rooms are relatively bare, but tidy. An inviting ground-floor communal area encourages meeting and chatting.

@Hua Lamphong　　　　HOSTEL $
(Map p648; ☑0 2639 1925; www.at-hualamphong. com; 326/1 Th Phra Ram IV; dm 400-450B, r 690-950B; ❋ @ 🛜; ⊜ Tha Ratchawong, Ⓜ Hua Lamphong) Plain but clean hostel across the street from the train station.

⌂ Siam Square

If you need to be centrally located, then opt for Siam Square, which is on both BTS (Skytrain) lines. Accommodation in Siam Square is more expensive than Banglamphu but you'll save in cab fare. You can also bypass rush-hour traffic between here and Th Khao San by hopping on the *klorng* (canal) taxi at Tha Ratchathewi.

★Lub*d　　　　HOSTEL $
(Map p660; ☑0 2634 7999; siamsquare.lubd.com; Th Phra Ram I; dm 750B, r 1800-2400B; ❋ @ 🛜;

S National Stadium exit 1) The title is a play on *làp dee,* meaning 'sleep well', but the fun atmosphere at this backpacker hostel encourages late nights. There are 14 dorms (including ladies-only rooms), each with four beds, and a few private rooms, both with and without bathrooms. If this one's full, there's another **branch** (Map p648; ☑ 0 2634 7999; silom. lubd.com; 4 Th Decho; dm 550-650B, r 1400-1800B; ✳ @ 🛜; S Chong Nonsi exit 2) just off Th Silom.

Wendy House   HOSTEL $$
(Map p660; ☑ 0 2214 1149; www.wendyguesthouse. com; 36/2 Soi Kasem San 1; r incl breakfast 1100-1490B; ✳ @ 🛜; S National Stadium exit 1) Wendy is a cheery place with small, basic rooms.

Sukhumvit

Th Sukhumvit is a high-end international neighbourhood that isn't the most budget-friendly crash pad. But it is near the Eastern (Ekamai) bus station and on the BTS and MRT lines; the MRT links to the Hualamphong train station. Be warned that the lower-numbered *soi* attract sex tourists visiting the nearby go-go bars.

Suk 11   HOTEL $
(Map p648; ☑ 0 2253 5927; www.suk11.com; 1/33 Soi 11, Th Sukhumvit; r incl breakfast 500-1600B; ✳ @ 🛜; S Nana exit 3) Extremely well run and equally popular, this rambling building is a green oasis in the urban jungle. The cheaper rooms have shared bathrooms. Advance bookings recommended.

Bed Bangkok   HOSTEL $
(Map p648; ☑ 0 2655 7604; www.bedbangkok.com; 11/20 Soi 1, Th Sukhumvit; dm 390B, r 800-1200B; ✳ @ 🛜; S Phloen Chit exit 3) This hostel manages to be cosy despite the industrial design. The friendly service makes up for the rather hard dorm beds.

Atlanta   HOTEL $
(Map p648; ☑ 0 2252 1650; www.theatlantahotel bangkok.com; 78 Soi 2, Th Sukhumvit; incl breakfast r 690-800B, ste 950-1950B; ✳ @ 🛜 ⍻; S Nana exit 2) The perfectly preserved midcentury lobby, complete with old-fashioned writing desks and a grand staircase, is a charming time capsule. Unfortunately, the simple rooms (the cheapest of which are fan-cooled) don't live up to the standard set by the lobby. But the pool and the restaurant (guests only) provide perks for paupers. Note: the Atlanta is forthright about not welcoming sex tourists.

Silom, Lumphini & Riverside

The financial district around Th Silom has a handful of budget hostels, though the neighbourhood is mainly for bigger budgets. The bonus is that the MRT links with the Hualamphong train station. The old backpacker hood near Lumphini Park has some cheapies too.

Silom Art Hostel   HOSTEL $
(Map p648; ☑ 0 2635 8070; www.silomarthostel. com; 198/19-22 Soi 14, Th Silom; dm 400-550B, r 1200-1500B; ✳ @ 🛜; S Chong Nonsi exit 3) Bright and fun, Silom Art Hostel combines recycled materials, bizarre furnishings and colourful wall paintings to create a unique and artsy home-away-from-home. Beds and rooms are functional and comfortable, with lots of communal areas.

HQ Hostel   HOSTEL $
(Map p648; ☑ 0 2233 1598; www.hqhostel.com; 5/3-4 Soi 3, Th Silom; dm 380-730B, r 1300-1700B; ✳ @ 🛜; M Si Lom exit 2, S Sala Daeng exit 2) A flashpacker hostel combines basic but stylish private rooms and dorms with inviting communal areas, smack dab in the middle of Bangkok's financial district.

River View Guest House   HOTEL $
(Map p648; ☑ 0 2234 5429; www.riverviewbkk.com; 768 Soi Phanurangsi, Th Songwat; dm 250B, r 400-1500B; ✳ 🛜; ⍿ Tha Marine Department) After 20 years, this budget staple is finally receiving a much-needed renovation. To get there, heading north on Th Charoen Krung from

---

SLEEPING NEAR THE AIRPORT

If you're still in transit and don't want to bed in central Bangkok, there are more and more options on the eastern outskirts of town within striking distance of the Suvarnabhumi International Airport.

Refill Now! (☑ 0 2713 2044; www.refill now.co.th; 191 Soi Pridi Bhanom Yong 42, Soi 71, Th Sukhumvit; dm 325B, r 899-2077B; ✳ @ 🛜 ⍻; S Phra Khanong exit 3 & taxi) The closest, cheapest, and chicest hostel near the airport.

Grand Inn Come Hotel (☑ 0 2738 8189; www.grandinncome-hotel.com; 99 Moo 6, Th Kingkaew; r 1400-2300B, ste 4500-5000B; ✳ @ 🛜) Solid midranger, 10km from the airport, with airport shuttle.

Siam Square & Pratunam

THAILAND

Th Phetchaburi

Ratchathewi S

Soi 15

Soi 17

9

Pantip
Plaza

Th Phayathai

**Jim
Thompson
House**
1

Tha Saphan
Hua Chang

Soi Kasem San 2

4

Soi Kasem San 1

Sra
Pathum
Palace

Siam
Kempinski
Hotel

3

Bangkok Art
& Culture
Centre

Siam
Discovery
Center

6

**National
Stadium**

S

8

Siam
Center

5

Siam
S

Wat
Patum

Th Phra Ram I

**SIAM
SQUARE**

Soi 2

Soi 3

Siam
Square

Soi 4

Soi 5

Soi 6

7

British
Council

Soi 11

Soi 7

Soi Chulalongkorn 64

Th Henri Dunant

Th Chulalongkorn

Th Phayathai

PATHUMWAN

Royal Bangkok
Sports Club

Chulalongkorn
University

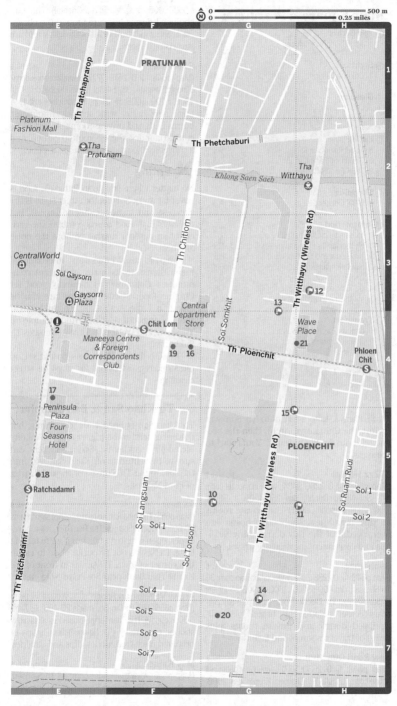

THAILAND

Siam Square & Pratunam

Th Si Phraya, take a left onto Th Songwat (before the Chinatown Arch), then the second left onto Soi Phanurangsi. You'll start to see signs.

ETZzz Hostel   HOSTEL $
(Map p648; ☑ 0 2286 9424; www.etzhostel.com; 5/3 Soi Ngam Duphli; dm 250-450B, r 900B; ❇ @ 🛜; Ⓜ Lumphini exit 1) The private rooms at this brand-new shophouse hostel are overpriced, but the tidy dorm, shiny facilities and convenient location are draws.

Saphaipae   HOSTEL $
(Map p648; ☑ 0 2238 2322; www.saphaipae.com; 35 Th Surasak; dm 400-550B, r 1800-2500B; ❇ @ 🛜; Ⓢ Surasak exit 1) Decked out in a playful primary colour palette, this hostel has well-equipped dorms and private rooms, plus heaps of travel resources and facilities.

New Road Guesthouse   HOSTEL $
(Map p648; ☑ 0 2630 9371; www.newroadguest house.com; 1216/1 Th Charoen Krung; dm 250B,

r 550-1600B; ❇ @ 🛜; Ⓔ Tha Oriental) The fan-equipped dorms here are among the cheapest accommodation in all of Bangkok and are surprisingly clean.

S1 Hostel   HOSTEL $
(Map p648; ☑ 0 2679 7777; www.facebook.com/S1hostelBangkok; 35/1-4 Soi Ngam Duphli; dm 330-380B, r 700-1300B; ❇ @ 🛜; Ⓜ Lumphini exit 1) A huge new hostel with stylishly minimalist dorms beds and private rooms. A host of facilities (laundry, kitchen, rooftop garden) and a convenient location make it great value.

✕ Eating

No matter where you go in Bangkok, food is never far away. Surfing the street stalls is the cheapest and tastiest culinary pursuit, but the city's mall food courts combine the variety of an outdoor market without the noise and heat.

Bangkok also offers an international menu thanks to its many immigrant communities. Chinatown is naturally good for Chinese food; Middle Eastern fare can be found in Little Arabia, off Th Sukhumvit; Indian hangs out near the Hindu temple on Th Silom; and Western cuisine dominates Th Sukhumvit.

Do note that food vendors do not set up on Mondays, ostensibly for citywide street cleaning.

✕ Th Khao San & Banglamphu

Th Khao San is lined with restaurants, but the prices tend to be higher and the quality incredibly inauthentic. Serial snackers can survive by venturing off Khao San and into the *soi* around Th Samsen or the old district of Phra Nakhon.

Pa Aew   THAI $
(Map p656; Th Maha Rat, no roman-script sign; mains 20-60B; ☺ 10am-5pm; Ⓔ Tha Tien) Yes, it's a bare-bones, open-air curry stall, but if we're talking taste, Pa Aew is our favourite place to eat in this corner of town. Pa Aew is in front of the Krung Thai Bank near Soi Pratu Nokyung.

Arawy Vegetarian Food   VEGETARIAN, THAI $
(Map p656; 152 Th Din So; mains 20-40B; ☺ 7am-8.30pm; ☑; Ⓔ Tha Phan Fah) Housed in a narrow shophouse, Arawy ('Delicious') has heaps of prepared meat-free curries, dips and stir-fries

May Kaidee's   VEGETARIAN, THAI $
(Map p656; www.maykaidee.com; 33 Th Samsen; mains 50-100B; ☺ 9am-10pm; ☑; Ⓔ Tha Phra

Athit (Banglamphu)) A longstanding restaurant that also houses a vegie Thai cooking school.

Shoshana   ISRAELI **$$**
(Map p656; 88 Th Chakraphong; mains 70-240B; ⊙10am-midnight; 🚲; 🚤Tha Phra Athit (Banglamphu)) One of Khao San's longest-running Israeli restaurants, Shoshana does gut-filling chips-falafel-and-hummus plates that leave nothing to be desired.

Hemlock   THAI **$$**
(Map p656; 56 Th Phra Athit; mains 75-280B; ⊙4pm-midnight Mon-Sat; 🚲; 🚤Tha Phra Athit (Banglamphu)) This perennial favourite has enough style to feel like a special night out but doesn't skimp on flavour or indulge in price. The menu does the usual suspects with some surprises.

🍴 Chinatown

Old Siam Plaza   THAI SWEETS **$**
(Map p656; cnr Th Phahurat & Th Triphet; mains 30-90B; ⊙6am-7pm; 🚤Tha Saphan Phut (Memorial Bridge)) Sugar junkies, be sure to include this stop on your Bangkok eating itinerary. The ground floor of this shopping centre is a candy land of traditional Thai sweets and snacks, most made right before your eyes.

Samsara   JAPANESE, THAI **$$**
(Map p648; 1612 Th Songwat; mains 110-320B; ⊙4pm-midnight Tue-Thu, to 1am Fri-Sun; 🚲; 🚤Tha Ratchawong, Ⓜ Hua Lamphong exit 1 & taxi) Combining Japanese-Thai dishes, Belgian beers and a retro/artsy atmosphere, Samsara is easily Chinatown's most eclectic place to eat. The generous riverside breezes and views simply add to the package. The restaurant is at the end of tiny Soi Khang Wat Pathum Khongkha, just west of the temple.

Royal India   INDIAN **$$**
(Map p648; 392/1 Th Chakraphet; mains 70-195B; ⊙10am-10pm; 🚲; 🚤Tha Saphan Phut (Memorial Bridge)) A windowless dining room of 10 tables in a dark alley may not be everybody's ideal lunch destination, but this legendary North Indian place continues its decades-long reign. Try any of the delicious breads or curries, and finish with a homemade Punjabi sweet.

🍴 Siam Square

Mall food courts, which are better than you would expect, are this neighbourhood's primary food troughs.

★MBK Food Island   THAI **$**
(Map p660; 6th fl, MBK Center, cnr Th Phra Ram I & Th Phayathai; mains 35-150B; ⊙10am-10pm; 🚲; Ⓢ National Stadium exit 4) The granddaddy of the genre, MBK's expansive food court offers vendors selling dishes from virtually every corner of Thailand and beyond. Exchange cash for a card and head for the tasty vegetarian food stall (stall C8) or the decent northeastern Thai food vendor (C22). Any money you don't use can be refunded at another desk.

Gourmet Paradise   THAI **$**
(Map p660; ground fl, Siam Paragon, 991/1 Th Phra Ram I; mains 35-500B; ⊙10am-10pm; Ⓢ Siam exits 3 & 5) The perpetually busy Gourmet Paradise unites international fast-food chains, domestic restaurants and food court–style stalls, with a particular emphasis on the sweet stuff.

Food Republic   INTERNATIONAL **$**
(Map p660; 4th fl, Siam Center, cnr Th Phra Ram I & Th Phayathai; mains 30-200B; ⊙10am-10pm; 🚲; Ⓢ Siam exit 1) The city's newest food court has a good mix of Thai and international (mostly Asian) outlets, all in an open, modern-feeling locale. We particularly fancied the Thai-Muslim dishes at the stall called 'Curry Rice'.

🍴 Sukhumvit

Fine dining is Sukhumvit's strong suit but you can find a few modest places too.

Soi 38 Night Market   THAI **$**
(Map p648; cnr Soi 38 & Th Sukhumvit; mains 30-60B; ⊙8pm-3am; Ⓢ Thong Lo exit 4) This late-night market does basic Thai-Chinese standards for the post-drinking crowd.

Muslim Restaurant   MUSLIM, THAI **$**
(Map p648; 1354-6 Th Charoen Krung; mains 40-140B; ⊙6.30am-5.30pm; 🚤Tha Oriental, Ⓢ Saphan Taksin exit 1) Plant yourself in any random wooden booth of this ancient eatery for a glimpse into what Bangkok restaurants used to be like. The menu, much like the interior design, doesn't appear to have changed much in the restaurant's 70-year history, and the biryanis, curries and samosas are still more Indian-influenced than Thai.

Pier 21   THAI **$**
(Map p648; 5th fl, Terminal 21, cnr Th Sukhumvit & Soi 21 (Asoke); mains 39-200B; ⊙10am-10pm; 🚲; Ⓜ Sukhumvit exit 3, Ⓢ Asok exit 3) Ascend a seemingly endless number of escalators to arrive at this buzzy food court made up

from vendors across the city. The selection is vast and the dishes are exceedingly cheap, even by Thai standards.

Nasir Al-Masri
MIDDLE EASTERN $$$

(Map p648; 4/6 Soi 3/1, Th Sukhumvit; mains 160-370B; ⊙24hr; 🖉; S Nana exit 1) This popular Egyptian joint simply can't be missed (so much stainless steel). This is Muslim food, with an emphasis on meat and more meat, but the kitchen also pulls off some brilliant vegie meze as well. Enhance your postprandial digestion with a hookah in the streetside patio.

Soul Food Mahanakorn
THAI $$$

(Map p648; 🖉0 2714 7708; www.soulfoodmahanakorn.com; 56/10 Soi 55 (Thong Lor), Th Sukhumvit; mains 220-300B; ⊙5.30pm-midnight; 🖉; S Thong Lo exit 3) Soul Food remains top of the restaurant heap thanks to its dual nature as both a restaurant – the menu features upscale takes on rustic Thai dishes – and a bar serving deliciously boozy, Thai-influenced cocktails. Reservations recommended.

Bo.lan
THAI $$$

(Map p648; 🖉0 2260 2962; www.bolan.co.th; 42 Soi Rongnarong Phichai Songkhram, Soi 26, Th Sukhumvit; set dinner 1980B; ⊙6pm-midnight Tue-Sun; S Phrom Phong exit 4) Upscale Thai is usually more garnish than flavour, but Bo.lan, started up by two former chefs of London's Michelin-starred nahm, is the exception. Reservations recommended.

Riverside, Silom & Lumphini

Bangkok's financial district does a bustling lunchtime business. The Muslim and Indian restaurants, offshoots of their respective ethnic enclaves, are worth an evening outing.

Chennai Kitchen
INDIAN $

(Map p648; 10 Th Pan; mains 70-150B; ⊙10am-3pm & 6-9pm; 🖉; S Surasak exit 3) This thimble-sized restaurant near the Hindu temple does solid southern Indian vegetarian food. Yard-long *dosai* (a crispy southern Indian bread) is always a good choice, or opt for

---

OUTSMARTING THE SCAM ARTISTS

Commit these classic rip-offs to memory and join us in our ongoing crusade to outsmart Bangkok's scam artists.

Closed today Ignore any 'friendly' local who tells you that an attraction is closed for a Buddhist holiday or for cleaning. These are set-ups for trips to a bogus gem sale or shopping.

Túk-túk rides for 10B Say goodbye to your day's itinerary if you climb aboard this ubiquitous scam. These 'tours' bypass the sights and instead cruise to the overpriced tailor and gem shops that pay commissions.

Flat-fare taxi ride Flatly refuse any driver who quotes a flat fare, which will usually be three times more than the meter rate. Head out to the street and flag down a cab. If the driver 'forgets' to turn on the meter, just say, 'Meter, *kâ/kráp*'.

Long-distance tourist buses Buy your long-distance bus tickets from the government-run bus stations instead of tourist-centre agents selling private tourist bus tickets. Sometimes agents will inflate their commission fees or charge for VIP service but deliver cut-rate vehicles. Readers have consistently reported thefts from personal bags and stowed luggage from private buses.

Bus-boat combination tickets A popular way for getting to the islands is to buy one of these combo tickets; just double-check that you've got both a bus and boat ticket as you'll be left on dry land without proof of payment for the second leg of the journey. Also buy from a reputable company.

Friendly strangers Be wary of smartly dressed locals who approach you asking where you're from and where you're going. Their opening gambit is usually followed with: 'Ah, my son/daughter is studying at university in (your city)'. This sort of behaviour is out of character for Thais and is usually a prelude for the notorious gem scam.

Unset Gems Bangkok is no place to be an amateur gem trader. Never accept an invitation to visit a gem shop and refuse to purchase unset stones that can supposedly be resold in your home country.

the banana-leaf *thali* that incorporates just about everything in the kitchen.

Somtam Convent
NORTHEASTERN THAI **$**
(Hai; Map p648; 2/4-5 Th Convent; mains 30-100B; ⊙11am-9pm Mon-Fri, to 5pm Sat; Ⓜ Si Lom exit 2, Ⓢ Sala Daeng exit 2) Northeastern Thai food is usually relegated to less-than-hygienic stalls perched by the side of the road with no menu or English-speaking staff. But this is a less intimidating introduction to the wonders of *lâhp* (a minced meat 'salad') *sôm đam* and other Isan dishes.

Bonita Cafe & Social Club
VEGETARIAN **$$**
(Map p648; 56/3 Th Pan; mains 160-250B; ⊙11am-10pm Wed-Mon; 🛜 🖉; Ⓢ Surasak exit 3) Resembling grandma's living room, this restaurant serves vegan and raw, mostly Western-style dishes.

★nahm
THAI **$$$**
(Map p648; 🖉 0 2625 3388; www.comohotels.com/metropolitanbangkok/dining/nahm; ground fl, Metropolitan Hotel, 27 Th Sathon Tai (South); set lunch 1100B, set dinner 2000B, mains 180-700B; ⊙noon-2pm Mon-Fri, 7-10.30pm daily; Ⓜ Lumphini exit 2) Australian chef-author David Thompson is behind what is quite possibly the best Thai restaurant in Bangkok. Dinner takes the form of a multicourse set meal, while lunch means *kà·nŏm jeen*, thin rice noodles served with curries. If you're expecting bland, gentrified Thai food, prepare to be disappointed. Reservations recommended.

🍷 Drinking & Nightlife

Most backpackers are pleased to find that the party finds them on Th Khao San, where night-time equals the right time for a drink. If you feel like a wander there are hip watering holes sprinkled throughout the city.

Bangkok's curfew (midnight to 1am for bars, 2am for clubs) is strictly enforced, though there are always loopholes. Smoking is banned from all indoor bars and clubs and some open-air places as well.

Cover charges for clubs range from 100B to 800B and usually include a drink or two. Most clubs heat up after 11pm; bring your ID.

Bangkok's party people are fickle and dance clubs are used up like tissues. To chase down the crowds check out **Bangkok Invaders** (www.facebook.com/the.bangkok.invaders), **Club Soma** (www.facebook.com/clubsomaparty) or **Dudesweet** (www.dudesweet.org), which organise popular monthly parties.

★WTF
BAR
(Map p648; www.wtfbangkok.com; 7 Soi 51, Th Sukhumvit; ⊙6pm-1am Tue-Sun; Ⓢ Thong Lo exit 3) No, not that WTF – Wonderful Thai Friendship is a bar-cum-gallery. Old-school cocktails, live music and DJ events, poetry readings, art exhibitions and tasty bar snacks attract an equally eclectic crowd.

Center Khao Sarn
BAR
(Map p656; Th Khao San; ⊙24hr; 🚤 Tha Phra Athit (Banglamphu)) One of many front-row views of the human parade on Th Khao San. The upstairs bar hosts late-night bands.

Hippie de Bar
BAR
(Map p656; www.facebook.com/hippie.debar; 46 Th Khao San; ⊙3pm-2am; 🚤 Tha Phra Athit (Banglamphu)) Popular with locals, Hippie boasts a funky retro vibe, indoor and outdoor seating, and a soundtrack you're unlikely to hear elsewhere in town.

Rolling Bar
BAR
(Map p656; Th Prachathipatai; ⊙5pm-midnight; 🚤 klorng boat to Tha Phan Fah) An escape from hectic Th Khao San is a good-enough excuse to schlep to this quiet canal-side boozer. Live music and capable bar snacks are good reasons to stay.

Cheap Charlie's
BAR
(Map p648; Soi 11, Th Sukhumvit; ⊙4.30-11.45pm Mon-Sat; Ⓢ Nana exit 3) There's never enough seating and the design concept can be diplomatically described as 'junkyard' but it is a perennially chummy beer corner.

Wong's Place
BAR
(Map p648; 27/3 Soi Si Bamphen; ⊙9pm-late Tue-Sun; Ⓜ Lumphini exit 1) An odd choice for an institution, this dusty den is a time warp into the backpacker world of the early 1980s. The namesake owner died several years ago, but a relative removed the padlock and picked up where Wong left off. Wong's works equally well as a destination or a last resort, but don't bother knocking until midnight, and it stays open until the last person crawls out.

Badmotel
BAR
(Map p648; www.facebook.com/badmotel; Soi 55 (Thong Lor), Th Sukhumvit; ⊙5pm-1.30am; Ⓢ Thong Lo exit 3 & taxi) The new Badmotel combines the modern and the cosmopolitan, and the kitschy and the Thai, in a way that has formed a devout Bangkok hipster following. Hale's Blue Boy, a Thai childhood drink staple, is served with rum, and *'naam*

prik ong' a northern-style dip, is served with pappadum.

Iron Fairies
BAR
(Map p648; www.theironfairies.com; 394 Soi 55 (Thong Lor),Th Sukhumvit; ⊙6pm-2am; ⑤Thong Lo exit 3 & taxi) Imagine, if you can, an abandoned fairy factory in Paris c 1912, and you'll begin to get an idea of the vibe at this popular pub/wine bar. If you manage to wangle one of a handful of seats, you can test its claim of serving Bangkok's best burgers. There's live music after 9.30pm.

RCA
NIGHTCLUB
(Royal City Avenue; Map p648; Royal City Ave, off Th Phra Ram IX; Ⓜ Phra Ram 9 exit 3 & taxi) RCA is well and truly Club Alley. Formerly a bastion of the teen scene, this Vegas-like strip has finally graduated from high school and hosts partiers of every age. Worthwhile destinations include Slim/Flix (Map p648; www.facebook.com/slimbkk; Royal City Ave, off Th Phra Ram IX; ⊙8pm-2am; Ⓜ Phra Ram 9 exit 3 & taxi) and Route 66 (Map p648; www.route66club.com; 29/33-48 Royal City Ave (RCA), off Th Phra Ram IX; ⊙8pm-2am; Ⓜ Phra Ram 9 exit 3 & taxi).

Arena 10
NIGHTCLUB
(Map p648; cnr Soi Ekamai 5 & Soi 63 (Ekamai), Th Sukhumvit; ⑤ Ekkamai exit 2 & taxi) This open-air entertainment zone is the destination of choice for Bangkok's young and beautiful – for the moment at least. Demo (Map p648; www.facebook.com/demobangkok; admission free; ⊙6pm-2am; ⑤ Ekkamai exit 2 & taxi) combines blasting beats and a NYC warehouse vibe, while Funky Villa (Map p648; www.facebook.com/funkyvillabkk; ⊙7pm-2am; ⑤ Ekkamai exit 2 & taxi), with its outdoor seating and Top 40 soundtrack, is more chilled.

Q Bar
NIGHTCLUB
(Map p648; www.qbarbangkok.com; 34 Soi 11, Th Sukhumvit; admission from 600B; ⊙8pm-2am; ⑤ Nana exit 3) In club years, Q Bar is fast approaching retirement age, but a recent renovation ensures that it still rules over Bangkok's club scene.

☆ Entertainment

★ Brick Bar
LIVE MUSIC
(Map p656; www.brickbarkhaosan.com; basement, Buddy Lodge, 265 Th Khao San; ⊙8pm-2am; ⊛ Tha Phra Athit (Banglamphu)) This basement pub hosts a nightly revolving cast of bands for an almost exclusively Thai crowd. Teddy Ska is the big act.

Ad Here the 13th
LIVE MUSIC
(Map p656; 13 Th Samsen; ⊙6pm-midnight; ⊛ Tha Phra Athit (Banglamphu)) Located beside Khlong Banglamphu, Ad Here is everything a neighbourhood joint should be: lots of regulars, cold beer and heart-warming tunes delivered by a masterful house band starting at 10pm.

Brown Sugar
LIVE MUSIC
(Map p656; www.brownsugarbangkok.com; 469 Th Phra Sumen; ⊙5pm-1am Mon-Thu, to 2am Sat & Sun; ⊛ Tha Phra Athit (Banglamphu)) This long-standing, live-music staple has found a cosy new home in Old Bangkok.

Lumpinee Boxing Stadium
BOXING
(www.muaythailumpinee.net/en/index.php; Th Ramintra; tickets 3rd class/2nd class/ringside 1000/2000/3000B; Ⓜ Chatuchak Park exit 2 & taxi, ⑤ Mo Chit exit 3 & taxi) One of Bangkok's premier boxing rings has moved to fancy new digs north of town. Matches occur on Tuesday and Friday from 6.30pm to 10.30pm,

---

HIGH CULTURE, LOW COST

Thai classical dance is typically promoted among package tourists as a dinner-theatre experience, but baht-minded travellers can see performances in free, or nearly free, venues.

➡ **Lak Meuang** (ศาลหลักเมือง; Map p656; cnr Th Sanam Chai & Th Lak Meuang; ⊙6.30am-6.30pm; ⊛ Tha Chang) **FREE** , near Wat Phra Kaew, showcases shrine dances to the guardian spirits by merit-makers whose wishes have been granted.

➡ **Erawan Shrine** (p654), next to Grand Hyatt Erawan hotel, also features shrine dances.

➡ **Artist's House** (บ้านศิลปิน; Khlong Bang Luang, Thonburi; ⊙10am-6pm; ⑤ Wongwian Yai exit 2 & taxi) **FREE** has free traditional Thai puppets shows on weekends at 2pm.

➡ **National Theatre** (Map p656; ☏ 0 2224 1342; 2 Th Ratchini; tickets 60-100B; ⊛ Tha Chang) hosts traditional dance performances on the first and second Sundays of the month and on the first Friday of the month, while Thai musical performances are held on the third Friday of the month.

GAY & LESBIAN BANGKOK

Bangkok's gay community is loud, proud and knows how to party. A newcomer might want to visit the websites **Utopia** (www.utopia-asia.com) and **Lesbian Guide to Bangkok** (www.bangkoklesbian. com) for nightlife tips.

Bangkok's 'pink alleys' branch off Th Silom. Reliable standards include **Balcony** (Map p648; www.balconypub.com; 86-88 Soi 4, Th Silom; ⊙5.30pm-1am; 🛜; Ⓜ Si Lom exit 2, Ⓢ Sala Daeng exit 1) and **Telephone** (Map p648; www.telephonepub.com; 114/ 11-13 Soi 4, Th Silom; ⊙6pm-1am; 🛜; Ⓜ Si Lom exit 2, Ⓢ Sala Daeng exit 1), while dance clubs cluster on Soi 2, Th Silom.

and Saturday at 4pm to 8pm and 8.30pm to midnight. There are plans underway for a Thai boxing museum and school for foreign fighters.

Ratchadamnoen Stadium BOXING
(Map p656; off Th Ratchadamnoen Nok; tickets 3rd class/2nd class/ringside 1000/1500/2000B; 🚤klorng boat to Tha Phan Fah, Ⓢ Phaya Thai exit 3 & taxi) Ratchadamnoen Stadium, Bangkok's oldest and most venerable venue for *muay thai* (Thai boxing), hosts matches on Monday, Wednesday, Thursday and Sunday starting at 6.30pm. Be sure to buy tickets from the official ticket counter, not from the touts who hang around outside the entrance.

🛍 Shopping

Bangkok is a great shopping destination but smart travellers opt for a shopping spree right before their return flight to avoid hauling extra cargo across Southeast Asia.

★**Chatuchak Weekend Market** MARKET
(ตลาดนัดจตุจักร, Talat Nat Jatujak; www.chatuchak. org; Th Phahonyothin; ⊙9am-6pm Sat & Sun; Ⓜ Chatuchak Park exit 1, Kamphaeng Phet exits 1 & 2, Ⓢ Mo Chit exit 1) Among the largest markets in the world, Chatuchak Weekend Market sells everything buyable, from used vintage sneakers to baby squirrels. The market is roughly divided into thematic sections; the best guide to these is *Nancy Chandler's Map of Bangkok*. Food also plays a significant role here should you suffer from shopping-induced hunger. Plan to spend a full day, as there's plenty to see, do and buy. But come early,

around 9am to 10am, to beat the crowds and the heat.

★**MBK Center** SHOPPING CENTRE
(Map p660; www.mbk-center.com; cnr Th Phra Ram I & Th Phayathai; ⊙10am-10pm; Ⓢ National Stadium exit 4) This immense shopping mall is a tourist destination in its own right. You can buy everything you need here: mobile phones, accessories, shoes, name brands, wallets, handbags and T-shirts. The 6th-floor food court is one of the city's most expansive.

Patpong Night Market SOUVENIRS
(Map p648; Soi Patpong 1 & 2, Th Silom; ⊙6pm-midnight; Ⓜ Si Lom exit 2, Ⓢ Sala Daeng exit 1) You'll be faced with the competing distractions of strip-clubbing and shopping on this infamous street. And true to the area's illicit leanings, pirated goods (in particular watches) make a prominent appearance even amid a wholesome crowd of families and straight-laced couples. Bargain with determination, as first-quoted prices tend to be astronomically high.

ℹ Information

EMERGENCY

Police (☑191)

Tourist Police (☑24hr hotline 1155) This English-speaking unit investigates criminal activity involving tourists and can act as a bilingual liaison with the regular police.

INTERNET ACCESS

Internet cafes are ubiquitous. Wi-fi is mostly free of charge and is becoming increasingly available at hotels, guesthouses and public hot spots.

MEDIA

Austin Bush Food Blog (www.austinbush photography.com) Food blog by Bangkok-based Lonely Planet author.
Bangkok 101 (www.bangkok101.com) A monthly lifestyle and city primer magazine.
Bangkok Post (www.ban7gkokpost.com) English-language newspaper.
Nation (www.nationmultimedia.com) English-language daily with a heavy focus on business.

MEDICAL SERVICES

There are several outstanding hospitals in Bangkok with English-speaking staff.
Bangkok Christian Hospital (Map p648; ☑0 2235 1000; www.bangkokchristianhospital.org; 124 Th Silom; Ⓜ Si Lom exit 2, Ⓢ Sala Daeng exit 1)

BNH (Map p648; ☑0 2686 2700; www.bnh hospital.com; 9 Th Convent; Ⓜ Si Lom exit 2, Ⓢ Sala Daeng exit 2)

Bumrungrad International Hospital (Map p648; ☑0 2667 1000; www.bumrungrad.com; 33 Soi 3, Th Sukhumvit; Ⓢ Phloen Chit exit 3)

MONEY
Thai banks have currency-exchange kiosks that have extended hours (usually 8am to 8pm) in many parts of Bangkok, especially tourist areas. ATMs are conveniently located. Go to 7-Eleven shops or other reputable places to break 1000B bills; don't expect a vendor or taxi to able to make change on a note 500B or larger.

POST
Main Post Office (Map p648; ☑0 2233 1050; Th Charoen Krung; ⊘8am-8pm Mon-Fri, to 1pm Sat & Sun; ⊠ Tha Oriental) Poste restante and a packing service for parcels. Branch post offices also offer similar services.

TOURIST INFORMATION
Official tourist offices distribute maps, brochures and sightseeing advice. Don't confuse these free services with the licensed travel agents that make bookings on a commission basis. Often, travel agencies incorporate elements of the national tourism organisation name (Tourism Authority of Thailand; TAT) into their business name to confuse tourists.

Bangkok Information Center (Map p656; ☑0 2225 7612-4; www.bangkoktourist.com; 17/1 Th Phra Athit; ⊘9am-7pm Mon-Fri, 9am-5pm Sat-Sun; ⊠ Tha Phra Athit (Banglmaphu)) Municipal tourism office that provides maps, brochures and directions.

Tourism Authority of Thailand (TAT; Map p648; ☑0 2250 5500, nationwide call centre 1672; www.tourismthailand.org; 1600 Th Phetchaburi Tat Mai; ⊘8.30am-4.30pm; Ⓜ Phetchaburi exit 2). Also has offices in Banglamphu (Map p656; cnr Th Ratchadamnoen Nok & Th Chakrapatdi-pong) and at Suvarnabhumi International Airport (☑0 2134 0040; 2nd fl, btwn Gates 2 & 5, Suvar-nabhumi International Airport; ⊘24hr).

VISAS & IMMIGRATION
Bangkok Immigration Office (☑0 2141 9889; Bldg B, Government Center, Soi 7, Th Chaeng Watthana; ⊘8.30am-noon & 1-4.30pm Mon-Fri; 🚇 Mo Chit & access by taxi) In Bangkok, exten-sions are handled by the Immigration Bureau office. A fee of 1900B will be charged, and you'll need the usual mug shots.

❶ Getting There & Away

AIR
Bangkok is the air-travel hub for Thailand and mainland Southeast Asia.

Suvarnabhumi International Airport (☑0 2132 1888; www.suvarnabhumiairport.com), 30km east of Bangkok, handles all international air traffic and most domestic routes. The airport name is pronounced 'sù·wan·ná·poom,' and its airport code is BKK.

Don Muang Airport (DMK; ☑0 2535 1111; www.donmuangairportonline.com), 25km north of central Bangkok, handles domestic routes with budget airlines Nok Air, Orient Thai and Air Asia; some international routes are available through Air Asia.

BUS
Eastern Bus Terminal (Ekamai; Map p648; ☑0 2391 2504; Soi 40, Th Sukhumvit; Ⓢ Ekkamai exit 2) The departure point for buses to Pattaya, Rayong, Chanthaburi and other points east, except for Aranya Prathet. It is pronounced 'sà·tăh·nee èk·gà·mai' (Ekamai station), and is accessible via BTS Ekkamai.

Northern & Northeastern Bus Terminal (Mo Chit; ☑ for northeastern routes 0 2936 2852, ext 602/605, for northern routes 0 2936 2841, ext 325/614; Th Kamphaeng Phet; Ⓜ Kam-phaeng Phet exit 1 & taxi, Ⓢ Mo Chit exit 3 & taxi) Located just north of Chatuchak Park, it is commonly called kŏn sòng mŏr chít (Mo Chit station). Buses depart to all northern and northeastern destinations as well as Aranya Prathet and international destinations, such as Siem Reap (Cambodia), Pakse (Laos) and Vientiane (Laos). Take BTS to Mo Chit or MRT to Chatuchak Park and transfer to city bus 3, 77 or 509, or hop on a motorcycle taxi.

Southern Bus Terminal (Sai Tai Mai; ☑0 2894 6122; Th Boromaratchachonanee) Commonly called săi đài mài, this station is far from the centre. It serves all of the south as well as the west, including Kanchanaburi. Take a taxi, bus 79, 159, 201 or 516 from Th Ratch-adamnoen Klang or bus 40 from the Victory Monument.

Suvarnabhumi Public Transport Centre (☑0 2132 1888; Suvarnabhumi Airport) Lo-cated 3km from Suvarnabhumi International Airport, this terminal has departures to points east and northeast including Aranya Prathet (for the Cambodian border), Chanthaburi, Ko Chang, Nong Khai (for the Lao border), Pattaya, Rayong, Trat and Udon Thani. It can be reached from the airport by a free shuttle bus.

TRAVEL HINTS
Skip the long-distance bus services that originate out of Bangkok's Th Khao San; these often have hidden costs, commission-generating hassles and a high rate of theft from stowed luggage.

MINIVAN

Privately run minivans *(rót dôo)* are increasingly replacing buses for fast and comfortable service between Bangkok and its neighbouring provinces as they travel directly into town (usually the central market) instead of to the out-of-town bus stations. In Bangkok, Victory Monument is surrounded by various minivan depots.

TRAIN

Hualamphong Train Station (☑ 0 2220 4334, nationwide call centre 1690; www.railway.co.th; off Th Phra Ram IV; Ⓜ Hua Lamphong exit 2) is the terminus for the main rail services to the south, north, northeast and east.

Bookings can be made in person at the advance booking office (8.30am to 4pm) or from windows 2 to 11 at certain times. Avoid smiling 'information' staff who try to direct all arrivals to a travel agency on the mezzanine level.

Hualamphong has the following services: shower room, mailing centre, luggage storage, cafes and food courts. To get to the station from Sukhumvit take the MRT to the Hua Lamphong stop. From western points (Banglamphu, Thewet), take bus 53.

Bangkok Noi (off Th Itsaraphap; Ⓢ Wongwian Yai exit 4 & taxi) handles infrequent (and overpriced for foreigners) services to Kanchanaburi. The station can be reached by river ferry to Tha Rot Fai.

ⓘ Getting Around

Bangkok is nearly always choked with traffic. You will need a good map and a lot of patience to get around. If you plan to use Bangkok's economical bus system, check out www.transitbangkok.com.

TO/FROM THE AIRPORTS
Suvarnabhumi International Airport

Airport Rail Link There are two rail services linking the airport to central Bangkok.

➟ **Local service** (45B, 30 minutes, every 15 minutes from 6am to midnight) Six stops between airport and Phaya Thai terminal connected to BTS Phaya Thai. Disembark at Phaya Thai and flag a cab to Th Khao San.

➟ **Express service** (90B, 15 minutes, hourly from 6am to midnight) Nonstop between airport and Makkasan/Bangkok City Air Terminal, accessible to MRT Phetchaburi. The MRT links to Silom and Sukhumvit. The train continues to Phaya Thai terminal.

Local Bus Local buses travel between central Bangkok and the airport's public transport centre, a 3km ride on a free shuttle bus from the airport. Buses run roughly from 6am to 10pm and fares start at 35B. Useful routes include the following:

➟ Bus 551 (Victory Monument)

➟ Bus 554 (Don Muang); allow at least two hours transfer because of traffic

➟ Bus 552 (On Nut BTS station)

➟ Minivan to Don Muang; direct route, slightly faster than local bus.

Intercity Bus The airport's public transport centre has services to other eastern cities within Thailand.

Taxi Public meter taxis (not the 'official airport taxis') queue outside of the baggage claim area. Taxi lines tend to be long; you can always dodge the line by flagging a cab from the arrivals hall. Touts often offer flat fares (usually inflated), but you can try to bargain for a fare closer to the meter rate. For meter taxis you must also pay a 50B airport surcharge to the driver and toll charges (usually about 75B). Politely insist that the meter is used ('Meter, *na kha/khrap*') if the driver suggests otherwise. Depending on traffic, meter rates should be as follows:

➟ Banglamphu/Khao San: 350B to 400B

➟ Th Sukhumvit: 200B to 250B

➟ Th Silom: 300B to 350B

Don Muang Airport

Airport Bus/Minivans These services depart from the airport to various points in central Bangkok. Fares are 30B and buses run hourly from 9am to midnight.

➟ A1 (BTS Mo Chit, Northern and Northeastern Bus Terminal)

➟ A2 (BTS Mo Chit, BTS Victory Monument)

➟ Minivan to Suvarnabhumi airport (50B, 40 minutes, from 5.30am to 5pm)

Local Bus The following air-con buses stop on the highway in front of the airport; fares are typically 30B and buses 59 and 29 run 24 hours:

➟ Bus 59 (Th Khao San)

➟ Bus 29 (Victory Monument and Hualamphong train station)

➟ Bus 555 (Suvarnabhumi airport)

Taxi There is a 50B airport surcharge added to the meter fare and tolls are paid by the passenger. Sample fares:

➟ Banglamphu/Th Khao San: 300B

➟ Sukhumvit or Silom: 200B to 300B

Train Exit Terminal 1 towards the Amari Airport Hotel to connect to Don Muang train station with service to Hualamphong train station (5B to 10B, one hour, roughly every hour from 4am to 11.30am and 2pm to 9.30pm).

BOAT

Chao Phraya Express Boat (☑ 0 2623 6001; www.chaophrayaexpressboat.com) is a scenic and efficient way of exploring the sights in Ko Ratanakosin, Banglamphu and parts of Silom. The boats ply a regular route along the Mae Nam

THAILAND BANGKOK

Chao Phraya between Tha Wat Ratchasingkhon in the south and Nonthaburi in the north, and overlap with BTS Saphan Taksin at Tha Sathon. During rush hour pay close attention to the boat's colour-coded flags to avoid boarding an express line. The company operates the following services:

⇒ **Express** Indicated by an orange, yellow or green flag; 15B to 32B, morning and evening rush hour till about 7pm.

⇒ **Local** Without a flag; 10B to 14B, morning and evening rush hour till 5.30pm Monday to Friday.

⇒ **Tourist** Larger boat; 40B, one-day pass 150B, 9.30am to 10pm.

Klorng taxis (10B to 20B, 5.30am to 8.30pm) zip up and down Khlong Saen Saep, a narrow waterway connecting eastern and western Bangkok. The canals are something akin to an open sewer so try not to get splashed and take care when boarding and disembarking as the boats stop for mere seconds. Useful piers include the following:

⇒ **Tha Phan Fah** Eastern terminus, Banglamphu.

⇒ **Tha Hua Chang** Siam Square area.

⇒ **Tha Pratunam** Interchange pier, BTS Chitlom.

BTS (SKYTRAIN)

The elevated **BTS** (Skytrain; ☑ 0 2617 7300; www.bts.co.th) is a slick ride through the modern parts of town. There are two lines: the Sukhumvit and Silom lines. Trains run frequently from 6am to midnight; fares vary from 15B to 40B, or 120B for a one-day pass. Staffed booths provide change for the fare-card machines but do not sell single-fare tickets. You can buy value-stored tickets from the booths. Trains are labelled with the line and the terminal station (indicating the direction the train is travelling). There are also interchange stations with MRT (Metro).

BUS

The Bangkok bus service is frequent and frantic and is operated by **Bangkok Mass Transit Authority** (☑ 0 2246 0973; www.bmta.co.th). Fares for ordinary buses start at 7B and air-con buses at 10B. Most buses operate between 5am and 10pm or 11pm; a few run all night.

Bangkok Bus Guide, by thinknet, is the most up-to-date route map available. The following bus lines are useful:

Bus 15 Sanam Luang (accessible to Wat Phra Kaew), Th Ratchadamnoen Klang (accessible to Th Khao San), MBK (connect to BTS).

Bus 47 Sanam Luang, Th Ratchadamnoen, MBK.

MRT (METRO)

Bangkok's subway or underground (depending on your nationality) is operated by the **MRT** (www.bangkokmetro.co.th), the Metropolitan Rapid Transit Authority. For visitors the MRT is most useful if travelling from Silom or Sukhumvit to the Hualamphong train station. Trains operate from 6am to midnight and cost 15B to 40B, or 120B for

a one-day pass. The following MRT stations provide interchange to BTS (Skytrain):

Chatuchak (BTS Chatuchak)

Sukhumvit (BTS Asoke)

Silom (BTS Sala Daeng)

TAXI

Most taxis in Bangkok are meter taxis, though some drivers 'forget' to use their meters or prefer to quote a flat (and grossly inflated) fare to tourists. Skip the cabs that park in front of hotels (they operate on a charter basis) and instead flag down a roving cab on one of the main streets. Unless it is a rainy rush hour, cabs are plentiful. Fares should generally run from 60B to 100B, depending on distance.

Motorcycle taxis camp out at the mouth of a *soi* to shuttle people from the main road to their destinations down the lane. *Soi* trips cost 10B to 15B; don't ask the price, just pay them as you disembark.

TÚK-TÚK

The Thai version of a go-kart is Bangkok's most iconic vehicle and its most enduring hassle. Túk-túk chatter like a chainsaw; drivers take corners at an angle and are relentless in drumming up business. There are so many túk-túk scams that you really need some tenure in the city to know how much your trip should cost before bargaining for a ride and to know when a túk-túk is handier and cheaper than a cab.

If you climb aboard just for the fun of it, you might end up being taken for a ride, literally. Beware of túk-túk drivers who offer to take you on a sightseeing tour for 10B or 20B – it's a touting scheme designed to pressure you into purchasing overpriced goods. You must fix fares in advance for all túk-túk rides.

AROUND BANGKOK

Floating Markets

Photographs of Thailand's famous floating markets – wooden canoes laden with multicoloured fruits and vegetables – have become an iconic and alluring image for the kingdom. They are also a sentimental piece of history. Like all good nations do, Thailand has modernised, replacing canals with roads, and boats with motorcycles and cars. The floating markets, which were once lively trading posts for produce farmers and local housewives, have crawled ashore. But there are still vestiges of this ancient commerce at riverside markets just outside of Bangkok.

Just across the river from Bangkok, **Taling Chan Floating Market** (ตลาดน้ำตลิ่งชัน; Khlong Bangkok Noi, Thonburi; ☺7am-4pm Sat & Sun) is an ordinary produce market with a few floating twists. Vendors in canoes serve food to customers on floating docks. The market can be reached by longtail tours along Khlong Bangkok Noi or by air-con bus 79 (16B, 25 minutes) from Ratchadamnoen Klang.

Amphawa Floating Market (ตลาดน้ำ อัมพวา; Amphawa, Samut Songkhram; dishes 20-40B; ☺4-9pm Fri-Sun) is a weekend market popular with Bangkok tourists thanks to its scenic canalside setting. For a cultural immersion, spend the night in one of the village's homestays (200B to 1000B per person) and experience the after-dark firefly display on a canal tour. To get here, take a minivan from Bangkok's Victory Monument to Samut Songkhram (also known as Mae Klong; 73B, 1½ hours, 5.30am to 9pm) and then transfer to a *sŏrng·tăa·ou* (pick-up truck) to Amphawa (8B, 10 minutes).

Damnoen Saduak Floating Market (ตลาดน้ำดำเนินสะดวก; Damnoen Saduak, Ratchaburi Province; ☺7am-noon) is the most famous of them all, though it is really a floating souvenir stand catering to tourists. The unique shopping setting makes for a good story back home. You can reach Damnoen Saduak (80B, two hours, frequent) from Bangkok's Southern Bus Terminal. Boats at the market can be hired for 100B per person.

CENTRAL THAILAND

Thailand's heartland, the central region is a fertile river plain that birthed the country's history-shaping kingdoms of Ayuthaya and Sukhothai and crafted the culture and language that defines the mainstream Thai identity. The nationally revered river Mae Nam Chao Phraya is the lifeblood of the region and connects the country's interior with the Gulf of Thailand. Geographically, central Thailand is a necessary thoroughfare for any Chiang Mai–bound traveller, but culturally it is a worthwhile stop.

Ayuthaya   พระนครศรีอยุธยา
POP 137,553

The fabled city, the fallen city: Ayuthaya crowned the pinnacle of ancient Thai history and defined the country's ascendancy to regional domination. It was built at the conflu-

MINIATURE WONDERS

The industrial town of Samut Prakan is an unlikely place for the open-air architectural museum of the **Ancient City** (เมืองโบราณ, Muang Boran; www.ancient city.com; 296/1 Th Sukhumvit, Samut Prakan; adult/child 500/250B; ☺8am-5pm), a unique intersection of entertainment, artistry and curatorship. More than 100 scaled-down models of Thailand's famous architectural monuments have been re-created here in an attempt to preserve traditional craftsmanship and to consolidate the country's artistic heritage into an afternoon's outing.

The museum is 12km south of Samut Prakan (also known as Pak Nam). From Bangkok take air-con bus 511 from the eastern side of Th Sukhumvit to Samut Prakan's bus station. From there board minibus 36, which will pass the entrance of the Ancient City.

ence of three rivers (Mae Nam Lopburi, Chao Phraya and Pa Sak) on a unique island and was auspiciously named after the home of Rama in the Indian epic Ramayana.

The rivers formed both a natural barrier to invasion and an invitation to trade, allowing the city-state to flourish into a fully fledged nation from 1350 to 1767. Though the Thai kings outmanoeuvred Western power plays, it was repeated assaults by the Burmese that eventually sacked the city and ended Ayuthaya's reign. After two years of war the capital fell in 1767; the Burmese looted the city and the Thais re-established their power centre near present-day Bangkok.

Today the ruins of the old city survive with many battle scars amid a modern provincial town, a slight distraction for imagining what Ayuthaya once was. To its credit, the kingdom's history is well preserved and very accessible here.

The modern town still clings to the old ways of the river, which acts as transport, bath and kitchen sink for its residents. The holiday of **Loi Krathong**, when tiny votive boats are floated on rivers as a tribute to the River Goddess, is celebrated with great fanfare in Ayuthaya.

⊙ Sights

A Unesco World Heritage Site, Ayuthaya's historic temples are scattered throughout

THAILAND AYUTHAYA

THAILAND

Ayuthaya

1 km
0.5 miles

N

Mae Nam Pa Sak

Th Dusit

5

11

Train Station

Main (5km)

Chao Phrom Pier

Bank of Ayuthaya

Th Watkluay

Saphan Pridi Damrong

13

14

Th U Thong

Ferry Pier

Wat Phanan Choeng

3

Provincial Bus Station

Ferry Landing

Siam City Bank

Phom Phet Fortress

Chao Phraya

16
19
15
18

Soi 2

Th Naresuan

Th Pamaphrao

Th Khlong Makhamriang

Mae Nam

7

Chinese Shrine

Buses to Bangkok

17

Minivans to Bangkok

Th Bang Ian

Th Dechawat

Th Rotchana

Muslim District

20

Th U Thong

Mosque

21

Th Chee Kun

Th Chee Kun

23

10

9

Th Naresuan (Chao Phrom)

Beung Phra Ram

Th Pa Thon

6

Th U Thong

Wat Kuti Thong

Mae Nam Lopburi

Old Royal Palace

Ayuthaya Historical Park

Wat Phra Si Sanphet

4

12

Wat Phra Ram

8

Th Si Sanphet

22

Tourism Authority of Thailand

Ayuthaya Tourist Center

1

Phra Nakorn Si Ayuthaya Hospital

Th Khlong Thaw

Th Ayuthaya – Pa Mok

Wat Chetharam

Wat Lokayasutharam

Queen Suriyothai Memorial Pagoda

Th U Thong

Wat Kasatthirat

Mae Nam Chao Phraya

Wat Chai Wattanaram

2

Ayuthaya

◉ Top Sights
1 Ayutthaya Tourist Center C3
2 Wat Chai Wattanaram.....................A4
3 Wat Phanan Choeng........................F4
4 Wat Phra Si Sanphet C2

◉ Sights
5 Ayuthaya Floating Market G1
6 Ayuthaya Historical Study
   Centre...D3
7 Chantharakasem National
   Museum E1
8 Chao Sam Phraya National
   Museum C3
9 Wat Phra Mahathat D2
10 Wat Ratburana D2
11 Wat Yai Chai Mongkhon...................G4
12 Wihaan Phra Mongkhon Bophit.........C3

◉ Sleeping
13 Baan Are Gong F2
14 Baan Khun Pra F3
15 Baan Lotus Guest House E2
16 Chantana Guest House F2
17 Grandparent's Home........................E2
18 PU Inn Ubonpon.............................E2
19 Tony's Place F2

◉ Eating
20 Hua Raw Night Market E1
21 Lung Lek......................................D2
22 Roti Sai Mai Stalls C4
23 Sai Thong......................................D4

the city and along the encircling rivers. The ruins are divided into two geographical areas: ruins 'on the island', in the central part of town between Th Chee Kun and the western end of Th U Thong, which are best visited by bicycle; and those 'off the island' on the other side of the river, which are best visited on an evening boat tour or by motorbike.

Most temple ruins are open from 8am to 4pm; the more famous sites charge an entrance fee. A one-day pass for most sites on the island is available for 220B and can be bought at the museums or ruins. The ruins are symbols of royalty and religion, and require utmost respect and proper attire (cover to elbows and knees).

◉ On the Island

★**Ayutthaya Tourist Center**   MUSEUM
(☎0 3524 6076; www.tourismthailand.org/ayut thaya; ⊙8.30am-4.30pm) **FREE** This should

be your first stop in Ayuthaya, as the excellent upstairs exhibition hall puts everything in context and describes the city's erstwhile glories. Also upstairs is the tiny but interesting **Ayutthaya National Art Museum**. Downstairs, the TAT office has lots of maps and good advice.

★**Wat Phra Si Sanphet**   RUIN
(วัดพระศรีสรรเพชญ์; admission 50B; ⊙8am-6pm; **P**) The three magnificent *chedi* (stupas) at Wat Phra Si Sanphet are the most iconic image in Ayuthaya. Built in the late 15th century, it was the city's largest temple and was used by several kings. It contained a 16m-high standing Buddha (Phra Si Sanphet) covered with 250kg of gold, which was melted down by Burmese conquerors.

**Wihaan Phra
Mongkhon Bophit**   BUDDHIST TEMPLE
(วัดพระมงคลบพิตร; ⊙8.30am-4.30pm) **FREE** Next to Wat Phra Si Sanphet is this sanctuary hall, which houses one of the largest bronze Buddha images in Thailand. This 17m-high figure has undergone several facelifts due to lightning strikes and fire.

Wat Phra Mahathat   RUIN
(วัดพระมหาธาตุ; cnr Th Chee Kun & Th Naresuan; admission 50B; ⊙8am-6pm) The most photographed image in Ayuthaya is here: a sandstone Buddha head that lies mysteriously tangled within a tree's entwined roots. Built in 1374 during the reign of King Borom Rachathirat I, Wat Phra Mahathat also has a central *prang* (Khmer-style *chedi*) and rows of headless Buddha images.

Wat Ratburana   RUIN
(วัดราชบูรณะ; admission 50B; ⊙8am-6pm) The *prang* in this temple is one of the best extant versions in the city, with detailed carvings of lotuses and mythical creatures. The temple, just north of Wat Phra Mahathat, was built in the 15th century by King Borom Rachathirat II on the cremation site for his two brothers who died while fighting each other for the throne.

**Ayutthaya Historical
Study Centre**   MUSEUM
(ศูนย์ศึกษาประวัติศาสตร์อยุธยา; Th Rotchana; adult/child 100/50B; ⊙9am-4.30pm; **P**) This well-designed, open-plan museum features a diorama of the city's former glories, replica vessels and an exhibition on how traditional villagers used to survive.

ⓘ **TEMPLE GUIDES**

Audio guides (150B) can be hired at Wat Phra Si Sanphet, Wat Phra Mahathat and Wat Chai Wattanaram. The English-language guides provide excellent background information and vivid detail that help visitors imagine exactly what once stood on these sites.

Chantharakasem National Museum MUSEUM

(พิพิธภัณฑสถานแห่งชาติจันทรเกษม; Th U Thong; admission 100B; ⊙9am-4pm Wed-Sun) Inside this national museum is a collection of Buddhist art, sculptures, ancient weapons and lacquered cabinets. The museum is within the grounds of Wang Chan Kasem (Chan Kasem Palace), which was built for King Naresuan by his father in 1577.

Chao Sam Phraya National Museum MUSEUM

(พิพิธภัณฑสถานแห่งชาติเจ้าสามพระยา; cnr Th Rotchana & Th Si Sanphet; adult/child 150B/free; ⊙9am-4pm Wed-Sun; Ⓟ) The largest museum in the city has 2400 items on show, ranging from a 2m-high bronze-cast Buddha head to glistening treasures found in the crypts of Wat Phra Mahathat and Wat Ratburana.

◉ Off the Island

★ Wat Phanan Choeng BUDDHIST TEMPLE

(วัดพนัญเชิง; admission 20B; ⊙8am-7pm) Merit-making ceremonies, firecrackers and ritualistic fish feeding make this a hectic temple. The signature attraction is the 19m-high Phra Phanan Choeng, which was created in 1324 and sits in the *wí·hǎhn* (sanctuary), surrounded by 84,000 Buddha images that line the walls. The statue's broad shape is typical of the U Thong period.

Wat Phanan Choeng, southeast of the old city, can be reached by ferry (5B) from the pier near Phom Phet Fortress. Your bicycle can accompany you across.

★ Wat Chai Wattanaram BUDDHIST TEMPLE

(วัดไชยวัฒนาราม; admission 50B; ⊙8am-6pm) Just 40 years ago this temple and one-time garrison was immersed in thick jungle. Today it is one of Ayuthaya's most-photographed sites thanks to its impressive 35m-high Khmer-style central *prang*. Built in 1673 by King Prasat Thong, the temple is a great place to watch sunsets. The site is west of the

island and can be reached by bicycle via a nearby bridge.

Wat Yai Chai Mongkhon BUDDHIST TEMPLE

(วัดใหญ่ชัยมงคล; admission 20B) A 7m-long reclining Buddha is the highlight at Wat Yai Chai Mongkhon. If you can get a coin to stick to the Buddha's feet, it is thought good luck will come your way. King U Thong built the monastery in 1357 to house monks from Sri Lanka. The bell-shaped *chedi* was built later to honour King Naresuan's victory over Burma.

Ayuthaya Floating Market MARKET

(ตลาดน้ำอโยธยา; www.ayutthayafloatingmarket. com; ⊙9am-7pm; Ⓟ) **FREE** A touch kitsch, but popular with locals and visitors, the floating market sells snacks, artwork and clothes. Set on wooden platforms above the water, longboats (20B) offer rides through the waterways. Traditional performances take place throughout the day. Avoid the neighbouring Ayodia Inter Market as it has some dubious animal attractions.

The market is to the east of the old city off Th Dusit, near Wat Kudi Dao.

Wat Tha Ka Rong BUDDHIST TEMPLE

(⊙6am-5pm; Ⓟ) **FREE** Just to the northwest of the island sits this bizarre temple. If you aren't dazzled by the fairy lights, you may notice the skeleton models that *wâi* (greet you with palms together) as you pass by, the room full of life-size monk statues and the superfancy bathrooms, which are an attraction in themselves.

The display of differing Buddhas from neighbouring countries is worth a look. To the rear is a modest **floating market** that focuses on food.

🛏 Sleeping

Budget travellers can walk from the bus stop to the guesthouses, most of which are located on Soi 2, Th Naresuan.

★ Baan Lotus Guest House GUESTHOUSE $

(☏0 3525 1988; 20 Th Pamaphrao; s 200B, d 450-600B; Ⓟ❀🛜🏊) The gorgeous, green grounds surrounding this converted teak schoolhouse make staying here a treat. Staff are as charmingly old-school as the building itself.

PU Inn Ubonpon GUESTHOUSE $

(☏0 3525 1213; www.puguesthouse.com; 20/1 Soi Thaw Kaw Saw; s 200-300B, d 400-900B, tr 700B; ❀@🛜) Knowledgeable staff and neat, if not spectacular, rooms have made this spot so popular the owners had to open a sister hotel right opposite. Some staff speak Japanese.

Grandparent's Home
GUESTHOUSE $

(📞08 3558 5829; 19/40 Th Naresuan; r 550B; ❄ 🛜 🍴) Simple little touches and splashes of colour give the rooms in this deceptively large guesthouse a warm vibe. A good-value place right next to the Historical Park.

Chantana Guest House
GUESTHOUSE $

(📞0 3532 3200; chantanahouse@yahoo.com; 12/22 Soi 2, Th Naresuan; r 500-650B; P ❄ @ 🛜 🍴) Chantana is a well-established guesthouse with sparse but clean rooms. Staff are friendly and the location is excellent. Splash out an extra 50B to snag a room with a balcony.

Baan Khun Pra
GUESTHOUSE $

(📞0 3524 1978; www.bannkunpra.com; 48/2 Th U Thong; dm/d 250/600B; ❄ @ 🛜) Meaning 'Bureaucrat's Home', this riverside teak property, built around 100 years ago, is in a wonderful charismatic time warp, with antiques dotted everywhere. Dorms sleep up to four.

Baan Are Gong
GUESTHOUSE $

(📞0 3523 5592; siriporntan@yahoo.com.sg; off Th Rotchana; s 220B, d 500-600B; ❄ 🛜) Walking distance from the train station, Baan Are Gong is an imposing 100-year-old teak guesthouse, run by a welcoming Thai-Chinese family. The 4B ferry to the island is nearby.

★Tony's Place
GUESTHOUSE $$

(📞0 3525 2578; www.tonyplace-ayutthaya.com; 12/18 Soi 2, Th Naresuan; r 300-1200B; ❄ 🛜 🍴) Tony's remains the flashpackers' top choice thanks to well-renovated rooms, a mini pool and the chance to swap travel trips with fellow visitors. Cheaper rooms have fans and shared bathrooms.

✕ Eating

The range of restaurants in Ayuthaya can come as a disappointment after living it up in Bangkok. But there is a modest collection of culinary traditions, including Muslim and European fare, that survive from ancient times.

★Sai Thong
THAI $

(Th U Thong; dishes 90-150B; ⏱9.30am-10pm; P 🚗 🍴) The number of cars vying for parking spaces each night is testament to how much locals love Sai Thong. The 180 menu items include classics as well as some slight variations, so browse before picking.

Hua Raw Night Market
MARKET $

(Th U Thong) This evening market offers simple riverside seating and a range of Thai and Muslim dishes; for the latter look for the green star and crescent.

Roti Sai Mai Stalls
THAI SWEETS $

(Th U Thong; ⏱10am-8pm) The Muslim dessert of *roh- đee săi măi* is famous in these parts. Buy a bag then make your own by by rolling together thin strands of melted palm sugar and wrapping them inside the roti. Stalls can be found opposite Ayuthaya Hospital.

Lung Lek
NOODLES $

(Th Chee Kun; dishes 30-40B; ⏱8.30am-4pm) Everybody's favourite noodle emporium, Uncle Lek still serves the most notable noodles in town. Opposite Wat Ratburana, this is the perfect pit stop between temples.

ℹ Information

Main Post Office (Th U Thong; ⏱8.30am-4.30pm Mon-Fri, 9am-noon Sat & Sun) Has an international telephone service, open 8am to 8pm, upstairs.

Phra Nakorn Si Ayuthaya Hospital (📞0 3532 2555-70, emergency 1669; cnr Th U Thong & Th Si Sanphet) Has an emergency centre and English-speaking doctors.

Tourism Authority of Thailand (TAT; 📞0 3524 6076; 108/22 Th Si Sanphet; ⏱8.30am-4.30pm Mon-Fri) If you would like in-depth coverage of Ayuthaya history, talk to TAT about hiring a guide. TAT's office at Ayutthaya Tourist Center (p673) is open daily.

Tourist Police (📞emergency 1155; Th Si Sanphet)

ℹ Getting There & Away

BUS

Ayuthaya has two bus terminals. The **provincial bus station** is on Th Naresuan, a short walk from the guesthouse area. Minivans depart nearby. For long-distance travel to the north, the terminal is 5km east of the centre on the Asia Hwy. For Kanchanaburi-bound travellers, catch the Suphanburi bus and transfer from there.

TRAIN

Ayuthaya's train station is on the eastern banks of the Mae Nam Pa Sak and is an easy walk from the city centre via a short ferry ride (4B). *Sŏrngtăaou* to the guesthouse area should cost 50B. If you're headed to Khao Yai, catch the train to Pak Chong. For Bangkok's Th Khao San area by train, get off at Bang Sue.

TRANSPORT FROM AYUTHAYA

DESTINATION	BUS & MINIVAN	TRAIN
Bangkok	60B, 1½hr, every 25min (Victory Monument, minivan); 56-60B, 1½hr, every 25min (Northern & Northeastern bus station; bus)	15-345B, 1½hr, frequent (Hualamphong); 14-345B, 1½hr, frequent (Bang Sue)
Chiang Mai	438-876B, 8hr, frequent	586-1198B, 12hr, 6 daily departures
Lopburi	50B, 1½hr, every 15min (minivan)	13-34B, 1½hr, frequent
Pak Chong	23-173B, 4hr, 7 departures	N/A
Phitsanulok	304-473B, 5hr, 4 daily	75-300B, 4½hr, frequent
Sukhothai	279-387B, 7hr, frequent	N/A
Suphanburi	80B, 1½hr, frequent (minivan)	N/A

ⓘ Getting Around

Bikes can be rented at most guesthouses (30B). Túk-túk can be hired for the day to tour the sites; a single trip within the city should be about 30B or 40B.

Lopburi ลพบุรี

POP 26,500

This small, low-key town is a delightful respite from the rigours of the tourist trail. No aggressive túk-túk drivers, no grumpy guesthouse staff and few foreigners making you feel that you flew a long way to be with familiar faces. Lopburi is an ancient town with plenty of old ruins to prove its former occupation by almost every Southeast Asian kingdom: Dvaravati, Khmer and Ayuthaya. The old city is presently occupied by ordinary Thai life: noodle stands, motorcycle stores and, most importantly, a gang of monkeys. The city celebrates its resident monkeys with an annual festival during the last week of November.

⊙ Sights

Lopburi's old ruins are easy to walk to from the town centre and a 150B day pass (available at Phra Narai Ratchaniwet) allows entry to all sights.

★ Phra Narai Ratchaniwet   MUSEUM

(วังนารายณ์ราชนิเวศน์; entrance Th Sorasak; admission 150B; ☉ gallery 8.30am-4pm Wed-Sun, palace grounds 8am-5pm) Start your tour of Lopburi at this former royal palace. Inside the palace grounds is the **Lopburi Museum** (officially called Somdet Phra Narai National Museum), which houses displays of local history. The museum is divided into three separate buildings. In Phiman Mongkut Pavilion there are sculptures and art from the Lopburi, Khmer, Dvaravati, U Thong and Ayuthaya periods.

A 150B one-day pass to the main ruins can be bought here.

★ Prang Sam Yot   MONUMENT

(ปรางค์สามยอด; Th Wichayen; admission 50B; ☉ 6am-6pm) Prang Sam Yot and its resident troop of monkeys are the most famous attraction in Lopburi. The three linked towers originally symbolised the Hindu Trimurti of Shiva, Vishnu and Brahma. Now two of them contain ruined Lopburi-style Buddha images. The towers are accessible and offer relief from the heat and monkeys.

Young guides show visitors around for a small donation. Their English is minimal, but their catapults keep the monkeys at bay.

Wat Phra Si Ratana Mahathat   RUIN

(วัดพระศรีรัตนมหาธาตุ; Th Na Phra Kan; admission 50B; ☉ 7am-5pm) Opposite the train station is this 13th-century Khmer wat. Once the town's largest monastery, it has been heavily renovated and makes for a great photo opportunity. The central Phra Prang has basrelief depicting the life of the Buddha while its arched gate has images in the style of the Lawo period.

🛏 Sleeping

In the old town most hotels are old and basic, but they are within walking distance of the ruins.

★ Noom Guesthouse   GUESTHOUSE $

(☏ 0 3642 7693; www.noomguesthouse.com; 15-17 Th Phraya Kamjat; r 150-500B; ✴ 🛜 ♨) Easily the most *faràng*-friendly (foreigner-friendly) spot in town, Noom's rooms are either bamboo bungalows or simple pads with shared bathrooms. A nearby sister guesthouse takes any overspill.

Nett Hotel GUESTHOUSE $
(☑ 0 3641 1738; netthotel@hotmail.com; 17/1-2 Th Ratchadamnoen; r 260-570B; ❄ 🛜) The Nett remains a good option, as rooms are reasonable and you are walking distance from the ruins. Cheaper rooms are fan-only and have cold-water showers.

Sri Indra Hotel GUESTHOUSE $
(☑ 0 36411261; 3-4 Th Na Phra Kan; r 200-350B; ❄) As long as you don't mind monkeys peering in your room, this is a good, centrally located guesthouse that is near the train station and San Phra Kan. Cheaper options are fan-only.

🍴 Eating & Drinking

⭐**Khao Tom Hor** CHINESE-THAI $
(cnr Th Na Phra Kan & Th Ratchadamnoen; dishes 30-80B) Constantly busy Khao Tom Hor offers Thai-Chinese dishes, including *salid tôrd* (deep-fried salted fish) and *pàd gàprow gài* (chicken stir-fried with basil). Service is speedy and efficient.

Central Market MARKET $
(off Th Ratchadamnoen & Th Surasongkhram; ⊙6am-5pm) Wander through the narrow alleyways and take in the sights and smells of this local market. Blood-red strawberries, orange prawns and silver fish are laid out alongside *kôw đom mùd* (rice wrapped in coconut leaves), *đa·go peu·ak* (taro custard with coconut milk) and *gài tôrt* (fried chicken). In the centre is a vegetarian pavilion.

Teu THAI $
(Th Pratoo Chai; dishes 40-70B; ⊙3pm-12.30am) To eat with the locals, pull up a plastic stool and snack on the fantastic *gaang 'bàh nêua* (jungle curry with beef) and slushy frozen beer. Seating is opposite the restaurant by a grassy verge or inside, next to the chaotic kitchen. Look for the big red sign.

Matini WESTERN $
(www.matinirestaurant.com; Th Phraya Kamjat; dishes 80-130B; ⊙noon-midnight; 🛜☑🔖) Free pool,

> ### MONKEY TROUBLE
>
> Lopburi residents are ambivalent about the town's iconic macaques. According to Hindu-Buddhist beliefs, the monkeys have divine connections and should not be harmed. To dissuade them from raiding shops, a feeding station (10am and 4pm daily) next to **San Phra Kan** (Kala Shrine; Th Wichayen) provides heaps of vegetables and fruit. And they are given a huge banquet in November during the annual monkey festival.
>
> But there are rumours that shopkeepers are fed up with the monkey antics and that some troupes might be rounded up and taken to an out-of-town location. In the meantime, tourists should exercise caution when visiting San Phra Kan and Prang Sam Yot, the monkeys' favourite hangouts. Avoid interacting with them as they are wild animals and do bite; don't carry bottles of water, cameras, bags or anything that can be grabbed out of your hands.

a Blues Brothers' motif on the wall and great Western food make this Lopburi's hippest place. And though the name may look like a typo, 'Matini' means 'come here' in Thai.

Sahai Phanta BAR
(Th Sorasak) To party with the locals, check out this town-centre venue with its Carabao-style house band.

ℹ Information

Muang Narai Hospital (☑ 0 3661 6300; Th Pahonyohtin)
Post Office (Th Phra Narai Maharat)
Tourism Authority of Thailand (TAT; ☑ 0 3642 2768-9; Th Phra Narai Maharat; ⊙8.30am-6.30pm Mon-Fri) The office is a rather inconvenient 5km east of the old town, along Th Phra Narai Maharat, but is worth finding for TAT's excellent free map.
Zon Coffee Bar (Th Naresuan) Free wi-fi.

TRANSPORT FROM LOPBURI

DESTINATION	BUS & MINIVAN	TRAIN
Ayuthaya	50B, 1½hr, every 15min (minivan)	13-340B, 1½hr, frequent
Bangkok	100B, 1½hr, every 30min (Northern & Northeastern bus station); 120B, 2hr, every 20min (Victory Monument, minivan)	28-374B, 2½hr, frequent

ℹ️ Getting There & Away

Lopburi's bus station is nearly 2km outside of the old town. Minivans to Bangkok depart from Th Na Phra Kan. The **train station** (Th Na Phra Kan) is near the old town and it has luggage storage if you just want to do a brief layover en route to points north.

ℹ️ Getting Around

Sǎhmlór (pedicabs) go anywhere in old Lopburi for 30B. *Sǒrngtǎaou* run a regular route between the old and new towns for 10B and can be used to travel between the bus station and the old town.

Phitsanulok พิษณุโลก

POP 84,000

Because of its convenient location on an important train route, some travellers use Phitsanulok as a base for visiting the ancient city of Sukhothai. As an attraction in itself, Phitsanulok (often abbreviated as 'Philok') boasts a famous Buddha and a few minor curiosities.

🅾️ Sights

⭐ Wat Phra Si Ratana Mahathat
BUDDHIST TEMPLE

(วัดพระศรีรัตนมหาธาตุ; Th Phutta Bucha; ⊙6am-9pm, museum 9am-5.30pm Wed-Sun) **FREE** The main *wí·hǎhn* (sanctuary) at this temple, known by locals as Wat Yai, appears small from the outside, but houses the Phra Phuttha Chinnarat, one of Thailand's most revered and copied Buddha images. This famous bronze statue is probably second in importance only to the Emerald Buddha in Bangkok's Wat Phra Kaew. Dress appropriately: cover to elbows and knees.

⭐ Sergeant Major Thawee Folk Museum
MUSEUM

(พิพิธภัณฑ์พื้นบ้าน จ่าทวี; 26/43 Th Wisut Kasat; admission adult/child 50/25B; ⊙8.30am-4.30pm) This museum displays a remarkable collection of tools, textiles and photographs from Phitsanulok Province. Spread throughout five traditional-style Thai buildings with well-groomed gardens, the displays are all accompanied by informative and legible English descriptions. The museum is on Th Wisut Kasat, about 1km south of Phitsanulok's train station; a túk-túk here should cost about 80B.

🛏️ Sleeping

Lithai Guest House
HOTEL **$**

(📞0 5521 9626; 73/1-5 Th Phayarithai; r incl breakfast 300-580B; ※@🛜) The light-filled 60 or so rooms here don't have much character but they are clean. Air-con rooms include perks such as large private bathrooms with hot water, cable TV, fridge and breakfast.

Kraisaeng Place
HOTEL **$**

(📞0 5521 0509; www.facebook.com/kraisaeng place45; 45 Th Thammabucha; r incl breakfast 400-450B; ※🛜) Having more in common with a small apartment building than a hotel, the well-equipped rooms here are a super bargain, although traffic noise can be an issue.

🍽️ Eating

Night Market
MARKET **$**

(Th Phra Ong Dam; mains 30-60B; ⊙5pm-midnight) This night market lines either side of Th Phra Ong Dam north of Th Authong.

Rim Nan
THAI **$**

(5/4 Th Phutta Bucha, no roman-script sign; mains 20-35B; ⊙9am-4pm) Rim Nan serves *gǒoay·děe·o hôy kǎh*, literally meaning, 'legs-hanging' noodles,' named for the way customers sit on the floor facing the river, with their legs dangling below.

⭐ Ban Mai
THAI **$$**

(93/30 Th Authong, no roman-script sign; mains 100-200B; ⊙11am-10pm) Dinner at this local favourite is like a meal at your grandparents' place: opinionated conversation, frumpy furniture and an overfed resident cat. The likewise homey dishes include *gaeng phed ped yang* (grilled duck curry) and *yam tra krai* (herbal lemongrass 'salad'). Look for the yellow compound across from Ayara Grand Palace Hotel.

Paknang
CHINESE, THAI **$**

(Th Sairuthai; mains 40-280B; ⊙10am-10pm) This corner of old Phitsanulok has a distinctly old-world Chinese feel – an excellent pairing with the tasty Chinese-style dishes at this long-standing restaurant.

Fah-Ke-Rah
MUSLIM, THAI **$**

(786 Th Phra Ong Dam, no roman-script sign; mains 20-60B; ⊙6am-9pm) Near the Pakistan Mosque on Th Phra Ong Dam, this Muslim restaurant serves *gaang mát·sà·màn* (Muslim curry) with thick *roh·đee* (roti) instead of rice.

Night Bazaar
MARKET

(Th Phutta Bucha; ⊙7pm-midnight) Distinctly workday, the night bazaar is a tourist attraction for the restaurant serving the town's signature dish: *pàk bûng loy fáh* (literally 'floating-in-the-sky morning glory vine'), in which the cook fires up a batch of *pàk bûng*

TRANSPORT FROM PHITSANULOK

DESTINATION	AIR	BUS & MINIVAN	TRAIN
Bangkok	520-2700B, 55min, 6 daily (Don Muang Airport)	304-416B, 5-6hr, hourly 6.20am-12.30am	69-1664B, 5-7hr, 10 daily
Chiang Mai	N/A	299-349B, 6hr, hourly 5.40am-1.30am	65-1645B, 7-9hr, 6 daily
Chiang Rai	N/A	273-410B, 7-8hr, hourly 8am-12.40am	N/A
Kamphaeng Phet	N/A	59-83B, 3hr, hourly 5am-6pm	N/A
Lampang	N/A	220-265B, 4hr, hourly 8am-midnight	158-1042B, 5hr, 5 daily
Mae Sot	N/A	163-168B, 4hr, hourly 7am-3pm	N/A
Sukhothai	N/A	43-60B, 1hr, hourly 7.20am-6.15pm	N/A
Sukhothai Historical Park	N/A	70B, 1½hr, half-hourly 5am-6pm	N/A

in the wok and then flings it through the air to a waiting server who catches it on a plate.

🍷 Drinking

Wood Stock BAR
(148/22-23 Th Wisut Kasat; ⊙7pm-midnight) It's, like, 1969 all over again, man. Wood Stock combines funky '60s- and '70s-era furniture, live music and a brief and cheap menu of *gàp glâam* (Thai-style nibbles). Groovy.

Camper BAR
(Th Baromtrilokanart; ⊙7pm-midnight) An open-air, ramshackle convocation of falling-apart retro furniture, local hipsters, draft beer and live music, Camper is as loose and fun as it sounds.

ℹ️ Information

@net (off Th Baromtrilokanart; per hr 10B; ⊙24hr) Twenty-four-hour internet access.
Tourism Authority of Thailand Office (TAT; ☑ 0 5525 2742, nationwide 1672; tatphlok@tat.or.th; 209/7-8 Th Baromtrilokanart; ⊙8.30am-4.30pm) Off Th Baromtrilokanart, with helpful staff who hand out free maps of the town and a walking-tour sheet.
Tourist Police (☑1155; Th Akatossaroth)

ℹ️ Getting There & Away

If you're in a real hurry, Phitsanulok is linked by air to Bangkok's Don Muang Airport through **Air Asia** (☑ 0 2515 9999; www.airasia.com; Phitsanulok Airport) and **Nok Air** (☑ 0 5530 1051, nationwide 1318; www.nokair.co.th; Phitsanulok Airport; ⊙8am-5pm).

Bus transport options out of Phitsanulok are good as it's a cross-country junction. Phitsanulok's **bus station** (☑ 0 5521 2090; Rte 12) is

2km east of town. Túk-túk and motorcycle taxis to/from town cost 60B.

The **train station** (☑ 0 5525 8005, nationwide 1690; www.railway.co.th; Th Akatossaroth) is in the centre of town within walking distance of accommodation.

ℹ️ Getting Around

Rides on the town's Darth Vader–like sǎhmlór start at about 60B.

Sukhothai สุโขทัย

POP 37,000

The ruins of Sukhothai are a mini version of the architectural styles found in Angkor with a few Thai flourishes. Considered the first independent Thai kingdom, Sukhothai emerged as the Khmer empire was crumbling in the 13th century and subsequently ruled over parts of the empire's western frontier for 150 years. This new Thai kingdom took artistic inspiration from its former overseers and the resulting city of temples is now a compact and pleasant collection of gravity-warped columns, serene Buddha figures and weed-sprouting towers.

Though Ayuthaya has a more interesting historical narrative, Sukhothai's ancient city is better preserved and architecturally more engaging. No surprise since Sukhothai (meaning 'Rising Happiness') is regarded as the blossoming of a Thai artistic sensibility.

The modern town of Sukhothai (often referred to as New Sukhothai; 12km from the ruins) is a standard, somewhat bland, provincial town but it is close and convenient.

Sukhothai Historical Park

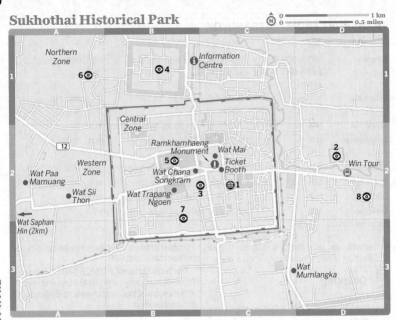

Sukhothai Historical Park

Sights
1 Ramkhamhaeng National Museum....C2
2 Wat Chang Lom D2
3 Wat Mahathat...C2
4 Wat Phra Phai Luang............................B1
5 Wat Sa Si..B2
6 Wat Si Chum..A1
7 Wat Si Sawai...B2
8 Wat Trapang Thong..............................D2

Sights & Activities

Ranked as an Unesco World Heritage Site, the **Sukhothai Historical Park** (อุทยาน ประวัติศาสตร์สุโขทัย), known in Thai as *'meuang kào'* or 'old city', comprises most of the ancient kingdom, which was surrounded by three concentric ramparts and two moats bridged by four gateways – important celestial geometry. Inside the old walls are the remains of 21 historical buildings; there are an additional 70 sites within a 5km radius. The ruins are divided into five geographic zones, each of which charges a 100B admission fee.

The historical park also hosts a beautiful version of Thailand's popular **Loi Krathong** festival in November.

Central Zone

This is the historical park's main **zone** (admission 100B, plus per bicycle/motorcycle/car 10/30/50B; ⊙ 6.30am-7pm Sun-Fri, to 9pm Sat) and is home to what are arguably some of the park's most well-preserved and impressive ruins. An audio tour can be rented at the ticket booth for 150B. This zone is best reached from town by *sŏrngtăaou*. Once at the park, renting a bicycle is ideal; shops nearby rent bikes for 30B per day.

Wat Mahathat   BUDDHIST TEMPLE
(วัดมหาธาตุ) Completed in the 13th century, the largest wat in Sukhothai is surrounded by brick walls (206m long and 200m wide) and a moat that is believed to represent the outer wall of the universe and the cosmic ocean.

The *chedi* spires feature the famous lotus-bud motif, and some of the original stately Buddha figures still sit among the ruined columns of the old *wí·hăhn* (sanctuary). There are 198 *chedi* within the monastery walls – a lot to explore in what is believed to be the former spiritual and administrative centre of the old capital.

Ramkhamhaeng National Museum
MUSEUM

(พิพิธภัณฑสถานแห่งชาติรามคำแหง; admission 150B; ⊘9am-4pm) A good starting point for exploring the historical park ruins is this museum. A replica of the famous Ramkhamhaeng inscription, said to be the earliest example of Thai writing, is kept here among an impressive collection of Sukhothai artefacts. Admission to the museum is not included in the ticket to the central zone.

Wat Si Sawai
BUDDHIST TEMPLE

(วัดศรีสวาย) Just south of Wat Mahathat, this Buddhist shrine (dating from the 12th and 13th centuries) features three Khmer-style towers and a picturesque moat. It was originally built by the Khmers as a Hindu temple.

Wat Sa Si
BUDDHIST TEMPLE

(วัดสระศรี) Also known as 'Sacred Pond Monastery', Wat Sa Si sits on an island west of the bronze monument of King Ramkhamhaeng (the third Sukhothai king). It's a simple, classic Sukhothai-style wat containing a large Buddha, one *chedi* and the columns of the ruined *wí·hǎhn*.

Wat Trapang Thong
BUDDHIST TEMPLE

(วัดตระพังทอง) Next to the museum, this small, still-inhabited wat with its fine stucco reliefs is reached by a footbridge across the large lotus-filled pond that surrounds it. This

---

THE EMPIRE'S SUBURBS

The Sukhothai empire expanded its administrative centre and monument-building efforts to Si Satchanalai and Chaliang, two satellite cities about 70km away. Today the historic park containing the remaining temple ruins is set amid rolling hills and offers a more pastoral experience than Old Sukhothai.

An all-inclusive admission fee (220B) allows entry to Si Satchanalai, Chaliang's Wat Chao Chan and the Si Satchanalai Centre for Study & Preservation of Sangkhalok Kilns.

Si Satchanalai

This historic **zone** (admission 100B, plus car 50B; ⊘8am-5pm) covers roughly 720 hectares and is surrounded by a 12m-wide moat along the banks of Mae Nam Yom. An information centre distributes useful maps, and bicycles can be rented (30B) near the entrance gate. **Wat Chang Lom** (วัดช้างล้อม; off Rte 12) `FREE` has a *chedi* (stupa) surrounded by Buddha statues set in niches and guarded by the remains of well-preserved elephant buttresses. Climb to the top of the hill supporting **Wat Khao Phanom Phloeng** (วัดเขาพนมเพลิง) for a view over the town and river. **Wat Chedi Jet Thaew** (วัดเจดีย์เจ็ดแถว) has a group of stupas in classic Sukhothai style.

Chaliang

Chaliang is an older city site, dating to the 11th century, and sits 1km from Si Satchanalai. **Wat Phra Si Ratana Mahathat** (วัดพระศรีรัตนมหาธาตุ; admission 20B; ⊘8am-4.30pm) contains a classic walking Buddha, a hallmark of the Sukhothai era. **Wat Chao Chan** (วัดเจ้าจันทร์; admission 100B; ⊘8am-5pm) has a large Khmer-style tower probably constructed during the reign of Khmer King Jayavarman VII (1181–1219). The roofless *wíhǎhn* (sanctuary) contains the laterite outlines of a large standing Buddha that has all but melted away from exposure.

Sangkhalok Kilns

The Si Satchanalai-Chaliang area was famous for its beautiful pottery, much of which was exported. The Chinese and Indonesians were once keen collectors, and some fine specimens can still be seen in the National Museum in Jakarta, Indonesia. **Si Satchanalai Centre for Study & Preservation of Sangkhalok Kilns** (ศูนย์ศึกษาและอนุรักษ์เตาสังคโลก; admission 100B; ⊘8.30am-5pm), 5km northwest of Si Satchanalai, has large excavated kilns and intact pottery samples documenting the area's pottery traditions.

Getting There & Away

Si Satchanalai-Chaliang Historical Park is off Rte 101 between Sawankhalok and new Si Satchanalai. From Sukhothai, take a Si Satchanalai bus (46B, 1½ hours, 11am) and ask to get off at 'meuang gòw' (old city). The last bus back to New Sukhothai leaves at 4.30pm.

WORTH A TRIP

SANGKHALOK MUSEUM

This small but comprehensive **museum** (พิพิธภัณฑ์สังคโลก; Rte 1293; admission adult/child 100/50B; ☺8am-5pm) is an excellent introduction to ancient Sukhothai's most famous product and export, ceramics. It displays an impressive collection of original 700-year-old Thai pottery found in the area, plus pieces traded from Vietnam, Burma and China. The 2nd floor features examples of non-utilitarian pottery made as art, including some rare and beautiful ceramic Buddha statues. The museum is about 2.5km east of the centre of New Sukhothai; a túk-túk here will run about 100B.

reservoir, the original site of Thailand's Loi Krathong festival, supplies the Sukhothai community with most of its water.

◉ Northern Zone

This **zone** (admission 100B, plus per bicycle/motorcycle/car 10/30/50B; ☺7.30am-5.30pm) is located 500m north of the old city walls and is easily reached by bicycle.

Wat Si Chum   BUDDHIST TEMPLE
(วัดศรีชุม) This wat contains an impressive *mon·dòp* (pavilion) with a 15m, brick-and-stucco seated Buddha. This Buddha's elegant, tapered fingers are much photographed. Archaeologists theorise that this image is the 'Phra Atchana' mentioned in the famous Ramkhamhaeng inscription.

Wat Phra Phai Luang   BUDDHIST TEMPLE
(วัดพระพายหลวง) This somewhat isolated wat features three 12th-century Khmer-style towers, bigger than those at Wat Si Sawai. This may have been the centre of Sukhothai when it was ruled by the Khmers of Angkor prior to the 13th century.

◉ Western Zone

This **zone** (admission 100B, plus per bicycle/motorcycle/car 10/30/50B; ☺8am-4.30pm) is 2km west of the old city walls but contains largely featureless ruins. A bicycle or motorcycle is necessary to explore this zone.

Wat Saphan Hin   BUDDHIST TEMPLE
(วัดสะพานหิน) Located on the crest of a hill that rises about 200m above the plain, the name of the wat, which means 'stone bridge',

is a reference to the slate path and staircase that leads up to the temple, which are still in place. The site is 3km west of the former city wall and gives a good view of the Sukhothai ruins to the southeast and the mountains to the north and south. All that remains of the original temple are a few *chedi* and the ruined *wí·hǎhn*, consisting of two rows of laterite columns flanking a 12.5m-high standing Buddha image on a brick terrace.

☞ Tours

Cycling Sukhothai   BICYCLE TOURS
(☏08 5083 1864, 0 5561 2519; www.cycling-sukhothai.com; off Th Jarot Withithong; half-/full day 650/750B, sunset tour 350B) Belgian cycling enthusiast Ronny Hanquart has been a Sukhothai resident for nearly 20 years, and his rides follow themed historical itineraries. The office is based about 1.2km west of Mae Nam Yom in New Sukhothai, and free transport can be arranged.

🛏 Sleeping

The accommodation listed here are in New Sukhothai.

TR Room & Bungalow   GUESTHOUSE $
(☏0 5561 1663; www.sukhothaibudgetguesthouse.com; 27/5 Th Prawet Nakhon; r 250-450B, bungalows 400-550B; ✳@🛜) The rooms here are basic and lack character, but figure among the tidiest we've encountered in northern Thailand. For those needing leg room, there are five wooden bungalows out back.

Sabaidee House   HOTEL $
(☏0 5561 6303; www.sabaideehouse.com; 81/7 Th Jarot Withithong; r 200-600B; ✳🛜) This cheery guesthouse in a semi-rural setting spans seven attractive bungalows and rooms in the main structure. Sabaidee is off Th Jarot Withithong about 200m before the intersection with Rte 101; look for the sign.

Hangjeng   GUESTHOUSE $
(☏0 5561 0585; viyada_sethvanich@hotmail.com; 44/10 Th Prawet Nakhon; r 200-400B; ✳@🛜) A sign here reads 'Welcome with open arms', and one gets the impression they really mean it. Maintained by an exceptionally lovely family, the basic rooms are in a rambling house and share toilets and balconies.

Ban Thai   HOTEL $
(☏0 5561 0163; banthai_guesthouse@yahoo.com; 38 Th Prawet Nakhon; r 200-500B, bungalows 350-550B; ✳@🛜) None of the rooms here is particularly remarkable, but the convergence of

a friendly atmosphere, an attractive garden setting and low prices culminate in a winner.

4T Guesthouse
HOTEL **$**

(📞 0 5561 4679; fourthouse@yahoo.com; 122 Soi Mae Ramphan; r 300-400B, bungalows 600-700B; ✴ @ 🛜 ☒) Hardly a leaf is out of place at this expansive budget-level resort. There's a smorgasbord of bungalows and spacious rooms to consider, and the swimming pool makes the decision even easier.

Baan Thit
GUESTHOUSE **$**

(📞 08 1532 6400; www.baantit.com; 31/6 Th Jarot Withithong; r incl breakfast 450-600B; ✴ @ 🛜) The modern-feeling home of a former English teacher has been turned into this comfortable guesthouse. The four rooms are basic but stylish, and most feature quasi-outdoor bathrooms and small balconies.

J&J Guest House
GUESTHOUSE **$**

(📞 0 5562 0095; jjguest-house@hotmail.com; 12 Th Kuhasuwan; bungalows 500-600B; ✴ @ 🛜) Located in a manicured garden by the river, the eight bungalows here are attractive, cool and relatively spacious. They're also identical, and price depends on whether you go with fan or air-con.

✘ Eating & Drinking

Thai towns love to claim a signature dish and Sukhothai weighs in with its own version of *kŭaytǐaw* (noodle soup), featuring a sweet broth, pork, ground peanuts and thinly sliced green beans. The dish is available at **Jayhae** (Th Jarot Withithong; dishes 25-40B; ⊙ 8am-4pm) and **Ta Pui** (Th Jarot Withithong, no roman-script sign; dishes 25-35B; ⊙ 7am-3pm), located across

from each other on Th Jarot Withithong, about 1.3km west of the Mae Nam Yom.

Night Market
MARKET **$**

(Th Jarot Withithong; mains 30-60B; ⊙ 6-11pm) At Sukhothai's evening market, most vendors are accustomed to accommodating foreigners and even provide bilingual menus.

Chula
CHINESE, THAI **$**

(Th Jarot Withithong; dishes 30-120B; ⊙ 10am-11pm) It has all the charm of an airport hangar, but the food at this local favourite is solid. Pick and choose from prepared dishes, or do the same with the raw ingredients displayed out front.

Dream Café
THAI **$$**

(86/1 Th Singhawat; mains 120-250B; ⊙ 5-11pm; 📋) A meal at Dream Café is like dining in an antique shop. Eclectic but tasteful furnishings and knick-knackery abound, staff are equal parts competent and friendly, and most importantly of all, the food is good. Try one of the well-executed *yam* (Thai-style 'salads'), or one of the dishes that feature freshwater fish, a local speciality.

Chopper Bar
BAR

(Th Prawet Nakhon; mains 30-150B; ⊙ 10am-12.30am; 🛜) Both travellers and locals congregate at this restaurant/bar from morning till hangover for food, drinks and live music. Take advantage of Sukhothai's cool evenings on the rooftop terrace.

ℹ Information

There are banks with ATMs in New Sukhothai and a few in Old Sukhothai.

THAILAND SUKHOTHAI

TRANSPORT FROM SUKHOTHAI

DESTINATION	AIR	BUS & MINIVAN	SŎRNGTǍAOU
Bangkok	2500B, 1hr, 2 daily	279-416B, 6-7hr, half-hourly 7.50am-10.40pm	N/A
Chiang Mai	N/A	239-308B, 5-6hr, half-hourly 6.15am-5.30pm	N/A
Chiang Rai	N/A	266B, 9hr, 4 daily	N/A
Kamphaeng Phet	N/A	60-77B, 1½hr, frequent 7.50am-11pm	43B, 2hr, frequent 7am-4.30pm
Mae Sot	N/A	130B, 3hr, 4 daily	N/A
Phitsanulok	N/A	43B, 1hr, hourly 6am-6pm	N/A
Sawankhalok	N/A	29-38B, 1hr, hourly 6.40am-6pm (bus); 85B, 2hr, half-hourly 7.10am-4.30pm (minivan)	N/A
Si Satchanalai	N/A	50B, 1½hr, 11am	N/A

Sukhothai Hospital (☑ 0 5561 0280; Th Jarot Withithong) Located just west of New Sukhothai.

Tawan Hi-Speed (Th Jarot Withithong, no roman-script sign; per hr 10B; ☺ 9.30am-midnight) Internet cafe near the bridge in New Sukhothai.

Tourism Authority of Thailand (TAT; ☑ 0 5561 6228, nationwide 1672; Th Jarot Withithong; ☺ 8.30am-4.30pm) Near the bridge in New Sukhothai, this new office has a pretty good selection of maps and brochures.

❶ Getting There & Away

The airport is an inconvenient 27km from town; **Bangkok Airways** (☑ 0 5564 7224, nationwide 1771; www.bangkokair.com; Sukhothai Airport; ☺ 7.30am-5.30pm) operates flights to Bangkok's Suvarnabhumi International Airport.

The **bus station** (☑ 0 5561 4529; Rte 101) is 1km northwest of the new town centre. A motorcycle taxi between the bus station and New Sukhothai should cost around 50B, to Sukhothai Historical Park, 120B. Alternatively, you can hop on any *sŏrngtăaou* bound for Sukhothai Historical Park (30B, 10 minutes, frequent departures from 6am to 5.30pm).

If you're staying near the historical park, **Win Tour** (Rte 12; ☺ 6am-9.40pm) runs buses to Bangkok (356B, six hours, three daily) and Chiang Mai (239B, five hours, hourly from 6.30am to 1.40pm) from its office near Wat Trapang Thong.

❶ Getting Around

Sŏrngtăaou run between New Sukhothai and Sukhothai Historical Park (30B, 30 minutes, 6am to 5.30pm); vehicles leave from Th Jarot Withithong near Poo Restaurant. A *săhmlór* ride within New Sukhothai should cost no more than 40B.

Kamphaeng Phet กำแพงเพชร

POP 30,000

An easy detour from the tourist trail, Kamphaeng Phet (Diamond Wall) is a peaceful provincial town known for its whitewashed city walls. Historically it played a protective role on the front lines of defence for the Sukhothai kingdom. It's a nice place to spend a day or so wandering around the ruins and experiencing daily Thai life.

◉ Sights

Kamphaeng Phet Historical Park HISTORICAL PARK
(อุทยานประวัติศาสตร์กำแพงเพชร; ☺ 8am-6pm) An Unesco World Heritage Site, this park features the ruins of structures dating back

to the 14th century, roughly the same time as the better-known kingdom of Sukhothai. Kamphaeng Phet's Buddhist monuments continued to be built until the Ayuthaya period, nearly 200 years later, and thus possess elements of both Sukhothai and Ayuthaya styles, resulting in a school of Buddhist art quite unlike anywhere else in Thailand.

The historical park comprises two sections: the **walled city** (admission 100B; ☺ 8am-4pm), just north of modern Kamphaeng Phet, and ruins **outside of town** (admission 100B; ☺ 8am-6pm), about 1.5km north. A combination ticket of 150B allows entry to both. You'll need to charter transport to these two sections: a motorcycle taxi should cost 40B and 80B respectively.

Kamphaeng Phet National Museum MUSEUM
(พิพิธภัณฑสถานแห่งชาติกำแพงเพชร; Th Pindamri; admission 100B; ☺ 9am-noon & 1-4.30pm Wed-Sun) This worthwhile museum was being renovated when we stopped by. Previously, it has been home to an expansive collection of artefacts from the Kamphaeng Phet area, including an immense Shiva statue that is the largest bronze Hindu sculpture in the country.

Kamphaeng Phet Regional Museum MUSEUM
(พิพิธภัณฑ์เฉลิมพระเกียรติกำแพงเพชร; Th Pindamri; admission 10B; ☺ 9am-4.30pm) The regional museum is a series of Thai-style wooden structures on stilts set among nicely landscaped grounds. There are three main buildings in the museum featuring displays ranging from history and prehistory to the various ethnic groups that inhabit the province.

🛏 Sleeping & Eating

A busy night market sets up every evening near the river, just north of the Navarat Hotel.

Three J Guest House GUESTHOUSE $
(☑ 08 1887 4189, 0 5571 3129; www.threejguesthouse.com; 79 Th Rachavitee; r 250-800B; ✳ @ 🛜) The cheapest bungalows at this welcoming guesthouse are fan-cooled and share a clean bathroom while the more expensive have air-con. There's heaps of local information, and bicycles and motorcycles are available for hire.

Grand View Resort HOTEL $
(☑ 0 5572 1104; 34/4 Moo 2, Nakhon Chum; r & bungalows incl breakfast 290-590B; ✳ 🛜) One of a handful of semi-rural 'resorts' on the west

BUSES FROM KAMPHAENG PHET

DESTINATION	PRICE	DURATION	DEPARTURES
Bangkok	230-344B	5hr	frequent 8.30am-1.30
Chiang Mai	228-342B	5hr	8 departures 11.30am-1am
Chiang Rai	305-773B	7hr	frequent noon-10.30pm
Mae Hong Son	509-905B	11hr	10pm & 11pm
Mae Sot (minivan)	140B	3hr	frequent 8am-6pm
Phitsanulok	59-83B	2½hr	hourly 6am-6pm
Sukhothai	65-77B	1hr	hourly

bank of Mae Nam Ping, the highlights here are the six floating raft bungalows.

★ **Bamee Chakangrao** THAI $
(Th Ratchadamnoen 1; mains 25-30B; ☺8.30am-3pm) Thin wheat and egg noodles (bà-mèe) are a speciality of Kamphaeng Phet. The noodles are made fresh every day behind the restaurant. There's no English-language sign; look for the green banners on the corner.

ⓘ Getting There & Around

The bus station is 1km west of Mae Nam Ping. Motorcycle taxis (50B) and sŏrngtăaou (20B, frequent from 7.30am to 5pm) run between the station and town. If coming from Sukhothai or Phitsanulok, get off in the old city or at the roundabout on Th Thesa 1 to save yourself the trouble of backtracking into town.

NORTHERN THAILAND

Forming the crown of the country is a mountainous region loved for its lush forest and unique cultural and natural attractions. This cascade of peaks and valleys unites northern Thailand with the peoples and the cultures of neighbouring Myanmar, Laos and southwestern China. The region's ancient kingdom, known as Lanna Thai (Million Thai Rice Fields), established its capital in Chiang Mai, which retains its connection to the past. Wanderers, such as the autonomous hill-tribe peoples, traversed the range, limited only by altitude rather than political boundaries.

Chiang Mai เชียงใหม่

POP 200,000

Chiang Mai is a cultural darling: it is a cool place to kick back and relax, the streets of the old city are filled with monks (and a ton of Chinese tourists), bookshops outnumber glitzy shopping centres and the region's Lanna heritage is worn with pride. For culture vultures, Chiang Mai is a vibrant classroom to study Thai language, cooking, meditation and massage.

The old city of Chiang Mai is a neat square bounded by a moat and remnants of a medieval-style wall built 700 years ago to defend against Burmese invaders. A furious stream of traffic flows around the old city, but inside the old district narrow soi lead to a quiet world of family-run guesthouses and leafy gardens.

Th Moon Muang, along the east moat, is the main traveller centre but there is also a vibrant scene along Th Ratchaphakhinai, in the southern corner. Intersecting with Th Moon Muang, Th Tha Phae runs east from the exterior of the moat towards the Mae Nam Ping. Once it crosses the river, the road is renamed Th Charoen Muang and eventually arrives at the main post office and train station.

Finding your way around Chiang Mai is fairly simple. A copy of Nancy Chandler's Map Guide to Chiang Mai is a good investment; pick one up at bookshops or guesthouses.

◉ Sights

Chiang Mai's primary attractions are the old city's historic and holy temples that show off distinctive northern Thai architecture. A few stand-out features include intricate carved gables, colourful exterior mosaics, Singha lions guarding the entrances and octagonal high-based chedi.

★ **Wat Phra Singh** BUDDHIST TEMPLE
(วัดพระสิงห์; Th Singharat; admission 20B; ☺6am-6pm) Chiang Mai's most revered temple, Wat Phra Singh draws pilgrims and sightseers for its resident Buddha and its classic Lanna art and architecture. Visitors should dress modestly (clothing covering shoulders and knees).

Chiang Mai

0.25 mi
0   0.5 km

Akha Ama Cafe (400m);
UniTEFL International (1.6km);
Lanna Muay Thai Boxing Camp (2.3km);
Wat Phra That Doi Suthep (16km)

Th Huay Kaew

Th Hutsadisawee

32

Th Mani Nopharat
Th Si Phum

Chang Pheuak Bus Terminal

Th Chotana (Th Chang Pheuak)

Pratu Chang Pheuak

Th Sanan Kila

Th Ratanakosin

Th Chaiyaphum

Th Muang Samut

Indian Consulate (400m)

Thai Tribal Crafts (300m);
McCormick Hospital (600m);
Payap University (600m);
Arcade (3km)

Soi 3

UK Consulate (350m)

Th Kaew Nawarat

Th Wat Ket

Th Charoenrat

Mae Nam Ping

49
51 (1.4km)

Th Tha Phae

Chiang Mai–Lamphun

Th Praisani

Talat Warorot

Wat Saen Fang

Chinese Arch

59

Th Ratchawong

Wat Chompu

Th Chang Moi

Wat U Sai Kham

6
16
53
56
13

Soi 1
Soi 6

Th Chang Khlan

Wat Loi Khroh

Soi 3
Soi 4
Soi 5
Soi 6

Wat Phan Tawng

Pratu Tha Phae

Th Tha Phae

43
Wat Dokaueng
22
52
54
55
14
23
30
38
40
24
15
36
10
34
35
17
29
47
48
25
Wat Lam Chang
27
18
37

Th Moon Muang
Th Chaiyaphum

50

Th Ratchaphakhinai

Soi 1
Soi 7
Soi 6

Soi 9
7

Lanna Folklife Museum
Kasat 1
5
Anusawari Sam

Sunday Walking Street

Wat Pan Ping
Wat Phan An

Soi 5
Soi 8
21
28
26
33

Th Phra Pokklao

Th Ratchamankha

Wat Chedi Luang
3
8
2

Th Ratchadamnoen

Duang Di
Wat Chai Phra Kiat
41
11
19
Wat Thung Yu

District Offices
Former Chiang Mai Women's Prison

Soi 8

Th Jhaban

Wat Hua Khwang
20

Soi 4

Wat Chai
Wat Si Koet
45
39
12

Wat Phra Singh
4

Th Singharat

Th Inthawarorot

Th Bureuangrit
Th Arak

Th Suthep

Wat Suan Dok (900m);
Din Dee Cafe (1.4km);
Warm-Up (1.8km);
Khun Churn (1.9km)

Chiang Mai Ram Hospital

Malaria Centre

Best Friend Library (500m)

46
42

Phra Singh (Lion Buddha), the temple's famous image, is housed in Wihan Lai Kham, a small chapel to the rear of the temple grounds next to the *chedi*. The building boasts a Lanna-style three-tiered roof and carved gables. Inside are sumptuous *lai·krahm* (gold-pattern stencilling) and murals.

★Wat Chedi Luang   BUDDHIST TEMPLE

(วัดเจดีย์หลวง; Th Phra Pokklao; donations appreciated; ☉6am-6pm) A historic and venerable temple, Wat Chedi Luang is built around a crumbling Lanna-style *chedi* (built in 1441) that was one of the tallest structures in ancient Chiang Mai.

The famed Phra Kaew (Emerald Buddha), now held in Bangkok's Wat Phra Kaew, resided in the eastern niche in 1475. Today there is a jade replica, given as a gift from the Thai king in 1995 to celebrate the 600th anniversary of the *chedi* and the 700th anniversary of the city.

Wat Phan Tao   BUDDHIST TEMPLE

(วัดพันเตา; Th Phra Pokklao; donations appreciated; ☉6am-6pm) This pretty little temple evokes mist-shrouded forests and the largess of the teak trade. The main *wí·hăhn* is constructed entirely of moulded teak panels supported by 28 gargantuan teak pillars. Coloured mirror mosaics decorate *naga* (mythical serpent being) bargeboards, and the facade's primary ornamentation of a peacock over a dog, represents the astrological year of the former royal resident's birth.

Wat Chiang Man   BUDDHIST TEMPLE

(วัดเชียงมั่น; Th Ratchaphakhinai; donations appreciated; ☉6am-6pm) Chiang Mai's oldest temple, Wat Chiang Man, was established by the city's founder, Phaya Mengrai, sometime around 1296. The temple contains two famous Buddhas, which reside in the small sanctuary to the right of the main chapel. **Phra Sila** is a marble bas-relief Buddha that stands about 30cm high and reportedly came from Sri Lanka or India. **Phra Sae Tang Khamani**, a 10cm high, crystal image, is thought to have come from Lavo (Lopburi) 1800 years ago.

Wat Suan Dok   BUDDHIST TEMPLE

(วัดสวนดอก; Th Suthep; donations appreciated; ☉6am-6pm) Built on a former flower garden in 1373, this plain-jane temple has a photogenic collection of whitewashed *chedi* that pose in front of the blue peaks of Doi Suthep and Doi Pui.

THAILAND CHIANG MAI

Chiang Mai

According to legend, a relic was brought to Wat Suan Dok, miraculously duplicated itself and was then used as a 'guide' for the founding of Wat Phra That Doi Suthep. The relic is enshrined in the temple's central *chedi*.

Chiang Mai City Arts & Cultural Centre
MUSEUM

(หอศิลปวัฒนธรรมเชียงใหม่; ☎0 5321 7793; Th Phra Pokklao; adult/child 90/40B; ☉8.30am-5pm Tue-Sun) This museum offers a fine primer on Chiang Mai history. The 1st floor has engaging and informative historical and cultural displays. The 2nd-floor rooms have life-sized exhibits of bygone eras, including an early Lanna village.

Nearby are two sister museums: Chiang Mai Historical Centre and Lanna Folklife Museum. A combination ticket for all three costs 180B.

The Arts & Culture Centre is housed in a lovely 1920s building that used to be Chiang Mai's former Provincial Hall.

★ Lanna Folklife Museum
MUSEUM

(พิพิธภัณฑ์พื้นถิ่นล้านนา; Th Phra Pokklao; adult/child 90/40B; ☉8.30am-5pm Tue-Sun) This new and professional museum is a sister site to the other cultural attractions near Anusawari Sam Kasat (Three Kings Monument). Life-size dioramas explain northern Thai religious beliefs and customs, temple

MONK CHAT

If you're curious about Buddhism, many Chiang Mai temples offer 'monk chat', monks get to practise their English by fielding questions from visitors.

Wat Suan Dok (p687) has a dedicated room just beyond the main sanctuary hall a. holds its chats from 5pm to 7pm, Monday, Wednesday and Friday. Wat Sisuphan holds its sessions from 5.30pm to 7pm just before its meditation course. Wat Chedi Luang (p687) has a table under a shady tree where monks chat from 9am to 6pm daily.

paraphernalia and symbolism, traditional crafts and other features of ordinary life. The displays have artistic merit and informative English signage and the atmospheric building, once a former royal residence and later used by the court system, is a pleasure to stroll around.

Chiang Mai Historical Centre MUSEUM
(ทอประวัติศาสตร์เมืองเชียงใหม่; Th Ratwithi; 8.30am-5pm Tue-Sun; adult/child 90/40B) This new museum covers the area's history with professional and well-signed displays. Topics cover the founding of the capital, the Burmese occupation and the modern era of trade and unification with Bangkok. The bottom floor contains an archaeological dig of an ancient temple wall.

Chiang Mai National Museum MUSEUM
(พิพิธภัณฑสถานแห่งชาติเชียงใหม่; 0 5322 1308; www.thailandmuseum.com; off Th Superhighway; admission 100B; 9am-4pm Wed-Sun) Operated by the Fine Arts Department, this museum is the primary caretaker of Lanna artefacts and northern Thai history. The museum is a nice complement to the municipally run Chiang Mai City Arts & Cultural Centre with more art and artefacts that extend beyond the city limits. The best curated section is **Lanna art**, which displays a selection of Buddha images in all styles. Apart from this exhibit, the museum is a bit lacklustre. Unfortunately it is inconveniently located outside of the old city.

Wat Sisuphan BUDDHIST TEMPLE
(วัดศรีสุพรรณ; Soi 2, Th Wualai; donations appreciated; 6am-6pm) The district's silver craftsmanship is given a spectacular setting at this neighbourhood temple. The prime attraction is the 'silver' *ubosot* (ordination hall), covered entirely with silver, nickel and aluminium embossed panels. The temple also hosts local silver artisans, monk chat, meditation courses and Poy Luang Festival (a Shan ordination in March).

★ **Wat Phra That Doi Suthep** BUDDHIST TEMPLE
(วัดพระธาตุดอยสุเทพ; Th Huay Kaew, Doi Suthep; admission 30B; 6am-6pm) Overlooking the city from its mountain throne, Wat Suthep is one of the north's most sacred temples.

The temple was established in 1383 under King Keu Naone and enjoys a mystical birth story. A visiting Sukhothai monk instructed the Lanna king to establish a temple with the twin of a miraculous Buddha relic (enshrined at Wat Suan Dok). The relic was mounted on a white elephant, which wandered the mountain until it died at this spot, interpreted as the 'chosen' location.

The temple is reached by a strenuous, 306-step staircase, intended as an act of meditation. (For the less fit, there's a tram for 20B.)

🏃 **Activities**

Chiang Mai is one of the easiest and most popular places in Thailand to arrange a hill-tribe trek, so competition for business is fierce. It is difficult for Lonely Planet to recommend a specific company because guides often float between companies and the standards fluctuate. Also note that most businesses in Chiang Mai are merely booking agents, not tour operators.

Relying on the travellers' grapevine is a good start, though opinions often diverge wildly. The differences often come down to the trek's social dynamic. Although it is a tour of the outdoors, the social camaraderie is the unexpected highlight. For this reason, try to team up with travellers you enjoy hanging out with as you'll spend more time with them than the elephants or the hill-tribe villagers.

Most companies offer the same itinerary: about an hour trekking, another hour riding an elephant, some waterfall-spotting then spending the night in a hill-tribe village. Repeat if it is a multiday tour. Some trekkers have complained that the hike was too short, others report that it was too strenuous. Keep in mind that the humidity makes physical exertion feel more demanding.

n't expect to have any meaningful con-tions with the hill-tribe villagers; in most ases, the trekking tours stay in rudimentary lodging outside the village and travellers have reported that the village hosts were most un-welcoming. Instead a trek is a good time to get to know Thailand through the Thai guide, who is usually young and charismatic. If you want meaningful interaction with hill-tribe villagers, donate your time to one of the non-profits working with these communities.

We don't advise prebooking in Bangkok as the potential for rip-off is too great. Instead shop around locally to find the lowest com-mission rates.

It is also possible to go trekking in Mae Hong Son and Chiang Rai; the latter has trekking companies with an economic and educational development component.

Chiang Mai has also developed a fairly so-phisticated soft-adventure scene for travellers looking for more of a workout than the hill-tribe treks.

Chiang Mai Mountain
Biking & Kayaking   MOUNTAIN BIKING
(✆08 1024 7046, 0 5381 4207; www.chiangmaikayak ing.com; 1 Th Samlan; tours 1550-2000B) A variety of guided mountain-biking and kayaking trips head into the jungles and rivers, respectively, for fresh air, a workout and mountain scenery. Tours are suited for all levels and adjusted for the seasons. There is a second branch (28 Th Kamphaeng Din) near the night market.

Click and Travel   CYCLING
(✆0 5328 1553; www.clickandtravelonline.com; tours 1050-1200B; 🚲) Click and Travel offers a pedal-powered, cultural trip with full- and half-day tours, visiting temples and attrac-tions outside of the city centre.

Elephant Nature Park   ELEPHANT ENCOUNTER
(✆0 5381 8754; www.elephantnaturepark.org; 1 Th Ratchamankha; 1-/2-day tour 2500/5800B) 🐘 A pioneer in the new wave of elephant tour-ism, Khun Lek (Sangduen Chailert) runs this sanctuary for injured and rescued elephants. The park is in the Mae Taeng valley, 60km from Chiang Mai, and provides a semi-wild environment for the animals. Visitors help wash the elephants and watch the herd, but there is no show or riding. Volunteering is also available.

Baan Chang Elephant
Park   ELEPHANT ENCOUNTER
(✆0 5381 4174; www.baanchangelephantpark. com; 147/1 Th Ratchadamnoen; tours 2400-4200B)

Educating visitors about elephants and their preservation, Baan Chang is a solid choice in the conservation tourism model. Tours involve a day of mahout training, including guiding, riding and bathing. Less-expensive tours are for two people to one elephant. It is located in Mae Taeng, 50 minutes north of Chiang Mai.

Peak Adventure Tour   ADVENTURE SPORTS
(✆0 5380 0567; www.thepeakadventure.com; tours 1800-2500B) The Peak offers a variety of ad-venture trips, including quad biking, abseil-ing, trekking, white-water rafting and rock climbing.

Siam River Adventures   RAFTING
(✆08 9515 1917; www.siamrivers.com; 17 Th Rat-withi; tours from 1800B) With more than a dec-ade of experience, this white-water rafting outfit has a well-regarded safety reputation. The guides have swiftwater rescue training and additional staff are located at danger-ous parts of the river with throw ropes. Trips can be combined with elephant trekking and village overnight stays.

Vocational Training Center of Chiang
Mai Women's Correctional
Institution Centre   MASSAGE
(100 Th Ratwithi; foot/traditional massage 150/180B; ⊘8am-4.30pm Mon-Fri, 9am-4.30pm Sat & Sun) When you tire of sightseeing in the old city, just duck into the women's prison for a massage. Seriously. It offers body and foot massages by inmates participating in a job-training program.

🍴 Courses

Cooking

Cooking classes typically include a tour of a local market, hands-on cooking instruction and a recipe booklet. Classes range from 900B to 1100B and are held at either an in-town location for those with limited time or at an out-of-town garden setting for more ambience. There are dozens of schools.

Gap's Thai Culinary Art School   COOKING
(✆0 5327 8140; www.gaps-house.com; 3 Soi 4, Th Ratchadamnoen; course 900B; ⊘closed Sun) Af-filiated with the guesthouse Gap's House, classes are held out of town at the owner's house. The student-to-teacher ratio is an in-timate 6:1.

Thai Farm Cooking School   COOKING
(✆08 7174 9285, 08 1288 5989; www.thaifarm cooking.com; Soi 9, Th Moon Muang; course 1100B)

MEDITATION COURSES & RETREATS

The seekers and the curious often come to Thailand to explore the spiritual discipline of meditation.

Bangkok's **Wat Mahathat** (Map p656; 3 Th Maha Rat; 🚢 Tha Chang) offers daily meditation instruction amidst Ko Ratanakosin's famous temples.

The sacred city of Chiang Mai is home to **Wat Suan Dok** (📞 08 4609 1357; www.monk chat.net; Th Suthep; ⊘ Tue & Wed), which conducts monthly meditation retreats.

Daen Maha Mongkol Meditation Centre (แดนมหามงคล; ⊘ 8-11am & 1-5pm) is a forest temple outside of Kanchanaburi that runs daily meditation retreats. The centre is off Hwy 323 and is well signposted. By train, get off at Maha Mongkol station.

Wat Pa Nanachat (www.watpahnanachat.org; ⊘ dawn-dusk) **FREE**, in Ubon Ratchathani, was founded by renowned forest monk Phra Ajahn Chah. The temple is geared toward serious monastic trainees who speak English.

Thailand's most famous retreat is run by **Wat Suanmok** (www.suanmokkh.org; Wat Suanmokkh), near the southern town of Chaiya. It is a forest temple founded by Ajahn Buddhadasa Bhikkhu.

You can merge your beach needs with your spiritual needs at Ko Pha-Ngan's **Wat Khao Tham**. Periodic meditation retreats are held by an American-Australian couple.

Teaches cooking classes at its organic farm, 17km outside of Chiang Mai.

Language

Being a university town, Chiang Mai fosters continuing education opportunities in Thai language.

Payap University   LANGUAGE
(http://ic.payap.ac.th; Th Kaew Nawarat, Kaew Nawarat Campus; classes from 8000B) A private university founded by the Church of Christ of Thailand; offers intensive Thai-language courses in 60-hour or 120-hour modules. There is also a three-day course in Thai language, culture and professional ethics (5000B) offered to foreign teachers.

American University Alumni   LANGUAGE
(AUA; 📞0 5327 8407; www.learnthaiinchiangmai. com; 73 Th Ratchadamnoen; group course 4800B) Conducts six-week and eight-week Thai courses that work on mastering tones, small talk and basic reading and writing. Classes meet for two hours, Monday to Friday. Private instruction is also available.

Massage

Lek Chaiya   MASSAGE
(📞0 5327 8325; www.nervetouch.com; 27-29 Th Ratchadamnoen; courses 5000-7000B) Courses run from two to three days and cover about 50% of a traditional Thai massage course, with the remainder dedicated to the nervetouch technique and herbal therapies.

Old Medicine Hospital   MASSAGE
(OMH; 📞0 5327 5085; www.thaimassageschool. ac.th; 78/1 Soi Siwaka Komarat, Th Wualai; courses 5000-6000B) The government-accredited curriculum is very traditional, with a northern-Thai slant, and was one of the first to develop massage training for foreigners. There are two 10-day massage courses a month, as well as shorter foot and oil massage courses.

Muay Thai (Thai Boxing)

Lanna Muay Thai Boxing Camp   BOXING
(Kiatbusaba; 📞0 5389 2102; www.lannamuaythai. com; 161 Soi Chang Khian, Th Huay Kaew; day/month 400/8000B) Offers *muay thai* instruction to foreigners and Thais. The gym is famous for having trained the title-winning, transvestite boxer Parinya Kiatbusaba.

Chai Yai Gym   BOXING
(📞08 2938 1364; www.chaiyaigym.com; 30/17 Th Sunpiliang, Nong Hoi; day/month 550/8000B) This 30-year veteran trains Thai and foreign fighters of all levels. The gym is southeast of town.

TEFL Training

Teaching English as a foreign language (TEFL) is big business in Chiang Mai. Quality TEFL schools should offer the following: trainers with several years of experience and a training diploma, accreditation from one of the international governing boards (either CELTA or TEFL International), a final exam and school practicums.

A HELPING HOLIDAY

Thailand hosts about three million migrants from Myanmar living and working in Thai cities. Many of these workers are undocumented and are vulnerable to arrest and deportation. Their illegal status means they are paid less and are often exploited by their employers and by the police.

The following groups work on issues related to displaced peoples, including education and health care; some also have volunteer positions:

Best Friend Library (302/2 Soi 13, Th Nimmanhaemin; ⊙ 11.30am-8pm Mon-Sat) A community space that offers English-language courses to people from Myanmar, maintains a lending library to educate the international community about Myanmar and works on positive change within Myanmar.

Thai Freedom House (www.thaifreedomhouse.org) Offers education programs.

We Women Foundation (www.wewomenfoundation.org) Assists women from Myanmar to be leaders within their country and communities through scholarships and career development.

MAP Foundation (www.mapfoundationcm.org) An advocacy group working on labour rights, immigration policies and legal representation for the migrant population.

UniTEFL International   TEFL
(📞 08 8402 8217; www.unitefl.com; 123/1 Th Huay Kaew; certificate program 45,000B) Offers 120-hour certificate program with six practicums in Thai schools; uses TEFL International (TI) standards with access to other TI centres and job networks.

International House   TEFL
(www.ihbangkok.com; Vdara Resort & Spa, Mae Hia; certificate program 48,000B) International network of schools using CELTA standards; the school is headquartered in Bangkok with branches in Chiang Mai and Phuket.

✴️ Festivals & Events

Flower Festival   AGRICULTURAL
(⊙ early Feb) This agricultural celebration is held over a three-day period in early February and includes displays of flower arrangements, cultural performances and beauty pageants. The festival highlight is the parade down Th Tha Phae.

Songkran   NEW YEAR
(⊙ mid-Apr) The traditional Thai New Year (12 to 14 April) is celebrated in Chiang Mai with boozy enthusiasm. Thousands of revellers line up along all sides of the moat to throw water on any passersby in the city (and each other). Prior to the start of the pandemonium, more traditional Songkran rituals are held at Wat Phra Singh.

Loi Krathong   RELIGIOUS
(⊙ Oct/Nov) This lunar holiday (usually October or November) is celebrated along Mae Ping with small lotus-shaped boats honouring the spirit of the river. Northern Thais call it Yi Peng, which is traditionally celebrated by launching illuminated lanterns into the night sky.

🛏️ Sleeping

Thanks to the boom in Chinese tourists, new accommodation is springing up all over the city. Vacancies disappear during European and Chinese holiday periods.

Most guesthouses make their 'rice and curry' from booking trekking tours and reserve rooms for those customers. Free wi-fi is standard in Chiang Mai guesthouses.

★ **Awanahouse**   GUESTHOUSE $
(📞 0 5341 9005; www.awanahouse.com; 7 Soi 1, Th Ratchadamnoen; r 375-1000B; 🖲️ 🛜 🌐 🛗) Popular with families, this multistorey building has bright and well-decorated rooms, ranging from basic to just right. The ground-level pool and the rooftop chill-out area are added bonuses.

Gap's House   GUESTHOUSE $
(📞 0 5327 8140; www.gaps-house.com; 3 Soi 4, Th Ratchadamnoen; r 550-850B; 🖲️ 🛜) A matron among guesthouses, good old Gap's still has a jungle-like garden and budget rooms in old-fashioned wooden houses. Bring your mozzie spray. No advance reservations.

Aoi Garden Home   GUESTHOUSE $
(📞 08 3574 8174; 51/1 Soi 4, Th Singharat; dm 150, r 300-380B; 🖲️ 🛜) This self-described 'homey

hostel' is set in a traditional wooden house with an ample garden and lots of shady nooks. Five-bed dorms are mixed; private rooms share bathrooms.

Lamchang House GUESTHOUSE $
(☎0 5321 0586; 24 Soi 7, Th Moon Muang; r 200-300B) One of Chiang Mai's cheapest, this old wooden house has basic fan rooms with shared bathrooms and simple, ascetic charm.

Julie Guesthouse GUESTHOUSE $
(☎0 5327 4355; www.julieguesthouse.com; 7 Soi 5, Th Phra Pokklao; dm 80B, r 100-350B; 🛜) Ever popular Julie is Chiang Mai's sleep and be-seen scene. Rooms boast little to no mod cons (shared bathrooms, cold showers) but the cafe is full of enthusiastic first-timers.

Diva Guesthouse GUESTHOUSE $
(☎0 5327 3851; www.divaguesthouse.com; 84/13 Th Ratchaphakhinai; dm 110B, r 250-800B; 🌬@🛜) One of many new hostels in town, Diva does communal sleeping with a hip attitude. Rooms range from dorms to family suites. The downstairs cafe is a happening scene.

Smile House 1 GUESTHOUSE $
(☎0 5320 8661; www.smilehousechiangmai.com; 5 Soi 2, Th Ratchamankha; r 300-1000B; 🌬🛜⚊⛹) A little backpacker village flourishes around this old house tucked away on a tranquil *soi*. The rooms are basic boxes popular with young backpackers and families because of the lounge-worthy pool.

Thong Ran's House GUESTHOUSE $
(☎0 532 77307; www.thongranhouse.com; 105 Th Ratchamankha; r 600B; 🌬🛜) This new guest-house has cosy, stylish rooms in a quiet *soi* off of the main road. The location is slightly removed from the usual tourist hubbub but still central.

Rendezvous Guest House GUESTHOUSE $
(☎0 5321 3763; 3/1 Soi 5, Th Ratchadamnoen; r 350-900B; 🌬🛜) On a *soi* filled with budget options, Rendezvous stands out from the pack with clean, adequate rooms. It flaunts its backpacker credentials with handy travel-ler info.

Daret's House GUESTHOUSE $
(☎0 5323 5440; 4/5 Th Chaiyaphum; s/d 170/220B) Dependable Daret's has stacks of basic, well-worn but clean rooms at a smidge more than what dorms charge for herd sleeping. You can even splurge for hot-water showers.

Jonadda Guest House GUES[
(☎0 5322 7281; 23/1 Soi 2, Th Ratwithi; r 25
🌬) This reliable cheapie has spotle[
rooms.

VIP House GUESTHOUSE $
(☎08 1366 5625; Soi 1, Th Ratchadamnoen; r 250-500B; 🌬🛜) What VIP lacks in personality it makes up for in budget value: rooms are basic and clean with en suites.

Siri Guesthouse GUESTHOUSE $
(☎0 5332 6550; 31/3 Soi 5, Th Moon Muang; r 350-450B; 🌬) This low-key guesthouse has an assortment of quality budget rooms in a cen-tral location. The upstairs rooms are more spacious and airy than the cheaper ground-floor rooms.

Soho Hostel HOSTEL $
(☎0 5320 6360; 64/2 Th Loi Kroh; dm 200-300B, r 1000-1800; 🌬🛜) Loi Kroh is better known for girly bars than backpacker bunks, but that hasn't prevented this huge hostel from winning fans. It has six- to 12-bed dorms and private rooms.

Spicythai Backpackers HOSTEL $
(☎08 3477 9467; www.spicyhostels.com; 14 Th Hut-sadisawee; dm 250B; 🌬@🛜) Recommended by readers, this place offers single-sex dorms in a converted residence. It is north of the city and has a garden with hammocks, free conti-nental breakfast and a homey setting.

🍴 Eating

Dining in Chiang Mai is homey and healthy with an emphasis on vegetarianism. The city is also well known for its covered markets. **Talat Pratu Chiang Mai** (Th Bamrungburi; ⏱4am-noon & 6pm-midnight) is a busy morning market selling fresh fruit, piles of fried food and fistfuls of sticky rice. After its midday si-esta, the market caters to the dinner crowd.

Northern Thai specialities can be found near the Night Bazaar at the string of res-taurants around **Ban Haw Mosque** (Soi 1, Th Charoen Khlan), the anchor for Chiang Mai's Yunnanese Muslim community. But honestly, the atmosphere is way better than the food.

★ Kow Soy Siri Soy THAI $
(Th Inthawarorot; mains 40-50B; ⏱7am-3pm Mon-Fri) Well known among locals, this is an easy and tasty lunch stop for *kôw soy*. Order *kôw man gài* (chicken and rice) for children and the chilli-averse.

NORTHERN CUISINE

Thanks to northern Thailand's cooler climate, familiar vegetables such as broccoli and cauliflower might make an appearance in a stir-fry. Forest herbs and mushrooms are also incorporated into regional dishes, imparting a distinct flavour of mist-shrouded hills. Even coffee grows here. Day-market vendors sell blue sticky rice, which is dyed by a morning glory–like flower and topped with an egg custard.

Showing its Burmese, Chinese and Shan influences, the north prefers curries that are milder and more stewlike than the coconut milk–based curries of southern and central Thailand. Sour notes are enhanced with the addition of pickled cabbage and lime. The most famous example is *kôw soy*, a mild chicken curry with flat egg noodles. A Burmese expat, *gaang hang·lair* is another example of a northern-style curry. Like the Chinese, northern Thais love pork and vendors everywhere sell *kâap mǔu* (deep-fried pork rind) as a snack and side dish.

Khun Churn
VEGETARIAN $

(Soi 17, Th Nimmanhaemin; buffet 129B; ⊘8am-10pm; ✐) The 'professor' of vegetarian, Khun Churn is best known for its all-you-can-eat meatless buffet (11am to 2pm) boasting dozens of dishes, salads, herbal drinks and Thai-style desserts. Dining with the Churn is a Chiang Mai ritual for expats and Thais.

Angel's Secrets
INTERNATIONAL $

(Soi 1, Th Ratchadamnoen; mains 90-150B; ⊘Tue-Sun 7am-4pm; ✿✐) True to its name, this sweet little restaurant is shielded by a fence of greenery from peeping appetites. Inside you'll find creative and wholesome Western breakfasts, including crusty homemade bread, crepes and omelettes, and made-to-order vegetarian Thai food.

Heuan Phen
THAI $$

(✐0 5327 7103; 112 Th Ratchamankha; mains 80-200B; ⊘11am-10pm) True northern food is difficult to find in a restaurant setting, but this tourist-friendly place does its best to introduce visitors to regional specialities. During the day, pre-made dishes are set up in a large canteen out front. In the evenings, an antique-cluttered dining room offers more of a culinary experience.

AUM Vegetarian Food
VEGETARIAN $

(66 Th Moon Muang; mains 75-150B; ⊘8am-5pm; ✿✐) One of the original health-food peddlers, AUM (pronounced 'om') creates a meditative space to enjoy fresh and original vegetarian dishes.

Dada Kafe
VEGETARIAN $

(Th Ratchamankha; mains 60-100B; ⊘8am-10pm; ✿✐) Tasty health food marches from the kitchen to the dining room of this busy restaurant. Cure-all fruit juices, hearty breakfasts and stir fries with tofu and brown rice become daily rituals for many visitors.

Blue Diamond
VEGETARIAN $

(35/1 Soi 9, Th Moon Muang; mains 70-150B; ⊘7am-9pm Mon-Sat; ✿✐) Chock-full of fresh produce and baked goods, this backpacker kitchen is a jack-of-all health trends: big salads sopped up with slices of bread, veg stir-fries, and 'inter' food such as fish-sauce spaghetti.

Juicy 4U
VEGETARIAN $

(5 Th Ratchamankha; mains 90-120B; ⊘8.30am-5.30pm; ✿✐) This funky cafe does vegan and veg dishes, hangover-fighting juices and make-your-own vegetarian sandwiches – all to a cool techno soundtrack.

Lemontree
THAI $

(Th Huay Kaew; mains 70-110B; ⊘11am-10pm) The well-worn dining room tells you it's been around for a long time and it still garners praise for its cheap, quick and generous portions of Thai standards.

Swan
BURMESE $

(Th Chaiyaphum; mains 70-150B; ⊘11am-10pm; ✐) This grubby restaurant east of the old city offers a trip across the border with its Burmese menu. The backyard courtyard provides an escape from the moat traffic.

Din Dee Cafe
ASIAN $

(Th Nimmanhaemin; mains 70-120B; ⊘9am-6pm Tue-Sun) In the middle of the parking lot of Chiang Mai University Art Center is this outpost to healthy living, housed in a mud hut. Japanese-owned Din Dee does fresh baked bread, herbal salads and bean curries, plus coffee and fruit shakes.

Drinking & Nightlife

The ale flows fast and furious at the tourist bars in the old city. West of the old city, Th Nimmanhaemin is where Thai uni students go bar-hopping.

Zoe In Yellow

BAR

(40/12 Th Rathwithi; ☺5pm-2am) Everybody's party pal, Zoe In Yellow is a beer garden, club and live-music venue. Start off in the garden for sobriety cure-alls then stumble over to the dance floor with your new-found confidence.

UN Irish Pub

PUB

(24/1 Th Ratwithi; ☺10am-midnight) Chiang Mai's leading pub ambassador, this is *the* place for international sport matches and Thursday quiz nights. There's Guinness on tap, a backyard garden and a bakery.

Small House Kafe

BAR

(18/1 Th Sermsuk; ☺5pm-midnight Tue-Sat) A groovy place to howl at the moon with expats and Thais alike. There's hip-hop on Friday nights, periodic book swaps and lots of built-in friends.

Warm-Up

NIGHTCLUB

(☏0 5340 0676; 40 Th Nimmanhaemin; ☺9pm-2am) Still going strong, this hi-so dance club attracts the young and the beautiful. Hip-hop is spun in the main room, electronic house reverberates in the lounge, and rock/indie bands jam in the garden.

CHIANG MAI CAFES

Chiang Mai has gone coffee crazy, with cafes serving locally grown Arabica beans popping up everywhere. Here are a few of our faves:

Libernard Cafe (36 Th Chaiyaphum; dishes 50-110B; ☺8am-5pm Tue-Sun) One of the original brew masters and still does a smooth latte in a slightly ramshackle garden.

Akha Ama Cafe (9/1 Soi 3, Th Hutsadisawee, Mata Apartment; coffee drinks from 50B; ☺9am-9pm) Has a heartwarming backstory: the owner is an Akha tribal member and the first in his village to graduate from college. The old-city branch (www.akhaama.com; 175/1 Th Ratchadamnoen; ☺8am-8pm; ☎) is easier to get to.

Entertainment

Riverside Bar & Restaurant

LIVE MUSIC

(9-11 Th Charoenrat; ☺noon-midnight) Long-running Riverside does dining, drinking and music with a view of the twinkly Mae Ping. Bands range from classic-rock, jazz and even pop, and a recent expansion across the road adds more elbow room.

Good View

LIVE MUSIC

(13 Th Charoenrat; ☺5pm-2am) Cover bands, 20-somethings and a pretty riverside location keeps Good View in everyone's good graces.

Le Brasserie

LIVE MUSIC

(Th Chaiyaphum; ☺5pm-2am) A popular late-night spot has recently moved from its riverside location to this convenient spot near Pratu Tha Phae. Devotees come to hear local guitarist Took pay homage to all the rock and blues legends.

Shopping

Chiang Mai has long been an important centre for handicrafts. Th Tha Phae and the small *soi* near Talat Warorot are filled with interesting antique and textile stores.

Elements

JEWELLERY

(Red Ruby; 400-402 Th Tha Phae; ☺10am-9pm) An eclectic and fun collection of sterling silver and stone jewellery and other trinkets fill this unsigned store near Pratu Tha Phae. Its shop next door sells silks and decorative items.

Praewphun Thai Silk

TEXTILES

(83-85 Th Tha Phae; ☺10am-6pm) This 50-year-old shop sells silks of all ilks, and the octogenerian owner is a spry and dedicated saleswoman.

Thai Tribal Crafts

TEXTILES

(☏0 5324 1043; www.ttcrafts.co.th; 208 Th Bamrungrat; ☺10am-6pm) Peruse the ornate needlework of various hill tribes at this missionary-backed, fair-trade shop near the McCormick Hospital. There is an old-town branch called **Fair Trade** (25/9 Th Moon Muang).

Backstreet Books

BOOKS

(2/8 Th Chang Moi Kao; ☺9am-8pm) Backstreet has a good selection of crime and thriller novels in a rambling shop along 'book alley'.

Information

DANGERS & ANNOYANCES

The majority of guesthouses in town subsidise their cheap room rates through commissions on booking trekking tours. For this reason, they

PEDESTRIAN COMMERCE

Once upon a time Chiang Mai was a destination for itinerant Yunnanese merchants trading goods along an ancient route from China all the way to Burma. Today the city's pedestrian markets tap into this tradition and expertly merge commerce and culture.

Sunday Walking Street (ถนนเดินวันอาทิตย์; Th Ratchadamnoen; ⊘4pm-midnight Sun) A festive night bazaar that takes over the old city. The temples along the way host food stalls selling northern Thai cuisine and other shopping-stamina boosts. The market is extremely popular and gets very crowded.

Saturday Walking Street (ถนนเดินวันเสาร์; Th Wualai; ⊘4pm-midnight Sat) A smaller version of the Sunday Walking Street that unfolds along the traditional silver-smithing neighbourhood south of the old city. Vendors peddling many of the same wares and Thai snacks give everyone a reason to wander, nibble and shop.

Chiang Mai Night Bazaar (Th Chang Khlan; ⊘7pm-midnight) The leading night-time tourist attraction occupying an old Yunnanese trading post. The market offers a huge variety of ordinary souvenirs, some northern Thai handicrafts, and lots of people-watching and people-dodging on the congested footpaths.

might limit nontrekkers to a three-day stay, but ask at check-in.

Avoid the private bus and minivan services from Bangkok's Th Khao San to Chiang Mai because they are full of commission-generating schemes to subsidise the cut-rate fares.

Dengue has become a major concern in Chiang Mai province, especially during the wet season. Use DEET-insect repellent throughout the day and night to avoid mosquito bites.

EMERGENCY

Chiang Mai Immigration Office (☑0 5320 1755; chiangmaiimm.com; Th Mahidon; ⊘8.30am-4.30pm Mon-Fri) Visa extensions available.

Tourist Police (☑0 5324 7318, 24hr emergency 1155; Th Faham; ⊘6am-midnight) Has a volunteer staff of foreign nationals who speak a variety of languages. It's on the eastern side of the river, just south of the superhighway.

INTERNET ACCESS

Most guesthouses and restaurants have free wi-fi, resulting in fewer internet shops.

MEDIA

1 Stop Chiang Mai (www.1stopchiangmai.com) Comprehensive website about tourist attractions and amenities.

Chiangmai Mail (www.chiangmai-mail.com) Weekly English-language newspaper covering local and regional news and politics.

Citylife (www.chiangmainews.com) Lifestyle magazine profiling restaurants, bars, local culture, politics and people; also has a classified section.

Irrawaddy News Magazine (www.irrawaddy.org) A well-respected journal covering news in Myanmar, northern Thailand and other parts of Southeast Asia.

MEDICAL SERVICES

Chiang Mai Ram Hospital (☑0 5322 4880; www.chiangmairam.com; 8 Th Bunreuangrit) The most modern hospital in town, though expats often complain that prices are inflated for travel insurance plans.

Malaria Centre (☑0 5322 1529; 18 Th Bunreuangrit) Offers blood checks for malaria.

McCormick Hospital (☑0 5392 1777; www.mccormick.in.th; 133 Th Kaew Nawarat) Former missionary hospital; good for minor treatments.

MONEY

All major Thai banks have branches and ATMs throughout Chiang Mai; many are along Th Tha Phae and Th Moon Muang.

TOURIST INFORMATION

Tourism Authority of Thailand (TAT; ☑0 5327 6140; www.tourismthailand.org; Th Chiang Mai-Lamphun; ⊘8.30am-4.30pm) English-speaking staff provide maps and recommendations for tour guides. It's just over Saphan Lek on the eastern side of the river. At the time of writing the office had temporarily relocated to 164/94-95 Th Chang Khlan while a new building was being constructed on the original site.

ⓘ Getting There & Away

Regularly scheduled international and domestic flights arrive at **Chiang Mai International Airport** (www.chiangmaiairportonline.com), 3km south of the old city. Domestic airlines include Nok Air, Air Asia, Bangkok Airways and Kan Air. Direct flights linking Chinese cities to Chiang Mai are expanding. Airport taxis cost a flat 120B. If you aren't in a hurry, you can also walk out to the main road and flag down a túk-túk or *rót daang* (literally 'red truck' or *sŏrngtăaou*), which should cost 60B or 80B to your hotel.

There are two bus stations in Chiang Mai. **Arcade bus station** (Th Kaew Nawarat), 3km northeast of town, covers long-distance destinations. From the town centre, a túk-túk should cost 80B to 100B; *rót daang*, about 60B. **Chang Pheuak bus station** (Th Chang Pheuak), north of the old city, handles buses to nearby provincial towns (Tha Ton); to reach the bus station catch a *rót daang* (20B).

The **train station** (Th Charoen Muang) is 2.5km east of the old city. Transport to the station should cost 40B to 60B. Overnight trains from Bangkok's Hualamphong station are a popular way to reach Chiang Mai but bookings need to be made in advance as sleeping berths fill up quickly. In 2013 a portion of the northern line was closed for repairs after several derailments; check local media about current conditions.

ℹ Getting Around

Red *sŏrngtăaou* (called *rót daang*) circulate around the city operating as shared taxis. Flag one down and tell them your destination; if they are going that way, they'll nod and pick up other passengers along the way. The starting fare is 20B, with longer trips 40B. Túk-túk rides around town cost about 60B to 80B; negotiate the fare beforehand.

You can rent bicycles (60B to 150B a day) or 100cc motorcycles (from 200B) to explore Chiang Mai. Bicycles are a great way to get around the city.

Around Chiang Mai

Doi Inthanon National Park
อุทยานแห่งชาติดอยอินทนนท์

The highest peak in the country, Doi Inthanon (2565m), and the surrounding national park (☑ 0 5328 6730; adult/child 200/100B, car/motorbike 30/20B; ⊘ 8am-sunset) have hiking trails, waterfalls and two monumental stupas erected in honour of the king and queen. It's a popular day trip from Chiang Mai for tourists and locals, especially during the New Year's holiday when there's the rarely seen phenomenon of frost.

Most visitors come on a tour from Chiang Mai but the park is accessible via public transport and a lot of patience. Buses leave from Chang Pheuak terminal and

TRANSPORT FROM CHIANG MAI

DESTINATION	AIR	BUS & MINIVAN	TRAIN
Bangkok	1750B, 1½hr, daily (Don Muang Airport); 1750-2000B, daily (Suvarnabhumi)	438-876B, 9-10hr, frequent	491-881B, 12hr, 5-6 daily (sleeper train)
Chiang Khong	N/A	190-351B, 6½hr, 2 daily	N/A
Chiang Rai	N/A	144-288B, 3-4hr, hourly	N/A
Chiang Saen	N/A	232B, 4hr, 1 daily	N/A
Khorat (Nakhorn Ratchasima)	N/A	600-700B, 12hr, 11 daily	N/A
Luang Prabang	Lao Airlines: 5000B, 6 weekly	1200B, 20hr, 2 daily	N/A
Mae Hong Son (via Mae Sariang)	N/A	192-346B, 5-6hr, 6 daily	N/A
Mae Hong Son (via Pai)	1500B, 35min, daily	138B, 7-8hr, hourly; 250B, 6hr, hourly (minivan)	N/A
Mae Sai	N/A	182-364B, 5hr, 2-3 daily	N/A
Mae Sariang	N/A	100-200B, 4-5hr, 6 daily	N/A
Mae Sot	1200B, 1hr, daily	259-330B, 6hr, 2 daily	N/A
Pai	1900B, 1½hr, 3 weekly	138B, 4hr, hourly; 150B, 3hr, hourly (minivan)	N/A
Sukhothai	N/A	239-308B, 5-6hr, 6 daily	N/A
Tha Ton	N/A	90B, 4hr, 6 daily	N/A

rngtăaou leave from Pratu Chiang
hom Thong (70B), 58km from Chi-
nd the closest town to the park.

's go directly to the park's entrance
near Nam Tok Mae Klang, and some are
bound for Hot and will drop you off in Chom
Thong.

From Chom Thong there are regular
sŏrngtăaou to the park's entrance gate
(50B), about 8km north. *Sŏrngtăaou* from
Mae Klang to the summit of Doi Inthanon (100B) leave almost hourly until late
afternoon.

Mae Sa Valley Loop   แม่สา

One of the easiest mountain escapes, the
Mae Sa Valley loop travels from the lowland's concrete expanse into the highlands'
forested frontier. The 100km route makes
a good day trip with private transport.
Golden Triangle Rider (www.gt-rider.com)
publishes a detailed map of the area.

Head north of Chiang Mai on Rte 107 (Th
Chang Pheuak) toward Mae Rim, then left
onto Rte 1096. The road becomes more rural but there's a steady supply of tour-bus
attractions: orchid farms, butterfly parks,
snake farms, you name it.

The road eventually starts to climb and
twist into the fertile **Mae Sa Valley**, once
a high-altitude basin for growing opium
poppies. Now the valley's hill-tribe farmers
have re-seeded their terraced fields with
sweet peppers, cabbage, flowers and fruits,
which are then sold to the royal agriculture
projects under the Doi Kham label.

On the outskirts of the valley, the road
swings around the mountain ridge and
starts to rise and dip until it reaches the
conifer zone. Beyond, the landscape unfolds in a cascade of mountains and eventually the road spirals down into **Samoeng**,
a pretty Thai town, and then arcs back into
Chiang Mai.

Chiang Rai   เชียงราย

POP 68,000

Leafy and well groomed, Chiang Rai is more
liveable than visitable. The town itself is a
convenient base for touring the Golden
Triangle and an alternative to Chiang Mai
for arranging hill-tribe treks. Don't assume
you'll be the only foreigner in town; Chiang
Rai is well-loved by well-heeled package
tourists.

◉ Sights

Wat Phra Kaew   BUDDHIST TEMPLE
(วัดพระแก้ว; Th Trairat; ⊘temple 7am-7pm, museum 9am-5pm) FREE This is the city's most
revered Buddhist temple. Legend has it that
in 1434 lightning struck the temple's *chedi*,
which fell apart to reveal the Phra Kaew
Morakot (Emerald Buddha), now housed in
Bangkok's Wat Phra Kaew and considered a
national talisman.

Oub Kham Museum   MUSEUM
(พิพิธภัณฑ์อูบคำ; www.oubkhammuseum.com; Th
Nakhai; adult/child 300/100B; ⊘8am-5pm) This
slightly zany museum houses an impressive
collection of paraphernalia from virtually
every corner of the former Lanna kingdom.
The items, some of which truly are one of a
kind, range from a monkey-bone food tast-
er used by Lanna royalty to an impressive
carved throne from Chiang Tung, Myanmar.

The Oub Kham Museum is 2km west of
the town centre and can be a bit tricky to
find; túk-túk will go here for about 50B.

**Hilltribe Museum &
Education Center**   MUSEUM
(พิพิธภัณฑ์และศูนย์การศึกษาชาวเขา; www.pdacr.org;
3rd fl, 620/25 Th Thanalai; admission 50B; ⊘9am-
6pm Mon-Fri, 10am-6pm Sat & Sun) This museum
and cultural centre is a good place to visit
before undertaking any hill-tribe trek. Run
by the nonprofit Population & Community
Development Association (PDA), the displays
are underwhelming in their visual presenta-
tion, but contain a wealth of information on
Thailand's various tribes and the issues that
surround them.

**Mae Fah Luang Art &
Culture Park**   MUSEUM
(ไร่แม่ฟ้าหลวง; www.maefahluang.org/rmfl; 313 Moo
7, Ban Pa Ngiw; admission 200B; ⊘8.30am-4.30pm
Tue-Sun) In addition to a museum that houses
one of Thailand's biggest collections of Lanna
artefacts, this meticulously landscaped compound includes antique and contemporary
Buddhist temples, art and other structures.
Mae Fah Luang Art & Culture Park is located
about 4km west of the centre of Chiang Rai;
a túk-túk or taxi here will run around 100B.

**Tham Tu Pu &
Buddha Cave**   BUDDHIST TEMPLE
(ถ้ำตูปู/ถ้ำพระ; ⊘daylight hours) FREE If you
follow Th Winitchaikul across the bridge to
the northern side of Mae Nam Kok, you'll
come to a turn-off for Tham Tu Pu and the

Chiang Rai

Buddha Cave, two caves about 1.5km and 4km, respectively, from town.

Neither attraction is particularly amazing on its own, but the surrounding country is beautiful and would make an ideal destination for a lazy bike ride.

🏃 Activities

Most two-day tours (starting at 2500B) typically cover the areas of Doi Tung, Doi Mae Salong or Chiang Khong. The following are primarily nonprofit community development organisations working in hill-tribe communities that use trekking as an awareness campaign and fundraiser.

Mirror Foundation   TREKKING
(📞0 5373 7616; www.thailandecotour.org) Although its rates are higher than others, trekking with this nonprofit NGO helps support the training of its local guides. Treks range from one to three days and traverse the Akha,

Karen and Lahu villages of Mae Yao District, north of Chiang Rai.

PDA Tours & Travel   TREKKING
(📞0 5374 0088; www.pda.or.th/chiangrai/pack age_tour.htm; 3rd fl, Hilltribe Museum & Education Center, 620/25 Th Thanalai; ⊙9am-6pm Mon-Fri, 10am-6pm Sat & Sun) One- to three-day treks are available through this NGO. Profits go back into community projects that include HIV/AIDS education, mobile health clinics, education scholarships and the establishment of village-owned banks.

Rai Pian Karuna   TREKKING
(📞08 7186 7858, 08 2195 5645; www.facebook.com/raipiankaruna) This new, community-based social enterprise conducts one- and multiday treks and homestays at Akha, Lahu and Lua villages in Mae Chan, north of Chiang Rai. Other activities, from week-long volunteering stints to cooking courses, are also on offer.

Chiang Rai

🛏 Sleeping

Baan Bua Guest House   GUESTHOUSE **$**
(🖉0 5371 8880; www.baanbua-guesthouse.com; 879/2 Th Jetyod; r 300-500B; ❋ @ ☎) This quiet guesthouse consists of a strip of 17 bright green rooms surrounding an inviting garden. Rooms are simple, but clean and cosy.

The North   HOTEL **$**
(🖉0 5371 9873; www.thenorth.co.th; 612/100-101 Sirikon Market; dm 200B, r with fan/air-con 350/450B; ❋ @ ☎) This hotel has provided the drab market/bus station area with a bit of colour. The 15 rooms here combine both Thai and modern design, some attached to inviting chill-out areas.

Moon & Sun Hotel   HOTEL **$**
(🖉0 5371 9279; www.moonandsun-hotel.com; 632 Th Singhaclai; r incl breakfast 500-600B; ste incl breakfast 800B; ❋ ☎) Bright and sparkling clean, this little hotel offers large modern rooms. Some feature four-poster beds, while all come with desk, cable TV and refrigerator. Suites have a separate, spacious sitting area.

Chook Dee Guest House   GUESTHOUSE **$**
(🖉08 6027 8529; Th Jetyod; dm 100B, r 200-250B) The rooms are basic, and the hyper-chilled reggae vibe doesn't exactly suggest sky-high standards of service, but for those who fancy a social backpacker scene, this is your place.

Jansom House   HOTEL **$**
(🖉0 5371 4552; 897/2 Th Jetyod; r incl breakfast 450-500B; ❋ ☎) This three-storey hotel offers tidy rooms set around a small courtyard filled with plants. Go for the slightly more expensive air-con rooms, as the ground-floor fan rooms can be a bit musty.

★Bamboo Nest de Chiang Rai   GUESTHOUSE **$$**
(🖉08 9953 2330, 08 1531 6897; www.bamboonest-chiangrai.com; bungalows incl breakfast 650-1300B) The Lahu village that's home to this unique accommodation is only 23km from Chiang Rai but feels a world away. Bamboo Nest takes the form of simple but spacious bamboo huts perched on a hill overlooking tiered rice fields. The only electricity is provided by solar panels. Free transport to/from Chiang Rai is available for those staying two nights or more.

Ben Guesthouse   GUESTHOUSE **$$**
(🖉0 5371 6775; www.benguesthousechiangrai.com; 351/10 Soi 4, Th Sankhongnoi; r 350-850B, ste 1500-3000B; ❋ @ ☎ ❄) Ben is one of the best budget-to-midrange places we've encountered in the north. The absolutely spotless compound has a bit of everything, from fan-cooled cheapies to immense suites. It's 1.2km from the centre of town, at the end of Soi 4 on Th Sankhongnoi (the street is called Th Sathanpayabarn where it intersects with Th Phahonyothin) – a 60B túk-túk ride away.

✕ Eating

The **night bazaar** has a decent collection of food stalls offering snacks and meals as well as post-noshing shopping.

Khao Soi Phor Jai   THAI **$**
(Th Jetyod, no roman-script sign; mains 30-60B; ☉7.30am-5pm) Phor Jai serves mild but tasty bowls of the eponymous curry noodle dish, as well as a few other northern Thai staples.

Rosprasert Muslim Food   MUSLIM, THAI **$**
(Th Itsaraphap; mains 25-50B; ☉7am-8pm) This open-air restaurant next to the mosque on Th Itsaraphap dishes up delicious Thai-Muslim favourites, including *kôw mòk gài*, the Thai version of chicken biryani.

Nam Ngiaw Paa Nuan   VIETNAMESE, THAI **$**
(Vietnamese Restaurant; Th Sanpannard, no roman-script sign; mains 10-120B; ☉9am-5pm) This

WAT RONG KHUN & BAAN DUM

Modern art meets religious symbolism in two of Chiang Rai's bizarre but beloved attractions.

Known as the White Temple, **Wat Rong Khun** (วัดร่องขุ่น; off Asia 1 Hwy; ⊗ 8am-5pm Mon-Fri, 8am-5.30pm Sat & Sun) `FREE` is the artistic vision of noted Thai painter-turned-architect Chalermchai Kositpipat. The temple has a stunning whitewashed facade and several avant-garde sculpture installations representing Buddhist principals. Contemporary historic scenes as well as pop culture references have replaced the typical images of village life and Buddha figures found in temple murals.

Wat Rong Khun is located about 13km south of Chiang Rai. To get to the temple, hop on one of the regular buses that run from Chiang Rai to Chiang Mai or Phayao (20B).

Nearby is the visual counterpoint of **Baan Dum** (Black House; off Asia 1 Hwy; ⊗ 9am-noon & 1-5pm) `FREE`, the bizarre brainchild of Thai National Artist Thawan Duchanee. The 'Black House' unites several northern Thai–style houses into an exhibit of the macabre, decorated with animal pelts and bones. Baan Dum is located 13km north of Chiang Rai in Nang Lae; any Mae Sai–bound bus will drop you off here for around 20B.

quasi-concealed place serves a unique mix of Vietnamese and northern Thai dishes. Tasty food, friendly service and a fun barnlike atmosphere make us wish they were open for dinner as well.

Phu-Lae NORTHERN THAI $$
(673/1 Th Thanalai; mains 80-320B; ⊗ 11.30am-3pm & 5.30-11pm) This air-conditioned restaurant is exceedingly popular with Thai tourists for its tasty but somewhat gentrified northern Thai fare. Recommended local dishes include the *gaang hang·lair* (pork belly in a rich Burmese-style curry), here served with pickled garlic, and *sâi òo·a*, herb-packed pork sausages.

🍷 Drinking

Th Jetyod is Chiang Rai's bar strip thanks to popular **Cat Bar** (1013/1 Th Jetyod; ⊗ 5pm-1am) and **Easy House** (cnr Th Jetyod & Th Pemavipat; ⊗ 5pm-midnight).

BaanChivitMai Bakery CAFE
(www.baanchivitmai.com; Th Prasopsook; ⊗ 8am-9pm Mon-Sat; 🛜) In addition to a very well prepared cup of local joe, you can snack on amazingly authentic Swedish-style sweets (and Western-style meals and sandwiches) at this popular bakery. Profits go to BaanChivitMai, an organisation that runs homes and education projects for vulnerable, orphaned or AIDS-affected children.

🛍 Shopping

Walking Street MARKET
(Th Thanalai; ⊗ 4-10pm Sat) If you're around

on a Saturday evening check out this street market focusing on all things Chiang Rai, from handicrafts to local dishes. The market spans Th Thanalai from the Hilltribe Museum to the morning market.

Thanon Khon Muan MARKET
(Th Sankhongnoi; ⊗ 6-9pm Sun) Come Sunday evening, the street becomes a pedestrian market filled with vendors selling clothes, handicrafts and local food. Th Sankhongnoi is called Th Sathanpayabarn where it intersects with the southern end Th Phahonyothin.

Orn's Bookshop BOOKS
(off Soi 1, Th Jetyod; ⊗ 8am-8pm) Although Orn's feels like the private library of a conspiracy theorist, the general selection is decent and spans many languages.

ℹ️ Information

Banks can be found along Th Thanalai and along Th Phahonyothin. Internet access is readily available for about 30B.

Overbrook Hospital (📞 0 5371 1366; www.overbrookhospital.com; Th Singhaclai) English is spoken at this modern hospital.

Tourism Authority of Thailand (TAT; 📞 0 5374 4674, nationwide 1672; tatchrai@tat.or.th; Th Singhaclai; ⊗ 8.30am-4.30pm) English is limited, but staff here do their best to give advice and can provide a small selection of maps and brochures.

Tourist Police (📞 0 5374 0249, nationwide 1155; Th Utarakit; ⊗ 24hr) English is spoken and police are on stand-by 24 hours a day.

TRANSPORT FROM CHIANG RAI

DESTINATION	AIR	BUS & MINIVAN
Bangkok	2135-3590B, 1¼hr, 2 daily (Don Muang Airport); 2600B, 1¼hr, 3 daily (Suvarnabhumi International Airport)	487-980B, 11-12hr, hourly 7-9.40am & 5-7.30pm
Chiang Khong	N/A	65B, 2hr, frequent 6am-5pm
Chiang Mai	N/A	144-288B, 3-7hr, hourly 6.30am-7.30pm
Chiang Saen	N/A	39-45B, 1½hr, frequent
Kunming (China)	7500B, 1hr, 3 weekly	N/A
Lampang	N/A	112-157B, 4-5hr, hourly
Luang Prabang (Laos)	N/A	950B, 16hr, 1pm
Mae Sai	N/A	39-46B, 1½hr, frequent
Phitsanulok	N/A	273-410B, 6-7hr, hourly 6.30am-10.30pm
Sop Ruak (Golden Triangle)	N/A	50B, 2hr, hourly 6.20am-5.40pm
Sukhothai	N/A	300B, 8hr, hourly 7.30am-2.30pm
Tha Ton	N/A	350B, 4hr, 10.30am

ⓘ Getting There & Away

Chiang Rai International Airport (Mae Fah Luang; ☑ 0 5379 8000) is 8km north of town. **Air Asia** (☑ 0 5379 3543, nationwide 0 2515 9999; www.airasia.com; ⊙ 8am-9pm) and **Nok Air** (☑ 0 5379 3000, nationwide 1318; www.nokair.co.th; ⊙ 8am-7pm) fly to Bangkok's Don Muang and Thai Airways International flies to Suvarnabhumi. **China Eastern** (☑ 0 5379 3688; www.flychinaeastern.com; ⊙ 8.30am-5pm) flies to Kunming. From town, a metered taxi will cost 120B.

Chiang Rai's **provincial bus station** (Th Prasopsook) is in the heart of town; it also has ordinary (fan) buses to nearby provinces. The **long-distance bus station** (☑ 0 5377 3989) is 5km south of town on Hwy 1. *Sŏrngtăaou* link the old station (15B).

Chiang Rai is accessible by boat along Mae Nam Kok from Tha Ton, the northern tip of Chiang Mai province.

Golden Triangle

The three-country border between Thailand, Myanmar and Laos forms the legendary Golden Triangle, once a mountainous frontier where the opium poppy was a cash crop for the region's ethnic minorities. Thailand has successfully stamped out its cultivation through infrastructure projects, crop-substitution programs and aggressive law enforcement.

But the porous border and lawless areas of the neighbouring countries have switched production to the next generation's drug of choice: methamphetamine and, to a lesser extent, heroin. Much of this illicit activity is invisible to the average visitor and the region's heyday as the leading opium producer is now marketed as a tourist attraction.

Mae Salong   แม่ สลอง
POP 20,000

Built along the spine of a mountain, Mae Salong is more like a remote Chinese village in Yunnan than a Thai town. It was originally settled by the 93rd Regiment of the Kuomintang Nationalist Party (KMT), which fled from China after the 1949 revolution. The ex-soldiers and political exiles initially settled in Myanmar but later were forced to Thailand, where they supported themselves as middlemen between the opium growers and the opium warlords. The modern-day descendants still carry on the language and traditions (minus the profession) of their forefathers: Chinese is more frequently spoken here than Thai and the land's severe incline boasts tidy terraces of tea and coffee plantations.

An interesting **morning market** (⊙ 6-8am) convenes at the T-junction near Shin Sane Guest House. The market attracts town residents and tribespeople from the surrounding

SLOW BOATS TO CHIANG RAI

Escape the daredevil highway antics of Thailand's bus drivers with a slow ride on the Mae Nam Kok departing from Tha Ton, north of Chiang Mai. The river ride is a big hit with tourists and includes stops at hill-tribe villages that specialise in Coca-Colas and souvenirs. This isn't uncharted territory but it is scenic and relaxing.

Chiang Rai–bound boats (☑ 0 5305 3727; ticket 350B; ⊘ departs 12.30pm) leave from Tha Ton and make stops along the way at Mae Salak, a large Lahu village, and Ban Ruammit, a Karen village. The trip takes three to five hours; the boat carries 12 passengers.

In order to catch the boat on time, you'll need to overnight in Tha Ton; there are several pretty riverside guesthouses, including Apple Resort (☑ 0 5337 3144; r 500-1200B; ❄). Buses from Chiang Mai to Tha Ton leave from Chang Pheuak bus station.

You can also do the trip in reverse (from Chiang Rai to Tha Ton), a less popular option because it takes much longer. Boats leaving Chiang Rai disembark from CR Pier (☑ 0 5375 0009; ⊘ 6am-4.30pm) in the northwest corner of town at 10.30am.

Adding to your indecision, you could skip the river and backdoor to Chiang Rai via the ridgetop village of Mae Salong.

districts. An all-day market sets up at the southern end of town. Most of the guesthouses in town can arrange treks to nearby hill-tribe villages; some also distribute maps for self-guided tours.

Shin Sane Guest House (☑ 0 5376 5026; www.maesalong-shinsane.blogspot.com; r 100B, bungalows 300B; @ ❁) is Mae Salong's original guesthouse, boasting the standards and prices of decades past. Saeng A Roon Hotel (☑ 0 5376 5029; r 300-400B; ❄ ❁) is a newcomer to these parts. Little Home Guesthouse (☑ 0 5376 5389; www.maesalonglittlehome.com; bungalows 800B; @ ❁) has a collection of bungalows near the market intersection; the friendly owner produces an accurate map of the area.

Getting to Mae Salong is an adventure in transport: take a Chiang Rai–Mae Sai bus and get off at Ban Pasang (20-25B, 30 minutes, frequent 6am to 8pm). From there, sŏrngtăaou climb the mountain to Mae Salong (60B, one hour, when full from 6am to 5pm); you can also charter a vehicle for 500B. Mae Salong can also be reached from the scenic western road via Tha Ton (50B).

Mae Sai   เเม่สาย

POP 22,000

Thailand's northernmost town is a busy trading post for gems, jewellery, cashews and lacquerware, and is also a legal border crossing into Myanmar. Many travellers make the trek here to extend their Thai visa or to dip their toes into Myanmar. The town is also a convenient base for exploring the surrounding Golden Triangle area.

Most guesthouses line the street along the Mae Nam Kok to the left of the border checkpoint. Maesai Guest House (☑ 0 5373 2021; 688 Th Wiengpangkam; bungalows 200-600B; ❁) has a collection of A-frame bungalows with varying amenities. Yeesun Guesthouse (☑ 0 5373 3455; www.yeesunguesthouse.com; 816/13 Th Sailomjoy; r 400B; ❄ ❁) is a good-value, family-run hotel. Little Bear (☑ 0 5364 0933; www. littlebear-house.com; off Soi 6, Th Phahonyothin; r 280-480B; ❄ @ ❁) has basic but tidy rooms and a social bar-cafe.

Mae Sai has a night market (Th Phahonyothin; mains 30-60B; ⊘ 5-11pm) with an excellent mix of Thai and Chinese dishes. Bismillah Halal Food (Soi 4, Th Phahonyothin; mains 30-60B; ⊘ 5am-5pm) does an excellent biryani.

The bus station (☑ 0 5371 1224; Rte 110) is 4km from the immigration office. Destinations include Bangkok (673B to 943B, 12 hours, frequent), Chiang Mai (182B to 364B, five hours, nine departures), Chiang Rai (39B to 69B, 1½ hours, frequent) and Tha Ton (74B, two hours, 7am).

On Th Phahonyothin by Soi 8 there's a bus stop from which sŏrngtăaou run to Sop Ruak (40B, frequent) and terminate in Chiang Saen (50B). Sŏrngtăaou around town cost 15B.

Chiang Saen   เชียงแสน

POP 11,000

A sedate river town, Chiang Saen is famous in the Thai history books as the 7th-century birthplace of the Lanna kingdom, which later moved to Chiang Mai. Today, huge river

THAILAND GOLDEN TRIANGLE

GETTING TO MYANMAR: MAE SAI TO KYAINTONG

Getting to the border The Thai immigration office at the Mae Sai/Tachileik border is just before the bridge over the Mae Nam Sai in the centre of town.

At the border If you're approaching from Thailand and haven't already obtained a Myanmar visa, it's relatively straightforward to cross to Tachileik for the day, and slightly more complicated to get a two-week visa and permission to visit Kyaingtong and/or Mong La.

The Thai immigration office is open from 6.30am to 6.30pm. After taking care of the usual formalities, cross the bridge and head to the Myanmar immigration office. There, you must pay a fee of 500B and your picture is taken for a temporary ID card that allows you to stay in town for the day; your passport will be kept at the office. The border town of Tachileik looks a lot like Mae Sai, except with more teashops and Burmese restaurants.

Moving on If you'd like to visit Kyaingtong and/or Mong La on the Chinese border, proceed directly to the MTT office. There, you'll need to inform the authorities exactly where you're headed, and you'll need three photos and US$10 or 500B to process a border pass valid for 14 days; your passport will be kept at the border during this time, and you're expected to exit Myanmar at Tachileik. It's also obligatory to hire a guide for the duration of your stay. Guides cost 1000B per day, and if you haven't already arranged for a Kyaingtong-based guide to meet you at the border, you'll be assigned one by MTT and will also have to pay for your guide's food and accommodation during the duration of your stay. Recommended guides include **Leng** (+95 9490 31470; sairoctor.htunleng@gmail.com), **Freddie** (Sai Yot; +95 9490 31934; yotkham@gmail.com) and **Paul** (Sai Lon; +95 842 2812, +95 9490 30464). Note that if you're crossing this way, advance permission from MTT is required to visit other destinations in Myanmar.

At research time, foreign travellers were allowed to travel by road between Tachileik and Mong La, and by air between Kyaingtong and Tachileik and the rest of Myanmar, but the 280 miles of NH4 between Kyaingtong and Taunggyi remained completely off-limits.

For information on making the crossing in the other direction, see p510.

---

barges from China moor in town, reviving an old interior Asian trade route.

You can wander around the kingdoms' ruins at **Wat Pa Sak** (วัดป่าสัก; off Rte 1290; historical park admission 50B; ⊙8.30am-4.30pm Wed-Sun) `FREE`, about 200m from Pratu Chiang Saen, along with other ruins scattered throughout town. Or survey the artefacts at **Chiang Saen National Museum** (พิพิธภัณฑสถานแห่งชาติเชียงแสน; 702 Th Phahonyothin; admission 100B; ⊙8.30am-4.30pm Wed-Sun).

An easy day trip from Chiang Saen is the 'official' centre of the Golden Triangle, **Sop Ruak**, an odd souvenir and museum stop for package tourists. The **House of Opium** (บ้านฝิ่น; www.houseofopium.com; Rte 1290; admission 50B; ⊙7am-7pm), across from the giant Buddha statue known as Phra Chiang Saen Si Phaendin, has historical displays pertaining to opium culture. Another drug-themed museum is the **Hall of Opium** (หอฝิ่น; Rte 1290; admission 200B; ⊙8.30am-4pm Tue-Sun), 1km south of town opposite the Anantara Resort & Spa. The facility includes a fascinating history of opium and

examines the effects of abuse on individuals and society. Sop Ruak is accessible from Chiang Saen via **Mekong River Trips** (Th Rimkhong; ⊙8am-3pm), for 500/600B one way/return per boat (five passengers). Or you can catch a blue *sŏrngtǎaou* (20B, frequent 7am to noon) at the eastern end of Th Phahonyothin.

Sleeping options in Chiang Saen include **Chiang Saen Guest House** (☑0 5365 0196; 45/2 Th Rimkhong; r & bungalows 100-500B; ❋⌖), opposite the river and night stalls, and **Sa Nae Charn Guest House** (☑0 5365 1138; 641 Th Nhongmoon; r 300-450B; ❋⌖). **Riverside food vendors** (Th Rimkhong; mains 30-60B; ⊙4-11pm) set up each evening along the bank of the Mekong River in the dry months. There are also **evening food vendors** (Th Phahonyothin; mains 30-60B; ⊙4-10pm) and a **Walking Street** (Th Rimkhong; mains 20-60B; ⊙4-9pm Sat).

Chiang Saen has an informal bus terminal at the eastern end of Th Phahonyothin. Destinations include Chiang Rai (37B, 1½ hours, frequent) and Chiang Mai (232B, five hours, one morning departure).

Sŏrngtăaou go to Mae Sai (50B) and Chiang Khong (80B). The Mekong River Trips also continue to Chiang Khong (2500/3000B per boat one way/return).

Chiang Khong
เชียงของ

POP 12,000

Remote yet lively Chiang Khong is historically important as a market town for local hill tribes and for trade with northern Laos. Travellers pass through en route to Laos and southern China.

🛏 Sleeping

PP Home
GUESTHOUSE $

(Baan Pak Pon; ☑ 0 5365 5092; baanpakpon@hotmail.co.th; off Th Sai Klang; r 350-600B; ✳@🛜) One of a dwindling number of accommodation options still owned by locals, this rambling wooden house features large rooms with wood panelling and a couple of new rooms in an adjacent cement add-on.

Funky Box
HOSTEL $

(☑08 2765 1839; Soi 2, Th Sai Klang; dm 100B; ✳🛜) In addition to 16 dorm beds, this new and lively hostel also has a bicycle-themed pub and museum.

Rimnaum Guest House
HOTEL $

(☑0 5365 5680; abu_bumpbump@sanook.com; off Th Sai Klang; r 350-500B; ✳🛜) This riverside place unites 20 mostly identical, spacious and clean budget rooms, the more expensive of which have air-con.

Chiang Khong Green Inn
HOTEL $

(☑0 5379 1009; www.chiangkhong-greeninn.com; 89/4 Th Sai Klang; r 200-500B; ✳@🛜) The cheaper rooms in this modern-feeling backpacker joint are tight, fan-cooled and share bathrooms, but the rooms with air-con have a bit more leg room and TVs.

Baanrimtaling
GUESTHOUSE $

(☑0 5379 1613; maleewan_th@yahoo.com; 99/2 Soi 19, Th Sai Klang; dm 100-120B, r 150-450B; @🛜) The rooms here are pretty run-of-the-mill for this price range, and the location isn't exactly ideal, but the homelike atmos-

phere and gentle service may have you staying a bit longer than you planned.

🍴 Eating

Street eats can be found at the twice-weekly **Walking Street** (Th Sai Klang; mains 30-60B; ⊙6-10pm Wed & Sat Nov-May).

Khao Soi Pa Orn
THAI $

(Soi 6, Th Sai Klang, no roman-script sign; mains 15-30B; ⊙8am-4pm) You may think you know *kôw soy*, the famous northern curry noodle soup, but the version served in Chiang Khong forgoes the coconut milk and replaces it with a rich minced pork and tomato mixture.

Bamboo Mexican House
INTERNATIONAL $$

(Th Sai Klang; mains 70-250B; ⊙7.30am-8.30pm; 🖉) Run by the manager of a now-defunct guesthouse, the chef of this tiny restaurant and bakery learned to make Mexican dishes from her American and Mexican guests. To be honest, though, we never got past the coffee and delicious homemade breads and cakes. Opens early, and boxed lunches can be assembled for the boat ride to Luang Prabang.

ⓘ Getting There & Away

Buses pick up and drop off passengers at various points near the market, south of the centre of town. *Sŏrngtăaou* to Chiang Saen (80B, two hours, 8.30am) involve a transfer in Ban Hat Bai.

Pai
ปาย

POP 2000

This cool corner of the northern mountains started out as a hippie enclave for Chiang Mai bohos who would come to hang out beside the rambling river and strum out blues tunes at night. Word spread and the dusty little town now does a thriving trade in mountain scenery and laid-back living. Urban Thais have joined the Pai altar for its stress-reducing setting and the oddity of 'winter' (from December to January). The town itself – a modest mixture of Shan, Thai and Muslim Chinese

THAILAND PAI

BUSES FROM CHIANG KHONG

DESTINATION	PRICE (B)	DURATION (HR)	DEPARTURES
Bangkok	688-963	14	several late afternoon
Chiang Mai	144-288	3	frequent 8am-5.30pm
Chiang Rai	65	2½	half-hourly 4.30am-3.45pm

residents – can be explored in a matter of minutes, but the real adventure lies along the paths in the hills beyond. Some might sniff that Pai is played out, but remember folks, this isn't a race.

◉ Sights & Activities

Since Pai is more of a 'state of mind', it is lean on fully fledged tourist attractions. If you need an outing, head to **Wat Phra That Mae Yen** (วัดพระธาตุแม่เย็น; ⊘daylight hours) **FREE**, 1km east of town, for its hilltop vista. The other main contender is **Tha Pai Hot Springs** (บ่อน้ำ ร้อนท่าปาย; adult/child 200/100B; ⊘7am-6pm), a well-kept park featuring a scenic stream and pleasant hot-spring bathing pools. The park is 7km southeast of town across Mae Nam Pai.

The rest of your time will be spent on various wanderings or pamperings (traditional massage is big here). All the guesthouses in town can provide information on **trekking** (from 800B per day).

Thai Adventure Rafting   RAFTING
(⧉0 5369 9111; www.thairafting.com; Th Chaisongkhram; ⊘8am-5pm) This French-run outfit leads one- and two-day rafting excursions. On the way, rafters visit a waterfall, a fossil reef and hot springs; one night is spent at the company's permanent riverside camp.

Pai Traditional Thai Massage   MASSAGE
(PTTM; ⧉0 5369 9121; www.pttm1989.com; 68/3 Soi 1, Th Wiang Tai; massage per 1/1½/2hr 180/270/350B, sauna per visit 100B, 3-day massage course 2500B; ⊘9am-9pm) This longstanding and locally owned outfit offers very good northern Thai massage, as well as a sauna (cool season only) where you can steam yourself in sà·mǔn·prai (medicinal herbs). Three-day massage courses begin every Monday and Friday and last three hours per day. The friendly couple that do the massages and teach the course are accredited and are graduates of Chiang Mai's Old Medicine Hospital.

Thom's Pai Elephant Camp   ELEPHANT RIDES
(⧉0 5369 9286; www.thomelephant.com; Th Rangsiyanon; elephant rides per person 500-2000B; ⊘9am-6pm) Pai's most established elephant outfitter has an office in town. You can choose between

riding bareback or in a seat, and some rides include swimming with the elephants – a barrel of laughs on a bouncing elephant in the river. Rides include a soak in the hot-spring-fed tubs afterwards.

Mam Yoga House   YOGA
(⧉08 9954 4981; www.mamyoga.paiexplorer.com; 27 Th Rangsiyanon; lessons 200-550B; ⊘10am-noon & 3-5pm) Just north of the police station, Mam offers Hatha Yoga classes and courses in small groups.

🛏 Sleeping

Pai's accommodation continues to boom and trend upscale. There are still some budget spots in town, though out-of-town lodging is more idyllically rural. During the cool season (November to April) it can be difficult to find a room and prices increase with demand.

Tayai's Guest House   GUESTHOUSE $
(⧉0 5369 9579; off Th Raddamrong; r & bungalows 200-500B; ❄🖥) Simple but clean fan and air-con rooms and bungalows in a leafy compound just off the main drag.

Charlie's House   GUESTHOUSE $
(⧉0 5369 9039; Th Rangsiyanon; r 150-600B; ❄🖥) This long-standing, locally run place offers a range of options in a clean, suburban-feeling compound in town.

Breeze of Pai Guesthouse   HOTEL $
(⧉08 1998 4597; suthasinee.svp@gmail.com; Soi Wat Pa Kham; r 400B, bungalows 800B; ❄🖥) This well-groomed compound near the river consists of nine attractive and spacious rooms and six large A-frame bungalows. It's close to the action without the noise pollution. A loyal customer base means you'll probably have to book ahead.

Pai Country Hut   HOTEL $
(⧉08 7779 6541; www.facebook.com/paicountry bungalows; Ban Mae Hi; bungalows incl breakfast 200-500B; 🖥) The bamboo bungalows here are utterly simple, but are tidy and most have bathrooms and inviting hammocks. Although it's not exactly riverside, it's the most appealing of several similar budget places in the area.

TRANSPORT FROM PAI

DESTINATION	AIR	BUS	MINIVAN
Chiang Mai	1990B, 20min, daily	80B, 3-4hr, noon	150B, 3hr, hourly 7am-4.30pm
Mae Hong Son	N/A	75B, 3-4hr, 11am	150B, 2½hr, 8.30am

GETTING TO LAOS: NORTHERN BORDERS

Chiang Rai to Huay Xai

The Chiang Khong/Huay Xai crossing is the most popular crossing for Chiang Mai–Luang Prabang (Laos) travellers. Since the completion of the Thai-Lao Friendship Bridge 4 in late 2013, the former boat crossing across the Mekong is only for locals.

Getting to the Border The bridge is 11km south of Chiang Khong, a 200B túk-túk ride from town.

At the Border The border is open from 6am to 10pm. After going through the usual formalities on the Thai side, board the bus (20B to 30B) that crosses the bridge to Lao immigration, where visas are available on arrival.

Moving On On the Lao side, túk-túk charge 80B per person to Huay Xai. Destinations from Huay Xai's bus station include Luang Nam Tha (350B, 4½ hours, 9am and 12.30pm), Luang Prabang (700B to 900B, 12 hours, 2pm and 5pm), Udomxai (500B to 700B, nine hours, 3pm) and Vientiane (1800B, 24 hours, 3pm). Alternatively, the daily slow boat (950B, 10.30am) to Luang Prabang takes two days, including a night in the village of Pak Beng. Avoid the noisy fast boats (1600B, six to seven hours, frequent 9am to 11am) as there have been reports of bad accidents. Huay Xai also has transit connections to China (though Chinese visas need to be arranged beforehand). Buses from Huay Xai go directly to the Xishuangbanna town of Mengla or Kunming.

Phrae to Hongsa

The Ban Huay Kon/Muang Ngeun border crossing is 140km north of Nan.

Getting to the border To Ban Huay Kon, there are four daily minivans originating in Phrae and stopping in Nan at 5am, 6.50am, 8am and 9.30am (100B, three hours). The only other option is to hop on a bus from Nan to Pon (85B, 2½ hours, hourly from 6am to 6pm), at which point you'll need to transfer to the infrequent *sŏrngtăaou* (pick-up truck) that go the remaining 30km to Ban Huay Kon (100B, one hour, from 9am to 6pm).

At the border After passing the Thai immigration booth (open 8am to 6pm), foreigners can purchase a 30-day visa for Laos for US$30 to US$42, depending on nationality. There is an extra US$1 or 50B charge after 4pm and on weekends.

Moving on You can then proceed 2.5km to the Lao village of Muang Ngeun. *Sŏrngtăaou* leave from the tiny passenger car station beside the market for Hongsa (40,000K, 1½ hours) between 2pm and 4pm, and to Pak Kaen (35,000K, one hour) at around 7.30am and 2pm arriving in time for the Mekong slowboats to Huay Xai and Pak Beng respectively. Once the new bridge north of Pak Beng is open, there will also be a bus service and ostensibly, more frequent transport links.

For information on making these crossings in the opposite direction, see p345.

Spicypai Backpackers HOTEL $

(☑ 08 5263 5147; Mae Yen; dm 100-150B, bungalows 500B; ✳ @ 🛜) The bamboo dorms here look like they could have featured in an episode of *Survivor*. Communal areas ranging from kitchen to fire pit continue the rustic feel, and there are a few air-con bungalows for those with loftier standards. It's about 750m east of Mae Nam Pai, just off the road that leads to Thai Pai Hot Springs.

★ **Bueng Pai Farm** GUESTHOUSE $$

(☑ 08 9265 4768; www.paifarm.com; Ban Mae Hi; bungalows 500-2000B; 🛜 ✉) Uniting yoga enthusiasts and fisherfolk, the 12 simple bungalows here are strategically and attractively positioned between a functioning farm and a vast pond stocked with freshwater fish. During the tourist season, Run and Orn serve meals made with their own organic produce. Bueng Pai is 2.5km from Pai, off the road leading to Tha Pai Hot Springs; look for the sign.

🍴 Eating

During the day there's takeaway food at **Saengthongaram Market** (Th Khetkelang; mains 30-60B; ⊙ 6-11am). For tasty local eats, try the **evening market** (Th Raddamrong; mains 30-60B; ⊙ 3-7pm). Night vendors turn Th Chaisongkhram and Th Rangsiyanon into an open-air buffet during tourist season.

★ **Larp Khom Huay Poo** THAI $

(Ban Huay Pu; mains 30-70B; ⊙9am-8pm) Escape the wheat-grass-and-tofu crowd and get your meat on at this unabashedly carnivore eatery. The house special is *lâhp kôo·a*, minced meat (beef or pork) fried with local herbs and spices. Accompanied by a basket of sticky rice, a plate of bitter herbs and an ice-cold Singha, it's the best meal in Pai. The restaurant is on the road to Mae Hong Son, about 1km north of town, just past the well-posted turn-off to Sipsongpanna.

★ **Yunnanese Restaurant** CHINESE $

(no roman-script sign; mains 30-180B; ⊙8am-8pm) This open-air place in the Chinese village of Ban Santichon serves the traditional dishes of the town's Yunnanese residents. Standouts include *màntŏ* (steamed buns) served with stewed pork leg with Chinese herbs. Or you could go for the excellent noodles, made by hand and topped with a delicious mixture of minced pork, garlic and sesame. The restaurant is behind the giant rock in Ban Santichon, about 4km west of Pai.

Good Life INTERNATIONAL $

(Th Wiang Tai; mains 40-170B; ⊙🌱) Trays of wheat grass and secondhand books (sample title: *The Aloe Answer*) function as interior design at this eclectic and popular cafe.

Mama Falafel ISRAELI $

(Soi Wanchalerm; set meals 80-90B; ⊙11am-8pm Mon-Sat; 🌱) This friendly native of Pai has been cooking up tasty falafel, hummus, schnitzel and other Jewish and Israeli faves since 2002; the set meals win in both quality and quantity.

 Drinking

Alfresco drinking convenes along Th Chaisongkhram, live-music venues line Th Wiang Tai and guesthouse-style bars and restaurants can be found on Th Rangsiyanon. Reggae bars hang out at the eastern end of Th Raddamrong.

Edible Jazz LIVE MUSIC

(www.ediblejazz.com; Soi Wat Pa Kham; ⊙8.30-11pm) Probably Pai's cosiest place for live music. Stroke a cat and nurse a beer while listening to acoustic guitar performances. Depending on who's in town, the open-mic nights on Thursdays and Sundays can be surprisingly good.

Bebop LIVE MUSIC

(Th Rangsiyanon; ⊙8pm-1am) This legendary box is popular with both locals and travellers and has live music nightly (from about 10pm), emphasising blues, R&B and rock.

ℹ **Information**

Several places around town offer internet services (20B to 30B per hour). Banks and ATMs can be found along Pai's two main streets, Th Rangsiyanon and Th Chaisongkhram.

ℹ **Getting There & Around**

Pai's airport is 1.5km north of town and offers a daily connection to Chiang Mai.

The **bus stop** (Th Chaisongkhram) is in a dirt lot in the centre of town. The road from Chiang Mai to Pai and on to Mae Hong Son is savagely steep.

Mae Hong Son แม่ฮ่องสอน

POP 7000

Northern Thai aficionados prefer the far-flung border feel of Mae Hong Son to that of Pai. Mae Hong Son is a quiet provincial capital that practically peers into Myanmar and is skirted by forested mountains. The local trekking scene in Mae Hong Son is the primary draw but the daily market and local eats further impress its fan base. November to February are cool and pleasant times to visit.

⊙ **Sights & Activities**

Mae Hong Son's temples are surviving monuments to their Burmese and Shan artisans and benefactors and hint at the town's past as

TRANSPORT FROM MAE HONG SON

DESTINATION	AIR	BUS	MINIVAN
Bangkok	N/A	796-905B, 15hr, 3 departures 2-4pm	N/A
Chiang Mai	1590B, 35min, 3 daily	145B, 8hr, 8.30am & 12.30pm (northern route); 178-319B, 9hr, frequent 6am-9pm (southern route)	250B, 6hr, hourly 7am-3pm
Mae Sariang	N/A	95-187B, 4hr, frequent 6am-9pm	N/A
Pai	N/A	80B, 4½hr, 8.30am & 4pm	150B, 2½hr, hourly 7am-4pm

a logging and elephant-training centre. **Wat Jong Klang & Wat Jong Kham** (วัดจองคำ/ วัดจองกลาง; Th Charm-naan Satit; museum admission by donation; ☺ temple daylight hours, museum 8am-6pm) **FREE** boast whitewashed stupas and glittering zinc fretwork. The temples are often lit at night, reflecting in the still waters of Nong Jong Kham (Jong Kham Lake).

Glimpse the misty morning fog from **Wat Phra That Doi Kong Mu** (วัดพระธาตุดอยกองมู; ☺ daylight hours), which sits on a hilltop west of town.

The **Poi Sang Long Festival** in March takes place at Wat Jong Klang and Wat Jong Kham. It's a Shan custom in which young boys entering the monastery as novice monks are dressed in ornate costumes and paraded around the temple under festive parasols.

Treks to nearby hill-tribe villages and **longtail boat trips** on the Mae Nam Pai are all popular pastimes. Guesthouses can handle bookings for outdoor trips, which start at 1000B for the day.

Friend Tour TREKKING
(☑ 0 5361 1647; PA Motor, 21 Th Pradit Jong Kham; ☺ 7.30am-7.30pm) With nearly 20 years' experience, this recommended outfit offers trekking, elephant riding and rafting, as well as day tours. Located at PA Motor.

Nature Walks TREKKING
(☑ 08 9552 6899, 0 5361 1040; www.trekkingthai land.com) Although the treks here cost more than elsewhere, John, a native of Mae Hong Son, is the best guide in town. Treks range from day-long nature walks to multiday journeys across the province. John can also arrange custom nature-based tours, such as the orchid-viewing tours he conducts from March to May.

🛏 Sleeping

Coffee Morning HOTEL $
(☑ 0 5361 2234; 78 Th Singha-nat Barm Rung; r 500-600B; @ 🛜) This old wooden house unites a cafe-bookshop and three basic rooms. Considering that bathrooms are shared, the rates aren't exactly a steal, but free internet and an artsy atmosphere make up for it.

Friend House GUESTHOUSE $
(☑ 0 5362 0119; 20 Th Pradit Jong Kham; r 150-500B; 🛜) The super-clean though characterless rooms here run from the ultra basic, which share hot-water bathrooms, to larger rooms with private bathrooms.

Palm House GUESTHOUSE $
(☑ 0 5361 4022; 22/1 Th Charm-naan Satit; r 350-700B; ❄ 🛜) This two-storey cement building offers several characterless but clean rooms with TV, fridge, hot water and fan/air-con. The helpful owner speaks English and can arrange transport.

🍴 Eating & Drinking

Mae Hong Son's **morning market** (off Th Phanit Wattana; mains 10-30B; ☺ 6-9am) is a cultural and culinary adventure. Several vendors at the north end of the market sell *tòoa òon,* a Burmese noodle dish with thick chickpea porridge. Others sell a local version of *kà·nŏm jeen nám ngée·o* (thin white noodles) topped with Shan-style deep-fried vegetables.

There are two **night markets**: the one near the airport is mostly takeaway northern Thai food, while the market on Th Khunlumprapas has seating and serves standard Thai food. There is also an evening **Walking Street** (Th Pradit Jong Kham; ☺ 5-10pm Oct-Feb) with eats and more.

Mae Si Bua THAI $
(cnr Th Pradit Jong Kham & Th Singha-nat Barm Rung, no roman-script sign; mains 20-30B; ☺ lunch) Like the Shan grandma you never had, Auntie Bua prepares a huge variety of curries, soups and dips on a daily basis.

Chom Mai Restaurant THAI $
(www.sesamebar.com; off Rte 108, no roman-script sign; mains 35-180B; ☺ 8.30am-3.30pm; 🛜 ✍) The English-language menu here is limited, but don't miss the deliciously rich *kôw soy* or *kôw mòk gài* (chicken biryani). Chom Mai is about 4km south of Mae Hong Son along the road that leads to Tha Pong Daeng – look for the Doi Chaang coffee sign.

Salween River Restaurant & Bar INTERNATIONAL, THAI $
(www.salweenriver.com; 23 Th Pradit Jong Kham; mains 40-240B; ☺ 8am-10pm; 🛜 ✍) Salween is your typical travellers' cafe: a few old guidebooks, free wi-fi and a menu ranging from burgers to Burmese. Yet unlike most travellers' cafes, the food here is good; don't miss the Burmese green tea salad.

La Tasca ITALIAN $$
(Th Khunlumprapas; mains 149-209B; ☺ 11am-10pm; ✍) This cosy place has been serving homemade pasta, pizza and calzone for as long as we can remember and is one of the few places in town to do relatively authentic Western food.

Sunflower Café BAR

(Th Pradit Jong Kham; ☺ 7.30am-10pm) This open-air place combines draught beer, live lounge music and views of the lake. Sunflower also does meals (mains 35B to 180B) and runs tours.

ⓘ Information

Most banks on Th Khunlum Praphat have ATMs.

Mae Hong Son Internet (88 Th Khunlumprapas; per hr 30B; ☺ 8.30am-10pm)

Maehongson Living Museum (27 Th Singha-nat Barm Rung; ☺ 7am-5pm; 🛜) This attractive wooden building has been turned in a museum, primarily in Thai. There are a few maps and brochures in English, and there's also free wi-fi and bike rental (15B per day).

Tourism Authority of Thailand (TAT; ☏ 0 5361 2982, nationwide 1672; www.travelmaehongson. org; Th Ni-wet Pi-sarn; ☺ 8.30am-4.30pm) Basic tourist brochures and maps can be picked up here.

Tourist Police (☏ 0 5361 1812, nationwide 1155; Th Singhanat Bamrung; ☺ 8.30am-4.30pm)

ⓘ Getting There & Around

Mae Hong Son is 368km from Chiang Mai, but the terrain is so rugged that the trip takes at least eight long, but scenic, hours. For this reason, many people opt for the 35-minute flight to/from Chiang Mai with **Nok Air** (☏ 0 5361 2057, nationwide 1318; www.nokair.co.th; Mae Hong Son Airport; ☺ 9am-5pm). The airport is near the centre of town.

Mae Hong Son's bus station is 1km south of the city. A túk-túk or motorcycle ride into town costs 60B. The centre of Mae Hong Son can be covered on foot. Motorbike rental is available from **PA Motor** (☏ 0 5361 1647; 21 Th Pradit Jong Kham; ☺ 8am-6.30pm), opposite Friend House.

Mae Sariang   แม่สะเรียง

Little-visited Mae Sariang is gaining a low-key buzz among adventurous travellers. There's

natural beauty, ethnic and cultural diversity as well as a new breed of community-based trekking outfits.

Dragon Sabai Tours (☏ 08 9555 8715, 08 9956 9897; www.thailandhilltribeholidays.com; Th Mongkolchai), **Mae Sariang Tours** (☏ 08 8404 8402; www.maesariangtours.com) and **Salawin Tour & Trekking** (☏ 08 1024 6146; River Bank Guesthouse, Th Laeng Phanit) are all recommended for their eco-conscious and culturally sensitive tours.

🛏 Sleeping

Northwest Guest House GUESTHOUSE $

(☏ 08 9700 9928; www.northwestgh.blogspot. com; 81 Th Laeng Phanit; r 250-450B; ❄ @ 🛜) The rooms in this cosy wooden house are mattress-on-the-floor simple, but get natural light and are relatively spacious.

Pang Sariang GUESTHOUSE $

(☏ 0 5368 2333; 2 Th Laeng Phanit, no roman-script sign; r 300B; ❄ @ 🛜) A villa with four homey-feeling yet simple rooms. Look for the sign that says 'Guest House & Restaurant'.

🍴 Eating & Drinking

Local eats can be found at the **Sunday Market** (Th Wiang Mai; mains 20-60B; ☺ 3-8pm).

Inthira Restaurant THAI $

(Th Wiang Mai; mains 30-150B; ☺ 8am-10pm) Probably the town's best all-around restaurant, this place features a thick menu of dishes using unusual ingredients such as locally grown shiitake mushrooms and fish from the Mae Nam Moei.

Sawaddee Restaurant & Bar THAI $

(Th Laeng Phanit; mains 40-150B; ☺ 7am-10pm; 🛜 🍴) Like a beachside bar, this is a great place to recline with a beer and watch the water (in this case Mae Nam Yuam). There's a lengthy menu with lots of options for vegetarians.

TRANSPORT FROM MAE SARIANG

Destination	Bus	Minivan	Sŏrngtăaou
Bangkok	482-722B, 12hr, 4 departures 4pm-7.30pm	N/A	N/A
Chiang Mai	105-187B, 4-5hr, 5 departures 7am-3pm	200B, 3½hr, 5 departures 8am-5pm	N/A
Mae Hong Son	105-187B, 3-4hr, 6 departures 7am-1am	N/A	N/A
Mae Sot	N/A	N/A	200B, 6hr, frequent 6.30am-12.30pm

Lee Lawadee THAI $

(cnr Th Wiang Mai & Th Mae Sariang; mains 40-180B; ⊙7am-9pm; 🛜) This friendly place has an English-language menu of both one-dish meals and mains, as well as real coffee and free wi-fi.

WESTERN THAILAND

Tall rugged mountains rise up from the central plains to meet Thailand's western border with Myanmar. Though the distances from population centres are minor, much of the region remains remote and undeveloped with an undercurrent of border intrigue. Kanchanaburi, just a few hours' bus ride from Bangkok, is a convenient and historical gateway to the region.

Kanchanaburi   กาญจนบุรี

POP 47,147

If you don't have time for Chiang Mai and its surrounding mountain scenery, head to Kanchanaburi, west of Bangkok, quietly lounging alongside Mae Nam Khwae (known in English as Kwai River). The town has a healthy soft-adventure scene – elephant rides and bamboo rafting – and is a peaceful place to relax if Bangkok made you dizzy. It also has an unlikely claim on WWII history as the site of a Japanese-operated WWII prisoner-of-war camp made famous by the movie *The Bridge Over the River Kwai*. Today visitors come to pay their respects to fallen Allied soldiers or to learn more about this chapter of the war.

⦿ Sights

★**Death Railway Bridge** HISTORIC SITE

(สะพานข้ามแม่น้ำแคว, Bridge Over the River Kwai; Th Mae Nam Khwae) The famous 300m railway bridge still retains its power and symbolism. The centre span was destroyed by Allied bombs in 1945 so only the outer spans are original. Every 30 minutes a train rolls through – stand in one of the safety points along the bridge when one appears.

The bridge is 2.5km from the centre of Kanchanaburi, you can walk here along Th Mae Nam Khwae or jump on a northbound *sŏrngtăaou* (10B) along Th Saengchuto. A mini rainbow-coloured train runs regular trips (20B, 8am to 10am and noon to 2pm) over the bridge from the nearby train station. On the other side, pop in to the Chinese temple on the right and view the bridge from its tranquil garden.

During the last week of November and first week of December a nightly sound-and-light show marks the Allied attack on the Death Railway in 1945.

★**Thailand–Burma Railway Centre Museum** MUSEUM

(ศูนย์รถไฟไทย-พม่า; www.tbrconline.com; 73 Th Jaokannun; adult/child 120/60B; ⊙9am-5pm) This informative museum uses video footage, models and detailed displays to explain Kanchanaburi's role in WWII. Nine galleries tell the history of the railway, how prisoners were treated and what happened after the line was completed. Upstairs is a display of wartime artefacts, including one POW's miniature chess set. A poignant video from POW survivors ensures that the deaths remain a tragedy, not a statistic. Half-/full-day tours (2400/4900B) can be arranged from here.

★**Allied War Cemetery** HISTORIC SITE

(สุสานทหารพันธมิตรดอนรัก; Th Saengchuto; ⊙24hr) FREE Across the street from the Thailand–Burma Railway Centre is the Allied War Cemetery, which is immaculately maintained by the War Graves Commission. Of the 6982 POWs buried here, nearly half were British; the rest came mainly from Australia and the Netherlands.

It is estimated at least 100,000 people died while working on the railway, the majority being labourers from nearby Asian countries, though not one of these has an identifiable grave. If you are looking for the resting place of a loved one, a small office to the side has lists of names and locations within the cemetery. As you stand at the cemetery entrance, the front left area contains Australian graves, the rear left honours Dutch soldiers and the entire right side contains British victims.

WWII Museum MUSEUM

(พิพิธภัณฑ์สงครามโลกครั้งที่สอง; Th Mae Nam Khwae; admission 40B; ⊙8am-6.30pm) Perhaps the best thing to say about this museum is that the view of the Death Railway Bridge is great. Otherwise, this is an eclectic, ramshackle collection of artefacts. The museum is divided into two buildings. On one side is a collection of Japanese vehicles, along with press cuttings and waxwork POWs.

The larger building resembles a Chinese temple and is far more opulent, or garish, depending on your viewpoint, though the collection of weapons and amulets is

Kanchanaburi

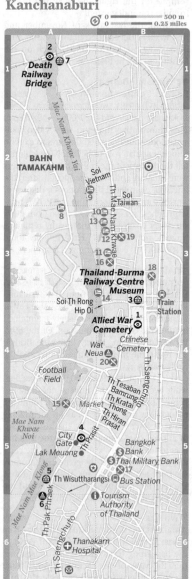

Jeath War Museum　　　　　　　　　MUSEUM
(พิพิธภัณฑ์สงคราม; Th Wisuttharangsi; admission 30B; ☺8am-5pm) This small museum contains cuttings, correspondence and artwork from WWII. Located in bamboo *ata,* similar to the shelters used for POWs, it details the harsh punishments meted out by Japanese troops. The museum is run by the monks of the adjacent **Wat Chaichumphon** (Wat Chai).

Chung Kai Allied War Cemetery　　　　　　　　HISTORIC SITE
(สุสานทหารพันธมิตรช่องไก่; ☺7am-6pm) FREE
Chung Kai was the site of a major prisoner camp during WWII, and Allied prisoners built their own hospital and church close to here. Most graves have brief, touching epitaphs for the 1400 Commonwealth and 300 Dutch soldiers buried here.

The cemetery is 4km south of central Kanchanaburi across the Mae Nam Khwae Noi and can be reached by bicycle.

Heritage Walking Street　　　　　HISTORIC STREET
Set near the City Gate, this wonderful old street offers a glimpse of a bygone Kanchanaburi. More than 20 yellow signs reveal the history and architecture of this

impressive. The top level is the best place to see the nearby Death Railway Bridge.

Between the two buildings is a pyramid-shaped family shrine with coloured bowls decorating the exterior. The museum is immediately south of the Death Railway Bridge.

WHY BRIDGE THE RIVER KHWAE

The construction of the 'Death Railway' was an astonishing feat of engineering. However, the prisoners and conscripted workers who toiled to build it paid a terrible price. Around 100,000 labourers died due to the extreme conditions.

The railway was built during the WWII-era Japanese occupation of Thailand (1942–43) and its objective was to link 415km of rugged terrain between Thailand and Burma (Myanmar) to secure an alternative supply route for the Japanese conquest of other west Asian countries.

Japanese engineers estimated that the project would take five years but the Japanese army forced the POWs to complete the 1m-gauge railway in 16 months. Much of the work was done by hand with simple tools. Food supplies were meagre and spoilt, infectious diseases were rampant, and punishments were cruel.

The bridge that spans the river near Kanchanaburi (dubbed the 'Death Railway Bridge') was used for just 20 months before the Allies bombed it in 1945. The route quickly became an escape path for Japanese troops rather than a supply line.

fascinating area. Leave at least an hour to stroll and note the variety of buildings, which include Sino-Portuguese, Thai and Chinese styles. Coffee and art shops are now also here.

Many shops date from the turn of the 20th century and are still owned by the same family. Look out for the erstwhile hotel that, back in the good old days, charged 1B per night.

🛌 Sleeping

The most atmospheric places to stay are built along the river. The once-noisy karaoke barges are now limited to weekend evenings.

Blue Star Guest House　　GUESTHOUSE $
(📞 0 3451 2161; bluestar_guesthouse@yahoo.com; 241 Th Mae Nam Khwae; r 200-850B; 🅿️❄️📶) Arguably the best of the raft-house options. Nature wraps itself around Blue Star, creating a feeling of remoteness and tranquillity. Cheaper rooms have cold showers.

Bamboo House　　GUESTHOUSE $
(📞 0 3462 4470; www.bamboohouse.host.sk; 3-5 Soi Vietnam, Th Mae Nam Khwae; r 200-1100B; 🅿️❄️📶) A new block of smart, airy rooms has breathed fresh life into this place. Set in spacious grounds, the cheaper raft rooms have stunning sunset views.

Jolly Frog　　GUESTHOUSE $
(📞 0 3451 4579; 28 Soi China; s 70B, d 150-290B; f 400B; 🅿️❄️📶🚲) Despite the un-jolly welcome we received, the Frog remains a backpackers' favourite thanks to the hammock-laden garden, lively restaurant and good-value but grungy rooms.

VN Guest House　　GUESTHOUSE $
(📞 0 3451 4082; www.vnguesthouse.net; 44 Soi Th Rong Hip Oi; r 280-450B; ❄️📶) One of the few remaining choices along this strip, VN has great river views from its floating raft houses. Prepare for a few passing karaoke boats.

Apple's Retreat　　GUESTHOUSE $
(📞 0 3451 2017; www.applenoi-kanchanaburi.com; 153/4 Moo 4, Ban Tamakham; r 790-990B; 🅿️❄️📶🚲) 🍃 Almost like a chic homestay, the super-friendly Apple and Noi offer simple but stylish rooms, bags of local knowledge and well-maintained grounds. To be ecofriendly, rooms lack a TV and fridge. Cheaper rooms do not include breakfast, but it is worth the extra just for the mango jam.

Sam's House　　GUESTHOUSE $$
(📞 0 3451 5956; www.samsguesthouse.com; 14/2 Moo 1, Th Mae Nam Khwae; d 400-800B; 🅿️❄️📶) A walkway beside a bed of hyacinths leads to basic but clean bungalows and raft houses. The A-frame designs and gnarly wood patterns add character.

Pong Phen　　GUESTHOUSE $$
(📞 0 3451 2981; www.pongphen.com; Th Mae Nam Khwae; r 400-1300B; ❄️📶🏊) Pong Phen has a range of comfortable wooden bungalows and raft houses, plus a restaurant that offers decent Western and Thai dishes – but the real bonus is the pool.

🍴 Eating

The **night market** (Th Saengchuto; dishes 30-60B; ⏱️6-11pm) near the train station is packed with stalls serving fried treats and smoothies. Several good-quality **floating restaurants** (Th Song Khwae; dishes 80-200B;

THAILAND KANCHANABURI

6-11pm) are often full of Korean or Thai package tourists. The **market** (Th Saengchuto) near the bus station is well known for its excellent *hŏy tôrt* (fried mussels in an egg batter).

★ **Blue Rice**   THAI $

(153/4 Moo 4 Ban Tamakahm; dishes 95-150B; P 🛜 🍽 ⓦ) A perfect riverside setting, brilliant menu and fantastic flavours make this a winner. Chef Apple puts a fresh spin on Thai classics, such as the eponymous rice, *yam sôm oh* (pomelo salad) and chicken soup with banana plant.

★ Mangosteen Cafe   CAFE $

(📋 08 1793 5814; www.mangosteencafe.net; 13 Th Mae Nam Khwae; dishes 70-150B; 🕘 9.30am-10pm; 🛜 🍽 ⓦ) Browse the 1000 or so books on offer while munching through the divine pizza toasties and sipping real coffee.

Saisowo   NOODLES $

(Th Chaokunen; dishes 20-30B; 🕘 8am-4pm) When a place is this popular with locals, it must be doing something right. This long-established noodle spot has a few surprise options, such as the excellent *gŏoay dĕeo dôm yam kài kem* (noodle soup with salty eggs).

On's Vegetarian Restaurant   VEGETARIAN $

(📋 08 7364 2264; www.onsthaiissan.com; Th Mae Nam Khwae; dishes 40B; 🕘 10am-10pm; 🍽) If you happen to like the northeastern-style vegie food on offer here, On can teach you how to make it. A two-hour, three-dish cookery course costs 600B.

ℹ️ Information

Several major Thai banks can be found along Th Saengchuto near the market and bus terminal. Internet cafes can be found along Th Mae Nam Khwae. Check out www.kanchanaburi-info.com for general information.

Main Post Office (Th Saengchuto; 🕘 8.30am-4.30pm Mon-Fri, 9am-noon Sat & Sun)

Thanakarn Hospital (📋 0 3462 2366, emergency 0 3462 2811; Th Saengchuto) Near the junction of Th Chukkadon, this is the best-equipped hospital to deal with foreign visitors.

Tourism Authority of Thailand (TAT; 📋 0 3451 1200; Th Saengchuto; 🕘 8.30am-4.30pm) Provides free maps of the town and province, along with advice on what to do and where to stay.

Tourist Police (📋 0 3451 2795, 1155; Th Saengchuto)

ℹ️ Getting There & Away

BUS

Kanchanaburi's **bus station** (📋 0 3451 5907; Th Saengchuto) is south of town. If you're headed to Hua Hin, transfer at Ratchaburi. If you're headed to Ayuthaya, transfer at Suphanburi.

TRAIN

Kanchanaburi's train station is 500m from the river, near the guesthouse area. Kanchanaburi is on the Bangkok Noi–Nam Tok rail line, which includes a portion of the historic Death Railway. The SRT promotes this as a historic route, and charges foreigners 100B for any one-way journey, regardless of the distance.

Destinations include the following:

Bangkok Noi station (three hours, departs 7.19am, 2.48pm and 5.41pm) Located in Thonburi, across the river from Bangkok.

Nam Tok (two hours, departs 6.07am, 10.35am and 4.26pm) Terminus station.

ℹ️ Getting Around

Săhmlór within the city cost 50B a trip. Regular *sŏrngtăaou* ply Th Saengchuto for 10B, but be careful you don't accidentally 'charter' one. There are plenty of places hiring motorbikes along Th Mae Nam Khwae. The going rate is 200B per day. Bicycles can be hired from most guesthouses for around 50B a day.

Around Kanchanaburi

Head out of town to explore Kanchanaburi's forests and rivers. Most of the guesthouses will book minivan tours that do a little bit of everything in a hurry.

Erawan National Park (อุทยานแห่งชาติ เอราวัณ; admission 200B; 🕘 8am-4pm) is the home of the seven-tiered Erawan Falls, which makes for a refreshing day swimming in pools and climbing around the trails. Go early as this is a popular tour spot. Buses from Kanchanaburi stop at the entrance to the falls (50B, 1½ hours, every 1½ hours from 8am to 5.20pm). The last bus back to Kanchanaburi leaves at 4pm.

Hellfire Pass Memorial (ช่องเขาขาด; Rte 323; museum admission by donation; 🕘 grounds 9am-4.30pm, museum to 4pm) curates a section of the Death Railway that was carved out of unforgiving mountain terrain under breakneck speed. The pass was so named for the fire-light shadows cast by the night-labouring POWs. A portion of the walking trail follows the old railbed. Located near the Km 66 marker on the Sai Yok–Thong Pha Phum road, Hellfire Pass can be reached by

BUSES FROM KANCHANABURI

DESTINATION	PRICE (B)	DURATION (HR)	FREQUENCY
Bangkok (Northern & Northeastern bus station/Mo Chit)	105-135	2	every 1½hr 6am-6pm
Bangkok (Southern bus station/Sai Tai Mai)	95-110	2	frequent 4am-8pm
Bangkok (Victory Monument)	120	2	hourly until 8pm
Ratchaburi	50-70	2	frequent
Sangkhlaburi	130	4	frequent 7.30am-4.30pm
Suphanburi	50	2	frequent

a Sangkhlaburi-bound bus (80B, 1½ hours, last bus back at 4.45pm). Inform the attendant of your destination so that the bus stops en route.

Sangkhlaburi สังขละบุรี

Few tourists know the scenic but small town of Sangkhlaburi, but for international aid workers this is one of many remote outposts for refugee relief work. Many displaced people, whether they be Mon, Karen or Burmese, arrive in Thailand with few belongings and fewer rights. The town consists of a few paved roads overlooking the enormous Kheuan Khao Laem (Khao Laem Dam). The surrounding wilderness is an underappreciated natural attraction boasting one of the largest conservation areas in Southeast Asia. Guesthouses in town can arrange outdoor outings.

🏃 Activities

Scenns (📱09 1281 6441; www.scenns.com) runs an informal cultural centre teaching classical Thai dance, language and cooking.

Volunteer opportunities are available through the following:

Children of the Forest VOLUNTEERING
(www.childrenoftheforest.org) A foundation that helps stateless ethnic minorities.

Ban Thor Phan VOLUNTEERING
(📱08 1824 3369; banthorphan@gmail.com) A health resort that funds a children's home.

Hilltribe Learning Centre VOLUNTEERING
(ศูนย์การศึกษาตามอัธยาศัยไทยภูเขา) Provides English lessons to Karen children.

Baan Unrak VOLUNTEERING
(บ้านอุ่นรักษ์, House of Joy; www.baanunrak.org) Runs an orphanage and animal sanctuary.

Sleeping & Eating

Travellers tend to eat at the main guesthouses, which all have lakefront restaurants. The day market is across from the bus stop and is good for sampling Mon-style curries (look for the large metal pots). **Baan Unrak Bakery** (snacks 25-90B) is a meatless cafe with excellent pastries and Thai dishes and is run by a local charitable organisation.

★P Guest House GUESTHOUSE $
(📱0 3459 5061; www.p-guesthouse.com; 81/2 Mu 1; r 250-950B; P🌫🛜🛖) Has lovely lake-view rooms. Fan rooms are plain and have shared bathrooms. Book in advance as rooms fill up.

Oh Dee Hostel HOSTEL $$
(📱0 3459 5626; www.ohdee-hostel.com; 147/1 Mu 3; dm 590B, d 1400-1500B; 🌫🛜) A new and surprisingly hip hostel for sleepy Sangkhlaburi.

ℹ️ Getting There & Away

The bus stop is across from the day market; destinations include the following:

Bangkok's Northern & Northeastern bus terminal (Mo Chit) 249B, seven hours, four daily departures.

Kanchanaburi 150-175B, five hours, frequent.

Mae Sot แม่สอด

POP 120,000

Mae Sot is a scruffy border town preoccupied with trading and cross-border traffic. But it's the population's diversity that is most striking – Indo-Burmese, Chinese, Karen, Hmong and Thai – an ethnic mix that makes border towns so intriguing. The town also hosts a relatively large population of foreign doctors and NGO aid workers, dealing with the consequences of the clashes between Myanmar's central government and ethnic minorities.

There aren't a lot of official sights to lure tourists this far west, but the recent relaxing of border regulations makes this crossing one of the most convenient land entries into Myanmar. Some travellers also come with a charitable spirit to lend a hand with the various volunteer organisations. Other selling points include underdeveloped nature preserves, diverse hill-tribe communities and its location off the usual tourist trail.

◉ Sights & Activities

Border Market
MARKET

(ตลาดริมน้ำเมย; Rte 105; ◎ 7am-7pm) Alongside the Mae Nam Moei on the Thai side is an expansive market that sells a mixture of workaday Burmese goods, black-market clothes, cheap Chinese electronics and food, among other things.

The market is 5km west of Mae Sot; *sŏrngtăaou* depart from a spot on Th Bun Khun between about 6am and 6pm (20B).

Herbal Sauna
SAUNA

(Wat Mani, Th Intharakhiri; admission 20B; ◎ 3-7pm) Wat Mani has separate herbal sauna facilities for men and women. The sauna is towards the back of the monastery grounds, past the monks' *gù·đì* (living quarters).

▭ Sleeping

Phan Nu House
GUESTHOUSE $

(☑ 08 1972 4467; 563/3 Th Intharakhiri; r 250-500B; 🅐🅦🆁) This place consists of 29 large rooms in a residential strip just off the street. Most are equipped with air-con, TV, fridge and hot water, making them a good deal.

Ban Pruk Sa Guesthouse
GUESTHOUSE $

(☑ 0 5553 2656; www.banpruksa.com; 740 Th Intharakhiri; r 200-800B; 🅐🆁) This tidy villa unites a handful of unassuming but spacious and comfortable budget rooms.

@ Baan Tung
GUESTHOUSE $

(☑ 0 5553 3277; www.baantungguesthouse.com; 63/4 Soi Ban Tung; r 350-500B; 🅐@🆁) Located on a quiet street, this place features vast rooms in polished concrete, beds on an elevated platform and tight, round-shaped bathrooms. The price depends on whether you opt for fan or air-con.

Bai Fern Guesthouse
HOTEL $

(☑ 0 5553 1349; www.bai-fern.com; 660 Th Intharakhiri; r 150-350B; 🅐🆁) Set just off the road in a large house, the shared-bathroom budget rooms here are tidy but plain. Service is friendly, and a stay includes use of a kitchen, fridge and wi-fi in the communal area.

✕ Eating

Mae Sot is a culinary crossroads. For breakfast head to the area south of the mosque where several Muslim restaurants serve sweet tea, roti and *nanbya* (a tandoori-style bread). The town's vibrant day market is the place to try Burmese dishes such as *mohinga*, a noodle dish. And Mae Sot's night market, at the eastern end of Th Prasat Withi, features mostly Thai-Chinese dishes. The Saturday Walking Street (Soi Rong Chak; ◎ 5-9pm Sat) convenes near the police station.

Khrua Canadian
INTERNATIONAL, THAI $$

(3 Th Sri Phanit; dishes 40-280B; ◎ 7am-10pm; 🆁✍) This is the place to go if you want to forget you're in Asia for one meal. Dave, the Canadian, brews his own coffee and also offers homemade bagels, deli meats and

---

GETTING TO MYANMAR: MAE SOT TO HPA-AN

The Mae Sot/Myawaddy border is one of four open land borders with Myanmar.

Getting to the border The border is 5km west of Mae Sot; *sŏrngtăaou* make the trip to the border (20B, frequent 6am to 6pm).

At the border The **Thai immigration booth** (☑ 0 5556 3004; ◎ 6.30am-6.30pm) sits at the foot of the Friendship Bridge. If you have a pre-arranged visa, you can proceed through the **Myanmar immigration booth** (☑ 95 0585 0100; ◎ 6am-6pm) and on to your next destination. Without a visa, you can buy a 500B temporary ID, which allows you to stay in Myawaddy until 6pm the same day; your passport will be held at the border and returned upon departure.

Moving on About 200m from the border crossing are white share taxis that depart when full on even-numbered days to the following destinations: Mawlamyine (K10,000 to K15,000, six hours), Hpa-an (K10,000 to K15,000, six hours) and Yangon (K40,000, 14 hours). There's also a bus to Yangon (K12,000, 16 hours, 5am).

For information on making this crossing in the opposite direction, see p502.

TRANSPORT FROM MAE SOT

DESTINATION	AIR	BUS	MINIVAN	SŎRNGTĂAOU
Bangkok	1590B, 65min, 4 daily (Don Muang Airport)	333-666B, 7-8hr, frequent 8am-9.45pm	N/A	N/A
Chiang Mai	1290B, 40min, 1 daily	259-333B, 5-6hr, 6am & 8am	N/A	N/A
Kamphaeng Phet	N/A	140B, 3hr, frequent 8am-3.30pm	N/A	N/A
Mae Sariang	N/A	N/A	N/A	200B, 6hr, hourly 6am-noon
Mawlamyine (Myanmar)	1590B, 30min, 9.45am	N/A	N/A	N/A
Phitsanulok	N/A	N/A	185B, 4hr, 4 departures 7am-1pm	N/A
Sukhothai	N/A	N/A	150B, 3hr, 4 departures 7am-1pm	N/A
Yangon (Myanmar)	1590B, 55min, 11.35am	N/A	N/A	N/A

cheeses. The servings are large, the menu is varied, and when you finally remember you're in Thailand again, local information is also available.

Lucky Tea Garden
BURMESE $

(Th Bun Khun; mains 10-50B; ⊗6am-6pm) For the authentic Burmese teashop experience without crossing over to Myawaddy, visit this friendly cafe equipped with sweet tea, tasty snacks and bad Burmese pop music.

Aiya
BURMESE, THAI $

(533 Th Intharakhiri; mains 50-250B; ⊗noon-11.30pm;) Aiya is a simple place that serves good Burmese food, which is particularly strong on vegetarian options; don't miss the delicious Burmese tea-leaf salad.

 Drinking

For a night on the town, head to the bars at the western end of Th Intharakhiri.

Mali Bar
BAR

(Th Intharakhiri; ⊗6pm-midnight) Staffed by Burmese and popular with the NGO set, this rather dark bar has a pool table and a world music soundtrack.

 Shopping

Borderline Shop
HANDICRAFTS

(www.borderlinecollective.org; 674/14 Th Intharakhiri; ⊗10am-6pm Tue-Sat, 2-6pm Sun, tea garden 9am-6pm Tue-Sun) Selling arts and crafts items made by refugee women, the profits from this shop go back into a women's collective and a child-assistance foundation. Upstairs, a gallery sells paintings and the house is also home to a tea garden and cookery course.

ℹ Information

There are several banks with ATMs in the town centre.

Tourist Police (☑1155; 738/1 Th Intharakhiri) Located east of the centre of town.

ℹ Getting There & Away

Mae Sot has an airport with service to Bangkok and Chiang Mai via Nok Air; international destinations include Mawlamyine and Yangon, Myanmar.

NORTHEASTERN THAILAND

Thailand's other regions have natural beauty, but the northeast has soul. The main event in this undervisited region is the people, friendly folks who might invite you over to share their picnic under a shade tree.

That's not to say there isn't beauty in the flat, sun-beaten landscape of rice fields punctuated by shade trees and lonely water buffaloes. Indeed, you've never seen such a vivid green until you've trundled through in the wet season when rice shoots are newly born.

Also referred to as Isan, the northeast is one of Thailand's most rural and agricultural regions. It is a tapestry of Lao, Thai and Khmer

THAILAND NORTHEASTERN THAILAND

traditional cultures, which meandered across the shifting borders much like the mighty Mekong River. The Mekong defines a wide arc across the northern reaches of the region passing small riverfront towns. Local festivals display the region's unique fusion of cultures, and magnificent mini–Angkor Wats were left behind by the Khmer empire.

There's little in the way of guesthouse culture and few English speakers. Indeed, this is the end of the tourist trail and the beginning of the Thailand trail.

Nakhon Ratchasima (Khorat) นครราชสีมา (โคราช)

POP 2 MILLION

To most shoestringers, Nakhon Ratchasima (more commonly known as 'Khorat') is just a transit hub. Bland concrete development has buried much of its history, and its status as Thailand's second-largest city makes Bangkok look exponentially more interesting. But if you're curious, Khorat is a part of the urban Isan puzzle, where village kids grew up to be educated bureaucrats living comfortable middle-class lives – an economic success story.

⊙ Sights

Thao Suranari Monument MONUMENT
(อนุสาวรีย์ท้าวสุรนารี; Th Rajadamnern) FREE
Thao Suranari, wife of the city's assistant governor during the reign of Rama III, is something of a wonder woman in these parts. Ya Mo (Grandma Mo), as she's affectionately called, became a hero in 1826 by organising

AT HOME WITH THE HERD

Thailand's rural northeast is flush with village homestay programs, mainly aimed at urban Thais who didn't grow up beside a rice paddy. One of the few that can accommodate English-speaking visitors is **Ban Kham Pia** (✆08 7861 0601; www.thailandwildelephanttrekking. com; r 200-300B, meals 50-90B), which is located within walking distance of the 186-sq-km Phu Wua Wildlife Reserve. The reserve has nature trails and a resident herd of elephants. Ban Kham Pia is 190km east of Nong Khai, just 3km off Hwy 212. Buses from Nong Khai (150B, 3½ hours) will drop you at Ban Don Chik, 3km away.

a successful prisoner revolt after Chao Anou of Vientiane had conquered Khorat during his rebellion against Siam. As one version of the legend has it, she convinced the women to seduce the Lao soldiers and then the Thai men launched a surprise attack, which saved the city.

Though much of the story lacks historical backing, Thais flock to the monument in adoring droves to burn incense and leave offerings of flowers and food. Those whose supplications have been honoured hire singers to perform *pleng koh·râht* (Khorat folk songs) on small stages.

Dan Kwian HANDICRAFTS VILLAGE
Just a quick trip out of town, Dan Kwian has been producing pottery for hundreds of years and is something of a magnet for Thailand's artistic hippies. The ceramic creations are famous for their rough texture and rust-like hue derived from local kaolin sources. The village is essentially a row of art-gallery shops lining the highway. To get here, hop on a bus (14B, 30 minutes) from Khorat's southern city gate or Bus Terminal 2.

🛏 Sleeping

★**Sansabai House** HOTEL $
(✆0 4425 5144; www.sansabai-korat.com; Th Suranaree; r 300-550B; P❄✿✿) Walk into the welcoming lobby and you half expect the posted prices to be a bait-and-switch ploy. But no, all rooms are bright and cheerful and come with good mattresses, mini-fridges and little balconies.

Assadang Hotel HOTEL $
(✆0 4424 2514; Th Assadang; r 400-500B; P✿✿) There's no escaping the fact that this is just an old concrete box with small rooms, but a two-tone paint job and various little decorations boost it past the jailhouse vibe. Wi-fi only reaches the 500B rooms.

Sri Ratna Hotel HOTEL $
(✆0 4424 3116; Th Suranaree; r 200-350B; P) The centrally located Sri Ratna has the ambience of an insane asylum, but the owners run it with the care and efficiency of a four-star resort. The 200B fan rooms have cold-water showers and squat toilets. If you want aircon, choose another hotel.

🍴 Eating

Khorat is famous for *pàt mèe khorâht*, a local twist on the ubiquitous *pàt tai*.

Nakhon Ratchasima (Khorat)

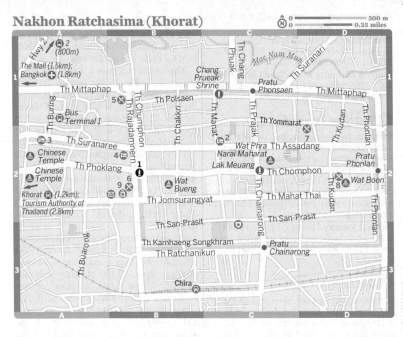

Nakhon Ratchasima (Khorat)

Wat Boon Night Bazaar   THAI **$**
(Th Chumphon; ⊘5-9.30pm) This night market
is less popular than Night Bazaar Korat, but
it's the better choice for eating. Offers Thai,
as well as northeastern Thai food.

Ming Ter   VEGAN **$**
(Th Rajadamnern; dishes 35-80B; ⊘7.30am-6pm;
🍴) There's little English at this homey
vegan affair, but since it does mock-meat
versions of Thai and Chinese standards
you can just order your favourites and the
message will get through. Or, just point to
something in the buffet tray.

Gai Yang Saang Thai   THAI **$**
(Th Rajadamnern; whole free-range chicken 150B;
⊘7.30am-8pm) Has served some of the best

gài yâhng (grilled chicken) in Khorat for
half a century.

★ **Rabieng Kaew**   THAI **$$**
(Th Yommarat; dishes 80-300B; ⊘11am-5pm; 🅿)
This lovely spot has an antique-filled din-
ing room and a leafy garden in back. But
it's not all about the atmosphere. The food,
all big dishes meant to be shared, is simply
excellent.

ⓘ Information

Bangkok Hospital (📞0 4442 9999; Th
Mittaphap)

Banks (Th Mittaphap) Has many extended-
hours banks and AEON ATM.

Klang Plaza 2 (Th Jomsurangyat) This
shopping centre has a Bangkok Bank open

10.30am to 7pm daily, and an AEON ATM outside by the alley entrance.

Post Office (Th Jomsurangyat; ⊗8.30am-10.30pm Mon-Fri, 9am-noon & 4-10.30pm Sat, 4-10.30pm Sun & holidays)

Tourism Authority of Thailand (TAT; ☑0 4421 3666; tatsima@tat.or.th; Th Mittaphap; ⊗8.30am-4.30pm) Next to Sima Thani Hotel.

ℹ Getting There & Away

Khorat has two bus stations: **Bus Terminal 1** (☑0 4424 2899; Th Burin) in the city centre serves Bangkok and towns within Nakhon Ratchasima Province. **Bus Terminal 2** (bor kŏr sŏr sŏrng; ☑0 4429 5271; Hwy 2), known locally as *bor kŏr sŏr sŏrng*, is north of downtown and serves all other destinations and has minivan service. White No 15 *sŏrngtăaou* goes to Terminal 2.

Khorat Railway Station (☑0 4424 2044) sees a lot of traffic but buses are faster. The smaller **Chira Railway Station** is closer to town.

ℹ Getting Around

Sŏrngtăaou (8B) run fixed routes through the city, but even locals complain about how difficult it is to figure out the numbers and colours assigned to the routes. Most pass down Th Suranaree near the market, which is a good place to start. Heading west on Th Suranaree, the yellow *sŏrngtăaou* No 1 with white and green stripes will take you to the train station and the Mall.

Túk-túk and motorcycle taxis cost between 40B and 70B around town.

Phimai พิมาย

Of the many Khmer temples that pepper Isan, **Phimai Historical Park** (อุทยาน ประวัติศาสตร์พิมาย; ☑0 4447 1568; Th Anantajinda; admission 100B; ⊗7.30am-6pm) is an easy day trip from Khorat, making it an ideal ruin for those pressed for time.

The temple was built a century before its strikingly similar cousin Angkor Wat and marked one of the westernmost outposts of the Khmer empire's holy highway of laterite temples. The site was originally started by King Jayavarman V in the late 10th century and finished by King Suryavarman I (r 1002–49). The majestic structure boasts a 28m-tall main shrine of cruciform design and made of white sandstone, while the adjunct shrines are of pink sandstone and laterite. The sculptures over the doorways to the main shrine depict Hindu gods and scenes from the Ramayana.

Phimai National Museum (พิพิธภัณฑสถาน แห่งชาติพิมาย; Th Tha Songkhran; admission 100B; ⊗9am-4pm Wed-Sun), outside the main complex, has a fine collection of Khmer sculpture, including temple lintels and other architectural ruins; closed for renovations until 2016.

Sai Ngam (ไทรงาม; ⊗dawn-dusk) is a 350-plus-year-old tree that blankets an island east of town where food vendors serve *pàt phimai*, which is basically *pàt mèe khorâht*, which is basically *pàt tai*.

There are several places to stay in Phimai if Khorat is too busy for you; these include **Khru Pom** (☑08 6648 9383; Th Anantajinda; s without bathroom 150B, r 350-450B; ▣⊖✲@⬤) and **Moon River Homestay** (☑08 5633 7097; www.moon-river-phimai.com; Ban Sai Ngam Patana Soi 2; r 400-600B, f 1200B; ▣⊖✲⬤).

All buses to Phimai leave from Khorat's Bus Terminal 2 (50B, 1¼ hours, frequent departures).

TRANSPORT FROM NAKHON RATCHASIMA (KHORAT)

DESTINATION	BUS	MINIVAN	TRAIN
Aranya Prathet	165B, 4hr, 5 daily	N/A	N/A
Ayuthaya	N/A	132B, 4hr, frequent	15-350B, 2hr, hourly
Khon Kaen	120-250B, 3-4hr, frequent	129B, 2½hr, hourly 7am-5pm	38-170B, 3½hr, 3 daily
Lopburi	N/A	120B, 3½hr, every 30min 6am-7pm	N/A
Nang Rong	75-95B, 2hr, frequent	75B, 1½hr, every 30min 5am-8pm	N/A
Nong Khai	220-435B, 6hr, hourly	N/A	64B-301B, 6½hr, 1 daily
Surin	136-175B, 4hr, 6 daily	N/A	38-250B, 3hr, 5 daily
Ubon Ratchathani	286-445B, 5-6hr, frequent	58-106B, 5-6hr, 6 daily	N/A
Vientiane (Laos)	540B, 6½hr, 12.30am	N/A	N/A

WEIRD & WONDERFUL ISAN

From ghouls to gunpowder, Isan dominates in the bizarre attractions category.

Dan Sai's Spirit Festival

The raucous **Phi Ta Khon Festival** is a cross between the revelry of Carnival and the ghoulishness of Halloween. The festival coincides with the subdued Buddhist holy day of Bun Phra Wet (Phra Wet Festival), honouring the penultimate life of Buddha, Phra Wessandara (often shortened in Thai to Phra Wet). But in Dan Sai the main event is a rice-whisky-fuelled parade in which villagers don masks to transform themselves into the spirits who welcomed Phra Wet's return. The shop **Kawinthip Hattakham** (กวินทิพย์ หัตถกรรม; Th Kaew Asa; ☉ 8am-7pm) can help arrange homestay accommodation. Dan Sai sits between Loei (65B to 70B, 1½ hours) and Phitsanulok (73B to 102B, three hours) and the festival usually occurs in June.

Yasothon's Kaboom Fest

Rocket Festivals (Bun Bâng Fai) are held across Isan in May and June to tell Phaya Thaen, a pre-Buddhist rain god, that it's time for him to send down the wet stuff; but no place celebrates as fervently as Yasothon, where the largest rockets, called *bâng fai síp láhn,* are 3m long and packed with 500kg of gunpowder. The festival is held on the second weekend of May. **BM Grand** (☏ 0 4571 4262; Th Rattanakhet; s/d 400/450; P ⊟ ✳ 🛜) has cheap sleeps in the city centre. Yasothon can be reached by bus from Nakhon Ratchasima (175B to 230B, four hours) and Ubon Ratchathani (73B to 109B, 1½ hours) and by minivan from Mukdahan (84B, two hours, every half-hour).

Si Saket's Glass Temple

Before recycling was in vogue, the idea for **Wat Lan Khuat** (☉ dawn-dusk), better known as the Million Bottle Temple, was born from a religious vision. In 1982 the abbot dreamt of a sanctuary in heaven made of diamonds and gems. Wishing to replicate this divine splendour he set about covering the temple buildings in the most sparkly material he could find: green bottles. And today the temple shines *sort of* gemlike. The temple sits outside of Si Saket in Khun Han, 11km south of Hwy 24 via Rte 2111. Public transport is limited so you'll have to rent a motorbike in Surin.

Khao Yai National Park

อุทยานแห่งชาติเขาใหญ่

Thailand's oldest and most remarkable national park, Khao Yai (อุทยานแห่งชาติเขาใหญ่; ☏ 08 6092 6529; adult/child 400/200B, car 50B) is a vast wilderness astonishingly close to the country's major population centres. This is one of the largest intact monsoon forests in mainland Asia and, along with neighbouring forest complexes, it is now a Unesco World Heritage Site.

The park surrounds a 1351m-high mountain on the western edge of the Dangrek range, which forms a natural boundary between Thailand and Cambodia. There are more than 50km of trekking trails (many of them formed by the movement of wildlife), some wild elephant herds, majestic waterfalls (for part of the year) and impressive bird life.

The most beautiful time to visit is just after the monsoon rains in November through to the start of the hot season (around April) when the landscape is green and the waterfalls are full. But this is also when leeches are at their fiercest.

The park headquarters has some general trail information but doesn't have an accurate trail map. For the major highlights it is easy enough to visit on your own but you'll need a guide for minor trails and to spot wildlife. The guesthouses in Pak Chong can arrange transport and day tours. Greenleaf Guesthouse has long enjoined enthusiastic praise and **Bobby's Apartments & Jungle Tours** (☏ 08 6262 7006; www.bobbysjungletourkhaoyai.com) is a relative newcomer earning high marks.

🍴 Sleeping & Eating

Staying within the park cuts out your commute, though access to food and transport are limited. Park restaurants at the visitor centre close at 7pm. Most backpackers base themselves in the nearby town of Pak Chong.

★ **Greenleaf Guesthouse** GUESTHOUSE **$**
(☏0 4436 5073; www.greenleaftour.com; Th Thanarat, Km 7.5; r 200-300B; ⓟ📶) Step past the slightly chaotic common areas and you'll be surprised by the good-value rooms (with cold-water private bathrooms) at the back of this long-running family-owned place. Note they'll probably be 'full', if you don't book a tour.

Park Accommodation CAMP SITES **$**
(☏0 2562 0760; www.dnp.go.th/parkreserve; camp sites 30B, r from 800B) Within the park there are camp sites and a variety of rooms and bungalows, which require advance reservation. Camping gear is also available for rent.

Khaoyai Garden Lodge HOTEL **$$**
(☏0 4436 5178; www.khaoyaigardenlodgekm7.com; Th Thanarat, Km 7; r 250-2500B, f 2800B; ⓟ😊❄@📶🐾) This friendly, family-run place offers a variety of rooms (the cheapest are sterile, have shared hot-water bathrooms, and fans), all spread out around a garden. It's a bit worn, but it's still good value and the restaurant-lounge in front encourages interaction with your fellow guests. There's a Thai dance show on Friday nights.

ℹ Getting There & Around

Pak Chong, the primary base town for the park, is served by buses and minivans from the following destinations:

Bangkok (Northern and Northeastern bus terminal/Mo Chit) 128B to 150B, three hours.

Bangkok (Victory Monument) 180B, 2½ hours, hourly.

Nakhon Ratchasima (Khorat): 60B to 80B, 1½ hours.

Pak Chong is also on the rail line, but this is only a good option if you're coming from Ayuthaya (23B to 363B, two to three hours, nine daily).

Sŏrngtăaou travel the 30km from Pak Chong to the park's northern gate (40B, 45 minutes, every half-hour from 6am to 5pm); hop aboard on Th Thanarat in front of the 7-Eleven store and hop off at the ticket gate. From here it is another 14km to the visitor centre; hitchhiking this stretch is quite common. There are also motorcycle rentals at the gate (500B) and in Pak Chong town (300B).

Phanom Rung Historical Park

อุทยานประวัติศาสตร์ ขาพนมรุ้ง

Spectacularly located atop an extinct volcano, **Phanom Rung Historical Park** (☏0 4466 6251; admission 100B, combined ticket with Prasat Muang Tam 150B; ☉6am-6pm) is the largest and best restored of the ancient Khmer sanctuaries in Thailand. Dating from the 10th to 13th centuries, the complex faces east towards the sacred capital of Angkor in Cambodia. It was

---

GETTING TO LAOS: EASTERN BORDERS

Ubon Ratchathani to Pakse

The busy Chong Mek/Vang Tao border crossing connects to Laos' Si Phan Don (Four Thousand Islands) region via Pakse; it is also the only Thai–Lao border where you don't have to cross the Mekong.

Getting to the border Direct Ubon Ratchathani–Pakse buses stop at the border for visa formalities.

At the border The border is open 6am to 8pm and is largely hassle-free, save for the occasional practice of a 'stamping' levy by Lao officials. Lao visas are available on the spot for US$30 to US$44, depending on nationality; a passport photo is needed.

Moving on The southern Lao city of Pakse is about an hour away.

Mukdahan to Savannakhet

The Thai-Lao Friendship Bridge links Mukdahan and Savannakhet, where onward transport continues to the Vietnamese coast.

Getting to the border From Mukdahan, buses to Savannakhet (45B, hourly from 7.30am to 7pm) make the crossing.

At the border Border formalities are handled on the bridge. A 30-day Lao visa is available for US$30 to US$44, depending on nationality; bring a passport photo.

Moving on On the Lao side there are buses to Vietnam, a journey of about seven hours.

For information on making these crossings in the opposite directions, see p363.

first built as a Hindu monument and features sculpture relating to Vishnu and Shiva. Later it was converted into a Buddhist temple.

The craftsmanship at Phanom Rung represents the pinnacle of Khmer artistic achievement, on par with the bas-reliefs at Angkor Wat in Cambodia. One of the most striking design features is the promenade, an avenue sealed with laterite and sandstone blocks and flanked by sandstone pillars with lotus-bud tops. It leads to the first and largest of three *naga* bridges, which are the only surviving architectural features of their kind in Thailand.

The central *prasat* (tower) has a gallery on each of its four sides, and the entrance to each gallery is a smaller incarnation of the main tower. The galleries have curvilinear roofs and windows with false balustrades. Once inside the temple walls, check out the galleries and the *gopura* (entrance pavilion); pay particular attention to the lintels over the doors.

If you can, plan your visit for one of the four times of the year when the sun shines through all 15 sanctuary doorways. This solar alignment happens during sunrise on 3 to 5 April and 8 to 10 September and sunset on 5 to 7 March and 5 to 7 October (one day earlier in leap years).

🛏 Sleeping

Phanom Rung is a day trip from Nakhon Ratchasima (Khorat) and Surin, but some people spend the night in Nang Rong, the nearest town to the temple.

★P California Inter Hostel   GUESTHOUSE $
(☑08 1808 3347; www.pcalifornianangrong.webs.com; Th Sangkakrit; s 250-500B; d 300-600B; P ☺ ❄ ☎) This great place, which isn't actually a hostel, on the east side of town offers bright, good-value rooms. English-speaking owner Khun Wicha is knowledgable and leads tours. Bikes are free of charge. A motorcycle taxi from the bus station costs 50B.

Honey Inn   GUESTHOUSE $
(☑08 1264 7144; Soi Si Kun; r 250-350B; ❄ @ ☎) This family-run veteran, 1km north of the bus station, is a bit dated but has the necessary services: motorcycle hire and guided tours.

❶ Getting There & Away

For day-trippers from Nakhon Ratchasima (Khorat) or Surin, take a bus to Ban Tako (75B to 80B, two hours, hourly), a well-marked turn-off 14km east of Nang Rong, the closet village to the

historic site. From here the easiest option is to hire a motorcycle taxi (300B return).

Nang Rong can be reached via bus from Khorat and Pak Chong. From Nang Rong there's a *sŏrngtăaou* (25B, 30 minutes, every half-hour) that leaves from the old market at the east end of town and goes to Ban Ta Pek, where motorcycle taxis charge 200B return to Phanom Rung Historical Park. It is probably easier to rent a motorcycle in Nang Rong.

Surin & Around

POP 41,200

There's not a lot to see in sleepy Surin until the annual Elephant Round-up comes to town in November. The rest of the year, a few travellers trickle through en route to the Khmer temples that line the Cambodian border. Culturally, Surin has a strong Khmer influence, and the province is renowned for its silk-weaving villages.

Surin is also a launching point for a little-used border-crossing point for Siem Reap–bound travellers.

◉ Sights

Elephant Study Centre   ELEPHANT ENCOUNTER
(☑0 4414 5050; admission 100B; ⊗8.30am-4pm) To see Surin's elephants outside of festival time, visit this centre in Ban Tha Klang, a Suai (traditional elephant-herder ethnic group) village about 50km north of Surin. During Visakha Bucha (usually in May), an elephant procession delivers the young men entering the monastery.

Sŏrngtăaou run from Surin's bus terminal (60B, 1½ hours, hourly) with the last one returning at 4pm.

Queen Sirikit Sericulture Center   HANDICRAFT CENTRE
(ศูนย์หม่อนไหมเฉลิมพระเกียรติสมเด็จพระนางเจ้าสิริกิติ์ พระบรมราชินีนาถ (สุรินทร์); ☑0 4451 1393; Rte

226; ◎ 8am-4.30pm) **FREE** The easiest place to see the entire silk-making process, from larva to loom, is at this research centre 4km west of town. Various displays can be seen any time, but the silk makers only work on weekdays.

Craft Villages HANDICRAFT CENTRES
There are many silk and silvercraft villages within striking distance of Surin. These traditional crafts, especially the silk patterns, display Khmer influences and are not widely available in the rest of the country. **Ban Tha Sawang**, 8km from Surin, is known for its exquisite brocade fabrics *(pâh yók torng)*. *Sŏrngtăaou* (15B, 20 minutes) depart from Surin's fresh market.

Ban Khwao Sinarin and **Ban Chok**, about 18km north of Surin, are known for silk and silver respectively. The OTOP handicrafts mall at the east end of the villages displays the making of Surin-style beaded silver jewellery (claiming Khmer heritage). Big blue *sŏrngtăaou* to Ban Khwao Sinarin (25B, 30 minutes, hourly) leave from near Surin's train station.

Prasat Ta Meuan KHMER RUIN
(◎ dawn-dusk) **FREE** One of three Khmer temples that linked Angkor Wat (in Cambodia) to Phimai (in Nakhon Ratchasima province), Prasat Ta Meuan was built in the Jayavarman VII period (AD 1181–1219) as a rest stop for pilgrims. Just 300m south, **Prasat Ta Meuan Toht** was a healing station and 1km further on is **Prasat Ta Meuan Thom**, a Shiva shrine. The ruins are 10.3km south of Ban Ta Miang on Rte 224 and you'll need private transport.

✯✯ Festivals

The annual **Elephant Round-up** showcases the elephants in mock battles and various feats of strength and dexterity, and all of the hotels fill up with foreigners – an astonishing feat in itself.

VOLUNTEERING IN SURIN

LemonGrass (p789) is a well-run volunteer program in Surin that places English-speaking volunteers in local schools. The **Surin Project** (🖉 08 4482 1210; www.surinproject.org), based in Ban Tha Klang, offers volunteering opportunities for visitors who would like to spend quality time with elephants in a traditional elephant-herding village.

🛏 Sleeping & Eating

During the Elephant Round-up, every hotel in town is booked and rates can triple; reserve well in advance.

★ **Baan Chang Ton** HOMESTAY $
(🖉 08 7459 8962; www.baanchangton.com; Th Suriyarart; r 400-500B; 🅿 🖨 ❄ @ 🛜) The friendly owners have rescued an old wooden house and created one of Isan's most charming (but simple) places to stay. Guests can use the kitchen or join the family for dinner. Bring your own towel. It's south of the *săh·lah glahng* (provincial hall).

Pirom-Aree's House GUESTHOUSE $
(🖉 0 4451 5140; Soi Arunee; s/d 120/200B; 🅿 🖨 🛜) This long-time budget favourite, 1km west of the city, has simple wooden rooms with shared bathrooms, and a shady garden overlooking a rice paddy. Aree does the cooking and Pirom knows about the region. A túk-túk from the train/bus station costs 60/70B.

Maneerote Hotel HOTEL $
(🖉 0 4453 9477; www.maneerotehotel.com; Soi Poi Tunggor, Th Krungsri Nai; r 400-450B; 🅿 ❄ @ 🛜) This quiet hotel southwest of the fresh market scores off the charts in the high-quality-to-low-price ratio, though it's a little out of the way.

Night Market THAI $
(Th Krungsri Nai; ◎ 5-10pm) A block south of the fountain, this night market whips up a wide selection of Thai and Isan dishes.

Petmanee 2 THAI $
(Th Murasart; dishes 20-80B; ◎ 9am-3pm) This simple spot south of Ruampaet Hospital by Wat Salaloi (look for the large chicken grill) is Surin's most famous purveyor of *sôm·đam* and *gài yâhng*. The *súp nòr mái* (bamboo shoot salad) is good too. There's little English, spoken or written, but it's worth stumbling through an order.

Larn Chang THAI $
(Th Siphathai Saman; dishes 35-280B; ◎ 10am-midnight; 🛜) Tasty and low-priced Thai and Isan food is served in an old wooden house that overlooks a surviving stretch of the city moat called *Sŭan Rák* (Love Park). The food and the setting are lovely, especially at sunset. It's a longish walk south of the centre, on the east side of the park.

TRANSPORT FROM SURIN

DESTINATION	BUS	TRAIN
Aranya Prathet	234B, 6hr, 5 daily	N/A
Bangkok	272-543B, 7hr, 9 daily	73-1146B, 7-9hr, 9 daily
Khon Kaen	182B, 4hr, hourly	N/A
Khorat	125-175B, 4hr, every 30min	38-250B, 3hr, 5 daily
Ubon Ratchathani	105-200B, 3hr, every 2hr	31-382B, 2-4hr, 10 daily

ⓘ Getting There & Away

The **bus terminal** (⌨ 0 4451 1756; Th Jitrbumrung) is one block from the **train station** (⌨ 0 4451 1295); both are centrally located.

Ubon Ratchathani อุบลราชธานี

POP 115,000

Although it is one of the bigger cities in the region, Ubon still retains a small-town feel thanks to the relaxing nature of the Mae Nam Mun, Thailand's second-longest river, and its palpable Lao heritage. It is easily traversed by foot and easily appreciated by aimless wandering. Ubon doesn't see a lot of foreign visitors because it is in an odd corner of the country, but there is a nearby Thai–Lao border crossing that provides an alternative route into southern Laos.

◎ Sights

★**Wat Thung Si Meuang**　BUDDHIST TEMPLE
(วัดทุ่งศรีเมือง; Th Luang; ◎ dawn-dusk) FREE Wat Thung Si Meuang was built during the reign of Rama III (1824–51) and has a classic *hŏr đrai* (Tripitaka hall) in excellent shape. Like many *hŏr đrai,* it rests on tall, angled stilts in the middle of a pond to protect the precious scriptures (written on palm-leaf paper) from termites. It's kept open so you can look inside. The original murals in the little *bòht* beside the *hŏr đrai* show life in that era and are in remarkably good condition.

Wat Si Ubon Rattanaram　BUDDHIST TEMPLE
(วัดศรีอุบลรัตนาราม; Th Uparat; ◎ dawn-dusk) FREE The 7cm-tall topaz Buddha, Phra Kaew Butsarakham, is this temple's primary draw; it was reportedly brought here from Vientiane at Ubon's founding and is one of the city's holiest possessions.

Ubon Ratchathani National Museum　MUSEUM
(พิพิธภัณฑสถานแห่งชาติอุบลราชธานี; Th Kheuan Thani; admission 100B; ◎ 9am-4pm Wed-Sun) Occupying the former city hall, this is a very informative museum displaying Dvaravati-era artefacts and a 2500-year-old bronze drum and Ubon textiles. The museum's most prized possession is a 9th-century Ardhanarisvara, a composite statue combining Shiva and his consort Uma into one being; one of just two ever found in Thailand.

✯✯ Festivals

Candle Parade　CULTURAL
(Kabuan Hae Tian) In preparation for Khao Phansaa (the start of Buddhist Lent, usually in July) it was customary to offer candles to the temples as a source of light. Ubon took the tradition and supersized it into huge wax sculptures depicting Buddhist iconography. The creations are then paraded through town during this annual festival. Prize winners are displayed afterwards and pre-festival construction occurs on the temple grounds.

🛏 Sleeping & Eating

Rates shoot up and availability goes down during the Candle Parade.

★**Sri Isan Hotel**　HOTEL $
(⌨ 0 4526 1011; www.sriisanhotel.com; Th Ratchabut; r incl breakfast 450-800B; P ❄ ✱ @ ☎) The exception to the rule of Isan's uninspired budget hotels is this cheerful spot. The rooms are small, and rather ordinary (look at several before deciding), but it has a great location for exploration.

★**Outside Inn**　GUESTHOUSE $$
(⌨ 08 8581 2069; www.theoutsideinnubon.com; Th Suriyat; r incl breakfast 450-790B; P ❄ ✱ ☎) A nice little garden lounge sets the relaxed, communal vibe at this new hotel. The rooms are large and comfy though street noise does drift in. The Thai-American owners are great hosts and cook Thai and Mexican dishes in the attached cafe. It's a long walk to the town's main attractions, but bikes (50B per day) and motorcycles (250B to 300B per day) can be hired and *sŏrngtăaou* No 10 can deliver you from the bus station.

★ **Rung Roj** THAI $
(Th Nakhonban; dishes 45-280B; ⊙9.30am-8.30pm; 🛜) What this Ubon institution lacks in service, it more than makes up for with excellent food using family recipes and fresh ingredients. Many people swear by the ox-tongue stew. Look for the bold plate, fork and spoon sign.

Night Market THAI, VIETNAMESE $
(Th Kheuan Thani; ⊙4-11pm) Though it's smaller than you'd expect, Ubon's city-centre night market makes an excellent dining destination, especially when paired with the weekend **Walking Street** (Th Ratchabut; ⊙6-11pm Fri-Sun). Vendors sell Thai, Isan and Vietnamese food.

Porntip Gai Yang
Wat Jaeng THAI $
(Th Saphasit; dishes 20-130B; ⊙8am-8pm) It looks like a tornado has whipped through this no-frills spot, but the chefs cook up a storm of their own. This is considered by many to be Ubon's premier purveyor of *gài yâhng, sôm-đam,* sausages and other classic Isan foods.

❶ Information

Tourism Authority of Thailand (TAT; ☑0 4524 3770; tatubon@tat.or.th; Th Kheuan Thani; ⊙8.30am-4.30pm) Has helpful staff.

Ubonrak Thonburi Hospital (☑0 4526 0285; Th Phalorangrit) Has a 24-hour casualty department.

❶ Getting There & Around

Ubon has an airport serviced by **Air Asia** (☑0 2515 9999; www.airasia.com) and **Nok Air** (☑0 2900 9955; www.nokair.com) with flights to Bangkok's Don Muang; **Thai Airways International** (THAI; ☑0 4531 3340; www.thaiairways.com) flies to Bangkok's Suvarnabhumi Airport. Ubon's **bus terminal** (☑0 4531 6085) is at the far northern end of town, 3km from the centre. It is accessible via *sŏrngtăaou* No 2, 3 or 10.

The **railway station** (☑0 4532 1588) is in Warin Chamrap, south of central Ubon, accessible via *sŏrngtăaou* No 2.

Numbered *sŏrngtăaou* (10B) run throughout town. A túk-túk trip will cost 30B to 50B.

Mukdahan มุกดาหาร

POP 34,300

Mukdahan is linked to Savannakhet in Laos by the Thai-Lao Friendship Bridge 2, part of the ambitious Trans-Asia Hwy that continues by road all the way to the Vietnamese port town of Danang. Though the world has arrived at Mukdahan's doorstep, the town provides little distraction between arrival and departure.

If you need to overnight here, **Ban Rim Suan** (☑0 4263 2980; www.banrimsuan.weebly.com; Th Samut Sakdarak; r 350B; P🚗❄@🛜) is the best budget deal in the city. For something quite unique, splurge a little at **Thai House-Isaan** (☑08 7065 4635; www.thaihouse-isaan.com; r incl breakfast 750-1500B; P🚗❄@🛜🏊🐕) 🛵, a village-based guesthouse with cultural tours and cooking lessons; it is about an hour from Mukdahan by bus to Ban Kham Pok. Reservations required.

Wine Wild Why? (Th Samran Chaikhongthi; dishes 40-150B; ⊙9am-10pm; P🛜) is an atmospheric eatery for Thai and Isan food. **Goodmook*** (Th Song Nang Sathit; dishes 70-450B; ⊙9am-10pm Tue-Sun; 🛜) has all the ingredients of a travellers' cafe: an international menu, free wi-fi and actual decor. The **night market** (Th Song Nang Sathit; ⊙4-9pm) provides Vietnamese food along with the usual suspects.

❶ Getting There & Away

Mukdahan's bus terminal is on Rte 212, west of town. Take a yellow *sŏrngtăaou* (10B) from Th Phitak Phanomkhet near the fountain. Destinations include the following:

TRANSPORT FROM UBON

DESTINATION	AIR	BUS	TRAIN
Bangkok	1350-2500B, 2-5 daily	420-603B, 8½-10hr, frequent	95-691B, 11½hr, six daily
Khon Kaen	N/A	180-277B, 4½hr, every 30min	N/A
Mukdahan	N/A	75-135B, 3½hr, every 30min	N/A
Nakhon Ratchasima	N/A	286-445B, 5-6hr, 14 daily	58-106B, 5-6hr, 6 daily
Pakse (Laos)	N/A	200B, 3hr, 9.30am & 3.30pm	N/A
Surin	N/A	105-200B, 3hr, every 2hr	31-382B, 2-4hrs, 10 daily

Bangkok's Northern & Northeastern bus terminal 420B to 533B, 10 hours, evening departures.

Nakhon Phanom 80B, two hours, frequent.

That Phanom 40B, one hour.

Ubon Ratchathani 75B to 135B, 3½ hours, frequent.

That Phanom ธาตุพนม

This drowsy hamlet is a little piece of Laos on the wrong side of the Mekong River. It is not a place you'd chart a course to on purpose but if you're headed to Nong Khai from the Mukdahan border crossing, That Phanom is a lovely detour. The highlight in town is **Wat Phra That Phanom** (วัดพระ ธาตุพนม; Th Chayangkun; ☺ 5am-8pm) **FREE**, crowned by an iconic *tâht,* a needle-like Lao-style *chedi* that is loudly celebrated during the **That Phanom Festival** (☺ late Jan or early Feb). A lively **Thai-Lao market** gathers by the river north of the pier on Monday and Thursday from 7am to 2pm, where Lao merchants sell herbal medicines, forest roots and river crabs.

Kritsada Rimkhong Hotel (☎ 08 1262 4111; www.ksdrimkhong-resort.com; Th Rimkhong; r 400-600B; P ⊖ ❋ @ ☜) has rooms that range from plain to attractive and **Baan-Ing-Oon Guesthouse** (☎ 0 4254 0111; Th Phanom Phanarak; r 450-550B; ⊖ ❋ ☜) supplies some

much-needed guesthouse culture. There's a small **night market** (☺ 4-10pm) for dinner.

That Phanom's bus station is west of town with bus and minivan services to Mukdahan (47B to 50B, one hour), Nakhon Phanom (40B to 50B, one hour, seven daily) and Ubon Ratchathani (150B to 185B, 4½ hours, frequent).

You can also take one of the frequent *sŏrngtăaou* that park in town to Nakhon Phanom (40B, 90 minutes).

Nakhon Phanom นครพนม

POP 31,700

This tidy provincial capital has a picturesque setting beside the Mekong River overlooking the asymmetrical peaks of Laos. With its French colonial buildings and Vietnamese influences, this is a little piece of Indochina on the far northeastern fringes of Siam. There's also a legal border crossing into Laos should you be looking for an escape hatch.

The neighbouring village of Ban Na Chok, 3km west of town, gave refuge to Vietnamese liberator Ho Chi Minh. He planned the resistance movement in what is now called **Uncle Ho's House** (บ้านโฮจิมินห์; ☎ 0 4252 2430; entry by donation; ☺ dawn-dusk), which served as his residence in 1928–29. More Uncle Ho memories are kept at the **Ho Chi Minh Museum** (☎ 08 0315 4630; admission free; ☺ 8am-4pm).

POIPET TRANSPORT SCAMS

It's worth mastering the transport tricks of the scam-ridden Poipet/Aranya Prathet border to save both hassle and money.

Rule number one: coming in from Thailand, under no circumstances should you deal with any 'Cambodian' immigration officials who might approach you on the Thai side – this is a pure scam. Entering Cambodia you should not have to pay more than the US$20 visa fee, but again they will likely try to charge you at least 100B extra as a 'stamp' or 'overtime' fee.

Once you're through immigration, your next challenge is dealing with the Poipet transport mafia. Poipet has two bus stations: the Poipet Tourist Passenger International Terminal, situated 9km east of town in the middle of nowhere, and the main bus station, which is at the main market, one block north of Canadia Bank off NH5. Touts will try to shepherd you towards the international tourist terminal, where rates for onward buses and share taxis cost double what they should.

Instead of giving these scam artists your business, stay solo and walk or take a moto (2000r) 1km along NH5 to the bus company offices near Canadia Bank, or to the main bus station nearby. You'll get 'real' bus fares here. Unfortunately, the vast majority of buses depart in the morning (before 10.30am). If you can't get a bus, just take a share taxi – these also depart from the NH5 around Canadia Bank – onwards to Siem Reap (seat/whole taxi US$5/35), Battambang (seat/whole taxi US$4.25/30) or Phnom Penh (seat/whole taxi US$8/42). Don't take the taxis that hang out near the roundabout by the border – these charge tourists at least double.

For transport information from Bangkok and omward to Siem Reap, see p735

see p735

GETTING TO LAOS: REMOTE BORDERS

Nakhon Phanom to Tha Khaek

Though not the most convenient crossing, Nakhon Phanom feeds into the Lao town of Tha Khaek.

At the border Buses cross the Thai-Lao Friendship bridge to Tha Khaek (70B to 75B, eight daily from 8am to 5pm). Lao visas are available at the border for US$30 to US$42, depending on nationality; bring a passport photo.

Moving on Savannakhet is a two-hour bus ride from Tha Khaek.

For information on making this crossing in the other direction, see p353.

Bueng Kan to Paksan

You can cross the border to Paksan, but only if you already have a Lao visa.

Getting to the border Buses to Bueng Kan leave from Nong Khai (100B to 150B, 3½ hours, eight daily) and Nakhon Phanom (140B, three hours, four daily). The border crossing is 2.5km northwest of town; a túk-túk costs 60B.

At the border You'll need a pre-arranged Lao visa in order to cross.

Moving on Boats cross the river to Paksan (60B, 8.30am to noon and 1pm to 4.30pm).

For information on making this crossing in the other direction, see p353.

Loei to Pak Lai

Foreigners can get Lao visas at the seldom-used Thai-Lao Nam Heuang Friendship Bridge at the Tha Li/Kaen Thao border crossing in Amphoe Tha Li, 60km northwest of Loei. But the road from Kaen Thao to Luang Prabang is rough and public transport is scarce.

For information on making this crossing in the other direction, see p345.

The city runs an hour-long **sunset cruise** (☑ 0 4251 4436; per person 50B) along the Mekong on *Thesaban*, which docks across from the Indochina Market.

Nakhon Phanom is famous for its October **Illuminated Boat Procession**, a modern twist on the ancient tradition of floating offerings to the Mekong *naga,* a mythical serpent that appears in Buddhist art and iconography.

SP Residence (☑ 0 4251 3500; Th Nittayo; r 450-800B; P ⊜ ⊛ @ ☎) has plain but modern rooms and the **Grand Hotel** (☑ 0 4251 3788; Th Si Thep; r 200-400B; P ⊛) is grandly spartan. The outdoor terrace at the **Indochina Market** (Th Sunthon Wijit; ⊙ 7am-7pm) has choice seats that frame the mountain views. The **night market** (Th Fuang Nakhon; ⊙ 4-9pm) cooks up a variety of take-away food. **Luk Tan** (Th Bamrung Meuang; dishes 39-149B; ⊙ 5-10pm Wed-Sun), in the centre of town, is a quirky spot featuring international dishes.

The **bus terminal** (☑ 0 4251 3444; Th Fuang Nakhon) is west of the town centre. Destinations include Nong Khai (210B, six hours, four daily departures), Mukdahan (80B, 2½ hours), That Phanom (40B, one hour) and Bangkok (447B to 574B, 12 hours, three daily).

Nong Khai หนองคาย

POP 61,500

Adorable Nong Khai has a winning recipe: a sleepy setting beside the Mekong River, enough tourist amenities to dispel isolation and enough attractions to fill a day with sightseeing and snacking. It's an easy overnight train ride from Bangkok and sits on a convenient border crossing into Vientiane, Laos.

⊙ Sights

★ Sala Kaew Ku   SCULPTURE PARK
(admission 20B; ⊙ 8am-6pm) This quasireligious sculpture park is a 3D journey into the mind of a mystic shaman. Built over a period of 20 years by Luang Pu Boun Leua Sourirat, who died in 1996, the park features a weird and wonderful array of gigantic sculptures ablaze with Hindu-Buddhist imagery. To get to Sala Kaew Ku, board a bus heading east and ask to get off at Wat Khaek (10B), as the park is also known; it's about a five-minute walk from the highway. Chartered túk-túk cost 150B return with a one-hour wait. Or you can reach it by bike in about 30 minutes.

Tha Sadet Market
MARKET

(ตลาดท่าเสด็จ; Th Rimkhong; ⊙8.30am-6pm)
Everyone loves a stroll through this covered
riverside market. It offers the usual mix of
clothes, electronic equipment, food and assorted bric-a-brac, most of it imported from
Laos and China, but there are also a few
shops selling quirky quality stuff.

★★ Festivals

The **Rocket Festival** (Bun Bâng Fai) begins on
Visakha Bucha day in late May/early June.

The end of Buddhist Lent (Ork Phansaa)
in late October/early November ushers in a
variety of river-based events, including **longtail boat races** and the mysterious **naga
fireballs** (when illuminated, seemingly gase-
ous balls rise out of the river on the night of
the full moon).

⊨ Sleeping

Nong Khai is the only Isan town with a fully
fledged backpacker scene.

★ Mut Mee
Garden Guesthouse
GUESTHOUSE $

(✍0 4246 0717; www.mutmee.com; Soi Mutmee; r
180-1500B; ❀❂🛜) Occupying a sleepy stretch
of the Mekong, Nong Khai's budget old-timer
has a garden so relaxing it's intoxicating, and
most nights it's packed with travellers. A
huge variety of rooms are clustered around a
thatched-roof restaurant.

Ruan Thai Guesthouse
GUESTHOUSE $

(✍0 4241 2519; Th Rimkhong; r 300-400B, f
1200B; P❀❂@🛜) Long popular due to
its good prices, convenient location, regular maintenance and friendly vibe. There's
a mix of fan and air-con rooms plus one
wooden cottage and some flower-filled
garden greenery.

Sawasdee Guesthouse
GUESTHOUSE $

(✍0 4241 2502; www.sawasdeeguesthouse.com;
Th Meechai; s 180B, d 200-450B; P❀@🛜) If
you could judge a hotel by its cover, this
charismatic guesthouse in an old Franco-
Chinese shophouse would come up trumps.
The tidy rooms (the fan options share bathrooms) mostly lack the old-school veneer
of the exterior and lobby, but they're fairly
priced. The owner is quite a character.

✕ Eating

★ Dee Dee Pohchanah
THAI $

(Th Prajak; dishes 45-250B; ⊙10.30am-2am) How
good is Dee Dee? Just look at the dinner-
time crowds – but don't be put off by them.
Despite having a full house every night, this
simple place is a well-oiled machine and you
won't be waiting long.

★ Saap Lah
THAI $

(Th Meechai; dishes 25-150B; ⊙7am-8pm) For excellent gài yâhng, sôm·đam and other Isan
foods, follow your nose to this no-frills shop.

Daeng Namnuang
VIETNAMESE $

(Th Rimkhong; dishes 60-130B; ⊙8am-8pm; P🛜)
This massive river restaurant has grown into
an Isan institution, and hordes of out-of-
towners head home with car boots and carry-
on bags stuffed with năam neu·ang (pork
spring rolls).

Nagarina
THAI $$

(✍0 4241 2211; Th Rimkhong; dishes 40-400B;
⊙10am-9pm; 🛜✎) The floating restaurant
affiliated with Mut Mee guesthouse special-
ises in fish with true Thai flavours. There's
a sunset cruise (100B) most nights around
5pm; order food at least 30 minutes before
departure.

THAILAND NONG KHAI

GETTING TO LAOS: NONG KHAI TO VIENTIANE

The Nong Khai/Tha Na Long crossing is one of the most popular Thai–Lao border crossings.

Getting to the border If you already have your Lao visa, a direct bus from Nong Khai to
Vientiane (55B, one hour, six daily) leaves from the bus station. If you're getting a visa at
the border, take a túk-túk (50B to 100B) to the bridge. Don't let the driver take you to a
visa-service agency.

At the border The border is open 6am to 10pm. **Thai immigration office** (✍0 4299
0935; ⊙8.30am-noon & 1-4.30pm Mon-Fri) is south of the bridge. After getting stamped out of
Thailand, you'll need to take a minibus (20B to 30B) across the bridge. Lao visas are avail-
able upon arrival for US$32 to US$42, depending on nationality; bring a passport photo.

Moving on It is 22km to Vientiane, via buses, túk-túk and taxis.

For information on making this crossing in the other direction, see p323.

Drinking

There are several pubs along Th Rimkhong, the riverfront road. Two standouts are **Gaia** (⊙7pm-late) and **Warm Up**, which has a pool table and is popular with Thais and travellers.

Shopping

Nong Khai Walking Street Market MARKET
(⊙4-10pm Sat) This street festival featuring music, handmade items, and food takes over the promenade every Saturday night.

Hornbill Books BOOKS
(Soi Mut Mee; ⊙10am-7pm Mon-Sat) Buys, sells and trades English-language books. Has internet access too.

Village Weaver Handicrafts HANDICRAFTS
(Th Prajak) This place sells high-quality, hand-woven fabrics and clothing (ready-made or made to order) that help fund development projects around Nong Khai. The *mát-mèe* cotton is particularly good here.

ℹ Information

There is no shortage of banks with ATMs in town. For a wealth of information on Nong Khai and the surrounding area, visit www.mutmee.com.
Nong Khai Hospital (☑0 4241 3456; Th Meechai) Has a 24-hour casualty department.
Tourism Authority of Thailand (TAT; ☑0 4242 1326; tat_nongkhai@yahoo.com; Hwy 2; ⊙8.30am-4.30pm) Located outside of town.

ℹ Getting There & Away

Nong Khai's main **bus terminal** (☑0 4242 1264) is just off Th Prajak, by the Pho Chai market, about 1.5km from the riverfront guesthouses. Nearby is Udon Thani, a major bus hub with more transport options.

The **train station** (☑0 4241 1592; Hwy 212) is 2km west of town. Two express trains connect to **Bangkok** (103B to 498B, 11 to 12 hours, one morning and one afternoon departure).

EASTERN GULF COAST

Thailand's east coast isn't as stunning as the postcard-famous southern coast, but it is an ideal beach jaunt from jostling Bangkok if you're pinched for time or travelling overland to/from Cambodia. While your friends are still packed into buses en route to Ko Pha-Ngan, you'll be sun-kissed and sandy-toed.

Ko Samet เกาะเสม็ด

Bangkok's beachy backyard, Ko Samet is close enough for a weekend escape, yet worlds away from the urban bustle. Traffic-weary Thais, Russian and Chinese package tourists and Bangkok expats are Samet's steady clientele – and everyone squeezes into the petite east-coast beaches. It's been a **national park** (admission 200B) since 1981 and is still surprisingly rustic considering Thailand's penchant for urban makeovers of its seaside parks. Walking trails connect the beaches and the rocky headlands, the interior road isn't paved and coconut trees tower over the buildings. However, there is talk of paving the interior road and the 2013 oil spill on the island's west coast means changes ahead.

Bring mosquito spray as the forested island is home to everyone's favourite blood suckers.

🛏 Sleeping & Eating

Most bungalows have restaurants offering mixed menus of Thai and traveller food. Weekday rates don't rank well on the value scale (fan rooms start at 800B) but are better than weekend and holidays rates, which increase by as much as 100%. Eat at the noodle bars and stir-fry joints in Na Dan, the small village next to the pier.

BUSES FROM NONG KHAI

DESTINATION	PRICE (B)	DURATION (HR)	DEPARTURES
Bangkok's Northern & Northeastern (Mo Chit) station	380-490	11	afternoon & evening
Bangkok's Suvarnabhumi (Airport) bus station	495	9	8pm
Nakhon Phanom	210	6½	4 daily
Udon Thani	50	1	frequent
Vang Vieng (Laos)	270	4	10am
Vientiane (Laos)	55	1	6 daily

Ko Samet

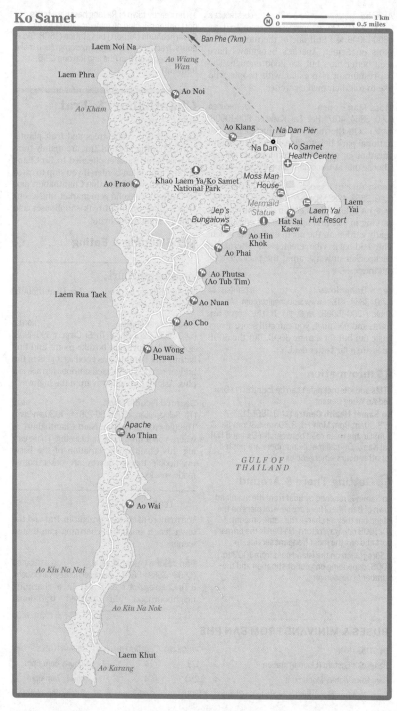

N
0 — 1 km
0 — 0.5 miles

Ban Phe (7km)

Laem Noi Na

Ao Wiang Wan

Laem Phra

Ao Noi

Ao Kham

Ao Klang

Na Dan Pier

Na Dan

Ko Samet
Health Centre

Ao Prao

Khao Laem Ya/Ko Samet
National Park

Moss Man
House

Mermaid
Statue

Laem
Yai

Jep's
Bungalows

Laem Yai
Hut Resort

Hat Sai
Kaew

Ao Hin
Khok

Ao Phai

Ao Phutsa
(Ao Tub Tim)

Laem Rua Taek

Ao Nuan

Ao Cho

Ao Wong
Deuan

Apache
Ao Thian

GULF OF
THAILAND

Ao Wai

Ao Kiu Na Nai

Ao Kiu Na Nok

Laem Khut

Ao Karang

Apache
GUESTHOUSE $

(☑ 08 1452 9472; www.apachesamed.com; Ao Thian; r 800-1300B; ❄) Still one of the most chilled spots on Samet, Apache's bungalows have seen better days but are good enough. The bar-restaurant is popular with people who like to roll their own cigarettes.

Moss Man House
GUESTHOUSE $

(☑0 3864 4017; Hat Sai Kaew; r 800-1000B; ❄ ☎) On the main street, just before the national park ticket office, is this very sound guesthouse, with large, comfortable rooms. Choose one at the back for peace and quiet.

Laem Yai Hut Resort
GUESTHOUSE $$

(☑0 3864 4282; Hat Sai Kaew; r 1000-2000B; ❄ ☎) A colourful collection of 25 bungalows varying in size and age are camped out in a shady garden on the north end of the beach. The laid-back vibe creates an alternative backpacker universe amid the package-tour madness.

Jep's Bungalows
GUESTHOUSE $$

(☑0 3864 4112; www.jepbungalow.com; Ao Hin Khok; r 300-1800B; ❄ @ ☎) If the stars are right, and it's quiet, you can still score a very basic fan hut for a mere 300B. But the 600B ones are a far better deal.

❶ Information

ATMs and internet cafes can be found in Na Dan and Ao Wong Deuan.

Ko Samet Health Centre (☑0 3861 1123; ⊙8.30am-9pm Mon-Fri, 8.30am-4.30pm Sat & Sun) On the main road between Na Dan and Hat Sai Kaew. On-call mobile numbers are posted for after-hours emergencies.

❶ Getting There & Around

Ko Samet is reached by boat from the mainland town of Ban Phe. There are several piers on the island but they all charge the same amount: 70/100B one way/return. Na Dan is the primary port and has the most frequent service.

Sŏrngtǎaou on the island cost from 100B to 400B, depending on your destination and the number of passengers.

The nearby town of Rayong has more transport options, including minivans to Bangkok's Suvarnabhumi (Airport) bus station (160B, 3½ hours, frequently 5am to 8pm); sŏrngtǎaou make the trip between Ban Phe and Rayong (25B, frequent).

Chanthaburi & Trat
จันทบุรี / ตราด

Surrounded by palm trees and fruit plantations, Chanthaburi and Trat are mainly transit points for travellers headed to Ko Chang or the Cambodian border. If you stop to catch your breath, you'll find that Chanthaburi dazzles with its weekend gem market, and sleepy Trat is filled with old teak shophouses and genuine small-town living.

🛌 Sleeping & Eating

🛏 Chanthaburi

You're unlikely to need a bed in Chanthaburi, but just in case...

River Guest House
HOTEL $

(☑0 3932 8211; 3/5-8 Th Si Chan; r 190-490B; ❄ @ ☎) Lumpy beds, boxlike rooms and tiny bathrooms, but this is as good as it gets in the budget range. The relaxed outdoor terrace is a plus. Ask for a room away from the highway.

Seafood Noodle Shop
THAI $

(Th Sukhaphiban; dishes 50-70B; ⊙10.30am-9pm) The old city, along Mae Nam Chanthaburi, is where you'll find most sightseeing Thais eating this Chanthaburi variation of the basic rice-noodle theme; nearby are other home-made snacks.

🛏 Trat

You're more likely to overnight in Trat and the town has a small but charming guesthouse scene.

Ban Jaidee Guest House
GUESTHOUSE $

(☑08 3589 0839; banjaideehouse@yahoo.com; 6 Th Chaimongkol; r 200B; ☎) In a charming neighbourhood, this relaxed traditional

BUSES & MINIVANS FROM BAN PHE

DESTINATION	PRICE (B)	DURATION (HR)	DEPARTURES
Bangkok's Eastern (Ekamai) station	173	4	hourly 6am-6pm
Bangkok's Victory Monument	250	4	hourly 7am-6pm
Laem Ngo (mainland pier for boats to Ko Chang)	300	4-5	2 daily departures

wooden house has simple rooms with shared bathrooms (hot-water showers). Paintings and objets d'art made by the owners decorate the common spaces. It's very popular and booking ahead is essential.

NP Guest House GUESTHOUSE **$**
(☑0 3951 2270; Soi Yai On; r 150-400; ❄🛜) Tucked down a quiet *soi* running between Th Lak Meuang and Th Thana Charoen, this newcomer offers simple rooms with a few nice, decorative touches. The cheapest rooms have shared bathrooms.

★Cool Corner Cafe INTERNATIONAL, THAI **$**
(☑08 4159 2030; 49-51 Th Thana Charoen; dishes 60-160B; ☺8am-10pm) Run by Khun Morn, a modern Renaissance woman (writer, artist and traveller) from Bangkok, Cool Corner is an anchor for Trat's expats.

ⓘ Information

Bangkok Hospital Trat (☑0 3953 2735; www. bangkoktrathospital.com; 376 Moo 2, Th Sukhumvit; ☺24hr) Best health care in the region. It's 400m north of the town centre.

ⓘ Getting There & Away

Most buses originating in Bangkok stop in Chanthaburi and Trat.

CHANTHABURI

For travellers heading to/from the northeast, Chanthaburi is the transfer station. The bus station is on Th Saritidet. Minivans park near the market. Sa Kaew is the transfer point for Aranya Prathet–bound travellers.

TRAT

Trat has an airport served by Bangkok Airways with flights to Suvarnabhumi International Airport.

The bus station is outside of town; *sŏrngtăaou* leave from Th Sukhumvit near the market to the bus station (20B to 60B, depending on number of passengers).

Minivans to Chanthaburi leave when full from a stop on Th Sukhumvit north of the indoor market. **Family Tour** (☑08 1940 7380; cnr Th Sukhumvit & Th Lak Meuang) runs minivans to Bangkok's Victory Monument and Th Khao San.

There are three piers outside of Trat that handle ferries to/from Ko Chang; the area is collectively known as Laem Ngop. Inquire about transfers to the pier when buying ferry tickets in Trat.

TRANSPORT FROM CHANTHABURI & TRAT

Chanthaburi

DESTINATION	BUS	MINIVAN
Bangkok Eastern (Ekamai) Bus Terminal	250B, 4hr, 25 daily	N/A
Bangkok Northern (Mo Chit) Bus Terminal	214B, 4hr, 2 daily	N/A
Nakhon Ratchasima (Khorat)	292B, 4hr, hourly	N/A
Rayong	N/A	100B, 2½hr, frequent
Sa Kaew	150B, 2hr, hourly	N/A
Trat	74B, 1hr, every 30min	70B, 50min, frequent

Trat

DESTINATION	AIR	BUS	MINIVAN
Bangkok Suvarnabhumi International Airport	from 2550B, 1hr, 3 daily	272B, 5-6hr, 5 daily	N/A
Bangkok Eastern (Ekamai) Bus Terminal	N/A	265B, 5hr, 17 daily	N/A
Bangkok Northern (Mo Chit) Bus Terminal	N/A	272B, 5-6hr, 5 daily	
Chanthaburi	N/A	80B, 1hr, hourly 7.30am-11.30pm	70B, 50min, frequent 5am-7pm
Hat Lek (for Cambodia)	N/A	N/A	120B, 1½hr, hourly 5am-6pm
Rayong/Ban Phe (for Ko Samet)	N/A	N/A	200B, 2½hr, hourly 5am-7pm

Sŏrngtăaou leave from a stop on Th Sukhumvit to Laem Ngop's piers (50B per person for six passengers, 45 minutes).

Ko Chang   เกาะช้าง

Jungle-clad Ko Chang sits firmly in Thailand's package-tourism industry, with an assortment of sophisticated resorts, bars and daily flights from the capital to nearby Trat. Despite its recent incarnation, plenty of backpackers still make the Ko Chang–Cambodia tour because it has an array of outdoor activities for the hyperactive visitor. Diving and snorkelling spots are nearby, the forested interior can be explored by foot or by elephant, and kayaks can survey sea coves and mangrove bays. Ko Chang is part of a larger **national park** that includes neighbouring islands.

◉ Sights & Activities

Mainly the west coast has been developed for tourism. In the northwest is **Hat Sai Khao**, by far the biggest, busiest and brashest beach. The backpacker fave is **Lonely Beach**, which is lonely no more, especially at night. An old-fashioned fishing community in **Bang Bao** has become a bustling tourist market. The east coast is largely undeveloped.

In a forested setting in the northern interior, **Ban Kwan Chang** (บ้านควาญช้าง; ☑08 1919 3995; changtone@yahoo.com; ☺8am-5pm) offers a quiet experience with its nine resident elephants.

Ko Chang cuts an impressive and heroic profile when viewed from the sea aboard a kayak. Most hotels rent open-top kayaks (from 300B per day) that are convenient for near-shore outings and non-committal kayakers. For more serious paddlers, **KayakChang** (☑0 3955 2000; www.kayakchang. com; Amari Emerald Cove Resort, Khlong Prao) rents closed-top kayaks (from 1000B per day) and leads day and multiday trips.

On the east side of the island, explore the mangrove swamps of Ao Salak Kok while supporting an award-winning eco-tour program. The **Salak Kok Kayak Station** (☑08 1919 3995; kayak rentals per hr 100B) rents self-guided kayaks and is a village-work project designed to protect the traditional way of life. The kayak station can also arrange hiking tours.

The **dive sites** near Ko Chang offer a variety of coral, fish and beginner-friendly shallow waters on par with other Gulf of Thailand dive sites.

🛌 Sleeping

Accommodation prices on Ko Chang are higher than the quality because of the package-tour industry. Prices and crowds increase around the Christmas holiday period.

Independent Bo's   GUESTHOUSE $
(☑08 5283 5581; Hat Sai Khao; r 400-850B; ❄🛜) This place on the jungle hillside exudes a creative, hippy-ish vibe. All bungalows are funky and different. No reservations.

Starbeach Bungalows   GUESTHOUSE $
(☑09 2575 7238; Hat Sai Khao; bungalows 700B; 🛜) Ramshackle in appearance, these simple bungalows wind up the hillside and are solid enough. Close to the prime part of the beach.

Arunee Resort   GUESTHOUSE $
(☑0 3955 1075; aruneeresorttour@hotmail.com; Hat Sai Khao; r 250-500B; 🛜) Digs don't come much cheaper than this anywhere on the island, and you're a 50m walk from the beach, but the rooms are basic and cramped.

Tiger Huts   GUESTHOUSE $
(☑08 4109 9660; Ao Khlong Prao; r 300-600B) Basic wooden huts, rock-hard beds and cold-water showers, but this is the prettiest part of the beach. You'll need the attached restaurant; it's over 1km to the main road from here.

Buzza's Bungalows   GUESTHOUSE $
(☑08 7823 6674; Hat Kaibae; r 400-450B; 🛜) Simple fan-only bungalows with porches that face each other, creating a laid-back travellers ambience. But this is the rocky part of the beach.

Porn's Bungalows   GUESTHOUSE $
(☑08 0613 9266; www.pornsbungalows-kohchang. com; Hat Kaibae; r 550-1500B) Very chilled spot at the far western end of the beach. All bungalows are fan-only. The 900B beachfront bungalows are a great deal.

Little Eden   GUESTHOUSE $
(☑08 4867 7459; www.littleedenkohchang.com; Lonely Beach; r 600-1100B; ❄🛜) Fifteen bungalows here, all connected by an intricate series of wooden walkways. They're a decent size with better bathrooms than the price indicates. Pleasant communal area and staff.

Paradise Cottages   HOTEL $
(☑08 1773 9337; www.paradisecottagekochang. com; Lonely Beach; r 400-1000B; ❄🛜) Stylishly minimalist rooms and a mellow atmosphere with hammocks for guests to swing their worries away. It's oceanfront, but the beach is too rocky for swimming.

GETTING TO CAMBODIA

Many travellers undertaking the Angkor pilgrimage start this epic journey in Bangkok and cross the border at Aranya Prathet/Poipet. There is now a direct government bus from Bangkok to Siem Reap that relieves some of the transport hassles from previous years. There are also other remote and little-used crossings with access to Siem Reap.

Bangkok to Siem Reap

Getting to the border Buses to the Aranya Prathet/Poipet border and to Siem Reap leave from Bangkok's Northern and Northeastern (Mo Chit) bus terminal. There are also buses to Aranya Prathet from Suvarnabhumi (Airport) bus station and minivans to Aranya Prathet from Bangkok's Victory Monument. Aranya Prathet is also accessible by bus from Chanthaburi and Khorat. Most buses and minivans go all the way to the Rong Kluea Market at the border sparing you the hassle of transferring to local transport in Aranya Prathet town. We do not recommend the tourist buses that leave from Th Khao San road.

There are also daily trains from Bangkok's Hualamphong station to Aranya Prathet town.

At the border Thai immigration is open 7am to 8pm. It is advisable to reach the border as early as possible, especially on weekends when casino-bound Thais and guest workers clog the immigration lines. Cambodian visas are available on arrival from Cambodian immigration with the usual formalities (passport photo and US$20 visa fee). Ignore any touts or money-exchange services on both sides of the border and watch out for pickpockets.

Moving on If you didn't opt for the direct Bangkok–Siem Reap bus, the best way to continue to Siem Reap is by share taxi departing from the main bus station, 1km from the border near the main market. A motorcycle taxi from the border to the main bus station should cost 2000r.

For information on making this crossing in the other direction, see p93.

Surin to Samraong

Getting to the border Minibuses leave from Surin's bus terminal to the Chong Chom/O Smach border (60B, 1½ hours, frequent).

At the border The border is open 7am to 8pm and Cambodian visas (US$20 and passport photo) are available on arrival. Cambodian officials will try to get you to pay for your visa in baht – usually 1000B. If you insist on paying in dollars you should be able to pay close to the real price of US$20. Politely decline any hired help in the process.

Moving on Deal directly with the drivers on the Cambodian side instead of taxi agents on the Thai side of the border. Bargain a fare on the shared taxis to Siem Reap: usually 350B to 500B per person or 1500B to 1800B for the whole car; it is a two-hour ride. Alternatively, take a moto (US$5) to Samraong, where morning share taxis depart to Siem Reap (US$7.50, two hours).

For information on making this crossing in the other direction, see p110.

Chong Sa-Ngam to Anlong Veng

The Chong Sa-Ngam/Choam border sees less traffic than the nearby Chong Chom/O Smach border.

Getting to the border Cambodian casinos occasionally run free shuttles to this border from a host of Thai towns, including Ku Khan (45 minutes), Si Sa Ket (1¼ hours) and Kantharalak (1½ hours), but schedules are sporadic. Otherwise, make your way by bus to Phusing, which is 30 minutes from the border by taxi, motorcycle taxi or casino shuttle.

At the border The border is open from 7am to 8pm. Entering Cambodia, note that they charge a premium for visas on arrival – US$25 instead of the normal US$20. Try to talk them down to the normal rate.

Moving on Motos are readily available at the border to take you 16km to Anlong Veng (US$5). In Anlong Veng share taxis do the run to Siem Reap (20,000r, 1½ hours).

For information on making this crossing in the other direction, see p110.

Siam Hut   GUESTHOUSE $
(✆0 3961 9012; Lonely Beach; r 480-680B; ❄ 🖥) Party central for backpackers. This is the only budget option right on the sandy stretch of the beach. Smallish wooden huts, but then you won't be spending much time in them.

Jungle Way   GUESTHOUSE $
(✆08 9247 3161; www.jungleway.com; Khlong Son Valley; r 300-500B) Ko Chang's un-sung attribute is its jungle interior and the English-speaking guides who grew up playing in it. Lek, a local guide, and his family run this friendly guesthouse, deep in the woods and beside a babbling brook. Bungalows are simple but adequate and the on-site restaurant will keep you well fed. Free pier pick-up.

Blue Lagoon Bungalows   GUESTHOUSE $$
(✆0 3955 7243; www.kochangbluelagoon.com; Khlong Prao; r 650-1300B; ❄ 🖥 🌐) An exceedingly friendly garden spot with a range of bungalows to suit different budgets beside a peaceful estuary. A wooden walkway leads to the beach. Yoga, a cooking school, kids' playground and activities are on offer too.

✗ Eating

Nid's Kitchen   THAI $
(nidkitchen@hotmail.com; Hat Kaibae; dishes 50-150B; ⊙6pm-midnight) Nid's does all the Thai standards like a wok wizard in a hut festooned with rasta imagery. Equally fine for a drink or three.

Magic Garden   THAI $
(✆0 3955 8027; Lonely Beach; dishes 60-220B; ⊙11am-late) Still a popular Lonely Beach hang-out, but better for a drink than a meal. The menu covers Thai and Western standards.

★ Phu-Talay   SEAFOOD $$
(Khlong Prao; 100-320B; ⊙10am-10pm) Cute, homey feel at this wooden-floored, blue-and-white decorated place perched over the lagoon. Sensible menu of Ko Chang classics (lots of fish) and far more reasonably priced than many other seafood places.

KaTi Culinary   THAI $$
(✆08 1903 0408; Khlong Prao; dishes 120-550B; ⊙11am-10pm; 🍴🌐) Seafood, and a few Isan dishes and its famous, homemade curry sauce. The menu features creative smoothies, such as lychee, lemon and peppermint, and there's a kids menu too.

Kaotha   INTERNATIONAL, THAI $$
(Lonely Beach; dishes 50-300B; ⊙9am-midnight; 🖥) One of the hot spots on the Lonely Beach

dining scene, with an excellent selection of pizzas and nice and spicy Thai dishes, this airy venue is a popular hang-out for coffee too. There's live music on Saturdays.

❶ Information

Internet cafes and banks with ATMs are plentiful on the island, especially in Hat Sai Khao.
I Am Koh Chang (www.iamkohchang.com)
Ko Chang Hospital (✆0 3952 1657; Ban Dan Mai) Public hospital with a good reputation and affordably priced care; south of the ferry terminal.
Tourist Police Office (✆1155) Based north of Ban Khlong Prao. Also has smaller police boxes in Hat Sai Khao and Hat Kaibae.

❶ Getting There & Away

Beware of the cheap minibus tickets from Siem Reap to Ko Chang; these usually involve some sort of time- and money-wasting commission scam.

Ko Chang–bound boats depart from the mainland piers collectively referred to as Laem Ngop, southwest of Trat. You'll arrive in Ko Chang at either Tha Sapparot or Tha Centrepoint, depending on which pier and boat company you used on the mainland. The ferry prices are the same at both piers (80B, 30 to 45 minutes, frequent 6.30am to 7pm).

Tha Sapparot is the closest to the west-coast beaches and receives vehicle ferries from the mainland pier of Tha Thammachat. **Koh Chang Ferry** (✆0 3955 5188) runs this service.

Tha Centrepoint is further west from the west-coast beaches and is served by a mainland pier of the same name by the **Centrepoint Ferry** (✆0 3953 8196) company.

Tha Bang Bao is at the southern end of the island and Bang Bao Boats runs to nearby islands of Ko Wai, Ko Mak and Ko Kut.

A direct bus from Bangkok's Eastern (Ekamai) station (27B, seven hours, three daily) goes all the way to a mainland pier on Laem Ngop; this route includes a stop at Suvarnabhumi (Airport) bus station as well as Trat's bus station.

Another option is a minivan service from Bangkok's Victory Monument that goes all the way to Ko Chang's Tha Sapparot (one way 300B, four hours, hourly departures).

❶ Getting Around

Sŏrngtăaou on the island will shuttle you from the pier to the various beaches (50B to 200B).

It is not recommended to drive a motorcycle between Ban Khlong Son south to Hat Sai Khao as the road is steep and treacherous with several hairpin turns and occasional mudslides during storms. If you do rent a motorbike, stick to the west coast beaches and wear protective clothing when riding to reduce injury.

SOUTHERN GULF COAST

Palm-fringed beaches, warm lazy days, jewel-toned seas: the southern gulf coast pours an intoxicating draught of paradise that attracts a steady crowd of sun worshippers. Most are bound for one or more of the islands in the Samui archipelago: resorty Ko Samui, hippie Ko Pha-Ngan and dive-centric Ko Tao.

If the Vitamin D treatments have you recharged, stop off at the mild-mannered provincial capitals that live and work by the sea for a glimpse at the rhythms of coastal Thailand. Even further south, Thailand starts to merge with Malaysia: onion-domed mosques peep over the treeline; the diction is fast and furious as southern Thais are legendary speed talkers; and a roti seller can be found on every corner.

The best time to visit Thailand's southern reaches is from March to May, when the rest of the country is practically melting from the angry sun.

Hua Hin
หัวหิน

POP 42,000

Within reach of Bangkok, Hua Hin is considered the elegant alternative to seedy Pattaya. It is a city by the sea long favoured by older Europeans and hi-so Bangkok Thais, and oft neglected by backpackers searching for rustic island living. But as the bamboo beach hut goes the way of the do-do bird, it is time to reconsider Hua Hin and its old fishing port charm, lively seafood night market and long silky sand beaches.

Hua Hin's best **beaches** are south of town heading towards Khao Takiab (Chopstick Mountain; accessible by green *sŏrngtăaou* leaving from the market) and Khao Tao (Turtle Mountain; accessible by Pranburi bus, transfer to motorcycle taxi).

🛏 Sleeping

Most of the budget options are in town, an atmospheric location but you'll have to 'commute' to the beach.

Victor Guest House
GUESTHOUSE **$**
(☏ 0 3251 1564; victorguesthouse@gmail.com; 60 Th Naresdamri; r 390-790B; ✳@🛜) This newish guesthouse has solid rooms, a small garden and a central location. Helpful staff and a good source of travel tips.

Fulay Guesthouse
GUESTHOUSE **$**
(☏0 3251 3145; www.fulayhuahin.net; 110/1 Th Naresdamri; r 550-900B; ✳🛜) With the waves

crashing underneath and the floorboards creaking, this is a fine old-school pier guesthouse. Good beds, OK bathrooms and flowering plants in the common area.

Pattana Guest House
GUESTHOUSE **$**
(☏0 3251 3393; 52 Th Naresdamri; r 390-590B; ✳🛜) Located in a simple teak house tucked away down a *soi*. There's a lovely garden here filled with little reading nooks. The rooms are small and basic, but the more expensive ones have private bathrooms.

Euro-Hua Hin City Hotel YHA
HOSTEL **$**
(☏0 3251 3130; www.huahineuro.com; 5/15 Th Sasong; r 179-999B; ✳@🛜) Some dorms are fan-only, all are cramped and it feels a tad institutional, but the price is right for Hua Hin and the staff are helpful. The private rooms are sizeable, though the bathrooms could do with an overhaul. Add 50B to these prices if you don't belong to HI. It's off the road; look for the sign.

Tong-Mee House
GUESTHOUSE **$$**
(☏0 3253 0725; tongmeehuahin@hotmail.com; 1 Soi Raumpown, Th Naebkehardt; r 550-950B; ✳@🛜) Hidden away in a quiet residential *soi*, this smart guesthouse has cosy and clean rooms with balconies. Book ahead.

Rahmahyah Hotel
GUESTHOUSE **$$**
(☏0 3253 2106; Rahmahyah@yahoo.co.uk; 113/10 Soi Hua Hin 67, Th Phetkasem, South Hua Hin; r 800-1200B; ✳🛜🏊) Across the street from Market Village, about 1km south of town, is a small guesthouse enclave tucked between the high-end resorts, with beach access. The Rahmahyah is the best of the bunch with clean, functional rooms. Guests can use the communal swimming pool opposite.

🍴 Eating

Night Market
THAI **$**
(Th Dechanuchit btwn Th Phetkasem & Th Sasong; dishes from 50B; ⏰5pm-midnight) An attraction that rivals the beach, Hua Hin's night market tops locals' lists of favourite spots to eat. Ice-packed displays of spiny lobsters and king prawns appeal to the big spenders but the simple stir-fry stalls are just as tasty. Try *pàt pŏng gà-rèe ‌boo* (crab curry), *gûng tôrt* (fried shrimp) and *hŏy tôrt* (fried mussel omelette). In between, souvenir stalls cater to Thai's favourite digestive activity: shopping.

Thanon Chomsin Food Stalls
THAI **$**
(cnr Th Chomsin & Th Naebkehardt; dishes 30-40B; ⏰9am-9pm) If you're after 100% authentic eats, check out the food stalls that congregate

GETTING TO CAMBODIA: COASTAL BORDERS

Trat to Koh Kong

The Hat Lek/Cham Yeam crossing is the most convenient border crossing between Ko Chang and Sihanoukville in coastal Cambodia.

Getting to the border Take a minivan from Trat's bus station to the border at Hat Lek (120B, 1½ hours, departs when full, more frequently in the morning).

At the border Cambodian tourist visas are available at the border for 1200B (as opposed to the standard US$20); payment is only accepted in baht. Bring a passport photo and avoid the runner boys who want to issue a health certificate or other 'medical' paperwork. The border closes at 8pm.

Moving on From the Cambodian border, take a taxi (US$10) or moto (US$3) to Koh Kong where you can catch onward transport to Sihanoukville and Phnom Penh; arriving in the morning ensures more onward transport options.

Chanthaburi to Pailin

If you're heading to Siem Reap (or Battambang) from Ko Chang, you don't have to schlep up to Aranya Prathet/Poipet border. The Pong Nam Ron/Psar Pruhm crossing isn't crowded and shaves off some travel time.

Getting to the border Take a minivan from Chanthaburi to Ban Pakard/Pong Nam Ron (150B, 1½ hours, three times daily); the Chanthaburi minivan stop is across the river from River Guesthouse.

At the border Cross the border with the usual formalities (a passport photo and US$20 visa fee) to Psar Pruhm.

Moving on From the border, arrange a motorbike taxi to Pailin, which has connections to Battambang and from there to Siem Reap. If you cross early enough, the 7.30am public buses from the border straight to Phnom Penh via Battambang are an option. A private taxi from the border to Battambang costs US$40.

at this popular lunch corner. Though the setting is humble, Thais are fastidious eaters and use a fork (or their fingers with a pinch of *kôw nĕe·o*) to remove the meat from the bones of *gài tôrt* (fried chicken) rather than putting teeth directly to flesh.

Chatchai Market THAI **$**
(Th Phetkasem; dishes from 30B; ☺ daylight hours) The city's day market resides in an historic building built in 1926 with a seven-eaved roof in honour of Rama VII. There are the usual market refreshments: morning vendors selling *ʰbah·tôrng·gŏh* (Chinese-style doughnuts) and *gah·faa boh·rahn* (ancient-style coffee spiked with sweetened condensed milk); as well as all-day noodles with freshly made wontons; and fresh tropical fruit.

★ **Hua Hin Koti** THAI **$$**
(☑ 0 3251 1252; 16/1 Th Dechanuchit; dishes 120-300B; ☺ 11am-10pm) Across from the night market, this Thai-Chinese restaurant is a national culinary luminary. Thais adore the

fried crab balls, while foreigners swoon over *dôm yam gûng* (shrimp soup with lemon grass). And everyone loves the spicy seafood salad *(yam tá-lair)* and deep-fried fish with ginger. Be prepared to queue for a table.

ℹ Information

Hospital San Paolo (☑ 0 3253 2576; 222 Th Phetkasem) Just south of town with emergency facilities.

Municipal Tourist Information Office (☑ 0 3251 1047; cnr Th Phetkasem & Th Damnoen Kasem; ☺ 8.30am-4.30pm Mon-Fri) Provides maps and information about Hua Hin. There's another branch (☑ 0 3252 2797; Th Naebkehardt; ☺ 9am-7.30pm Mon-Fri, 9.30am-5pm Sat & Sun) near the clock tower.

Tourism Authority of Thailand (TAT; ☑ 0 3251 3885; 39/4 Th Phetkasem; ☺ 8.30am-4.30pm) Staff here speak English and are quite helpful; the office is north of town near Soi Hua Hin 70.

Tourist Police (☑ 0 3251 5995; Th Damnoen Kasem) At the eastern end of the street.

ⓘ Getting There & Around

Hua Hin's **bus station** (Th Phetkasem btwn Soi Hua Hin 94 & 98) is south of town and includes services to long-distance destinations as well as Bangkok's Suvarnabhumi Airport bus station. Buses to Bangkok's Southern bus station (Sai Tai Mai) leave from a bus company's in-town **office** (Th Sasong), near the night market. Minivans to Bangkok's Victory Monument leave from an office at the corner of Th Phetkasem and Th Chomsin. Ordinary buses depart from north of the market on Th Phetkasem. Hua Hin's historic train station is on Th Phrapokklao. **Lomprayah** (☑ 0 3253 3739; Th Narasdamri) offers a bus-boat combination from Hua Hin to Ko Tao.

ⓘ Getting Around

Green *sǒrngtǎaou* depart from the corner of Th Sasong and Th Dechanuchit, near the Night Market, and travel south on Th Phetkasem to Khao Takiab (20B). Túk-túk fares in Hua Hin are outrageous (starting at 100B). Motorcycle taxis are more reasonable (40B to 50B) for short hops.

Prachuap Khiri Khan
ประจวบคีรีขันธ์

POP 86,870

A prettier-than-average seaside town, Prachuap Khiri Khan is relaxed and untouristed with only a few minor attractions, a draw in itself if you're looking to escape 'Khao San' culture.

The bus dumps you off in the centre of town – not a pushy motorcycle taxi in sight. At the base of town is a sparkling blue bay sprinkled with brightly coloured fishing boats. To the north is **Khao Chong Krajok** (Mirror Tunnel Mountain), topped by a wat

with spectacular views; the hill is claimed by a clan of monkeys who supposedly hitched a ride into town on a bus from Bangkok to pick up some mangoes. There isn't much else to do except walk along the waterfront promenade or rent a motorcycle and explore the northern bays, fishing villages and the cave temple at **Wat Ao Noi**. You'll find a swimming beach at **Ao Manao**, 6km south of the city within the grounds of a Thai air-force base. It is popular with local Thais who swim fully clothed.

🛏 Sleeping & Eating

You can always find a place to stay near the sea as many of the oceanfront residences rent out rooms. The **night market** (Th Kong Kiat; ⊙5-9pm) has evening meals.

Maggie's Homestay GUESTHOUSE $
(☑ 08 7597 9720; 5 Soi Tampramuk; r 180-550B; ❀@🐱) In the old-fashioned backpacker tradition, lovely owner Maggie oversees an eclectic collection of travellers who call her house home. Comfortable rooms, all with shared bathrooms, occupy a converted house with a shady garden and shared kitchen facilities.

Yuttichai Hotel GUESTHOUSE $
(☑ 0 3261 1055; 115 Th Kong Kiat; r 160-350B; @🐱) Yuttichai has simple budget rooms (with cold-water showers) close to the train station. The cheapest rooms are cell-like and share OK bathrooms. Its old-school Thai-Chinese cafe is decent and patronised by the local fuzz.

Suan Krua VEGETARIAN $
(Soi Tampramuk; dishes 20-60B; ⊙6.30am-3pm; 🍴) Super vegetarian, buffet-style eatery. Choose from an array of dishes, but they go fast and

TRANSPORT FROM HUA HIN

DESTINATION	BUS	MINIVAN	TRAIN
Bangkok Hualamphong	N/A	N/A	44-421B, 5-6hr, 13 daily 12.45am-4.01pm
Bangkok Southern Bus Terminal	175B, 4½hr, 8 daily 3am-9pm	N/A	N/A
Bangkok Suvarnabhumi Airport	305B, 5hr, 6 daily 7am-6pm	N/A	N/A
Bangkok Victory Monument	N/A	180B, 4hr, every 30min 6am-7pm	N/A
Chiang Mai	851B, 12hr, 3 daily 8am, 5pm & 6pm	N/A	N/A
Ko Tao	1000B, 8½hr, 1 daily	N/A	N/A
Phuket	823B, 9-10hr, 3 nightly	N/A	N/A
Surat Thani	413-829B, 7-8hr, 4 daily	N/A	N/A

TRANSPORT FROM PRACHUAP KHIRI KHAN

DESTINATION	BUS	MINIVAN	TRAIN
Bang Saphan Yai	N/A	80B, 1½hr, hourly 6am-5pm	8 daily
Bangkok Hualamphong	N/A	N/A	168-455B, 7-8hr, 8 daily 2.41am-11.26pm
Bangkok Southern Bus Terminal	200B, 6-7hr, 7 daily 9am-1am	200B, 5-6hr, hourly 7am-5pm	N/A
Bangkok Victory Monument	N/A	240B, 6hr, hourly 6am-5pm	N/A
Hua Hin	N/A	80B; 1½hr, hourly 6am-5pm	8 daily

then it shuts. Be here promptly and with an appetite.

★**Rim Lom**   SEAFOOD **$$**
(5 Th Suanson; dishes 120-290B; ⊙10am-10pm)
Still the go-to place in town for the locals, the *pàt pŏng gà·rèe ʰboo* (crab curry) comes with big chunks of sweet crab meat and the *yam ta-lair* (seafood salad) is spicy and zesty. It's 200m past the bridge on the left.

Ma Prow   INTERNATIONAL, THAI **$$**
(48 Th Chai Thaleh; dishes 120-395B; ⊙10am-10pm)
An airy wooden pavilion, Ma Prow is more foreigner-orientated than other places on the promenade. It's the best option in town if craving a steak rather than seafood, although the tamarind fish goes down a treat here.

ℹ Getting There & Around

Prachuap's bus station is 2km northwest of town on the main highway; motorcycle taxis make the trip for 40B to 50B. Buses to Bangkok use an in-town office on Th Phitak Chat. Minivans to Bangkok leave from the corner of Th Thetsaban Bamrung and Th Phitak Chat. There is also a train station on Th Maharat.

Prachuap is small enough to get around on foot but a motorcycle (250B) is handy for exploring the nearby beaches and traffic is minimal so it is safer to drive here than in other places.

Chumphon   ชุมพร
POP 55,835

Chumphon is a jumping-off point for boats to Ko Tao. The transition from bus to boat is fairly painless and travel agencies, such as **Fame Guesthouse** (🖉0 7757 1077; 188/20-21 Th Sala Daeng; r 200-300B; @🖸), can help with onward travel to the Andaman coast and provide all sorts of day-use amenities (such as luggage storage, shower and toilet).

If you need to spend the night, try **Suda Guest House** (🖉08 0144 2079; 8 Soi Sala Daeng

3; r 250-650B; ❋@🖸) or **San Tavee New Rest House** (🖉0 7750 2147; 4 Soi Sala Daeng 3; r 250-300B) two doors down. The **night market** (Th Krom Luang Chumphon) is a good spot for meals and entertainment.

ℹ Getting There & Away

BOAT
You have many boat options to Ko Tao, though departure times are limited to mainly morning and night. Most ticket prices include pier transfer. If you buy a combination ticket, make sure you have a ticket for both the bus and the boat.

Lomprayah (www.lomprayah.com) runs high-speed catamarans from Chumphon to Ko Tao and on to Ko Pha-Ngan and Ko Samui as well as from Surat Thani to Ko Samui. This is one of the fastest services and the most likely to run during choppy seas. It also has bus-boat combination tickets from Bangkok and Hua Hin.

Songserm (www.songserm-expressboat.com) and runs an express boat from Chumphon to the islands with relatively fast, morning options. **Seatran Discovery** (www.seatrandiscovery.com) also does the circuit but in reverse from Surat Thani.

The cheapest but slowest option is the nightly slow boat that leaves from Chumphon to Ko Tao and from Surat Thani to Samui. The boats are simple cargo ships where everyone stretches out on the open deck with the stars twinkling overhead. These boats don't run in rough seas or inclement weather.

There are also car ferry services from Chumphon to Ko Tao and from Surat Thani to Samui. From Chumphon, the boat travels through the night with bunk or mattress options.

BUS
The main bus terminal is on the highway, an inconvenient 16km from Chumphon. To get there you can catch a *sŏrngtăaou* (50B) from Th Nawamin Ruamjai. You'll have to haggle with the taxi drivers for night transit to/from the station; it shouldn't cost more than 200B.

TRANSPORT FROM CHUMPHON

DESTINATION	BOAT	BUS	MINIVAN	TRAIN
Bangkok Hualamphong	N/A	N/A	N/A	192-1162B, 8hr, 11 daily
Bangkok Southern Bus Terminal	N/A	380-590B, 8hr, 11 daily	N/A	N/A
Hat Yai	N/A	400B, 4 daily, 7hr	N/A	6 daily
Ko Pha-Ngan	1000B, 3¼hr, 7am & 1pm (Lomprayah); 900B, 5½hr, 7am (Songserm)	N/A	N/A	N/A
Ko Samui	1100B, 4½hr, 7am & 1pm (Lomprayah); 1000B, 7hr, 7am (Songserm)	N/A	N/A	N/A
Ko Tao	600B, 1½hr, 7am & 1pm (Lomprayah); 400B, 7hr, 11pm (car ferry); 250B, 6hr, midnight (slow boat)	N/A	N/A	N/A
Phuket	N/A	350B, 3½hr, 4 daily	N/A	N/A
Prachuap Khiri Khan	N/A	N/A	180B, 4hr, 3pm	10 daily
Ranong	N/A	120B, 2½hr, 4 daily	130B, 2hr, frequent	N/A
Surat Thani	N/A	N/A	170B, 3hr, hourly 6am-5pm	12 daily

There are several in-town bus stops. **Choke Anan Tour** (☑ 0 7751 1757; soi off of Th Pracha Uthit), in the centre of town, has departures to Bangkok, Phuket and Ranong. Suwannatee Tour serves Bangkok and Prachuap Khiri Khan. Buses to Hat Yai depart from near the petrol station on Th Nawamin Ruamjai. Minivans to Surat Thani, Bang Saphan Yai and Prachuap Khiri Khan leave from the no-name *soi* opposite Salsa Guesthouse.

TRAIN

The **train station** (Th Krom Luang Chumphon) is within walking distance of the centre of town. Southbound rapid and express trains – the only trains with 1st- and 2nd-class cars – are less frequent and can be difficult to book out of Chumphon from November to February.

Ko Samui   เกาะสมุย

POP 50,000

One of the original islands that started the backpacker migration to Thailand, Ko Samui has matured into an all-purpose beach resort. The hotels have international standards, the guests are mainly package tourists and the transition from home to deck chair involves little culture shock. Families and honeymooners put Ko Samui at the top of their lists for its conveniences and impressive stoles of sand.

But for all the 'too-touristy' talk, Samui is underappreciated for its size and variety of beaches: with one cab ride you can travel from brash and beautiful to sleepy and rustic. Plus there is a thriving Thai community on the island, and you can nosh at roadside curry shacks or grab a cup of thick coffee at the morning market. Samui is a unique hybrid for beach people who also want to see Thailand.

◎ Sights

Ko Samui is quite large – the island's ring road is almost 100km in total. **Chaweng** is the most popular spot – it's the longest and most beautiful beach on the island. At the south end of **Lamai**, the second-largest beach, you'll find the infamous **Hin-Ta** and **Hin-Yai** stone formations providing endless mirth to giggling tourists. **Hua Thanon**, just beyond, is home to a vibrant Muslim fishing community.

Ko Samui

Although the **northern beaches** have coarser sand, they have a laid-back vibe and stellar views of Ko Pha-Ngan. **Bo Phut** stands out with its charming Fisherman's Village.

🛏 Sleeping

🛏 Chaweng

Lucky Mother GUESTHOUSE **$**
(☑ 0 7723 0931; 60 Moo 2; r & bungalows 800-1500B; ✳ 🛜) First, let's take a moment to giggle at the name. OK, now let's appreciate the action-filled beachfront location, clean, bright, polished-cement detailed rooms and popular bar out front that's prime for mingling with your toes in the sand. In all it's a great deal if you avoid the sour lemons on staff.

P Chaweng HOTEL **$**
(☑ 0 7723 0684; r from 600B, ste 1000B; ✳ @ 🛜) Off the main drag and a short walk to the beach, this vine-covered cheapie has extra-clean, pink-tiled or wood-floored spacious rooms, decked out with air-con, hot water, TVs and fridges. It's a 10-minute walk to the bar zone and not particularly hip, but good luck finding a better room in the area for this price.

Loft Samui HOSTEL **$**
(☑ 0 7741 3420; www.theloftsmaui.com; r 700-1500B; ✳ @ 🛜) The doubles and deluxe rooms in the new building have a warm, butter-yellow style, but bungalows across from reception are musty and dark. This place is popular despite the thin walls and proximity to the bars; if you're not up all night on purpose, bring earplugs.

Pott Guesthouse
GUESTHOUSE **$**

(r fan/air-con 300/500B; ❄️ 🛜) The big, bright cement rooms all with attached hot-water bathrooms in this nondescript apartment block are a steal. Reception is at an unnamed restaurant on the main drag across the alley.

Akwa
GUESTHOUSE **$**

(🖋️ 08 4660 0551; www.akwaguesthouse.com; r from 700B; ❄️ @ 🛜) Akwa has a few funky rooms decorated with bright colours but there's little natural light and everything is a bit past its prime.

Samui Hostel
HOSTEL **$**

(🖋️ 08 9874 3737; dm 200B; ❄️ @) It doesn't look like much from the front, but the three dorm rooms here are surprisingly spic and span and each has its own hot-water bathroom and air-conditioning. The staff are sweet too.

★ Jungle Club
BUNGALOW **$$**

(🖋️ 08 1894 2327; www.jungleclubsamui.com; huts 800-1800B, houses 2700-4500B; ❄️ @ 🛜 🏊) The perilous drive up the slithering road is totally worthwhile once you take in the incredible views from the top. This isolated mountain getaway is a huge hit among locals and tourists alike. Call ahead for a pick-up.

Lamai

Beer's House
BUNGALOW **$**

(🖋️ 0 7723 0467; 161/4 Moo 4, Lamai North; bungalows 600-700B, r 1000B) One of the last of a dying breed on Ko Samui, this old-school backpacker village of coconut bark huts sits right on a beautiful, sandy beach. Some huts have a communal toilet, but all have plenty of room to sling a hammock.

New Hut
BUNGALOW **$**

(🖋️ 0 7723 0437; newhutlamai@yahoo.co.th; Lamai North; huts 300-500B; 🛜) A-frame huts right on the beach all share a big, clean block of bathrooms. There's a lively restaurant, friendly staff and one of the most simple and happy backpacker vibes on the island.

Amarina Residence
HOTEL **$**

(www.amarinaresidence.com; r 900-1200B; ❄️ 🛜) A two-minute walk to the beach, this excellent-value small hotel has two storeys of big, tastefully furnished, tiled rooms encircling the lobby and an incongruous dipping pool.

Spa Resort
BUNGALOW **$$**

(🖋️ 0 7723 0855; www.spasamui.com; Lamai North; bungalows 1000-3500B; ❄️ 🛜) Programs at this practical, not glamorous, spa include colonics, massage, aqua detox, hypnotherapy and yoga, just to name a few. Accommodation books up quickly. Nonguests are welcome to partake in the programs and dine at the excellent (and healthy) restaurant.

Northern Beaches

Khuntai
GUESTHOUSE **$**

(🖋️ 0 7724 5118; r fan/air-con 600/750B; ❄️ 🛜) A block away from the beach, right in the Fisherman's Village, Khuntai's massive 2nd-floor fan rooms are drenched in afternoon sunshine and sea breezes. All rooms have hot-water bathrooms, fridges and TVs.

Shangri-la
BUNGALOW **$**

(🖋️ 0 7742 5189; Mae Nam; bungalows fan/air-con from 500/1300B; ❄️) A backpacker's Shangri La indeed – these are some of the cheapest huts around and they're on a sublime part of the beach. The basic concrete bungalows, all with attached bathrooms (only air-con rooms have hot water), are well-kept and the staff are pleasant.

✖ Eating & Drinking

Chaweng

Dozens of the restaurants on the 'strip' serve a mixed bag of local bites, international cuisine and greasy fast food. Market oglers should not miss the opportunity to check out **Laem Din** (dishes from 35B; ☺ 4am-6pm, night market 6pm-2am).

Ninja Crepes
THAI **$**

(dishes from 75B; ☺ 11am-midnight) Even though this basic food hall gets packed nightly, the owners welcome and chat with nearly every-one; it's a miracle of friendly service. The food, from Thai seafood to sweet and savoury pancakes, is a delectable bargain.

DON'T MISS

WALKING STREETS

Dine, shop and people-watch at the weekly Walking Streets, which occupy the beach villages main drag starting around 4pm till 11pm or midnight. Check with your guesthouse about the walking street schedules.

> **DON'T MISS**
>
> ### ANG THONG MARINE NATIONAL PARK
>
> The 40-some jagged jungle islands of Ang Thong Marine National Park stretch across the cerulean sea like a shattered emerald necklace – each piece a virgin realm featuring sheer limestone cliffs, hidden lagoons and perfect peach-coloured sands. These dream-inducing islets inspired Alex Garland's cult classic *The Beach*, about dope-dabbling backpackers.
>
> The best way to reach the park is to catch a private day-tour from Ko Samui, such as **Blue Stars** (☏ 0 7741 3231; www.bluestars.info; Hat Chaweng; kayak & snorkelling tours 2200B). Although the islands sit between Samui and the mainland pier at Don Sak, there are no ferries that stop off along the way. The park officially has an admission fee, although it should be included in the price of every tour (verify this when buying tickets).
>
> February, March and April are the best months; crashing monsoon waves means that the park is almost always closed during November and December.

Khaosan Restaurant
& Bakery   INTERNATIONAL **$**
(dishes from 70B; ⊘ breakfast, lunch & dinner) From filet mignon to flapjacks and everything in between, this chow house is popular for cheap nosh. Hang around after your meal and catch a newly released movie on the big TV. It's everything you'd expect from a place called 'Khaosan'.

Wave Samui   INTERNATIONAL **$**
(dishes from 60B; ⊘ breakfast, lunch & dinner; 🛜) This jack-of-all-trades (guesthouse-bar-restaurant) serves honest food at honest prices and fosters a travellers' ambience with an in-house library and a popular happy hour (3pm to 7pm).

Bar Solo   BAR
(Hat Chaweng) A future-fitted outdoor beer hall in an urban setting with sleek cubist decor and a cocktail list that doesn't scream holiday hayseed. The evening drink specials lure in the front-loaders preparing for a late, late night at the dance clubs.

Ark Bar   BAR
(www.ark-bar.com; Hat Chaweng) Drinks are dispensed from the multicoloured bar draped in paper lanterns, guests recline on loungers on the beach, and the party is on day and night.

Green Mango   BAR
(Hat Chaweng) Samui's favourite power drinking house is very big, very loud and very *faràng*. Green Mango has blazing lights, expensive drinks and masses of sweaty bodies swaying to dance music.

Reggae Pub   BAR
(Hat Chaweng) This fortress of fun sports an open-air dance floor with music spun by foreign DJs. It's a towering two-storey affair with long bars, pool tables and a live-music stage. The whole place doubles as a shrine to Bob Marley.

🍴 Lamai

The **Lamai Day Market** (dishes from 30B; ⊘ 6am-8pm) or the Muslim **Hua Thanon Market** (dishes from 30B; ⊘ 6am-6pm) are both local spots for local eats.

French Bakery   BAKERY **$$**
(set breakfasts from 120B; ⊘ breakfast & lunch) The expat's breakfast choice is away from the main zone, near Wat Lamai on Rte 4169, but it's worth the 10-minute walk. Choose from fresh bread and pastries or unusually good set breakfasts.

🍴 Northern Beaches

The Hut   THAI **$**
(mains 80-300B; ⊘ dinner) You'll find basic Thai specialities at reasonable prices (for the area) as well as more expensive fresh seafood treats. There are only about a dozen tables and they fill fast so get here early or late if you don't want to wait.

Karma Sutra   INTERNATIONAL **$$**
(mains 180-700B; ⊘ breakfast, lunch & dinner; 🛜) A haze of purples and pillows, this charming chow spot straddles the heart of Bo Phut's Fisherman's Village and serves up very good international and Thai eats.

Starfish & Coffee   THAI **$$**
(mains 150-280B; ⊘ breakfast, lunch & dinner) This streamer-clad eatery was probably named after the Prince song, since we couldn't find any starfish on the menu (there's loads of coffee

though). Evenings feature standard Thai fare and sunset views of rugged Ko Pha-Ngan.

 West Coast

The quiet west coast features some of the best seafood on Samui. Na Thon has a giant **day market** on Th Thawi Ratchaphakdi where you can grab snacks before your ferry ride.

★**Ging Pagarang** SEAFOOD **$**
(Thong Tanote; meals from 50B; ⊙ 11.30am-8pm) Locals know this is one of the island's best Samui-style seafood huts. It's simple and family-run, but the food and views are extraordinary.

About Art & Craft Café VEGETARIAN **$$**
(Na Thon; dishes 80-180B; ⊙ breakfast & lunch) An artistic oasis in the midst of hurried Na Thon, this cafe serves an eclectic assortment of healthy and wholesome food, gourmet coffee and, as the name states, art and craft, made by the owner and her friends.

Coco Tam's BAR
(Bo Phut; shesha pipes 500B) Plop yourself on a beanbag on the sand, order a giant cocktail served in a jar and take a toke on a *sheesha* (water pipe). It's a bit pricey, but this boho spot oozes relaxation.

ⓘ Information

Road accidents and fatalities in Samui are very high, in part because inexperienced motorcycle drivers take to the crowded and poorly maintained roads. If you've never driven a motorbike before don't learn on Samui. If you do rent a motorcycle, do the customary inspection with the rental associate and document (with photos) any pre-existing damage to avoid incurring responsibility.

Bangkok Samui Hospital (☑ 0 7742 9500, emergency 0 7742 9555) Your best bet for just about any medical problem.

Hyperbaric Chamber (☑ 0 7742 7427; Big Buddha Beach) The island's dive medicine specialists.

Immigration Office (☑ 0 7742 1069; ⊙ 8.30am-noon & 1-4.30pm Mon-Fri) Offers seven-day tourist visa extensions. Located about 2km south of Na Thon.

Main Post Office Near the TAT office; not always reliable.

Tourism Authority of Thailand (TAT; ☑ 0 7742 0504; Na Thon; ⊙ 8.30am-4.30pm) At the northern end of Na Thon; this office is friendly, helpful and has handy brochures and maps, although travel agents throughout the island can provide similar information.

Tourist Police (☑ 0 7742 1281, emergency 1155) Based at the south of Na Thon.

ⓘ Getting There & Away

AIR

Samui's airport is located in the northeast of the island near Big Buddha Beach. **Bangkok Airways** (www.bangkokair.com) operates direct flights to Bangkok's Suvarnabhumi Airport, Phuket and Chiang Mai; there are also direct flights to Singapore and Hong Kong but the fares are crazy expensive. **Firefly** (www.fireflyz.com.my) flies to Kuala Lumpur's Subang airport.

If Samui flights are full, check out prices and availability of flights to Surat Thani on the mainland.

BOAT

There are a variety of boats from the mainland town of Surat Thani. Check which pier is being used in Surat Thani and if transfer to/from the

TRANSPORT FROM KO SAMUI

DESTINATION	AIR	BOAT	BUS-BOAT COMBO
Bangkok	3800B, 50min, frequent (Suvarnabhumi International Airport)	N/A	1450B, 13½hr, 2 daily
Chiang Mai	6590B, 2hr, 1 morning	N/A	N/A
Chumphon	N/A	1100B, 4hr, 1 daily	N/A
Hua Hin	N/A	N/A	1400B, 10hr, 1 daily
Ko Pha-Ngan	N/A	200-300B, 20min-1hr, 12 daily	N/A
Kuala Lumpur	5600B, 3hr, 1 daily	N/A	N/A
Phuket	3000B, 1hr, 5 daily	N/A	N/A
Surat Thani	N/A	350-450B, 45min-2hr (Lomprayah); 150B (car ferry), hourly 5am-7pm; 200B, 6hr, 9pm (slow boat)	N/A

bus or train station is included in the price. There are also bus-boat combinations from Bangkok and Hua Hin through Lomprayah. Inter-island ferries are also an option; expect pier transfer to be included in the ticket price. When heading to Ko Pha-Ngan or Ko Tao you can avoid a trip to Na Thon (Samui's main pier) by using one of the companies that departs from the northern beaches of Big Buddha Beach or Mae Nam.

ⓘ Getting Around

You can rent motorcycles (200B) from almost every resort on the island. *Sŏrngtăaou* (50B to 100B) run a loop between the popular beaches during daylight hours. Taxis typically charge around 500B for an airport transfer.

Ko Pha-Ngan

เกาะพะงัน

POP 12,500

Swaying coconut trees, brooding mountains, ribbons of turquoise water: Ko Pha-Ngan has held fast to its title as favourite backpacker idyll despite modernisation and the installation of an airport.

Every sunburnt face you meet in Khao San's bars will tell you all about the most brilliant beaches on Ko Pha-Ngan, which means you won't be alone in paradise, but nobody really wants a really lonely planet. Ko Pha-Ngan's Full Moon parties transform the island into a college campus of drunken abandon.

⚕ Activities

With Ko Tao, the high-energy diving behemoth, just a few kilometres away, Ko Pha-Ngan enjoys a much quieter, more laid-back diving scene focused on fun dives; it also now competes in price with Tao for Open Water certifications. The favourite snorkelling spot is **Ko Ma**, a small island in the northwest connected to Ko Pha-Ngan by a charming sandbar.

A major perk of diving from Ko Pha-Ngan is the proximity to **Sail Rock** (Hin Bai), the best dive site in the Gulf of Thailand and a veritable beacon for whale sharks. Three-dive day trips cost around 3650B to 3800B.

Chaloklum Diving   DIVING
(☑ 0 7737 4025; www.chaloklum-diving.com) One of the more established dive shops on the island with quality equipment and high standards; based on the main drag in Ban Chalok Lam.

Reefers   DIVING
(☑ 08 6471 4045; www.reefersdiving.com) Vic, the owner, and his gaggle of instructors are chilled and professional. Recommended.

🛏 Sleeping

Hat Rin

During Full Moon events, bungalow operations expect you to stay for a minimum number of days (around four or five). We strongly suggest booking in advance.

★**Lighthouse Bungalows**   BUNGALOW $
(☑ 0 7737 5075; www.lighthousebungalows.com; Hat Seekantang; bungalows 500-1200B; ❄ 🛜) This hidden, low-key collection of huts gathers along a bouldered terrain. The fan options are rustic but the newest, spacious air-con bungalows are terrific value. Every room has a terrace and sweeping view of the sea. To get there, follow the boardwalk southeast from Hat Leela.

Blue Marine   BUNGALOW $
(☑ 0 7737 5079; www.bluemarinephangan.com; Hat Rin Nai; bungalows 600-1200B; ❄ 🛜) This cluster of identical concrete bungalows surrounds a manicured green lawn; the best have dreamy views over Sunset Beach. Every unit is spacious, clean and has air-con, fridge, hot water and TV. Staff are helpful and friendly.

Seaview Sunrise   BUNGALOW $
(www.seaviewsunrise.com; Hat Rin Nok; r 500-1400B; ❄ 🛜) Sleep inches from the tide. The beachfront models have bright, polished wooden interiors often splashed with bursts of neon paint from the ghosts of parties past.

Paradise Bungalows   BUNGALOW $
(☑ 0 7737 5244; Hat Rin Nok; bungalows 650-2500B; ❄) The original Full Moon Party was hatched at this scruffy batch of bungalows, and the place has been living on its fame ever since.

Same Same   GUESTHOUSE $
(☑ 0 7737 5200; www.same-same.com; Ban Hat Rin; dm 500B, r 550-850B; ❄ 🛜) A super-sociable spot for Scandinavians during the full moon madness, Same Same offers simple but bright rooms and plenty of party preparation fun.

Southern Beaches

These aren't the most stunning beaches but lodging options are well priced compared to other parts of the island, and you're not too far from Hat Rin. Many of the copy-cat moon parties happen in these parts.

★ Coco Garden   BUNGALOW $
(☑08 6073 1147, 0 7737 7721; www.cocogardens. com; Thong Sala; bungalows 450-1250B; ❄🛜) The best budget hang-out along the southern coast, Coco Garden one-ups the nearby resorts with well-manicured grounds and sparkling bungalows. As such, it's really popular with the backpacker set and is a fun scene.

Blue Parrot   BUNGALOW $
(☑0 7723 8777; www.theblueparrotphangan.com; Thong Sala; r fan/air-con 450/750B; ❄🛜) Two cute lines of good-sized, clean bungalows – some tiled with burnt-yellow exteriors and others of grey polished cement – lead to the beach. There's a little on-site cafe that travellers say serves great Western and Thai food.

Boom's Cafe Bungalows   BUNGALOW $
(☑0 7723 8318; www.boomscafe.com; Ban Khai; bungalows 600-1200B; ❄) Staying at Boom's is like visiting the Thai family you never knew you had. No one seems to mind that there's no swimming pool, since the curling tide rolls right up to your doorstep. Boom's is at the far eastern corner of Ban Khai, near Hat Rin.

West Coast Beaches

The west coast is an upmarket outpost, though there are a few cheapies in the mix. The atmosphere is a middle ground between the seclusion of the east coast and hypersocial Hat Rin.

Tantawan Bungalows   BUNGALOW $
(☑0 7734 9108; www.tantawanbungalow.com; Hat Son; bungalows 600-1200B; ❄) This charming teak nest, tucked among jungle fronds, is dripping with clinking chandeliers made from peach coral and khaki-coloured seashells. It had changed management and big changes were planned when we passed.

High Life   BUNGALOW $
(☑0 7734 9114; www.highlifebungalow.com; Hat Yao; fan bungalows 500B, air-con bungalows 800-2200B; ❄🛜❄) We can't decide what's more conspicuous: the dramatic ocean views from the infinity-edged swimming pool, or the blatant double entendre in the resort's name. True to its moniker, the 25 bungalows sit on an outcropping above the cerulean sea.

Shiralea   BUNGALOW $
(☑08 0719 9256; www.shiralea.com; Hat Yao; bungalows 600-1000B; ❄🛜❄) The fresh-faced

poolside bungalows here are simple but the ambience, with an on-site bar that pours draught beer, is convivial. It's about 100m away from the beach and it fills up every few weeks with Contiki student tour groups.

Shambhala Bungalow Village   BUNGALOW $$
(☑08 9875 2100; www.shambhala-phangan.com; Ao Nai Wok; bungalows 850-2300B; ❄🛜) The owners of Shambhala have lovingly restored a batch of huts. Expect fresh linen, carved wood, artistic lighting and neatly designed bathrooms, but also isolation and a very small beach.

Northern Beaches

Ao Mae Hat on the northwestern tip has ocean vistas, plenty of sand and access to petite Ko Ma. Chalok Lam is a pleasant fishing village where locals outnumber tourists. Thong Nai Pan on the northeast of the island has beautiful and remote (though there are plans for a paved road) beaches split between budget and upscale.

Island View Cabana   BUNGALOW $
(☑0 7737 4173; islandviewcabana@gmail.com; Ao Mae Hat; bungalows 400-1500B; 🛜) It's a bit overpriced but the bungalows here are really big, relatively new and on a truly wonderful slice of beach right at the isthmus to Ko Ma. The copious staff seem to have been trained to be exuberant although not necessarily helpful.

Fantasea   BUNGALOW $
(☑08 9443 0785; www.fantasea.asia; Chalok Lam; bungalows fan/air-con 400/700B; 🛜) One of the better of a string of family-run bungalows along the eastern part of Chalok Lam. There's a thin beach out front with OK swimming, an elevated Thai-style restaurant, and you might

ⓘ DANGERS & ANNOYANCES

There is a lot of trouble mixed up with all of Ko Pha-Ngan's fun. Don't buy drugs on the street; usually this is an extortion set-up (or worse, a sting operation) with the local police.

Women travellers should not travel alone on the island – rapes and assaults are common and increase during the Full Moon party.

Motorcycle accidents on the island's rutted and steep roads are also common; don't drive here if you don't have serious skills.

Ko Pha-Ngan

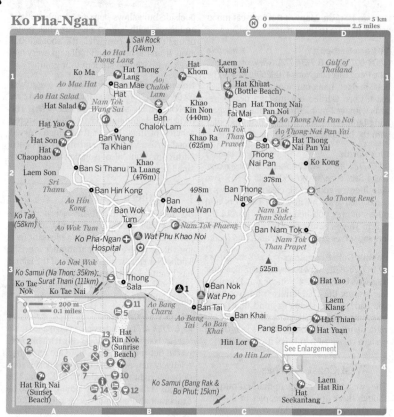

Ko Pha-Ngan

◎ Sights
1 Wat Khao Tham.....................................B3

⌂ Sleeping
2 Blue Marine..A4
3 Paradise Bungalows............................B4
4 Same Same..A4
5 Seaview Sunrise..................................B3

✕ Eating
6 Lazy House...A4
7 Little Home..A4

8 Mama Schnitzel...................................A4
Mr K Thai Food................................(see 8)

◎ Drinking & Nightlife
9 Cactus Bar..B4
10 Drop-In Bar..B4
11 Mellow Mountain................................B3
12 Rock..B4
13 Sunrise...B4

ℹ Information
14 Backpackers Information Centre..........B4

be adopted by a local a dog who sleeps on your terrace and barks at passersby.

Smile Bungalows   BUNGALOW $
(☎ 08 1956 3133; smilebeach@hotmail.com; Bottle Beach/Hat Khuat; bungalows 400-700B) At the far western corner of Bottle Beach, Smile features an assortment of wooden huts that

climb up a forested hill. The two-storey bungalows are our favourite.

Bottle Beach II   BUNGALOW $
(☎ 0 7744 5156; Bottle Beach/Hat Khuat; bungalows 300-500B; 🐾) At the far eastern corner of the beach, this double string of very basic, turquoise bungalows is the ideal place

to chill out – for as long as you can – if you don't need many creature comforts.

Dolphin   BUNGALOW $
(Thong Nai Pan; bungalows 500-1800B; ※ 🛜) This hidden retreat gives you a chance to rough it in style. But lodging is only available on a first-come, first-served basis.

Longtail Beach Resort   BUNGALOW $
(✆0 7744 5018; www.longtailbeachresort.com; Thong Nai Pan; bungalows fan/air-con from 490/890B; ※ 🛜) Tucked at the lovely, southern end of the beach and effortlessly adorable, Longtail offers backpackers charming thatch-and-bamboo abodes that wind up a lush garden path. The lounge area is strewn with cushions and very busy.

East-Coast Beaches

Robinson Crusoe, eat your heart out! For the most part, you'll have to hire a boat to get to these beaches; water taxis are available in Hat Rin and Chalok Lam and there's direct service from Samui. A 4WD taxi leaves from Thong Sala to Than Sadet (200B, 1pm).

Mai Pen Rai   BUNGALOW $
(✆0 7744 5090; www.thansadet.com; Than Sadet; bungalows 500-1200B; 🛜 ⅰ) This quiet, beachy bay elicits nothing but sedate smiles. Trek up to Nam Tok Than Sadet falls, hike an hour to Thong Nai Pan or explore by sea kayak. There's a friendly on-site restaurant.

Bamboo Hut   BUNGALOW $
(✆08 7888 8592; Hat Yuan; bungalows 350-1000B; 🛜) Beautifully lodged on the outcrops overlooking Hat Yuan, this groovy, hippie village is a favourite for yoga retreats and relaxation. Dark-wood bungalows are small and have terraces and the patrons all float around the property high on fasting.

★**Sanctuary**   BUNGALOW $$
(✆08 1271 3614; www.thesanctuarythailand.com; Hat Thian; dm 220B, bungalows 770-6000B) A friendly forested enclave, the Sanctuary is a haven of splendid lodgings, yoga classes and detox sessions. Accommodation, in various manifestations of twigs, is scattered along a tangle of hillside jungle paths. You'll want to Nama-stay forever.

✗ Eating

Ko Pha-Ngan is no culinary capital, especially since most visitors quickly absorb the lazy lifestyle and wind up eating at their accommodation.

✗ Hat Rin

The infamous **Chicken Corner** is a popular intersection stocked with several faves such as **Mr K Thai Food** (Ban Hat Rin; dishes 30-80B) and **Mama Schnitzel** (Ban Hat Rin; dishes 40-100B) who promise to cure any case of the munchies, be it noon or midnight.

Little Home   THAI $
(Ban Hat Rin; mains from 40B; ⊘breakfast, lunch & dinner) Little Home woos the masses with cheap, flavourful Thai grub that's gobbled up with alacrity among wooden tables and flimsy plastic chairs.

Lazy House   INTERNATIONAL $$
(Hat Rin Nai; dishes 90-270B; ⊘ lunch & dinner) Back in the day, this joint was the owner's apartment – everyone liked his cooking so much that he turned it into a restaurant and hangout spot.

✗ Southern Beaches

A **Walking Street** (4pm to 10pm Saturday) sets up on a side street in the eastern part of Thong Sala.

Night Market   MARKET $
(Thong Sala; dishes 25-180B; ⊘dinner) Thong Sala's night market is a must for a dose of culture and snacking.

Ando Loco   MEXICAN $
(Ban Tai; mains from 59B; ⊘dinner) This outdoor Mexican hang-out looks like an animation cell from a vintage Hanna-Barbera cartoon, with kitschy accoutrements like papier-mâché cacti. Down a super-sized margarita and show your skills on the beach volleyball court.

★**Fisherman's Restaurant**   SEAFOOD $$
(✆08 4454 7240; Thong Sala; dishes 50-600B; ⊘1-10pm) Lit up at night it's one of the island's nicest settings and the food, from the addictive yellow crab curry to the massive seafood platter (with an assortment of critters; 800B to 900B), is wonderful too.

✗ Other Beaches

★**Sanctuary**   HEALTH FOOD $$
(Hat Thian; mains from 130B) Forget what you know about health food: the Sanctuary's restaurant proves that wholesome eats can also

be delicious. Don't forget to wash it all down with a shot of neon-green wheatgrass. Yum!

 Cucina Italiana　ITALIAN $$
(Jenny's; Chalok Lam; pizzas 180-200B; ⊙dinner) The friendly Italian chef is passionate about his food, and creates everything from his pasta to his tiramisu daily, from scratch. The rustic, thin-crust pizzas are out-of-this-world good.

Drinking & Nightlife

Hat Rin is the beating heart of the legendary Full Moon fun, and the area can get pretty wound up even without the lunar influence. The following party venues flank Hat Rin's infamous Sunrise Beach from south to north:

Rock　BAR, NIGHTCLUB
Great views of the party from the elevated terrace on the far south side of the beach. Also, the best cocktails in town.

Drop-In Bar　BAR, NIGHTCLUB
This dance shack blasts the chart toppers that we all secretly love. This is one of the liveliest places and even non-full-moon nights can get boisterous.

Cactus Bar　BAR, NIGHTCLUB
Smack in the centre of Hat Rin Nok, Cactus pumps out a healthy mix of old school tunes, hip-hop and R&B. It's also very popular and always happening.

Sunrise　BAR, NIGHTCLUB
A spot on the sand where trance beats shake the graffiti-ed walls.

Mellow Mountain　BAR, NIGHTCLUB
Also called 'Mushy Mountain' (you'll know why when you get there), this trippy hang-out sits at the northern edge of Hat Rin Nok delivering stellar views of the shenanigans below. One of those places you need to at least see if you're on Hat Rin.

ⓘ Information

Backpackers Information Centre (☎0 7737 5535; www.backpackersthailand.com; Hat Rin) A reliable outfit for tour bookings and traveller info.

Ko Pha-Ngan Hospital (☎0 7737 7034; Thong Sala; ⊙24hr) About 2.5km north of Thong Sala; offers 24-hour emergency services.

Main Police Station (☎191, 0 7737 7114) The police station in Hat Rin (near Hat Rin school) will not file reports; to do so you must go to the main station in Thong Sala. Local police have sometimes charged a 200B filing 'fee'. Politely decline to pay this. If you are arrested you do have the right to an embassy phone call; you do not have to agree to use their 'interpreter'.

Main Post Office (⊙8.30am-4.30pm Mon-Fri, 9am-noon Sat) In Thong Sala; there's a smaller office right near the pier in Hat Rin.

ⓘ Getting There & Away

Ko Pha-Ngan's airport is expected to open in 2014 and will be served by **Kan Air** (www.kanairlines.com) with flights to Bangkok. The main pier on Ko

---

THE 10 COMMANDMENTS OF FULL MOON FUN

On the eve of every full moon, tens of thousands of bodies converge on the kerosene-soaked sands of Sunrise Beach for an epic trance-a-thon. Though people come for fun, having a good time is serious business. There is a 100B entrance fee that is charged to help with beach clean-up and much-needed security. Visitors need to secure their valuables and be vigilante about their physical safety. Thefts, assaults and injuries are common.

➡ Thou shalt arrive in Hat Rin at least three days early to nail down accommodation.

➡ Thou shalt double-check the party dates as sometimes they are rescheduled.

➡ Thou shalt secure all valuables, especially when staying in budget bungalows.

➡ Thou shalt savour some delicious fried fare in Chicken Corner before the revelry begins.

➡ Thou shalt wear protective shoes, unless ye want a tetanus shot.

➡ Thou shalt cover thyself with swirling patterns of neon body paint.

➡ Thou shalt visit Mellow Mountain or The Rock for killer views of the heathens below.

➡ Thou shalt not sample the drug buffet, nor shall thou swim in the ocean under the influence.

➡ Thou shalt stay in a group of two or more people, especially if thou art a woman.

➡ Thou shalt party until the sun comes up and have a great time.

TRANSPORT FROM KO PHA-NGAN

DESTINATION	BOAT	BUS-BOAT COMBO
Bangkok	N/A	1500B, 17hr
Chumphon	N/A	800-1000B, 2½hr
Ko Samui	200-300B, 20-30min, frequent from 7am-6pm	N/A
Ko Samui (east coast of Ko Pha-Ngan–Mae Nam)	200-400B (Thong Nai Pan Express)	N/A
Ko Samui (Hat Rin-Big Buddha Beach)	200B, 50min, 4 daily (Haad Rin Queen)	N/A
Ko Tao	350-500B, 1½-2hr, 5 daily	N/A
Surat Thani	350-550B, 3-4½hr, 8 daily from 7am-8pm; 350B, 7hr, 10pm (slow boat)	N/A

Pha-Ngan is Thong Sala, though some companies run boats to Hat Rin and the east coast from Samui.

❶ Getting Around

Motorbike rental is widely available for 200B to 250B. It is not recommended to rent a motorbike on the island if you're a novice.

Sŏrngtǎaou chug along the island's major roads, charging 100B between Thong Sala to Hat Rin and 150B to 200B for other beaches. Rates double after sunset. Ask your accommodation about free or discount transfers when you leave the island.

Longtail boats depart from Thong Sala to various beaches throughout the day. Rates range from 50B to 300B.

Ko Tao   เกาะเต่า

POP 1500

The smallest of the Samui islands, Ko Tao has long attracted visitors for its nearshore reefs, cheap dive certificates and jungle-clad coves. It has firmly moved into upscale territory but it still remains one of the cheapest places to learn how to scuba.

◉ Sights & Activities

Diving

Ko Tao is *the* place to lose your scuba virginity. The shallow bays scalloping the island are perfect for beginners. Over 40 dive centres are ready to saddle you up with some gear and teach you the ropes in a 3½-day Open Water certification course (from 9800B). Stiff competition means prices are low and standards are high.

Expect large crowds and booked-out beds throughout the months of December, January, June, July and August, and a monthly glut of wannabe divers after every Full Moon Party on Ko Pha-Ngan next door.

Dive schools typically have affiliated accommodation with discounted rates for diving guests.

Ban's Diving School   DIVING

(☑0 7745 6466; www.amazingkohtao.com; Sairee Beach) A well-oiled machine that's relentlessly expanding, Ban's conducts sessions in large groups, but there's a reasonable amount of individual attention in the water. A breadth of international instructors means that students can learn to dive in their native tongue.

Big Blue Diving   DIVING

(☑0 7745 6772, 0 7745 6415; www.bigbluediving. com; Sairee Beach) If Goldilocks were picking a dive school, she'd probably pick Big Blue – a midsize operation with a sociable vibe and high standard of service.

Buddha View   DIVING

(☑0 7745 6074; www.buddhaview-diving.com; Chalok Ban Kao) Another big dive operation, Buddha View offers the standard fare.

New Heaven   DIVING

(☑0 7745 6587; www.newheavendiveschool.com; Chalok Ban Kao) A small dive shop with an environmental niche.

Snorkelling

Most snorkellers opt for the do-it-yourself approach – hiring a longtail boat to putter around the various bays. Equipment can be rented for 100B to 200B per day from guesthouses, though the quality is not superb.

THAILAND KO TAO

Ko Tao

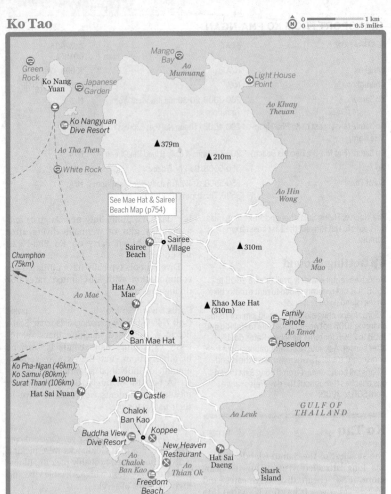

🛏 Sleeping

🛏 Sairee Beach

Tao's longest strip of sand is its dive training zone coupled with decompression bars and restaurants.

Blue Wind   BUNGALOW **$**
(📞0 7745 6116; bluewind_wa@yahoo.com; bungalows 350-1400B; ❄️📶) Blue Wind offers a breath of fresh air from the high-intensity dive resorts. Sturdy bamboo huts are peppered along a dirt trail behind the beachside bakery. It's rustic but relaxing.

Spicytao Backpackers   HOSTEL **$**
(📞08 1036 6683; www.spicyhostels.com; dm 200-250B; ❄️📶) Like your own country hangout, Spicytao is hidden off the main drag in a rustic garden setting. Backpackers rave about the ambience and staff. Book in advance!

Ban's Diving Resort   RESORT **$$**
(📞0 7745 6466; www.amazingkohtao.com; r 600-29,700B; ❄️@📶🏊) This dive-centric party palace offers a wide range of quality accom-

modation. Post-scuba chill sessions happen on Ban's prime slice of beach or at one of the two swimming pools.

Palm Leaf & Bow Thong BUNGALOW $$
($\square$0 7745 6266; www.bowthongresort.com; bungalows 700-4900B; ✴ ☎ ⛱) Palm Leaf is the swankier part of these conjoined resorts; Bow Thong has more popular lower-priced digs. The lowest-priced bungalows are on a first-come, first-served basis.

Big Blue Resort BUNGALOW $$
($\square$0 7745 6050; www.bigbluediving.com; dm 400B, r 2000-7000B; ✴ @) This scuba resort has a summer-camp vibe – diving classes during the day, socialising at night. Both the basic fan bungalows and motel-style air-con rooms offer little when it comes to views.

Mae Hat

The island's primary village and pier doesn't have much in the way of a beach but is central if all you want to do is dive. These lodgings are accessed by water taxi from the Mae Hat pier.

Sai Thong Resort BUNGALOW $
($\square$0 7745 6868; Hat Sai Nuan; bungalows 500-2000B; ✴) Sai Thong Resort emerges along quiet, sandy Hat Sai Nuan. Bungalows, in various rustic incarnations of bamboo and wood, have colourful porch hammocks and palm-filled vistas.

Tao Thong Villa BUNGALOW $
($\square$0 7745 6078; Ao Sai Nuan; bungalows 400-1800B; ✴ @ ☎) Popular with long-termers seeking peace and quiet, these funky, no-frills bungalows have killer views. Tao Thong actually straddles two tiny beaches on a craggy cape about halfway between Mae Hat and Chalok Ban Kao.

Chalok Ban Kao

Tropicana GUESTHOUSE $
($\square$0 7745 6167; www.koh-tao-tropicana-resort.com; r 500-1500B) Low-rise, basic hotel units peppered across a sandy, shady garden campus that provide fleeting glimpses of the ocean between fanned fronds and spiky palms.

JP Resort GUESTHOUSE $
($\square$0 7745 6099; r from 600-1300B; ✴ @ ☎) A colourful (some may say old-fashioned) menagerie of prim motel-style rooms stacked on a small scrap of jungle across the street from the sea.

East-Coast Beaches

The less-developed east coast has scenic boulder-strewn coves perfect for castaways. Ao Tanot, which is accessed by a paved road, is the east coast's 'commercial' centre.

Hin Wong Bungalows BUNGALOW $
($\square$0 7745 6006; Hin Wong; bungalows 350-700B; ☎) It all feels a bit like *Gilligan's Island*. A rickety dock, jutting out just beyond the restaurant, is the perfect place to dangle your legs and watch black sardines slide through the cerulean water.

View Rock BUNGALOW $
($\square$0 7745 6549, 0 7745 6548; viewrock@hotmail.com; Hin Wong; bungalows 500-2000B; ✴ ☎) Follow the signs as they lead you north of Hin Wong Bungalows. View Rock is precisely that: views and rocks; the hodgepodge of wooden huts looks like a secluded fishing village built upon the steep cliff.

Poseidon BUNGALOW $
($\square$0 7745 6735; poseidonkohtao@hotmail.com; Ao Tanot; bungalows 400-1200B; ☎) Poseidon keeps the tradition of the budget bamboo bungalow alive with a dozen basic-but-sleepable huts scattered near the sand.

Family Tanote BUNGALOW $$
($\square$0 7745 6757; Ao Tanot; bungalows 800-3500B; ✴ @ ☎) As the name suggests, these hillside bungalows are cared for by a local family who take pride in providing comfy digs to solitude seekers. There's snorkelling right at your doorstep and pleasant views of the bay.

✗ Eating

✗ Sairee Beach

Su Chili THAI $
(dishes 70-150B; ☺lunch & dinner; ☎) Fresh and tasty Thai food served by friendly waitstaff who always ask how spicy you want your food and somehow get it right. Try the delicious northern Thai specialities or Penang curries.

ZanziBar CAFE $
(sandwiches 90-150B; ☺breakfast, lunch & dinner) The island's outpost of sandwich yuppie-dom slathers an array of yummy ingredients between two slices of wholegrain bread.

Mae Hat & Sairee Beach

0 — 500 m
0 — 0.25 miles

Gulf of Thailand

Sairee Beach

Chumphon (75km)

Ao Mae

Hat Ao Mae

Ko Pha-Ngan (46km)

Diver Safety Support

Surat Thani (106km)

Mae Hat & Sairee Beach

✕ Mae Hat

Pim's Guesthouse
THAI $

(curry 70B; ☺ lunch) Every day Pim makes a daily curry (the massaman is everyone's favourite) at this humble spot, and every day she sells out before the lunch hour is over.

Safety Stop Pub
INTERNATIONAL $

(mains 60-250B; ☺ breakfast, lunch & dinner; 🛜) A haven for homesick Brits, this pierside restaurant and bar feels like a tropical beer garden. Stop by on Sundays to stuff your face with an endless supply of barbecued goodness; and the Thai dishes also aren't half bad.

Pranee's Kitchen
THAI $

(dishes 50-150B; ☺ breakfast, lunch & dinner; 🛜) An old Mae Hat fave, Pranee's serves scrumptious curries and other Thai treats in an open-air pavilion sprinkled with lounging pillows, wooden tables and TVs. English movies (with hilariously incorrect subtitles) are shown nightly at 6pm.

Food Centre
THAI $

(mains from 30B; ☺ breakfast, lunch & dinner) An unceremonious gathering of hot-tin food stalls, Food Centre lures lunching locals with veritable smoke signals rising up from the

Blue Wind Bakery
INTERNATIONAL $

(mains 50-180B; ☺ breakfast, lunch & dinner) This beachside shanty dishes out Thai favourites, Western confections and freshly blended fruit juices. Enjoy thick fruit smoothie and flaky pastry while reclining on tattered triangular pillows and watching the waves roll in.

★Barracuda Restaurant & Bar
ASIAN FUSION $$

(📞 08 0146 3267; mains 180-400B; ☺ dinner) Chef Ed Jones caters for the Thai princess when she's in town but you can sample his exquisite cuisine for pennies. Locally sourced ingredients create fresh, fusion masterpieces.

Chopper's Bar & Grill
INTERNATIONAL $$

(dishes 60-200B; ☺ breakfast, lunch & dinner) So popular that it has become a local landmark, Chopper's is a two-storey hang-out where divers and travellers can widen their beer bellies. There's live music, sports on the TVs, billiards and a cinema room.

TRANSPORT FROM KO TAO

DESTINATION	BOAT	BUS-BOAT COMBINATION
Bangkok	N/A	1000B, 12hr
Chumphon	500-600B, 1½-3hr, 3 daily; 250B, 8hr, nightly (slow boat)	N/A
Ko Pha-Ngan	430-500B, 1¾hr, 4-5 daily	N/A
Ko Samui	450-600B, 2hr, 4-5 daily	N/A

concrete parking lot abutting Mae Hat's petrol station.

★ **Whitening**　　　　　　　　INTERNATIONAL $$
(dishes 150-400B; ☺ dinner; ☏) This starched white, beachy spot falls somewhere between being a restaurant and a chic seaside bar – foodies will appreciate the tasty twists on indigenous and international dishes.

⚔ Chalok Ban Kao

I Salad　　　　　　　　　　CAFE $$
(salads 160-200B; ☺ breakfast & lunch; ☏) A healthy array of salads and wraps use fresh ingredients and are big and filling. There are also real fruit juices and healthy egg-white-only breakfasts.

Long Pae　　　　　　　　STEAKHOUSE $$$
(mains 100-430B; ☺ dinner) Off the radar from most of the island's tourist traffic, 'Uncle Pae' sits on a scruffy patch of hilly jungle with distant views of the sea below. The speciality here is steak, which goes oh-so-well with pan-Asian appetisers.

☕ Drinking & Entertainment

After diving, Ko Tao's favourite pastime is drinking, and there's definitely no shortage of places to get tanked. In fact, the island's three biggest dive centres each have bumpin' bars: **Fish Bowl, Crystal Bar** and **Buddha on the Beach**. Stop in even if you aren't a diver.

Castle　　　　　　　　　　NIGHTCLUB
(www.thecastlekohtao.com; Mae Hat) Located along the main road between Mae Hat and Chalok Ban Kao, the Castle is a beloved party venue, luring an array of local and international DJs to its monthly parties.

Lotus Bar　　　　　　　　　　BAR
(Sairee Beach) Lotus is the de-facto late-night hang-out spot along the northern end of Sairee. Muscular fire twirlers toss around flaming batons, and the drinks are so large there should be a lifeguard on duty.

Office Bar　　　　　　　　　　BAR
(Sairee Beach) With graffiti proudly boasting 'No Gaga, and no Black Eyed Peas', this hexagonal hut lures regulars with grunge beats and rickety wooden seats.

ℹ Information

The ubiquitous Ko Tao info booklet lists loads of businesses and covers the island's history, culture and social issues.

The island's roads are not safe enough for novice motorbike drivers. Dengue is a problem on the island, so use mosquito repellent day and night.

Diver Safety Support (☏ 08 1083 0533; kohtao@sssnetwork.com; Mae Hat; ☺ on call 24hr) Has a temporary hyperbaric chamber and offers emergency evacuation services.

Police Station (☏ 0 7745 6631) Between Mae Hat and Sairee Beach along the rutted portion of the beachside road.

Post Office (☏ 0 7745 6170; ☺ 9am-5pm Mon-Fri, 9am-noon Sat) A 10- to 15-minute walk from the pier; at the corner of Ko Tao's main inner-island road and Mae Hat's 'down road'.

ℹ Getting There & Away

Chumphon is the mainland jumping-off point for Ko Tao. Inter-island ferries connect Tao to its neighbours and on to Surat Thani.

ℹ Getting Around

Sŏrngtăaou, pick-up trucks and motorbikes haul passengers from the pier in Mae Hat to their hotels. Rates to Sairee Beach and Chalok Ban Kao cost 100/200B, for one/two passengers; try to hook up with other travellers to keep the transfer inexpensive. Water taxis leave from Mae Hat to Chalok Ban Kao to the northern part of Sairee Beach. Chartered boats start at 1500B per day.

Surat Thani 　อำเภอเมืองสุราษฎร์ธานี

POP 128,990

Surat Thani was once the seat of the ancient Srivijaya empire, which ruled much of southern Thailand, Malaysia and Sumatra. Today it is an important transport hub that

THAILAND SURAT THANI

TRANSPORT FROM SURAT THANI

DESTINATION	AIR	BOAT	BUS	TRAIN
Bangkok	from 1000B, 1½hr, frequent	421-856B, 10hr, frequent	380-800B, 11-14hr	107-1379B, 8½hr
Ko Pha-Ngan	N/A	350-550B, 3-4½hr, 8 daily; 350B, 7hr, 10pm (slow boat)	N/A	N/A
Ko Samui	N/A	150-450B, 1½hr; 200B, 6hr, 11pm (slow boat)	N/A	N/A
Ko Tao	N/A	8hr, 10pm (slow boat)	N/A	N/A
Krabi	N/A	150B, 2½hr, hourly	N/A	
Phuket	N/A	N/A	200B, 6hr, hourly	N/A

indiscriminately moves cargo and people around the country. Travellers rarely linger here as they make their way to Ko Samui, Ko Pha-Ngan and Ko Tao.

If you need to stay the night, **My Place @ Surat Hotel** (☏0 7727 2288; www.myplace surat.com; 247/5 Na Meuang Rd; fan r with/without bathroom 260/199B, air-con r with bathroom 490B; ❋❞) is central and clean. Near the out-of-town Tesco Lotus is **100 Islands Resort & Spa** (☏0 7720 1150; www.roikoh.com; 19/6 Moo 3, Bypass Rd; r 900-1800B; ❋@❞❋), which surprisingly has almost-budget options.

Go to the **night market** (Sarn Chao Ma; Th Ton Pho; dishes from 35B; ☺6-11pm) for fried, steamed, grilled or sautéed delicacies. There are additional evening food stalls near the departure docks for the night boats to the islands, and a **Sunday market** (☺4-9pm) near the TAT office. During the day many food stalls near the downtown bus terminal sell *kôw gài òp* (marinated baked chicken on rice).

ⓘ Information

Th Na Meuang has a bank on virtually every corner in the heart of downtown. If you're staying near the 'suburbs', the Tesco-Lotus has ATMs as well.

Taksin Hospital (☏0 7727 3239; Th Talat Mai) The most professional of Surat's three hospitals. Just beyond the Talat Mai Market in the northeast part of downtown.

Tourism Authority of Thailand (TAT; ☏0 7728 8817; tatsurat@samart.co.th; 5 Th Talat Mai; ☺8.30am-4.30pm) Friendly office southwest of town. Distributes plenty of useful brochures and maps, and staff speak English very well.

ⓘ Getting There & Away

In general, if you are departing from points north (such as Bangkok or Hua Hin) for the Samui islands, use Chumphon rather than Surat as a jumping-off point.

AIR

Although flights from Bangkok to Surat Thani are cheaper than the flights to Samui, it takes a significant amount of time to reach the gulf islands from the airport. Surat's airport receives Bangkok flights from Air Asia, which has transfer shuttles to the boat pier, Nok Air and **Thai Airways International** (THAI; ☏0 7727 2610; 3/27-28 Th Karunarat).

BOAT

Most boats leave from Surat's Don Sak pier (about one hour from Surat; bus transfers are included in the ferry ticket); but Songserm and the slow night boats leave from central Surat.

BUS & MINIVAN

Frequent buses and minivans depart from two main locations in town. Talat Kaset 1, on the north side of Th Talat Mai (the city's main drag) offers speedy service to Nakhon.

Talat Kaset 2, on the south side of Th Talat Mai, has minivans to Krabi and buses to Phuket.

The 'new' bus terminal (which is now old, but still referred to as 'new' by locals) is located 7km south of town and serves Bangkok.

TRAIN

Surat's train station is in Phun Phin, 14km west of town. From Phun Phin, there are buses to Phuket, Phang-Nga and Krabi, some via Takua Pa, the stopping point for Khao Sok National Park.

ⓘ Getting Around

Airport minivans will drop you off at your hotel for 100B per person. *Sŏrngtăaou* around town cost 10B to 30B (15B to Tesco-Lotus). Orange ordinary buses run from Phun Phin train station to Surat Thani (15B, 25 minutes, frequent). Taxis from the train station charge 200B for a maximum of four people.

Hat Yai

หาดใหญ่

POP 191,696

Welcome to southern Thailand's urban hub. In addition to its shopping malls and modern amenities, it is also a favourite weekend trip for Malaysian men looking for prostitutes, giving it a slightly rough border town image. Occasionally the low-scale insurgent war in Thailand's nearby Deep South provinces spills over to Hat Yai with bomb attacks on high-profile targets (such as shopping malls, hotels and the airport). However, these violent attacks do not mean that Hat Yai is off-limits to foreign tourists, in fact it is still an important and necessary transit link.

Hat Yai has dozens of hotels within walking distance of the train station. The city is the unofficial capital of southern Thailand's cuisine, offering Muslim roti and curries, Chinese noodles and dim sum, and fresh Thai-style seafood from both the Gulf and Andaman coasts.

ⓘ Information

Immigration Office (Th Phetkasem) Near the railway bridge, it handles visa extensions.

Tourism Authority of Thailand (TAT; www.tourismthailand.org/Hat-Yai; 1/1 Soi 2, Th Niphat Uthit 3; ⊙8.30am-4.30pm) The very helpful staff here speak excellent English and have loads of info on the entire region.

Tourist Police (Th Niphat Uthit 3; ⊙24hr) Near the TAT office.

ⓘ Getting There & Away

AIR

Thai Airways International (182 Th Niphat Uthit 1), Air Asia and Nok Air operate flights to Bangkok.

BUS

Most inter-provincial buses and south-bound minivans leave from the bus terminal, 2km southeast of the town centre. Most northbound minivans leave from a minivan terminal 5km west of town at Talat Kaset, a 60B túk-túk ride from the centre of town. **Prasert Tour** (Th Niphat Uthit 1) and **Cathay Tour** (93/1 Th Niphat Uthit 2) run minivans to many destinations in the south.

TRAIN

Hat Yai is a convenient place to catch the train south to Butterworth (Malaysia), and then transfer to Penang. The train station is central.

ⓘ Getting Around

Airport Taxi Service (☏ 0 7423 8452; 182 Th Niphat Uthit 1) makes the run to the airport (80B per person, four times daily). A private taxi for this run costs 320B.

Sŏrngtăaou run along Th Phetkasem (10B per person). Túk-túk and motorcycle taxis around town cost 20B to 40B per person.

THE ANDAMAN COAST

The Andaman is Thailand's turquoise coast, that place on a 'Travel to Paradise' poster that makes you want to leave your job and live in flipflops. White beaches, cathedral-like limestone cliffs, neon corals and hundreds of jungle-covered isles extend down the Andaman Sea from the border of Myanmar to Malaysia. It is a postcard-perfect destination firmly rooted in the package-tourist industry, and finding budget spots takes some searching.

Ranong

ระนอง

POP 29,096

On the eastern bank of the Sompaen River's turbid, tea-brown estuary, Ranong is a short boat ride – or a filthy swim – from Myanmar. This border town *par excellence* (shabby, frenetic, slightly seedy) has a thriving population of people from Myanmar, nearby hot springs (Th Petchkasem; ⊙8am-5pm) FREE and tremendous street food.

Today the town is a transit point to Ko Phayam, a popular southern visa run and even an 'open' border into Myanmar.

TRANSPORT FROM HAT YAI

DESTINATION	AIR	BUS	TRAIN
Bangkok	from 1100B, 1½hr, 8 daily	688-1162B, 15hr, hourly	146-825B, 16hr, 4 daily
Butterworth (Malaysia)	N/A	N/A	3hr, 100B, 7 daily
Krabi	N/A	182-535B, 5hr	N/A
Surat Thani	N/A	160-240B, 6hr	N/A

TRANSPORT FROM RANONG

DESTINATION	AIR	BUS & MINIVAN
Bangkok	from 1100B, 2hr, 2 daily	360-725B, 10hr
Chumphon	N/A	130B, 3hr
Hat Yai	N/A	420B, 5hr
Khao Lak	N/A	180B, 3½hr
Krabi	N/A	210B, 6hr
Phuket	N/A	260B, 5-6hr
Surat Thani	N/A	190B, 4-5hr

Meanwhile, dive operators specialising in live-aboard trips to the Surin or Similan Islands and Burma Banks are establishing themselves here. Try **A-One-Diving** (☎0 7783 2984; www.a-one-diving.com; 256 Th Ruangrat; 3-night packages from 16,900B; ⊙Oct-Apr) or **Aladdin Dive Safari** (☎08 7288 6908; www.aladdindivesafari.com; Ko Phayam Pier; live-aboard trips from 14,900B; ⊙Oct-Apr).

Sleeping & Eating

If you are doing a visa run through an agency, they'll ship you in and out of town without having to sleep over. If you decide to spend the night, try the remodelled **Luang Poj** (☎08 7266 6333, 0 7783 3377; www.facebook.com/luangpojhostel; 225 Th Ruangrat; r 500B; ❄📶).

For some grub, there's a **night market** on Th Kamlangsap not far from Hwy 4. The **day market** on Th Ruangrat offers inexpensive Thai and Burmese meals. **Pon's Place** (☎08 1597 4549; www.ponplace-ranong.com; Th Ruangrat; ⊙7.30am-midnight) is Ranong's one-stop-shop for food, tourist information and everything in between. Expats hang out at **Sophon's Hideaway** (☎0 7783 2730; www.sophonshideaway.asia; 323/7 Th Ruangrat; mains 45-350B; ⊙10am-11pm; 📶), which has a bit of everything, including a free pool table, a pizza oven and rattan furnishings aplenty.

Information

Internet can be found along Th Ruangrat for 20B per hour and there's a cluster of ATMs at the Th Tha Meuang and Th Ruangrat intersection.

Main Post Office (Th Chonrau; ⊙9am-4pm Mon-Fri, to noon Sat)

Getting There & Away

AIR

Happy Air (☎08 1891 5800; www.happyair.co.th) and **Nok Air** (☎0 2900 9955; www.nokair.com) run flights to Bangkok's Suvarnabhumi and Don Muang airports, respectively. The airport is 22km south of town.

BUS

The **bus terminal** is on Th Petchkasem, 1km from town, though some Bangkok-bound buses stop at the main market. Minivans travel to the Gulf Coast towns of Chumphon and Surat Thani.

Getting Around

Motorcycle taxis will take you almost anywhere in town for 50B and to the pier for 70B. Airport shuttles (350B) transfer passengers into town and to the pier.

Ko Chang เกาะช้าง

If you're looking for the big Ko Chang, you've come to the wrong place. But if you're seeking a lonely stretch of sand, then you've chosen the right Chang. Unlike most of the Andaman's islands, Ko Chang enjoys its back-to-basics lifestyle – there are no ATMs, no 24-hour electricity and no cars.

Sleeping & Eating

★**Crocodile Rock** GUESTHOUSE $
(☎08 0533 4138; tonn1970@yahoo.com; Ao Yai; bungalows 400-500B; @) Outstanding bamboo bungalows perched on Ao Yai's serene southern headland. It's not 'on' the beach but it has superb views. The kitchen turns out homemade yoghurt, breads, espresso and a variety of vegie and seafood dishes. This place has its own pier, so ask to be dropped here by longtail. Three-night minimum.

Sawasdee GUESTHOUSE $
(☎08 1803 0946, 08 6906 0900; www.sawadeekohchang.com; Ao Yai; bungalows 350-600B) A-frame wooden bungalows have vented walls to keep things cool, sunken bathrooms painted bright colours and hammocks on the terraces.

ℹ Getting There & Away

From Ranong's day market, take a *sŏrngtăaou* to Tha Ko Phayam (25B) or a shuttle (50B to 100B) run by most guesthouses. Speedboats go to Ao Yai (350B, 45 minutes, two daily from late October to April). Longtail boats make the same trip (150B, two hours, twice daily). In the dry season, longtails stop at all the west-coast beaches. During the monsoon months service is limited.

Ko Phayam   เกาะพยาม

Technically part of Laem Son National Park, little Ko Phayam is a beach-laden isle that has gone mainstream without selling out. Spectacular beaches are dotted with beach bungalows and the wooded interior has some rudimentary concrete motorbike paths.

The main drawback of Ko Phayam is that the snorkelling isn't great, but the Surin Islands are relatively close by. For dive trips and PADI courses try **Phayam Divers** (☑08 6995 2598; www.phayamlodge.com; Ao Yai).

🍴 Sleeping & Eating

★ **June Horizon**   BUNGALOWS **$**
(☑08 0145 9771; Ao Khao Kwai; bungalows 450-600B; ☺Nov-May) A joyful addition tucked into a mangrove inlet at the south end of the beach. Bunk in one of its creatively styled circular concrete bungalows brushed with fanciful murals, or grab a beach hut nailed together with reclaimed and distressed wood. All have outdoor baths. The wonderful 'gypsy bar' is worth a tipple.

Aow Yai Bungalows   GUESTHOUSE **$**
(☑08 9819 8782, 0 7787 0216; Ao Yai; bungalows 200-400B) The thatched bamboo bungalow pioneer that started it all 24 years ago. Choose between small wooden-and-bamboo bungalows in the palm grove and a larger beachfront model on the southern end of Ao Yai.

PP Land   HOTEL **$**
(☑08 1678 4310; www.payampplandbeach.com; Ao Hin-Khow; bungalows from 650B) This eco-lodge, north of the pier on the little-visited east side of the island, offers stylish concrete bungalows powered by the wind and sun with terraces that overlook the sea.

ℹ Getting There & Around

From Ranong's Saphan Plaa, ferries (150B, 1½ to two hours, one morning departure) and speed-boats (350B, 45 minutes, four daily) go to Ko Phayam's main pier.

A motorcycle taxi from the pier to the main beaches costs 50B to 80B per person. Motorbike and bicycle rentals are available in the village and from most of the larger resorts.

Khao Sok National Park
อุทยานแห่งชาติเขาสก

If your leg muscles have atrophied after one too many days of beach-bumming, consider venturing inland to the wondrous Khao Sok National Park. Many believe this lowland jungle – the wettest spot in Thailand – to be more than 160 million years old, or one of the oldest rainforests on the globe. It features dramatic limestone formations and waterfalls that cascade through juicy thickets drenched with rain. A network of dirt trails snakes through the quiet park, allowing visitors to spy on the exciting array of indigenous creatures.

🍴 Sleeping

We recommend the two-day, one-night trips (2500B per person) to Chiaw Lan, where you sleep in floating huts on the lake and go on a variety of canoeing excursions.

Art's Riverview Jungle Lodge   GUESTHOUSE **$$**
(☑09 0167 6818; http://krabidir.com/artsriverview lodge; 54/3 Moo 6; bungalows 650-1500B) In a monkey-filled jungle bordering a limestone cliff-framed swimming hole, this is the prettiest guesthouse property in Khao Sok. Wood bungalows are simple but big.

Tree House   GUESTHOUSE **$$**
(☑0 7739 5169; ww.khaosok-treehouse.com; 233 Moo 6; r with fan/air-con 1000/2000B; ✳🛜💺) Don't be dissuaded by the Disney-esque facade, here is a complex of excellent and spacious bungalows connected by raised paths and bridges. The best nests have flat screens, air-con and two terraces. Fan rooms are simpler and smaller but clean.

ℹ Information

The park headquarters and visitors centre are 1.8km off Rte 401, close to the Km 109 marker.

There's an ATM outside the Morning Mist Mini-Mart and internet (2B) is available near the park entrance.

ⓘ Getting There & Around

Minivans to/from Surat Thani (250B, one hour), Krabi (300B, two hours) and a handful of other destinations leave daily from the park. Otherwise, Surat–Takua Pa buses can drop you off along the highway (Rte 401), 1.8km from the visitors centre. If guesthouse touts don't meet you, you'll have to walk to your chosen nest (from 50m to 2km). To explore Chiaw Lan lake on your own, charter a longtail (2000B per day) at the dam's entrance.

Khao Lak & Around

Hat Khao Lak is a beach for folks who shun the glitzy resorts of Phuket, but still crave beach civilisation (comfort, shopping and amenities). With warm waves to frolic in, long stretches of golden sand backed by forested hills, and easy day trips to nearby national parks, the area is a central base for exploring the North Andaman – above and below the water.

🏃 Activities

Diving or snorkelling day excursions to the Similan and Surin islands are immensely popular, but if you can, opt for a live-aboard trip since the islands are around 60km from the mainland (about three hours by boat). All dive shops offer live-aboard trips from around 17,000/29,000B for three-/five-day packages and day trips for 4900B to 6500B.

★**Wicked Diving**   DIVING
(📞0 7648 5868; www.wickeddiving.com) An exceptionally well-run and environmentally conscious outfit that books diving and snorkelling overnight trips, as well as a range of live-aboards. Conservation trips are run in conjunction with **Ecocean** (www.whaleshark.org). It does all the PADI courses, too.

★**Fantastic**   SNORKELLING
(📞0 7648 5998; www.fantasticsimilan.com; adult/child 3200/2200B) This is a campy frolic of a Similans snorkelling tour featuring players from a cross-dressing cabaret as guides. No booking office; meet at the pier or Fantastic can arrange pick-ups from your hotel.

Sea Dragon Diver Centre   DIVING
(📞0 7648 5420; www.seadragondivecenter.com; Th Phetkasem) One of the older operations in Khao Lak, Sea Dragon has maintained high standards throughout the years.

🛏 Sleeping

For the cheapest sleeps in town, head to Sea Dragon Diver Center and ask about the dorm beds at **Tiffy's Café** (per night 180B).

GETTING TO MYANMAR: RANONG TO KAWTHOUNG (VICTORIA POINT)

This is a popular visa run for beach bums who have stayed too long in the kingdom. Most travellers opt for the organised 'visa trips' (from 1000B per person including visa fees) offered by travel agencies in Ranong. But the trip could just as easily be arranged independently. Do note that Myanmar is 30 minutes behind Thailand.

This border now also allows land entry into Myanmar (with a pre-arranged visa) or you could visit the tumbledown port city of Kawthoung as a day trip.

Getting to the border Boats to Kawthoung leave from the Saphan Plaa pier, 5km from Ranong. Sŏrngtăaou No 3 from Ranong goes to the pier (20B).

At the border Longtail boat drivers will meet you at the pier and negotiate a fare; trips to Myanmar should cost 150/300B one way/return. You'll get stamped through **Thai immigration** (⊙8.30am-4.30pm), board the boat to the other side and go through Myanmar's checkpoint. Upon arriving at the Myanmar immigration office, you'll most likely be greeted by an English-speaking tout who insists on 'helping' by translating and making photocopies in return for an exorbitant fee; you can ignore this, but it might complicate things.

As a day visitor, you will pay a US$10 fee (crisp, untorn bills) for a border pass, which will allow you to stay in a 24-mile radius of Kawthoung for up to 14 days; your passport will be kept at the border. There are some well-meaning border 'helpers' who will carry your bag and collect forms for a tip. As a visa-runner the whole process should take two hours.

Moving On Tour Kawthoung for the day or continue to Myanmar with a pre-arranged visa.

For information about making this trip in the opposite direction, see p502.

GETTING TO MALAYSIA: SUNGAI KOLOK TO KOTA BHARU

Getting to the Border The Thai immigration post (open 5am to 9pm) at the Sungai Kolok/Rantau Panjang border is about 1.5km from the centre of Sungai Kolok or the train station. Motorbike taxis charge 30B.

At the Border This is a hassle-free, straightforward border crossing. After completing formalities, walk across the Harmony Bridge to the Malaysian border post.

Moving On Shared taxis and buses to Kota Bharu, the capital of Malaysia's Kelantan State, can be caught 200m beyond the Malaysian border post. Shared taxis cost RM8 per person (80B) or RM40 (400B) to charter the whole car yourself. The ride takes around 40 minutes. Buses make the hour-long journey for RM5.10 (50B).

It's possible to continue south by the so-called 'jungle train', but the closest station is at Pasir Mas, located along taxi/bus routes to Kota Bharu.

For information on making this trip in the opposite direction, see p429.

Walker's Inn   GUESTHOUSE **$**
(☑ 08 6281 7668, 08 4840 2689; www.walkersinn. com; Th Phetkasem; dm/r 200/600B; ☀☺) A long-running backpacker fave that offers bright and spacious air-con rooms, decent dorms, and a fine downstairs pub.

Khaolak Banana Bungalows   BUNGALOWS **$**
(☑ 0 7648 5889; www.khaolakbanana.com; 4/147 Moo 7; r 500-1200B; ☀☺) These adorable little bungalows have swirls painted on the cement floors and sun-filled indoor-outdoor bathrooms. A cute pool with deckchairs sweetens the deal.

Fasai House   GUESTHOUSE **$**
(☑ 0 7648 5867; r 500-700B; ☀@) The best budget choice in Khao Lak, Fasai has immaculate motel-style rooms and smiling staff members who coyly giggle like geishas.

Greenbeach   HOTEL **$$**
(☑ 0 7648 5845; www.khaolakgreenbeachresort. com; bungalows 1400-2300B; ☀☺) On an excellent stretch of beach and extending back into a garden, this place has a warm, family-style soul. Even the cheapest rooms have sea views.

🍴 Eating & Drinking

Early-morning divers will be hard-pressed to find a place to grab a bite before 8.30am.

Go Pong   THAI **$**
(Th Phetkasem; dishes 30-100B; ☺noon-10pm) Get off the tourist taste-bud tour at this terrific little streetside diner where they do stir-fried noodles and spicy rice dishes. If you dig the pig, try the stewed pork leg with rice or maybe the Chinese broccoli with crispy pork.

Jumbo Steak & Pasta   ITALIAN **$**
(☑ 08 7269 3928; Th Phetkasem, Ban Khukkhuk; mains 70-220B; ☺10.30am-10pm Thu-Tue) This hole-in-the-wall, just past the police boat, was launched by a former line chef at Le Meridian who does beautiful pasta dishes. Dishes are good value, though portions aren't huge.

Phu Khao Lak   INTERNATIONAL, THAI **$$**
(☑ 0 7648 5141; Th Phetkasem; dishes 80-300B; ☺8am-10pm) It's a hard restaurant to miss. And you shouldn't because there's a huge menu of Western and Thai dishes with ample descriptions, all well prepared.

Happy Snapper   BAR
(☑ 0 7648 5500; www.happysnapperbar.com; Th Phetkasem) The bar is stocked with good liquor, and there's a rockin' house band led by the owner, Pitak, a Bangkok-born bass legend.

ℹ Information

For emergencies (included dive-related) call the **SSS Ambulance** (☑ 08 1081 9444), which rushes injured persons to Phuket.

There are numerous travel agencies scattered about – the best is **Khao Lak Land Discoveries** (☑ 0 7648 5411; www.khaolaklanddicovery.com; Th Petchkasem).

ℹ Getting There & Away

Any bus running along Hwy 4 between Takua Pa and Phuket will stop at Hat Khao Lak (60B to 100B), if you ask the driver.

Khao Lak Discoveries runs hourly minivans to/ from Phuket International Airport (600B, one hour). Or take a Phuket-bound bus and ask for the airport; you'll be dropped off at an intersection where motorcycle taxis will complete the journey (10 minutes, 100B). It works, we promise.

THAILAND KHAO LAK & AROUND

Surin Islands Marine National Park

อุทยานแห่ง ชาติหมู่ เกาะสุรินทร์

The five gorgeous islands that make up this national park (www.dnp.go.th; admission adult/child 500/300B; ☺mid-Nov–mid-May) sit about 60km offshore and a measly 5km from the Thai–Myanmar marine border. Healthy rainforests, pockets of white-sand beach in sheltered bays and rocky headlands that jut into the ocean characterise these granite-outcrop islands. The clearest of water makes for great marine life, with underwater visibility often up to 35m. Park headquarters and all visitor facilities are on Ko Surin Neua, near the jetty.

Khuraburi, on the mainland, is the jumping-off point for the park. The pier is 9km north of town, as is the national park office (☑0 7649 1378; ☺8am-5pm) with good information, maps and helpful staff.

◉ Sights & Activities

Dive sites in the park include Ko Surin Tai and HQ Channel between the two main islands. Richelieu Rock (a seamount 14km southeast) is also technically in the park and happens to be one of the best, if not the best, dive sites on the Andaman coast. There's no dive facility in the park itself, so dive trips must be booked from the mainland. Bleaching has damaged the hard corals but you'll see plenty of fish and soft corals.

Snorkelling trips (140B per person, two hours, 9am and 2pm) leave from the park headquarters.

Ban Moken at Ao Bon on the South Island welcomes visitors and runs snorkel tours as well. Post-tsunami, Moken people have settled in this sheltered bay where a major ancestral worship ceremony (Loi Reua) takes place in April. The national park offers a Moken Village Tour (per person 300B).

🛏 Sleeping & Eating

Decent Park accommodation (www.dnp.go.th) includes bungalows (weekday/weekend 1400/2000B) and a campground (2-/4-person 300/450B, bedding per person 60B), but because of the island's short, narrow beaches it can feel seriously crowded when full (around 300 people).

❶ Getting There & Away

Tour operators use speedboats (return 1700B, one hour, 9am). Several tour operators run day trips from Khao Lak. The Surin Islands are also accessible via live-aboard boats that depart from the mainland.

Similan Islands Marine National Park

อุทยานแห่ง ชาติหมู่ เกาะสิมิลัน

Known to divers the world over, beautiful Similan Islands Marine National Park (www.dnp.go.th; admission adult/child 400/200B ; ☺Nov-May) is 60km offshore. Its smooth granite islands are as impressive above water as below, topped with rainforests, edged with white-sand beaches and fringed with coral reefs.

Two of the nine islands, Island 4 (Ko Miang) and Island 8 (Ko Similan), have ranger stations and accommodation; park headquarters and most visitor activity centres are on Island 4. The park has expanded to include Ko Bon and Ko Tachai, and both are unscarred by coral bleaching. Khao Lak is the jumping-off point for the park. The pier is at Thap Lamu, about 10km south of town.

◉ Sights & Activities

The Similans offer diving for all levels of experience, at depths from 2m to 30m. There are dive sites at each of the six islands north of Ko Miang; the southern part of the park (Islands 1, 2 and 3) is off-limits to divers and is a turtle nesting ground. No facilities for divers exist in the national park itself, so you'll need to take a dive tour from the mainland or Phuket.

You can hire snorkelling gear (per day 150B) from the park headquarters. Day trippers from Khao Lak usually visit three or four different snorkelling sites (trips from 3000B).

The islands also have some lovely walking trails where you can spot a variety of bird life.

🛏 Sleeping & Eating

Park accommodation (www.dnp.go.th) can also be booked through the national park office (☑0 7645 3272) at Khao Lak. Ko Miang has bungalows (2000B; ❊🖙), longhouses (r 1000B; ❊) and camp sites (2-/4-person 300/450B); there's electricity from 6pm to 6am. There is also a restaurant near the headquarters.

❶ Getting There & Away

There's no public transport to the park so you'll have to join a tour; most tours spend the night in the park so it is almost like you did it yourself. The most common way to visit is on a multiday liveaboard dive trip from Khao Lak.

Phuket ภูเก็ต

POP 94,325

The island of Phuket has long been misunderstood. First of all, the 'h' is silent. Ahem. And second, Phuket doesn't feel like an island at all. It's so huge (the biggest in the country) that one can never really get the sense that they're surrounded by water. Dubbed the 'pearl of the Andaman' by savvy marketing execs, this is Thailand's original tailor-made fun-in-the-sun resort.

Phuket's beating heart can be found in Patong, a 'sin city' that is the ultimate gong show where podgy beachaholics sizzle like rotisserie chickens and go-go girls play pingpong – without paddles...

These days, however, Phuket's affinity for luxury far outshines any of its old-school hedonism. Jet-setters touch down in droves, getting pummelled at swanky spas and swigging sundowners at fashion-forward nightspots.

Shoestringers should treat Phuket as a splurge for its seaside setting and high-end dining.

Sights

Phuket's stunning west coast, scalloped by sandy bays, faces the Andaman Sea. **Patong** is the eye of the tourist storm, with **Kata** and **Karon** – Patong's little brothers – south. The island's quieter east coast features gnarled mangroves. **Phuket Town**, in the southeast, is the provincial capital and home to most of the locals.

Big Buddha BUDDHIST TEMPLE
(พระใหญ่; mingmongkolphuket.com; off Hwy 402) **FREE** This massive, alabaster stone Buddha is an awe-inspiring sight, offering spiritual energy and spectacular views to match. It sits on a hilltop just northwest of Chalong circle.

Phuket Town NEIGHBOURHOOD
Phuket Town has an interesting collection of Sino-Portuguese architecture dating back to the island's shipping days. The most magnificent examples are the **Standard Chartered Bank** (Th Phang-Nga), **Thai Airways International office** (Th Ranong) and **Phuket Philatelic Museum** (Th Montri; ⊘9.30am-5.30pm) **FREE**, housed in the old post office. The **Phuket Thaihua Museum** (พิพิธภัณฑ์ภูเก็ตไทยหัว; 28 Th Krabi; admission 200B; ⊘9am-5pm) provides a glimpse into Phuket's past with

historic photos and, because this is Thailand, an exhibit on local dishes.

Phuket Gibbon Rehabilitation Centre ANIMAL SHELTER
(☑0 7626 0492; www.gibbonproject.org; admission 10B; ⊘9am-4pm) This tiny sanctuary in the park near Nam Tok Bang Pae is open to the public. The centre adopts gibbons that have been kept in captivity in the hopes they can be reintroduced to the wild. There are also volunteer opportunities and the animals are cared for through donations (1500B to 'adopt' a gibbon for a year).

Activities

Diving & Snorkelling
Phuket isn't the cheapest place to dive but it is centrally located to many renowned sites in the Andaman. Decent snorkelling spots can be found in Hat Nai Yang and Hat Kamala, or it's possible to day trip to nearby islands.

Sea Fun Divers DIVING
(☑0 7634 0480; www.seafundivers.com; 29 Soi Karon Nui, Patong; 2/3 dives per day 4100/4500B, open-water course 18,400B) An outstanding and very professional diving operation. Standards are extremely high and service is impeccable. There's an office at Le Meridien resort in Patong, and a second location at Katathani Resort in Kata Noi.

Sea Kayaking
★ **John Gray's Seacanoe** KAYAKING
(☑0 7625 4505; www.johngray-seacanoe.com; 124 Soi 1, Th Yaowarat; adult/child from 3950/1975B) The original, the most reputable and by far the most ecologically sensitive company on the island. Like any good brand in Thailand, John Gray's 'Seacanoe' name and itineraries have been frequently copied. Located north of Phuket Town.

Surfing
Decent surfing occurs from June to September. **Phuket Surf** (☑08 1611 0791, 08 7889 7308; www.phuketsurf.com; Th Koktanod, Kata; lessons 1500B, board rental per hr/day 150/500B; ⊘Apr-late Oct) is a good spot for rentals and information.

Kiteboarding
The best spots are in Hat Nai Yang, Karon and Rawai (ideal for beginners). Phuket's kiteboarding operators – **Kiteboarding Asia** (☑08 1591 4594; www.kiteboardingasia.com; lessons from 4000B), **Kite Zone** (☑08 3395 2005; www.kitesurfingphuket.com; 1hr beginner lessons from 1100B, half-day lesson 4400B; ⊘May-late Oct) and **Bob's Kite School Phuket** (www.

Phuket

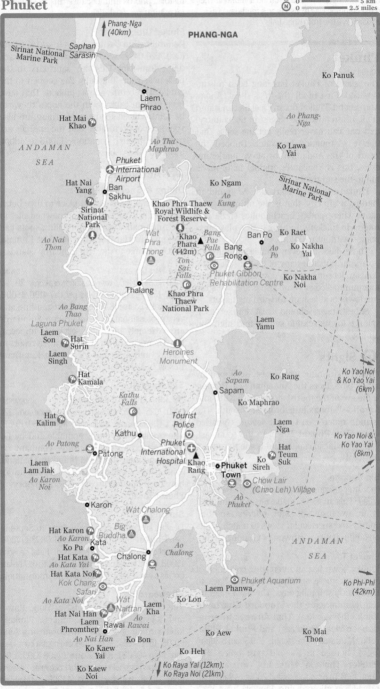

PHANG-NGA

Phang-Nga (40km)

Sirinat National Marine Park

Saphan Sarasin

Ko Panuk

Laem Phrao

Ao Phang-Nga

Hat Mai Khao

ANDAMAN SEA

Ao Tha Maphrao

Ko Lawa Yai

Phuket International Airport

Ko Ngam

Sirinat National Marine Park

Hat Nai Yang
Ban Sakhu

Ao Kung

Sirinat National Park

Khao Phra Thaew Royal Wildlife & Forest Reserve

Ban Po
Ko Raet

Ao Nai Thon

Wat Phra Thong

Khao Phara (442m)

Bang Pae Falls

Bang Rong

Ao Po

Ko Nakha Yai

Ton Sai Falls

Phuket Gibbon Rehabilitation Centre

Ko Nakha Noi

Thalang

Khao Phra Thaew National Park

Ao Bang Thao
Laguna Phuket

Laem Yamu

Laem Son
Hat Surin

Heroines Monument

Laem Singh

Hat Kamala

Kathu Falls

Ao Sapam
Sapam

Ko Rang

Ko Yao Noi & Ko Yao Yai (6km)

Hat Kalim

Ko Maphrao

Laem Nga

Tourist Police

Ao Patong

Kathu

Phuket International Hospital

Ao Sapam

Hat Teum Suk

Ko Yao Noi & Ko Yao Yai (8km)

Laem Lam Jiak
Ao Karon Noi

Patong

Khao Rang

Ko Sireh

Phuket Town

Chow Lair (Chao Leh) Village

Karon

Wat Chalong

Ao Phuket

Hat Karon
Ao Karon
Kata
Ko Pu

Big Buddha

Ao Chalong

ANDAMAN SEA

Hat Kata
Ao Kata Yai
Hat Kata Noi
Kok Chang Safari
Ao Kata Noi

Chalong

Phuket Aquarium

Ko Phi-Phi (42km)

Wat Naittan

Laem Kha

Laem Phanwa

Hat Nai Han
Laem Phromthep
Ao Nai Han

Rawai
Ao Rawai

Ko Lon

Ko Kaew Yai

Ko Bon

Ko Aew

Ko Mai Thon

Ko Heh

Ko Kaew Noi

Ko Raya Yai (12km);
Ko Raya Noi (21km)

THAILAND

kiteschoolphuket.com; Nai Yang; 1hr discovery lesson 1000B, 3hr course 3300B) – are affiliated with the International Kiteboarding Organization.

Tours

Amazing Bike Tours
CYCLING
(☑ 0 7628 3436; www.amazingbiketoursthailand.asia; 32/4 Moo 9, Th Chaofa, Chalong; day trips adult/child from 1600/1400B) Amazing Bike Tours leads small groups on half-day bicycle tours through the Khao Phra Thaew Royal Wildlife & Forest Reserve and offers terrific day trips around Ko Yao Noi and the gorgeous beaches and waterfalls in nearby Phang-Nga province.

Festivals

The annual **Vegetarian Festival** takes place in late September or October and is a cacophonous and colourful street procession of trance-like worshippers performing acts of self-mortification.

Sleeping

Phuket Town

Phuket Town has a healthy assortment of budget-friendly lodging options, but you'll have to commute to the beach.

Al Phuket Hostel
HOSTEL $
(☑ 0 7621 2881; www.aiphukethostel.com; 88 Th Yaowarat; dm 299B, d 699B; ❄ @ ☎) Double rooms are spacious with wood floors, greenhouse windows and funky papered ceilings. Dorms are bright, clean and sleep eight. All share polished concrete baths and a cramped downstairs lounge for movies and hang time.

Phuket 346
GUESTHOUSE $
(☑ 08 0146 2800; www.phuket346.com; 15 Soi Romanee; r with fan/air-con from 400/800B; ❄ ☎) This romantic old shophouse has been exquisitely restored to look like a cosy art gallery. Downstairs are fish ponds and a street-side cafe playing sultry jazz tunes.

Southern Beaches

Some of the prettiest beaches, like Hat Nai Han, can be found in this corner of the island. Hat Kata has a social but relaxed vibe, while Hat Karon is more hyperactive.

Ao Sane Bungalows
HOTEL $
(☑ 0 7628 8306; 11/2 Moo 1, Th Viset, Hat Nai Han; bungalows 600-1200B) Rickety cold-water, fan-cooled wooden bungalows sit on a secluded beach, with million-dollar views of Ao Sane

and Ao Nai Han. There's a beachside restaurant, a dive centre and an old-hippy vibe.

Rumblefish Adventure
HOSTEL $
(☑ 0 7633 0315; http://scubatuna.com; 98/79 Th Kata, Hat Kata; dm 250B, s/d 600/700B; P ❄ ☎) A dive-company flophouse offering reasonably clean doubles with private baths, hot water and air-con. Dorms sleep six. There's a mini living area upstairs too. It's in the Beach Center complex.

Chanisara Guesthouse
GUESTHOUSE $
(☑ 08 5789 5701; 48/5 Soi Casa del Sol, Hat Kata; r from 1000B; ❄ ☎) Rooms are super bright, tiled affairs with air-con, flat-screen TVs, recessed lighting and a little balcony. Low-season rates drop to 600B per night.

Fantasy Hill Bungalow
HOTEL $
(☑ 0 7633 0106; fantasyhill@hotmail.com; 8/1 Th Patak West, Hat Kata; r with fan 600B, air-con 1000-1200B; P ❄ ☎) Sitting in a lush garden on a hill, the older but well-maintained bungalows here are great value. It's peaceful but central and the staff are super sweet. Angle for a corner air-con room with a view.

★Bazoom Haus
GUESTHOUSE $$
(☑ 08 9533 0241; www.bazoomhostel.com; 269/5 Karon Plaza, Hat Karon; dm 300B, r 2700B; ❄ @ ☎) The fabulous private rooms offer wood floors and furnishings, recessed lighting, flat screens and mosaic showers. There's a Jacuzzi and barbecue on the roof deck, DJ decks in the in-house Korean restaurant (the owners are from Korea), and a dive shop too. Dorms have six beds to a room.

Kangaroo Guesthouse
GUESTHOUSE $$
(☑ 0 7639 6517; www.kangarooguesthouse.com; 269/6-9 Karon Plaza, Hat Karon; r 1200B; ❄ ☎) Basic, but very clean, sunny tiled rooms with hot water, air-con, a cute breakfast nook, and balconies overlooking a narrow, slightly seedy *soi*.

Patong

Patong is crammed with tourists and tourist schlock – you'll either love it or hate it. Budget digs are disappearing but rates drop in the low season.

Patong Backpacker Hostel
HOSTEL $
(☑ 0 7625 6680; www.phuketbackpacker.com; 140 Th Thawiwong; dm 250-450B; ❄ ☎) This has a great location near the beach and the owner offers info on all the best, cheapest places to eat in town. Dorm prices vary depending

on the number of beds in the room (four to 10). The top floor is the brightest, but dorm rooms on the lower floors each have their own attached bathrooms.

Tune Hotel   HOTEL **$$**
(☑0 7634 1936; www.tunehotels.com; 56 Th Rat Uthit; r 1500B; P ✳) The Tune is a budding new Southeast Asian brand. It offers small but comfy rooms with wood floors, satellite TV and plush linens. It's no frills but it works.

Northern Beaches

Sirinat National Park   CAMP SITES, BUNGALOWS **$**
(☑0 7632 7152; www.dnp.go.th/parkreserve; camp sites 30B, bungalows 700-1000B) There are camp sites (BYO tent) and large, concrete bungalows at the park headquarters on a gorgeous, shady, white-sand bluff. Check in at the visitors centre or book online.

Discovery Beach Resort   GUESTHOUSE **$**
(65/17 Moo 5, Hat Nai Yang; r with fan/air-con 800/1500B; ✳ 🛜) With wooden Thai accents on the facade and lacquered timber handrails and furnishings, this spotless budget spot has enough motel kitsch to make it interesting, and its location – right on the beach – makes it a terrific value.

Clear House   HOTEL **$$**
(☑0 7638 5401; www.clearhousephuket.com; 121/2, 121/10 Th Rimhaad, Hat Kamala; r 1300B; ✳ 🛜) Shabby chic with a mod twist, white-washed rooms have pink-accent walls, plush duvets, flat-screen TVs, wi-fi and huge pebbled baths. This place just feels good.

 Eating

Phuket Town

There's good food in Phuket Town, and meals here cost a lot less than those at the beach.

Kopitiam by Wilai   THAI **$**
(☑08 3606 9776; www.facebook.com/kopitiamby wilai; 18 Th Thalang; mains 70-120B; ⊘11am-10pm Mon-Sat; 🛜) Phuket soul food. It does Phuketian *pàt tai* with some kick to it, and a fantastic *mee sua:* think noodles sautéed with egg, greens, prawns, chunks of sea bass, and squid. Wash it down with fresh chrysanthemum juice.

Cook   FUSION **$**
(☑0 7625 8375; 101 Th Phang-Nga; pasta dishes 90-160B, pizzas 160-240B) The Thai owner-chef used to cook Italian at a megaresort, so when

he opened this ludicrously inexpensive Old Town cafe he fused the two cultures. Order the sensational green curry pizza with chicken or the pork curry coconut milk pizza.

★**Suay**   FUSION **$$**
(☑08 1797 4135; www.suayrestaurant.com; 50/2 Th Takuapa; most dishes 90-350B; ⊘5-11pm) Fusion at this converted house just south of Old Town means salmon carpaccio piled with a tart and bright pomelo salad, an innovative take on *sôm·dam* featuring mangosteen, a yellowfin tuna *larb*, smoked eggplant served with roast chilli paste and crab meat, and a massaman curry with lamb chops.

Southern Beaches

★**Pad Thai Shop**   THAI **$**
(Th Patak East, Hat Karon; dishes 50-60B; ⊘9am-8pm) On the busy main road just north of Ping Pong Bar is this glorified local food stand that spills forth from the owners' home. Rich and savoury chicken-noodle stew, beef-bone soup, spicy basil stir-fries and the best *pàt tai*.

Roti House   THAI **$**
(81/6 Soi Sameka, Rawai; mains 20-40B; ⊘7-11am) If you like French toast or croissants, you'll love roti, Thailand's Muslim morning delicacy accompanied by a breakfast curry. Dunk, munch, repeat. It also does *martabak* (stuffed roti), tea and sugary, milky coffee.

Som Tum Lanna   THAI **$**
(☑08 6593 2711; 2/16 Th Sai Yuan, Rawai; mains 50-150B; ⊘8am-5pm Tue-Sun) When it comes to *sôm·dam*? Don't be a hero. Order it mild. And don't forget the chicken: heed the words of another blissed-out, greasy-mouthed customer: 'This is some killer chicken!'

Mama Noi's   THAI, ITALIAN **$**
(Karon Plaza, Hat Karon; mains 60-185B; ⊘8am-10pm; 🛜) A simple tiled cafe with a handful of plants out front that has been feeding the expat masses for nearly a generation. It does all the Thai dishes and some popular pasta dishes, too.

★**Sabai Corner**   INTERNATIONAL, THAI **$$**
(☑0 9875 5525; www.sabaicorner.com; Th Karon Lookout, Hat Kata; mains 200-499B; ⊘10am-10pm; P 🛜) There is no better view on the island than from the deck at this superlative pub. You'll find it downhill and around a bend from the Karon Lookout, a little over halfway between Rawai and Kata.

★ **Rum Jungle** INTERNATIONAL $$$
(☑ 0 7638 8153; 69/8 Th Sai Yuan, Rawai; meals 300-500B; ☺ 11.30am-10.30pm) The best restaurant in the area is family-run and spearheaded by a terrific Aussie chef. The New Zealand lamb shank is divine, as are the steamed clams, and the pasta sauces are all made from scratch.

★ **Boathouse Wine & Grill** INTERNATIONAL $$$
(☑ 0 7633 0015; www.boathousephuket.com; 2/2 Th Kata (Patak West), Hat Kata; mains 450-950B; ☺ 11am-11pm) The perfect place to wow a fussy date, the Wine & Grill is the pick of the bunch for most local foodies. The atmosphere can be a little stuffy, but the Mediterranean fusion food is fabulous, the wine list expansive and the sea views sublime.

✖ Patong

Bargain seafood and noodle stalls pop up across town at night – try the lanes on and around Th Bangla, or venture over to the **Patong Food Park** (Th Rat Uthit; meals 100-200B; ☺ 4pm-midnight) once the sun drops.

Chicken Rice Briley THAI $
(☑ 0 7634 4079; Patong Food Park, Th Rat Uthit; meals 35-45B; ☺ 9am-3pm) The only diner in the Patong Food Park to offer sustenance when the sun shines. Steamed chicken served on a bed of rice accompanied by a fantastic chilli sauce. There's a reason it's forever packed with locals.

Mengrai Seafood SEAFOOD $$
(☑ 08 7263 7070; Soi Tun; meals 120-300B) Located down a sweaty *soi* off Th Bangla, Mengrai is in a wonderful food court serving fresh, local food that local expats swear by.

✖ Northern Beaches

Beach Restaurants THAI, INTERNATIONAL $
(Hat Kamala; dishes 50-250B; ☺ 11am-9pm) One of Kamala's highlights is its long stretch of eateries where you can dine in a swimsuit with your feet in the sand. There's everything from Thai to pizza, and plenty of cold beer. **Ma Ma Fati Ma**, at the far northern part of the beach, is our favourite.

★ **Ban Ra Tree** THAI $$
(Hat Nai Yang; mains 90-350B; ☺ 11am-10.30pm) The best choice on the Hat Nai Yang beach strip, its plastic tables are elegantly dressed in linens and parasols. The seafood is dynamite: green curry fried rice is topped with a whole, meaty cracked crab for just 220B!

♟ Drinking & Entertainment

Th Bangla is Patong's beer and bar-girl mecca and features a number of spectacular go-go extravaganzas, where you can expect the usual mix of gyrating Thai girls and often red-faced Western men.

★ **Sanaeha** BAR
(☑ 08 1519 8937; 83, 85 Th Yaowarat, Phuket Town; ☺ 6pm-late) Sanaeha is an upscale bohemian joint lit by seashell chandeliers, with plenty of dark corners where you can sip, snuggle, snack and dig that soulful crooner on stage.

★ **Ska Bar** BAR
(186/12 Th Koktanod, Kata; ☺ noon-late) At Kata's southernmost cove, Ska is our choice for oceanside sundowners. The Thai bartenders add to the funky Rasta vibe, and the canopy dangles with buoys, paper lanterns and flags. Friday nights brings fire spinners to the beach.

★ **Seduction** NIGHTCLUB
(www.facebook.com/seductiondisco; 39/1 Th Bangla, Patong; ☺ 10pm-4am) International DJs, a professional-grade sound system and the best dance party on Phuket, without question. Winner and still champion.

Timber Hut NIGHTCLUB
(☑ 0 7621 1839; 118/1 Th Yaowarat, Phuket Town; ☺ 6pm-2am) Thai and expat locals have been filling this clubhouse every night for nearly 20 years. They gather at long wooden tables on two floors, converge around thick timber columns, swill whiskey, and sway to live bands.

Barefoot Beach Shack BAR
(☑ 08 9697 2337; www.facebook.com/Barefoot BeachShack; Th Thawiwong, Patong; ☺ 10am-10pm; ◉) A whimsically decorated retro bar with a Caribbean feel, crafted from reused corrugated tin and reclaimed wood. It's right on the beach, pulses with pop tunes and is irrigated with middling cocktails and Chang draught.

Sound Phuket NIGHTCLUB
(☑ 0 7636 6163; www.soundphuket.com; Jung Ceylon complex, Unit 2303, 193 Th Rat Uthit, Patong; admission varies; ☺ 10pm-4am) When internationally renowned DJs come to Phuket, they are usually gigging amid the rounded, futuristic environs of Patong's hottest (and least sleazy) nightclub. Expect to pay up to 300B entry fee for big-name DJs.

Phuket Simon Cabaret CABARET
(☑ 0 7634 2011; www.phuket-simoncabaret.com; Th Sirirach; admission 700-800B; ☺ performances 6pm, 7.45pm & 9.30pm) About 300m south of Patong

TRANSPORT FROM PHUKET

DESTINATION	AIR	BUS
Bangkok	from 1480B, 1¾hr, frequent	543-1058, 13-15hr, frequent
Chiang Mai	1600B, 2 daily (Air Asia)	N/A
Hong Kong	5000-10,740B, 3hr, daily (Air Asia)	N/A
Jakarta	from 2730B, 3 weekly (Air Asia)	N/A
Ko Samui	N/A	430B, 8hr (bus-boat combo)
Krabi	N/A	150B, 3½hr
Kuala Lumpur	1712B, 20min, 4 daily (Air Asia)	N/A
Ranong	N/A	209-270B, 5-6hr
Seoul	23,000B, 7hr, 3 daily (Korean Air & Thai Airways)	N/A
Singapore	1400B, 40min, daily (Air Asia)	N/A
Surat Thani	N/A	195-220B, 6hr

town, this cabaret offers entertaining transvestite shows. The 600-seat theatre is grand, the costumes are gorgeous and the ladyboys are convincing. Though the show is brief, the house is often full – book ahead.

Bangla Boxing Stadium   BOXING
(🖉0 7282 2348; 198/4 Th Rat Uthit; admission 1000-1500B; ⊗9-11.30pm Tue, Wed, Fri & Sun) Old name, new stadium, same game: a packed line-up of competitive *muay thai* (Thai boxing) bouts.

ℹ Information

During May to October, large waves and fierce undertows make it too dangerous to swim, especially at certain beaches; red-flag warnings are posted when conditions are rough.

Phuket's roads are congested with erratic road rules. It is not advised to rent a motorcycle, especially for inexperienced drivers, as vehicle accidents and fatalities are common. If you do drive a motorbike, wear a helmet and protective clothing and keep your belongings on your person, not in the basket. Do not drink drive.

The English-language *Phuket Gazette* (www.phuketgazette.net) is a news and lifestyle weekly.
Main Post Office (Th Montri; ⊗8.30am-4pm Mon-Fri, 9am-noon Sat)

Phuket International Hospital (🖉0 7624 9400; www.phuketinternationalhospital.com; Th Chalermprakiat) International doctors rate this hospital as the best on the island.

Tourism Authority of Thailand Office (TAT; 🖉0 7621 2213; www.tat.or.th; 73-75 Th Phuket, Phuket Town; ⊗8.30am-4.30pm) Has maps, information brochures, a list of standard *sŏrngtăaou* fares and charter costs.

Tourist Police (🖉1699; cnr Th Thawiwong & Th Bangla, Patong)

ℹ Getting There & Away

AIR
Phuket International Airport (🖉0 7632 7230; www.phuketairportonline.com) is 30km northwest of Phuket Town; it takes around 45 minutes to an hour to reach the southern beaches from here. Flights to Bangkok are handled by Air Asia, Bangkok Airways, Nok Air and Thai Airways International. Direct international destinations, in Asia, are also served; frequencies and destinations often increase during high season.

An orange **airport bus** (🖉0 7623 2371; www.airportbusphuket.com; tickets 90B) runs between the airport and Phuket Town via the Heroines Monument about every hour between 6am and 7pm. A minivan service goes to Phuket Town (150B) and the beaches (1800B), if there are enough passengers. Metered taxis should cost no more than 550B (including airport tax).

BOAT
Tha Rasada, north of Phuket Town, is the main pier for boats to Ko Phi-Phi with other southern Andaman islands. Boats to Krabi and Ao Nang via the Ko Yao Islands leave from Tha Bang Bong north of Tha Rasada.

BUS & MINIVAN
The **bus terminal** (🖉0 7621 1977; Th Thepkrasattri) is in Phuket Town. Minivans to the Gulf Coast and the southern Andaman leave from Phuket Town as well.

ℹ Getting Around

Large *sŏrngtăaou* run from Th Ranong near Phuket Town's day market to the beaches (25B to 40B, regularly 7am to 5pm).

Túk-túk and taxis should cost about 500B to 600B from Phuket Town to the beaches. Motorcycle rentals (300B) are widely available but are not recommended for novice riders.

Krabi Town   กระบี่

POP 30,882

Krabi Town is the jumping-off point to the karst-studded Krabi peninsula. The town is well-versed in transit travels with lodging, amenities and transport.

🛏 Sleeping

Krabi has an exceptional and always-improving guesthouse scene; flashpackers should head to Ao Nang.

★ Pak-up Hostel   HOSTEL $

(📞 0 7561 1955; www.pakuphostel.com; 87 Th Utarakit; dm 220-270B, d 500-600B; ❋ @ 🛜) This is the grooviest hostel on the Andaman coast; occupying a converted school house (Krabi's first) and featuring several uber-hip eight- and 10-bed dorms, all co-ed and named for school subjects.

Chan Cha Lay   GUESTHOUSE $

(📞 0 7562 0952; www.chanchalay.com; 55 Th Utarakit; r without/with bathroom 200/400B; ❋ 🛜) The en-suite rooms here, all decorated in tasteful Mediterranean blues and whites with white-pebble and polished-concrete semi-outdoor bathrooms, are among Krabi's most comfortable. Shared-bathroom, fan-only rooms are plain but spotless.

Hometel   HOTEL $

(📞 0 7562 2301; 7 Soi 2, Th Maharat; r 750B; ❋ 🛜) A modern and funky boutique sleep. Abstract art brings the colour, there are rain showers, some rooms have two terraces and all have high ceilings.

🍴 Eating & Drinking

Krabi Town has great market eats. Try the night market (Th Khong Kha; meals 20-50B) near the Khong Kha pier. Relax coffee (Th Chao Fah; mains 45-220B; ⏱ 7.30am-6pm; 🛜) has a relaxing storefront near the river. Playground (87 Th Utarakit; 🛜) is Pak-up's cool courtyard bar.

ℹ Information

Immigration Office (📞 0 7561 1350; Th Chamai Anuson; ⏱ 8.30am-4pm Mon-Fri) Handles visa extensions.

Krabi Hospital (📞 0 7561 1210; Th Utarakit) Located 1km north of town.

Post Office (Th Utarakit) Just south of the turn-off to Khong Kha pier.

ℹ Getting There & Away

AIR

Most domestic carriers offer flights between Bangkok and Krabi International Airport.

Bangkok Air (www.bangkokair.com) has a daily service to Ko Samui. To get to/from the airport, a taxi will cost 400B. A tourist airport bus costs 100B and a motorcycle taxi costs 300B.

BOAT

Boats to Ko Phi-Phi and Ko Lanta leave from the passenger pier at Khlong Chilat, about 4km southwest of Krabi. Travel agencies will arrange free transfers.

The largest boat operator is **PP Family Co** (📞 0 7561 2463; www.phiphifamily.com; Th Khong Kha), which has a ticket office right beside the pier in town. High-season service has more frequent departures to more islands.

For Railay, take a longtail boat from Krabi's Khong Kha pier.

BUS & MINIVAN

The **Krabi bus terminal** (📞 0 7561 1804; cnr Th Utarakit & Hwy 4) is in nearby Talat Kao, about 4km north of Krabi. *Sŏrngtǎaou* run from the bus station to central Krabi (50B, frequently 6am to 6.30pm).

Minivans run to popular tourist destinations in southern Thailand but they tend to be uncomfortably overcrowded.

THAILAND KRABI KRABI TOWN

TRANSPORT FROM KRABI TOWN

DESTINATION	AIR	BUS	BOAT
Bangkok	4400B, 1¼hr	720-1100B, 12hr, 4 daily	N/A
Hat Yai	N/A	170B, 3hr	N/A
Ko Lanta	N/A	N/A	400-450B, 2hr, 1 daily
Ko Phi-Phi	N/A	N/A	300B, 1½hr, 4 daily
Phuket	N/A	145B, 3½hr	N/A
Railay	N/A	N/A	150B, 45min, 2 daily
Surat Thani	N/A	140B, 2½hr	N/A

Ao Nang

อ่าวนาง

POP 12,400

The closest of the Krabi peninsula's beaches, Ao Nang provides 'civilisation' instead of scenery. It's convenient for a 'night out' but not the tropical hideaway that most people are looking for.

Activities and tours abound – from the sea lagoon at Ko Hong (1500B to 1800B) to bike trips with **Krabi Eco Cycle** (✎0 7563 7250; www.krabiecocycle.com; 41/2 Moo 5; half-/full-day tour 800/1700B). Diving trips (from 2500B) visit submarine tunnels and other features of the local karst scenery, and local island tours (2500B) are a popular day trip; snorkelling can also be arranged.

Rates in Ao Nang drop by 50% during the low season. Budgetarians should try **Glur** (✎08 9001 3343, 0 7569 5297; www.krabiglurhostel.com; 22/2 Moo 2, Soi Ao Nang; dm 600B, d 1300-1500B; Ⓟ✱@🖥️🏊), a stylish hostel.

Ao Nang is full of mediocre international food. Walk along **Soi Sunset** (✎0 7569 5260; Soi Sunset; dishes 60-400B; ⏰noon-10pm) – a narrow pedestrian-only alley housing several seafood joints – to find the catch of the day. Glur has a tasty sandwich shop.

ⓘ Getting There & Around

Sŏrngtǎaou run to/from Krabi Town (50B, 20 minutes). Airport buses from Krabi Town go to Ao Nang (80B to 100B). Minibuses go to Phuket (350B to 400B, 3½ hours), Pak Bara (300B, 3½ hours) and Ko Lanta (400B, two hours). Boats go to Hat Railay West (100/150B day/night, 15 minutes, minimum of six passengers). **Ao Nang Long-tail Boat Service** (✎0 7569 5313; www.aonangboatco-op.com) operates this service.

Railay

ไร่เล

Krabi's fairytale limestone crags come to a dramatic climax at Railay, the ultimate jungle gym for rock-climbing fanatics. Towering karst poke out of the azure waters and from the forested interior and in between are quiet sandy patches from which to view the splendour. The atmosphere is fittingly reverential.

◉ Sights

Tham Phra Nang (Princess Cave) is an important shrine for local fishers. About halfway along the path from Hat Railay East to Hat Phra Nang, a crude path leads up the jungle-cloaked cliff wall to a hidden lagoon known as **Sa Phra Nang** (Holy Princess Pool) with a killer viewpoint. **Tham Phra Nang Nai** (Inner Princess Cave; adult/child 40/20B; ⏰5am-8pm) is another large cave above Hat Railay East.

✦ Activities

Railay is one of the most scenic spots to go **rock climbing**, with nearly 500 bolted routes, ranging from beginner to advanced climbs, all with unparalleled cliff-top vistas of a marine garden of karst islands. The going rate for climbing courses is 800B to 1000B for a half-day and 1500B to 2000B for a full day. Snorkelling trips and overnight kayaking trips to deserted islands can also be arranged.

★ Base Camp Ton Sai   ROCK CLIMBING
(✎08 1149 9745; www.tonsaibasecamp.com; Hat Ton Sai; ⏰8am-9.30pm) Arguably the most professional outfit in the area.

Highland Rock Climbing   ROCK CLIMBING
(✎08 0693 0374; highlandrockclimbingthailand.weebly.com; Hat Railay East) If you're bunking on the mountain, this is the man to climb with.

Hot Rock   ROCK CLIMBING
(✎0 7562 1771; www.railayadventure.com; Hat Railay West) Has a very good reputation and is owned by one of the granddaddies of Railay climbing.

King Climbers   ROCK CLIMBING
(✎0 7563 7125; www.railay.com; Hat Railay East) One of the biggest, oldest, most reputable and commercial schools.

🛏️ Sleeping & Eating

Railay's three beaches (Hat Railay West, Hat Railay East and Hat Phra Nang) are the domain of midrange and top-end hotels and resorts. Budget spots occupy Railay Highlands (500m up the hills from Hat Railay East) and nearby Hat Ton Sai (the next cove over from Hat Railay West).

Railay Cabana   GUESTHOUSE $
(✎08 45341928, 0 7562 1733; Railay Highlands; bungalows 350-600B) Superbly located in the karst cliffs, this is your hippy mountain hideaway. Rustic yet clean thatched-bamboo bungalows are surrounded by an orchard.

Paasook   HOTEL $
(✎08 9648 7459; Hat Ton Sai; bungalows 200-900B) The cheaper, cinder-block cells are clean and doable, but the wooden cottages are far more appealing. It's at the far western end of the beach, beneath Groove Tube.

Railay Garden View BUNGALOWS $$

(📞08 5888 5143; www.railaygardenview.com; Hat Railay East; bungalows 1300B) A collection of tin-roof, woven-bamboo bungalows, stilted high above the mangroves on the east beach. They look weather-beaten from the outside, but are spacious and clean on the inside.

Sand Sea Resort HOTEL $$

(📞0 7562 2608; www.krabisandsea.com; Hat Railay West; bungalows 1950-5950B; ❄@☲) The lowest-priced resort on this beach offers everything from ageing fan-only bungalows to newly remodelled cottages. The grounds aren't as swank as the neighbours, but there's a karst-view pool – and of course the sublime beach.

Mama's Chicken THAI $

(Hat Ton Sai; 50-90B; ⊙7.30am-10pm) Beach stall serving Western breakfasts, fruit smoothies and cheap Thai dishes, including massaman tofu. Grab a table and watch management battle with a mango-thieving mob of macaques.

ℹ Getting There & Around

Longtail boats to Railay run from Khong Kha pier in Krabi (150B, 45 minutes, every 1½ hours from 7.45am to 6pm with six to 10 passengers).

Boats run from Ao Nang to Hat Railay West and Hat Ton Sai (100/150B day/night, 15 minutes, with eight passengers).

The *Ao Nang Princess* runs from nearby Hat Noppharat Thara National Park headquarters to Ko Phi-Phi with a stop at Hat Railay West (350B, 9.15am October to May).

Ko Phi-Phi เกาะพีพีดอน

With movie-star good looks, Ko Phi-Phi lives life in the fast lane with hedonistic parties and a drunken abandon. The island is still a stunner: craggy cliffs, curvy, blonde beaches and bodacious jungles. But it isn't a peaceful idyll: boats unload tons of package tourists and bars terrorise the night's slumber. On the plus side there are still cheap places to stay

Ko Phi-Phi

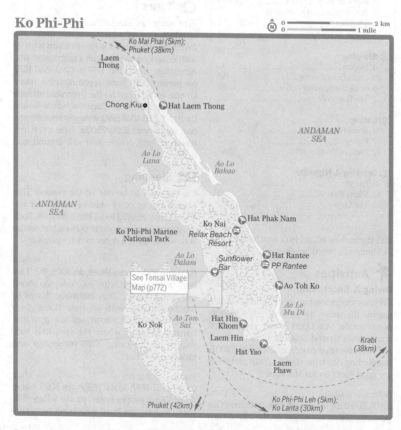

0 — 2 km
0 — 1 mile

Ko Mai Phai (5km);
Phuket (38km)

Laem Thong

Chong Kiu ● ⊗Hat Laem Thong

ANDAMAN SEA

Ao Lo Lana

Ao Lo Bakao

ANDAMAN SEA

Ko Nai ⊗Hat Phak Nam

Ko Phi-Phi Marine National Park

Relax Beach Resort

Ao Lo Dalam

Sunflower Bar

⊗Hat Rantee
⊗PP Rantee

See Tonsai Village Map (p772)

⊗Ao Toh Ko

Ao Lo Mu Di

Ko Nok

Ao Tom Sai

Hat Hin Khom

Laem Hin

Hat Yao

Krabi (38km)

Laem Phaw

Ko Nok

Phuket (42km)

Ko Phi-Phi Leh (5km);
Ko Lanta (30km)

Tonsai Village

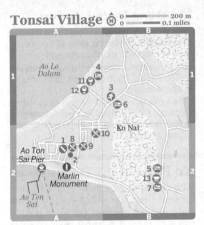

0 ———— 200 m
0 ———— 0.1 miles

Tonsai Village

and the carless island isn't nearly as chaotic as Thailand's paved beaches.

Activities

Diving & Snorkelling

Crystal-clear Andaman water and abundant marine life make the perfect recipe for top-notch scuba. An Open Water certification course costs around 12,900B, while the standard two-dive trips cost from 2500B to 3200B. Snorkelling day trips start at 600B and there are good spots on Ko Mai Phai.

Adventure Club   DIVING
(08 1970 0314; www.phi-phi-adventures.com) Our favourite diving operation on the island runs

an excellent assortment of educational, eco-focused tours, including the recommended shark-watching snorkel trips.

Rock Climbing

There are some good rock-climbing outfitters on the island, with most places charging around 1200B for a half-day of climbing.

Try **Spider Monkey** (0 7581 9384; www.spidermonkeyphiphi.com) or **Ibex Climbing & Tours** (08 4309 0445, 0 7560 1423; www.ibexclimbingandtours.com).

Courses

**Pum Restaurant &
Cooking School**   COOKING
(08 1521 8904; www.pumthaifoodchain.com; classes 399-1200B; classes 1pm & 4pm) Thai-food fans can take cooking courses here in the Tourist Village. You'll learn to make some of the excellent dishes that are served in the restaurant and go home with a cookbook.

Tours

Ever since Leo smoked a spliff in the movie adaptation of Alex Garland's novel *The Beach*, uninhabited **Ko Phi-Phi Leh** with its scenic lagoons has become a pilgrimage site. Adventure Club and **U-Rip** (0 7560 1075; per person 600B) have recommended tours. Or you could forgo all the overrated athletic torture in favour of **Captain Bob's Booze Cruise** (08 4848 6970; www.phiphiboozecruise.com; men/women 3000/2500B; departs at 1pm, returns at 7pm), where you sail around and drink.

Sleeping

Phi-Phi used to be one of the priciest Thai islands before every slice of sand went upscale. Today Phi-Phi looks like a bargain. Book in advance during holiday periods and secure your windows and doors to deter break-ins.

Blanco   HOSTEL $
(0 7562 8900; Tonsai Village; dm 300B;) This bare bones (better bring your own top sheet) yet stylish hostel offers eight-bed dorms in bamboo chalets with concrete floors. Digs are cramped and mattresses are gym-mat hard, but this is where the cool kids stay, thanks to fun-loving Thai ownership and groovy beach bar.

Rock Backpacker   HOSTEL $
(08 1607 3897; Tonsai Village; dm 300B; r from 400-600B) A proper hostel on the village hill, with clean dorms lined with bunk beds, tiny

BOATS FROM KO PHI-PHI

DESTINATION	PRICE (B)	DURATION (HR)	FREQUENCY
Ao Nang	350	1½	1 daily Oct-Apr
Ko Lanta	350	1½	3 daily Oct-Apr
Krabi	300	1½	4 daily, year-round
Phuket	250-350	2	3 daily year-round

private rooms, an inviting restaurant-bar and a rugged, graffiti-scrawled exterior.

Oasis Guesthouse GUESTHOUSE $
(☑ 0 7560 1207; Tonsai Village; r 800-900B; ✴) It's worth the walk up the side road east of the village centre to find this cute guesthouse surrounded by trees. It's first-come, first-served only.

Tee Guesthouse GUESTHOUSE $
(☑ 08 4851 5721; Tonsai Village; r with fan/air-con 800/1200B; ✴) A fun and funky choice tucked down a side road. Rooms are simple with graceful touches like exposed brick and lavender walls, queen beds, mosaic-tiled baths, and a welcome blast of graffiti on the exterior. They have a darling little cafe (⊙8am-4pm) here, too.

PP Rantee BUNGALOWS $$
(☑ 08 1597 7708; Hat Rantee; bungalow with fan 1200-1600B, air-con 2000B; ⊙restaurant 7am-10pm; ✴☏) Here are basic yet acceptable bamboo bungalows and newer, clean tiled bungalows with wide porches. It also has the best restaurant on this beach, and a big wooden swing on the tree out front.

★**Relax Beach Resort** HOTEL $$$
(☑ 08 9475 6536, 08 1083 0194; www.phiphirelax resort.com; bungalows 1800-4900B; @✴) There are 47 unpretentious lacquered Thai-style bungalows with wood floors, two-tiered terraces with lounging cushions and mosaic baths in the sweetest nests. Some suffer from a tinge of must and scuffed-up walls. You can walk to Hat Rantee at low tide.

✗ Eating & Drinking

All of your partying needs will be met at Slinky Bar (Ao Lo Dalam), Ibiza (Ao Lo Dalam) or the mellow Sunflower Bar (Ao Lo Dalam).

Local Food Market THAI $
(Ao Ton Sai; meals 30-60B; ⊙8am-8pm) The cheapest and most authentic eats are at the market. The walls are scrawled with the blessings of a thousand travellers.

Papaya Restaurant THAI $
(☑ 08 7280 1719; dishes 80-300B; ⊙11am-11pm) Cheap, tasty and spicy. Here's some real-deal Thai food served in heaping portions. They're so popular they decided to open a second cafe (☑ 08 7280 1719; Ton Sai Village; dishes 80-300B) a block away.

❶ Getting There & Away

Boats moor at Ao Ton Sai though a few Phuket boats use the northern pier at Laem Thong. To get to Railay, use the boat bound for Ao Nang.

❶ Getting Around

There are no roads on Phi-Phi Don so transport on the island is mostly by foot. Longtails can be chartered from Ao Ton Sai pier to the different beaches for 100B to 500B, depending on distance.

Ko Lanta เกาะลันตา

POP 20,000

Once the domain of backpackers and sea gypsies, Lanta has morphed into a mid-range, package-tour getaway. But it is infinitely more relaxed than party-hard Ko Phi-Phi and there are still a few cheapies sprinkled throughout the island.

Ko Lanta is relatively flat compared to the karst formations of its neighbours, so the island can be easily explored by motorbike. A quick trip around reveals a colourful crucible of cultures – fried-chicken stalls sit below slender minarets, creaking *chow lair* (sea gypsy) villages dangle off the island's side, and small Thai wats hide within green-brown tangles of curling mangroves. Don't miss a visit to Ban Ko Lanta (Old Town), which was the original port and commercial centre for the island that retains many 100-year-old wooden stilt houses.

Ko Lanta Marine National Park (อุทยาน แห่งชาติเกาะลันตา; www.dnp.go.th; adult/child 200/100B) – which protects 15 islands in the Ko Lanta group – can be explored on sea kayak tours.

Just off-shore are some of Thailand's top diving and snorkelling spots, including the undersea pinnacles of Hin Muang and Hin Daeng. Dive trips cost 4500B to 5500B. **Scubafish** (☑ 0 7566 5095; www.scuba-fish.com; Ban Sala Dan) is a recommended dive operator.

Time for Lime (☑ 0 7568 4590; www.timeforlime.net; per class 1800B) is a cooking school on Hat Khlong Dao, which funds Lanta Animal Welfare with its profits.

🛏 Sleeping

Some resorts close down from May to October (low season), while others drop their rates by 50% or more. The recent building boom means that there are now new roadside accommodations with more affordable rates.

Hutyee Boat GUESTHOUSE $
(☑ 08 9645 1083, 08 3633 9723; Hat Phra Ae; bungalows 350-400B) A hidden, hippy paradise of big, solid bungalows with tiled bathrooms and mini fridges in a forest of palms and bamboo. It's just back from the beach behind Nautilus. It's run by a sweet Muslim family.

Sanctuary GUESTHOUSE $
(☑ 08 1891 3055; sanctuary_93@yahoo.com; Hat Phra Ae; bungalows 600-1200B) The original Phra Ae resort is still a delightful place to stay. There are artistically designed wood-and-thatch bungalows with a hippy-ish atmosphere. The restaurant offers Indian and vegetarian eats and the Thai usuals. It also holds yoga classes.

Andaman Sunflower BUNGALOWS $
(☑ 0 7568 4668; Hat Phra Ae; bungalows 850B; ☉ Oct-Apr; 🗲) Set back from the beach, these are some of the best budget bungalows around.

Somewhere Else GUESTHOUSE $
(☑ 08 1536 0858; Hat Phra Ae; bungalows 600-1200B; 🗲) Choose among small, basic and clean thatched bamboo bungalows. All are fan-cooled and steps from the best stretch of Long Beach.

★ **Bee Bee Bungalows** BUNGALOWS $
(☑ 08 1537 9932; www.beebeebungalows; Hat Khlong Khong; bungalows 900B; @ 🗲) One of the best budget spots on the island, Bee Bee's super-friendly staff care for a dozen creative bamboo cabins – every one is unique and a few are stilted in the trees.

Where Else? BUNGALOWS $
(☑ 0 756 67173, 08 1536 4870; www.lanta-where-else.com; Hat Khlong Khong; bungalows 300-800B) One of Ko Lanta's little slices of bohemia. The bungalows may be a bit shaky but there is great mojo here and the place buzzes with backpackers.

Round House GUESTHOUSE $
(☑ 08 1606 0550; www.lantaroundhouse.com; Hat Khlong Nin; r/bungalow/house 800/1000/2400B; ✳ 🗲) A cute little find on the north end of this beach. The wooden and bamboo bungalows are closest to the beach, just behind the breezy restaurant.

Baan Phu Lae BUNGALOWS $
(☑ 08 5474 0265, 0 7566 5100; www.baanphu-lae.com; Ao Mai Pai; bungalows 800-1000B) Set on the rocks at the end of this tiny beach are a collection of romantic, canary-yellow concrete bungalows with thatched roofs, bamboo beds and private porches. The restaurant's rickety deck juts over the sea.

Mu Ko Lanta Marine National Park Headquarters CAMP SITES $
(☑ in Bangkok 0 2561 4292; www.dnp.go.th; with own tent per person 30B, with tent hire 225B, 2-/4-room bungalows 1500/3000B) The secluded grounds of the national park headquarters are a wonderfully serene place to camp.

There are toilets and running water, but you should bring your own food.

Sriraya GUESTHOUSE $
(☑ 0 7569 7045; Ban Ko Lanta; r with shared bathroom 500B) Sleep in a simple but beautifully restored, thick-beamed Chinese shophouse,

TRANSPORT FROM KO LANTA

DESTINATION	MINIVAN	BOAT
Ko Lipe	N/A	1500-1900B, 3-4hr
Ko Phi-Phi	N/A	300B, 1½hr, 2 daily
Krabi	250-300B, 1½hr, hourly 7am-3.30pm (airport & Krabi Town)	400B, 2hr, 1 daily (Khlong Chilat pier)

that's possibly the very best value on the island. Walls are brushed in earth tones and bathrooms are shared. Angle for the streetfront balcony room that overlooks the old town's ambient centre.

Eating

Ban Sala Dan has plenty of restaurants and minimarts. Don't miss the seafood restaurants, like Lanta Seafood (0 7566 8411; Ban Sala Dan; mains 80-300B), along the northern edge of the village. In Ban Ko Lanta, try Beautiful Restaurant (0 7569 7062; www.beautifulrestaurantkolanta.com; Ban Ko Lanta; mains 100-200B;), where tables are scattered on four piers that extend into the sea.

Drinking & Nightlife

If you're looking for roaring discotheques, pick another island. If you want a low-key bar scene head to Hat Phra Ae. Opium Bar supports the guest DJ scene.

❶ Information

Ban Sala Dan village has internet cafes (1B per minute), travel agencies and other tourist amenities.

Ko Lanta Hospital (0 7569 7085) The hospital is 1km south of Ban Ko Lanta (Old Town).

Police Station (0 7569 7017) North of Ban Ko Lanta.

❶ Getting There & Away

There are two piers at Ban Sala Dan. The passenger jetty is about 300m from the main strip of shops; vehicle ferries leave from a second jetty several kilometres further east. Ferry service varies with the weather and the tourist season. Minivans are your best option for year-round travel.

❶ Getting Around

Most resorts provide transfer from the piers. In the opposite direction expect to pay 80B to 350B. Alternatively, you can take a motorcycle taxi from opposite the 7-Eleven in Ban Sala Dan; fares vary from 50B to 350B depending on distance.

Motorcycles (250B per day) can be rented all over the island.

Ko Tarutao Marine National Park

อุทยานแห่ง ชาติหมู่ เกาะตะรุเตา

One of the most exquisite and unspoilt regions in all of Thailand, Ko Tarutao Marine National Park (0 7478 1285; adult/child 400/200B; Nov–mid-May) encompasses 51 barely developed islands surrounded by healthy coral reefs and radiant beaches. There are no foreign-exchange facilities on the islands – you can change cash and travellers cheques at travel agencies in Pak Bara and there's an ATM at La-Ngu.

Ko Tarutao is the biggest island in the group but it is still rustic. The park headquarters and government accommodation (camp sites from 375B and bungalows 600B to 1000B) are here. Bookings can be made at the park office in Pak Bara or online. The island closes from the end of May to mid-September.

Ko Lipe has more civilisation and stays open year-round. Budget accommodations are lean, though. Forra Dive (08 0545 5012; www.forradiving.com; Sunrise Beach; bungalows 600-1400B) provides discounts for diving guests.

❶ Getting There & Away

Boats from Pak Bara stop at Ko Tarutao (450B, 4 daily) and Ko Lipe (550B to 650B, 1½ hours,

---

GETTING TO MALAYSIA: KO LIPE TO PULAU LANGKAWI

It is easy to island-hop to the Malaysian island of Pulau Langkawi from Ko Lipe. Note Malaysia is one hour ahead of Thailand.

Getting to the border From Ko Lipe, Tigerline and Satun-Pak Bara Speedboat have services to Pulau Langkawi (1400B, one hour, 7.30am, 10.30am and 4pm).

At the border Before departing on the boat, get stamped out of Thailand from the immigration office at the Bundhaya Resort in Ko Lipe. Border formalities on Pulau Langkawi are straightforward and most European nationals receive a visa on arrival.

Moving on Pulau Langkawi has transport connections to the mainland and to Penang.

For information on making this crossing in the other direction, see p414.

4 daily). Service runs from 21 October to the end of May.

Tigerline offers the cheapest service to from Ko Lipe to Ko Lanta (1700B, 5½ hours), stopping at some of the Trang Islands (1400B to 1600B, 3½ to 4½ hours). It departs from Ko Lipe's Pattaya Beach at 9.30am. The Satun-Pak Bara Speedboat Club offers similar service.

UNDERSTAND THAILAND

Thailand Today

Political tensions dog Thailand. The opposition groups are frequently rebranded but the disagreement remains the same: the political involvement of ousted prime minister Thaksin Shinawatra. Removed from office by the 2006 coup and now living in self-imposed exile after being convicted of abuse of powers, Thaksin is believed to rule the country via his sister Yingluck Shinawatra, who was elected as prime minister in 2011. His politically aligned party controls the popularly elected portion of the parliament. Though he is despised by the urban elite, he is almost worshipped by the urban and rural working class and his political proxies handily win elections.

In 2013 the parliament attempted to pass an amnesty bill which would absolve Thaksin and other political figures of criminal wrongdoing during the political crisis of the last decade. The bill did not pass the upper chamber, which is partially composed of anti-Thaksin appointments. The counter campaign by Thaksin's political allies was to amend the constitution so that the senate would be 100% elected, allowing them to remove legislative opposition in the next round of elections. This sparked massive and sometimes violent street protests in Bangkok and southern provincial capitals. Anti-government protestors demanded that Yingluck step down as prime minister; she politely refused and instead called for general elections in 2014. The new round of elections were fraught with problems: polling stations were blocked by anti-government groups, the opposition Democrat party refused to participate in the ballot and many seats went unregistered. The only certainty is that Thailand's political discord will continue.

History

Rise of Thai Kingdoms

It is believed the first Thais migrated southwest from modern-day Yúnnán and Guangxi, China, to what is today known as Thailand. They settled along river valleys and formed small farming communities that eventually fell under the dominion of the expansionist Khmer empire of present-day Cambodia. What is now southern Thailand, along the Malay peninsula, was under the sway of the Srivijaya empire based in Sumatra.

By the 13th and 14th centuries, what is considered to be the first Thai kingdom, Sukhothai (meaning 'Rising Happiness'), emerged and began to chip away at the crumbling Khmer empire. The Sukhothai king-

---

COLOURS: MORE THAN MEETS THE EYE

Colours in Thailand have always had meaning. Each day of the week is associated with a colour, which in turn symbolises a person's birth day. (Thai astrology is based on the day of the week not the month or date of a person's birth.)

Starting in 2006 anti-Thaksin demonstrators donned yellow shirts showing their allegiance to the king (Thaksin was viewed as having designs on the crown); yellow is the colour associated with the present king because of his birth day. This group was dubbed 'Yellow Shirts' and soon the colour became entwined with the political movement. In the most recent anti-government flare-up, protesters have rebranded themselves and now wear the colours of the Thai flag and carry whistles (to represent whistleblowing against corruption).

The pro-Thaksin camp adopted the colour red as a symbol of democracy and they became known as the 'Red Shirts'. Red Shirts were primarily working class or rural class hailing originally from the north and northeast.

To some degree the ongoing political crisis is a class struggle, though there are left-leaning intellectuals and pro-democracy advocates within the ranks of the Red Shirts, as well as avid anti-Thaksin Yellow Shirts from humble backgrounds. In the middle of the extremes are the un-colour-coded Thais who hope for a political truce.

dom is regarded as the cultural and artistic kernel of the modern state.

Sukhothai was soon eclipsed by another Thai power, Ayuthaya, established by Prince U Thong in 1350. This new centre developed into a cosmopolitan port on the Asian trade route, courted by various European nations. The small nation managed to thwart foreign takeovers, including one orchestrated by a Thai court official, a Greek man named Constantine Phaulkon, to advance French interests. For 400 years and 34 successive reigns, Ayuthaya dominated Thailand until the Burmese led a successful invasion in 1765, ousting the monarch and destroying the capital.

The Thais eventually rebuilt their capital in present-day Bangkok, established by the Chakri dynasty, which continues to occupy the throne today. As Western imperialism marched across the region, King Mongkut (Rama IV, r 1851–68) and his son and successor, King Chulalongkorn (Rama V, r 1868–1910), successfully steered the country into the modern age without becoming a colonial vassal. In return for the country's continued independence, King Chulalongkorn ceded huge tracts of Laos and Cambodia to French-controlled Indochina – an unprecedented territorial loss in Thai history.

A Struggling Democracy

In 1932 a peaceful coup converted the country into a constitutional monarchy, loosely based on the British model. What has followed has been a near-continuous cycle of power struggles among three factions – the elected government, military leaders and the monarchy backed by the aristocrats. These groups occasionally form tenuous allegiances based on mutual dislike for the opposition and the resulting power grab is often a peaceful military takeover sometimes dubbed 'smooth as silk' coups.

During the mid-20th century the military dominated the political sphere with an anticommunist tenure that is widely regarded as being ineffectual except in the suppression of democratic representation and civil rights. In 1973 student activists staged demonstrations calling for a real constitution and the release of political dissidents. A brief respite came, with reinstated voting rights and relaxed censorship. But in October 1976 a demonstration on the campus of Thammasat University in Bangkok was brutally quashed, resulting in hundreds of casualties and the reinstatement of authoritarian rule. Many activists went underground to join armed communist insurgency groups hiding in the northeast.

In the 1980s, as the regional threat of communism subsided, the military-backed Prime Minister Prem Tinsulanonda stabilised the country and moved towards a representative democracy. The military reemerged in 1991 to overthrow the democratically elected government; this was the country's 10th successful coup since 1932. In May 1992 huge demonstrations led by Bangkok's charismatic governor Chamlong Srimuang erupted throughout the city and the larger provincial capitals. The bloodiest confrontation occurred at Bangkok's Democracy Monument, resulting in nearly 50 deaths, but it eventually led to the reinstatement of a civilian government.

Same, Same but Different

Through the turn of this century, Thailand's era of coups seemed to have ended. Democratically elected governments oversaw the 1997 enactment of Thailand's 16th constitution, commonly called the 'people's constitution' because it was the first charter in the nation's history not written under military order. The country pulled through the 1997 Asian currency crisis and entered a stable period of prosperity in the early 2000s. Telecommunications tycoon Thaksin Shinawatra and his populist Thai Rak Thai party were elected into power in 2001 and over the next five years effectively engineered one-party rule. With little political opposition, Thaksin consolidated power in all ranks of government, stifling press criticism and scrutiny of his administration.

In 2006 Thaksin was accused of abusing his powers and conflicts of interest, most notably in his family's sale of their Shin Corporation to the Singaporean government for 73 billion baht (US$1.88 billion), a tax-free gain thanks to telecommunications legislation that he helped craft. Meanwhile Thaksin's working-class and rural base rallied behind him, spotlighting longstanding class divides within Thai society.

Behind the scenes the military and the aristocrats forged an allegiance that resulted in the 2006 coup of the Thaksin government, forcing the charismatic prime minister into exile. At first the military takeover was heralded as a necessary step in ridding the country of an elected dictator and cleptocracy. The military spent the next year attempting to 'clean house' of Thaksin's political party (Thai Rak Thai), only to have the regenerated (and re-christened) party win the 2007 reinstatement of democratic elections. In response, the aristocrats, organised under the group calling itself the People's Alliance for Democracy (PAD) but often dubbed 'Yellow Shirts', were unhappy with the return of Thaksin's political proxies and staged massive protests in Bangkok that took over the parliament building and closed down the city's two airports for a week in November 2008. This dealt a blow to Thailand's economy just as the US financial crisis was morphing into a global recession.

The Constitutional Court sided with PAD's demands and dissolved the ruling (and popularly elected) party due to a technicality. A new coalition was formed in December 2008, led by Oxford-educated Abhisit Vejjajiva, leader of the Democrat party and Thailand's fourth prime minister of the year. It was viewed by pro-Thaksin factions as a silent coup.

The pro-Thaksin faction (known as 'Red Shirts') retaliated with a crippling demonstration after Thailand's Supreme Court ordered the seizure of US$46 billion of Thaksin's assets and charged him with abusing his powers as prime minister. Starting in March 2010, thousands of Red Shirts occupied Bangkok's central shopping district for two months. Protest leaders demanded the dissolution of the government and reinstatement of elections. In May 2010 the military used force to evict the protestors, resulting in bloody clashes (91 people were killed) and a smouldering central city (US$1.5 billion of crackdown-related arson damage was estimated). In an effort to avoid future civilian-military showdowns, elections were held in 2011 and Thaksin's politically allied party won a clear majority and his sister, Yingluck Shinawatra, became Thailand's first female prime minister.

Her first two years in office were peaceful, though not without scandal. She fulfilled her campaign promise of raising the minimum wage to 300B per day and was blamed for the mishandling of the government's response to the devastating floods of 2011.

The Monarchy

Revered King Bhumibol Adulyadej (Rama IX, r 1946–) defined the post-absolute monarch role as a paternal figure who acted with perceived wisdom in times of political crisis. Now 86 years old, the king is the world's longest-serving monarch but as his health has declined, his role in the society at large has diminished. The heir apparent is Crown Prince Vajiralongkorn, the king's son.

People & Culture

Thais are laid-back, good-natured people whose legendary hospitality has earned their country a permanent place on the global travel map.

The National Psyche

Paramount to the Thai philosophy of life is *sànùk* (fun) – each day is celebrated with food and conversation, foreign festivals are readily adopted as an excuse for a party and every task is measured on the *sànùk* meter.

The social dynamics of Thai culture can be perplexing. The ideals of the culture are based on Buddhist principles and include humility, gratitude and filial piety. These golden rules are translated into such social conventions as saving face *(nâa)*, in which confrontation is avoided and people endeavour not to embarrass themselves or other people.

An important component of saving face is knowing one's place in society: all relationships in Thai society are governed by conventions of social rank defined by age, wealth, status and personal and political power. Thais 'size up' a Westerner's social status with a list of common questions: Where are you from? How old are you? Are you married? These questions to a Thai are matters of public record and aren't considered impolite.

Religion and the monarchy, which is still regarded by many as divine, are the culture's sacred cows. Whatever you do, don't insult the king or disrespect his image, especially in this new era of ultra-sensitivity towards the institution.

Lifestyle

Thailand straddles the divide between the highly Westernised urban life in major cities and the traditional rhythms of rural, agricultural life. But several persisting customs offer a rough snapshot of daily life. Thais wake up early, thanks in part to the roosters that start crowing sometime after sunset. In the grey stillness of early morning,

THAILAND'S HILL-TRIBE COMMUNITIES

Thailand's hill-tribe communities (referred to in Thai as *chao khao,* literally 'mountain people') are ethnic minorities who have traditionally lived in the country's mountainous frontier. Most tribes migrated from Tibet and parts of China some 200 years ago and settled along Southeast Asia's mountain belt from Myanmar to Vietnam. The Tribal Research Institute in Chiang Mai recognises 10 different hill tribes, but there may be up to 20 in Thailand.

Hill-Tribe Groups

The **Karen** are the largest hill-tribe group in Thailand and number about 47% of the total tribal population. They tend to live in lowland valleys and practise crop rotation rather than swidden agriculture. Their numbers and proximity to the mainstream society has made them the most integrated and financially successful of the hill-tribe groups. Thickly woven V-neck tunics of various colours are traditional dress.

The **Hmong** are Thailand's second-largest hill-tribe group and are especially numerous in Chiang Mai province. They usually live on mountain peaks or plateaus above 1000m. Traditional dress is a simple black jacket and indigo or black baggy trousers. Sashes may be worn around the waist, and embroidered aprons draped front and back.

The **Akha** are among the poorest of Thailand's ethnic minorities and live mainly in Chiang Mai and Chiang Rai provinces, along mountain ridges or steep slopes 1000m to 1400m in altitude. They are regarded as skilled farmers but are often displaced from arable land by government intervention. Their traditional garb is a headdress of beads, feathers and dangling silver ornaments.

Other minority groups include the Lisu, Lahu and Mien.

Village Etiquette

The minority tribes have managed to maintain their own distinct cultural identity despite increased interaction with the majority culture, conversion to Christianity or Buddhism and adoption of second-hand clothing instead of traditional garb. If you're planning on visiting hill-tribe villages, talk to your guide about dos and don'ts.

➡ Always ask permission before taking photos, especially at private moments inside dwellings. Many traditional belief systems view photography with suspicion. Also some tribespeople will ask for money in exchange for a photo; honour their request.

➡ Show respect for religious symbols and rituals. Don't touch totems at village entrances or sacred items. Don't participate in ceremonies unless invited to join.

➡ Avoid cultivating a tradition of begging, especially among children. Instead talk to your guide about donating to a local school.

➡ Avoid public nudity and be careful not to undress near an open window where village children might be able to peep in.

➡ Don't flirt with members of the opposite sex unless you plan to marry them. Don't drink or do drugs with the villagers; altered states sometimes lead to culture clashes.

➡ Smile at villagers even if they stare at you; ask your guide how to say 'hello' in the tribal language.

➡ Avoid public displays of affection, which in some traditional systems is viewed as offensive to the spirit world.

➡ Don't interact with the villagers' livestock; these creatures are valuable possessions not curiosities. Also avoid interacting with jungle animals, which may be viewed as visiting spirits.

➡ Don't litter.

➡ Adhere to the same feet taboos of Thai culture (see p783).

THAILAND PEOPLE & CULTURE

barefoot monks carrying large round bowls travel through the town to collect their daily meals from the faithful. The housewives are already awake steaming rice and sweep-ing their front porches with stiff bristled brooms. Soon business is in full swing: the vendors have arrived at their favourite corner to feed the uniformed masses, be they

MODERN MIGRANTS

Refugees from Myanmar first crossed into Thailand in 1984, when the Myanmarese army penetrated the ethnic Karen state and began a campaign of forced relocation. Today there are refugee camps around Mae Sot and elsewhere along the two countries' border, and the UN High Commissioner for Refugees (UNHCR) estimates that 140,000 people from Myanmar, mainly ethnic Karen, live in these camps. Refugees are assured protection from the military, but have little opportunities to gain an education, employment or an independent life because the Thai government does not recognise them as citizens or residents. Some have lived in this limbo state for decades. With the recent liberalisation of Myanmar, the two countries are working on repatriation agreements, though some of the camp residents have never been to Myanmar. There are also approximately three million economic migrants, predominately from Myanmar, working in Thailand; a minority of them have work permits and legal protection from exploitation.

khaki-clad civil servants or white-and-black-wearing university students.

Eating appears to make up the rest of the day. Notice the shop girls, ticket vendors or even the office workers: they can be found in a tight circle swapping gossip and snacking (or *gin lên,* literally 'eat for fun'). Then there is dinner and after-dinner and the whole seemingly chaotic, yet highly ordered, affair starts all over again.

Population

About 75% of citizens are ethnic Thais, further divided by geography (north, central, south and northeast). Each group speaks its own Thai dialect and to a certain extent practises customs unique to its region or influenced by neighbouring countries. Politically and economically the central Thais are the dominant group. People of Chinese ancestry make up roughly 14% of the population, many of whom have been in Thailand for generations. Ethnic Chinese probably enjoy better relations with the majority population here than in any other country in Southeast Asia. Other large minority groups include the Malays in the far south, the Khmers in the northeast and the Lao, spread throughout the north and east. Smaller non-Thai-speaking groups include the hill tribes living in the northern mountains.

Religion

Alongside the Thai national flag flies the yellow flag of Buddhism – Theravada Buddhism (as opposed to the Mahayana schools found in East Asia and the Himalaya). Country, family and daily life are all married to religion. Every Thai male is expected to become a monk for a short period in his life, since a family earns great merit when a son 'takes robe and bowl'.

More evident than the philosophical aspects of Buddhism is the everyday fusion with animist rituals. Monks are consulted to determine an auspicious date for a wedding or the likelihood of success for a business. Spirit houses *(phrá phuum)* are constructed outside buildings and homes to encourage the spirits to live independently from the family but to remain comfortable so as to bring good fortune to the site.

Roughly 95% of the population practises Buddhism, but in southern Thailand there is a significant Muslim minority community.

Arts

MUSIC

Classical Thai music was developed for the royal court as an accompaniment to classical dance-drama and other forms of theatre. Traditional instruments have more pedestrian applications and can often be heard at temple fairs or provincial festivals. Whether used in the high or low arts, traditional Thai music has an incredible array of textures and subtleties, hair-raising tempos and pastoral melodies.

In the north and northeast there are several popular wind instruments with multiple reed pipes, which function like a mouth organ. Chief among these is the *khaen,* which originated in Laos; when played by an adept musician it sounds like a calliope organ. It is used chiefly in *măw lam* music, a rural folk tradition often likened to the American blues. A near cousin to *măw lam* is *lûuk thûng* (literally 'children of the fields'), which enjoys a working-class fan base much like country music does in the US.

Popular Thai music has borrowed rock-and-roll's instruments to create perky teeny-bop hits, hippie protest ballads and even urban indie anthems. It is an easy courtship with Thai classic rock, like the decades-old group Carabao and the folk style known as *phleng phêua chii-wít* (songs for life). Alternative rock groups such as Modern Dog and Aparment Khunpa have defined Thailand's new millennial sound and a host of new-indie bands carry on the tradition.

SCULPTURE & ARCHITECTURE

Thailand's most famous sculptural output has been its bronze Buddha images, coveted the world over for their originality and grace. Traditional architecture is more visible as it is applied to simple homes and famous temples. Ancient Thai homes consisted of a single-room teak structure raised on stilts, since most Thais once lived along river banks or canals. The space underneath also served as the living room, kitchen, garage and barn. Rooflines in Thailand are steeply pitched and often decorated at the corners or along the gables with motifs related to the *naga* (mythical sea serpent), long believed to be a spiritual protector. Temple buildings demonstrate more formal aspects of traditional architecture and artistic styles.

THEATRE & DANCE

Traditional Thai theatre consists of six dramatic forms, including *khŏhn,* a formal masked dance-drama depicting scenes from the Ramakian (the Thai version of India's Ramayana) that were originally performed only for the royal court. Popular in rural villages, *li-gair* is a partly improvised, often bawdy folk play featuring dancing, comedy,

melodrama and music. The southern Thai equivalent is *mánohraa,* which is based on a 2000-year-old Indian story. Shadow puppet plays *(năng)* found in southern Thailand demonstrate that region's cultural heritage with Malaysia and Indonesia.

Food & Drink

Food

Thai food is a complex balance of spicy, salty, sweet and sour. The ingredients are fresh and zesty with lots of lemongrass, basil, coriander and mint. Chilli peppers pack a nose-running, tongue-searing burn. And pungent *nám Ъlah* (fish sauce; generally made from anchovies) adds a touch of the sea. Throw in a little lime and a pinch of sugar and the ingredients make a symphony of flavours.

Day and night markets, pushcart vendors, makeshift stalls, open-air restaurants – Thais eat most of their meals outside of the home as prices are relatively low and local cooks are famous for a particular dish. No self-respecting shoestringer would shy away from the pushcarts in Thailand for fear of stomach troubles.

For breakfast and late-night snacks, Thais nosh on *gŏo·ay đĕe·o,* a noodle soup with chicken or pork and vegetables. There are two major types of noodles: *sên lek* (thin) and *sên yài* (wide and flat). Before you dig into your steaming bowl, first use the chopsticks and a spoon to cut the noodles into smaller segments so they are easier to pick up. Then add to taste a few teaspoonfuls of the provided spices: dried red chilli, sugar, fish sauce and vinegar. Now you have the true taste of Thailand in front of you. The weapons of choice when eating noodles

THAILAND FOOD & DRINK

ISAN CUISINE: PUTTING THE FIRE IN SPICY

The holy trinity of Isan cuisine – *gài yâhng* (grilled chicken), *sôm·đam* (papaya salad) and *kôw nĕe·o* (sticky rice) – is integral to the identity of hard-working farmers and a de facto national dish for the region. The Isan diaspora has been so widespread that the triumvirate has now gone mainstream.

Every Isan town wakes to a veritable chicken massacre, in which side-of-the-road grills are cluttered with marinated carcasses, and wafts of smoke lure appetites. Beside the grill is an earthenware *khrók* (mortar) and wooden *sàak* (pestle) beating out the ancient rhythm of *sôm·đam* preparation: in go grated papaya, sliced limes, a fistful of peppers, sugar and a host of preferential ingredients. People taste the contents and call out adjustments: more *nám Ъlah* (fish sauce) or *Ъlah ráa* (fermented fish sauce, which looks like rotten mud). Everything is eaten with the hands, using sticky rice as a 'spoon', and a plate of fresh, chalky-tasting vegetables help offset the chilli burn.

> ### ℹ EAT LIKE A PRO
>
> In Thailand, chopsticks are used for noodle dishes and a spoon and fork for rice dishes. Many curries and soups are served in bowls but should be ladled on to a bed of rice rather than eaten directly from the bowl.

(either *gŏo·ay dĕe·o* or *pàt taı̂*) are chopsticks and a rounded soup spoon.

Thais are social eaters: meals are rarely taken alone and dishes are meant to be shared. Usually a small army of plates will be placed in the centre of the table, with individual servings of rice in front of each diner. The protocol goes like this – ladle a spoonful of food at a time on to your plate of rice. Dishes aren't passed in Thailand; instead you reach across the table to the different items. When you are full, leave a little rice on your plate (an empty plate is a silent request for more rice) and place your fork so that it is cradled by the spoon in the centre of the plate.

Even when eating with a gang of *faràng*, it is still wise to order 'family style', as dishes are rarely synchronised. Ordering individually will leave one person staring politely at a piping hot plate and another staring wistfully at the kitchen.

Drink

Water purified for drinking is simply called *náam dèum* (drinking water), whether boiled or filtered. All water offered in restaurants, offices or homes will be purified. Ice is generally safe in Thailand. *Chaa* (tea) and *kaa-fae* (coffee) are prepared strong, milky and sweet – an instant morning buzz.

Thanks to the tropical bounty, exotic fruit juices are sold on every corner. Thais prefer a little salt to cut the sweetness of the juice; the salt also has some mystical power to make a hot day tolerable.

Cheap beer appears hand-in-hand with backpacker ghettos. Beer Chang and Beer Singha (pronounced 'sing', not 'sing-ha') are a couple of local brands. Thais have created yet another innovative method for beating the heat; they drink their beer with ice to keep the beverage cool and crisp.

More of a ritual than a beverage, Thai whisky usually runs with a distinct crowd – soda water, Coke and ice. Fill the short glass with ice cubes, two-thirds whisky, one-third soda and a splash of Coke. Thai tradition dictates the youngest in the crowd is responsible for filling the other drinkers' glasses. Many travellers prefer to go straight to the ice bucket with shared straws, not forgetting a dash of Red Bull for a cocktail to keep them going.

Environment

Thailand's shape on the map has been likened to the head of an elephant, with its trunk extending down the Malay peninsula. The country covers 517,000 sq km, which is slightly smaller than the US state of Texas. The centre of the country, Bangkok, sits at about 14° north latitude – level with Madras, Manila, Guatemala and Khartoum. Because the north–south reach spans roughly 16 latitudinal degrees, Thailand has perhaps the most diverse climate in Southeast Asia.

The Land

The country stretches from dense mountain jungles in the north to the flat central plains to the southern tropical rainforests. Covering the majority of the country, monsoon forests are filled with a sparse canopy of deciduous trees that shed their leaves during the dry season to conserve water. The landscape becomes dusty and brown until the rains (from July to November) transform everything into a fecund green. As the rains cease, Thailand enters its 'winter', a period of cooler temperatures, virtually unnoticeable to a recent arrival except in the north, where night-time temperatures can drop to 13°C. By March, the hot season begins and the mercury climbs to 40°C or more at its highest, plus humidity.

In the south, the wet season lasts until January, with months of unrelenting showers and floods. Thanks to the rains, the south supports the dense rainforests more indicative of a 'tropical' region. Along the coastline, mangrove forests anchor themselves wherever water dominates.

Thailand's national flower, the orchid, is one of the world's most beloved parasites.

Wildlife

Thailand is particularly rich in bird life: more than 1000 resident and migrating species have been recorded and approximately 10% of all world bird species dwell here. Thailand's most revered indigenous mammal, the elephant, once ran wild in the country's dense virgin forests. Since ancient times,

DON'T GET TIED-UP BY THAI ETIQUETTE

Master this simple list of dos and don'ts (mainly don'ts) and you'll be an honoured guest.

➡ The king's anthem is played before every movie in a theatre and the national anthem is played twice a day (in the morning and evening) in public places. You are expected to stand respectfully during both.

➡ Thailand is a nonconfrontational culture. Don't get angry; keep your cool and things will work out.

➡ Feet are the lowest and 'dirtiest' part of the body. Keep your feet on the floor, not on a chair. Never touch anyone or point with your foot; never step over someone (or something) sitting on the ground. Take your shoes off when you enter a home or temple.

➡ Dress modestly (cover shoulders and knees) and don't sunbathe topless.

➡ Women aren't allowed to touch or sit next to a monk or his belongings. The very back seat of the bus and the last row on public boats are reserved for monks.

➡ A neat and clean appearance complements Thais' persistent regard for beauty. Frequent daily showers provide natural air-conditioning and a pleasing scent to your neighbours.

➡ Traditionally, Thais greet each other with a *wâi,* a prayerlike gesture. In general, if someone *wâis* you, then return the *wâi* (unless *wâi*-ed by a child or a service person). The placement of the fingertips in relation to the facial features varies with the recipient's social rank and age. The safest, least offensive spot is to place the tips of your fingers to nose level and slightly bow your head.

➡ All images of the king (on money, coins, stamps) are treated like holy objects.

annual parties led by the king would round up young elephants from the wild to train them as workers and fighters. Integral to Thai culture, the elephant symbolises wisdom, strength and good fortune. White elephants are even more auspicious and by tradition are donated to the king. Sadly, elephants, both wild and domesticated, are now endangered, having lost their traditional role in society and much of their habitat.

Environmental Issues

Like all countries with a high population density, there is enormous pressure on Thailand's ecosystems: in the middle of last century about 70% of the countryside was forest; by 2000 an estimated 20% of the natural forest cover remained.

In response to environmental degradation, the Thai government created protected natural areas and outlawed logging. Thailand designated its first national park (Khao Yai) in the 1960s and has added over 100 parks, including marine environments, to the list since. Together these cover 15% of the country's land and sea area, one of the highest ratios of protected to unprotected areas of any nation in the world. Since the turn of the millennium, forest loss has slowed to

about 0.2% per year according to the World Bank.

Though the conservation efforts are laudable, Thailand's national parks are poorly funded and poorly protected from commercial development, illegal hunting and logging, or swidden agriculture. The passing of the 1992 Environmental Act was an encouraging move by the government, but standards still lag behind Western nations. Thailand is a signatory to the UN Convention on International Trade in Endangered Species (CITES). Forty of Thailand's 300 mammal species are on the International Union for Conservation of Nature (IUCN) list of endangered species.

SURVIVAL GUIDE

ⓘ Directory A–Z

ACCOMMODATION

There is a healthy selection of budget accommodation in Thailand, starting at around 300B to 400B for a dorm bed or a bed-in-a-box single with fan and shared (cold water) bathroom. In Bangkok and the beach resorts it is hard to find anything under 700B.

PARTS OF A WAT

Planning to conquer Thailand's temples and ruins? With this handy guide, you'll be able to sort out your wats (Thai temple complex) from your what's that:

Chedi Large bell-shaped tower usually containing five structural elements symbolising (from bottom to top) earth, water, fire, wind and void; relics of Buddha or a Thai king are housed inside the *chedi;* also known as a stupa.

Prang Towering phallic spire of Khmer origin serving the same religious purpose as a *chedi.*

Wíhaan Main sanctuary for the temple's Buddha sculpture and where laypeople come to make offerings; sometimes it is translated as the 'assembly hall'; typically the building has a three-tiered roofline representing the triple gems (Buddha, the teacher; Dharma, the teaching; and Brotherhood, the followers).

Guesthouses are the primary budget options. These converted family homes or multistorey apartment-style buildings usually subsidise their low room rates with an attached restaurant, which cultivates a sense of community accompanied by lots of travel advice.

More impersonal are the Thai-Chinese hotels that cater to a local clientele and are sometimes the only option in non-touristed places.

During Thailand's peak season (December to February and June to August) prices increase and availability decreases, especially on the island and beach resorts.

Unless otherwise noted, reservations at the guesthouses are not recommended as standards vary from room to room and year to year. It is recommended to inspect the room beforehand since refunds are not a common practice. Advance payment to secure a reservation is also discouraged.

In our listings, high-season prices have been quoted. Enquiries for discounts can be made during low-tourist seasons.

Price Ranges

In big cities and beach resorts, the following prices ranges refer to a double room.

$ less than 1000B (US$30)

$$ 1000B to 3000B (US$30 to US$92)

$$$ more than 3000B (US$92)

In small towns, the following prices ranges are used:

$ less than 600B (US$18)

$$ 600B to 1500B (US$18 to US$46)

$$$ more than 1500B (US$46)

CUSTOMS REGULATIONS

Thailand allows the following items to enter duty free:

➻ reasonable amount of personal effects (clothing and toiletries)

➻ professional instruments

➻ 200 cigarettes

➻ 1L of wine or spirits

Thailand prohibits import of the following:

➻ firearms and ammunition (unless preregistered with the police department)

➻ illegal drugs

➻ pornographic media

When leaving Thailand, you must obtain an export licence for any antique reproductions or newly cast Buddha images (except personal amulets). Submit two front-view photos of the object(s), a photocopy of your passport, the purchase receipt and the object(s) in question, to the **Department of Fine Arts** (⌨ 0 2628 5032). Allow four days for the application and inspection process to be completed.

DRIVING LICENCE

An International Driving Permit is necessary to drive vehicles in Thailand, but this is rarely enforced for motorcycle hire.

ELECTRICITY

Thailand uses 220V AC electricity; power outlets most commonly feature two-prong round or flat sockets.

EMBASSIES & CONSULATES

Foreign embassies are located in Bangkok; some nations also have consulates in Chiang Mai, Phuket or Pattaya.

Australian Embassy (Map p648; ⌨ 0 2344 6300; www.thailand.embassy.gov.au/ bkok/home.html; 37 Th Sathon Tai (South); ⌚ 8.30am-4.30pm Mon-Fri; Ⓜ Lumphini exit 2)

Cambodian Embassy (⌨ 0 2957 5851; 518/4 Th Pracha Uthit/Soi Ramkhamhaeng 39; ⌚ 9am-noon Mon-Fri; Ⓜ Phra Ram 9 exit 3 & taxi)

Canadian Embassy (Map p648; ⌨ 0 2646 4300; www.canadainternational.gc.ca; 15th fl, Abdulrahim Pl, 990 Th Phra Ram IV; ⌚ 7.30am-12.15pm & 1-4.15pm Mon-Thu, to 1pm Fri; Ⓜ Si Lom exit 2, Ⓢ Sala Daeng exit 4)

Canadian Consulate (📞0 5385 0147; 151 Superhighway, Tambon Tahsala)

Chinese Embassy (Map p648; 📞0 2245 7044; www.fmprc.gov.cn; 57 Th Ratchadaphisek)

Chinese Consulate (📞0 5327 6125; chiangmai.chinsesconsulate.org; 111 Th Chang Lor, Tambon Haiya)

Danish Embassy (Map p648; 📞0 2343 1100; thailand.um.dk; 10 Soi 1, Th Sathon Tai) Consulate in Phuket.

French Embassy (Map p648; 📞0 2657 5100; www.ambafrance-th.org; 35 Soi 36, Th Charoen Krung; ⏰8.30am-noon Mon-Fri; 🚤Tha Oriental)

French Consulate (📞0 5328 1466; 138 Th Charoen Prathet) Consulates also in Phuket and Surat Thani.

French Bangkok Visa & Culture Services (📞0 2627 2150; ambafrance-th.org; 29 Th Sathon Tai)

German Embassy (Map p648; 📞0 2287 9000; www.bangkok.diplo.de; 9 Th Sathon Tai (South); ⏰8.30-11am Mon-Fri; Ⓜ Lumphini exit 2)

Indian Embassy (Map p648; 📞0 2258 0300-6; indianembassy.in.th; 46 Soi Prasanmit/Soi 23, Th Sukhumvit)

Indian Consulate (📞0 5324 3066; 33/1 Th Thung Hotel, Wat Gate)

Indian Visa Centre (Map p648; 📞0 2664 1200; www.indiavisathai.com; IVS Global Services, 22nd fl, 253 Soi 21/Asoke, Th Sukhumvit)

Indonesian Embassy (Map p660; 📞0 2252 3135; www.kemlu.go.id/bangkok; 600-602 Th Phetchaburi)

Irish Honorary Consulate (Map p648; 📞0 2632 6720; www.irelandinthailand.com; 62 Th Silom, 4th fl, Thaniya Bldg) Consulate only; the nearest Irish embassy is in Kuala Lumpur.

Israeli Embassy (Map p648; 📞0 2204 9200; bangkok.mfa.gov.il; 25 Soi 19, Th Sukhumvit, Ocean Tower 2, 25th fl)

Japanese Embassy (Map p648; 📞0 2207 8500; www.th.emb-japan.go.jp; 177 Th Witthayu/Wireless Rd)

Japanese Consulate (📞0 5320 3367; 104-107 Th Mahidon, Airport Business Park)

Laotian Embassy (📞0 2539 6678; www.lao embassybkk.com; Th Ramkamhaeng, 502/1-3 Soi Sahakarnpramoon, Pracha Uthit/Soi 39)

Malaysian Embassy (Map p648; 📞0 2629 6800; www.kln.gov.my/web/tha_bangkok/home; 35 Th Sathon Tai (South); ⏰8am-4pm; Ⓜ Lumphini exit 2)

Myanmar Embassy (Map p648; 📞0 2233 7250; www.myanmarembassybkk.com; 132 Th Sathon Neua (North); ⏰9am-4.30pm (embassy), 9am-noon & 1-3pm Mon-Fri (visa section); 🚤Surasak exit 3)

Nepalese Embassy (📞0 2391 7240; nepalem bassybangkok.com; 189 Soi 71, Th Sukhumvit)

Netherlands Embassy (Map p660; 📞0 2309 5200; thailand.nlembassy.org; 15 Soi Tonson; ⏰8.30-11.30am Mon-Wed, 8.30-11.30am & 1.30-3pm Thu (consular office); 🚤Chit Lom exit 4)

New Zealand Embassy (Map p660; 📞0 2254 2530; www.nzembassy.com/thailand; 14th fl, M Thai Tower, All Seasons Pl, 87 Th Witthayu (Wireless Rd); ⏰8am-noon & 1-2.30pm Mon-Fri; 🚤Phloen Chit exit 5)

Philippine Embassy (Map p648; 📞0 2259 0139; www.bangkokpe.com; 760 Th Sukhumvit)

Russian Embassy (Map p648; 📞0 2234 9824; www.thailand.mid.ru; 78 Soi Sap, Th Surawong) Consulate in Phuket.

Singaporean Embassy (Map p648; 📞0 2286 2111; www.mfa.gov.sg/bangkok; 129 Th Sathon Tai)

Spanish Embassy (Map p648; 📞0 2661 8284; es.embassyinformation.com; 193 Th Ratchadaphisek, 23 fl, Lake Ratchada Office Complex)

Swiss Embassy (Map p660; 📞0 2674 6900; www.eda.admin.ch/bangkok; 35 Th Witthayu/Wireless Rd)

UK Embassy (Map p660; 📞0 2305 8333; www.gov.uk/government/world/organisations/british-embassy-bangkok; 14 Th Witthayu (Wireless Rd); ⏰8am-4.30pm Mon-Thu, to 1pm Fri; 🚤Phloen Chit exit 5)

UK Consulate (📞0 5326 3015; www.british-consulate.net; 198 Th Bamrungrat)

US Embassy (Map p660; 📞0 2205 4049; http://bangkok.usembassy.gov; 95 Th Witthayu/Wireless Rd)

US Consulate (📞0 5310 7700; chiangmai.usconsulate.gov; 387 Th Wichayanon)

Vietnamese Embassy (Map p660; 📞0 2251 5838, 0 2251 5836; www.vietnamembassy-thailand.org; 83/1 Th Witthayu/Wireless Rd)

FESTIVALS & EVENTS

Many Thai festivals are linked to Buddhist holy days and follow the lunar calendar. Thus they fall on different dates each year. Many provinces hold annual festivals or fairs to promote their agricultural specialities.

Businesses typically close and transport becomes difficult preceding any public holiday or national festival. The following are popular national festivals:

Songkran Festival From 12 to 14 April, Buddha images are 'bathed', monks and elders have their hands respectfully sprinkled with water and a lot of water is wildly tossed about on everyone else. Bangkok and Chiang Mai are major battlegrounds.

Loi Krathong On the night of the full moon in November, small lotus-shaped boats made of banana leaves and decorated with flowers and candles are floated on waterways in honour of the river goddess.

FOOD

Our restaurant reviews are organised into the following categories:

$ less than 150B (US$4.50)

$$ 150B to 350B (US$4.50 to US$11)

$$$ more than 350B (US$11)

GAY & LESBIAN TRAVELLERS

Gays and lesbians won't have a problem travelling through Thailand as long as they are respectful of the culture and remain somewhat discreet. Prominent gay communities exist in large cities such as Bangkok and Chiang Mai, and gay-pride events are celebrated in Bangkok, Pattaya and Phuket. Although public displays of affection are common (and are usually platonic) between members of the same sex, you should refrain from anything beyond friendly hand-holding.

Gay, lesbian and transsexual Thais are generally tolerated in day-to-day life, though they face institutional discrimination and are often labelled as 'sexual deviants' and barred from studying to become teachers or from joining the military.

Utopia (www.utopia-asia.com) is a good starting point for more information on Thailand for gay or lesbian travellers.

INTERNET ACCESS

You'll find plenty of internet cafes, though they are in decline as smartphones become more prolific. The going rate is anywhere from 40B to 100B an hour. Connections tend to be pretty fast. Free wi-fi is available in guesthouses, restaurants and some hot spots. Mobile 3G networks are available, mainly in urban centres.

LEGAL MATTERS

In general, Thai police don't hassle foreigners, especially tourists. One major exception is in regard to drugs.

If you are arrested for any offence, the police will allow you the opportunity to make a phone call to your embassy or consulate in Thailand, if you have one, or to a friend or relative if not. Thai law does not presume an indicted detainee to be either 'guilty' or 'innocent' but rather a 'suspect', whose guilt or innocence will be decided in court. Trials are usually speedy.

MONEY

The Thai baht (B) is divided into colour-coded notes as well as coins of various sizes.

Coins come in 1B, 2B (gold-coloured), 5B and 10B denominations. There are 100 satang to 1B and occasionally you'll see 25 and 50 satang coins at department stores or supermarkets.

Notes are in colour-coded denominations of 20B, 50B, 100B, 500B and 1000B. In the dark it can be easy to mix up a 50B note with a 500B note so take care to segregate your bills by denomination. ATM withdrawals dispense cash in 1000B notes, which can be impossible for a taxi driver or market vendor to change. Break your big bills at 7-Elevens.

POST

The Thai postal system is relatively efficient and few travellers complain about undelivered mail or lost parcels. Never send cash or small valuable objects through the postal system, even if the items are insured. Poste restante can be received at any town that has a post office.

PUBLIC HOLIDAYS

Government offices and banks close on the following days:

New Year's Day 1 January

Makha Bucha Day, Buddhist holy day February (date varies)

Chakri Day, commemorates founder of the Chakri dynasty, Rama I 6 April

Songkran Festival, traditional Thai New Year and water festival 13–14 April

Coronation Day, commemorating the 1946 coronation of HM the King and HM the Queen 5 May

Labour Day 1 May

Visaka Bucha, Buddhist holy day May/June (date varies)

Asahna Bucha, Buddhist holy day July (date varies)

Queen's Birthday 12 August

Chulalongkorn Day 23 October

Ork Phansaa, the end of Buddhist 'lent' October/November (date varies)

King's Birthday 5 December

Constitution Day 10 December

New Year's Eve 31 December

SAFE TRAVEL

Although Thailand is not a dangerous country, it's wise to be cautious, particularly if travelling alone. Most tourist-oriented towns will have a **tourist police office** (☎1155), with officers who can speak English and liaise with the Thai police. The tourist police can also issue official documentation for insurance purposes if valuables are stolen.

It is not recommended to travel into Thailand's southernmost provinces of Yala, Narathiwat, Pattani and remote corners of Songkhla because of a low-level war between the national government and ethnic separatists.

Here are a few pointers to avoid problems:

➡ Avoid arguments with Thais (especially about money or matters of the heart and if alcohol is involved). Thais who feel that they've been embarrassed occasionally retaliate with violence.

➡ Don't wander around alone at night intoxicated, especially women and especially on Ko Samui and Ko Pha-Ngan.

➡ Don't buy, sell or possess drugs (opium, heroin, amphetamines, hallucinogenic mushrooms and marijuana); there are strict punishments for drug possession and trafficking that are not relaxed for foreigners.

➡ Don't accept an invitation to go shopping or play cards with a stranger you've met on the street. This is the lead-up to a well-rehearsed scam.

➡ Carry your personal effects (money, credit cards, passport) on your person to avoid theft or loss, especially during long-distance travel when stowed luggage can be accessed by thieves.

TELEPHONE

The telephone numbers in listings are written for domestic dialling; to call a Thai telephone number from outside the country, omit the initial '0'.

If you want to call an international number from Thailand, dial an international access code then the country code then the subscriber number. There are various international access codes with different rates per minute. Do an internet search to find out the promotional codes associated with your wireless provider.

TOILETS

Increasingly, the Asian-style squat toilet is less of the norm in Thailand. There are still specimens in provincial bus stations, older homes and modest restaurants. Some modern toilets also come with a small spray hose – Thailand's version of the bidet.

TOURIST INFORMATION

The **Tourist Authority of Thailand** (www. tourismthailand.org) has offices throughout the country that distribute maps and sightseeing advice. TAT offices do not book accommodation, transport or tours.

TRAVELLERS WITH DISABILITIES

Thailand presents one large, ongoing obstacle course for the mobility-impaired. The book *Exotic Destinations for Wheelchair Travelers* by Ed Hansen and Bruce Gordon contains a useful chapter on seven locations in Thailand.

VISAS

The Ministry of Foreign Affairs oversees immigration and visas issues. Check the Thai embassy or consulate for application procedures and costs. Changes to visa requirements are often monitored by **Thaivisa** (www.thaivisa.com).

Visa Exemptions & Tourist Visas

The Thai government allows citizens from most of Europe, Australia, New Zealand and the USA to enter the country without a prearranged visa. Arrivals by air receive a 30-day visa. Arrivals by land receive either a 30- or 15-day visa, depending on their nationality. Passport holders from UK, USA, Japan, Germany, France, Canada and

OPENING HOURS

The following are standard business hours in Thailand. Government offices and banks are closed public holidays.

BUSINESS	OPENING HOURS	EXCEPTIONS
Bars	6pm-midnight (officially)	Closing times vary due to local enforcement of curfew laws; bars close during elections and certain religious public holidays.
Banks	9.30am-3.30pm Mon-Fri	ATMs accessible 24hr
Clubs (discos)	6pm-2am	Closing times vary due to local enforcement of curfew laws; clubs close during elections and certain religious public holidays.
Government offices	8.30am-4.30pm Mon-Fri	Some close for lunch (noon-1pm), while others are open Saturday (9am-3pm).
Live-music venues	6pm-1am	Closing times vary due to local enforcement of curfew laws; clubs close during elections and certain religious public holidays.
Restaurants	8am-10pm	Some shops specialise in morning meals and close by 3pm.
Stores	local stores 10am-6pm; department stores 10am-8pm	In some small towns, local stores close on Sunday.

Italy receive the recently instated 30-day visa at all land borders.

Technically, without proof of an onward ticket and sufficient funds, any visitor can be denied entry but this is rarely enforced.

If you plan to stay in Thailand longer than your arrival visa allows, you should apply for the 60-day tourist visa from a Thai consulate or embassy before entering the country.

Visa Extensions

If you have already arrived in Thailand and wish to stay longer than your visa allows, you have two options for extension. You can cross a land border and receive a new 30-/15-day visa upon reentry (at no charge); or you can apply for a visa extension at a Thai immigration office and receive seven to 10 days with a fee.

The fee for a visa extension is 1900B and the number of days (seven to 10) depends on the discretion of the immigration officer. Bring two passport-sized photos and one copy each of the photo and visa pages of your passport. Dress neatly and do not hire a third-party proxy.

If you overstay your visa, the penalty is 500B per day, with a 20,000B limit. Fines can be paid at the airport or in advance at an immigration office. If you've overstayed only one day, you don't have to pay.

There are immigration offices in Bangkok, Chiang Mai, Ko Samui, Krabi Town, among other Thai cities and border towns.

VOLUNTEERING

Voluntary and paid positions with charitable organisations can be found in the education, development or public-health sectors. Volunteers typically work with marginalised communities – like migrants from Myanmar, hill-tribe villagers or rural northeastern Thais. There are also opportunities to work at animal sanctuaries or on environmental issues.

The following are volunteering organisations:

Andaman Discoveries (08 7917 7165; www.andamandiscoveries.com; Phang-Nga) Manages a learning centre for children of migrants from Myanmar, an orphanage and a school for disabled children in southern Thailand.

Cultural Canvas Thailand (www.culturalcanvas.com; Chiang Mai) Places volunteers in migrant learning centres, art programs and other social-justice projects in northern Thailand.

Isara (0 4246 0827; www.isara.org) Places teachers in underprivileged schools around Thailand; one of the few volunteer programs that is free and placements include housing and some meals.

LemonGrass (08 1977 5300; www.lemongrass-volunteering.com) A well-run Surin-based outfit places native English-speakers in local

primary schools where they work alongside the regular teachers.

Open Mind Projects (08 7233 5734; www.openmindprojects.org) Offers volunteer positions in IT, health care, education and community-based ecotourism throughout Thailand.

Wild Animal Rescue Foundation (WARF; www.warthai.org) Operates the Phuket Gibbon Rehabilitation Centre; job placements include assisting with the daily care of gibbons that are being rehabilitated for life in the wild.

WORKING

Teaching English is one of the easiest ways to immerse yourself into a Thai community. Those with academic credentials, such as teaching certificates or degrees in English as a second language (ESL) or English as a foreign language (EFL), get first crack at the better-paying jobs at universities and international schools. But there are hundreds of language schools for every variety of native English speaker. Ajarn.com has job listings and tips on teaching. TEFL certificate programs are increasingly popular, especially in popular tourist towns like Chiang Mai.

Getting There & Away

AIR

Thailand has one primary international airport (Suvarnabhumi International Airport) plus a budget carrier airport (Don Muang Airport) with some international connections in Bangkok. Chiang Mai and Phuket also have some international flights from nearby countries, especially China.

The following airlines fly to and from Bangkok:

Air Asia (0 2515 9999; www.airasia.com)

Air Berlin (001 800 12 0666 375; www.airberlin.com)

Air Canada (Map p648; 0 2718 1839; www.aircanada.com)

Air China (Map p648; 0 2108 1888; www.airchina.com)

Air France (001 800 441 0771; www.airfrance.fr)

Air New Zealand (Map p648; www.airnewzealand.com)

Bangkok Airways (1771; www.bangkokair.com)

British Airways (Map p648; 001 800 441 5906; www.britishairways.com)

Cathay Pacific Airways (Map p660; 0 2263 0606; www.cathaypacific.com)

China Airlines (Map p660; 0 2250 9898; www.china-airlines.com)

Delta Airlines (001 800 658 228; www.delta.com)

Emirates (Map p648; 0 2664 1040; www.emirates.com)

Eva Air (Map p648; 0 2269 62300; www.evaair.com)

Garuda Indonesia (Map p648; ☎ 0 2285 6470; www.garuda-indonesia.com)

Japan Airlines (Map p660; ☎ 001 800 811 0600; www.jal.co.jp)

Jetstar Airways (☎ 0 2267 5125; www.jetstar. com)

KLM Royal Dutch Airlines (Map p648; ☎ 001 800 441 5560; www.klm.com)

Korean Air (Map p648; ☎ 0 2620 6900; www. koreanair.com)

Lao Airlines (☎ 0 2236 9822; www.laoairlines. com)

Lufthansa Airlines (Map p648; ☎ 0 2264 6800; www.lufthansa.com)

Malaysia Airlines (Map p660; ☎ 0 2263 0565; www.mas.com.my)

Myanmar Airways International (Map p648; ☎ 0 2261 5060; www.maiair.com)

Nepal Airlines (☎ 0 2266 7146; www.nepalair lines.com.np)

Philippine Airlines (Map p648; ☎ 0 2633 5713; www.philippineairlines.com)

Qantas Airways (Map p648; ☎ 0 2632 6611; www.qantas.com.au)

Royal Brunei Airlines (Map p648; ☎ 0 2638 3050; www.bruneiair.com)

Scandinavian Airlines (Map p648; ☎ 0 2693 7888; www.flysas.com)

Singapore Airlines (Map p648; ☎ 0 2353 6000; www.singaporeair.com)

South African Airways (Map p648; ☎ 0 2635 1414; www.flysaa.com)

Thai Airways International (THAI; Map p648; ☎ 0 2288 7000; www.thaiair.com; 485 Th Silom; ⊗8am-5pm Mon-Sat; Ⓢ Chong Nonsi exit 3)

United Airlines (Map p660; ☎ 0 2353 3939; www.united.com)

Vietnam Airlines (Map p660; ☎ 0 2655 4137; www.vietnamair.com)

LAND

Thailand enjoys open and safe border relations with Cambodia, Laos and Malaysia and increasingly with Myanmar thanks to that country's recent democratic reforms.

Cambodia

Cambodian tourist visas are available at the border for US$20, though some borders charge 1500B. Bring a passport photo and decline offers from 'helpers' who want to issue a health certificate or exchange money.

Laos

It is fairly hassle-free to cross into Laos. Lao visas (US$35 to US$50) can be obtained on arrival and applications require a passport photo.

Malaysia

Malaysia, especially the west coast, is easy to reach via bus, train and even boat.

Myanmar

As of 2013, Myanmar opened four of its land borders to foreign tourists; meaning that you can now enter the country via these crossings and exit via others. In order to cross into Myanmar by land, you must have a pre-arranged visa. Some borders also have additional travel restrictions so make the necessary arrangements in advance. If you don't have a pre-arranged visa, you can do a 'day trip' to the border town for a fee.

❶ Getting Around

AIR

More and more provincial routes through budget carriers are making travel by air competitively priced with bus travel.

BICYCLE

Bikes are an ideal form of local transport because they're cheap, nonpolluting and keep you moving slowly enough to see everything. Carefully note the condition of the bike before hiring; most have dodgy brakes.

BOAT

Being a riverine people, Thais have colourful boats of traditional design. With a long graceful breast that barely skims the water and an elongated propeller, longtail boats are used as island-hoppers, canal coasters and river ferries. Small wooden fishing boats sometimes shuttle tourists out to nearby islands. Cargo boats and high-speed ferries make the island voyage as well. Boat services are often suspended during the wet season and schedules are subject to weather conditions.

BUS & MINIVANS

The Thai bus service is widespread, convenient and phenomenally fast – nail-bitingly so. Reputable companies operate out of the government bus stations not the tourist centres. Starting at the top, VIP buses are the closest you will come to a rock star's tour bus. The seats recline, the air-con is frosty and an 'air hostess' dispenses refreshments. Various diminishing classes of air-con buses begin to strip away the extras until you're left with a fairly beat-up bus with an asthmatic cooling system.

For trips to nearby cities, minivans are a convenient option. They depart from the market instead of an out-of-town bus station and, in some cases, offer hotel drop-off.

For long-distance trips, check out schedules and/or purchase tickets the day before.

CAR & MOTORCYCLE

Cars and motorcycles can be rented in most tourist towns. Inspect the vehicle beforehand, as fleets are often poorly maintained, and document any existing damage to avoid being charged for it. Always verify that the vehicle is insured for

THAILAND GETTING AROUND

ROAD SAFETY

Thailand rates as one of the most dangerous places to be on the road and many Western nations issue travel advisories for highway safety.

Fatal bus crashes make headlines, but more than 80% of vehicle accidents in Thailand involve motorcycles. Many tourists are injured riding motorcycles because they don't know how to handle the vehicles and are unfamiliar with local driving conventions.

If you are a novice motorcyclists, familiarise yourself with the vehicle in an uncongested area of town and stick to the smaller 100cc automatic bikes. Drive slowly, especially when roads are slick or when there is loose gravel. Remember to distribute weight as evenly as possible across the frame of the bike to improve handling. And don't expect that other vehicles will look out for you. Wear a helmet and protective clothing.

It is not advised for novice motorcyclists to drive in Ko Samui, Ko Pha-Ngan and other places where road conditions are poor.

liability before signing a rental contract, and ask to see the dated insurance documents.

Motorcycle travel is a popular way to get around Thailand. Motorcycle rental usually requires that you leave your passport as a deposit.

Thais drive on the left-hand side of the road – most of the time. Every two-lane road has an invisible third lane in the middle that all drivers use as a passing lane. The main rule to be aware of is that 'might makes right' and smaller vehicles always yield to bigger ones. Drivers usually use their horns to indicate that they are passing.

HITCHING

It is uncommon to see people hitching, since bus travel is inexpensive and reliable. Hitching becomes an option where public transport isn't available. In this case you can usually catch a ride, but remember to use the Asian style of beckoning: hold your arm out towards the road, palm-side down and wave towards the ground.

That said, hitching is never entirely safe, and travellers who do so should understand that they are taking a small but potentially serious risk.

LOCAL TRANSPORT
Săhmlór & Túk-Túk

Săhmlór (also written 'samlor'), meaning 'three wheels', are pedal rickshaws found mainly in small towns for short hops. Their modern replacements are the motorised túk-túk, named for the throaty cough of their two-stroke engines. In Bangkok, túk-túk drivers give all local transport a bad name. In other towns they tend to be more reliable.

You must bargain and agree on a fare before accepting a ride.

Sŏrngtăaou

Sŏrngtăaou (literally, 'two benches') are small pick-up trucks with a row of seats down each side. In some towns, sŏrngtăaou serve as public buses running regular, fixed-fare routes. But in tourist towns, sŏrngtăaou act as shared taxis or private charter; in this case, agree on a fare beforehand.

TRAIN

The **State Railway of Thailand** (SRT; ☑1690; www.railway.co.th) operates comfortable and moderately priced, but rather slow, services. All rail travel originates in Bangkok and radiates north, south and northeast. Trains are convenient for overnight travel between Bangkok and Chiang Mai and south to Chumphon or Surat Thani. The train can also dodge Bangkok traffic to Ayuthaya.

The SRT operates passenger trains in three classes – 1st, 2nd and 3rd – but each class varies depending on the train type (ordinary, rapid or express). Rapid and express trains make fewer stops than ordinary trains.

Fares are calculated from a base price with surcharges added for distance, class and train type. Extra charges are added for air-con and for sleeping berths (either upper or lower).

Advance bookings can be made from one to 60 days before your intended date of departure. You can make bookings in person from any train station. Train tickets can also be purchased at travel agencies, which usually add a service charge to the ticket price. If you are planning long-distance train travel from outside the country, you should email the State Railway of Thailand at least two weeks before your journey. You will receive an email confirming the booking. Pick up and pay for tickets an hour before leaving at the scheduled departure train station.

Timor-Leste

☑ 670 / POP 1.17 MILLION

Why Go?

With mountains to climb and untouched reefs to dive, Asia's newest country, Timor-Leste, is a winner. It's home to a youthful population and a diverse international presence that adds just the right amount of spice. Its capital, Dili, has all the bright lights, but venture out for wild cultural experiences. Stay in a grand Portuguese *pousada* (traditional Portuguese lodging) on a misty hilltop, or at a quiet island ecolodge. Get rowdy dancing the night away at a Timorese wedding, journey down roads alongside herds of buffalo, then wind up through rainforests dotted with coffee plants. Keep an eye out for whales as you grip the cliffs along the north-coast road. Photogenic white-sand beaches with aqua waters tempt swimmers, and for those who want to delve deeper, Dili-based dive companies have spent the past decade discovering world-class dive sites. Trailblaze your way through this amazing country; it's adventure with a smile.

Best Colonial Relics

➡ Pousada de Maubisse (p802)

➡ Pousada de Baucau (p800)

➡ Maubara Fort (p801)

➡ Balibo Fort (p798)

Best Places for Cultural Connections

➡ Australia Flag House (p801)

➡ Resistance Museum (p795)

➡ Santa Cruz Cemetery (p795)

➡ Chega! Exhibition (p794)

When to Go

Dili

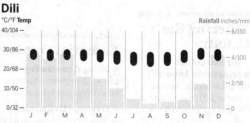

| **May–Aug** Dry season – there's little rainfall and good weather – though Dili gets a little dusty. | **Sep–Oct** As the heat builds up it's whale-watching season in Timor. | **Nov–Mar** Heavy rain makes the landscape lush but some roads are impassable in the districts. |

DON'T MISS

Even if you're not a scuba diver, getting under the water in Timor-Leste is a must. Grab a snorkel and ask around for the best spot for **snorkelling**. You won't believe your eyes.

Fast Facts

➡ **Area** 15,007 sq km

➡ **Capital** Dili

➡ **Emergency** police ☑121, ☑333 1283, ambulance ☑110, fire ☑115, ☑333 1031

Exchange Rates

Australia	A$1	US$0.90
Euro Zone	€1	US$1.37
Indonesia	10,000Rp	US$0.86
Singapore	S$1	US$0.79
UK	UK£1	US$1.66

Set Your Budget

➡ **Dorm bed** US$15–20

➡ **Local restaurant meal** US$3–$10

➡ **Snorkelling** US$10

Entering the Country

➡ **Nicolau Lobato International Airport** Taxi to centre US$10, airport transfer $10 (five minutes). *Microlet* (local bus) from main road US$0.25.

➡ **Dili Seaport** In central Dili, taxis around the city US$2.

At a Glance

➡ **Currency** US dollars. Anything under US$1 can be paid for in East Timorese Centavos (cv).

➡ **Language** Tetun and Portuguese (official languages), Bahasa Indonesian, other local languages.

➡ **Money** International ATMs in Dili only. Expensive hotels take credit cards.

➡ **Visas** Visa on arrival at Dili airport or seaport; US$30 for 30 days. Most nationalities need a visa in advance for land border arrivals.

➡ **Mobile Phones** Good coverage throughout major population centres. Timor Telecom, Telkomsel and Digicel SIM cards can be used in unlocked phones.

ITINERARIES

One Week

From Dili it's off to the eastern end of the island, stopping along the spectacular coast before overnighting in Baucau. Head to Ossu and trek to Mundo Perdido (The Lost World) before spending the night by a surging river at Hotel Wailakurini. Next, to Com for lunch then onto Tutuala, from where you can reach the sacred Jaco Island the next day for magnificent snorkelling. Return to Dili to explore museums and markets and cap off your trip by heading out to Atauro Island for a night.

One Month

As above, then head west to Liquiçá for luxury camping at Caimeo Beach. Head to the Indonesian border then turn inland to reach Balibo for a slice of history. Stay in Maliana and visit the enchanting Marobo hot springs. The next day head south via Bobonaro to Suai, with its pretty villages and beach, then turn east and head back into the mountains via either Ainaro or Same to Hatubuilico to climb Mr Ramelau. Next stop is Maubisse with its old Portuguese *pousada*, then back to Dili.

Essential Outdoor Activities

➡ **Diving & snorkelling** Visit the sacred Jaco Island to snorkel and swim in turquoise waters, or trek through Atauro Island's remote villages to Adara for magical snorkelling.

➡ **Trekking, Mt Ramelau** Watch the sunrise from Timor-Leste's highest peak; on a clear day you can see both coasts.

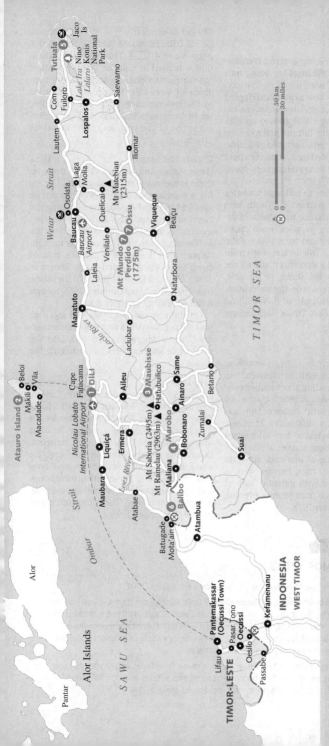

Timor-Leste Highlights

1 Go diving in **Dili** (p795) and enjoy being in one of the few cities where the reef is just steps away from the centre

2 Snorkel and relax daytrip-style on **Atauro Island** (p799),

or stay awhile in a beach bungalow at **Barry's Place** (p799) in Beloi

3 Venture to an *uma lulik* (sacred house) or to a

terraced waterfall outside **Maubisse** (p802)

4 Recharge at the **Marobo Hot Springs** (p802), a former Portuguese mountain retreat with breathtaking views

5 Peek over at Jaco Island from open-air thatched rooms on Walu beach, **Tutuala** (p801)

6 Make the pilgrimage to Australia Flag House in **Balibo** (p801), near where five

Australian-based journalists were killed in 1975

7 Relax in a bungalow overlooking a surging river in **Ossu** (p800) or trek to **Mt Mundo Perdido** (p800)

DILI

POP 234,000

Dili is a city undergoing a rapid transformation. Burnt-out buildings are being torn down and replaced with the city's first skyscrapers, and there's now a cinema, shopping mall and an array of stylish restaurants catering to Timor-Leste's new cashed-up elite and expat community. But the juxtaposition between haves and have-nots is inescapable. Throngs of unemployed men sit on the street gazing away while luxury Hummers speed past with tinted windows.

Dili is a good place to recharge batteries (literally) and base yourself for jaunts into the districts; it's a chance to indulge in international food, buy supplies, learn about Timor-Leste's history and meet some of the locals and the expats. Dili itself spreads from the airport, along the waterfront and all the way to the Christo Rei statue in the east. Most of the action occurs on the waterfront, or one or two blocks south of it. You'll find travellers' hubs at East Timor Backpackers and Castaway Bar.

◉ Sights

Waterfront
WATERFRONT

From children covered in seaweed to serious boatmen reading the weather conditions opposite the grand Palácio do Governo (Government Palace), Dili has a waterfront with a distinctive Timorese personality. It stretches for kilometres in a quasi-boomerang shape, with Farol lighthouse beaming at one end, and Lita Supermarket at the other. Further west is an esplanade dotted with gigantic 'look at me' embassies, which front vibrant evening fish & chicken stalls (p797).

Chega! Exhibition
MUSEUM

(☑ 331 0315; Estrada de Balide; ⊘ 9am-noon & 2-5pm Mon-Fri) FREE This must-see exhibition is housed in a prison where countless human rights violations occurred and hundreds of resistance figures were interned by the Indonesian military. The exhibition, set in the prison buildings and cells, gives a glimpse of the realities of the notorious prison.

Christo Rei Statue
STATUE

(Jesus Statue) Around 7km east of town on Cape Fatucama is the hard-to-miss Christo Rei, a popular morning and evening exercise spot for locals and expats. From the cape, the views of turquoise bays and green-covered mountains are stunning. As you climb the well-marked path up to Jesus, look for a little path after the last of 14 grottoes. It leads down to an often-deserted beach, known as Jesus Backside beach. A taxi to the statue from town should cost around US$6, though it can be difficult getting back.

On the way out to Christo Rei you'll go past the popular Areia Branca, a restaurant-lined beach where you can sink into the sand while sipping beers and watching the sunset.

Arte Moris
ART GALLERY

(☑ 331 0346; Av dos Mártires de Pátria, Comoro; admission free; ⊘ 9am-6pm Mon-Sat) FREE There's a distinct Bob Marley/boho feel to Arte Moris, a residential art gallery in what was Dili's domed Indonesian-era museum. Downstairs the collection features creative woodcarvings and paintings sprayed onto *tais* (woven cloth). Those with artistic bones and a yearning to hang around are welcome to impart knowledge. The compound is just west of the Comoro bridge.

LOCAL KNOWLEDGE

WHY DIVE TIMOR-LESTE?

Expat Kym Smithies has been diving Timor-Leste's sites since 2002.

What's so good about diving in Timor-Leste? Only 40 minutes from Dili you can dive pristine reefs filled with small colourful marine life. Healthy, colourful coral, small shoals of fish, the occasional reef shark and turtle, and a wonderful variety of macro-life are guaranteed. Nudibranch lovers will enjoy spotting a large variety of different species as well as frogfish, seahorses, mimic octopus and more.

Any particular highlights? Atauro Island is one of the few places where you may see large pelagic creatures like turtles, hammerhead sharks, whales and dolphins (mostly from the boat). Strong currents mean that most dives are drift dives.

Santa Cruz Cemetery CEMETERY
On 12 November 1991, Indonesian soldiers fired on a peaceful memorial procession at the Santa Cruz Cemetery. Although exact figures aren't known, it's estimated by experts that at least 280 civilians died, many of them after they were rounded up and trucked away by the military. British journalist Max Stahl filmed the bloody attack, and his footage features in the documentary *In Cold Blood*. The massacre at the Santa Cruz Cemetery is cited as a turning point in the independence struggle.

Xanana Cultural Centre MUSEUM
(☑ 331 2890; Rua Belarmino Lobo; ⊙ 10am-6pm Mon-Fri, to 4pm Sat) FREE This complex houses loads of memorabilia from Xanana Gusmão, and there is a library, free internet cafe, bookshop and exhibition. Artwork on display includes those Xanana Gusmão painted while imprisoned in Jakarta.

Resistance Museum MUSEUM
(☑ 333 1159; Rua Formosa; admission US$1; ⊙ 9am-5pm Tue-Sat) This museum commemorates the 24-year struggle against the Indonesians. The story of Falintil's resistance is brought to life with a timeline, photos, and exhibits of the weapons and tools of communication the East Timorese used in their fight for independence.

🏃 Activities
The reef fringing the entire north coast of Timor-Leste provides spectacular diving and snorkelling opportunities. Many sites, including the legendary K41 (located 41km east of town), are easily accessed by walking in from the beach, with dramatic drop-offs just 10m offshore in parts.

Compass Charters WHALE-WATCHING, DIVING
(☑ 7723 0965; www.compassadventuretours.com; Av dos Mártires de Pátria) Compass specialises in boat dives to the premier Atauro Island and north coast sites. Guided shore dives are US$50 each, while trips to Atauro Island including two dives and lunch start at US$150. Also offers a range of PADI courses with experienced dive instructors. It's next to Tiger Fuel.

Dive Aquatica DIVING
(☑ 7803 8885; www.aquaticadiveresort.com) The newest dive operator on the block, Dive Aquatica has brand new gear and offers US$45 shore dives, a range of courses and day trips to Atauro Island for US$180 (two dives and lunch). It's behind the Ocean View Beach Hotel in Bebonuk, just east of the Comoro River.

Dive Timor Lorosae DIVING
(☑ 7723 7092; www.divetimor.com; Av de Portugal) This dive centre offers shore dives (US$45) and day-trip diving around Atauro Island, including two dives from US$165 per person. It also has a training pool and runs the full range of PADI courses.

Dili City of Peace Marathon RUNNING
(www.dilimarathon.com) This full (42km) and half (21km) marathon is held each May, beginning at the Palacio Governu. It's not for the faint hearted, though there is a 7km fun run.

Tour de Timor CYCLING
(www.tourdetimorlorosae.com; registration US$500) Each September up to 300 cyclists make their way along the roads of Timor-Leste. Cheer them on or join in the rugged five-day challenge.

🛏 Sleeping
Dili doesn't have many cheap beds, and until the influx of UN and NGO staff wanes, prices will remain high.

East Timor Backpackers HOSTEL $
(☑ 7723 9821; info@easttimorbackpackers.com; Av dos Mártires de Pátria; dm US$12; ❄ @) This hostel is *the* meeting place for backpackers in Dili. Rooms are simple and there's a chilled-out bar out the back, free wifi and a kitchen for self-caterers. It also rents bikes (guests/nonguests US$3/5).

SPLURGE
The Esplanada (☑ 331 3088; www.hotelesplanada.com; Av de Portugal; r incl breakfast US$110; ❄ @ 🏊) has a great location right on the water and a restaurant that makes the most of the views. Two-storey blocks surround a pleasant pool oasis at this modern and stylish compound. After lounging about the spacious grounds, head up to the bar-restaurant for a cool drink as the sun sets over the sea.

Dili

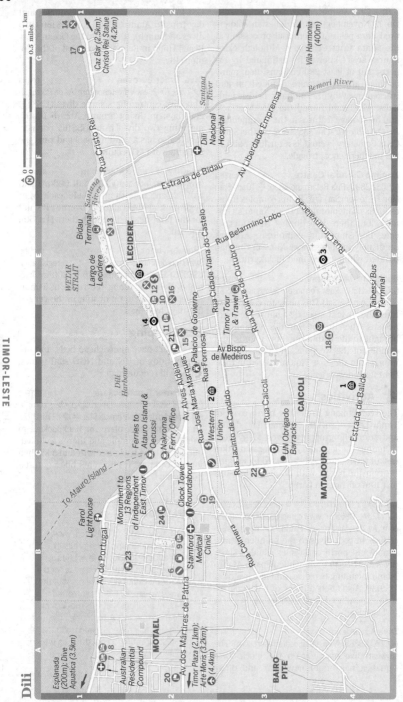

TIMOR-LESTE

N 0 0.5 miles
0 1 km

Esplanada (200m); Dive Aquatica (3.5km)

Caz Bar (2.5km); Cristo Rei Statue (4.2km)

Vila Harmonia (400m)

Bemori River

Santana River

Rua Cristo Rei

Dili Nacional Hospital

Av Liberdade Emprensa

Estrada de Bidau

Rua Circunvalação

WETAR STRAIT

Santana River

Bidau Terminal

LECIDERE

Largo de Lecidere

Rua Belarmino Lobo

Rua Cidade Viana do Castelo

Taibessi Bus Terminal

Dili Harbour

Palacio de Govierno

Rua Formosa

Timor Tour & Travel

Rua Quinze de Outubro

Av Bispo de Medeiros

Ferries to Atauro Island & Oecussi

Nakroma Ferry Office

Av Alves Aldeia

Rua José Maria Marques

Western Union

Rua Jacinto de Candido

Rua Caicoli

CAICOLI

To Atauro Island

Farol Lighthouse

Monument to 13 Regions of Independent East Timor

Clock Tower Roundabout

Rua Colmera

UN Obrigado Barracks

Estrada de Balide

MATADOURO

Av de Portugal

Stamford Medical Clinic

MOTAEL

Australian Residential Compound

Av dos Mártires de Pátria

Timor Plaza (2.1km); Arte Moris (3.2km); (4.4km)

BAIRO PITE

Dili

Rocella HOTEL $$
(📞7723 7993; Rua Presidente Nicolau Lobato 18; r incl breakfast & internet US$45; ❄@) Rooms here are comfortable and clean, and by far the best in this price range. There's a pleasant bar downstairs and the family who runs the place can cook up a Portuguese storm (meals US$7 to US$20).

Dive Timor Lorosae Guest House & Apartments GUESTHOUSE $$
(📞7723 7092; www.divetimor.com; Av de Portugal; dm US$30, r US$40-100; ❄@≋) The dorms at DTL have a sharehouse vibe and come with a shared bathroom, kitchen and lounge. The stylish apartments are set around the pool and are good value if shared.

Hotel Dili HOTEL $$
(📞331 3958; www.hoteldili.com; Av dos Direitos Humanos; r incl breakfast & internet US$50-150; ❄@) Hotel Dili offers pretty basic rooms but has good tropical fruit breakfasts and a waterfront location. The cheapest rooms are tiny and share bathrooms; all rooms have high-speed internet and satellite TV.

Dili Beach Hotel HOTEL $$
(📞331 0493; www.dilibeachhotel.com; Av de Portugal; dm US$20, r US$45-90 incl breakfast & internet; ❄@≋) The rooms are a little dark and the lime green walls don't do any favours but the pool is a bonus and the restaurant upstairs has a great range of pub-style meals (US$7 to US$14).

✖ Eating

Fish on a Stick MARKET $
(opposite the Australian Residential Compound; ⊙dinner) After sunset this stretch of road is a-smokin' (literally); fill up on delicious and simple chicken and fish dishes from the various stalls for US$0.25 to US$3.

Starco INDONESIAN, CHINESE $
(Rua Presidente Nicolau Lobato; meals US$4-5; ⊙11am-2pm & 5-9pm) You'll find tasty and fresh Indonesian and Chinese fare at good prices. It is located next to the Plaza Hotel.

Padaria Brasao BAKERY $
(Rua Presidente Nicolau Lobato; lunch US$1.50-7; ⊙7am-6pm) This Portuguese bakery has some of the best bread in town and the cafe serves coffee and cheap toasted sandwiches.

★Castaway Bar INTERNATIONAL $$
(📞7733 9000; Av de Portugal; mains US$6-16; ⊙6.30am-9.30pm Sun-Thu, to 1am Fri & Sat) A very popular two-storey joint overlooking the western waterfront. Crowds enjoy pizzas, steaks, burgers and Asian fare while taking in the cool breezes. Don't miss the lunch and dinner specials. Expats flock here for live music and drinks on Friday nights.

Little Pattaya THAI, LEBANESE $$
(Rua Christo Rei; mains US$5-12; ⊙noon-9.30pm) Located right on the beach, this Thai and Lebanese restaurant is a consistent favourite. It's half way to Areia Branca.

TRIVIA NIGHTS

Dili's social event of the week is Trivia Night. Test your knowledge every second Tuesday at 7.30pm at Dili Beach Hotel. It costs $5 per person and profits go to a local medical clinic.

Kebab Club TURKISH **$$**
(73089642; Rua Belarmino Lobo; mains US$4-7; ☺8am-9.30pm) Darn authentic Turkish fare, including delicious kebabs, velvety hummus and perfect baklava.

Lita Supermarket SUPERMARKET **$**
(Av dos Direitos Humanos; ☺9am-8pm) Sells a wide range of groceries and homewares and there's a fresh fruit & veg market across the road.

🍷 Drinking

Caz Bar BAR
(🕿7723 3961; Area Branca; ☺7am-9pm Mon-Fri, to 10pm Sat & Sun) Sink back in your chair on the beach at this popular place that tops the line-up of beachside joints east of town. At sunset, it's a toss-up between a beer and a fresh coconut milk.

Di Za BAR
(🕿7808 9877; Metiaut; ☺10am-midnight) Di Za effortlessly blends classy Balinese-styled decor with a West-African-inspired menu. Try the cocktails; they're the best in Dili.

🛍 Shopping

Alola Foundation HANDICRAFTS
(www.alolafoundation.org; Av Bispo de Medeiros) Alola sells *tais* (a piece of East Timorese woven cloth), sculptures, soaps and other crafts from around the country to support its work with the women and children of Timor-Leste.

Tais Market HANDICRAFTS
(Rua Sebastiao da Costa) Each region in Timor-Leste possesses its own distinctive style of *tais*. This market has *tais*, of varying quality, from all over the country.

Timor Plaza MALL
(Rua Presidente Nicolau Lobato, Comoro) Timor's first shopping mall is bustling with activity. There's a food court, an arcade and even a cinema. Timorese families flock here on weekends for events, while students hang around to use the free wifi.

ⓘ Information

As yet there's no tourist office, however, hotel staff are always a good source of info.

DANGERS & ANNOYANCES

Be aware that violent outbreaks can and do occur quickly, so stay clear of simmering trouble. Theft can be a problem. The city is all but deserted after dark, when you should take extra care.

INTERNET ACCESS

For free internet, head to the Xanana Cultural Centre or use the free wifi at Timor Plaza. Those staying in Timor-Leste longer may want to purchase a 3G USB dongle (US$25 to US$50) from one of three internet providers. Prepaid access starts at around $18 for 1GB.

MEDICAL SERVICES

Medical services in Timor-Leste are limited; serious cases may require evacuation to Darwin. Check with your embassy for other options.

Australian Residential Compound (🕿331 1555; Av de Portugal, Marconi) You don't have to be Australian to see the doctor here.

Dili Nacional Hospital (🕿331 1008; Rua Cidade Viana do Castelo) A cadre of Western volunteers assists locals at this busy place just east of Estrada de Bidau.

Stamford Medical Clinic (🕿after hr emergencies 7772 1111, 331 0141; Rua Mártires da Pátria; ☺9am-6pm Mon-Fri, 9am-1pm Sat) This spotless, Western clinic also opens after hours for emergencies.

MONEY

Banks are generally open between 9am and 3.30pm Monday to Friday.

ANZ (🕿332 4800; www.anz.com/timorleste; Timor Plaza) The ATM dispenses US dollars. Also has ATMs at the airport, Tiger Fuel, Lecidere and outside Hotel Dili.

Western Union (🕿332 1586; Rua José Maria Marques) Transfers funds internationally.

POST & TELEPHONE

Post Office (Av Bishop de Medeiros; ☺8am-5pm Mon-Fri) This new central post office is opposite the Alola Foundation.

The three telecom companies all offer phone and internet services.

Timor Telecom (🕿332 2245; www.timortelecom.tp; Timor Plaza; ☺8am-6.30pm Mon-Sat) Has phone and internet services.

Telemor (🕿7551 1555; www.telmor.tl; Landmark Plaza; ☺8am-8pm)

Telkomsel (🕿7373 7373; www.telkomcel.tl; Timor Plaza; ☺8am-7pm) Offers phone and internet services.

ⓘ Getting There & Away

The **Nakroma ferry office** (Av de Portugal; ⊙8.30am-5.30pm) is in the large building at the port. Buy your tickets one day in advance. When the Nakroma is running (at the time of writing it was on a much needed maintenance break) ferries for Oecussi (US$14, 12 hours) leave at 3pm Monday and Thursday, returning Tuesday and Friday.

Dili's bus 'terminals' (which are actually more like shabby shelters) are served by taxis and *mikrolet* (small minibuses). Buses are more frequent in the morning.

Tasitolu Terminal, west of the airport, is the hub for destinations to the west of the country (Ermera, Maliana and Liquiçá). Buses travelling to the east (Baucau, Lospalos, Viqueque etc) leave from Bidau Terminal, on the waterfront near Santana River. The Taibessi Terminal, at the huge Hali-laran market, is the stop for transport to Maubisse, Same and Suai.

ⓘ Getting Around

Mikrolet (US$0.25) buzz about on designated routes during daylight hours. They stop frequently over relatively short distances, so choosing a taxi might be quicker.

Cars are useful for night travel, but walking and using taxis should suffice otherwise.

Decrepit yellow (unmetered) taxis abound in Dili, and if you negotiate before you get in, most trips cost US$2. If you find a good driver, ask for their mobile number and see if they'll be your night driver, as streets as usually taxi-free by 9pm.

ATAURO ISLAND

After busy Dili, Atauro Island seems positively deserted. Its sandy beaches are gateways to broad fringing reefs and there's great snorkelling to be found all around the island. Walking trails lead through savannah and remnants of tropical forest.

Atauro Island's location, 30km from Dili over a section of sea 3km deep in parts, made it perfect for use as a jail by both the Portuguese and Indonesian governments. Dili's dive shops (p792) arrange underwater tours; you can arrange snorkelling trips with local fishing boats from US$15, or swim out. Ask the locals about the many hiking possibilities.

🏃 Activities

Hike through traditional villages in Atauro Island's interior (four to five hours) to reach a pristine white-sand beach at **Adara**, where you'll find some of the best snorkelling on the island. Underwater there's a beautiful coral drop-off and diverse marine life. Barry's Place can organise lunch (US$5) and a fishing boat (US$80 for one to five people) to get you back to Beloi.

🛌 Sleeping

Manukoko-Rek Guesthouse   GUESTHOUSE $
(☑7748 7301; r per person incl breakfast US$15) Located in Vila, this guesthouse has basic rooms with bunk beds and shared bathrooms. The Italian restaurant, run by an Italian priest, serves up delicious homemade gnocchi and pizza (meals US$5 to US$15).

Barry's Place   GUESTHOUSE $$
(☑7723 6084; www.barrysplaceonatauro.com; tent/r per person incl meals US$30/45) Just north of the ferry dock in Beloi, this ecolodge is the best place to unwind on Atauro Island. The sun-drenched thatched bungalows and tents are right on the beach, set up with hammocks to laze the day away on. Book ahead.

ⓘ Getting There & Around

Compass Charters (☑7723 0965; svscdili@telstra.com; Av dos Mártires de Pátria, Dili) next to Tiger Fuel, it runs a daily water-taxi service to Atauro Island (US$45 one way, 90 minutes). This is the most reliable way to get to the island.

The **Nakroma ferry** (☑728 09638; Av de Portugal, Dili) departs from Dili every Saturday at 9am and returns at 4pm, taking two hours each way. Fares for foreigners are US$5 each way.

The **Atauro Roo** (☑7747 8280; one way per person US$35) boat, run by an Australian couple, also travels to and from Atauro Island when there are enough people to justify the trip.

EAST OF DILI

With your own wheels (or on painfully slow public transport) you'll stumble across lime-green rice paddies, mangroves and idyllic beaches where buffalos (and the occasional crocodile) roam. Some of the best diving in the country is found just off shore.

Baucau

Baucau is a charming colonial town located 123km east of Dili. The Old Town boasts a Portuguese-era *mercado municipal* (municipal market) and a roadside town market where pyramid-shaped piles of potatoes, neat bunches of greens and mounds of maize form a colourful patchwork on the pavement. Head down through the market and take a left to spot the pink *pousada*. A clear natural spring runs from Old Town to the swimming pool (entry US$0.50) and down through the lush ravine to the delightful palm-fringed **Oso-lata beach**. The bland, Indonesian-built New Town (Kota Baru) is 2km from Old Town.

◉ Sights

Afalyca Community Art Centre   GALLERY
(afalyca@gmail.com) This is a small gallery and can arrange traditional dance perform-ances. It's on the left heading into Old Town from Dili.

🛏 Sleeping & Eating

Melita Guesthouse   GUESTHOUSE $
(✎ 7725 0267; Rua Vao Redi Bahu, Old Town; r per person US$15) With clean rooms, friendly staff and a huge open-air deck, Melita is one of the best budget options. Rooms have fans and private bathrooms. To find it take a left at the Pousada roundabout.

Baucau Beach Bungalows   BUNGALOW $
(✎ 7739 7467; Osolata; r per person incl breakfast US$15) Choose from a simple thatched bun-galow that sleeps five, or one of three rooms in a neighbouring Indonesian-style house (with shared kitchen and lounge). Meals can be arranged for US$6, with fish sourced from the local fishing boats.

Pousada de Baucau   HOTEL $$
(✎ 7724 1111; www.pousadadebaucau.com; Rua de Catedral, Old Town; r incl breakfast US$75; ❋ @) Despite its eerie history as a torture centre during Indonesian times, this large, salmon-pink building is still one of Timor-Leste's nicest hotels, with *tais* bedheads, timber floorboards and air con. The restaurant has good Portuguese food (meals from US$6).

Restaurante Amalia   PORTUGUESE $
(✎ 7726 2330; Old Town; mains US$4-7; ⊙ noon-10pm) Take a shady spot on the outdoor terrace and enjoy the sea views, along with delicious Portuguese-style meals served with a smile.

❶ Information

The characterless New Town overlooks the Old Town. On the road linking the two, **Timor Telecom** (internet per hr US$1; ⊙ 9am-5pm) has internet access and there's currency ex-change next door. There are no international ATMs, so don't forget to bring cash from Dili.

❶ Getting There & Away

Numerous buses drive the 123km between Dili and Baucau (US$5; four hours) each day. Buses also head to Viqueque (US$3, three hours) and Lospalos (US$5, four hours).

South of Baucau

South of Baucau are the lush hills where Fretilin members hid during the Indonesian occupation.

After 28km of rugged road you come to the large and impressive buildings of **Veni-lale**, a town wedged between Mt Matebian in the east and Mt Mundo Perdido (Lost World; 1775m) in the west. The road dete-riorates along the 16km to the misty village of **Ossu**. Some 9km south of here take a sharp left at the sign for **Hotel Wailakurini** (✎ 7741 3487; www.villagehotelstl.com; Loi Hunu; r incl breakfast US$25-50), a quaint ecolodge set up on a hillside near a surging river and wa-terfall. The meals are delicious and you can arrange hiking guides and cooking classes. Stay in the bungalow, which has breathtak-ing views. Travel past roadside waterfalls and white cliffs to the sprawling town of **Viqueque**, 63km from Baucau. The new town has a market and an abundance of Indonesian monuments. **Finlos Restaurant & Guesthouse** (✎ 7725 2827; r incl breakfast US$15) is a spotless place to stay about 2km north of the centre.

Buses and *mikrolet* run daily between Viqueque and Baucau (US$3, three hours) and on to Dili (US$5, four hours).

Around Baucau

South of Baucau is **Mt Matebian** (2315m). Topped with a statue of Christ and known as 'Mountain of the Souls', this holy place attracts thousands of pilgrims annually for All Souls Day (2 November). About 15km from Baucau is **Molia**, turn-off point for the end-of-the-road village of **Quelicai**. On the right-hand side of the road between the market and the church is the green **Mate-bian Guesthouse** (✎ 7726 8812; whitehead. simon@ymail.com; r per person incl meals US$25), a family-run guesthouse that offers walk-ing tours to Matebian and the family's *uma adat* (traditional house).

One or two *mikrolet* make the 33km jour-ney from Baucau to Quelicai in the mornings and early afternoons (US$2, two hours), or you can charter one from Baucau for US$17.

Com

You're literally at the end of the road in Com, a town focused on fishing and tourism. There's excellent snorkelling and a good, long beach (although it's beaten by the one at the 171km marker to the west).

Guesthouses line this stretch, as does the shell-studded **Com Beach Resort** (✆7728 3311; r US$25-120; ❄ @). Better value is the beachside, *uma adat*-styled **Kati Guesthouse** (✆7732 4294; r US$20), which has 10 small rooms (with shared bathrooms) and meals.

You'll be eating at the resort's **Ocean View Restaurant** (mains US$5-15) unless you book ahead at a guesthouse.

There are regular *mikrolet* from Lospalos to Com (US$2, one hour).

Tutuala & Jaco Island

The 50km of road from Lautem to Tutuala ventures past the shimmering waters of Lake Ira Lalaro, a few stilted Fataluku houses and through Nino Konis Santana National Park. The road ends on a bluff in Tutuala village, where there are sweeping views out to sea from a renovated Portuguese **pousada** (✆7806 9300; r US$25-35). You'll need a 4WD to tackle the steep 8km track down to **Walu**, a stunning white-sand beach. Turn left after the descent and you'll find thatched cabins at the community-run **Walu Sere** (✆7729 9076; r US$20). Fall asleep listening to waves lapping and wake to the stunning vision of Jaco Island, just offshore across the turquoise waters. Considered sacred by the Timorese, no one lives on Jaco Island or can stay there overnight, but fishers will take you across for US$8. Once you arrive, it's like being on a deserted tropical island. The water is crystal clear and there's an array of sea creatures and a beautiful coral reef.

Staff at Walu Sere can organise tours of the local rock-art caves.

You can take a daily *mikrolet* from Lospalos to Tutuala (US$3, three hours), or you can charter one from Com for about US$20, but you'll have to walk the last 8km down to the beach.

Lospalos

Lospalos, home to the Fataluku-language speakers, is mostly of interest for its market, nearby caves and Fataluku houses. A good budget choice for accommodation is

27@ (✆7796 8051; r per person US$15). Look for the traditional roof behind the office of the Plan children's charity. The five clean rooms have mosquito nets and a shared bathroom. The name derives from the day in August 1999 when the owner's husband was among scores of locals killed by the retreating Indonesians.

The **Lospalos Cultural Centre** (✆7799 7661; www.manyhands.org.au) is set to open its doors in early 2014, with a small gallery and cultural presentations available on request. It's in the centre of town at the old market.

Buses and *mikrolet* run between Lospalos and Baucau (US$5, four hours).

WEST OF DILI

The border with Indonesian West Timor is four hours west of Dili along a coast-gripping road punctuated by small villages selling differing wares.

Liquiçá has some grand Portuguese-era buildings, and its bustling market is a few kilometres east of the main town. **Caimeo Beach Camping** (✆7725 3339; www.caimeo beach.com; tents US$25-60) is the best place to stay west of Dili. Located right on the beach, the luxurious tents come with ready-made beds, fans, lights and hot showers. The attached **Black Rock Restaurant** (meals US$6-12, ◷ 8am-8pm) has tasty food and daybeds to lounge around on. The turnoff is just west of Liquiçá town.

At beachside **Maubara**, 40km from Dili, there's a Portuguese restaurant in the rejuvenated 17th-century Dutch **fort** and a handicraft market. *Mikrolets* depart Dili

TIMOR-LESTE AROUND BAUCAU

BALIBO

Inland from Batugade is the mountain town of **Balibo**, where five Australia-based journalists were killed by Indonesian soldiers in 1975.

The Australian flag the journalists painted for protection is still visible on **Australia Flag House**, which is now a community centre with a memorial inside.

A restored 18th-century Portuguese fort stands high on the hill, housing a visitor centre, and in 2014 this should be open as the Balibo Fort Hotel (www.balibofort.com).

and stop at both villages (US$1, one hour). Buses from Dili pass through the skimpy border town of Batugade (111km from Dili).

The hills of West Timor are in plain view over the rice fields adjoining Maliana, 26km inland from Balibo. The place to stay here is the Pousada Maliana (☑7742 2436; r incl breakfast US$25), which has clean rooms with shared bathrooms and sweeping views of the plains. From Maliana head south to Marobo and follow the signs to the *bee manas* (hot springs). You'll need a 4WD for the steep 6km track down. Once a former Portuguese mountain resort, the hot springs flow into a an old Portuguese-style pool surrounded by aqueducts covered in lime-green algae. The views are spectacular. Continue on to Suai (though roads can be diabolical during the wet season). You can also do a round trip to Same and Maubisse from here.

SOUTH OF DILI

From bare winding passes to rainforest canopies that shade coffee beans, the area south of Dili shows how diverse this country is. Coffee-country grabs you in Aileu before you hit the true cloud-dwelling town of Maubisse.

Maubisse

ELEV 1400M

Waking up in chilly Maubisse, 70km from Dili, and watching clouds rising, uncovering the village below, is a highlight of travelling in Timor-Leste. There are several restaurants near the buzzing market on the southern side of town.

Buses depart from Dili for Maubisse (US$3, three hours) each morning.

🛏 Sleeping

Hakmatek Cooperative GUESTHOUSE $
(☑7771 4410; r per person incl breakfast US$15) This is the place for basic thatched huts with sweeping views. Ask for permission to visit the *uma lulik* (sacred house) or stunning terraced waterfall nearby. Located in the village of Tartehi just south of Maubisse.

Café Maubisse GUESTHOUSE $
(☑7727 4756; r per person US$10) A cheap weekend option opposite Maubisse's elaborate church.

Pousada de Maubisse HOTEL $$
(☑7734 5321; r Mon-Thu & Sun US$20, Fri & Sat US$56) The historic, hilltop Pousada de Maubisse was formerly the governor's residence. While today it is a little rundown, it has good food (mains US$6) and gorgeous grounds that make for great-value weekday stays.

Hatubuilico & Mt Ramelau

Wild roses grow by the road and mountain streams trickle through the teeny town of Hatubuilico, located at the base of Mt Ramelau (2963m). Stay at the eight-room Pousada Alecrim Namrau (☑7730 4366; Rua Gruta Ramelau Hun 1; r per person US$10), where meals can be arranged for US$2.50. The uniquely decorated guesthouse is run by the village chief, who can arrange a guide (US$10) to get you up the mountain – and up at 3am in time to reach the peak for sunrise.

Hiking from the village to the Virgin Mary statue at the top of Mt Ramelau takes around three hours; with a 4WD you can drive 2.5km to a meadow from where it's a two-hour walk to the top. The trail is a

---

GETTING TO INDONESIA

Getting to the border Catch a direct Dili–Kupang bus through Timor Tour & Travel (☑7723 5093; Rua Quinze de Outubro 17, Dili; US$20); if booking from Kupang, call +62 9133 713 5720. Paradise Tour & Travel (☑728 6673, 723 5678; Rua Mártires da Pátria, Dili; US$23) offers the same service; if booking from Kupang, call +62 0394 4715423. Services depart each morning (12 hours); book in advance.

It's slightly cheaper but harder work to catch a local bus to Batugade (US$5). Walk through both border checkpoints and catch local transport on the other side (US$3 to Atambua, then US$7 Kupang; eight hours).

At the border You'll need an Indonesian visa, available from the Indonesian Embassy (p809) in Dili. Usual business hours apply.

wide walking path, with plenty of evidence of use by horses, and is very easy to follow. An open-air church sits on a plateau at the 2700m mark. From the peak the south and north coast is visible. Sunrise will give you chills, both down your spine and up your arms (temperatures average 5°C).

From Maubisse, the Hatubuilico turn-off is at the 81km post; you'll reach the village after 18km. If the road is passable, *angguna* (tray trucks) travel from Maubisse to Hatubuilico on Wednesdays and Saturdays. The price depends on the number of passengers, but the trip should cost around US$4 and take three hours.

Same & Betano

Same (Sar-may), 43km south of Maubisse, is a lush town at the base of a picturesque valley. There's a great little handicrafts market in the centre and a couple of good places to stay.

If you've got this far, it is worth making the simple 45-minute journey to the quiet black-sand beach at Betano (27km). From here, in dry season, you can journey east over narrow tracks through crocodile-infested mangroves to Viqueque (this takes six or more hours).

Mikrolets run frequently between Maubisse and Same (US$5, three hours) and between Same and Betano (US$1.50, 30 minutes).

🛏 Sleeping

Hotel Umaliurai HOTEL **$$**
(☑ 7725 3849; bmonagh@yahoo.com; r incl breakfast US$30-70) Hotel Umaliurai has the best beds in Same. Rooms have teak furniture, air con, cable TV and fridges. Meals (US$6 to US$12) are delicious.

Suai

Suai, the south coast's main town, sprawls 5km inland and is a confusing collection of villages. The main town, Debos, is dominated by a recently rebuilt cathedral, where, in September 1999, East Timorese were pushed to their deaths from the balcony. The now-demolished Our Lady of Fatima Church, also the scene of a massacre, is today the site of a memorial to 'Black September'. Sleep at the Fronteria Guesthouse (r per person US$10) and dine on Malaysian at chic Kamenasa Restaurant (meals US$10).

Angguna run between Suai and Maubisse (around US$4, at least five hours), via Ainaro (with its colourful church) or Same. You can also get here via Maliana.

OECUSSI

POP 63,000
The remote enclave of Oecussi is a Cinderella-in-waiting. Surrounded on all sides by Indonesian West Timor, Oecussi can be tricky to get to. But if you make the journey, you'll be rewarded with long stretches of beach and reef, some of the most beautiful *tais* in the country and pools of hot mud bubbling in its southernmost region. Relax into the slow pace of this beautiful and secluded district.

Pantemakassar, aka Oecussi town, is (literally) a one-taxi town. It's a flat, spread-out town with so little going on that any movement seems surprising. There are frequent sightings of dugong in the waters here, and the sheer coral drop-off about 20m offshore augurs well for snorkelling, though a 'croc watch' is essential. Just 1.5km to its south you can climb up to the old Portuguese fort Fatusuba, which is a whisper of its former self. Travel 5km along the coast west of Pantemakassar and you'll find Lifau, the site of the original Portuguese settlement. A rock-studded monument commemorates the first landing. The best beach begins 2km east of town on Pantai Mahata, which ends at a stunning red-rock headland.

Hot mud (for bathing in!) is found near the southern town of Passabe.

The pricier rooms at Rao Homestay & Restaurant (☑ 7755 6255; r US$15-40; ❄) are worth a look. Oecussi Amasat (☑ 7732 9755; oe-cusseamasat@hotmail.com; r incl breakfast US$55), run by an Australian owner and his wife from Oecussi, has the best beds in town. Restaurant Aries does a filling *nasi rendang* for US$1.25. Internet is available at Timor Telecom (Rua Francisco Mousino; ⊙ 8am-3pm Mon-Fri) east of the traffic circle. The Nakroma ferry (☑ 7728 0963; Av de Portugal, Dili; economy/business class US$4/14; ⊙ 9am-5pm) travels from Dili to Oecussi (12 hours) on Monday and Thursday nights. The return departure is around 5.30pm the following evening. In Pantemakassar the office is opposite the dock.

You'll need an Indonesian visa to get from Oecussi to West Timor overland (available in Dili). *Ojeks* (boys on motorbikes) can give you a lift from the border to town for a few dollars.

UNDERSTAND TIMOR-LESTE

Timor-Leste Today

Life after independence was turbulent, with a series of violent events (communal conflict, violence between the army and police and an assumed attempted coup) leaving many wondering: when do the good times start?

Well, finally, for many, the good times *have* started. The nation is playing host to international events and petroleum revenues are flowing from the Timor Sea. Timorese-owned businesses are in operation. The international presence is still here and newcomers arrive daily.

Fretilin, which led the struggle for independence during the Indonesian occupation, suffered from divisions in 2005. Prime Minister Mari Alkatiri sacked one third of the army in March 2006 and, in the ensuing months of rioting, more than 150,000 people fled their homes. Relative peace only returned after public demonstrations forced Alkatiri to resign, and the UN force was beefed up again. In 2007, after a year as acting prime minister, José Ramos-Horta was elected president of Timor-Leste with 70% of the vote. The vote for prime minister was not as clear-cut. Xanana Gusmão's National Congress for Timorese Reconstruction (CNRT) came second to Fretilin, winning 24% of the votes to Fretilin's 29%. However, CNRT quickly formed a coalition with other parties and Gusmão was sworn in as prime minis-

ter. Angry Fretilin supporters rioted, causing damage around the country and boosting the numbers of the more than 100,000 people already living in crowded internally displaced persons camps. In February 2008, Ramos-Horta was shot and injured near his home during an alleged attempted coup led by former naval commander and Timor-Leste Defence Force (F-FDTL) Major Alfreido Reinado. Reinado, who had been playing a cat-and-mouse game with Australian forces since escaping from jail in 2006, was killed at the scene by Ramos-Horta's security. Since 2008 Timor-Leste has been a safer and more stable country. Elections in 2012 were peaceful and the UN and International Stabilisation Force (Australian and New Zealand forces) both withdrew without any problems. The nation's focus is now on development rather than security, but with the charismatic Gusmão set to retire in the near future, this could be a new test for democracy in Timor.

History

Portugal Settles In

Little is known of Timor before AD 1500, although Chinese and Javanese traders visited the island from at least the 13th century, and possibly as early as the 7th century. These traders searched the coastal settlements for aromatic sandalwood and beeswax. Portuguese traders arrived between 1509 and 1511, but it wasn't until 1642 that the Topasses (descendents of Dominicans from nearby islands) established the first Portuguese set-

---

CAST OF CHARACTERS

Two men form the face of modern-day Timor-Leste.

Xanana Gusmão is Timor-Leste's charismatic prime minister. Gusmão was a leader of guerrilla forces from 1978 until 1992, when he was captured and imprisoned in Jakarta. He became the first president of the country, and earned the enmity of many of his old Fretilin brethren by breaking with the party after independence. Following the troubled 2007 parliamentary elections, Gusmão was named prime minister, leading the National Congress for Timorese Reconstruction (CNRT) party. His wife is Australian-born Kirsty Sword Gusmão, who runs the prominent charity the Alola Foundation. Gusmão has announced his retirement in 2014 and it remains unclear who will replace him.

José Ramos-Horta is the magnetic Nobel Prize winner who spent 20 years in exile during the Indonesian occupation. He took over as prime minister after Alkatiri was forced from office in 2006, and was elected president in 2007 with a huge margin. In 2008 he was shot during an alleged assassination attempt and recovered in Darwin, Australia. In 2012 the widely respected Taur Matan Ruak, a former leader of the resistance army FALINTIL, defeated him at the polls.

tlement at Lifau in Oecussi and set about converting the Timorese to Catholicism.

To counter the Portuguese, the Dutch established a base at Kupang in western Timor in 1653. The Portuguese appointed an administrator to Lifau in 1656, but the Topasses went on to become a law unto themselves, driving out the Portuguese governor in 1705.

By 1749 the Topasses controlled central Timor and marched on Kupang, but the Dutch won the ensuing battle, expanding their control of western Timor in the process. On the Portuguese side, after more attacks from the Topasses in Lifau, the colonial base was moved east to Dili in 1769.

The 1859 Treaty of Lisbon divided Timor, giving Portugal the eastern half, together with the north-coast pocket of Oecussi; this was formalised in 1904. Portuguese Timor was a sleepy and neglected outpost ruled through a traditional system of *liurai* (local chiefs). Control outside Dili was limited and it wasn't until the 20th century that the Portuguese intervened in a major way in the interior.

World War II

In 1941, Australia sent a small commando force into Portuguese Timor to counter the Japanese, deliberately breaching the colony's neutral status. Although the military initiative angered neutral Portugal and dragged Portuguese Timor into the Pacific War, it slowed the Japanese expansion. Australia's success was largely due to the support it received from the locals, including young *creados* (young Timorese boys who assisted Australian servicemen during WWII). In 1942 the Portuguese handed control of Portuguese Timor to the Japanese. Japanese soldiers razed villages, seized food and killed Timorese in areas where Australians were operating. By the end of the war, between 40,000 and 60,000 Timorese had died.

Portugal Pulls Out, Indonesia Invades

After WWII the colony reverted to Portuguese rule. After the Carnation Revolution in Portugal on 25 April 1974, Lisbon set about discarding its colonial empire. Within a few weeks political parties had formed in Timor-Leste, and the Timorese Democratic Union (UDT) attempted to seize power in August 1975. A brief but brutal civil war saw UDT's rival Fretilin (previously known as the Asso-

ciation of Timorese Social Democrats) come out on top, and it urgently declared the independent existence of the Democratic Republic of Timor-Leste on 28 November, amidst an undeclared invasion by Indonesia. On 7 December Indonesia finally launched their full-scale attack on Dili after months of incursions (including at Balibo, where five Australia-based journalists were killed).

Anti-communist Indonesia feared an independent Timor-Leste governed by a left-leaning Fretilin would bring communism to its door, and commenced its invasion of Timor-Leste just a day after Henry Kissinger and Gerald Ford departed Jakarta, having tacitly given their assent. (Indeed, the Americans urged the Indonesians to conduct a swift campaign so that the world wouldn't see them using weapons the US had provided). Australia and Britain also sided with Indonesia.

Falintil, the military wing of Fretilin, fought a guerrilla war against Indonesian troops (which numbered 35,000 by 1976) with marked success in the first few years, but weakened considerably thereafter, though the resistance continued. The cost of the takeover to the Timorese was huge; it's estimated that up to 183,000 died in the hostilities, and the ensuing disease and famine.

By 1989 Indonesia had things firmly under control and opened Timor-Leste to limited controlled tourism. On 12 November 1991, Indonesian troops fired on protesters who'd gathered at the Santa Cruz Cemetery in Dili to commemorate the killing of an independence activist. With the event captured on film and aired around the world, the Indonesian government admitted to 19 killings (later increased to more than 50), although it's estimated that over 280 died in the massacre. While Indonesia introduced a civilian administration, the military remained in control. Aided by secret police and civilian pro-Indonesian militia to crush dissent, reports of arrest, torture and murder were commonplace.

Independence

After Indonesia's President Soeharto resigned in May 1998, his replacement BJ Habibie unexpectedly announced a referendum for autonomy in Timor-Leste. January 1999 marked the commencement of attacks by Indonesian military-backed militias who began terrorising the population to coerce them to reject independence.

Attacks peaked in April 1999, just prior to the arrival of the UN Electoral Mission, when, according to a report commissioned by the UN Office of the High Commissioner for Human Rights, up to 60 people were massacred near Liquiçá church. Other attacks occurred in Dili and Maliana while Indonesian authorities watched on. Attacks escalated in the weeks prior to the vote, with thousands seeking refuge in the hills away from the reach of the TNI and militia.

Despite threats, intimidation and brutality, on 30 August 1999, Timor-Leste voted overwhelmingly (78.5%) for independence from, rather than autonomy within, Indonesia. Though the Indonesian government promised to respect the results of the UN-sponsored vote, militias and Indonesian forces went on a rampage, killing people, burning and looting buildings and destroying infrastructure.

While the world watched in horror, the UN was attacked and forced to evacuate, leaving the Timorese defenceless. On 20 September, weeks after the main massacres in Suai, Dili, Maliana and Oecussi, the Australian-led International Force for East Timor (INTERFET) arrived in Dili. The Indonesian forces and their militia supporters left for West Timor, leaving behind an incomprehensible scene of destruction. Half a million people had been displaced, and telecommunications, power installations, bridges, government buildings, shops and houses were destroyed. Today these physical scars remain.

The UN set up a temporary administration during the transition to independence, and aid and foreign workers flooded into the country. As well as physically rebuilding the country, Timor-Leste has had to create a civil service, police, judiciary, education, health system and so on, with staff recruited and trained from scratch.

The UN handed over government to Timor-Leste on 20 May 2002. Falintil leader Xanana Gusmão was elected president of the new nation, and the long-time leader of Fretilin, Mari Alkatiri, who ran the party from exile in Mozambique, was chosen as prime minister.

Birth Pangs

In December 2002, Dili was the scene of riots as years of poverty and frustration proved too much for the nascent democracy. The economy was in a shambles and people were ready for things to start improving – and fast. But without any viable industry or employment potential, Timor-Leste was reliant almost entirely on foreign aid.

Only a small UN contingent remained in Timor-Leste by mid-2005. As the number of outsiders shrank, the challenges of creating a new nation from the ground up became all too apparent. Parliamentary factions squabbled while the enormous needs of the people festered.

The Future

Timor-Leste continues to rely partly on foreign money, and proceeds from its petroleum fields are filtering through.

In 2006 Australia and Timor-Leste signed an agreement to give US$10 billion in oil revenue to each country over the next 40 years, but Timor-Leste is attempting to annul the treaty, claiming Australian intelligence agencies bugged Timor's cabinet room during negotiations. During the negotiations, Australia's Howard government was accused of using bullying tactics to deny the struggling and poor country its fair share of the money (initially offering only 20%, later agreeing on a 50/50 split). The arbitration case is a David and Goliath battle, and one that could monumentally impact Timor-Leste's oil revenues.

High in the hills outside Dili is another natural resource: coffee. Some 100,000 people work seasonally to produce arabica beans, noted for their cocoa and vanilla character. Shade-grown and organic, Timorese coffee is prized by companies such as Starbucks, and production is increasing.

Timor-Leste's tourism industry has great potential, although there needs to be a perception of stability for numbers to grow beyond the 1500 or so people who visit annually.

People & Culture

The National Psyche

Timor-Leste's identity is firmly rooted in its survival of extreme hardship and foreign occupation. As a consequence of the long and difficult struggle for independence, the people of Timor-Leste are profoundly politically aware – not to mention proud and loyal. While there is great respect for elders and church and community leaders, there lurks a residual suspicion surrounding foreign occupiers, most recently in the form of the UN. In a country where Catholicism cloaks animistic beliefs and practices, religious beliefs also greatly inform the national consciousness.

Lifestyle

Most East Timorese lead a subsistence lifestyle: what is farmed (or caught) is eaten. Large families are common (the birth rate is 7.7 children per woman) and infant mortality remains high. According to the World Food Program, food insecurity is widespread – one third of the population regularly experience food shortages. Infrastructure remains limited; only a few towns have 24-hour electricity and running water. Roads are particularly dismal.

Family life exists in simple thatched huts, though rising wages have meant that satellite dishes are appearing beside even the most basic huts, beaming Indonesian TV into homes. NGOs and aid projects have worked to create self sufficiency, but the ability to rise above poverty seems to be impossible for many as bad roads and drought or floods play havoc. Motorised vehicles remain rare; on weekends, buses are packed with those heading to the family events that form the backbone of Timorese life.

Population

Timor-Leste has at least a dozen indigenous groups, the largest being the Tetun (about 25% of the total population), who live around Suai, Dili and Viqueque. The next largest group (around 10%) is the Mambai, who live in the mountains of Maubisse, Ainaro and Same. Other groups each account for 5% or less of the total population. The Kemak live in the Ermera and Bobonaro districts; the Bunak also live in Bobonaro, and their territory extends into West Timor and the Suai area. The Fataluku people are famous for their high-peaked houses in the area around Lospalos. More groups are scattered among the interior mountains.

Religion

Religion is an integral part of daily life for most Timorese. Recent estimates indicate 98% of Timor-Leste's population is Catholic (underpinned by animist beliefs), 1% is Muslim and 1% Protestant.

LANGUAGE? WHICH LANGUAGE?

Most Timorese speak four or five languages. On the street you'll hear Tetun (also known as Tetum), one of two official languages, and most people also speak a regional dialect (one of 16). Some older folk speak Portuguese (the other official language), while those who were educated or working between 1975 and 1999 speak Bahasa Indonesia. Any attempt to communicate in Tetun will be greeted with big smiles. Lonely Planet's *East Timor Phrasebook* is a handy (and compact) introduction.

Indigenous religions revolve around an earth mother, from whom all humans are born and shall return to after death, and her male counterpart, the god of the sky or sun. These are accompanied by a complex web of spirits from ancestors and nature. The *matan d'ok* (medicine man) is the village mediator with the spirits; he can divine the future and cure illness. Many people believe in various forms of black magic and it's not uncommon for people to wish evil spells upon their rivals.

Arts

MUSIC & DANCE

The Timorese love a party, and celebrate with *tebe* (dancing) and singing. They're serious about their dancing; weddings often involve all-night three-step sessions. Music has been passed down through the years and changed little during Indonesian times. Traditional trancelike drumming is used in ceremonies, while Timorese rock and hip-hop groups are popular. Country-and-western style is popular, too, and features plenty of guitar use and the usual lovelorn themes.

TEXTILES

Throughout the country, women weave *tais* using small back-strap looms. Each region has its own style of *tais* and they're usually used as skirts or shawls for men (*tais mane*) or sewn up to form a tube skirt/dress for women (*tais feto*). Some are made with organic dyes. Some weavers have cottoned on that a *tais* with the words 'Timor-Leste 2014' or similar woven into it makes a good souvenir.

TIMOR-LESTE PEOPLE & CULTURE

Environment

The Land

With an area of 15,007 sq km, Timor-Leste consists of the eastern half of the island of Timor, Atauro and Jaco Islands, and the enclave of Oecussi on the north coast, 70km to the west and surrounded by Indonesian West Timor.

Once part of the Australian continental shelf, Timor fully emerged from the ocean only four million years ago, and is therefore composed mainly of marine sediment, principally limestone. Rugged mountains, a product of the collision with the Banda Trench to the north, run the length of the country, the highest of which is Mt Ramelau (2963m).

Wildlife

Timor-Leste is squarely in the area known as Wallacea, a kind of crossover zone between Asian and Australian plants and animals, and one of the most biologically distinctive areas on earth.

Timor-Leste's north coast is a global hot spot of whale and dolphin activity, and its coral reefs are home to a diverse range of marine life. Species spotted include dugongs, blue whales, whale sharks and dolphins. More than 240 species of bird have been recorded in its skies. The Lautem district was declared a national park partly because of its rich bird life: it's home to honeyeaters, critically endangered yellow-crested cockatoos and endangered *wetar* ground-doves. The number of mammals and reptiles in the wild is limited, though crocodiles and snakes make appearances.

Environmental Issues

Timor-Leste's first national park, the Nino Konis Santana National Park, was declared in 2008 – a 123,000-hectare parcel of land (including some tropical forest) and sea at the country's eastern tip, also incorporating Jaco Island and Tutuala. Most of the country, however, is suffering from centuries of deforestation, and erosion is a huge problem. Roads and even villages have been known to slip away.

SURVIVAL GUIDE

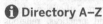 **Directory A–Z**

ACCOMMODATION

Dili's accommodation is nothing to write home about, expect sit-down loos and air conditioning and, well, little more. Accommodation with adjoining restaurants/bars is a good idea for those who'd prefer not to travel around at night. Elsewhere, don't expect anything swank – if you get a clean room with good mosquito nets and a few hours of electricity for reading and a fan, you're doing well.

In most places you will be able to find some sort of accommodation, even if it is a homestay (offer US$10 a night). Washing facilities are likely to be Indonesian *mandi* style. A *mandi* is a large concrete water tank from where you scoop water to wash yourself. Don't jump in!

The costs per room are indicated in our reviews by the following categories:

$ less than US$15
$$ US$15 to US$100
$$$ more than US$100

ACTIVITIES

There are many opportunities for the adventure traveller; think limestone caves, rugged mountain tracks and secret waterfalls. For many activities it will be BYO equipment, or check with Dili's adventure-travel company.

Diving

The diving is sublime in Timor-Leste, and there are three companies that can show you what's out there. Dive Timor Lorosae (p795) runs a range of PADI courses; Compass Charters (p795) has its own boat and takes dive trips out to Atauro Island, while new kid on the block Dive Aquatica (p795) has brand new gear. Conditions are best during the dry season (May to November), when visibility is at around 20m to 30m.

Hiking

Serious hikers are popping up in villages around the country (and surprising the locals), and 10-day north-to-south coast hikes are not unheard of. Popular day-long hikes include those to the summit of Mt Ramelau (from where you can see the south and north coasts of Timor-Leste) and to the sacred peak of Mt Matebian. Both mountains have accommodation nearby that can provide guides. There's also hiking in Atauro's interior. Check www.trekkingeasttimor.org for more information.

CUSTOMS REGULATIONS

You can bring the following into Timor-Leste:
Alcohol 1.5L of any type
Cigarettes 200

Money Up to US$10,000 per person but amounts over US$5000 must be declared. No restrictions on taking cash out of the country.

DANGERS & ANNOYANCES

Malaria and dengue are concerns for those staying in Timor-Leste; take precautions. Stick to bottled water, avoid tap water and ice, and wipe off water from the tops of beverage cans before drinking. Antibiotics and other pharmaceuticals are easily bought in Dili but are hard to find elsewhere.

Drivers should always be on the lookout for vehicles speeding around corners, roaming children and livestock, potholes, speed humps and landslides. Cases of theft occur most frequently from cars, with mobile phones a prime target. Women should be wary of exercising in isolated spots in Dili, as there have been attacks. Given the regular bouts of political instability in Timor-Leste, check the current situation before you visit (although government travel advisories are usually cautious in the extreme).

ELECTRICITY

At hotels you can often plug in Australian flat three-pin plugs, in other places two-pin (round) plugs are used.

EMBASSIES & CONSULATES

A number of countries have embassies in Dili. Citizens of the UK should contact their embassy in Indonesia.

Australian Embassy (332 2111; www.timorleste.embassy.gov.au; Av dos Mártires de Pátria) They also assist Canadian citizens.

European Commission (331 1580; delegation-timor-leste@eeas.europa.eu; Casa Europa, Av Presidente Nicolau Lobato)

French Representative Office (731 4081; frcoopedili@gmail.com; Casa Europa, Av Presidente Nicolau Loboto)

Indonesian Embassy (331 7107; www.kbri dili.com; Rua Gov Maria de Serva Rosa)

Irish Representative Office (332 4880; www.irishaid.gov.ie; Rua Alferes Duartre Arbiro 12, Dili)

New Zealand Embassy (331 0087; dili@mfat.govt.nz; Rua Geremias)

US Embassy (332 4684; www.timor-leste.usembassy.gov; Av de Portugal)

FOOD

As an approximate guide, the following price ranges refer to the price of a main course.

$	less than US$5
$$	US$5 to US$15
$$$	more than US$15

GAY & LESBIAN TRAVELLERS

There is no organised network for gays and lesbians in Timor-Leste, but it's also unlikely that there will be any overt discrimination. While there is no law against homosexuality it's wise to be less demonstrative in the more conservative rural areas outside of Dili.

INSURANCE

Travel insurance is vital in Timor-Leste. Medical facilities outside Dili are limited and any serious cases generally get evacuated from the country to Darwin or Singapore. Accordingly, travellers need to ensure that they have full evacuation coverage.

Worldwide insurance is available at www.lonelyplanet.com/travel_services. You can buy, extend and claim online anytime – even if you're already on the road.

INTERNET ACCESS

There are plenty of internet cafes, and many hotels in Dili have relatively reliable, albeit slow, access, averaging US$1 an hour. All Timor Telecom offices in the district capitals have access, as do hotels attracting foreigners outside of Dili, such as those in Baucau and Com.

LEGAL MATTERS

If you are the victim of a serious crime, go to the nearest police station and notify your embassy. If arrested, you have the right to a phone call and legal representation, which your embassy can help locate.

OPENING HOURS

In Dili most of the budget and midrange eateries are open from morning until late, with the high-end restaurants only doing lunch (noon to 2pm) and dinner (6pm to 10pm). Expect smaller shops to be open from 9am to 6pm and closed on Sundays. The larger supermarkets are generally open 8am to 8pm everyday. Apart from Dili there are only a handful of places that keep business hours, typically 9am to 6pm Monday to Friday, sometimes with a long lunchtime siesta as a reminder of the old Portuguese influence, and maybe with a few Saturday hours to keep busy.

Exceptions to these hours are noted in individual reviews.

PUBLIC HOLIDAYS

Timor-Leste has a large list of public holidays. Many special days of commemoration are declared each year. November seems to be the front-runner with five holidays.

New Year's Day 1 January

Good Friday March/April (variable)

World Labour Day 1 May

Restoration of Independence Day 20 May (the day in 2002 when sovereignty was transferred from the UN)

Corpus Christi Day May/June (variable)
Popular Consultation Day 30 August (marks the start of independence in 1999)
Idul Fitri End of Ramadan (variable)
All Saints' Day 1 November
All Souls' Day 2 November
Idul Adha Muslim day of sacrifice (variable)
National Youth Day 12 November (commemorates the Santa Cruz Cemetery massacre)
Proclamation of Independence Day 28 November
National Heroes' Day 7 December
Day of Our Lady of Immaculate Conception and Timor-Leste Patroness 8 December
Christmas Day 25 December

TELEPHONE
International access code ☑0011
International country code ☑670
Landline numbers All start with ☑3 or ☑4

International & Local Calls
Can be made from every Timor Telecom office in the country. They can be found in Dili and in every district capital.

Mobile Phones
To get set up with a mobile phone, simply bring an unlocked handset with you to Timor-Leste and buy a SIM card from **Timor Telecom** (www.timortelecom.tp), Telkomsel (p798) or Digicel.

TOILETS
Hotels and restaurants recommended in this book will have toilet facilities ranging from modern Western flush toilets down to a well-kept hole in the ground with a handy bucket of water.

TOURIST INFORMATION
Timor-Leste doesn't have a tourist office. However, the expat community is especially generous with information. Drop by any of the popular bars, restaurants or dive shops and soon you'll be hooked into all sorts of info. Language differences aside, locals are also very happy to help.

VISAS
Dili International Airport & Dili Seaport Arrivals
An entry visa (US$30; up to 30 days) is granted to holders of a valid passport on arrival. Always ask for a 30-day visa, even if you don't plan on staying that long. Tourist visas can be extended for 30 days (US$35) or 60 days (US$75) with a Timorese sponsor. If needing a multiple-entry visa or to stay between 30 and 90 days, you can apply for the Visa Application Authorisation before arrival.

Land-Border Arrivals From Indonesia
East Timorese Consulates (caetanoguterres@hotmail.com) Bali (☑62 2 8133 855 8950; caetanoguterres@hotmail.com; Denpasar);

Kupang (☑8133-9367 558; Jl El Tari) All nationalities (other than Indonesian and Portuguese nationals) must apply for a Visa Application Authorisation prior to their arrival at the border – most travellers apply for them at these consulates. Check the Immigration Service's website (http://migracao.gov.tl). You need a photograph and the US$30 fee; it takes 10 working days.

VOLUNTEERING
Many organisations take on volunteers to assist in a wide variety of roles. Check the links page at www.etan.org for a voluminous listing.
Alola Foundation (☑332 3855; www.alolafoundation.org; Rua Bispo de Medeiros, Dili)
Australian Volunteers International (☑332 2815; www.australianvolunteers.com; Apartment 204, Plaza Hotel, Av Presidente Nicolau Lobato)

WOMEN TRAVELLERS
Women travellers need to be aware of personal security issues, particularly in Dili. Do not walk or take taxis after dark, unless you're in a group.

❶ Getting There & Away
There are no passenger boat services to Timor-Leste from other countries.

AIR
Airports & Airlines
You can fly to Dili from Denpasar (Bali), Jakarta, Darwin and Singapore. Dili's Nicolau Lobato International Airport is a five-minute drive from town. A 24-hour **Airport Shuttle** (Flybus; ☑7750 8585; kijoli@bigpond.com; per person one way US$10) can pick you up and drop you off, or catch a taxi for US$10. *Mikrolets* (local buses) charge $US0.25 from the main road into town.
Air North (☑in Australia 1800 627 474; www.airnorth.com.au) Flies twice daily between Darwin and Dili (return fares from US$400, 1½ hours).
Air Timor (☑331 2777; www.air-timor.com) Flies Singapore to Dili return each Tuesday, Thursday and Saturday (return from US$800, 2½ hours).
Merpati (☑332 1881; www.merpati.co.id) Flies daily between Denpasar (Bali) and Dili (return fares from US$200, two hours) and between Jakarta and Dili (return fares from US$500).
Sriwijaya Air (☑331 1355; www.sriwijayaair.co.id) Flies daily between Denpasar (Bali) and Dili (return fares from US$160) and between Jakarta and Dili (return fares from US$500).

BORDER CROSSINGS
Overland travellers to Timor-Leste (including Oecussi) need to apply for a visa in advance unless they have a multiple-entry visa.

ℹ️ Getting Around

BICYCLE

New bikes can be purchased in Dili for around US$200. Road conditions away from the north coast can be brutal, which may appeal to mountain bikers.

BOAT

Ferry transport is available between Dili and Atauro Island, and Dili and Oecussi. Book in advance. In practice business-class tickets are for foreigners and economy tickets are for locals, but people freely mix across the ship. **Compass Charters** (☑ 7723 0965; svscdili@telstra.com; Av dos Mártires de Pátria, Dili), next to Tiger Fuel, runs a daily water-taxi service to Atauro Island (US$45 one way, 90 minutes).

BUS

Mikrolet (small minibuses) operate around Dili and to some towns, often roaming villages looking for passengers. Crowded buses do the main routes from Dili to Lospalos, Viqueque, Maliana and Suai. More rugged routes are covered by *angguna* (tray trucks where passengers, including the odd buffalo or goat, all pile into the back). If *angguna* aren't covering their usual turf you can be assured the road conditions are exceptionally dire. Trip times in this chapter are a rough guide only – times depend on how bad the roads are and the whim of the driver when it comes to stops/visits to family members along the way.

CAR & MOTORCYCLE

There's nothing easy about driving in Timor-Leste; the roads are a minefield of chickens, goats, sleepy dogs and children, and locals congregate on the side of roads in what seems to be a national pastime (moving off the road is optional). Dips, ditches and entire missing sections of road are common, as are very fast *karetta estadu* (government car) drivers. There are plenty of blind corners.

While conventional cars can handle Dili, a 4WD is recommended for the roads elsewhere. Better

---

DEPARTURE TAX

There's an additional departure tax of US$10 when leaving Dili's airport.

---

roads include those east to Com (but not to Tutuala) and west to Batugade, and the inland road to Maubisse. Motorcycles can be quite handy, breezing over bumps at a respectable pace.

EDS Car Rentals (☑ 7723 0880; edsdili@dynamictrade.ch) Offers a good range of high-quality cars, 4WDs, trucks and buses. They also have a team of experienced drivers who know Dili and the back blocks of Timor-Leste. When you are driving toward Dili it is the last right-hand turn before you go over the bridge; follow the river for 1.5km and it is on your left. Rates start at US$90 for 4WDs.

Tiger Fuel (☑ 7723 0965; Av dos Mártires de Pátria, Comoro) Tiger rents motorcycles from US$35 per day, negotiable price for more than four days.

Fuel

Petrol (gasoline) in Portuguese is *besin*, diesel fuel is *solar*; expect to pay around US$1.30 to US$1.65 per litre.

HITCHING

Locals on long walks into towns may ask for a ride. Waiting for a lift may be the only option if you're leaving Oecussi and heading into Kefamenanu in West Timor, and it's likely your payment will be in cigarettes. However, hitchhiking is never entirely safe, so it's not recommended.

TOURS

A tour can allow you to visit places not easily accessible by public transport, and a guide can bridge the language barrier. The following agency is based in Dili:

Eco Discovery (☑ 332 2454; www.eco discovery-easttimor.com; Landmark Plaza, Av dos Mártires de Pátria) Tours range from around Dili to explorations by 4WD and boat.

TIMOR-LESTE GETTING AROUND

Vietnam

Includes ➡

Best Places to Eat

➡ Nha Hang Ngon (p887)

➡ Hill Station Signature Restaurant (p842)

➡ Mermaid Restaurant (p866)

➡ KOTO (p825)

➡ Lac Canh Restaurant (p872)

Best Markets

➡ Bac Ha (p839)

➡ Sapa (p840)

➡ Ben Thanh, HCMC (p889)

➡ Phong Dien (p896)

Why Go?

Astonishingly exotic and utterly compelling, Vietnam is a kaleidoscope of vivid colours and subtle shades, grand architecture and deeply moving war sites. The nation is a budget traveller's dream, with inexpensive transport, outstanding street food, good-value accommodation and *bia hoi* – perhaps the world's cheapest beer.

Nature has gifted Vietnam soaring mountains in the north, emerald-green rice paddies in the Mekong Delta and a sensational, curvaceous coastline of ravishing sandy beaches. Travelling here you'll witness children riding buffalo, see the impossibly intricate textiles of hill-tribe communities, taste the super-fresh and incredibly subtle flavours of Vietnamese cuisine and hear the buzz of a million motorbikes.

This is a dynamic nation on the move, where life is lived at pace. Prepare yourself for the ride of your life.

When to Go
Hanoi

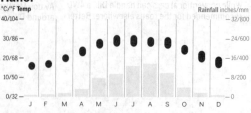

| Dec–Mar Expect cool weather north of Hué as the winter monsoon brings cloud, mist and drizzle. | Apr Danang's river front explodes with colour and noise during the city's fireworks festival. | Jul–Aug Perfect beach-time on the central coastline, with balmy sea and air temperatures. |

Don't Miss

Northern Vietnam comprises one of the world's most impressive limestone landmasses, a vast swathe of spectacular scenery that has been eroded into ethereal rock formations. The myriad pinnacle-like islands of Halong Bay are one superb example of this spectacular karst scenery, or head to neighbouring Lan Ha Bay (p833) for less crowds.

Near Ninh Binh, the jagged limestone mountains of Tam Coc are a surreal sight, while further south the extraordinary Phong Nha-Ke Bang National Park (p846) is home to three gargantuan cave systems (including the world's largest cave) set in tropical forest studded with towering peaks.

ITINERARIES

One Week

Begin in Hanoi, immerse yourself in Old Quarter life and tour the capital's sights. Then it's a day trip to Halong Bay to lap up the surreal karst scenery. Move down to Hué to explore the imperial citadel and then shift to Hoi An for two days of foodie treats, old world ambience and beach time. Finish off with a night in Ho Chi Minh City (Saigon).

Two Weeks

Check out the capital, seeing the sights and experiencing Hanoi's unique streetlife. Tour incomparable Halong Bay, followed by the highland mountains and epic mountain scenery around Sapa. Then it's the extraordinary caves and karst hills of Phong Nha. Hué, city of pagodas and tombs, beckons next. Push on to charming Hoi An, where you can rest up for a day or two. Continue south along the coast via party capital Nha Trang. Round things off Saigon-style in Vietnam's liveliest metropolis, Ho Chi Minh City.

Essential Food & Drink

→ **White rose** An incredibly delicate, subtly flavoured shrimp dumpling topped with crispy onions.

→ **Pho** Rice-noodle soup. A good *pho bo* (beef noodle soup) hinges on the broth, which is made from beef bones boiled for hours in water with shallot, ginger, fish sauce, black cardamom, star anise and cassia.

→ **Banh xeo** This giant crispy, chewy rice crepe is made in 12- or 14-inch skillets or woks and amply filled with pork, shrimp, mung beans and bean sprouts.

→ **Bia hoi** 'Fresh' or draught beer brewed daily, without additives or preservatives, to be drunk within hours.

→ **Vietnamese coffee** Often served iced, with condensed milk.

AT A GLANCE

→ **Currency** Dong (d)

→ **Language** Vietnamese

→ **Money** ATMs are widespread

→ **Visas** Mostly required in advance

→ **Mobile phones** Prepay SIM cards available for a few dollars

VIETNAM

Fast Facts

→ **Area** 329,566 sq km

→ **Capital** Hanoi

→ **Emergency** Police ☏113

Exchange Rates

Australia	A$1	19,045d
Cambodia	10,000r	53,250d
Euro Zone	€1	28,960d
Laos	10,000K	26,330d
UK	UK£1	35,110d
US	US$1	21,085d

Set Your Budget

→ **Budget room** US$8–18

→ **Filling meal** US$2–4

→ **Coffee** from US$0.75

→ **Short taxi ride** US$2

Entering the Country

Fly into Hanoi or Ho Chi Minh City, or cross at one of the many land borders with Cambodia, China and Laos.

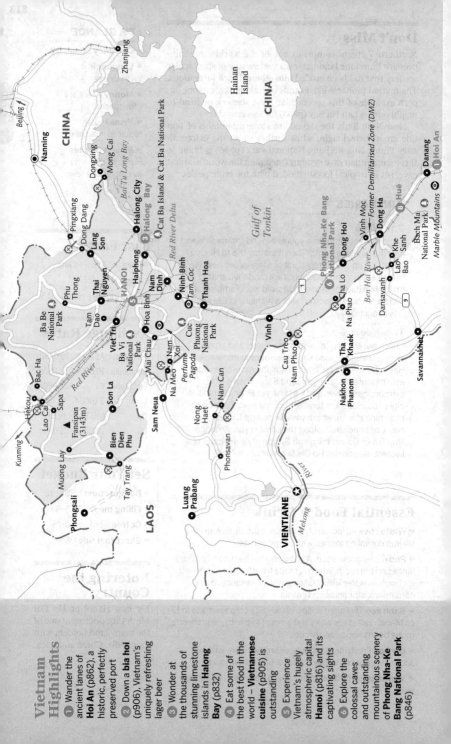

Vietnam Highlights

1 Wander the ancient lanes of **Hoi An** (p862), a historic, perfectly preserved port

2 Down a **bia hoi** (p906), Vietnam's uniquely refreshing lager beer

3 Wonder at the thousands of stunning limestone islands in **Halong Bay** (p832)

4 Eat some of the best food in the world – **Vietnamese cuisine** (p905) is outstanding

5 Experience Vietnam's hugely atmospheric capital **Hanoi** (p816) and its captivating sights

6 Explore the colossal caves and outstanding mountainous scenery of **Phong Nha-Ke Bang National Park** (p846)

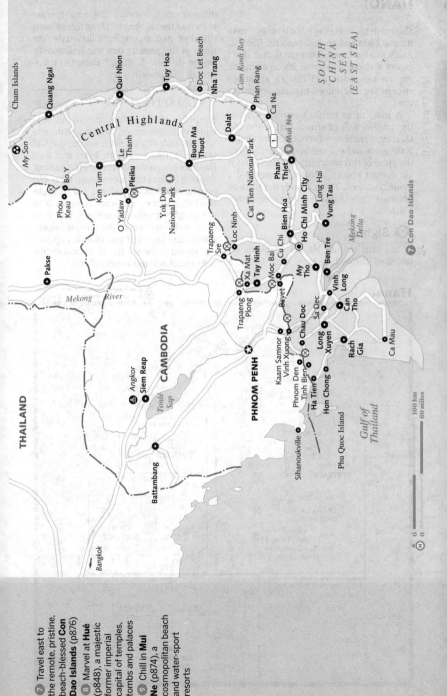

⑦ Travel east to the remote, pristine, beach-blessed **Con Dao Islands** (p876)

⑧ Marvel at **Hué** (p848), a majestic former imperial capital of temples, tombs and palaces

⑨ Chill in **Mui Ne** (p874), a cosmopolitan beach and water-sport resorts

HANOI

☑ 04 / POP 6.8 MILLION

Showcasing sweeping boulevards, tree-fringed lakes and ancient pagodas, Hanoi is Asia's most atmospheric capital. Just don't expect a sleepy ambience: it's an energetic city on the move, and Hanoi's ambitious citizens are determined to make up for lost time.

A mass of motorbikes swarms through the tangled web of streets that is the Old Quarter, a cauldron of commerce for almost 1000 years and still the best place to check the pulse of this resurgent city. Hanoi has it all: ancient history, a colonial legacy and a modern outlook. There is no better place to untangle the paradox that is contemporary Vietnam.

◉ Sights

In the 13th century Hanoi's 36 guilds established themselves here, each taking a different road – hence the area became known as the '36 Streets'. *Hang* means 'merchandise' and is usually followed by the name of the product that was traditionally sold in that street. Thus, P Hang Gai translates as 'Silk Street'.

◉ Old Quarter

Steeped in history, pulsating with life, bubbling with commerce, buzzing with motorbikes and rich in exotic scents, the Old Quarter is Hanoi's historic heart and soul. Hawkers pound the streets bearing sizzling, smoking baskets that hide a cheap meal. *Pho* (noodle soup) stalls and *bia hoi* (draught beer) dens hug every corner, resonant with the sound of gossip and laughter. Take your time and experience the unique sights, sounds and smells of this chaotic, captivating warren of lanes – this is Asian streetlife at its purist and most atmospheric.

Hanoi

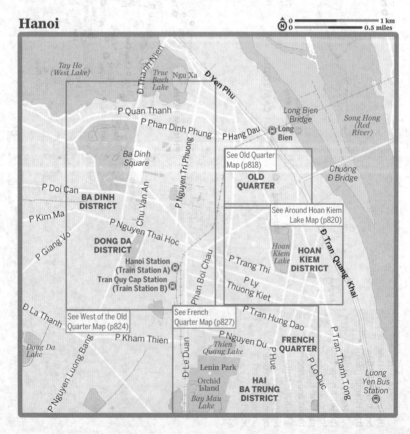

The flip side is that it's also a notoriously chaotic and polluted enclave, and tough to explore on foot, as you pick your way through an urban assault course of motorbikes (parked and speeding) and cracked pavements. One day the authorities will get round to a pedestrianisation program, but for now enjoy the chaos.

★**Bach Ma Temple**   BUDDHIST TEMPLE
(Map p818; cnr P Hang Buom & P Hang Giay; ⊕8-11am & 2-5pm Tue-Sun) **FREE** In the heart of the Old Quarter, the small Bach Ma Temple is said to be the oldest temple in the city, though much of the current structure dates from the 18th century and a shrine to Confucius was added in 1839. It was originally built by Emperor Ly Thai To in the 11th century to honour a white horse that guided him to this site, where he chose to construct his city walls.

Memorial House   HISTORIC BUILDING
(Map p818; 87 P Ma May; admission 5000d; ⊕8.30am-5pm) One of the Old Quarter's best-restored properties, this traditional merchants' house is sparsely but beautifully decorated, with rooms set around two courtyards and filled with fine furniture. Note the high steps between rooms, a traditional design incorporated to stop the flow of bad energy around the property.

◉ **Around Hoan Kiem Lake**

★**National Museum of
Vietnamese History**   MUSEUM
(Map p820; www.nmvnh.org.vn; 1 P Trang Tien; adult/student 20,000/10,000d; ⊕8am-noon & 1.30-5pm, closed 1st Mon of the month) The wonderful architecture of the history museum was formerly home to the École Française d'Extrême-Orient in Vietnam. An elegant, ochre-coloured structure, it was built between 1925 and 1932. French architect Ernest Hébrard was among the first in Vietnam to incorporate a blend of Chinese and French design elements. Highlights include bronzes from the Dong Son culture (3rd century BC to 3rd century AD), Hindu statuary from the Khmer and Champa kingdoms, and beautiful jewellery from imperial Vietnam.

More recent history includes the struggle against the French and the story of the Communist Party. The breezy garden cafe is a lovely spot for a drink.

★**Hoa Lo Prison
Museum**   HISTORIC BUILDING
(Map p820; ☑04-3824 6358; cnr P Hoa Lo & P Hai Ba Trung; admission 15,000d; ⊕8am-5pm) This thought-provoking site is all that remains of the former Hoa Lo Prison, ironically nicknamed the 'Hanoi Hilton' by US POWs during the war in Vietnam. Most exhibits relate to the prison's use up to the mid-1950s, focusing on the Vietnamese struggle for independence from France. A gruesome relic is the French guillotine, used to behead Vietnamese revolutionaries.

There are also displays focusing on the American pilots who were incarcerated at Hoa Lo during the war in Vietnam. These include Pete Peterson (the first US ambassador to a unified Vietnam in 1995) and Senator John McCain (the Republican nominee for the US presidency in 2008).

★**Hoan Kiem Lake**   LAKE
(Map p820) Legend claims that in the mid-15th century, Heaven sent Emperor Le Thai To (Le Loi) a magical sword which he used to drive the Chinese from Vietnam. After the war a giant golden turtle grabbed the sword and disappeared into the depths to restore it to its divine owners, inspiring the name Ho Hoan Kiem (Lake of the Restored Sword). Every morning at around 6am local residents practise traditional t'ai chi on the shore.

Ngoc Son Temple   BUDDHIST TEMPLE
(Jade Mountain Temple; Map p820; Hoan Kiem Lake; adult/student 20,000/10,000d; ⊕7.30am-5.30pm) Hanoi's most visited temple sits pretty on a delightful little island in the northern part of Hoan Kiem Lake. An elegant scarlet bridge, Huc (Rising Sun) Bridge, constructed in classical Vietnamese style and lined with flags, connects the island to the lake shore. Surrounded by water and shaded by trees, the small temple is dedicated to General Tran Hung Dao (who defeated the Mongols in the 13th century), La To (patron saint of physicians) and the scholar Van Xuong. Inside you'll find some fine ceramics, a gong or two, some ancient bells and a glass case containing a stuffed lake turtle, which is said to have weighed a hefty 250kg.

Vietnamese Women's Museum   MUSEUM
(Map p820; www.baotangphunu.org.vn; 36 P Ly Thuong Kiet; admission 30,000d; ⊕8am-5pm) This excellent museum showcases the role of women in Vietnamese society and culture. Labelled in English and French, it's

Old Quarter

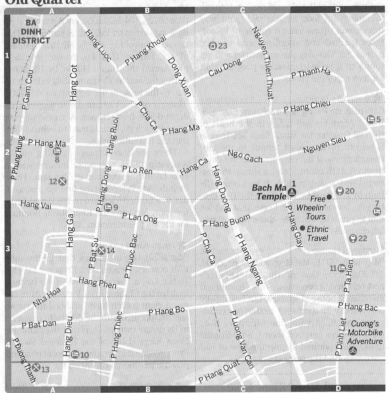

the memories of the wartime contribution by individual heroic women that are most poignant. There is a stunning collection of propaganda posters, as well as costumes, tribal basketware and fabric motifs from Vietnam's ethnic minority groups. Check the website for special exhibitions.

St Joseph Cathedral CHURCH
(Map p820; P Nha Tho; ⊙main gate 5am-noon & 2-7.30pm) **FREE** The striking neo-Gothic St Joseph Cathedral was inaugurated in 1886, and boasts a soaring facade that faces a little plaza. Its most noteworthy features are its twin bell towers, elaborate altar and fine stained-glass windows. Mass times are listed on a sign on the gates to the left of the cathedral. The main gate is open when Mass is held.

Guests are welcome at other times of the day, but must enter via the compound of the Diocese of Hanoi, the entrance to which is a block away at 40 P Nha Chung.

⦿ West of the Old Quarter

★**Temple of Literature** TEMPLE
(Map p824; ☑04-3845 2917; P Quoc Tu Giam; adult/student 20,000/10,000d; ⊙8am-5pm) This highly impressive, well-preserved temple was dedicated to Confucius in 1070 by Emperor Ly Thanh Tong, and later established as a university for the education of mandarins. Its roofed gateways, low-eaved buildings and five courtyards are typical of 11th-century courtly architecture.

In 1484, Emperor Le Thang Tong ordered the establishment of stelae honouring the men who had received doctorates in triennial examinations dating back to 1442. Each of the 82 stelae that stands here is set on a stone tortoise.

★**Ho Chi Minh's Mausoleum** TOMB
(Map p824; ⊙8-11am Tue-Thu, Sat & Sun Dec-Sep, last entry 10.15am) **FREE** In the

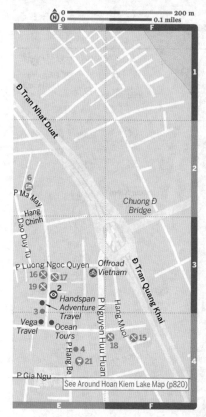

tradition of Lenin, Stalin and Mao, Ho Chi Minh's Mausoleum is a monumental marble edifice. Contrary to his desire for a simple cremation, the mausoleum was constructed from materials gathered from all over Vietnam between 1973 and 1975. Set deep in the bowels of the building in a glass sarcophagus is the frail, pale body of Ho Chi Minh. The mausoleum is closed for about two months each year while his embalmed body goes to Russia for maintenance.

➡ Ho Chi Minh Museum

(Map p824; ☎ 04-3846 3757; www.baotang hochiminh.vn; admission 25,000d; ◷ 8-11.30am daily & 2-4.30pm Tue-Thu, Sat & Sun) The huge concrete Soviet-style Ho Chi Minh Museum is a triumphalist monument dedicated to the life of the founder of modern Vietnam and to the onward march of revolutionary socialism. Mementos of Ho's life are showcased, and there are some fascinating pho-

tos and dusty official documents relating to the overthrow of the French and the rise of communism.

➡ Ho Chi Minh's Stilt House

(Nha San Bac Ho; Map p824; admission 25,000d; ◷ summer 7.30-11am & 2-4pm, winter 8-11am & 1.30-4pm, closed Mon, closed Fri afternoon) This humble stilt house is where Ho lived intermittently from 1958 to 1969. Set in a well-tended garden, the house is an interpretation of a traditional rural dwelling, and has been preserved just as Ho left it. In an adjacent building a sign proclaims, 'Ho Chi Minh's Used Cars' – in reality, automobiles he used during his life.

➡ One Pillar Pagoda

(Map p824; P Ong Ich Kiem; admission 25,000d; ◷ summer 7.30-11am & 2-4pm, winter 8-11am & 1.30-4pm, closed Mon, closed Fri afternoon) The One Pillar Pagoda was originally built by

Around Hoan Kiem Lake

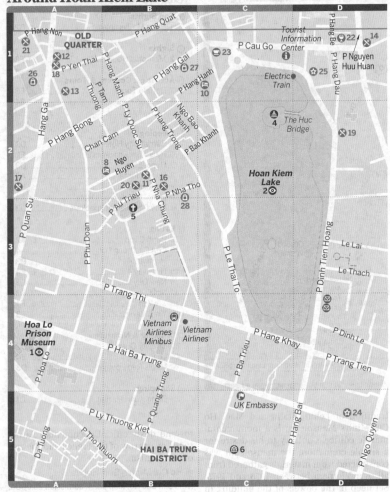

Emperor Ly Thai Tong, who ruled from 1028 to 1054. According to the annals, the heirless emperor dreamed that he met Quan The Am Bo Tat, the Goddess of Compassion, who handed him a male child. Ly Thai Tong then married a young peasant girl, who bore him a son and heir. As a way of expressing his gratitude for this event, he constructed a pagoda here in 1049.

Built of wood on a single stone pillar, the pagoda is designed to resemble a lotus blossom, the symbol of purity, rising out of a sea of sorrow.

Imperial Citadel   HISTORIC SITE
(Map p824; www.hoangthanhthanglong.vn; 19C P Hoang Dieu, main entrance; ☉8.30-11.30am & 2-5pm, closed Mon & Fri) FREE Added to Unesco's World Heritage List in 2010 and reopened in 2012, Hanoi's Imperial Citadel was the hub of Vietnamese military power for over 1000 years. Ongoing archaeological digs of ancient palaces, grandiose pavilions and imperial gates are complemented by fascinating military command bunkers from the war in Vietnam. The leafy grounds are also an easygoing and quiet antidote to Hanoi's bustle.

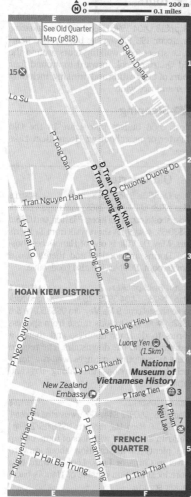

★ Vietnam Military History Museum

MUSEUM

(Map p824; ☎ 04-3823 4264; www.btlsqsvn.org. vn; P Dien Bien Phu; admission 30,000d, camera fee 20,000d; ⊙8-11.30am & 1-4.30pm, closed Mon & Fri) Easy to spot thanks to a large collection of weaponry out front, the Military Museum displays Soviet and Chinese equipment alongside French- and US-made weapons captured during years of warfare. The centrepieces are a Soviet-built MiG-21 jet fighter, triumphant amid the wreckage of French aircraft downed at Dien Bien Phu, and a US F-111.

★ Fine Arts Museum

MUSEUM

(Map p824; www.vnfam.vn; 66 P Nguyen Thai Hoc; adult/concession 20,000/7000d; ⊙8.30am-5pm) Hanoi's excellent Fine Arts Museum is housed in two buildings that once comprised the French Ministry of Information. Artistic treasures from Vietnam abound, including ancient Champa stone carvings and some astonishing effigies of Quan Am, the thousand-eyed, thousand-armed Goddess of Compassion. Look out too for the remarkable lacquered-wood statues of robed Buddhist monks from the Tay Son dynasty.

○ Greater Hanoi

★ Vietnam Museum
of Ethnology | MUSEUM

(☑04-3756 2193; www.vme.org.vn; Đ Nguyen Van Huyen; admission 40,000d, guide 100,000d, camera fee 50,000d; ⊗8.30am-5.30pm Tue-Sun) Occupying a modern structure, the collection here features well-presented tribal art, artefacts and everyday objects gathered from across the nation. Displays are well labelled in Vietnamese, French and English. For anyone with an interest in Vietnam's minorities, it's an essential visit – though it is located way out in the suburbs, 7km northwest of central Hanoi.

Bus 14 (3000d) departs from P Dinh Tien Hoang (east side of Hoan Kiem Lake) and passes within a couple of blocks of the museum – get off at the Nghia Tan bus stop and head to Đ Nguyen Van Huyen. Or it's around 200,000d each way in a taxi.

Tay Ho | LAKE

(West Lake; Map p824) The city's largest lake, Tay Ho is 15km in circumference and ringed by upmarket suburbs. On the south side, along Đ Thuy KHué, are seafood restaurants, and to the east, the Xuan Dieu strip is lined with restaurants, cafes, boutiques and luxury hotels. You'll also find two temples on its shores: the Tay Ho and Tran Quoc pagodas. A pathway circles the lake, making for a great bicycle ride. To rent a bike contact the Hanoi Bicycle Collective (www.thbc.vn; 44 Ngo 31, Xuan Dieu, Tay Ho; bike rental per day from 100,000d; ⊗8am-8pm Tue-Sun).

🏃 Activities

MOD Palace Hotel | SWIMMING POOL

(Map p820; ☑04-3825 2896; 33C P Pham Ngu Lao; admission 65,000d; ⊗6am-8pm) In central Hanoi, the MOD Palace offers day use of its pool, which is big enough for laps and open all year. It gets very busy with children in the afternoon.

🎓 Courses

Highway 4 | COOKING

(Map p818; ☑04-3715 0577; www.highway4.com; 3 Hang Tre; per class US$50) Classes incorporate a *cyclo* ride and market tour, and continue on to Highway 4's Tay Ho restaurant, the House of Son Tinh (☑04-3715 0577; www.highway4.com; 31 P Xuan Dieu, Tay Ho; meals 100,000-200,000d; ⊗10am-11.30pm). Also on offer are cocktail-making classes using Highway 4's traditional Son Tinh liquors.

☞ Tours

Food on Foot | WALKING TOUR

(Map p818; ☑04-3990 1733; www.vietnamawesome travel.com; 19B P Hang Be; US$25) Excellent-value street-food walking tours around the Old Quarter. Look forward to around four hours of tasty eating and drinking, including beer and rice wine.

🛏 Sleeping

Most good budget places are in the Old Quarter or neighbouring Hoan Kiem Lake area.

Old Quarter

May De Ville Backpackers | HOSTEL $

(Map p818; ☑04-3935 2468; www.maydevilleback packershostel.com; 1 Hai Tuong, P Ta Hien; dm US$6, d US$30-35; 🌬@🛜) A short walk from Ta Hien's bars, May De Ville is one of Hanoi's best hostels. Dorms are spotless and there's also a movie room. Doubles are also good value.

Hanoi Backpackers 2 | HOSTEL $

(Map p818; ☑04-3935 1890; www.hanoiback packershostel.com; 9 Ma May; dm US$7.50, tw & d US$25; 🌬@🛜) Options range from spotless dorms to designer doubles, and there's a restaurant and bar downstairs. The relaxed team at reception arranges well-run tours including excursions to Halong Bay and Sapa.

Hanoi Hostel 1 | HOSTEL $

(Map p818; ☑0972 844 804; www.vietnam-hostel. com; 91C P Hang Ma; dm/d/tr US$6/16/21; 🛜) Well-run and clean with lots of tours on tap and plenty of information about onward travel to China or Laos. Look forward to a more local location outside of Hanoi's backpacker scrum.

Hanoi Hostel 2 | HOSTEL $

(Map p818; ☑0972 844 804; www.vietnam-hostel. com; 32 P Hang Vai; dm/d/tr US$6/18/21; 🛜) More tours, traveller information and clean rooms at the Hanoi Hostel's second Old Quarter location. A private family room for four people (US$25) is also available.

Hanoi Rendezvous Hotel | HOTEL $

(Map p818; ☑04-3828 5777; www.hanoi rendezvoushotel.com; 31 Hang Dieu; dm/s/d/tr US$7.50/25/30/35; 🌬@🛜) Deliciously close to several brilliant street-food places, Hanoi Rendezvous features spacious rooms, friendly staff and well-run tours to Halong Bay, Cat Ba Island and Sapa.

Camel City Hotel GUESTHOUSE $
(Map p818; ☎04-3935 2024; www.camelcityhotel.com; 8/50 Dao Duy Tu; r $17-30; ❄@📶) A family-owned operation in a quiet lane just a short walk from the after-dark attractions on P Ta Hien. Rooms are trimmed with Asian design touches and service is friendly.

★**Hanoi Elite** BOUTIQUE HOTEL $$
(Map p818; ☎04-3828 1711; www.hanoielitehotel.com; 10/5032 Dao Duy Tu; r US$50-55; ❄@📶) Features cool and classy decor, top-notch staff and stylish touches like rainforest shower-heads, breakfasts cooked to order and in-room computers.

Around Hoan Kiem Lake

Madame Moon Guesthouse GUESTHOUSE $
(Map p820; ☎04-3938 1255; www.madammoonguesthouse.com; 17 Hang Hanh; r US$23-27; ❄@📶) Keeping it simple just one block from Hoan Kiem Lake, Madame Moon has surprisingly chic rooms and a (relatively) traffic-free location in a street filled with local cafes and bars.

Hanoi Backpackers Hostel HOSTEL $
(Map p820; ☎04-3828 5372; www.hanoibackpackershostel.com; 48 P Ngo Huyen; dm US$7.50, r US$25; ❄@📶) A perennially popular hostel now occupying two buildings on a quiet lane. It's impressively organised, with custom-built bunk beds and lockers, and dorms all have en suite bathrooms.

Eating

Hanoi offers cuisine from all over the world, but as the capital's grub is so tasty, fragrantly spiced and inexpensive you're best sticking to local fare. Don't miss the street food either.

Old Quarter

Zenith Cafe CAFE $
(Map p820; www.zenithyogavietnam.com; 16 P Duong Thanh; mains 45,000-100,000d; ⏲9am-6pm; 🌿) Relaxing and peaceful haven under a yoga studio with excellent juices, salads and vegetarian mains, including felafel and hummus, goat-cheese pizzas and healthy breakfasts like homemade muesli.

THE OLD QUARTER'S TOP STREET FOOD

When in Hanoi, chow down with the masses. Most of these stalls specialise in just one dish and have somewhat flexible opening hours.

Bun Cha Nem Cua Be Dac Kim (Map p820; 67 P Duong Thanh; ⏲11am-7pm) The *bun cha* at this place is a heady combination of grilled pork patties, crab spring rolls, vermicelli noodles and fresh herbs.

Banh Cuon (Map p818; 14 P Hang Ga; ⏲8am-3pm) Gossamer-light *banh cuon* (steamed rice crepes filled with minced pork, mushrooms and ground shrimp).

Pho Thin (Map p820; 61 Dinh Tien Hoang; ⏲6am-3pm) Excellent *pho bo* (beef noodle soup). A classic Hanoi experience that hasn't changed in decades.

Banh Ghoi (Map p820; 52 P Ly Quoc Su; ⏲10am-7pm) Under a banyan tree near St Joseph Cathedral, this stall turns out *banh ghoi*, deep-fried pastries crammed with pork, vermicelli and mushrooms.

Bun Oc Saigon (Map p820; cnr P Nguyen Huu Huan & Hang Thung; ⏲11am-11pm) Shellfish specials here include *bun oc* (snail noodle soup) with a hearty dash of tart tamarind.

Bun Bo Nam Bo (Map p820; 67 P Hang Dieu; ⏲11am-10pm) *Bu bo nam bo* (dry noodles with beef) is a zingy southern Vietnamese dish mixed with bean sprouts, garlic, lemongrass and green mango.

Xoi Yen (Map p818; cnr P Nguyen Huu Huan & P Hang Mam; ⏲7am-11pm) Specialises in sticky rice topped with goodies including sweet Asian sausage, gooey fried egg and slow-cooked pork.

Mien Xao Luon (Map p820; 87 P Hang Dieu; ⏲7am-2pm) Crunchy fried eels prepared three different ways.

Bun Rieu Cua (Map p820; 40 P Hang Tre; ⏲7-9am) A Hanoi breakfast classic, *bun rieu cua* (crab noodle soup) is noodle broth laced with fried shallots and garlic, and topped with shrimp paste and chilli.

West of the Old Quarter

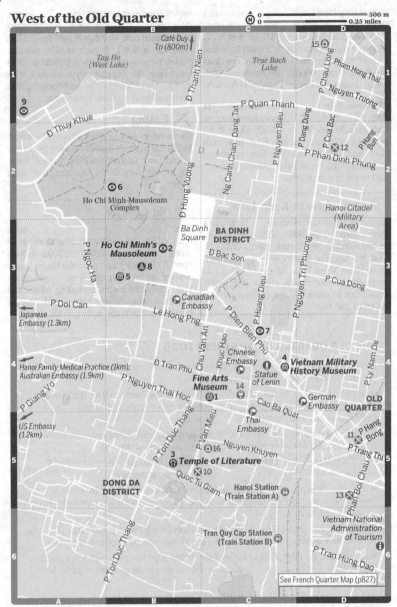

See French Quarter Map (p827)

New Day VIETNAMESE $
(Map p818; 72 P Ma May; mains 70,000-100,000d;
⊙8am-late) Attracts locals, expats and travellers. The eager staff always find space for new diners, so look forward to sharing a table with some like-minded fans of Vietnamese food.

Nola CAFE $
(Map p818; 89 P Ma May; snacks 30,000-60,000d;
⊙9am-midnight) Retro furniture is mixed and matched in this bohemian labyrinth tucked away from Ma May's tourist bustle. Pop in

West of the Old Quarter

for a coffee and banana bread, or return after dark for one of Hanoi's best little bars.

Highway 4   VIETNAMESE $$
(Map p818; ☑ 04-3926 0639; www.highway4.com; 3 P Hang Tre; mains 125,000-275,000d; ◎ noon-late) The legendary Highway 4 popularised unusual northern and minority cuisine in the capital. Try bite-sized snacks like *nem ca xa lo* (catfish spring rolls) or meatier satay-style dishes. There's another **branch** (Map p818; 25 P Bat Su) in the Old Quarter.

Yin & Yang   VIETNAMESE $$
(Map p818; 78 P Ma May; mains 100,000-130,000d; ◎ 8am-late; ☎) This atmospheric spot along touristy Ma May stands out with well-priced versions of Vietnamese classics like *bun cha* and banana flower salad.

Cha Ca Thang Long   VIETNAMESE $$
(Map p818; ☑ 04-3824 5115; 21 P Duong Thanh; cha ca fish 180,000d; ◎ 10am-3pm & 5-10pm) Bring along your DIY cooking skills here and grill your own succulent fish with a little shrimp paste and plenty of herbs.

✗ Around Hoan Kiem Lake

Hanoi House   CAFE $
(Map p820; www.thehanoihouse.com; 48A P Ly Quoc Su; snacks 40,000-60,000d; ◎ 8.30am-

11pm; ☎) A chic and bohemian cafe with superb upstairs views of St Joseph Cathedral. Chill out on the impossibly slim balcony with excellent juices and Hanoi's best ginger tea.

Cart   CAFE $
(Map p820; www.thecartfood.com; 10 Tho Xuong; snacks & juices 40,000d-80,000d; ◎ 7.30am-5pm; ☎✍) Superlative pies, excellent juices and smoothies, and interesting baguette sandwiches feature at this little haven of Western comfort food tucked away near St Joseph Cathedral.

Hanoi Social Club   CAFE $$
(Map p820; www.facebook.com/TheHanoiSocial Club; 6 Hoi Vu; mains 95,000-160,000d; ◎ 8am-11pm) On three funky levels with retro furniture, this is the city's most cosmopolitan cafe. Also works as a good spot for a beer or glass of wine and hosts regular gigs and events (check the Facebook page).

✗ West of the Old Quarter

Net Hue   VIETNAMESE $
(Map p824; cnr P Hang Bong & P Cam Chi; snacks & mains from 35,000d; ◎ 11am-9pm) Net Hue is well-priced for such comfortable surroundings. Head to the top floor for the nicest ambience and enjoy Hué-style dishes such as *banh nam* (steamed rice pancake with minced shrimp).

Quan An Ngon   VIETNAMESE $
(Map p824; www.ngonhanoi.com.vn; 15 Phan Boi Chau; dishes 60,000-120,000d; ◎ 11am-11pm) A number of small kitchens turn out street-food specialities from across Vietnam. Try and visit just outside the busy lunch and dinner periods, or consider Quan An Ngon's newest **branch** (Map p824; 34 P Phan Đinh Phung) in a lovely French villa just north of the Old Quarter.

★KOTO   CAFE $$
(Map p824; ☑ 04-3747 0338; www.koto.com. au; 59 P Van Mieu; meals 120,000-160,000d; ◎ 7.30am-10pm, closed dinner Mon; ☎) Stunning four-storey modernist cafe-bar-restaurant overlooking the Temple of Literature, where the short menu has everything from excellent Vietnamese food to beer-battered fish & chips. KOTO is a not-for-profit project providing career training and guidance to disadvantaged children and teens.

🍷 Drinking

With dive bars, congenial pubs, sleek lounges and clubs and *bia hoi* joints by the barrel-load you won't go thirsty in Hanoi. Cafes come in every persuasion too.

Cafes

Coffee meccas include P Trieu Viet Vuong, around 1km south of Hoan Kiem Lake, which has scores of cafes.

Café Duy Tri   CAFE
(43A P Yen Phu) In the same location since 1936, this caffeine-infused labyrinth is a Hanoi classic. Try the delicious *caphe sua chua* (iced coffee with yoghurt).

Cafe Pho Co   CAFE
(Map p820; 11 P Hang Gai) This place has plum views over Hoan Kiem Lake. Enter through the silk shop and then via a courtyard. For something deliciously different, try the *caphe trung da,* coffee topped with a silkily smooth beaten egg white.

Cong Caphe   CAFE
(Map p827; 152 P Trieu Viet Vuong) Settle in to the eclectic beats and kitsch communist memorabilia at Cong Caphe.

Bars

Ha Tien in the Old Quarter has a choice of bars and is a good starting or finishing point for a crawl.

Bar Betta   BAR, CAFE
(Map p824; www.facebook.com/barbetta34; 34 Cao Ba Quat; ⊙9am-midnight) Retro decor and a jazz-age vibe combine with good cocktails, coffee and cool music in this breezy French colonial villa. Two-for-one beers are available from 3pm to 7pm.

Cama ATK   BAR
(Map p827; www.cama-atk.com; 73 P Mai Hac De; ⊙6pm-midnight Wed-Sat) A bohemian bar run by CAMA (Hanoi's Club for Art and Music Appreciation). Check the website for what's on, which includes everything from Japanese funk and dancehall DJs to experimental short films.

Quan Ly   BAR
(Map p827; 82 P Le Van Hu; ⊙10am-9pm) Owner Pham Xuan Ly has lived on this block since 1950, and now runs one of Hanoi's most traditional *ruou* (Vietnamese liquor) bars. Kick off with the ginseng one, and work your way up to the gecko variation. There's also cheap beer and good Vietnamese food.

Blah Blah   BAR
(Map p820; 59B P Hang Be; ⊙7am-late) The unpretentious Blah Blah is Hanoi's cosiest bar, so you'll definitely have to chat to other fellow travellers. The music's decent and we're big fans of the Friday night pub quiz at 8pm.

Cheeky Quarter   BAR
(Map p818; ☑0936 143 3999; 1 P Ta Hien; ⊙noon-4am) This sociable bar comes complete with patterned wallpaper and intriguing framed portraits (that look vaguely like they're depicting some eccentric titled family). The tunes are contemporary: drum 'n' bass or house music.

Mao's Red Lounge   BAR
(Map p818; 5 P Ta Hien; ⊙noon-late) Classic dive bar with dim lighting and air that's thick with tobacco smoke. Drinks are well priced and the music's usually good. If you don't like what's playing, just ask if you can hook up your own tunes to the sound system.

Le Pub   PUB
(Map p818; ☑04-3926 2104; 25 P Hang Be; ⊙7am-late) Le Pub is a great place to meet others. There's a cosy, tavernlike interior (with big screens for sports fans), a street-facing terrace and a rear courtyard. Bar snacks are served and the service is slick.

☆ Entertainment

Cinematheque   CINEMA
(Map p820; ☑04-3936 2648; 22A P Hai Ba Trung) This Hanoi institution is a hub for art-house film lovers, and there's a great little cafe-bar here too. It's nominally 'members only', but a 50,000d one-off membership usually secures visitors an always-interesting themed double bill.

Hanoi Rock City   LIVE MUSIC
(www.hanoirockcity.com; 27/52 To Ngoc Van, Tay Ho) Hanoi Rock City is tucked away down a residential lane about 7km north of the city near Tay Ho, but it's a journey well worth taking for an eclectic mix including reggae, Hanoi punk and regular electronica nights.

Municipal Water Puppet Theatre   THEATRE
(Map p820; ☑04-3824 9494; www.thanglong waterpuppet.org; 57B P Dinh Tien Hoang; admission 60,000-100,000d, camera fee 20,000d, video fee 60,000d; ⊙performances 3.30pm, 5pm, 6.30pm, 8pm & 9.15pm daily, 10.30am Sat, 9.30am Sun) Performances are held at the Municipal Water Puppet Theatre. These shows are a real treat for children. Multilingual

French Quarter

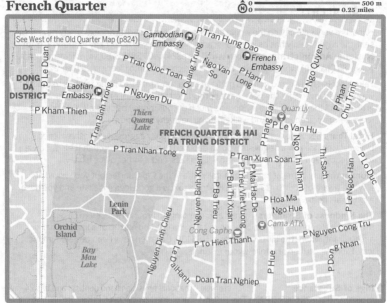

programs allow the audience to read up on each vignette as it's performed. Book well ahead, especially during high season.

🛍 Shopping

The Old Quarter is brimming with temptations. As you wander around you'll find cosmetics, fake sunglasses, luxury food, T-shirts, musical instruments, herbal medicines, jewellery, spices, propaganda art, fake English Premier League football kits and much, much more.

Art & Handicrafts

For ethnic minority garb and handicrafts P Hang Bac and P To Tich are good hunting grounds.

North and northwest of Hoan Kiem Lake around P Hang Gai, P To Tich, P Hang Khai and P Cau Go are dozens of shops offering handicrafts (lacquerware, mother-of-pearl inlay and ceramics) as well as artwork and antiques.

Private art galleries are concentrated on P Trang Tien, between Hoan Kiem Lake and the Opera House.

Craft Link (Map p824; ☑ 04-3843 7710; www. craftlink.com.vn; 43 P Van Mieu; ⊘ 9am-6pm) sells quality tribal handicrafts and weavings at fair-trade prices.

Bookshops

Bookworm   BOOKS

(Map p824; www.bookwormhanoi.com; 44 Chau Long; ⊘ 9am-7pm) Stocks over 10,000 new and used English-language books with plenty of fiction; it's also good for Southeast Asian history and politics.

Markets

Dong Xuan Market   MARKET

(Map p818; ⊘ 6am-7pm) With hundreds of stalls, this market is fascinating to explore if you want to catch the flavour of Hanoian street life.

Hang Da Market   MARKET

(Map p820; Yen Thai) Small, but good for imported foods, wine, beer and flowers.

Silk Products & Clothing

P Hang Gai, about 100m northwest of Hoan Kiem Lake, and its continuation, P Hang Bong, are good places to look for embroidery and silk (including tailored clothes).

Tan My Design   CLOTHING

(Map p820; www.tanmydesign.com; 61 P Hang Gai; ⊘ 8am-8pm) Stylish clothing, jewellery and accessories, with the added bonus of a hip cafe when you need a break from shopping. The homewares and bed linen are definitely worth a look.

SCAM ALERT!

Hanoi is a very safe city on the whole and crimes against tourists are extremely rare. That said, the city certainly has its share of scams. Make sure you report any to the **Vietnam National Administration of Tourism** (Map p824; ☑ 04-3942 3760; www.vietnamtourism. gov.vn; 80 Quan Su), who might well pressure the cowboys into cleaning up their act.

Fake Hotels The taxi and minibus mafia at the airport take unwitting tourists to the wrong hotel. Invariably, the hotel has appropriated the name of another popular property and will then attempt to swindle as much of your money as possible. Check out a room before you check in. And walk on if you have any suspicions.

Hotel Tours Some budget hotel staff have been verbally aggressive and threatened physical violence towards guests who've declined to book tours through their in-house tour agency. Don't feel pressured, and if it persists, find another place to stay.

Women Walking alone at night is generally safe in the Old Quarter, but you should always be aware of your surroundings. Hailing a taxi is a good idea if it's late and you have a long walk home.

The Kindness of Strangers There's a scam going on around Hoan Kiem Lake. A friendly local approaches you, offering to take you out. You end up at a karaoke bar or a restaurant, where the bill is upwards of US$100. Gay men have been targeted in this way. Exercise caution and follow your instincts.

Things of Substance CLOTHING (Map p820; ☑ 04-3828 6965; 5 P Nha Tho; ⊙9am-6pm) Tailored fashions and some off-the-rack items at moderate prices. The staff are professional and speak decent English.

ⓘ Information

EMERGENCY
Ambulance (☑115)
Fire (☑114)
Police (☑113)

INTERNET ACCESS
Virtually all budget and midrange hotels offer free internet access, with computers in the lobby and wi-fi. You'll find several cybercafes on P Hang Bac in the Old Quarter; rates start at 5000d per hour.

INTERNET RESOURCES
Hanoi Grapevine (www.hanoigrapevine.com) Information about concerts, art exhibitions and cinema.

The Word (www.wordhanoi.com) Online version of the excellent, free monthly magazine *The Word*.

TNH Vietnam (www.tnhvietnam.xemzi.com) The premier online resource for visitors and expats; good for up-to-date restaurant and bar reviews.

MEDICAL SERVICES
Hanoi Family Medical Practice (☑04-3843 0748; www.vietnammedicalpractice.com; Van Phuc Diplomatic Compound, 298 P Kim Ma; ⊙24hr) Includes a team of well-respected international physicians and dentists and has 24-hour emergency cover. Prices are high, so check that your medical travel insurance is in order.

SOS International Clinic (☑04-3826 4545; www.internationalsos.com; 51 Xuan Dieu; ⊙24hr) English, French, German and Japanese are spoken and there is a dental clinic. It's near Tay Ho Lake.

MONEY
Hanoi has many ATMs, and around Hoan Kiem Lake are international banks where you can change money and get cash advances on credit cards.

POST
Domestic Post Office (Buu Dien Trung Vong; Map p820; ☑ 04-3825 7036; 75 P Dinh Tien Hoang; ⊙7am-9pm) For internal postal services in Vietnam.

International Postal Office (Map p820; ☑04-3825 2030; cnr P Dinh Tien Hoang & P Dinh Le; ⊙7am-8pm) The entrance is to the right of the domestic office.

TELEPHONE
Guesthouses and internet cafes are convenient for local calls. For international services, internet cafes using Skype offer the cheapest rates.

TOURIST INFORMATION
Tourist Information Center (Map p820; ☑04-3926 3366; P Dinh Tien Hoang; ⊙9am-7pm) Offers city maps and brochures, but it's privately run with an emphasis on selling tours. The excellent local magazine *The Word* is a better source of info.

TRAVEL AGENCIES

Hanoi has hundreds of budget travel agencies. It's not advisable to book trips or tickets through guesthouses and hotels. Dealing directly with tour operators gives you a much better idea of what you'll get for your money; seek out those operators that stick to small groups.

Successful tour operators often have their names cloned by others looking to trade on their reputation, so check addresses and websites carefully.

Ethnic Travel (Map p818; ☑04-3926 1951; www.ethnictravel.com.vn; 35 P Hang Giay; ⊗9am-6pm Mon-Sat, 10am-5pm Sun) Off-the-beaten-track trips across the north in small groups. Some trips are low-impact using public transport and homestays, others are activity-based (including hiking, cycling and cooking).

Handspan Adventure Travel (Map p818; ☑04-3926 2828; www.handspan.com; 78 P Ma May; ⊗9am-8pm) Sea-kayaking trips around Cat Ba Island, and jeep tours, mountain biking and trekking. Includes remote areas such as Moc Chau, community-based tourism projects in northern Vietnam, and the *Treasure Junk* for cruises in Halong Bay.

Ocean Tours (Map p818; ☑04-3926 0463; www.oceantours.com.vn; 22 P Hang Bac; ⊗8am-8pm) Well-organised tour operator with Halong Bay and Ba Be National Park options, and 4WD road trips around the northeast.

Vega Travel (Map p818; ☑04-3926 2092; www.vegatravel.vn; cnr P Ma May & 24A P Hang Bac; ⊗8am-8pm) Excellent tours around the north and throughout Vietnam. The company also supports ethnic minority kindergartens and schools around Sapa and Bac Ha.

❶ Getting There & Away

AIR

Hanoi has fewer international flights than Ho Chi Minh City (HCMC), but with a change of aircraft in Hong Kong or Bangkok you can get almost anywhere.

Vietnam Airlines (Map p820; ☑1900 545 486; www.vietnamair.com.vn; 25 P Trang Thi; ⊗8am-5pm Mon-Fri) Links Hanoi to destinations including Dalat, Danang, Dien Bien Phu, HCMC, Hué and Nha Trang, all served daily.

Jetstar Airways (☑1900 1550; www.jetstar.com) Operates low-cost flights to Danang, HCMC and Nha Trang.

VietJet Air (☑1900 1886; www.vietjetair.com) Low-cost airline with flights to Danang, Dalat, Hué and Bangkok.

BUS

Hanoi has four long-distance bus stations, each serving a particular area. It's a good idea to arrange your travel the day before you want to leave. The stations are pretty well organised with ticket offices, displayed schedules and fixed prices.

Gia Lam bus station (☑04-3827 1569; Đ Ngoc Lam) Located 3km northeast of the centre, is the place for buses to points east and northeast of Hanoi.

Luong Yen bus station (Map p816; ☑04-3942 0477; cnr Tran Quang Khai & Nguyen Khoai) Located 3km southeast of the Old Quarter, serves destinations to the south and the east, including sleeper buses to Hué, Dalat and Nha Trang and transport to Cat Ba Island. Note that taxis at Luong Yen are notorious for their dodgy meters. Walk a couple of blocks and hail one off the street.

My Dinh bus station (☑04-3768 5549; Đ Pham Hung) Located 7km west of the city, provides

TRAINS FROM HANOI

Eastbound & Northbound Trains

DESTINATION	STATION	DURA-TION (HR)	HARD SEAT OR SLEEPER	SOFT SEAT OR SLEEPER	DEPARTURE
Beijing	Tran Quy Cap	18	US$224	US$328	6.30pm Tue & Fri
Haiphong	Gia Lam	2	55,000d	65,000d	6am
Haiphong	Long Bien	2½-3	55,000d	65,000d	9.20am, 3.30pm, 6.10pm
Nanning	Gia Lam	12	US$23	US$35	9.40pm

Southbound Trains

DESTINATION	HARD SEAT	SOFT SEAT	HARD SLEEPER	SOFT SLEEPER
Danang	From 418,000d	From 615,000d	From 773,000d	From 942,000d
HCMC	From 776,000d	From 1,140,000d	From 1,300,000d	From 1,672,000d
Hué	From 364,000d	From 535,000d	From 665,000d	From 884,000d
Nha Trang	From 678,000d	From 996,000d	From 1,237,000d	From 1,607,000d

services to the west and the north, including sleeper buses to Dien Bien Phu.

Giap Bat bus station (☎04-3864 1467; Đ Giai Phong) Located 7km south of the Hanoi train station, is used by some buses from Ninh Binh and the south.

Most travellers prefer the convenience of open-tour buses (hop-on, hop-off bus services that connect the capital with HCMC). From Hanoi, these services stop at all main destinations heading south, including Ninh Binh and Hué.

Tourist-style minibuses can be booked through most hotels and cafes. Popular destinations include Halong Bay and Sapa. Prices are usually about 30% to 40% higher than the regular public bus, but include a hotel pick-up.

Buses also connect Hanoi with Nanning in China. Two daily services (at 7.30am and 7.30pm) to Nanning (450,000d, eight hours) leave from the private terminal of **Hong Ha Tourism** (Map p820; ☎04-3824 7339; 204 Đ Tran Quang Khai). Tickets should be purchased in advance and you may be asked to show your Chinese visa.

BUSES FROM HANOI

Gia Lam Bus Station

DESTINATION	PRICE (D)	DURATION (HR)	FREQUENCY
Ba Be	180,000	6	noon
(Bai Chay) Halong City	120,000	3½	every 30min
Haiphong	70,000	2	frequent
Lang Son	100,000	4	every 45min
Lao Cai	250,000	9	6.30pm, 7pm (sleeper)
Mong Cai	260,000	8	hourly (approx)
Sapa	300,000	10	6.30pm, 7pm (sleeper)

Luong Yen Bus Station

DESTINATION	PRICE (D)	DURATION (HR)	FREQUENCY
Cat Ba Island	240,000	5	5.20am, 7.20am, 11.20am, 1.20pm
Haiphong	70,000	3	frequent
HCMC	920,000	40	7am, 10am, 2pm, 6pm
Lang Son	100,000	3½	frequent

My Dinh Bus Station

DESTINATION	PRICE (D)	DURATION (HR)	FREQUENCY
Cao Bang	190,000	10	every 45min
Dien Bien Phu	375,000	11	11am, 6pm
Ha Giang	140,000	7	frequent
Hoa Binh	55,000	3	frequent
Son La	170,000	7	frequent to 1pm

Giap Bat Bus Station

DESTINATION	PRICE (D)	DURATION (HR)	FREQUENCY
Dalat	450,000	35	9am, 11am
Danang	380,000	12	frequent sleepers noon-6.30pm
Dong Ha	380,000	8	frequent sleepers noon-6.30pm
Dong Hoi	380,000	8	frequent sleepers noon-6.30pm
Hué	380,000	10	frequent sleepers noon-6.30pm
Nha Trang	700,000	32	10am, 3pm, 6pm
Ninh Binh	70,000	2	frequent 7am-6pm

CAR & MOTORCYCLE

Car hire is best arranged via a travel agency or tour operator. The roads in the north are in pretty good shape but expect an average speed of 35km to 40km per hour. You'll definitely need a 4WD. Daily rates start at about US$110 a day (including driver and petrol).

TRAIN

The main **Hanoi train station** (Ga Hang Co; Train Station A; ☎04-3825 3949; 120 Đ Le Duan; ⊙ticket office 7.30am-12.30pm & 1.30-7.30pm) is at the western end of P Tran Hung Dao. Trains from here go to destinations south.

To the right of the main entrance of the train station is a separate ticket office for northbound trains to Lao Cai (for Sapa) and China. Note that all northbound trains leave from a separate station (just behind the main station) called **Tran Quy Cap station** (Train Station B; ☎04-3825 2628; P Tran Quy Cap; ⊙ticket office 4-6am & 4-10pm).

To make things even more complicated, some northbound (Lao Cai and Lang Son included) and eastbound (Haiphong) trains depart from **Gia Lam** (Đ Ngoc Lam) on the eastern side of the Song Hong (Red River), and Long Bien on the western (city) side of the river. Be sure to ask just where you need to go to catch your train.

Schedules, fares, information and advance bookings are available at **Vietnam Railway** (https://vietnam-railway.com) and **Vietnam Impressive** (www.vietnamimpressive.com), two dependable private booking agents.

It's best to buy tickets at least one day before departure to ensure a seat or sleeper. Travel agents will book train tickets for a commission.

ⓘ Getting Around

BICYCLE

Many Old Quarter guesthouses and cafes rent bikes for about US$2 per day. Good luck with that traffic.

BUS

Plenty of local buses (fares from 3000d) serve routes around Hanoi but very few tourists bother with them.

CYCLO

A few *cyclo* (pedicab) drivers still frequent the Old Quarter. Settle on a price first and watch out for overcharging. Aim to pay around 50,000d for a shortish journey.

ELECTRIC TRAIN

Hanoi's ecofriendly **electric train** (Map p820; per car (6 passengers) 250,000d; ⊙8.30am-10.30pm) is actually a pretty good way to get your bearings. It traverses a network of 14 stops in the Old Quarter and around Hoan Kiem Lake.

Catch one at the northern end of Hoan Kiem Lake; a circuit takes around 40 minutes.

MOTORCYCLE

Offers for *xe om* (motorbike taxi) rides are incessant. A short ride should be about 30,000d, about 5km around 70,000d.

Forget getting around Hanoi by motorbike – traffic is relentless, road signs are missing, road manners are nonexistent and it's dangerous.

TAXI

Taxis are everywhere. Flag fall is around 20,000d, which takes you 1km or 2km; every kilometre thereafter costs around 15,000d. Some dodgy operators have high-speed meters, so use the following reliable companies:
Mai Linh Taxi (☎04-3822 2666)
Thanh Nga Taxi (☎04-3821 5215)

NORTHERN VIETNAM

The roof of Vietnam, the north delivers spectacular scenery and outstanding cultural interest. For trekking and exploring minority villages, the attractive old French hill station of Sapa remains popular, but nearby Bac Ha is a less-visited alternative. Expect a riot of colour in the markets as you're dazzled by the scarlet headdresses of the Dzao, the indigo fabrics of the Black Hmong and the Flower Hmong's brocaded aprons.

Bizarre but beautiful, Halong Bay is geology gone wild, with hundreds of limestone pinnacles emerging from the waters. North of Halong Bay is less-visited Bai Tu Long Bay, where nature's spectacular show continues all the way to the Chinese border. Or head to rugged Cat Ba, a verdant island renowned for its hiking, biking, sailing and world-class rock climbing.

> **WORTH A TRIP**
>
> ### BAI TU LONG BAY
>
> The area immediately northeast of Halong Bay is part of **Bai Tu Long National Park** (☎033-379 3365), which is blessed with spectacular limestone islands every bit as beautiful as its more famous neighbour Halong.
>
> Hanoi travel agencies including Ethnic Travel run trips into the Bai Tu Long area. Or for more flexibility head overland to Cai Rong and visit the outlying islands by boat from there.

Halong Bay

Majestic, mysterious, inspiring and imperious, Halong Bay's 3000 or more incredible islands rise from the emerald waters of the Gulf of Tonkin. A Unesco World Heritage Site, this mystical seascape of limestone islets is a vision of breathtaking beauty. The islands are dotted with wind- and wave-eroded grottoes, many now illuminated with technicolour lighting effects. Sadly, litter and trinket-touting vendors are now also part of the experience.

From February through until April, the weather is often cold and drizzly, and the ensuing fog can cause low visibility, although the temperature rarely falls below 10°C. Tropical storms are frequent during the summer months (July to September).

Most visitors sensibly opt for tours that include sleeping on a boat in the bay. Some dodge the humdrum gateway Halong City completely and head independently for Cat Ba Town, from where trips to the less-visited, equally alluring Lan Ha Bay are easily set up.

Halong Bay Management Department (☑033-384 6592; http://halong.org.vn; 166 Ð Le Thanh Tong), 2km west of Halong City, regulates independent cruises on the bay. It's easy here to hook up with other people to share a boat with; rates start at about 50,000d an hour.

Halong City

☑033 / POP 201,000

Halong City is the main gateway to Halong Bay. Its seafront is blighted by high-rise hotels, but you will find good budget accommodation here.

An elegant suspension bridge connects the western, touristy side of town (known as Bai Chay) with the much more Vietnamese entity (Hon Gai) to the east.

🛏 Sleeping & Eating

The 'hotel alley' of Ð Vuon Dao has more than 50 minihotels, most of them almost identical

and costing US$15 a double room. For cheap, filling food there are modest places at the bottom of Ð Vuon Dao with English menus.

Thanh Hué Hotel   HOTEL **$**
(☑033-384 7612; Ð Vuon Dao; r US$12-18; 🌢 @ 🛜) Look for the powder-blue paint job on this good-value hotel. Most rooms have cracking views of the bay from their balconies. It's a bit of a walk uphill.

Tung Lam Hotel   HOTEL **$**
(☑033-364 0743; 29 Ð Vuon Dao; r US$10-16; 🌢 🛜) This minihotel is making a little more effort than most. The rooms all have two beds, a TV, a minibar and en suite bathrooms, and those at the front are spacious and include a balcony.

ℹ Getting There & Away

The bus station is 6km south of central Bai Chay, just off Hwy 18.

Cat Ba Island

☑031 / POP 14,000

Rugged, craggy and jungle-clad, Cat Ba is northern Vietnam's adventure sport and ecotourism mecca. There's a terrific roll-call of activities here – sailing trips, birdwatching, biking, hiking and rock climbing – and some fine tour operators organising them.

Lan Ha Bay, off the southeastern side of the island, is especially scenic and offers numerous beaches to explore. You could spend a year here discovering a different islet every day while swimming and snorkelling the bay's turquoise waters. Cat Ba Island has a few fishing villages, as well as a fast-growing town.

Much of Cat Ba Island was declared a national park in 1986 to protect the island's diverse ecosystems and wildlife, including the endangered golden-headed langur, the world's rarest primate. There are beautiful beaches, numerous lakes, waterfalls and grottoes in the spectacular limestone hills.

In recent years Cat Ba Town has experienced a hotel boom, and a chain of ugly con-

BUSES FROM HALONG CITY

DESTINATION	PRICE (D)	DURATION (HR)	FREQUENCY
Haiphong	50,000	2	every 20min
Hanoi	120,000	3½	every 15min
Lang Son	110,000	5½	11.45am & 12.45pm
Mong Cai	90,000	4	every 40 min till 3pm
Ninh Binh	94,000	3	every 1½hr

CRUISING THE KARSTS: TOURS TO HALONG BAY

Halong Bay tours sold out of Hanoi start from US$50 per person for a dodgy day trip, rising to around US$200 for two nights on the bay with kayaking. For around US$90 to US$110, you should get a worthwhile overnight cruise.

We get many complaints about poor service, bad food and rats running around on the boats, but these tend to be on the ultra-budget tours. Spend a little more and enjoy the experience a whole lot more.

Most tours include transport, meals and, sometimes, island hikes or kayaking. Boat tours are sometimes cancelled in bad weather – ascertain in advance what a refund will be. You should also take real care with your valuables if on a day trip (most overnight cruises have lockable cabins).

If you've got more time and want to experience Halong Bay without the crowds, consider heading to Cat Ba Island. From there, tour operators concentrate on Lan Ha Bay, which is relatively untouched and has sublime sandy beaches.

crete hotels now frames a once-lovely bay. That said, its ugliness is skin deep, as the rest of the island and Lan Ha Bay are so alluring.

◉ Sights

Lan Ha Bay   BAY
(admission 30,000d) The 300 or so karst islands of Lan Ha Bay are south and east of Cat Ba Town; geologically they are an extension of Halong Bay. The limestone pinnacles and scenery are just as beautiful as Halong Bay, but these islands have the additional attraction of numerous white-sand beaches.

Lan Ha Bay is a fair way from Halong City, so not so many tourist boats venture here and it has a more isolated, off-the-beaten-track appeal.

Sailing and kayak trips are best organised in Cat Ba Town. With hundreds of beaches to choose from, it's easy to find your own private patch of sand for the day. Camping is permitted on gorgeous Hai Pai Beach (also known as Tiger Beach). Lan Ha Bay also offers superb rock climbing and is the main destination for trips run by Asia Outdoors.

Cat Ba National Park   PARK
(☑ 031-216 350; admission 30,000d; ☺ sunrise-sunset) This accessible national park is home to 32 types of mammal and 70 bird species. Mammals in the park include langurs and macaques, wild boar, deer, civets and several species of squirrel, including the giant black squirrel. The golden-headed langur is officially the world's most endangered primate with only around 65 remaining, most in this park. Birds include hawks, hornbills and cuckoos.

There's good trekking including a challenging 18km hike through the park up to one of the mountain summits. This is not

an easy walk, and is much harder and more slippery after rain. Shorter hiking trails are less hardcore.

To reach the **park headquarters** at Trung Trang, take a green QH public bus from the docks at Cat Ba Town (20,000d, 20 minutes). Buses leave at 8am and 11am. *Xe om* (motorbike taxis) charge 80,000d one-way.

Hospital Cave   HISTORIC SITE
(☑ 031-368 8215; admission 15,000d; ☺ 7am-4.30pm) Hospital Cave served both as a secret, bomb-proof hospital during the war in Vietnam and as a safe house for VC leaders. Built between 1963 and 1965 this incredibly well-constructed three-storey feat of engineering was in constant use until 1975. The cave is about 10km north of Cat Ba Town.

A guide will show you around the 17 rooms, point out the old operating theatre and take you to the huge natural cavern that was used as a cinema (and even had its own small swimming pool).

Cat Co Cove   BEACH
A 15-minute walk southeast from Cat Ba Town, the three Cat Co Cove beaches boast white sand and good swimming, although debris and rubbish in the water can be problem on some days. The prettiest is Cat Co 2, backed by limestone cliffs and the site of Cat Ba Beach Resort. Cat Co 1 and 3 also have resorts.

⚡ Activities

Cat Ba is a superb base for adventure sports.

Mountain Biking

Hotels can arrange Chinese mountain bikes (around US$6 per day), and Blue Swimmer rents Trek bikes for US$15 per day.

One possible route traverses the heart of the island, past Hospital Cave down to the west coast's mangroves and crab farms.

Rock Climbing

Cat Ba Island and Lan Ha Bay's spectacular limestone cliffs make for world-class rock climbing amid stunning scenery. Asia Outdoors uses fully licensed and certified instructors and remains the absolute authority.

Full-day climbing trips including instruction, transport, lunch and gear start at US$60 per person. Climbing and boat trips incorporate kayaking, beach stops and exploring the amazing karst landscape.

Sailing & Kayaking

Blue Swimmer offers sailing excursions to myriad islands around Cat Ba, often including kayaking and sleeping on a private beach.

Plenty of hotels in Cat Ba Town rent kayaks (half-day around US$8); Blue Swimmer's cost a little more but are ideal for exploring the Cat Ba coast independently. Sailing excursions on gorgeous Lan Ha Bay and full-day trips on a Chinese junk to Long Chau lighthouse, built by the French in the 1920s, are also possible.

Trekking

Most of Cat Ba Island consists of protected tropical forest. For details of trekking routes see Cat Ba National Park (p833). Asia Outdoors and Blue Swimmer both offer a great hike around Cat Ba Island, taking in Butterfly Valley.

⛳ Tours

Tours of the island and boat trips around Halong Bay are offered by nearly every hotel in Cat Ba, costing around US$20 for day trips including kayaking and US$80 for two-day, one-night tours.

We have received unfavourable feedback – cramped conditions and dodgy food – about some of these trips. The following adventure tour operators will steer you to really special areas of Cat Ba, Lan Ha Bay and beyond.

★ **Asia Outdoors**   ROCK CLIMBING
(✐ 031-368 8450; www.asiaoutdoors.com.vn; 222 1-4, Cat Ba Town) Climbing instruction is Asia Outdoors' real expertise, but it also offers excellent, well-structured boating, kayaking, biking and hiking trips. Rock up to its office in Noble House (at 6pm every night) to see what's planned.

★ **Blue Swimmer**   SAILING, KAYAKING
(✐ 0915 063 737, 031-368 8237; www.blueswimmer sailing.com; Ben Beo Harbour) A well-organised, environmentally conscious outfit with superb sailing and kayak trips, and trekking and mountain biking excursions.

Cat Ba Ventures   BOAT TOUR, KAYAKING
(✐ 0912 467 016, 031-388 8755; www.catba ventures.com; 223 Đ 1-4, Cat Ba Town) Locally owned, professionally run company offering boat trips to Halong Bay, kayaking and hiking.

🛌 Sleeping

Most hotels are in Cat Ba Town. Room rates fluctuate greatly between high-season summertime and the slower winter months. The following are low-season prices.

🛌 CAT BA TOWN

Thu Ha   HOTEL $
(✐ 031-388 8343; Đ 1-4, Cat Ba Town; r US$12-20; ❇ 🛜) With air-con, wi-fi and a seafront location, the Thu Ha offers great value. Negotiate hard for a front room and wake up to sea views.

Le Pont   HOSTEL $
(✐ 0165 662 0436; jim.lepontcatba@gmail.com; 62-64 Đ Nui Ngoc; dm US$5, d & tw US$15-20; @ 🛜) The best spot in town for budgetwise backpackers with cheap dorms and OK double and twin rooms. The rooftop bar and terrace is a handy place to meet fellow travellers.

Duc Tuan Hotel   HOTEL $
(✐ 031-388 8783; www.catbatravelservice.com; 210 Đ 1-4, Cat Ba Town; r US$12-20; ❇ 🛜) Simple but colourfully furnished rooms feature at this family-owned spot on the main drag. The rooms at the back are quieter, but lack windows.

Cat Ba Dream   HOTEL $
(✐ 031-388 8274; www.catbadream.com.vn; 226 Đ 1-4, Cat Ba Town; r US$15-25; ❇ @ 🛜) Slightly more expensive than Cat Ba's ultra cheapies, Cat Ba Dream is a good addition to the town's seafront cavalcade of accommodation. Angle for a front room with sea views.

🛌 AROUND CAT BA ISLAND

Ancient House Homestay   HOMESTAY $
(✐ 0916 645 858, 0915 063 737; www.catba-homestay.com; Ang Soi Village; shared house s/d US$17/25, private house d US$50; 🛜) Located around 3km from Cat Ba Town, this beautiful wooden heritage home has a high-ceilinged

HALONG BAY TO CAT BA ISLAND (WITHOUT THE HASSLE)

Warning! Travelling from Halong City to Cat Ba Island can be fraught with hassles.

Tourist boats (US$10, four hours) depart from Halong Bay around 1pm for Cat Ba Island, but they dock at Gia Luan (40km from Cat Ba Town) and local taxi and *xe om* operators frequently demand up to US$50 for the ride. There *is* actually a local bus (20,000d) – the QH Green Bus – at 5pm, but this usually departs just before the boats arrive. Funny that...

Many boat owners in Halong Bay are part of the scam, so check if onward transport to Cat Ba Town is included. Some operators including Cat Ba Ventures (p834) do include it.

An alternative route is taking the **passenger and vehicle ferry** (per person 40,000d; 1hr; ⊙ on the hour 5am-5pm May-Sep & 8am, 11.10am & 3pm Oct-Apr) that travels from the resort island of Tuan Chau to Gia Luan. (A taxi from Halong City to Tuan Chau is around 150,000d, *xe om* 50,000d.) You can then catch a QH Green bus (departures at 6am, 9.30am, 1.10pm, 4pm & 5pm for 15,000d) to Cat Ba Town.

To travel in the other direction, contact Cat Ba Ventures (p834) in Cat Ba Town for the latest information.

interior. A second adjacent house is available for more private use. Cookery classes, biking, sailing and kayaking can all be arranged.

Whisper of Nature   GUESTHOUSE $
(☑ 031-265 7678; www.vietbungalow.com; Viet Hai Village; dm US$12, d US$28) Offers concrete-and-thatch bungalows grouped around a stream on the edge of the forest. Getting there is an adventure in itself, with the final stage a bike ride through lush scenery. Ask about transport when you book.

✗ Eating & Drinking

There are a few good places dotted along Cat Ba Town's seafront strip, and the floating restaurants offshore are also worth a visit. For a cheaper feed, head to the food stalls in front of the market.

On the seafront, two good places for a drink are **Good Bar** (Ð 1-4, Cat Ba Town; ⊙noon-late), which is a social HQ for travellers, with pool tables and a lively vibe, and the tiny Kiwi-owned **Flightless Bird** (☑031-388 8517; Ð 1-4, Cat Ba Town; ⊙noon-11pm; 🖐). Just inland, **Rose Bar** (15 Ð Nui Ngoc; ⊙noon-3am; 🖐) has lots of happy-hour specials and shisha (water pipe) action.

Green Bamboo Forest   VIETNAMESE $
(Ð 1-4; meals 80,000-120,000d; ⊙7am-11pm) Friendly and well-run waterfront eatery that also acts as a booking office for Blue Swimmer. Our pick of the restaurants along the seafront, and the quieter location is also a bonus.

Family Bakery   BAKERY $
(196 Ð 1-4, Cat Ba Town; dishes 80,000-120,000d; ⊙7am-4pm) Friendly spot that opens early for goodies like Turkish bread and almond pastries. Pop in for a coffee, crème caramel or croissant before the bus-ferry-bus combo back to Hanoi.

Phuong Nung   VIETNAMESE $
(184 Ð 1-4, Cat Ba Town; meals 45,000d; ⊙7-10am) Bustling breakfast spot that's the most popular place in town for a hearty bowl of *pho bo* (beef noodle soup) – just the thing you need before a day of climbing or kayaking.

Bamboo Café   VIETNAMESE $
(☑031-388 7552; Ð 1-4, Cat Ba Town; dishes 80,000-120,000d) A good option for a casual bite on the seafront, this enjoyable little place has a small harbour-facing terrace and an intimate bamboo-walled interior.

❶ Information

There are internet cafes and an **Agribank** (☑ 031-388 8227) ATM on the harbourfront. The best impartial travel information is at Asia Outdoors (p834).

❶ Getting There & Away

Cat Ba Island is 45km east of Haiphong and 30km south of Halong City. Various boat and bus combinations make the journey, starting in either Hanoi or Haiphong. Boat connections from Halong City to Cat Ba Island are blighted by scams.

TO/FROM HANOI

The easiest way to/from Hanoi is via the city's Luong Yen bus station. Here, **Hoang Long** (☑ 031-268 8008) offers a combined bus-boat-bus ticket (240,000d, five hours) straight through to Cat Ba Town. Buses depart Hanoi at 5.20am, 7.20am, 11.20am and 1.20pm, and return from Cat Ba Town at 7.15am, 9.15am, 1.15pm and 3.15pm.

GETTING TO CHINA: NORTHEAST BORDERS

Dong Dang to Pingxiang

Getting to the border This is the most popular border crossing. The border post itself is at Huu Nghi Quan (Friendship Gate), 3km north of Dong Dang. Take a bus from Hanoi to Dong Dang (150,000d, 3¼ hours) and a *xe om* (30,000d) to the border. International trains that run direct from Hanoi to Nanning and Beijing also pass through this border, but it's not possible to jump aboard these services in Lang Son or Dong Dang.

At the border Open 24 hours. Visas must be arranged in advance.

Moving on On the Chinese side, it's a 20-minute drive from the border to Pingxiang by bus or shared taxi. Pingxiang is connected by train and bus to Nanning.

Mong Cai to Dongxing

Mong Cai and Dongxing straddle the Chinese border in the extreme northeastern corner of Vietnam, but this crossing is rarely used by foreigners. It's about 3km between the border and Mong Cai bus station; aim to pay around 20,000d on a *xe om* or 40,000d in a taxi. The border crossing is open from 7am to 7pm daily and visas must be arranged in advance.

TO/FROM HAIPHONG

A fast hydrofoil departs Haiphong's Ben Binh Harbour and goes straight to Cat Ba Town. This takes around 50 minutes (200,000d). Cat Ba–bound hydrofoils depart from Haiphong at 7am, 9am, 1pm and 3pm, and return from Cat Ba Town at 8am, 10am, 2pm and 4pm.

❶ Getting Around

Rented bicycles are a good way to explore the island. Motorbike rentals (with or without driver) are available from most of the hotels from US$5 per day.

Haiphong

📱 031 / POP 1.89 MILLION

Vietnam's third-largest city, Haiphong has a graceful air, and its verdant tree-lined boulevards conceal some classic colonial-era structures. It's an important seaport, industrial centre and transport hub, but very few visitors linger long.

◉ Sights & Activities

★ **Haiphong Museum** MUSEUM
(66 P Dien Bien Phu; admission 5000d; ⊙8am-12.30pm & 2-4pm Mon-Fri, 7.30-9.30pm Wed & Sun) In a splendid colonial building, the Haiphong Museum concentrates on the city's history. Some displays have English translations and the museum's garden harbours a diverse collection of war detritus.

🛏 Sleeping & Eating

Duyen Hai Hotel HOTEL $
(📱031-384 2134; 6 Đ Nguyen Tri Phuong; r 250,000-400,000d; ❄️🛜) With a recently renovated reception area and decent rooms, the Duyen Hai offers fair value and is handily near Lac Long bus station and Ben Binh harbour.

Com Vietnam VIETNAMESE $
(📱031-384 1698; 4A P Hoang Van Thu; mains 40,000-60,000d; ⊙11am-9pm) This restaurant hits the spot for its affordable local seafood and Vietnamese specialities. Diminutive, unpretentious and with a small patio.

❶ Information

There are internet cafes on P Dien Bien Phu; many cafes have free wi-fi. ATMs dot the city centre.

❶ Getting There & Away

Vietnam Airlines (📱031-3810 890; www.vietnamair.com.vn; 30 P Hoang Van Thu), **Jetstar Pacific** (📱1900 1550; www.jetstar.com) and **VietJet** (📱1900 1886; www.vietjetair.com) all offer flights to cities across the nation.

Buses for Hanoi (100,000d, two hours, every 10 minutes) leave from the **Tam Bac bus station** (P Tam Bac), 4km from the waterfront. Buses heading to points south, including Ninh Binh (110,000d, 3½ hours, every 30 minutes), leave from **Niem Nghia bus station** (Đ Tran Nguyen Han). **Lac Long bus station** (P Cu Chinh Lan) has buses to Halong City (70,000d, 1½ hours).

There are four trains a day to Hanoi (from 48,000d, two to three hours) from **Haiphong train station** (Đ Pham Ngu Lao).

Ba Be National Park

🏛 0281 / ELEV 145M

Boasting mountains high, rivers deep, and waterfalls, lakes and caves, **Ba Be National Park** (🏛 0281-389 4014; admission per person 20,000d) is an incredibly scenic spot. The region is surrounded by steep peaks (up to 1554m) while the park contains tropical rainforest with more than 400 plant species. Wildlife in the forest includes bears, monkeys, bats and lots of butterflies. Surrounding the park are Tay minority villages.

Ba Be (Three Bays) is in fact three linked lakes, with a total length of 8km and a width of about 400m. The Nang River is navigable for 23km between a point 4km above Cho Ra and the **Dau Dang Waterfall** (Thac Dau Dang), which is a series of spectacular cascades between sheer walls of rock. River cave **Puong Cave** (Hang Puong) is about 30m high and 300m long.

Park staff can organise **tours**, starting at about US$35 per day for solo travellers, less for a group. **Boat trips** (hire around 650,000d) take around seven hours to take in most sights; canoe, cycling, boating and walking excursions are also possible. Tay-owned **Ba Be Center Tourism** (🏛 0281-389 4721; www.babe centertourism.com; Bolu Village) arranges home-stays, boat trips and trekking and kayaking.

🛏 Sleeping & Eating

There are two accommodation options not far from the park headquarters.

Park Guesthouse   GUESTHOUSE $
(🏛 0281-389 4026) Offers semi-detached bungalows (350,000d) and rooms (220,000d) that are fairly basic. Meals (from 50,000d) are available here – place your order a few hours ahead.

EXPLORING THE FAR NORTH

With spectacular scenery and relatively minimal traffic, the northwest loop from Hanoi to Lao Cai, over to Dien Bien Phu and back to the capital is a truly memorable motorbike ride.

Hanoi is the place to start making arrangements. Consider joining a tour or hiring a guide, who will know the roads and can help with mechanical and linguistic difficulties. Get acquainted with your bike first and check current road conditions and routes.

Most motorbikes in Vietnam are under 250cc. Japanese road and trail bikes (around US$20 to US$30 per day) are good choices as they tend to be reliable and have decent shock absorbers and seat cushioning. You'll suffer on a moped given the rough roads.

Essentials include a good helmet, local mobile phone for emergencies, rain gear, a spare parts and repair kit (including spark plugs, spanners, inner tube and tyre levers), air pump and decent maps. Knee and elbow pads and gloves are also a good idea.

Highways can be hell in Vietnam, so let the train take the strain on the long route north to Lao Cai. Load your bike into a goods carriage while you sleep in a berth. You'll have to (almost) drain it of petrol.

If you're planning on riding from Dien Bien Phu via Muong Lay and Lai Chau on Hwy 12 to Sapa, check road conditions first. At the time of writing, the 40km after Muong Lay to Lai Chau was very rough with many roadworks. Highway 12 was scheduled to be completed by August 2014, so it should be OK once this edition is published.

Take it slowly, particularly in the rain. Do not ride during or immediately after heavy rainstorms as this is when landslides might occur; many mountain roads are quite new and the cliff embankments can be unstable. Expect to average about 35km per hour. Only use safe hotel parking. Fill up from petrol stations where the petrol is less likely to have been watered down.

If running short on time or energy, remember that many bus companies will let you put your bike on the roof of a bus, but get permission first from your bike rental company.

Recommended specialists in Hanoi include **Cuong's Motorbike Adventure** (Map p818; 🏛 0913 518 772; www.cuongs-motorbike-adventure.com; 46 P Gia Ngu; ⊗ 8am-6pm) and **Offroad Vietnam** (Map p818; 🏛 0913 047 509; www.offroadvietnam.com; 36 P Nguyen Huu Huan; ⊗ 8am-6pm Mon-Sat).

Stilt House Homestays HOMESTAY $
(per person 70,000d) Homestays are available in Pac Ngoi village on the lakeshore; the park office can help organise this. Meals cost 40,000d to 60,000d. Only cash is accepted; the nearest ATM and internet access are in Cho Ra.

❶ Getting There & Around

Ba Be National Park is 240km from Hanoi and 18km from Cho Ra.

Most visitors get here by chartered vehicle from Hanoi (six hours) or on a tour.

A noon bus (180,000d, six hours) leaves Hanoi's Gia Lam bus station for Cho Ra, where you'll have to overnight before continuing to Ba Be by *xe om* (100,000d).

Mai Chau

☑ 0218 / POP 47,500

In an idyllic valley, Mai Chau is surrounded by lush paddy fields and the rural soundtrack is defined by gurgling irrigation streams and birdsong.

Dozens of local families have signed up to a highly successful homestay initiative, and for visitors the chance to sleep in a traditional stilt house is a real appeal – though note that the villages are on the tour-group agenda. If you're looking for hardcore exploration, this is not the place, but for biking, hiking and relaxation, Mai Chau fits the bill nicely.

◉ Sights & Activities

You can **walk** past rice fields and **trek** to minority villages; a local guide costs about US$10. Most homestays also rent bikes.

A popular 18km trek is from **Lac village** (Ban Lac) in Mai Chau to the Hmong **Xa Linh village**, near a mountain pass (elevation 1000m) on Hwy 6. This trek takes in a 600m climb in altitude and usually involves an overnight stay.

Many travel agencies in Hanoi run inexpensive trips to Mai Chau.

🛏 Sleeping & Eating

Most visitors stay in **Thai stilt houses** (per person incl breakfast around 200,000d) in the villages of Lac or Pom Coong, just a five-minute stroll apart. All homestays have electricity, running water, hot showers, mosquito nets and roll-up mattresses. **Mai Chau Nature Lodge** (☑ 0946 888 804; www.maichaunatureplace.com; Lac Village; dm US$5, d US$40) in Lac village offers dorms, private bungalows with bamboo furniture and free bikes.

Most people eat where they stay. Establish the price of meals first as some families charge up to 150,000d for dinner. Warning: cheesy song-and-dance routines follow dinner at some places.

❶ Getting There & Around

Direct buses to Mai Chau leave Hanoi's My Dinh bus station at 6am, 8.30am and 11am (100,000d, 3¾ hours). Alternatively, catch a regular Son La or Dien Bien Phu bus to Tong Dau junction (100,000d, 3½ hours) from where it's 25,000d in a *xe om*.

Lao Cai

☑ 020 / POP 47,000

One of the gateways to the north, Lao Cai lies at the end of the train line, 3km from the Chinese border. The town has no sights but is a major hub for travellers journeying between Hanoi, Sapa and the Chinese city of Kunming.

There are ATMs next to the train station, plus internet cafes close by. You'll find inexpensive hotels around the station including the clean **Nga Nghi Tho Huong** (☑ 020-383 5111; 342A P Nguyen Hué; r 180,000-300,000d; ❈ 🗢).

❶ Getting There & Around

Nine daily buses (250,000d, nine hours) ply the Hanoi–Lao Cai route, but virtually everyone pre-

---

GETTING TO CHINA: HANOI TO KUNMING

Getting to the border The Lao Cai/Hekou crossing connects northern Vietnam with Yunnan Province in China. The border is about 3km from the Lao Cai train station; *xe om* charge 25,000d.

At the border The border crossing is open from 7am to 10pm. Travellers have reported Chinese officials confiscating *Lonely Planet China* guides at this border, so you may want to try masking the cover. Visas must be arranged in advance.

Moving on Trains do not currently run from Hekou to Kunming, but there are several 'sleeper' buses (Y175); two leaving at 7.20pm and 7.30pm for the 12-hour journey to Kunming.

fers the train. Minibuses for Sapa (50,000d, one hour) wait by the train station, while services to Bac Ha (60,000d, 2½ hours) leave at 6.30am, 8.15am, 9am, 11.30am, noon, 2pm and 3pm from a terminal next to the Red River bridge.

Rail tickets to Hanoi (8½ to 10 hours) start at 135,000d for a hard seat (bad choice) to 515,000d for an air-con soft sleeper, and rise by about 15% at weekends. There are three night trains and two day trains in either direction.

Bac Ha

☎ 020 / POP 7400

An unhurried and friendly town, Bac Ha makes a relaxed base to explore the northern highlands and hill-tribe villages. The atmosphere is very different from Sapa, and you can walk the streets freely without being accosted by hawkers. The climate here is also noticeably warmer than in Sapa.

Bac Ha has a certain charm, though its stock of traditional old adobe houses is dwindling and being replaced by concrete structures. Wood smoke fills the morning air and chickens and pigs poke around the back lanes. For six days a week Bac Ha slumbers, but its lanes fill up to choking point each Sunday when tourists and Flower Hmong flood in for the weekly market.

◎ Sights

Bac Ha's Sunday market is a riot of colour and commerce. The *ruou* corn hooch produced by the Flower Hmong is so potent it can ignite; there's an entire area devoted to it at the Sunday market.

While you're here, check out the outlandish **Vua Meo** ('Cat King' House; ◎ 7.30-11.30am & 1.30-5pm) **FREE** a palace constructed in a kind of bizarre 'oriental baroque' architectural style.

Beyond town lie several interesting markets; tour operators in Bac Ha can arrange day trips to all the following.

Can Cau Market   MARKET
(◎ 6am-1pm Sat) A Saturday morning market, 20km north of Bac Ha that spills down a hillside with food stalls on one level and livestock at the bottom of the valley, includ-

ing plenty of dogs. Locals will implore you to drink the local *ruou* with them and you can't fail to be impressed with the costumes of the Flower Hmong and Blue Hmong (look out for the striking zigzag costume of the latter).

Coc Ly Market   MARKET
(◎ 6am-1pm Tue) The impressive Coc Ly market attracts Dzao, Flower Hmong, Tay and Nung people from the surrounding hills. It's about 35km southwest of Bac Ha along reasonably good roads.

Lung Phin Market   MARKET
(◎ 6am-1pm Sun) About 12km from town, this Sunday market has a really local feel, and is a good place to move on to once the tour buses arrive in Bac Ha from Sapa.

✦ Activities

There's great hiking to hill-tribe villages around Bac Ha. The Flower Hmong village of **Ban Pho** is one of the nearest to town. Other nearby villages include **Trieu Cai**, an 8km return walk, and **Na Ang**, a 6km return walk; it's best to set up a trip with a local guide.

Tour guides in Bac Ha can arrange visits to rural schools as part of a motorbike or trekking day trip. There's also a **waterfall** near Thai Giang Pho village, about 12km east of Bac Ha, which has a pool big enough for swimming.

Consult www.bachatourist.com for inspiration; it's operated by English-speaking **Mr Nghe** (☎ 0912 005 952; www.bachatourist.com; Green Sapa Tour, Đ Tran Bac), Bac Ha's one-man tourism dynamo. All hotels recommended here offer excursions too.

🛏 Sleeping & Eating

Room rates increase on weekends; weekday rates are quoted here.

Hoang Vu Hotel   GUESTHOUSE $
(☎ 020-388 0264; www.bachatourist.com; 5 Đ Tran Bac; r from US$8) It's nothing fancy, but the spacious rooms offer good value (all have TV and fan). The best spot in town for budget travellers.

BUSES FROM BAC HA

DESTINATION	PRICE (D)	DURATION (HR)	FREQUENCY
Hanoi	400,000	11	8pm
Lao Cai	60,000	2½	6 daily

Ngan Nga Bac Ha
HOTEL **$**

(☑ 020-380 0286; www.nganngabachahotel.com; 117 Ngoc Uyen; r US$18-20; ☎) This friendly place is above a popular restaurant that does a roaring trade in tasty hotpots. Tours to homestays and markets can be arranged.

Congfu Hotel
HOTEL **$$**

(☑ 020-388 0254; www.congfuhotel.com; 152 Ngoc Uyen; r US$30; ✳ @ ☎) This place has 21 attractive rooms and its restaurant (meals from 60,000d) is one of the best in town. Book rooms 205, 208, 305 or 308 for a floor-to-ceiling window overlooking Bac Ha Market.

Hoang Yen Restaurant
VIETNAMESE **$**

(Đ Tran Bac; mains 60,000-100,000d; ⊘ 7am-10pm; ☎) Hoang Yen's menu includes decent breakfast options and a good-value set menu for 140,000d. Cheap beer and wi-fi access are both available. You'll find it right on Bac Ha's main square.

ⓘ Information

There's an ATM at the Agribank and wi-fi access at Hoang Yen Restaurant.

ⓘ Getting There & Away

Tours to Bac Ha from Sapa cost from US$20 per person; on the way back you can bail out in Lao Cai and catch the train back to Hanoi.

A motorbike/taxi to Lao Cai costs US$25/70, or to Sapa US$30/80.

Sapa

☑ 020 / POP 37,300 / ELEV 1650M

Sapa overlooks a plunging valley of cascading rice terraces, with mountains towering above the town on all sides. Founded as a French hill station in 1922, it's the premier tourist destination in northern Vietnam. Views of this epic scenery are often subdued by thick mist rolling across the peaks, but even if it's cloudy, Sapa is still a fascinating place, especially when local hill-tribe people fill the town with colour.

The town's colonial villas fell into disrepair during successive wars, but Sapa has experienced a recent renaissance – the downside of which is a hotel-building boom.

Inherent in this prosperity is cultural change for the hill-tribe people. Many have little formal education but have a good command of several languages, and are canny (and persistent) traders, urging you to buy handicrafts.

Sapa is known for its cold, foggy winters (down to 0°C). The dry season for Sapa is approximately January to the end of June.

◉ Sights & Activities

Surrounding Sapa are the Hoang Lien Mountains, including Fansipan, which at 3143m is Vietnam's highest peak. The trek from Sapa to the summit and back can take several days. Some of the better-known sights around Sapa include the epic Tram Ton Pass; the pretty Thac Bac (Silver Falls); and Cau May (Cloud Bridge), which spans the Muong Hoa River.

Treks can be arranged at many guesthouses and travel agencies.

★ Sapa Market
MARKET

(⊘ 6am-2pm) Hill-tribe people go to the Sapa market most days to sell handicrafts and ethnic-style clothing. Saturday is the busiest day, but every day the market's food stalls are popular for breakfast and lunch. The location of the town's market may change in the next few years.

Sapa Museum
MUSEUM

(103 Đ Xuan Vien; ⊘ 7.30-11.30am & 1.30-5pm) **FREE** Excellent showcase of the history and ethnology of the Sapa area including the colonial period. Exhibitions demonstrate the differences between the various ethnic minority people of the area.

★ Sapa O'Chau
HIKING

(☑ 020-377 1166; www.sapaochau.com; 8 Đ Thac Bac; ⊘ 6.30am-6.30pm) Excellent day walks, longer homestay treks and Fansipan hikes are offered. Profits from this tour agency provide training to Hmong children in a learning centre. Volunteers are welcome.

🛏 Sleeping

Green Valley Hotel
HOSTEL **$**

(☑ 0979 110 800; sapagreenvalleyhotel@gmail.com; 45 Đ Muong Hoa; dm US$4, s US$7-10, d & tw US$10-15; @ ☎) Sapa's only true backpacker hostel is this welcoming spot with great views. Motorcycles can be rented for US$5 per day, and there's a cosy on-site bar with pool table. It's also a good source of information for onward travel to Laos or China.

Casablanca Sapa Hotel
BOUTIQUE HOTEL **$**

(☑ 0974 418 111; www.casablancasapahotel.com; 26 Dong Loi; r US$22-30; @ ☎) One of Sapa's first boutique hotels has a new lease on life thanks to the friendly owners. Look forward to colourful decor and good hospitality from Mr Tom.

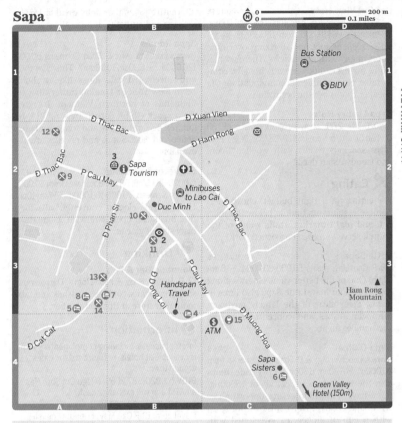

Sapa

⊙ Sights
1 Sapa Church..B2
2 Sapa Market..B3
3 Sapa Museum.......................................B2

🛈 Activities, Courses & Tours
Sapa O'Chau................................(see 12)

🛏 Sleeping
4 Casablanca Sapa Hotel.......................B4
5 Cat Cat View Hotel..............................A3
6 Luong Thuy Family Guesthouse..........C4
7 Phuong Nam Hotel..............................A3
8 Sapa Luxury Hotel...............................A3

🍴 Eating
9 Baguette & Chocolat............................A2
10 Little Sapa..B2
11 Sapa Market...B3
12 Sapa O'Chau..A2
13 Sapa Rooms...A3
14 The Hill Station Signature
    Restaurant...A3

🍸 Drinking & Nightlife
15 Mountain Bar & Pub..............................C4

**Luong Thuy Family
Guesthouse** GUESTHOUSE **$**
(📞 020-387 2310; www.familysapa.com; 28 Đ
Muong Hoa; s/d from US$15/18; @🛜) This
friendly guesthouse is slightly away from the
hubbub of downtown Sapa. Motorcycles and
bikes can be rented, trekking and transport

arranged, and there are valley views from
front balconies.

Phuong Nam Hotel GUESTHOUSE **$**
(📞 0975 055 199; hanghai289@gmail.com; 33 Đ Phan
Si; dm/s/d/tr US$5/12/15/18; @🛜) Cheap rooms
and dorms with access to lots of good restaurants nearby. Motorcycles can be rented.

Cat Cat View Hotel   HOTEL $$

(☑ 020-387 1946; www.catcathotel.com; 46 Đ Phan Si; budget r US$10, s/d from US$30/35; @ 🛜) This excellent spot has 40 rooms over nine floors, many with great views. There's something for every budget, with homely, comfortable pine-trimmed accommodation; the cheaper rooms are the best value.

Sapa Luxury Hotel   HOTEL $$

(☑ 020-387 2771; www.sapaluxuryhotel.com; 36 Đ Phan Si; s/d/tr from US$28/28/35; @ 🛜) Features spacious rooms with wooden floors and trendy Asian decor.

Eating

For eating on a tight budget, cheap Vietnamese restaurants huddle below the market, and **night-market stalls** south of the church serve *bun cha* (barbecued pork).

Little Sapa   VIETNAMESE $

(18 P Cau May; mains 50,000-80,000d; ⊗ 8am-10pm) One of the better-value eateries along touristy P Cau May, Little Sapa also lures in locals. Steer clear of the largely mediocre European dishes and concentrate on the Vietnamese menu.

Sapa O'Chau   CAFE $

(www.sapaochau.org; 8 Đ Thac Bac; snacks from 20,000d; ⊗ 6.30am-6.30pm) Cosy cafe that's also the best place to ask about trekking, homestays and volunteering opportunities with Sapa O'Chau. Don't miss warming up with a cup of ginger tea sweetened with Sapa mountain honey.

Sapa Market   VIETNAMESE $

(P Cau May; dishes around 30,000d; ⊗ 6am-1pm; 🥢) Lots of local food stalls and a good

---

SPLURGE

Cool Zen decor and superb views showcase Hmong ethnic minority cuisine at the **Hill Station Signature Restaurant** (www.thehillstation. com; 37 Đ Phan Si; meals 90,000-180,000d; ⊗ 7am-10.30pm). Dishes include chicken with wild ginger, ash-baked trout in banana leaves, and traditional Hmong-style black pudding. Tasting sets of local rice and corn wine are also of interest to curious travelling foodies. Don't miss trying the delicate rainbow-trout rolls; think of them as 'Sapa sushi'.

---

alternative to another hotel breakfast or for a cheap and authentic lunch.

Sapa Rooms   CAFE $$

(www.saparooms.com; Đ Phan Si; mains 60,000-120,000d; ⊗ 6.30am-10.30pm) This flamboyantly decorated cafe looks like it should be in New York or London rather than the highlands of northern Vietnam. It's great for a snack (think corn fritters or BLT baguette), decent burgers and soups, and great coffee and cake. Soups and noodles are also available.

Baguette & Chocolat   CAFE $$

(☑ 020-387 1766; Đ Thac Bac; cakes from 30,000d, snacks & meals 70,000-160,000d; ⊗ 7am-10pm) Head to this elegant converted villa for a fine breakfast, open sandwich, baguette or tasty slab of gateau.

🍷 Drinking

Mountain Bar & Pub   BAR

(2 Đ Muong Hoa; ⊗ noon-11pm) Dangerously strong cocktails, cold beer, shishas and table football feature at this popular bar.

ℹ Information

Internet access, including complimentary wi-fi, is available at hotels, restaurants and cafes around town.

BIDV (☑ 020-387 2569; Đ Ngu Chi Son) Has an ATM and will exchange cash.

Duc Minh (☑ 020-387 1881; www.ducminh travel.com; 10 P Cau May) Friendly English-speaking operator organising transport, treks to hill-tribe villages and ascents of Fansipan.

Handspan Travel (☑ 020-387 2110; www. handspan.com; Chau Long Hotel, 24 Dong Loi) Offers trekking and mountain-biking tours to villages and markets.

Main Post Office (Đ Ham Rong) International phone calls can also be made here.

Sapa Sisters (www.sapasisters.webs.com; Luong Thuy Family Guesthouse, 28 Đ Muong Hoa) Trekking and homestays with a group of savvy and knowledgeable Hmong girls.

Sapa Tourism (☑ 020-387 3239; www.sapa-tourism.com; 103 Đ Xuan Vien; ⊗ 7.30-11.30am & 1.30-5pm) Helpful English-speaking staff offering details about transport, trekking and weather. Internet access is free for 15 minutes, and the organisation's website is also a mine of useful information.

ℹ Getting There & Away

The gateway to Sapa is Lao Cai, 38km away to the west. Minibuses (50,000d, one hour) make the trip regularly until mid-afternoon.

A minibus to Bac Ha for the Sunday market is around US$30 per person; departure from Sapa is at 6am and from Bac Ha at 1pm. It's cheaper to go by public minibus, changing in Lao Cai. Direct sleeper buses for Hanoi (300,000d, 10 hours) depart from Sapa's main square, and there's a 5pm sleeper bus to Halong City (500,000d, 13 hours). Services to Dien Bien Phu will resume when highway improvements are finished (scheduled for late 2014).

Most hotels and travel agencies can book train tickets from Lao Cai to Hanoi.

❶ Getting Around

Downtown Sapa can be walked in 20 minutes. You can hire a motorbike for per day, or take one with a driver from US$12.

Dien Bien Phu

📞 0230 / POP 77,400

On 7 May 1954 French colonial forces were defeated by the Viet Minh in a decisive battle at Dien Bien Phu (DBP), and the days of their Indochine empire were numbered.

Previously just a minor settlement, DBP only became a provincial capital in 2004. Boulevards and civic buildings have been constructed and the airport now has daily flights from Hanoi.

⊙ Sights

★ **Dien Bien Phu Museum** MUSEUM
(📞 0230-382 4971; Đ 7-5; admission 5000d; ⊙ 7-11am & 1.30-5pm) Commemorating the 1954 battle, this well-laid-out museum features eclectic content. Alongside weaponry and guns, there's a bicycle capable of carrying 330kg of ordnance, and photographs and documents, some with English translations. At the time of writing, a new modern structure to house the collection was under construction.

★ **Bunker of Colonel de Castries** MONUMENT
(admission 5000d; ⊙ 7-11am & 1.30-5pm) Across the river the command bunker of Colonel Christian de Castries has been recreated. You'll probably see Vietnamese tourists mounting the bunker and waving the national flag.

★ **A1 Hill** MONUMENT
(admission 3000d; ⊙ 7-11am & 1.30-5pm) There are more tanks and a monument to Viet Minh casualties on this former French position. The elaborate trenches at the heart of the French defences have also been recreated.

🍽 Sleeping & Eating

Dining options are limited in DBP. You'll find *pho* stalls and simple restaurants opposite the bus station.

Viet Hoang 2 GUESTHOUSE $
(📞 0989 797 988; 69 Đ Phuong Thanh Binh; r 250,000-350,000d; ❄ @ 🛜) Tucked away opposite the bus station, this guesthouse is the newer (and much cleaner) offshoot of the older, nearby Viet Hoang 1 (rooms 150,000d to 200,000d). The extra dong are definitely worth it.

Binh Long Hotel GUESTHOUSE $
(📞 0230-382 4345; 429 Đ Muong Thanh; d & tw US$10; ❄ 🛜) Another small, friendly, family-run place, but on a busy junction in the thick of things. The twin rooms aren't exactly huge, but the owners know about onward transport to Sapa and Laos.

Lien Tuoi Restaurant VIETNAMESE $
(📞 0230-382 4919; Đ Hoang Van Thai; mains 60,000-90,000d) A long-running place famous for its filling Vietnamese and Chinese food, Lien Tuoi has a menu in English and French with some imaginative translations.

Bia Hoi VIETNAMESE $
(Đ Hoang Van Thai; ⊙ noon-10pm) You can meet the locals at the *bia hoi* gardens along Đ Hoang Van Thai. There's also decent and cheap grilled food if you're tired of rice and noodles.

❶ Information

Internet cafes are on Đ Hoang Van Thai.
Agribank (📞 0230-382 5786; Đ 7-5) Has an ATM and changes US dollars.
Main Post Office (Đ 7-5) Post and phone services.

BUSES FROM DIEN BIEN PHU

DESTINATION	PRICE (D)	DURATION (HR)	FREQUENCY
Hanoi	375,000	11½	frequent 4.30am-9pm
Lai Chau	130,000	6-7	frequent 5am-1.15pm
Son La	97,000	4	4.30am, 8am, noon, 2pm

ⓘ Getting There & Away

Vietnam Airlines (☑0230-382 4948; www. vietnamairlines.com; Nguyen Huu Tho; ⊙7.30-11.30am & 1.30-4.30pm) Operates one flight daily between Dien Bien Phu and Hanoi. The office is near the airport, about 1.5km from the town centre.

NORTH-CENTRAL VIETNAM

With ancient history, compelling culture, incredible food and terrific beaches, north-central Vietnam has real allure. This is an area that packs in the serene city of Hué (Vietnam's former imperial capital), DMZ battle sites, booming Danang and Hoi An, an exquisite architectural gem that time forgot. Chuck in the ruins of My Son, extraordinary cave systems of Phong Nha, the karst scenery around Ninh Binh and numerous nature reserves and the region's appeal is overwhelming.

Ninh Binh

☑030 / POP 130,000

The city of Ninh Binh, 93km south of Hanoi, isn't a destination in itself, but it's a good base for exploring some quintessentially Vietnamese karst scenery and bucolic countryside (including Tam Coc and Cuc Phuong National Park). However, Ninh Binh has become a massive destination for domestic travellers, and many of its attractions are heavily commercialised.

🛏 Sleeping & Eating

Accommodation is excellent value here. All the places listed can arrange tours and hire out motorbikes and bicycles.

Restaurant choices are limited. Try the local speciality, *de* (goat meat); there are also lots of snail restaurants serving delicious *oc luoc xa* (snails cooked with lemongrass and chilli) in the lanes north of Ð Luong Van Tuy.

GETTING TO LAOS: NORTHERN BORDERS

Dien Bien Phu to Muang Khua

Getting to the border Buses from Dien Bien Phu to Muang Khua (110,000d, seven to eight hours) leave daily at 5.30am, crossing at the Tay Trang/Sop Hun border. It's advisable to book your ticket the day prior to travelling. The journey can be longer depending on the roads and border formalities. Other destinations in Laos from DBP include Luang Prabang (495,000d, 6am), Nam Tha (350,000d, 6.30am) and Udomxai (230,000d, 7.30am).

At the border Open daily from 7am to 7pm. Most travellers can get a 30-day visa on arrival (US$20 to US$42, depending on your nationality). Have photo ID and additional cash (around US$5) on hand for occasional local administrative fees.

Moving on From Muang Khua there are buses to Udomxai.

Thanh Hoa to Sam Neua

Getting to the border Those seeking a backwoods adventure can try the Na Meo/Nam Soi border crossing. If at all possible take a direct bus and avoid getting onward transport on the Vietnamese side of the border where foreigners are seriously ripped off. There's a daily 8am bus from Thanh Hoa's western bus station (Ben Xe Mien Tay) to Sam Neua (310,000d), but expect overcharging.

At the border The border is open from 7am to 5pm. Lao visas are available on arrival from Vietnam, for US$30 to US$40 depending on nationality. Bring a passport photo, otherwise pay an extra 40B. Readers have reported no hassle from border officials, but they may try to offer you bad rates for all currencies – you'll get a better deal in Na Meo hotels. It's best not to get stuck on the Laos side of the border as transport is extremely irregular and there's no accommodation. Na Meo has several basic, serviceable guesthouses.

Moving on There's unbelievable overcharging on this route (unless you're on a direct bus). Vietnamese bus drivers demand up to US$50 for the trip to Thanh Hoa (it should cost about US$8).

Thanh Thuy's Guest House & New Hotel

GUESTHOUSE $

(☑030-387 1811; www.hotelthanhthuy.com; 53 Đ Le Hong Phong; r with fan/air-con from 150,000/250,000d; ❋@🛜) Set well back from the road, this guesthouse's courtyard and restaurant are a great place to meet other travellers. Offers good-value, clean rooms, some with balcony. It also runs tours.

Kinh Do Hotel

HOTEL $

(☑030-389 9152; http://kinhdohotel.vn; 18 Đ Phanh Dinh Phung; s/d 140,000/250,000d; ❋@🛜) The service here is excellent, as management goes the extra mile (even offering free pick-ups from the bus/train station). Spacious, clean rooms with high ceilings represent fine value.

★Thuy Anh Hotel

HOTEL $$

(☑030-387 1602; www.thuyanhhotel.com; 55A Đ Truong Han Sieu; r old wing US$15-25, r new wing US$25-35; ❀❋@🛜) A well-run place with good-value rooms in the old wing and spotless, tastefully furnished and comfortable rooms in the new wing. The restaurant serves Vietnamese and Western-style food (including hearty complimentary breakfasts).

ℹ Information

You'll find a cluster of internet cafes on Đ Luong Van Tuy and several ATMs on Đ Tran Hung Dao.

ℹ Getting There & Away

Public buses leave very regularly from Giap Bat and Luong Yen bus terminals in Hanoi (70,000d, 2½ hours). The bus station is on the east side of the Van River. The city is on the open-tour bus route too.

Ninh Binh is a scheduled stop for some trains travelling between Hanoi and HCMC.

Around Ninh Binh

Guesthouses in Ninh Binh can arrange transport and tours to all the sights around town.

Tam Coc

Famed for huge limestone rock formations that loom over rice paddies, Tam Coc (per boat 1/2 people 110,000/140,000d) boasts breathtaking scenery, though it is touristy.

The only way to see Tam Coc is by rowboat on the Ngo Dong River. The boats pass through karst caves on this beautiful two-hour trip. Boats seat two passengers (and have no

shade). Arrive before 9am to beat the crowds, and prepare yourself for pushy vendors.

Tam Coc is 9km southwest of Ninh Binh. By car or motorbike, follow Hwy 1 south and turn west at the turn-off.

Chua Bai Dinh

A vast (modern) Buddhist temple complex, Chua Bai Dinh (◷7am-5.45pm) FREE attracts thousands of Vietnamese visitors. Cloisterlike walkways pass 500 stone *arhats* (statues of enlightened Buddhists). They line the route up to the triple-roofed Phap Chu pagoda, which contains a 10m, 100-tonne bronze Buddha. Chua Bai Dinh is 11km northwest of Ninh Binh.

Hoa Lu

Hoa Lu was the capital of Vietnam under the Dinh (968–80) and Le dynasties (980–1009). The ancient citadel (admission 10,000d), most of which, sadly, has been destroyed, once covered an area of about 3 sq km. Hoa Lu is 12km north of Ninh Binh.

Cuc Phuong National Park

☑030 / ELEV 150-648M

This national park (☑030-384 8006; www.cucphuongtourism.com; adult/child 40,000/20,000d) is one of Vietnam's most important nature preserves, and was declared the nation's first national park in 1963. The climate is subtropical at the park's lower elevations.

Excellent trekking opportunities abound in the park, including a hike (8km return) to an enormous 1000-year-old tree (*Tetrameles nudiflora*, for botany geeks), and to a Muong village, where you can also go rafting. A guide is mandatory for longer treks.

The Endangered Primate Rescue Center (☑030-384 8002; www.primatecenter. org; ◷9.30-11.30am & 1.30-4.30pm) is home to around 150 rare monkeys bred in captivity or confiscated from illegal traders. These gibbons, langurs and lorises are rehabilitated, studied and, whenever possible, released into semi-wild protected areas.

There's also a Turtle Conservation Center (☑030-384 8090; www.asianturtlenet work.org; ◷9-11am & 2-4.45pm). You'll find excellent information displays, and there are incubation and hatchling viewing areas. The centre successfully breeds and releases turtles of 11 different species.

During the rainy season (July to September) leeches are common in Cuc Phuong.

Sleeping & Eating

There are three accommodation areas.

At the visitor centre are dark, **basic rooms** (per person US$8) and decent en suite **guesthouse rooms** (US$25-30); 2km away you'll find attractive **bungalows** (US$35) overlooking Mac Lake.

The main park centre, 18km from the gate, has simple **rooms** (per person US$8), large **four-bed rooms** (US$25) and a few **bungalows** (r US$32).

You'll find **restaurants** (meals 25,000-50,000d) in all three locations. It's important to call ahead and place your order for each meal (except breakfast).

Cuc Phuong can get very busy at weekends and holiday time, when you should make a reservation.

❶ Getting There & Away

Cuc Phuong National Park is 45km west of Ninh Binh, with irregular bus connections (28,000d, 1½ hours).

Phong Nha-Ke Bang National Park

A Unesco World Heritage Site, the remarkable **Phong Nha-Ke Bang National Park** FREE contains the oldest karst mountains in Asia and is riddled with hundreds of cave systems. Its collection of stunning dry caves, terraced caves, towering stalagmites and glistening crystal-edged stalactites represent nature on a very grand scale indeed.

Serious exploration only began in the 1990s, led by the British Cave Research Association and Hanoi University. Cavers first penetrated deep into Phong Nha Cave, one of the world's longest systems. In 2005 Paradise Cave was discovered, and in 2009 a team found the world's largest cave – Son Doong. Huge caverns and unknown cave networks are being discovered each year.

Above the ground, most of this mountainous 885-sq-km national park is near-pristine tropical evergreen jungle, over 90% of which is primary forest. More than 100 types of mammal (including 10 species of primate, tigers, elephants and the saola, a rare Asian antelope), 81 types of reptile and amphibian, and more than 300 varieties of bird have been logged in Phong Nha.

Until recently, access was strictly controlled by the Vietnamese military. Things are relaxing, but remain quite tight: officially you are not allowed to hike here without a licensed tour operator.

The Phong Nha region is changing fast, with more and more accommodation options opening. **Son Trach** village (population 3000) is the main centre, but it's a tiny place – there's only one ATM and transport connections are poor.

◉ Sights & Activities

Paradise Cave   CAVE
(Thien Dong; adult/child under 1.3m 120,000/60,000d; ⊙ 7.30am-4.30pm) Deep in the national park, surrounded by forest and karst peaks, this remarkable cave system extends for 31km, though most people only visit the first kilometre or so. Once you're inside, the sheer scale of Paradise Cave is truly breathtaking, as wooden staircases descend into a cathedral-like space replete with colossal stalagmites and glimmering stalactites of white crystal that resemble glass pillars.

Commendably, development has been sensitive. But in the last few years, visitor numbers have soared – spoiling the whole experience. Try to get here as early as you can to beat the crowds.

Paradise Cave is about 14km southwest of Son Trach.

Tu Lan Caves   CAVE
An outstanding excursion, the Tu Lan cave trip begins with a countryside hike then a swim (with headlamps and life jackets) through two spectacular river caves before emerging in an idyllic river valley. Then there's more hiking through dense forest to a 'beach' where rivers merge that's an ideal campsite. There's more wonderful swimming here into vast river caverns. Tu Lan is 65km north of Son Trach and can only be visited on a guided tour. Oxalis (p848) is the specialist.

Phong Nha Caves & Boat Trip   CAVE
(adult/child 50,000/25,000d, boat 300,000d; ⊙ 7am-4pm) The spectacular boat trip through Phong Nha Cave is a highly enjoyable, though quite touristy, experience beginning in Son Trach village. You cruise along the Son River past bathing buffalo, jagged limestone peaks and church steeples to the cave's gaping mouth. Then the engine is cut and you're transported to another world as you're paddled through cavern after garishly illuminated cavern.

Hang En
CAVE

This gigantic cave is very close to Hang Son Doong. Getting here involves a trek through dense jungle, valleys and the Ban Doong minority village. You stay overnight in the cave or the minority village.

Tours (4,600,000d per person, minimum two people) are run by park rangers.

🛏 Sleeping & Eating

There are a dozen or so guesthouses (all 200,000d) and cheap eateries in Son Trach village.

Easy Tiger
HOSTEL $

(☑052-367 7844; www.easytigerphongnha.com; Son Trach; dm 160,000d; ❄ @ �🢒) Owned by the Farmstay crew, this great new hostel has comfortable dorms, an inviting bar-resto area, pool table and excellent travel info and tours. There's a real vibe developing here and a swimming pool is planned.

Thanh Dat
GUESTHOUSE $

(☑052-367 7069; Son Trach; r 250,000d; ❄ �🢒) This is the most welcoming locally owned place. Rooms are clean and the family speaks a little English.

★ Phong Nha Farmstay
GUESTHOUSE $$

(☑052-367 5135; www.phong-nha-cave.com; Cu Nam village; r 500,000-900,000d, f 1,500,000d; ⊝ ❄ @ ⟬ ✉) The Farmstay has views overlooking an ocean of rice paddies, and smallish but neat rooms, with high ceilings and shared balconies. The bar-restaurant with pool table has tasty Asian and Western grub (meals 40,000d to 120,000d) and a gregarious vibe.

VIETNAM PHONG NHA-KE BANG NATIONAL PARK

GETTING TO LAOS: CENTRAL BORDERS

Vinh to Lak Sao

Getting to the border The Cau Treo/Nam Phao border crossing is 96km west of Vinh and about 30km east of Lak Sao in Laos. This border has a dodgy reputation with travellers, who report chronic overcharging and hassles on local buses (such as bus drivers ejecting foreigners in the middle of nowhere unless they cough up extra bucks). Stick to direct services. Buses leave Vinh at 6am (on Mondays, Wednesdays, Fridays and Saturdays) for Vieng Khan in Laos (280,000d). There are also regular local buses from Vinh to Tay Son (70,000d, two hours) and then irregular services from Tay Son on to the border at Cau Treo. Otherwise *xe om* (motorbike taxi) ask around 170,000d for the ride.

At the border The border is open from 7am to 6pm. Laos issues 30-day visas (costing between US$30 and US$40) on arrival. There's an exchange booth on the Laos side with ungenerous rates and, inconveniently, the Vietnam border post is another 1km up the road. Bring a passport photo if you're headed into Laos, otherwise pay an extra 40B.

Moving on On the Laos side, a jumbo or *sŏrngtǎaou* (small pick-up truck) between the border and Lak Sao runs to about 50,000 kip (bargain hard).

Vinh to Phonsavan

Getting to the border The often mist-shrouded Nam Can/Nong Haet border crossing is 250km northwest of Vinh. Direct buses from Vinh's marketplace leave daily for Phonsavan in Laos (320,000d, 12 hours). It's possible to travel independently from Vinh to Muong Xen by bus and then take a motorbike (around 170,000d) uphill to the border, but we strongly recommend you take the direct option due to overcharging and hassle.

At the border Open daily from 8am to 5pm. Laos issues 30-day visas (costing between US$30 and US$40) on arrival. There's an exchange booth on the Laos side with ungenerous rates and, inconveniently, the Vietnam border post is another 1km up the road. Bring a passport photo if you're headed into Laos, otherwise pay an extra 40B.

Moving on Transport on the Laos side to Nong Haet is erratic, but once you get there, you can pick up a bus to Phonsavan.

Dong Hoi to Tha Khaek

Buses leave Dong Hoi for the Lao towns of Vien Chan and Savannakhet (430,000d, 12 hours, both at 6.30am Monday to Saturday only) via the quiet Cha Lo/Na Phao border crossing where Lao visas are available.

HANG SON DOONG

Ho Khanh, a hunter, stumbled across gargantuan **Hang Son Doong** (Mountain River Cave) in the early 1990s, but the sheer scale and majesty of the principal cavern (more than 5km long, 200m high and, in some places, 150m wide) was only confirmed as the world's biggest cave when British explorers returned with him in 2009.

Sections of the cave are pierced by skylights that reveal formations of ethereal stalagmites (some up to 80m high) that cavers have called the Cactus Garden. Colossal cave pearls have been discovered, measuring 10cm in diameter. Magnificent rimstone pools are present too.

Hang Son Doong is one of the most spectacular sights in Southeast Asia, and the only specialist operator permitted (by the Vietnamese president no less) to lead tours here is Son Trach–based Oxalis. Seven-day expeditions cost a backpacking blowout US$3000 per person.

Tours are outstanding. There are no dorms. It's in Cu Nam village, 9km east of Son Trach.

Phong Nha Lake House Resort HOTEL **$$**
(☑052-367 5999; http://phongnhalakehouse.com; Khuong Ha; dm/d/villas US$10/35/50; ❀ 🜚) Impressive new lakeside resort owned by an Australian-Vietnamese couple with an excellent dorm (with quality beds, mossie nets, en suite bathroom and high ceilings), spacious and stylish rooms and lovely villas. A pool, Jacuzzi and spa are planned. It's 7km east of Son Trach.

★ **Jungle Bar** CAFE **$**
(Son Trach; meals 25,000-50,000d; ⊙7am-midnight; 🜚) Run by Hai, a switched-on, English-speaking local, this cool bar-cafe offers cheap grub (including breakfasts and vegetarian choices), fresh juices, travel info and a welcoming atmosphere. In the evening it's more of a bar, with lounge music, cocktails and an open mic some nights.

❶ Information

In Son Trach, head to the Jungle Bar where owner Hai (an ecologist) is a superb source of independent travel information, can book train and bus tickets, organise tours and rent bikes and motorbikes. Staff at Phong Nha Farmstay and Easy Tiger hostel are also extremely well informed and can assist with information and transport.

There's an ATM in Son Trach and some places have wi-fi.

❶ Getting There & Around

The coastal city of Dong Hoi, 166km north of Hué on Hwy 1 and on the north–south train line, is the main gateway to Phong Nha. The national park abuts Son Trach village, which is 50km northwest of Dong Hoi.

Local buses (45,000d, two hours) offer irregular connections between Dong Hoi and Son Trach. There's also a bus connection (120,000d, 1hr 15min) between Dong Hoi train station, the Farmstay and Son Trach. It leaves Dong Hoi daily at 6.30am and 8am and returns from Son Trach (via Farmstay) at 6pm and 8pm. A tour bus (500,000d, five hours) also links Son Trach, the Farmstay and Hué, stopping at the Ben Hai River Museum and Vinh Moc Tunnels. It leaves Son Trach at 6.30am daily and returns from Hué at 1pm. Tickets on these buses to/from Hué and Dong Hoi can be booked via the Farmstay, Easy Tiger or Hué Backpackers.

Hotels can organise lifts in private cars from Dong Hoi (400,000d to 500,000d); they work together so rides can be shared between travellers to cut costs.

Organised tours are an excellent way to explore the park – those run by Phong Nha Farmstay are recommended (1,000,000d by minibus). Oxalis (☑052-367 7678; www.oxalis.co.vn; Son Trach) is a highly professional adventure tour operator specialising in caving and trekking expeditions, and is the only outfit licensed to conduct tours to Hang Son Doong.

It's possible to rent a bike and explore the region yourself, though road signs are lacking. But with a sense of adventure, some wheels and a map (ask at Jungle Bar) it's perfectly do-able.

Hué

☑054 / POP 348,000

Palaces and pagodas, tombs and temples, culture and cuisine, history and heartbreak – there's no shortage of poetic pairings to describe the graceful city of Hué. A World Heritage Site, the capital of the Nguyen emperors is where tourists come to see opulent royal tombs and the grand, crumbling Citadel. Most of these architectural attractions lie along the northern side of the Song Huong (Perfume River). For rest and recreation, plus a little refreshment, the south bank is where it's at.

The city hosts a biennial arts festival, the Festival of Hué (www.Huéfestival.com), every even-numbered year, featuring local and international artists and performers.

◉ Sights & Activities

Most of Hué's principal sights reside within the moats of its Citadel, including the Imperial Enclosure. Other museums and pagodas are dotted around the city. All the principal royal tombs are some distance south of Hué.

◉ Inside the Citadel

Built between 1804 and 1833, the Citadel (Kinh Thanh) is still the heart of Hué. Heavily fortified, it consists of 2m-thick, 10km-long walls; a moat (30m across and 4m deep); and 10 gateways.

The Citadel has distinct sections. The Imperial Enclosure and Forbidden Purple City formed the epicentre of Vietnamese royal life. On the southwestern side were temple compounds. There were residences in the northwest, gardens in the northeast and in the north the Mang Ca Fortress (still a military base).

★ Imperial Enclosure   HISTORIC SITE

(admission 105,000d; ◷ 7am-5.30pm) The Imperial Enclosure is a citadel-within-a-citadel, housing the emperor's residence, temples and palaces and the main buildings of state within 6m-high, 2.5km-long walls. Today much of it is in ruins. What's left is only a fraction of the original – the enclosure was badly bombed during the French and American wars, and only 20 of its 148 buildings survived. Restoration and reconstruction of damaged buildings is ongoing.

We've organised the sights inside the Imperial Enclosure as you'll encounter them inside the compound, beginning at the Ngo Mon Gate entrance and moving anticlockwise around the enclosure.

Ngo Mon Gate   GATE

The principal entrance to the Imperial Enclosure is Ngo Mon Gate. The central passageway with its yellow doors was reserved for the use of the emperor, as was the bridge across the lotus pond. Others had to use the gates to either side and the paths around the pond.

Thai Hoa Palace   PALACE

This palace (Palace of Supreme Harmony; 1803) is a spacious hall with an ornate timber roof supported by 80 carved and lacquered columns. It was used for the emperor's official receptions and important

---

OFF THE BEATEN TRACK

TOMBS AND DUNES

From the centre of Hué it's only 15km north to the sands of **Thuan An Beach** where there's a large resort hotel. If you continue southeast from here there's a beautiful, quiet coastal road to follow with very light traffic (so it's ideal for bikers). The route actually traverses a narrow coastal island, with views of the Tam Giang-Cau Hai lagoon on the inland side and simply stunning sandy beaches and dunes on the other. This wonderful coastal strip is virtually undeveloped, but between September and March the water's often too rough for swimming.

From Thuan An the road winds past villages alternating with shrimp lagoons and vegetable gardens. Thousands and thousands of garishly colourful and opulent graves and family temples line the beach, most the final resting places of Viet Kieu (overseas Vietnamese). Little tracks cut through the tombs and sand dunes to the ocean. Just pick a spot and the chances are you'll have a beach to yourself.

At glorious **Phu Thuan beach** (about 7km southeast of Thuan An) you pass the lovely Beach Bar Hue (p856), then 8km from there are the remains of **Phu Dien**, a small Cham temple half-buried in a sand dune.

Continuing southeast a narrow but paved road weaves past fishing villages, shrimp farms, more giant sand dunes and the settlement of Vinh Hung until you reach the mouth of another river estuary at Thuon Phu An, where there's a row of seafood restaurants. This spot is 40km from Thuan An. Cross the Tu Hien bridge here and you can continue around the eastern lip of the huge Cau Hai lagoon and link up with Hwy 1.

Hué

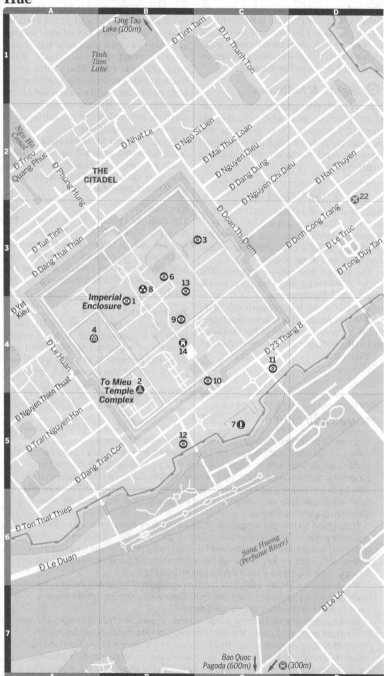

- Tang Tau Lake (100m)
- Tinh Tam Lake
- Ngu Ha Canal
- Đ Triêu Quang Phục
- Đ Phung Hung
- Đ Tinh Tam
- Đ Le Thanh Ton
- Đ Nhat Le
- Đ Ngo Si Lien
- Đ Mai Thuc Loan
- Đ Nguyen Dieu
- Đ Dang Dung
- Đ Nguyen Chi Dieu
- Đ Han Thuyen
- THE CITADEL
- Đ Doan Thi Diem
- Đ Dinh Cong Trang
- Đ Le Truc
- Đ Tue Tinh
- Đ Dang Thai Than
- Đ Tong Duy Tan
- 3
- 6
- 8
- 13
- **Imperial Enclosure** 1
- 9
- Đ Yet Kieu
- 4
- 14
- Đ Le Huan
- Đ 23 Thang 8
- 11
- **To Mieu Temple Complex** 2
- 10
- Đ Nguyen Thien Thuat
- 7
- Đ Tran Nguyen Han
- 12
- Đ Dang Tran Con
- Đ Ton That Thiep
- Đ Le Duan
- Song Huong (Perfume River)
- Đ Le Loi
- Bao Quoc Pagoda (600m)
- (300m)
- 22

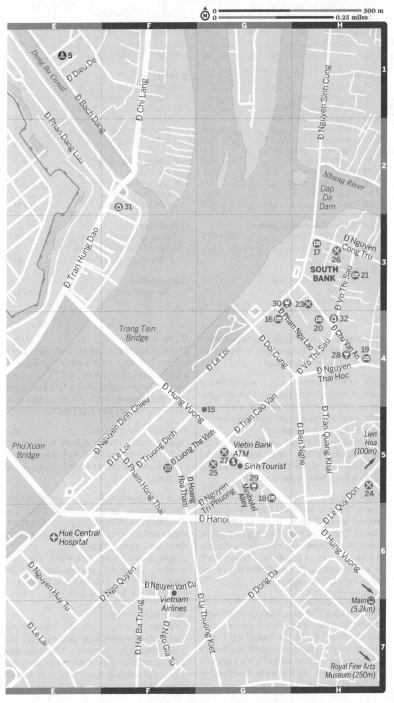

VIETNAM

0 ____ 500 m
0 ____ 0.25 miles

Đ Dieu De
Đ Bach Dang
Dong Ba Canal
Đ Phan Dang Luu
Đ Chi Lang

⛩5

🏧31

Đ Tran Hung Dao

Nhung River

Dap
Da
Dam

Đ Nguyen Sinh Cung

Đ Nguyen
Cong Tru

17 ⊗26   21

SOUTH
BANK

Đ Vo Thi Sau

Trang Tien
Bridge

30 📷 23 ⊗
16 📷   Đ Pham Ngu Lao
        20
28 📷   Đ Chu Van An   📷32
              19

Đ Le Loi
Đ Doi Cung
Đ Vo Thi Sau
Đ Nguyen
Thai Hoc

Đ Hung Vuong

●15

Đ Tran Cao Van

Đ Ben Nghe

Đ Tran Quang Khai

Lien
Hoa
(100m)

Phu Xuan
Bridge

Đ Nguyen Dinh Chieu
Đ Le Loi
Đ Truong Dinh
Đ Luong The Vinh
Đ Pham Hong Thai

✉   ⊗27 💲
    25   Sinh Tourist

Vietin Bank
ATM

29
18 📷

⊗24

Đ Le Quy Don

Đ Nguyen
Tri Phuong
Đ Hoang
Hoa Tham
Minihotel
Alley

Đ Hanoi

Đ Hung Vuong

✚ Hue Central
  Hospital

Đ Nguyen Huy Tu
Đ Ngo Quyen
Đ Hai Ba Trung
Đ Nguyen Van Cu
Đ Ngo Gia Tu
Đ Ly Thuong Kiet
Đ Dong Da

Vietnam
Airlines ●

Main 🚌
(5.2km)

Đ Le Lai

Royal Fine Arts
Museum (250m)

Hué

ceremonies. On state occasions the emperor sat on his elevated throne, facing visitors entering via the Ngo Mon Gate.

Halls of the Mandarins HISTORIC BUILDING
Located immediately behind Thai Hoa Palace on either side of a courtyard, these halls were used by mandarins as offices and to prepare for court ceremonies.

Behind the courtyard are the ruins of the Can Chanh Palace, where two wonderful long galleries, painted in gleaming scarlet lacquer, have been reconstructed.

Royal Theatre HISTORIC BUILDING
(Duyen Thi Duong; ☎ 054-351 4989; www.nhanhac. com.vn; tickets 70,000d; ☺performances 9am, 10am, 2.30pm & 3.30pm) The Royal Theatre, begun in 1826 and later home to the National Conservatory of Music, has been rebuilt on its former foundations. Cultural performances here last 30 minutes.

Emperor's Reading Room HISTORIC BUILDING
(Thai Binh Lau) The exquisite (though crumbling) two-storey Emperor's Reading Room was the only part of the Forbidden Purple City to escape damage during the French reoccupation of Hué in 1947. It's currently being renovated, but it's worth checking out the Gaudí-esque roof mosaics.

Co Ha Gardens GARDENS
These delightful gardens were developed by the first four emperors of the Nguyen dynasty but fell into disrepair. They've been beautifully recreated in the last few years, and are dotted with little gazebo-style pavilions (one a cafe) and ponds.

Forbidden Purple City RUIN
(Tu Cam Thanh) There's almost nothing left of the once-magnificent Forbidden Purple City, which was almost entirely destroyed in wartime.

Dien Tho Residence HISTORIC BUILDING
The stunning, partially ruined Dien Tho Residence (1804) once comprised the apartments and audience hall of the Queen Mothers of the Nguyen dynasty.

Just outside is an enchanting pleasure pavilion, a carved wooden building set above a lily pond. This has now been transformed into a delightful little cafe.

★ To Mieu Temple Complex BUDDHIST TEMPLE
This highly impressive walled complex has been beautifully restored. The imposing three-tiered Hien Lam Pavilion on the south side of the complex dates from 1824. On the other side of a courtyard is the solemn To

Mieu Temple, housing shrines to each of the emperors, topped by their photos.

Between these two temples are Nine Dynastic Urns (dinh), cast between 1835 and 1836, each dedicated to one Nguyen sovereign.

Nine Holy Cannons   CANNON

Located just inside the Citadel ramparts, near the gates to either side of the Flag Tower, are the Nine Holy Cannons (1804), symbolic protectors of the palace and kingdom. Each brass cannon is 5m long and weighs about 10 tonnes.

Outside the Citadel

★ Royal Tombs   HISTORIC BUILDINGS

(◎ 6.30am-5.30pm summer, 7am-5pm winter) The tombs of the rulers of the Nguyen dynasty (1802-1945) are extravagant mausoleums, spread out along the banks of the Perfume River between 2km and 16km south of Hué. The following three are particularly impressive, but there are many more.

The Tomb of Tu Duc (admission 80,000d), constructed between 1864 and 1867 is one of the most impressive. Emperor Tu Duc designed it himself, but the enormous expense and the forced labour used in its construction spawned a coup plot that was discovered and suppressed. Tu Duc lived a life of imperial luxury and carnal excess – he had 104 wives and countless concubines, though no offspring.

Renowned for its architecture and sublime natural setting, the Tomb of Minh Mang (admission 80,000d) was planned during his reign (1820-40) but built by his successor, Thieu Tri. It's on the west bank of the Perfume River, about 12km from Hué, and surrounded by a forest.

The hillside Tomb of Khai Dinh (admission 80,000d), 10km south of Hué, is a synthesis of Vietnamese and European elements. Most of the tomb's grandiose exterior is covered in blackened concrete, creating an unexpectedly Gothic air, while the interiors resemble an explosion of colourful mosaics.

While many of the tombs can be reached by boat, you'll have more time to enjoy them by renting your own bicycle or motorbike. Alternatively hire a xe om or car and driver for the day.

★ Thien Mu Pagoda   BUDDHIST TEMPLE

FREE Built on a hill overlooking the Perfume River, 4km southwest of the Citadel, this pagoda is an icon of Vietnam and as potent a symbol of Hué as the Citadel. The 21m-high octagonal tower, Thap Phuoc Duyen, was constructed under the reign of Emperor Thieu Tri in 1844. Each of its seven storeys is dedicated to a manushi-buddha (a Buddha that appeared in human form).

Since the 1960s it has been a flashpoint of political demonstrations.

Royal Fine Arts Museum   MUSEUM

(150 Đ Nguyen Hué; ◎ 6.30am-5.30pm summer, 7am-5pm winter) FREE This museum is located in the baroque-influenced An Dinh Palace, commissioned by Emperor Khai Dinh in 1918 and full of elaborate murals, floral motifs and trompe l'œil details. Inside you'll find some outstanding ceramics, paintings, furniture, silverware, porcelain and royal clothing, though information is a little lacking.

Dieu De National Pagoda   BUDDHIST TEMPLE

(Quoc Tu Dieu De; 102 Đ Bach Dang) FREE Overlooking Dong Ba Canal, this pagoda was

---

GETTING TO LAOS: DONG HA TO SAVANNAKHET

Getting to the border The Lao Bao/Dansavanh border is the most popular and least problematic Vietnam–Laos border crossing. Buses to Savannakhet in Laos run from Hué via Dong Ha and Lao Bao. From Hué, there's a 7am air-con bus (340,000d, 9½ hours), on odd days only, that stops in Dong Ha at the Sepon Travel office around 8.30am to pick up more passengers. It's also easy to cross the border on your own; Dong Ha is the gateway. Buses leave the town to Lao Bao (55,000d, two hours) roughly every 15 minutes. From here, xe om charge 12,000d to the border.

At the border The border is open from 7am to 6pm. Laos 30-day visas are granted on entry and cost between US$30 and US$40 depending on your nationality. Bring a passport photo.

Moving on Entering Laos, sŏrngtǎaou (small pick-up trucks) to Sepon leave fairly regularly.

Hué's Imperial Enclosure

EXPLORING THE SITE

An incongruous combination of meticulously restored palaces and pagodas, ruins and rubble, the Imperial Enclosure is approached from the south through the outer walls of the Citadel. It's best to tackle the site as a walking tour, winding your way around the structures in an anticlockwise direction.

You'll pass directly through the monumental **Ngo Mon Gateway ❶** where the ticket office is located. This dramatic approach quickens the pulse and adds to the sense of occasion as you enter this citadel-within-a-citadel. Directly ahead is the **Thai Hoa Palace ❷** where the emperor would greet offical visitors from his elevated throne. Continuing north you'll step across a small courtyard to the twin **Halls of the Mandarins ❸**, where mandarins once had their offices and prepared for ceremonial occasions.

To the northeast is the Royal Theatre, where traditional dance performances are held several times daily. Next you'll be able to get a glimpse of the Emperor's Reading Room built by Thieu Tri and used as a place of retreat. Just east of here are the lovely Co Ha Gardens. Wander their pathways, dotted with hundreds of bonsai trees and potted plants, which have been recently restored.

Guarding the far north of the complex is the Tu Vo Phuong Pavilion, from where you can follow a moat to the Truong San residence and then loop back south via the **Dien Tho Residence ❹** and finally view the beautifully restored temple compound of To Mieu, perhaps the most rewarding part of the entire enclosure to visit, including its fabulous **Nine Dynastic Urns ❺**.

TOP TIPS

Allow half a day to explore the Citadel. Drink vendors are dotted around the site, but the best places to take a break are the delightful Co Ha Gardens, the Tu Vo Phuong Pavilion and the Dien Tho Residence (the latter two also serve food).

Dien Tho Residence
This pretty corner of the complex, with its low structures and pond, was the residence of many Queen Mothers. The earliest structures here date from 1804.

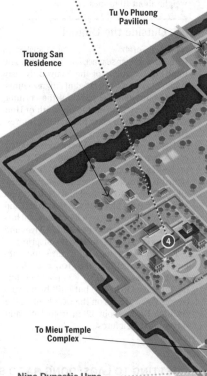

Tu Vo Phuong Pavilion

Truong San Residence

To Mieu Temple Complex

Nine Dynastic Urns
These colossal bronze urns were commissioned by Emperor Minh Mang and cast between 1835 and 1836. They're embellished with decorative elements including landscapes, rivers, flowers and animals.

Tu Vo Phuong Pavilion

The two-storey Tu Vo Phuong Pavilion, elevated above a moat, was once a defense bastion for the northern part of the Imperial Enclosure. It combines both European and Vietnamese architectural styles (note the elaborate roof dragons).

Halls of the Mandarins

Unesco-sponsored conservation work is ongoing in the eastern hall here to preserve the elaborate ceiling and wall murals.

Emperor's Reading Room

Co Ha Gardens

Royal Theatre

③

②

①

⑤

Ngo Mon Gateway

A huge, grandiose structure that guards the main approach to the Imperial Enclosure, this gateway has a fortified lower level and a more architecturally elaborate upper part. It dates from 1833.

Thai Hoa Palace

Be sure to check out this palace's incredible ironwood columns, painted in 12 coats of brilliant scarlet and gold lacquer. The structure was saved from collapse by restoration work in the 1990s.

built under Emperor Thieu Tri's rule (1841–47) and is famous for its four low towers, one to either side of the gate and two flanking the sanctuary.

Bao Quoc Pagoda BUDDHIST TEMPLE
(Ham Long Hill) `FREE` Founded in 1670, this hilltop pagoda is on the southern bank of the Perfume River and has a striking triple-gated entrance reached via a wide staircase.

⎈ Tours

Most hotels and travellers' cafes offer shared tours covering the main sights (from as little as US$4 to around US$18 per person). These tours usually run from 8am to 4pm. There are many different itineraries; some of the better ones start with a morning river cruise, stopping at pagodas and temples, then after lunch you transfer to a minibus to hit the main tombs and then return to Hué by road. On the cheaper options you'll often have to hire a motorbike to get from the moorings to the tombs, or walk (in the intense heat of the day).

It's perfectly possible to rent a *xe om* or your own bike and do a DIY tour.

Cafe on Thu Wheels TOUR
(☑054-383 2241; minhthuHué@yahoo.com; 10/2 Đ Nguyen Tri Phuong) Inexpensive cycle, motorcycle (from US$10 per person) and car tours run by Minh, who is a great character.

Stop & Go Café TOUR
(☑054-382 7051; www.stopandgo-Hué.com; 3 Đ Hung Vuong) Personalised motorbike and car tours.

🛏 Sleeping

All the following places are in the city, except Beach Bar Hue.

SPLURGE

The **Orchid** (☑054-383 1177; www.orchidhotel.com.vn; 30A Đ Chu Van An; r US$30-75; ⊝ ❋ @ 🛜 🖶) is a well-run modern hotel rightly renowned for its warm service; staff really make an effort. The accommodation is excellent (some pricier rooms even have a Jacuzzi with city views) as is the complimentary breakfast, with eggs cooked to order.

★ Huenino GUESTHOUSE $
(☑054-625 2171; www.Huénohotel.com; 14 Đ Nguyen Cong Tru; r US$14-24; ⊝ ❋ @ 🛜) Family-owned, this warm, welcoming guesthouse has an artistic flavour with stylish furniture, artwork and smallish rooms with minibar, cable TV and good-quality beds. A generous breakfast is included.

★ Jade Hotel GUESTHOUSE $
(☑054-393 8849; http://jadehotelHué.com; 17 Đ Nguyen Thai Hoc; r US$15-25; ⊝ ❋ @ 🛜) You'll find simply excellent service standards at this fine place; staff are very sweet and welcoming indeed. Rooms enjoy soft comfy mattresses and there's a nice lobby-lounge for hanging out.

★ Beach Bar Hue HOTEL $
(☑0908 993 584; www.beachbarhue.com; Phu Thuan beach; dm/bungalow 250,000/600,000d, meals 100,000d; ⊝ 🛜) Set on gorgeous Phu Thuan beach 22km east of Hué, this new place has excellent backpacker-geared dorms and bungalows. There's a funky little bamboo-and-thatch bar for drinks and snacks.

Star City Hotel HOTEL $
(☑054-383 1358; http://starcityhotelhue.com; 2/36 Đ Vo Thi Sau; r US$12; ❋ @ 🛜) Offering really cheap rates, this five-storey hotel has a lift, and clean, spacious rooms all with TV and air-con. It's set off the street so traffic noise isn't an issue.

Hue Backpackers HOSTEL $
(☑054-382 6567; www.vietnambackpackerhostels.com; 10 Đ Pham Ngu Lao; dm US$8-12, r US$18; ❋ @ 🛜) Backpackers' mecca thanks to its central location, eager-to-please staff, good info and sociable bar-restaurant. Dorms (some with queen-sized beds) are well designed and have air-con and lockers.

Hung Vuong Inn HOTEL $
(☑054-382 1068; truongdung2000@yahoo.com; 20 Đ Hung Vuong; r US$11-17; ❋ @ 🛜) Nine spacious rooms with cable TV and attractive bathrooms, plus a convenient location, although it's on a busy road. There's a restaurant that's popular with travellers here too.

🍴 Eating

Hué's culinary variety is amazing, with many unique local dishes, including lots of vegie creations. Royal rice cakes, the most common of which is *banh khoai,* are well worth seeking out.

Lien Hoa
VEGETARIAN $
(3 Đ Le Quy Don; meals 30,000-55,000d; ⊙11am-9.30pm; ✍) No nonsense, very local Viet vegie restaurant renowned for providing filling food at rock-bottom rates. Fresh *banh beo* (steamed rice pancakes), noodle dishes, crispy fried jackfruit and aubergine with ginger all deliver. The menu has very rough English translations to help you order (staff speak little or no English).

Take
JAPANESE $
(34 Đ Tran Cao Van; meals 60,000-140,000d; ⊙11.30am-9.30pm) An authentic Japanese restaurant with tasteful furnishings (including lanterns, calligraphy wall hangings and even fake cherry blossoms) and a winsome menu that takes in sushi, tempura and yakitori dishes.

Restaurant Bloom
CAFE $
(14 Đ Nguyen Cong Tru; meals 35,000-80,000d; ⊙7am-9.30pm; 🖥) Ideal for pasta, a sandwich, baguette or homemade cake (baked on the premises), this likeable little cafe employs disadvantaged youths and graduates of the ACWP (Aid to Children Without Parents) training program. Food is MSG-free.

Mandarin Café
VIETNAMESE $
(🖉 054-382 1281; 24 Đ Tran Cao Van; mains from 26,000d; 🖥✍) Owner-photographer Mr Cu, whose inspirational pictures adorn the walls, has been hosting backpackers here for years, and his relaxed restaurant has lots of vegetarian and breakfast choices. Also operates as a tour agency.

Japanese Restaurant
JAPANESE $
(🖉054-382 5146; 12 Đ Chu Van An; dishes US$1.50-9; ⊙6-9pm) Offers all your usual Japanese faves (including teriyaki and udon and soba noodles). It's a little lacking in ambience, but does employ former street children and supports a home for them.

Caphé Bao Bao
VIETNAMESE $
(38 Đ Le Thanh Ton; meals 20,000-35,000d; ⊙10.30am-8pm) A simple courtyard place serving delicious and very cheap barbecued pork kebabs, served with noodles and vegetables.

🍷 Drinking

⭐ Brown Eyes
BAR
(Đ Chu Van An; ⊙5pm-late; 🖥) The most popular late-night bar in town, with a good blend of locals and traveller-revellers and a party vibe. DJs drive the dance floor with R&B, hip-hop and house music anthems, and staff rally the troops with free shots. It's open 'till the last one passes out'.

DMZ Bar
BAR
(www.dmz.com.vn; 60 Đ Le Loi; ⊙7am-1am; 🖥) Ever-popular riverside bar with a free pool table, cold Huda beer, cocktails (try a watermelon mojito) and a good craic most nights. Also serves Western and local food till midnight, smoothies and juices. Happy hour is 3pm till 8pm.

Hue Backpackers
BAR
(10 Đ Pham Ngu Lao; ⊙6am-11pm; 🖥) There's always a buzz about this backpackers' spot, which packs 'em in with its infused vodkas, cocktail list and happy hour (8pm to 9pm).

TRANSPORT FROM HUÉ

DESTINATION	AIR	BUS	CAR & MOTORBIKE	TRAIN
Danang	N/A	US$3.50, 3hr, frequent	2½-4hr	US$3.50-6, 2½-4hr, 7 daily
Dong Hoi	N/A	US$4-7, 4hr, 12 daily	3½hr	US$5-11, 3-5½hr, 7 daily
Hanoi	from US$30, 1hr, 3 daily	US$20-32, 13-16hr, 9 daily	16hr	US$24-42, 12-15½hr, 6 daily
HCMC	from US$34, 1¼hr, 4 daily	US$26-42, 19-24hr, 9 daily	22hr	US$32-55, 19½-23hr, 5 daily
Ninh Binh	N/A	US$14-22, 10½-12hr, 8 daily	11hr	US$19-35, 10-13hr, 5 daily

WORTH A TRIP

BACH MA NATIONAL PARK

A French-era hill station known for its cool weather, **Bach Ma National Park** (Vuon Quoc Gia Bach Ma; ☑054-387 1330; adult/child/under 6yr 40,000/20,000d/free) is 45km southeast of Hué. The road to the summit has recently been upgraded.

There's some decent trekking in the lower levels through subtropical forest to villages on the fringes of the park. You can book village and birdwatching tours and English- or French-speaking guides (250,000d per day) at the visitor centre. Unexploded ordnance is still in the area, so stick to the trails.

There's a **guesthouse** (☑054-387 1330; bachmaeco@gmail.com; campsites per person 10,000d, r with fan/air-con 180,000/270,000d) at the park entrance.

Café on Thu Wheels　　　　　　BAR
(10/2 Đ Nguyen Tri Phuong; ⊙6.30am-11pm; 🛜)
Hole-in-the-wall bar par excellence. Graffiti-splattered walls, a sociable vibe and good info from the feisty owner, Thu, and her family. It also offers good tours, serves cheap grub and has books and mags to browse.

Shopping

Hué produces the finest conical hats in Vietnam and is renowned for rice paper and silk paintings. As ever, bargain hard.

**Spiral Foundation Healing
the Wounded Heart Center**　　HANDICRAFTS
(☑054-383 3694; www.hwhshop.com; 23 Đ Vo Thi Sau; ⊙8am-6pm) Generating cash from trash, this store stocks lovely handicrafts – such as quirky bags from plastic, and picture frames from recycled beer cans – made by artists with disabilities. Profits aid heart surgery for children in need.

Dong Ba Market　　　　　　MARKET
(Đ Tran Hung Dao; ⊙6.30am-8pm) Just north of Trang Tien Bridge, this is Hué's largest market, selling anything and everything.

❶ Information

Wi-fi is very widespread and internet cafes abound on Đ Hung Vuong and Đ Le Loi.
Hué Central Hospital (Benh Vien Trung Uong Hué; ☑054-382 2325; 16 Đ Le Loi; ⊙6am-10pm)
Mandarin Café (☑054-382 1281; www.mrcumandarin.com; 24 Đ Tran Cao Van) Mr Cu (who speaks English and French) offers great information, transport and tours.
Post Office (8 Đ Hoang Hoa Tham; ⊙7am-5.30pm Mon-Sat)
Sinh Tourist (☑054-382 3309; www.thesinhtourist.vn; 7 Đ Nguyen Tri Phuong) Books open-tour buses and buses to Laos.
Vietin Bank ATM (12 Đ Hung Vuong)

❶ Getting There & Away

AIR

Vietnam Airlines (☑054-382 4709; 23 Đ Nguyen Van Cu; ⊙closed Sun) has two daily flights to both Hanoi and HCMC. **VietJet** (☑1900 1886; www.vietjetair.com) also connects Hué daily with the capital and HCMC.

Hué's Phu Bai Airport is 14km south of the city. Metered taxis meet all flights and cost about 190,000d to the centre, or use the minibus service for 50,000d. Vietnam Airlines also runs an airport shuttle, which can collect you from your hotel (tickets 60,000d).

BUS

The main bus station, 4km southeast of the centre, has connections to Danang and south to HCMC. **An Hoa bus station** (Hwy 1), northwest of the Citadel, serves northern destinations. From here, one daily bus at 11.15am (look for 'Phuc Vu' in the windscreen) heads for Phong Nha Farmstay and Son Trach (150,000d, four hours).

There's also a useful minibus connection (500,000d, five hours) between Hue Backpackers and Phong Nha Farmstay/Son Trach village, leaving the hostel in Hué at 1pm and stopping at the Vinh Moc Tunnels and the Ben Hai River museum. Entrance tickets and a guide at the tunnels are included.

Hué is a regular stop on open-tour bus routes. Most drop off and pick up passengers at central hotels.

Mandarin, Sinh and Stop & Go Café can arrange bookings for buses to Savannakhet, Laos.

TRAIN

Hué train station (☑054-382 2175; 2 Đ Phan Chu Trinh) is at the southwestern end of Đ Le Loi.

❶ Getting Around

Bicycles (US$1 to US$2), motorbikes (US$5 to US$10) and cars (from US$40 per day) can be hired through hotels all over town. **Mai Linh**

(☑ 054-389 8989) has taxis with meters. Cyclos and *xe om* will find you whether you need them or not.

Around Hué

Demilitarised Zone (DMZ)

From 1954 until 1975, the Ben Hai River served as the dividing line between South Vietnam and North Vietnam. The DMZ, 90km north of Hué, consisted of the area 5km on either side of the line.

Many of the 'sights' around the DMZ may not be worthwhile unless you're into war history. To make sense of it all, and to avoid areas where there's still unexploded ordnance, a guide is essential. Group day tours from Hué cost from US$15 for a budget bus trip to as much as US$120 for a specialised car tour with a Viet vet.

◉ Sights

Vinh Moc Tunnels　　　　HISTORIC SITE
(admission 20,000d; ⊘ 7am-4.30pm) A highly impressive complex of tunnels 110km from Hué, **Vinh Moc** is the remains of a coastal North Vietnamese village that literally went underground in response to unremitting American bombing. More than 90 families disappeared into three levels of tunnels and continued to live and work while bombs rained down around them.

MUSEUM OF CHAM SCULPTURE

Danang's jewel is its famed **Museum of Cham Sculpture** (Bao Tang; 1 Ð Trung Nu Vuong; admission 30,000d; ⊘ 7am-5pm). This classic, colonial-era building houses the finest collection of Cham sculpture to be found anywhere on earth. There are more than 300 pieces on display, including altars, *lingas*, garudas, *apsaras*, Ganeshas and images of Shiva, Brahma and Vishnu – all dating from the 5th to 15th centuries. These intricately carved sandstone pieces come from Cham sites all over Vietnam.

Guides hang out at the museum's entrance.

Khe Sanh Combat Base　　　HISTORIC SITE
(museum 20,000d; ⊘ museum 7am-5pm) The site of the most famous siege of the war in Vietnam, about 500 Americans, 10,000 North Vietnamese troops and uncounted civilian bystanders died around this remote highland base. Today the site is occupied by a small **museum**. Khe Sanh is 3km north of the small town of Huong Hoa.

Truong Son National Cemetery　　CEMETERY
An evocative memorial to the North Vietnamese soldiers who died along the Ho Chi Minh Trail, this cemetery is a sobering sight. More than 10,000 graves dot these hillsides, each marked by a simple white tombstone headed by the inscription *liet si* (martyr). It's 27km northwest of Dong Ha.

Danang

☑ 0511 / POP 944,000

Nowhere in Vietnam is changing as fast as Danang. Vietnam's fifth-biggest city, for decades it had a reputation as a slightly mundane provincial backwater, but a major facelift is in the works. The Han riverfront is resplendent with gleaming new modernist hotels and restaurants. Beachside, five-star hotel developments are emerging on the My Khe strip. Oh, and a revamped international airport opened in 2012.

That said, the city itself still has few conventional sightseeing spots except for a decent museum. For most travellers, a day or two is probably enough.

⨼ Sleeping

Good budget places are tough to find, but there are some excellent midrange mini-hotels close to the river.

Zion Hotel　　　　　　　HOTEL $
(☑ 0511-382 8333; http://sion.com.vn; 121/7 Hoang Van Thu; s US$15, d US$20-25; ❋@⊛) There's a scarlet theme running through this new excellent-value hotel, from the lobby to the inviting modern rooms. It boasts a convenient location and staff are eager to please.

Eena Hotel　　　　　　　HOTEL $
(☑ 0511-222 5123; www.geocities.jp/eenahotel; Khu An Cu 3, My Khe; s150,000-400,000d, d&tw350,000-800,000d; ❋@⊛) Beachside about 4km from the centre, this Japanese-owned mini-hotel is a great base with its immaculately

Danang

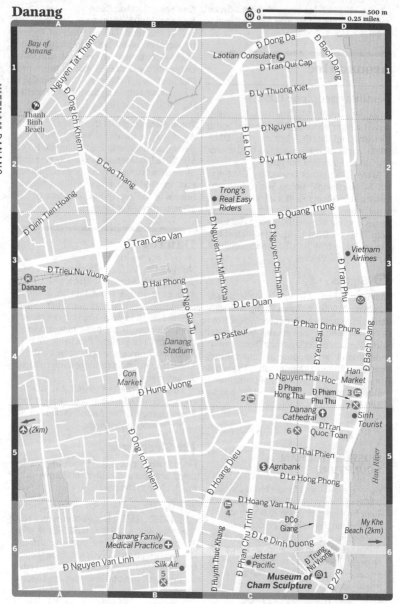

clean and spacious white rooms. There's a good complimentary breakfast.

Bao Ngoc Hotel
HOTEL **$**
(📞 0511-381 7711; baongochotel@dng.vnn.vn; 48 Đ Phan Chu Trinh; r US$18-22; ❄ @ 🛜) Spacious,

carpeted and comfortable rooms full of solid, dark-wood furniture; some have sofas. The ageing five-storey building also retains a glint of colonial character, with its chocolate-brown French-style shutters.

Danang

◎ Top Sights
1 Museum of Cham Sculpture D6

⬢ Sleeping
2 Bao Ngoc Hotel C4
3 New Moon Hotel................................. D4
4 Zion Hotel.. C6

⊗ Eating
5 Com Tay Cam Cung Dinh B6
6 Quan Com Hue Ngon C5
7 Waterfront D4

New Moon Hotel   HOTEL $$
(☑ 0511-382 8488; http://newmoonhotel.vn; 126 Đ
Bach Dang; r 440,000-1,100,000d; ❈@✿) Mod-
ern minihotel with a selection of inviting
rooms in different price categories, all with
flat-screen TV, minibar, wi-fi and en suite
marble bathrooms, while the river-view
options enjoy incredible vistas.

✖ Eating & Drinking

Quan Com Hué Ngon   VIETNAMESE, BARBECUE $
(65 Tran Quoc Toan; meals 50,000-80,000d; ⊙3-
9pm) Fab new barbecue place, all charcoal
smoke and sizzling meats, where you grill
your own. There's a street terrace and the
welcoming English-speaking owner will
help with the menu.

Com Tay Cam Cung Dinh   VIETNAMESE $
(K254/2 Đ Hoang Dieu; dishes 15,000-40,000d;
⊙11am-8pm) This simple place is good for
local dishes including *hoanh thanh* – a
wonton-like combination of minced pork
and shrimp. It's down a little alley.

❶ Information

There are internet cafes scattered all over Dan-
ang. Consult the website www.indanang.com for
reviews and information.

Agribank (202 Đ Nguyen Chi Thanh; ⊙7.30am-
3.30pm Mon-Sat)

Danang Family Medical Practice (☑0511-
358 2700; www.vietnammedicalpractice.com;
50-52 Đ Nguyen Van Linh; ⊙7am-6pm)

Main Post Office (64 Đ Bach Dang; ⊙7am-
5.30pm)

Sinh Tourist (☑0511-384 3258; www.thesinh-
tourist.vn; 154 Đ Bach Dang) Books open-tour
buses and tours, and offers currency exchange.

Trong's Real Easy Riders (☑0903 597 971;
www.easyridervn.com; 12/20 Nguyen Thi Minh
Khai) A motorbike collective. Four-day trips to
the central highlands cost US$280.

❶ Getting There & Away

AIR
Danang's international airport has **Silk Air**
(☑0511-356 2708; www.silkair.com; HAGL Plaza
Hotel, 1 Đ Nguyen Van Linh) flights to Singapore
and Siem Riep, Lao Airlines flights to Pakse,
Savannakhet and Vientiane, and there are a
few connections to China including a Dragon
Air flight to Hong Kong. For domestic destina-
tions, **Jetstar Pacific** (☑0511-358 3538; www.
jetstar.com; 307 Đ Phan Chu Trinh) and **VietJet**
(☑1900 1886; www.vietjetair.com) have daily
flights from Danang to HCMC and Hanoi, while
Vietnam Airlines (☑0511-382 1130; www.
vietnamairlines.com; 35 Đ Tran Phu) flies to lots
of cities nationwide.

BUS
Danang's **intercity bus station** (☑0511-382
1265; Đ Dien Bien Phu) is 3km west of the centre
and has services to all major towns.

For Laos, there are three weekly buses to
Savannakhet at 8pm (340,000d, 14 hours) and
a daily service to Pakse at 6.30am (330,000d,
13 hours). Buses to the Lao Bao border alone are
128,000d (six hours); you may have to change
buses at Dong Ha.

Yellow public buses to Hoi An (18,000d, one
hour, every 30 minutes) travel along Đ Bach Dang.

Sinh Tourist open-tour buses operate twice
daily to both Hué (80,000d to 89,000d, 2½
hours) and Hoi An (70,000d, one hour).

TAXI & MOTORBIKE
A taxi to Hoi An officially costs around
400,000d, but most will drop to 330,000d,
while *xe om* charge around 120,000d. A ride to
the airport is around 55,000d. Call **Mai Linh**
(☑0511-356 5656) for a cab.

SPLURGE

The **Waterfront** (☑0511-384 3373;
www.waterfrontdanang.com; 150-152 Đ
Bach Dang; meals 95,000-360,000d;
⊙10am-11pm; ✿) is a riverfront lounge-
cum-restaurant that gets everything
right on every level. It works as a stylish
bar for a chilled glass of NZ Sauvignon
Blanc and also as a destination restau-
rant for a memorable meal (book the
terrace deck for a stunning river vista).
The menu features imported meats,
Asian seafood and also terrific 'gour-
met' sandwiches.

TRANSPORT FROM DANANG

DESTINATION	AIR	BUS	CAR & MOTORBIKE	TRAIN
Dong Hoi	N/A	US$8-13, 6½hr, 7 daily	6-7hr	US$10-17, 5½-8½hr, 6 daily
Hanoi	from US$36, 70min, 9 daily	US$24-34, 16-19hr, 7 daily	19hr	US$28-45, 14½-18hr, 6 daily
HCMC	from US$33, 75min, 18 daily	US$24-39, 19-25hr, 9 daily	18hr	US$31-50, 17-22hr, 5 daily
Hué	N/A	US$3-4, 3hr, every 20min	2½-4hr	US$3.50-6, 2½-4hr, 6 daily
Nha Trang	from US$38, 30min, 2 daily	US$15-22, 10-13hr, 8 daily	13hr	US$18-29, 9-12hr, 5 daily

TRAIN

Danang's **train station** (202 Đ Hai Phong) has services to all destinations on the north–south main line.

The train ride to Hué is one of the best in the country – it's worth taking as an excursion in itself.

Around Danang

About 10km south of Danang are the striking **Marble Mountains** (admission 15,000d; ⊙ 7am-5pm), which consist of five craggy marble outcrops topped with jungle and pagodas. With natural caves sheltering small Hindu and Buddhist sanctuaries and stunning views of the ocean and surrounding countryside, they're worth taking the time to explore.

China Beach (Bai Non Nuoc), once an R'n'R hang-out for US soldiers during the war, is actually a series of beaches stretching 30km between Hoi An and Danang.

For surfers, China Beach's break gets a decent swell from mid-September to December. There's a mean undertow, so take care.

Hoi An

📱 0510 / POP 126,000

Graceful, historic Hoi An is Vietnam's most atmospheric and delightful town. Once a major port, it boasts the grand architecture and beguiling riverside setting that befits its heritage, and the 21st-century curses of traffic and pollution are almost entirely absent.

In the Old Town, an incredible legacy of tottering Japanese merchant houses, Chinese temples and ancient tea warehouses has been preserved and converted into stylish restaurants, wine bars and a glut of tailor shops. And yet down by the market and over

in neighbouring An Hoi, peninsula life has changed little.

Travel a few kilometres further – you'll find some superb bicycle, motorbike and boat trips – and some of central Vietnam's most enticing bucolic scenery and beaches are within easy reach.

⊙ Sights

◎ Hoi An Old Town

A Unesco World Heritage Site, Hoi An Old Town levies an admission fee to most of its historic buildings, which goes towards funding the preservation of the town's architecture. Buying the ticket (admission 90,000d) gives you a choice of five heritage sites to visit – Chinese Assembly Halls, pagodas and temples, historic houses and museums. Booths dotted around the Old Town sell tickets.

★ **Japanese Covered Bridge**   BRIDGE
(Cau Nhat Ban) FREE This beautiful little bridge is emblematic of Hoi An. A bridge was first constructed here in the 1590s by the Japanese community in order to link them with the Chinese quarters across the stream.

The structure is very solidly constructed because of the threat of earthquakes. Over the centuries the ornamentation has remained relatively faithful to the original understated Japanese design.

★ **Assembly Hall of the Fujian Chinese Congregation**   TEMPLE
(Phuc Kien Hoi Quan; opposite 35 Đ Tran Phu; admission by Old Town ticket; ⊙ 7am-5.30pm) Originally a traditional assembly hall, this structure was later transformed into a temple for the worship of Thien Hau (Tianhou), a deity

Hoi An

VIETNAM

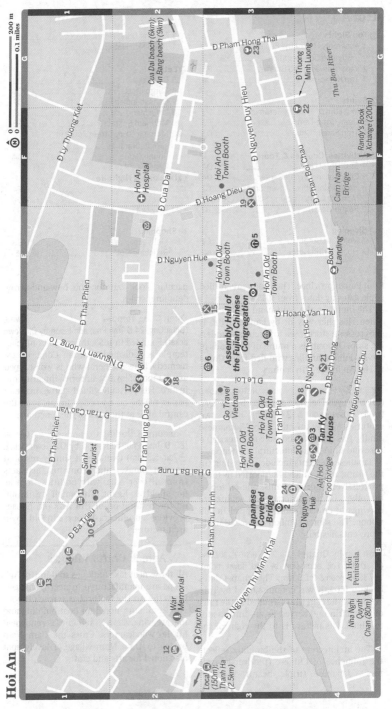

0   200 m
0   0.1 miles

Cua Dai beach (6km);
An Bang beach (9km)

Đ Pham Hong Thai
23

Đ Truong
Minh Luong
22

Thu Bon River

Đ Ly Thuong Kiet

Randy's Book
Xchange (200m)

Hoi An
Hospital

Đ Cua Dai

Hoi An Old
Town Booth

Đ Hoang Dieu
19

Đ Nguyen Duy Hieu

Đ Phan Boi Chau

Cam Nam
Bridge

Đ Nguyen Hue

Hoi An Old
Town Booth

5

Hoi An Old
Town Booth

Boat
Landing

Đ Thai Phien

Assembly Hall of
the Fujian Chinese
Congregation

1

Đ Hoang Van Thu

15

Đ Nguyen Truong To

Agribank

6

4

Đ Le Loi

Đ Nguyen Thai Hoc

21

Đ Bach Dang

17

18

Go Travel
Vietnam

Hoi An Old
Town Booth

8

7

Đ Nguyen Phuc Chu

Đ Tran Cao Van

Đ Tran Hung Dao

Đ Tran Phu

Sinh
Tourist

11

9

Đ Hai Ba Trung

Hoi An Old
Town Booth

Tan Ky
House

20

16

3

An Hoi
Footbridge

Đ Thai Phien

Đ Ba Trieu

10

Japanese
Covered
Bridge

24

2

Đ Nguyen Hue

An Hoi
Peninsula

14

Đ Phan Chu Trinh

Đ Nguyen Thi Minh Khai

13

War
Memorial

Church

Nha Nghi
Quynh
Chan (80m)

12

Local (150m);
Thanh Ha
(2.5km)

Hoi An

from Fujian province. The gaudy, green-tiled triple gateway dates from 1975.

The mural on the right-hand wall depicts Thien Hau, her way lit by lantern light as she crosses a stormy sea to rescue a foundering ship. Opposite is a mural of the heads of the six Fujian families who fled from China to Hoi An in the 17th century.

★ **Tan Ky House** HISTORIC BUILDING
(101 Đ Nguyen Thai Hoc; admission by Old Town ticket; ⊙ 8am-noon & 2-4.30pm) Built two centuries ago by an ethnically Vietnamese family, this gem of a house combines Japanese and Chinese architectural influences.

Japanese elements include the ceiling (in the sitting area), which is supported by three progressively shorter beams, one on top of the other. Under the crab-shell ceiling are carvings of crossed sabres wrapped in silk ribbon. The sabres symbolise force, the silk represents flexibility.

Tran Family Chapel HISTORIC BUILDING
(21 Đ Le Loi; admission by Old Town ticket; ⊙ 7.30am-noon & 2-5.30pm) This chapel dates back to 1802. It was commissioned by Tran Tu, one of the clan who ascended to the rank of mandarin and served as an ambassador to China. His picture is to the right of the chapel.

The architecture of the building reflects the influence of Chinese (the 'turtle' style roof), Japanese (triple beam) and ver-

nacular (look out for the bow-and-arrow detailing) styles.

Quan Cong Temple TEMPLE
(Chua Ong; 24 Đ Tran Phu; admission by Old Town ticket) Founded in 1653, this small Confucian temple is dedicated to Quan Cong, an esteemed Chinese general who is worshipped as a symbol of loyalty, sincerity, integrity and justice. His partially gilded statue, made of papier-mâché on a wooden frame, is on the central altar at the back of the sanctuary.

Museum of Trading Ceramics MUSEUM
(80 Đ Tran Phu; admission by Old Town ticket; ⊙ 7am-5.30pm) Occupies a simply restored wooden house and contains artefacts from all over Asia, with oddities from as far afield as Egypt. The small exhibition on the restoration of Hoi An's old houses provides a useful crash course in Old Town architecture.

◎ Arts & Crafts Villages

All those neat fake antiques sold in Hoi An's shops are manufactured in nearby villages. Cross the An Hoi footbridge to reach the **An Hoi Peninsula**, noted for boat building and mat weaving. **Cam Kim Island** is renowned for its woodcarvers. Cross the Cam Nam bridge to **Cam Nam** village, a lovely spot also noted for arts and crafts.

✈ Activities

Two reputable dive schools offer trips to the Cham Islands. Both charge almost exactly the same rates: two fun dives are US$75 to US$80. The diving is not world class, but can be intriguing, with good macro life – and the day trip to the Cham islands is superb.

Snorkellers pay US$30 to US$40. Trips only leave between February and September; conditions are best in June, July and August.

Diving & Snorkelling

Cham Island Diving Center　DIVING
(☑0510-391 0782; www.chamislanddiving.com; 88 Đ Nguyen Thai Hoc) Run by a friendly, experienced team, this dive shop's mantra is 'no troubles, make bubbles'. They have a large boat and also a speedboat for zippy transfers. Overnight snorkelling and camping trips cost US$80.

Blue Coral Diving　DIVING
(☑0510-627 9297; www.divehoian.com; 77 Đ Nguyen Thai Hoc) Friendly, professional outfit with an 18m dive boat and additional speedboat. Chief instructor is Steve Reid from the UK.

Massage & Spa

★Palmarosa　SPA
(☑0510-393 3999; www.palmarosaspa.vn; 90 Đ Ba Trieu; 1hr massage from US$21; ◑10am-9pm) A cut above the competition, this highly professional spa offers a full range of massages (including Thai and Swedish), scrubs, facials as well as hand and foot care. A mineral mud wrap is US$17.

✍ Courses

Vietnamese cooking classes are offered all over Hoi An.

Green Bamboo Cooking School　COOKING
(☑0905 815 600; www.greenbamboo-hoian.com; 21 Đ Truong Minh Hung, Cam An; per person US$35) Directed by Van, a charming local lady, these courses are more personalised than most. Groups are limited to a maximum of 10, and take place in Van's spacious home (5km east of the centre).

Morning Glory Cooking School　COOKING
(☑0510-224 1555; www.restaurant-hoian.com; 106 Đ Nguyen Thai Hoc; half-day course US$27) Directed by the acclaimed Trinh Diem Vy, owner of several restaurants in town, or one of her protégés, these classes concentrate on local recipes. Note that classes can have up to 30 people.

Red Bridge Cooking School　COOKING
(☑0510-393 3222; www.visithoian.com/redbridge; Thon 4, Cam Thanh) At this school, going to class involves a relaxing 4km cruise down the river. There are half-day (US$29) and full-day (US$47) courses, both of which include market visits. Located 4km east of town.

🛏 Sleeping

Hoi An is awash with excellent accommodation options, though no hostels.

Nhi Trung Hotel　HOTEL $
(☑0510-386 3436; 700 Đ Hai Ba Trung; r US$17-27; ✲@☎) Around 1.5km north of the Old Town, this well-run hotel has spacious rooms, some with balconies, that represent excellent value. The free breakfast (pancakes, omelettes, fruit) is superb.

Sunflower Hotel　HOTEL $
(☑0510-393 9838; http://sunflowerhotelhoian.com; 397 Cua Dai; dm US$7, r US$20-22; ✲@☎⛱) Popular place 2km east of the centre with a hostel vibe that draws lots of young backpackers. Dorms are decent and the buffet breakfast will set you up for the day.

Phuong Dong Hotel　HOTEL $
(☑0510-391 6477; www.hoianphuongdonghotel.com; 42 Đ Ba Trieu; s/d/tr US$13/16/20; ✲@☎) It's nothing fancy, but a safe budget bet: plain, good-value rooms with comfortable mattresses, reading lights, fridge and aircon. The owners rent motorbikes at fair rates too.

Hoang Trinh Hotel　HOTEL $
(☑0510-391 6579; www.hoianhoangtrinhhotel.com; 45 Đ Le Quy Don; s/d/tr US$20/25/30; ✲@☎) Well-run hotel with helpful, friendly staff where travellers are made to feel welcome. Rooms are quite 'old school' Vietnamese but spacious and clean. A generous breakfast and pick-up are included.

Hoa Binh Hotel　HOTEL $
(☑0510-391 6838; www.hoianbinhhotel.com; 696 Đ Hai Ba Trung; dm US$9, r US$15-25; ✲@☎⛱) A good selection of modern rooms, all with minibar, cable TV and air-con, and a reasonable dorm. The inclusive breakfast is good, but the pool is covered by a roof.

Nha Nghi Quynh Chan GUESTHOUSE $
(0510-353 3977; 9 Đ Nguyen Phuc, An Hoi; r US$15-20; ✳ 🛜) Owned by a friendly lady, these five modern, well-kept rooms (all with fridge and some with balcony) are located in a block opposite the Vung Hung Riverside Resort.

Thien Nga Hotel HOTEL $$
(✆ 0510-391 6330; thienngahotel@gmail.com; 52 Đ Ba Trieu; r US$35; ✳ @ 🛜 ☒) This place has a fine selection of rooms; most are spacious, light and airy and have a balcony and a minimalist feel. Book one at the rear for garden views. Staff are smiley and breakfast is generous, but the pool is covered by a roof.

🍴 Eating

Hoi An offers a culinary tour de force, including several amazing local specialities. Be sure to try *banh bao* ('white rose'), an incredibly delicate dish of steamed dumpling stuffed with minced shrimp. *Cao lau* – doughy flat noodles mixed with croutons, bean sprouts and greens, topped with pork slices and served in a savoury broth – is also delicious. The other two culinary treats are fried *hoanh thanh* (won ton) and *banh xeo* (crispy savoury pancakes rolled with herbs in fresh rice paper).

★Mermaid Restaurant VIETNAMESE $
(✆ 0510-386 1527; www.restaurant-hoian.com; 2 Đ Tran Phu; most dishes 38,000-95,000d; ⏱ 10.30am-10pm) For local specialities, you can't beat this modest little restaurant, owned by local legend Vy, who chose the location because it was close to the market, ensuring the freshest produce was directly at hand. Hoi An's holy culinary trinity (*cao lau*, white rose and *banh xeo*) are all superb, as are the special fried wontons.

Bale Well VIETNAMESE $
(45-51 Đ Tran Cao Van; meals 45,000-85,000d; ⏱ 11.30am-10pm) Down a little alley near the famous well, this local place is renowned for one dish: barbecued pork, served up satay-style, which you then combine with fresh greens and herbs to create your own fresh spring roll. Nontouristy, and with plenty of atmosphere in the evenings.

Little Menu VIETNAMESE $
(www.thelittlemenu.com; 12 Đ Le Loi; dishes 50,000-135,000d; ⏱ 7am-9.30pm; 🛜) English-speaking owner Son is a fantastic host at this great little restaurant with an open kitchen and short menu – try the fish in banana leaf or duck spring rolls.

Phone Café VIETNAMESE $
(80b Đ Bach Dang; dishes 22,000-62,000d; ⏱ 7am-9pm) This humble-looking place serves up the usual faves, plus good clay-pot specialities.

★Morning Glory
Street Food Restaurant VIETNAMESE $$
(✆ 0510-224 1555; www.restaurant-hoian.com; 106 Đ Nguyen Thai Hoc; dishes 45,000-130,000d; ⏱ 8am-11pm; 🛜 ✍) An outstanding restaurant in historic premises that concentrates on street food and traditionally prepared dishes. Highlights include the pork-stuffed squid, and shrimp mousse on sugarcane skewers. There's an excellent vegetarian selection including many wonderful salads.

★Cargo Club INTERNATIONAL, VIETNAMESE $$
(✆ 0510-391 0489; www.restaurant-hoian.com; 107 Đ Nguyen Thai Hoc; dishes 35,000-105,000d; ⏱ 8am-11pm; 🛜) Remarkable cafe-restaurant, serving mainly Western food, with a terrific riverside location – the upper terrace has stunning views. The breakfasts are legendary (try the eggs benedict), the patisserie and cakes are to die for, and fine dining dishes seriously deliver, too.

Ganesh Indian Restaurant INDIAN $$
(✆ 0510-386 4538; www.ganeshindianrestaurant. com; 24 Đ Tran Hung Dao; meals 65,000-135,000d; ⏱ noon-10.30pm; 🛜 ✍) Highly authentic, fine-value North Indian restaurant where the tandoor oven pumps out perfect naan bread and the chefs' fiery curries don't pull any punches. Also offers plenty of vegetarian choices.

🍷 Drinking

★Dive Bar BAR
(88 Đ Nguyen Thai Hoc; ⏱ 8am-midnight; 🛜) The best bar in town, with a great vibe thanks to the welcoming service, contemporary electronic tunes and sofas for lounging. There's also a cocktail garden and bar at the rear, pool table and pub grub.

Why Not? BAR
(10B Đ Pham Hong Thai; ⏱ 5pm-late; 🛜) Great late-night bar 1km east of the centre, run by a friendly local character. Choose a tune from YouTube and it'll be beamed over the sound system. There's a popular pool table and usually a party vibe in the air.

3 Dragons PUB
(51 Đ Phan Boi Chau; ⏱ 7.30am-midnight; 🛜) Half sports bar (where you can watch everything from Aussie Rules to Indian cricket), half restaurant (burgers, steaks and local food).

🛍 Shopping

Tailor-made clothing is one of Hoi An's best trades, and there are more than 200 tailor shops in town that can whip up suits, shirts, dresses and much more.

Hoi An also boasts a growing array of interesting art galleries, especially on the west side of the Japanese Covered Bridge.

★**Metiseko**   CLOTHING
(www.metiseko.com; 86 Đ Nguyen Thai Hoc; ⊙9am-9.30pm) This eco-minded store stocks gorgeous clothing, accessories and homeware such as cushions using natural silk and organic cotton.

★**Reaching Out**   SOUVENIRS, CLOTHING
(www.reachingoutvietnam.com; 103 Đ Nguyen Thai Hoc; ⊙8am-8pm) Excellent fair-trade gift shop that stocks good-quality silk scarfs, clothes, jewellery, hand-painted Vietnamese hats, handmade toys and teddy bears. The shop employs and supports artisans with disabilities.

Randy's Book Xchange   BOOKS
(www.randysbookxchange.com; To 5 Khoi Xuyen Trung; ⊙9.30am-6pm Mon-Sat) Head to Cam Nam Island and take the first right to get to this bookshop. Stocks over 5000 used books and offers digital downloads too.

ℹ Information

The website www.livehoianmagazine.com is excellent for cultural content, features and reviews. Virtually all hotels have lobby computers and free wi-fi.

For the most part, Hoi An is very safe at any hour. However, late-night bag snatchings in the unlit market have been known, and women should avoid walking home alone late at night.

Agribank (Đ Cua Dai; ⊙8am-4.30pm Mon-Fri, 8.30am-1pm Sat)

Hoi An Hospital (✆0510-386 1364; 4 Đ Tran Hung Dao; ⊙6am-10pm) If it's anything serious, make for Danang.

Hoi An Police Station (✆0510-386 1204; 84 Đ Hoang Dieu)

Main Post Office (6 Đ Tran Hung Dao; ⊙7am-5pm)

Rose Travel Service (✆0510-391 7567; www.rosetravelservice.com; 37-39 Đ Ly Thai To; ⊙7.30am-5.30pm) Offers tours all over Vietnam, car rental and bus bookings.

Sinh Tourist (✆0510-386 3948; www.thesinhtourist.vn; 587 Đ Hai Ba Trung; ⊙7.30am-6pm) Books reputable open-tour buses.

ℹ Getting There & Away

Most north–south bus services do not stop at Hoi An, but you can head for Vinh Dien (10km to the west) and catch one there. If you're heading for Hué or Nha Trang, open-tour buses are easier.

Hoi An bus station (96 Đ Hung Vuong), 1km west of the centre, mainly serves local destinations, including Danang (18,000d, one hour).

The nearest airport and train station are both in Danang. **Go Travel Vietnam** (✆0510-392 9115; info@go-travel-vietnam.com; 61A Phan Chau Trinh; ⊙9am-9pm) offers shuttle bus transfers between Hoi An and Danang airport and train station five times per day (80,000d, one hour).

ℹ Getting Around

Metered taxis and motorbike drivers wait for business over the footbridge in An Hoi. Call **Hoi An Taxi** (✆0510-391 9919) or **Mai Linh** (✆0510-392 5925) for a pick-up.

Many hotels offer bicycles/motorbikes for rent from 20,000/100,000d per day.

Around Hoi An

Beaches

The nearest beach to Hoi An, **Cua Dai**, is subject to intense development and the domain of hard-selling beach vendors. There are seafood restaurants here.

Just 3km north of Cua Dai, **An Bang** is fast emerging as one of Vietnam's most happening and enjoyable beaches. It's easy to see what all the fuss is about – you're greeted with a wonderful stretch of fine sand, a huge empty ocean and an enormous horizon, with only the distant Cham Islands interrupting the seaside symmetry. You'll find lots of little cool little beachfront bar-restaurants serving European cuisine. **Le Banyan Bar** (An Bang beach; meals 130,000-240,000d; ⊙10am-10pm; 🕸), **Soul Kitchen** (✆0906 440 320; www.soulkitchen.sitew.com; meals 80,000-180,000d; ⊙10am-10pm Tue-Sun, 10am-6pm Mon; 🕸) and **La Plage** (✆0510-392 8244; www.laplagehoian.com; snacks/meals 70,000/130,000d; ⊙8am-10pm; 🕸) are all quite pricey but worth a splurge.

The coastline immediately to the north of An Bang remains pristine, a glorious broad beach lined with casuarina and pandan trees and dotted with the curious coracles of local fisherfolk.

Cham Islands

✆ 0510 / POP 2750

A breathtaking cluster of granite islands offshore from Hoi An, the beautiful Cham islands make a wonderful excursion. In the last year or two the serenity of the islands has been compromised (on weekends and Vietnamese holidays) by boatloads of day-tripping tourists from the mainland, so try to plan your visit accordingly. It'll have to be between March to September, as the ocean is usually too rough at other times.

The best trips include diving or snorkelling at Cham's (modest) coral reefs, and a visit to the main island of Hon Lao. The islands are protected as a marine park; the underwater environment includes 135 species of soft and hard coral and varied macro life.

Bai Lang, Hon Lao's pretty little port, is the only real settlement. Drop by the curious temple Ong Ngu, which is dedicated to whales (locals worshipped them as oceanic deities). There are two good, simple guesthouses in town, Luu Ly (✆ 0510-393 0240; r with shared bathroom 220,000d) and Thu Trang (✆ 0510-393 0007; r with shared bathroom 220,000d), and both places serve meals.

A dirt track heads southwest from Hon Lao for 2km past coves to a fine, sheltered beach, home to Cham Restaurant (✆ 0510-224 1108; meals 50,000-120,000d; ◷ 10am-5pm).

Tiny Bai Huong, a fishing village 5km southeast of Bai Lang, is an idyllic but isolated spot where an excellent new homestay (✆ 0120 237 8530; www.homestaybaihuong.com; per person 100,000d, meals 30,000-70,000d) initiative has been set up. Facilities are basic and little or no English is spoken by locals, but it's certainly the perfect place to get away from it all.

❶ Getting There & Away

Most visitors arrive on tours (US$25 to US$40) organised in Hoi An; those run by the dive schools are recommended. There's also a scheduled daily boat connection from the boat landing on Đ Bach Dang in Hoi An (20,000d, two hours, 7am daily), but note foreigners are routinely charged more. Boats do not sail during heavy seas. Bring a copy of your passport and visa.

My Son

Set under the shadow of Cat's Tooth Mountain are the enigmatic ruins of My Son (admission 100,000d; ◷ 6.30am-4pm), the most important remains of the ancient Cham empire and a Unesco World Heritage Site. Although Vietnam has better-preserved Cham sites, none are as extensive and few have such beautiful surroundings, with brooding mountains and clear streams running between the temples.

The ruins are 55km southwest of Hoi An. Day tours to My Son can be arranged in Hoi An for between US$4 and US$8, not including admission, and some trips return to Hoi An by boat. Independent travellers can hire a motorbike, xe om or car. Get here early in order to beat the tour groups, or later in the afternoon.

SOUTHEAST COAST

Vietnam has an incredibly curvaceous coastline and on this coast it's defined by sweeping sands, towering cliffs and concealed bays.

Nha Trang, Mui Ne and the Con Dao islands are key destinations, but the beach breaks come thick and fast here. If your idea of paradise is reclining in front of turquoise waters, weighing up the merits of a massage or a mojito, then you have come to the right place.

On hand to complement the sedentary delights are activities to set the pulse racing, including scuba diving, snorkelling, surfing, windsurfing and kitesurfing. Action or inaction, this coast bubbles with opportunities.

Nha Trang

✆ 058 / POP 394,000

Welcome to the beach capital of Vietnam. Loud and proud (say it!), the high-rise, high-energy resort of Nha Trang enjoys a stunning setting – ringed by a necklace of hills, with a sweeping crescent beach and turquoise bay dotted with tropical islands.

Nha Trang is a party town at heart, like any self-respecting resort should be. Forget the curfews of the capital; people play late here. Or if cocktail buckets and shooters aren't your flavour, try the natural mud baths or visit the imposing Cham towers.

◉ Sights

★ Nha Trang Beach   BEACH

Forming a magnificent sweeping arc, Nha Trang's 6km-long golden-sand beach is the city's trump card. The cobalt water is fabulously inviting and the promenade a delight to stroll.

Two popular lounging spots are the Sailing Club and Louisiane Brewhouse. If you head south of here, the beach gets quieter and it's possible to find a stretch of sand to yourself.

★ **Po Nagar Cham Towers**   BUDDHIST TEMPLE
(Thap Ba, Lady of the City; admission 21,000d; ☺ 6am-6pm) Built between the 7th and 12th centuries, these four Cham Towers are still actively used for worship by Cham, ethnic Chinese and Vietnamese Buddhists. Originally the complex had seven or eight towers, but only four towers remain, of which the 28m-high North Tower (Thap Chinh), which dates from AD 817, with its terraced pyramidal roof, vaulted interior masonry and vestibule, is the most magnificent.

The towers stand on a granite knoll 2km north of central Nha Trang on the banks of the Cai River.

Long Son Pagoda   BUDDHIST TEMPLE
(☺ 7.30-11.30am & 1.30-5.30pm) FREE This striking pagoda was founded in the late 19th century. The entrance and roofs are decorated with mosaic dragons constructed of glass and ceramic tile, while the main sanctuary is a hall adorned with modern interpretations of traditional motifs.

Behind the pagoda is a huge white **Buddha** (Kim Than Phat To) seated on a lotus blossom. Around the statue's base are fire-ringed relief busts of Thich Quang Duc and six other Buddhist monks who died in self-immolations in 1963.

The pagoda is 400m west of the train station, just off Đ 23 Thang 10.

Alexandre Yersin Museum   MUSEUM
(☑ 058-382 2355; 10 Đ Tran Phu; admission 28,000d; ☺ 7.30-11am & 2-4.30pm Mon-Fri, 8-11am Sat) Dr Alexandre Yersin (1863–1943) founded Nha Trang's Pasteur Institute in 1895. He learned to speak Vietnamese fluently, introduced rubber and quinine-producing trees to Vietnam, and discovered the rat-borne microbe that causes bubonic plague.

You can see Yersin's library and office at this small, interesting museum; displays include laboratory equipment (such as astronomical instruments) and a fascinating 3-D photo viewer.

Tours are conducted in French, English and Vietnamese.

Hon Chong Promontory   LANDMARK
(admission 11,000d) The narrow granite promontory of Hon Chong offers fine views of the mountainous coastline north of Nha Trang and the nearby islands.

TRIPPING THE BAY BY BOAT

The 71 offshore islands around Nha Trang are renowned for their remarkably clear water. Boat trips to these islands – booze cruises and snorkelling excursions, from just 150,000d – are wildly popular with young backpackers.

Frankly, most of these trips are extremely touristy, involving whistle-stop visits to the Tri Nguyen **Aquarium** (Ho Ca Tri Nguyen; admission 50,000d), some snorkelling on a degraded reef and a bit of beach time (beach admission 30,000d). The booze cruises feature (very) organised entertainment with a DJ on the deck (or a cheesy boy band) and lots of drinking games.

Keep the following tips in mind:

➡ Choose the right tour. Some are geared towards Asian families, others are booze cruises.

➡ Remember sunscreen and drink plenty of water.

➡ Entrance charges are not usually included.

➡ If you're more interested in snorkelling than drinking, the dive schools' trips will be more appropriate.

Some decent boat-trip operators include the following:

Funky Monkey (☑ 058-352 2426; www.funkymonkeytour.com.vn; 75A Đ Hung Vuong; cruise incl pick-up 100,000d) Backpacker fun-filled trip including live entertainment.

Nha Trang Tours (☑ 058-352 4471; www.nhatrangtour.com.vn; 1/24 Đ Tran Quang Khai) Budget party-themed booze cruises for US$8 or snorkelling trips for around US$15.

Khanh Hoa Tourist Information (☑ 058-352 8000; khtourism@dng.vnn.vn; Đ Tran Phu; cruise incl lunch 349,000d) Boat trips to beautiful Van Phong Bay.

Central Nha Trang

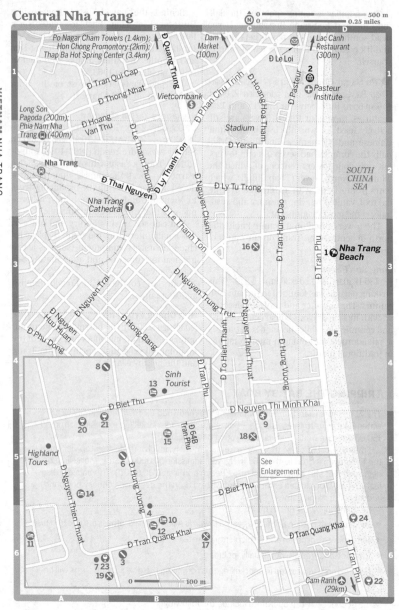

0 — 500 m
0 — 0.25 miles

Po Nagar Cham Towers (1.4km);
Hon Chong Promontory (2km);
Thap Ba Hot Spring Center (3.4km)

Đ Quang Trung

Dam Market (100km)

Đ Le Loi

Lac Canh Restaurant (300m)

Đ Tran Qui Cap

Đ Thong Nhat

Đ Phan Chu Trinh

Đ Pasteur

Pasteur Institute

Vietcombank

Đ Hoang Hoa Tham

Long Son Pagoda (200m);
Phia Nam Nha Trang (400m)

Đ Hoang Van Thu

Đ Le Thanh Phuong

Đ Ly Thanh Ton

Stadium

Đ Yersin

Nha Trang

Đ Thai Nguyen

Đ Nguyen Chanh

Đ Ly Tu Trong

SOUTH CHINA SEA

Nha Trang Cathedral

Đ Le Thanh Ton

Đ Tran Hung Dao

16

Đ Tran Phu

1 Nha Trang Beach

Đ Nguyen Trung Truc

Đ Nguyen Trai

Đ Nguyen Huu Huan

Đ Hong Bang

Đ To Hien Thanh

Đ Nguyen Thien Thuat

Đ Hung Vuong

5

Đ Phu Dong

8

Sinh Tourist

13

Đ Tran Phu

Đ Biet Thu

20

21

15

Đ 64B Tran Phu

Đ Nguyen Thi Minh Khai

9

18

Highland Tours

6

Đ Hung Vuong

See Enlargement

Đ Biet Thu

Đ Nguyen Thien Thuat

14

4

10

12

Đ Tran Quang Khai

17

24

11

7 23

3

19

Cam Ranh (29km)

22

Đ Tran Phu

Đ Tran Quang Khai

0 — 100 m

🏃 Activities

Diving

Nha Trang is Vietnam's most popular scuba-diving centre. February to September is considered the best time to dive, while October to December is the worst time of year.

There are around 25 dive sites in the area. Some sites have good drop-offs and there are small underwater caves to explore. It's not world-class diving, but the waters support a reasonable number of small reef fish.

Central Nha Trang

A two-dive boat trip costs between US$60 and US$85; snorkellers typically pay US$15 to US$20.

Most dive operators also offer a range of dive courses. Watch out for dodgy dive shops not following responsible diving practices and even using fake PADI/SSI accreditation – stick to reputable operators.

Mark Scott Dive Center DIVING
(📞 0122 903 7795; www.divingvietnam.com; 24/4 Đ Hung Vuong) Owned by a larger-than-life Texan, this new school has quickly established an excellent reputation. SSI courses are offered.

Angel Dive DIVING
(📞 058-352 2461; www.angeldivevietnam.info; 1/33 Đ Tran Quang Khai) Reliable operator with English, French and German instruction, plus the choice of PADI or SSI certification.

Rainbow Divers DIVING
(📞 058-352 4351; www.divevietnam.com; 90A Đ Hung Vuong) Large, well-established PADI dive school that's part of a nationwide chain. There is also a popular restaurant and bar.

Other Activities

Vietnam Active ADVENTURE SPORTS
(📞 058-351 5821; www.vietnamactive.com; 47 B1 Nguyen Thien Thuat) Activities include mountain-biking trips (from US$45 for four people), scuba-diving courses and yoga.

Shamrock Adventures RAFTING, KAYAKING
(📞 058-352 7548; www.shamrockadventures.vn; Đ Tran Quang Khai; trips per person incl lunch from US$40) Offers white-water rafting, mountain biking and kayak and fishing trips.

Thap Ba Hot Spring Center THERMAL BATHS
(📞 058-383 4939; www.thapbahotspring.com.vn; 25 Ngoc Son; ⊙ 7am-7.30pm) The original hot thermal mud centre. For 250,000/500,000d you get a single/double wooden bathtub full of gooey mud, or it's 120,000d per person for a communal slop-up. Located 7km northwest of Nha Trang (130,000d in a taxi).

🛏 Sleeping

★ Sunny Sea HOTEL $
(📞 058-352 5244; http://sunnyhotel.com.vn; 64B/9 Đ Tran Phu; r US$10-15; ✴@🛜) An exceptional place managed by welcoming people. Recently renovated, the rooms boast new mattresses, a minibar, modern bathrooms and some have a balcony. The location is great, on a quiet lane just off the beach, and there's a lift.

Sao Mai Hotel HOTEL $
(📞 058-352 6412; www.saomainhatranghotel.com; 99 Đ Nguyen Thien Thuat; dm US$6, r US$12-25; ✴@🛜) Long-standing budget favourite that's moved a little upmarket but remains superb value, with friendly management and 32 immaculately clean, spacious rooms. The five-bed dorm has air-con, en suite bathroom and lockers.

Mojzo Inn HOSTEL $
(📞 0988 879 069; 120/36 Đ Nguyen Thien Thuat; dm US$7, r US$16-19; ✴@🛜) The name is more cocktail list than hotel bed, but this funky new hostel gets most things right, with well-designed dorms and a lovely cushion-scattered lounge area.

Ngoc Thach
HOTEL $

(📞 058-352 5988; ngocthachhotel@gmail.com; 6I Quan Tran, Đ Hung Vuong; r US$15-18; ❄🛜) A great deal, the spacious, modern rooms (some with balcony) here are in excellent shape and have a real sparkle considering the modest tariffs. There's a lift.

Perfume Grass Inn
HOTEL $

(📞 058-352 4286; www.perfume-grass.com; 4A Đ Biet Thu; r US$14-35; ❄@🛜) This welcoming inn has plenty of character, particularly the pricier rooms with their wooden panelling and floors. Free breakfast, a slim garden and friendly English-speaking management add to the appeal.

Le Duong
HOTEL $$

(5 & 6 Quan Tran, Đ Hung Vuong; r 450,000-700,000d; ❄🛜) New in 2013, this inviting modern hotel has 50 beautifully presented, spacious rooms with pale furniture and white linen that represent excellent value. Prices are flexible to a degree.

🍴 Eating

For inexpensive, authentic Vietnamese food, head to **Dam Market** (Đ Trang Nu Vuong; ⊙6am-4pm), which has good stalls and lots of vegie choices.

Nha Hang Yen's
VIETNAMESE $

(3/2A Tran Quang Khai; dishes 55,000-120,000d; ⊙7am-9.30pm; 🛜) Stylish restaurant with a hospitable atmosphere and a winning line-up of flavoursome clay-pot, noodle and rice dishes. Lilting traditional music and waitresses in *ao dai* add to the vibe.

Hy Lap
GREEK $

(1 Đ Tran Quang Khai; meals 30,000-75,000d; ⊙noon-10pm) Casual, inexpensive hole-in-the-wall Greek place run by an extremely welcoming Cretan couple. Only has six tables (all outside) but good for moussaka, souvlaki or a salad.

Au Lac
VEGETARIAN $

(28C Đ Hoang Hoa Tham; meals 15,000-30,000d; ⊙11am-7pm; 🖉) Long-running vegan/vegetarian eatery near the corner of Đ Nguyen Chanh. A mixed plate is just about the best value meal you can find in Nha Trang.

★ Lac Canh Restaurant
VIETNAMESE $$

(44 Đ Nguyen Binh Khiem; dishes 30,000-150,000d; ⊙11am-8.45pm) A totally local experience, this bustling, smoky, scruffy and highly enjoyable place is crammed most nights with groups firing up the table-top barbecues (beef is the speciality, but there are other meats and seafood, too). Closes quite early.

Lanterns
VIETNAMESE $$

(www.lanternsvietnam.com; 34/6 Đ Nguyen Thien Thuat; dishes 48,000-158,000d; ⊙7.30am-9.30pm; ⊖🛜🖉) Now in superb new premises with an expansive terrace, this restaurant supports local orphanages and provides scholarships. Flavours are predominantly Vietnamese, such as lemon and chilli pork and tofu curry, with set menus available (from 108,000d), plus a few international offerings. Cooking classes and tours are also offered.

Louisiane Brewhouse
INTERNATIONAL $$

(www.louisianebrewhouse.com.vn; 29 Đ Tran Phu; mains 62,000-360,000d; ⊙7am-1am; 🛜) It's not only the beer that draws a crowd here, as there is an eclectic menu with breakfast classics, superb salads, fish and seafood (red snapper is 140,000d) and Vietnamese, Japanese and Italian dishes. The beachside setting is superb, with tables grouped around a pool and giant copper beer vats.

🍷 Drinking

★ Guava
LOUNGE

(www.guava.vn; 17 Đ Biet Thu; ⊙7am-1am; 🛜) Groovy Guava is the only game in town for quality electronic music – DJs spin house and lounge here on weekends. Expect a friendly vibe, good service, pub grub and a busy pool table.

Sailing Club
BAR, CLUB

(www.sailingclubnhatrang.com; 72-74 Đ Tran Phu; ⊙7am-2am) Sailing Club is the definitive Nha Trang nightspot with a good mix of locals and foreigners. It's an upmarket venue, with expensive drinks, DJs and bands, and draws the city's beautiful crowd.

DRINK SPIKING

There have been a number of reports of laced cocktail buckets doing the rounds in popular night spots. This might mean staff using homemade moonshine instead of legal spirits or could mean the addition of drugs of some sort by other punters. While buckets are fun and communal, take care in Nha Trang and try and keep an eye on what goes into the bucket. You don't want your night to end in paranoia or robbery.

Louisiane Brewhouse   BREWERY
(058-352 1948; 29 Đ Tran Phu; per glass 40,000d;
 7am-midnight;) Microbreweries don't get much more sophisticated than this. There are six brews to try, including a red ale and a dark lager, or for 110,000d you can sample the lot.

Oasis   BAR
(3 Đ Tran Quang Khai; 7am-2am;) Buzzing bar on a corner plot with large garden terrace that's popular for bucket-downing and shisha-puffing. Happy hour runs right through from 4pm to midnight. It's a good choice for big sporting events.

Crazy Kim Bar   BAR
(http://crazykimvietnam.wordpress.com; 19 Đ Biet Thu; 8am-midnight;) With more of a pub atmosphere, this place is home to the commendable 'Hands off the Kids!' campaign, working to prevent paedophilia. Hosts regular themed party nights, devilish cocktail buckets, shooters, cheap beer (from 25,000d), good tunes and tasty grub.

ⓘ Information

Though Nha Trang is generally a safe place, be very careful on the beach during the day (theft) and at night (robbery). Pickpocketing is a perennial problem. Bags with valuables left behind bars for 'safekeeping' are regularly relieved of cash and phones. Drive-by bag snatching is on the rise. And note the warning about spiked cocktail buckets. (See the boxed text opposite).

Nha Trang has lots of internet cafes and most hotels and bars have free wi-fi. ATMs are widespread.

Highland Tours (058-352 4477; www.highlandtourstravel.com; 54G Đ Nguyen Thien Thuat) An extensive program of affordable tours in the Nha Trang area, to the central highlands and along the coast. A day trip along the Cai River costs from US$27.

Main Post Office (4 Đ Le Loi; 6.30am-8pm)

Pasteur Institute (058-382 2355; 10 Đ Tran Phu; 7-11am & 1-4.30pm) Offers medical consultations and vaccinations. Located inside the Alexandre Yersin Museum.

Sinh Tourist (058-352 2982; www.thesinhtourist.vn; 2A Đ Biet Thu) Inexpensive local tours as well as open-tour buses.

Vietcombank (17 Đ Quang Trung; 7.30am-4pm Mon-Fri) Has an ATM.

ⓘ Getting There & Away

AIR
Vietnam Airlines (058-352 6768; www.vietnamairlines.com; 91 Đ Nguyen Thien Thuat) connects Nha Trang with Hanoi (three daily) and to HCMC and Danang daily. **VietJet Air** (1900 1886; www.vietjetair.com) flies to both Hanoi and HCMC daily. **Jetstar** (www.jetstar.com) offers five weekly connections with Hanoi.

BUS
Phia Nam Nha Trang bus station (Đ 23 Thang 10) has services to Danang. Heading south, there are sleeper buses to HCMC from 7pm. Open-bus tours are the best option for Mui Ne (four to five hours). Open buses also head to Dalat (five hours) and Hoi An (11 hours).

TRAIN
Nha Trang train station (058-382 2113; Đ Thai Nguyen; ticket office 7-11.30am, 1.30-6pm & 7-9pm) is in the middle of town.

ⓘ Getting Around

Cam Ranh international airport is 30km south of the city via a beautiful coastal road. A shuttle bus runs the route (60,000d), leaving from the site of the old airport (near 86 Đ Tran Phu) two hours before scheduled departure times, taking about 40 minutes. Taxis cost 380,000/300,000d to/from the airport.

Cyclos and xe om cost 20,000d for a short ride. Hotels and cafes rent bicycles from 30,000d per day. **Mai Linh** (058-382 2266) taxis are safe and reliable.

TRANSPORT FROM NHA TRANG

DESTINATION	AIR	BUS	CAR & MOTORBIKE	TRAIN
Dalat	N/A	US$7, 5hr, 17 daily	4hr	N/A
Danang	from US$55, 1hr, 1 daily	US$11-14, 12hr, 13-16 daily	11hr	US$16-26, 9-11hr, 5 daily
HCMC	from US$28, 1hr, 6 daily	US$10-14, 11hr, 13 daily	10hr	US$11-17, 7-9hr, 6 daily
Mui Ne	N/A	US$8, 6hr, open buses only	5hr	N/A

Mui Ne

062 / POP 15,000

Once upon a time, Mui Ne was an isolated stretch of sand, but it was too beautiful to be ignored – now it's a string of resorts. Mercifully, most of these are low-rise and set amid pretty gardens by the sea. The area is definitely moving upmarket, as more exclusive resorts open their doors, but a (kite) surfer vibe still sets the scene.

Windsurfing and kitesurfing are huge here – surf's up from August to December. It's also the 'Sahara' of Vietnam, with the most dramatic sand dunes in the region looming large.

Virtually everything is spread along a 10km stretch of highway. Most accommodation lines the beachfront, while restaurants and shops flank the inland side.

⊙ Sights

Sand Dunes
BEACH

Mui Ne is famous for its enormous red and white sand dunes. The white dunes are the more impressive, the near-constant oceanic winds sculpting the sands into wonderful Saharaesque formations. But as this is Vietnam (not deepest Mali) there's little chance of experiencing the silence of the desert.

Prepare yourself for the hard-sell as children press you to hire a plastic sledge to ride the dunes. Quad bikes and dune buggies also destroy the peace. Expect some litter too.

Po Shanu Cham Towers
TEMPLE

(Km 5; admission 5000d; ⊙7.30-11.30am & 1.30-4.30pm) West of Mui Ne, the Hindu Po Shanu Cham towers occupy a hill near Phan Thiet, with sweeping views of the town and a cemetery filled with candylike tombstones.

SPLURGE

An outstanding hotel-restaurant, **Sandals** (24 Đ Nguyen Dinh Chieu, Mia Resort; meals 90,000-350,000d; ⊙7am-10pm; 🛜) has tables set around a shoreside pool (or in elegant adjacent dining rooms). Staff are knowledgeable, attentive and welcoming. The menu is superb with everything from pasta dishes to Malay-style *laksa* executed and presented beautifully.

🏃 Activities

Surfpoint Kiteboarding School
KITESURFING, SURFING

(☑0167 342 2136; www.surfpoint-vietnam.com; 52A Đ Nguyen Dinh Chieu; 5hr course incl all gear US$250; ⊙7am-6pm) Offers well-trained instructors and a friendly vibe. A three-hour taster costs US$145. Surfing lessons on softboards are also offered (from US$50) when waves permit.

Jibes
KITESURFING

(☑062-384 7405; www.windsurf-vietnam.com; 84-90 Đ Nguyen Dinh Chieu; ⊙7.30am-6pm) Set up in 2000, this is the original kitesurfing school, offering lessons and renting state-of-the-art gear, including windsurfs, surfboards, kitesurfs and kayaks.

Sankara Kitesurfing Academy
KITESURFING

(☑0914 910 607; http://muinekiteschool.com; 78 Đ Nguyen Dinh Chieu) This school is run by experienced kitesurfers and offers kitesurfing lessons and equipment rentals. Lessons start at US$99 for two hours, or US$270 for five hours.

🎓 Courses

Taste of Vietnam
COOKING

(☑0916 655 241; www.c2skykitecenter.com/cooking-school; Sunshine Beach Resort, 82 Đ Nguyen Dinh Chieu; ⊙9am-12.30pm) Well-regarded Vietnamese cooking classes by the beach. Pay US$30 and a market visit is included.

🛏 Sleeping

Coco Sand Hotel
GUESTHOUSE $

(☑0127 364 3446; cocosandcatdua@yahoo.com.vn; 119 Đ Nguyen Dinh Chieu; r US$12-15; 🌬🛜) Down a lane on the inland side of the main drag, these simple, clean rooms are quite spacious and excellent value. The owners are all smiles and there's a little garden with hammocks.

Mui Ne Backpackers
GUESTHOUSE $

(☑062-384 7047; www.muinebackpackers.com; 88 Đ Nguyen Dinh Chieu; dm US$6-10, r US$20-60; 🌬@🛜🏊) Popular with young travellers for its sociable vibe and shoreside location, the dorms (with en suite bathrooms and good mattresses) are a good bet, though the rooms are a little pricey and quite plain. Lots of tours offered; transport tickets can be arranged.

Mui Ne Beach

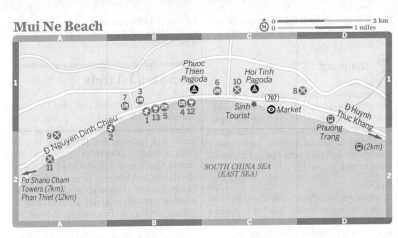

N 0 ——————— 2 km
0 ——————— 1 miles

SOUTH CHINA SEA
(EAST SEA)

Po Shanu Cham
Towers (7km);
Phan Thiet (12km)

Song Huong Hotel HOTEL **$**
(☑062-384 7450; www.songhuonghotel.com; 241 Đ Nguyen Dinh Chieu; r US$12-20; ❄ 🛜) Run by welcoming family owners, this hotel is set well back from the road and boasts spacious, airy rooms in a modern house. Breakfast is included.

Lu Hoang Guesthouse HOTEL **$**
(☑062-350 0060; 106 Đ Nguyen Dinh Chieu; r US$16-22; ❄ @ 🛜) This guesthouse has been lovingly decorated and several rooms include a sea view and breezy balconies, plus all have spotless bathrooms. The charming owners really make an effort here.

Xin Chao BOUTIQUE HOTEL **$$**
(☑062-374 3086; www.xinchaohotel.com; 129 Đ Nguyen Dinh Chieu; r US$20-50; ❄ @ 🛜 ▨) Impressive new hotel (owned by kitesurfers) set well back from the busy coastal road. Rooms are grouped around a pool at the rear, and a small lounge area (with pool table) and roadside bar-restaurant add to its appeal.

✖ Eating

★Com Chay Phuoc VEGETARIAN **$**
(15B Đ Huynh Thuc Khang; meals 20,000d; ⊙7am-9pm; ✐) An exceptional little roadside vegetarian place owned by Di, the ever-helpful English-speaking owner. There are always four or five freshly cooked Vietnamese dishes and you eat on bamboo tables in very clean surrounds. Located on the far east part of the strip.

Phat Hamburgers INTERNATIONAL **$**
(253 Đ Nguyen Dinh Chieu; burgers 55,000-95,000d; ⊙11am-9.30pm; 🛜) Roadside burger joint with variety of options, from gourmet to classic, served with great fries. Sip on a shake (try the chocolate and mint) for the full experience.

Peaceful Family Restaurant VIETNAMESE **$**
(Yen Gia Quan; 53 Đ Nguyen Dinh Chieu; dishes 30,000-70,000d; ⊙7am-9.30pm) A long-running local restaurant, the family here serve up traditional Vietnamese cuisine under a

breezy thatched roof. Prices are pretty reasonable and the service is always efficient and friendly.

 Drinking

Joe's Café   BAR
(www.joescafegardenresort.com; 86 Đ Nguyen Dinh Chieu; ⊙7am-1am; 🛜) Mui Ne's premier live music (every night at 7.30pm) hangout with a sociable bar area, tables under trees, lots of drinks specials, an extensive food menu and pool table. Draws a slightly older crowd.

Fun Key   BAR
(124 Đ Nguyen Dinh Chieu; ⊙10am-1am; 🛜) With a faintly boho ambience, this bar is popular with backpackers. Overlooks the ocean and has drink promotions to rev things up.

Dragon Beach   BAR, CLUB
(120-121 Đ Nguyen Dinh Chieu; ⊙8am-2am) With a great shoreside location that catches the sea breeze, this place is the most happening dance floor in town. Western and local DJs playing deep house, techno and drum 'n' bass. Happy hour is 8pm to 10pm.

ℹ️ **Information**

Head to www.muinebeach.net for online information.

Internet and wi-fi is widely available and there are numerous ATMs.

Main Post Office (348 Đ Huynh Thuc Khang; ⊙7am-5pm)

Sinh Tourist (www.thesinhtourist.vn; 144 Đ Nguyen Dinh Chieu) Books open-tour buses, trips around Mui Ne and offers credit card cash advances.

ℹ️ **Getting There & Around**

Mui Ne is connected to Hwy 1 via branch roads to the north and south, but few regular buses serve the town.

Open-tour buses are the best option for Mui Ne; several companies have daily services to/from HCMC (120,000d to 149,000d, six hours), Nha Trang (120,000d, five hours) and Dalat (110,000d, four hours). Sleeper buses usually cost more: Sinh Tourist's prices are HCMC (209,000d), Nha Trang (209,000d), Hoi An (378,000d) and Hué (477,000d).

Phuong Trang (www.futabuslines.com.vn; 97 Đ Nguyen Dinh Chieu) has four to five comfortable buses a day running between Mui Ne and HCMC (135,000d).

Local buses run from nearby Phan Thiet to Mui Ne, or take a *xe om* (60,000d). **Mai Linh**

(📞062-389 8989) operates metered taxis. *Xe om* charge 20,000d to 40,000d for rides up and down the coast.

Con Dao Islands

📞 064 / POP 5500

Isolated from the mainland, the Con Dao Islands are one of the star attractions in Vietnam. Long an outpost for political prisoners and undesirables, this place is now turning heads thanks to its striking natural beauty. Con Son, the largest of this chain of 15 islands and islets, is ringed with lovely beaches, coral reefs and scenic bays and remains partially covered in thick forests. Hiking, diving and deserted beaches are all a big draw.

More than three-quarters of the land area in the island chain is part of Con Dao National Park, which protects Vietnam's most important **sea turtle nesting grounds**.

👁️ **Sights**

All the following sights are in Con Son town, share the same opening hours and are covered by a single ticket costing 20,000d, which you can purchase in the museum. There are 11 former prisons on Con Son.

Phu Hai Prison   HISTORIC BUILDING
(⊙7-11.30am & 1-5pm) The largest jail on the island, Phu Hai dates from 1862. Thousands of prisoners were held here, with up to 200 crammed into each detention building. During the French era all prisoners were kept naked, chained together in rows, with one small box serving as a toilet for hundreds. One can only imagine the squalor and stench. Today, emaciated mannequins that are all too lifelike recreate the era.

Tiger Cages   HISTORIC BUILDING
The notorious cells dubbed tiger cages were built in 1940 by the French to incarcerate nearly 2000 political prisoners. There are 120 chambers with ceiling bars, where guards could poke at prisoners like tigers in a Victorian zoo. Prisoners were beaten with sticks from above and sprinkled with quick lime and water (which burnt their skin and caused blindness).

Hang Duong Cemetery   CEMETERY
Some 20,000 Vietnamese prisoners died on Con Son and 1994 graves can be seen at

this cemetery on the eastern edge of town. Vietnam's most famous heroine, Vo Thi Sau (1933–52), was buried here, the first woman executed by a firing squad on Con Son, on 23 January 1952.

Revolutionary Museum   MUSEUM
(⊙7-11am & 1.30-5pm) Located in the former French commandant's residence, this museum has exhibits on the Vietnamese resistance against the French, communist opposition to the Republic of Vietnam and the treatment of political prisoners.

Coastline   BEACH
The best beach on the island, **Bai Dot Doc** is a simply beautiful cove, consisting of a kilometre-long crescent of pale sand backed by green hills. It's fringed by the exclusive Six Senses resort but is *not* a private beach. Reached via a dirt track 1km before the airport, **Bai Dram Trau** is a sublime but remote 700m half-moon crescent of soft sand. On the north side of Con Son town, **Bai Loi Voi** is a broad sand-and-shingle beach with casuarinas for shade.

CAT TIEN NATIONAL PARK

One of the outstanding natural spaces in Vietnam, Unesco-listed **Cat Tien National Park** (☑061-366 9228; www.cattiennationalpark.vn; adult/child 50,000/20,000d; ⊙7am-10pm) 🍃 comprises an amazingly biodiverse area of lowland tropical rainforest. The hiking, mountain biking and birdwatching are outstanding.

Fauna in the park includes 326 bird species, 100 mammals (including elephants) and 79 reptiles. Leopards are also believed to be present, though the last rhino was killed by poachers in 2010.

Call ahead for reservations, as the park can accommodate only a limited number of visitors.

Sights & Activities
Cat Tien National Park can be explored on foot, by mountain bike, by 4WD and also by boat along the Dong Nai River. There are many well-established hiking trails in the park, though you'll need a **guide** (from 250,000d), who should be booked in advance.

Trips to the **Crocodile Swamp** (Bau Sau; admission 140,000d, guide fee 300,000d, boat trip 350,000d), taking in a three-hour jungle trek, are popular. **Night safaris** (from 300,000d) are another option. There's also a small bear sanctuary for animals rescued from the bile trade.

Dao Tien Endangered Primate Species Centre (www.go-east.org; adult/child incl boat ride 150,000/50,000d; ⊙8am & 2pm) is located on an island in the Dong Nai River. This rehabilitation centre hosts gibbons, langurs and lorises that have been confiscated as pets or from traffickers.

Wild Gibbon Trek (ecotourism@cattiennationalpark.vn; per person US$60, maximum 4 people) involves a 4am start to hear the gibbons in time for their dawn chorus and a fully guided tour of the Primate Species Centre. Book ahead.

Sleeping & Eating
Cat Tien National Park (☑061-366 9228; namcattien@yahoo.com.vn; small/big tents 220,000/350,000d, bungalows from 580,000d; ❋) offers basic bungalow rooms and tented accommodation close to the park headquarters. There are two small **restaurants** (mains from 25,000d; ⊙7am-9pm) here. In Jun village by the park entrance, **Sinthai Ho Lak** (☑0905 424 239; Jun Village; per person US$5) offers comfortable communal longhouse accommodation and meals. Avoid weekends and holidays if possible.

Getting There & Around
Cat Tien is 175km south of Dalat; turn off Hwy 20 at Tan Phu and it's another 25km up a paved access road to the entrance.

Buses between Dalat and HCMC pass the access road. Waiting motorbikes (around 170,000d) will then take you to the park entrance.

Bicycles are available for hire in the park, from 20,000d per day.

SOUTHWEST HIGHLANDS

It's easy to get off the beaten track in the wonderfully scenic highlands. This is a great part of the country to see from the back of a motorbike.

The upgrading of the historic **Ho Chi Minh Trail** has made it easier to visit out-of-the-way places such as **Kon Tum**, one of the friendliest cities in Vietnam.

Buon Ma Thuot is the major city in the region, but the biggest buzz you'll get is from the coffee beans. Nearby **Yok Don National Park** (✆0500-378 3049; www.yokdon nationalpark.vn; admission free as part of package) is home to 38 endangered mammal species, including plenty of elephants. Stunning waterfalls in this area include **Gia Long** (✆363 8456; admission 10,000d) and **Dray Nur Falls** (✆0500-321 3194; admission 20,000d) along the Krong Ana River.

Northeast of Dalat, the **high road to Nha Trang** offers spectacular views, hitting 1700m at Hon Giao mountain, following a breathtaking 33km pass.

And 43km southeast of Dalat, it's possible to see the ocean from the spectacular **Ngoan Muc Pass**.

🏃 Activities

Con Dao offers the most pristine marine environment in the country. **Diving** is possible year-round, but for ideal conditions and good visibility, January to June is considered the best time.

There are lots of treks around forested Con Son Island; it's necessary to take a national park guide (180,000d to 300,000d). Trekking destinations include **Bamboo Lagoon** (Dam Tre), **Ong Dung Bay** and former fruit plantations at **So Ray**.

★**Dive! Dive! Dive!**   DIVING
(✆064-383 0701; www.dive-condao.com; Đ Nguyen Hué; ⊙8am-9pm) A conservation-minded, American-run operation with plenty of experience, offering both PADI and SSI courses. Two dives are US$160 and snorkelling tours cost US$40 (including equipment).

🛏 Sleeping & Eating

Accommodation and eating prices are about double mainland rates.

Nha Nghi Thanh Xuan   GUESTHOUSE $
(✆064-383 0261; 44 Đ Ton Duc Thang; r 350,000-450,000d; 🛜) Painted in marine blue, this guesthouse has rooms with good mattresses and duvets, and the upstairs rooms are light and airy. The owners speak little to no English.

Hai Nga Mini Hotel   HOTEL $
(✆064-363 0308; 7 Đ Tran Phu; r 400,000-600,000d; ❄@🛜) A tempting option for sharers, some rooms here sleep up to five people, and all have air-con. It's run by a friendly family who can speak some English and German.

Thu Tam   VIETNAMESE $$
(Đ Nguyen Hué; mains 25,000-170,000d; ⊙11.30am-9pm) On the Con Son strip, offering fresh seafood from bubbling tanks. Shells in many shapes and sizes, or go for a huge fish to feed a family.

Quan Thanh Huyen   VIETNAMESE $$
(Khu 3, Hoang Phi Yen; meals 70,000-160,000d; ⊙noon-9pm) South of town by a water-lily-filled lake, this lovely little restaurant enjoys a great setting. Serves authentic Vietnamese cuisine including hotpots and snakehead fish straight from the lake.

ℹ Information

Speak to Larry at Dive! Dive! Dive! for independent information. The **National Park HQ** (✆064-383 0669; www.condaopark.com. vn; 29 Đ Vo Thi Sau; ⊙7-11.30am & 1.30-5pm daily) has information about excursions and hikes.

There are three ATMs in Con Son town. Internet access and wi-fi are available at hotels.

ℹ Getting There & Around

Vasco (✆064-383 1831; www.vasco.com.vn; 44 Đ Nguyen Hué) offers three flights daily from HCMC for US$75 one-way, and connections to Can Tho for US$65. The tiny airport is about 15km from the town centre. You can hitch a ride to town on hotel shuttle minibuses for about 50,000d.

Ferries connect Con Son Island with Vung Tau, with sailings three to four times a week. Facilities are basic and the crossing can be very rough, leading to frequent cancellations. The ferries (at 5pm, seat/berth 145,000/275,000d, 12 hours) depart from Ben Dam port, 12km south of Con Son town.

Boat trips (2,000,000d to 5,000,000d per day) can be arranged through the national park office or Dive! Dive! Dive! Bicycles (US$2) and motorbikes (from US$7) are available for rent from hotels.

SOUTHWEST HIGHLANDS

There's a rugged charm to this distinctly rural region, with pine-studded hilltops soaring over intensively farmed fields and remote, bumpy roads meandering through coffee plantations.

Looking for big nature? Check out Cat Tien National Park, where there are gibbons, crocodiles and elusive tigers.

Dalat, a former French hill station that still boasts plenty of colonial charm, makes a great base. An adventure sports mecca, it offers myriad biking and hiking trips for daytime thrills and atmospheric restaurants and bars for after-dark chills.

Dalat

◢ 063 / POP 208.000 / ELEV 1475M

Dalat is the alter-ego of lowland Vietnam. The weather is springlike cool instead of tropical hot. The town is dotted with elegant French-colonial villas, and farms are thick with strawberries and flowers, not rice.

Dalat is small enough to remain charming, and the surrounding countryside is blessed with lakes, waterfalls, evergreen forests and gardens.

The town is a big draw for domestic tourists, for whom it's a honeymoon capital. For travellers, the moderate climate is ideal for adrenaline-fuelled activities – mountain biking, forest hiking, canyoning and climbing.

◉ Sights

Perhaps there's something in the cool mountain air that fosters the distinctly artistic vibe that veers towards cute kitsch in Dalat.

Hang Nga Crazy House NOTABLE BUILDING
(◢ 063-382 2070; 3 Đ Huynh Thuc Khang; admission 40,000d; ⊗ 7am-7pm) A free-wheeling architectural exploration of surrealism, Hang Nga Crazy House defies definition. Joyously designed, outrageously artistic, this private home is a monument to the creative potential of concrete, with sculptured rooms connected by super-slim bridges and an excess of cascading lava-flowlike shapes. Think Gaudí on acid.

Wander around as you please; getting lost is definitely part of the experience.

Bao Dai's Summer Palace HISTORIC BUILDING
(off Đ Trieu Viet Vuong; admission 15,000d; ⊗ 7am-5pm) A faded art-deco-influenced villa, this was one of three palaces Bao Dai (the last emperor of the Nguyen dynasty) kept in Dalat. The building's design is striking, though it's in serious need of restoration and the once-modern interior is distinctly scruffy today.

Bao Dai's imposing office, with its royal and military seals and flags, is still impressive. The palace is set in a pine grove, 2km southwest of the city centre.

Crémaillère Railway
Station HISTORIC BUILDING
(Ga Da Lat; 1 Đ Quang Trung; ⊗ 6.30am-5pm) **FREE**
Dalat's wonderful art deco train station is no longer connected to the Vietnamese rail network, though you can turn back the clock by riding one of the five scheduled trains that run to Trai Mat (return 124,000d, 30 minutes) daily between 7.45am and 4pm. Arrive early and note that the train won't leave without at least two passengers.

EASY DOES IT

For many travellers, the highlight of their trip to the central highlands is an off-the-beaten-track motorcycle tour with an Easy Rider (driver-guide). The flip side to the popularity of the Easy Riders is that now everyone claims to be one. In central Dalat, you can't walk down the street without being invited (sometimes harassed) for a tour.

Rider-guides can be found in hotels and cafes in Dalat. Read testimonials from past clients. Check the bike over. Test-drive a rider first before committing to a longer trip. Then discuss the route in detail – for scenery, the new coastal highways that link Dalat to Mui Ne and Nha Trang, plus the old road to the coast via Phan Rang, are wonderful. Rates start at US$25 for a day tour, or US$50 to US$70 per day for longer journeys.

Central Dalat

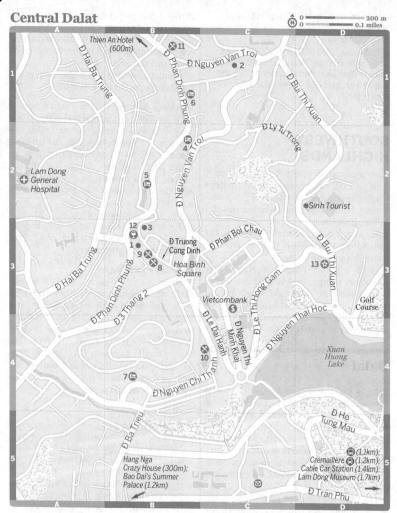

Lam Dong Museum
MUSEUM

(☎ 063-382 0387; 4 Đ Hung Vuong; admission 10,000d; ☉ 7.30-11.30am & 1.30-4.30pm Mon-Sat) Housed in a pink building 2.5km east of the centre, this hillside museum displays ancient artefacts and pottery, as well as costumes and musical instruments of local ethnic minorities.

🏃 Activities

★ Phat Tire Ventures
ADVENTURE TOUR

(☎ 063-382 9422; www.ptv-vietnam.com; 109 Đ Nguyen Van Troi) A highly professional operator with mountain biking trips from US$49,

trekking from US$31, kayaking from US$39, canyoning from US$45 and white-water rafting (US$72) in the rainy season. Combined bike-riding/rafting trips to Mui Ne (US$115) are definitely the best way to hit the coast.

Groovy Gecko Adventure Tours
ADVENTURE TOUR

(☎ 063-383 6521; www.groovygeckotours.net; 65 Đ Truong Cong Dinh) Experienced agency operated by a lively young team with prices starting at US$35 for rock climbing, canyoning or mountain biking, and two-day treks from US$59.

Central Dalat

Pine Track Adventures ADVENTURE TOUR
(063-383 1916; www.pinetrackadventures.com; 72B Đ Truong Cong Dinh) Run by an enthusiastic team, offering canyoning, trekking, biking and some excellent multi-sport packages. A six-day trip from Dalat to Mui Ne is US$510.

Sleeping

★**Dreams Hotel** GUESTHOUSE $
(063-383 3748; dreams@hcm.vnn.vn; 138-140 Đ Phan Dinh Phung; r US$20-25; ♨@🛜) An incredibly hospitable place owned by a family that looks after its guests with affection and care. Boasts spotless rooms, a legendary breakfast spread and hot tub and sauna.

Thien An Hotel HOTEL $
(063-352 0607; thienanhotel@vnn.vn; 272A Đ Phan Dinh Phung; s US$18, d US$22-25; @🛜) Superb, very welcoming family hotel providing spacious and well-equipped rooms, glorious breakfasts (including Vegemite and Marmite), a cosy atmosphere and high levels of cleanliness. Free bicycles provided.

Le Phuong Hotel HOTEL $
(063-382 3743; www.lephuonghotel.com; 80 Đ Nguyen Chi Thanh; s 300,000d, d 350,000-500,000d; ❄@🛜) From the gleaming lobby to the stylish, spacious, minimalist rooms, this family run hotel is a great deal. Cleanliness standards are high and it's conveniently located.

Green City HOTEL $
(063-382 7999; www.dalatgreencityhotel.com; 172 Đ Phan Dinh Phung; s/d/tw US$17/19/21; ❄@🛜) New place switched on to travellers' needs with attractive, well-presented rooms, all with fine wooden beds, fresh linen, TV and minibar. Loafers will love the sofa-strewn lobby.

★**Dreams 3** HOTEL $$
(063-383 3748, 063-382 5877; dreams@hcm.vnn.vn; 138-140 Đ Phan Dinh Phung; r US$30-35; ♨❄@🛜) This commodious new venture offers incredibly tasteful accommodation. All rooms have high-quality mattresses and modish bathrooms, and some have a balcony. There's a Jacuzzi, steam room and sauna; a restaurant is planned. The only downer is the location on a traffic-heavy street.

Eating

There are vegetarian food stalls and cheap eats in the market area.

★**Trong Dong** VIETNAMESE $
(063-382 1889; 220 Đ Phan Dinh Phung; mains 40,000-80,000d; ⏱11.30am-9.30pm) Intimate restaurant run by a very hospitable team where the menu has been creatively designed – shrimp paste on a sugarcane stick and beef wrapped in *la lut* leaf excel.

GETTING TO LAOS: KON TUM TO ATTAPEU

Getting to the border The Bo Y/Phou Keua border connects Kon Tum and Attapeu (Laos). From Pleiku bus station, Mai Linh buses leave daily at 6.30am for Attapeu (250,000d, seven hours), continuing to Pakse (420,000d, 11½ hours). **Kon Tum Tourist** (060-386 1626; ktourist@dng.vnn.vn; 2 Đ Phan Dinh Phung) can arrange for you to join the bus when it passes through Kon Tum at around 8.15am. Crossing the border independently can be a challenge as traffic is light on both sides of the border.

At the border Lao visas are available on arrival.

Moving on On the Laos side, things are very quiet and you'll be at the mercy of passing traffic to hitch a ride onwards.

★ **Goc Ha Thanh**   VIETNAMESE **$**
(53 Đ Truong Cong Dinh; mains 35,000-119,000d;
⊘ 7am-10pm; 🛜) Casual new place with attractive bamboo furnishings owned by a welcoming Hanoi couple. Strong on dishes such as coconut curry, hotpots, clay pots, stir-fries and noodles.

Lan Mot Nguoi   VIETNAMESE **$**
(58 Đ Nguyen Chi Thanh; meals 32,000-68,000d;
⊘ 10am-10pm) Specialising in steaming hotpots, this modern place has a casual air and draws a faithful local clientele. Try the spicy seafood hotpot.

Da Quy   VIETNAMESE, WESTERN **$**
(Wild Sunflower; 49 Đ Truong Cong Dinh; dishes 30,000-72,000d; ⊘ 8am-10pm) Run by Loc, a friendly English speaker, Da Quy has a sophisticated ambience and wallet-friendly prices. Try the traditional clay-pot dishes, a hotpot or something from the Western menu.

🍷 Drinking & Entertainment

Hangout   BAR
(71 Đ Truong Cong Dinh; ⊘ 11am-11pm; 🛜) Popular hang-out for some of Dalat's Easy Riders, as well as visiting backpackers, with a relaxed vibe and a popular pool table. The owner, a fluent English speaker, is an excellent source of local information.

★ **Escape Bar**   LIVE MUSIC
(Basement, Blue Moon Hotel, 4 Đ Phan Boi Chau; ⊘ 4pm-midnight; 🛜) Outstanding live-music bar, owned by blues guitarist Curtis who performs here virtually every night with a rotating band (from 9pm). Sunday is a jam session. The bar's decor, all 1970s chic and 'groovy baby' furnishings, suits the sonics perfectly.

🛍 Shopping

Hoa Binh Sq and the market building adjacent to it are the places to purchase ethnic handicrafts, including Lat rush baskets that roll up when empty.

ℹ️ Information

Dalat has numerous ATMs and internet cafes; wi-fi is widely available.

Lam Dong General Hospital (📲 063-382 1369; 4 Đ Pham Ngoc Thach; ⊘ 24hr)

Main Post Office (14 Đ Tran Phu; ⊘ 7am-6pm)

Sinh Tourist (📲 063-382 2663; www.thesinh tourist.vn; 22 Đ Bui Thi Xuan) Tours, including city sightseeing trips, and open-tour bus bookings.

Vietcombank (6 Đ Nguyen Thi Minh Khai; ⊘ 7.30am-3pm Mon-Fri, to 1pm Sat)

ℹ️ Getting There & Around

Vietnam Airlines (📲 063-383 3499; www. vietnamairlines.com; 2 Đ Ho Tung Mau) has daily services to HCMC, Danang and Hanoi. **Vietjet Air** (📲 1900 1886; www.vietjetair.com) also flies daily to Hanoi. Lien Khuong Airport is 30km south of the city.

Dalat's modern **long-distance bus station** (Đ 3 Thang 4) has timetables and booking offices; it's about 1.5km south of Xuan Huong Lake. From here there are express buses to HCMC, other cities in the highlands, Danang and Nha Trang. **Phuong Trang** (📲 063-358 5858) operates smart double-decker buses, including several sleeper services, to HCMC (US$11, seven to eight hours, roughly hourly).

Dalat is a major stop for open-tour buses. Sinh Tourist has daily buses to Mui Ne (129,000d, four hours), Nha Trang (129,000d, five hours) and HCMC (179,000d, eight hours).

Full-day tours with motorbike guides (from US$20) are a great way to see the area. Many hotels offer bicycle and motorbike hire. For a taxi call **Mai Linh** (📲 063-352 1111).

Around Dalat

👁 Sights

Truc Lam Pagoda & Cable Car   BUDDHIST TEMPLE
(Ho Tuyen Lam; cable car adult one-way/return 50,000/70,000d, child 30,000/40,000d; ⊘ cable car 7.30-11.30am & 1.30-5pm) For a spiritual

TRANSPORT FROM DALAT

DESTINATION	AIR	BUS	CAR & MOTORBIKE
Buon Ma Thuot	N/A	US$6, 5hr, 9 daily	4hr
Danang	from US$49, 1hr, 1 daily	US$15, 12hr, 3 daily	13hr
HCMC	from US$34, 1hr, 4 daily	US$9-11, 7-9hr, every 30min	9hr
Mui Ne	N/A	N/A	5hr
Nha Trang	N/A	US$6.50, 4-5hr, 17 daily	4hr

recharge, visit Truc Lam Pagoda, which enjoys a hilltop setting and has splendid gardens. It's an active monastery (ask about meditation sessions) and the grounds are expansive enough to escape the odd tour group. Be sure to arrive by cable car (the terminus is 3km south of the centre), which soars over majestic pine forests.

Waterfalls   WATERFALL
There are a number of waterfalls around Dalat, though none are royally spectacular and the focus tends to be on commerce rather than nature. If you're exploring the countryside, others include **Ankroët Falls**, **Gougah Falls** (admission 7000d; ⊙7am-4pm) and **Pongour Falls** (admission 10,000d; ⊙7am-4pm).

HO CHI MINH CITY (SAIGON)

🎵 08 / POP POP 7.4 MILLION

Ho Chi Minh City (HCMC) is Vietnam at its most dizzying: a high-octane city of commerce and culture that has driven the whole country forward with its pulsating energy. A chaotic whirl, the city breathes life and vitality into all who settle here – visitors cannot help but be hauled along for the ride.

Wander through alleys to ancient pagodas or teeming markets, past ramshackle wooden shops selling silk and spices, before fast-forwarding into the future beneath skyscrapers and mammoth malls. The ghosts of the past live on in the churches, temples, former GI hotels and government buildings that one generation ago witnessed a city in turmoil.

Put simply, there's nowhere else quite like it. Saigon has it all.

🔾 Sights

🔾 Dong Khoi Area

This well-heeled area, immediately west of the Saigon River, is a swish enclave of designer stores and fashionable restaurants, concrete towers and tree-lined boulevards.

★Notre Dame Cathedral   CHURCH
(Map p886; Đ Han Thuyen; ⊙mass 9.30am Sun) Built between 1877 and 1883, Notre Dame Cathedral rises up romantically from the heart of HCMC's government quarter. A brick, neo-Romanesque church with two

---

GETTING TO CAMBODIA: PLEIKU TO BAN LUNG
....

Getting to the border Remote and rarely used by foreigners, the Le Thanh/O Yadaw border crossing links Pleiku with Ban Lung, Cambodia. From Pleiku there's a daily Noi Thinh bus at 7.30am (60,000d, two hours) from the main marketplace on Đ Tran Phu direct to the Cambodian border at Le Thanh.

At the border Open 7am to 5pm. Visas are available on arrival in Cambodia. Vietnamese visas need to be organised in advance.

Moving on From O Yadaw, on the Cambodia side of the border, local buses (US$8) or motorbikes (around US$25) head to Ban Lung. There are far fewer transport options in the afternoon. For information on making this trip in the opposite direction see p137

40m-high square towers, it looks like it's been beamed in from Normandy.

HCMC Museum   MUSEUM
(Bao Tang Thanh Pho Ho Chi Minh; Map p886; www.hcmc-museum.edu.vn; 65 Đ Ly Tu Trong; admission 15,000d; ⊙8am-5pm) A grand, neoclassical structure built in 1885, HCMC's city museum is a singularly beautiful and impressive building, telling the story of the city through archaeological artefacts, ceramics, old city maps and displays on the marriage traditions of its various ethnicities.

★Central Post Office   HISTORIC BUILDING
(Map p886; 2 Cong Xa Paris) HCMC's striking French post office was designed by Gustave Eiffel and built between 1886 and 1891. Painted on the walls of its grand concourse are fascinating historic maps of South Vietnam and Saigon.

🔾 Da Kao & Around

★Jade Emperor Pagoda   TEMPLE
(Phuoc Hai Tu, Chua Ngoc Hoang; Map p888; 73 Đ Mai Thi Luu; ⊙7am-6pm, on 1st & 15th of lunar month 5am-7pm) FREE Built in 1909 in honour of the supreme Taoist god this is one of the most spectacularly atmospheric temples in HCMC, stuffed with statues of phantasmal divinities and grotesque heroes. The pungent smoke of incense *(huong)* fills the air, obscuring the exquisite woodcarvings.

Ho Chi Minh City

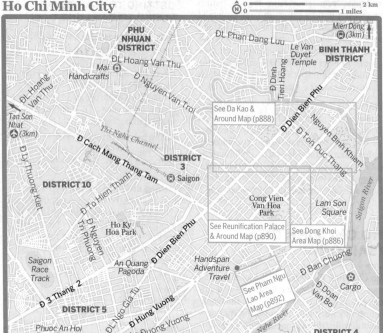

★**History Museum** MUSEUM
(Bao Tang Lich Su; Map p888; Đ Nguyen Binh Khiem; admission 15,000d; ⊙8-11.30am & 1.30-5pm Tue-Sun) This notable Sino-French museum houses a rewarding collection of artefacts illustrating the evolution of the cultures of Vietnam, from the Bronze Age Dong Son civilisation onwards.

Botanic Gardens GARDENS
(Thao Cam Vien; Map p888; 2 Đ Nguyen Binh Khiem; 8000d; ⊙7am-7pm) These fantastic, lush gardens are very agreeable for strolling beneath giant tropical trees. Avoid the miserable zoo.

◉ Reunification Palace & Around

★**War Remnants Museum** MUSEUM
(Bao Tang Chung Tich Chien Tranh; Map p890; ☎08-3930 5587; 28 Đ Vo Van Tan, cnr Đ Le Quy Don; admission 15,000d; ⊙7.30am-noon & 1.30-5pm)

Once known as the Museum of Chinese and American War Crimes, this museum effectively drives home the brutality of war and its many civilian victims. Many of the atrocities documented here were well publicised but rarely do Westerners get to hear the victims tell their own stories.

While the displays are one-sided, many of the most disturbing photographs illustrating US atrocities are from US sources, including those of the infamous My Lai Massacre.

Upstairs, look out for the **Requiem Exhibition** compiled by legendary war photographer Tim Page.

★**Reunification Palace** HISTORIC BUILDING
(Dinh Thong Nhat; Map p890; ☎08-3829 4117; Đ Nam Ky Khoi Nghia; adult/child 30,000/3000d; ⊙7.30-11am & 1-4pm) Built in 1966 to serve as South Vietnam's Presidential Palace, today this landmark is known as the Reunification Palace. It's an outstanding example of

1960s architecture, with an airy and open design.

The first communist tanks in Saigon crashed through the gates of this building on the morning of 30 April 1975 when Saigon surrendered to the North. The building is a time warp, having been left just as it looked on that momentous day.

English- and French-speaking guides are available.

Mariamman Hindu Temple TEMPLE
(Chua Ba Mariamman; Map p890; 45 Đ Truong Dinh; ☉7.30am-7.30pm) This colourful slice of southern India is also considered sacred by many ethnic Vietnamese and Chinese. Indeed, it is reputed to have miraculous powers. The temple was built at the end of the 19th century and dedicated to the Hindu goddess Mariamman.

◎ Cholon

Cholon, 5km southwest of the centre, forms the city's Chinatown. The district has a wealth of wonderful Chinese temples including **Thien Hau Pagoda** (Ba Mieu, Pho Mieu, Chua Ba Thien Hau; Map p884; 710 Đ Nguyen Trai) **FREE**, dedicated to Thien Hau (Tianhou), the Chinese goddess of the sea, and the fabulously ornamental **Phuoc An Hoi Quan Pagoda** (Map p884; 184 Đ Hong Bang) **FREE**, built in 1902 by the Fujian Chinese congregation. **Quan Am Pagoda** (Chua Quan Am; Map p884; 12 Đ Lao Tu) **FREE** has a roof decorated with fantastic scenes, rendered in ceramic, from traditional Chinese plays and stories.

🏃 Activities

Vietnamese Traditional Massage Institute MASSAGE
(Map p892; ☎08-3839 6697; 185 Đ Cong Quynh, District 1; per hr in fan/air-con room 50,000/60,000d, per hr sauna 40,000d; ☉8.30am-8pm) Inexpensive, no-nonsense massages performed by well-trained blind masseurs from the HCMC Association for the Blind.

Workers' Club POOL
(Map p890; 55B Đ Nguyen Thi Minh Khai, District 3; admission 18,000d; ☉6am-7pm) This swimming pool still has some art deco charm.

🍲 Courses

Saigon Cooking Class COOKING
(Map p886; ☎08-3825 8485; www.saigoncookingclass.com; 74/7 ĐL Hai Ba Trung, District 1; per

adult/child under 12yr US$39/25; ☉10am & 2pm Tue-Sun) Watch and learn from the chefs at Hoa Tuc as they prepare three mains and one dessert.

Vietnam Cookery Centre COOKING
(Map p886; ☎08-3512 7246; www.vietnamcookery.com; 362/8 Đ Ung Van Khiem, Binh Thanh District) Introductory classes and market visits.

Cyclo Resto COOKING
(Map p890; ☎08-6680 4235; www.cycloresto.com; 3-3a Đ Dang Tran Con; US$23) Fun and informative three-hour cooking class including a trip to **Thai Binh Market** (Map p892) by cyclo.

🧭 Tours

Bach Dang jetty is the place to arrange a boat to tour the Saigon River. Small boats cost around US$10 per hour, larger boats US$15 to US$30.

XO Tours TOUR
(☎0933 083 727; www.xotours.vn; from US$38) Wearing *ao-dai* (traditional dress), these girls run fun foodie, sightseeing and Saigon-by-night tours on scooters/motorbikes.

Back of the Bike Tours TOUR
(☎0935 046 910; www.backofthebiketours.com) Wildly popular four-hour street-food tours, or lasso in the sights of Saigon. Excellent guides.

🛏 Sleeping

Virtually all budget travellers head straight to the Pham Ngu Lao area. Saigon's backpacker precinct has more than 100 places to stay, most between US$10 and US$35, and even the odd dorm. Some hotels with Đ Pham Ngu Lao or Đ Bui Vien addresses are located in alleys off those main streets.

★Madame Cuc 127 GUESTHOUSE $
(Map p892; ☎08-3836 8761; www.madamcuchotels.com; 127 Đ Cong Quynh; s US$20, d US$25-30; ❀@☎) The original and by far the best of the three hotels run by the welcoming Madame Cuc and her friendly and fantastic staff. Rooms are clean and spacious.

Giang Son GUESTHOUSE $
(Map p892; ☎08-3837 7547; www.guesthouse.com.vn; 283/14 Đ Pham Ngu Lao; r US$16-28; ❀@☎) Tall and thin, with three rooms on each floor, a roof terrace and charming service, Giang Son's sole downer is that there's no lift. Consider upgrading to a room with a window.

Dong Khoi Area

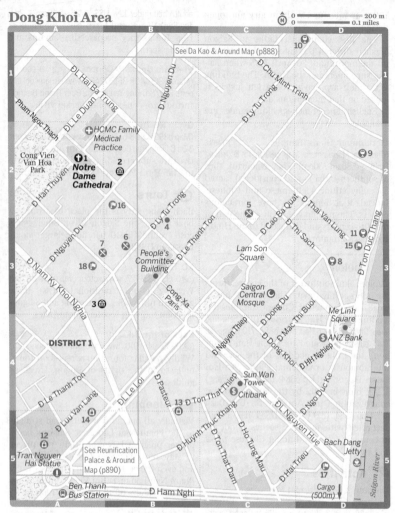

See Da Kao & Around Map (p888)

DISTRICT 1

See Reunification Palace & Around Map (p890)

Hong Han Hotel   GUESTHOUSE $

(Map p892; ☎08-3836 1927; www.honghan.net firms.com; 238 Đ Bui Vien; r US$20-25; ❄@☎) Another corker guesthouse (seven floors, no lift), Hong Han has front rooms with ace views and smaller, quieter and cheaper rear rooms. Free breakfast served on the 1st-floor terrace.

Bich Duyen Hotel   GUESTHOUSE $

(Map p892; ☎08-3837 4588; bichduyenhotel@ yahoo.com; 283/4 Đ Pham Ngu Lao; r US$17-30; ❄@☎🐾) On the same slender lane as Giang Son, this spruce 15-room place follows a similar template. The US$25 rooms are worth the extra money for a window. No lift.

Giang Son 2   GUESTHOUSE $

(Map p892; ☎08-3920 9838; www.guesthouse. com.vn; 283/24 Pham Ngu Lao; r US$18-25) Son of Giang Son some may say, with a more contemporary finish. Two double rooms come with balcony and staff are excellent. No lift.

PP Backpackers   HOSTEL $

(Map p892; ☎1262 501 823; Đ 283/41 Pham Ngu Lao; dm US$6, d US$16-18; ❄@☎) Very helpful, friendly and efficient staff at this cheap and welcoming hostel where you can nab a dorm bed for US$6 or fork out a bit more for an affordable double room.

Dong Khoi Area

◎ **Top Sights**
1 Notre Dame Cathedral A2

◎ **Sights**
2 Central Post Office B2
3 HCMC Museum A3

◉ **Activities, Courses & Tours**
Saigon Cooking Class .... (see 5)
4 Vietnam Cookery Centre B3

◎ **Eating**
5 Hoa Tuc C2
6 Huong Lai B3
7 Nha Hang Ngon A3

◎ **Drinking & Nightlife**
8 Apocalypse Now D3
9 Fuse D2
10 Lush D1
Vasco's .... (see 5)
11 Vesper D3

◎ **Shopping**
12 Ben Thanh Market A5
13 Dogma B4
14 Mekong Quilts A5

◉ **Information**
15 Australian Consulate D3
16 Canadian Consulate B2
Central Post Office .... (see 2)
17 Japanese Consulate D5
18 Laotian Consulate A3
New Zealand Consulate .... (see 16)

Diep Anh GUESTHOUSE $
(Map p892; ☏ 08-3836 7920; dieptheanh@hcm.vnn.
vn; 241/31 Đ Pham Ngu Lao; r US$20; ❈ @ ☎) A
step above most PNL guesthouses, figurative-
ly and literally (think thousand-step stairs),
Diep Anh's tall and narrow shape makes for
light and airy upper rooms. The gracious staff
ensure they're kept in good nick.

Blue River Hotel HOTEL $$
(Map p892; ☏ 08-3837 6483; www.blueriverhotel.
com; 283/2C Đ Pham Ngu Lao; US$25-40; ❈ @ ☎)
Welcoming and well-run 10-room place of-
fers clean, spacious rooms, each with neat
furnishings and a safe. A kitchen for guests'
use is available, as is a piano (and more
brand-new rooms across the way).

✗ Eating

HCMC is the reigning culinary king of
Vietnam. Restaurants here range from dirt-
cheap sidewalk stalls to atmospheric villas,
each serving a unique interpretation of

Vietnam sustenance. Besides brilliant native
fare, Saigon offers world cuisine, with Indi-
an, Japanese, Thai, French, Spanish, Korean
and Argentinian all on offer.

Good foodie neighbourhoods include the
Dong Khoi area, which has many top-quali-
ty restaurants, as well as nearby District 3.
Pham Ngu Lao's eateries are generally less
memorable.

✗ Dong Khoi Area

★ **Nha Hang Ngon** VIETNAMESE $
(Map p886; ☏ 08-3827 7131; 160 Đ Pasteur; mains
35,000-205,000d; ◷ 7am-10pm; ◉ ☎) Throng-
ing with locals and foreigners, this is one
of HCMC's most popular spots, with a large
range of the very best street food in stylish
surroundings. Set in a leafy garden ringed by
food stalls, each cook serves up a specialised
traditional dish, ensuring an authentic taste.

Huong Lai VIETNAMESE $
(Map p886; 38 Đ Ly Tu Trong; mains 49,000-
150,000d) A must for finely presented, tra-
ditional Vietnamese food. The airy and
high-ceilinged loft of an old French-era sho-
phouse is the setting for dining with a differ-
ence. Staff are from disadvantaged families
or are former street children and receive
on-the-job training, education and a place
to stay.

Hoa Tuc VIETNAMESE $
(Map p886; ☏ 08-3825 1676; 74/7 ĐL Hai Ba Trung;
mains 50,000-190,000d; ◷ 10.30am-10.30pm;
◉ ☎) In the trendy courtyard of the former
opium refinery, Hoa Tuc offers atmosphere
and style to match the excellence of its food.
Signature dishes include spicy beef salad
with kumquat, baby white eggplant and
lemongrass.

✗ Da Kao & Around

Pho Hoa VIETNAMESE $
(Map p888; 260C Đ Pasteur; mains 45,000-
50,000d; ◷ 6am-midnight) This long-running
establishment is more upmarket than most
but is definitely the real deal – as evidenced
by its popularity with regular local patrons.

Banh Xeo 46A VIETNAMESE $
(Map p888; ☏ 08-3824 1110; 46A Đ Dinh Cong
Trang; mains 25,000-50,000d; ◷ 10am-9pm; ☞)
Locals will always hit the restaurants that
specialise in a single dish and this renowned
spot serves some of the best *banh xeo* in
town.

Da Kao & Around

Da Kao & Around

◎ Top Sights
1 History Museum D1
2 Jade Emperor Pagoda........................ C1

◎ Sights
3 Botanic Gardens D1

✖ Eating
4 Banh Xeo 46A.................................... B1
5 Pho Hoa..A2
6 Tib B2
7 Tib A1

◎ Drinking & Nightlife
8 Decibel...C1
9 Hoa Vien...C2

🛍 Shopping
10 Orange...B2
11 Thu Quan Sinh Vien C2

ℹ Information
12 Cambodian Consulate B2
13 French Consulate.............................C2
14 German Consulate............................B2
15 Netherlands Consulate C2
16 UK Consulate....................................C2
17 US Consulate....................................C2

Tib VIETNAMESE $
(www.tibrestaurant.com.vn) **Hai Ba Trung** (Map p888; ☑ 08-3829 7242; 187 Đ Hai Ba Trung; mains 70,000-285,000d; 🛜); **Express** (Map p890; 162 Đ Nguyen Dinh Chieu; mains 28,000-50,000d; ☑); **Vegetarian** (Map p888; 11 Đ Tran Nhat Duat; mains 30,000-40,000d; ☑) Justifiably famous atmospheric old house that showcases imperial Hué cuisine in a wonderful

setting. Tib Express and Tib Vegetarian offer a cheaper, more relaxed take on the same.

✖ Pham Ngu Lao Area

★ Baba's Kitchen INDIAN $
(Map p892; ☑ 08-3838 6661; 164 Đ Bui Vien; mains 50,000-210,000d; ⏰ 11am-11pm; ☑) Baba's has set Bui Vien alight with its fine flavours, aromas and spices of India. There's ample vegetarian choice and the atmosphere is as inviting as the cuisine is delectable.

Coriander THAI $
(Map p892; 16 Đ Bui Vien; mains 40,000-180,000d; ⏰ 11am-2pm & 5-11pm) The menu here is stuffed with authentic Siamese delights: lovely fried *doufu* (tofu) is almost a meal in itself, the green curry is zesty and the clay-pot seafood fried rice is excellent.

Five Oysters VIETNAMESE $
(Map p892; 234 Bui Vien; mains from 35,000d; ⏰ 9.30am-11pm) Light and bright Five Oysters is frequently packed with travellers feasting on oysters (25,000d), grilled octopus, seafood soup, snail pie, *pho*, fried noodles, grilled mackerel with chilli oil and more.

Dinh Y VEGETARIAN $
(Map p892; 171B Đ Cong Quynh; mains from 25,000d; ⏰ 6am-9pm; ☑) Run by a friendly Cao Dai family, this humble eatery is in a very 'local' part of PNL near Thai Binh Market. The food is delicious and cheap.

🍸 Drinking & Nightlife

Action is concentrated around the Dong Khoi area, with everything from dives to designer bars. However, places in this area generally close around 1am while Pham Ngu Lao rumbles on into the wee hours.

HCMC's hippest club nights include the semi-regular **Everyone's a DJ** (www.everyonesadjvietnam.wordpress.com) loft party, **dOSe** and the **Beats Saigon** (www.thebeats-saigon.com).

🍷 Dong Khoi Area

★Vesper
BAR
(Map p886; Ground fl, Landmark Bldg, 5B Đ Ton Duc Thang; ⏰10am-late Mon-Sat) From the curve of the hardwood bar to the smoothly arranged bottles on the shelves, soft chill-out rhythms, funky caramel leather furniture and fine tapas menu, Vesper is a cool spot by the river.

Apocalypse Now
CLUB
(Map p886; 🗷08-3824 1463; 2C Đ Thi Sach; ⏰7pm-2am) A sprawling place with a big dance floor and an outdoor courtyard, it's quite a circus, with a cast comprising travellers, expats, Vietnamese movers and shakers, plus the odd hooker (some odder than others).

Vasco's
BAR, CLUB
(Map p886; www.vascosgroup.com; 74/7D ĐL Hai Ba Trung; ⏰4pm-late; 📶) Hip hang-out for cocktails, while the upstairs nightclub-like space regularly hosts DJs and live bands.

Lush
BAR, CLUB
(Map p886; www.lush.vn; 2 Đ Ly Tu Trong; ⏰7.30pm-late) This bar's decor is very manga, with cool graphics plastering the walls. DJs spin most nights, with Fridays devoted to hip-hop.

Fuse
CLUB
(Map p886; 3A Đ Ton Duc Thang; ⏰7pm-late) Small club, loud techno.

🍷 Da Kao & Around

★Decibel
BAR
(Map p888; 79/2/5 Đ Phan Kê Bính; ⏰7.30am-midnight Mon-Sat) This small restaurant-cafe-bar is a super-relaxed choice for a coffee or cocktail, with a fine cultural vibe, film night and art events.

Hoa Vien
BREWERY
(Map p888; www.hoavien.vn; 18 bis/28 Nguyen Thi Minh Khai; ⏰8am-midnight; 📶) An unexpected find in the backstreets of HCMC, this Czech restaurant brews up fresh pilsner daily.

🍷 Pham Ngu Lao Area

Le Pub
PUB
(Map p892; 🗷08-3837 7679; www.lepub.org; 175/22 Đ Pham Ngu Lao; ⏰9am-2am; 📶) Ranging three floors Le Pub has an extensive beer list, nightly promotions, cocktail jugs and good grub.

Go2
BAR
(Map p892; 187 Đ De Tham; ⏰24hr; 📶) There's no better street theatre than watching the crazy Bui Vien goings-on from the outside seats of this all-night venue, which also has a trashy club upstairs.

☆ Entertainment

Pick up the *Word HCMC, Asialife HCMC* or the *Guide* to find out what's on during your stay in Saigon, or log onto www.anyarena.com or www.thewordhcmc.com.

★Acoustic
LIVE MUSIC
(Map p890; 🗷08-3930 2239; 6E1 Đ Ngo Thoi Nhiem; ⏰7pm-midnight; 📶) The city's leading live-music venue. It's at the end of the alley, by the upended VW Beetle.

★Cargo
LIVE MUSIC
(Map p884; Đ 7 Nguyen Tat Thanh; ⏰3pm-midnight Wed-Sun) Hugely popular spacious warehouse venue in District 4. Hosts up-and-coming local acts, regional bands and DJ events.

Golden Dragon Water Puppet Theatre
WATER PUPPETS
(Map p890; 🗷08-3930 2196; www.goldendragon waterpuppet.com; 55B Đ Nguyen Thi Minh Khai; US$7.50) The main water-puppet venue, with shows starting at 5pm, 6.30pm and 7.45pm and lasting about 50 minutes.

🛍 Shopping

Among the tempting wares to be found in Saigon are embroidered silk shoes, miniature *cyclos* and fake Zippos. Boutiques along Đ Le Thanh Ton and Đ Pasteur sell handmade ready-to-wear fashion. In Pham Ngu Lao, shops sell ethnic-minority fabrics, handicrafts, T-shirts and various appealing accessories.

Ben Thanh Market (Cho Ben Thanh; Map p886; ĐL Le Loi, ĐL Ham Nghi, ĐL Tran Hung Dao & Đ Le Lai) has both everyday items and a lucrative tourist trade.

Mekong Quilts
HANDICRAFTS
(Map p886; 🗷08-2210 3110; www.mekong-quilts.org; 1st fl, 68 Đ Le Loi, District 1; ⏰9am-7pm) For beautiful handmade silk quilts, sewn by the rural poor in support of a sustainable income.

VIETNAM HO CHI MINH CITY (SAIGON)

Reunification Palace & Around

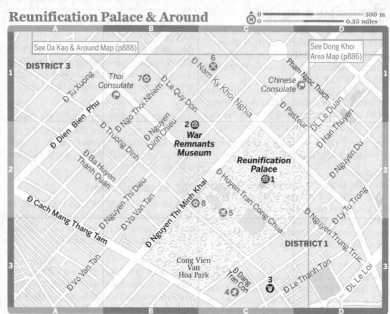

Reunification Palace & Around

Dogma SOUVENIRS
(Map p886; www.dogmavietnam.com; 1st fl, 43 Đ Ton That Thiep; ⊙9am-10pm) Specialises in reproduction propaganda art, emblazoning their revolutionary motifs on posters, coffee mugs, coasters, jigsaws and T-shirts.

Thu Quan Sinh Vien BOOKS
(Map p888; 2A ĐL Le Duan; ⊙8am-10pm; 🛜) This upmarket store stocks imported books and magazines in English, French and Chinese.

Orange CLOTHING, ACCESSORIES
(Map p888; 238B Đ Pasteur; ⊙9am-10pm) Funky T-shirts and bags.

Hanoi Gallery PROPAGANDA POSTERS
(Map p892; 79 Đ Bui Vien; ⊙9am-10pm) Both original (or so we're told) revolutionary propaganda posters (US$600) and A3 prints (US$8).

Blue Dragon HANDICRAFTS
(Map p892; 1B Đ Bui Vien; ⊙8.30am-10.30pm) Souvenirs including ethnic bags, jewellery, horn bracelets and clothing.

Mai Handicrafts HANDICRAFTS
(Map p884; 🕿08-3844 0988; www.maihandicrafts.com; 298 Đ Nguyen Trong Tuyen, Tan Binh District; ⊙10am-7pm Mon-Sat) 🍃 A fair-trade shop dealing in ceramics and ethnic fabrics.

🛈 Information

For up-to-date information on what's going on in town, check out the **Word HCMC** (www.word hcmc.com) or **Asialife HCMC** (www.asialife hcmc.com), both quality listings magazines.

DANGERS & ANNOYANCES

Be careful in the Dong Khoi area and along the Saigon riverfront, where motorbike 'cowboys' operate and specialise in bag, phone, tablet and camera snatching.

EMERGENCY
Ambulance (☎115)
Police (☎113)

INTERNET ACCESS
Most hotels, cafes, restaurants and bars have free wi-fi. Internet cafes are everywhere.

MEDICAL SERVICES
HCMC Family Medical Practice (Map p886; ☎24hr emergency 08-3822 7848; www. vietnammedicalpractice.com; rear, Diamond Department Store, 34 ĐL Le Duan; ☺24hr)
International SOS (☎08-3829 8424; www. internationalsos.com; 167A Đ Nam Ky Khoi Nghia; ☺24hr) Has an international team of doctors who speak English, French, Japanese and Vietnamese.

MONEY
ANZ Bank (Map p886; ☎08-3829 9319; 11 Me Linh Sq) With ATM.
Citibank (Map p886; 115 Đ Nguyen Huế)

POST
Central Post Office (Map p886; 2 Cong Xa Paris; ☺7am-9.30pm)

TRAVEL AGENCIES
Dozens of travel agents offer tours of the Mekong Delta and other jaunts beyond HCMC. Some of the better ones include the following:
Handspan Adventure Travel (Map p884; ☎08-3925 7605; www.handspan.com; 10th fl, Central Park Bldg, 208 Nguyen Trai) Excellent, high-quality and innovative tours from this HCMC branch of the Hanoi-based agency.
Sinh Tourist (Map p892; ☎08-3838 9593; www.thesinhtourist.vn; 246 Đ De Tham; ☺6.30am-10.30pm) Budget tour agency and operates good open-tour buses.
Sinhbalo Adventures (Map p892; ☎08-3837 6766; www.sinhbalo.com; 283/20 Đ Pham Ngu Lao) For customised tours, this is a great choice. Their most popular package trips include a two-day Mekong tour and three-day Mekong cycling tour.

ⓘ Getting There & Away

AIR
Jetstar Pacific Airlines (☎1900 1550; www. jetstar.com) Flies to/from Hanoi, Hai Phong, Vinh, Hué and Danang
VietJet Air (☎1900 1886; www.vietjetair.com) Flies to/from cities including Hanoi, Dalat and Danang.
Vietnam Airlines (☎08-3832 0320; www. vietnamairlines.com) Flies to/from Hanoi,

Hai Phong, Vinh, Dong Hoi, Hué, Danang, Quy Nhon, Nha Trang, Dalat, Buon Ma Thuot, Pleiku, Rach Gia and Phu Quoc Island.
Vietnam Air Service Company (VASCO; www. vasco.com.vn) Flies to/from Con Dao Islands and Ca Mau.

BUS
Intercity buses operate from three main bus stations around HCMC. Local buses (3000d) travelling to the intercity bus stations leave from the local bus station opposite Ben Thanh Market.
An Suong Bus Station (Ben Xe An Suong) Buses to Tay Ninh and points northeast of HCMC; in District 12, west of the centre. Buses to/from Cu Chi leave from here but tours are far more convenient.
Mien Dong Bus Station (Ben Xe Mien Dong; ☎08-3829 4056) Buses heading north of HCMC; about 5km from downtown on Hwy 13. Express buses depart from the east side of the station, and local buses connect with the west side of the complex.
Mien Tay Bus Station (Ben Xe Mien Tay; ☎08-3825 5955; Đ Kinh Duong Vuong) Serves all the main Mekong Delta towns; located about 10km southwest of Saigon in An Lac.

CAR & MOTORCYCLE
Hotels and travellers' cafes can arrange car rentals (from US$40 per day). Pham Ngu Lao is the neighbourhood to look for motorbike rentals (US$5 to US$10 per day).

GETTING TO CAMBODIA: HCMC TO PHNOM PENH

Getting to the border The busy Moc Bai/Bavet border crossing is the fastest land route between HCMC and Phnom Penh. Pham Ngu Lao traveller cafes sell through bus tickets (US$10 to US$15) to Phnom Penh; buses leave from Pham Ngu Lao between 6am and 3pm. Reliable companies include **Mekong Express** (www.catmekongexpress. com), **Sapaco** (www.sapacotourist. vn) and the cheaper **Kumho Samco** (www.kumhosamco.com.vn). Allow six hours for the entire trip, including time spent on border formalities.

At the border Cambodian visas (US$20) are issued at the border (you'll need a passport-sized photo).

Moving on Most travellers have a through bus ticket from HCMC to Phnom Penh, a further four-hour bus ride away.

Pham Ngu Lao Area

Pham Ngu Lao Area

◎ Sights
1 Thai Binh Market	A6

◆ Activities, Courses & Tours
2 Vietnamese Traditional Massage Institute	A6

🛏 Sleeping
3 Bich Duyen Hotel	A4
4 Blue River Hotel	A4
5 Diep Anh	A3
6 Giang Son	A4
7 Giang Son 2	A4
8 Hong Han Hotel	B5
9 Madame Cuc 127	B6
10 PP Backpackers	A4

✖ Eating
11 Baba's Kitchen	B3
12 Coriander	B5
13 Dinh Y	A6
14 Five Oysters	B5

🍸 Drinking & Nightlife
15 Go2	B2
16 Le Pub	A1

🛍 Shopping
17 Blue Dragon	B1
18 Hanoi Gallery	B3

There are plenty of international bus services connecting HCMC and Cambodia, most with departures from the Pham Ngu Lao area. **Sapaco** (Map p892; ☑ 08-3920 3623; www.sapaco tourist.vn; 309 Pham Ngu Lao) has nine direct daily services to Phnom Penh (230,000d, six hours, departing between 6am and 3pm), as well as one to Siem Reap (430,000d, 12 hours, 6am).

TRAIN

Trains from **Saigon train station** (Ga Sai Gon; ☑ 08-3823 0105; 1 Đ Nguyen Thong, District 3; ⏰ ticket office 7.15-11am & 1-3pm) head north to various destinations.

In Pham Ngu Lao, purchase tickets from **Hoa Xa Agency** (Map p892; ☑ 08-3836 7640; 275C Đ Pham Ngu Lao; ⏰7.30am-6pm) or from most travel agents for a small fee.

ℹ Getting Around

TO/FROM THE AIRPORT

Tan Son Nhat Airport is 7km northwest of central HCMC. Metered taxis cost around 180,000d to/from the centre. English-speaking controllers will shuffle you into a waiting cab and tell the driver your destination. The driver may try to claim your hotel of choice is closed, burned

Open-tour buses depart and arrive in the Pham Ngu Lao area. Many travellers buy a ticket to Hanoi (US$25 to US$50) but you can also do short hops to destinations including Mui Ne, Nha Trang and Dalat. Sinh Tourist (p891) is a good company.

down, is dirty and dangerous, or anything to steer you somewhere else for a commission. Stick to your guns.

Air-conditioned buses (route 152; 5000d, every 15 minutes, 6am to 6pm) also run to and from the airport. These make regular stops along Đ De Tham (Pham Ngu Lao area) and at international hotels along Đ Dong Khoi.

BICYCLE
Bicycles are available for hire (US$2) from many budget hotels and cafes. Use parking lots to safeguard against theft.

CAR & MOTORCYCLE
HCMC is *not* the place to learn to ride a motorbike, but they are available in Pham Ngu Lao for US$5 to US$10 per day.

CYCLO
Cyclos are an interesting way to get around town, but overcharging tourists is the norm. Short hops are 20,000d to 25,000d.

TAXI
Metered taxis are very affordable; short rides cost just two or three bucks. These are reliable companies:

Mai Linh Taxi (☑ 08-3838 3838)
Vinasun Taxi (☑ 3827 2727)

XE OM
Xe om drivers hang out on parked bikes touting for passengers. A short ride is 20,000d, more at night.

AROUND HO CHI MINH CITY

Cu Chi
If the tenacious spirit of the Vietnamese could be symbolised by a single place, then Cu Chi might be it. Its fame is such that it's become a place of pilgrimage for many Vietnamese, and a must-see for travellers.

◉ **Sights**

Cu Chi Tunnels   HISTORIC SITE
(www.cuchitunnel.org.vn; adult/child 80,000/20,000d) These tunnels are the stuff of legend due to their role facilitating Viet Cong control of a large rural area only 30km from Saigon. At its height, the tunnel system stretched from Saigon to the Cambodian border.

Two sections of this remarkable tunnel network (which are enlarged and upgraded versions of the real thing) are open to the public. Most tourists head to Ben Dinh, as it's easier for tour buses to reach.

Visits start with an extremely dated propaganda video before guides in army greens lead small groups through some short sections of tunnel.

Both sites have gun ranges where you can fire machine guns. You pay per bullet, so if you're firing an automatic weapon, be warned.

Cu Chi Wildlife Rescue Station   WILDLIFE
(www.wildlifeatrisk.org; adult/child US$5/free; ☺ 7.30-11.30am & 1-4.30pm) A few kilometres past the Ben Dinh tunnels, this small rescue centre includes bears, otters and gibbons. There is an informative display on the rather depressing state of wildlife in Vietnam, including the 'room of death' featuring a host of traps and baits. It's tough to navigate these back roads solo, so talk to a travel agent about incorporating it into a Cu Chi Tunnels trip.

Tay Ninh
☑ 066 / POP 127,000
Tay Ninh town serves as the headquarters of Cao Dai, one of Vietnam's most interesting indigenous religions. The **Cao Dai Great Temple** was built between 1933 and 1955. Victor Hugo is among the Westerners especially revered by the Cao Dai; look for his likeness at the Great Temple.

VIETNAM CU CHI

TRANSPORT FROM HCMC

DESTINATION	AIR	BUS	TRAIN
Dalat	from US$39, 50min	US$8-15, 7hr	N/A
Hanoi	from US$70, 2hr	US$35-49, 41hr	US$49-93, 30hr
Hué	from US$37, 80min	US$26-37, 29hr	US$26-64, 18hr
Nha Trang	from US$44, 55min	US$10-20, 12hr	US$17-31, 6½hr

Tay Ninh is 96km northwest of HCMC. The Cao Dai Holy See complex is 4km east of Tay Ninh. One-day tours from Saigon, including Tay Ninh and the Cu Chi Tunnels, cost from US$7.

Beaches

There are several beach resorts within striking distance of downtown Saigon, although most travellers make for Mui Ne. If time is short and you want a quick fix, consider the city-resort Vung Tau, which you can reach by hydrofoil.

MEKONG DELTA

The 'rice bowl' of Vietnam, the Mekong Delta is a landscape carpeted in a dizzying variety of greens. It's also a water world where boats, houses, restaurants and even markets float upon the innumerable rivers, canals and streams that flow through like arteries.

Visitors can experience southern charm in riverside cities where few tourists venture and dine on home-cooked delicacies before overnighting as a homestay guest. There are also bird sanctuaries and impressive Khmer pagodas.

Those seeking a tropical hideaway will find it on Phu Quoc, an island lined with white-sand beaches.

By far the easiest and cheapest way to see the delta is by taking a tour with a travel agency in Ho Chi Minh City. It's also possible to travel independently, although sometimes time-consuming.

My Tho

074 / POP 221,000

Gateway to the Mekong Delta for day-trippers to the region, the slow-paced capital of Tien Giang Province is an important market town, but to visit floating markets you'll need to continue on to Can Tho.

On the riverfront, the **My Tho Tourist Boat Station** (8 Đ 30 Thang 4) is home to several tour companies offering river cruises. Destinations usually include a coconut-candy workshop, a honey farm (try the banana wine) and an orchid garden. A 2½-hour boat tour costs around 350,000d for one person or 450,000d for two. Prices drop if you join a group.

Sleeping & Eating

My Tho is well-known for a special vermicelli soup called *hu tieu My Tho*, which is richly garnished with fresh and dried seafood, pork, chicken, offal and fresh herbs.

Song Tien Annex   HOTEL $
(073-387 7883; www.tiengiangtourist.com; 33 Đ Thien Ho Duong; r 450,000-500,000d;) Rooms at this becalming, clean and tidy hotel have hardwood floors, lovely bathrooms with freestanding claw-footed bathtubs and modern furniture.

Getting There & Around

The **bus station** (Ben Xe Tien Giang; 42 Đ Ap Bac) is 3km west of the town centre on Đ Ap Bac, the main road to HCMC. Buses head to HCMC's Mien Tay bus station (35,000d, around 75 minutes), Can Tho (50,000d), Cao Lanh (32,000d), Chau Doc and Ca Mau (123,000d).

Ben Tre

075 / POP 147,000

Famous for its *keo dua* (coconut candy), Ben Tre's sleepy waterfront is lined with ageing villas and is easy to explore on foot. It's a relatively peaceful city that makes a lovely stop on a Mekong tour.

Ben Tre Tourist (075-382 9618; www.bentretourist.vn; 65 Đ Dong Khoi; 7-11am & 1-5pm) rents out bikes and motor boats (per hour US$12) and arranges excursions, including a bike tour to coconut, guava and grapefruit groves.

Hung Vuong (075-382 2408; 166 Đ Hung Vuong; d/tw/ste 350,000/370,000/530,000d;) has an attractive riverfront plot plus large clean rooms while **Nam Son** (075-382 2873; 40 Đ Phan Ngoc Tong; mains 20,000-60,000d) is famous for grilled chicken.

Buses leave regularly from the bus terminal 5km northwest of town for HCMC (67,000d, last bus around 5pm), Can Tho (55,000d), Ca Mau (103,000d) and Ha Tien (134,000d).

Slow boats can be rented at the public pier near the market for around 100,000d per hour.

Vinh Long

070 / POP 151,000

Vinh Long is a noisy, chaotic transit hub, but the riverfront has plenty of cafes and restaurants. Close by are several worthwhile sites including the Cai Be floating market, beautiful islands, abundant orchards and atmospheric homestays (which can be a highlight of a Mekong journey).

Cuu Long Tourist (☑ 070-382 3616; www.cuulongtourist.com; 2 Đ Phan B Chau; ⏱ 7am-5pm) offers boat tours ranging from three hours (from US$14 per person) to three days.

Bustling **Cai Be floating market** (⏱ 5am-5pm) is worth including on a boat tour from Vinh Long. Arrive early in the morning to see huge boats packed with tropical fruit and vegetables.

We suggest you don't stay in town; instead opt for a homestay. **Dong Khanh** (49 Đ 2 Thang 9; mains from 30,000d; ⏱ 6am-6pm) offers lots of hotpots and rice dishes.

Frequent buses go between Vinh Long and HCMC (90,000d, three hours) from the terminal in the middle of town. Buses to other locations, including Can Tho (40,000d), leave from a provincial bus station 3km south of town.

Can Tho

☑ 071 / POP 1.2 MILLION

Can Tho is the political, economic, cultural and transportation epicentre of the Mekong Delta. It's a buzzing city with a waterfront lined with gardens and an appealing blend of narrow backstreets and wide boulevards.

CanThoTourist (☑ 071-3821852; www.canthotourist.com.vn; 50 Đ Hai Ba Trung) has helpful English- and French-speaking staff. Tours are available, and there's a booking desk for both Vietnam Airlines and Jetstar. ATMs and internet cafes are dotted around town.

Cai Rang is the biggest floating market in the Mekong Delta, 6km from Can Tho; it's a morning affair. You can hire boats (about 100,000d per hour) on the river near the Can Tho market. It's one hour by boat, or you can drive to Cau Dau Sau boat landing, where you can get a **rowing boat** (per hr around 90,000d) to the market, 10 minutes away.

Mekong Delta

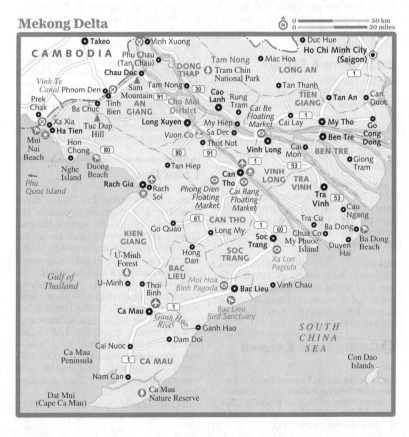

OFF THE BEATEN TRACK

MORE OF THE MEKONG DELTA

It's not hard to get off the beaten track in the Mekong Delta, as most tourists are on hit-and-run day trips from HCMC or passing through on their way to or from Cambodia. Here are some lesser-known regional gems:

➡ Check out some Khmer culture in **Tra Vinh**, home to a significant population of Cambodians and their beautiful temples.

➡ The Khmer kingdom of Funan once held sway over much of the lower Mekong; its principal port was at **Oc-Eo**, located near Long Xuyen. Archaeologists have found ancient Persian and Roman artefacts here.

➡ Birdwatching enthusiasts will want to make a diversion to **Tram Chin National Park** (⊙7am-4pm) near Cao Lanh, a habitat for the rare eastern sarus crane. These huge birds are depicted on the bas-reliefs at Angkor and are only found here and in northwest Cambodia.

➡ The small and secluded beach resort of **Hon Chong** has the most scenic stretch of coastline on the Mekong Delta mainland. The big attractions here are Chua Hang Grotto, Duong Beach and Nghe Island.

Less crowded and less motorised is the **Phong Dien market**, 20km from Can Tho by road, which has more stand-up rowboats. It's best between 6am and 8am. You can hire a boat on arrival.

🛏 Sleeping & Eating

Kim Lan Hotel HOTEL $
(☑071-381 7049; www.kimlancantho.com.vn; 138A Đ Nguyen An Ninh; r US$20-48; ☀@🛜) 🍃 Offers chic rooms with contemporary furnishings and artwork. Even the small, windowless standard rooms (US$20) are perfectly adequate, and deluxe rooms are lovely.

Xuan Mai Minihotel HOTEL $
(☑071-382 3578; tcdac@yahoo.com; 17 Đ Dien Bien Phu; r US$12; ☀🛜) Located down a small lane, this place has spacious, clean and surprisingly quiet rooms with TVs, fridges and hot showers.

Mekong VIETNAMESE, INTERNATIONAL $
(38 Đ Hai Ba Trung; mains from 25,000d; ⊙7am-8pm; 🖋) A terrific blend of local and international food at reasonable prices. Try the sour soup with fish (40,000d); there's also a good vegie selection.

ℹ Getting There & Around

AIR
Can Tho's new airport 10km northwest of the centre has **Vietnam Airlines** (www.vietnamair-lines.com) flights to Phu Quoc (from 610,000d, daily), Con Dao (1,300,000d, four per week), Ho Chi Minh City, Danang and Hanoi.

BOAT
Boat services include hydrofoils to Ca Mau (150,000d, three to four hours), passing through Phung Hiep.

BUS
Can Tho has two bus stations. The **old bus station** (Ben Xe Khach Can Tho; cnr Đ Nguyen Trai & Đ Hung Vuong) on the northern edge of the city centre has regular buses to HCMC's Mien Tay bus station (100,000d to 110,000d), Ben Tre (70,000d), My Tho (70,000d) and Chau Doc (60,000d). The **new bus station** in the southwest has buses to HCMC (110,000d) and Dalat (320,000d).

Chau Doc

☑076 / POP 112,000

Perched on the banks of the Bassac River, Chau Doc is a charming town near the Cambodian border, with sizeable Chinese, Khmer and Cham communities. Its cultural diversity – apparent in the mosques, temples, churches and nearby pilgrimage sites – makes it a fascinating place to explore.

The popular nearby river crossing between Vietnam and Cambodia means many travellers pass through. Nearby Sam Mountain is a local beauty spot with views over Cambodia.

War remnants near Chau Doc include Ba Chuc, the site of a Khmer Rouge massacre with a bone pagoda, and Tuc Dup Hill, where an expensive American bombing campaign in 1963 earned it the nickname Two Million Dollar Hill.

It's also possible to visit fish farms set up underneath floating houses on the river.

Mekong Tours (☎ 076-356 2828; www .mekongvietnam.com; 14 Đ Nguyen Huu Canh; ⊗ 8am-8pm) is a reliable travel agent offering boat or bus transport to Phnom Penh, car rentals and boat trips on the Mekong.

Sleeping & Eating

Local eateries in Chau Doc include **Bay Bong** (22 Đ Thuong Dang Le; mains 40,000-80,000d; ⊗ 9am-8pm) with excellent hotpots and soups, and **Thanh Tinh** (42 Đ Quang Trung; mains 30,000-80,000d; ⊗ 6am-7pm; 🍴) for vegetarian food.

⭐ **Trung Nguyen Hotel**   HOTEL **$**
(☎ 076-386 6158; trunghotel@yahoo.com; 86 Đ Bach Dang; s/d/tw US$14/16/20; ❄ @ 🛜) Good budget place with balconies overlooking the market. It's a busy corner site, so pack earplugs.

Hai Chau   HOTEL **$**
(☎ 076-626 0066; www.haichauhotel.com; 61 Đ Thuong Dang Le; r US$18-28; ❄ 🛜) Sixteen well-kept rooms with dark wooden furniture, some with a balcony. Above a restaurant, with a lift.

ℹ Getting There & Around

Buses to Chau Doc depart HCMC's Mien Tay station (130,000d, six hours).

Ha Tien

☎ 077 / POP 94,000
Ha Tien may be part of the Mekong Delta, but lying on the Gulf of Thailand it feels a world away from the rice fields and rivers that typify the region. Dramatic limestone formations define the area, pepper tree plantations dot the hillsides and the town itself has a sleepy tropical charm. It's a transport hub for road links to the Cambodia border at Xa Xia–Prek Chak and boats to Phu Quoc.

The **post office** (☎ 077-385 2190; 3 Đ To Chau; ⊗ 7am-5pm) has internet access and **Agribank** (☎ 077-385 2055; 37 Đ Lam Son), one block from the waterfront, has an ATM.

Sleeping

Hai Phuong   HOTEL **$**
(☎ 077-385 2240; So 52, Đ Dong Thuy Tram; r 200,000-700,000d; ❄ 🛜) Friendly and family-run, this smart six-level hotel is in good nick and some rooms have excellent river views from the balconies.

Anh Van Hotel   HOTEL **$**
(☎ 077-395 9222; So 2, Đ Mach Thien Tich; d/tw/f 200,000/400,000/500,000d; ❄ 🛜) Near the bridge, this large hotel has windowless and small cheaper rooms – it's worth paying extra for those with river views and smarter bathrooms.

🍴 Eating & Drinking

Xuan Thanh (20 Đ Tran Hau; mains 35,000-200,000d; ⊗ 6am-9pm) boasts a range of Vietnamese favourites including good shrimp dishes.

Be sure to try the local coconut. Its flesh is mixed with ice and sugar and served all over town. For a beer, try **Oasis** (☎ 077-370 1553; www.oasisbarhatien.com; 42 Đ Tuan Phu Dat; ⊗ 9am-9pm; 🛜) run by an expat and his Vietnamese wife; it's also a great source of impartial travel information.

A NIGHT ON THE MEKONG

For many travellers, the chance to experience river life and to share a home-cooked meal with a local family is a highlight of a Mekong visit. Vinh Long offers many homestay options.

Ba Linh (☎ 0939 138 142, 070-385 8683; balinhhomestay@gmail.com; 95 An Thanh, An Binh; r 350,000d) A traditional-looking, popular place with six simple partitioned rooms. Breakfast and dinner are included.

Ngoc Sang (☎ 070-385 8694; 95/8 Binh Luong, An Binh; per person US$15) Friendly, canal-facing homestay where free bikes are available. You can even help out in the family's orchard.

Ut Trinh (☎ 0919 002 505, 070-395 4255; vinhlongmekongtravel@yahoo.com; Hoa Qui, Hoa Ninh, An Binh; r US$15-25) A pleasant, fresh and clean homestay with excellent rooms in two buildings on a vegie and fruit farm.

Nam Thanh (☎ 070-385 8883; namthanhhomestayvn@gmail.com; 172/9 Binh Luong, An Binh; from US$12) Friendly homestay with single beds in a communal space and sturdier doubles.

ⓘ Getting There & Away

Ferries stop across the river from the town.

Buses connect HCMC (from 140,000d, 10 hours) and Ha Tien; they also run to destinations including Chau Doc (70,000d), Rach Gia (50,000d) and Can Tho (from 110,000d). Ha Tien bus station is on the road to Mui Nai Beach and the Cambodian border.

Rach Gia

☎ 077 / POP 210,000

Rach Gia is something of a boom town, flush with funds from its thriving port, and has significant numbers of ethnic Chinese and Khmers. Few travellers linger, heading straight to Phu Quoc Island, but the waterfront is lively and the backstreets hide inexpensive seafood restaurants.

Banks, ATMs and internet cafes are scattered around town. **Kien Giang Tourist** (Du Lich Lu Hanh Kien Giang; ☎ 077-386 2081; ctycpdu-lichkg@vnn.vn; 5 Đ Le Loi; ☺ 7am-5pm) is the provincial tourism authority. Head to **Kim Co Hotel** (☎ 077-387 9610; www.kimcohotel.com; 141 Đ Nguyen Hung Son; r 350,000-400,000d; ❉ 🛜) for bright, cheerful rooms.

Vietnam Airlines flies daily between HCMC (from 600,000d) and Rach Gia, continuing on to Phu Quoc Island. The airport is about 10km outside town; taxis cost about 130,000d.

For Phu Quoc ferries, drop by the **Rach Gia hydrofoil terminal** (☎ 077-387 9765) the day before, or phone ahead to book a seat.

There are regular services to Ca Mau (50,000d, three hours), Ha Tien (38,000d, two hours) and other cities in the region

---

GETTING TO CAMBODIA: SOUTHERN BORDERS

Chau Doc to Phnom Penh

Getting to the border One of the most enjoyable ways to enter Cambodia is via the Vinh Xuong/Kaam Samnor border crossing located just northwest of Chau Doc along the Mekong River. Several companies in Chau Doc sell boat journeys from Chau Doc to Phnom Penh via the Vinh Xuong border. **Hang Chau** (☎ Chau Doc 076-356 2771, Phnom Penh 855-12-883 542; www.hangchautourist.com.vn; per person US$24) boats depart Chau Doc at 7.30am from a pier at 18 Đ Tran Hung Dao, arriving at 12.30pm.

At the border Cambodian visas are available at the crossing, but minor overcharging is common (plan on paying around US$24).

Ha Tien to Kep

Getting to the border The Xa Xia/Prek Chak border crossing connects Ha Tien with Kep and Kampot on Cambodia's south coast. Direct minibuses leave Ha Tien for Cambodia at around 1pm, heading to Kep (US$12, one hour, 47km), Kampot (US$15, 1½ hours, 75km), Sihanoukville (US$20, four hours, 150km) and Phnom Penh (US$18, four hours, 180km). Bookings can be made through Ha Tien Tourism (which also operates through the Oasis bar in Ha Tien), which can also arrange the Cambodian visa. It's far better to change money in Ha Tien than at the border.

At the border Cambodian visas are available at the border.

Moving on As it costs only slightly more than taking local transport and is far comfier, most travellers opt for a through minibus ticket.

Chau Doc to Takeo

Getting to the border Eclipsed by the newer crossing of Xa Xia near Ha Tien, the Tinh Bien/Phnom Den border crossing is less convenient for Phnom Penh–bound travellers, but may be of interest for those who savour the challenge of obscure border crossings. Buses from Chau Doc to Phnom Penh (US$15 to US$21, five hours) depart at 7.30am and can be booked through Mekong Tours in Chau Doc. The roads leading to the border are terrible.

At the border Cambodian visas can be obtained here, although it's not uncommon to be charged US$25, several dollars more than the official rate.

Moving on Most travellers opt for a through bus ticket from Chau Doc.

from the **central bus station** (260A Đ Nguyen Binh Khiem) north of town. A taxi into town will cost around 20,000d.

Phu Quoc Island

📱 077 / POP 88,000

Fringed with idyllic beaches and with large tracts still covered in dense, tropical jungle, Phu Quoc is morphing from a sleepy backwater into a favoured escape. Beyond the chain of resorts lining Long Beach, it's still largely undeveloped. Dive the reefs, kayak bays, explore backroads by motorbike – or live the life of a lotus eater by lounging on the beach, indulging in a massage and dining on fresh seafood.

Despite increasing development (including a new international airport), close to 70% of the island is protected as Phu Quoc National Park.

Phu Quoc's rainy season is from July to November; the peak season for tourism is between December and March.

👁 Sights

Deserted white-sand beaches ring Phu Quoc.

Duong Dong   TOWN
The island's main town and chief fishing port is not that exciting, though the filthy, bustling market is interesting. The old bridge in town is a great vantage point to photograph the island's fishing fleet crammed into the narrow channel. Take a peek at **Cau Castle** (Dinh Cau; Đ Bach Dang, Duong Dong) FREE, actually more of a temple-cum-lighthouse, built in 1937 to honour Thien Hau (Tianhou), the Chinese goddess of the sea.

Phu Quoc is famous for the quality of its fish sauce, and the factory **Nuoc Mam Hung Thanh** (⏱8-11am & 1-5pm) FREE exports all over the world.

Long Beach   BEACH
(Bai Truong) Long Beach is draped invitingly along the coast from Duong Dong almost to An Thoi port. Development concentrates in the north near Duong Dong, where the recliners and rattan umbrellas of the various resorts rule. With its west-facing aspect, sunsets can be stupendous.

Sao Beach   BEACH
(Bai Sao) With white sand like powdered ivory, the delightful curve of beautiful Sao Beach bends out alongside a sea of mineral-water clarity just a few kilometres from An Thoi, the main shipping port at the southern tip of the island. There are a couple of beachfront restaurants, where you can settle into a deckchair or partake in water sports.

Phu Quoc National Park   PARK
About 90% of Phu Quoc is forested and the trees and adjoining marine environment enjoy official protection (in 2010 it was declared a Unesco Biosphere Reserve). There are a few primitive dirt roads, but no real hiking trails.

An Thoi Islands   ISLAND
(Quan Dao An Thoi) Just off the southern tip of Phu Quoc, these 15 islands and islets can be visited by chartered boat. It's a fine area for sightseeing, fishing, swimming and snorkelling. Hon Thom (Pineapple Island) is about 3km in length and is the largest island in the group.

Vung Bau, Dai & Thom Beaches   BEACH
(Bai Vung Bau, Bai Dai, Bai Thom) Still retaining their isolated, tropical charm, these northern beaches are rarely peopled, let alone crowded. A newer road follows the coast along **Vung Bau** (Bai Vung Bau) and **Dai** (Bai Dai) beaches, cutting down on motorbike time and red dust in your face. The road from Dai to **Thom** (Bai Thom) via Ganh Dau is very beautiful, passing through dense forest with tantalising glimpses of the coast below.

🏊 Activities

Diving & Snorkelling

There's plenty of underwater action around Phu Quoc, but only during the dry months (from November to May). Two fun dives cost from US$40 to US$80; four-day PADI Open Water certification runs between US$320 and US$360; and snorkelling trips are US$20 to US$30. The following schools are based in the Duong Dong area.

Rainbow Divers   DIVING, SNORKELLING
(📱0913 400 964; www.divevietnam.com; 11 Đ Tran Hung Dao; ⏱9am-6pm) A PADI outfit with a wide range of diving and snorkelling trips.

Flipper Diving Club   DIVING
(www.flipperdiving.com; 60 Đ Tran Hung Dao; ⏱9am-9pm) Multilingual PADI dive centre for everything from novice dive trips to full instructor courses.

Fishing & Boat Trips

Anh Tu's Tours
BOAT TOUR

(☑ 077-399 6009; anhtupq@yahoo.com) Snorkelling, squid fishing, island tours and motorbike rental.

John's Tours
BOAT TOUR

(☑ 0919 107 086; www.johnsislandtours.com; 4 Đ Tran Hung Dao) Snorkelling, island-hopping and squid-fishing trips.

🛏 Sleeping

Most beachside accommodation options are at Long Beach. Expect to pay more here than elsewhere in Vietnam; accommodation prices also yo-yo depending on the season.

🛏 Duong Dong

Sea Breeze
HOTEL $

(Gio Bien; ☑ 077-399 4920; www.seabreezephuquoc.com; 62A Đ Tran Hung Dao; r fan from US$15, air-con US$25-40; ❋ 🛜) Clean, modern and attractive rooms, though accommodation road-side is noisier at this curvaceous hotel.

Hiep Phong Hotel
GUESTHOUSE $

(☑ 077-384 6057; nguyet_1305@yahoo.com; 17 Đ Nguyen Trai; r US$15-20; ❋ @ 🛜) A very friendly, family-run minihotel in the middle of town. The rooms include satellite TV, fridge and hot water.

🛏 Long Beach

Mushrooms
GUESTHOUSE $

(☑ 0126 471 4249; 170 Đ Tran Hung Dao; dm US$6, d US$10-15) This spruce, clean and colourful outfit has spic-and-span six- and four-bed dorms, and a couple of decent doubles, one without shower.

Lien Hiep Thanh Hotel
HOTEL $

(☑ 077-384 7583; lienhiepthanh2007@yahoo.com.vn; 118/12 Đ Tran Hung Dao; r with fan US$15-20, air-con US$30-60; ❋ 🛜) Simple rooms and bungalows amid trees on a great strip of beach. Beachfront rooms include air-con and hot water, and there's a small restaurant.

🛏 Around the Island

Lang Toi
GUESTHOUSE $$

(☑ 077-397 2123; Sao Beach; r US$35-45; 🛜) Also known as Gecko Jack's, this simple place on Sao Beach has four fan-cooled rooms, each with spacious bathrooms. Two rooms come with sea view and verandah, two with a garden setting. Book ahead.

Freedomland
HOMESTAY $$

(☑ 077-399 4891; www.freedomlandphuquoc.com; 2 Ap Ong Lang, Xa Cua Duong; bungalow US$30-60; ⊙ Oct-Jun; @ 🛜) With an emphasis on socialising – fun, communal dinners are a mainstay – Freedomland has 11 basic bungalows (mosquito nets, fans, no hot water) scattered around a shady plot. It's a popular choice, particularly with solo budget travellers; it's best to call first. Shut in the rainy season.

🍴 Eating & Drinking

Most hotels have their own lively cafes or restaurants in-house.

Duong Dong's **night market** (Đ Vo Thi Sau; ⊙ 5pm-midnight) is one of the most atmospheric (and affordable) places to dine with a delicious range of Vietnamese seafood, grills and vegetarian options.

The seafood restaurants in the fishing village of Ham Ninh also offer an authentic local experience and taste; try **Kim Cuong I** (☑ 077-384 9978; mains 30,000-300,000d).

🍴 Duong Dong

★ Buddy Ice Cream
ICE CREAM $

(www.visitphuquoc.info; 26 Đ Nguyen Trai; mains 25,000-130,000d; ⊙ 8am-10pm; 🛜) With the coolest music in town, this cafe is excellent for sides of free internet and tourist info with its New Zealand ice-cream combos, toasted sandwiches, fish and chips, thirst-busting fruit juices, shakes, smoothies, all-day breakfasts, comfy sofas and book exchange.

🍴 Long Beach

★ Spice House at Cassia Cottage
VIETNAMESE $

(www.cassiacottage.com; 100C Đ Tran Hung Dao; mains from 74,000d; ⊙ 7-10am & 11am-10pm) Nab a beachside high-table, order a papaya salad, grilled garlic, a cinnamon-infused okra or a delectable fish curry and time dinner to catch the sunset at this excellent restaurant.

Alanis Deli
CAFE $

(98 Đ Tran Hung Dao; pancakes from 75,000d; ⊙ 8am-10pm) Fab caramel pancakes and coffees plus ace breakfasts and friendly service.

ℹ Information

There are ATMs in Duong Dong and in many resorts on Long Beach. Buddy Ice Cream offers free internet and wi-fi.

ⓘ Getting There & Away

AIR

Demand can be high in peak season, so book ahead. **Vietnam Airlines** (☏ 077-399 6677; www.vietnamairlines.com; 122 Đ Nguyen Trung Truc) flies to/from Rach Gia, Can Tho, Hanoi and HCMC (from 450,000d, 10 daily). Vietjet flies to/from HCMC.

BOAT

Fast boats connect Phu Quoc to both Ha Tien (1½ hours) and Rach Gia (2½ hours). Phu Quoc travel agents have the most up-to-date schedules and can book tickets. The ferry port on Phu Quoc is at Bai Vong on the east coast.

Also from Ha Tien, a massive 400-passenger car ferry (departing 8.20am from Ha Tien and 2pm from Phu Quoc; per passenger/motorbike/car 165,000d/100,000d/US$50) departs every day.

Savanna Express (☏ 077-369 2888; www.savannaexpress.com; adult/child 330,000/250,000d) Departs Rach Gia at 8.05am and Phu Quoc at 1.05pm; 2½ hours.

Superdong (☏ Phu Quoc 077-398 0111, Rach Gia 077-387 7742; www.superdong.com.vn; to Rach Gia adult/child 320,000/250,000d, to Ha Tien adult 215,000-230,000d, child 160,000d) Departs Rach Gia and Phu Quoc at 8am, 9am, 12.40pm and 1pm. Departs Ha Tien at 8am and 1pm and leaves Phu Quoc at 8.30am and 1.30pm.

ⓘ Getting Around

The island's new Phu Quoc International Airport is 10km from Duong Dong; a taxi costs around US$8 to Long Beach.

Bicycle rentals are available through most hotels from US$3 per day.

There is a skeletal bus service (every hour or two) between An Thoi and Duong Dong. A bus (20,000d) waits for the ferry at Bai Vong to take passengers to Duong Dong.

Rental motorbikes cost US$7 to US$10 (automatic) per day. Motorbike taxis are everywhere. Short hops cost 20,000d; figure on around 50,000d for about 5km.

Call **Mai Linh** (☏ 077-397 9797) for a taxi.

UNDERSTAND VIETNAM

Vietnam Today

Vietnam's had a good couple of decades: a period of rising, sustained growth has benefited most. The standard of living has risen markedly, as cities have been transformed, education and healthcare have improved and the tourism sector continues to thrive. Yet a growing disconnection between a heavy-handed state and its people is evident, with widespread resentment regarding rampant corruption and evidence of growing, if limited, political dissent.

Politics & Economy

Vietnam's political system could not be simpler: the Communist Party is the sole source of power. Officially, according to the Vietnamese constitution, the National Assembly (or parliament) is the country's supreme authority, but in practice it's a tool of the party and carefully controlled elections ensure 90% of delegates are Communist Party members.

The state still controls around two-fifths of the economy. More than 100 of the 200 biggest companies in Vietnam are state-owned and the key sectors of oil production, shipbuilding, cement, coal and rubber are government controlled. Many of these state-controlled businesses are in deep trouble and are haemorrhaging money.

Corruption scandals are frequent: Vietnam Electricity's head honcho was sacked after losses of over US$1 billion were reported.

Dissent & the Net

Dubbed the 'bamboo firewall', the entire nation's internet operates behind a state-controlled security system that blocks anything – including Facebook – that might potentially lead to trouble.

In September 2013 the Vietnamese government introduced new rules restricting all use of websites and online social media to the exchange of 'personal information' only. Political dissent is a complete no-no and arrests and trials are common.

Bloggers are particularly vulnerable, with 46 sentenced to prison for 'anti-state propaganda' in 2013, including Le Quoc Quan, a democracy activist and prominent Catholic.

All newspapers and television channels are state-run.

North & South

The Vietnamese economy has been buoyant for 20 years, but some areas are more buoyant than others. In 2013, Ho Chi Minh City's economy was growing at almost double the national rate (8.1% compared to 4.3%). It's the south that's benefited most from inward investment as Viet Kieu (overseas Vietnamese, the vast majority of whom are southerners) have returned and invested in the region.

The government is aware of these divisions and tries to balance the offices of state, so if the prime minister is from the south, the head of the Communist Party is from the north.

When it comes to the older generation, the south has never forgiven the north for bulldozing their war cemeteries, imposing communism and blackballing whole families. The north has never forgiven the south for siding with the Americans against their own people. Luckily for Vietnam, the new generation seems to have less interest in the country's harrowing history.

Vietnam's Place in the World

Today, relations with the USA are politically cordial and economically vibrant (bilateral trade was worth US$24.9 billion in 2012). United States and Vietnamese militaries hold annual Defense Policy Dialogue talks. Vietnam's suppression of political dissent and issues of freedom of speech and religion remain areas of contention though. For the Vietnamese, the legacy of Agent Orange and dioxin poisoning remains unresolved – the USA has never paid compensation to the up to four million victims of dioxin poisoning resulting from aerial bombing during the American War.

The situation with Vietnam's traditional historic enemy, China, is far more complicated and occasionally fraught. On the plus side trade is booming (though more one-way than the Vietnamese would like) and borders are hyper busy. Chinese is the second-most-popular foreign language studied in Vietnam. However, the Spratly Islands, rich in oil deposits, remain a potential flashpoint, with both nations – in addition to several others – claiming sovereignty. There have been regular protests in Hanoi against the Chinese occupation of the islands.

Vietnam enjoys cordial relations with most Southeast Asian countries, but there are ongoing tensions with Laos over the construction of dams on the Mekong River.

State of the Nation

Overall, most Vietnamese are pretty happy with their lot – for now. The last couple of decades have transformed the nation as

blue-chip finance has flooded into a red-flag communist society and comrades have become entrepreneurs. The country is stable. However, this status quo is very much dependent on the economy and with declining rates of growth, the situation is less rosy than it was a few years ago.

History

Early Vietnam

The Vietnamese trace their roots back to the Red River delta where farmers first cultivated rice. Millennia of struggle against the Chinese then followed. Vietnam only became a united state in the 19th century, but quickly faced the ignominy of French colonialism and then the devastation of the American intervention. The Vietnamese nation has survived tempestuous, troubled times, but its strength of character has served it well. Today, the signs are it's continuing to grow with some promise.

The sophisticated Indianised kingdom of Funan flourished from the 1st to 6th centuries AD in the Mekong Delta area. Archaeological evidence reveals that Funan's busy trading port of Oc-Eo had contact with China, India, Persia and even the Mediterranean. Between the mid-6th century and the 9th century, the Funan empire was absorbed by the pre-Angkorian kingdom of Chenla.

Meanwhile, around present-day Danang, the Hindu kingdom of Champa emerged in the late 2nd century AD. Like Funan, it adopted Sanskrit as a sacred language and borrowed heavily from Indian art and culture. By the 8th century Champa had expanded to include what is now Nha Trang and Phan Rang. The Cham warred constantly with the Vietnamese to the north and the Khmers to the south and ultimately found themselves squeezed between these two great powers.

Chinese Occupation

The Chinese conquered the Red River Delta in the 2nd century BC and over the following centuries attempted to impress a centralised state system on the Vietnamese. There were numerous small-scale rebellions against Chinese rule – which was characterised by tyranny, forced labour and insatiable demands for tribute – between the 3rd and 6th centuries, but all were defeated.

However, the early Viets learned much from the Chinese, including advanced irrigation for rice cultivation and medical knowledge as well as Confucianism, Taoism and Mahayana Buddhism. Much of the 1000-year period of Chinese occupation was typified by both Vietnamese resistance and the adoption of many Chinese cultural traits.

In AD 938 Ngo Quyen destroyed Chinese forces on the Bach Dang River, winning independence and signalling the start of a dynastic tradition. During subsequent centuries the Vietnamese successfully repulsed foreign invaders, including the Mongols, and absorbed the kingdom of Champa in 1471 as they expanded south.

Contact with the West

In 1858 a joint military force from France and the Spanish colony of the Philippines stormed Danang after several missionaries were killed. Early the next year, Saigon was seized. By 1883 the French had imposed a Treaty of Protectorate on Vietnam. French rule often proved cruel and arbitrary. Ultimately, the most successful resistance came from the communists, first organised by Ho Chi Minh in 1925.

During WWII, the only group that significantly resisted the Japanese occupation was the communist-dominated Viet Minh. When WWII ended, Ho Chi Minh – whose Viet Minh forces already controlled large parts of the country – declared Vietnam independent. French efforts to reassert control soon led to violent confrontations and full-scale war. In May 1954, Viet Minh forces overran the French garrison at Dien Bien Phu.

The Geneva Accords of mid-1954 provided for a temporary division of Vietnam at the Ben Hai River. When Ngo Dinh Diem, the anti-communist, Catholic leader of the southern zone, refused to hold the 1956 elections, the Ben Hai line became the border between North and South Vietnam.

The War in Vietnam

Around 1960, the Hanoi government changed its policy of opposition to the Diem regime from one of 'political struggle' to one of 'armed struggle'. The National Liberation Front (NLF), a communist guerrilla group better known as the Viet Cong (VC), was founded to fight against Diem.

An unpopular ruler, Diem was assassinated in 1963 by his own troops. When the Hanoi government ordered North

UNCLE OF THE PEOPLE

Father of the nation, Ho Chi Minh (Bringer of Light) was the son of a fiercely nationalistic scholar-official. Born Nguyen Tat Thanh near Vinh in 1890, he was educated in Hué and adopted many pseudonyms during his momentous life. Many Vietnamese affectionately refer to him as Bac Ho (Uncle Ho) today.

In 1911 he signed up as a cook's apprentice on a French ship, sailing the seas to North America, Africa and Europe. While odd-jobbing in England and France as a gardener, snow sweeper, waiter, photo-retoucher and stoker, his political consciousness developed.

Ho Chi Minh moved to Paris, where he mastered languages including English, French, German and Mandarin and began to promote the issue of Indochinese independence. He was a founding member of the French Communist Party in 1920.

In 1941 Ho Chi Minh returned to Vietnam for the first time in 30 years, and established the Viet Minh (whose goal was independence from France). As Japan prepared to surrender in August 1945, Ho Chi Minh led the August Revolution, and his forces then established control throughout much of Vietnam.

The return of the French compelled the Viet Minh to conduct a guerrilla war, which ultimately led to victory against the colonists at Dien Bien Phu in 1954. Ho then led North Vietnam until his death in September 1969 – he never lived to see the North's victory over the South.

Since then the party has worked hard to preserve the image and reputation of Bac Ho. His image dominates contemporary Vietnam. This cult of personality is in stark contrast to the simplicity with which Ho lived his life. For more Ho, check out Ho Chi Minh, the excellent biography by William J Duiker.

BEST FILMS

Apocalypse Now (1979) The American War depicted as an epic 'heart of darkness' adventure.

The Deer Hunter (1978) Examines the psychological breakdown suffered by small-town servicemen.

Platoon (1986) Based on the first-hand experiences of the director, it follows idealistic volunteer Charlie Sheen to 'Nam.

Cyclo (1995) Visually stunning masterpiece that cuts to the core of HCMC's underworld.

The Quiet American (2002) Atmospherically set in Saigon during the French colonial period, with rebellion in the air.

Vietnamese Army (NVA) units to infiltrate the South in 1964, the situation for the Saigon regime became desperate. In 1965 the USA committed its first combat troops, soon joined by soldiers from South Korea, Australia, Thailand and New Zealand, in an effort to bring global legitimacy to the conflict.

As Vietnam celebrated the Lunar New Year in 1968, the VC launched a surprise attack, known as the Tet Offensive, marking a crucial turning point in the war. Many Americans, who had for years believed their government's insistence that the USA was winning, started demanding a negotiated end to the war. The Paris Agreements, signed in 1973, provided for a ceasefire, the total withdrawal of US combat forces and the release of American prisoners of war.

Reunification

Saigon surrendered to the NVA on 30 April 1975. Vietnam's reunification by the communists meant liberation from more than a century of colonial oppression, but was soon followed by large-scale internal repression. Hundreds of thousands of southerners fled Vietnam, creating a flood of refugees for the next 15 years.

Vietnam's campaign of repression against the ethnic Chinese, plus its invasion of Cambodia at the end of 1978, prompted China to attack Vietnam in 1979. The war lasted only 17 days, but Chinese-Vietnamese mistrust lasted for well over a decade.

Post-Cold War

After the collapse of the Soviet Union in 1991, Vietnam and Western nations sought rapprochement. The 1990s brought foreign investment and Association of Southeast Asian Nations (Asean) membership. The US established diplomatic relations with Vietnam in 1995, and Bill Clinton and George W Bush visited Hanoi. Vietnam was welcomed into the World Trade Organization (WTO) in 2007.

People & Culture

The Vietnamese are battle-hardened, proud and nationalist, as they have earned their stripes in successive skirmishes with the world's mightiest powers. But that's the older generation, who remember every inch of the territory for which they fought. For the new generation, Vietnam is a place to succeed, a place to ignore the staid structures set in stone by the communists, and a place to go out and have some fun.

As in other parts of Asia, life revolves around the family; there are often several generations living under one roof. Poverty, and the transition from a largely agricultural society to that of a more industrialised nation, sends many people seeking their fortune to the bigger cities, and is changing the structure of the modern family unit. Women make up 52% of the nation's workforce but are not well represented in positions of power.

Vietnam's population is 84% ethnic Vietnamese (Kinh) and 2% ethnic Chinese; the rest is made up of Khmers, Chams and members of more than 50 minority people, who mainly live in highland areas.

Religion

Over the centuries, Confucianism, Taoism and Buddhism have fused with popular Chinese beliefs and ancient Vietnamese animism to form what's collectively known as the Triple Religion (Tam Giao). Most Vietnamese people identify with this belief system, but if asked, they'll usually say they're Buddhist. Vietnam also has a significant percentage of Catholics (8% to 10% of the total population).

Cao Daism is a unique and colourful Vietnamese sect that was founded in the 1920s. It combines secular and religious philosophies of the East and West, and is based on seance messages revealed to the group's founder, Ngo Minh Chieu.

There are also small numbers of Muslims (around 60,000) and Hindus (50,000).

Arts

CONTEMPORARY ART & MUSIC

It is possible to catch modern dance, classical ballet and stage plays in Hanoi and Ho Chi Minh City (HCMC).

The work of contemporary painters and photographers covers a wide swathe of styles and gives a glimpse into the modern Vietnamese psyche; there are good galleries in Hanoi, HCMC and Hoi An.

Youth culture is most vibrant in HCMC and Hanoi, where there's more freedom for musicians and artists. There are small hip-hop, rock, punk and DJ scenes. Hot bands include rock band Microwave, metal merchants Black Infinity, the punk band Giao Chi and alt-roots band 6789.

ARCHITECTURE

The Vietnamese were not great builders like their neighbours the Khmer. Early Vietnamese structures were made of wood and other materials that proved highly vulnerable in the tropical climate. The grand exceptions are the stunning towers built by Vietnam's ancient Cham culture. These are most numerous in central Vietnam. The Cham ruins at My Son are a major draw.

SCULPTURE

Vietnamese sculpture has traditionally centred on religious themes and has functioned as an adjunct to architecture, especially that of pagodas, temples and tombs.

The Cham civilisation produced exquisite carved sandstone figures for its Hindu and Buddhist sanctuaries. The largest single collection of Cham sculpture is at the Museum of Cham Sculpture in Danang.

WATER PUPPETRY

Vietnam's ancient art of *roi nuoc* (water puppetry) originated in northern Vietnam at least 1000 years ago. Developed by rice farmers, the wooden puppets were manipulated by puppeteers using water-flooded rice paddies as their stage. Hanoi is the best place to see water-puppetry performances, which are accompanied by music played on traditional instruments.

Food & Drink

Food

Vietnamese food is one of the world's greatest cuisines; there are said to be nearly 500 traditional dishes. It varies a lot between north, centre and south. Soy sauce, Chinese influence and hearty soups like *pho* typify northern cuisine. Central Vietnamese food is known for its prodigious use of fresh herbs and intricate flavours; Hué imperial cuisine and Hoi An specialities are key to this area. Southern food is sweet, spicy and tropical – its curries will be familiar to lovers of Thai and Cambodian food. Everywhere you'll find that Vietnamese meals are superbly prepared and excellent value.

Most restaurants trade seven days a week, opening around 7am or 8am and closing around 9pm, often later in the big cities.

FRUIT

Aside from the usual delightful Southeast Asian fruits, Vietnam has its own unique *trai thanh long* (green dragon fruit), a bright fuchsia-coloured fruit with green scales. Grown mainly in the coastal region near Nha Trang, it has white flesh flecked with edible black seeds, and tastes something like a mild kiwifruit.

MEALS

Pho is the noodle soup that built a nation and is eaten at all hours of the day, but especially for breakfast. *Com* are rice dishes.

> ### THERE'S SOMETHING FISHY AROUND HERE...
>
> *Nuoc mam* (fish sauce) is the one ingredient that is quintessentially Vietnamese, and it lends a distinctive character to Vietnamese cooking. The sauce is made by fermenting highly salted fish in large ceramic vats for four to 12 months. Connoisseurs insist high-grade sauce has a much milder aroma than the cheaper variety. Dissenters insist it is a chemical weapon. It's very often used as a dipping sauce, and takes the place occupied by salt on a Western table.

You'll see signs saying *pho* and *com* everywhere. Other noodle soups to try are *bun bo Hué* and *hu tieu*.

Spring rolls (*nem* in the North, *cha gio* in the South) are a speciality. These are normally dipped in *nuoc mam* (fish sauce), though many foreigners prefer soy sauce (*xi dau* in the North, *nuoc tuong* in the South).

Because Buddhist monks of the Mahayana tradition are strict vegetarians, *an chay* (vegetarian cooking) is an integral part of Vietnamese cuisine.

SNACKS

Street stalls or roaming vendors are everywhere, selling steamed sweet potatoes, rice porridge and ice-cream bars even in the wee hours.

There are also many other Vietnamese nibbles to try including the following:

Bap xao Made from stir-fried fresh corn, chillies and tiny shrimp.

Bo bia Nearly microscopic shrimp, fresh lettuce and thin slices of Vietnamese sausage rolled up in rice paper and dipped in a spicy-sweet peanut sauce.

Sinh to Shakes made with milk and sugar or yoghurt, and fresh tropical fruit.

SWEETS

Many sticky confections are made from sticky rice, like *banh it nhan dau,* which also contains sugar and bean paste and is sold wrapped in banana leaf.

Most foreigners prefer *kem* (ice cream) or *yaourt* (yoghurt), which is generally of good quality.

Try *che,* a cold, refreshing sweet soup made with sweetened black bean, green bean or corn. It's served in a glass with ice and sweet coconut cream on top.

Drink

ALCOHOLIC DRINKS

Memorise the words *bia hoi,* which mean 'draught beer'. Probably the cheapest beer in

BEWARE YOUR BLEND

Some consider *chon* to be the highest grade of Vietnamese coffee. It is made of beans fed to a certain species of weasel and later collected from its excrement.

the world, *bia hoi* starts at around 4000d a glass, so anyone can afford a round and you can get 'off yer heed' for just a few bucks. Places that serve *bia hoi* usually also serve cheap food.

Several foreign labels brewed in Vietnam under licence include Tiger, Carlsberg and Heineken.

National and regional brands include Halida and Hanoi in the north, Huda and Larue in the centre, and BGI and 333 (*ba ba ba)* in the south of the country.

Wine and spirits are available but at higher prices. Local brews are cheaper but not always drinkable.

NONALCOHOLIC DRINKS

Whatever you drink, make sure that it's been boiled or bottled. Ice is generally safe on the tourist trail, but may not be elsewhere.

Vietnamese *cà phê* (coffee) is fine stuff and there is no shortage of cafes in which to sample it.

Foreign soft drinks are widely available in Vietnam. An excellent local treat is *soda chanh* (carbonated mineral water with lemon and sugar) or *nuoc chanh nong* (hot, sweetened lemon juice).

Environment

Environmental consciousness is low in Vietnam. Rapid industrialisation, deforestation and pollution are major problems facing the country.

Unsustainable logging and farming practices, as well as the extensive spraying of defoliants by the US during the war, have contributed to deforestation. This has resulted not only in significant loss of biological diversity, but also in a harder existence for many minority people.

The country's rapid economic and population growth over the last decade – demonstrated by the dramatic increase in industrial production, motorbike numbers and helter-skelter construction – has put additional pressure on the already stressed environment.

The Land

Vietnam stretches more than 1600km along the east coast of the Indochinese peninsula. The country's land area is 329,566 sq km, making it slightly larger than Italy and a bit smaller than Japan.

As the Vietnamese are quick to point out, it resembles a *don ganh,* or the ubiquitous bamboo pole with a basket of rice slung from each end. The baskets represent the main rice-growing regions of the Red River Delta in the north and the Mekong Delta in the south.

Of several interesting geological features found in Vietnam, the most striking are its spectacular karst formations (limestone peaks with caves and underground streams). The northern half of Vietnam has a spectacular array of karst areas, particularly around Halong Bay and Phong Nha.

Wildlife

We'll start with the good news. Despite some disastrous bouts of deforestation, Vietnam's flora and fauna is still incredibly exotic and varied. The nation has an estimated 12,000 plant species, only 7000 of which have been identified; more than 275 species of mammal, 800 species of bird, 180 species of reptile and 80 species of amphibian. The other side of the story is that despite this outstanding diversity, the threat to Vietnam's remaining wildlife has never been greater due to poaching, hunting and habitat loss. Three of the nation's iconic animals – the elephant, saola and tiger – are on the brink. It's virtually certain that the last wild Vietnamese rhino was killed inside Cat Tien National Park in 2010. And for every trophy animal there are hundreds of other less 'headline' species that are being cleared from forests and reserves for the sake of profit (or hunger).

Many officials still turn a blind eye to the trade in wildlife for export and domestic consumption, though laws are in place to protect the animals. Poachers continue to profit from meeting the demand for exotic animals for pets and traditional medicines.

National Parks

There are 31 national parks, covering about 3% of Vietnam's total territory. In the north the most interesting and accessible include Cat Ba, Bai Tu Long, Ba Be and Cuc Phuong. Heading south Phong Nha-Ke Bang, Bach Ma National Park, Yok Don National Park and Cat Tien National Park are well worth investigating.

SURVIVAL GUIDE

ℹ Directory A–Z

ACCOMMODATION

In general, accommodation in Vietnam offers superb value for money and excellent facilities. In big cities and the main tourism centres you'll find everything from hostel dorm beds to uberluxe hotels. Cleanliness is generally good and there are very few real dumps.

Most hotels in Vietnam quote prices in Vietnamese dong and/or US dollars. Prices are quoted in dong or dollars in reviews based on the preferred currency of the particular property.

Hostel dorm beds (around US$4 to US$7) are usually the cheapest options, but these only exist in a few backpacker centres such as Nha Trang, Ho Chi Minh City, Hué and Hanoi. Guesthouses are the next level up, and rooms here often have private bathrooms and cost from around US$8 to US$20. A class above guesthouses, minihotels typically come with more amenities, such as satellite TV.

When it comes to midrange places, flash a bit more cash and three-star touches are available,

---

RHINO HORN & VIETNAM

In 2013 the WWF and Traffic (the wildlife trade monitoring network) launched a campaign in Vietnam to counter rhino horn sale and consumption, declaring that the country needed to 'clean up its act'.

Some Vietnamese still believe rhino horn can do everything from increasing libido to curing cancer.

Even the tragic news about the extinction of the rhino in Vietnam has failed to curb domestic demand. Vietnamese gangs have stolen antique rhino horns from museum displays across Europe, and provoked a rhinopoaching crisis in South Africa.

A media campaign was launched in 2013 to try to change mindsets and make the consumption of rhino horn unacceptable. **ENV** (Education for Nature-Vietnam; www.envietnam.org) is coordinating the efforts.

For more information consult **Save the Rhino** (www.savetherhino.org) and the **Rhinose Foundation** (http://rhinosday.com).

HOMESTAYS

Homestays are popular in parts of Vietnam. These are usually well-organised in specific villages, including several minority areas. Often the accommodation is in a longhouse or communal space with people sleeping on roll-up mattresses.

Areas that are well set up include Vinh Long in the Mekong Delta, the Cham islands, Mai Chau and Ba Be National Park.

such as chic decor or access to a swimming pool.

Be aware that some hotels apply a 10% sales tax. Check carefully before taking a room to avoid any unpleasant shocks on departure.

Accommodation is at a premium during Tet (late January or early February), when the whole country is on the move and overseas Vietnamese flood back into the country. Prices can rise by 25% or more. Christmas and New Year represent another high season.

Price Ranges

The following price ranges refer to a double room with bathroom in high season. Dorm-bed prices are given individually.

$　less than 525,000d (US$25)

$$　525,000d to 1,575,000d (US$25 to US$75)

$$$　more than 1,575,000d (US$75)

BOOKS

The Quiet American (Graham Greene) Classic novel set in the 1950s as the French empire is collapsing.

The Sorrow of War (Bao Ninh) The North Vietnamese perspective, retold in novel form via flashbacks.

Vietnam: Rising Dragon (Bill Hayton) A candid assessment of the nation that's one of the most up-to-date sources available.

Catfish & Mandala (Andrew X Pham) Beautifully written and thought-provoking biographical tale of a Vietnamese-American.

CHILDREN

Children get to have a good time in Vietnam. There are some great beaches, but pay close attention to any playtime in the sea.

Kids generally enjoy local cuisine, which is rarely too spicy; the range of fruit is staggering. Comfort food from home (pizzas, pasta, burgers and ice cream) is available in most places too.

With babies and infants, the main worry is keeping an eye on what they're putting in their mouths: dysentery, typhoid and hepatitis are common.

Keep hydration levels up, and slap on the sunscreen.

ELECTRICITY

Voltage is 220V, 50 cycles. Sockets are two pin, round head.

EMBASSIES & CONSULATES

Australian Embassy (☑ 04-3774 0100; www.vietnam.embassy.gov.au; 8 Đ Dao Tan, Ba Dinh District, Hanoi)

Australian Consulate (Map p886; ☑ 08-3521 8100; 5th fl, 5B Đ Ton Duc Thang, HCMC)

Cambodian Embassy (Map p827; camemb.vnm@mfa.gov.kh; 71A P Tran Hung Dao, Hanoi)

Cambodian Consulate (Map p888; ☑ 08-3829 2751; 41 Đ Phung Khac Khoan, HCMC)

Canadian Embassy (Map p824; www.canadainternational.gc.ca/vietnam; 31 Đ Hung Vuong, Hanoi)

Canadian Consulate (Map p886; ☑ 08-3827 9899; www.canadainternational.gc.ca/vietnam; 10th fl, 235 Đ Dong Khoi, HCMC)

Chinese Embassy (Map p824; ☑ 04-8845 3736; http://vn.china-embassy.org/chn; 46 P Hoang Dieu, Hanoi)

Chinese Consulate (Map p890; ☑ 08-3829 2457; 39 Đ Nguyen Thi Minh Khai, HCMC)

French Embassy (Map p827; ☑ 04-3944 5700; www.ambafrance-vn.org; P Tran Hung Dao, Hanoi)

French Consulate (Map p888; 27 Đ Nguyen Thi Minh Khai, HCMC)

German Embassy (Map p824; ☑ 04-3845 3836; www.hanoi.diplo.de; 29 Đ Tran Phu, Hanoi)

German Consulate (Map p888; ☑ 08-3829 1967; www.hanoi.diplo.de; 126 Đ Nguyen Dinh Chieu, HCMC)

Japanese Embassy (☑ 04-3846 3000; www.vn.emb-japan.go.jp; 27 P Lieu Giai, Ba Dinh District, Hanoi)

Japanese Consulate (Map p886; ☑ 08-3822 5341; 13-17 ĐL Nguyen Hué, HCMC)

Laotian Embassy (Map p827; ☑ 04-3942 4576; www.embalaohanoi.gov.la; 22 P Tran Binh Trong, Hanoi)

Laotian Consulate (Map p886; ☑ 08-3829 7667; 93 Đ Pasteur, HCMC)

Laotian Consulate (☑ 0511-382 1208; 12 Đ Tran Qui Cap, Danang)

Netherlands Embassy (☑ 04-3831 5650; www.netherlands-embassy.org; 6th fl, Daeha Office Tower, 360 Kim Ma St, Ba Dinh, Hanoi)

Netherlands Consulate (Map p888; ☑ 08-3823 5932; Saigon Tower, 29 ĐL Le Duan, HCMC)

New Zealand Embassy (Map p820; ☑04-3824 1481; www.nzembassy.com/viet-nam; Level 5, 63 P Ly Thai To, Hanoi)

New Zealand Consulate (Map p886; ☑08-3827 2745; 8th fl, The Metropolitan, 235 Đ Dong Khoi, HCMC)

Thai Embassy (Map p824; ☑04-3823 5092; www.thaiembassy.org; 3-65 P Hoang Dieu, Hanoi)

Thai Consulate (Map p890; ☑08-3932 7637; 77 Đ Tran Quoc Thao)

UK Embassy (Map p820; ☑04-3936 0500; http://ukinvietnam.fco.gov.uk; Central Bldg, 31 P Hai Ba Trung, Hanoi)

UK Consulate (Map p888; ☑08-3829 8433; 25 ĐL Le Duan, HCMC)

US Embassy (☑04-3850 5000; http://vietnam.usembassy.gov; 7 P Lang Ha, Ba Dinh District, Hanoi)

US Consulate (Map p888; ☑08-3822 9433; http://hochiminh.usconsulate.gov; 4 ĐL Le Duan, HCMC)

FOOD

The range of prices in reviews for dining out are based on a typical meal, excluding drinks.

$ less than 105,000d (US$5)

$$ 105,000d to 315,000d (US$5 to US$15)

$$$ more than 315,000d (US$15)

GAY & LESBIAN TRAVELLERS

Vietnam is pretty hassle-free for gay travellers. There's not much in the way of harassment, nor are there official laws on same-sex relationships. Hanoi's first Gay Pride march was held in 2012. Indeed, in 2013 the government started a consultation process about legalising same-sex marriages. Checking into hotels as a same-sex couple is perfectly OK. But be discreet – public displays of affection are not socially acceptable whatever your sexual orientation.

Check out **Utopia** (www.utopia-asia.com) to obtain contacts and useful travel information.

INSURANCE

Insurance is a *must* for Vietnam, as the cost of major medical treatment is prohibitive. A travel-insurance policy to cover theft, loss and medical problems is the best bet.

Some insurance policies specifically exclude such 'dangerous activities' as riding motorbikes, diving and even trekking. Check that the policy covers an emergency evacuation in the event of serious injury.

Worldwide travel insurance is available at www.lonelyplanet.com/travel_services. You can buy, extend or claim anytime – even if you're already on the road.

INTERNET ACCESS

Internet and wi-fi is widely available throughout Vietnam. However, be aware that the government regularly blocks access to social networking sites, including Facebook, Twitter and Yahoo Messenger.

Something like 98% of hotels and guesthouses have wi-fi; it's almost always free of charge. Cybercafes charge from 3000d to 8000d per hour for internet access.

Connection speeds in towns and cities are normally quite good.

LEGAL MATTERS

If you lose something really valuable such as your passport or visa, you'll need to contact the police. Very few foreigners experience any hassle from police. The Vietnamese government is seriously cracking down on the burgeoning drug trade. You may face imprisonment and/or large fines for drug offences, and drug trafficking can be punishable by death.

MAPS

The road atlas *Tap Ban Do Giao Thong Duong Bo Viet Nam* is the best available, but the latest roads are not included. It's available in bookstores including Fahasa and costs 220,000d.

MONEY

The Vietnamese currency is the dong (abbreviated to 'd'). US dollars are also widely used.

For the last few years the dong has been fairly stable at around 21,000d to the dollar.

ATMs are widespread and present in virtually every town in the country.

Tipping is not expected, but is appreciated.

Credit & Debit Cards

Visa and MasterCard are accepted in many tourist centres, but don't expect budget guesthouses or noodle bars to take plastic. Commission charges (around 3%) sometimes apply.

For cash advances, try branches of Vietcombank in cities or Sinh Tourist travel agencies. Expect at least a 3% commission for this service.

OPENING HOURS

Vietnamese people rise early and consider sleeping in to be a sure indication of illness. Lunch is taken very seriously and many government offices close between 11.30am and 2pm.

Banks 8am to 3pm weekdays, to 11.30am Saturday

Offices and museums 7am or 8am to 5pm or 6pm; museums generally close on Monday

Restaurants 11.30am to 9pm

Shops 8am to 6pm

Temples and pagodas 5am to 9pm

PHOTOGRAPHY

Memory cards are pretty cheap in Vietnam. Most internet cafes can also burn photos onto a CD or DVD to free up storage space. Photo-processing shops and internet cafes in bigger cities can burn digital photos onto DVDs. Colour print film is widely available; slide film is available in HCMC and Hanoi.

PUBLIC HOLIDAYS

If a Vietnamese public holiday falls on a weekend, it is observed on the following Monday.

New Year's Day (Tet Duong Lich) 1 January

Vietnamese New Year (Tet) A three-day national holiday; late January or February

Founding of the Vietnamese Communist Party (Thanh Lap Dang CSVN) 3 February

Hung Kings Commemorations (Hung Vuong) 10th day of the 3rd lunar month; late March or April

Liberation Day (Saigon Giai Phong) 30 April

International Workers' Day (Quoc Te Lao Dong) 1 May

Ho Chi Minh's Birthday (Sinh Nhat Bac Ho) 19 May

Buddha's Birthday (Phat Dan) Eighth day of the fourth lunar month (usually June)

National Day (Quoc Khanh) 2 September

SAFE TRAVEL

All in all, Vietnam is an extremely safe country to travel. Sure, there are scams and hassles in some cities, particularly in Hanoi and Nha Trang. But overall the police keep a pretty tight grip on social order and we very rarely receive reports about muggings, armed robberies and sexual assaults.

Watch out for petty theft. Drive-by bag snatchers on motorbikes are not uncommon, and thieves patrol buses, trains and boats. Don't be flash with cameras and jewellery.

Since 1975 many thousands of Vietnamese have been maimed or killed by rockets, artillery shells, mortars, mines and other ordnance left over from the war. Stick to defined paths and *never* touch any suspicious war relic you might come across.

TIME

Vietnam is seven hours ahead of Greenwich Mean Time/Universal Time Coordinated (GMT/UTC). There's no daylight-saving or summer time.

TOILETS

Western-style sit-down toilets are the norm, but the odd squat bog still survives in some cheap hotels and bus stations. Hotels usually supply a roll, but it's wise to bring your own while on the road.

TOURIST INFORMATION

Tourist offices in Vietnam have a different philosophy from the majority of tourist offices worldwide. Most are really travel agencies whose primary interests are booking tours and turning a profit.

Travellers' cafes, travel agencies and your fellow travellers are a much better source of information than most of the so-called tourist offices.

TRAVELLERS WITH DISABILITIES

Vietnam is not the easiest of places for disabled travellers. Tactical problems include the chaotic traffic, a lack of lifts in smaller hotels and pavements (sidewalks) that are routinely blocked by parked motorbikes and food stalls.

That said, with some careful planning it is possible to enjoy your trip. Find a reliable company to make the travel arrangements. Many hotels in the midrange and above category have elevators, and disabled access is improving. Bus and train travel is tough, but rent a private vehicle with a driver and almost anywhere becomes instantly accessible.

The hazards for blind travellers in Vietnam are pretty acute, with traffic coming at you from all directions, so you'll definitely need a sighted companion.

The Travellers with Disabilities forum on Lonely Planet's Thorn Tree (www.lonelyplanet.com) is a good place to seek the advice of other disabled travellers.

You might also try contacting the following organisations:

Accessible Journeys (☑610-521 0339; www.disabilitytravel.com)

Mobility International USA (☑541-343 1284; www.miusa.org)

Royal Association for Disability Rights (Radar; ☑020-7250 3222; http://disability rightsuk.org)

Society for Accessible Travel & Hospitality (SATH; ☑212-447 7284; www.sath.org)

VISAS

Most nationalities have to endure the hassle of arranging a visa (or approval letter) to enter Vietnam. Entry and exit points include Hanoi, HCMC and Danang airports or any of Vietnam's plentiful land borders, shared with Cambodia, China and Laos.

Tourist visas are valid for a 30- or 90-day stay (and can be single or multiple entry). Online visa agents provide a more efficient, cheaper and quicker service than Vietnamese embassies for those flying into Vietnam.

If you plan to exit Vietnam and enter again from Cambodia or Laos, arrange a 90-day multiple-entry visa (around US$110).

In our experience, personal appearance influences the reception you'll receive from airport immigration – try your best to look 'respectable'.

Visa on Arrival

Citizens of the following countries do not need to apply in advance for a Vietnamese visa if arriving by air. Always double-check visa requirements before you travel as policies change regularly.

COUNTRY	DAYS
Myanmar, Brunei	14
Thailand, Malaysia, Singapore, Indonesia, Laos, Cambodia	30
Philippines	21
Japan, South Korea, Russia, Norway, Denmark, Sweden, Finland	15

Visa Extensions

If you've got the dollars, they've got the rubber stamp. Tourist visa extensions officially cost as little as US$10, and have to be organised via agents. The procedure can take seven days and you can only extend the visa for 30 or 90 days depending on the visa you hold.

You can extend your visa in any provincial capital, but if it's done in a different city from the one you arrived in (oh, the joys of Vietnamese bureaucracy!) it'll cost you around US$30. In practice, extensions work most smoothly in major cities, such as HCMC, Hanoi, Danang and Hué.

Multiple-Entry Visas

It's possible to exit Vietnam and then re-enter without having to apply for another visa. However, you must hold a multiple-entry visa *before* you leave Vietnam.

If you arrived in Vietnam on a single-entry visa, multiple-entry visas are easiest to arrange in Hanoi or HCMC, but you will have to ask a visa or travel agent to do the paperwork for you.

Agents charge about US$45 for the service and visa fees are charged on top of this – the procedure takes up to seven days.

VOLUNTEERING

Opportunities for voluntary work are quite limited in Vietnam.

The **NGO Resource Centre** (☑ 04-3832 8570; www.ngocentre.org.vn; Room 201, Bldg E3, 6 Dang Van Ngu, Trung Tu Diplomatic Compound, Dong Da, Hanoi) keeps a database of all of the NGOs assisting Vietnam. **Service Civil International** (www.sciint.org) has links to options in Vietnam.

You can donate your skills, time or money to **KOTO** (www.koto.com.au), which helps give street children career opportunities in its restaurants in Hanoi or HCMC; a three-month minimum commitment is required.

Volunteers for Peace (www.vpv.vn) is always looking for volunteers to help in an orphanage on the outskirts of Hanoi.

WEBSITES

Vietnam Coracle (http://vietnamcoracle.com) Excellent independent travel advice.

The Word (www.wordhcmc.com) Based in HCMC, this superb magazine has comprehensive coverage and excellent features.

Thanh Nien News (www.thanhniennews.com) Government-approved news, but includes diverse and interesting content.

Lonely Planet (www.lonelyplanet.com/vietnam) Destination information, hotel bookings, traveller forum and more.

WORK

At least 90% of foreign travellers seeking work in Vietnam end up teaching English. Pay can be as low as US$7 per hour at a university and up to US$20 per hour at a private academy.

Jobs in the booming private sector or with NGOs are usually organised outside Vietnam before arriving.

VIETNAM VISA AGENTS

If you're flying into Vietnam it's usually easiest and cheapest to get your visa approved through an online visa-service company. This system does *not* operate at land border crossings.

They will need passport details, and will email you an approval document two to three days later (one day for rush service), which you need to print and bring with you to the airport. On arrival, present the approval document and passport picture, then pay a stamping fee (US$45 for single-entry, US$65 to US$95 for multiple-entry visas). Many travellers prefer this method since they don't have to deal with bureaucratic hassles or give up their passport, and it's usually cheaper than using a Vietnamese embassy based in the West.

Recommended companies include **Vietnam Visa Choice** (www.vietnamvisachoice.com) and **Vietnam Visa Center** (www.vietnamvisacenter.org).

ⓘ Getting There & Away

Most travellers enter Vietnam by plane or bus, but there are also train links from China and boat connections from Cambodia via the Mekong River.

Flights, tours and rail tickets can be booked online at lonelyplanet.com/bookings.

ENTERING VIETNAM

Formalities at Vietnam's international airports are generally smoother than at land borders. That said, crossing overland from Cambodia and China is now relatively stress-free. Crossing the border between Vietnam and Laos can be slow.

Passport

Your passport must be valid for six months upon arrival in Vietnam. Most nationalities have to arrange a visa in advance.

AIR
Airports

There are three main international airports in Vietnam and a few others (Hué, Phu Quoc) which see the odd charter.

Tan Son Nhat International Airport (☑08-3848 5383; www.tsnairport.hochiminhcity.gov.vn/vn; Tan Binh District) For Ho Chi Minh City.
Noi Bai Airport (☑04-3827 1513; www.hanoi-airportonline.com) Serves Hanoi.
Danang Airport (☑0511-383 0339) International flights to China, Laos and Cambodia.

BORDER CROSSINGS

Vietnam shares land border crossings with Cambodia, China and Laos. Vietnam visas were not available at any land borders at the time of research. Officials at border crossings occasionally ask for an 'immigration fee' of a dollar or two.

Cambodia

Cambodia and Vietnam share a long frontier with seven (and counting) border crossings. One-month Cambodian visas are issued on arrival at all border crossings for US$20, but overcharging is common at all borders except Bavet.

Cambodian border crossings are officially open daily between 8am and 8pm.

China

There are currently three borders where foreigners are permitted to cross between Vietnam and China: Huu Nghi Quan (the Friendship Pass), Lao Cai and Mong Cai. It is necessary to arrange a Chinese visa in advance.

China time is one hour ahead.

Laos

There are seven (and counting) overland crossings between Vietnam and Laos. Thirty-day Lao visas are available at all borders.

The golden rule is to try to use direct city-to-city bus connections between the countries, as potential hassle will be greatly reduced. If you travel step-by-step using local buses expect hassle and transport scams (eg serious overcharging) on the Vietnamese side. Devious drivers have even stopped in the middle of nowhere to renegotiate the price.

Transport links on both sides of the border can be hit and miss, so don't use the more remote borders unless you have plenty of time, and patience, to spare.

ⓘ Getting Around

AIR

Vietnam has good domestic flight connections, and very affordable prices (if you book early). Airlines accept bookings on international credit or debit cards. However, note that cancellations are not unknown.

Vietnam Airlines, Jetstar and Vietjet are the main carriers, while Vasco provides additional services.

Jetstar Airways (☑1900 1550; www.jetstar.com) Budget airline with affordable fares, but serves a limited number of destinations.
Vasco (☑038 422 790; www.vasco.com.vn) Connects HCMC with the Con Dao Islands and the Mekong Delta.
Vietjet Air (☑1900 1886; www.vietjetair.com) An expanding number of internal flights.
Vietnam Airlines (www.vietnamairlines.com.vn) The leading local carrier is the most reliable and has the most comprehensive network.

BICYCLE

Bikes are a great way to get around Vietnam, particularly when you get off the main highways.

The main hazard is the traffic, and it's wise to avoid certain areas (notably Hwy 1). Some of the best cycling is along quiet coastal roads in Central Vietnam, in the Southwest Highlands and up in the northern mountains (although you'll have to cope with some big hills here). The Mekong Delta is a rewarding option for those who like it flat.

Purchasing a good bicycle in Vietnam is hit-and-miss. It's recommended that you bring one from abroad, along with a quality helmet and spare parts.

Bicycles can be rented from guesthouses for about US$2 per day while good-quality mountain bikes cost US$10 to US$12.

BOAT

In the north, cruises on Halong Bay or Lan Ha Bay area are extremely popular and should not be missed. Hydrofoils also connect Haiphong with Cat Ba Island (near Halong Bay). Day trips by boat to islands off the coast of Nha Trang and to the Chams off Hoi An are also worthwhile.

The extensive network of canals in the Mekong Delta makes getting around by boat feasible. Travellers to Phu Quoc Island can catch ferries from Ha Tien or Rach Gia.

BUS

Vietnam has an extensive network of buses that reach the far-flung corners of the country. Modern buses, operated by myriad companies, run on all the main highways.

Many travellers (perhaps the majority) never actually visit a Vietnamese bus station at all, preferring to stick to the convenient, tourist-friendly open-tour bus network.

Whichever class of bus you're on, bus travel in Vietnam is never speedy; reckon on just 50km/h on major routes including Hwy 1.

Bus Stations

Many cities have several bus stations – make sure you go to the right one! Bus stations all look chaotic, but many now have ticket offices with official prices and departure times displayed.

Reservations & Costs

Always buy a ticket from the office, as bus drivers are notorious for overcharging. Reservations aren't usually required for most of the frequent, popular services between towns and cities.

On rural runs foreigners are typically charged anywhere from twice to 10 times the going rate. As a benchmark, a typical 100km ride should be between US$2 and US$3.

Bus Types

On most popular routes, modern air-conditioned Korean and Chinese deluxe buses offer comfortable reclining seats, while sleeper buses have padded flat beds for really long trips.

Deluxe buses are nonsmoking. On the flip side, most of them are equipped with blaring TVs.

Connecting backpacker haunts across the nation, open-tour buses are wildly popular in Vietnam. These air-con buses use convenient, centrally located departure points and allow you to hop-on, hop-off at any major city along the main north to south route. Prices are reasonable. An open-tour ticket from Ho Chi Minh City to Hanoi costs between US$25 and US$45, Nha Trang to Hoi An around US$12. Travellers' cafes, tour agencies and budget hotels sell tickets. **Sinh Tourist** (✍ 08-3838 9597; www.thesinh-tourist.com) started the concept and has a good reputation.

Local buses in the countryside are slow and stop frequently. Conductors tend to routinely overcharge foreigners on these local services.

CAR & MOTORCYCLE

Having your own set of wheels gives you maximum flexibility to visit remote regions and stop when and where you please. Car hire always includes a driver. Motorbike hire is good value and this can be self-drive or with a driver.

Driving Licence

In order to drive in Vietnam, you officially need a Vietnamese licence and an International Driving Permit (IDP). However, all rental companies only rent out cars with drivers.

When it comes to renting motorbikes, the whole situation is a grey area. An IDP and motorbike licence (which includes a test in the Vietnamese language) is officially required, but the reality on the ground is that foreigners are never asked for it by police, and no rental places ever ask to see one.

Car & Minibus

Renting a vehicle with a driver is a realistic option (even for budget travellers) if you share the cost.

Costs per day:

Standard model US$60 to US$100
4WD/minibus US$90 to US$130

Motorbike

Motorbikes can be rented from virtually anywhere, including cafes, hotels and travel agencies. Some places will ask to keep your passport as security. Ask for a signed agreement stating what you are renting, how much it costs, the extent of compensation and so on.

It is compulsory to wear a helmet when riding a motorbike in Vietnam, even when travelling as a passenger.

Costs per day:

Moped (semi-auto) US$4 to US$6
Moped (fully auto) US$6 to US$10
Trail and road bikes From US$15 to US$30

Plenty of local drivers will be willing to act as a chauffeur and guide for US$10 to US$20 per day too.

Insurance

If you are travelling in a tourist vehicle with a driver, then it is almost guaranteed to be insured. When it comes to motorbikes, many rental bikes are not insured, and you may have to sign a contract agreeing to a valuation for the bike if it is stolen.

Road Conditions & Hazards

Road safety is definitely not one of Vietnam's strong points. Vehicles drive on the right-hand side (in theory). Size matters and small vehicles get out of the way of big vehicles. Even Hwy 1 is only a two-lane highway for most of its length and collisions are common.

MOTORBIKE & 4WD TOURS

Specialised motorbike tours offer an unrivalled way to explore Vietnam's scenic excesses on traffic-light backroads. Many of the leading companies also offer tuition for first-timers.

Explore Indochina (☎ 09-1309 3159; www.exploreindochina.com) Expertly arranged trips on vintage Urals or modified Minsks. Jeep tours are also offered.

Free Wheelin' Tours (Map p818; ☎ 04-3926 2743; www.freewheelin-tours.com; 2 P Ta Hien, Hoan Kiem District, Hanoi; ⊙ 10am-7pm) Motorbike and 4WD tours around the north.

Hoi An Motorbike Adventures (☎ 0510-391 1930; www.motorbiketours-hoian.com; 111 Ba Trieu) Specialises in short tours and day trips (from US$40) on cult Minsk motorbikes. The guides really know the terrain.

Offroad Vietnam (☎ 04-3926 3433; www.offroadvietnam.com) Well-organised tours to remote areas. Also rents quality Honda road bikes (from US$20).

In general, the major highways are hard surfaced and reasonably well maintained, but seasonal flooding can be a problem. Nonpaved roads are best tackled with a 4WD vehicle or motorbike. Mountain roads are particularly dangerous: landslides, falling rocks and runaway vehicles can add an unwelcome edge to your journey.

LOCAL TRANSPORT
Cyclos
These are bicycle rickshaws. Drivers hang out in touristy areas and some speak broken English. Bargaining is imperative; settle on a fare before going anywhere. A short ride should be 10,000d to 20,000d in most places.

Taxis
Metered taxis are found in all cities and are very, very cheap by international standards and a safe way to travel around at night. Average tariffs are about 10,000d to 15,000d per kilometre. Only travel with reputable or recommended companies, **Mai Linh** (www.mailinh.vn) and **Vinasun** (www.vinasuntaxi.com) are two excellent nationwide firms.

Xe Om
Motorbike taxis are everywhere. Fares are comparable with those for a *cyclo*. Drivers hang around street corners, markets, hotels and bus stations. They will find you before you find them.

TOURS
The following are Vietnam-based travel agencies that offer tours throughout Vietnam:

Handspan Adventure Travel (☎ 04-3926 2828; www.handspan.com) Expert locally owned company.

Ocean Tours (☎ 04-3926 0463; www.oceantours.com.vn) Halong Bay and Ba Be National Park options.

Buffalo Tours (Map p818; www.buffalotours.com) Diverse and customised trips.

TRAIN
The railway system, operated by **Vietnam Railways** (Duong Sat Viet Nam; ☎ 04-3747 0308; www.vr.com.vn), is an ageing, slow, but pretty dependable service, and offers a relaxing way to get around the nation. Travelling in an air-con sleeping berth sure beats a hairy overnight bus journey along Hwy 1. And there's spectacular scenery to lap up too.

Routes
The main line connects HCMC with Hanoi. Three rail-spur lines link Hanoi with other parts of northern Vietnam: Haiphong, Lang Son and Lao Cai.

The train journey between Hanoi and HCMC takes from 30 to 41 hours, depending on the train.

Classes & Costs
Trains classified as SE are the smartest and fastest. There are four main ticket classes: hard seat, soft seat, hard sleeper and soft sleeper. These classes are further split according to whether or not they have air-conditioning. Presently, air-con is only available on the faster express trains. Hard-seat class is usually packed. It's tolerable for day travel, but expect plenty of cigarette smoke.

Ticket prices vary depending on the train; the fastest trains are the most expensive.

Reservations
You cannot buy tickets in advance from Vietnam Railways, but agencies can make bookings. Reservations for all trips should be made at least one day in advance. For sleeping berths, it's wise to book several days before the date of departure.

Schedules, fares, information and advance bookings are available at Vietnam Railway (p831) and Vietnam Impressive (p831), two dependable private booking agents. They'll deliver tickets to your hotel in Vietnam free of charge (or can send them abroad using DHL for a fee).

Many travel agencies, hotels and cafes will also buy you train tickets for a small commission.

Understand Southeast Asia

Southeast Asia Today

The Southeast Asian nations sailed through the global economic downturn but are now facing an uncertain future as once hot-blooded economies are developing cold feet. In general, though, the region continues to develop better infrastructure, more modern economies, a higher standard of living and a better educated, cosmopolitan population even if the economic tea leaves are unpromising.

Best in Print

Eat, Pray, Love (2006) Elizabeth Gilbert's book that kindled a love affair with Bali.

The Killing Fields (1984) Based on a real-life tale of the Khmer Rouge takeover.

Burmese Days (1934) George Orwell's classic tale of close-minded colonials living in Burma.

Saving Fish From Drowning (2009) Amy Tan's deceased main character leads readers on a 'guided' tour from San Francisco to Burma.

The Beach (1998) Alex Garland's now-classic tale about a backpacker utopia in southern Thailand.

Best on Film

Apocalypse Now (1979) Set in Vietnam, filmed in the Philippines; it is the classic-rock of war flicks.

The Lady (2011) A French-directed biopic about Myanmar's democracy leader Aung San Suu Kyi.

Fable of the Fish (2011) A Filipino film set in the slums of Manila with a magic-realism plot.

36 (2012) Experimental Thai film about lost love through recovered memories.

Berbagi Suamia (2006) An Indonesian film-fest winner about a polygamous marriage.

The Region's Economic Temperature

On average, Southeast Asian economies rack up an impressive 5% growth rate, but the end of 2013 brought some disappointing financial news.

Vietnam's economy, once turbo-charged, is slowing, with a two-year period of less growth than Indonesia and the Philippines. No stranger to the economic roller coaster, Indonesia is the region's largest economy but it has gone from being heralded as a global star to a potential invalid. Growth has slowed to 5.8% and rising fuel prices and a weakening currency have economists worrying about a potential bubble burst.

Super-typhoon Yolanda (Haiyan) has damaged more than just lives and livelihoods in the Philippines. It has destroyed a third of the country's rice fields and nearly drowned the country's economic growth prospects. Losses are estimated at US$12 to US$15 billion, an insurmountable sum in a country that lacks comprehensive property insurance that would underwrite rebuilding efforts.

Thailand's economy fell into recession in 2013. Government stimulus after the devastating 2011 floods tapered off and rising costs of living along with increased consumer debt have cut into consumer demand. Political tensions have also heated up with yet another round of large-scale protests occupying Bangkok and worrying foreign investors.

For the region's poorest countries, the economic outlook is bright. Cambodia's economy continues to expand with a strong textile industry, growing tourism and service sector, and even a profitable year for agriculture. Cambodia is expected to be reclassified as a lower-middle income economy (based on GDP per capita). Laos still saunters on the outskirts of the global marketplace. It's economy remains dominated by subsistence agriculture.

Ever-capable Singapore posted strong economic growth, heralded as a sign that the global recession is lessening since the city-state is the region's largest trader.

Malaysia, the region's third-largest economy, fared better than expected but has one of the region's highest debt-to-GDP ratios.

Open Wide

Coming in 2015, the Asian Economic Community (AEC) will unite the association's 10 Southeast Asian countries into a liberalised marketplace to increase competitiveness. The AEC will remove restrictions on the movement of goods, services and skilled workers and streamline customs. AEC was inspired by the European Union model but there are no plans for a regional central bank, single currency or governing body.

Myanmar is poised to be one of the largest recipients of regional investment. Thailand and Myanmar have enjoyed commercial cooperation since the turn of the millennium and that relationship will increase as the two countries work to secure funding for the Dawei Port Project, a deep-sea port in southern Myanmar, and build infrastructure linking it with Bangkok.

To meet AEC requirements, Myanmar has lifted some of its border regulations, allowing foreigners to cross into the country at land borders with Thailand and exit through a different land or air border. Previously Myanmar funnelled visitors through the airport in Yangon. As a result, international flights have begun to service Mandalay and Nay Pyi Taw. Relaxed border regulations are just one of Myanmar's exciting new developments.

Moving Towards a Single Visa?

As the AEC introduces visa-free entry for Asean nationals, there have been talks about a single visa for the region, but presently only Thailand and Cambodia have reached a bilateral agreement.

The Era of Natural Disasters

Tsunamis, typhoons, cyclones – the ocean has not been kind to the land masses of Southeast Asia lately. And then there are earthquakes, erupting volcanoes and seasonal flooding. It is a disaster movie without the fantasy. The deadliest natural disaster of recorded time was the 2004 Indian Ocean tsunami. A massive 9.0 magnitude earthquake struck off the coast of Sumatra (Indonesia) and triggered a tsunami that travelled across the entire Indian Ocean, killing 230,000 people and affecting five Southeast Asian countries (Indonesia, Thailand, Malaysia, Myanmar and Singapore) as well as South Asia and the east coast of Africa. The earthquake was so powerful that the entire planet vibrated from its force.

Smaller but costly disasters have occurred on an almost annual basis since. In 2010 there were six natural disasters that affected five countries in the region. In 2011, the world suffered US$270 billion of economic losses associated with natural disasters, 90% of which was in Asia due in large part to massive flooding in Thailand's manufacturing centre. In 2013, super-typhoon Yolanda (Haiyan) was yet another sad instalment in the disaster saga.

POPULATION:
593,400,000

COMBINED GDP:
US$1.9 TRILLION

GDP PER CAPITA:
SINGAPORE US$51,709
CAMBODIA US$946

UNEMPLOYMENT:
CAMBODIA 0.1%
PHILIPPINES 7.3%

ANNUAL INFLATION:
SINGAPORE 1.60%
INDONESIA 8.32%

economy
(% of GDP)

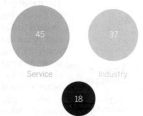

45 Service

37 Industry

18 Agriculture

if Southeast Asia were 100 people

39 would be Muslim
36 would be Buddhist
18 would be other
7 would be Christian

population per sq km

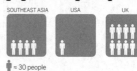

SOUTHEAST ASIA   USA   UK

= 30 people

History

Sitting at the crossroads of land and sea routes, the Southeast Asian nations share unifying historic themes: they have traded, adopted religions, paid tribute, repulsed invaders, become colonies of foreign interests and declared independence. The mainland is united by religious associations and historic empires, while the island nations struggle with diversity within their respective archipelagos. Today they are dynamic economies transitioning with various rates of speed from subsistence farming into modern and prosperous nations with expanding tourism sectors.

Early Kingdoms

The mainland Southeast Asian countries owe much of their early historical happenings to the more dominant civilisations of China and India. As early as 150 BC, China and India interacted with the scattered Southeast Asian communities for trade and tribute. Vietnam, within short reach of China, was a subject, student and reluctant offspring of its more powerful neighbour for more than 1000 years. India, on the other hand, conquered by spiritual means, spreading Hinduism, Buddhism and later Islam across the region, and influencing art and architecture.

Several highly organised states emerged in the region as a result of contact with India. From the 7th to the 9th centuries AD, the Srivijaya empire controlled all shipping through the Java Sea from its capital at Palembang in southeast Sumatra. The Srivijaya capital was also a religious centre for Mahayana Buddhism (Greater Vehicle Buddhism) and attracted scholars as well as merchants.

But the region's most famous empire emerged in the interior of present-day Cambodia. The Khmer empire ruled the land for four centuries, consuming territory and labour to build unparalleled and enduring Hindu-Buddhist monuments to its god-kings. Eventually the Khmer empire included most of what is now Thailand, Laos and Cambodia. Its economy was based on agriculture, and a sophisticated irrigation system cultivated vast tracts of land around Tonlé Sap (Great Lake). Attacks from emerging city-states on the Thai frontier contributed to the decline of the empire and the abandonment of the Angkor capital.

Ancient Capitals

Angkor (Cambodia)

Sukhothai (Thailand)

Bagan (Myanmar)

My Son (Vietnam)

TIMELINE	2800–100 BC	AD 802	1025
	Ancestors of modern Southeast Asians begin to migrate south from China and Tibet, populating river valleys and coastal areas and organising small city-states.	King Jayavarman consolidates the Khmer empire in parts of present-day Cambodia, Thailand, Myanmar and Malaysia that supplants the local Funan state.	Srivijaya empire is toppled by the Chola kingdom of South India, creating a power vacuum for the rise of smaller regional entities and the introduction of Islam.

The Classical & Colonial Period

As the larger powers withered, Southeast Asia entered an age of cultural definition and international influence. Regional kingdoms created distinctive works of art and literature, and joined the international sphere as important ports. The Thais expanded into the dying Khmer empire and exerted control over parts of Cambodia, Laos and Myanmar. Starting around 1331, the Hindu kingdom of Majapahit united the Indonesian archipelago from Sumatra to New Guinea and dominated the trade routes between India and China. The kingdom's reign continued until the advent of Islamic kingdoms and the emergence of the port town of Melaka on the Malay peninsula in 1402. Melaka's prosperity soon attracted European interest, and it fell first to the Portuguese in 1511, then the Dutch and finally the English.

Initially these European nations were only interested in controlling shipping in the region, usually brokering agreements and alliances with local authorities. Centred on Java and Sumatra, the Dutch monopolised European commerce with Asia for 200 years. The Spanish, French and later the English had civilisation and proselytising on their minds. Spain occupied the Philippines archipelago, Britain steadily rolled through India, Myanmar and the Malay peninsula, while the Dutch grasped Indonesia to cement a presence in the region. And France, with a foothold in Vietnam, usurped Cambodia and Laos to form Indochina.

Although its sphere of influence was diminished, Thailand was the only Southeast Asian nation to remain independent. One reason for this was that England and France agreed to leave Thailand as a 'buffer' between their two colonies. Credit is also frequently given to the Thai kings who Westernised the country and played competing European powers against each other.

Independence Movements

The 20th century and WWII signalled an end to European domination in Southeast Asia. As European power receded, the Japanese expanded control throughout the region, invading Thailand, Malaysia and Indonesia. After the war, the power vacuums in formerly colonised countries provided leverage for a region-wide independence movement. Vietnam and Indonesia clamoured most violently for freedom, resulting in long-term wars with their respective colonial powers. For the latter half of the 20th century, Vietnam fought almost uninterrupted conflicts against foreign powers. After the French were defeated by communist nationals, Vietnam faced civil war and the intervention of the USA, which hoped to contain the spread of communism within the region. Cambodia's civil

European Hill Stations

Sapa
(Vietnam)

Cameron Highlands
(Malaysia)

Bokor National Park
(Cambodia)

13th century	1511	1939–45	1946–65
The beginning of the decline of the Khmer empire and rise of powerful states in modern-day Thailand and Vietnam.	Melaka falls to the Portuguese and marks the beginning of colonial expansion in the region by such European powers as the Dutch, Spanish, French and British.	WWII; Japan occupies much of Southeast Asia using Thailand as a cooperative base and Malaysia and Indonesia as a source of conscripts.	Post-war Europe withdraws from the region, ushering in independence movements. First, the Philippines gains independence followed by Myanmar, Indonesia, the countries of Indochina, Malaysia and Singapore.

war ended in one of the worst nightmares of modern times, with the ascension of the Khmer Rouge. The revolutionary army evacuated the cities, separated families into labour camps and closed the country off from the rest of the world. An estimated 1.7 million people were killed by the regime during its brief four-year term (1975–79).

Many of the newly liberated countries struggled to unite a land mass that shared only a colonial legacy. Dictatorships in Myanmar, Indonesia and the Philippines thwarted the populace's hopes for representative governments and civil liberties. Civilian rioters, minority insurgents and communist guerrillas further provoked the unstable governments, and the internal chaos was usually agitated by the major superpowers: China, the Soviet Union and the USA.

Modern Industrial Era

Near the turn of the current millennium, the region entered a period of unprecedented economic growth. Singapore, along with Hong Kong and South Korea, was classified as an 'Asian Tiger' economy – export-driven countries experiencing as much as 7% annual growth in gross domestic product. Emerging tigers included Thailand, Malaysia, Indonesia and, to a lesser extent, the Philippines. These countries were quickly industrialising and beginning to dominate sophisticated manufacturing sectors such as automobile, machinery and electronics production.

Born in 1967, the Association of Southeast Asian Nations (Asean) is a regional cooperation organisation that includes 10 member countries (excluding Timor-Leste).

In 1997, the upward trend was derailed by a currency crisis. Thailand's baht was the first currency to crash (falling from 50B/US$1 to 25B/US$1); neighbouring currencies soon followed. A period of economic retraction and financial austerity restored these developing economies to a more sustainable footing. More than a decade since the economic crash of 1997, many of the former tigers have become house cats, enjoying respectable GDP growth of about 5%, foreign investment, and an increasingly affluent and educated population.

The formerly cloistered countries of Vietnam, Laos and Cambodia began to open up in the mid- to late 1990s and have experienced various degrees of economic success and industrialisation. Vietnam continues to be a determined capitalist engine with an ever-expanding economy and a youthful optimism that counteracts government inefficiencies.

Laos woke up from its backwater slumber to find that China needed it for natural resources; the landlocked country is quickly becoming a trading crossroads with neighbouring markets. Increased infrastructure is helping Laos and its comrade-in-tragedy Cambodia develop a thriving tourism sector that has matured from low-budget adventurers to high-end jet-setters. In addition to tourism, the two countries still depend largely on small-scale agriculture with some industrialisation in the textile industry. Both lag behind their neighbours in terms of economic

1955–1975	1999	2002	2004
The US becomes involved in Vietnam's civil war as an anti-communism effort. Laos and Cambodia become peripherally involved. The US withdraws after the fall of Saigon to North Vietnamese troops.	Timor-Leste votes for independence from Indonesian occupiers. An international peace-keeping force enters the country to prevent violence.	Bombing of a tourist district in Bali by members of the anti-Western Islamic group Jemaah Islamiyah kills 202 people, mostly Australians.	An Indian Ocean earthquake with its epicentre near Sumatra (Indonesia) triggers a giant tsunami that affects four Southeast Asian countries.

growth and standard of living and are still classified by the UN as being among the poorest countries in the world.

Indonesia and the Philippines rode the first wave of post-colonial development, stalled during the 1997 economic crisis and then became the region's classic underachievers. Both have incredible natural resource wealth but are hampered by ethnic conflicts, corruption, political instability, vast geography and a diverse populace.

Trouble Spots

In general, Southeast Asia is safer now than it was during the communist era of the mid-20th century or during the Islamic terror attacks in the early 2000s.

Between 2002 and 2005, Indonesia suffered civilian-targeted, allegedly Jemaah Islamiyah (JI) linked bombings on an annual basis. The militant Islamic group JI, which was formed in the 1990s with a mission to establish a pan-Islamic state, was believed to have links with Al Qaeda and its global jihad. The group turned to civilian terror tactics in the 2000s and allegedly orchestrated multiple bombing attacks in Indonesia and the Philippines.

The worst event occurred in October 2002 on the island of Bali, where suicide bombers targeted a crowded nightclub, killing 202 people and injuring hundreds more, mostly Australian tourists. After massive arrests, the mainstream faction of JI has since turned away from Western targets and many senior leaders are evading joint Philippines and Indonesian manhunts. In 2010, Abu Bakar Bashir, alleged to be the spiritual leader of JI, was sentenced to 15 years in jail for his involvement in a terror-training camp in Aceh. The Muslim cleric had previously served reduced, almost nominal, sentences on conspiracy charges for the 2002 Bali bombing. This latest conviction is viewed by Western allies as a restoration of justice.

In the southern Philippines, mainly the island of Mindanao and the Sulu Archipelago, there are several active Islamic insurgency groups. In 2012, the Filipino government reached a preliminary peace deal with one of the nationalist groups, but rival factions that oppose government negotiations waged a week-long streak of violence that displaced 100,000 people.

Since 2004, the Muslim-dominated areas of southern Thailand (Narathiwat, Pattani, Yala and parts of Songkhla) have waged an ethnonationalist struggle. In 2013, talks between the self-proclaimed leaders of the insurgency and the government began, followed by an upturn in violence.

Historical Reads
....

Southeast Asia: An Introductory History (Milton Osborne)
....
In Search of Southeast Asia: A Modern History (David P Chandler, et al)
....
Southeast Asia: Past and Present (DR SarDesai)

2008	2012	2013	2015
Cyclone Nargis kills 138,000 people and causes US$10 billion in damages, qualifying as Myanmar's worst natural disaster.	Western leaders begin visiting Myanmar in support of the country's ongoing normalisation. Tourism expands with record numbers of visitors, increasingly from China.	Super-typhoon Yolanda (Haiyan) crushes central Philippines, leaving an estimated 6200 dead and four million displaced.	Asean Economic Community (AEC) goes into effect, uniting the region into a common marketplace.

People & Culture

Southeast Asia is a culturally rich region that encompasses most of the world's religions with a special tropical flair. Colourful artistic traditions date back to a period of regional empires, when kings and sultans were cultural patrons. Akin to the region's personality, each country's culture chest is generously shared with curious outsiders. There is also a fascinating interplay between ancient traditions and modern sensibilities in the rural villages and dense urban cities that provide insightful perspectives.

People

Within the dominant cultures of Southeast Asia are minority groups that remain in isolated pockets or cultural islands. Regarded as the Jews of Asia, ethnic Chinese have long filtered into the region as merchants and labourers, establishing distinct neighbourhoods within their host communities and perpetuating their mother country's language and customs.

Every small town has a Chinatown (typically the main business district). In places such as Malaysia and Singapore, the Chinese diaspora has morphed into a distinct entity, termed Straits Chinese, which refers to the inter-marrying of Chinese and Malay couples. This union is most obvious in the kitchen, where traditional Chinese dishes have a distinctly Malay flair. Lunar Chinese festivals are celebrated throughout the region and Chinese temples appear alongside the dominant religious buildings. While most countries derive cultural and commercial strength from Chinese immigrants, in times of economic hardship, especially in Malaysia and Indonesia, ethnic Chinese have been targets of abuse for their prosperity and ethnic differences. Ethnic Indians from the southern provinces of Tamil Nadu have also settled along the Malay peninsula and Bangkok.

High up in the mountains that run through Myanmar, Laos, Thailand and Vietnam, a diverse mix of minority groups, collectively referred to as hill tribes, maintain ancient customs, speak their own tribal languages and wear traditional clothing. Believed to have migrated from the Himalayas or southern China, hill-tribe communities such as the Akha, Karen and Hmong were isolated from the dominant

INVASION OF PERSONAL SPACE

Southeast Asia might be known for its easy-going nature but it is a pressure cooker when it comes to personal space. Tight quarters are everywhere – public transport, city streets and markets – and people are always squeezing into spaces that already seem filled to capacity. You might think that the minivan is full but the driver will shoehorn in three more sweaty bodies before he careens off towards the horizon.

There are no queues. Customers crowd around the vendor, handing over money or barking orders. And they think Westerners are dim for standing around wide-eyed waiting for someone to pay attention to them. Southeast Asians fill empty spaces like flowing water, never leaving a gap, and they exhibit a Zen-like calm on cheek-to-jowl bus rides.

culture until the latter half of the 20th century. They were often considered nuisances by the central governments because of their cultural non-conformity, their involvement in illicit poppy cultivation (used to make opium and heroin) and their political opposition, which was leveraged by outsiders during the war in Vietnam. Myanmar has the largest concentration of hill-tribe groups and until recently many of these groups were engaged in a long-standing resistance war against the central government.

A host of minority tribes occupies the diverse archipelago nations of Indonesia and the Philippines. In some islands, a bus ride to the next town places the visitor in an entirely new ethnically dominated place. Maintaining a cohesive identity from such diversity is crucial to the character of these two countries.

Lifestyle

The diverse countries of Southeast Asia share the unifying characteristics of developing nations. Foreign visitors have varying reactions to the Third World's low standard of living and the great disparity that exists between the haves and the have-nots.

In the rural areas, life is still tied to the agricultural clock with deep roots in a home village. In these communities multi-generational households are the norm and distinct animistic customs are ingrained in daily life. Rice farming, especially with crude tools such as ploughs drawn by water buffalo, is difficult work that typically affords only a subsistence lifestyle.

Increasingly, though, the region is moving towards a more urban and industrialised way of life. Southeast Asian cities, except for Singapore, are studies in disorder and dysfunction, and are fascinating places for their faults. In the cities, the rich live modern air-conditioned lives while the poor huddle in makeshift slums in abandoned land that lacks proper sewage or water treatment. In between is the middle class, usually educated government workers who can afford terrace house apartments.

Thailand and Vietnam, Malaysia and Singapore are considered lower-middle, upper-middle and high-income countries, respectively. In real terms, these countries have enjoyed half a millennium of stable governments and relatively prosperous economies. Laos and Cambodia are still tipped toward the poorer end of the scale.

Indonesia and the Philippines are both lower-middle economies but they are stories unto themselves because of their diverse geography and ethnic make-up. Certain islands are prosperous and modern while others are remote and undeveloped. Myanmar is just beginning its voyage into the global economy as it emerges from its decades-long isolation.

Identity

Like a symphony orchestra, Southeast Asian society focuses on group identity rather than the independent self-determination favoured by Western cultures. Social harmony is ensured by the concept of 'face' – avoiding embarrassing yourself or others by being non-confrontational. This translates into everyday life by not showing anger or frustration and avoiding serious debates that could cause offence. Keeping calm in stressful situations is a cultural ideal. Once you've spent time in the region you will appreciate the undercurrent of peace that this approach provides to an otherwise chaotic landscape.

Religion

Religion is a fundamental component of the national and ethnic identities of the people in Southeast Asia. Buddhism and Islam are the

PEOPLE & CULTURE RELIGION

Top Flicks

Opera Jawa (2006, Indonesia)

Living In Fear (2005, Vietnam)

Thy Womb (2012, Philippines)

The Missing Picture (2013, Cambodia)

Uncle Boonmee Who Can Recall His Past Lives (2011, Thailand)

Bayanihan is a Filipino term meaning 'communal work', a beloved term evoked during the relief efforts following super-typhoon Yolanda (Haiyan).

PRINCELY TALES

The literary epic of the Ramayana serves as cultural fodder for traditional art, dance and shadow puppetry throughout the region. In this fantastic tale, Prince Rama (an incarnation of the Hindu god Vishnu) falls in love with beautiful Sita and wins her hand in marriage by completing the challenge of stringing a magic bow. Before the couple can live in peace, Rama is banished from his kingdom and his wife is kidnapped by Ravana. With the help of the monkey king, Hanuman, Sita is rescued, but a great battle ensues. Rama and his allies defeat Ravana and restore peace and goodness to the land.

region's dominant religions and both have absorbed many of the traditional animistic beliefs of spirit and ancestor worship that predate the region's conversions. Christianity is present in former colonies of Catholic European countries and among ethnic minorities converted by the missionaries.

Buddhism

Buddhism is the majority religion in most of mainland Southeast Asia, and because many of these countries are cultural cousins the religion has a specific regional identity. Outside of the Buddhist majority countries, there are also minority Buddhist populations, mainly ethnic Chinese, in the Philippines, Indonesia, Malaysia and Brunei.

History & Fundamentals of Buddhism

Buddhism begins with the story of an Indian prince named Siddhartha Gautama in the 6th century BC, who left his life of privilege at the age of 29 on a quest to find the truth. After years of experimentation and ascetic practices, he meditated under a bodhi tree for 49 days, reaching final emancipation and breaking the cycle of birth, death and rebirth. He returned as Buddha, the 'Awakened One', to teach the 'middle way' between extremes. Passion, desire, love and hate are regarded as extremes, so Buddhism counsels that constant patience, detachment, and renouncing desire for worldly pleasures and expectations brings peace and liberation from suffering.

The ultimate end of Buddhism is nirvana, which literally means the 'blowing out' or extinction of all grasping and thus of all suffering (*dukkha*). Effectively, nirvana is also an end to the cycle of rebirths (both moment-to-moment and life-to-life) that is existence.

ANIMIST BELIEFS

Animist beliefs were absorbed into Buddhism and comprise many religious rituals, from tending family altars and spirit houses to consulting monk astrologers.

Conversion to Buddhism

The adoption of Buddhism followed the same route into Southeast Asia as Hinduism – through traders and missionaries from India and Sri Lanka. The Khmer empire's adoption of Buddhism during King Jayavarman's reign in the 12th century marked the beginning of the religion's dominance. The subsequent Thai and Lao kings promoted the religion and were often viewed as divine religious figures as well as national leaders. Most of the monarchies did not survive into the modern era but the religion did, with 90% or more of the population in each mainland Southeast Asian country identifying as Buddhist.

Thailand, Cambodia, Laos and Myanmar practise Theravada Buddhism (Teaching of the Elders), which travelled to the region via Sri Lanka. Vietnam adopted Mahayana Buddhism (Greater Vehicle), which took a northern route through Tibet, China and Japan. Though in practice, most Vietnamese practise a fusion of Confucianism, Taoism and Buddhism, collectively known as the Triple Religion.

One of the major theological differences between the two types of Buddhism lies in the outcome of a devout life. In Theravada, followers strive to obtain nirvana (release from the cycle of existence) over the course of many reincarnations, the final one of which is as a member of the monastic order. The emphasis is on self-enlightenment. But in Mahayana tradition, nirvana can be achieved within a single lifetime and emphasis is on helping other sentient beings become enlightened. With this emphasis on teaching, more attention is given to bodhisattva (one who has almost reached nirvana but renounces it in order to help others attain it).

This doctrinal difference and country of origin can be viewed in the two schools' places of worship. Theravada temples typically have one central hall of worship containing a central (Gautama) Buddha image. Hindu elements inherited from South Asia infuse the Theravada religious art and architecture. Mahayana temples conform more to inherited aesthetics from China. Temples contain a hall dedicated to the three Buddhas (including modern incarnations Amitabha and Medicine Buddha) and another hall to the three important bodhisattvas.

Buddhist Monuments

Temples of Angkor, Cambodia

Borobudur, Indonesia

Bagan, Myanmar

Sukhothai Historical Park, Thailand

PEOPLE & CULTURE RELIGION

Islam

Islam in Southeast Asia is characterised by the region's unique cultural, historical and philosophical landscape. For this reason, many Westerners notice a vast difference between the way Islam is practised in Southeast Asia compared with the way it is practised in other parts of the Muslim world (such as the Middle East).

History & Fundamentals of Islam

Islam is a monotheistic religion that originated in Arabia in the 7th century. The religion's primary prophet is Mohammed, who received and promoted the word of God (the Quran, the holy book of the faith). Islam means 'submission' in Arabic, and it is the duty of every Muslim to submit to Allah (God). This profession of faith is the first of the five pillars of Islam; the other four are to pray five times a day, give alms to the poor, fast during Ramadan and make the pilgrimage to Mecca.

Conversion to Islam

Trade played an important role in the introduction of the religion. Many Southeast Asian communities converted to Islam in order to join a brotherhood of merchants (Muslim Arabs, Indians and Chinese) and to escape the inflexible caste system of the Srivijaya kingdom, a Hindu-Buddhist empire that controlled the Malay peninsula and parts of Indonesia. It is believed that Muslim conversions and settlements first occurred in northern Sumatra's Aceh province and then spread to the port cities, including the important trade and cultural centre of Melaka (Malaysia). Starting around the 12th century, Islam gained in popularity,

THE FACE OF MODERN ISLAM

Just going by the numbers, modern Islam is a lot more Asian than Arab. In fact only 15% of the world's Muslims are Arab, while the majority are South and Southeast Asians. If the media were looking for a model citizen, they could choose Indonesia, which has the largest population of Muslims in the world (it's home to 12% of the world's Muslims). It is a devout country and sends the largest national delegation of pilgrims to Mecca every year. But it is also a multinational, multi-ethnic and multi-religious democratic country – more like Turkey than Saudi Arabia.

Top Museums

Asian Civilisations Museum (Singapore)

Islamic Arts Museum (Malaysia)

Vietnam Museum of Ethnology (Vietnam)

Jim Thompson's House (Thailand)

spreading through Malaysia to southern Thailand, Indonesia and parts of the Philippines.

The mystical traditions of Sufism are often credited for this widespread adoption of Islam. Sufis were itinerant holy men ('suf' is an Arabic word for the 'coarse wool' worn by a religious ascetic) who were believed to have magic abilities and encouraged a personal expression of the religion instead of a strict orthodoxy and adherence to the law. Scholars believe that Sufis helped mould traditional beliefs and folk practices stemming from the region's Hindu-Buddhist past around an Islamic core, instead of forcing local communities to abandon pre-Islamic practices. Chanting and drumming remain a component of Southeast Asia's Islamic prayer tradition; shadow puppetry adopted Arabic and Islamic stories as well as the original Hindu myths; the ideas of the annihilation of the ego and of nirvana were tweaked to fit Islamic theology. Women were never cloistered and retained their traditional roles outside the home. In the past, the older generation did not wear headscarves, but the younger generation has adopted the practice, much to the concern of non-Muslim observers who fear an increased regional fundamentalism.

Political Islam

The practice of Islam in Southeast Asia has been characterised by many of the same tensions that have emerged in Muslim communities around the world. Debates continue to rage about the interpretation of various passages in the Quran, and their implications for legal, social and financial institutions. As the region's colonial era was waning, the reform movement of Wahhabism became a popular political tool. Wahhabism promoted a literal interpretation of the Quran and intended to purge the religion of its pagan practices. It also emphasised the development of an Islamic political state.

Integral to an Islamic political state is Sharia (Islamic law or God's law), which regulates criminal, civil and personal conduct. There are debates within the Muslim world as to the exact extents of Sharia and how to overlap contradictory elements within a modern pluralistic state. A few indisputable components are the abstinence from pork products, drinking and gambling, as well as modesty in dress, though the last is also subject to local and generational interpretation.

Within Southeast Asia, Sharia justice systems are on the rise. Malaysia has long maintained a parallel Sharia system applied to Muslim Malays only, though there are censorship rules that often cross over into mainstream film and print media. Indonesia does not have national Sharia, but it does allow the province of Aceh to enforce partial Sharia under the terms of the 2005 peace deal. The Philippines government has proposed a similar agreement with the Moro people on the southern island of Mindanao as part of its 2013 peace agreement.

Most of Brunei's criminal system is based on a British model, but over the last five years it has increasingly adopted Islamic laws and punishments, including hand amputation for thefts and public stoning.

Violent low-scale wars exist in the Muslim-majority region of southern Thailand and the southern Philippines. These conflicts are considered to be ethnic independence struggles rather than jihad.

Christianity

Catholicism was introduced to Vietnam by the French, to the Philippines by the Spanish and to Timor-Leste by the Portuguese. Parts of Indonesia are Christian, mainly Protestant, due to the efforts of Western missionary groups. In each of these converted groups there are remnants of the original animistic beliefs and an almost personal emphasis on preferred aspects of the liturgy or the ideology. The local adaptations can often be so pronounced that Westerners of the same faith might still observe the practice as foreign.

Hinduism

Hinduism ruled the spiritual lives of Southeast Asians more than 1500 years ago, and the great Hindu empires of Angkor and Srivijaya built grand monuments to their pantheon of gods. The primary representations of the multiple faces of the one omnipresent god are Brahma (the creator), Vishnu (the preserver) and Shiva (the destroyer or reproducer). All three gods are usually shown with four arms, but Brahma has the added advantage of four heads to represent his all-seeing presence.

Although Buddhism and Islam have filtered across the continent, Hinduism has filtered through these mainstream religions and Buddhism regards the Hindu deities with respect. Also, the Hindu island of Bali is a spiritual anomaly in the region. Within the last 100 years, the influx of Indian labourers to Southeast Asia has bolstered the religion's followers.

Arts & Architecture

Southeast Asia's most notable artistic endeavours are religious in nature. The Buddhist countries have distinctive artistic depictions of the Hindu deities and symbols of Buddhism. Both an artistic and architectural wonder, the temples of Angkor in Cambodia defined much of mainland Southeast Asia's artistic interpretation of religious iconography. The temples' elaborate sculptured murals pay homage to Hindu gods Brahma (represented as four-headed, four-armed figure) and Shiva (styled either in an embrace with his consort or as an ascetic), while also recording historical events and creation myths. Angkor-inspired monuments were built by the Khmers in neighbouring countries and were adopted by later regional empires, such as the Thai kingdoms of Sukhothai and Ayuthaya.

Statues of Buddha reflect an individual country's artistic interpretations of an art form governed by highly symbolic strictures. Buddha is depicted sitting, standing and reclining – all representations of historic moments in his life. In Vietnam, representations of the Buddha are more akin to Chinese religious art, rather than India or Angkor. Also found decorating many temple railings is the mythical water serpent, known as *naga*, which represents the life-giving power of water.

In Indonesia, Malaysia, Brunei and the Philippines, Islamic art and architecture intermingled with animist traditions. Every town in Malaysia has a grand fortressed mosque with an Arabic minaret and Moorish tile work. Indonesia is home to the region's biggest mosque

Religious Reads

Living Faith: Inside the Muslim World of Southeast Asia, by Steve Raymer

Buddhism for Beginners, by Thubten Chodron

PEOPLE & CULTURE ARTS & ARCHITECTURE

BUDDHA IMAGES

Buddha images are visual sermons. Elongated earlobes, no evidence of bone or muscle, arms that reach to the knees, a third eye: these non-human elements express Buddha's divine nature. Periods within Buddha's life are also depicted in the figure's 'posture' or pose:

Reclining Exact moment of Buddha's enlightenment and death.

Sitting Buddha teaching or meditating. If the right hand is pointed towards the earth, Buddha is shown subduing the demons of desire; if the hands are folded in the lap, Buddha is turning the wheel of law.

Standing Buddha bestowing blessings or taming evil forces.

Walking Buddha after his return to earth from heaven.

(Istiqlal Mosque in central Jakarta, designed by a Christian architect), as well as stunning mosques that incorporate palace-like features from international inspirations.

Food

Southeast Asia's tropical climate creates a year-round bounty. Food is central to every cultural celebration. Many traditional holidays revolve around the region's staple: rice. Village festivals mark the beginning of rice-planting season, with rituals and customs designed to ensure a bountiful harvest. Even the invisible spirits who guide good luck in the Buddhist countries require daily offerings of food to sate their mischievous nature.

Traces of Southeast Asia's cultural parents – India and China – can be detected in the individual nation's cuisines. In Myanmar, Malaysia and southern Thailand, Indian-style flatbreads accompany curries as the meal's staple, instead of rice. Throughout the region, the Indian creation of curry receives much reinvention, drawing on such local ingredients as coconut milk and a penchant for chillies. As the centre of the ancient spice trade, Indonesia became a global kitchen, adopting recipes from India, Arabia, Europe and China, and fashioning them into such dishes as buffalo curries and peanut sauces for satay (peanuts were brought by Spanish and Portuguese traders).

Among many other dishes, the Chinese donated noodles, which are fried, drowned in broth or tossed in salads. Noodle soups are the quintessential comfort food, eaten in the morning, after a night carousing or at midday when pressed for time. Much of the Chinese cuisine that has become comfortably settled in Southeast Asia is from southern China, but it has been reinvented, imported to neighbouring countries and reproduced so many times that some dishes' pedigrees are totally obscured.

Thailand and Laos share many common dishes, often competing for the honour of spiciest cuisine (Laos wins in our humble opinion). Green papaya salad is a mainstay of both – the Thais like theirs with ground peanuts, fresh tomatoes and dried shrimp; the Lao version uses fermented fish sauce, field crabs and lots of chillies (it is more delicious than it sounds). In Laos and neighbouring Thai provinces, the local people eat 'sticky rice' (a shorter grain than the standard fluffy jasmine rice). This kind of rice is eaten with the hands and usually rolled up into balls and dipped into spicy sauces.

Spicy food is beloved by Southeast Asian cultures and each country has a spicy condiment, consisting of ground chillies, lime juice and sometimes, but not always, fish sauce or paste. The Spanish are often credited for introducing chillies to the region.

As dictated by the strictures of Islam, Muslim communities throughout the region don't eat pork, creating a culinary culture clash with their Chinese neighbours who adore pork dishes.

Top Noodle Dishes

laksa (Malaysia)

pho (Vietnam)

pàt tai (Thailand)

mie goreng (Indonesia)

mee kola (Cambodia)

lard na (Laos)

pancit bihon (Philippines)

char kway teow (Singapore)

Survival Guide

Responsible Travel

In Southeast Asia, tourism brings blessings and curses. Small-scale tourism fosters family-owned businesses and one-on-one cultural exchanges that broaden people's perspective, and help preserve cultural and environmental assets. But tourism also puts environmental and cultural pressures on the host country. To ensure that your trip is a gift, not a burden, mind your manners, be green, learn everything you can about the host country and be a conscientious consumer.

ENVIRONMENTAL CONCERNS

Southeast Asia has some of the greatest biodiversity on the planet, containing species that do not exist anywhere else – particularly in mega-diverse countries such as Indonesia, Malaysia and the Philippines. Environmental superlatives include: reefs regarded as the world's most abundant (75% of the world's coral species are found here), including the 6-million-sq-km Coral Triangle, which stretches all the way from Malaysia to the Solomon Islands; the Mekong River, which rivals the Amazon for biodiversity; the world's largest lizard (the Komodo dragon); and numerous endemic bird species (the region is also an important stopover for migratory species).

But the region is also densely populated and environmental degradation is immediately tangible. Smoke fills the air as the forests are cleared for beach bungalows, small-scale farms, palm-oil plantations or logging. Major cities are choked with smog and pollution from vehicle emissions. The waterways are clogged with trash, and raw sewage is dumped into turquoise waters because of inadequate waste treatment facilities.

Deforestation

Due to deforestation and associated forest fires, Indonesia is the world's third-largest greenhouse gas emitter. Destruction of the mangrove forests, which act as tidal buffer zones, mean coastal storms have had a disastrous effect on the local population, contributing to the death toll of the 2004 Boxing Day tsunami and 2013 super-typhoon Yolanda (Haiyan).

INTERNET RESOURCES

Responsible Travel (www.responsible-travel.org) General tips on how to be a 'better' tourist regarding environmental issues, begging and bargaining, as well as ethical holidays.

Mekong Responsible Tourism (www.mekong-responsibletourism.org) Online guide promoting community-based and socially responsible tourism in the Mekong region. Homestays, cultural attractions and eco-lodges are often featured.

WWF International (www.panda.org) Read up on WWF's environmental campaigns to protect Southeast Asia's threatened species and landscapes.

Mongabay (www.mongabay.com) Environmental science and conservation news site with a focus on tropical rainforests, including Indonesia.

Ecology Asia (www.ecologyasia.com) Facts and figures about Southeast Asia's flora and fauna.

Sealang Projects (http://sealang.net) Academic resource for learning Southeast Asian languages.

Water Systems

Water systems are suffering as well. Environmental degradation of coral reefs is caused by overfishing, sediment run-off from coastal development, as well as climate change. Along the Mekong River, hydroelectric dams are significantly altering the river's ecosystem, from sediment transport to fish migration, as well as water levels downstream.

Habitat Loss

Habitat loss is a serious threat to the region's indigenous wildlife. The few remaining natural areas are also subject to poaching. Thailand is one of the primary conduits through which live wildlife and harvested wildlife parts travel to overseas markets.

Solutions

Though the environmental problems are apparent, obvious answers are not. Conserving wild lands requires political convictions undeterred by moneyed interests, a tall order in a region with limited national budgets and a culture of corruption. Of all of the Southeast Asian nations, Brunei leads the conservationist charge with approximately 70% of its original forest cover still intact, but its oil wealth allows it to overlook the profits of undeveloped lands.

What You Can Do

There are many environmental problems that the average tourist has zero control over, but on a local level visitors can strive to reduce their individual 'footprint' by putting as little pressure on the natural environment and the localities' inadequate infrastructure

RESPONSIBLE DIVING

The popularity of Southeast Asia's diving industry places immense pressure on fragile coral sites. To help preserve the ecology, adhere to these simple rules:

➡ Avoid touching living marine organisms, standing on coral or dragging equipment (such as fins) across the reef. Coral polyps can be damaged by even the gentlest contact.

➡ When treading water in shallow reef areas, be careful not to kick up clouds of sand, which can easily smother the delicate reef organisms.

➡ Reduce time in underwater caves where air bubbles can be caught within the roof and leave previously submerged organisms high and dry.

➡ Join a coral clean-up campaign, sponsored by dive shops.

➡ Don't feed the fish or allow your dive operator to dispose of excess food in the water. The fish become dependent on this food source and don't tend to the algae on the coral, causing harm to the reef.

➡ Don't collect souvenirs (corals, shells or shipwreck debris) from the sea.

as possible. Here are some modest steps:

➡ Live like a local: opt for a fan instead of an air-con room; shower with cold water instead of hot.

➡ Use biodegradable soap to reduce water pollution.

➡ Eat locally sourced meals instead of imported products.

➡ Dispose of plastic packaging before leaving home so that it doesn't end up in overburdened refuse systems.

➡ Dispose of cigarette butts in rubbish bins, not on the beach or into the water.

➡ Choose unplugged modes of transit (walking tour over minivan tour, bicycle over motorbike, kayak over jet ski).

➡ Volunteer with a local conservation or animal-welfare group.

➡ Be a responsible diver.

➡ Dispose of your rubbish in a proper receptacle, even if the locals don't.

➡ Don't eat or drink food products made from endangered animals or plants.

➡ Refill plastic bottles whenever possible.

➡ Patronise businesses with ecotourism models (designated with a sustainable icon in this book).

CULTURAL & SOCIAL CONCERNS

Most Southeast Asians don't expect tourists to know very much about them and for this reason they overlook innocent breaches of social etiquette. But each culture has a host of taboos and sacred beliefs that should not be disrespected. Before arriving, figure out the touchy subjects and tread gingerly.

Tourists also encounter problems when they show anger over money disputes or miscommunication and

PROSTITUTION

Prostitution is technically illegal but common and tolerated in many parts of Southeast Asia. While some sex workers are adults, some are also minors who have been sold or recruited by family members and are exploited by the business owner through intimidation and abuse. Unicef estimates that there are close to one million child prostitutes in all of Asia – one of the highest figures in the world.

Sex with minors is a serious offence that is enforced with severe penalties by Southeast Asian countries. Many Western countries also prosecute and punish citizens for paedophile offences committed abroad. For more information contact **End Child Prostitution & Trafficking** (Ecpat; www.ecpat.net), a global network that works to stop child prostitution, child pornography and the trafficking of children for sexual purposes. **Childsafe International** (www.childsafe-international. org) aims to educate businesses and individuals to be on the lookout for children in vulnerable situations.

during drunken escapades. Being polite and patient is better than being right and belligerent.

What You Can Do

Here are some pointers to keep you on everyone's good side:

➡ Always ask for permission before you take a picture of someone, especially during private moments; asking in the local language is even better.

➡ Take a language course or at least learn a few stock phrases in the local language.

➡ Treat religious objects, no matter how old or decrepit, with the utmost respect; don't clamber on temple ruins or pose behind headless Buddha statues.

➡ Learn about the country's history, current events and social problems.

➡ Share your snacks or cigarettes with your neighbour on long bus rides.

➡ Tip here and there as daily wages are pitifully small.

➡ Smile while bargaining; your beauty will distract them from opportunistic pricing.

➡ Keep a thick skin and a sense of humour.

POVERTY & ECONOMIC DISPARITY

The disparity between rich and poor is one of Southeast Asia's most pressing social concerns. Only a few of the region's countries have well-developed social safety nets to catch people left homeless or jobless by debt mismanagement, rapid industrialisation or institutionalised discrimination.

Remote villagers, including ethnic minorities, often live precarious subsistence lives without access to health care, economic opportunity or basic education. In some cases, their traditional lifestyles are incompatible with the modern marketplace, and many villages lose their young people to jobs in the cities. Urban migrants often do menial labour for menial wages; some turn to more profitable enterprises, such as prostitution or other illicit ventures. When a family is financially compromised, children are often expected to work, either formally in a factory or informally as a street hawker. They often don't have the luxury of time or money to receive an education.

There is also an ongoing problem of human trafficking, mainly economic migrants who are lured to a neighbouring country for work to find that they are vulnerable to exploitation.

What You Can Do

➡ Volunteer as an English teacher at a local school or NGO; education is an important tool for economic success.

➡ Support businesses with a social-justice mission, such as fair-trade weaving cooperatives or job-skills development sites.

➡ Stay at village homestays to support traditional lifestyles.

➡ Discourage child labour by not patronising child vendors or hawkers.

➡ Make a donation to a local school or charity instead of handing out money or gifts to beggars, especially children.

➡ Hire local guides to encourage village-based employment opportunities.

➡ Avoid all-inclusive purchases (lodging, transport, tours, food); instead spread your spending so that more local people benefit.

Directory A–Z

Accommodation

The accommodation listed in reviews occupies the low end of the price and amenities scale. Basic rooms typically have four walls, a bed and a fan (handy for keeping mosquitoes at bay). In the cheapest instances, the bathroom is shared. Most places geared to foreigners have Western-style toilets, but hotels that cater to locals usually have Asian squat toilets. Air-con, private bathrooms and well-sealed rooms cost more. Camping is not a widespread option, but dorms are becoming a more economical option – especially in the Philippines, Singapore and Thailand, where accommodation tends to be more expensive.

Be a smart shopper when looking for a room. Always ask for the price first, then ask to see a room to inspect it for cleanliness, comfort and quiet. Don't feel obligated to take a room just because the place is mentioned in Lonely Planet. Sometimes the quality of a guesthouse plummets after gaining a mention in Lonely Planet, but this can be corrected by diligent travellers who exercise their own judgement.

Each hotel or guesthouse has its own convention for payment. Some require payment in advance, while others collect the money upon check out. Before you pay for numerous nights in advance, make sure that you find the accommodation acceptable, as getting a refund will be impossible. Be sure to settle your bill on your last evening if you're leaving early the next day.

Activities

Ocean sports and jungle trips are the major outdoor activities in Southeast Asia. For casual enthusiasts most tourist businesses rent out gear. If you're not a beginner, consider bringing the required gear from home, as equipment here can be substandard.

Diving & Snorkelling

Southeast Asia is a diving and snorkelling paradise with inexpensive dive certificate training and a myriad of undersea environments. Thailand, Malaysia, Indonesia and the Philippines are all famous dive destinations.

Diving and snorkelling put unique pressures on the natural environment. Select reputable and environmentally conscious operators.

Rock Climbing

Southeast Asia's limestone cliffs have been transformed into climbing routes for vertical challenges and spectacular views. Thailand, Laos and Vietnam boast several rock-climbing centres for beginners and experts.

Trekking

Trekking in Southeast Asia includes hikes through a diminutive offshoot of the Himalaya, into soggy rainforests and around smouldering volcanoes. Trekking requires a guide, as trails aren't well marked, transport to the trail-head is difficult to arrange, and foreigners are unfamiliar with the region's climate and microclimates. Hiring a guide also provides income for local villagers who regard the natural areas as their own backyards. You should also be aware of local laws, regulations and etiquette about wildlife and the environment.

In Thailand and Laos, elephant trekking is also popular but standards and conditions of the elephants and camps vary greatly.

Sometimes camps doing bulk-business in tourism will put profits ahead of the animals. Do your homework about the elephants' living and working conditions before signing up for a trek.

Be prepared for a trek with proper clothing: long pants, adequate hiking shoes and leech socks (during and after the rainy season). Bring along rain gear (for yourself and your pack) even if the skies are clear. Drink lots of water and pace yourself, as the humidity can make even minimal exercise feel demanding.

Water Sports

Surfing and kitesurfing are big draws in Southeast Asia. Indonesia is the region's surfing capital, though the Philippines isn't too far behind. Vietnam and Thailand have consistent winds for seasonal kitesurfing. Laos is known for tubing and kayaking. Be sure to go with a company with a good safety record and avoid river travel during the monsoon when conditions can be dangerous.

Bathing

In remote corners or basic accommodation, you'll meet the Southeast Asian version of a shower: a large basin that holds water for bathing. Water should be scooped out of the basin with a smaller bowl and poured over the body. Resist the urge to climb in like a bathtub or avoid washing directly over the basin, as this is your source for clean water.

Modern facilities might have a cold-water shower that is a star-rated environmental choice, but it can be difficult to adequately rinse off soap and shampoo. Consider travelling with an easy-to-rinse, biodegradable soap.

More expensive accommodation, large cities and colder regions will offer hot-water showers, usually point-of-use heaters, for an extra charge.

Many rural people bathe in rivers or streams. If you choose to do the same, be aware that public nudity is not acceptable. Do as the locals do and bathe while wearing a sarong.

Customs Regulations

Customs regulations vary little around the region. Drugs and arms are strictly prohibited – death or a lengthy stay in prison are common sentences. Pornography is also a no-no.

Discount Cards

The International Student Identity Card (ISIC) is moderately useful in Southeast Asia, with limited success in gaining the holder discounts. Some domestic and international airlines provide discounts to ISIC cardholders, but the cards carry little bargaining power because knock-offs are so readily available.

Discrimination

Skin colour may be a factor in Southeast Asia. White foreigners stand out in a crowd. Children will often point, prices may double and a handful of presumptions may precede your arrival. In general, these will seem either minor nuisances or exotic elements of travel. If you are a Westerner of Asian descent, most Southeast Asians will assume that you are a local until the language barrier proves otherwise. With the colour barrier removed, many Westerners with Asian heritage are treated like family and sometimes get charged local prices.

Many Asians might mistake people of African heritage with fairly light complexions for locals or at least distant cousins. People

with darker complexions will be regarded to be as foreign as white visitors, but may also be saddled with the extra baggage of Africa's perceived inferior status in the global hierarchy.

Electricity

Most countries work on a voltage of 220V to 240V at 50Hz (cycles); note that 240V appliances will happily run on 220V.

You should be able to pick up adaptors in electrical shops in most Southeast Asian cities.

Embassies & Consulates

It's important to realise what your own embassy – the embassy of the country of which you are a citizen – can and can't do to help you if you get into trouble.

Generally speaking, it won't be much help in emergencies if the trouble you're in is remotely your own fault. You are bound by the laws of the country you are in. Your embassy will not be sympathetic if you end up in jail after committing a crime locally, even if such actions are legal in your own country.

In genuine emergencies you might get some assistance if other channels have been exhausted. For example, if you need to get home urgently, a free ticket home is exceedingly unlikely – the embassy would expect you to have insurance. If you have all your money and documents stolen, it might assist with getting a new passport, but a loan for onward travel is out of the question.

Most travellers should have no need to contact their embassy while in Southeast Asia, although if you're travelling in unstable regions or going into uncharted territory, it may be worth letting your embassy know upon departure and return. In this way valuable time, effort and money won't be wasted looking for you while you're relaxing on a beach somewhere.

For details on embassies in Southeast Asia see Embassies & Consulates in the individual country directories.

Gay & Lesbian Travellers

Southeast Asia could easily be ranked as one of the most progressive regions regarding homosexuality outside the Western world. In general most urban centres have gay communities, and attitudes towards same-sex relationships are tolerant, though travellers should still mind the region-wide prescription of refraining from public displays of affection.

Utopia Asian Gay & Lesbian Resources (www.utopia-asia.com) has an excellent profile of each country's record on acceptance, as well as short reviews on gay nightspots and handy travel guides to the various Southeast Asian countries.

For more details on gay and lesbian travel, see the specific country directories.

Insurance

A travel-insurance policy to cover theft, loss and medical problems is a necessity. There's a wide variety of policies available, so check the small print. For more information about the ins and outs of travel insurance, contact a travel agent or travel insurer.

Some policies specifically exclude 'dangerous activities', which can include scuba diving, motorcycling and even trekking. A locally acquired motorcycle licence is also not valid under some policies. Check that the policy covers ambulance rides, emergency flights home and, in the case of death, repatriation of a body.

Internet Access

In metropolitan areas, Southeast Asia is incredibly well wired, with internet cafes, fast connections and cheap prices, Skype headsets and even wi-fi access. Outside the big cities, things start to vary. Good internet connections are usually commensurate with a destination's road system: well-sealed highways usually mean speedy travel through the information superhighway as well. Increasingly 3G mobile access is available in large urban centres.

Censorship of some sites is in effect across the region.

Legal Matters

Be sure to know the national laws so that you don't unwittingly commit a crime. In all of the Southeast Asian countries, using or trafficking drugs carries stiff punishments that are enforced even if you're a foreigner.

If you are a victim of a crime, contact the tourist police, if available; they are usually better trained to deal with foreigners and foreign languages than the regular police force.

Maps

Country-specific maps are usually sold in English-language bookstores in capital cities. Local tourist offices and guesthouses can also provide maps of smaller cities and towns.

Money

Check www.xe.com for current exchange rates. Check the specific destination chapters for the availability of ATMs and any other pre-arrival concerns about money.

Bargaining

Most Southeast Asian countries practise the art of bargaining. Remember that it is an art, not a test of wills, and the trick is to find a price that makes everyone happy.

Bargaining is acceptable in markets and in shops where the prices aren't displayed. Here are some basic 'dance moves' for bargaining for goods. First ask the price and then ask for a discount. If the discount isn't acceptable offer something slightly lower but be prepared to accept an amount in between. Once you counter you can't lower your price. Don't start to haggle unless you're serious about buying. If you become angry or visibly frustrated, you've lost the game.

It is also customary (and mandatory) to bargain for chartered transport as tourists are often taken advantage of by local taxi drivers. Ask at your guesthouse how much a trip should cost before chartering a vehicle. Then head out to the street and start negotiations with a driver, counter with your own offer and accept something in between. If the driver won't budge, then politely decline the service and move on. Don't fight with the driver – they are famous for their tempers.

Opening Hours

In the Buddhist countries of Southeast Asia, businesses are typically open seven days a week. In the Muslim countries some businesses close during Friday afternoon prayers.

Refer to the Opening Hours in the individual country directories for details.

Passports

To enter most countries your passport must be valid for at least six months from your date of entry, even if you're only staying for a few days.

It's probably best to have at least a year left on your passport if you are heading off on a trip around Southeast Asia.

Testy border guards may refuse entry if your passport doesn't have enough blank pages available. Before leaving get more pages added to a valid passport (if this is a service offered by your home country). Once on the road, you can apply for a new passport in most major Southeast Asian cities from your home embassy or consulate.

Photography

Digital photo files can be offloaded from your device to a cloud-storage site or other device via a wi-fi connection, often available at hotels and guesthouses. USB drives can also be used to store photos; internet cafes usually have desktops that can interface with your components if you aren't travelling with a laptop. Before leaving home, determine whether your battery charger will require a power adapter by visiting the website of the **World Electric Guide** (www. kropla.com/electric.htm).

The best places to buy camera equipment or have repairs done are Singapore, Bangkok and Kuala Lumpur. Be aware that the more equipment you travel with, the more vulnerable you are to theft.

You should always ask permission before taking a person's photograph. Many hill-tribe villagers seriously object to being photographed, or they may ask for money in exchange; if you want the photo, you should honour the price. Also respect people's privacy even if they are in public; guesthouses and small restaurants serve double-duty as the owner's living space and they deserve to have family time without being a photo-opportunity.

Post

Postal services are generally reliable across the region. There's always an element of risk in sending parcels home by sea, though as a rule they eventually reach their destination. If it's something of value, you're better off mailing home your dirty clothes to make room in your luggage for precious keepsakes.

Don't send cash or valuables through government-run postal systems.

Poste restante is widely available though infrequently used and is the best way of receiving mail. Ask the senders to leave plenty of time for mail to arrive and to print your name very clearly. Underlining the surname also helps.

Safe Travel

It is safer in Southeast Asia than you might think. But you still need to keep your wits about you to avoid scams, injury, assault and even embarrassment.

Assaults

Violent assaults in Southeast Asia are not common, but instances of attacks on foreigners generate media attention and corresponding anxiety. Travellers should exercise basic street smarts: avoid lonely areas at night, excessive drinking or angering locals. Police enforcement of local laws and investigations into crimes are often inadequate so don't assume that a country's general friendliness equals a crime-free zone.

Avoid confrontations with locals, in general, but especially when alcohol is involved. What might seem like harmless verbal sparring to you might be regarded as injurious by the local and might provoke disproportionately violent acts of retribution

thanks to the complicated concept of 'saving face'.

Special caution should be exercised at big parties, likes Thailand's Full Moon raves, where criminal gangs with political connections take advantage of intoxicated revellers. Other party places, Sihanoukville and Bali, both have seedy underbellies that should be avoided.

Drugs

The risks associated with recreational drug use and distribution are serious even in places with illicit reputations. Just down the road from Kuta Beach in Bali is a jail where travellers are enjoying the tropical climate for much longer than they had intended. In Indonesia you can be jailed because your travel companions had dope and you didn't report them. A spell in a Thai prison can be very grim; in Malaysia and Singapore, possession of certain quantities of dope can lead to hanging. Even laidback Laos seriously prosecutes drug trafficking. With heightened airport security, customs officials are zealous in their screening of both luggage and passengers.

The death penalty, prison sentences and huge fines are given as liberally to foreigners as to locals; no one has evaded punishment because of ignorance of local laws. In Indonesia in 2005, nine Australians (dubbed the 'Bali Nine') were arrested on charges of heroin possession: seven received life sentences and two were sentenced to death by firing squad. In 2009 a UK citizen was sentenced to life in prison in Laos for drug trafficking; her sentence was downgraded from the death penalty and her custody transferred to a British jail after she became pregnant while in custody.

Recreational drug use is often viewed in the same league as drug trafficking and can result in prison terms. In Thailand, sometimes the drug dealers are in cahoots with the police and use a drug transaction as an opportunity to extract a huge bribe. You also never know what you're really getting. In Cambodia, what is sold as methamphetamine is often a homemade concoction of cheap and toxic chemicals and what is sold as cocaine is heavy-duty heroin that is easily consumed in overdose levels.

Political Unrest

Avoid all political demonstrations, no matter how benign or celebratory they may appear. Mass rallies can quickly turn into violent clashes between rival factions or the military. With that said, just because there are rallies in one corner of a massive city, like Bangkok, doesn't mean that the whole country, or even the whole city, is off limits. Your home country's embassy will issue the safest possible travel warnings, which should be juxtaposed with coverage by the local press in order to gauge the best-possible outcome. No-go zones experiencing low-scale independence wars exist in parts of southern Thailand and the Philippines.

Scams

Every year we get letters and emails from travellers reporting that they've been scammed in Southeast Asia. In most cases, the scams are petty rip-offs, in which a naive traveller pays too much for a ride to the bus station, to exchange money, buy souvenirs etc. Rip-offs are in full force at border crossings, popular tourist attractions, bus and rail stations and wherever travellers might get confused.

Here are some tips for avoiding scams:

➡ Be diplomatically suspicious of over-friendly locals.

➡ Avoid super-cheap, inclusive transport packages, which often include extra commission-generating fees.

➡ Don't accept invitations to play cards or go shopping with a friendly stranger; this is a prelude to a well-rehearsed and expensive scam.

➡ Understand that commissions are common business practices in the region and are levied wherever there is a third party.

Theft

Theft in Southeast Asia is usually by stealth rather than by force. Violent theft is rare but can occur late at night and often after the victim has been drinking. Be sure that you are with people whom you trust if you are going to drink your weight in Thailand's famous booze buckets or Vietnam's endless supply of draught beer. Travel in groups late at night, especially after a night of carousing, to ensure safety in numbers. Women should be especially careful about returning home late at night from a bar.

Clandestine theft is a concern, especially on overnight buses, in communal dorms or in lodging with inadequate locks on windows and dorms. In Malaysia, petty thieves have been known to check into a guesthouse and then rob the other guests in the middle of the night.

Snatch thieves are an increasing problem, especially in Vietnam and Cambodia. Typically the thieves aboard a motorcycle pull up alongside a tourist, usually a woman, just long enough to grab a bag or camera and then they speed away. This can happen when the tourist is walking along the street or riding in a vehicle like a moto or túk-túk.

Here are some tips for keeping your stuff safe:

➡ Keep your money and valuables in a money belt (worn underneath your clothes).

➡ Don't carry valuables in a bag that can be grabbed by snatch thieves and don't carry your camera by its strap.

➡ Place your bag in between you and the driver when riding on a motorcycle or between your legs when riding in a túk-túk to prevent snatch thieves.

➡ Don't store valuables in easily accessible places such as backpack pockets or packs that are stored in the luggage compartment of buses.

➡ Don't put valuables in the baskets of a motorcycle or bicycle, easy pickings for snatch thieves.

➡ Be especially careful about your belongings when sleeping in dorms.

Unexploded Ordnance & Landmines

The legacy of war lingers on in Cambodia, Laos and Vietnam. Laos suffered the fate of being the most heavily bombed country per capita in the world, while all three countries were on the receiving end of more bombs than were dropped by all sides during WWII. There are still many undetonated bombs and explosives out there, so be careful walking off the trail in areas near the Laos–Vietnam border or around the Demilitarised Zone (DMZ). Cambodia suffers the additional affliction of landmines, some four to six million of them according to surveys. Many of these are located in border areas with Thailand in the north and west of the country, but it pays to stick to marked paths anywhere in Cambodia.

Toilets

As tourism continues to grow in the region, Western-style sit-down toilets are increasingly common. However, in rural areas it is another story and squat toilets are widespread.

If you encounter a squat, here's what you should do. Straddle the two footpads and face the door. To flush use the plastic bowl to scoop water out of the adjacent basin and pour into the toilet bowl. Some places supply a small pack of toilet paper available for purchase at the entrance; otherwise bring your own stash or wipe the old-fashioned way with water.

Even in places where sit-down toilets are installed, the septic system may not be designed to take toilet paper. In such cases there will be a waste basket where you're supposed to place used toilet paper and feminine hygiene products.

Tourist Information

Most of the Southeast Asian countries have government-funded tourist offices of varying usefulness. Better information is sometimes available through guesthouses and fellow travellers. Do be aware that official tourist offices don't make accommodation and transport bookings. If a so-called tourist office provides this service, then they are a travel agency that charges a commission.

Travellers with Disabilities

Travellers with serious disabilities will likely find Southeast Asia to be a challenging place to travel. Even the more modern cities are very difficult to navigate for mobility- or vision-impaired people. Generally speaking, the various countries' infrastructure is often inadequate for those with disabilities.

International organisations that can provide information on mobility-impaired travel include the following:

Disability Alliance (www.disabilityrightsuk.org)

Mobility International USA (www.miusa.org)

Society for Accessible Travel & Hospitality (SATH; www.sath.org)

Visas

Before arriving in a country (either by air, land or sea), find out if you need to pre-arrange a visa or if one is available for your nationality upon arrival. Here are some additional visa tips:

➡ Plan your trip around the length of stay mandated by the visa.

➡ If you plan on staying longer than the typical allotment, apply for a longer visa from the embassy in your home country or from an embassy in a neighbouring country or investigate the ease of extending a visa within the country.

➡ Stock up on passport photos, as you'll probably need at least two pictures each time you apply for a visa.

➡ Have the correct amount of local currency (or US dollars) to pay the on-arrival visa fee.

➡ Dress smartly when you're visiting embassies, consulates and borders; Southeast Asians appreciate appearance.

Women Travellers

While travel in Southeast Asia for women is generally safe, solo women should exercise caution when travelling at night or returning home by themselves from a bar or a party. While physical assault is rare, local men often consider foreign women to be exempt from their own society's rules of conduct. Be especially careful in party towns, especially the Thai islands and Bali, where drunken abandon may be exploited by opportunists.

Travelling in Muslim areas introduces some challenges for women. In conservative areas, local women rarely go out unaccompanied and are usually modestly dressed. Foreign women doing the exact opposite are observed first as strange and second as searching for a local boyfriend. While the region is very friendly, be careful about teaming up with young men who may not respect certain boundaries.

Keep in mind that modesty in dress is culturally important right across Southeast Asia. Covering past the shoulders and above the knees helps define you as off limits, while spaghetti-strap singlets inadvertently send the message that you're sexually available.

Finally, you can reduce hassles by travelling with other backpackers. You can often pair up with other travellers you meet on the way.

Work

Teaching English is the easiest way to support yourself in Southeast Asia. For short-term gigs, Bangkok, Ho Chi Minh City (Saigon) and Jakarta have language schools and a high turnover of staff. In the Philippines, English speakers are often needed as language trainers for call centres. In Indonesia and Thailand you may be able to find some dive-school work. TEFL programs, especially in Thailand, are popular ways to prepare for an international job and live in a foreign country.

Payaway (www.payaway.co.uk) provides a handy online list of language schools and volunteer groups looking for recruits for its Southeast Asian programs.

Transitions Abroad (www.transitionsabroad.com) is a web portal that covers all aspects of overseas life, including landing a job in a variety of fields.

Transport

GETTING THERE & AWAY

Step one is to get to Southeast Asia, and flying is the easiest option. The only overland possibilities from outside the region are from Papua New Guinea into Indonesia – an unlikely scenario – and from China into Vietnam or Laos. Flights, tours and rail tickets can be booked online at lonelyplanet.com/bookings.

Air

The major Asian gateways for cheap flights are Bangkok, Kuala Lumpur, Singapore, Denpasar (Bali) and Manila. Thanks to the proliferation of budget carriers, there are often cheap fares between China and Southeast Asian cities or beach resorts.

When pricing flights compare the cost of flying to an East Asian city (such as Hong Kong) from your home country and then connecting to a budget carrier, to the cost of flying directly to your destination on a long-haul airline. Fares on budget carriers don't usually factor into online search engines, but if you have more time than money, may the budget forces be with you.

Also be flexible with travel dates and know when to buy a ticket. Trips longer than two weeks tend to be more expensive. Buying a ticket too early or too close to your departure will affect the price as well. The ticket-purchasing sweet spot is 21 to 15 days before departure. When researching airline fares, dump your computer's cookies, which track your online activity and can sometimes result in a higher fare upon subsequent searches.

The following online resources can help you research bargain airfares:

Attitude Travel (www.attitudetravel.com) A guide to low-cost carriers in Asia.

Lonely Planet (www.lonelyplanet.com) Click on Travel Services to research multi-destination trips.

Round-the-World & Circle Asia Tickets

If Asia is one of many stops on a worldwide tour, consider a round-the-world (RTW) ticket, which allows a certain number of stops within a set time period as long as you don't backtrack. Circle Asia passes are offered by various airline alliances for a circular route originating in the USA, Europe or Australia and travelling to certain destinations in Asia.

Before committing, check the fares offered by the budget regional carriers to see if either of these multistop tickets offer enough of a savings over à la carte fares. Contact airlines or a travel agent for more information or try **Air Treks** (www.airtreks.com).

CLIMATE CHANGE & TRAVEL

Every form of transport that relies on carbon-based fuel generates CO_2, the main cause of human-induced climate change. Modern travel is dependent on aeroplanes, which might use less fuel per kilometre per person than most cars but travel much greater distances. The altitude at which aircraft emit gases (including CO_2) and particles also contributes to their climate change impact. Many websites offer 'carbon calculators' that allow people to estimate the carbon emissions generated by their journey and, for those who wish to do so, to offset the impact of the greenhouse gases emitted with contributions to portfolios of climate-friendly initiatives throughout the world. Lonely Planet offsets the carbon footprint of all staff and author travel.

Land

The land borders between Southeast Asia and the rest of Asia include those between Myanmar and India and Bangladesh, and the Chinese border with Myanmar, Laos and Vietnam. Of these, it is possible to travel overland from China into Laos and Vietnam. There is a possibility that the Mu-Se–Ruili border between Myanmar and China will soon open to travellers without special permits.

Another international crossing is between Indonesia and Papua New Guinea, though this isn't a feasible international gateway.

Sea

Ocean approaches to Southeast Asia can be made aboard cargo ships plying routes around the world. Ridiculously expensive and hopelessly romantic, a trip aboard a cargo ship is the perfect chance for you to write that novel that never writes itself. Some freighter ships have space for a few noncrew members, who have their own rooms but eat meals with the crew. Prices vary depending on your departure point, but costs start at around US$150 a day plus additional fees.

GETTING AROUND

Border Crossings

It is easier than ever to travel overland (or over water) between neighbouring Southeast Asian countries. There are some well-trodden routes, especially within mainland Southeast Asia, that have straightforward public transport options and plenty of migrating travellers to share the road with. In some cases overland travel is the cheapest, though not always the fastest, route between major destinations. However, with the increasing affordability of flights, sometimes an airfare is equivalent to a long-distance bus ticket.

With the inception of the Asean Economic Community (AEC), border relations between most countries have normalised, but there are still visa regulations and minor scams to be prepared for beforehand.

Do be aware that some border crossings are not recommended due to political violence and instability in the region. Those areas to avoid include the west coast of Thailand crossing to Malaysia (Sungai Kolok to Rantau Panjang) as well as boat crossings from Malaysian Borneo to the southern Philippines' port of Zamboanga.

Ask around or check the Lonely Planet Thorn Tree (www.lonelyplanet.com/thorntree) for border-crossing trip reports for further information and transport recommendations.

Other considerations when planning the border crossings for your trip include the following:

➡ Know which borders offer visas on arrival and which ones require prearranged visas.

➡ When arriving at borders that do issue visas upon arrival, be prepared with two passport photos and enough cash in the required currency to pay the visa fee and complete border formalities.

➡ Plan your trip so that you arrive at the border during opening hours to avoid being stranded overnight or needing to make last-minute arrangements in a small border town.

➡ There are few legal money-changing facilities at some border crossings (even at crossings that do not seem remote, such as Cambodia's Poipet crossing with Thailand) so be sure to have some small-denomination US dollars handy.

➡ The black-market money changers are an option for local currencies, but remember that black marketeers have a well-deserved reputation for short-changing customers and offering unfavourable exchange rates.

➡ Be aware of border-crossing scams, like dodgy transport schemes and pesky runner boys.

➡ At some border crossings staff may request or demand extra processing fees, like overtime surcharges or other nonstandard charges, in addition to the legitimate visa-issuing fees. Resisting might result in some savings but it will not make the crossing speedier or smoother. Whatever approach you take, just remember to stay calm and don't get angry.

➡ For more details on border crossings, refer to destination chapters in On the Road.

Air

Air travel can be a bargain within the region, especially from transit hubs such as Bangkok, Singapore and Kuala Lumpur. No-frills regional carriers have made travelling between capital cities cheaper than taking land transport in some cases. Some airports in Southeast Asia charge a departure tax, so make sure you have a bit of local currency left. The following airlines often have affordable fares between cities and capitals:

Air Asia (www.airasia.com)

Cebu Pacific Air (www.cebupacificair.com)

Jetstar/ValueAir (www.jetstar.com)

Tigerair (www.tigerair.com)

SOUTHEAST ASIAN BORDER CROSSINGS

From Brunei Darussalam

TO	BORDER CROSSING	CONNECTING TOWNS	SEE MORE
Malaysia	Kuala Berait (B)/Miri (M)	Bandar Seri Begawan (B)/Miri (M)	p58
Malaysia	Muara (B)/Bandar Labuan (M)	Bandar Seri Begawan (B)/Kota Kinabalu (M)	p58

From Cambodia

TO	BORDER CROSSING	CONNECTING TOWNS	
Laos	Trapeang Kriel (C)/Nong Nok Khiene (L)	Stung Treng (C)/Si Phan Don (L)	p130
Thailand	Poipet (C)/Aranya Prathet (T)	Siem Reap (C)/Bangkok (T)	p93
Thailand	Cham Yeam (C)/Hat Lek (T)	Koh Kong (C)/Trat (T)	p111
Thailand	O Smach (C)/Chong Chom (T)	Samraong (C)/Surin (T)	p109
Thailand	Psar Pruhm (C)/Pong Nam Ron (T)	Pailin (C)/Chanthaburi (T)	p111
Thailand	Choam (C)/Chong Sa-Ngam (T)	Anlong Veng (C)/Chong Sa-Ngam (T)	p110
Vietnam	Bavet (C)/Moc Bai (V)	Phnom Penh (C)/Ho Chi Minh City (V)	p83
Vietnam	Kaam Samnor (C)/Vinh Xuong (V)	Phnom Penh (C)/Chau Doc (V)	p83
Vietnam	Prek Chak (C)/Xa Xia (V)	Kep (C)/Ha Tien (V)	p126
Vietnam	Phnom Den (C)/Tinh Bien (V)	Takeo (C)/Chau Doc (V)	p83
Vietnam	O Yadaw (C)/Le Thanh (V)	Ban Lung (C)/Pleiku (V)	p136
Vietnam	Trapeang Sre (C)/Loc Ninh (V)	Snuol (C)/Binh Long (V)	p136
Vietnam	Trapeang Plong (V)/Xa Mat (V)	Kompong Cham (C)/Tay Ninh (V)	p136

From Indonesia

TO	BORDER CROSSING	CONNECTING TOWNS	
Malaysia	Dumai (I)/Melaka (M)	Bukittinggi (I)/Melaka (M)	p250
Malaysia	Riau Islands (I)/Johor Bahru (M)	Riau Islands (I)/Johor Bahru (M)	p250
Malaysia	Entikong (I)/Tebedu (M)	Pontianak (I)/Kuching (M)	p273
Malaysia	Tarakan (I)/Tawau & Nunukan (M)	Sabah (M)/Kalimantan (I)	p273
Papua New Guinea	Skouw (I)/Wutung (P)	Jayapura (I)/Vanimo (P)	p293
Singapore	Riau Islands (I)/Singapore	Riau Islands (I)/Singapore	p250
Timor-Leste	Kupang (I)/Dili (T)	Kupang (I)/Dili (T)	p247

From Laos

TO	BORDER CROSSING	CONNECTING TOWNS	
Cambodia	Nong Nok Khiene (L)/Trapeang Kriel (C)	Si Phan Don (L)/Stung Treng (C)	p369
China	Boten (L)/Mohan (Ch)	Luang Namtha (L)/Mengla (Ch)	p347
Thailand	Tha Na Long (L)/Nong Khai (T)	Vientiane (L)/Nong Khai (T)	p323
Thailand	Paksan (L)/Bueng Kan (T)	Paksan (L)/Bueng Kan (T)	p353
Thailand	Huay Xai (L)/Chiang Khong (T)	Huay Xai (L)/Chiang Rai (T)	p345
Thailand	Tha Khaek (L)/Nakhon Phanom (T)	Tha Khaek (L)/Nakhon Phanom (T)	p353
Thailand	Savannakhet (L)/Mukdahan (T)	Savannakhet (L)/Mukdahan (T)	p363
Thailand	Vang Tao (L)/Chong Mek (T)	Pakse (L)/Ubon Ratchathani (V)	p363
Thailand	Kaen Thao (L)/Tha Li (T)	Pak Lai (L)/Loei (T)	p345

Thailand	Muang Ngeun (L)/Ban Huay Kon (T)	Hongsa (L)/Phrae (T)	p345
Vietnam	Dansavanh (L)/Lao Bao (V)	Savannakhet (L)/Dong Ha (V)	p359
Vietnam	Phou Keua (L)/Bo Y (V)	Attapeu (L)/Kon Tum (V)	p359
Vietnam	Na Phao (L)/Cha Lo (V)	Tha Khaek (L)/Dong Hoi (V)	p354
Vietnam	Nong Haet (L)/Nam Can (V)	Phonsavan (L)/Vinh (V)	p340
Vietnam	Nam Phao (L)/Cau Treo (V)	Lak Sao (L)/Vinh (V)	p354
Vietnam	Nam Soi (L)/Na Meo (V)	Sam Neua (L)/Thanh Hoa (V)	p340
Vietnam	Sop Hun (L)/Tay Trang (V)	Muang Khua (L)/Dien Bien Phu (V)	p340

From Malaysia

TO	BORDER CROSSING	CONNECTING TOWNS	
Brunei Darussalam	Bandar Labuan (M)/Muara (B)	Pulau Labuan (M)/Bandar Seri Begawan (B)	p449
Brunei Darussalam	Miri (M)/Kuala Berait (B)	Miri (M)/Bandar Seri Begawan (B)	p466
Indonesia	Melaka (M)/Dumai (I)	Melaka (M)/Bukittinggi (I)	p399
Indonesia	Johor Bahru (M)/Riau Islands (I)	Johor Bahru (M)/Riau Islands (I)	p416
Indonesia	Tawau (M)/Tarakan & Nunukan (I)	Tawau (M)/Tarakan & Nunukan (I)	p448
Indonesia	Tebedu (M)/Entikong (I)	Kuching (M)/Pontianak (I)	p456
Philippines	Sandakan (M)/Zamboanga (P)	Sandakan (M)/Zamboanga (P)	p443
Singapore	Johor Bahru (M)/Singapore	Johor Bahru (M)/Singapore	p417
Thailand	Bukit Kayu Hitam (M)/Sadao (T)	Alor Setar (M)/Hat Yai (T)	p413
Thailand	Padang Besar (M)/Hat Yai (T)	Kangar (M)/Hat Yai (T)	p413
Thailand	Pulau Langkawi (M)/ Satun & Ko Lipe (T)	Pulau Langkawi (M)/ Satun & Ko Lipe (T)	p414
Thailand	Rantau Panjang (M)/Sungai Kolok (T)	Kota Bharu (M)/Bangkok (T)	p429

From Myanmar

TO	BORDER CROSSING	CONNECTING TOWNS	
China	Mu-Se (M)/Ruili (C)	Mu-Se (M)/Ruili (C)	p532
Thailand	Tachileik (M)/Mae Sai (T)	Kyaintong (M)/Mae Sai (T)	p510
Thailand	Kawthoung (M)/Saphan Pla Pier (T)	Kawthoung (M)/Ranong (M)	p502
Thailand	Myawaddy (M)/Mae Sot (T)	Hpa-an (M)/Mae Sot (T)	p502

From Thailand

TO	BORDER CROSSING	CONNECTING TOWNS	
Cambodia	Aranya Prathet (T)/Poipet (C)	Bangkok (T)/Siem Reap (C)	p735
Cambodia	Hat Lek (T)/Cham Yeam (C)	Trat (T)/Koh Kong (C)	p738
Cambodia	Chong Chom (T)/O Smach (C)	Surin (T)/Samraong (C)	p735
Cambodia	Pong Nam Ron (T)/Psar Pruhm (C)	Chanthaburi (T)/Pailin (C)	p738
Cambodia	Chong Sa-Ngam (T)/Choam (C)	Chong Sa-Ngam (T)/Anlong Veng (C)	p735
Laos	Nong Khai (T)/Tha Na Long (L)	Nong Khai (T)/Vientiane (L)	p729
Laos	Bueng Kan (T)/Paksan (L)	Bueng Kan (T)/Paksan (L)	p728
Laos	Chiang Khong (T)/Huay Xai (L)	Chiang Rai (T)/Huay Xai (L)	p707
Laos	Nakhon Phanom (T)/Tha Khaek (L)	Nakhon Phanom (T)/Tha Khaek (L)	p728
Laos	Mukdahan (T)/Savannakhet (L)	Mukdahan (T)/Savannakhet (L)	p722
Laos	Chong Mek (T)/Vang Tao (L)	Ubon Ratchathani (T)/Pakse (L)	p722
Laos	Tha Li (T)/Kaen Thao (L)	Loei (T)/Pak Lai (L)	p728
Laos	Ban Huay Kon (T)/Muang Ngeun (L)	Phrae (T)/Hongsa (L)	p707

Malaysia	Ko Lipe (T)/Pulau Langkawi (M)	Ko Lipe (T)/Pulau Langkawi (M)	p775
Malaysia	Rantau Panjang (M)/Sungai Kolok (T)	Kota Bharu (M)/Sungai Kolok (T)	p761
Myanmar	Mae Sai (T)/Tachileik (M)	Mae Sai (T)/Kyaintong (M)	p704
Myanmar	Saphan Pla Pier (T)/Kawthoung (M)	Ranong (T)/Kawthoung (M)	p760
Myanmar	Mae Sot (T)/Myawaddy (M)	Mae Sot (T)/Hpa-an (M)	p716

From Vietnam

TO	BORDER CROSSING	CONNECTING TOWNS	
Cambodia	Moc Bai (V)/Bavet (C)	Ho Chi Minh City (V)/ Phnom Penh (C)	p891
Cambodia	Vinh Xuong (V)/Kaam Samnor (C)	Chau Doc (V)/Phnom Penh (C)	p898
Cambodia	Xa Xia (V)/Prek Chak (C)	Ha Tien (V)/Kep (C)	p898
Cambodia	Tinh Bien (V)/Phnom Den (C)	Chau Doc (V)/Takeo (C)	p898
Cambodia	Le Thanh (V)/O Yadaw (C)	Pleiku (V)/Ban Lung (C)	p883
China	Lao Cai (V)/Hekou (Ch)	Hanoi (V)/Kunming (Ch)	p838
China	Huu Nghi Quan (V)/Pingxiang (Ch)	Dong Dang (V)/Pingxiang (Ch)	p836
China	Mong Cai (V)/Dongxing (Ch)	Mong Cai (V)/Dongxing (Ch)	p836
Laos	Lao Bao (V)/Dansavanh (L)	Dong Ha (V)/Savannakhet (L)	p853
Laos	Bo Y (V)/Phou Keua (L)	Kon Tum (V)/Attapeu (L)	p881
Laos	Na Phao (L)/Cha Lo (V)	Dong H4 (V)/Savannakhet (L)	p853
Laos	Nam Can (V)/Nong Haet (L)	Vinh (V)/Phonsavan (L)	p847
Laos	Cau Treo (V)/Nam Phao (L)	Vinh (V)/Lak Sao (L)	p847
Laos	Nam Soi (V)/Na Meo (L)	Thanh Hoa (V)/Sam Neua (L)	p844
Laos	Tay Trang (V)/Sop Hun (L)	Dien Bien Phu (V)/Muang Khua (L)	p844

Air Passes

National airlines of Southeast Asian countries frequently run promotional deals from select Western cities or for regional travel. Airline alliances also offer regional air passes. You'll have to do a generic web search for 'air passes' to find the most up-to-date information, as monitoring sites aren't always current.

Bicycle

Touring Southeast Asia on a bicycle has long had many supporters. Long-distance cyclists typically start in Thailand and head south through Malaysia to Singapore. Road conditions are good enough for long-haul touring in most places, but mountain bikes are definitely recommended for forays off the beaten track.

Vietnam is a great place to travel by bicycle – you can take bikes on buses, and the entire coastal route is feasible. If flat-land cycling is not your style, then Indonesia might be the challenge you're looking for. Roads here are bad and inclines steep, but the Sumatran jungle is still deep and dark. In Laos and Cambodia, road conditions are improving and the traffic is still light.

Top-quality bicycles and components can be bought in major cities such as Bangkok, but fittings are hard to find. Bicycles can travel by air; check with the airline about charges and specifications.

Boat

Ferries and boats travel between Singapore and Indonesia, Malaysia and Indonesia, Thailand and Malaysia, and the Philippines and Malaysia. You also have the option of crossing the Mekong River from Thailand to Laos and from Cambodia to Vietnam. Guesthouses or travel agents sell tickets and provide travellers with updated departure times. Check visa regulations at port cities; some don't issue visas on arrival.

Bus

In most cases, land borders are crossed via bus. In some cases, direct buses connect two major towns with a stop for border formalities, while in other cases buses terminate at the border towns and you'll need to negotiate onward travel on the other side. Bus travellers will enjoy a higher standard of luxury in Thailand, the Philippines and Malaysia, where roads are well paved, and reliable schedules exist. Be aware that theft does occur on some long-distance buses; keep all valuables on your person, not in a stowed locked bag.

MOTORCYCLE SAFETY

Road traffic accidents are a leading cause of death in Southeast Asia, especially in Thailand, and motorcycles are among the most vulnerable vehicles on the road, in part because of no (or unenforced) helmet laws, reckless driving, poor road conditions and inadequate emergency response systems. The World Health Organization has begun a region-wide campaign trying to reduce these accidental deaths.

Foreigners who rent motorbikes in the region expose themselves to greater risk because they don't have prior experience driving motorcycles and don't understand the local road rules (or lack of rules). Foreign consulates in Indonesia and Thailand are often inundated with requests to assist nationals injured in motorcycling accidents.

If you accept the risks, be sure to take the following precautions:

➜ Wear a helmet and protective clothing (long pants and long shirts).

➜ Drive carefully and defensively.

➜ Yield to bigger vehicles; might makes right here.

➜ Slow down in rainy conditions, around curves or where there is loose gravel.

➜ Get in the habit of climbing off a moto to your left, stepping clear of the scorching exhaust pipe. Singed flesh doesn't smell very nice and, in the tropical humidity, takes a long time to heal.

Most Asians are so adept at riding motorcycles that they can balance the whole family on the front bumper or even take a quick nap as a passenger. Foreigners unaccustomed to motorcycles are not as graceful. If you're riding on the back of a motorcycle, remember to relax so that the driver can balance your body. Tall people should keep long legs tucked in as most drivers are used to shorter passengers. Women wearing skirts should collect loose material so it doesn't catch in the wheel or drive chain. On older motorcycles, watch out for the exposed exhaust pipe when riding and disembarking; it gets hot enough to barbecue exposed flesh.

Car & Motorcycle

What is the sound of freedom in Southeast Asia? The 'put-put' noise of a motorcycle. For visitors, motorcycles are convenient for getting around the beaches or touring the countryside. Car hire is also available in most countries and is handy for local sightseeing or long-haul trips. You could hit Thailand and Malaysia by car pretty easily, enjoying well-signposted, well-paved roads. Road conditions in Laos and Cambodia vary, although sealed roads are becoming the norm. Indonesia and the Philippines have roads that vary between islands, but most are in need of repair. Vietnam's major highways are in relatively good health.

Driving Licences

Parts of Southeast Asia, including Malaysia, Indonesia and Thailand, are good spots for exploring by car and motorcycle. If you are planning to do any driving, get an International Driving Permit (IDP) from your local automobile association before you leave your home country; IDPs are inexpensive and valid for one year. Read up on road safety as road accidents are a serious concern in Southeast Asia.

Insurance

Get insurance with a motorcycle if at all possible. The more reputable motorcycle-rental places insure all their motorcycles; some will do it for an extra charge. Without insurance, you're responsible for anything that happens to the bike. To be absolutely clear about your liability, ask for a written estimate of the replacement cost for a similar bike – and take photos as a guarantee. Some agencies will accept only the replacement cost of a new motorcycle. Insurance for a rented car is also necessary. Be sure to ask the car-rental agent about liability and damage coverage.

Rental

Western car-rental chains camp out at Southeast Asian airports, capitals and major tourist destinations. Mum-and-Dad shops also rent motorcycles and cars, but these fleets are often poorly maintained. Before renting a vehicle, do a walk around with the proprietor, noting any existing damage so that you won't be charged for old wounds. Taking pictures of the vehicle before driving it off the premises is another safeguard. Check the tyre treads and brakes to make sure that the vehicle is in good working order.

Road Rules & Safety

Drive carefully and defensively. Motorcycle accidents

are a leading cause of injury in Southeast Asia. Remember, too, that smaller vehicles yield to bigger vehicles regardless of the circumstances – on the road, might is right. The middle of the road is used as a passing lane, even in oncoming traffic. Your horn notifies other vehicles that you intend to pass.

Hitching

Hitching is never entirely safe and is not recommended. Travellers who hitch should understand that they are taking a small but potentially serious risk. People who do choose to hitch will be safer if they travel in pairs and let someone know where they are planning to go.

Local Transport

Because personal ownership of cars in Southeast Asia is limited (though this is changing in middle-income countries such as Malaysia and Thailand, where car ownership is increasing), local transport within towns is a roaring business. For the right price, drivers will haul you from the bus station to town, around town, around the corner or around in circles. The bicycle rickshaw still survives in the region, assuming such aliases as săhmlór in Thailand and cyclo in Vietnam. Anything motorised is often modified to carry passengers – from Thailand's obnoxious three-wheeled chariot, the túk-túk, to the Philippines' altered US Army jeeps. In large cit-

ies, extensive bus systems either travel on fixed routes or do informal loops around the city, picking up passengers on the way. Bangkok, Kuala Lumpur and Singapore boast state-of-the-art light-rail systems that make zipping around town feel like time travel.

Train

The *International Express* train runs from Bangkok all the way through the Malay peninsula, ending its journey in Singapore. Trains also serve Nong Khai, on the Thailand–Cambodia border, and Aranya Prathet, on the Thailand–Laos border. Thailand and Malaysia have the most extensive rail systems, although trains rarely run on time.

Health

Health issues and the quality of medical facilities vary enormously depending on where you travel in Southeast Asia.

Travellers tend to worry about contracting infectious diseases when in the tropics, but infections are a rare cause of serious illness or death in travellers.

Accidental injury (such as traffic accidents) and pre-existing medical conditions account for most life-threatening problems. Becoming ill in some way, however, is relatively common and may include respiratory infections, diarrhoea and dengue fever. Fortunately, most common illnesses can be either prevented or treated.

BEFORE YOU GO

Pack medications in their original, clearly labelled containers. A signed, dated letter from your physician describing your medical conditions and medications, including generic names, is recommended. If carrying syringes or needles, have a physician's letter stating their medical necessity. If you have a heart condition, bring a copy of your ECG.

If you take any regular medication, bring a double supply in case of loss or theft. In most Southeast Asian countries, excluding Singapore, you can buy many medications over the counter, but it can be difficult to find some of the newer drugs, particularly the latest antidepressants, blood-pressure medications and contraceptive pills.

Insurance

Even if you are fit and healthy, don't travel without health insurance – accidents do happen. Adventure activities, such as rock climbing, often require extra coverage. If your existing health insurance doesn't cover you for medical expenses abroad, consider purchasing travel insurance that includes emergency evacuation.

Find out in advance if your insurance plan will make payments directly to providers or reimburse you later for overseas health expenditures. (In many countries doctors expect payment in cash.) If you have to claim later, make sure you keep all documentation. Some policies ask you to call a centre in your home country, where an immediate assessment of your problem is made.

Divers should ensure their insurance covers them for decompression illness – get specialised dive insurance through an organisation, such as **Divers Alert Network** (DAN; www.diversalert-network.org). Have a dive medical before you leave your home country; there are certain medical conditions that are incompatible with diving.

Recommended Vaccinations

Specialised travel-medicine clinics can advise on which vaccines are recommended for your trip. Some vaccines require multiple injections spaced out over a certain period of time; start the process six weeks prior to departure.

The World Health Organization (WHO) recommends the following vaccinations for travellers to Southeast Asia:

➡ Adult diphtheria and tetanus

FURTHER READING

Centers for Disease Control & Prevention (www.cdc.gov) Country-specific advice.

International Travel & Health (www.who.int/ith) Health guide published by the WHO.

MD Travel Health (www.mdtravelhealth.com) Travel-health recommendations for every country.

- Hepatitis A
- Hepatitis B
- Measles, mumps and rubella (MMR)
- Polio
- Typhoid
- Varicella

The following immunisations are recommended for long-term travellers (more than one month) or those at special risk:

- Japanese B Encephalitis
- Meningitis
- Rabies
- Tuberculosis (TB)

Required Vaccinations

The only vaccine required by international regulations is for yellow fever. Proof of vaccination will be required only if you have visited a country in the yellow-fever zone within the six days before entering Southeast Asia. If you are travelling to Southeast Asia from Africa or South America you should check to see if you require proof of vaccination.

IN SOUTHEAST ASIA

Availability of Health Care

Most capital cities in Southeast Asia have clinics that cater specifically to travellers and expats. These clinics are more expensive than local medical facilities but offer a superior standard of care and the staff speaks English.

It is difficult to find reliable medical care in rural areas. Your embassy and insurance company are good contacts.

The standard of care in Southeast Asia varies from country to country:

Brunei General care is reasonable. There is no local medical university, so expats and foreign-

trained locals run the health-care system. Serious or complex cases are better managed in Singapore.

Cambodia There are international clinics in Phnom Penh and Siem Reap and an NGO-run surgical hospital in Battambang that provide primary care and emergency stabilisation. Elsewhere, government hospitals should be avoided. For more serious conditions, including dengue fever, it is advisable to be evacuated to Bangkok.

MEDICAL CHECKLIST

Recommended items for a personal medical kit:

- antibacterial cream, eg mupirocin
- antibiotic for skin infections, eg amoxicillin/clavulanate or cephalexin
- antibiotics for diarrhoea, eg norfloxacin or ciprofloxacin; azithromycin for bacterial diarrhoea; tinidazole for giardiasis or amoebic dysentery
- antifungal cream, eg clotrimazole
- antihistamine, eg cetirizine for daytime and promethazine for night
- anti-inflammatory, eg ibuprofen
- antiseptic, eg Betadine
- antispasmodic for stomach cramps, eg Buscopan
- contraceptives
- decongestant, eg pseudoephedrine
- DEET-based insect repellent
- diarrhoea treatment, including an oral rehydration solution (eg Gastrolyte), diarrhoea 'stopper' (eg loperamide) and antinausea medication (eg prochlorperazine)
- first-aid items, eg scissors, plasters, bandages, gauze, thermometer (but not one with mercury), sterile needles and syringes, safety pins and tweezers
- indigestion medication, eg Quick-Eze or Mylanta
- iodine tablets to purify water
- laxative, eg Coloxyl
- paracetamol
- permethrin to impregnate clothing and mosquito nets
- steroid cream for allergic or itchy rashes, eg 1% to 2% hydrocortisone
- sunscreen and hat
- throat lozenges
- thrush (vaginal yeast infection) treatment, eg Clotrimazole pessaries or Diflucan tablet
- Ural or equivalent if you're prone to urine infections
- Divers and surfers should seek specialised advice stocking medical kits for coral cuts and tropical ear infection treatments.

East Timor No private clinics. The government hospital is basic and should be avoided.

Indonesia Local medical care in general is not yet up to international standards. Foreign doctors are not allowed to work in Indonesia, but some clinics catering to foreigners have 'international advisers'. Almost all Indonesian doctors work at government hospitals during the day and in private practices at night. This means that private hospitals often don't have their best staff available during the day. Serious cases are evacuated to Australia or Singapore.

Laos There are no good facilities in Laos; the nearest acceptable facilities are in northern Thailand. The Australian Embassy Clinic in Vientiane treats citizens of Commonwealth countries.

Malaysia Medical care in the major centres is good and most problems can be adequately dealt with in Kuala Lumpur.

Myanmar (Burma) Local medical care is dismal and local hospitals should be used only in desperation. There is an international medical clinic in Yangon.

Philippines Good medical care is available in most major cities.

Singapore Excellent medical facilities and referral centre for most of Southeast Asia.

Thailand After Singapore, Bangkok is the city of choice for expats living in Southeast Asia who require specialised care.

Vietnam Government hospitals are overcrowded and basic. In order to treat foreigners, the facility needs to obtain a special licence, and so far only a few have been provided. The private clinics in Hanoi, Ho Chi Minh City and Danang should be your first choice.

Infectious Diseases

Cutaneous Larva Migrans

Risk areas All countries except Singapore.

This disease, caused by dog hookworm, is particularly common on the beaches of Thailand. The rash starts as a small lump then slowly spreads in a linear fashion. It is intensely itchy, especially at night. It is easily treated with medications and should not be cut out or frozen.

Dengue

Risk areas All countries.

This mosquito-borne disease is increasingly problematic throughout Southeast Asia, especially in the cities. There is no vaccine, only prevention. The mosquito that carries dengue bites day and night, so use DEET-mosquito cream periodically throughout the day. Symptoms include high fever, severe headache and body ache (dengue used to be known as breakbone fever). Some people develop a rash and experience diarrhoea. There is no specific treatment, just rest and paracetamol – do not take aspirin as it increases the likelihood of haemorrhaging. See a doctor to be diagnosed and monitored.

Don't assume this is a rural issue: Southeast Asia's cities, such as Bangkok and Singapore, as well as Thailand's southern islands and Chiang Mai Province are high-risk areas.

Hepatitis A

Risk areas All countries.

A problem throughout the region, this food- and water-borne virus infects the liver, causing jaundice (yellow skin and eyes), nausea and lethargy. There is no specific treatment for hepatitis A; you just need to allow time for the liver to heal. All travellers to Southeast Asia should be vaccinated against hepatitis A.

Hepatitis B

Risk areas All countries.

The only serious sexually transmitted disease that can be prevented by vaccination, hepatitis B is spread by body fluids. In some parts of Southeast Asia, up to

---

RARE BUT BE AWARE

The following diseases are common in the local population (in all countries except Singapore) but rare in travellers.

➡ **Filariasis** – a mosquito-borne disease prevented by mosquito-avoidance measures.

➡ **Typhus** – murine typhus is spread by the bite of a flea and scrub typhus is spread via a mite; symptoms include fever, muscle pains and a rash. Prevention is through general insect-avoidance measures or doxycycline.

➡ **Tuberculosis** – medical and aid workers and long-term travellers should take precautions and consider pre- and post-travel testing; symptoms are fever, cough, weight loss and tiredness.

➡ **Meliodosis** (Thailand only) – an infection contracted by skin contact with soil; symptoms are similar to tuberculosis.

➡ **Japanese B Encephalitis** (Vietnam, Thailand and Indonesia are highest risk areas) – a viral disease, transmitted by mosquitoes; most cases occur in rural areas and vaccination is recommended for travellers spending more than one month outside cities.

20% of the population carry hepatitis B, and usually are unaware of it. The long-term consequences can include liver cancer and cirrhosis.

Hepatitis E

Risk areas All countries.
Hepatitis E is transmitted through contaminated food and water, and has similar symptoms to hepatitis A but is far less common. It is a severe problem in pregnant women, and can result in the death of both mother and baby. There is currently no vaccine; prevention is by following safe eating and drinking guidelines.

HIV

Risk areas All countries.
HIV is now one of the most common causes of death in people under the age of 50 in Thailand. The Southeast Asian countries with the worst and most rapidly increasing HIV problem are Cambodia, Myanmar, Thailand and Vietnam. Heterosexual sex is now the main method of transmission in these countries.

Influenza

Risk areas All countries.
Present year-round in the tropics, influenza (flu) symptoms include high fever, muscle aches, runny nose, cough and sore throat. It can be very severe in people over the age of 65, and in those with underlying medical conditions such as heart disease or diabetes; vaccination is recommended for these individuals. There is no specific treatment, just rest and paracetamol.

Leptospirosis

Risk areas Thailand and Malaysia.
Leptospirosis is most commonly contracted after river rafting or canyoning. Early symptoms are very similar to the flu, and include headache and fever. The disease can vary from very mild to fatal. Diagnosis is through blood tests and it is easily treated with doxycycline.

Malaria

Risk areas All countries except Singapore and Brunei.
Many parts of Southeast Asia, particularly city and resort areas, have minimal to no risk of malaria, and the risk of side effects from the prevention tablets may outweigh the risk of getting the disease.

For most rural areas, however, the risk of contracting the disease is increased and malaria can be fatal. Before you travel, seek medical advice on the right medication and dosage.

Malaria is caused by a parasite transmitted by the bite of an infected mosquito. The most important symptom of malaria is fever, but general symptoms such as headache, diarrhoea, cough or chills may also occur. Diagnosis can only be made by taking a blood sample.

Two strategies are combined to prevent malaria – mosquito avoidance and antimalarial medications.

Travellers are advised to prevent mosquito bites by taking the following steps:

➡ Use an insect repellent containing DEET on exposed skin.

➡ Sleep under a mosquito net that is impregnated with permethrin.

➡ Choose accommodation with screens and fans (if not air-conditioned).

➡ Impregnate clothing with permethrin when in high-risk areas.

➡ Wear long sleeves and trousers in light colours.

➡ Use mosquito coils.

➡ Spray your room with insect repellent before going out for your evening meal.

Measles

Risk areas All countries except Singapore and Brunei.
Measles remains a problem in some parts of Southeast Asia. This highly contagious bacterial infection is spread via coughing and sneezing. Most people born before 1966 are immune as they had the disease during childhood. Measles starts with a high fever and rash, and can be complicated by pneumonia and brain disease. There is no specific treatment.

Rabies

Risk areas All countries except Singapore and Brunei.
Still a common problem in most parts of Southeast Asia, this uniformly fatal disease is spread by the bite or lick of an infected animal, most commonly a dog or monkey. You should seek medical advice immediately after any animal bite and commence post-exposure treatment. Having a pre-travel vaccination means the post-bite treatment is greatly simplified. If an animal bites you, gently wash the wound with soap and water, and apply iodine-based antiseptic. If you are not pre-vaccinated you will need to receive rabies immunoglobulin as soon as possible.

Schistosomiasis

Risk areas Philippines, Vietnam and Sulawesi (Indonesia).
Schistosomiasis is a tiny parasite that enters your skin after you've been swimming in contaminated water. Travellers usually only get a light infection and hence develop no symptoms. On rare occasions, travellers may develop 'Katayama fever'. This occurs some weeks after exposure, as the parasite passes through the lungs and causes an allergic reaction; symptoms are coughing and fever. Schistosomiasis is easily treated with medications.

STDs

Risk areas All countries.
Sexually transmitted diseases most commonly found in Southeast Asia include herpes, warts, syphilis, gonorrhoea and chlamydia. People carrying these diseases

FOOD & WATER

Food and water contamination are the biggest risk factor for contracting traveller's diarrhoea. Here are some safety considerations:

➡ Eat only freshly cooked food and fruit that can be peeled.

➡ Avoid food that has been sitting around for hours.

➡ Eat in busy restaurants with a high turnover of customers.

➡ Never drink tap water; opt for bottled or filtered water instead.

➡ Avoid ice.

➡ Avoid fresh juices that may have been watered down.

➡ Boil water or use iodine tablets as a means of purification; pregnant women or those with thyroid problems should avoid iodine use.

often have no signs of infection. Condoms will prevent gonorrhoea and chlamydia but not warts or herpes. If after a sexual encounter you develop any rash, lumps, discharge or pain when passing urine, seek immediate medical attention. If you have been sexually active during your travels, have an STD check on your return home.

Strongyloides

Risk areas Cambodia, Myanmar and Thailand.

This parasite, transmitted by skin-contact with soil, is common in travellers but rarely affects them. It is characterised by an unusual skin rash called larva currens – a linear rash on the trunk that comes and goes. Most people don't have other symptoms until their immune system becomes severely suppressed, when the parasite can cause an overwhelming infection. It can be treated with medications.

Typhoid

Risk areas All countries except Singapore.

This serious bacterial infection is spread via food and water. It gives a high and slowly progressive fever and a headache, and may be accompanied by a dry cough and stomach pain. It is diagnosed by blood tests and treated with antibiotics. Vaccination is recommended for all travellers spending more than a week in Southeast Asia, or travelling outside the major cities. Vaccination is not 100% effective so you must still be careful about what you eat and drink.

Traveller's Diarrhoea

Traveller's diarrhoea is by far the most common problem that affects travellers – between 30% and 50% of people will suffer from it within two weeks of starting their trip. In over 80% of cases, traveller's diarrhoea is caused by bacteria (there are numerous potential culprits), and therefore responds promptly to treatment with antibiotics. Treatment will depend on your situation – how sick you are, how quickly you need to get better etc.

Traveller's diarrhoea is defined as the passage of more than three watery bowel actions within 24 hours, plus at least one other symptom such as fever, cramps, nausea, vomiting or feeling generally unwell.

Treatment consists of staying well hydrated; rehydration solutions such as Gastrolyte are the best for this. Antibiotics such as norfloxacin, ciprofloxacin or azithromycin will kill the bacteria quickly.

Loperamide is just a 'stopper'. It can be helpful if you have to go on a long bus ride. Don't take loperamide if you have a fever, or blood in your stools. Seek medical attention quickly if you do not respond to an appropriate antibiotic.

Amoebic Dysentery

Amoebic dysentery is very rare in travellers but is often misdiagnosed by poor-quality labs in Southeast Asia. Symptoms are similar to bacterial diarrhoea – fever, bloody diarrhoea and generally feeling unwell. You should always seek reliable medical care if you have blood in your diarrhoea.

Treatment involves two drugs: tinidazole or metronidazole to kill the parasite in your gut, and then a second drug to kill the cysts. If left untreated, complications such as liver or gut abscesses can occur.

Giardiasis

Giardia lamblia is a relatively common parasite in travellers. Symptoms include nausea, bloating, excess gas, fatigue and intermittent diarrhoea. 'Eggy' burps are often attributed solely to giardiasis, but work in Nepal has shown that – are not specific to this infection. The parasite will eventually go away if left untreated but this can take months.

The treatment of choice is tinidazole, with metronidazole being a second option.

Environmental Hazards

Heat

Many parts of Southeast Asia are hot and humid. For most people it takes at least two weeks to adapt to the climate. Swelling of the feet and ankles is common, as are muscle cramps caused by excessive sweating. You can prevent these by avoiding dehydration and excessive activity; you should also take it easy when you first arrive. Treat cramps by stopping activity, resting, rehydrating with double-strength rehydration solution and gently stretching.

Dehydration is the main contributor to heat exhaustion. Symptoms include weakness, headache, irritability, nausea or vomiting, sweaty skin, a fast pulse, and a normal or slightly elevated body temperature. Treatment involves getting out of the heat, fanning and applying cool wet cloths to the skin, lying flat with legs raised, and rehydrating with water containing a quarter of a teaspoon of salt per litre. Recovery is usually rapid, though it is common to feel weak afterwards.

Heat stroke is a serious medical emergency. Symptoms come on suddenly and include weakness, nausea, a hot dry body with a body temperature of over 41°C, dizziness, confusion, loss of coordination, seizures, and eventually collapse and loss of consciousness. Seek medical help and commence cooling by getting out of the heat, removing clothes, fanning and applying cool wet cloths or ice to the body, especially to the groin and armpits.

Prickly heat is a common skin rash in the tropics caused by sweat being trapped under the skin. The result is an itchy rash of tiny lumps. Treat by moving out of the heat and into an air-conditioned area for a few hours and by having cool showers. Creams and ointments clog the skin so they should be avoided. Locally bought prickly-heat powder can be helpful.

Insect Bites & Stings

Bedbugs don't carry disease but their bites are very itchy. They live in the cracks of furniture and walls, and then migrate to the bed at night to feed on you. You can treat the itch with an antihistamine.

Lice inhabit various parts of your body, but most commonly your head and pubic area. Transmission is via close contact with an infected person. Lice can be difficult to treat and you may need numerous applications of an anti-lice shampoo. Pubic lice are usually contracted from sexual contact.

Ticks are contracted after walking in rural areas. They are commonly found behind the ears, on the belly and in armpits. If you have had a tick bite and experience symptoms such as a rash at the site of the bite or elsewhere, or fever or muscle aches, you should see a doctor. Doxycycline prevents tick-borne diseases.

Leeches are found in humid rainforest areas. They do not transmit any disease but their bites are often intensely itchy for weeks afterwards and can easily become infected. Apply an iodine-based antiseptic to any leech bite to help prevent infection.

Bee and wasp stings mainly cause problems for people who are allergic to them. Anyone with a serious bee or wasp allergy should carry an injection of adrenaline (eg an Epipen) for emergency treatment. For others, pain is the main problem – apply ice to the sting and take painkillers.

Most jellyfish in Southeast Asian waters are not dangerous, just irritating. First aid for jellyfish stings involves pouring vinegar onto the affected area to neutralise the poison. Do not rub sand or water onto the stings. Take painkillers, and if you feel ill in any way after being stung seek medical advice. Take local advice if there are dangerous jellyfish around and keep out of the water.

Parasites

Numerous parasites are common in local populations in Southeast Asia; however, most of these are rare in travellers. The two rules for avoiding parasitic infections are to wear shoes and to avoid eating raw food, especially fish, pork and vegetables. A number of parasites are transmitted via the skin by walking barefoot, including *Strongyloides*, hookworm and cutaneous larva migrans.

Skin Problems

Fungal rashes are common in humid climates. There are two common fungal rashes that tend to affect travellers. The first occurs in moist areas that get less air, such as the groin, armpits and between the toes. It starts as a red patch that slowly spreads and is usually itchy. Treatment involves keeping the skin dry, avoiding chafing and using an antifungal cream such as clotrimazole or Lamisil. *Tinea versicolor* is also common – this fungus causes small, light-coloured patches, most commonly on the back, chest and shoulders. Consult a doctor.

Cuts and scratches become easily infected in humid climates. Take meticulous care of them to prevent complications such as abscesses. Immediately wash all wounds in clean water and apply antiseptic. If you develop signs of infection (increasing pain and redness), see a doctor. Divers and surfers should be particularly careful with coral cuts as they can be easily infected.

Snakes

Southeast Asia is home to many species of both poisonous and harmless snakes.

Assume that all snakes are poisonous and never try to catch one. Wear boots and long pants if walking in an area that may have snakes. First aid in the event of a snakebite involves pressure immobilisation using an elastic bandage firmly wrapped around the affected limb, starting at the bite site and working up towards the chest. The bandage should not be so tight that the circulation is cut off, and the fingers or toes should be kept free so the circulation can be checked. Immobilise the limb with a splint and carry the victim to medical attention. Do not use tourniquets or try to suck the venom out. Antivenin is available for most species.

Sunburn

Even on a cloudy day sunburn can occur rapidly. Always use a strong sunscreen (at least factor 30), making sure to reapply after a swim, and always wear a wide-brimmed hat and sunglasses outdoors. Avoid lying in the sun during the hottest part of the day (10am to 2pm). If you become sunburnt, stay out of the sun until you have recovered, apply cool compresses and take painkillers for the discomfort. One per cent hydrocortisone cream applied twice daily is also helpful.

Women's Health

In the urban areas of Southeast Asia, supplies of sanitary products are readily available. Birth-control options may be limited so bring adequate supplies of your own form of contraception. Heat, humidity and antibiotics can all contribute to thrush. Treatment is with antifungal creams and pessaries such as clotrimazole. A practical alternative is a single tablet of fluconazole (Diflucan). Urinary tract infections can be precipitated by dehydration or long bus journeys without toilet stops; bring suitable antibiotics.

Pregnant women should receive specialised advice before travelling. The ideal time to travel is in the second trimester (between 16 and 28 weeks), when the risk of pregnancy-related problems is at its lowest and women generally feel at their best. During the first trimester there is a risk of miscarriage and in the third trimester complications such as premature labour and high blood pressure are possible. It's wise to travel with a companion. Always carry a list of quality medical facilities available at your destination and ensure you continue your standard antenatal care at these facilities. Avoid rural travel in areas with poor transport and medical facilities. Most of all, ensure travel insurance covers all pregnancy-related possibilities.

Malaria is a high-risk disease during pregnancy. WHO recommends that pregnant women do *not* travel to areas with chloroquine-resistant malaria. None of the more effective antimalarial drugs are completely safe in pregnancy.

Traveller's diarrhoea can quickly lead to dehydration and result in inadequate blood flow to the placenta. Many of the drugs used to treat various diarrhoea bugs are not recommended in pregnancy. Azithromycin is considered safe.

Language

This chapter offers basic vocabulary to help you get around Southeast Asia. Read our coloured pronunciation guides as if they were English, and you'll be understood. The stressed syllables are in italics. The polite and informal forms are indicated by the abbreviations 'pol' and 'inf' where needed. The abbreviations 'm' and 'f' indicate masculine and feminine gender respectively.

BURMESE

In Burmese, there's a difference between aspirated consonants (pronounced with a puff of air) and unaspirated ones. These consonants are said with a puff of air after the sound: ch (as in 'church'), k (as in 'kite'), ş (as in 'sick'), t (as in 'talk'); the following ones are pronounced with a puff of air before the sound: hl (as in 'life'), hm (as in 'me'), hn (as in 'not'), hng (as in 'sing'), hny (as in 'canyon'). Note also that the apostrophe (') represents the sound heard between 'uh-oh', th is pronounced as in 'thin' and ṭh as in 'their'.

There are three distinct tones in Burmese (the raising and lowering of pitch on certain syllables). They are indicated in our pronunciation guides by the accent mark above the vowel: high creaky tone, as in 'heart' (á), plain high tone, as in 'car' (à), and the low tone (a). Note also that ai is pronounced as in 'aisle', aw as in 'law', and au as in 'brown'.

WANT MORE?

For in-depth language information and handy phrases, check out Lonely Planet's *Southeast Asia Phrasebook*. You'll find it at **shop.lonelyplanet.com**, or you can buy Lonely Planet's iPhone phrasebooks at the Apple App Store.

Basics

Hello.	မင်္ဂလာပါ။	ming·guh·la·ba
Goodbye.	သွားမယ်နော်။	thwà·me·naw
Excuse me.	ဆောရီးနော်။	sàw·rì·naw
Sorry.	ဆောရီးနော်။	sàw·rì·naw
Please.	တဆိတ်လောက်။	duh·şay'·lau'
Thank you.	ကျေးဇူး တင်ပါတယ်။	jày·zù ding·ba·de
Yes.	ဟုတ်ကဲ့။	hoh'·gé
No.	ဟင့်အင်း။	híng·ìn
Help!	ကယ်ပါ။	ge·ba

Numbers – Burmese

1	တစ်	di'
2	နှစ်	hni'
3	သုံး	thòhng
4	လေး	làv
5	ငါး	ngà
6	ခြောက်	chau'
7	ခုနစ်	kung·ni'
8	ရှစ်	shi'
9	ကိုး	gòh
10	တစ်ဆယ်	duh·şe

What's your name?
နာမည် ဘယ်လို
ခေါ် သလဲ။
nang·me be·loh
kaw·ṭhuh·lè

My name is ...
ကျနော်/ကျမ
နာမည်က- - -ပါ။
juh·náw/juh·má
nang·me·gá ... ba (m/f)

Do you speak English?
အင်္ဂလိပ်လို
ìng·guh·lay'·loh

ပြောတတ်သလား။ byàw·da'·thuh·là

I don't understand.
နားမလည်ဘူး။ nà·muh·le·bòo

How much is it?
ဒါဘယ်လောက်လဲ။ da be·lau'·lè

Where are the toilets?
အိမ်သာ ဘယ်မှာလဲ။ ayng·ţha be·hma·lè

I'd like the ..., please.	- - - ပေးပါ။	... bày·ba
bill	ဘောက်ချာ	bau'·cha
menu	မီးနူး	mì·nù
Call ...	- - - ခေါ်ပေးပါ။	... kaw·bày·ba
a doctor	ဆရာဝန်	şuh·ya·wung
the police	ရဲ	yèh

FILIPINO

Filipino is easy to pronounce and most sounds are familiar to English speakers. In addition, the relationship between Filipino sounds and their spelling is straightforward and consistent, meaning that each letter is always pronounced the same way. Note that ai is pronounced as in 'aisle', ay as in 'say', ew like ee with rounded lips, oh as the 'o' in 'go', ow as in 'how' and ooy as the 'wea' in 'tweak'. The r sound is stronger than in English and rolled. The glottal stop, pronounced like the pause between the two syllables in 'uh-oh', is indicated in our pronunciation guides by an apostrophe (').

Basics

Good day.	*Magandáng araw pô.* (pol)	ma·gan·*dang* a·row po'
	Magandáng araw. (inf)	ma·gan·*dang* a·row
Goodbye.	*Paalam na pô.* (pol)	pa·a·lam na po'
	Babay. (inf)	*ba*·bai

Numbers – Filipino

1	*isá*	ee·*sa*
2	*dalawá*	da·la·*wa*
3	*tatló*	tat·*lo*
4	*apat*	*a*·pat
5	*limá*	lee·*ma*
6	*anim*	*a*·neem
7	*pitó*	pee·*to*
8	*waló*	wa·*lo*
9	*siyám*	see·*yam*
10	*sampû*	sam·*poo'*

Yes.	*Opò.* (pol)	*o*·po'
	Oo. (inf)	*o*·o
No.	*Hindí pô.* (pol)	heen·*dee'* po'
	Hindî. (inf)	heen·*dee'*
Thank you.	*Salamat pô.* (pol)	sa·*la*·mat po'
	Salamat. (inf)	sa·*la*·mat
Help!	*Saklolo!*	sak·*lo*·lo

What's your name?
Anó pô ang pangalan ninyó? a·*no* po' ang pa·*nga*·lan neen·*yo*

My name is ...
Ang pangalan ko pô ay ... ang pa·*nga*·lan ko po' ai ...

Do you speak English?
Marunong ka ba ng Inglés? ma·*roo*·nong ka ba nang eeng·*gles*

I don't understand.
Hindí ko náiintindihán. heen·*dee* ko *na*·ee·een·teen·dee·*han*

How much is it?
Magkano? mag·*ka*·no

Where are the toilets?
Násaán ang kubeta? na·sa·*an* ang koo·*be*·ta

I'd like the menu.
Gustó ko ng menú. goos·*to* ko nang me·*noo*

Please bring the bill.
Pakidalá ang tsit. pa·kee·da·*la* ang tseet

Call ...!	*Tumawag ka ng ...!*	too·*ma*·wag ka nang ...
a doctor	*doktór*	dok·*tor*
the police	*pulís*	poo·*lees*

INDONESIAN & MALAY

Indonesian and Malay are very similar, so in this section we've provided translations in both languages – indicated by (I) and (M) respectively – only where the differences are significant enough to cause confusion. Most letters are pronounced more or less the same as their English counterparts, except for the letter c which is always pronounced as the 'ch' in 'chair'. Nearly all syllables carry equal emphasis, but a good approximation is to lightly stress the second-last syllable.

Basics

Hello.	*Salam./Helo.* (I/M)
Goodbye.	*Selamat tinggal/jalan.* (by person leaving/staying)
Excuse me.	*Maaf.*
Sorry.	*Maaf.*
Please.	*Silakan.*
Thank you.	*Terima kasih.*
Yes.	*Ya.*

Numbers – Indonesian/Malay	
1	*satu*
2	*dua*
3	*tiga*
4	*empat*
5	*lima*
6	*enam*
7	*tujuh*
8	*delapan* (I)
	lapan (M)
9	*sembilan*
10	*sepuluh*

No.	*Tidak.*
Help!	*Tolong!*
What's your name?	*Siapa nama anda/kamu?* (I/M)
My name is ...	*Nama saya ...*
Do you speak English?	*Anda bisa Bahasa Inggris?* (I) *Adakah anda berbahasa Inggeris?* (M)
I don't understand.	*Saya tidak mengerti.* (I) *Saya tidak faham.* (M)
How much is it?	*Berapa harganya?*
Where are the toilets?	*Kamar kecil di mana?* (I) *Tandas di mana?* (M)
I'd like the menu.	*Saya minta daftar makanan.*
Bring the bill, please.	*Tolong bawa kuitansi/bil.* (I/M)
Call a doctor!	*Panggil doktor!*
Call the police!	*Panggil polis!*

KHMER

In our pronunciation guides, vowels and vowel combinations with an h at the end are pronounced hard and aspirated (with a puff of air). The symbols for vowels are as follows: aa as the 'a' in 'father'; a and ah shorter and harder than aa; i as in 'kit'; uh as the 'u' in 'but'; ii as the 'ee' in 'feet'; eu like 'oo' (with the lips spread flat); euh as eu (short and hard); oh as the 'o' in 'hose' (short and hard); ow as in 'glow'; u as the 'u' in 'flute' (short and hard); uu as the 'oo' in 'zoo'; ua as the 'ou' in 'tour'; uah as ua (short and hard); œ as 'er' in 'her' (more open); ia as the 'ee' in 'beer' (without the 'r'); e as in 'they'; ai as in 'aisle'; ae as the 'a' in 'cat'; ay as ai (slightly more nasal); ey as in 'prey'; o as the 'ow' in 'cow'; av like a nasal ao (without the 'v'); euv like a nasal eu (without the 'v'); ohm as the 'ome' in 'home'; am as the 'um' in 'glum'; ih as the 'ee' in 'teeth'

(short and hard); eh as the 'a' in 'date' (short and hard); awh as the 'aw' in 'jaw' (short and hard); and aw as the 'aw' in 'jaw'.

Some consonant combinations in our pronunciation guides are separated with an apostrophe for ease of pronunciation, eg 'j-r' in j'rook and 'ch-ng' in ch'ngain. Also note that k is pronounced as the 'g' in 'go'; kh as the 'k' in 'kind'; p as the final 'p' in 'puppy'; ph as the 'p' in 'pond'; r as in 'rum' but hard and rolling; t as the 't' in 'stand'; and th as the 't' in 'two'.

Basics

Hello.	ជម្រាបសួរ	johm riab sua
Goodbye.	លាសិនហើយ	lia suhn hao-y
Excuse me.	សូមទោស	sohm toh
Sorry.	សូមទោស	sohm toh
Please.	សូម	sohm
Thank you.	អរគុណ	aw kohn
Yes.	បាទ/ចាស	baat/jaa (m/f)
No.	ទេ	te
Help!	ជួយខ្ញុំផង!	juay kh'nyohm phawng
What's your name?		
អ្នកឈ្មោះអី?		niak ch'muah ei
My name is ...		
ខ្ញុំឈ្មោះ...		kh'nyohm ch'muah ...
Does anyone speak English?		
ទីនេះមានអ្នកចេះ		tii nih mian niak jeh
ភាសាអង់គ្លេសទេ?		phiasaa awngle te
I don't understand.		
ខ្ញុំមិនយល់ទេ		kh'nyohm muhn yuhl te
How much is it?		
នេះថ្លៃប៉ុន្មាន?		nih th'lay pohnmaan

Numbers – Khmer		
1	មួយ	muy
2	ពីរ	pii
3	បី	bei
4	បួន	buan
5	ប្រាំ	bram
6	ប្រាំមួយ	bram muy
7	ប្រាំពីរ	bram pii
8	ប្រាំបី	bram bei
9	ប្រាំបួន	bram buan
10	ដប់	dawp

Where are the toilets?

ບ່ອນຂ່ນໂນໃຈໄດທຶໃ?   bawngkohn neuv ai naa

Do you have a menu in English?

ມານມ້ນຸຍຫຈ

ພາສາອັງກຈໂຮເຫ?   mien menui jea

piasaa awnglay te

The bill, please.

ສຸມກິຕລຸຍ   sohm kuht lui

Call a doctor!

ຈວຍເຫາະທ່ະເພເລຍມກ!   juay hav kruu paet mao

Call the police!

ຈວຍເຫາະບ໋ລິສມກຄ!   juay hav polih mao

LAO

Lao is a tonal language, meaning that many identical sounds are differentiated only by changes in the pitch of a speaker's voice. Pitch variations are relative to the speaker's natural vocal range, so that one person's low tone isn't necessarily the same pitch as another person's. There are six tones in Lao, indicated in our pronunciation guides by accent marks on letters: low tone (eg dẹe), high (eg héu·a), rising (eg sǎhm), high falling (eg sôw) and low falling (eg kòw). Note that no accent mark is used for the mid tone (eg het).

The pronunciation of vowels goes like this: i as in 'it'; ee as in 'feet'; ai as in 'aisle'; ah as the 'a' in 'father'; a as the short 'a' in 'about'; aa as in 'bad'; air as in 'air'; er as in 'fur'; eu as in 'sir'; u as in 'put'; oo as in 'food'; ow as in 'now'; or as in 'jaw'; o as in 'phone'; oh as in 'toe'; ee·a as in 'Ian'; oo·a as in 'tour'; ew as in 'yew'; and oy as in 'boy'. Most consonants correspond to their English counterparts. The exceptions are đ (a hard 't' sound, a bit like 'dt') and ƀ (a hard 'p' sound, a bit like 'bp').

In our pronunciation guides, the hyphens indicate syllable breaks, eg àng-gít (English). Some syllables are divided with a dot to help pronounce compound vowels, eg kěe·an (write).

Basics

Hello.	ສະບາຍດີ	sábai-děe
Goodbye.	ສະບາຍດີ	sábai-děe
Excuse me.	ຂໍໂທດ	kǒr tôht
Sorry.	ຂໍໂທດ	kǒr tôht
Please.	ກະລຸນາ	ga-lú-náh
Thank you.	ຂອບໃຈ	kòrp jai
Yes.	ແມນ	maan
No.	ບໍ່	bor
Help!	ຂ່ວຍແດ່	soo·ay daa

Numbers – Lao

1	ໜຶ່ງ	neung
2	ສອງ	sǒrng
3	ສາມ	sǎhm
4	ສີ່	see
5	ຫ້າ	hàh
6	ຫກ	hók
7	ເຈັດ	jét
8	ແປດ	ƀàat
9	ເກົ້າ	gòw
10	ສິບ	síp

What's your name?

ເຈົ້າຂື່ຫຍັງ   jôw seu nyǎng

My name is ...

ຂ້ອຍຂື່ ...   kòy seu ...

Do you speak English?

ເຈົ້າປາກ

ພາສາອັງກິດໄດ້ບໍ່   jôw ƀàhk

páh-sǎh ang·kít dâi bor

I don't understand.

ບໍ່ເຂົ້າໃຈ   bor kòw jai

How much (for) ...?

... ເທົ່າໃດ   ... tow dại

Where are the toilets?

ຫ້ອງນ້ຳຢູ່ໃສ   hòrng nâm yoo sǎii

  menu

ລາຍການອາຫານ   lái-gạhn ạh·hǎhn

Please bring the bill.

ຂໍແຊັກແດ່   kǒr saak daa

Call a doctor!

ຂ້ອຍຕາມຫາໝໍ

ໃຫ້ແດ່   soo·ay đạhm hǎh mǒr

hài daa

Call the police!

ຂ້ອຍເອີ້ນຕຳລວດແດ່   soo·ay êrn đam-lòo·at daa

TETUN

Tetun pronunciation is pretty straightforward. Letters always have the same sound value, and are generally pronounced just like in English, with the following exceptions: j is pronounced as the 's' in 'pleasure' (and sometimes as the 'z' in 'zebra'), x is pronounced as the 'sh' in 'ship' (sometimes as the 's' in 'summer'), while lh and nh are pronounced as the 'ly' in 'million' and the 'ny' in 'canyon' respectively (and outside Dili they are often reduced to l and n respectively).

Word stress is fairly regular and usually falls on the second-last syllable of a word; if it falls on another syllable, we've indicated this with an accent mark on the vowel (eg *polísia*).

Basics

Numbers – Tetun	
1	*ida*
2	*rua*
3	*tolu*
4	*hat*
5	*lima*
6	*nen*
7	*hitu*
8	*ualu*
9	*sia*
10	*sanulu*

Hello.	*Haló./Olá.* (pol/inf)
Goodbye.	*Adeus.*
Excuse me.	*Kolisensa.*
Sorry.	*Disculpa.*
Please.	*Favór ida./Faz favór.*
Thank you.	*Obrigadu/a.* (m/f)
Yes.	*Sin./Diak./Los.*
No.	*Lae.*
Help!	*Ajuda!*

What's your name?	*Ita-nia naran saida?*
My name is ...	*Hau-nia naran ...*
Do you speak English?	*Ita koalia Inglés?*
I don't understand.	*Hau la kompriende.*
How much is it?	*Folin hira?*
Where are the toilets?	*Sintina iha nebé?*
Please bring the menu/bill.	*Favór ida lori hela menu/konta mai.*
Call a doctor!	*Bolu dotór!*
Call the police!	*Bolu polísia!*

THAI

In Thai the meaning of a syllable may be altered by means of tones. In standard Thai there are five tones: low (eg *bàht*), mid (eg *dee*), falling (eg *mâi*), high (eg *máh*) and rising (eg *săhm*). The range of all tones is relative

to each speaker's vocal range, so there is no fixed 'pitch' intrinsic to the language.

In our pronunciation guides, the hyphens indicate syllable breaks within words, and for ease of pronunciation some compound vowels are divided with a dot (eg *mêu·a-rai*).

The vowel a is pronounced as in 'about', aa as the 'a' in 'bad', ah as the 'a' in 'father', ai as in 'aisle', air as in 'flair' (without the 'r'), eu as the 'er' in 'her' (without the 'r'), ew as in 'new' (with rounded lips), oh as the 'o' in 'toe', or as in 'torn' (without the 'r') and ow as in 'now'.

Note also the pronunciation of the following consonants: b (a hard 'p' sound, almost like a 'b', eg in 'hip-bag'); d (a hard 't' sound, like a sharp 'd', eg in 'mid-tone'); and r (as in 'run' but flapped; often pronounced like 'l').

Basics

Hello.	สวัสดี	sà-wàt-dee
Goodbye.	ลาก่อน	lah gòrn
Excuse me.	ขออภัย	kŏr à-pai
Sorry.	ขอโทษ	kŏr tôht
Please.	ขอ	kŏr
Thank you.	ขอบคุณ	kòrp kun
Yes.	ใช่	châi
No.	ไม่	mâi

Help!	ช่วยด้วย	chôo·ay dôo·ay
What's your name?		
คุณชื่ออะไร		kun chêu à-rai
My name is ...		
ผม/ดิฉัน		pŏm/dì-chăn
ชื่อ...		chêu ... (m/f)

Numbers – Thai		
1	หนึ่ง	nèung
2	สอง	sŏrng
3	สาม	săhm
4	สี่	sèe
5	ห้า	hâh
6	หก	hòk
7	เจ็ด	jèt
8	แปด	bàat
9	เก้า	gôw
10	สิบ	sìp

Do you speak English?

คุณพูดภาษา
อังกฤษได้ไหม   kun pôot pah-săh
    ang-grìt dâi măi

I don't understand.

ผม/ดิฉันไม่
เข้าใจ   pŏm/dì-chăn mâi
    kôw jai (m/f)

How much is it?

เท่าไร   tôw-rai

Where are the toilets?

ห้องน้ำอยู่ที่ไหน   hôrng nám yòo têe năi

I'd like the menu, please.

ขอรายการ
อาหารหน่อย   kŏr rai gahn
    ah-hăhn nòy

Please bring the bill.

ขอบิลหน่อย   kŏr bin nòy

Call a doctor!

เรียกหมอหน่อย   rêe·ak mŏr nòy

Call the police!

เรียกตำรวจหน่อย   rêe·ak đam·ròo·at nòy

VIETNAMESE

Numbers – Vietnamese

1	*một*	mạwt
2	*hai*	hai
3	*ba*	baa
4	*bốn*	báwn
5	*năm*	nuhm
6	*sáu*	sóh
7	*bảy*	bảy
8	*tám*	dúhm
9	*chín*	jín
10	*mười*	muhr·eè

Vietnamese is written in a Latin-based phonetic alphabet, which was declared the official written form in 1910.

In our pronunciation guides, a is pronounced as in 'at', aa as in 'father', aw as in 'law', er as in 'her', oh as in 'doh!', ow as in 'cow', u as in 'book', uh as in 'but' and uhr as in 'fur' (without the 'r'). We've used dots (eg dee·úhng) to separate the combined vowel

sounds. Note also that d is pronounced as in 'stop', đ as in 'dog', and ğ as in 'skill'.

Vietnamese uses a system of tones to make distinctions between words – so some vowels are pronounced with a high or low pitch. There are six tones in Vietnamese, indicated in the written language (and in our pronunciation guides) by accent marks on the vowel: mid (ma), low falling (mà), low rising (mả), high broken (mã), high rising (má) and low broken (mạ). The mid tone is flat.

The variation in vocabulary between the Vietnamese of the north and the south is indicated by (N) and (S) respectively.

Basics

Hello.	*Xin chào.*	sin jòw
Goodbye.	*Tạm biệt.*	daạm bee·ụht
Excuse me.	*Xin lỗi.*	sin lõy
Sorry.	*Xin lỗi.*	sin lõy
Please.	*Làm ơn.*	laàm ern
Thank you.	*Cảm ơn.*	ğaảm ern
Yes.	*Vâng./Dạ.* (N/S)	vuhng/yạ
No.	*Không.*	kawm
Help!	*Cứu tôi!*	ğuhr·oó doy

What's your name?

Tên là gì?   den laà zeè

My name is ...

Tên tôi là ...   den doy laà ...

Do you speak English?

Bạn có nói tiếng
Anh không?   baạn ğó nóy dee·úhng
    aang kawm

I don't understand.

Tôi không hiểu.   doy kawm heé·oo

How much is this?

Cái này giá bao nhiêu?   ğaí này zaá bow nyee·oo

Where is the toilet?

Nhà vệ sinh ở đâu?   nyaà vẹ sing ẻr đoh

I'd like the menu.

Tôi muốn thực đơn.   doy moo·úhn tụhrk đern

The bill, please.

Xin tính tiền.   sin díng dee·ùhn

Please call a doctor.

Làm ơn gọi bác sĩ.   laàm ern gọy baák sẽ

Please call the police.

Làm ơn gọi công an.   laàm ern gọy ğawm aan

Behind the Scenes

SEND US YOUR FEEDBACK

We love to hear from travellers – your comments keep us on our toes and help make our books better. Our well-travelled team reads every word on what you loved or loathed about this book. Although we cannot reply individually to your submissions, we always guarantee that your feedback goes straight to the appropriate authors, in time for the next edition. Each person who sends us information is thanked in the next edition – the most useful submissions are rewarded with a selection of digital PDF chapters.

Visit **lonelyplanet.com/contact** to submit your updates and suggestions or to ask for help. Our award-winning website also features inspirational travel stories, news and discussions.

Note: We may edit, reproduce and incorporate your comments in Lonely Planet products such as guidebooks, websites and digital products, so let us know if you don't want your comments reproduced or your name acknowledged. For a copy of our privacy policy visit lonelyplanet.com/privacy.

OUR READERS

Many thanks to the travellers who used the last edition and wrote to us with helpful hints, useful advice and interesting anecdotes:

A Alison Aspden **B** Balthazar Breij, Brendan McKenzie **C** Caroine Peters, Chelsea-Rae Abbate **E** Edouard Gendreau, Elise Petitjean & Yda Gough, Emily Ford, Erik Visscher **G** Gabrielle Innes, Goncalo Franca **I** Inka Kukkamaki **J** Jacqueline Piper, Jess Jennison, Joakim Carbonnier, Julia Simonelli **L** Len Pillen **M** Marcos Mendonca, Mark Candey, Markus Koller, Martina Roos, Matthias Hatzak, Maurizio Geri **N** Natalie Davidson **O** Orianna Rubin **P** Peter Howard **R** Rahel Bücheler **S** Santiago Creixell, Sebastià Mas Alòs, Sebastian Myrus, Susan Duncan

AUTHOR THANKS

China Williams

Many thanks to my good buddy Nong, the gals at TJR, Candyhome nursery school, Pong at Libernard Café, Andrew Bond, Pim of CityLife, Aidan from Chiang Mai Mountain Bikes, Pat of Patara Elephant Farm. In Bangkok, much thanks to Ruengsang, Mai, Jane, Kanchana and Austin. Thanks to Matt and Felix for taking care of each other and to Mandy for taking care of them. Applause to the co-authors, Lorna, Elin

and to those Lonely Planet production staff who have left. I heart old-fashioned publishing.

Greg Bloom

The cumulative knowledge of my *barkada* in Manila was elemental as usual. A special nod to Wilipino for the nightlife tips, and to Johnny Weekend, who joined me for some surfing, snorkelling, hiking and motorbiking on Camiguin and Siargao. In Cambodia, thanks to Anna for being my 'travel with children' guinea pig in Anlong Veng, Preah Viheah, Stung Treng and Ratanakiri. And thanks to Lucy for dutifully joining me for Phnom Penh restaurant research and rolling with this crazy lifestyle.

Celeste Brash

On the ground, big thanks to Eawasain, Gerard and Jay, David Hogan, Anna Kamininski, Peck Choo Ho, Brandan Tan, Narelle McMurtrie, Joan Khaw, Aril Zainal, Michael Chick and Ben Phillips. Always a pleasure to work with Lonely Planet folks Daniel Robinson and China Williams. At home big thanks to my family for holding up the fort.

Stuart Butler

Thank you to Yuono Tartousodo from Jogja Trans for helping me out so much in Yogya and eastern Java, and to my various drivers, guides and other people who helped out in so many ways throughout Java and Sumatra. Finally, thank you as always to my wife Heather and my children, Jake and Grace, for putting up with me vanishing to the other side of the world for so long.

Shawn Low

As always thanks to the commisioning editor: Ilaria for believing and more importantly, hiring! Good luck in your new role. Cheers also to coordinating author: China (yet another one done and dusted!). Thanks to the Lonely Planet crew who are working on this: editors, cartographers, layout designers etc. I've been behind the scenes and know how hard you all work. Despite all the Lonely Planet shake-ups, you all remain some of the best people I've worked with and I miss you all and the old days at Lonely Planet already. Much love to Wyn-Lyn: to future adventures.

Simon Richmond

Many thanks to my fellow authors and the following: William Myatwunna, Thant Myint-U, Edwin Briels, Jessica Mudditt, Greg Klemm, Vicky Bowman, Marcus Allender, Tun Lin Htaik (Tom Tom), Andrea Martini Rossi, Amelie Chan, Aung Soe Min, Wanna Aung, Allison Morris, Pete Silverster, New Ni Thien (Nina), Soe Moe Aung, Nay Aung, Patrick Kyaw Khin, Patrick Winn and Sean Turnell.

Daniel Robinson

Special thanks to Rosalind Tsang, Dr Stephen Sutton, Katie King, Tom Hewitt, Jessica Hegarty, Joe Chapman, Kennesh Manokaran, Rohan Perkins, Leslie Chiang, Danny Hardini, Dr Supry Ladi, Mary Maroney, Eric and Annie Yap, Kelvin Egay, Philip Yong, Robert Basiuk, Jacqueline Fong, Jo-Lynn Liao, Paul Chuo Kong Yu, Mrs Lee (Miri), Sally Bungan Bat, John Tarawe, Rebita Lupong, Tine and Stephen Baya, Rhonwyn Hagedorn, Sue and Jeremy Clark, Kat and Glenn van Zutphen, Michael Ewing-Chow, Seng Beng Yeo, Geok Cheng, Leonard Koh, Belinda Foo, Michelle and David Solomon, Lenny Thal, Harvey Goldstein and Melanie Hildebrandt.

Iain Stewart

Thanks to Vinh Vu, Chien, Dzung, Neil and Caroline, Mark Wyndham, Ben and Bich, Howard and Deborah Limbert, the Nha Trang boys and Mark and Jason in HCMC. And to China Williams and all the Lonely Planet editors and cartographers for their professionalism and help on this title.

Ryan Ver Berkmoes

This list just seems to grow. Many thanks to friends like Hanafi, Cat Wheeler, Patticakes Miklautsch, Pascal and Pika (who can really engage), the incomparable Marg Toohey, Alex Laviosso and Amélie, Maite and her love shack, Nengah, Edy Sudrajat and the tireless Abba and Michael. At LP, thanks the entire publishing and production teams – especially Bruce Evans – who ignored turmoil and personal concerns to produce a great book. And Alexis Averbuck, who's golden, sometimes languid and always glistens.

Richard Waters

Special thanks go to Alex for his zeal and generosity, as well to Vianney for his much needed wisdom, Elizabeth for her fiery Bloody Marys at the inspiring Icon Bar, Mr Somkiad for his patience, DC for fixing my bike, Thierry for the sturdy Baja, Lao Heritage Hotel, Scandy Bakery for keeping me awake, Don Duvall for his excellent help, my friend Adri Berger, and as ever to the Lao people who make me wonder why the rest of the planet can't possess a little more of their gentle essence.

ACKNOWLEDGMENTS

Climate map data adapted from Peel MC, Finlayson BL & McMahon TA (2007) 'Updated World Map of the Köppen-Geiger Climate Classification', *Hydrology and Earth System Sciences*, 11, 163344.

Illustrations p100-1, p652-3 and p854-5 by Michael Weldon.

Cover photography: (main) Sunset, Mrauk U, Myanmar (Burma)/Dennis Walton/Getty Images ©; (inset top) Boat, Krabi Province, Thailand/JS Callahan/Tropicalpix/Alamy ©; (inset centre) Tarsier, Philippine Tarsier Sanctuary, Bohol, Philippines/Bruno Morandi/SIME/4Corners ©; (inset bottom) Monks, Luang Prabang, Laos/Otto Stadler/4Corners ©

THIS BOOK

This is the 17th edition of Lonely Planet's *Southeast Asia* guidebook. The 1st edition was written by Tony and Maureen Wheeler in 1975, funded by the cult success of their first guidebook, *Across Asia on the Cheap*, a compilation of journey notes put together back in 1973. This 17th edition was written by China Williams, Greg Bloom, Celeste Brash, Stuart Butler, Shawn Low, Simon Richmond, Daniel Robinson, Iain Stewart, Ryan Ver Berkmoes, Meagan Weymes and Richard Waters. Original research for Brunei Darussalam was provided by Daniel Robinson. Original research for Cambodia was provided by Nick Ray and Greg Bloom. Original research for Indonesia was provided by Ryan Ver Berkmoes and Stuart Butler. Original research for Laos was provided by Nick Ray, Greg Bloom and Richard Waters. Original research for Malay-

sia was provided by Celeste Brash, Daniel Robinson and Simon Richmond. Original research for Myanmar (Burma) was provided by Simon Richmond, Austin Bush, David Eimer, Mark Elliott and Nick Ray. Original research for the Philippines was provided by Greg Bloom. Original research for Singapore was provided by Shawn Low. Original research for Thailand was provided by China Williams, Mark Beales, Tim Bewer, Celeste Brash, Austin Bush, David Eimer and Adam Skolnick. Original research for Vietnam was provided by Iain Stewart, Brett Atkinson and Damian Harper. This guidebook was commissioned in Lonely Planet's Melbourne office, and produced by the following:

Commissioning Editor
Ilaria Walker

Associate Product Director Angela Tinson

Coordinating Editors
Elin Berglund, Lorna Parkes, Amanda Williamson

Senior Cartographer
Diana Von Holdt

Assisting Editors Carolyn Bain, Judith Bamber, Michelle Bennett, Penny Cordner, Melanie Dankel, Andrea Dobbin, Kate Evans, Carly Hall, Anne Mulvaney, Rosie Nicholson, Chris Pitts, Katie O'Connell

Assisting Cartographers Mick Garrett, Sophie Hatcher, Corey Hutchison, Rachel Imeson, James Leversha, Alison Lyall

Book Designer
Clara Monitto

Cover Researcher
Naomi Parker

Language Content
Branisalava Vladisavljevic

Thanks to Anita Banh, Bruce Evans, Ryan Evans, Larissa Frost, Briohny Hooper, Genesys India, Jouve India, Kate James, Elizabeth Jones, Claire Naylor, Karyn Noble, Catherine Naghten, Martine Power, Alison Ridgway, Dianne Schallmeiner, Luna Soo, Tracy Whitmey

Index

INDEX C-G

Map Legend

Sights
- Beach
- Bird Sanctuary
- Buddhist
- Castle/Palace
- Christian
- Confucian
- Hindu
- Islamic
- Jain
- Jewish
- Monument
- Museum/Gallery/Historic Building
- Ruin
- Sento Hot Baths/Onsen
- Shinto
- Sikh
- Taoist
- Winery/Vineyard
- Zoo/Wildlife Sanctuary
- Other Sight

Activities, Courses & Tours
- Bodysurfing
- Diving
- Canoeing/Kayaking
- Course/Tour
- Skiing
- Snorkelling
- Surfing
- Swimming/Pool
- Walking
- Windsurfing
- Other Activity

Sleeping
- Sleeping
- Camping

Eating
- Eating

Drinking & Nightlife
- Drinking & Nightlife
- Cafe

Entertainment
- Entertainment

Shopping
- Shopping

Information
- Bank
- Embassy/Consulate
- Hospital/Medical
- Internet
- Police
- Post Office
- Telephone
- Toilet
- Tourist Information
- Other Information

Geographic
- Beach
- Hut/Shelter
- Lighthouse
- Lookout
- Mountain/Volcano
- Oasis
- Park
- Pass
- Picnic Area
- Waterfall

Population
- Capital (National)
- Capital (State/Province)
- City/Large Town
- Town/Village

Transport
- Airport
- Border crossing
- Bus
- Cable car/Funicular
- Cycling
- Ferry
- Metro/MRT station
- Monorail
- Parking
- Petrol station
- Skytrain/Subway station
- Taxi
- Train station/Railway
- Tram
- Underground station
- Other Transport

Note: Not all symbols displayed above appear on the maps in this book

Routes
- Tollway
- Freeway
- Primary
- Secondary
- Tertiary
- Lane
- Unsealed road
- Road under construction
- Plaza/Mall
- Steps
- Tunnel
- Pedestrian overpass
- Walking Tour
- Walking Tour detour
- Path/Walking Trail

Boundaries
- International
- State/Province
- Disputed
- Regional/Suburb
- Marine Park
- Cliff
- Wall

Hydrography
- River, Creek
- Intermittent River
- Canal
- Water
- Dry/Salt/Intermittent Lake
- Reef

Areas
- Airport/Runway
- Beach/Desert
- Cemetery (Christian)
- Cemetery (Other)
- Glacier
- Mudflat
- Park/Forest
- Sight (Building)
- Sportsground
- Swamp/Mangrove